Industrial Market Structure

Industrial Market Structure and Economic Performance

F. M. Scherer
INTERNATIONAL INSTITUTE OF MANAGEMENT
BERLIN, GERMANY

RAND McNALLY & COMPANY · Chicago

RAND McNALLY ECONOMICS SERIES

Fourth Printing, 1973

Preface

When a person spends the better part of four years writing a book, he ought to have some compelling reason. Mine was relatively simple. Although much progress has been made in our understanding of how real-world industrial markets function, there was no single work which put all the pieces together to my satisfaction or to the satisfaction of other industrial organization economists with whom I exchanged laments. This book, then, is a case of demand-pull innovative response.

For whom should the fragments of knowledge be assembled? I resolved the audience question early in the game by deciding to pull no punches in using the relevant tools of economic analysis, but to present the material in a way which could be comprehended by bright, well-motivated laymen with no more background than a basic undergraduate price theory course. Most of the time I had in mind Supreme Court clerks as the reader. Needless to say, few publishers these days can work up much enthusiasm about a market of some two dozen copies per year. I hasten to add therefore that the book can serve as a text for courses in Industrial Organization and Public Policy offered to graduate students or to strong undergraduates. It is in fact based upon my lectures in a two-semester undergraduate sequence at the University of Michigan —the first semester emphasizing positive explanation and theory, the second policy. It could also be used for a breathless one-semester dash through both areas or (somewhat less economically) for either component alone. Al-though I try to minimize the use of jargon and relegate mathematics to footnotes and appendices, some of the book's more novel contributions and the overall conceptual scheme may even prove stimulating to professional economists. Certainly, I intended to achieve that by-product.

In any attempt to cover such a broad canvas there are bound to be lacunae and blemishes. The manuscript was completed, except for revisions, in August 1968. Since then there have been a number of noteworthy additions to the industrial organization literature, not all of which could be covered adequately during rewriting. Also, as I turn to new lines of research, I discover almost weekly some older but significant contribution of which I had been unaware. Life is too short to read everything. To those who find a favorite hypothesis or analysis overlooked, I hope this will be an adequate apology.

For mistakes I have no excuse other than human frailty. Following the example of certain industries, I am tempted to offer only a one-year warranty against defects. After that, full responsibility would pass to those who have read the book and failed to find any errors and (all the more) to those who found them but failed to report them to me. But this is the age of consumerism, so I am compelled to shoulder the burden alone.

That this load is not oppressive is due in no small measure to the constructive criticism I obtained from many colleagues and friends. Valuable comments on the whole manuscript or major parts were provided by William Comanor, Shorey Peterson, Jesse Markham, Thomas Kauper, and the students in my Fall 1967 graduate industrial organization course, among whom Ben Branch and Darius Gaskins deserve special mention. From John Cross, Saul Hymans, Harold Levinson, Sidney Winter, Ronald Teigen, Michael Klass, Erich Kaufer, and James Denny I received helpful criticisms concerning particular chapters. Geoffrey Shepherd helped fill in many gaps in my knowledge as writing was in progress. Louis Hawkins, Lowell Seyburn, and Thomas Schick performed yeoman service as research assistants, gathering data and checking out countless details. To all I am heavily indebted. I am grateful also to the University of Michigan's Institute of Public Policy Studies, whose financial support permitted me to devote full time to research and writing during the summers of 1967 and 1968.

My greatest debt is, as always, to my wife Barbara and to my son Thomas and daughters Karen and Christina, who bore in good spirits my excessive absence from the hearth. My obligation to them, like the national debt, never seems to get repaid. Yet happily, the union survives and prospers.

I should like to dedicate this volume to three individuals who had much to do with my being in a position to write it—to Shorey Peterson, who first stirred the fires of interest; to Jesse Markham, whose 1961–1962 industrial organization seminar at Harvard influenced nearly every chapter; and to Richard Heflebower, who taught me the power of the profit maximization hypothesis.

F. M. Scherer

Ann Arbor, Michigan
January 1970

Table of Contents

List of Figures

List of Tables

Industrial Market Structure

Chapter 1

Introduction

This book explores systematically the field of economics known as *industrial organization*. The name is a curious one, distinctive mainly in its inability to communicate to outsiders what the subject is all about. It has little or nothing to say about how one organizes and directs a particular industrial enterprise, although there are industrial organization courses in business and engineering schools which deal with such matters. Rather, the field is concerned with how productive activities are brought into harmony with society's demands for goods and services through some organizing mechanism such as a free market, and how variations and imperfections in the organizing mechanism affect the degree of success achieved by producers in satisfying society's wants.

Any economy, whatever its cultural and political traditions may be, must solve three fundamental problems:

(a) What end products to produce, and how much of each to produce both in current and future time periods (the *what* problem);

(b) How to produce each end product, and specifically, how to apportion society's scarce resources in producing each (the *how* problem); and

(c) How to divide up the end products among the various members of society (the *for whom*, or *distribution* problem).

To solve this whole bundle of problems is called *the economic problem*. There are three main alternative ways of going about the job. First, decisions can be made to conform with *tradition*. The economic organization of manors in Europe during feudal times and the caste system of occupational choice in India are prominent examples. Second, the economic problem can be solved through *central planning*. Illustrations include output and input planning for most heavy industry in the Soviet Union and China, and the elaborate controls the U. S. Department of Defense imposes over its contractors. Finally, there is the *market system* approach under which consumers and producers make their decisions in response to price signals generated by the interplay of supply and demand forces in more or less freely operating markets, each participant seeking to make the best of the market conditions he faces (i.e., by maximizing profit or subjective utility).

The field of industrial organization is concerned primarily with the third of these approaches—the market system approach. This is not to deny the existence of a substantial overlap with other fields, such as the field of comparative economic systems, which specializes in analyzing the operation of centrally planned, hybrid socialist, and traditional economies. Many of the structural features we shall examine are of equal concern to the central planner. Likewise, our understanding of free market processes can be sharpened by studying the resource allocation processes of socialist and centrally planned economies, just as one may gain new insights into the incentive problems of centrally planned econo-

1

mies by analyzing the synthetic market incentives employed by the U. S. defense authorities. Still to remain within manageable scope, this book respects the traditional division of intellectual labor, confining its coverage to market processes.

On similar grounds of manageability and convenience, our focus must be narrowed even further. We shall have very little to say about the operation of labor markets, whose study is the domain of the labor specialist, and even less about the banking, finance, and insurance industries, which belong conventionally to the field of money and banking. Primary emphasis will be placed on the manufacturing sector of industrialized economies, with secondary emphasis on the transportation, public utility, distribution, and service sectors. Manufacturing will occupy the center ring, partly because of further division of labor traditions (e.g., public utility and transportation economics are often considered separate specialties) and partly because of its sheer size and strategic position in the economy. Finally, the empirical analyses in this volume will for the sake of convenience and data availability relate mainly to the United States economy, although comparisons with other nations will be drawn frequently, and there is no reason to believe that the theories we shall develop cannot be applied equally well in explaining the operation of other industrialized economies.

THE SCOPE AND METHOD OF INDUSTRIAL ORGANIZATION ANALYSIS

In the field of industrial organization, we try to determine how market processes direct the activities of producers in meeting consumer demands, how these processes may break down, and how they can be adjusted (i.e., through government intervention) to make actual performance conform more closely to the ideal. Many of these questions are also the concern of pure microeconomic theory, or at least, of the market theory and welfare economics branches of microeconomic theory. How does industrial organization analysis differ from pure theory? In fact, there is a fair amount of overlap, but there are also significant differences in goals and methodology.

Both are concerned with explaining why things happen—why, for instance, prices are lower under one set of conditions than under another, and how some variable such as price will change in response to changes in other (independent) variables. Both view the type of market organization linking producers with consumers as an important variable. They differ mainly in the richness of the independent variables they attempt to subsume, and in their concern for applying predictions and explanations to concrete real-world cases. The pure microeconomic theorist thrives on simplicity and rigor; he is happiest when he can strip his model to the barest few essential assumptions and variables. The industrial organization economist is more inclined toward explanations rich in both quantitative and institutional detail. To be sure, he should prefer a simpler theory to a more complex one when the two have equal explanatory power. But when a tradeoff must be made, the pure theorist will sacrifice some explanatory power for elegance, while the industrial organization specialist bends in the opposite direction.

Another useful perspective on the differences between industrial organization economics and pure microeconomic theory is provided by Joseph A. Schumpeter's concept of "economic analysis." A science, wrote Schumpeter, is any field of knowledge that has developed specialized techniques of factfinding and interpretation or analysis.[1] What distinguishes the scientific economic analyst from other people who think, talk, and write about economic topics, according to Schumpeter, is a command over three main techniques: history, statistics, and theory— theory being defined as a "box of tools" or a set of models which permits one to deal analytically with broad classes of cases by focusing on certain properties or aspects they have in common.[2] As

[1] *History of Economic Analysis* (New York: Oxford University Press, 1954), p. 7.
[2] *Ibid.*, pp. 12–16. See also Joan Robinson, *The Economics of Imperfect Competition* (London: Macmillan, 1933), p. 1.

we shall see repeatedly in later chapters, the industrial organization economist must have a command over all three techniques to make the most of his trade. He must be at home in pure microeconomic theory to forge rigorous predictive links between fundamental assumptions and their behavioral consequences. He must use modern statistical methods to extract appropriate generalizations from data on industrial structure and performance without plunging into the many pitfalls which line the quantitative analyst's path. And he needs some familiarity with the methods and results of historical research, both to put his findings in broader perspective and to extract from a tangle of institutional detail the causes of departures from the norm. In short, all three horses in Schumpeter's methodological troika are required to pull the industrial organization cart; pure theory is only one member of the team.

Why should an economist be interested in industrial organization problems? There seem to be two main reasons. First, studies in the field have a direct and continuing influence on the formulation and implementation of public policies in such areas as the choice between private and public enterprise, the regulation and coordination of transportation systems and public utilities, the promotion of competition through antitrust, the stimulation of technological progress through patent grants and subsidies, etc. The field's attraction to policy-oriented economists was especially strong between 1887 and 1915, when the antitrust laws and the first federal regulatory agencies were in their infancy; and between 1933 and 1940, when new developments in economic theory interacted with depression psychosis to stimulate a reassessment of the proper role for competition. Since 1950 the excitement has died down somewhat, and industrial organization studies have lost some of their magnetism to economists eager to grapple with weighty public policy questions. This shift followed naturally from an ascendance of other issues on the ladder of social priorities (e.g., achieving growth in underdeveloped nations and the problems of the urban ghetto). Reallocation of intellectual resources in favor of problems more urgent socially is obviously desirable. Still the agenda of unsettled or inadequately resolved policy issues in industrial organization continues to be impressive. And because the law of diminishing marginal returns operates pervasively, many economists find their marginal contribution to social welfare in industrial organization studies higher than in work on problems which, while more important in some absolute sense, are being subjected to an intensive attack by scholarly hordes.

A second reason for toiling in the industrial organization vineyard is that it is intellectually exciting. One thing which should become clear as this volume unfolds is the vastness of our ignorance concerning many facets of an industrialized market economy's functioning. As a symptom, the pure theories of firm and market behavior have been bogged down on a broad front, awaiting an injection of new insights and evidence before further advances are set in motion. The data, methodology, and financial support needed to explore these voids are gradually becoming available. It is likely therefore that an able person doing research on industrial organization problems will advance the frontiers of knowledge, and lucky ones may achieve or trigger major breakthroughs. To those who relish the quest for knowledge, this is an attractive prospect.

AN INTRODUCTORY PARADIGM

Before turning to the tasks at hand, it is useful to have a simple model of our overall approach to industrial organization analysis. We begin from the fundamental assumption that what society wants from producers of goods and services is good performance. Good performance is a multidimensional attribute. It embodies at least the following goals, not necessarily listed in order of social importance or priority:

(a) Decisions as to *what, how much*, and *how* to produce should be efficient in two respects: scarce resources should not be wasted outright, and production decisions should be responsive qualitatively and quantitatively to consumer demands.

(b) The operations of producers should be progressive, taking advantage of opportunities opened up by science and technology for increasing output per unit of input and making available to consumers superior new products, in both ways contributing to the long-run growth of per capita real income.

(c) The operations of producers should facilitate stable full employment of resources, especially human resources. Or at the very minimum, they should not make maintenance of full employment through macroeconomic policy instruments excessively difficult.

(d) The distribution of income should be equitable. Equity in economics is a notoriously slippery concept, but it implies at least that producers do not secure rewards far in excess of those needed to call forth the amount of services supplied. A sub-facet of this goal is the desire to achieve reasonable price stability, for rampant inflation distorts the distribution of income in widely disapproved ways.

These goals may not always be completely consistent with one another, and later chapters will identify conflicts which cannot be resolved without invoking basic value judgments. Still, to the extent possible, good industrial performance implies maximum satisfaction of all four goals. Measuring the degree to which the goals have been satisfied is also not easy, but operational approximations can be achieved by using data on price-cost margins, the relationship of actual costs to technologically feasible minima, rates of change of prices and output per manhour, variability of employment over the business cycle, etc.

With this ultimate focus, we seek to identify sets of attributes or variables which influence economic performance and to build theories detailing the nature of the links between those attributes and end performance. The broad descriptive model of these relationships used in most industrial organization studies was conceived by Edward S. Mason at Harvard during the 1930s and extended by numerous scholars.[8] It is illustrated schematically in Figure 1.1. *Performance* in particular industries or markets is said to depend upon the *conduct* of sellers and buyers in those markets in such matters as pricing policies and practices, overt and tacit cooperation among firms, product line strategies, research and development commitments, advertising strategies, legal tactics (e.g., in enforcing patent rights), and so on. Conduct depends in turn upon the *structure* of the relevant market, embracing such features as the number and size distribution of sellers and buyers, the degree of physical or subjective differentiation prevailing among competing sellers' products, the presence or absence of barriers to the entry of new firms, the ratio of fixed to total costs in the short run for a typical firm, the degree to which firms are vertically integrated from raw material production to retail distribution, the amount of diversity or conglomerateness characterizing individual firms' product lines, and the geographic dispersion or concentration of buyers and sellers.

Market structure and conduct are also influenced by various *basic conditions*. On the supply side, for example, basic conditions include the location and ownership of essential raw materials, the character of the available technology (e.g., batch vs. process production, or high vs. low elasticity of input substitution), the durability of the product, the value-weight characteristics of the product, etc. A list of significant basic conditions on the demand side must include at least the price elasticity of demand at various prices; the rate of growth of demand; the availability of (and cross elasticity of demand for) substitute products; the methods employed by buyers in purchasing (e.g., acceptance of list prices as given vs. solicitation of sealed bids vs. haggling); the marketing characteristics of the product

---

[8]Mason's seminal works are "Price and Production Policies of Large-Scale Enterprise," *American Economic Review*, Supplement, March 1939, pp. 61–74; and "The Current State of the Monopoly Problem in the United States," *Harvard Law Review*, June 1949, pp. 1265–1285. Important extensions include Joe S. Bain, *Industrial Organization* (New York: Wiley, 1959), especially Chapter 1; Richard B. Heflebower, "Toward a Theory of Industrial Markets and Prices," *American Economic Review*, May 1954, pp. 121–139; and Steven H. Sosnick, "A Critique of Concepts of Workable Competition," *Quarterly Journal of Economics*, August 1958, pp. 416–423. See also L. J. Zimmerman, *The Propensity To Monopolize* (Amsterdam: North Holland, 1952); and J. M. Clark, *Competition as a Dynamic Process* (Washington: Brookings, 1961), pp. 98–116 and 419–425.

sold (e.g., specialty vs. convenience vs. shopping goods)[4]; and the time pattern of production and sales (i.e., whether goods are produced to order or delivered from inventory). Other germane basic conditions are the environment of laws and government policies within which industries operate and the dominant socioeconomic values of the business community (i.e., whether sympathies run toward aggressive individualism or cooperation).

As the heavy arrows in Figure 1.1 suggest, we shall be primarily concerned in this volume with those relationships or tendencies involving a causal flow from market structure and/or basic conditions to conduct and performance. That is, we seek theories which permit us to predict ultimate market performance from the observation of structure, basic conditions, and conduct. To cite an example which will be pursued further in Chapter 7, we may find that the current technology calls for a capital intensive production process, which implies a short-run cost structure with high fixed and low variable costs, which encourages aggressive pricing conduct even in oligopolistic industries when demand is price inelastic and cyclically volatile, which in turn has important ramifications in terms of price-cost margins and other performance indicators. Or for a less complex illustration to be elaborated in Chapter 5, durability of an industry's product may have a marked impact on price-cost margins, other things being equal, because it affects the ability of firms to deal with demand uncertainties by taking inventory positions.

To be sure, not all influences flow from basic conditions or market structure toward performance. There are also feedback effects (broken lines in Figure 1.1). For example, vigorous research and development efforts may alter an industry's technology, and hence its cost conditions and/or the degree of product differentiation. Or the policies pursued by sellers in coordinating their mutual price interactions may either

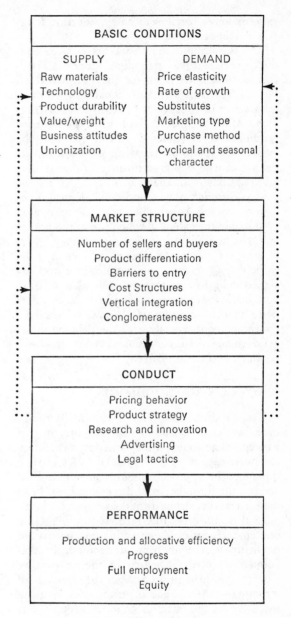

Figure 1.1
A Model of Industrial Organization Analysis

---

[4]Convenience goods, such as toothpaste, razor blades, and cigarettes, are items which are purchased with little shopping around because the costs of obtaining price comparisons outweigh the benefits. Shopping goods, such as furniture, major items of clothing, and mortgages, are items whose purchase is infrequent and whose value is high, so that price and quality comparison shopping trips are warranted. Specialty goods are high-value items on which the buyer has been pre-sold, so that he will go to considerable trouble to obtain the particular brand he wants. Examples include high-priced cameras and major appliances purchased by *Consumer Reports* readers. Cf. Heflebower, *op. cit.*, pp. 128–129; and R. H. Holton, "The Distinctions Between Convenience Goods, Shopping Goods, and Specialty Goods," *Journal of Marketing*, July 1958, pp. 53–56.

raise or lower barriers to entry, affecting long-run market structure.

This basic conditions – market structure – conduct – performance paradigm provides both theme and counterpoint for the analysis which follows. The book's organizational thrust centers on a structure – conduct – performance trichotomy. After Chapter 2 lays some preliminary groundwork, Chapters 3 and 4 examine the existing structure of American industry and its determinants. Chapters 5 through 17 then undertake an extended analysis of conduct in the pricing, product policy, and technological innovation spheres, concluding with an integrated appraisal of the extent to which present structure and conduct yield satisfactory economic performance. Chapters 18 through 22 conclude the work with a survey of public policy measures designed to improve performance by manipulating both market structure and conduct. As counterpoint to this sequence of themes, we shall be concerned continuously with the detailed interactions among basic conditions, market structure, conduct, and performance.

A NOTE ON METHODOLOGY

Readers already acquainted with the literature of industrial organization will recognize in this conceptual scheme a heavy intellectual debt to the pioneering work of Joe S. Bain. Yet a major difference in approach should be noted. Bain stresses the formulation of direct empirical links between market structure and economic performance, deemphasizing intermediate conduct. Only one chapter out of fifteen in his text is devoted explicitly to the analysis of conduct. In this volume, by contrast, much of the analysis in Chapters 5 through 16 attacks the question of structure—performance associations by focusing intensely on the business conduct which spans those phenomena. If the difference in approaches had to be characterized by means of labels, it could be said that Bain is predominantly a structuralist, while the author of the present work is a behaviorist.

Bain's case for his approach can be summarized in three main propositions.[5] First, the inclusion of conduct variables is not essential to the development of an operational theory of industrial organization. Acceptable predictions of actual performance can be generated by using only structural indices as independent variables. Second, a priori theory based upon structure – conduct and conduct – performance links yields ambiguous predictions. Widely divergent conduct may follow from given structural conditions, or varying qualities of performance may result from presumably similar conduct patterns. Third, even if satisfactory a priori structure – conduct – performance hypotheses could be formulated, the person attempting to test those hypotheses would encounter serious obstacles. Much published information on business conduct is incomplete and unreliable, and business firms have been less than hospitable in allowing well-trained students of industrial organization access to the requisite internal information. Even if this last hurdle could be surmounted, research which penetrates the decision-making processes of firms is so costly and time consuming that few company studies could be accomplished, and one might be placed in the unhappy position of generalizing from an 'inadequate sample of special cases.

All three arguments have merit. None is unassailable. On the first, it is true that much progress has been made in explaining industrial performance using only structural variables. We shall honor these contributions by frequent citation in coming chapters, and we can expect even better results in the future as improved data become available and as students of industrial organization grow in methodological sophistication. But it would be possible to make still better predictions, eliminating some statistical variance that would otherwise go unexplained, by probing intermediate structure-conduct and conduct-performance associations. To this claim, the structuralist might reply that predictions using only structure variables are already 'good enough' or, on a more sophisticated plane, that

---

[5] See *Industrial Organization*, pp. 36–38, 295–301, and 310–315. I have also benefitted from a discussion of this problem with Professor Bain.

the cost of introducing explicit conduct hypotheses would exceed the value of the increases in predictive accuracy. Such an objection cannot be proved or disproved in the present state of knowledge, but even if it were valid, it would overlook an important point. While science may be construed narrowly as nothing more than systematically verified prediction, surely the joy of science involves something more: finding out *why* things happen, and not just that they do happen when certain levers are pulled. To stop short of learning what we can about conduct linkages would be to deny man's urge to know. And for reasons stated earlier, failure to explore these linkages may also hinder the achievement of needed advances in pure microeconomic theory.

The second argument can be disposed of more brusquely. Bain's observation that traditional *a priori* theories yield ambiguous predictions is largely correct. But the problem lies in the naiveté of these theories, not in theorizing per se. The predictions are ambiguous because significant variables have been excluded from the models. By introducing a much richer complement of independent variables, we should be able to predict conduct from structure and performance from conduct with greater precision and confidence.

Bain's third objection can also be contested. To begin at the end of the chain, the increased financial support of social science research likely in the future will, among other things, make it possible to carry out numerous in-depth studies of firms' pricing, product policy, and innovative responses to alternative market environments. To be sure, some firms have been reluctant to cooperate in research of this nature, partly through fear of investigative bias and sometimes because they fear the truth will out. But in the author's experience, many other companies cooperate gladly when the investigator enters without preconceived conclusions, and the more recalcitrant organizations can then be pulled in through a kind of bandwagon effect. Perhaps a more serious obstacle is the characteristic indolence of economists. It is hard work to plow through file after file of company documents and to interview dozens of executives, cross-checking each observation to guard against bias and misinterpretation. It is much easier to work with census data punched into IBM cards which can be interrogated in the comfort of home, answer all questions without evasion, and never complain when bent or spindled. Yet despite these difficulties, the job can be done, and there are undoubtedly scholars willing to rise to the challenge—given a little encouragement and financial support.

In any event, we sum up the defense for the methodological tack taken in this book as follows: Industrial organization economists have done well using Bain's structure-performance dichotomy. But we can do still better with a richer model which includes intermediate behavioral links. Opportunities for progress exist, and there are substantial payoffs to be attained, if not from improved public policies, then at least from the joy of knowing.

Chapter 2

The Welfare Economics of Competition and Monopoly

Competition has long been viewed as a force which leads to an optimal solution of the economic problem, just as monopoly has been condemned throughout recorded history for frustrating attainment of the competitive ideal. To Adam Smith, the vital principle underlying a market economy's successful functioning was the pursuit of individual self interest, channelled and controlled by competition. As each individual strives to maximize the value of his own capital, said Smith, he

> ... necessarily labours to render the annual revenue of society as great as he can. He generally, indeed, neither intends to promote the public interest, nor knows how much he is promoting it. . . . [H]e intends only his own gain, and he is in this, as in many other cases, led by an invisible hand to promote an end which was no part of his intention.[1]

Smith's "invisible hand" is the set of market prices emerging in response to competitive forces. When these forces are thwarted by "the great engine . . . of monopoly," the tendency for resources to be allocated "as nearly as possible in the proportion which is most agreeable to the interest of the whole society" is frustrated.[2]

Much of Smith's detailed analysis is obsolete. Yet his arguments on the efficacy of free competition remain intact, a philosophical foundation stone to nations which rely upon competitive market processes to solve their economic problem. Economists have, to be sure, amended their view of competition since the time of Smith, and they have developed more elegant models of how competitive markets do their job of allocating resources and distributing income. One objective of this chapter is to survey these modern views on the nature of and rationale for a competitive market system. In addition, we shall examine some of the qualifications and doubts which have led to the partial or complete rejection of Smith's gospel in many parts of the world.

COMPETITION DEFINED

Let us begin by making clear what is meant by *competition* in economic analysis. Two broad conceptions, one emphasizing the conduct of sellers and buyers and the other market structure, can be distinguished. Adam Smith's widely scattered comments, dealing with both conduct and structural features, typify the dominant strain of economic thought during the 18th and

---

[1] *An Inquiry into the Nature and Causes of the Wealth of Nations* (Modern Library edition), p. 423.
[2] *Ibid.*, pp. 594–595. See also pp. 61, 147, and 712.

8

19th centuries.[3] On the conduct side, competition to Smith was essentially an *independent striving* for patronage by the various sellers in a market. The short-run structural prerequisites for competitive conduct were left ambiguous. Smith observed that independent action might emerge with only two sellers, but it was more likely (i.e., collusion among the sellers was much less likely) with twenty or more sellers.[4] However, competition in Smith's schema also had a long-run dimension which could be satisfied, despite short-run aberrations, as long as it was possible for resources to move from industries in which their returns were low to those in which they could earn comparatively high returns. This in turn depended upon a structural condition: the absence of artificial barriers to resource transfers. Recognizing that resources were often fairly immobile in the short run, Smith and his followers conceded that the full benefit of competitive market processes might be realized only in a long-run context.

As mathematical reasoning began to penetrate economics at the close of the 19th century, a different, essentially structural, concept of competition came to the forefront. In modern economic theory, an industry is said to be competitive (or more precisely, purely competitive) only when the number of firms selling a homogeneous commodity is so large, and each individual firm's share of the market so small, that no individual firm finds itself able to influence the commodity's price significantly by varying the quantity of output it sells. In mathematical jargon, price is a *parameter* to the competitive seller —it is determined by market forces, and not subject to the individual seller's conscious control. The parametric character of price to the competitive firm is fundamentally a subjective phenomenon. If industry demand curves are smooth and continuous, it is not strictly true that a small seller's output changes have *no* effect on the market price. They simply have such a minute effect that the influence is *imperceptible* to the seller, who can therefore act as if the effect were in fact zero.[5]

This technical definition of competition differs markedly from the usage adopted by businessmen who, following Adam Smith's lead, are apt to perceive competition as a conscious striving against other businessmen for patronage, perhaps on a price basis but possibly also (or alternatively) on non-price grounds. Failure to recognize these implied semantic distinctions has often led to confusion in policy discussions. To keep such confusion at a minimum, we adopt the term 'rivalry' to characterize much of the activity businessmen commonly call 'competition.' The essence of rivalry is a striving for potentially incompatible positions (i.e., if Firm A sells 100 units of output to Mr. X, Firm B cannot satisfy that part of X's demand); combined with a clear *awareness* by the parties involved that the positions they seek to attain may be incompatible.[6] Under this dichotomy, it is possible for there to be vigorous rivalry which cannot be called pure competition; the jockeying for position in the automobile market among General Motors, Ford, and Chrysler is an obvious example. At the same time, there can be pure competition without rivalry. For instance, two Iowans growing corn on adjacent farms are pure competitors, but not rivals in the sense implied here. Since the market for corn is so large relative to the two farmers' potential supply, it can readily absorb their offerings with scarcely a ripple in the Chicago Board

[3]For admirable surveys of the development of economic thought on the nature of competition, see George J. Stigler, "Perfect Competition, Historically Contemplated," *Journal of Political Economy*, February 1957, pp. 1–17; J. M. Clark, *Competition as a Dynamic Process* (Washington: Brookings, 1961), Chapters 2 and 3; Paul J. McNulty, "A Note on the History of Perfect Competition," *Journal of Political Economy*, August 1967, Part 1, pp. 395–399; and *idem*, "Economic Theory and the Meaning of Competition," *Quarterly Journal of Economics*, November 1968, pp. 639–656.

[4]*The Wealth of Nations*, p. 342.

[5]This definition is given for the sellers' side of an industry. The definition of buyers' competition is symmetric. Pure competition exists among buyers when the number of entities buying a homogeneous product is so large, and each buyer's share of the market so small, that each buyer believes variations in the quantity he buys have an imperceptible effect on the market price.

[6]For a more extended analysis using different terminology, see Kenneth E. Boulding, *Conflict and Defense* (New York: Harper, 1962), Chapter 1.

of Trade price, and so neither farmer can sensibly consider his neighbor's output decisions as having any perceptible adverse impact on his own economic position.

Violations of the principal structural preconditions for pure competition give rise to a rich variety of sellers' market types. For present purposes it suffices to identify the five most important types, using the following two-way classification based upon the number of sellers and the nature of the product:

Number of Sellers

	One	A Few	Many
Homogeneous Product		HOMOGENEOUS OLIGOPOLY	PURE COMPETITION
	PURE MONOPOLY		
Differentiated Product		DIFFERENTIATED OLIGOPOLY	MONOPOLISTIC COMPETITION

The distinction between homogeneity and differentiation in this classification hinges on the degree of substitutability among competing sellers' products. Homogeneity prevails when, in the minds of buyers, products are perfect substitutes. Products are differentiated when, due to differences in physical attributes, ancillary service, geographic location, and/or subjective image, one firm's products are clearly preferred by at least some buyers over rival products at a given price. The distinguishing trait of a differentiated product is the ability of its seller to raise the product's price without sacrificing his entire sales volume. Obviously, infinite gradations in the degree of product differentiation may exist, and it is difficult in practice to draw a precise line where homogeneity ends and differentiation begins. Similarly, although pure monopoly ends and oligopoly begins when the number of sellers rises from one to two, it is hard to specify on *a priori* grounds exactly where oligopoly shades into a competitive market structure. The key to the distinction is subjective—whether or not the sellers consider themselves conscious rivals in the sense defined earlier. If the sellers are sufficiently few in number so that each believes his

economic fortunes are perceptibly influenced by the market actions of other individual firms, and that those firms are in turn affected significantly by his own actions, then the market can be said to be oligopolistic.

Pure monopolists, oligopolists, and monopolistic competitors share a common characteristic: each recognizes that its output decisions have a perceptible influence on price or, in other words, each can increase the quantity of output it sells under given demand conditions only by reducing its price. All three types of firms possess some degree of power over price, and so we say that they possess *market power* or *monopoly power*.

Homogeneity of the product and insignificant size of individual sellers relative to their market (i.e., atomistic market structure) are sufficient conditions for the existence of pure competition —the only basic structural type under which sellers possess no market power. It is conventional, however, to add several additional characteristics in describing the 'ideal' competitive market of economic theory. When these are present, competition is said to be not only *pure* but also *perfect*.[7] The most important is the absence of barriers to the entry of new firms, combined with mobility of resources employed or potentially employable in an industry. Conversely, significant entry barriers are the *sine qua non* of monopoly and oligopoly, for as we shall see in later chapters, sellers have little or no enduring power over price when entry barriers are non-existent. Other conditions sometimes associated with perfect competition include continuous divisibility of inputs and outputs and perfect knowledge of both present and future market conditions. These are less important, as well as less realistic, for their violation does not necessarily alter the main conclusions generated by the theoretical model of a purely and perfectly competitive market system's operation.

One final terminological point deserves mention, since it is a common source of confusion. The power over price possessed by a monopolist or oligopolist depends upon the firm's size *relative to* the market in which it is operating. It is

---

[7]This distinction is essentially that adopted by E. H. Chamberlin in *The Theory of Monopolistic Competition* (Cambridge: Harvard University Press, 1933), Chapter 1.

entirely possible for a firm to be very small in absolute terms, but nonetheless to have considerable monopoly power. The physician in an isolated one-doctor town is an excellent example. So is the Besser Manufacturing Co., which was found guilty in 1951 of illegally monopolizing the concrete block machinery industry, even though it employed only 465 persons at the time and had sales of less than $15 million.[8] On the other hand, a firm may be enormous in absolute terms, but possess little monopoly power in its principal markets. A good illustration is the Cities Service Oil Company, which had sales of $1.2 billion in 1965, but accounted for less than 3 per cent of U. S. crude petroleum refining. Market power depends upon size relative to the market, not on absolute size, although relative and absolute bigness may of course co-exist. To postulate a 1:1 relationship between monopoly power and absolute size is like confusing pregnancy with obesity. Some superficial manifestations may be similar, but the underlying phenomena could hardly differ more.

THE CASE FOR COMPETITION

We proceed now to the principal questions on our agenda. Why is a competitive market system held in such high esteem by statesmen and economists alike? Why is competition the ideal in a market economy, and what is wrong with monopoly?

POLITICAL ARGUMENTS

We begin with the political arguments for competition, not merely because they are sufficiently obvious to be treated briefly, but also because, when all is said and done, they and not the economist's abstruse models have tipped the balance of social consensus toward competition. One of the most important arguments is that the atomistic structure of buyers and sellers required for competition decentralizes and disperses power. The economic problem is solved through the almost mechanical interaction of supply and demand forces on the market, and not through the conscious exercise of power held in private hands (i.e., under monopoly) or government hands (i.e., under state enterprise or government regulation). Limiting the power of both government bodies and private individuals to make decisions shaping people's lives and fortunes is one of the oldest and most fundamental goals in the liberal ideology, which in turn was the guiding spirit underlying the design of the American governmental system. As Carl Kaysen has observed:

> If the regime of competition and the arguments of *laissez faire* ever commended themselves widely, it has been primarily on political rather than economic grounds. The replacement of the all-too-visible hand of the state by the invisible hand of the marketplace, which guided each to act for the common good while pursuing his own interests and aims without an overt show of constraint, was what attracted general ideological support to the liberal cause.[9]

A closely related benefit is the fact that competitive market processes solve the economic problem *impersonally*, and not through the personal control of big businessmen or bureaucrats. There is nothing more galling than to have the achievement of some desired objective frustrated by the decision of an identifiable individual or group of persons. Who, on the other hand, can work up much outrage about a setback administered by the impersonal interplay of competitive market forces? To illustrate, we need only consider the wrath of President John F. Kennedy in April of 1962, when the chairman of the United States Steel Corporation informed him that U. S. Steel would lead a potentially inflationary price increase. No such anger was displayed over the contemporaneous behavior of the middle Atlantic coast construction industry, where hundreds of decentralized negotiations led to arranged wage bargains which deviated by a much wider margin from the President's anti-inflation guidelines.

---

[8] *U.S.* v. *Besser Mfg. Co.,* 96 F. Supp. 304 (1951); affirmed, 343 U.S. 444 (1952).

[9] "The Corporation: How Much Power? What Scope?" in E. S. Mason, ed., *The Corporation in Modern Society* (Cambridge: Harvard University Press, 1960), pp. 98–99. See also Carl Kaysen and Donald F. Turner, *Antitrust Policy* (Cambridge: Harvard University Press, 1959), pp. 14–18.

A third political merit of a competitive market system is its freedom of opportunity. When the no-barriers-to-entry condition of perfect competition is satisfied, individuals are free to choose whatever trade or profession they prefer, limited only by their own talent and skill and by their ability to raise the (presumably modest) amount of capital required.

THE EFFICIENCY OF COMPETITIVE
MARKETS

Admitting the salience of these political benefits, our main concern will nonetheless be with the economic case for competitive market processes. Figure 2.1 reviews the conventional textbook analysis of equilibrium in a competitive industry (panel [b]) and in a representative firm belonging to that industry (panel [a]). Suppose we begin observing the industry when the short-run industry supply curve is S_1, which in turn embodies the horizontal summation of all member firms' marginal cost curves. The short-run market equilibrium price is OP_1, which is viewed

as a parameter or 'given' by our representative firm, so that the firm's subjectively perceived demand curve is a horizontal line at the level OP_1. The firm maximizes its profits by expanding output until marginal cost (MC) rises into equality with the price OP_1. It produces OX_1 units of output and earns profits equal to the per-unit profit GC_1 times the number of units OX_1. Because economic profits are positive for the representative firm, this cannot be a long-run equilibrium position. New firms will enter the industry, attracted by the profit lure, adding their new marginal cost functions to the industry's supply curve and thereby shifting the supply curve to the right. Entry will continue, expanding industry output and driving the price down, until price has fallen into equality with average total cost (ATC) for the representative firm.[10] In the figures shown, this zero-profit condition emerges with the short-run supply curve S_2, yielding the market price OP_2. The representative firm maximizes its profits by equating marginal cost with price OP_2, barely

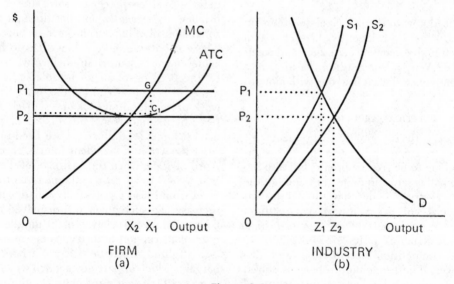

Figure 2.1
Equilibrium under Pure Competition

[10]We assume perfect imputation of all factor scarcity rents here. If the imputation process is imperfect, only the marginal firm—the firm just on the borderline between entering and not entering—will realize zero profits.

covering its total unit costs at the output OX_2.

The long-run equilibrium state of a competitive industry has three general properties with important normative implications:

(a) The cost of producing the last unit of output—the marginal cost—is equal to the price paid by consumers for that unit. This is a necessary condition for profit maximization, given the competitive firm's perception that price is unaffected by its output decisions. It implies efficiency of resource allocation in a sense to be explored momentarily.

(b) With price equal to average total cost for the representative firm, supra-normal economic profits are absent. Investors receive a return just sufficient to induce them to maintain their investment at the level required to produce the industry's equilibrium output efficiently. Avoiding a surplus return to capital is generally considered a favorable result vis-à-vis the equity of income distribution.

(c) In long-run equilibrium, each firm is producing its output at the minimum point on its average total cost curve. Firms which fail to operate at the lowest possible unit cost will incur losses and eventually be driven from the industry. Thus, resources are employed at maximum production efficiency under competition.

One further benefit is sometimes attributed to the working of pure competition, although with less logical compulsion. Because of the pressure of prices on costs, entrepreneurs may have especially strong incentives to seek and adopt cost-saving technological innovations. Indeed, if industry capacity is correctly geared to demand at all times, the *only* way competitive firms can earn positive economic profits is through leadership in innovation. We might expect therefore that technological progress will be more rapid in competitive industries. However, some doubts concerning the correctness of this hypothesis must be raised in a moment.

THE INEFFICIENCY OF MONOPOLY PRICING

Monopolists and monopolistic competitors differ from purely competitive firms in only one really essential respect: they face a downward sloping demand curve for their product. Given this fact of its economic life, the firm with market power knows that to sell an additional unit (or block) of output, it must reduce its price to the customer(s) for that unit; and if it is unable to practice price discrimination (as we shall generally assume, unless otherwise indicated) the firm must also reduce the price to all customers who would have made their purchases even without the price reduction. The net addition to the non-discriminating monopolist's revenue from selling one more unit of output, or its *marginal revenue*, is equal to the price paid by the marginal customer, minus the change in price required to secure the marginal customer's patronage multiplied by the number of units which would have been sold without the price reduction in question.[11] Except at prices so high as to choke off all demand, the monopolist always sacrifices something to gain the benefits of increased patronage: the higher price it could have extracted had it limited its sales only to more eager customers. Marginal revenue must therefore be less than the price paid by the marginal customer. Or to state this vital condition more generally, when demand functions are continuous and smooth, *marginal revenue under monopoly is necessarily less than price* for finite quantities sold. When the monopolist's demand function can be represented by a straight line, marginal revenue for any desired output is given by the ordinate of a straight line intersecting the demand curve where the latter intersects the vertical axis, and with twice the slope of the demand curve, as illustrated in

---

[11]Generally, for the monopolist price is a function $P = f(X)$ of the quantity X sold. Total sales revenue $R = P \cdot X$. Marginal revenue is the change in total revenue associated with a unit change in quantity sold; thus:

$$MR = dR/dX = P + X(dP/dX).$$

P here is the price paid by the marginal consumer, dP/dX is the change in price necessary to attract him (usually with a negative sign); and X corresponds approximately to the quantity which would be sold without the price reduction.

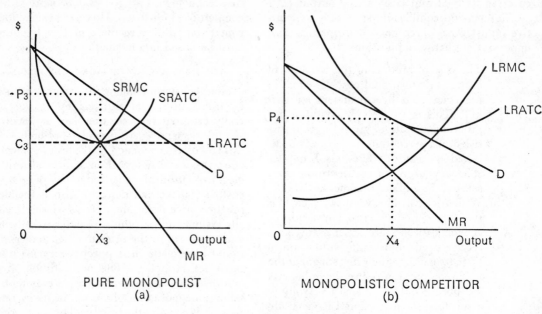

Figure 2.2
Equilibrium under Monopoly

Figures 2.2(a) and 2.2(b).[12] We will normally use straight-line demand curves in subsequent illustrations because they greatly simplify derivation of the associated marginal revenue curves.

Now the profit-maximizing firm with market power will expand its output only as long as the net addition to revenue from selling an additional unit (the marginal revenue) exceeds the addition to cost from producing that unit (the marginal cost). At the monopolist's profit-maximizing output, marginal revenue equals marginal cost. But as long as output is positive, marginal revenue is necessarily less than the monopoly price. Price, therefore, exceeds marginal cost. This equilibrium condition for firms with market power necessarily differs from the competitive firm's equilibrium position. For the competitor, price equals marginal cost; for the monopolist, price exceeds marginal cost. This behavioral difference has important implications to which we shall

return in a moment, after considering some other possible differences between monopoly and competition.

The competitive firm earns zero economic profit in long-run equilibrium. Is the firm with market power different? Perhaps, but not necessarily. Figure 2.2(a) illustrates one out of the many possible cases in which positive monopoly profits are reaped: specifically, the per-unit profit margin P_3C_3 times the number of units OX_3 produced. As long as entry into the monopolist's domain is barred, there is no reason why this profitable equilibrium cannot continue indefinitely. Figure 2.2(b), on the other hand, illustrates the standard long-run equilibrium position of a monopolistic competitor.[13] The crucial distinguishing assumptions are that monopolistic competitors are small relative to the market for their general class of differentiated products, and that entry into the market is free.

---

[12]Proof: Let the demand curve have the equation $P = a - bX$, where X is the quantity demanded. Total revenue $R = P \cdot X = aX - bX^2$. Marginal revenue $dR/dX = a - 2bX$. At $X = O$, $P = MR$. The slope $(-2b)$ of the marginal revenue function is twice the slope $(-b)$ of the demand curve.

[13]Cf. Chamberlin, *op. cit.*, Chapter 5.

Then if positive profits are earned, new firms will squeeze into the industry, shifting the typical firm's demand curve to the left until, in long-run equilibrium, it is tangent to the firm's long-run unit cost function *LRATC*. The best option left for the firm then is to produce output OX_4, where marginal revenue equals marginal cost (as in any monopolistic situation) and the average revenue or price OP_4 is barely sufficient to cover unit cost. Thus, while firms with market power *may* earn monopoly profits, they need not, especially under the plausible conditions of monopolistic competition.

We found earlier that in long-run equilibrium the purely and perfectly competitive firm produces at minimum average total cost. Is this true also of monopoly? Many textbooks imply that it is not, or that it will be true only by accident. Again consider Figure 2.2(a). It assumes that the monopolist operates under constant long-run cost conditions; i.e., that plants (or plant complexes) designed to produce at high outputs give rise to roughly the same cost per unit as those designed to produce at low outputs. We shall see in Chapter 4 that many real-world cost functions exhibit this property over substantial output ranges. If so, the firm will invest in a plant or plant complex characterized by the short-run cost function *SRATC*, with minimum short-run unit costs identical to the minimum long-run unit cost OC_3 at the optimal output OX_3. We conclude that it is perfectly conceivable theoretically and empirically that monopolists will operate in such a way as to minimize average total cost, like their competitive brethren. This is also not necessary, however. Figure 2.2(b) presents the most widely discussed exception. Since the monopolistic competitor in Chamberlinian equilibrium operates with its demand curve tangent to its *LRATC* curve, and since the demand curve is downward sloping, the *LRATC* curve must also have a negative slope at the equilibrium output. It follows that average total cost is *not* minimized, for lower unit costs could be realized by expanding the firm's scale. The monopolistic

competitor does not do so because price (read off the demand curve) falls more rapidly than unit cost beyond the Chamberlinian equilibrium output, so that a higher output would spell negative profits.

In sum, firms with market power may deviate from the zero-profit and minimum-cost conditions associated with purely and perfectly competitive equilibrium, but they need not do so.[14] The only distinction necessarily implied by the pure theory of competition and monopoly is the fact that the monopolist's price exceeds marginal cost, while the competitor's price equals it. This seeming technicality, so trivial at first glance, is the basis of the economist's most general condemnation of monopoly: it leads to an allocation of resources which is inefficient, in the sense of satisfying consumer wants with less than maximum effectiveness.

To see this, we must think more deeply about the meaning of price, as it affects the decisions of a consumer just on the margin between buying one more unit of a commodity and not buying it. A numerical illustration is especially helpful, so let us consider Figure 2.3(a). It assumes that the production of a composite commodity 'manufactured goods' with the demand curve D_M is monopolized. The industry is assumed (for simplicity) to produce under constant cost conditions, with long-run average total cost and marginal cost equal to $5 per unit at any output level chosen. The manufactured goods monopolist maximizes its profits by setting marginal cost equal to marginal revenue, which for the assumed cost and demand conditions requires producing 2 million units and setting a market-clearing price of about $9.70 per unit.

Now in setting this price, the monopolist chokes off the demand of consumers who would have been willing to purchase units (or additional units) at prices below $9.70. Consider some consumer who would purchase an extra unit at $9.60, but not at $9.70. We say that $9.60 is his *reservation price*—the price just low enough to overcome his reservations about purchasing an

---

[14]But firms with monopoly power cannot normally be free simultaneously of both deviations. If they earn zero or negative profits, they will necessarily find it optimal to operate at higher than minimum average total cost. And (ignoring some dynamic complications to be introduced in Chapter 8) if they find it optimal to operate at minimum average cost, they will earn positive monopoly profits.

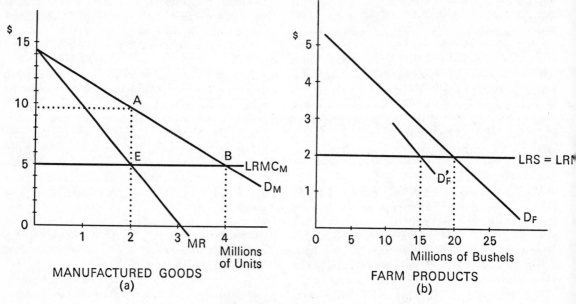

Figure 2.3
Resource Allocation with Competition and Monopoly

extra unit. He buys the extra unit at $9.60 because it is worth that much to him; he refrains from purchasing at $9.70 because he considers the unit not worth the higher price. The consumer's reservation price for any incremental unit of consumption indicates in monetary terms how much that unit is worth to him; it is an index of the value of an extra unit of consumption from the consumer's viewpoint and hence, in a social system honoring consumer sovereignty, from the viewpoint of society.[15]

The extra unit of manufactured goods required to satisfy the demand of this marginal consumer can be produced with resources costing $5. The marginal social value of the extra unit is $9.60. Marginal value exceeds marginal cost, so it would appear eminently worthwhile to produce that unit. The same can be said for all other units of manufactured goods which would be demanded at prices from $9.60 down to $5;

their value to the marginal consumer exceeds their marginal cost, and so they ought to be produced. They are not produced—that is, output is unduly restricted—because the monopolist is unwilling to sacrifice the profits it can secure by charging the higher price ($9.70) and selling fewer units.

Of course, the resources needed to expand production of manufactured goods must come from somewhere, which (assuming full employment) means that consumption of some other end product must be reduced. The problem of efficient resource allocation is a *general equilibrium* problem, involving the balance of all sectors in the economy. Unfortunately, the analysis of general equilibrium takes us between Scylla and Charybdis: the rigorous models lack intuitive appeal and the intuitive models lack rigor. Because it is so important to understand the common sense of monopoly resource allocation, we

[15]Indirectly, the reservation price measures the utility of a marginal unit to the consumer, for when a utility-maximizing consumer is in equilibrium, the price of each commodity included in his market basket equals the marginal utility of that commodity divided by the marginal utility of money.

opt for an intuitive approach here. A more rigorous approach is pursued in the mathematical appendix to this chapter.[16]

Suppose the economy consists of only two industries, a monopolized manufactured goods industry and a competitive farm products industry. Figure 2.3 shows these two industries in general equilibrium, given the assumed demand functions D_M and D_C, constant-cost production conditions in each industry, and the assumed market structures. (Note that the diagrams are not drawn to the same scale.) The output of manufactured goods is (as before) 2 million units per year; the output of farm products 20 million bushels per year. Now suppose we could arrange to transfer resources valued at $100 from the farm products industry to the manufactured goods industry. Since the marginal cost of manufactured goods is $5 per unit, it will be possible to produce 20 extra units with these resources. To sell this extra production, price will have to be reduced infinitesimally—e.g., to $9.699. The value of the extra manufactured output from the viewpoint of marginal consumers barely willing to pay this new, lower price is 20 units $\times$ $9.699 $\cong$ $194. However, the loss of farm products due to the resource transfer must be weighed against this gain. Since the marginal cost of a bushel of farm produce is $2, the transfer of $100 in resources forces society to sacrifice 50 bushels of output. To choke off the demand for this output (at least as a first approximation) the price of farm products must be raised slightly—e.g., to $2.001 per bushel. This reduction in quantity demanded comes at the expense of consumers who were willing to buy an extra bushel at $2 but not at $2.001. Since they would rather abstain from consuming that bushel than pay $2.001, the value of the farm products foregone at the margin must be about $2 per bushel. The total value of farm products sacrificed as a result of the resource transfer is approximately $2 $\times$ 50 bushels = $100. Recapitulating, society (consumers) has benefited from the resource reallocation by a net increase in output value of approximately $194 − $100 = $94.

If it is possible through such a reallocation to increase the value of the overall output bundle, it must follow that the value of output was not maximized in the original (monopoly) equilibrium. Too few resources were allocated to the monopolized sector, and too many to the competitive sector, relative to that allocation which maximizes the value of output to society. Because it leads to an allocation of resources which fails to maximize the value of the overall output bundle, we say that monopoly *misallocates* resources, or that it leads to an *inefficient allocation* of resources.

Obviously, if significant value gains can be made by reallocating $100 worth of resources, additional gains can be achieved by carrying the process further. Let us go all the way, breaking up the manufactured goods monopoly into numerous independent production units and eliminating any barriers to the entry of new resources. With the manufactured goods price initially well above the cost of production, resources will flow (or be drawn) into manufacturing, where the lure of positive profits beckons, and out of farming, where a zero-profit competitive equilibrium prevailed. It might seem that the price of farm products must rise above marginal cost as resources are pulled away and output contracts. This is true as a first approximation, but not as a second, for two reasons. First, a competitive industry simply cannot be in long-run equilibrium if price exceeds cost. Something must give to restore the equality between price and cost. Second, as the price of manufactured goods is reduced to sell an expanding output, a substitution effect in favor of manufactured goods and adverse to farm products is induced. Assuming for the moment that the price of farm products hovers near the marginal cost of $2, the *ceteris paribus* assumption on which the manufactured goods sector's demand function was constructed remains valid, so there will be no shift in D_M. But because of the fall in the manufactured goods

[16]For different approaches to the problem, see William J. Baumol, *Welfare Economics and the Theory of the State* (London: Bell, 1952), Chapters 1–6; M. W. Reder, *Studies in the Theory of Welfare Economics* (New York: Columbia University Press, 1947), Chapters 1–4; and Francis Bator, "The Simple Analytics of Welfare Maximization," *American Economic Review*, March 1957, pp. 22–59.

price there must be a leftward shift in the farm products demand curve—i.e., to D'_F. Temporarily ignoring some complications, let us assume that D'_F represents the final farm products demand curve after all adjustments have taken place, and D_M the manufactured products demand curve. To be in final equilibrium, each competitive industry must have price equal to long-run marginal cost. This implies an output of 4 million units of manufactured goods with a price of $5 per unit, and an output of 15 million bushels of farm products at a price of $2 per bushel. Resources originally valued at $10 million have been transferred from farm products to manufactured goods production, increasing the value of the aggregate output to society by a substantial amount—specifically, by the triangular area ABE in Figure 2.3(a).

Now let us attempt a further reallocation of resources. If we transfer resources valued at $100 from farm products to manufactured goods production, we sacrifice 50 bushels of farm output. These would have been bought by consumers with reservation prices of $2 or slightly higher, so the value of farm output sacrificed is at least $100 and perhaps a bit more. We gain 20 extra units of manufactured goods saleable only at prices slightly less than $5, so the value of the additional manufactured output is less than $100. The value of the output gained is less than the value of the output sacrificed, and thus the transfer reduces the overall value of output to society. If we transfer $100 in resources in the opposite direction, we obtain 50 more bushels of farm output saleable only at prices slightly less than $2, for a gain of less than $100. We give up 20 units of manufactured goods which would have been bought by consumers with reservation prices of $5 or higher, implying a value sacrifice exceeding $100. The value of the output added in the farm sector is less than the value of the manu-

factured goods sacrificed, and so this transfer too reduces the total value of output. Thus, a transfer of resources in *either* direction away from the competitive equilibrium allocation reduces the total value of output. It follows that the value of output must have been at a (local) maximum in competitive equilibrium. Quite generally, when all sectors of an economy are in competitive equilibrium, with price equal to marginal cost for each firm, the total value of the output, measured in terms of each commodity's equilibrium price, is at a maximum. It is impossible to make any small resource reallocations which yield a higher output value. Because it maximizes the social value of output, a fully competitive market system is said to allocate resources efficiently.[17] Because it fails to do so, a system shot through with monopoly elements is inefficient. This, in a nutshell, is the heart of the economic theorist's case for competition and against monopoly.

The analysis thus far has ignored a few complications. To describe the final equilibrium we need a third approximation. One loose end is that the fall in manufactured goods prices increases the real income of all consumers. This income effect will shift both sector demand curves to the right (unless one of the commodities happens to be an inferior good). Monopoly profits are also wiped out, freeing part of the money supply to support these increases in demand.[18] The increased demand for products will be transmitted into increased demand for productive inputs, whose wages will be bid up.[19] This leads to an upward shift in the industry cost functions. With the present model, it is not possible to specify exactly where the final equilibrium will occur, after all these effects have worked their way through the system, and therefore the shifted curves are not shown in Figure 2.3. One thing is certain, however. In each sector price will be equal to marginal cost for every producer, and

[17]It is remarkable how acute Adam Smith's insight was on this point, when he observed that the individual producer in a competitive economy necessarily labors to render "the exchangeable value of the whole annual produce . . . as great as possible." *Wealth of Nations*, p. 423.

[18]Under the previous (second) approximation, payments to all income claimants were $50 million, compared to $59.4 million when the manufacturing sector was monopolized. For monetary equilibrium to be restored, there must either be an input and output price increase, or a contraction of the money supply.

[19]Unless supply functions are perfectly inelastic, the rise in wages will also call forth increased input supplies, which in turn will permit a general expansion of output, *ceteris paribus*.

so no further resource transfers can increase the aggregate value of output. Efficiency in the allocation of resources will have been achieved.

While this end result of eliminating monopoly is clearly desirable, another effect is more difficult to assess. Income will have been redistributed, with former monopoly profit recipients losing and other claimants (such as laborers) gaining. Whether this is good or bad cannot be decided without a value judgment over which reasonable men may disagree. There are at least two reasons for thinking that the competitive equilibrium may be preferred to the monopolistic one on equitable grounds, but the case is not air-tight.[20] First, society may object to monopoly profits as unearned gains and place a high ethical value on seeing them eliminated. The trouble with this objection is that the original builders of the monopoly may already have reaped their gains by selling out their ownership interests at high capitalized values, leaving secondary and tertiary stock-buyers, who are receiving no more than a normal return on their money investment, holding the bag if the monopoly is atomized. Second, the ownership of industrial enterprises is concentrated among a few hundred thousand wealthy individuals. If all persons have similar income utility functions, the marginal utility of income must be higher for the multitudes who supply only their labor services to industry than for the wealthy few with monopoly shareholdings. A redistribution of income away from monopolists and toward labor suppliers will therefore add to total society-wide utility. Still, however appealing this may appear intuitively, there is no scientific way of making the interpersonal utility comparisons required to support the assertion. Therefore, we tread warily when we say that competition is beneficial not only because it allocates resources efficiently, but also in terms of income distribution equity.

This completes the case based upon orthodox economic theory against monopoly and for competition. Some other more institutional criticisms of monopoly can be mentioned briefly. In the absence of competitive pressure, firms may not exercise diligence in controlling their costs and therefore waste resources. As Adam Smith observed, "Monopoly . . . is a great enemy to good management."[21] For similar reasons, monopolists may display a lethargic attitude toward technological innovation and progress, although contrary suggestions will be considered shortly. And finally, firms with market power may engage in wasteful advertising or establish pricing systems which lead to unnecessarily high transportation costs through 'cross-hauling.' These alleged flaws, we shall find, may be even more serious than the resource misallocation problem. It is only for reasons of orderly presentation that we defer a more detailed examination until later.

QUALIFICATIONS AND DOUBTS

General equilibrium analysis reveals the superiority of a competitive market system in solving society's *what* and *how* problems under certain assumptions. But can we expect real-world economies to conform to the assumptions of the theorist's abstract model? Might there not be violations of assumptions stated explicitly or implicitly, or additional considerations not taken into account, which would cause us to modify our judgment? Several qualifications and doubts come to mind.

For one, the whole concept of efficient resource allocation is built upon the fundamental belief that the consumer is sovereign; that individual preferences are what count in the ledger of social values.[22] If, for example, consumers freely choosing in the market demonstrate that they would prefer at the margin to give up 50 bushels of grain to get an additional 20 hair shirts, we conclude that society is really better off because of

---

[20]For another rather involved set of income distribution considerations, see Joan Robinson, *The Economics of Imperfect Competition* (London: Macmillan, 1934), p. 319.

[21]*Wealth of Nations*, p. 147.

[22]For perceptive explorations of the consumer sovereignty issue in welfare economics, see Tibor Scitovsky, "On the Principle of Consumers' Sovereignty," and Jerome Rothenberg, "Consumers' Sovereignty Revisited and the Hospitality of Freedom of Choice," both in *American Economic Review*, May 1962, pp. 262–290.

the transfer. Yet in practice our respect for consumer sovereignty is by no means universal—not, in any event, for infants, convicted criminals, dope addicts, the insane, and others whose preferences cannot be trusted to lead to rational choices. And in this age of widespread neurosis and psychosis, the line between rationality and irrationality is not at all easy to draw. One might even entertain doubts about the soundness of consumption decisions made by presumably normal, rational adults who through ignorance pass up choices which would really yield them higher satisfaction, or whose tastes (assumed in the conventional theory of consumer behavior to be stable) have been remolded under a barrage of advertising messages. Further qualms intrude when we recognize that there are external diseconomies in consumption, i.e., that the purchase of a new hair shirt by Mr. Willoughby may not only increase his utility, but simultaneously reduce the utility of envious neighbors. All this warns us that the theorems of welfare economics which, among other things, assert the superiority of competitive resource allocation are erected upon shaky foundations. This does not mean that their conclusions are wrong. The demonstration of a competitive system's allocative efficiency makes considerable sense even when complications related to advertising, ignorance, and the like are introduced. But blind faith is also uncalled for.

A second common assault on the economist's conventional wisdom holds that only through monopoly can firms be large enough to realize all economies of scale. Under monopolistic (or oligopolistic) organization of an industry, then, costs are lower than they would be if the industry includes many small-scale producers. The consequences are illustrated in Figure 2.4. A monopolist's long-run average total cost curve is assumed to be $LRATC_M$, with associated marginal costs $LRMC_M$. If on the other hand the industry were atomistically structured, with each member firm operating a plant designed to produce OF units of output at a unit cost of OA, the long-run supply curve would be AS_C. Given these assumptions, the profit-maximizing monopolist produces output OX_M, which is higher than the competitive supply OX_C. Clearly, it cannot be

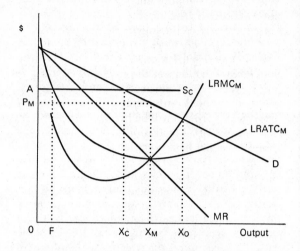

Figure 2.4
Monopoly with Scale Economies

said that consumer demands are satisfied less fully under monopoly in this case than they would be under competition (although resource allocation could be still better if the monopolist could be induced to expand his production to OX_0, where marginal cost is equal to price). By realizing scale economies, the monopolist also conserves resources which inefficiently small competitive firms would require, and which have worthwhile alternative uses elsewhere in the economy. Nevertheless, the conclusion drawn here depends entirely upon the shapes assumed for the monopoly and competitive cost curves. Whether monopolists in fact enjoy such a decided cost advantage (or indeed any at all) is an empirical question. We shall deal with it thoroughly in Chapter 4.

Previously it was suggested that monopolists, sheltered from the stiff gale of competition, might be sluggish about developing and introducing technological innovations which increase productivity (reducing costs) or enhance product quality. Yet some economists, led by the late Professor Joseph A. Schumpeter, have argued exactly the opposite: firms need protection from competition before they will bear the risks and costs of invention and innovation, and that a monopoly affords an ideal platform for shooting at the rapidly and jerkily moving targets of new technology.[23] If this is true, then progress will be more rapid under monopoly than under competition. And it is the rate of technical progress, not the efficiency of resource allocation at any particular moment in time, that in the long run determines whether per capita real incomes will be high or low. Suppose, for purposes of illustration, that real gross national product this year could be $1 trillion under pure and perfect competition, but that the misallocation caused by monopoly elements reduces it at any moment in time by 10 per cent—i.e., to $900 billion this year. Suppose furthermore that a purely competitive economy can sustain growth of 3 per cent per annum, so that in five years the GNP under competition will be $1.16 trillion. How much more rapid must growth be under monopoly to catch up to the competitive potential in five years, starting from the lower monopoly base of $900 million? The answer is, a monopolistic economy growing at 5 per cent will catch up in five years, and it will surpass the competitive system by an increasing margin from then on. Or if a monopolistic economy starting from a 10 per cent static allocation disadvantage could grow at the rate of 3.5 per cent per annum, it would overtake the competitive system in 20 years. If in fact growth is more rapid under monopoly than competition, sooner or later the powerful leverage of compound interest will put the monopolistic system in the lead, despite any plausible starting handicap due to static misallocation. The basic empirical question is, of course, Was Schumpeter right? Is progress really more rapid under monopoly? Orderly presentation demands that we leave the issue unsettled here, returning to it in Chapters 15 and 16.

Another question concerned with dynamic performance is whether monopolistic industry organization might be more conducive to the macroeconomic stability of employment, listed in Chapter 1 as an important performance goal.

It is conceivable that the hair-trigger price adjustments of purely and perfectly competitive markets could intensify tendencies toward instability, making it more difficult to combat the waste and human misery of cyclical unemployment through fiscal and monetary policy measures. If so, a tradeoff between static efficiency and dynamic stability might be required. The economic arguments are too complex to be summarized here, but they will be investigated in Chapters 7 and 13.

The discussion of allocative efficiency has thus far emphasized the monopoly and monopolistic competition cases, studiously ignoring oligopolistic market structures. We now ask, how much competition is necessary to bring prices into rough equality with marginal cost? Will rivalry among the few, or oligopoly, suffice? This turns out to be an extraordinarily difficult question, for the theory of oligopoly pricing does not yield the neat, confident generalizations about price-cost relationships provided by the pure theories of monopoly and monopolistic competition. We shall spend several chapters exploring the theory and evidence on oligopoly pricing before answers can be ventured. In a similar vein is Professor Galbraith's contention that countervailing power —the power of a few large buyers dealing with monopolistic sellers—offers an effective substitute for competition.[24] Market power on the buyer's side and its effects on economic performance will be the subject matter of Chapter 9.

Of all the qualifications to the purely competitive model of resource allocation, the most damaging arises from the theory of monopolistic competition. The monopolistic competitor faces a downward-sloping demand curve, and therefore maximizes his profits at an output which leaves marginal cost below price, because his product is differentiated physically or through service, advertising, location, etc. from the products of other sellers. Our earlier analysis told us that this departure of price from marginal cost is bad in terms of allocative efficiency, and when entry is free, monopolistic competitors in addition end

[23]J. A. Schumpeter, *Capitalism, Socialism, and Democracy* (New York: Harper, 1942), especially pp. 88 and 103.
[24]John K. Galbraith, *American Capitalism: The Concept of Countervailing Power* (Cambridge: Houghton Mifflin, 1952), Chapter 9.

up producing at higher than minimum average cost per unit. But the consumer gets something in exchange: greater *variety* in the available bundle of goods and services. This poses a dilemma. To satisfy the desire for variety, we may have to sacrifice homogeneity of products; but in sacrificing homogeneity, we find each firm facing demand conditions which contribute to resource misallocation. Professor Chamberlin's reaction is devastatingly unambiguous:

> The explicit recognition that product is differentiated brings into the open the problem of variety and makes it clear that *pure competition may no longer be regarded as in any sense an "ideal" for purposes of welfare economics.* In many cases it would be quite impossible to establish it, even supposing it to be desirable. Retail shops, for example, could not all be located on the same spot, and personal differences between actors, singers, professional men, and business men could not be eliminated. But even where possible, it would not be desirable to standardize products beyond a certain point. Differences in tastes, desires, incomes, and locations of buyers, and differences in the uses which they wish to make of commodities all indicate the need for variety and the necessity of substituting for the concept of a "competitive ideal" an ideal involving both monopoly and competition. How much and what kinds of monopoly, and with what measure of social control, become the questions.[25]

Chamberlin is undeniably correct. Consumers *are* willing to sacrifice some allocative nicety for variety, and so the social ideal must be not pure competition but some alloy of pure and monopolistic competition. The question of market organization then becomes a quantitative one: How much purity to sacrifice in order to maximize social welfare? And on this question, economic theory has no operational answers. We know only that the purely competitive model is not ideal, but we do not know how well it serves as an approximation to the ideal.

THE PROBLEM OF SECOND BEST

Having heaped doubt upon doubt, let us advance forthwith to the summit of Mount Agnostica—the problem of second best. Its underlying motivation is as follows: There are many reasons why, in the real world, it is impossible or undesirable to satisfy all the assumptions of the purely competitive general equilibrium model. The desire for variety, and hence the emergence of monopolistic competition, is one. Economies of scale may necessitate monopolistic or oligopolistic industry organization. External diseconomies, such as the air pollution effects of coal-fired electrical generating plants, or external economies, such as the spillover from individual firms' basic research discoveries, cause divergences between private and social costs or benefits, leading the invisible hand astray. Given the fact that competition cannot be pure and perfect in all sectors, what should policy be toward the remaining sectors? With the best economic organization out of reach, is the second best solution to encourage maximum conformity to the competitive model, whenever and wherever we can? The answer suggested by the theory of second best is: Quite possibly not, but it is difficult to say on *a priori* grounds, since the answer depends upon circumstances peculiar to each case.

To put the problem in perspective, we return to Figure 2.3. We assume an economy consisting of two sectors, manufactured goods and farm products. The manufactured goods sector is monopolized; there is misallocation of resources; and we want to improve matters. Suppose, however, that there is no feasible way of breaking up the monopoly, i.e., because of scale economies or a recalcitrant Supreme Court. If something is to be done, it must be done in the farm products sector. What to do? Let us, out of desperation, organize the farmers into a monopoly. The farm price will be raised. This will set off a chain of repercussions. Due to the change in relative prices, a substitution effect will shift the manufactured goods demand curve to

---

[25] *The Theory of Monopolistic Competition*, (Sixth ed., 1948), pp. 214–215 (italics in original). See also his "Product Heterogeneity and Public Policy," *American Economic Review*, May 1950, pp. 85–92; and Lawrence Abbott, *Quality and Competition* (New York: Columbia University Press, 1955).

the right, drawing resources out of the farming sector. Income effects may induce further shifts and price changes; monopoly profits will rise; the wages of some productive inputs will probably fall, shifting marginal cost curves downward, etc. Suppose, after all the necessary adjustments have been made, the economy settles down into the equilibrium illustrated in Figure 2.5. The price of manufactured goods is $7, with 4.25 million units supplied at a cost of $4 per unit; and the price of farm products is $2.80, with 11 million bushels supplied at $1.60 cost per unit.[26]

Now let us try, as before, to increase the aggregate value of the economy's output by further resource transfers. Suppose we transfer resources valued at $160 out of the farm monopoly into manufacturing. This entails a sacrifice of 100 bushels of farm produce (since the marginal cost is $1.60) and a gain of 40 manufactured good units. The additional manufactured goods can be sold only to consumers with reservation prices below $7, and so the value gain must be slightly less than $280. So far, so good. But the farm produce given up has a value to consumers of $2.80 or slightly more per unit, implying a total value sacrifice *exceeding* $280. The value sacrifice exceeds the gain, and hence the transfer is not worth while. It can be seen by similar reasoning that a transfer of resources from manufacturing into farming will reduce the value of output slightly. It follows that the aggregate value of output must be at a (local) maximum in the equilibrium attained by monopolizing both sectors! By abandoning our effort to maintain a world of competition and moving instead to a world of monopolies, we have apparently secured an equilibrium which, like the ideal competitive equilibrium, maximizes the aggregate value of the economy's output.[27]

This happens to be a special case. The curves in Figure 2.5 were constructed so that the ratio of the equilibrium price to marginal cost in the manufactured goods sector (7 to 4) equals the

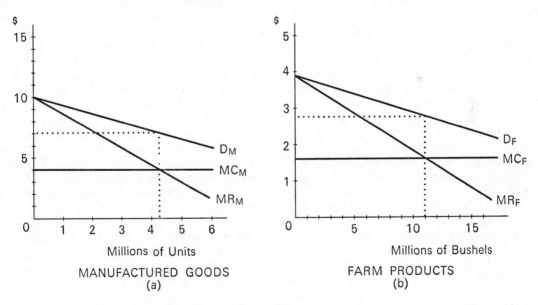

Figure 2.5
Resource Allocation in a World of Monopolies

[26]Marginal costs have fallen by 20 per cent, reflecting a commensurate decline in input wages. The diagrams assume a 13 per cent average decline in the quantity of inputs supplied.

[27]Cf. Joan Robinson, *op. cit.*, Chapter 27.

price/marginal cost ratio in the farming sector (2.80 to 1.60). Quite generally, when the supply of productive inputs is fixed, and when all producers sell their end products directly and only to consumers, it is possible to arrive at a completely efficient (first best) allocation of resources by equalizing the ratio of price to marginal cost for each and every producer. This *rule of proportionality* was proposed by some economists during the 1930s as a possible solution to the monopoly problem, to be enforced by direct government intervention in pricing decisions.[28] Adherence to the rule will follow automatically, even without government intervention, if (as assumed in Figure 2.5) all producers happen to have identical price elasticities of demand at their equilibrium prices.

The odds against the equal elasticities happenstance are so high as to make the possibility unworthy of serious attention. Moreover, enforcing the equal P/MC rule through public authority will also not lead to an efficient allocation of resources under certain highly probable conditions. For one, there are always some commodities which are almost necessarily sold under competitive conditions, frustrating attainment of a true world of monopolies. The most prominent example is leisure. The price of leisure to a typical consumer is the opportunity cost he incurs by not supplying additional hours of labor services—that is, the wage he receives. From the viewpoint of firms, the marginal cost of labor is equal to the wage paid, unless the labor market is imperfect, in which case it exceeds the wage paid. For the world-of-monopolies solution to be achieved, the price of leisure must be raised above the marginal cost of labor services to firms in the same proportion as all other commodity prices exceed their marginal costs. It is extremely difficult to find a practical way of doing this; direct per-hour subsidy payments by the government to each and every worker obviously fail to meet the practicality test. But unless the price of leisure is raised relative to the wage paid by producers, or unless all workers' labor supply curves are completely

inelastic, workers will consume too much leisure and supply too little labor relative to the quantities required for an efficient allocation of resources. In other words, the total quantity of labor supplied, and hence the size of the output bundle available to society, will be smaller under a world-of-monopolies approach to product pricing than it would be if all products were supplied under competitive conditions.

Another complication stems from the elaborate vertical and horizontal interrelationships characterizing any modern economy. Many products are not sold exclusively to final consumers; they are also used in whole or in part by other firms as intermediates. Consider the case of common salt, and assume (merely to simplify matters) that the only scarce basic resource is labor, which receives an equilibrium wage of $2 per hour. Suppose that a hundredweight of salt can be produced using one hour of labor, and that monopolistic salt producers sell their product at $4 per CWT, so that the ratio of price to marginal cost is 2. Suppose in addition that the production of a barrel of pickles requires one CWT of salt (for which $4 is paid) and one hour of labor (for which the pickle-maker pays $2). The combined marginal cost, from the viewpoint of the pickle producer, is $6 per barrel. If the rule of proportionality is enforced, the pickles will be sold at a price twice their marginal cost; that is, at $12 per barrel. But since both salt and pickles enter directly into the market baskets of final consumers, a distortion emerges. Two hours of labor will produce salt valued at $8 by the marginal consumer, or pickles valued at $12. A reallocation of resources (labor) from the production of salt for final consumption to the production of pickles (requiring, of course, more intermediate salt) will raise the aggregate value of output. Thus, applying the 'rule of proportionality' fails to maximize the value of output when the products of individual firms serve as both final consumption goods and intermediates. Analogous difficulties arise when a particular intermediate good enters into the various end products' manufacturing processes at different

[28]See R. F. Kahn, "Some Notes on Ideal Output," *Economic Journal*, March 1935, pp. 1–35; and Abba P. Lerner, "The Concept of Monopoly and the Measurement of Monopoly Power," *Review of Economic Studies*, June 1934, pp. 157–175.

stages, or when the intermediate good accounts for varying proportions of the total cost for different end products.[29]

These and similar problems are assaulted head-on in the general theory of second best.[30] Since the theory does not lend itself readily to geometric presentation, we shall summarize the overall approach and its implications here, saving a full mathematical treatment for the appendix.

The starting point of any second best analysis is recognition that one or more of the conditions necessary for a first best optimum simply cannot be satisfied, i.e., because one sector of the economy is unavoidably monopolistic. In the monopoly case, it is necessary to assume in addition that one or more other sectors must remain competitive, or at least less monopolistic, so that the world-of-monopolies solution is unattainable. These violations of the first best optimum conditions are formulated and introduced as additional constraints upon the problem of maximizing the relevant criterion function—i.e., of maximizing social welfare or the aggregate value of output. The second best problem then is to find a new set of decision rules (e.g., set the price in a controlled sector equal to the marginal cost in that sector, times one plus the weighted average of the percentage differences between price and marginal cost in the violating sectors) which maximizes the value of the criterion function, *given* the violations barring attainment of the first best value as constraints.

The typical result is a set of formidably complex decision rules in place of the simple 'price-equals-marginal-cost' conditions customary in first best problems. Indeed, the general solutions are so complex that it is impossible to deduce unambiguously even the direction in which particular controlled prices should be adjusted in order to improve resource allocation. The main positive generalization reached by Lipsey and Lancaster is that when some first best optimum conditions cannot be attained, it is no longer desirable in general to fulfill the other first best optimum conditions.[31] But the departures called for in any given case depend upon the cost and demand relations particular to that case, and policy-makers are almost never blessed with sufficient information on these relationships to find an actual second best solution. A numerical illustration was computed by Lipsey and Lancaster for a simple monopoly distortion case, suggesting that the price/marginal cost ratio in sectors subject to control for second-best purposes will lie somewhere between the high ratio of the uncontrolled monopoly sector and the unit value of the uncontrolled competitive sector.[32] But this result is definitely not general, and we simply do not know how representative it is of more complex cases involving elaborate chains of substitution and complementarity in consumption and production, inferior goods, intermediate goods, and the like.[33]

Because it states that maintaining competition whenever possible is not necessarily optimal but offers no guidance toward improved policies in the absence of information which cannot be obtained, the theory of second best is a counsel of despair. Still policy decisions must be taken,

---

[29]See Lionel McKenzie, "Ideal Output and the Interdependence of Firms," *Economic Journal*, December 1951, pp. 785–803.

[30]The standard reference is R. G. Lipsey and Kelvin Lancaster, "The General Theory of Second Best," *Review of Economic Studies*, vol. 24, no. 1 (1956), pp. 11–32. An almost simultaneous and similar formulation is found in M. Boiteux, "Sur la gestion des monopoles publics astreints a l'equilibre budgetaire," *Econometrica*, 1956, pp. 22–40. Extensions, interpretations, and criticisms include M. McManus, "Comments on the General Theory of Second Best," *Review of Economic Studies*, June 1959, pp. 209–226; Albert Fishlow and Paul A. David, "Optimal Resource Allocation in an Imperfect Market Setting," *Journal of Political Economy*, December 1961, pp. 529–546; E. J. Mishan, "Second Thoughts on Second Best," *Oxford Economic Papers*, October 1962, pp. 205–217; Otto A. Davis and A. B. Whinston, "Welfare Economics and the Theory of Second Best," *Review of Economic Studies*, January 1965, pp. 1–13; Clarence C. Morrison, "The Nature of Second Best," *Southern Economic Journal*, July 1965, pp. 49–52; L. Athanasiou, "Some Notes on the Theory of Second Best," *Oxford Economic Papers*, March 1966, pp. 83–87; the collection of papers by P. Bohm, T. Negishi, McManus, Davis, and Whinston in the *Review of Economic Studies*, July 1967, pp. 301–331; and C. C. Morrison, "Generalizations on the Methodology of Second Best," *Western Economic Journal*, March 1968, pp. 112–120.

[31]Lipsey and Lancaster, *op. cit.*, p. 11.

[32]See *ibid.*, pp. 21–25.

[33]Large-scale computer simulation of second-best problems might yield useful insights.

and if the data needed for second-best solutions are lacking, rough and ready 'third-best' approximations will at least be better, as E. J. Mishan has advised, than "standing by and sadly sucking our thumbs under the sign of second best."[34]

There seem to be three possible ways out of the dilemma. First, we may search for circumstances under which competitive pricing rules continue to be optimal despite monopoly distortions in other sectors. In general, when there is little or no interdependence between the monopolized sectors and the demand and cost functions of all other sectors, enforcing competitive pricing in the nonmonopolized sectors is probably a good third-best policy. Consider as an example the prescription drug industry, in which notoriously high price/marginal cost ratios (on the order of 10 or more) prevailed for many important products during the 1950s and 1960s. Should the government try to adjust P/MC ratios in other sectors to achieve a better allocation of resources? Probably not, since the economic interdependence between drugs and other sectors (except perhaps the medical services industry) is weak. Prescription drugs are viewed by most consumers as a vital consumption item, and total expenditures on drugs constitute such a small part of the representative consumer's budget that altering the prices of all other commodities would not have much effect on drug consumption.[35] Similarly, drugs are a direct cost input into few other production processes, so vertical resource allocation would not be improved much by the optimal manipulation of non drug prices. Still this case is undoubtedly more the exception than the rule in a modern economy characterized by rich substitution possibilities in consumption and intricate vertical interdependence in production. Relying upon independence is therefore an escape route with only modest payoff potential.[36]

Second, we may conclude that we will never have the information required to deal optimally with particular cases in piecemeal fashion. If so, then the third-best course is to make a choice between alternative *general* policies, trying to adopt that policy which on the average has the most favorable resource allocation implications. In the present instance, the main practical alternatives boil down to letting monopoly increase in sectors not already monopolized vs. attempting to enforce as much competition as we can consistent with economies of scale, product differentiation, etc. When the issue is put this way, the case for competition gains renewed strength. On the positive side, if we have absolutely no prior information concerning the direction in which second-best solutions lie, eliminating avoidable monopoly power is as likely statistically to improve welfare as to reduce it. And on the negative side, it is easy for a policy which is permissive toward monopoly to get out of hand. Too much monopoly distortion may emerge in formerly competitive sectors, especially in view of the fact that some important sectors (such as the labor-leisure market) will by nature remain competitive. Weighing the possible gains from success in approximating a second-best solution against the risks of overshooting the desired degree of monopoly, I am inclined to believe that society will find itself in a superior third-best position on the average under a generally pro-competitive policy.[37]

Finally, one may decide that the whole question of allocative efficiency is so confused and uncertain, once second-best considerations are introduced, that policy-makers should give up trying to achieve the best possible allocation of resources and base their choices on other criteria, such as equity of income distribution, compatibility with political beliefs, conduciveness to production efficiency, and speed of technological progress. This is a step unpalatable to most economists. But if it must be taken, it is worth repeating that the first three alternative

---

[34]Cf. Mishan, *op. cit.*, p. 214.

[35]This is nearly the same as saying that the demand for drugs is highly inelastic with respect to changes in its own price. A pharmacist has estimated privately to the author that roughly one in fifty of his regular customers does without vital prescription drugs because of their high prices.

[36]Economists who have stressed independence of sectors include Davis and Whinston, *op. cit.*; Mishan, *op. cit.*, and W. J. Baumol, "Informed Judgment, Rigorous Theory, and Public Policy," *Southern Economic Journal*, October 1965, pp. 137–145.

[37]For an argument along similar lines, see Athanasiou, *op. cit.*, p. 86.

criteria generally favor a pro-competitive policy. Judgment is reserved on the progress issue until the relevant evidence can be examined.

DOUBTS CONCERNING THE PROFIT MAXIMIZATION HYPOTHESIS

The conclusions of economic theory regarding the allocation of resources and distribution of income under competition and monopoly are based, among other things, on the assumption that consumers strive to maximize their subjective satisfaction and firms seek to maximize profits. During the past three decades the profit maximization assumption has been attacked vigorously on several fronts.[38] The argument, in brief, is that profit maximization is at best unappealing and at worst meaningless to businessmen operating in an environment of dynamic uncertainty, organizational complexity, and conflicting goals. Since these charges emerging from the *managerial theory of the firm* may require modifications in both performance predictions based upon orthodox price theory and value judgments on the desirability of competition as opposed to monopoly, we must pay them careful heed.

THE EFFECTS OF UNCERTAINTY

Nearly all the interesting economic decisions made by business firms require some predictions about near or distant future events. These predictions are inherently uncertain. Decision-makers simply cannot know precisely how strong and how elastic demand will be in the next period, let alone ten years hence, or how far labor unions will carry their struggle for higher wages in forthcoming negotiations, or how rival sellers will react to a price increase, or what the prime interest rate will be next June. How should they behave in the face of these uncertainties? Economic theory usually assumes that businessmen formulate definite expectations about the future values of relevant variables, and then proceed to plug these expectations into their profit-maximizing decision rules. The expectations, presumably, include at least an estimate of the most-likely or best-guess value and perhaps also some notion about the probability of various departures from the anticipated central tendency. This is already assuming a lot. Critics have noted that many businessmen are poorly informed about business conditions in general, know almost nothing about the concept of probability, and understand only crudely the logic of profit maximization (i.e., what variables must be taken into account, such as marginal cost and marginal revenue, and how they must be related to maximize profits). It is hardly realistic to expect that profit-maximizing decisions will sprout through some magic from such barren soil, the skeptics continue. In defense of orthodoxy, Fritz Machlup has argued that businessmen have an *intuitive* understanding of what is required to maximize profits, even though they cannot articulate rules resembling the economist's price-equals-marginal-cost condition, just as automobile drivers who have never taken a course in differential equations are able intuitively to solve the problem of passing another car on a two-lane highway. He goes on to stress a subjective interpretation of the variables manipulated by businessmen:

> It should hardly be necessary to mention that all the relevant magnitudes involved—costs, revenue, profit—are subjective—that is, perceived or fancied by the men whose

[38]The literature is enormous. Especially useful contributions include K. E. Boulding, "The Theory of the Firm in the Last Ten Years," *American Economic Review*, December 1942, pp. 791–802; Fritz Machlup, "Marginal Analysis and Empirical Research," *American Economic Review*, September 1946, pp. 519–554; Andreas G. Papandreou, "Some Basic Problems in the Theory of the Firm," in B. F. Haley, ed., *A Survey of Contemporary Economics* (Homewood: Irwin, 1952), vol. 2, pp. 183–222; R. F. Lanzillotti, "Pricing Objectives in Large Companies," *American Economic Review*, December 1958, pp. 921–940; Herbert Simon, "Theories of Decision-Making in Economics and Behavioral Science," *American Economic Review*, June 1959, pp. 253–283; Edward S. Mason, ed., *The Corporation in Modern Society* (Cambridge: Harvard University Press, 1960); Robin Marris, "A Model of the 'Managerial' Enterprise," *Quarterly Journal of Economics*, May 1963, pp. 185–209; O. E. Williamson, "Managerial Discretion and Business Behavior," *American Economic Review*, December 1963, pp. 1032–1057; R. M. Cyert and J. G. March, *A Behavioral Theory of the Firm* (Prentice-Hall, 1963); Shorey Peterson, Adolf A. Berle, and Carl Kaysen, "Symposium on Corporate Capitalism," *Quarterly Journal of Economics*, February 1965, pp. 1–51; R. J. Monsen and Anthony Downs, "A Theory of Large Managerial Firms," *Journal of Political Economy*, June 1965, pp. 221–236; and John Kenneth Galbraith, *The New Industrial State* (Boston: Houghton Mifflin, 1967).

decisions or actions are to be explained . . . rather than "objective". . . . Marginal analysis of the firm should not be understood to imply anything but subjective estimates, guesses and hunches.[39]

This defense comes close to saying that whatever businessmen choose to do can be called profit maximization, however remotely it resembles the policies an omniscient maximizer would select. Carried so far, the theory of profit maximization becomes little more than tautology.

Yet even if we assume a close correspondence between businessmen's expectations and objective reality, further dilemmas appear. Imagine a decision-maker weighing two alternative policies, one offering a best-guess profit expectation of $1 million with a 10 per cent chance of bankrupting the firm (whose net worth is currently $4 million), the other an expected profit of $2 million with a 30 per cent chance of disaster. Which is the rational choice? It is really impossible to say without further information on the attitudes of the firm's owners toward increases in wealth vs. total loss of their equity. Rational behavior under uncertainty requires some tradeoff between average payoffs and variability of payoffs or, in the statistician's terms, between means and variances. Only the businessman who attaches no significance whatsoever to avoiding risk will always choose alternatives with the highest best-guess payoffs. And such businessmen, empirical studies suggest, are rare specimens.

Further complications are posed by the interactions among uncertainty, risk aversion, and the time horizon of the decision-maker. Economic theory normally assumes maximization of long-run profits; decision-makers are said to maximize the present value of the firm's current and future profit stream. But how far into the future? And at what rate shall future profits be discounted? Should distant profits be discounted more heavily than next year's profits, because the distant future is so much more uncertain? How these questions are resolved in practice—and unanimous agreement is lacking even in normative treatises on managerial economics—can have a substantial impact on conduct and performance in particular markets.

Consider, for example, the following problem. A firm with monopoly power must decide upon its pricing strategy. Because the future is uncertain, it may choose virtually to ignore the future repercussions of its current decisions and reap the highest possible profits it can today. This high-discount rate, short-horizon policy dictates a high price today. Alternatively, the firm may choose not to exploit its monopoly power fully today, hoping that a low current price will cement customer loyalties, increasing the probability that the firm will weather whatever storms the uncertain future holds. Either policy might be defended as the correct path to profit maximization under identical supply, demand, and market structural conditions. The only course open to the analyst confronted by such ambiguities is to amass as much evidence as he can on the attitudes of real-world businessmen toward risk and the future, and on how these attitudes are correlated with market structure. We shall return to this problem when we study the dynamics of industrial pricing behavior in Chapter 8.

Many other ambiguities or departures from the predictions of traditional theory arise because of uncertainty and firms' adaptation to it. Cyert and March, for instance, suggest that firms avoid uncertainty by using decision rules featuring short-run reaction to short-run feedbacks, circumventing the need to anticipate future events.[40] The use of such rules is almost certain to alter pricing behavior. Investment decisions cannot be made in this way, however, because of the long time spans involved in both implementation and realization of returns. Here risk aversion may lead to the rejection of some capital expenditure proposals, retarding the expansion of industry capacity and preventing price from falling to its long-run equilibrium level. But on the other hand, and especially under oligopoly conditions, entrepreneurs may consider a vigorous invest-

[39]Fritz Machlup, "Marginal Analysis and Empirical Research," *American Economic Review,* September 1946, pp. 521–522.
[40]*A Behavioral Theory of the Firm,* p. 119.

ment program the best possible hedge against unforeseeable future challenges, perhaps even carrying their investment beyond the level compatible with long-run competitive equilibrium. Once again, performance hinges on how businessmen react to uncertainty. Or to add one more example which by no means exhausts the list of possibilities, uncertainty about future business conditions may induce firms with market power to hedge by keeping their costs as low as possible (i.e., staying at fighting weight) when they would not be so inclined if the future could be predicted more confidently. Whereas reactions to uncertainty in the previous cases imply departures from strict profit maximization, in this last case risk aversion drives the firm closer to the profit maximization norm.

ORGANIZATIONAL COMPLEXITY

Another feature of the modern business enterprise which may prevent it from behaving in strict conformity to the profit maximization hypothesis is its organizational complexity. Responsibility is typically divided among functional components specializing in production, sales, materials procurement, finance, accounting, research and development, traffic, etc. In a large firm, an elaborate vertical chain of command extends from workers at the operating level to top management and the board of directors, who in turn represent stockholder interests. This whole structure must be tied together by a communication network, so that decisions taken at various levels and in the diverse functional components mesh. It is here that breakdowns occur. Conflicts among functional groups or hierarchical levels are bound to arise, demanding top management resolution. But the information transmission process is subject to attenuation. Top managers cannot possibly digest all the knowledge possessed by every operating-level employee, and so some grasp of special circumstances affecting particular cases must be sacrificed. Furthermore, the content of messages tends to become distorted to suit the prejudices and fears of both senders and receivers. (A production foreman is not, for example, going to tell his plant manager that he cannot enlist the wholehearted support of subordinates. He will

rationalize schedule delays as the result of understaffing. And the market researchers of Ford Motor Company during the 1950s did not question their superiors' basic assumption that the medium-priced car market would remain strong —an assumption which led to the Edsel disaster.) The more hierarchical filters through which information passes, the more distorted the information is likely to become, and the greater is the chance that incorrect decisions will be made. Or in the reverse flow from top management to operating levels, the more filters there are, the more likely misinterpretation or deliberate ignoring of instructions is.

Given this organizational complexity, it may prove very difficult for top management to arrive at and enforce choices which maximize profits, especially when personnel at the operating levels care little about profit maximization and care much about goals which conflict with profit maximization. And such clashes of goals are commonplace. Even the best-designed employee bonus and profit-sharing systems seldom succeed in instilling much zeal for profit maximization below the middle management level, for operating level employees see little correlation between their individual actions and the size of the profit pie in which they will share, just as firms in a competitive industry find their output decisions to have no perceptible effect on the market price. At the same time, these employees have many goals which conflict with profit maximization. Research and development engineers seek technical sophistication and product refinement for their own sake, even when these add more to costs than to revenues. Finance staff personnel oppose profitable investment proposals which threaten the firm's cash position. Production foremen find make-work jobs for redundant personnel to maintain a nice-guy reputation. And so on.

It is the classic responsibility of top management to ferret out these deviations and to establish a system of controls and incentives which ensures internal conformity with the firm's profit maximization goal. Organizational complexity, as we have seen, can cause the attempt to fall short of its mark. But an equally significant obstacle arises out of the very character of the modern business corporation. Like the functional specialists they command, top managers may be less than completely diligent in their stewardship, choosing to pursue goals which conflict with profit maximization.

This happens because, to an increasing degree, the control of American industrial enterprises has become divorced from ownership—a phenomenon to which Adolf A. Berle and Gardiner Means first directed serious attention in 1932.[41] There was a time, a century or more ago, when the individuals managing even the largest firms held, if not a majority, at least a substantial minority ownership interest in those companies. Gradually, this has changed. Big business has become bigger; the lion's share of all industrial output is produced by firms big by any reasonable definition of the word; and the ownership of large corporations has been dispersed among thousands of stockholders, no one of whom may own a sufficiently large proportion of the outstanding common stock to exercise a dominant controlling role. General Motors had 1.39 million stockholders in 1968. The median (250th) firm in terms of stockholder numbers on *Fortune*'s list of the 500 largest U. S. industrial corporations for 1956 recorded more than 9,000 shareholders. In their path-breaking study, Berle and Means found 88 of the 200 largest U. S. nonfinancial corporations to be "management controlled" in 1929 because no individual, family, corporation, or group of business associates owned more than a 20 per cent share of all outstanding voting stock, and because evidence of control by a smaller ownership group was lacking.[42] Only 22 of the 200 corporations were privately owned or controlled by a group of stockholders with a majority interest. Updating the Berle and Means analysis, R. J. Larner discovered that 169 of the

200 largest nonfinancial corporations had come to be management controlled by 1963, with no single ownership group holding 10 per cent or more of the outstanding voting stock. Out of the 200, only five were controlled by a majority ownership group.[43]

In a few of the corporations classified by Berle and Means and Larner as "management controlled," individuals or families holding one or two per cent of the stock have been able to obtain board of directors seats and to exercise significant influence on company decisions. But in a majority of the largest corporations, no stockholder group has such leverage, and by default management may possess considerable autonomous power to pursue its own goals. Top management personnel sit on the board of directors, often as a majority. Managers have a substantial and frequently decisive say in the nomination of non-management board members, and normally these nominations are validated by an overwhelming margin as stockholders docilely assign their proxy statements. The board of directors in turn approves management's recommendations on new managerial appointments and replacements. Through this process of reciprocal self-selection, the management group perpetuates its control.

As always, we must be wary of oversimplifying. There are constraints on managerial autonomy even in corporations with widely dispersed ownership. As we shall elaborate in the next chapter, substantial blocks of stock have come into the hands of mutual investment funds and banks serving as trustees for diverse individual stockholders or pension funds. When crises or proxy contests materialize, these financial intermediaries may wield decisive voting power. In more normal times they may quietly take the

[41] *The Modern Corporation and Private Property* (New York: Macmillan, 1932).

[42] *Ibid.*, pp. 90–118. Other studies of the separation of ownership and control prior to World War II include Raymond W. Goldsmith, *The Distribution of Ownership in the 200 Largest Nonfinancial Corporations*, Temporary National Economic Committee Monograph No. 29 (Washington: 1940); and R. A. Gordon, *Business Leadership in the Large Corporation* (Washington: Brookings, 1945). Both reach conclusions similar to those of Berle and Means.

[43] Robert J. Larner, "Ownership and Control in the 200 Largest Nonfinancial Corporations, 1929 and 1963," *American Economic Review*, September 1966, pp. 777–787. For slightly lower estimates, see Jean-Marie Chevalier, "The Problem of Control in Large American Corporations," *Antitrust Bulletin*, Spring 1969, pp. 163–180. See also Robert Sheehan, "Proprietors in the World of Big Business," *Fortune*, June 15, 1967, p. 179, who estimates that 150 industrial corporations on *Fortune*'s list of the 500 largest for 1966 were controlled by ownership groups with 10 per cent or more of the common stock outstanding.

initiative in prodding management to change its ways. A tradition of reticence and legal restrictions have limited the control which banks and other financial institutions have exercised over internal corporate decision-making, but as the volume of their holdings increases, their influence cannot help but rise accordingly.[44] It is uncertain, however, whether this additional element of control divorced from any conventional ownership role will necessarily channel managerial energies more consistently in profit-maximizing directions, or whether it might tolerate or even encourage some departures from profit maximization.

Another possible check on managerial autonomy is the threat of a raid or take-over by an acquisition-hungry outsider.[45] Take-overs used to be rare events, but in the late 1960s they proliferated so rapidly that management groups in both large corporations and small felt distinctly threatened. Again, the central issue for our present purposes is how these threats affect managerial behavior. They could stimulate profit maximization if companies which failed to take advantage of their profit-making opportunities were more vulnerable than others to successful raids. Three characteristics of corporations singled out for raids during the 1960s were slow earnings growth, high internal liquidity, and low dividend payout ratios. Of these, the first two might well be associated with failure to maximize profits. On the other hand, fear of a take-over could induce management to avoid risky investments, to seek sales growth for its own sake, and to adopt panicky defensive measures detrimental to long-run profits. Or managers might come to believe that take-over

attempts are so capricious there is little they can do to modify their behavior in a way which minimizes the threat, in which case their choices between profit maximization and non-maximization will be largely unaffected. We have little solid evidence on the relative frequency of these possible reactions. More research on the effects of financial intermediary intervention and take-over threats on managerial behavior is sorely needed.

THE MULTITUDE OF MANAGERIAL GOALS

Within certain imprecisely defined bounds, then, management may be free to pursue goals not necessarily consistent with maximizing stockholder earnings. What are these goals? How seriously do they conflict with profit maximization? These are key issues in the separation of ownership and control debate.

First, however, we must inquire whether firms as organizations can be said to have unambiguously defined goals at all. It is not clear in theory whether individuals with divergent preferences can somehow fuse those preferences into a consistent set of organizational goals.[46] Students of organizational behavior have suggested two ways out of this problem. First, it has been proposed that firms as organizations do not maximize the attainment of some well-defined objective function, but instead 'satisfice'—that is, seek choices which satisfy at least minimum levels of aspiration with respect to their several objectives.[47] For example, management may set a target rate of return on invested capital as its profit objective, and if that target is achieved, it turns to the satisfaction of other (nonprofit) objectives.[48] This satisficing hypothesis is far from universally accepted

---

[44]For a discussion of the substantial power German banks wield, see Philip Siekman, "Germany Catches Its Second Wind," *Fortune*, April 1969, pp. 147–148.

[45]A pioneer in recognizing the potential impact of take-overs on managerial behavior was Marris, *op. cit.* In a statistical exploration of the Marris hypotheses, D. A. Kuehn found that British corporations were more likely to be subjected to take-over raids if the market value of their common stock was depressed relative to the net book value stated in corporate accounts. "Stock Market Valuation and Acquisitions: An Empirical Test of One Component of Managerial Utility," *Journal of Industrial Economics*, April 1969, pp. 132–144.

[46]See Kenneth J. Arrow, *Social Choice and Individual Values* (New York: Wiley, 1951), for an analysis of paradoxes in democratic group decision-making; and Cyert and March, *op. cit.*, pp. 26–44, for a more general discussion of organizational goal formation.

[47]Cf. Simon, *op. cit.*, pp. 262–265; and Cyert and March, *op. cit.*, p. 10.

[48]Cf. R. F. Lanzillotti, "Pricing Objectives in Large Companies," *American Economic Review*, December 1958, pp. 921–940; Jesse W. Markham's review of a related book, *American Economic Review*, June 1959, pp. 262–263; and the comment by Alfred E. Kahn, *American Economic Review*, September 1959, pp. 671–676.

among economists, mainly because it is not evident how the targets are set in the first place and how they are modified dynamically in response to over-fulfillment or under-fulfillment. A second, related conjecture is that firms avoid facing up to goal conflicts by proceeding sequentially, satisfying one objective at a time before considering the fulfillment of others.[49] Still it is questionable whether the hard choices necessitated by a multitude of wants and a scarcity of means can be persistently dodged through any such technique. At this point we can only conclude that we know far too little about the methods of goal formation and conflict resolution within large organizations. It is clear at any rate that business managers are pulled in many directions, and that they must and do make choices among alternative objectives.

One possible departure from the direction of profit maximization is to seek a placid, comfortable, risk-free business existence. As J. R. Hicks put it in a much-quoted quip, "The best of all monopoly profits is a quiet life."[50] Such a characterization does considerable justice to the archetypal European businessman of past generations. Whether it reflects the psychology of his American counterpart or the new European generation is dubious.

Much closer to the mark is the assertion that managers without a significant ownership interest seek security of tenure in their jobs. The security motive does not necessarily conflict with profit maximization; a manager who keeps the profits rolling in is, after all, a good person to have around. Yet conflicts do arise, especially in decision-making under uncertainty. As Professor Fellner has pointed out, there tends to be an asymmetry in the rewards to managers.[51] If risky decisions turn out badly, stockholders lose their assets and managers their jobs. If they turn out well, the manager may be promoted or re-

ceive a bonus, but his rewards are seldom proportional to the stockholders' gains. Faced with this asymmetry, the hired manager is more apt to sacrifice higher expected profits for lower risk than an owner-manager under otherwise identical circumstances. A related manifestation is the hired manager's preference for lower, more stable earnings over high but fluctuating earnings, since minority stockholders may rise up and demand management changes in response to sharp profit declines whose end they cannot foresee due to their limited knowledge of company plans and prospects. Or, raiders may see a stock price slump as the signal to take over a corporation and, if successful, perhaps to reorganize its management.

Being human, most hired managers derive considerable satisfaction from achieving personal prestige and power. Both seem to be correlated more closely with the volume of a firm's sales than with the size or rate of profits it earns. Consequently, growth of sales for its own sake is a goal frequently attributed to hired managers.[52] In the static theory of the firm, maximizing sales is incompatible with maximizing profits except under improbable circumstances (i.e., when marginal cost is zero). In a dynamic context the conflict between sales growth and profitability is much less sharp, but increases in growth beyond some point must impose profit sacrifices as management's ability to control is over-strained, low-payoff investment projects are approved, and high-cost sources of capital funds are tapped. Whether the captains of management-controlled enterprises overstep this margin is an empirical question. There is some persuasive evidence (reviewed subsequently) that they do.

Statistical analyses reveal that the compensation (salaries plus bonuses) of top executives in large American corporations is somewhat more

[49]Cyert and March, *op. cit.*, pp. 35–36 and 118.

[50]"Annual Survey of Economic Theory: The Theory of Monopoly," *Econometrica*, January 1935, p. 8.

[51]William Fellner, *Competition Among the Few* (New York: Knopf, 1949), pp. 172–173.

[52]For various views, see Edith T. Penrose, *The Theory of Growth of the Firm* (Oxford: Blackwell, 1959); William J. Baumol, *Business Behavior, Value, and Growth* (Rev. ed.; New York: Harcourt, Brace & World, 1967), Chapters 5–10; Robin Marris, "A Model of the 'Managerial' Enterprise," *Quarterly Journal of Economics*, May 1963, pp. 185–209; and J. Williamson, "Profit, Growth and Sales Maximization," *Economica*, February 1966, pp. 1–16.

closely correlated with sales volume than with profits.[53] This is another reason why hired managers may find it worthwhile to sacrifice some profits in order to accelerate sales growth. Nor are executives necessarily content merely to enhance their direct pecuniary rewards at the expense of stockholders. They may also gain utility from empire-building and surrounding themselves with lavish office accommodations. Case studies by Oliver Williamson disclosed the existence in large corporations of considerable "managerial slack"—expenditures on staff and executive services which could be eliminated without any apparent adverse effect on production.[54] Such unnecessary expenditures may be quite large relative to total profit volume. In one case reported by Williamson, a curtailment of discretionary spending led to an increase in the affected firm's return on investment from 4 to 9 per cent.

Finally, managers may be motivated by the simple desire to do good—to pay their employees handsome salaries, to provide pleasant working conditions, to give consumers a square deal on price and product quality, to support worthwhile philanthropic and community causes, etc. All this is perfectly respectable, even if it does involve some sacrifice of profits, and it is clear that many closely-held corporations without an ownership-control separation problem have moved in the same direction. But if carried too far, corporate altruism can sabotage the market mechanism's functioning, for resources may be misallocated when price and wage signals are generated by managerial fiat rather than through the interplay of genuine market forces.[55]

To sum up, there is no shortage of ways in which businessmen *may* deviate from the behavioral norm assumed in the economist's pure theory of the firm. Nevertheless, an important counterforce has to be taken into account. Most large corporations have stock option plans which permit their top managers to realize substantial capital gains as earnings and stock prices rise. The share of the corporation's total outstanding common stock involved is typically minute, but for the participating manager, stock option gains often constitute a sizeable fraction of total compensation and (given an income tax structure preferential to capital gains) they quite possibly offer the only opportunity he has to amass a fortune. How completely stock option incentives counteract the temptation to depart from profit maximization is not known. It seems probable, however, that option plans have a really potent behavioral impact only at the very top of the managerial hierarchy, where the link between individual action and corporate gain is most immediate. At lower levels, where most day-to-day operating decisions are made, we should expect the lure of alternative managerial goals to be more compelling.

HOW MUCH DISCRETION DO FIRMS HAVE?

Several questions remain to be answered. How serious are the deviations induced by nonprofit goals? How much discretion do firms, owner-controlled and manager-controlled, have to pursue objectives other than profit maximization? And what are the implications of nonmaximization for the policy choice between competition and monopoly?

The work of illuminating these issues with hard evidence has barely begun. Three studies

[53]D. R. Roberts, *Executive Compensation* (Glencoe: Free Press, 1959); J. W. McGuire et al., "Executive Incomes, Sales, and Profits," *American Economic Review*, September 1962, pp. 753–761; and "For the Chief, Sales Set the Pay," *Business Week*, September 30, 1967, p. 174.

[54]"Managerial Discretion and Business Behavior," pp. 1051–1053; and Cyert and March, *op. cit.*, pp. 237–252. For similar evidence relating to the rather special case of defense contracting, see F. M. Scherer, *The Weapons Acquisition Process: Economic Incentives* (Boston: Harvard Business School, 1964), especially pp. 239–247 and 320–325.

[55]See Eugene V. Rostow, "To Whom and for What Ends Is Corporate Management Responsible?" in Mason, *op. cit.*, pp. 59–69; Milton Friedman, *Capitalism and Freedom* (Chicago: University of Chicago Press, 1962), pp. 133–136; and Fritz Machlup, "Corporate Management, National Interests, and Behavioral Theory," *Journal of Political Economy*, October 1967, pp. 772–774. Also apropos is Adam Smith's cynical comment, "I have never known much good done by those who affected to trade for the public interest." *Wealth of Nations*, p. 423.

deserve mention. Monsen, Chiu, and Cooley found for a sample of 72 carefully matched corporations that profit returns on stockholders' equity between 1952 and 1963 were about 75 per cent higher in owner-controlled firms than in manager-controlled entities, industry specialization being held constant.[56] There is reason to suspect that their sample is not completely representative, however, and since the differences in return on total assets and sales were much smaller for alternate control forms, it is conceivable that the degree of owner control affects financial structure decisions more than operating behavior. In a parallel study covering various subsamples of the 200 largest nonfinancial corporations, Kamerschen found a similar tendency toward higher profits in the owner-controlled as opposed to management-controlled firms, *ceteris paribus*, although the observed profit differences were not statistically significant.[57] Changes in the type of control between 1929 and 1963—in most instances, from owner to manager dominance—did show a significant *favorable* impact on profits —the opposite of what one might anticipate on *a priori* grounds. As in the Monsen work, however, Kamerschen's sampling approach leaves something to be desired, as do some of his variable definitions. A more limited but better controlled study by Shelton revealed that identical branch restaurants of a large chain were much more profitable when run by franchisee-owners than by hired managers, and that profits almost always increased with a change from hired manager to owner operation, while they fell with a change in the opposite direction.[58] Taken together, these studies provide a modest quantum of support for the hypothesis that profit maximization is pursued less diligently when ownership and management are divorced. Much more research

on the problem remains to be done, however.

A related issue is whether the pursuit of nonprofit goals goes so far as to invalidate the profit maximization hypothesis of theory. When driven into the trenches on this point, economists resort to the ultimate weapon in their arsenal: a variant of Darwin's natural selection theory.[59] Over the long pull, there is one very simple criterion for the survival of a business enterprise: profits must be nonnegative. No matter how strongly managers prefer to pursue other objectives, and no matter how difficult it is to find profit-maximizing strategies in a world of uncertainty and high information costs, failure to satisfy this criterion means ultimate disappearance from the economic scene. Profit maximization is therefore promoted in two ways. First, firms which depart too far from the optimum, either deliberately or by mistake, will disappear. Only those which do conform, knowingly or unknowingly, will survive, and if the process of economic selection is allowed to continue long enough, the only survivors will be firms which did a tolerably good job of profit maximization. The economic environment adopts the profit maximizers and discards the rest. Second, knowledge that only the fit will survive provides a potent incentive for all firms to *adapt* their behavior in profit-maximizing directions, learning whatever skills they need and emulating organizations which experience visible success in the survival game.

To be sure, the selection process operates a good deal less than perfectly. The environment is constantly changing, altering the behavior required for survival, so that adaptations learned today may not serve tomorrow. On the other hand, adaptation by industry members may be sufficiently slow to permit firms performing less than optimally to keep their heads above

[56]R. J. Monsen, John S. Chiu, and David E. Cooley, "The Effect of Separation of Ownership and Control on the Performance of the Large Firm," *Quarterly Journal of Economics*, August 1968, pp. 435–451.

[57]David R. Kamerschen, "The Influence of Ownership and Control on Profit Rates," *American Economic Review*, June 1968, pp. 432–447. Similar results were obtained by Robert Larner in his unpublished Ph.D. dissertation, "Separation of Ownership and Control and Its Implications for the Behavior of the Firm," University of Wisconsin, 1968.

[58]John P. Shelton, "Allocative Efficiency vs. 'X-Efficiency': Comment," *American Economic Review*, December 1967, pp. 1252–1258.

[59]The leading discussions are Armen A. Alchian, "Uncertainty, Evolution, and Economic Theory," *Journal of Political Economy*, June 1950, pp. 211–221; and Sidney G. Winter, "Economic 'Natural Selection' and the Theory of the Firm," *Yale Economic Essays*, Spring 1964, pp. 225–272.

water for a long time. Winter has demonstrated that even under conditions of pure competition, behavior which conforms only in special cases to the profit-maximizing norm may be consistent with survival.[60] Companies which satisfice, searching for optimal actions only when competitive pressures are unusually intense, are apt to be especially viable. And of course, if no firms in the industry happen to conform to the optimal pattern, the selection process can bog down altogether, for there will be no 'fit' to expand, multiply, and drive out the less fit.

Despite these qualifications, it seems reasonable to believe that the natural selection process is a stern master in a competitive environment. That it will work equally well under monopoly does not follow. If natural selection is to function in the economic sphere, its activating mechanism must be the competitive challenge of firms better adapted to their environment and opportunities. But when firms with market power are shielded by entry barriers, product differentiation, government favoritism, and the like, threats to their survival may be sufficiently blunted that they can survive for decades without ever maximizing profits or minimizing costs. On this point there is little dispute. The crucial question is, how sheltered from the forces of natural selection are firms with market power? How far can they depart from profit-maximizing rules and still remain viable? Here substantial differences of opinion appear.

One viewpoint is represented by Carl Kaysen, who writes:

> While the firm in the highly competitive market is constrained to seek after maximum profits, because the alternative is insufficient profit to insure survival, the firm in the less competitive market can choose whether to seek maximum profit or to be satisfied with some "acceptable" return and to seek other goals. . . . The more dominant the position of any particular firm in a single market . . . ,

the wider will be its range of significant choice.[61]

Shorey Peterson, on the other hand, has argued that profit margins are not large even for firms with undisputed market power, and that in a world of constant change and uncertainty, the Darwinian compulsion to strive for the maximum is no less applicable to such firms:

> The compelling constraint—obvious, but often forgotten—is that the firm's health, indeed its survival, depend on the relation within it of revenues and costs. Total revenues and total costs are large magnitudes in relation to the profit residual, so that management must be occupied overwhelmingly in keeping the elements in them moving in the right direction. . . . Competitors, though few, seem unrelenting; the commercial life of products is uncertain; capital needs, it is thought, must be met from profits; unions and public agencies threaten; so that both the feasible maximum seems lower and the minimum higher than in the outside view. What is feasible, moreover, cannot be divorced from conditions of efficiency, and it is hard to proceed vigorously toward the goal of not making too much money.[62]

The disagreement here is on an issue of fact: how much discretion firms with market power subjectively consider themselves to have. It cannot be resolved here, and we shall return repeatedly to aspects of the problem. At this point it is useful merely to add one fragment of evidence. In a study of some 30 firms leading their industries in sales for the years 1953, 1957, and 1961, Oliver Williamson found top executive compensation to be strongly and positively correlated with two indices of monopoly power, after taking into account differences in company profits and general and administrative expenses.[63] The more monopolistic the firms were, *ceteris paribus*, the more handsomely they paid their

[60]*Ibid.*, pp. 256–264.

[61]"The Corporation: How Much Power? What Scope?" in Mason, *op. cit.*, p. 90.

[62]"Corporate Control and Capitalism," *Quarterly Journal of Economics*, February 1965, pp. 9 and 16. See also Kaysen's counter-argument in the same issue, pp. 42–44.

[63]"Managerial Discretion and Business Behavior," pp. 1040–1047.

chief executive. This result lends support to the view that ability to pursue goals other than profit maximization increases with monopoly power.

IMPLICATIONS

From such theory and evidence, we can conclude with some confidence that firms with market power are not likely on the average to deviate *less* from profit maximization than competitive firms. If anything, we should expect them to depart further, as Williamson's results suggest. Tentatively assuming this to be so, we can identify three implications pertinent to the policy issue of monopoly vs. competition. First, to the extent that costs (especially marginal costs) are higher under monopoly than competition because monopolists pay excessive salaries, hire too large a staff, etc., monopolistic restriction of output will be even more serious than the pure theory of profit maximization predicts. On the other hand, monopolistic output restriction might be mitigated if managers tried to expand sales beyond the profit-maximizing level to enhance their personal power and prestige. How these potential effects balance out remains uncertain. Second, the amount of sheer resource waste will almost surely be higher under monopoly than competition. And third, to the extent that managers of monopolistic firms vote themselves salaries and fringe benefits exceeding what is required to call forth their services, income will be redistributed away from stockholders toward the managerial class. Since this involves a redistribution from one typically high income group to another, it is not obvious whether equity suffers or gains.

WORKABLE COMPETITION

We return now to our original question: How valid is the competitive ideal as a prescription for economic policy? Given all the qualifications and doubts unearthed in the foregoing pages,

extreme confidence in the purely and perfectly competitive model as a blueprint for Utopia is hardly in order. We may even experience an impulse to return to the womb—to Adam Smith's crude vision of how the market economy does its job. Smith was wrong in numerous details, but details of the system may be much less important than the broad scheme of operation. If one stands back and gazes astigmatically at the competitive model without worrying about the fine points, he sees that it does display generally greater responsiveness of product supplies to consumer demands, and it generates a more potent set of incentives for the frugal use of resources, than does the monopoly model. This, rather than the satisfaction of all optimal conditions in a general equilibrium system of 43 billion equations, may be the core of the case for competition.

Comparable doubts concerning the competitive model's utility as a policy guide prompted a search during the 1940s and 1950s for more operational norms of "workable competition." The coiner of this phrase was J. M. Clark, who observed in his seminal paper that perfect competition "does not and cannot exist and has presumably never existed" and that the competitive model of theory affords no reliable standard for judging real-world conditions.[64] Clark went on to argue that some departures from the purely and perfectly competitive norm are not as harmful in a long-run context as was commonly supposed and to formulate certain minimal criteria for judging the workability of competition. The criteria he chose were influenced by the depression psychosis of the times and are less important than the impact Clark's work had in stimulating other economists.

The result was an explosion of articles on workable competition, many in substantial disagreement with one another. We shall not attempt to review the literature here, since the job has been done admirably by Stephen Sosnick.[65]

[64] "Toward a Concept of Workable Competition," *American Economic Review*, June 1940, pp. 241–256. Extensions by Clark include "Competition: Static Models and Dynamic Aspects," *American Economic Review*, May 1955, pp. 450–462; and *Competition as a Dynamic Process* (Washington: Brookings, 1961), especially Chapters 2–4.

[65] "A Critique of Concepts of Workable Competition," *Quarterly Journal of Economics*, August 1958, pp. 380–423. See also C. E. Ferguson, *A Macroeconomic Theory of Workable Competition* (Durham: Duke University Press, 1964), especially pp. 26–31 and 48–82.

It suffices to outline some criteria of workability suggested especially frequently by diverse writers. Using Sosnick's scheme, these can be divided into structural, conduct, and performance categories.

Structural norms include the following:

(1) The number of traders should be at least as large as scale economies permit.
(2) There should be no artificial inhibitions on mobility and entry.
(3) There should be moderate and price-sensitive quality differentials in the products offered.

Conduct criteria include:

(4) Some uncertainty should exist in the minds of rivals as to whether price initiatives will be followed.
(5) Firms should strive to achieve their goals independently, without collusion.
(6) There should be no unfair, exclusionary, predatory, or coercive tactics.
(7) Inefficient suppliers and customers should not be shielded permanently.
(8) Sales promotion should not be misleading.
(9) Persistent, harmful price discrimination should be absent.

Last, we have a number of *performance criteria:*

(10) Firms' production operations should be efficient.
(11) Promotional expenses should not be excessive.
(12) Profits should be at levels just sufficient to reward investment, efficiency, and innovation.
(13) Output levels and the range of qualities should be responsive to consumer demands.
(14) Opportunities for introducing technically superior new products and processes should be exploited.
(15) Prices should not intensify cyclical instability.

(16) Success should accrue to sellers who best serve consumer wants.

While the items in this list are clearly unobjectionable, the list as a whole may be criticized for redundancy. In particular, the first two criteria might be considered a watered-down statement of the requisites for pure competition which if satisfied will lead almost automatically to satisfaction of most of the other criteria.

More fundamentally, critics of the workable competition concept have questioned whether the approach is as operational as its proponents intended.[66] On many of the variables, a line must be drawn separating enough from not enough or too much. How moderate should quality differentials be? When are promotional expenses excessive, and when not? How long must price discrimination persist before it is persistent? And so on. Value judgments can hardly fail to enter such determinations. Furthermore, fulfillment of many criteria is difficult to measure. For instance, to determine whether firms' production operations have been efficient, one needs a yardstick calibrated against what is possible; but the boundaries of what is possible may never have been probed in practice, and so the analyst must resort to subjective estimates. (This objection may be skirted if accurate international comparisons can be made, or if private and nationalized enterprises operate in the same field.) Finally and most important, how should the workability of competition be evaluated when some, but not all, of the criteria are satisfied? If, for example, performance but not structure conforms to the norms, should we conclude that competition is workable, since it is performance which in the end really counts? Perhaps not, because with an 'unworkable' market structure there is always a danger that future performance will deteriorate. If stress *is* placed on performance, what conclusion can be drawn when performance is good on some dimensions (such as technical progressiveness) but not on others (such as the level of promotional expenditures)? Here a decision cannot be reached without introducing subjective value judgments about the importance of

---

[66]See Sosnick, *op. cit.*, pp. 391–415; and Carl Kaysen and Donald F. Turner, *Antitrust Policy* (Cambridge: Harvard University Press, 1959), 53–56.

various performance dimensions. And as Professor Stigler warns with characteristic cynicism, embarrassing disagreements may result:

> To determine whether any industry is workably competitive, therefore, simply have a good graduate student write his dissertation on the industry and render a verdict. It is crucial to this test, of course, that no second graduate student be allowed to study the industry.[67]

Stigler's pessimism gains some support from scattered cases in which two students have simultaneously analyzed performance in the same industry and come to quite different conclusions. Still these may have been flukes, and the question of how significantly value biases affect performance judgments when performance is multidimensional has not been given the scientific attention it deserves. The only known systematic attempt to explore such a question yielded more hopeful results. A panel of 44 experts was asked to render paired comparisons judgments on the quality of the principal contractors' performance in eight widely differing military aircraft and guided missile research and development programs.[68] The level of agreement among the 44 judges proved to be fairly substantial, and the principal reasons for disagreement could be isolated. Some of the programs (notably those nearest the median) experienced performance which differed little by any reasonable set of criteria, and it was on these programs that the strongest disagreements appeared. It was also possible to determine through correlation analysis the subdimensions of overall performance to which the judges assigned the highest weight. Specifically, success in meeting the government's time schedule proved to be much more important than either cost control or magnitude of technical achievement.[69] There is no reason why similar methods could not be used to judge the workability of competition generally, and on particular performance dimensions, for a broad cross section of industries. Until some such attempt is made, we shall remain in the dark about the lethality of attacks on the workable competition concept.

One other approach to assessing the workability of competition must be mentioned. As an alternative to evaluating industry structure and performance against predetermined norms, some of which may be unattainable, Jesse Markham has proposed that:

> An industry may be judged to be workably competitive when, after the structural characteristics of its market and the dynamic forces that shaped them have been thoroughly examined, there is no clearly indicated change that can be effected through public policy measures that would result in greater social gains than social losses.[70]

Although this approach encounters the same measurement and value judgment difficulties as the more conventional methods, it does have the merit of focusing attention constructively on the policy problem of prescribing appropriate remedial actions.

CONCLUSION

Readers seeking a precise, certain guide to public policy are bound to be disappointed by this survey, for we have found none. The competitive norm does seem to serve as a good first approximation, but it is difficult to state *a priori* how much competition is needed to achieve desirable economic performance, nor can we formulate hard and fast rules for identifying cases in which a departure from competition is desirable. We therefore begin our journey into the following chapters with only a primitive map. Let us hope that we can avoid going too far astray, and end with experience useful in drawing a better map.

---

[67]Comment, *American Economic Review*, May 1956, p. 505.

[68]M. J. Peck and F. M. Scherer, *The Weapons Acquisition Process: An Economic Analysis* (Boston: Harvard Business School, 1962), pp. 543–580.

[69]Such an experiment covering 14 U. S. industries was under way as a Ph.D. dissertation by Steven Cox at the University of Michigan in late 1969.

[70]"An Alternative Approach to the Concept of Workable Competition," *American Economic Review*, June 1950, pp. 349–361.

Chapter *3*

The Structure of U. S. Industry

We begin our exploration of structure – conduct – performance links by surveying some structural features of modern industrial economies, with emphasis on the United States. In this chapter we cover four main facets of industry structure: the extent to which the economy as a whole is dominated by large firms, the extent to which particular markets are dominated by one or a few sellers, the extent to which firms are diversified across numerous product lines, and the degree to which firms are vertically integrated. Our main concern in this volume is with monopoly power, to which the second (market domination) dimension of structure is most closely related. In the present chapter we nevertheless take a more sweeping view which encompasses structural dimensions interacting with the orthodox bases of monopoly power. At the same time we shall neglect certain important aspects of market structure—notably, the height of entry barriers, the extent of product differentiation, and the degree of buyer concentration. These are handled more conveniently in later chapters.

THE POSITION OF THE LARGEST CORPORATIONS

Bigness and monopoly power are, as we have stressed previously, not necessarily synonymous. Still sheer size can complicate the economic performance problems associated with monopoly, and one may well be apprehensive on social and political grounds about the share of economic activity controlled by large corporations. It repays some labor, therefore, to examine the impressive position of the very largest industrial enterprises.

And impressive it is. In 1968, there were more than 1.5 million incorporated business enterprises operating in the United States, along with roughly 10 million sole proprietorships and partnerships. Yet a very few firms towered over all the rest. The biggest of the big in terms of both assets and employment was the American Telephone & Telegraph Company. Its 1968 assets of $40 billion represented four per cent of the assets of all nonfinancial corporations; its work force of 856,000 (including subsidiaries) exceeded the populations of eleven states of the Union and was almost as large as the industrial labor force of Austria, Switzerland, Sweden, or Mexico. The manufacturing corporation with the largest sales, General Motors, employed nearly as many workers (757,200) and had 1968 sales of $23 billion, but its assets amounted to only a paltry $14 billion. (Standard Oil of New Jersey, the largest manufacturer in terms of assets, had $16.8 billion in assets.)

Although A.T.&T. and General Motors are by most measures almost twice as large as their nearest neighbors in the industrial corporation size hierarchy, the neighbors are hardly small. In 1964 there were 325 nonfinancial corporations with assets valued at $250 million or more. These 325 firms controlled 42 per cent of the assets of all U. S. nonfinancial corporations. A further breakdown of the concentration of asset owner-

Table 3.1

The Percentage of All Corporate Assets Accounted for in 1964
by Corporations with Assets of $100 Million or More

Sector	Number of Corporations (All Sizes)	Sector Share of 1965 GNP*	Corporations With:			
			Assets Exceeding $100 Million		Assets Exceeding $250 Million	
			Number	Share of All Sector Assets	Number	Share of All Sector Assets
All nonfinancial corporations	1,249,446		739	50.6%	325	42.1%
Agriculture, forestry, and fisheries	25,933	3.7%	2	6.9	1	4.6
Mining	14,487	2.1	30	45.0	10	26.0
Construction	104,134	4.5	5	4.4	1	1.1
Manufacturing	184,961	28.9	393	61.3	171	51.0
Transportation, communications, electric and gas	56,338	8.8	214	84.6	118	75.5
Wholesale and retail trade	421,553	16.4	61	18.8	21	13.4
Services	176,902	10.4	17	10.1	3	2.8
Real estate	259,656	10.5	17	3.8	0	0
Banking, finance, and insurance	124,071	3.1	1,019	65.9	407	54.6

Source: U.S. Treasury Department, Internal Revenue Service, *Statistics of Income: 1964,* "Corporate Income Tax Returns, with Accounting Periods ended July 1964–June 1965" (Washington: 1969), Table 6.
*Includes contributions of unincorporated businesses and government.

ship by industrial sectors is given in Table 3.1. In the transportation-communications-electricity-gas, banking,[1] and manufacturing sectors, more than half of all corporate assets are controlled by firms with assets of $100 million or more. On the other hand, the construction, real estate, agriculture, and services sectors are the domain of enterprises relatively small as bigness in business goes.

Any analysis of this sort is affected by the choice of a size measure, since some measures show more concentration than others. To illustrate, in 1963 the 100 largest manufacturing corporations (ranked on the basis of value added in manufacture) accounted for the following shares of all domestic manufacturing activity on various dimensions:

Total domestic employees	25 per cent
Total domestic payroll	32 per cent
Value added in manufacture	33 per cent
Sales of domestic establishments	34 per cent
Assets of domestic establishments	36 per cent
After-tax profits	43 per cent[2]

[1] Asset sizes in banking and finance are not comparable with those in other sectors, since it is easier to put together and manage a large portfolio of financial assets than a large aggregation of physical assets. Also, financial enterprises must be segregated from nonfinancial corporations to avoid double counting, since a high fraction of financial firms' assets consists of claims against the assets of nonfinancial corporations.

[2] The data on employment, payrolls, sales, and value added are based on the 1963 census of manufactures and appear in U. S. Senate, Committee on the Judiciary, Subcommittee on Antitrust and Monopoly, Report, *Concentration Ratios in Manufacturing Industry: 1963* (Washington: 1966), p. 2. The asset figure was estimated

Employment is much less concentrated in the hands of the largest manufacturing corporations than value added and sales, which in turn are less concentrated than total assets and profits. This seems to be so for four main reasons. First, as a comparison of payroll and employment shares reveals, the largest corporations tend to pay higher salaries and/or wages. Second, the leading producers in particular industries on the average employ more capital-intensive production processes than their smaller compatriots. Third, the list of the 100 largest manufacturing corporations includes a disproportionate number of large petroleum refining firms which are much more capital-intensive than the typical manufacturing firm. And fourth, the largest firms evidently enjoy sufficient market power and/or scale economies to realize significantly higher profit margins.

Given these divergences, the analyst must choose with care his index of *aggregate concentration*—i.e., his measure of how large a share of economic activity the largest firms contribute. Value added is undoubtedly the best all-around indicator, since it takes into account the contributions of labor, capital, and the factors yielding supra-normal profits, giving each its due weight. But unfortunately, value added data comparable on a year-to-year or company-by-company basis are seldom available. Sales data serve as a tolerable substitute, especially for intercompany comparisons, as long as the degree of vertical integration does not vary too widely. However, the most common choice criterion is purely pragmatic: one uses the variable on which one can obtain the highest quality data, or maximum comparability, relevant to his hypotheses.

CHANGES IN AGGREGATE CONCENTRATION OVER TIME

The data problem becomes especially acute when we tackle the interesting question of trends over time in the aggregate concentration of manufacturing activity. A century ago, manufacturing was still predominantly the province of the relatively small firm serving local markets, and manufacturing industry was much less concentrated in the aggregate than it is today. (Transportation, on the other hand, already showed signs of growing dominance by large corporations.) At the time, Karl Marx stood alone among well-known economists in predicting that big business would come to dominate the industrial scene. This development Marx attributed to the corporate form of organization, then acquiring its modern trappings, and to the interaction of scale economies and bitter competition. "One capitalist always kills many," said Marx, leading to a "constantly diminishing number of the magnates of capital, who usurp and monopolise all advantages of this process of transformation."[3] The limit to the process was a state in which "the entire social capital would be united, either in the hands of one single capitalist, or in those of one single corporation," although Marx did not explicitly assert that the ultimate limit would ever be attained.[4]

During the next 60 years, the industrialized economies of the world evidently moved a considerable distance toward fulfilling Marx's prediction. It is less clear what has happened since then. The first systematic attempt to study trends in aggregate concentration was by Adolf Berle and Gardiner Means.[5] Using the best data

---

by assuming an aggregate production function of the Cobb-Douglas form with capital and labor shares of 30 and 70 per cent, respectively. The profit figure was estimated by assuming the same relationship between assets and profits as a Federal Trade Commission study found for 1962. See the testimony of W. F. Mueller in U. S. Senate, Committee on the Judiciary, Subcommittee on Antitrust and Monopoly, Hearings, *Economic Concentration* (hereafter cited by the short title *Economic Concentration*), Part 1 (Washington: 1964), p. 115.

None of the estimates above is comparable with the other estimates presented in this chapter, because the present estimates exclude sales, employment, assets, and profits of U. S. firms' overseas subsidiaries. Inclusion of overseas magnitudes leads to substantial changes in the leading firms' shares, since smaller firms have less extensive overseas subsidiary operations. For instance, the top 100 firms accounted for 38 per cent of all manufacturing sales when sales of overseas subsidiaries are included, compared to 34 per cent without.

[3] *Capital* (trans. by Ernest Untermann; Chicago: Kerr, 1912), vol. I, p. 836.

[4] *Ibid.*, p. 688. See also the more general discussion in Paul M. Sweezy, *The Theory of Capitalist Development* (New York: Monthly Review Press, 1942), pp. 254–269.

[5] *The Modern Corporation and Private Property* (New York: Macmillan, 1932).

they could secure, they discovered that the assets of the 200 largest nonfinancial corporations were growing considerably more rapidly on the average between 1909 and 1929 than the assets of all corporations taken together. Without committing themselves to a prediction of what would in fact occur, they noted that *if* the observed disparity in growth rates continued, the 200 largest nonfinancial corporations would account for 70 per cent of all industrial activity by 1950 and for practically all industrial corporation assets by 1972.[6] Obviously, this did not happen. Whether the extrapolation failed because of deficiencies in the original trend data, as some critics have charged,[7] or because the trend toward increasing aggregate concentration has abated since 1929, is a crucial but still unsettled question.

The most careful attempt to derive estimates comparable for benchmark years has been made by Gardiner Means. After consolidating balance sheets to ensure that the assets of subsidiaries in which a firm held a 50 per cent or greater common stock interest were included as part of the parent firm's assets, Means estimated that the 100 largest manufacturing corporations controlled 40 per cent of all manufacturing corporation assets in 1929, 44 per cent in 1933, and 49 per cent in 1962.[8] To obtain a more complete picture of the intervening time pattern, additional data from several sources have been adjusted and spliced into the Means series, using 1962 as the benchmark year.[9] The results are presented in Figure 3.1. From it we see that aggregate concentration has not been rising in an unbroken trend. By 1947, the share of the largest 100 manufacturers had dropped significantly below the level reached during the depths of the 1930s depression. The sharp rise in concentration between 1929 and 1933 was due to the greater vulnerability of smaller firms to financial crises of the times, while small corporations were apparently able to regain ground in the strong sellers' market following World War II. As the postwar boom faded, the largest firms began gaining again, moving from 40 per cent control of all manufacturing corporation assets in 1947 to 47 per cent in 1955. Since then the upward movement has been more gradual. We get the overall impression of a moderate upward trend, marred by deviations associated with sharp changes in business conditions.

That the concentration of manufacturing activity increased over the interval studied by Means has been disputed by Morris Adelman.[10]

Adelman's main argument is that any comparison of asset data between the 1930s and the 1960s is inherently uncertain because of changes in accounting for consolidations, depreciation, and stock watering. Means made a valiant effort to correct for the consolidation problem, but it is possible that biases of unknown magnitude have crept into his comparisons for other reasons. Using assumptions and data differing from those of Means, Adelman estimated that the share of all manufacturing corporation assets controlled by the 117 largest concerns actually declined from 45.6 per cent in 1933 to 44.6 per cent in 1960.[11] In contrast, Means found an increase for the top 100 firms from 44 per cent in 1933 to 49 per cent in 1962. While Means' data were apparently collected and adjusted with greater caution than Adelman's, the fact that different assumptions may lead to divergent estimates demonstrates the need for skepticism.

Nevertheless, Adelman clearly erred by implying that a comparison of the depressed 1930s with the moderately prosperous late 1950s is

[6]*Ibid.*, p. 40.

[7]See, for example, Edwin B. George, "Is Big Business Getting Bigger?" *Dun's Review*, May 1939.

[8]See his testimony in *Economic Concentration*, pp. 15–19 and 281–324.

[9]See the testimony of W. F. Mueller and John Blair in *ibid.*, pp. 120–123 and 203–207; and the Federal Trade Commission estimates in *Studies by the Staff of the Cabinet Committee on Price Stability* (Washington: January 1969), p. 92. The asset concentration estimates from the Mueller and Blair studies (and also those reported in Table 3.1) are lower than Means' figures mainly because Means has attempted to include the assets of controlled subsidiaries. Thus, Mueller's estimate of concentration for the top 100 in 1962 without consolidation is 45.7 per cent; Means' estimate after consolidation is 49 per cent.

[10]See his testimony in *Economic Concentration*, pp. 225–227, 234–240, and 339–341.

[11]*Ibid.*, pp. 236 and 339. See also his "The Measurement of Industrial Concentration," *Review of Economics and Statistics,* November 1951, pp. 285–290.

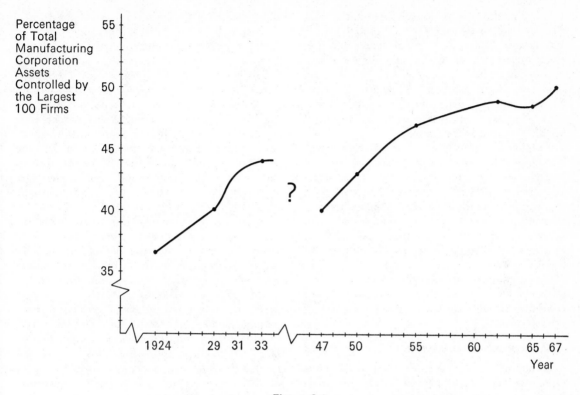

Figure 3.1
Estimated Changes in the Concentration of Manufacturing
Corporation Asset Control: 1924 to 1967

valid. In 1933, the share of the largest corporations was abnormally high. It is more meaningful to compare two relatively prosperous years, such as 1929 and 1962. When this is done, we find that the largest firms' share increased by 3 or 4 percentage points if Adelman's benchmark estimates are employed, even if not by the 9 percentage point margin found in Means' study. The rise in the relative position of the largest firms stands in even bolder relief when it is measured on the basis of *all* manufacturing assets, and not just the assets of manufacturing corporations. In 1929, about 10 per cent of all manufacturing assets were held by unincorporated enterprises; by 1962, the unincorporated firms' share had fallen to 1.8 per cent. Given these changes, we discover that the 100 largest manufacturing firms' share of all manufacturing assets rose between 1929

and 1962 by about 12 percentage points under Means' assumptions (e.g., from 36 per cent to 48 per cent) or by about 7 percentage points under Adelman's assumptions.

We still cannot be absolutely certain that the position of the largest corporations in the *domestic* economy has trended upward significantly. All the data used in these intertemporal comparisons include assets of foreign subsidiaries. The largest corporations have much higher investments abroad relative to their size than all other corporations, and therefore their share of all American manufacturing firms' assets is higher when overseas assets are included than when they are excluded. It is probable also that U. S. firms had higher investments abroad relative to their total assets in the period following World War II than they did around 1929 and

1933. Therefore, it is conceivable that a sub-stantial fraction of the apparent growth of the 100 largest firms' share of all manufacturing assets reflects those firms' expanding position in foreign markets, and not solely increasing dominance of the domestic manufacturing sector. No satisfactory evidence on this point has been marshalled, so we must remain in the dark until further research is conducted.

Despite these uncertainties, one thing is clear. The increasing domestic dominance of the 100 largest manufacturing firms since 1947 is no statistical illusion. We have excellent data from four censuses and a survey of manufactures, showing that the 100 largest producers' share of *value added* in manufacturing rose from 23 per cent in 1947 to 30 per cent in 1954, 30 per cent in 1958, 33 per cent in 1963, and 33 per cent in 1966, paralleling the upward movement of asset shares.[12] To learn whether this trend (?) will continue, we eagerly await the next exciting census episode.

AGGREGATE CONCENTRATION IN OTHER COUNTRIES

Is the role of big business in the United States typical or atypical, compared to other industrial-ized nations? The information on aggregate con-centration abroad is even more limited than U. S. data, but a few crude comparisons can be hazarded. All are based upon *Fortune* magazine's list of the 200 largest industrial companies out-side the United States, compiled annually since 1956 from published statements and private estimates of international business specialists.

One conclusion which stands out is that the biggest business in the United States is bigger by far than its nearest counterpart abroad. No pri-vate manufacturing firm overseas approaches the size of General Motors; the largest in terms of employment (Unilever) employs only a third as many people. Below this level the comparison is more even, if any matching of one nation against the rest of the world can be called even. There were 83 U. S. firms with sales exceeding $1 billion in 1967, compared to 38 abroad. But sales

data bias the comparison in favor of the United States, with its generally higher price and wage levels at prevailing currency exchange rates. When employment is taken as the size criterion, the balance tips: there were at least 68 firms abroad with 50,000 or more employees in 1967, compared to 51 industrial corporations in the United States. As one might expect, the heaviest concentration of big firms is found in the largest, most industrialized nations. England led the 1967 list with 53 out of the 200 largest foreign industrials; Japan was second with 43, Germany third with 26, France fourth with 23, and Canada fifth with 11.

A crude comparison of the degree to which industrial employment is concentrated among large firms in the United States and leading foreign nations can be made by combining *Fortune*'s lists with information from other sources.[13] There were 54 British firms on *For-tune*'s list for 1963. They employed approxi-mately 35 per cent of all workers in British manufacturing and mining occupations. The 54 largest U. S. corporations (by sales) on *Fortune*'s list for the same year accounted for 27 per cent of all U. S. manufacturing and mining employ-ment. This suggests that employment is some-what more concentrated in Great Britain. The comparison is misleading, however, since the British estimate is strongly influenced by in-clusion of the National Coal Board—a national-ized amalgamation of many formerly private mines, which in its consolidated form was Europe's largest employer. If the Coal Board is excluded, the remaining 53 largest British firms provide 29 per cent of all United Kingdom in-dustrial employment, compared to 27 per cent for the 53 largest American corporations. There were 33 German firms on *Fortune*'s 1963 list, responsible for 23 per cent of all manufacturing and mining employment in West Germany. This compares closely with the 33 largest U. S. firms' 22 per cent share of manufacturing and mining employment. The 25 French firms listed (in-cluding at least three nationalized enterprises)

[12]U. S. Senate, *Concentration Ratios in Manufacturing Industry: 1963, loc. cit.;* and U. S. Bureau of the Census, *Annual Survey of Manufactures: 1966*, "Value of Shipment Concentration Ratios by Industry," supplement to M66(AS)-8 (Washington: 1968).

[13]Notably, from the United Nations *Statistical Yearbook*, the International Labor Organization *Yearbook*, and various United Kingdom statistical abstracts.

employed 16 per cent of France's manufacturing and mining work force, compared to 18 per cent for the 25 largest U. S. industrials. The 37 Japanese firms accounted for only 11 per cent of all Japanese manufacturing and mining employment, compared to 23 per cent for the 37 largest American industrials.

Taking these estimates at face value, we find that, compared to an equal number of leading firms in the United States, industrial employment is somewhat more concentrated among large firms in Great Britain, at about the same level of concentration in Germany, slightly less concentrated in France, and much less concentrated in Japan. It is worth noting that the longer the nations in this small sample have enjoyed what Rostow calls technological maturity in their industrial sectors,[14] the more concentrated employment appears to be—a relationship to which we shall return in the next chapter.

Nevertheless, there is reason to believe that the data are less than perfectly comparable. Overseas subsidiaries are probably responsible for a higher fraction of the reported employment of the leading U. S. corporations than for the largest German, French, and Japanese firms, and so the comparisons tend to overstate the relative degree of U. S. domestic employment concentration. Viewed in this light, the concentration of industrial activity in the United States does not appear to be out of line with levels found in smaller but similarly industrialized nations. Still it is doubtful whether the foes of big business will rest easier, knowing that domination of industrial activity by a handful of large firms is not just a local phenomenon.

CONCENTRATION OF CONTROL THROUGH INTERLOCKING FINANCIAL TIES

The comparisons presented thus far may also mislead for another reason. Control over the activities of ostensibly independent firms may become concentrated further through interlocking financial and managerial ties. Consider, for instance, the case of Japan. We have estimated that the 37 largest Japanese industrial firms in 1963 hired only 11 per cent of all Japanese manufacturing and mining workers. But many of these and other smaller firms are linked together in *Zaibatsu* (literally, money clique) relationships. Before World War II, four Zaibatsu families with ownership interests in dozens of operating enterprises controlled a fourth of all paid-in capital in Japanese industry and finance.[15] The American occupation authorities instituted a Zaibatsu dissolution program after the war, but in recent years the old Zaibatsu firms have begun to reassemble through intercorporate stockholdings and strong financial affiliations with Zaibatsu banks. According to Eugene Rotwein, the three leading Zaibatsu groups in 1960 controlled 7.4 per cent of the paid-in capital of all Japanese corporations, if only firms with very close interrelations are counted, or 17.3 per cent if firms with weak and uncertain Zaibatsu ties are included.[16] From this, it is clear that the 37 firm – 11 per cent estimate substantially understates the actual degree to which the control of Japanese industry is concentrated.

A smaller nation, Sweden, provides an even more striking example. During the 1960s, eight of the 10 largest industrial firms were controlled by one family through strong minority stockholdings and family banking connections.[17] A still different form of concentration exists in France, where one wealthy capitalist—the central government—owns nearly a fourth of all manufacturing industry.[18]

Intricate ties among seemingly independent corporations are also found in the United States, although typically in more subtle form and on a less spectacular scale. Three main types of intercorporate linkage are of interest: control by

---

[14]Walt W. Rostow, *The Stages of Economic Growth* (Cambridge: Cambridge University Press, 1961), especially p. 59.

[15]A further discussion of Zaibatsu relationships before the war follows in Chapter 11.

[16]"Economic Concentration and Monopoly in Japan," *Journal of Political Economy*, June 1964, p. 268. On similar family ties in India, see Irene Till and Carl H. Fulda, "Concentration and Competitive Potential in India," *Antitrust Bulletin*, Fall 1968, pp. 1000–1006.

[17]"The 'Wallenberg Boys'—and How They Grew," *Business Week*, February 25, 1967, pp. 116–122.

[18]"Gaullists Call the Shots in Business, Too," *Business Week*, January 14, 1967, p. 96.

family groups, control by financial intermediaries, and interlocking directorates.

A survey made during the 1930s turned up several prominent examples of multi-corporation control by family groups possessing either majority or substantial minority stockholdings.[19] The du Pont family, through its various holding companies, owned roughly 25 per cent of the stock of the du Pont Company and about 20 per cent of the United States Rubber Company's stock. The du Pont Company in turn held a 23 per cent common stock interest in General Motors. To the Rockefeller family and its philanthropic institutions could be traced stock interests ranging between 7 and 24 per cent in six of the largest petroleum refining companies, along with the largest single share interest in the Chase National (now Chase Manhattan) Bank. The Mellon family had dominant ownership positions in the Gulf Oil Corporation, Alcoa, the Mellon National Bank, the Koppers Co., and the Pittsburgh Coal Co., as well as weaker affiliations with several other major corporations (including Westinghouse Electric). Since the 1930s, the control of these groups has been gradually attenuated as stock was distributed among multiplying heirs, as the heirs sold some of their shares to pay inheritance taxes, and as the corporations issued additional common stock to meet growing capital needs. The Mellon family's one-time majority interest in Gulf and Alcoa, for instance, has apparently eroded into a 25 to 30 per cent minority position.[20] Another important change came when a 1962 antitrust judgment required the du Pont family to eliminate its dominant ownership position in General Motors. As a result, the concentration of corporate control in a few family groups is probably not as extensive as it was three decades ago, although the evidence needed for a more precise assessment of the current situation is not readily available.

Another source of concentrated control—and one which is likely to become increasingly important in the future—is the stockholdings of financial intermediaries. In 1966, corporate pension funds, mutual stock funds, insurance companies, and other institutional investors owned more than 20 per cent of the common stock shares listed on the New York Stock Exchange, and Exchange officials predicted that this figure will rise to 30 per cent by 1980.[21] The proportion of any given firm's outstanding stock which these investors may acquire is generally limited by state and federal regulations. Still it is now commonplace for large institutional investors to become the principal minority stockholder in corporations with widely dispersed ownership, and from this position to compel management to listen carefully when they speak. During 1966, for example, the Fidelity Management and Research Co. of Boston, manager of ten mutual funds, held from 5 to 15 per cent of the outstanding common stock of 27 different corporations, including several firms (such as Raytheon, Sanders Associates, and General Precision Equipment) which are direct competitors in certain product lines.[22] Fidelity's 9 per cent stock interest in Metro-Goldwyn-Mayer was sufficient to determine the outcome of a 1967 proxy battle. An even larger (but in the case of pension funds, partly overlapping) mass of securities—more than $250 billion, or roughly one fourth the combined value of all state, local, and federal government debt plus the market value of all stocks and bonds listed on the New York Stock Exchange—was managed by the trust departments of commercial banks. A House of Representatives committee found that trust departments were using their fiduciary discretion to invest, among other things, in both their own stock and the stock of competing financial institutions.[23] The power to vote shares held in trust carries with it the power to influence the

---

[19]See U. S. National Resources Committee, *The Structure of the American Economy*, Part I (Washington: 1939), pp. 160–163 and 306–317.

[20]Charles J. V. Murphy, "The Mellons of Pittsburgh," *Fortune*, October 1967, pp. 121–122.

[21]"Big-Block Buyers May Speak Up," *Business Week*, November 26, 1966, p. 139.

[22]"The Mutual Funds Have the Votes," *Fortune*, May 1967, p. 151.

[23]U. S. House of Representatives, Banking and Currency Committee, Subcommittee on Domestic Finance, Report, *Bank Stock Ownership and Control* (Washington: 1966); and *Commercial Banks and Their Trust Activities: Emerging Influence on the American Economy*, two volumes (Washington: 1968).

decisions of company managements. An incomplete survey uncovered 33 instances of anti-management proxy votes by large bank trust departments in a single year.[24] That this power is in the hands of a relatively few trust officers clearly reduces the independence of firms which at first glance appear free of any unified control.

Interlocking directorates provide still another way of establishing ties where no direct financial connections exist. The simplest type of interlocking directorate occurs when one person sits on the boards of two or more corporations. Such multiple directorships are common. A House of Representatives study found that the 463 directors of 29 large industrial corporations held directorates in more than 1,200 different corporations during 1962.[25] Interlocking directorates among directly competing large firms were outlawed by the Clayton Act of 1914, and most of the interlocks revealed by the study undoubtedly had little or no direct effect on competition. However, the law was not vigorously enforced until 1968, and the study produced a long list of cases in which a single individual acted as director for two or more firms operating in similar product lines (typically, it would appear, representing only a small share of the implicated firms' total business).[26] The race by a few individuals from boardroom to boardroom also contributes to the maintenance of an industrial and commercial elite, to which one might object on political and social grounds.

An indirect interlock exists when separate directors of some firm (often a financial institution) individually hold seats on competing firms' boards. For example, the chairman of the board of Morgan Trust Company served in 1962 on the board of General Motors, while directors of both Ford Motor Company and Chrysler sat on the Morgan Trust board. The chairmen of both the New Jersey and California Standard Oil Companies sat on the board of the First National City Bank of New York, as did a director of Socony Mobil Oil. Banks take pains to ensure that their directors who also sit on competing clients' boards preserve confidences and engage in no unethical practices, and it is conceivable that the persons involved in these interlocks never discuss matters of mutual competitive interest when they meet. Nevertheless, the opportunity for abuse definitely exists. Whether or how frequently it blossoms from possibility into actuality, we simply do not know.

In sum, there are many formal and informal ties which, if exploited fully, could render domination of American industry by a few groups more monolithic than it appears in the bare statistics describing concentration. It is unlikely that a serious breakdown of corporate independence can be traced to these ties, partly because groups with weak minority voting positions may be unable to pull unwilling managers along, and partly because the officers of financial intermediaries have a tradition of reticence in exercising the power they possess. Yet our ignorance on this subject is great, and we can scarcely afford the complacent assumption that interlocking directorates and other intercorporate affiliations have no significant behavioral effects.

TURNOVER AMONG THE LARGEST CORPORATIONS

We have seen that the largest firms account for a sizeable share of all industrial activity, regardless of the size measure used. But is membership in this select group a stable condition, or something which slips readily from the grasp of those whose attention and zeal waver? In other words, is turnover among the ranks of the largest firms relatively high or low?

Several studies of turnover among the largest U. S. corporations have been published.[27] In the most comprehensive effort, Collins and Preston compiled lists of the 100 largest manufacturing, mining, and distribution firms, ranked by assets,

[24]"The Mutual Funds Have the Votes," p. 207.

[25]U. S. House of Representatives, Committee on the Judiciary, Antitrust Subcommittee, Staff Report, *Interlocks in Corporate Management* (Washington: 1965), pp. 115–116.

[26]*Ibid.*, pp. 159–164 and 234–255. See also Peter C. Dooley, "The Interlocking Directorate," *American Economic Review*, June 1969, pp. 314–323.

[27]A. D. H. Kaplan, *Big Enterprise in a Competitive System* (Washington: Brookings, 1954; Rev. ed., 1964), Chapter 7; Seymour Friedland, "Turnover and Growth of the Largest Industrial Firms, 1906–1950," *Review of Economics and Statistics*, February 1957, pp. 79–83; N. R. Collins and L. E. Preston, "The Size Structure of

for the years 1909, 1919, 1929, 1935, 1948, and 1958. They found that a total of 209 identifiable corporations appeared on these six lists at one time or another. Thirty-six of the top hundred firms in 1909 remained among the 100 leaders of 1958. On the average, 2.5 firms per year disappeared from the list.

Why did some firms drop off the list, while others ascended? A first impression can be gained by considering what happened to the leading ten firms on the 1909 list. They are ranked in order of 1909 assets, and the figure in parentheses indicates the firm's rank or status as of 1958:

1. United States Steel (3)
2. Standard Oil of New Jersey (1)
3. American Tobacco (37)
4. International Mercantile Marine (dropped)
5. International Harvester (24)
6. Anaconda (23)
7. United States Leather (dropped)
8. Armour (88)
9. American Sugar Refining (dropped)
10. Pullman (dropped)

Only two of the top 10 in 1909 remained among the top 10 of 1958, and four dropped from the list of the leading 100. Of these four, only one disappeared altogether.[28] After nearly succumbing in the 1921 recession and then struggling along for three more decades, United States Leather was liquidated in 1953. American Sugar Refining was 132nd on *Fortune*'s list of the 500 largest industrial firms for 1958 (ranked by sales); and Pullman was 119th. International Mercantile Marine, renamed United States Lines, was still plying the waterways in 1958, but with assets too meager to qualify for inclusion among the top 100. The disappearances and declines appear primarily to reflect the transition of the

American economy into the age of automobiles, aircraft, and appliances from an era in which food and basic clothing were the principal items in the average consumer's budget. Both Armour and American Sugar Refining were directly involved in the food processing industry, and International Harvester's indirect dependence on agriculture was heavy. Pullman and United States Lines, obviously, were victims of technological change. Other 1909 pacesetters who disappeared from the list of 100 leaders (and in a few cases, completely) for similar reasons include American Agricultural Chemical, American Cotton Oil, American Hide and Leather, American Ice, American Linseed Oil, Baldwin Locomotive Works, Cudahy Packing, General Cigar, Harbison-Walker Refractories, International Salt, U. S. Cast Iron Pipe and Foundry, United Shoe Machinery, Wilson Meat Packing, and Wells Fargo.

A similar, but not quite the same, picture emerges when we trace the ten largest firms of 1958 back to 1909:

1. Standard Oil of New Jersey (2)
2. General Motors (not listed in 1909)
3. United States Steel (1)
4. Gulf Oil (not listed)
5. Socony Mobil Oil (not listed)
6. The Texas Co. (91)
7. Ford Motor Co. (not listed)
8. Du Pont (29)
9. Standard Oil of Indiana (not listed)
10. Standard Oil of California (not listed)

The ascendance of General Motors and Ford (already listed among the top ten in 1919) was due, of course, to the automotive revolution in American consumption habits. It in turn propelled five additional petroleum refiners to the top in 1958—three of them fragments of the original New Jersey Standard Oil Company, broken off after a 1911 antitrust judgment.[29]

the Largest Industrial Firms," *American Economic Review*, December 1961, pp. 986–1011; the testimony by John Blair in *Economic Concentration*, pp. 86–88 and 207–210; and David Mermelstein, "Large Industrial Corporations and Asset Shares," *American Economic Review*, September, 1969, pp. 531–541.

[28]For an account of these and other disappearing firms' problems, see "The Dropouts," *Forbes*, September 15, 1967, pp. 149–172.

[29]The list of the top ten asset-holders includes such a predominance of petroleum refining companies partly because the petroleum industry is extremely capital-intensive. The top ten manufacturing and mining firms in order of *sales* for 1958 were General Motors, Standard Oil of New Jersey, Ford, General Electric, U. S. Steel, Socony Mobil Oil, Gulf Oil, Swift & Co., the Texas Co., and Western Electric.

That movement up and down on lists of the largest firms over time depends upon broad shifts in the pattern of demand is supported by the results of a statistical analysis. Seymour Friedland found a positive correlation between the rate of growth of 44 leading corporations' total assets and the rate of change of their home industry group's share of all manufacturing activity. The simple correlation coefficient was 0.87 for the 1906–1928 time period and 0.80 for the 1928–1950 period.[30]

Since there are no unambiguous criteria for judging, it is difficult to say whether the observed rate of turnover is high or low in some absolute sense. Whatever one's value judgments may be on this point, it is clear that the rate of turnover has declined over time. This is shown by the following tabulation of the average number of firms disappearing from the Collins and Preston lists per year for various time periods. Two measures are given: one showing the rate of exit for all reasons; and the second counting only 'natural' exits, excluding all primary and secondary effects of mergers and government antitrust actions:[31]

	TIME PERIOD				
	1909–19	1919–29	1929–35	1935–48	1948–58
Average number of exits per year for all causes	4.0	3.1	2.7	1.5	1.6
Average number of 'natural' exits per year	2.6	2.1	2.0	1.5	1.7

By either measure, a decline in the rate of turnover at least up to the 1940s is apparent. Four possible reasons for this change can be postulated. First, the largest firms may somehow have become more entrenched by virtue of the power their increased size confers, although it is difficult to think of a mechanism by which this entrenchment process could work. Second, the rate of technological change, or the rate of change in demand patterns, may have slowed. This too seems implausible, in view of the enormous scientific and technological changes wrought during the last three decades. Third, the management of large corporations may have become

[30]We shall use various types of correlation analysis often in this volume. The only really satisfactory background for comprehending the meaning and limitations of the correlation technique is a course in econometrics. For those (hopefully few) readers whose paths have not been crossed by that star, a brief explanatory note may be in order. The simple correlation coefficient r is a measure of the degree to which two variables vary in unison. Its maximum value is $+1.0$ (connoting perfect positive correlation), attained when increases in one variable are paralleled so uniformly by increases in the other that when the observations of the two variables are plotted on a scatter diagram (below), as in the first accompanying figure, they all lie precisely along a positively sloped straight line. The opposite extreme is perfect negative correlation ($r = -1.0$), when all plotted observations fall along a negatively sloped straight line. A correlation coefficient of zero means that there is no observable systematic relationship at all between the two variables, as in the second scatter diagram. Values of r between 0 and 1 (or between 0 and -1) signify imperfect systematic relationships, as in the third diagram. Variable Y appears to rise with increases in the value of X, but the observations are not tightly clustered along a single straight line characterizing that relationship. The square of the correlation coefficient indicates what fraction of the sum of the squared deviations of observations on a variable from their mean can be accounted for by the straight line best characterizing that variable's relationship with another variable. We shall also on occasion report *multiple correlation coefficients*, reflecting the relationship of one variable with another when further relationships with other variables are simultaneously taken into account. We conclude this brief explanation by cautioning that finding a correlation between two variables does not necessarily prove that there is a *causal* link between the two. It is possible that the observed correlation occurred purely by chance, although this is less likely when the correlation is found to be *statistically significant* at some high confidence level. It is also possible that a high correlation between X and Y means only that both are causally related to some third unmeasured variable Z.

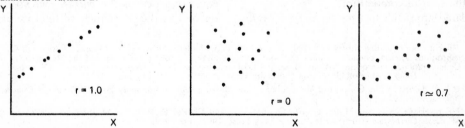

[31]See Collins and Preston, *op. cit.*, pp. 996–999 for further details.

more professionalized, taking a longer-run view of its role and identifying its function not as the production of certain products, but preservation of the firm *qua* organization. This implies among other things a willingness to adopt new product lines when the demand for traditional items declines. Such a change has probably occurred. Finally, as a by-product of their more professional managerial outlook and increased size, large corporations may have become more diversified, hedging against shifts in demand. This, we shall find later, has in fact happened.

CONCENTRATION IN PARTICULAR MARKETS

We turn now to the dimension of market structure most closely related to the main concern of this volume: the possession of monopoly power by sellers. To deal successfully with the problem, we must first identify several alternative means of measuring monopoly power.[32]

Alternative Measures of Monopoly Power

Some are performance-oriented. The best-known is the so-called *Lerner index*, defined as:[33]

$$M = \frac{\text{Price} - \text{Marginal Cost}}{\text{Price}}.$$

Its merit is that it directly reflects the departure of price from marginal cost associated with monopoly. Under pure competition, M is equal to 0. The more a firm's pricing decisions depart from the competitive norm, the higher is the associated Lerner index value. Unfortunately, it is difficult to derive marginal cost estimates from available accounting data; this is the chief drawback of the Lerner index. Measurement may also be thwarted if firms fail to maximize profits, incurring marginal costs higher than they would under the spur of competition.

A related approach focuses on the *net profits* realized by firms or industries. Ample profit data are available. But like the Lerner index, a profit index may understate the true degree of monopoly if firms with market power incur excessively high costs. The variability of reported profits over short-term business fluctuations and the diversity of accounting conventions on such matters as depreciation and loss writeoffs can also create ambiguities. A purely competitive industry may earn positive economic profits in disequilibrium; profit figures can therefore distinguish monopolistic from competitive situations at best only when they pertain to periods in which long-run equilibrium is approximated.

Other measures emphasize the sensitivity of sellers' sales or output to changes in rival product prices.[34] The simplest such index is the *cross elasticity of demand* between two firms, i.e., the percentage change in one firm's quantity sold associated with a given percentage change in another firm's price, holding the first firm's price constant. More complicated versions consider the amount of capacity firms have to exploit price advantages and the reactions of rivals to price changes. All suffer from the severe difficulty of getting the necessary data in specific situations.

A third and by far the most widely used approach is to focus on directly observable dimensions of industry structure. Economic theory suggests that the vigor of competition is related positively to the *number of firms* in the relevant industry, other things (such as the degree of product differentiation and the height of entry barriers) being equal. However, it makes a difference whether, in an industry with 100 firms, each firm controls 1 per cent of the industry's output, or four firms control 80 per cent while the remaining 96 account for only 20 per cent. An alternative, highly operational measure which copes more satisfactorily with the inequality aspect is the *market concentration ratio*, defined as the percentage of total industry sales

[32]For a more extended survey and analysis, see John Perry Miller, "Measures of Monopoly Power and Concentration: Their Economic Significance," and Tibor Scitovsky, "Economic Theory and the Measurement of Concentration," both in the National Bureau of Economic Research conference report, *Business Concentration and Price Policy* (Princeton: Princeton University Press, 1955), pp. 119–140 and 101–118.

[33]A. P. Lerner, "The Concept of Monopoly and the Measurement of Monopoly Power," *Review of Economic Studies*, June 1934, pp. 157-175.

[34]For various views, see Miller, *op. cit.*, pp. 124–127; and Charles E. Ferguson, *A Microeconomic Theory of Workable Competition* (Durham: Duke University Press, 1964), pp. 32–43.

(or physical output, or employment, or value added, or assets) contributed by the largest few firms, ranked in order of market shares. The most common variant in American studies (referred to as the four-firm sales concentration ratio and often as *the* concentration ratio) is the percentage of total industry sales made by the leading four firms. Concentration ratios are also published for U. S. manufacturing industries with respect to the leading eight, 20, and 50 firms.[35] Obviously, concentration data for several different numbers of firms provide more information on industry structure than the ratio for only one set (e.g., the top four), and so it is often useful to present a *concentration table*, like the following table for the U. S. semiconductor (transistor and diode) industry in 1963:

Group of Firms	Percentage of Total Industry Sales
Largest 4	46
Largest 8	65
Largest 20	90
Largest 50	99

A drawback to the concentration table approach is the awkwardness, both in verbal discourse and statistical analyses, of working with several sets of numbers.

There are various measures which summarize more succinctly the information provided by a concentration table. A common graphic technique is the *Lorenz curve*, which shows as a continuous function the percentage of total industry sales (or some other variable) accounted for by any given fraction of the total company population, with the firms ranked in order of market share or size. Lorenz curves can be characterized numerically by means of the *Gini coefficient*, which measures the departure between the Lorenz curve actually observed and the curve which would appear if all firms had equal market shares or sales.[36] A Gini coefficient of zero indicates perfect equality of firm shares; a coefficient of 1.0 reveals total inequality (with the leading firm producing the entire output). The Lorenz – Gini approach has two main disadvantages. As an index solely of inequality, the Gini coefficient may suggest paradoxical inferences when an industry is occupied by a small number of evenly matched firms. The Gini coefficient for duopolists or triopolists with equal market shares is zero, but one could hardly conclude that monopoly power is absent in such cases. Second, the shape of the Lorenz curve and the value of the Gini coefficient are quite sensitive to errors in defining the number of firms in the industry. The more borderline firms one includes, the higher the indicated degree of inequality tends to be.

A summary measure in the same spirit as the Gini coefficient, but without its serious flaws, is the so-called *Herfindahl index*, given by the formula:[37]

$$H = \sum_{i=1}^{N} S_i^2;$$

where S_i is the market share of the ith firm. When an industry is occupied by only one firm (a pure monopolist), the index attains its maximum value of 1.0. The value declines with increases in the number of firms and increases with rising inequality among any given number of firms. Thus, to the extent that monopoly power is correlated positively with both fewness of sellers and inequality in their sizes, the Herfindahl index

---

[35]The most recent complete compilation is U. S. Senate, *Concentration Ratios in Manufacturing Industry: 1963.* See also U. S. Bureau of the Census, *Annual Survey of Manufactures: 1966,* "Value-of-Shipment Concentration Ratios by Industry," M66(AS)-8 (Washington: 1968). Results of the 1967 census of manufactures will no doubt be available in 1970. For a summary of other U. S. concentration ratio sources, see Ralph L. Nelson, *Concentration in the Manufacturing Industries of the United States* (New Haven: Yale University Press, 1963), pp. 17–19. Nelson omitted one valuable source: U. S. Federal Trade Commission, *Report on Industrial Concentration and Product Diversification in the 1,000 Largest Manufacturing Companies: 1950* (Washington: 1957). It is the only report which identifies industry sales leaders by name.

[36]On techniques for computing the Gini coefficient, see Horst Mendershausen, *Changes in Income Distribution During the Great Depression* (New York: National Bureau of Economic Research, 1946), pp. 160–167.

[37]Cf. I. M. Grossack, "Toward an Integration of Static and Dynamic Measures of Industry Concentration," *Review of Economics and Statistics,* August 1965, pp. 301–308; A. O. Hirschman, "The Paternity of an Index," *American Economic Review,* September 1964, p. 761 (who implies that the index is misnamed); and M. A. Adelman, "Comment on the 'H' Concentration Measure as a Numbers-Equivalent," *Review of Economics and Statistics,* February 1969, pp. 99–101.

comes close to being an ideal composite measure.[38] Its main disadvantage is the scarcity of comprehensive market share data required for its computation.[39]

Finally, some economists have advocated using the variance of the logarithms of each industry member's sales or employment as a summary measure of concentration.[40] This index has desirable statistical properties. But like the Gini coefficient, it emphasizes inequality to the exclusion of differences in the number of firms. And the necessary data are again hard to come by.

With such a rich menu of alternative market structure measures, which should the analyst use? The most common choice criterion is a pragmatic one: use the best index possible, given data constraints. In a majority of cases, this means the humble four-firm concentration ratio. Fortunately, the chances of making a grievous analytic error in the choice of a market structure measure are slender, for the principal concentration indicators all display similar patterns. To illustrate, four structural indices—the four-firm sales concentration ratio, the eight-firm sales concentration ratio, the four-firm employment concentration ratio, and the Herfindahl index—were correlated for a sample of 91 industries on which comparable data were available.[41] For the six two-way comparisons of these four measures, the average correlation coefficient was 0.921, and the lowest of the six correlations was 0.859. The correlation between the four-firm sales concentration ratio (the most commonly used of all measures) and the Herfindahl index was 0.936. Similar results have been obtained in other studies of alternative market structure measures.[42]

Thus, if an industry has a high four-firm concentration ratio, it is likely also to have a high Herfindahl index, a high eight-firm concentration ratio, and a small number of firms. And although asset concentration ratios tend to be higher than sales concentration ratios, with sales ratios in turn somewhat higher than employment ratios, all tend to be *relatively* high for a given industry if any one is high. For most inter-industry comparison purposes, then, it is senseless to spend sleepless nights worrying about choosing the right concentration measure. Much more serious is the possibility that any structural index chosen, while suggesting about the same conclusion as alternative measures, will convey a false impression of the actual degree of monopoly power present.

THE LIMITATIONS OF CONCENTRATION RATIOS

To see this, we must consider more carefully some of the assumptions and limitations of the concentration index approach. The most widely used concentration ratio tells the percentage of all industry sales made by the leading four firms. When concentration ratios are computed, some difficulties may be encountered disentangling the four industry leaders' sales in the desired industry from their sales in other fields, for activities may be scrambled together under a single roof. But these are seldom serious. The main problem comes in defining the industry meaningfully—that is, so that all firms which are competitors, and only those firms, are included.

Most studies of market concentration use data collected through the Census of Manufactures, conducted twice each decade. The U. S. Census Bureau has developed an elaborate system—the

[38]The Herfindahl index does have one statistical peculiarity—a tendency to have a distribution strongly skewed toward low values. Whether this is undesirable theoretically is not clear—it depends on whether monopoly power is similarly distributed. The index may be popular among Chicago economists because of this property. If desired, the skewness can be eliminated by taking a logarithmic transformation of the index.

[39]The only source of Herfindahl indices for an extensive sample of American industries is Nelson, *op. cit.*

[40]P. E. Hart and S. J. Prais, "The Analysis of Business Concentration: A Statistical Approach," *Journal of the Royal Statistical Society*, 1956, Part 2, pp. 150–181. For a somewhat more skeptical view, see Irwin H. Silberman, "On Lognormality as a Summary Measure of Concentration," *American Economic Review*, September 1967, pp. 807–831.

[41]Cf. Nelson, *op. cit.*, Appendix Tables A:1 and A:3.

[42]See especially Gideon Rosenbluth, "Measures of Concentration," in National Bureau of Economic Research, *Business Concentration and Price Policy*, pp. 63–69 and 89–92; the testimony of John M. Blair in *Economic Concentration*, Part 5 (1966), pp. 1894–1902; and R. W. Kilpatrick, "The Choice Among Alternative Measures of Industrial Concentration," *Review of Economics and Statistics*, May 1967, pp. 258–260.

Standard Industrial Classification, or S.I.C.— for categorizing the output of each establishment (i.e., plant or store) of every business enterprise.[43] It is organized around a series of seven-digit numbers, each successive digit reflecting a finer degree of classification. Consider, for example, the seven-digit S.I.C. product line 2844511 (suntan lotions). The first digit (2) indicates that this set of commodities is produced in the manufacturing sector of the economy (as opposed to, say, 5 for trade or 0 for agriculture and forestry). The first two digits together (28) reveal that the commodity is produced in the 'chemicals and allied products' group of the manufacturing sector. There are 21 such two-digit groups altogether in manufacturing, numbered 19 through 39. The first three digits together (284) place our commodity in the 'cleaning and toilet products' field. Adding the fourth digit locates it more finely in four-digit *Census industry* 2844, covering 'toilet preparations.' Following from the 1963 Census of Manufactures, concentration ratios for some 430 four-digit manufacturing industries have been published. At a still finer level of detail is the five-digit *product class* 28445—in this case, a catch-all category covering 'other cosmetics and toilet preparations' (shaving preparations, perfumes, dentifrices, etc. having received separate five-digit codes). The 1963 Census of Manufactures covered roughly 1,000 such five-digit product classes, for most of which concentration ratios are available. Finally, we jump to the seven-digit *product* or *commodity* level. Examples in the five-digit class 28445 include suntan lotions, cosmetic and baby oils, hand lotions, liquid deodorants, face powder, etc. At this level of detail, the Census of Manufactures identifies some 7,500 different products. No concentration ratios are published at the seven-digit level.[44]

Unfortunately, Census Bureau industry and product class definitions do not always conform consistently to the criteria economists would like

to apply. To get its difficult job done at all, the Bureau must use definitions facilitating accurate reporting by business firms, which usually means that they must follow the way firms have grouped or segregated their production operations. Emphasis is often on similarity of production processes, which may not reflect competitive interrelationships. Consequently, four-digit census industries and even five-digit product classes are sometimes too broad relative to the economist's ideal industry definition, and sometimes they are too narrow.

The ideal definition of a market must take into account substitution possibilities in both consumption and production. On the demand side, firms are competitors or rivals if the products they offer are good substitutes for one another in the eyes of buyers. But how, exactly, does one draw the line between 'good' and 'not good enough' substitutes? One possibility is to consider cross elasticities of demand; if they are high between two products, the products should probably be grouped together in defining the relevant market. But how high is a high cross elasticity? Some element of arbitrariness is unavoidable in deciding. Also, the information necessary to make accurate cross elasticity estimates is seldom available. An alternative approach is to search for some clear gap in the chain of substitution, usually based on differences in physical attributes of the products in question. The results yielded by this method, it should be noted, may not always be consistent with the results of the cross-elasticities test.

Substitution on the production side must also be considered. Groups of firms producing completely noncompeting products may nevertheless be potential competitors if they employ essentially similar skills and machinery, and if there are no barriers preventing each group from entering the other's product lines should the profit lure beckon. The four-digit census 'screw machine products' industry is a good example

---

[43]On the census classification system, see M. R. Conklin and H. T. Goldstein, "Census Principles and Product Classification, Manufacturing Industries," in *Business Concentration and Price Policy*, pp. 15–36. For a broader, perceptive treatment of market definition problems in the census framework, see Dean A. Worcester, Jr., *Monopoly, Big Business, and Welfare in the Postwar United States* (Seattle: University of Washington Press, 1967), Chapters II, III, and IV.

[44]But see Worcester, *op. cit.*, pp. 70–81, who summarizes an analysis of concentration in selected seven-digit lines.

of a definition which satisfies this criterion, for screw machine shops produce an incredible variety of products with machines readily shifted from one product to another.

In view of these broad principles, how good are the Census Bureau's industry definitions for purposes of identifying structural monopoly power? What problems arise from the system? Are there consistent biases in the definitions, and if so, in what direction? And how can they be combatted operationally? As a backdrop for investigating these questions, Table 3.2 presents 1963 sales concentration data for a sample of 46 American manufacturing industries. All but two of the industries are defined at the four-digit level. The sample is fairly representative, except for favoring the larger, more prominent industries and excluding those which are catch-alls or otherwise vaguely defined.

The most important single source of problems is a definition excessively broad or narrow relative to the possibilities for substitution in consumption. Several of the industries in Table 3.2 are clearly too broad. The worst offender is pharmaceutical preparations, which lumps together dozens of drugs for which there are no adequate substitutes (except perhaps greatly extended medical care). Economically meaningful market definitions must generally be found in this case at the seven-digit level of detail, given that substitution in production is often blocked by patent barriers. Other industries defined too broadly include aircraft (involving a wide diversity of aircraft types requiring special production skills), motors and generators (with similar diversity of products and skills), and soaps and detergents (with several functionally distinct product lines, and with strong product differentiation enhancing market power even for firms producing functionally identical items). Farm machinery is another industry much too broadly defined in terms of substitution in consumption, although this criticism must be tempered by recognizing that producers can shift without great difficulty from one product line into others, as long as patented design features are circumvented. Industries defined too narrowly include the separate metal cans and glass containers groups (since cans and bottles are readily substitutable in many applications), broad woven cotton mills (since synthetic fabrics and wool compete in many uses), and synthetic rubber (for which natural rubber, accounting for about a fourth of total rubber use in 1963, may be substituted). Concentration ratios in the primary copper and aluminum (and to a lesser degree, steel) industries also tend to overstate market power, other things being equal, partly because these metals compete with one another in numerous applications and partly because the output of domestic scrap reprocessers is omitted from consideration. In 1963, resmelted copper scrap constituted about a third of all domestic copper production and reprocessed aluminum 20 per cent of all aluminum ingot production.

Industry definitions which segregate such basic materials as steel, copper, aluminum, plastics, etc. are becoming less and less suitable as technological changes accumulate, permitting producers of each to interpenetrate other raw material markets. In an input-output study of changes in the American economy between 1947 and 1958, Mrs. Carter found that raw materials were becoming increasingly interchangeable:

> . . . . The classical dominance of single kinds of material—metals, stone, clay and glass, wood, natural fibers, rubber, leather, plastics, and so on—in each kind of production has given way by 1958 to increasing diversification of the bill of materials consumed by each industry. This development comes from interplay between keenly competitive refinement in the qualities of materials and design backward from end-use specifications.[45]

To be sure, specific materials retain undisputed dominance in many applications, and so computation of concentration ratios for the traditional divisions is not altogether meaningless. Still, generalizations about the degree of monop-

---

[45]Anne P. Carter, "The Economics of Technological Change," *Scientific American*, April 1966, p. 27. Copyright © by Scientific American, Inc. All rights reserved. For a later, more technical version, see "Changes in the Structure of the American Economy, 1947 to 1958 and 1962," *Review of Economics and Statistics*, May 1967, pp. 209–224.

Table 3.2
1963 Concentration Ratios for Representative Industries

S.I.C. Code		4–Firm Ratio	8–Firm Ratio	Number of firms
37151	Passenger cars (five-digit)	99	100	n.a.
3741	Locomotives and parts	97	99	23
3334	Primary aluminum	96	100	7
3211	Flat glass	94	99	11
3511	Steam engines and turbines	93	98	17
3641	Electric lamps	92	96	52
3672	Cathode ray picture tubes	91	95	148
2073	Chewing gum	90	97	20
2111	Cigarettes	80	100	7
3331	Primary copper	78	98	13
3633	Household laundry equipment	78	95	31
3572	Typewriters	76	99	17
3411	Metal cans	74	85	99
2841	Soap and detergents	72	80	641
3011	Tires and inner tubes	70	89	105
2284	Thread mills	68	85	59
3721	Aircraft and parts	59	83	82
36512	Household television receivers (five-digit)	58	81	n.a.
2822	Synthetic rubber	57	80	16
3562	Ball and roller bearings	57	76	93
3221	Glass containers	55	72	40
3312	Blast furnaces and steel mills	50	69	162
3621	Motors and generators	50	59	316
3871	Watches and clocks	46	65	150
3522	Farm machinery and equipment	43	55	1,481
3552	Textile machinery	35	52	529
2041	Flour mills	35	50	510
2911	Petroleum refining	34	56	266
2082	Beer and malt liquors	34	52	171
2211	Broad woven cotton mills	30	46	229
3241	Cement	29	49	55
3141	Shoes, except rubber	25	32	785
2051	Bread and related products	23	35	4,339
2851	Paints and allied products	23	34	1,579
2026	Fluid milk	23	30	4,030
2834	Pharmaceutical preparations	22	38	944
3541	Metal-cutting machine tools	20	32	784
2256	Knit fabric mills	18	25	487
2711	Newspapers	15	22	7,982
2311	Men's and boys' suits and coats	14	23	1,031
3494	Valves and pipe fittings	13	22	580
3251	Brick and structural tile	12	19	401
2086	Bottled and canned soft drinks	12	17	3,569
2511	Wood furniture, not upholstered	11	16	2,927
2421	Sawmills and planing mills	11	14	11,931
3451	Screw machine products	5	8	1,861

Source: U.S. Senate, Committee on the Judiciary, Subcommittee on Antitrust and Monopoly, Report, *Concentration Ratios in Manufacturing Industry: 1963,* Part I (Washington: 1966).

oly power implied by those ratios must be made with caution.

Another historical development which affects the ability of concentration ratios to measure monopoly power is the apparent trend toward reduced tariffs and increased freedom of trade, combined with growing speed and efficiency of international transportation media. Thus far, this development is relatively unimportant in studies of the American economy, since imports represent only a small fraction (in 1963, about 8 per cent) of aggregate raw materials and finished goods production. Import competition, both actual and potential, is nevertheless a significant factor in some Table 3.2 industries, such as copper (with imports exceeding 20 per cent by value of domestic production in 1963), watches and clocks (with imports of 15 per cent), flat glass (with sheet glass imports amounting to 15 per cent of domestic output), typewriters (11 per cent), and primary aluminum (10 per cent, mostly from Canada).[46] For members of the European Common Market and other nations (like England and Switzerland) heavily dependent upon foreign trade, national concentration ratios for many industries are next to meaningless.

While failure to consider import competition causes concentration ratios to exaggerate the amount of monopoly power present, the implicit census assumption that all markets are nationwide in scope errs in the opposite direction. Certain bulky, low value commodities cannot economically be transported far from the site of production, and so the market definition must be local or regional to be meaningful. Cement is a classic example. Table 3.2 shows that the leading four firms account for 29 per cent of all nationwide sales. But 90 per cent of all cement is shipped 160 miles or less, and when the nation is divided into 51 regions (essentially on a state-wide basis), we find that in only three of the regions did the leading four producers account for less than 50 per cent of all sales.[47] Because of spatial isolation, the true level of concentration (and monopoly power) is also understated in such industries as newspaper publishing, beer brewing, milk supply, brickmaking, and (to a lesser degree) petroleum refining.

Finally, published concentration ratios may misrepresent the extent of structural monopoly power for various institutional reasons. The bottled and canned soft drinks industry, with a four-firm concentration ratio of 12, is an especially good illustration. Its ostensibly low concentration reflects the organization of the industry into numerous local bottling companies. But most bottlers operate under franchises from nationwide firms like Coca-Cola and Pepsi-Cola. A more meaningful index of concentration would be the proportion of the nationwide market commanded by products tied to the leading national firms. Some indication is provided by the fact that product class 20873—flavoring sirups for use by soft drink bottlers—had a four-firm concentration ratio of 89 in 1958.

To sum up, concentration ratios understate the true quantum of market power when markets are defined to include non-substitutes, when meaningful markets are local or regional rather than nationwide, when producers enjoy strong brand loyalties or other differentiation advantages within relevant product lines, and when special institutional features (like the soft drink franchise pattern) intrude. The degree of market power is overstated when substitutes are excluded from the industry definition and when import competition is significant.

How do these influences balance out? In an attempt to assess the average bias, the author carefully reviewed each of the industries in Table 3.2, determining whether the concen-

---

[46]U. S. Department of Commerce, Bureau of the Census, *U. S. Commodity Exports and Imports as Related to Output, 1964 and 1963* (Washington: 1966). Other U. S. product lines with high import ratios include canned seafood, liquors, carpets, cordage and twine, paper mill products, leather gloves, vitreous table ware, steel nails and spikes, still cameras, and jewels. It should be noted that the high import ratio for copper does not necessarily detract from the domestic concentration ratio's validity as an index of monopoly power, since the principal importers are firms dominating domestic production.

[47]U. S. Federal Trade Commission, *Economic Report on Mergers and Vertical Integration in the Cement Industry* (Washington: 1966), pp. 44–49. In many cases, statewide market definitions are unduly narrow, but the central point remains valid. See also Samuel Loescher, *Imperfect Collusion in the Cement Industry* (Cambridge: Harvard University Press, 1959), pp. 48–57.

tration ratios tended on balance either to understate or overstate the 'true' extent of concentration by 10 percentage points or more. The judgments were necessarily subjective, and the reader may wish to try his own hand at the game, but for what they are worth, true concentration was found to be understated in 18 industries and overstated in only eight. This conclusion cannot be extended directly to the entire population of census industries, since the Table 3.2 sample is not random. Very broadly defined industries like 'toilet preparations' and catch-all industries like 'organic chemicals, not elsewhere classified,' whose concentration ratios typically understate the actual degree of market power substantially, were deliberately excluded. Thus, it appears probable that the total population of four-digit manufacturing industries as classified for census purposes errs on the side of excessive breadth even more than the sample of industries in Table 3.2. However, five-digit definitions may be biased slightly in the opposite direction.

Given these deficiencies, what practical steps can be taken to avoid mistakes in the use and interpretation of concentration ratios? The most important is to recognize that pitfalls exist: that concentration indices are at best only a rough, one-dimensional indicator of monopoly power; and that their use must be governed by common sense. It is hard to inject common sense into an electronic computer, however, and so in statistical studies it is desirable to adjust misleading concentration ratios—e.g., by consolidating industries which have been defined too narrowly, and by employing five-digit concentration ratios when the four-digit industry has been defined too broadly.[48]

Another problem encountered in statistical work is a divergence in the degree of industry detail for which different variables are available. Concentration ratios are generally published at the four- and five-digit levels, while profit and advertising data may be available only for three-digit groups and research and development expenditures data only at the two-digit level. A standard practice in such cases is to compute weighted average concentration ratios for the broader groups, weighting each appropriately defined narrow industry's concentration index by employment or sales in that industry. We shall encounter this convention frequently in subsequent chapters.

THE OVERALL EXTENT OF MARKET CONCENTRATION IN THE AMERICAN ECONOMY

Forewarned and forearmed, we turn to the task of assessing how concentrated markets are in the American economy. For many sectors, we can only hazard impressionistic guesses, since adequate quantitative data are totally lacking. To put these guesses in perspective, Table 3.3 presents a breakdown of the U. S. gross national product by sector in 1967.

In the agriculture, forestry, and fisheries sectors, industry structures are overwhelmingly atomistic, but competition is moderated by a heavy overlay of government price supports, subsidies, and acreage restrictions. Mining presents a mixed picture. Some mining industries, such as limestone, common sand and gravel, gold, and phosphate, are atomistic nationally, although concentration may be high in some localized markets. Others, such as copper, iron ore, lead, zinc, and sulphur are highly concentrated even at the national level. Petroleum extraction is characterized by low concentration, but state production controls severely limit competition. Soft coal mining is atomistic in the important Appalachian Mountain region, but oligopolistic in the spatially isolated Midwestern region, where the four largest producers accounted for 55 per cent of total output in 1962.[49] Kaysen and Turner estimated that in total, roughly two thirds of all value added in mining originates from atomistically structured indus-

[48]For methodological guidance, see Leonard Weiss, "Average Concentration Ratios and Industrial Performance," *Journal of Industrial Economics,* July 1963, pp. 237–254; George J. Stigler, *Capital and Rates of Return in Manufacturing Industries* (Princeton: Princeton University Press, 1963), pp. 206–211; and Carl Kaysen and Donald F. Turner, *Antitrust Policy* (Cambridge: Harvard University Press, 1959), pp. 295–299.

[49]Cf. Reed Moyer, *Competition in the Midwestern Coal Industry* (Cambridge: Harvard University Press, 1964), pp. 10–37 and 68.

Table 3.3

U.S. Gross National Product in 1967, by Sector of Origin

Sector of Origin	Dollar Amount (Billions)	Percentage of Total
Agriculture, forestry, and fisheries	26.2	3.3
Mining	14.3	1.8
Contract construction	36.2	4.6
Manufacturing	224.6	28.3
Transportation	33.1	4.2
Communications	17.6	2.2
Electrical, gas, and sanitary services	18.9	2.4
Wholesale and retail trade	129.5	16.3
Finance, insurance, and real estate	106.9	13.5
Services	85.8	10.8
Government and government enterprise	95.5	12.0
Total	793.2	100.0

Source: U.S. Department of Commerce, Bureau of the Census. *Survey of Current Business,* April 1969, p. 14.

tries and one third from oligopolistic industries.[50] This judgment undoubtedly errs on the low side, since both coal and petroleum were viewed as atomistically competitive. Contract construction is characterized by large numbers of small firms and can be termed generally competitive in structure, despite pockets of localized oligopoly.

Competition in the transportation, communications, and electrical and gas utilities sectors is controlled and restrained by formal public regulation. Peering behind the regulatory veil, we would find that oligopoly is the prevailing market structure in railroading, air transport, intercity bus lines, parts of water transportation, and highway freight carriage between less densely travelled points, while large numbers of sellers operate in the high volume routes of trucking and in inland water transportation. Intermodal competition would also be strong in the absence of regulation. In telephone communications and the electric and gas industries, natural monopoly is the rule, while radio and television communi-

cations are oligopolistic except in very large metropolitan areas.

Wholesale and retail trade are more difficult to categorize. In metropolitan areas of substantial size (e.g., populations exceeding 100,000), market structures are characteristically atomistic or very loosely oligopolistic. Despite the rise of the chain store, single unit operations continue to predominate in retailing. Some 1.5 million single unit retailing firms accounted for 63 per cent of all retail sales in 1963. Chains with 101 or more units made 16 per cent of total 1963 sales, compared to 12 per cent in 1948.[51] Still elements of both spatial and subjective product differentiation are strong in retailing. The car-less, scooter-less student in Ann Arbor, Michigan, may find himself paying a price premium of 25 per cent to campus area grocers. And in small towns, high concentration is common. In Princeton, New Jersey, for example, the grocery trade during the mid-1960s consisted of two astonishingly lethargic national chain units, a small and higher-

[50]*Antitrust Policy*, pp. 37–39 and 286–288.

[51]U. S. Department of Commerce, Bureau of the Census. *1963 Census of Business*, vol. I, "Retail Trade Summary Statistics," Part 1, p. 4–2.

priced locally owned supermarket, and several very high-priced specialty shops. If a simple verdict must be rendered, however, it would be that high concentration is more the exception than the rule in retailing and wholesaling.

The pattern in banking is one of moderate oligopoly in nationwide credit markets and large cities, with very strong oligopoly or even monopoly confronting most customers in the smaller cities and towns. Competition in banking is regulated, as it is also in the insurance industries, which exhibit high to moderate concentration in the life and health insurance fields and low concentration in other fields. The real estate trades are atomistically structured, except in very small towns.

The service industries, including hotels and motels, laundry services, funeral parlors, barber shops, repair services, legal and medical services, and the like tend toward large numbers of sellers, except in small towns. Nevertheless, the amount of monopoly power present is much greater than a superficial analysis of market structure implies, due to, among other things, very strong product differentiation and in some fields (like medicine and barber services) cartelization. The extensive repair service trades pose special problems, for once the customer has left his auto or television set or whatever with a particular shop, a bilateral monopoly condition exists, and the customer typically lacks bargaining power because of his technical ignorance. Also included in the services sector are the various amusement and recreational industries, where concentration is high except in the largest cities.

The government services sector (including only activities directly carried out by government agencies, and not contracted-out work) is much too complex for any blanket statement. Many government services (law enforcement, legislation, and defense) are provided outside the market framework, and it makes little sense to discuss them in terms of monopoly vs. competi-

tion. In other areas, such as the Post Office service, the Government Printing Office, and the Navy's shipyards, government activities co-exist with more or less parallel private functions.

The manufacturing sector has been reserved for more thorough analysis in the next section, but one preliminary note is apropos. During the mid-1960s, the federal government was spending between \$25 and \$35 billion annually for the development and production of advanced weapon systems, space vehicles, and other technologically sophisticated military equipment. Because of the technological uncertainties, complexity, and unique applications associated with these defense and space projects, administrative supervision and controls have been substituted almost completely for the price system as a directing mechanism. It should be recognized therefore that between 10 and 15 per cent of all manufacturing industry activity, spread over numerous four-digit groups, occurs outside the market system. These nonmarket operations pose fascinating analytic problems which, unfortunately, we will not be able to examine in the present volume.[52]

It is futile to attempt a quantitative summary of how much structural monopoly power exists in the whole of the American economy. Suffice it to say that there is a modest amount of activity (not more than 6 or 7 per cent of gross national product) approximating pure monopoly, most of which is subject to government regulation or control; somewhat more activity approximating pure competition; and liberal quantities of oligopoly and monopolistic competition.[53]

CONCENTRATION IN MANUFACTURING INDUSTRY

Manufacturing is the largest single sector in the economy. It is also the only sector for which abundant data on market concentration exist, permitting detailed structural analyses.

Monopoly in the strict sense of a single seller is virtually nonexistent in nationwide manufactur-

[52]But see M. J. Peck and F. M. Scherer, *The Weapons Acquisition Process: An Economic Analysis* (Boston: Harvard Business School Division of Research, 1962); F. M. Scherer, *The Weapons Acquisition Process: Economic Incentives* (Boston: Harvard Business School Division of Research, 1964); and *idem*, "The Aerospace Industry," in Walter Adams, ed., *The Structure of American Industry* (Fourth ed.; New York: Macmillan, 1970).

[53]For other views on the overall incidence of competition and monopoly, see Kaysen and Turner, *op. cit.*, pp. 26–43; George J. Stigler, *Five Lectures on Economic Problems* (London: Longman, Green, 1949), pp. 46–62; and Clair Wilcox, "On the Alleged Ubiquity of Oligopoly," *American Economic Review*, May 1950, pp. 67–73.

Table 3.4

Distribution of Manufacturing Industries by Four–Firm
Sales Concentration Ratios: 1963

Four–Firm Concentration Ratio Range	Number of Industries	Percentage of All Industries	Percentage of Total Value Added
0–19	89	21.4	20.8
20–39	161	38.7	38.0
40–59	92	22.1	20.5
60–79	47	11.3	9.9
80–100	27	6.5	10.8

Source: U.S. Senate, Committee on the Judiciary, Subcommittee on Antitrust and Monopoly, Report, *Concentration Ratios in Manufacturing Industry: 1963* (Washington: 1966). Newspaper publishing has been excluded.

ing industries of appreciable size. The leading examples of firms which in recent decades have maintained positions even approaching monopoly for any significant length of time are General Motors (with about 85 per cent of the locomotive and intercity bus markets), Western Electric (with a comparable share of the telephone equipment market), United Shoe Machinery Corporation (which held roughly 85 per cent of its principal markets until a 1954 antitrust judgment reduced barriers to entry), Gillette (which controlled 90 per cent of the double-edged razor blade market until it lagged in the introduction of stainless steel blades), Dow Chemical Company (with 90 per cent of U. S. magnesium production until new entry took place in 1969), International Nickel (controlling about two thirds of non-Communist world nickel supplies), and International Business Machines Corporation (which had managed as of 1968 to retain more than 70 per cent of the turbulent digital electronic computer and data processing equipment market).

Oligopoly, on the other hand, is abundant. Table 3.4 shows the distribution of 416 four-digit manufacturing industries in 1963 by four-firm sales concentration classes. When the leading four firms control 40 per cent or more of the total market, it is fair to assume that oligopoly is beginning to rear its head. Inspection shows that 166 industries, accounting for 40 per cent of all industries by number and 41 per cent of value added, had four-firm concentration ratios of at least this magnitude.[54] Given the tendency for four-firm census industry definitions to be somewhat too broad on the average, these figures suggest that something on the order of half of all American manufacturing industry can be categorized as oligopolistic.

This conclusion, based on naive concentration data, is supported by the results of a more sophisticated analysis of 1954 data carried out by Kaysen and Turner.[55] Preferring to err on the side of defining industries too broadly, they consolidated 440 four-digit census industries into a total of 191 more inclusive industry groups. They made special adjustments to present a meaningful picture of concentration in 27 industry groups with regional or local markets. They then divided their sample into three categories: Type I oligopolies, in which the eight largest firms made at least 50 per cent of

[54]The share of value added breakdown for the 60–79 and 80–100 concentration classes is very sensitive to the disposition of the motor vehicles and parts industry, which had a value added concentration ratio of 79 but a sales concentration ratio of 84. Both understate the degree of concentration in the end product markets by including the activities of parts suppliers, dependent upon the major auto and truck makers for orders. If the industry were nevertheless reclassified into the 60–79 group, the share of value added associated with the 80–100 group falls to 4.2 per cent.

[55]*Antitrust Policy*, pp. 26–37.

industry sales and the 20 largest firms 75 per cent of sales; Type II oligopolies, in which the leading eight firms accounted for between 33 and 49 per cent and the top 20 less than 75 per cent of industry sales; and 'unconcentrated' industries with lower concentration levels. Relatively low concentration ratio floors were chosen in defining oligopoly because of the broad industry definitions used. On this basis, Kaysen and Turner arrived at the following distribution of industry categories:

	Number of Industries	Percentage of Total 1954 Manufacturing Sales
Type I Oligopolies	64	23
Type II Oligopolies	56	36
Unconcentrated	71	41

Altogether, industries found by Kaysen and Turner to be oligopolistic accounted for 59 per cent of total manufacturing industry sales in 1954. The incidence of oligopolistic structures was higher in durable and producers goods industries than in nondurables and consumer goods.

HISTORICAL TRENDS IN MANUFACTURING INDUSTRY CONCENTRATION

We conclude then that there is considerable market concentration in manufacturing industry, hastening to add that an appreciable fraction of manufactured goods output is produced in more or less atomistically structured industries. Has manufacturing industry always been as concentrated as it presently is? And is there an observable trend toward increasing or decreasing concentration?

Very long run analyses plunge us into the realm of incommensurables. During the first half of the 19th century, nationwide concentration of manufactured goods output was undoubtedly much lower than it is now. But markets were predominantly local then. The railroads had not been built on any significant scale, wagon roads were primitive, and the waterways system was circuitous, slow, and blocked in winter. As a result, competitive contact among geographically scattered manufacturers was modest, and the amount of market power possessed must have been high. As the railroads expanded their coverage from 9,000 miles of road operated in 1850 to 167,000 miles in 1890, and as the spread of telegraph and then telephone service greatly facilitated communications, something resembling a true national market emerged for the first time.[56] Firms interpenetrated each others' former home territory and competition flourished. Indeed, if we could measure monopoly power in manufacturing directly, we might well find it to have been at an all-time low between 1870 and 1890, for there was a sharp increase in concentration following 1880. This was due to the rapid internal growth of those firms which proved themselves fit for the competitive struggle, and even more to an enormous number of mergers among previously independent firms. We shall discuss this merger movement more fully in the next chapter. The main point for present purposes is that it ran its course shortly after the turn of the century, so that the economy of 1904 was structurally quite different from the economy of 1830 or 1870. Whether there was more or less monopoly power in 1904 than in 1830 no one can say with any confidence, because the whole economic environment had been transformed so radically.[57]

The gap between 1904 and the present can be bridged in less vague terms, thanks to the pains-

---

[56]For a more skeptical view of the impact of the railroad, see R. W. Fogel, *Railroads and American Economic Growth: Essays in Econometric History* (Baltimore: Johns Hopkins University Press, 1964).

[57]Another broader development deserves mention. Manufacturing has always been more concentrated than farming. From 1840 to 1900, value added in the farming sector fell from about 70 per cent of total agriculture, mining, manufacturing, and construction output to roughly 33 per cent, and since then it has fallen further to 10 per cent in 1965. This represents a long-run structural shift away from more competitively structured economic activity. See U. S. Bureau of the Census, *Historical Statistics of the United States, Colonial Times to 1957* (Washington: 1960), p. 139.

taking labors of G. Warren Nutter.[58] Utilizing a variety of published sources and a good deal of guesswork, Nutter estimated that 32.9 per cent of all national income originating in the manufacturing sector was attributable to industries in which the four largest firms accounted for 50 per cent or more of output at one time or another between 1895 and 1904.[59] Further processing of the data underlying Table 3.4 reveals that in 1963, 33.1 per cent of all value added originating in manufacturing came from four-digit industries with sales concentration ratios of 50 or more. The similarity is striking. As Professor Adelman concluded in a parallel study of concentration trends, "Any tendency either way, if it does exist, must be at the pace of a glacial drift."[60]

This impression of remarkable placidity is upset when we study the data available from four postwar censuses and a sample survey. The proportions of manufacturing value added originating in industries with four-firm sales concentration ratios of 50 or higher were as follows:[61]

1947	24.4 per cent
1954	29.9 per cent
1958	30.2 per cent
1963	33.1 per cent
1966	28.6 per cent

Were it not for Nutter's original benchmark, we might be inclined to conclude that a strong upward trend was operating, at least up to 1963. But since the 1963 high water mark barely exceeded Nutter's concentration estimate for 1895–1904, it seems more reasonable to assume that some sort of cyclical movement occurred, with market concentration falling to unusually low levels during the sellers' market immediately following World War II—a pattern analogous to the one observed for aggregate concentration.

Further analysis discloses that much of the postwar increase is the result of events in a few very large industries. Thus, about half the gain from 1947 to 1954 is due to a recorded rise in the steel industry's four-firm concentration ratio from 45 to 54, nudging it into the 'concentrated' group. A modification in Census Bureau classification assumptions was partly responsible for this change. The relative stability from 1954 to 1958 can be attributed in part to two offsetting sets of influences. The recession of 1958 significantly reduced the value added shares of large, concentrated industries like automobiles and steel. But the aircraft industry, which had expanded its value added share from 0.8 per cent in 1947 to 2.4 per cent in 1958 as a result of booming Cold War defense contracts, reentered the concentrated group when its four-firm ratio rose from 47 to 59. Then, of the 3 percentage point increase between 1958 and 1963, 2 points can be traced to the boom experienced by the automobile industry in 1963, although this gain was partly offset by a .5 percentage point decline in the aircraft industry's value added contribution. Of the 4.5 point decline from 1963 to 1966, 3.9 points were due to a fall in the steel industry's concentration ratio from 51 in 1963 to 49 in 1966.

From these few observations it should be clear that the Nutter-Adelman approach to identifying trends in concentration is extremely sensitive to relatively small concentration changes in key oligopolistic industries. An alternative view of the postwar experience is obtained by computing weighted average concentration ratios for all manufacturing industry, letting each individual

[58] *The Extent of Enterprise Monopoly in the United States: 1899-1939* (Chicago: University of Chicago Press, 1951), especially pp. 35–48 and 112–150. Nutter's aim was to determine whether the amount of monopoly in the *overall* economy was increasing. He concluded that it might or might not be, depending upon the quantitative assumptions taken. For a more recent attempt to play this game of blind man's bluff, see H. A. Einhorn, "Competition in American Industry, 1939–58," *Journal of Political Economy*, October 1966, pp. 506–511.

[59] *Ibid.*, p. 147. Note that one is likely to find more industries with a four-firm concentration ratio exceeding 50 at some time during a ten year period than in any single year. But there are so many other possibilities for error in a reconstruction job as difficult as Nutter's that it makes little sense to dwell heavily on this particular bias. See, for example, the comment by Stanley Lebergott and the rejoinder by Nutter in the *Review of Economics and Statistics*, November 1953, pp. 349–353.

[60] M. A. Adelman, "The Measurement of Industrial Concentration," pp. 295–296.

[61] Industries in the ordnance group (S.I.C. 19) are excluded from both numerator and denominator of these calculations, since no concentration data are published for them. For the 25 industries on which no 1966 concentration ratios were published, 1963 ratios were substituted.

industry's four-firm ratio be weighted by the value added originating in that industry.[62] The resulting concentration indices are as follows:

1947	35.3
1954	36.9
1958	37.0
1963	38.9
1966	39.0

This approach suggests a much more modest rise in concentration on the average between 1947 and 1963, with a continuing but very slight upward movement into 1966.

Additional insight is provided by an analysis of 184 four-digit industries whose definitions remained sufficiently static to permit a comparison over four postwar census years.[63] Although the sample covers 41 per cent of all 1963 manufacturing value added, it is not perfectly representative, since the industries not redefined were generally less dynamic technologically than those requiring redefinition. Nevertheless, the sample exhibits the same broad pattern of changes as does the whole of manufacturing industry.[64] Four different average four-firm sales concentration ratios were computed for each year, as follows:

	1947	1954	1958	1963
Simple (unweighted) average	41.7	41.7	41.4	42.7
Average (own year's value added weights)	40.2	44.4	44.0	46.2
Average (1947 value added weights)	40.2	42.8	42.2	43.1
Average (1963 value added weights)	42.8	46.2	45.6	46.2

All four comparisons show a rise in average concentration between 1947 and 1963, though most of the increase in weighted average concentration had already occurred by 1954, after which no strong trend is evident. The 16 year increase is greater when component industry concentration ratios are weighted than when not, indicating that concentration rose most in the relatively large industries. Changes in the relative sizes of industries between 1947 and 1963 worked in the direction of raising average concentration both absolutely and relative to the level with 1947 weights.

All in all, the patterns revealed are sufficiently complex and varied to mask evidence of an unambiguous long-term general trend. We are led to conclude that if market concentration is increasing in the manufacturing sector, it is not doing so in a spectacular, consistent fashion.

COMPARISONS WITH OTHER INDUSTRIAL NATIONS

Let us broaden our horizon. Three questions concerning the structure of industry in other industrialized nations are of special interest. Is market concentration greater or less on the average in manufacturing industries outside the United States? Are there consistent patterns in the degree of concentration observed in similar industries for diverse nations? And are there noticeable trends in market concentration in other countries? As one might expect, the problems of obtaining comparable data are formidable, but the available evidence does support the weight of some rough impressions.

First, it would appear that market concentration in the United States tends to be lower than in other major industrialized nations, with the possible exception of Great Britain and Japan. This was the gist of Joe S. Bain's conclusion from an analysis of market structures in eight

---

[62]The 1947, 1954, and 1958 figures are drawn from a table presented by Professor Adelman in *Economic Concentration*, p. 335.

[63]Some 30 other industries on which comparable concentration ratios were published have been excluded. Eight were catch-all categories, five were publishing industries, four were strongly defense-oriented and hence largely outside the market economy, and the remainder had other serious market definition deficiencies.

[64]See also W. G. Shepherd, "Trends of Concentration in American Manufacturing Industries," *Review of Economics and Statistics*, May 1964, pp. 200–212. Shepherd used employment-weighted data, which show less increase in concentration than value added – weighted data, since value added has risen relatively more rapidly than employment in the more concentrated industries, partly because of differential labor productivity growth rates and partly because wages have risen more rapidly in the more concentrated industries.

countries.[65] Relative to the levels existing in U. S. manufacturing industries as of 1954, Bain found average market concentration in Great Britain to be slightly lower, in Japan slightly higher, in France and Italy moderately higher, and in Canada, India, and Sweden much higher.

More detailed concentration data covering 26 industries in the United States, Canada, and Great Britain are presented in Table 3.5. The sample of industries is not random, being dictated largely by the availability of information on comparably defined industries. For Great Britain and Canada the concentration ratios pertain to the share of the three largest firms in each industry (except in one case), while all U. S. concentration ratios are on a four-firm basis. Taking this bias into account, concentration in Canada appears to be unquestionably higher than in the United States. The simple average concentration ratio for the United States is 36.3, compared to 50.4 for Canada, and if the Canadian data were to be adjusted to a four-firm basis, the average ratio would be closer to 56 or 58.[66] For Britain and the United States, the comparison is less definite. If the fourth firm in British industries added 2 per cent or more of total industry employment, average British concentration on a comparable four-firm basis would exceed the U. S. average. Still the differences are so small, and the sampling uncertainties sufficiently large, that we can safely conclude only that average manufacturing market concentration levels in the two nations are probably not greatly dissimilar.[67]

It does not follow that the average amount of monopoly power is about the same in Britain as in the United States. England and the other countries included in Bain's study are all exposed to more extensive import competition. On the other hand, formal cartel agreements among ostensibly independent firms were also more prevalent, at least during the 1950s. How these opposing forces balance out is difficult to say.

Casual inspection of Table 3.5 reveals a tendency for concentration in a given industry to be high in all three nations when it is high in one and to be low in all three when it is low in one, with only a few notable exceptions. This is verified by correlating the concentration ratios of the three nations. The correlation coefficient between U. S. and Canadian industry ratios is 0.72, between U. S. and British ratios 0.63, and between British and Canadian ratios 0.87.[68] When the three-firm concentration ratios for 23 Japanese industries are correlated with the four-firm ratios of comparable U. S. industries, a correlation coefficient of 0.55 is obtained.[69] These associations suggest that market structure must be influenced by basic technological and economic factors affecting all industrialized societies, and is not merely the result of historical accident. Chapter 4 searches further for such regularities.

Quantitative evidence on concentration trends outside the United States is much too meager to support broad generalizations. In Japan, concentration in manufacturing industries apparently declined on the average between 1937 and 1958, but may have begun to increase since then.[70] Shepherd found a marked increase in concentration in British industries between 1951 and 1958.[71] It is probable that similar increases would be observed on the European continent for the postwar period, if the data could be

---

[65]*International Differences in Industrial Structure* (New Haven: Yale University Press, 1966), especially pp. 67–122 and 138–139.

[66]See also Gideon Rosenbluth, *Concentration in Canadian Manufacturing Industries* (Princeton: Princeton University Press, 1957), pp. 75–87.

[67]Rosenbluth found in a comparison of 1935 concentration ratios for 57 industries that both weighted and unweighted average concentration ratios were slightly higher in England than in the United States. "Measures of Concentration," pp. 70–77.

[68]Rosenbluth obtained a 0.71 correlation between the concentration ratios of 41 comparable Canadian and U. S. industries. *Concentration in Canadian Manufacturing Industries*, pp. 89–92.

[69]The data are from Bain, *op. cit.*, p. 82.

[70]See Rotwein, *op. cit.*, pp. 264–265; and Kozo Yamamura, "Market Concentration and Growth in Postwar Japan," *Southern Economic Journal*, April 1966, pp. 451–464.

[71]W. G. Shepherd, "Changes in British Industrial Concentration, 1951–1958," *Oxford Economic Papers*, March 1966, pp. 126–132.

Table 3.5

Employment Concentration Ratios for Similar Industries
in the United States, Canada, and Great Britain

Industry	United States (4–Firm, 1950)	Canada (3–Firm, 1948)	Great Britain (3–Firm, 1951)
Automobiles	90	88	69
Cigarettes and cigars	70	85	70
Biscuits and crackers	66	42	34
Pig iron	57	92	45
Steel ingots and castings	55	76	40
Aircraft and parts	53	78	46
Shipbuilding	53	32	25
Abrasive products	52	82	76
Bicycles	52	81	64
Carpets and rugs	49	64	28
Petroleum refining	39	80	84
Cordage, rope, and twine	37	66	24
Woolen cloth	29	28	12
Cement	29	100	87
Flour mills	26	35	41
Paints and varnishes	23	32	19
Leather boots and shoes	22	9	8
Corsets and girdles	20	37	29
Pulp and paper mills	20	28	21
Beer and ale	19	49	14
Iron castings	18	20	13
Leather tanning	18	27	24
Bread and related products	16	21	15
Woolen yarn	15	39	21
Hosiery and knit goods	11	16	8
Sawmills and planing mills	4	5	6
Simple average for all industries	36.3	50.4	35.5

Sources: United States, U.S. Senate, Committee on the Judiciary, Subcommittee on Antitrust and Monopoly, Report, *Concentration in American Industry* (Washington, 1957), pp. 382–406; Canada, Gideon Rosenbluth, *Concentration in Canadian Manufacturing Industries* (Princeton: Princeton University Press, 1957), pp. 111-113; Great Britain, R. Evely and I.M.D. Little, *Concentration in British Industry* (Cambridge: Cambridge University Press, 1960), pp. 296–312. Some consolidations have been made to render industry definitions as comparable as possible. Data for the British cement industry are for four firms.

obtained.[72] However, the formation of the European Common Market raises problems for the interpretation of any such trends similar to those created by the expansion of American railroads and communication systems in the 19th century.

THE STABILITY OF LEADING POSITIONS

The concentration ratio is a static index, characterizing market structure for a specific,

typically short interval in time. We should not be surprised that the identity of the leading firms in an industry changes occasionally. And when turnover among the top firms is rapid, high concentration ratios may conceal or belie the real intensity of competition for two reasons. First, the shares of industry leaders, and hence the concentration ratio, will be lower when computed on, say, a five-year basis than the shares of

[72]For an account of some unsuccessful efforts, see M. A. Adelman, "Monopoly and Concentration: Comparisons in Time and Space," in *Essays in Honour of Marco Fanno* (Padova: 1966).

leaders identified for any shorter interval, since momentary leaders will tend to be firms enjoying market shares exceeding their long-run average shares. Second, the very rapidity of turnover suggests a competitive struggle for position. High turnover is said by some economists to be an indicator of dynamic competition, which may be present even when concentration ratios imply the absence of much competition in a static structural sense.

A first look at the available statistics on leading firm turnover lends some support to the claim that dynamic competition is vigorous. One early study of 262 product lines revealed that the four sales leaders of 1935 maintained their leadership positions during 1937 in only 19 per cent of the fields covered. In 40 per cent of the product lines, two or more of the 1935 leaders were replaced by other firms in 1937, and in 13 per cent, three or more of the 1935 leaders had been displaced.[73] An analysis of more recent data covering 204 four-digit industries yields the same magic number 19 as the percentage of all cases in which the four industry leaders of 1947 continued to be the leaders during 1958. In only 6 per cent of the 204 cases did the rank order of the four firms leading their industries in 1947 remain identical in 1958.[74]

However, these statistics may be misleading. Most of the market share changes which cause some firms to drop out of the top four and others to enter are small. If, for instance, the firms ranked 3 and 4 in an industry at some moment in time have market shares of 7.5 and 6.5 per cent, while the firms ranked 5 and 6 have shares of 6.2 and 5.7 per cent, it does not take a shakeup of dramatic proportions to let firms 3 and 4 be displaced from their positions. And most market shares, Michael Gort found in an analysis spanning the years 1947 through 1954, do not change drastically over such a seven year interval.[75] He obtained confidential census data on the market shares of all firms among the 15 sales leaders in 205 four-digit industries in 1947, 1954, or both. He then correlated, industry by industry, the market shares of those firms in 1954 with their 1947 market shares. In 74 per cent of the 205 cases, the inter-temporal correlation coefficient was 0.80 or higher. In only 10 per cent was the correlation coefficient less than 0.50. Thus, if a firm's market share was low relative to the pack in 1947, it was likely to be low also in 1954, and if it was high in 1947, it was likely to remain high in 1954.

Moreover, there is evidence that stability of market positions and concentration in the static sense are positively associated. The correlation between the inter-temporal correlation coefficients (serving as an index of relative stability) for the 205 industries in Gort's sample and 1947 four-firm concentration ratios was 0.52.[76] In another study, Preston found that industries with no change in the identity of their leading firms between 1947 and 1958 were on the average more concentrated than the industries in which at least one firm was displaced.[77]

From these results alone, we cannot be certain that a causal link exists between concentration and turnover (or lack of it), so that both indicators of monopoly power, one static and the other dynamic, point in the same direction. More trivial alternative explanations can be proposed. Notably, if there are more firms of about the same size as the largest four firms in unconcentrated than in concentrated industries, turnover among the top four will tend to be higher in the less concentrated industries for equal percentage variations over time in firm growth rates. By the same logic, if there is greater relative inequality of market shares in the more concentrated industries, inter-temporal market share correlations will also be higher for concentrated industries than for less concentrated industries experiencing similar variability in firm growth rates. These possibilities have not been adequately explored.

It is also possible that high instability of

---

[73]Cf. Rosenbluth, "Measures of Concentration," p. 93, citing and correcting mistakes in findings by Willard Thorp and Walter Crowder.

[74]See the testimony of Jules Backman in *Economic Concentration*, pp. 562–563.

[75]"Analysis of Stability and Change in Market Shares," *Journal of Political Economy*, February 1963, pp. 51–61.

[76]*Ibid.*, p. 56. See also Grossack, *op. cit.*

[77]Testimony of L. E. Preston in *Economic Concentration*, pp. 68–69.

market shares—to some economists a manifestation of competitive vigor—has the paradoxical long-run effect of increasing the level of static concentration. We shall explore this hypothesis in the next chapter.

DIVERSIFICATION OF AMERICAN FIRMS

Product line diversification is interesting for several reasons: as an increasingly prominent structural attribute; as a condition which can affect firms' pricing behavior (explored in Chapter 11) and research decisions (Chapter 15); as a potential target of the government's anti-merger policy (Chapter 20); and as a possible explanation of the largest firms' growing share of all manufacturing activity.

Even the most casual reader of the financial pages knows that large American firms have widely diversified interests. A more precise impression can be gleaned by analyzing the operations of the 1,000 largest industrial corporations during 1962.[78] Fifteen participated in more than 50 five-digit census product lines (out of a thousand possible lines in all); 236 participated in from 16 to 50 product lines; 477 in from 6 to 15 lines; 223 in from two to five lines; and 49 firms among the 1,000 largest confined themselves to one line. Another study showed that General Electric was the most highly diversified manufacturing company during 1954, operating in 74 different four-digit product classes (out of a possible total of 430), including 57 product classes outside the electrical equipment group.[79] Runners-up included United States Rubber, with 56 product classes; Westinghouse, with 54; General Motors, with 41; and Olin-Mathieson Chemical Corp., with 40 four-digit classes. A fresh look at the diversification scene, using much broader industry definitions, showed Litton Industries to be in the lead for 1966, participating in 18 out of a possible total of 54 industrial and nonindustrial categories.[80] Litton,

it is worth remarking, was founded only in 1954. It achieved its billion-dollar size and diversified status through an unusually ambitious program of mergers. General Electric had dropped to third place in the 1966 list, behind the General Tire and Rubber Co.

Merely counting product lines could exaggerate the overall significance of diversification, since many products may be only minor sidelines. However, company activities outside primary product lines are far from inconsequential. Using confidential Census Bureau data, Michael Gort found that 36 per cent of 111 large corporations' total manufacturing payrolls in 1954 were distributed outside the sampled firms' primary four-digit product class—that is, outside the class in which they had their highest sales.[81] For purposes of analyzing diversification, this four-digit definition of a firm's home base is perhaps too narrow. A more recent study showed that 24 per cent of the manufacturing employment of the 200 largest manufacturing firms in 1958 occurred in industry groups outside the firms' primary two-digit census groups.[82] The most diversified firms were those whose home bases were the fabricated metal products group (a catch-all classification), with 44 per cent of their employment in other groups; the electrical equipment group, with 37 per cent outside employment; and the rubber products group, with 33 per cent. The least diversified firms belonged to the tobacco products group (8 per cent outside employment), food products (8 per cent), and petroleum and coal products (13 per cent).

Diversification can be viewed statically as an element of market structure existing at some moment in time or as a dynamic process of movement by firms into new and different lines. In neither respect is diversification an entirely new phenomenon. However, both the amount and rate of diversification have apparently increased markedly since World War II. Gort observed that the 111 large firms in his sample collectively

[78]See the testimony of H. F. Houghton in *Economic Concentration*, pp. 155–158.

[79]Michael Gort, *Diversification and Integration in American Industry* (Princeton: Princeton University Press, 1962), pp. 155–157.

[80]Thomas O'Hanlon, "The Odd News about Conglomerates," *Fortune*, June 15, 1967, pp. 175–177.

[81]*Diversification and Integration in American Industry*, pp. 32–34.

[82]See the testimony of John M. Blair in *Economic Concentration*, pp. 83–86 and 388.

added 48 new four-digit product classes per year between 1929 and 1939, 43 new products per year between 1939 and 1950, and 108 products per year between 1950 and 1954.[83] He found also that between 1947 and 1954, the share of those 111 firms' total manufacturing payrolls associated with product lines outside their primary four-digit field of specialization increased from 31 per cent to 36 per cent, while the number of four-digit lines in which the companies operated rose by 30 per cent.[84] More recent evidence indicates that the trend toward increased diversification has continued and perhaps even accelerated. Five-digit product diversification patterns among the 1,000 largest industrial firms (ranked separately for each year) changed between 1950 and 1962 as follows:[85]

Number of Five-Digit Products Produced	Percentage of Firms in Class	
	1950	1962
1	7.8	4.9
2–5	35.4	22.3
6–15	43.2	47.7
16–50	12.8	23.6
Over 50	0.8	1.5

There was a clear movement into the more diversified groups; e.g., only 136 firms operated in 16 or more product lines in 1950, compared to 251 firms in 1962.

Some of this diversification was achieved through the acquisition of companies operating in different fields. We shall analyze merger patterns of the 1950s and 1960s in the next chapter. Internal growth, often based upon the development of new products originating from company research and development laboratories, was also an important route to diversification. Unfortunately, we have little information on the quantitative balance between mergers and internal growth

as contributors to increasing corporate diversification.

The very notion of diversification—movement into new fields—implies a breaking with past product specialization traditions. Still for most corporations this movement has not been totally unstructured. Much diversification effort has been directed into product lines not greatly different from existing lines. For example, electrical firms have expanded their coverage of the electrical product spectrum; firms like du Pont initially specializing in explosives have moved into other chemical products such as plastics, synthetic fibers, paints, and synthetic leather; and dairy products specialists like the Borden Company have broadened their coverage of the food products field by adding canned goods and confectionary lines. The trend, however, seems to be toward increasing crossing of two-digit industry group lines. Gort found that product line additions by the 111 firms in his sample were within the diversifying firms' two-digit field of primary interest in 43 per cent of all cases during the 1929–1939 period; in 35 per cent for the 1939–1950 period; and in only 32 per cent for the 1950–1954 period.[86] But even when firms have jumped two-digit industry lines, it has more often than not been into products with some technical or distributional link to existing products. Examples of technically related diversification include Armour's development of soaps and other chemical products using the by-products of its meat-packing operations, and General Electric's entry into the turbojet aircraft engine business, aided by its experience in steam turbine technology. Examples of diversification involving complementarities on the distribution side include the tin can manufacturers' migration into paper container and glass bottle production and the soap manufacturers' development of food product lines distributed through the same retail outlets as their traditional products. 'Pure conglomerate' diversification—diversification

---

[83]*Diversification and Integration in American Industry*, pp. 44–48.

[84]*Ibid.*, pp. 60–61.

[85]See *Economic Concentration*, p. 157. The 1950 product line count is based upon a Federal Trade Commission survey; the 1962 count on the listings in *Fortune*'s *Plant and Product Directory*. If there are biases in the inclusiveness of the listings, they probably run in favor of understating the growth of diversification.

[86]*Diversification and Integration in American Industry*, pp. 42–47.

with no technical or distributional complementarities at all—has been exceptional in the past, although its occurrence evidently increased rapidly during the late 1960s.

Certain additional patterns in the postwar diversification movement deserve notice. The new product lines entered by established firms have typically been growing rapidly, often as a result of technological advances. The dynamic chemicals, electronics, and aerospace fields have been especially frequent diversification targets. Gort discovered that diversification activity was more closely correlated with the ratio of engineers and chemists to total employment in the industries entered by diversifying firms than in the home base industries of those firms. He also found diversification to be positively associated with the four-firm concentration ratio in diversifying firms' primary industries—apparently because high concentration made it difficult to expand in traditional product lines without disrupting pricing relationships, forcing oligopolistic firms to turn outward in search of growth opportunities.[87]

Is the movement toward diversification responsible for observed increases in the share of all U. S. industrial activity controlled by the largest manufacturing firms? The only direct quantitative evidence presently available comes from Gort's study of 111 manufacturing companies. He found that their payrolls in non-primary (i.e., diversified) product lines rose from 31 per cent in 1947 to 36 per cent in 1954, while the share of the 100 largest manufacturers in all manufacturing value added rose from 23 per cent to 30 per cent. If we assume that the diversification pattern displayed by Gort's sample is representative of the 100 largest firms, then the 100 largest in 1954 originated 19.2 per cent of all manufacturing value added through operations in their primary product line (30 × .64) and 10.8 per cent through their diversification lines. Had their primary product share remained unaltered at 19.2 per cent, but their diversified product share been maintained at only 45 per cent of primary products (100 × $\frac{31}{69}$, as in 1947), the diversified product share would have been 8.6 per cent and their total share of 1954 value added 27.8 per cent, instead of 30 per cent. These calculations suggest that increased diversification accounted for only about a third of the value added share growth of the 100 largest firms between 1947 and 1954. And this estimate, Gort argues, is generous, since his sample was more diversification-prone than the 100 largest manufacturing firms, and since companies might have grown more in their primary product lines had they grown less through diversification.[88]

What of the remaining two thirds? Nelson's analysis indicates that it was due mainly to two factors: the extraordinarily rapid growth of the aircraft industry, seven of whose leading members joined the largest 50 manufacturers in 1954, and the less rapid but still impressive growth of auto makers General Motors, Ford, and Chrysler (partly in absolute terms, and significantly at the expense of other auto and parts manufacturers).[89] Thus, the rising share of the 100 largest manufacturing firms between 1947 and 1954 appears to have been the result of a concatenation of unusual changes in industry size, increases in concentration within a very large industry, and increased diversification.

At the time when this was written, no one had done the detective work required to explain the continued rise since 1954 in the largest firms' share of total manufacturing value added and assets. In all probability, diversification will turn out to play an even more prominent role.

VERTICAL INTEGRATION IN AMERICAN INDUSTRY

Vertical integration, like diversification, can be viewed both as a static dimension of market structure and as a process of altering market structures. Dynamically, firms which integrate 'upstream' or backward undertake to produce raw materials and semi-fabricated inputs which previously were supplied by independent pro-

---

[87]*Ibid.*, pp. 135–143.

[88]See Gort's testimony in *Economic Concentration*, pp. 673–676.

[89]*Concentration in the Manufacturing Industries of the United States*, pp. 99–108.

ducers. Firms which integrate 'downstream' or forward move toward further finishing of semi-fabricated products and the wholesaling and retailing operations which put manufactured goods into the hands of consumers. Vertical integration in the static sense, of course, describes the extent to which firms in fact cover the entire range of production and distribution stages.

The most obvious and pervasive motive for vertical integration is to reduce costs. A classic example is found in the steel industry: integration of diverse furnace with rolling mill operations eliminates the need for separate reheating steps. Vertical integration may also give producers enhanced control over their economic environment. Upstream integration, for example, can ensure that supplies of raw materials will be available in time of shortage and protect the firm from a price squeeze by monopolistic suppliers. Downstream integration gives the firm greater control over its markets, lessening the probability, among other things, of foreclosure (being shut out from the market) by powerful buyers or middlemen.[90]

With the opportunity for controlling markets through vertical integration goes the opportunity to abuse that control, and it is this element which makes vertical integration especially interesting. Firms integrated vertically may keep raw materials out of rival hands, or foreclose markets to rivals, or establish a vertical price structure (relating raw material to intermediate and end product prices) which squeezes profit margins of the less integrated competitor.[91] Integration may also affect pricing behavior in more subtle ways, e.g., by complicating price decisions to such an extent that rigidity ensues,[92] or by increasing overhead costs (through the internalization of costs which would have been fully

variable, if incurred by independent materials suppliers) and hence altering the integrated firm's susceptibility to local or general business downturns.

Thus, vertical integration is important. Unfortunately, we have little solid evidence on the extent of vertical integration in the American economy. Rough qualitative impressions are readily gained. We know, for example, that the major petroleum refiners are highly integrated, commanding extensive crude oil reserves, refining facilities, the pipelines through which crude and refined products flow to market, and in many instances networks of company-owned retail gasoline stations. Small transistor manufacturers, on the other hand, exhibit very little integration. They buy raw materials from chemicals and metals firms and sell their transistors to electrical equipment assemblers, who in turn utilize independent distributors to carry their television sets or tape recorders incorporating the transistors to the consumer. For any desired firm or industry, it is easy enough to make such an analysis. It is also possible to estimate the amount of vertical integration in the economy at a highly aggregated level. In 1962, for example, all private business enterprises reported combined sales of $1.146 trillion, to support their net output of final goods and services valued at roughly $525 billion. From this we compute that the 'typical' business firm generated value added of $46 for every $100 in sales, buying $54 worth of inputs from other firms.[93] But problems arise when we try to make systematic quantitative comparisons across industry lines and between firms within industries.

At first glance, the ratio of value added to sales might seem an appropriate measure of vertical integration at the microeconomic level too. How-

[90]On the strategy of downstream integration, see R. H. Holton, "The Role of Competition and Monopoly in Distribution," in J. P. Miller, ed., *Competition, Cartels and Their Regulation* (Amsterdam: North Holland, 1962), pp. 284–286.

[91]See W. S. Comanor, "Vertical Mergers, Market Power, and the Antitrust Laws," *American Economic Review*, May 1967, pp. 254–265; and Robert Crandall, "Vertical Integration and the Market for Repair Parts in the United States Automobile Industry," *Journal of Industrial Economics*, July 1968, pp. 212–234.

[92]See Walter Adams and Joel B. Dirlam, "Steel Imports and Vertical Oligopoly Power," *American Economic Review*, September 1964, pp. 626–655.

[93]Input-output tables also provide an indication of the amount of vertical integration and disintegration from an aggregate viewpoint, but the results they yield depend to some extent upon the degree of detail pursued in drawing up the tables. A 73 sector input-output table developed at Harvard indicates that the degree of vertical disintegration or "roundaboutness" in the U. S. economy increased slightly (by about 2 per cent) between 1947 and 1958. See Carter, "The Economics of Technological Change," p. 29.

ever, it gives misleading comparisons when firms or industries are located at varying stages in the stream of economic activity. Suppose, to use an example coined by Adelman, an economy consists of three disintegrated firms: a raw materials producer, a fabricator, and a distributor; and suppose each contributes one third of total value added.[94] Assuming further that the raw materials producer buys nothing from outside suppliers, his value added/sales ratio is 1.0, giving the misleading impression that he is totally integrated vertically. The fabricator (buying raw material valued at one third and adding his own labor etc. valued at one third) has a value added/sales ratio of .5, while the distributor will have a ratio of .33. The nearer the raw materials end of the production stream a specialist firm's (or industry's) operations are located, the higher its value added/sales ratio tends to be, *ceteris paribus*. Because of this bias, attempts to measure the degree of vertical integration in particular firms or industries using only the statistical data readily available to researchers give results which at best must be viewed with caution, and which at worst may be nonsensical.

An attempt to circumvent the conventional measurement problems was made by Gort in his study of 111 large corporations. Through qualitative analysis, he identified for each firm those four-digit product activities which were "auxiliary" to the firm's primary (largest) product class, namely, activities which either supplied inputs into the primary production operation or contributed to further downstream fabrication or distribution of the primary product. His index of integration was then defined as the percentage of employment in auxiliary industries to total company employment. Not surprisingly, he found petroleum industry firms to have by far the highest integration index—67 per cent. Distant runners-up were machinery, with 30.5 per cent of employment in auxiliary activities, and food products, with 30.3 per cent. The least integrated firms were found in the transportation equipment industry (9.7 per cent), electrical equipment (12.8 per cent), and fabricated metal products (15.0 per cent).[95]

Gort's study also shows that the ratio of auxiliary to total company employment is positively but only weakly related to firm size, with a rank correlation coefficient of 0.37.[96] Thus, the largest firms appear to be somewhat more integrated than medium-sized firms, but not strikingly or consistently so.

There is a modest amount of evidence on broad long-term trends in vertical integration. Examining value added/sales ratios for manufacturing industry as a whole between 1849 and 1939 and for selected steel firms between 1902 and 1952, Adelman found no clear trend toward either increased or reduced vertical integration.[97] Laffer computed similar ratios for all corporations in ten broad sectors of the economy between 1929 and 1965, concluding that there was no discernible time trend in the degree of integration.[98] In this respect as in others, the structure of American industry has apparently changed surprisingly little since the turn of the century.

[94]M. A. Adelman, "Concept and Statistical Measurement of Vertical Integration," in *Business Concentration and Price Policy*, pp. 281–283.

[95]*Diversification and Integration in American Industry*, pp. 80–82.

[96]*Ibid.*, pp. 81–84.

[97]"Concept and Statistical Measurement of Vertical Integration," pp. 308–311. See also George J. Stigler, "The Division of Labor Is Limited by the Extent of the Market," *Journal of Political Economy*, June 1951, pp. 189–190.

[98]Arthur B. Laffer, "Vertical Integration by Corporations, 1929–1965," *Review of Economics and Statistics*, February 1969, pp. 91–93.

Chapter 4

The Determinants of Market Structure

What accounts for the widespread differences in market structure found in diverse industries? Is it necessary for concentration to be as high as it is in many manufacturing industries? These questions are our concern in the present chapter. We shall explore several determinants of market structure, including economies of scale, mergers, various government policies, growth, and chance.

ECONOMIES OF SCALE

One condition which could lead to concentrated market structures is the existence of substantial scale economies, permitting relatively large producers to manufacture and market their products at lower average cost per unit than relatively small producers. The principal basis of scale economies in production is specialization, or the division of labor—a phenomenon Adam Smith deemed so central that he devoted the first three chapters of *Wealth of Nations* to it. In Smith's view, great increases in the productivity of labor (and hence great reductions in product cost) were due to three repercussions of the division of labor: an increase in worker dexterity, the saving of time commonly lost in "passing from one species of work to another," and "the invention of a great number of machines which facilitate and abridge labor, and enable one man to do the work of many."

Smith's observations are as pertinent today as they were two centuries ago, and they provide a natural starting point for any discussion of scale economies. In larger firms a richer division of labor is possible than in small firms. Specializa-tion may be achieved within a particular plant or production complex and also, when the firm operates more than one plant complex, across plant lines. This distinction between intra-plant and inter-plant economies must be kept in mind continually. As we shall see, there is reason to believe that most of the production cost savings attributable to specialization are realized within particular plants, and not through multiple plant operation.

The assembly line of an automobile plant is a classic illustration of intra-plant economies gained through worker specialization. Each worker on the line is assigned responsibility for one or a very few operations, and he is able to build up extraordinary proficiency at these tasks, even though he may lack any special mechanical aptitudes. A smaller auto maker could, of course, try to achieve a similar degree of specialization. But if there is just enough work at an output of 500 cars per day to employ, say, one left wheel nut tightener, a man assigned to that job in a plant whose output is only 250 cars per day will be idle half the time. To avoid this waste, the smaller plant may assign him other jobs, such as tightening right wheel nuts or placing left wheels on their lugs for bolting. But in the former case time is lost moving back and forth from one side of the assembly line to the other, and in the latter, time is lost as the worker shifts mental gears and fumbles for the correct tool and working position. The low-volume production line sacrifices either specialization or full utilization of specialized operatives, and therefore suffers some cost disadvantage.

Identical principles apply in the use of machinery. Special machines can be designed to perform certain tasks at a considerable savings of time and labor. But the small-scale producer may find no advantage in adopting them, because they cannot be scaled down and would therefore be idle much of the time, leaving a small number of units of output to bear the full burden of their capital costs. For instance, a large automobile engine plant can save millions of dollars annually by investing in automated cylinder boring, valve seating, and work-piece transfer machines, while the low-volume producer must opt for slower, more labor-intensive general-purpose machine tools.

Even when identical general-purpose machines are employed by both large producers and small, the larger entity often derives a cost advantage by virtue of its longer production runs. It takes from several hours to several days to set up a metal-stamping press to produce a particular automobile fender, roof, or door panel. The high-volume factory which can assign each press full time to a single part incurs this setup cost infrequently, while the low-volume plant which must produce numerous different parts on each press experiences much higher setup costs, and hence higher product costs.

A somewhat different basis of scale economies is found in the 'process' industries such as petroleum refining, chemical production, cement making, glass manufacturing, steam generation, and iron ore reduction. The output of a processing unit tends within certain physical limits to be roughly proportional to the volume of the unit, other things being equal, while the amount of materials and fabrication effort (and hence investment cost) required to construct the unit is more apt to be proportional to the surface area of the unit's reaction chambers, storage tanks, connecting pipes, etc. Since the area of a sphere or cylinder of constant proportions varies as the two thirds power of volume, the cost of constructing process industry plants can be expected to rise as the two thirds power of their output capacity, at least up to the point where they become so large that extra structural reinforcement and special fabrication techniques are required. There is considerable empirical support for the existence of this 'two thirds rule,' which is used by engineers in estimating the cost of new process equipment.[1]

Still another benefit of size arises from what E. A. G. Robinson calls "the economies of massed reserves."[2] A firm anxious to maintain continuity of production must hold equipment in reserve against machine breakdowns. A firm large enough to use only one specialized machine may be forced to double its capacity if it insists on hedging against breakdown; the larger firm with numerous machines can obtain virtually the same degree of protection by holding only a small proportion of its capacity in reserve. Likewise, the number of repairmen a company must employ to provide any stipulated amount of service in the event of random machine failures rises less than proportionately with the number of machines in operation.[3] Size also offers advantages in maintaining capacity sufficient to meet fluctuations in demand, for the more customers a given production complex serves, the more random peaks and valleys in individual customers' demands tend to cancel out, allowing the large firm to maintain less reserve capacity relative to the average level of demand.[4]

The cost-scale relationships identified thus far

[1]See F. T. Moore, "Economies of Scale: Some Statistical Evidence," *Quarterly Journal of Economics*, May 1959, pp. 232–245; the comment by S. C. Schuman and S. B. Alpert, *Quarterly Journal of Economics*, August 1960, pp. 493–497; and John Haldi and David Whitcomb, "Economies of Scale in Industrial Plants," *Journal of Political Economy*, August 1967, pp. 373–385.

[2]*The Structure of Competitive Industry* (Rev. ed.; Chicago: University of Chicago Press, 1958), pp. 26–27. Robinson's work continues to be the classic reference on the theory of scale economies.

[3]See T. M. Whitin and M. H. Peston, "Random Variations, Risk, and Returns to Scale," *Quarterly Journal of Economics*, November 1954, pp. 603–612.

[4]Similar economies have been hypothesized in the maintenance of cash balances sufficient to meet fluctuating payment demands, although more recent theoretical and empirical studies provide little support. See W. J. Baumol, "The Transactions Demand for Cash: An Inventory Theoretic Approach," *Quarterly Journal of Economics*, November 1952, pp. 545–556; and Karl Brunner and Allan H. Meltzer, "Economies of Scale in Cash Balances Reconsidered," *Quarterly Journal of Economics*, August 1967, pp. 422–436.

are of an essentially static character. That is, the plant or firm designed to produce a high volume of output will have lower unit costs in each time period (or over the average of all time periods) than the enterprise designed to produce a lower volume. But in many industries, unit costs are also related to volume in a dynamic way, falling as the *cumulative volume* of output increases due to the accumulation of experience and skill by production engineers, supervisors, and workers.[5] Studies of World War II aircraft production show that labor costs per unit declined by approximately 20 per cent on the average with every doubling of cumulative output. Similar relationships have been observed in the production of machine tools and electronic apparatus, and they undoubtedly hold for many other production processes requiring complex assembly operations. This 'learning by doing' phenomenon can have important structural implications in industries supplying moderate quantities of complex products, for the firm which gets in first and accumulates experience may be able to maintain a continuing cost advantage over later entrants producing roughly the same volume of output per time period. Whether similar advantages are sustained in mass-production industries such as television set and automobile manufacturing is less certain, since the rate of cost reduction evidently declines as cumulative output rises beyond several thousand units.[6]

WHAT CHECKS THE REALIZATION OF SCALE ECONOMIES?

It is quite clear that economies of scale do exist, and that unit costs decline with increases in plant and firm size, at least within limits. Does this decline in costs continue indefinitely? There are several reasons for believing that it does not.

In nearly all production and distribution operations the realization of scale economies appears to be subject to diminishing returns. Sooner or later a point is reached at which all opportunities for making further cost reductions through increased size are exhausted. This point is associated, although not necessarily in a simple way, with the scale at which the largest or most specialized machine or other input can be utilized fully. If, say, a particular stamping press can produce 120,000 units per year in continuous operation, and if every other specialized input has a lower operating rate, the stamping press is the bottleneck which governs the firm's *minimum optimal scale*—the smallest scale at which all economies of scale are realized. If all other inputs have quite small capacities relative to this bottleneck, 120,000 units per year will in fact be the minimum optimal scale. Complications arise, however, when other inputs also have high capacities. Suppose, for example, that the firm could benefit by employing an automated engine boring line fully utilized only at 80,000 units per year. If the production complex is designed for an annual volume of 120,000 units, either redundant engine boring capacity (two automated units) must be held, or 40,000 engines must be bored on inferior, less automated lines. Only at a scale of 240,000 units per year can stamping presses (two of them) and (three) engine boring lines all be utilized fully. This scale, at which all the discrete specialized processes dovetail perfectly, is then the minimum optimal scale. If no further complications intrude, equally low unit costs can be enjoyed at all outputs which are an integral multiple of the minimum optimal scale—i.e., in the present case, at annual outputs of 480,000 units, 720,000 units, etc.[7] Between these designed capacity levels, unit costs will be somewhat above their minimum value due to the

---

[5]See Armen Alchian, "Costs and Output," in Moses Abromovitz et al., *The Allocation of Economic Resources: Essays in Honor of B. F. Haley* (Stanford: Stanford University Press, 1959), pp. 23–40; Jack Hirshleifer, "The Firm's Cost Function: A Successful Reconstruction?" *Journal of Business*, July 1962, pp. 235–255; and L. E. Preston and E. C. Keachie, "Cost Functions and Progress Functions: An Integration," *American Economic Review*, March 1964, pp. 100–106.

[6]See Harold Asher, *Cost-Quantity Relationships in the Airframe Industry*, R–291 (Santa Monica: RAND Corporation, 1956), especially Chapters 4 and 7.

[7]These higher outputs can be achieved either by multiplying the number of separate plants or multiplying the scale of individual plants. Which approach is taken depends upon technological, managerial, transportation cost, and labor market variables.

imperfect dovetailing of processes, and the long-run cost curve of the firm will have a generally horizontal but scalloped shape.

A second set of considerations may modify this last assertion. It is possible that rising unit costs related to the difficulty of managing an enterprise of increasingly large scale will offset and eventually overwhelm the savings attributable to high-volume production and distribution. Two hypotheses in this vein have been advanced.[8]

For one, it is said that any enterprise must have a single individual who assumes ultimate authority and responsibility. Classical economists called him 'the entrepreneur'; or in President Truman's homelier simile, he is the man on whose desk rests the sign, "The buck stops here." The entrepreneur or chief executive is a fixed, indivisible input. And as every sophomore economics student has learned by heart, whenever increasing doses of variable inputs (workers, middle managers, technicians, stamping presses, etc.) are used in combination with some fixed input, sooner or later diminishing marginal returns take hold. Concretely, as the enterprise increases in size, the executive is confronted with more and more decisions, and he is removed further and further from the reality of front-line production and marketing operations, so that his ability to make sound decisions is attenuated, with a consequent rise in costs and/or fall in revenues. The problem is aggravated when the firm operates in a rapidly changing and uncertain environment, for it is the nonroutine decisions associated with change which press most heavily upon the chief executive's capacities.[9]

A related hypothesis asserts that as the enterprise increases in size, it becomes more and more difficult to keep each branch's operations in harmony with those of every other part. Hordes of middle managers, coordinators, and expediters[10] proliferate. The money cost of this bureaucracy is far from inconsequential and, in addition, organizational sluggishness rises with complexity. As Robinson puts it, a mistake by a platoon commander demands only an instantaneous "As you were!" A mistake by an army commander may require days of labor to set right.[11] The consequence of these management and coordination problems is upward pressure on costs which becomes increasingly intense as firm scales rise. At some critical point, the diseconomies of large-scale management overpower the economies of scale, and unit costs begin rising with output, giving the long-run average total cost curve its U-shape so familiar to readers of microeconomic theory texts. The downward segment of the 'U' is governed by conventional scale economies; the upward thrust by managerial diseconomies.

The concept of the U-shaped cost curve greatly simplifies many problems of economic theory. But is it valid? Quite possibly not. Some extremely able men have turned their inventive talents to overcoming the problem of large-scale management diseconomies, and they have enjoyed fair success. Staff functions have been designed to supply decision-making information to the chief executive in its most useful form and to round out a system of checks and balances which reduces the probability that important aspects of decisions will be overlooked. Communication has been simplified and accelerated by such technological innovations as the telephone, the teletype, and most recently, real-time electronic computer information systems. Techniques of cost accounting and budgetary control have been brought to a high state of perfection, giving the chief executive a clearer view of both the past per-

[8]See Robinson, *op. cit.*, Chapter 3; Nicholas Kaldor, "The Equilibrium of the Firm," *Economic Journal*, March 1934, pp. 60–76; R. H. Coase, "The Nature of the Firm," *Economica*, November 1937, pp. 386–405; and E. H. Chamberlin, "Proportionality, Divisibility, and Economies of Scale," *Quarterly Journal of Economics*, February 1948, pp. 229–262. For an interesting effort to make these basically simple ideas difficult, see O. E. Williamson, "Hierarchical Control and Optimum Firm Size," *Journal of Political Economy*, April 1967, pp. 123–138.

[9]For an ingenious attempt to test statistically the relationship between uncertainty and optimal firm size, see David Schwartzman, "Uncertainty and the Size of the Firm," *Economica*, August 1963, pp. 287–296. Schwartzman finds that the more uncertain the market environment is, as exemplified by the frequency and magnitude of price markdowns at the retail level, the smaller the largest manufacturing firms in the industry tend to be.

[10]For readers untutored in the ways of bureaucracy, an expediter is a man whose desk is between the desks of two coordinators.

[11]*Op. cit.*, p. 41.

formance and future plans of his organization. Electronic computers promise to contribute further here, making it possible to process and digest with great speed previously unimaginable quantities of information on costs, sales, inventories, etc. Perhaps most important of all, ways have been found to make the management of large organizations manageable through decentralization. Decentralization involves two vital features: the delegation of decision-making authority and responsibility to lower-level executives, so that the chief executive's capacity for handling key problems is not swamped; and the generation of pervasive incentives to spur lower-level executives toward profit-maximizing actions.

The classic model of a giant organization which has tried hard to ward off the managerial diseconomies of scale through decentralization is General Motors.[12] Substantial (but not total) decision-making authority and responsibility are delegated to the divisions and plants, and from them to the supervisors of narrower functional entities. Whenever feasible, operating entities are set up as semi-autonomous profit centers, with the stern, objective calculus of profit and loss simultaneously guiding the decisions of operating-level executives and providing top management with an indicator of good or bad performance. To round out the picture, incentives for vigorous effort are provided by a system under which some 15,500 salaried employees received bonuses averaging $7,000 in 1966, but varying widely to reflect supervisors' evaluations of each participant's contribution to the attainment of organizational objectives.[13] To be sure, the General Motors decentralization system works far from perfectly. Profit and loss calculations may send false signals to executives selling or buying component parts whose prices are set by interdivisional negotiation, and not in the market.[14] It remains to be seen whether General Motors' leaders will be able to free themselves from ingrown blind spots inhibiting adaptation to a changing environment.[15] Yet for nearly half a century, the system has passed the acid test of keeping large-scale managerial diseconomies in check. General Motors has been not only the largest private manufacturing corporation in the world, but also one of the most profitable. Executives of rival auto manufacturers concede that GM's unit costs are slightly to substantially lower than their own. Ford Motor Co. and large manufacturing firms in other industries have paid General Motors the supreme compliment of imitating its management system in detail. From this experience we must conclude that the long-run cost curve does not necessarily turn upward, at least for the largest private manufacturing enterprise we have been able to observe.

Still the GM example does not conclusively refute the U-shaped long-run cost curve hypothesis. There is another U. S. enterprise—the Department of Defense—much larger than General Motors in terms of employees (1.2 million civilians, plus 3.5 million military personnel), expenditures (about $80 billion in 1969), diversity of operations, or just about any other measure one might choose. The acute observer can hardly fail to notice the enormous difficulties the department has solving its problems efficiently, despite massive infusions of management technique, computers, and McNamaras. Whether this is due to gigantic scale or lack of a profit mechanism by which decision-making can be decentralized rationally is not clear; the truth probably contains a mixture of both explanations.

We need not rely only upon this pathological case, however. There are a number of large

---

[12]See Peter F. Drucker, *The Concept of the Corporation* (New York: Day, 1946), especially Part II; Alfred D. Chandler, Jr., *Strategy and Structure: Chapters in the History of the Industrial Enterprise* (Cambridge: MIT Press, 1962); Robert A. Gordon, *Business Leadership in the Large Corporation* (Washington: Brookings, 1945); and Richard Heflebower, "Observations on Decentralization in Large Enterprises," *Journal of Industrial Economics*, November 1960, pp. 7–22.

[13]"A Bonus Plan Where Performance Counts," *Business Week*, May 13, 1967, pp. 58–60.

[14]On this "transfer pricing" problem, see Heflebower, *op. cit.*; pp. 14–15; Jack Hirshleifer, "On the Economics of Transfer Pricing," *Journal of Business*, July 1956, pp. 172–184; and John A. Menge, "The Backward Art of Interdivisional Pricing," *Journal of Industrial Economics*, July 1961, pp. 215–232.

[15]See Drucker, *op. cit.*, pp. 85–97; and Dan Cordtz, "The Face in the Mirror at General Motors," *Fortune*, August 1966, pp. 117 ff.

private corporations which have been patently less successful than General Motors in avoiding the diseconomies of size. U. S. Steel is the most prominent example. The report of a management consulting firm hired during the 1930s to study U. S. Steel's operations has been summarized as follows:

> . . . [T]he report of the industrial engineers . . . pictured the Steel Corporation as a big sprawling inert giant whose production operations were improperly coordinated; suffering from a lack of a long run planning agency; relying on an antiquated system of cost accounting; with an inadequate knowledge of the costs or of the relative profitability of the many thousands of items it sold; with production and cost standards generally below those considered every day practice in other industries; with inadequate knowledge of its domestic markets and no clear appreciation of its opportunities in foreign markets; with less efficient production facilities than its rivals had; slow in introducing new processes and new products.[16]

Since World War II there has been some improvement, although many of the old problems persist.[17] Apparently, managerial diseconomies of scale can be avoided only through the exercise of organizational genius some firms are unable to call forth. And it is likely that in such volatile industries as fashion garment manufacturing, where rapid adaptation to changing demand conditions is of utmost importance, the burdens of management restrict much more severely the size firms can attain without experiencing rising unit costs.

We conclude then from *a priori* reasoning and a smattering of evidence that the long-run cost function of industrial firms has a shape something like that shown in Figure 4.1. Up to some minimum optimal scale *OA*, economies of scale facilitate reductions in unit cost as the

capacity of the enterprise is increased. Through decentralization and other management techniques, it is possible to increase the firm's size considerably beyond *OA* at more or less constant costs per unit. But if the enterprise expands too far—i.e., beyond scale *OB*—managerial diseconomies of scale take hold, leading to operation at higher-than-minimum cost per unit.

This analysis of the managerial cost-scale problem has been largely static in character. In a more dynamically-oriented analysis, Mrs. Penrose has shown that the relationship may be more complex, for one must take into account not only the choice of a particular size on the long-run cost curve, but also the process of moving from one scale to another.[18] Specifically, she argues that expansion during any short interval of time is constrained by the inability of the firm's management to cope with all the planning and leadership problems created by greatly increased size. Over the medium run of a few years, then, the firm's cost curve bends upward at a scale only slightly larger than its present scale.

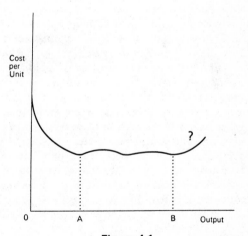

Figure 4.1
A Typical Long-Run Unit Cost Function

---

[16]Statement of George Stocking in U. S. House of Representatives, Committee on the Judiciary, Hearings, *Study of Monopoly Power* (Washington: 1950), pp. 966–967.

[17]See "A New Boss at The Corporation," *Business Week*, July 8, 1967, p. 140, in which U. S. Steel is dubbed "a bureaucratic dinosaur."

[18]Edith Tilton Penrose, *The Theory of Growth of the Firm* (Oxford: Basil Blackwell, 1959).

But as time passes, management digests the problems conferred by past growth and adapts its capabilities for dealing with new problems, making it possible to grow further without driving up unit costs. The managerial limit to efficient expansion recedes over time, and as a result, Mrs. Penrose argues, there is no single optimal firm size in the long run. This perceptive view of the firm's cost-scale relationships and the static model are not incompatible. Figure 4.1, for example, merely ignores the transitional problems of growth in assuming that the firm can operate anywhere within the output range *AB* at roughly constant cost per unit. Given sufficient time for managerial adaptation, the locus of cost-volume points within *AB* is indeed accessible.

TRANSPORTATION COSTS

A third major influence which may prevent economies of scale from being realized indefinitely is the cost of delivering output to customers. Transportation costs affect cost-scale relationships primarily at the level of a single plant or geographically clustered plant complex. If more output is produced in a plant complex, more must be sold. To sell more, it may be necessary to reach out to more distant customers. This in turn can lead to increased transportation costs per unit sold. The magnitude of the increase depends in a complex way upon a number of variables. One is the size of the plant in relation to the size of the market served. If the plant supplies only a small fraction of market demand, it may be able to increase sales substantially without expanding its geographic penetration. In this case transportation costs will be an insignificant constraint on plant size. A second factor is the nature of the pricing system. Transportation costs borne by the producer rise with output only if they cannot be passed along to customers in the form of higher prices. This will occur when prices are uniform in all markets, or when the price in more distant markets is set by more advantageously located rival producers. As we shall note further in Chapter 10, such situations, which require the producer to absorb freight in supplying more distant markets, are fairly commonplace. The third variable is the geographic structure of transportation costs. Usually the cost of transporting a given volume of freight rises less than proportionately with the distance shipped. The smaller the percentage increase in cost associated with shipping freight an extra 100 miles, the less will transportation costs constrain plant size. Fourth, the geographic distribution of potential customers matters. If customers are distributed evenly over the map, transportation costs will rise less than proportionately with the number of customers served, *ceteris paribus*, since shipping cost is related to the radius of shipment while volume of patronage is related to the square of the radius. If on the other hand customer density declines sharply away from the home market, transportation costs may even rise more than proportionately with the volume of output sold. Finally, the relationship of the commodity's production cost to its bulk is relevant. For bulky, low-value commodities like sand and milk bottles, unit transportation costs rise relatively rapidly with distance shipped. For compact, high-value items like transistors and machine tools, they rise only slowly.

The combined effect of these influences is illustrated in Figures 4.2a and 4.2b. We assume that increased output must be sold at greater distances by absorbing freight charges. For each diagram, an identical production cost-scale curve *UPC* is assumed. The minimum optimal scale in terms of production costs alone occurs at output *OX*. In Figure 4.2a, unit shipping costs *USC* rise slowly with increased output. Total cost per unit *LRATC* is the vertical sum of unit production costs and unit shipping costs. The minimum optimal scale, taking into account both production and transportation costs, occurs in Figure 4.2a at output *OY*. In Figure 4.2b, unit shipping costs rise much more rapidly, and this causes a reduction in the minimum optimal scale to *OZ*.

In industries with very low shipping costs relative to product value, or when the price structure is arranged so that customers absorb the cost of shipping output greater distances, the effect of transportation costs on optimal plant sizes will be negligible, and the unit cost curve may be quite flat beyond the minimum optimal scale, as

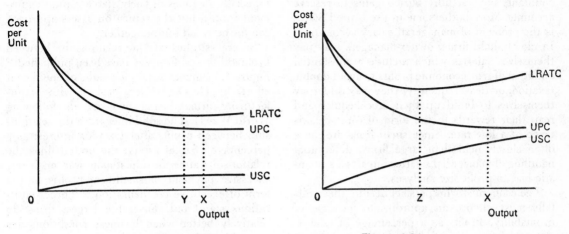

Figure 4.2a   Figure 4.2 b
The Effect of Transportation Costs on the Scale Optimum

illustrated in Figure 4.1. But when shipping costs which are high in relation to product value must be absorbed by the producer to sell more output, they can have an important impact, reducing optimal plant size and putting very large plants at a distinct cost disadvantage. Dynamic changes in transportation costs may also affect market structures. For instance, the expansion of the railroad networks during the second half of the nineteenth century caused a fall in unit transportation costs, moving many producers from a position like that of Figure 4.2b to one like 4.2a. The optimal scale of production thereupon rose, and firms took advantage by building new plants of unprecedented size.

THE MEASUREMENT OF COST-SCALE RELATIONSHIPS

Granting that economies of scale exist and that there is some minimum optimal scale (such as *OA* in Figure 4.1 or *OY* in Figure 4.2a) at which all economies of scale can be secured, the crucial question remains: Is the minimum optimal scale large or small relative to the demand for an industry's output? Whether there is room for many firms in the market, each large enough to enjoy all scale economies, for only one firm (a *natural monopoly* situation), or for just a few

(*natural oligopoly*) depends upon two key variables: the relevant production and distribution technology and the size of the market (i.e., the number of units which would be demanded at a price just sufficient to cover minimum unit cost). A number of techniques for measuring cost-scale relationships exist. Some are suitable mainly for ascertaining the minimum optimal *plant* size, some the minimum optimal *firm* size, and some for both.

An approach applicable primarily in studies at the firm level is to analyze profitability as a function of firm size. There are abundant data. However, some serious problems must be faced. The most important is that profitability is not necessarily related in any simple way to scale economies, as conventionally defined. Large firms may reap higher profits because they possess more monopoly power, or they may realize lower profits because they bear the burden of monopolistic output restriction. Profitability therefore reflects the overall suitability of firms' sizes to their market environment, and not just production and distribution cost advantages. Also, profit data are extremely sensitive to variations in accounting conventions with regard to depreciation, input rent imputations, etc. Indeed, many European firms report no profits or bare minimum profits year after year because their accountants have artfully buried gains in reserve accounts. More bothersome in the United States is the problem of managerial salary accounting. In closely-held firms, owner-managers may pay themselves salaries which include a substantial quantum of true economic profits to avoid double taxation, or (less frequently) they may underpay themselves to build up their stock equity and reap their rewards in the form of capital gains taxed at a low rate. Since small firms are more often closely-held than large firms, differential handling of managerial salaries imparts a systematic bias to profit-size analyses.

The economist who persists despite these pitfalls must choose an appropriate measure of profitability. Profits as a percentage of sales is clearly deficient, since it fails to take into account the process by which the market allocates capital among operations of widely varying capital intensity. Using profits as a percentage of net worth or stockholders' equity best satisfies the assumptions of economic theory that firms maximize equity ownership returns and that equity capital is allocated efficiently only when marginal returns (adjusted for risk differences) are equal in all industries. However, the return on equity index has the disadvantage of being highly sensitive to accounting quirks, inter-firm differences in the impact of inflation on asset values, and differences in the degree of capital structure leverage. Because it is somewhat less severely affected by these problems, an earnings measure consisting of profits plus interest on debt divided by total assets (net of depreciation) is sometimes employed. The return on stock-

holders' equity approach is probably preferable, especially in times of fairly stable capital equipment values, but the return on assets approach cannot be ruled out altogether.

Several studies of the relationship between profitability and firm size have been published.[19] Figure 4.3 summarizes some results of one recent effort, by H. O. Stekler, dealing with manufacturing firms during two periods following World War II. The solid lines trace the relationship between profits after tax plus interest as a percentage of total assets; the dotted lines the relationship after an adjustment was made for excessive payment of small-firm profits in the form of executive compensation.[20] Three implications stand out. First, the largest firms do relatively better when business conditions are normal or depressed than when business is booming, as it was during the 1947–1951 period of postwar readjustment and Korean war mobilization. This is undoubtedly the result of large firms' greater market power, and not economies of scale. Second, when earnings are adjusted for executive compensation biases, the disparity between large firms and small narrows and (for 1955–1957) disappears. However, the assumptions on which the adjustments were based are sufficiently tenuous to preclude a confident conclusion on this point. Third, a breakdown by two-digit industry groups showed that firms with assets exceeding $100 million had the most decisive earnings advantage over smaller rivals in the chemicals; paper products; stone, clay, and glass products; and transportation equipment (automobiles and aircraft) groups. These are for the most part fields in which, independent

[19]Leading examples include R. C. Epstein, *Industrial Profits in the United States* (New York: National Bureau of Economic Research, 1934); W. L. Crum, *Corporate Size and Earning Power* (Cambridge: Harvard University Press, 1939); Joseph Steindl, *Small and Big Business* (Oxford University Institute of Statistics, 1945); J. L. McConnell, "Corporate Earnings by Size of Firm," *Survey of Current Business*, May 1945, pp. 6–12; S. S. Alexander, "The Effect of Size of Manufacturing Corporation on the Distribution of the Rate of Return," *Review of Economics and Statistics*, August 1949, pp. 229–235; H. O. Stekler, *Profitability and Size of Firm* (Berkeley: University of California Institute of Business and Economic Research, 1963); Marshall Hall and Leonard W. Weiss, "Firm Size and Profitability," *Review of Economics and Statistics*, August 1967, pp. 319–331; and J. M. Samuels and D. J. Smyth, "Profits, Variability of Profits, and Firm Size," *Economica*, May 1968, pp. 127–139.

[20]Stekler adjusted compensation payments to match the rates reported by firms with zero or negative profits, on the assumption that such firms would have no incentive to restructure their payments so as to avoid the corporate profits tax. This assumption is vulnerable to criticism on numerous grounds. As just one example, firms showing losses in any given year do not necessarily incur losses in other years, and consistency is a virtue much admired by Internal Revenue auditors. It should be noted also that the use of after-tax earnings rates overstates the before-tax earning power of the smallest firms, which are subjected to lower tax rates on low profits.

evidence suggests, significant economies of scale exist. On the other hand, small firms were at their best in the printing, apparel, furniture, rubber products, petroleum, and primary metals fields. Economies of scale are known to be relatively unimportant in the first three, although the poor profit performance of large petroleum and metals producers is more difficult to reconcile with a scale economies hypothesis.

A more high-powered study of firm size and profitability by Marshall Hall and Leonard Weiss disclosed a large-firm profit advantage much greater than Stekler's results imply.[21] Confining their analysis to manufacturing corporations with assets of $50 million or more, they found that profitability was positively and significantly correlated with firm size during the 1956–1962 period after other variables reflecting home base industry concentration, the rate of past output growth, and capital structure leverage were simultaneously taken into account. After-tax profits as a percentage of both stockholders'

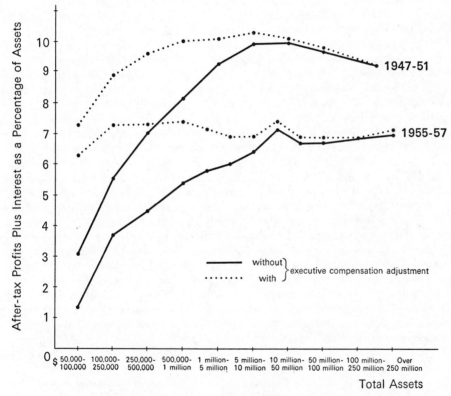

Figure 4.3
Return on Assets of Manufacturing Corporations in
Various Size Classes: 1947-51 and 1955-57 *

*Source: H. O. Stekler, *Profitability and Size of Firm* (Berkeley: University of California Institute of Business and Economic Research, 1963), pp. 37-39.

[21]"Firm Size and Profitability."

equity and total assets tended to be 30 per cent higher for firms with assets of $2 billion than for those with assets of $50 million, *ceteris paribus*. Whether their results diverge from the Stekler findings because of sample coverage differences or the focus by Hall and Weiss on a period of diminished prosperity and higher aggregate unemployment is not clear.[22] Further research is necessary before these issues are settled.

A second empirical approach to the optimal scale question is the so-called "survivor test," developed in its modern form by George Stigler.[23] The logic is simple: firm or plant sizes which survive and contribute increasing proportions of an industry's output are assumed to be optimal; those which supply a declining share of output are deemed too large or too small. This test of optimality clearly covers a much wider waterfront than mere production and physical distribution scale economies. As Stigler states, under the survivor test an efficient firm size "is one that meets any and all problems the entrepreneur actually faces: strained labor relations, rapid innovation, government regulation, unstable foreign markets, and what not"; and survival may reflect monopoly power or discriminatory legislation as well as conventional scale economies.[24] With this caveat more or less firmly in mind, several investigators have applied the survivor test to more than a hundred different industries.[25] The most prominent result has been the wide range of firm and plant sizes which seem to pass the test. This has been interpreted (somewhat misleadingly) by Stigler as evidence that "the long run marginal and average cost curves of the firm are customarily horizontal over a large range of sizes."[26] Applications of the test

also suggest that the minimum optimal plant or firm size is small relative to market size in most industries. This, for instance, was the conclusion of T. R. Saving, who found that 64 of the 91 industries for which he was able to make 1947–1954 survivorship estimates had minimum optimal plant sizes requiring the production of 1 per cent or less of industry value added.[27] Only four industries—piano and organ parts, pens and mechanical pencils, miscellaneous inorganic chemicals, and miscellaneous pressed and blown glass products—had estimated minimum optimal plant sizes exceeding 5 per cent of total industry output. Nevertheless, the survivor test is not free of ambiguities. Survival patterns are not always stable over time; curious patterns appear (such as survival of only the largest and smallest plants); and the criteria for distinguishing surviving from nonsurviving size groups contain a certain element of arbitrariness. Tests on the same industries by different analysts have sometimes yielded quite different estimates.[28] Because of these problems, the survivor method is better employed as a supplement to and check on other techniques than as one's sole or primary approach to analyzing optimal scale patterns.

Another more direct approach, appropriate mainly for plant studies, is statistical cost analysis. To determine the shape of the long-run plant cost curve, the analyst relates observations on average production cost for a broad cross-section of plants to observations on the output of those plants, taking into account such additional variables as the percentage of capacity utilization, differences in the age of the capital stock (and hence in the state of the technological art embodied), differences in input prices, differ-

---

[22]The inclusion by Hall and Weiss of additional variables affecting profitability is apparently not the explanation. According to a private communication from Weiss, the positive and statistically significant relationship between profitability and size persists when size is used as the sole explanatory variable.

[23]"The Economies of Scale," *Journal of Law and Economics*, October 1958, pp. 54–71.

[24]*Ibid.*, p. 56.

[25]See especially T. R. Saving, "Estimation of Optimum Size of Plant by the Survivor Technique," *Quarterly Journal of Economics*, November 1961, pp. 569–607; Leonard W. Weiss, "The Survival Technique and the Extent of Suboptimal Capacity," *Journal of Political Economy*, June 1964, pp. 246–261, with a correction, *Journal of Political Economy*, June 1965, pp. 300–301; and W. G. Shepherd, "What Does the Survivor Technique Show About Economies of Scale?" *Southern Economic Journal*, July 1967, pp. 113–122.

[26]*Op. cit.*, p. 71.

[27]"Estimation of Optimum Size of Plant by the Survivor Technique," p. 580.

[28]Cf. Shepherd, *op. cit.*

ences in output mixes, cumulative volume produced, etc. All this is easier said than done. Quantities of complete, reliable data sufficient for statistical generalization are hard to come by. When the data are obtained, comparability between plants may be impaired by differences in cost accounting conventions. One of the most serious problems relates to the imputation of rents attributable to specialized resources. If there are systematic differences in rent imputation between small plants and large, 'true' cost variations associated with scale differences may be either masked or exaggerated.

Despite these difficulties, there have been several dozen attempts to measure statistically the relationship between plant size and long-run unit cost for various industries, some executed at a high level of competence, others not.[29] If, any single typical result can be identified, it has been a cost curve similar to Figure 4.1, showing definite economies of scale at relatively small plant sizes, a range of intermediate sizes over which unit costs did not vary perceptibly, and (in a minority of cases) diseconomies of scale for very large plants. With few exceptions, the minimum optimal scale revealed in studies of American industries has been small relative to the size of the market. It would be hazardous to generalize from this last result, however, since industries with sufficiently many plants to permit a statistical approach to cost analysis should (assuming cost-minimizing behavior) be those with relatively small minimum optimal scales.

Finally, there is the *engineering approach* to scale economies measurement. Senior production engineers make their living by planning and designing new production plants, and in the process they accumulate considerable data on costs and on the plant designs required to achieve minimum costs. This knowledge is a potential gold mine for industrial organization students.

The principal disadvantages of the engineering approach are threefold: the heavy demands it places on both the investigator's and his informant's time, the tendency of some engineers to underemphasize the sensitivity of plant scale decisions to changes in input prices, and its applicability only to plants constructed using current, not past, technology. But no one disadvantage is serious, and carefully executed engineering estimates probably afford the best single source of information on the cost-scale question.

The leading engineering analysis study of plant scale economies for a substantial sample of industries has been made by Joe S. Bain.[30] He submitted detailed questionnaires to executives of 20 (mostly large) industries which originated roughly 20 per cent of all value added in manufacturing during 1947. The answers he received were supplemented with interviews and an array of evidence compiled by other scholars. The principal results of his research are summarized in Table 4.1. In the first column is an estimate, usually spanning a range of uncertainty, of the percentage of national capacity one plant of minimum optimal scale would supply during the early 1950s. In most of the 20 industries, economies of large plant scale clearly did not preclude a fairly competitive market structure, at least on a nationwide basis. In cement it was possible, given the technology and U. S. demand of 1951, to have 100 plants of optimal scale; in steel, at least 40; in rayon, at least 16; and in automobiles at least 10. Furthermore, firms building plants smaller than the size required to realize all scale economies were in several cases not seriously disadvantaged, as the second column of Table 4.1 suggests. For example, a cigarette plant producing enough to supply only 3 per cent of the national market would suffer a cost disadvantage of only 1 per cent compared to its larger, fully efficient counterparts when all costs (in-

[29]Perceptive surveys of the literature and discussions of the analytic hazards include J. Johnston, *Statistical Cost Analysis* (New York: McGraw-Hill, 1960); Caleb A. Smith, "Survey of the Empirical Evidence on Economies of Scale," with a comment by Milton Friedman, in National Bureau of Economic Research conference report, *Business Concentration and Price Policy* (Princeton: Princeton University Press, 1955), pp. 213–238; and A. A. Walters, "Production and Cost Functions: An Econometric Survey," *Econometrica*, January-April 1963, pp. 1–66, especially pp. 39–52.

[30]"Economies of Scale, Concentration, and the Condition of Entry in Twenty Manufacturing Industries," *American Economic Review*, March 1954, pp. 15–39 (hereafter, "Economies"); and *Barriers to New Competition* (Cambridge: Harvard University Press, 1956) (hereafter, *Barriers*).

Table 4.1

Estimates of Minimum Optimal Plant Scale Ranges for 20 U.S. Manufacturing Industries: 1951

Industry	Percentage of National Capacity Provided by One Plant Complex of Minimum Optimal Scale	Elevation of Unit Cost Due to Building a Plant One Half Minimum Optimal Scale	Number of Plants of Minimum Optimal Scale an Average Big Four Member Could Operate, Given 1947 Market Shares	Percentage of Major Regional or Product Submarkets Provided by One Plant of Minimum Optimal Scale
Flour Milling	0.1 to 0.5	n.a.	14 to 70	0.3 to 7
Shoe Manufacturing	0.14 to 0.5	1–10%	14 to 50	0.6 to 10
Canned Fruits and Vegetables	0.25 to 0.5	2– 5%	14 to 25	3 to 20
Cement Manufacturing	1	10%	7	4 to 34
Distilled Liquors	1.25 to 1.75	1%	11 to 15	—
Farm Machinery, exc. Tractors	1 to 1.5	"moderate"	6 to 9	4 to 6
Petroleum Refining	1.75	2%	5	4 to 12
Integrated Steel Mills	1 to 2.5	5%	4 to 11	3 to 50
Tin Can Manufacturing	0.3 to 2.0	n.a.	10 to 65	2 to 50
Diversified Meat Packing	2 to 2.5	"slight"	4 or 5	8 to 30
Rubber Tires and Tubes	1.4 to 2.75	3%	7 to 13	—
Gypsum Plaster and Plasterboard	2 to 3	n.a.	7 to 10	8 to 30
Rayon Yarn and Fibers	4 to 6	8%	3 to 5	—
Soap and Detergents	4 to 6	3%	3 to 5	—
Cigarettes	5 to 6	1%	4 or 5	—
Integrated Auto Production	5 to 10	5%	2 to 4	10 to 60
Fountain Pen Production	5 to 10	n.a.	1 or 2	10 to 15
Primary Copper Refining	10	n.a.	2	—
Tractor Manufacturing	10 to 15	"slight"	1	—
Typewriter Production	10 to 30	"substantial"	1	—

Source: Joe S. Bain, "Economies of Scale, Concentration, and the Condition of Entry in Twenty Manufacturing Industries," *American Economic Review*, March 1954, pp. 15–39; and *Barriers to New Competition* (Cambridge: Harvard University Press, 1956), pp. 7ⁿ–86,

cluding outbound and inbound freight, packaging, and federal excise taxes) were taken into account.

Plant economies of scale also provided little justification for the levels of national market concentration existing in 1947. The third column of Table 4.1 shows the number of fully efficient plants an average 'Big Four' member could operate, given the four-firm concentration ratios prevailing in 1947. In only two or three industries—typewriters, tractors, and perhaps fountain pens—was the average output of industry leaders such that it could be produced efficiently with just one plant large enough to reap all scale economies. Conversely, the average Big Four member in gypsum plaster had a market share sufficient to support seven or ten efficient plants; the average rayon industry leader could operate from three to six efficient plants; the average cigarette industry leader could operate four such plants, etc.

Only when markets are narrowly segmented due to physical differentiation of products or high transportation costs do economies of plant scale appear to compel or justify tightly-knit oligopolistic market structures. Several of the industries analyzed by Bain, such as flour-milling, cement, and plasterboard, are spatially differentiated because of product bulk and shipping costs; others have narrower, reasonably distinct qualitative submarkets (such as canned tomatoes and ball-point pens). The last column of Table 4.1 presents estimates of the share one plant of minimum optimal scale would supply in such segmented markets. The variation of high and low values for individual industries is wide, since the estimates cover both the minimum share supplied in the largest identifiable submarket and the maximum share supplied in the smallest significant submarket. Evidently, high concentration is required for efficient production in a few submarkets—e.g., in geographically isolated and sparsely populated regions consuming cement, steel, and plasterboard; and in the highest-price automobile lines. Still, the bulk of all output is sold in markets nearer the lower end of the range, and so the amount of segmented oligopoly required by scale economies is not as great as one might suppose from the maximum estimates.

To summarize the implications of Bain's research, economies of plant scale were responsible for oligopolistic national market structures in a few of the 20 industries studied, and for substantial degrees of oligopoly in segments of several additional industries. Nevertheless, in roughly half of the 20 industries a generous number of sellers could be maintained in national and all major segmented markets without sacrificing plant scale economies. And for all but a few industries, the degree of national market concentration was substantially in excess of what was needed merely to take advantage of production and physical distribution economies at the plant level.

These conclusions hold directly only for the limited sample studied by Bain. Indeed, Bain's sample was not representative of the overall manufacturing industry population. He intentionally selected a disproportionately large fraction of highly concentrated industries in order to give scale economies the maximum opportunity to show themselves. The simple average of the 20 industries' four-firm 1947 concentration ratios was 61, compared to 41 for all four-digit manufacturing industries in the same year. It seems reasonable to infer that for the complete population minimum optimal plant sizes were no larger (and probably even smaller) on the average in relation to national output. This conjecture is consistent with the results of plant survivor tests and statistical cost analyses for much larger samples of industries, and it is not contradicted by the smattering of published evidence from engineering analyses of a dozen or so other industries. Thus, we must look for some influence other than plant economies of scale to explain high concentration in most oligopolistic American manufacturing industries.

PLANT SCALE ECONOMIES AND VERTICAL INTEGRATION

One point deserves clarification and elaboration. Bain's minimum optimal plant scale estimates are not in all cases for a "plant" in the narrow sense of the word, but for an integrated production complex. The automobile industry provides the best illustration. His estimate that a plant of minimum optimal size had to produce

5 to 10 per cent of total output in the early 1950s assumed a complex manufacturing major components (engines, transmissions, metal stampings, trim, etc.) and assembling finished vehicles. Body component stamping and engine manufacturing were the bottleneck operations, requiring an annual volume of from 300,000 to 600,000 units to attain all economies of scale.[31] Bain's estimates are for such a "least common multiple" complex, which could support from three to ten efficient final assembly plants with market shares ranging from 1 to 3 per cent each.

The American automobile companies have integrated their production complexes vertically around such bottleneck stages as body stamping and engine and transmission manufacturing. But there is an alternative solution which might reduce the upward pressure of plant scale economies on market concentration. It is called "vertical disintegration," and it is best described by Robinson:

> Where some given process requires a scale of production considerably greater than the smaller firms in an industry can achieve, this process tends to be separated off from the main industry, and all the smaller firms to get this particular process performed for them by an outside specialist firm. Thus the industry becomes broken up into two or more industries, and each is enabled to work at its most convenient scale of production. The specialist firm, working for a number of the smaller firms, is on a larger scale than any of the individual firms could have achieved for that particural process or product. Examples of this principle may be found in the finishing stages of the textile industries, and in the manufacture of various component parts, such as radiators, electrical equipment, body shells, and crankshafts and other forgings, in the motor industry.[32]

Robinson's illustrations were drawn from Great Britain, where vertical disintegration of auto production has been more widespread than in the United States. For instance, the Pressed Steel Company, Ltd., was until 1965 an independent metal stamping specialist, with sales of $260 million, supplying major body components to several auto manufacturers. (In late 1965 it merged with the British Motors Corporation, the largest British automaker, which had consumed about 60 per cent of its output.)

Vertical disintegration of textile finishing operations also appears to be less prevalent in the United States than it is in England. But significant examples can be found in many other U. S. industries. Makers of molded plastic products, who ply their trade quite successfully on very small scales, turn to the large chemical companies for their plastic resins, which are produced efficiently only in plants of substantial size. The aircraft industry has come to depend upon only two domestic firms—the Pratt & Whitney Division of United Aircraft and General Electric—for large turbojet engines, and upon one—Wyman-Gordon—for a large share of its heavy forgings. And while the manufacturers of gasoline and consumer appliances sold in special outlets have frequently integrated downstream into retailing, makers of consumer convenience goods (such as cigarettes, soap, and chocolate bars) perforce rely upon vertically disintegrated distribution networks, since their products are marketed most efficiently by stores carrying a broad line of other items.

The very existence of vertical disintegration suggests several questions. Why is there not more, extending not only to bottleneck production and distribution operations, but also to any activity in which economies of specialization exist? If there are diseconomies of managing complex organizations, why isn't each component part of an automobile produced by independent specialists? On what grounds do entrepreneurs decide which operations will be integrated, and which disintegrated? And on a still

---

[31]*Barriers*, pp. 72 and 244–247. See also George Maxcy and Aubrey Silberston, *The Motor Industry* (London: Allen & Unwin, 1959), pp. 75–94, who place the body stamping bottleneck's minimum optimal scale at one million units per year; and U. S. Senate, Committee on the Judiciary, Subcommittee on Antitrust and Monopoly, Report, *Administered Prices: Automobiles* (Washington: 1958), pp. 11–18.

[32]*The Structure of Competitive Industry*, p. 20. See also George Stigler, "The Division of Labor is Limited by the Extent of the Market," *Journal of Political Economy*, June 1951, pp. 185–193.

more basic plane, what do economists mean by a 'firm,' when the components of an end product may be produced by a host of legally distinct entities?

Systematic answers to the last two questions were first supplied by R. H. Coase.[33] The distinguishing mark of a firm, he observes, "is the supersession of the price mechanism." Resource allocation in a market framework is normally guided and directed by the price mechanism, but within the firm the job is done through the conscious decisions and commands of management. The reason why vertical disintegration is not more widespread, and why it is profitable to collect a whole complex of activities within what we call a firm, is that there are costs in using the price mechanism. As a first approximation, activities are integrated within the firm when the cost of organizing those activities through direct managerial controls is less than under the impersonal controls of the price system.

There are many reasons why market transaction costs are not zero; only a few illustrations need be provided here. Price shopping, the communication of work specifications, and contract negotiation take time and effort. Especially when goods or services would have to be contracted for repeatedly in small quantities, it may be cheaper to bring them under the firm's direct span of managerial control. The payoffs from integration also increase with the complexity of product component interrelationships. It is easier to make the various parts of an automobile body fit together when all parties to the coordination effort work for the same boss than when design changes must be processed through a purchasing office.[34] In the automobile industry, too, the pace of competition is set by annual changes in body designs (and hence in metal stampings), and rapid adaptation to competitive developments (as well as maintaining secrecy of one's own designs) is facilitated under an integrated production approach.

Even more conductive to integration is a breakdown of competitive market processes due to external economies or monopoly. The latter is especially likely when bottleneck operations requiring a large scale of production are vertically disintegrated. Because scale economies are so important, the number of component sellers will tend to be small. From fewness follows monopoly or oligopoly pricing of the disintegrated components, driving up prices to the buyer. The buyer may then prefer to produce its own requirements, instead of being gouged by outsiders. We shall have more to say about vertical price relationships in Chapter 9.

While vertical integration often reduces transaction costs and dissolves monopolistic pricing stalemates for the integrating firm, it can simultaneously harm nonintegrated firms, which may find themselves foreclosed from sources of supply or markets, or locked into a price squeeze, by their integrated rivals. For example, one of the most serious problems faced by small, nonintegrated steel, copper, and aluminum producers in the United States is obtaining access on favorable price terms to supplies of ore. In all three industries, a few integrated firms command most of the supply, partly by having had the foresight and resources to buy up high-grade deposits as they were discovered, and partly because the development of new deposits often requires financial commitments beyond the reach of the independent small producer. As an extreme illustration, the consortia developing iron ore reserves in northwest Australia invested more than $600 million in towns, roads, ports, processing plants, and a 179 mile railroad before delivering significant quantities of ore.[35] Professor Robinson suggests that the high degree of vertical integration characterizing German industry was encouraged through the control of raw materials by large firms, while the paucity of vertical integration in Great Britain is attributed to her policy of free trade in raw materials.[36]

---

[33]"The Nature of the Firm," *Economica*, November 1937, pp. 386–405.
[34]On this aspect of the coordination problem in the advanced weapons industry, see M. J. Peck and F. M. Scherer, *The Weapons Acquisition Process: An Economic Analysis* (Boston: Harvard Business School, 1962), pp. 181–189.
[35]See "Australia's Iron Boom Comes Down to Earth," *Business Week*, August 13, 1966, pp. 98–101.
[36]*The Structure of Competitive Industry*, pp. 110–114.

The possibilities of market foreclosure through downstream vertical integration are illustrated by events in the cement industry.[37] Ready-mix concrete plants consume about 60 per cent of the industry's output. During the early 1960s a few cement manufacturers began purchasing ready-mix companies, quickly increasing their share of the acquired firms' orders from 35 per cent to 65 per cent. This foreclosed markets to other cement makers, who began acquiring independent ready-mix companies as a defensive measure, touching off a chain reaction eventually quenched by intervention of the antitrust authorities.

We shall return to this issue during our analysis of antitrust policy in Chapter 20. The main point for present purposes is that the breakdown of competition in vertical price relationships may lead some firms to integrate operations which might otherwise be vertically disintegrated. And when a few firms do so, fear of foreclosure induces others to follow suit, if they can, or makes survival more difficult for them if they are too small to do so. The result is an increase in the size of an optimal production complex, and hence upward pressure on market concentration.

THE IMPACT OF TECHNOLOGICAL CHANGE AND MARKET GROWTH

The minimum optimal scale depends, to be sure, on such institutional variables as incentives for vertical integration, but technology is the paramount determinant. Casual observation suggests that changes in technology can lead to greatly increased minimum optimal scales. Consider, for instance, the case of synthetic ammonia, which is used in large volume as a fertilizer.[38] Until the mid 1960s, the dominant production technology was a high-pressure process which required an output of roughly 125,000 tons per year to realize all economies of scale. Then the development of a computer-controlled low-pressure process using centrifugal compressors (in place of reciprocating pumps) made it possible to cut unit costs by more than 10 per cent, but only by building plants capable of producing at least 360,000 tons per year, or roughly 38 train carloads of ammonia per day. One might expect this increase in the minimum optimal scale to induce an increase in synthetic ammonia industry concentration. (In 1963, the four-firm concentration ratio was 38 per cent.) However, the market was already so large by 1965 that a plant attaining all scale economies with the new process needed to produce less than 4 per cent of total domestic output, and so if the leading four producers operated only one efficient plant each, their combined share of the market need not have exceeded 16 per cent. Moreover, the demand for fertilizer ammonia was expanding so rapidly that the industry was expected to have room for 30 or 50 plants of minimum optimal scale by 1970.

This pattern has been repeated again and again in American industry during the 20th century. There has been a general trend toward larger minimum optimal plant sizes. Sands analyzed 46 industries for which comparable data on physical output and the number of plants were available, and found that average physical output per plant increased between 1904 and 1947 by about 3 per cent per annum.[39] But while plants have been getting larger, so have the markets for their output. According to estimates by the National Bureau of Economic Research,

[37]Cf. U. S. Federal Trade Commission, *Economic Report on Mergers and Vertical Integration in the Cement Industry* (Washington: 1966), pp. 1–7 and 21–25. For a skeptical view, see M. J. Peck and John J. McGowan, "Vertical Integration in Cement: A Critical Examination of the FTC Staff Report," *Antitrust Bulletin*, Summer 1967, pp. 505–531. A rebuttal follows in Doris Wilk, "Vertical Integration in Cement Revisited," *Antitrust Bulletin*, Summer 1968, pp. 619–647.

[38]See "Ammonia's New World: More Plant, Less Crew," *Business Week*, November 13, 1965, pp. 134–139. On later developments, see "Oil Companies Bail Out of Fertilizer Surplus," *Business Week*, December 13, 1969, pp. 35–36.

[39]Saul S. Sands, "Changes in Scale of Production in United States Manufacturing Industry, 1904–1947," *Review of Economics and Statistics*, November 1961, pp. 365–368. It is important in such an analysis to use some measure of physical output, as Sands did, and not employment, as others have occasionally done. Plants may in a real sense be getting bigger while their employment declines because of capital-labor substitution and productivity increases. For example, the changes in synthetic ammonia production technology made it possible for a plant staffed by 32 persons to produce four times as much output as an old-style plant employing 71 persons.

physical output of all manufacturing industries increased by nearly 4 per cent per year between 1904 and 1947. If Sands's sample were representative of all manufacturing industries, this comparison would suggest a *decline* in average plant size relative to market size. The comparability is apparently not perfect, however, since Sands found in a related study that the largest 20 plants in 47 four-digit industries originated an (unweighted) average of 42 per cent of industry shipments by value in 1904, and 47 per cent in 1947.[40] This might be interpreted to mean that in his sample the long-run balance between increasing plant size and increasing market size ran slightly in favor of the former.

There is reason to believe that since World War II, the growth of plant scale has generally been slower than the growth of markets. A study of 125 four-digit industries for which comparable data were available revealed that the share of industry sales originating in the eight largest plants declined between 1947 and 1958 in 67 cases, while it increased in only 48.[41] According to John M. Blair, this seeming reversal of past trends was due to fundamental changes in the direction of technological change away from centralizing innovations and toward decentralizing techniques.[42] Examples include the replacement of central motive power units by individual electric motors; the rise to prominence of easily fabricated plastics and light metals; the replacement of highly specialized machines by more flexible and adaptable units, such as computer or tape-controlled contour milling machines; and the displacement of water and rail transportation by trucks, with greater flexibility and more economical accommodation of less-than-carload shipments. It has also been suggested that, while the electronic computer will help large firms conquer managerial diseconomies of scale, it will benefit small firms even more by permitting them (with the assistance of specialized programming and time-leasing firms) to solve analytic and control problems which previously lay completely beyond their grasp.[43]

While some developments in technology lead to smaller optimal plant scales relative to market volume, others are pushing in the opposite direction. It is too early to assess confidently how these forces balance out, and how they will affect scale economies and market concentration in decades to come. The problem is an important one, worthy of much more attention.

Given an industry's production technology, the level of market concentration required to attain all plant scale economies depends upon the other side of the coin we have been examining—the size of the market. Some industries are large, some small; some rapidly growing, some declining. The larger the market is, the less probable will it be that efficiency in production requires high concentration, *ceteris paribus*. The more rapidly a market is growing, the more likely it is that increases in market size will outstrip increases in minimum optimal plant size, and so the more feasible decreases in concentration will be.[44]

These are empirically testable hypotheses. On the first, Nelson reported a strong and persistent negative relationship between the 1954 sizes of four- and five-digit census industries and their

[40] *Idem*, "Concentration in United States Manufacturing Industry, 1904–1947," *International Economic Review*, January 1962, pp. 79–92.

[41] See the testimony of John M. Blair in *Economic Concentration*, Part 4 (1965), p. 1550.

[42] *Ibid.*, pp. 1536–1537; and his article, "Technology and Size," *American Economic Review*, May 1948, pp. 121–152.

[43] See the testimony of Walter W. Finke, President, Electronic Data Processing Division, Honeywell, Inc., in *Economic Concentration*, pp. 1575–1576.

[44] Technological changes are in part induced by market growth, and therefore the variables treated here cannot be considered entirely independent. See Jacob Schmookler, *Invention and Economic Growth* (Cambridge: Harvard University Press, 1967), especially Chapters 6–9. However, there is no evidence to show that changes in the minimum optimal scale of production are systematically and causally related to changes in market size.

It should be noted also that rapid market growth may lead to concentration decreases not only by outstripping the growth of optimal plant and firm sizes, but also by encouraging and facilitating the entry of new competitors. We shall discuss this point further in Chapter 8.

four-firm concentration ratios.[45] Some of this association was due to census classification biases which cause large industries to be large because they are defined too broadly, covering several economically meaningful markets, while small industries are less likely to be defined so broadly. However, after adjusting for such biases, Nelson found that the inverse relation between concentration and industry size persisted.

Several statistical studies have revealed the existence of an analogous dynamic relationship between changes in market size and changes in concentration. Nelson, for instance, found that each 100 percentage point increase in an industry's value added between 1935 and 1954 (i.e., from a 1935 index of 100 to a 1954 index of 200, and again from 200 to 300, etc.) was accompanied on the average by a 1.45 percentage point incremental decline in the four-firm concentration ratio.[46] For the period between 1947 and 1963, a government study group estimated that each 100 percentage point increase in industry sales induced an average concentration decline of 2.9 percentage points, *ceteris paribus*.[47] The changes in concentration associated with growth were obviously modest, and one may choose to conclude with Shepherd that "It would take a thumping amount of growth to reduce concentration by even a sliver."[48] Yet it is equally true that without the thumping amounts of growth actually experienced during past decades, market concentration probably would have risen a good deal more than it actually did, and that the vast differences in growth rates between industries were a significant determinant of their differential concentration trends.

ECONOMIES OF MULTI-PLANT OPERATION

The evidence from Bain's study examined thus far concerned economies of scale associated with operating a single plant or integrated production complex. Are further cost savings derived from operating several plants, each of minimum optimal scale? And if so, could these economies of multi-plant operation explain why so many markets are much more concentrated than they would be if leading firms operated only one plant of minimum optimal scale?

Before continuing, it is important to distinguish *real* economies of scale, which are realized by making better physical use of labor, materials, and capital inputs, from *pecuniary* economies, which result when large firms pay lower prices for their inputs than small firms, e.g., because of superior bargaining power or credit worthiness. Economists consider real economies of scale to be unambiguously beneficial, since the resources saved can be put to work satisfying other wants. The desirability of pecuniary economies is less clear-cut, since they lead mainly to a redistribution of income, benefitting large firms (and perhaps their customers) at the expense of input suppliers. In the present section we shall be concerned only with real economies of scale.

There are several features of multi-plant operation which could conceivably yield economies; whether they in fact do so is an empirical question. For one, a multi-plant operation may be able to economize on management services by sharing a common overhead pool of accountants, financial planners, market researchers, production planning specialists, labor relations specialists, purchasing agents, lawyers, etc. The prob-

[45]Ralph L. Nelson, *Concentration in the Manufacturing Industries of the United States* (New Haven: Yale University Press), 1963, pp. 46–48.

[46]*Ibid.*, pp. 52–56.

[47]*Studies by the Staff of the Cabinet Committee on Price Stability* (Washington: January 1969), pp. 63 and 96. For results that suggest that the relationship deteriorated in the 1958–1963 interval, see D. R. Kamerschen, "Market Growth and Industry Concentration," *Journal of the American Statistical Association*, March 1968, pp. 228–241.

[48]Testimony of W. G. Shepherd in *Economic Concentration*, p. 639. See also his "Trends of Concentration in American Manufacturing Industries, 1947–1958," *Review of Economics and Statistics*, May 1964, pp. 200–212. In a study of British industries, Shepherd was unable to find an analogous relationship. "Changes in British Industrial Concentration, 1951–1958," *Oxford Economic Papers*, March 1966, pp. 126–132. But this finding is disputed by K. D. George in "Changes in British Industrial Concentration: 1951–1958," *Journal of Industrial Economics*, July 1967, pp. 200–211.

lem here is that while there are economies of specialization in managerial services, there may also be diseconomies in coordinating a multi-plant operation. The net advantage of the multi-plant firm depends upon how these pluses and minuses average out. Second, there may be economies of scale in conducting centralized research and development which persist as the firm expands into a size range embracing several efficient plants. This is an important possibility which will be analyzed more conveniently in Chapter 15. Third, multi-plant operation may confer some *economies of massed reserves*, as suggested earlier. In the cement and tin can manufacturing industries, for example, it is sometimes cheaper to meet local peak demands by shipping products in from a neighboring plant, despite higher transportation costs, than to push local plant operations far beyond their designed capacity.

Other multi-plant cost-scale relationships are more complicated. Finding the most advantageous inventory policy involves tradeoffs among a number of variables, including frequency of out-of-stock situations due to random demand peaks, the clerical costs of frequent reordering and shipping, the cost of having capital tied up in inventory, and considerations of optimal production lot size. The extensive literature on inventory theory shows that as sales of an item rise, the optimal inventory level for that item increases less than proportionately.[49] This creates an incentive to centralize the warehousing function in a single location, and perhaps with it production. However, except in processing industries which use large quantities of bulky raw materials available only in certain geographic locations, transportation costs can be reduced by locating production and warehousing as near as possible to regional markets. This works for decentralization, and *if* the firm for some reason must operate on a nationwide plane, for multi-plant operation. The best solution to this locational problem depends upon a host of production, inventory, and transportation cost variables, and it is not clear that simple generalizations are possible. Still when decentralization is optimal, it might be achieved as efficiently by numerous independent regional specialists, unless there are advertising or other product differentiation advantages to nationwide distribution. We shall return to these advantages in a moment. *If* they dictate a nationwide posture for the firm, they, and not locational economies, should be credited (or blamed) as the cause of multi-plant operation.

Economies may also result when each of several plants specializes in producing part of a full-line firm's products—i.e., when an agricultural implement specialist produces harrows in one plant, harvesters in another, etc. Again, the key question is, why the broad line? There may be technical complementarities among various items in the firm's line, though this is rarely of great importance. More frequently, marketing variables play the decisive role. Selling costs per unit may be lower when regional sales office overhead costs can be pro-rated over several products, and when salesmen can push several items on each visit to customers. But there are clear limits here; the salesman's effectiveness undoubtedly declines with diffusion of focus. Equally important in encouraging full line merchandising are the advertising and 'image' benefits, which will be analyzed further in a moment. The main point is that economies of plant specialization enjoyed by a multi-product firm cannot be viewed in isolation from other advantages of multi-plant operation.

To sum up, some of the potential economies of multi-plant operation are straightforward, even if conjectural; others carry us into a tangle of interaction effects. Given the conceptual uncertainties, enlightenment must come from empirical studies. Unhappily, the evidence is meager.

The most comprehensive assault on the problem is again Bain's study of 20 industries.[50] He

[49]See, for example, J. F. Magee, *Production Planning and Inventory Control* (New York: McGraw-Hill, 1958); and T. M. Whitin, *The Theory of Inventory Management* (Second ed.; Princeton: Princeton University Press, 1957).

[50]"Economies," pp. 29–35; and *Barriers*, pp. 83–93 and 250–263.

questioned industry executives on the magnitude of cost savings attributable to multi-plant operation, excluding advantages of large-scale sales promotion. In six industries, multi-plant operation was believed to confer no economies. In eight others, no estimates of multi-plant cost advantages could be elicited, although Bain's further analysis of published materials turned up no evidence suggesting that such advantages were more than slight. Estimates of cost savings in the remaining six industries ranged from .5 per cent (for soap products, associated with operating two or three plants) to between 2 and 5 per cent (for steel, with estimates of the optimal number of plants running as high as eight). It is significant that some steel executives responding to Bain's questions denied that *any* economies of multi-plant operation existed. Respondents also had difficulty distinguishing between production and physical distribution benefits of multi-plant operation and sales promotional economies. The conclusion Bain draws from his pioneering effort is a modest, tentative one, but it is the best we have:

> The economies of large multi-plant firms are left in doubt by this investigation. In half the cases in which definite estimates were received, such economies were felt to be negligible or absent, whereas in most of the remainder of cases they seemed slight or small. Perhaps the frequently expressed suspicion that such economies generally are unimportant after all is supported, and perhaps we are justified in saying that we have had difficulty in accumulating convincing support for the proposition that in many industries production or distribution economies of large firms seriously encourage concentration....[51]

Despite the lack of convincing evidence associating substantial production and distribution cost economies with multi-plant operation, it is clear that existing levels of market concentration in the United States are attributable more to multiple plant control by large firms than to

some mandate that individual plants be large. As the third column of Table 4.1 shows, in all but four (typewriters, tractors, fountain pens, and copper) of the 20 industries in Bain's sample, the average Big Four member was large enough to have at least three plant complexes of approximately minimum optimal scale. In five industries (flour, shoes, canned fruits and vegetables, liquor, and tin cans) the four leaders were big enough to average 10 or more plants of minimum optimal size each.

Nelson's analysis of 83 four-digit industries responsible for 41 per cent of U. S. value added by manufacture during 1954 also points to multi-plant control as the principal basis of high market concentration.[52] The leading four firms each operated one plant in only four of these industries, while in more than half, they averaged more than three plants each. A detailed breakdown showed the following patterns:

Four-firm Concentration Ratio	Number of Industries	Average Number of Plants per Company	
		Four Leaders	Rest of Industry
70–100	16	7.2	1.11
50–69	24	4.0	1.12
30–49	25	5.8	1.11
0–29	18	4.3	1.06

Comparing the third and fourth columns, we see that industry leaders tended toward multi-plant operation much more than their smaller rivals. Reading down the third column, we note a slight tendency for the leading four firms to control more plants in highly concentrated industries than in industries of low or moderate concentration.

Nelson found that the four industry leaders operated not only more plants than their rivals, but also larger plants. In only one industry (cement) was the leading four firms' average plant size smaller than the overall industry aver-

---

[51]"Economies," pp. 38–39. See also *Barriers*, p. 89.

[52]*Concentration in the Manufacturing Industries of the United States*, pp. 62–77.

age, while in nearly a third of the industries the leaders' average plant size exceeded the industry average by a multiple of ten or more. However, exceptionally large Big Four plants were located as frequently in relatively unconcentrated industries as in the highly concentrated lines. In fact, Nelson discovered that four-firm concentration ratios for 1954 were lower, the higher the ratio of the leading companies' plant size to the average size of all industry plants, with a correlation coefficient (r) of -0.37. This result reinforces the conclusion that multi-plant control was a more important determinant of high concentration than large plant size.

Nelson observed that the fraction of all industry plants controlled by Big Four members and the ratio of average Big Four member plant size to average industry plant size were negatively correlated, with $r = -0.91$. This may mean that when minimum optimal plant scale is high, leading firms choose to operate relatively few large plants, while they gravitate toward multiplant operations when the minimum optimal plant scale is small in relation to the size of the market. The choices depend in turn upon the relevant production and transportation technology. Examples of industries with high concentration but little multi-plant operation include steam engines and turbines, transformers, locomotives, typewriters, chocolate products, sewing machines, photographic equipment, and aircraft propellers. In most of these cases, there is reason to believe that a plant of minimum optimal scale must produce a sizeable fraction of total market volume. Conversely, extensive multi-plant operation is found in the concentrated tin can, storage battery, compressed gas, electric lamp, and biscuit and cracker industries, among others. Here national markets tend to be large relative to the size of an efficient plant, but the products are bulky or difficult to transport. On the whole, there appear to be more industries of the latter type where tight oligopoly prevails. Out of 35 industries with four-firm concentration ratios of 60 or more studied by John Blair, in 22 the share of sales associated with the leading eight *firms* was at least 20 per-

centage points higher than the share of sales originating from the largest eight *plants*.[53] Again, we are drawn to the conclusion that multi-plant operation is a crucial contributor to high concentration.

ECONOMIES OF SCALE AND CONCENTRATION IN FOREIGN INDUSTRY

Those who read extensively in both the American and European industrial organization literature cannot avoid being struck by the contrast in emphasis. American economists seldom get very excited about scale economies, while for the typical European industry analyst, the day begins and ends with an impassioned tract on the advantages of size. One is tempted to advance a simple explanation for this divergence. The American market is very large and so, as we have seen, there is plenty of room for numerous firms enjoying all production and physical distribution economies. National markets in most other industrialized countries are much smaller, and so unless the logic of comparative advantage is respected more than it has been in the past, their policy-makers may be faced with choosing between the Scylla of oligopolistic or monopolistic industry structures and the Charybdis of inefficiently small firms. Only big affluent nations can avoid the dilemma most of the time; and only their economists can afford to be callous about scale economies.

This explanation overstates the conflict between competition and production efficiency—a sin shared by many overseas economists. Frequently, the minimum optimal plant scale is so small that even small nations can accommodate a sufficient number of independent producers to achieve some modicum of competition. Yet national market size does make a difference. The clearest indication comes from Bain's study of industrial structure in eight nations, summarized in the previous chapter, showing average levels of market concentration to be comparable to those of the United States only in Great Britain and Japan, while concentration was moderately higher in France and Italy and much higher in

---

[53]See *Economic Concentration*, pp. 1542–1548.

Canada, India, and Sweden.[54] Generally, the larger and more highly industrialized a nation is, the lower market concentration in its manufacturing industries tends to be.

Despite severe data limitations, Bain tried to go further in his study, identifying the direction of the choices taken when it was difficult or impossible simultaneously to enjoy scale economies and competitive market structures. The results, summarized in Table 4.2, are surprising. In Japan, France, Italy, and India, multi-plant operation by leading firms appeared to be about as prevalent as it was in the United States (although confidence in the comparisons is limited due to the paucity of observations). The extent of multi-plant operation was somewhat lower in England, and substantially lower only in Sweden and Canada—countries with less than a tenth the population of the United States. Thus, the emergence of multi-plant operations abroad does not appear to have been inhibited severely by market size limitations. Since multi-plant operation presumably confers few economies, this development cannot have added much to productive efficiency while exerting a multiplier effect on market concentration.

Where the impact of market size limitations shows up more sharply is in the choice of plant scales. Table 4.2 reveals that in all but England, plant sizes abroad (measured in terms of employment in the 20 largest plants for each industry) were much smaller on the average than in the United States—i.e., from 39 per cent of the U. S. median size down to only 13 per cent. And this difference in plant sizes may have imposed a significant burden of efficiency sacrifices. Assuming that the technological conditions governing cost – scale relationships were the same abroad as in the United States, and assuming further (on the basis of conclusions from his study of 20 U. S. industries) that at least 70 per cent of all output in U. S. industries is produced

Table 4.2

Extent of Multi-Plant Operation, Comparative Plant Size, and Extent of Efficient Plant Scales in Eight Nations During the 1950s

Nation	Mean Company/Plant Concentration Multiple[a]	Median Relative Size of 20 Largest Plants; U.S. Index=100[b]	Estimated Percentage of Workers Employed in Plants of "Reasonably Efficient Scale"
United States	$3.6_{(19)}$	$100_{(34)}$	$70_{(24)}$
United Kingdom	$2.6_{(17)}$	$78_{(32)}$	$54_{(22)}$
Japan	$3.9_{(12)}$	$34_{(31)}$	$46_{(23)}$
France	$4.3_{(9)}$	$39_{(31)}$	$48_{(20)}$
Italy	$3.6_{(5)}$	$29_{(32)}$	$42_{(23)}$
India	$4.3_{(3)}$	$26_{(22)}$	$33_{(16)}$
Canada	$2.0_{(5)}$	$28_{(14)}$	$46_{(8)}$
Sweden	$1.7_{(6)}$	$13_{(27)}$	$48_{(22)}$

Source: Joe S. Bain, *International Differences in Industrial Structure* (New Haven: Yale University Press, 1966), pp. 132, 139, and 164. Subscripted numbers in parentheses indicate the number of industries on which data were available.
[a] Ratio of the percentage of total industry employment accounted for by the three or four largest *firms* divided by the percentage of employment accounted for by the three or four largest *plants*.
[b] Median of industry ratios of employment in the 20 largest plants abroad to employment in the 20 largest U.S. plants.

[54] *International Differences in Industrial Structure* (New Haven: Yale University Press, 1966).

in plants whose costs exceed the feasible minimum by no more than 5 per cent, Bain estimated that less than half of all manufacturing employees worked in plants of "reasonably efficient scale" in Sweden, Canada, France, Japan, and Italy.[55] While this judgment is subject to considerable uncertainty, it does suggest rather strongly that smaller foreign nations have sacrificed *both* a certain amount of structural competition *and* production efficiency as a consequence of their smallness.

If this is so, why have large manufacturers abroad moved in the multi-plant direction? By foregoing the modest advantages of multi-plant operation, the largest firms could build larger, more efficient plants. The answer remains a mystery. It is conceivable that one or more of Bain's conclusions, on which we have been forced to rely so heavily, is wrong. That is, the typical plant abroad may be more efficient than he assumes, or there may be less multi-plant operation abroad than his sample implies, or multi-plant operation may confer greater production and distribution economies than the evidence from his 20 industry American research indicates. Alternately, multiple plant strategies may have been adopted abroad to gain economies of large-scale promotion or various monopolistic advantages. We shall proceed now to deal with the promotional economies aspect. Still it is not obvious why promotional advantages cannot be enjoyed as easily by big firms with one or two efficient plants as by big firms with numerous inefficient plants. We must close this section by admitting that we do not understand fully the reasons for the observed international differences in market structure. Again, a great deal of research remains to be done.

ECONOMIES OF LARGE-SCALE SALES PROMOTION

Economies of large-scale sales promotion pose special analytic problems. For one, they may show up not only in the form of lower costs, but also in the ability of firms to charge prices higher than those of smaller rivals for comparable products, or in some combination of price premiums and cost savings. Thus, both cost curves and demand curves are affected. A second complication is the element of chance associated with sales promotion. A massive advertising campaign may be a spectacular success or a resounding flop, depending upon the ingenuity and luck of the Madison Avenue men in charge. Third, there are dynamic ramifications. A million dollars spent on advertising this year will have different effects for the firm which has been spending large sums year after year than for the firm which is just entering the product differentiation game. And most important of all, the private benefits realized through large-scale promotion may not be mirrored by benefits to the public. It is not clear that society gains when one firm's monopoly power is bolstered by a successful promotional campaign, or whether the bleary-eyed television viewer is better off from the barrage of 'brief messages' to which he is subjected. These are matters of considerable controversy, and we shall progress best by dodging them for the present, scheduling a fuller debate for Chapter 14. Here we confine ourselves to the narrower question, to what extent is market concentration encouraged or entrenched by the private advantages of large-scale promotion?

The answer appears to be: substantially. There are definite economies of large-scale promotion and product differentiation, notably in the consumer goods industries. In his study of 20 American industries, Bain concluded that product differentiation was "of at least the same general order of importance . . . as economies of large-scale production and distribution" in giving established market leaders a price or cost advantage over rivals.[56] Moreover, when industry leaders possessed especially large price or cost

---

[55] *Ibid.*, p. 65. Using the survivor test on 66 industries, Leonard Weiss concluded that Bain's 20-industry sample was not representative, and that inefficient scales of operation are more widespread in U. S. industry. "The Survival Technique and the Extent of Suboptimal Capacity," *Journal of Political Economy*, June 1964, pp. 257–261. To the extent that the survivor estimates are reliable, this means that failure to achieve scale economies abroad is even more serious than Bain alleges.

[56] *Barriers*, pp. 142–143 and 216.

advantages over small rivals or potential industry entrants, it was typically because of successful product differentiation rather than production or distribution scale economies. Bain estimated that through their product differentiation advantages, established industry leaders could sustain price and/or cost differentials relative to potential new entrants of at least 5 per cent for ten years, or 10 per cent for five years, in six of his 20 industries: cigarettes, automobiles, typewriters, 'quality' fountain pens, liquor, and tractors.[57]

Advertising was found by Bain to be the single most important basis of these differentials. Large firms may enjoy several kinds of advertising advantages over small rivals.

First, an effective advertising campaign often needs to attain a certain saturation level before reaching maximum effectiveness. One message delivered to the average consumer may have no impact on his behavior; five or six are likely to, if advertising can move him at all. This means that there are increasing returns to advertising expenditures up to some possibly high absolute level, after which diminishing marginal returns set in. Experience in the automobile industry illustrates this point. To compete with General Motors and Ford for the consumer's attention, the smaller firms must mount a disproportionately large advertising campaign. Weiss calculated that GM and Ford each spent on advertising roughly $27 per car sold between 1954 and 1957, compared to $48 for Chrysler, $64 for Studebaker-Packard, and $58 for American Motors.[58]

Second, quantity discounts given by the principal advertising media may be available only to the relatively large firm. Full-page advertisements can be purchased at lower rates per square inch than quarter page or smaller insertions and probably have disproportionately high attention-getting power, *ceteris paribus*. The cost per reader for comparable space is higher when a firm advertises in the regional editions of national magazines than when it contracts for full national coverage. Up to 1966, the television networks offered quantity discounts to large advertisers willing to commit themselves to half-hour and hour-long programs over a full viewing season. However, these rates did not cover program production costs borne by the advertisers. There is some evidence that during the mid-1960s large advertisers enjoyed no systematic advantage over smaller advertisers in price paid per commercial minute, and they may in some cases have suffered a slight disadvantage.[59]

Third, certain effects of advertising tend to be cumulative. It takes a long time to build up a reputation, or to get consumers into the habit of requesting Prestone when what they want is ethylene glycol antifreeze. The small firm lacking such a reputation is limited in its choices to the least of several evils: selling its product at a discount relative to well-established lines; paying through the nose for current advertising to enhance its image among that subset of consumers who are highly receptive; or spending large sums year after year to build up lasting preferences. And for many small, thinly capitalized firms the third alternative, with its long-delayed payoffs and high risks, may appear out of the question.

To expand a bit on this last point, the dynamic properties of advertising as a determinant of firm size are not unlike those attributed by Mrs. Penrose to management in her theory of corporate growth.[60] In the short or medium run, the small firm trying to grow rapidly through vigorous advertising often runs into sharply diminishing returns in its efforts to dislodge customers from well-established large sellers. Only gradually, as it builds up its reputation, does this static barrier to expansion recede, raising the marginal efficiency of the firm's advertising expenditures and giving it an advantage over other sellers lacking product differentiation. It is also conceivable that barriers to

---

[57]*Barriers*, pp. 126–129. Bain's estimates for the last three industries are not entirely convincing.

[58]Leonard W. Weiss, *Economics and American Industry* (New York: Wiley, 1961), p. 342.

[59]See David M. Blank, "Television Advertising: The Great Discount Illusion, or Tonypandy Revisited," *Journal of Business*, January 1968, pp. 10–38; and the comment by William Leonard with rejoinder by Blank in the *Journal of Business*, January 1969, pp. 93–112.

[60]Cf. pp. 77–78 *supra*.

rapid growth through sales promotion will confine the small firm to a size at which it is unable to realize all production scale economies, putting it at a double disadvantage.[61] If so, it may take a great leap forward in promotion to achieve a scale at which the firm eventually enjoys both advertising and production scale economies, and of course, success in making the transition is never guaranteed.

Another quite different advantage of large scale is sometimes enjoyed by the sellers of complex durable goods and especially consumer durables. The automobile industry again affords the leading example. Most consumers are unwilling to buy a particular new car unless they are confident they can obtain prompt, reliable service not only at home, but wherever they may travel or migrate. This gives the manufacturer with a far-flung, high-quality dealer network a definite sales advantage. Establishing such a network is difficult for the smaller manufacturer, since there are economies of scale at the sales and service establishment level. A certain minimum investment in specialized testing equipment, tools, and spare parts is necessary. More important, the most able entrepreneurs are not apt to find the dealership for an auto brand attractive unless they can expect to sell a fairly high annual volume, and in smaller cities and towns, only the more popular brands offer this expectation. This sets up a vicious circle. Low-volume manufacturers cannot attract the most able dealers in smaller cities because of their limited volume potential. But they are unable to build up their volume potential because they lack a strong nationwide distribution network, and therefore suffer in the eyes of consumers. This advantage of large size is probably more important than any other scale economy in the automobile industry. Pashigian estimated that a manufacturer needs an annual volume of roughly 600,000 units before avoiding serious disadvantages of small scale distribution through franchised dealers, and additional advantages may accrue at volumes up to three times this level.[62] Inability to overcome its dealership problem broke the back of Studebaker, as well as several earlier postwar automobile industry casualties, and it is one of the most serious handicaps facing American Motors and (to a lesser degree) Chrysler. It is also the most important obstacle preventing many excellent foreign makes from penetrating the American market more extensively. Only Volkswagen has surmounted it with any conspicuous success.

Nevertheless, like many advantages of large-scale promotion, the nationwide dealership problem is a product of the institutional setting in which it exists, and it could be overcome through changes in those institutions. Most local automobile dealerships in the United States are tied to a particular manufacturer through an exclusive franchise. While such contracts offer certain benefits to both manufacturer and dealer, they are not essential, and they are somewhat less common in Europe. The sales promotional disadvantages of smaller automobile manufacturers could be reduced appreciably if dealers exceeding a certain size were required by law to accept orders for and service all auto makes, or if automobile distribution were organized along multi-brand supermarket lines. This last possibility may prove to be the wave of the future, if the understandable reluctance of the largest manufacturers (who stand to lose a major advantage) could be overcome (e.g., through legal compulsion). Until recently, the difficulty of managing a large-scale service operation has been a deterrent to auto supermarketing. But the development of computer-controlled diagnostic techniques is likely to make this problem more tractable. And in the longer run, the rise of electric propulsion could lead to simplified and perhaps better standardized engines and drive trains, further simplifying service operations. Should these changes come to fruition, there may well be a reversal in the half-century trend toward increasing automobile industry concentration.

Similar advantages of scale are found in other

[61]See *Barriers*, pp. 118–119

[62]See B. P. Pashigian, *The Distribution of Automobiles: An Economic Analysis of the Franchise System* (Englewood Cliffs: Prentice-Hall, 1961), especially pp. 238–239.

leading industries. IBM's dominance in the computer market, for instance, is attributable in large measure to the strength of its sales and service network. Because of its scale, IBM can provide an especially wide range of programming services to computer users, and it can afford to have trouble-shooters stationed in every part of the nation, ready to pounce upon unusual machine 'bugs' and in this way to minimize costly computing time losses. These are potent advantages in selling both to small, localized users and to nationwide firms anxious to standardize their decentralized computation facilities.[63] In the copying machine industry, Xerox found it necessary for several years to plow back profits into building an extensive sales and service network before it could successfully tap the market for high-volume copiers, where its technological advantage was greatest.[64] And in the tin can industry, only the largest manufacturers are able to maintain specialized service staffs to help canners solve unusual spoilage and corrosion problems. For this service many canners are apparently willing to pay a slight per-can price premium.[65]

Still another promotional advantage of large scale is found in durable goods industries selling products subject to rapid styling obsolescence. Again, the automobile industry is the classic case. Through some perverse quirk of human nature, the average consumer is decidedly unhappy driving around last season's assemblage of metal stampings. The automobile manufacturers have learned through experience that they can sell more cars by changing body designs regularly; or at least, that they will normally suffer market share losses if they fail to change their body designs while rivals do. As a result, almost every major American automobile model is subjected to a minor face-lifting once a year, and every two or three years complete style changes are effected. This is expensive. A face-lift involves design, testing, and retooling costs on the order of $15 million, and a full model redesign necessitates an investment ranging from $40 million to $120 million, depending upon the scope of the changes. The per-unit impact of these investments in styling change is obviously less for firms with high market volume. Suppose, for example, that $60 million is invested in model redesign every three years. The manufacturer with a sales volume of 200,000 units annually in the relevant line will incur design and retooling costs averaging $100 per unit, while the firm selling only 50,000 units finds its average model change costs four times as high. This again sets into motion a vicious circle against the smaller firm. If it keeps up the pace of model change, it is burdened by higher per-unit change costs than its larger rivals. If it falls behind, it suffers volume losses which cause it to sacrifice other economies of scale.

The strategic importance of model change scale economies in the auto industry depends upon a special interaction of technology, consumer tastes, and industry institutions. In most other consumer goods industries the phenomenon is less significant as a concentration-increasing force because consumers are less sensitive to style obsolescence or because model change costs are smaller in relation to total unit costs. Changes may also be in sight for automobiles. Computer-controlled pattern-making and milling could cut the cost of translating a stylist's designs into a completed production die. The development of new body materials (such as fiberglass) may permit smaller producers to use 'soft' body component dies with an average tooling cost per unit at low volumes not much greater than the unit costs incurred by large producers for their 'hard' dies. The result, again, may be a decline in the presently substantial promotional advantages enjoyed by large-scale auto manufacturers.

In sum, there are significant scale economies in many aspects of product differentiation. The implication conveyed thus far is that these advantages of size are a force contributing to market concentration far in excess of what is

---

[63] See "Control Data's Newest Cliffhanger," *Fortune*, February 1968, p. 176.

[64] Erwin A. Blackstone, "The Copying Machine Industry: A Case Study," unpublished Ph.D. dissertation, University of Michigan, 1968, pp. 58–67 and 138–139.

[65] J. W. McKie, *Tin Cans and Tin Plate* (Cambridge: Harvard University Press, 1959), pp. 127–129.

required to realize all production and physical distribution economies. This is correct, but it does not tell the whole story. The product differentiation sword can also cut in the opposite direction. Through successful product differentiation, smaller firms may be able to carve out for themselves a small but profitable niche in some special segment of a large market. Their sales volume may be too low to afford all production and promotional scale economies, but the higher costs associated with foregoing these advantages may be more than offset by the price premium consumers pay for the special product features they offer. Product innovation is one tactic by which smaller firms can survive despite conventional scale disadvantages. For example, economists studying the cigarette industry during the late 1940s concluded that the Big Three enjoyed a decisive advantage over smaller rivals due to economies of large-scale promotion; yet their share of the market fell from 85 per cent in 1947 to 69 per cent in 1959 as a consequence of successful king size and filter tip innovations by the smaller firms.

Another strategy is to cater to some narrow geographic market segment, or to some special consumer taste with a sales potential too small to interest the leading firms. Even in the automobile industry, where the disadvantages of small-scale production are so formidable, such niches can be found. In 1964, for example, one firm announced plans for yearly production of 2,000 fiberglass-body replicas of the 1936 Cord selling at $4,000 each, and another to produce 250 custom-built vehicles bearing the time-honored Duesenberg name offered at a minimum price of $18,000 each.[66] That the Cord venture failed two years later does not prove that its idea was unsound, for there are many automobile buyers able and willing to pay an impressive premium for the right kind of uniqueness. It is precisely for this reason that many high-priced European cars are able to penetrate the American market despite their inadequate distribution networks.

The success of a small firm pursuing a strategy of survival through differentiation depends in any given case upon the strength and elasticity of demand in the special market and the cost differential associated with producing at much less than the minimum optimal scale. As the American public grows more affluent and cultivates a more intense taste for variety, it is conceivable that an expanding fringe of small producers will find it possible to thrive despite the disadvantages of inefficiently low production volume. In this respect Americans will become more like European consumers. Although such comparisons are difficult to validate, casual observation suggests that the 'typical' middle-class European consumer is much less tolerant of standardized products than his American counterpart. This stronger European taste for differentiation may partly explain the high incidence of inefficiently small plants discovered by Bain in his international comparisons study.

Whether small-scale American firms selling differentiated consumer goods will prove increasingly viable in the future remains to be seen. It is more certain that in the past, and especially during the two decades following World War II, any tendency toward deconcentration due to a demand for greater variety was outweighed by tendencies toward concentration resulting from economies of scale in sales promotion. Willard Mueller divided 213 four-digit industries whose definitions remained comparable between 1947 and 1963 into two groups, consumer goods and producer goods.[67] In the producer goods category, he found that the four-firm sales concentration ratio declined by three percentage points or more in 62 industries, while it rose by three percentage points or more in only 38 industries. In sharp contrast, the four-firm concentration ratio declined by three points or more in only 24 consumer goods industries, increasing by a comparable amount in 43 industries. Although alternative hypotheses can be adduced, the most likely explanation for

---

[66]"Vintage Cars Return—Brand-New," *Business Week*, December 5, 1964, pp. 158–162; and "Special Cars for Special People," *Fortune*, February 1968, pp. 136–143.

[67]Testimony in U. S. Senate, Select Committee on Small Business, Hearings, *Status and Future of Small Business* (Washington: 1967), p. 479. For an extension to 1966 with essentially the same results, see *Studies by the Staff of the Cabinet Committee on Price Stability*, pp. 59–62.

these disparate trends appears to be the differential effect of large-scale sales promotional economies, applicable primarily in the consumer goods fields. The advent of television—a potent advertising medium subject to economies of intensive utilization—may have had much to do with the rising concentration in consumer goods industries. In an analysis of 36 consumer goods industries with television advertising outlays exceeding $250,000 in 1963, John Blair found four-firm concentration ratios to have fallen between 1947 and 1963 in only 11 fields, while they rose in 25 fields.[68] Increases of 6 percentage points or more were registered in 23 of the industries, while decreases of this magnitude occurred in only six industries.

All in all, the evidence points strongly toward a conclusion that economies of large-scale sales promotion are often substantial in consumer goods industries, and that they contribute prominently to market concentration. Whether such economies yield benefits to society commensurate with their structural impact is open to doubt.

PECUNIARY ECONOMIES OF SCALE

Finally, large size may confer advantages referred to as *pecuniary economies*, because they entail cost savings with no corresponding economies in the use of real resources. The simplest and most important case is that of large firms wresting price concessions from suppliers. If differential bargaining power is the cause, income is merely redistributed from the supplier to the buyer. Still the ability to obtain such concessions can solidify a large firm's position in the market, and so pecuniary economies in procurement are, like other scale economies, a concentration-increasing influence. Concrete illustrations will be presented in Chapters 9 and 10.

Large firms also enjoy a cost advantage in raising financial capital. They tend to pay lower interest rates on short- and long-term debt than smaller enterprises, and they can float equity issues at lower costs per dollar of useable funds received, other things being equal. This advantage of size has two main bases. First, certain more or less fixed transactions costs must be met in executing a loan or floating a stock or bond issue. The larger the size of the issue, the lower these costs are per dollar obtained. In a statistical analysis of 238 common stock issues floated by firms of widely varying sizes between 1960 and 1962, Archer and Faerber found that flotation costs ranged from 5 to 44 per cent of the total value of shares sold, and flotation cost as a percentage of total share value was inversely correlated with both size of firm and size of the issue.[69] These economies of large-scale financing are not solely pecuniary, but are backed by real managerial, promotional, and legal resource savings. Second, investors are evidently willing to buy the securities of large firms at lower interest and profit yields than similar securities of small firms, partly because the large firms are better known and have longer earnings histories, and partly because investments in large firms are demonstrably less risky, in the sense that earnings tend to be more stable and defaults rarer. Ferguson found, for instance, that the variability over time of firms' profit/asset ratios between 1947 and 1956 was negatively correlated with firm size in all 15 of the industries he studied.[70] Stekler estimated that the inter-firm standard deviation of the profit/asset ratio in manufacturing ranged from 5.3 per cent for firms with assets exceeding $250 million upward to 66 per cent for firms with assets of less than $25,000.[71] It is arguable whether this financing advantage should be labelled a strict pecuniary economy. Obviously, large firms offer something extra—greater security—in obtaining capital at lower costs from investors. Still the real resource savings are elusive; at best, investors save some

---

[68]Testimony in *Economic Concentration*, pp. 1902–1910.

[69]S. H. Archer and L. G. Faerber, "Firm Size and the Cost of Externally Secured Equity Capital," *Journal of Finance*, March 1966, pp. 69–83.

[70]C. E. Ferguson, *A Macroeconomic Theory of Workable Competition* (Durham: Duke University Press, 1964), pp. 172–174.

[71]*Profitability and Size of Firm*, p. 92. For similar British results, see J. M. Samuels and D. J. Smyth, "Profits, Variability of Profits, and Firm Size," *Economica*, May 1968, pp. 127–139.

subjective anguish by knowing their capital is in steady, time-tested hands.

A more interesting question is, why do the profits of large firms vary less than those of small firms? Two reasons can be suggested. First, large firms tend to possess greater monopoly power than smaller firms, *ceteris paribus*, and one manifestation of that power is the ability to stabilize earnings. In this respect size may beget size, for the lower capital costs attributable to the stability arising from market power constitute an advantage, helping the large firm maintain and perhaps increase its hold on the market. Second, ability to spread risks tends to increase with size. The large firm typically has more customers, so that the loss of any one or a few is a less disastrous blow. It may also operate in a larger number of local markets, or in a greater diversity of product lines, so that chance declines in some markets can be offset by booming sales and profits in others. This last benefit, it must be emphasized, is the result of conglomerate bigness, not of size in relation to particular markets, and therefore the links between size and monopoly power are fuzzier.

Indeed, the more distinct markets a firm of any given size serves and the less related they are, the less monopoly power that firm is likely to possess (ignoring some complications to be introduced in Chapter 11). But the more unrelated are the markets a conglomerate firm serves, the more stable will be its profits in the face of chance fluctuations within particular product lines. To put this point more rigorously, when a firm operates in two markets, the standard deviation of profits in Market 1 being σ_1 and in Market 2 σ_2, the standard deviation of the firm's *total* profits is given by the formula:

$$\sigma_t = \sqrt{\sigma_1^2 + \sigma_2^2 + 2r\sigma_1\sigma_2}$$

where r is the coefficient of correlation between profits in the two markets. Suppose, by way of illustration, that there are two plants serving distinct markets, each with a mean profit ex-

pectation of $1 million per year and a standard deviation of $400,000. If the plants are organized as independent firms, each finds the standard deviation of its profits to be 40 per cent of the mean. If the operations are combined under a single corporate roof, the relationship of profit variability to total combined profits depends upon the correlation between profits in the two markets. In the extreme case of a perfect *negative* correlation between profits in Market 1 and Market 2 ($r = -1.0$), the standard deviation of total corporate profits becomes zero, for each decline in one line's profits is exactly offset by an increase in the other's! A more plausible goal for the so-called pure conglomerate is a perfectly random relationship between profits in the two markets; that is, $r = 0$. For this assumption the standard deviation of the two-line firm's profits is about $566,000, or roughly 28 per cent of combined mean profits. The conglomerate enjoys profits relatively more stable than its divisions would as independent entities. The more markets with randomly related profits the conglomerate serves, *ceteris paribus*, the more its risks will be spread, and the smaller will be the standard deviation of total profits in relation to average total profits.[72] Finally, however, diversification fails to benefit the firm if variations in profits for the various lines are perfectly correlated positively, so that declines in one line are paralleled by declines in the others. With $r = +1.0$, we find from the above formula that the standard deviation of the two-line conglomerate firm's profits is $800,000, or 40 per cent of mean total profits.

From these relationships we might expect firms diversified into a host of unrelated markets to display especially low earnings variability, and hence to enjoy especially favorable treatment by investors. This conjecture has not been subjected to a careful test, partly because the pure conglomerate enterprise is a relatively recent phenomenon in America. The evidence readily at hand shows no consistent pattern. Up to the mid-1960s, investors tended to value the securi-

---

[72]Concretely, when $r = 0$ and the individual markets are of identical size, the ratio of the standard deviation to average total profits declines by the ratio $1/\sqrt{N}$ with increases in N, the number of markets served. Cf. T. R. Dyckman and H. O. Stekler, "Firm Size and Variability," *Journal of Industrial Economics*, June 1965, pp. 214–218.

ties of corporations stereotyped as pure conglomerates *less highly* than more narrowly based
firms. Then a conglomerate stock boom developed, fueled more by speculative motives than
by the risk-spreading qualities emphasized
here.[73] In 1968 disillusion began to set in,
however, and it was not clear at the time of
writing whether conglomerate stocks could
maintain investor favor. One reason for this
erratic record may be that the problems of
managing a conglomerate enterprise are particularly acute, making long-run stability and
success less likely. Alternatively, investors may
have been distressed by the paucity of information available on the operations of individual
conglomerate firm divisions. Or conceivably,
investors may prefer to hedge against risk by
diversifying their own stock portfolios, instead of
investing in a single stock and letting company
managers diversify for them internally.[74] More
research on the cost of capital to firms of
varying degrees of diversification, with its
obvious implications for the relative viability
of large vs. small enterprises, is needed. It is
evident in any event that larger firms do enjoy
at least moderately lower capital costs than their
smaller brethren, even though this advantage is
not related in any simple manner to the risk
spreading strategy pursued.

Thus far it has been implicitly assumed for
simplicity's sake that a firm of any given size and
degree of diversification faces a uniquely-defined
cost of capital, i.e., that capital markets are
perfect. This is not entirely true. A corporation
with assets of $200 million might be able to
borrow $10 million at very close to the prime
rate, but if it tries to double its assets suddenly
by borrowing, it will have to pay a steep interest
premium, and it may not be able to find any
willing lenders at all.[75] Such capital market
imperfections may contribute to concentration in
industries which demand a very high capital
investment for successful operation, since small
firms may be unable to raise the necessary funds.
The electronic computer industry affords an
excellent illustration. For a variety of reasons,
many computer users prefer to lease rather than
buy their machines, and IBM in developing the
market encouraged this practice. As a result,
one of the most difficult problems faced by small
rivals like Control Data, Scientific Data Systems,
and (in England) International Computers and
Tabulators has been securing funds to finance a
rapidly growing inventory of machines leased to
customers.[76] This condition has undoubtedly
contributed to IBM's dominance. Similarly, the
need to invest nearly a half billion dollars to
enter the automobile industry with a production
complex of minimum optimal scale, or $250
million to enter the steel industry on an efficient
scale, discourages the entry of new competitors.[77]

In a variation on this theme, Lance Davis has
argued that the rapid growth of industrial concentration in the United States during the late
19th century was partly the result of capital
market imperfections, engendering an environment in which only a few entrepreneurs (like
Carnegie, Morgan, Rockefeller, Swift, and
Armour) with especially good banking connections could mobilize the capital sums required to
exploit opportunities opened up by market
growth and technological change.[78] British in-

[73]See "Looking for a New Yardstick," *Business Week*, August 20, 1966, pp. 119–120; "Time of Testing for
Conglomerates," *Business Week*, March 2, 1968, p. 38; and "Changing Yardsticks," *Business Week*, March 8,
1969, p. 29.

[74]Cf. William W. Alberts, "The Profitability of Growth by Merger," in Alberts and J. E. Segall, ed., *The Corporate Merger* (Chicago: University of Chicago Press, 1966), pp. 271–272. See also M. R. Fisher, "Towards a
Theory of Diversification," *Oxford Economic Papers*, October 1961, pp. 293–311; Stephen Hymer and Peter
Pashigian, "Firm Size and Rate of Growth," *Journal of Political Economy*, December 1962, pp. 567–569; and
the comment by Herbert Simon, *Journal of Political Economy*, February 1964, p. 82.

[75]This is partly due to the "principle of increasing risk" articulated by Michal Kalecki in an article with the
same name, *Economica*, November 1937, pp. 440–447.

[76]See, for instance, "Personality: For Success, a Touch of Karate," *New York Times*, April 3, 1966; "Control
Data Digs Its Gold Mine," *Business Week*, September 28, 1968, pp. 59–60; and "Britain Presses Drive To
Develop Her Own Data Industry," *New York Times*, October 22, 1966.

[77]Cf. Bain, *Barriers*, pp. 162–163.

[78]Lance Davis, "The Capital Markets and Industrial Concentration: The U. S. and U. K., a Comparative
Study," *Economic History Review*, August 1966, pp. 255–272.

dustry experienced less concentration during the same period, Davis continues, because capital was more widely accessible; and the trend toward rising U. S. concentration ebbed in the early 20th century as capital markets were perfected. Although his handling of the evidence leaves something to be desired, there is probably more than a grain of truth in Davis' conjectures.

One final point must be mentioned. Because of its superior access to capital, the large firm may have greater staying power in periods of unusually sharp competition. This advantage includes the ability to weather a severe business recession successfully and to finance predatory ventures such as price wars against weaker rivals and lengthy court battles over patent rights. We shall have more to say about these activities in later chapters.

CONCLUSION

To conclude this long discussion of scale economies, let us attempt to put the evidence in perspective. Size confers advantages along such diverse dimensions as production costs, advertising costs, brand acceptance, input prices, and access to capital. What matters in analyzing the determinants of market concentration is not, however, the mere fact that scale economies exist. Rather, the important questions are quantitative ones: what size of plant or firm is needed to realize all scale economies; what cost and revenue penalties are associated with operation at suboptimal scale, and whether these penalties outweigh whatever additional managerial and coordinating costs large-scale operation imposes. We have found that, at least in the American economy, production and physical distribution scale economies seldom require very high seller concentration. Sales promotional and pecuniary economies of debatable social utility contribute by an unknown but probably substantial amount to higher concentration levels. Still we must guard against overemphasizing their significance. The illustrations presented here have been drawn mainly from industries in which the advantages of large-scale marketing and financing are ex-

ceptionally great. Promotional economies are of minor importance in nearly all producer goods and raw materials industries, and pecuniary economies are seldom sufficient to put smaller firms at an insuperable disadvantage. It is evident from studies of scale economies in particular industries and the observation of broad survival patterns that in many and perhaps most American industries high concentration is not a technological, marketing, or financial imperative.

MERGERS AND CONCENTRATION

Market structure is also affected by mergers, acquisitions, and other legal transformations through which two or more formerly independent firms come under common control. We defer discussion of whether the 'urge to merge' is independent of scale economies. It suffices by way of introduction to belabor the obvious: any merger among firms competing in the same market is a step, however large or small, toward increased concentration.

In assessing the impact of mergers on market structure, it is customary to distinguish three major merger waves which swept the American economy—the first between roughly 1887 and 1904, the second between 1916 and 1929, and the third following World War II and continuing through the 1960s. An overview of trends in manufacturing and mining industry mergers is provided by Figure 4.4, which combines tabulations developed by Ralph L. Nelson, Willard Thorp, and the Federal Trade Commission. The series are not completely comparable, especially before 1919, because of differences in the information sources tapped and changes in the size cutoff governing inclusion of acquired firms.[79] Still any imprecision is overwhelmed by the sharp fluctuations in merger activity. Each of the three identifiable merger waves warrants further comment.

THE GREAT MERGER WAVE OF 1887-1904

The merger wave which began with recovery from the world-wide depression of 1883 and

---

[79]The FTC series has been adjusted downward from 1962 on to increase comparability with the 1919–1961 segment.

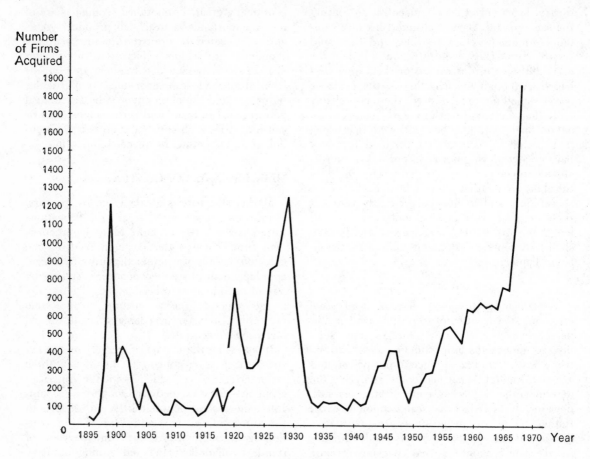

Figure 4.4
Number of Manufacturing and Mining Firms Acquired: 1895-1968 *

*Sources: Ralph L. Nelson. *Merger Movements in American Industry, 1895-1956* (Princeton: Princeton University Press, 1959), p. 37; U. S. House of Representatives, Select Committee on Small Business, Staff Report. *Mergers and Superconcentration* (Washington: 1962). pp. 10 and 266; and U. S. Federal Trade Commission. *Current Trends in Merger Activity, 1968* (Washington: March 1969).

ended with the depression of 1904 was a reaction of epic proportions to the vast changes in transportation, communications, manufacturing technology, competition, and legal institutions coin- ciding during the closing decades of the 19th century.[80] It involved at least 15 per cent of all plants and employees occupied in manufacturing at the turn of the century.[81] Its outstanding

[80]There is an extensive literature on this period. The best single survey and interpretation is Jesse W. Markham, "Survey of the Evidence and Findings on Mergers," in the National Bureau of Economic Research conference report, *Business Concentration and Price Policy* (Princeton: Princeton University Press, 1955), pp. 141–212. Other valuable recent sources include Ralph L. Nelson, *Merger Movements in American Industry, 1895–1956* (Princeton: Princeton University Press, 1959); and George Stigler, "Monopoly and Oligopoly by Merger," *American Economic Review*, May 1950, pp. 23–34.

[81]This is the estimate by Markham, *op. cit.*, p. 157.

characteristic was the simultaneous consolidation of numerous producers into firms dominating the markets they supplied. Nelson found that of the roughly 3,000 independent firm disappearances due to merger he counted for the 1895–1904 period, 75 per cent occurred in mergers involving at least five firms and 26 per cent in consolidations of ten or more firms. By way of contrast, 14 per cent of all 1915–1920 disappearances involved mergers of five or more firms and only 1.4 per cent consolidations of ten or more firms.[82] Multi-firm consolidations have been almost unheard of since World War II.

A pioneer in the market-dominance-by-merger game was the Standard Oil Company. Incorporated in 1870, it brought together 20 of the 25 existing Cleveland area petroleum refiners in early 1872. It then embarked upon a sustained program of acquiring competitors or driving them out of business, adding roughly 100 more affiliations by merger during the next two decades and capturing a 90 per cent share of U. S. petroleum refining capacity.

The pinnacle of the 1887–1904 merger wave was reached with the formation in 1901 of the United States Steel Corporation, combining an estimated 785 plants into the first American industrial corporation with a capitalization exceeding $1 billion. Actually, U. S. Steel is better described as a "combination of combinations." During the late 1890s, a series of mergers consolidated more than 200 formerly independent iron and steel makers into 20 much larger rival entities. Most of these new firms were confined to just a few facets of steel making, and after their formation many mapped out programs of integrating vertically to cover the whole spectrum from ore mining through fabrication. Charles Schwab, then president of Carnegie Steel, foresaw that this would lead to excess capacity and sharp price competition. He communicated his views to J. P. Morgan, who organized a merger among 12 of the prior consolidations and for his labor realized promotional profits estimated at $62.5 million. The end product was U. S. Steel, which at the time of its creation controlled roughly 65 per cent of all domestic blast furnace and finished steel output.

Similar developments reshaped many other industries, large and small. In an early study of 92 large consolidations, John Moody found that 78 gained control of at least 50 per cent of total output in their home industry, and 26 secured a market share of 80 per cent or more. While his figures are marred by slight inaccuracies, they have been shown to be substantially correct.[83] The industries affected included copper, lead, railroad cars, explosives, tin cans, tobacco products, electrical equipment, rubber products, paper, farm machinery, brick-making, chemicals, leather, sugar, business machines, photographic equipment, and shoe machinery. Many corporations which continue to dominate the American industrial scene were formed. General Electric, for instance, was created in 1892 through a merger of Thomson-Houston, which had previously bought out numerous rivals, and Edison General Electric, which had acquired several suppliers and major industrial customers in earlier mergers. The result was a virtual duopoly (with Westinghouse) in many lines of electrical equipment manufacturing. The American Can Company was organized in 1901 through one grand consolidation of some 120 firms with a combined 90 per cent share of the national market. American Tobacco, a consolidation of the leading five producers, had 90 per cent of the national cigarette market at its inception and added to its control by forcing small competitors to the wall and buying them out. DuPont achieved a virtual monopoly of the explosives industry by acquiring or merging with some 100 rivals between 1872 and 1912, and when forced in an antitrust action to divest some of its acquisitions, it pursued the merger route into other areas of the chemicals industry. Other firms whose formation or rise to prominence owes much to mergers during this period include National Lead, U. S. Rubber, United Shoe Machinery, Pittsburgh Plate Glass, International

---

[82]*Op. cit.*, pp. 28–29 and 53.

[83]Cf. Markham, *op. cit.*, pp. 158–162, commenting on John Moody, *The Truth About Trusts* (New York: 1904), and later studies. See also Nelson, *op. cit.*, p. 102.

Paper, United Fruit, Standard Sanitary, Allis-Chalmers, Eastman Kodak, International Salt, Corn Products Refining Co., International Harvester, and U. S. Gypsum. As Markham concluded, "The conversion of approximately 71 important oligopolistic or near-competitive industries into near monopolies by merger between 1890 and 1904 left an imprint on the structure of the American economy that fifty years have not yet erased."[84]

In his quantitative analysis of mergers during the 1895–1904 period, Ralph Nelson attempted to test several causal hypotheses. Two results are of special interest. First, we have suggested earlier that businessmen were motivated to seek mergers by the intensified competition resulting in part from improved transportation and communication networks. Nelson found that mergers around the turn of the century were in fact concentrated in industries with relatively high transportation costs per unit value. However, he discovered also that the producers in these industries tended to be clustered geographically, interacting competitively even before transportation methods were improved.[85] It is possible that transportation innovations were less important as a merger stimulus than we have inferred from the qualitative evidence, or that the links between those innovations and competition were quite complex. Second, it is often assumed that businessmen effected mergers to escape the bitter price competition developing during late 19th century recessions. However, Nelson demonstrated that merger activity peaks typically occurred during business upswings rather than downswings, periods of high merger activity correlating closely with stock market booms.[86] Still this does not necessarily undermine the recession hypothesis. A plausible interpretation is that the desire to escape competition in slack periods led businessmen to seek mergers which were consummated when capital was available on especially favorable terms. That is, long-run

restrictive goals underlay the desire for mergers, while short-run financial market conditions determined their timing.

Merger activity declined sharply in 1903 and 1904, coinciding with two major events—a severe recession, and a set of judicial pronouncements in the *Northern Securities* case which revealed for the first time that mergers leading to market dominance could be attacked successfully under the antitrust laws.[87] A period of relative quiet continued for a dozen years, interrupted occasionally by such ripples as the formation of International Business Machines Corporation (in 1911) and General Motors (combining Buick, Cadillac, Oldsmobile, and several other producers to gain a 22 per cent share of the market in 1909, and adding Chevrolet a few years later). In hindsight, the most spectacular episode appears to be 'the one that got away.' Twice Henry Ford was willing to sell out to General Motors—for $3 million in 1908 and for $8 million a year later. But GM was unable to raise the required cash, and so the two leading auto producers remained independent.

THE 1916–1929 MERGER MOVEMENT

The merger movement showed signs of reviving in 1916 and 1917, but was interrupted by the conversion to war production in 1918 and 1919 and the readjustment recession of 1921 and 1922. Then it rode the stock market boom of the 1920s to heights paralleling those of 1899. Markham has estimated that roughly 12,000 firms disappeared through mergers between 1919 and 1930.[88] However, this wave differed from its turn-of-the-century predecessor in several respects.

For one, a great deal of the activity, including many of the largest combinations, occurred in the electrical and gas utility sector. According to Markham, approximately 2,750 utilities, comprising 43 per cent of all public utility firms operating in 1929, were swallowed up to create

[84]*Ibid.*, p. 180.
[85]*Op. cit.*, pp. 85–88.
[86]*Ibid.*, pp. 6 and 74.
[87]*U. S. v. Northern Securities Co.*, 120 Fed. 721 (April 1903), 193 U. S. 197 (March 1904).
[88]*Op. cit.*, pp. 168–169.

the giant holding companies which collapsed so resoundingly during the depressed 1930s. Since these firms typically had a monopoly in their local markets before being acquired, and since most were regulated by state commissions, the public utility merger wave led at most to only peripheral increases in monopoly power.

In the manufacturing and mining sectors, the 8,000 mergers counted by Markham had a much less dramatic impact on market structure than a smaller number did in the 1887–1904 movement. Mergers creating a single dominant firm were evidently discouraged by the antitrust laws, even though the law was not stringently interpreted and enforced at the time. It is also possible that earlier merger activity had exhausted most of the promising opportunities for ascending to nationwide dominance through consolidation. Whatever the reason, simultaneous multi-firm consolidations were rare, and most of the mergers in manufacturing and mining involved relatively small market share accretions by the acquiring firms. Some of the most prominent manufacturing mergers created a relatively large 'number two' firm in an industry previously dominated by one giant—e.g., the rise of Bethlehem Steel by combining with the third, fourth, sixth, and eighth ranking steel producers of 1904; or Continental Can's absorption of 19 smaller companies between 1927 and 1930. The difference between the 1887–1904 and 1916–1929 merger waves has been depicted by George Stigler as the difference between "mergers for monopoly" and "mergers for oligopoly."[89]

Casual observation suggests that the wave of the 1920s was also characterized by a much higher incidence of vertical integration and conglomerate diversification mergers than its predecessor. Roughly 80 per cent of the recorded manufacturing sector mergers took place in the food products, chemicals, and metals industries.[90] Typifying developments in the food products industry was the experience of the National Dairy Co., which moved into (and sometimes came to dominate) numerous local areas, each a distinct market in the economic sense, through several hundred acquisitions of small milk and dairy products firms. In copper, mergers of refiners with fabricators were common, leading to an oligopolistic fabricated products market structure paralleling the primary metal smelting market structure. In chemicals, the formation of Allied Chemical in 1920 through a consolidation of five firms operating in largely noncompetitive lines set a pattern emulated frequently on a smaller scale. Although these conglomerate and product line extension mergers no doubt had some adverse effect on competition, it was an effect qualitatively different from the predominantly horizontal mergers of the 1887–1904 era.

THE MERGER MOVEMENT FOLLOWING WORLD WAR II

With the onset of the great depression in 1929, merger activity declined sharply and remained at low levels until the end of World War II was in sight. Then followed a revival which has persisted up to the present, with a marked acceleration in 1967 and 1968.

Its dimensions have been charted more completely than either of the earlier waves.[91] Some 11,668 manufacturing and mining mergers were recorded by the Federal Trade Commission in its compilation covering the 1945–1965 period. Another 4,933 were added from 1966 through 1968. Between 1948 and 1965, 814 manufacturing and mining corporations with assets of $10 million or more at the time of acquisition, whose total assets amounted to $27.2 billion, surrendered their independence through merger. Another 462 with assets of $10 million or more disappeared through merger from 1966 through 1968. Their combined assets amounted to $24.9 billion. To put these figures in perspective, there were 2,112 manufacturing and mining firms of this size in existence during 1964, with total assets valued at $266 billion. Thus, the firms acquired

---

[89]"Monopoly and Oligopoly by Merger."

[90]Cf. Markham, *op. cit.*, pp. 168–171, and the comment on his paper by George Stocking on pp. 207–209.

[91]See especially the testimony and exhibits presented by Willard Mueller, Director of the Federal Trade Commission's Bureau of Economics, in *Economic Concentration*, pp. 123–129, 508–520, and 2,020–2,024; and *Studies by the Staff of the Cabinet Committee on Price Stability*, pp. 69–81.

between 1948 and 1965 comprised 38 per cent by number of all firms with assets of $10 million or more at the end of the period, and their assets at the time of acquisition amounted to 10 per cent of the value of all such corporations' assets at the close of 1964. A further, almost equal share of the asset total was swallowed in the next three years, from 1966 through 1968. Of the 1,000 largest manufacturing corporations as of December 1950, 216 had disappeared through merger by 1963. And at least 68 of the firms on *Fortune*'s list of the 500 largest industrial corporations for 1955 had been acquired by 1965.

As common sense suggests, very large firms assimilated most of the acquired firms with assets of at least $10 million. Firms with assets of $100 million or more accounted for 59 per cent of the number of manufacturing and mining firms with assets exceeding $10 million acquired between 1948 and 1967, and 72 per cent of the value of assets acquired. Only 14 companies on *Fortune*'s list of the 500 largest industrials for 1961 participated in no mergers at all between 1955 and 1965. One of these 14, it is worth noting, was General Motors. The numerical champion was Beatrice Foods, a dairy products chain, with 204 acquisitions between 1951 and 1965.

Clearly, the postwar merger movement has been of more than inconsequential size. And it has caused considerable distress in government circles concerned with maintaining competition. One early reaction was a 1948 Federal Trade Commission report, which pointed to the importance of mergers in promoting concentration and concluded that:

> No great stretch of the imagination is required to foresee that if nothing is done to check the growth in concentration, either the giant corporations will ultimately take over the country, or the government will be impelled to step in and impose some form of direct regulation.[92]

Something *was* done, partly because of the report—passage in 1950 of a substantially strengthened amendment to the anti-merger provisions of the Clayton Act. Paradoxically, as Figure 4.4 reveals, merger activity rose steadily in the five years following passage of the new legislation.

Nor was this the only surprise. More careful analysis disclosed that the Federal Trade Commission erred in its interpretation of the postwar merger movement's implications.[93] It would be equally incorrect to say that the movement had no effect on concentration. But the effect was generally modest. For the most part, the firms acquired by large corporations have been small relative to the acquiring firm, in sharp contrast to the 1887–1904 pattern. And the larger the acquiring company was, the less important proportionately merger activity was relative to its total size. Counting only acquisitions of firms with assets of $10 million or more, the value of assets acquired between 1948 and 1967 by firms with assets of $250 million or more was 2 per cent of the value of all such giants' assets in 1967.[94] For firms with assets of from $100 million to $250 million, acquired assets amounted to 19 per cent of 1967 assets. The proportion rises with declining size, until for firms with assets between $10 million and $25 million, the acquired firms' assets were 50 per cent of the value of the acquiring firms' 1967 assets. It appears then that the volume of assets swallowed through merger between 1948 and 1967 by the largest firms was small relative to the size of those firms, and its contribution to their growth was modest compared to the contribution mergers made to the growth of medium-sized companies.

To the extent that size is correlated with market domination, this evidence implies also that mergers could not have led to a substantial increase in the dominance of large firms. More direct evidence concerning the effects of mergers on market concentration is meager. What we

---

[92]U. S. Federal Trade Commission, *The Merger Movement: A Summary Report* (Washington: 1948), pp. 25, 68.

[93]The most decisive attack was by John Lintner and J. K. Butters in "Effect of Mergers on Industrial Concentration, 1940–1947," *Review of Economics and Statistics*, February 1950, pp. 30–48, with various comments and rejoinders in the February 1951 issue, pp. 63–75.

[94]Cf. *Studies by the Staff of the Cabinet Committee on Price Stability*, p. 94, and the similar findings by Lintner and Butters, *op. cit.*

know is not particularly damning. The most careful study, by Leonard Weiss, is confined to six industries—autos, steel, petroleum, cement, flour milling, and beer brewing—for the period between 1929 through 1958.[95] Weiss found that mergers did lead to increases in concentration, but the effect was small—roughly 2 percentage points increase per decade in the four-firm concentration ratio. Broader but more casual observation turns up only a few fields in which market concentration increased significantly due to mergers during the postwar period. These include dairy products (which, however, is fragmented into local markets), paper products, textiles, and soft coal mining. All had characteristically low nationwide concentration ratios in 1947, and the effect of mergers was typically to establish some degree of oligopoly. Perhaps the most strikingly affected industry of any substantial size was the spatially isolated midwestern soft coal market, where mergers were the primary factor underlying an increase in the four-firm concentration ratio from 25 per cent in 1954 to 55 per cent in 1962.[96]

Although the number of recorded mergers rose distressingly after the anti-merger provisions of the Clayton antitrust act were strengthened in 1950, it cannot be said that the antitrust laws had no inhibiting effect. From 1950, if not earlier, to 1960, they were quite successful in discouraging mergers between competing firms, each with a substantial share of the relevant market. On the other hand, few acquisitions entailing a very small market share increase for the acquiring firm were deterred. But an accumulation of many such mergers can and did have a perceptible impact on concentration. Recognizing this, the antitrust authorities, backed by favorable Supreme Court interpretations, tightened their enforcement criteria during the 1960s. If this policy continues, we can confidently expect mergers to contribute virtually nothing to the future growth of concentration within individual markets.

Still such governmental pressure on business firms almost invariably elicits an adaptive response. One probable effect of the gradual turning of the antitrust screw was a redirection of businessmen's urge to merge. Table 4.3 presents the Federal Trade Commission's classification of the mergers between 1951 and 1968 involving manufacturing or mining firms with assets of $10 million or more when they were acquired. The proportion of assets changing hands through horizontal mergers (between firms operating at the time of acquisition in the same market) declined sharply as antitrust enforcement became tougher, while conglomerate mergers advanced in relative importance. The strongest relative gain occurred in the 'other,' or 'pure conglomerate,' category, covering mergers in which the acquired firm sold neither similar products in geographic market segments previously shunned by the acquiring firm (market extension mergers) nor different products complementary to the production operations or distribution channels of the acquiring firm (product extension mergers).

Further insight into the character of large-firm mergers is provided by an analysis of merger activity between 1950 and 1963 by 42 corporations belonging to two select groups: the 100 largest manufacturing companies by sales volume in 1950, and the 100 firms executing the largest number of mergers between 1950 and 1963.[97] Those 42 companies acquired a total of 181 firms with assets of at least $1 million each between 1950 and 1963, constituting a total asset transfer of $4.3 billion. Of the 181 companies acquired, 81 per cent operated primarily in four-digit industries in which the acquiring firm was *not* one of the four leading producers during 1950. In other words, the bulk of merger activity by the largest, most merger-prone firms following World War II was directed into fields outside those firms' traditional areas of dominance.

In view of this evidence, one might expect the merger activity of the largest firms to have contributed to a rise in aggregate concentration,

---

[95]"An Evaluation of Mergers in Six Industries," *Review of Economics and Statistics*, May 1965, pp. 172–181.

[96]Reed Moyer, *Competition in the Midwestern Coal Industry* (Cambridge: Harvard University Press, 1964), pp. 68 and 74–83.

[97]See the testimony of John M. Blair in *Economic Concentration*, p. 662.

Table 4.3

Classification of Large Manufacturing and Mining Firm Acquisitions by Period and Economic Type: 1951–68

Type of Merger	Number of Mergers					Percentage of Total Assets Acquired				
	1951–54	1955–58	1959–62	1963–66	1967–68	1951–54	1955–58	1959–62	1963–66	1967–68
Horizontal	30	60	44	54	26	40	34	19	14	8
Vertical	10	34	48	53	34	9	20	24	15	7
Conglomerate:										
Market Extension	5	9	22	17	1	4	2	8	13	4
Product Extension	30	101	104	189	216	43	39	27	43	46
Other	6	10	46	51	84	5	5	22	16	35
Total	81	214	264	364	361	100	100	100	100	100

Sources: U.S. House of Representatives, Committee on the Judiciary, Antitrust Subcommittee, Staff Report, *The Celler–Kefauver Act: Sixteen Years of Enforcement* (Washington: 1967), pp. 11 and 39; and U.S. Federal Trade Commission, Statistical Report, *Current Trends in Merger Activity. 1968* (Washington: March 1969).

even if not to concentration within individual markets. For this conjecture there is support. Between 1950 and 1962, the 200 largest manufacturing corporations increased their share of all manufacturing corporation assets from 48.9 per cent to 55.0 per cent. During the same interval, they acquired firms with assets valued at $13.8 billion at the date of acquisition.[98] Now suppose they had consummated no mergers at all, and that their 1962 assets were reduced by exactly the amount of the acquired assets, other things (such as the value of all manufacturing corporation assets) remaining equal. Then their share of all manufacturing corporation assets in 1962 would have been only 50.3 per cent, instead of 55.0 per cent, and their share would have risen by only 1.4 percentage points instead of 6.1 points. This suggests that mergers were responsible for the bulk—i.e., about 77 per cent—of the observed growth in the 200 largest manufacturing firms' share of all manufacturing corporation assets. However, the assumptions are vulnerable to two criticisms. First, the acquired firms must have contributed more than just the value of their assets at the time of acquisition to the acquiring firms' asset growth, since they undoubtedly continued to grow after being assimilated. Second, had the acquiring firms not used their resources to buy out the acquired firms, they probably could have used them instead to increase internal growth. Adjustments to take these criticisms into account would push in opposite directions. It is probable that the effect of correcting for the first would outweigh the second effect, since studies have shown that the industries into which the largest firms diversified were generally growing more rapidly than their home industries.[99] If so, then the 200 largest firms' aggregate share increase would have been even smaller than 1.6 percentage points under a no-merger policy.

We have seen earlier that the relative growth through merger of medium-sized firms was greater than the growth of firms with assets exceeding $100 million. This means that another effect of the postwar merger wave was to increase the equality of firm sizes within the population of the largest firms. It is doubtful, however, whether this tendency for already sizeable firms to get big faster than the biggest firms get bigger is much consolation to foes of big business.

To sum up, mergers during the two decades following World War II did have some impact in raising both aggregate and individual market concentration. But the effects were modest in comparison to the 1887–1904 merger wave.

MERGER CYCLES AND STOCK MARKET FLUCTUATIONS

An enticing byway in the study of mergers is the analysis of relationships between merger activity and the business cycle. Changes in the number of mergers per year appear to be especially closely related to the gyrations of the stock market. The discussion thus far implies, and more careful examination of Figure 4.4 confirms, that major declines in merger activity have usually coincided with stock market slumps— e.g., in 1904, 1907, 1921, and 1929–1931, with another pronounced decline occurring during the unsettled stock market conditions of 1948–1949 and modest downward dips taking place as the stock market receded in 1962 and 1966. In a statistical assault on the problem, Nelson found cyclical deviations in the number of mergers occurring per year between 1895 and 1954 to be positively correlated with deviations in stock prices, the correlation coefficient being 0.47. He obtained a much weaker correlation of 0.08 between trend-adjusted changes in the number of mergers and in the Federal Reserve Board's index of industrial production.[100]

A negative implication is that mergers are not

---

[98]See testimony of Willard Mueller in *Economic Concentration*, pp. 121–127.

[99]Cf Michael Gort, *Diversification and Integration in American Industry*, pp. 112–113; and John McGowan, "The Effect of Alternative Antimerger Policies on the Size Distribution of Firms," *Yale Economic Essays*, Fall 1965, especially pp. 465 and 471. Using more elaborate techniques, McGowan estimates that the share of the largest 100 manufacturing and mining firms would have risen from 41.0 per cent in 1950 to 41.9 per cent in 1960 under a no-merger policy, rather than to the 44.4 per cent level actually achieved.

[100]*Merger Movements in American Industry*, p. 118. See also Markham, *op. cit.*, pp. 146–154; and C. J. Maule, "A Note on Mergers and the Business Cycle," *Journal of Industrial Economics*, April 1968, pp. 99–105.

in general consummated as direct and immediate solutions to the intense competition prevailing during business slumps, even though such considerations may have been in the minds of businessmen as a longer-run objective, especially during the first great merger wave. On the positive side, the reasons why merger activity tends to rise with stock prices and to decline when they fall are evidently complex.[101] Owners and managers of firms expecting eventually to sell out find periods when stock prices are nearing a possible peak a particularly favorable time to execute their plans, whereas they may decide to hang on for a while longer when stock prices are falling. Acquiring firms find funds for acquisition easier and less costly to obtain when stock prices are high, and this may dominate their decisions, despite the fact that the prices they must pay to merger candidates are also higher. Behind this phenomenon may be a tendency for the price/earnings ratios of acquiring firms' stock to rise more sharply than those of acquisition prospects during a stock market boom. Or acquiring firms may hold more bullish expectations about the future, and are therefore more eager to expand through merger, when stock prices are high. At present, the relative importance of these and other factors governing the timing of mergers is not fully understood, and more research on the subject is needed.

THE MOTIVES FOR MERGER

Historically, mergers have had the effect of increasing market concentration by greater or lesser amounts. Was this merely a by-product of the urge to merge, or one of the primary goals? There are many possible reasons why businessmen might agree to a merger: to reduce competition, to gain promoter's profits, to realize economies of scale, to ameliorate the impact of tax laws, to build an empire, etc. In order to understand the merger phenomenon fully, we

must know the relative importance of these motives. This is not an easy assignment. For a host of reasons, businessmen are often less than candid about their motives in statements released for publication. And sometimes, given the complexity of merger decisions, they may be unconscious of deep-seated drives which affect their actions. Therefore, it is rash to place much reliance on the overt utterances of industrialists. One way out is to judge the motives for merger by the effects achieved, since the rational entrepreneur presumably intends what he brings about. This is the approach advocated by Markham.[102] Its main weakness is the fact that the correlation between achievement and intent is far from perfect. A firm may have tried hard to establish a monopoly, but failed. Or power over price might be an incidental and largely unintended result of a series of mergers undertaken for quite different reasons. Clearly, the best strategy is to combine both approaches, supplementing evidence on the effects of merger with whatever direct, credible evidence we have on motives.

Monopoly power was such a striking result of so many mergers around the turn of the century that one could hardly deny with a straight face that it was intended. Moreover, since monopolization through merger was a relatively new game at the time, it seems reasonable to suppose that other consolidations were formed in the hope of achieving market control, but failed to fulfill that hope.[103] The first inference is corroborated by statements of individuals involved in some of the more successful mergers. There is little doubt from the historical record that forestalling the competition bound to develop if each of several steel combinations pursued its independent expansion plans was uppermost in the minds of U. S. Steel's organizers, even though they were also concerned with such fringe benefits as the power to combat European steel cartels in their

---

[101]For various views, see Markham, *op. cit.*, pp. 153–154; Nelson, *op. cit.*, pp. 106–126; Nelson, "Business Cycle Factors in the Choice Between Internal and External Growth," in W. W. Alberts and J. E. Segall, ed., *The Corporate Merger* (Chicago: University of Chicago Press, 1966), pp. 52–66; the testimony of Willard Mueller in *Economic Concentration*, 505–508; and "Roadblocks Slow the Urge to Merge," *Business Week*, September 10, 1966, pp. 183–184.

[102]*Op. cit.*, pp. 158–162.

[103]Contrast Markham, *op. cit.*, pp. 158–162 and 180–181.

home territories. Similarly, market power was a motivating factor behind the formation of General Electric, as Thomas Edison's remark to a reporter at the time of the merger shows:

> Recently there has been sharp rivalry between [Thomson-Houston and Edison General Electric], and prices have been cut so that there has been little profit in the manufacture of electrical machinery for anybody. The consolidation of the companies . . . will do away with a competition which has become so sharp that the product of the factories has been worth little more than ordinary hardware.[104]

Those were days when businessmen had little fear of either public opinion or the wrath of trust busters, and the diligent student can uncover many such statements.

As we have seen, mergers were a much less prominent concentration-increasing force in recent decades, and from this change in effects it is reasonable to infer that the desire to build monopoly or oligopoly power has diminished in importance as a motive for merger. Still it has not disappeared completely. In the cement industry, for example, the president of one firm wrote in 1928 to the president of another concerning the acquisition of several price-cutting independents, "It is proven that the most effective way to cure a bad situation is to buy up the offenders."[105] And in coal, acquisition of the Nashville Coal Co. by the West Kentucky Coal Co. during 1955 not only hastened oligopolization of the midwestern market, but also eliminated the leading price cutter and brought a price war to an end.[106] It is hard to believe that there are not more cases of mergers motivated by the desire to establish pricing tranquility, even when market dominance of the 1890s variety is not attained.

Another important motive for merger has been the desire of parties to the deal to profit from their promotional efforts. The Morgan syndicate's $62.5 million profit in assembling U. S. Steel was only the most spectacular example of an almost everyday practice at the turn of the century. This motive for merger and the monopolization motive are related. The value of a company's common stock depends upon investor expectations regarding its future profits. If competition can be eliminated through merger, profits will presumably rise, and so the new consolidated firm's shares are worth more than the sum of the original competing companies' shares. Promoters sought to achieve such capital value transformations by arranging competition-reducing mergers, retaining a block of the new firm's stock as a reward for their trouble. However, many went further. Because investors were captivated by the prospect of pursuing this road to fortune, and because there were no effective controls on the quality of information disseminated in connection with new capital stock flotations, unscrupulous promoters arranged mergers with little chance of achieving real monopoly power, simultaneously issuing misleading prospectuses, planting rumors, and priming the market to convince investors otherwise. By exciting false expectations, the promoters were able to sell the stock of newly consolidated firms at prices far exceeding its true economic value—a practice known as *stock watering*.[107] As in honestly monopolistic consolidations, the promoters were paid in newly issued stock for their contribution. Only in this case, they hastened to sell their shares to unwary outsiders before the bubble burst. And burst it did. Livermore studied 328 mergers consummated between 1888 and 1905 and discovered that at least 141 were financial failures, 53 col-

---

[104]*New York Times*, February 21, 1892, p. 2, cited in H. C. Passer, *The Electrical Manufacturers: 1875–1900* (Cambridge: Harvard University Press, 1953), p. 326. See also p. 54 on the motives for several earlier Thomson-Houston mergers. Passer attempts to deny the obvious by observing that because Westinghouse remained independent, competition was not entirely eliminated.

[105]Quoted in Samuel M. Loescher, *Imperfect Collusion in the Cement Industry* (Cambridge: Harvard University Press, 1959), p. 120.

[106]See Moyer, *op. cit.*, pp. 82 and 157.

[107]Merely selling stock in the new firm at prices exceeding the sum of the old firms' share values is not necessarily stock watering, despite statements to this effect by many commentators. The crucial question is whether the new firm's earnings are sufficient to yield a normal return on the new, higher stock sale values.

lapsing shortly after their formation.[108] Analyzing a smaller sample, Markham found that consolidations promoted by outside banks, syndicates, and the like failed much more frequently than those put together by individuals with a continuing commitment to the affected industry.[109] From his survey of this and other evidence he concludes that the quest for promotional profits was the most important single motive for merger during the frenzied 1897–1899 and 1926–1929 periods.[110]

Alarm over such abuses led to passage of the Securities Act of 1933 and the Securities Exchange Act of 1934, establishing federal controls over the publication of security issue information and other promotional practices. They and the antitrust laws made it difficult for promoters to realize the kinds of gains typical of the 1890s, and so the promotional profit motive has lost some of its former potency. It has not died altogether, however. New ways have been invented to reap speculative gains through merger without breaking the law.

The most spectacular examples are the 'go-go' conglomerate mergers of the middle and late 1960s, through which merger impresarios like James Ling of Ling-Temco-Vought built substantial personal fortunes and corporate empires. To describe their financial tactics in detail would take a chapter, not the two paragraphs available. But in essence, the new breed of merger promoters profit by convincing investors they have invented a kind of perpetual growth machine. To illustrate, consider the hypothetical ZAM Corporation with current annual profits of $10 million, 1 million shares of common stock outstanding, earnings per share of $10, and (because investors are enthusiastic about its growth potential) the relatively high stock price/earnings ratio of 30. A share of ZAM common sells then at 30 × $10 = $300. ZAM then sets out to acquire the XYZ Corporation, with profits of $2 million, 200,000 shares of stock outstanding, earnings per share of $10, and a more conventional price/earnings ratio of 12, yielding a price per share of $120. To effect a take-over, ZAM offers XYZ stockholders six ZAM shares for each ten XYZ shares. If XYZ stockholders expect the ZAM stock price to hold firm, this is an irresistible offer, since they receive six shares valued at a total of $1,800 in exchange for ten shares valued at $1,200. To finance the deal, ZAM issues 120,000 new shares, conveying them to XYZ shareholders. Consolidated profits of the newly expanded ZAM Corporation are $12 million. With 1,120,000 shares outstanding, earnings per share are $10.71. If the market continues to evaluate ZAM stock at a price/earnings multiple of 30, the price per share rises to $321.30. Everyone is better off than before, even though total combined earnings have not increased at all!

This seeming Midas touch will turn to lead if the ZAM price/earnings ratio falls because ZAM becomes a different organization after the merger, having assimilated the less glamorous XYZ operation. But that need not happen if investors can be kept in the proper frame of mind. As long as ZAM can continue to make such deals, acquiring other firms with lower price/earnings ratios, and (more importantly) as long as investors believe it will continue to do so, earnings per share will rise. With rising earnings per share, investors' growth expectations are validated, and the price/earnings ratio remains high. Should those expectations for any reason be contradicted, however, the ZAM stock price will fall relative to earnings; ZAM will find it much more difficult to acquire other firms with lower price/earnings multiples; and the growth on which its high stock price depended must slow. The whole process, then, is fueled by self-reinforcing but inherently fragile speculative expectations. When they falter, the bubble bursts. And ultimately this type of speculation sows the seeds of its own undoing, for as the 'go-go' merger strategy is imitated by others, sooner or later the opportunities for making

---

[108]Shaw Livermore, "The Success of Industrial Mergers," *Quarterly Journal of Economics*, November 1935, pp. 68–96.

[109]*Op. cit.*, p. 163 note.

[110]*Ibid.*, p. 181.

attractive acquisitions dwindle as candidate firms' price/earnings ratios are bid up competitively, the ranks of acquirable firms are depleted, the acquiring firm develops managerial indigestion, and/or the government is sufficiently alarmed by the rise of merger activity to intervene and call a halt. Meanwhile, however, shrewd speculators and company executives with generous stock options have made a killing.

MORE ORTHODOX BENEFITS TO ACQUIRED FIRMS

A third set of motives for merger is that whole set of considerations Markham lumps together under the heading "ordinary business transactions among entrepreneurs."[111] These are considered most conveniently from the separate viewpoints of sellers and buyers.

Seller motives are clearly important. Butters and his colleagues found in a detailed study of 80 early post-World War II mergers that in more than two thirds of the cases, the initiative was taken by the acquired firms.[112] Although the proportion of seller-initiated mergers may have declined since then with the rise of the 'takeover,' there continue to be several normal, basically harmless reasons why the owners of a firm may wish to sell out.

First, they may find their ship sinking under them and seek rescue from a firm with new ideas, adequate financial resources, and able management. This seems to be an important consideration in relatively few large mergers, however. Only 17 out of 165 firms listed among the 1,000 largest manufacturing corporations for 1950 and acquired between 1951 and 1963 showed a loss in the year prior to their acquisition, and 90 of the 165 earned a healthy 7.5 per cent or more on net worth after taxes.[113]

Second, company owner-managers may be aging or weary of business pressures and lack heirs or other successors to take their place, and so they turn to merger as a means of selling out and perpetuating what they have started. This is one of the most common motives underlying small firm sales. The decision to sell out may be hastened if the firm has obsolete equipment for whose replacement owners are unable or unwilling to raise the necessary capital. Weiss estimated, using the survivor technique, that from 83 to 91 per cent of the capacity acquired through mergers in the steel, auto, petroleum, cement, flour, and brewing industries between 1929 and 1958 was of suboptimal scale.[114] A similar contributing element is growth of the firm to a size where new managerial philosophies and methods unattractive to present owner-managers are required.[115]

Third, and interacting with the second motive, income and estate tax ramifications often heighten the desire of individuals owning companies with unlisted or thinly traded stocks to sell out. By retaining earnings in his firm until he sells out, an entrepreneur can take advantage of the relatively low capital gains tax rates to build his fortune. Inheritance taxes, which ran as high as 77 per cent on bequests exceeding $10 million in 1963, create a twofold incentive to merge with a larger firm, since lack of a clear-cut market price for the small firm's common stock leaves heirs at the not-so-tender mercy of the Internal Revenue Service for estimation of their tax liability, and they may be forced to sell some of their stock on a thin market at distress prices to raise sufficient cash to pay their taxes. In an interview survey covering 89 mergers completed during the 1940s, Lintner and Butters found tax considerations to have been a major reason for selling out in roughly 40 per cent of mergers involving asset transfers of $15 million or more, but only rarely when the acquired firm had assets of less than $1 million.[116] In a questionnaire survey of 401 firms with unlisted stock

---

[111] *Loc. cit.*

[112] J. K. Butters, J. M. Lintner, and W. L. Cary, *Effects of Taxation on Corporate Mergers* (Boston: Harvard Business School, 1951), p. 309. See also Moyer, *op. cit.*, pp. 81–82.

[113] Cf. *Economic Concentration*, pp. 128–129.

[114] "An Evaluation of Mergers in Six Industries," *loc. cit.*

[115] Cf. Penrose, *op. cit.*, p. 161.

[116] John Lintner and J. K. Butters, "Effects of Taxes on Concentration," in *Business Concentration and Price Policy*, pp. 272–273, drawing upon Butters, Lintner, and Cary, *op. cit.*, Chapter 8.

acquired between 1955 and 1959, Bosland found company officers' concern over estate and gift tax problems to be the most important single incentive for merger, said to be of "substantial significance" in 63 per cent of all cases.[117]

Fourth, owners of firms too small or with too limited resources to diversify internally may seek to reduce risk by trading their stock for the shares of more diversified corporations listed on a major exchange. And, finally, owners may sell out because some buyer considers their firm worth a price too attractive to turn down. This leads us into the question of what benefits buyers hope to secure through merger.

ADVANTAGES TO THE ACQUIRING FIRM

For one profit-maximizing firm to make a merger bid which induces another to sell out, the capitalized value of the acquired firm when integrated into the acquiring firm's operations must exceed the capitalized value of the acquired firm operating independently, and the price paid by the acquirer must not exceed its cost of achieving the same result in some alternative way—e.g., by internal expansion. These conditions cover a lot of ground. To begin our analysis, let us focus on the first aspect. Why should a business entity be worth more after merger than before?

We have already considered one reason—because monopoly power results from the consolidation, increasing the surviving firm's control over demand and price. Let us try to leave this point behind (although we shall not be able to do so entirely). An analogous capital value increasing effect may occur on the cost side of the picture, if the merger leads to the realization of scale economies or to the exploitation of complementarities in production or distribution between the merging firms.

On the question of scale economies imparted by merger there has been an incredible amount of fuzzy thinking, so we must proceed cautiously. A good starting point is to recall that the bulk of all scale economies in production are realized at the plant level; multi-plant production and physical distribution economies of scale appear to be modest or nonexistent. Suppose then that two previously independent plants producing the same product are brought under the same corporate shell. What economies of scale will be realized? The answer must be: little or none. The plants are already built; not much can be done to unbuild them in order to increase their scale. Perhaps some overlapping functions can be eliminated, but these are seldom of great moment. For example, a merger of two poorly integrated steel-making firms was expected to yield savings amounting to no more than $\frac{1}{2}$ per cent of sales.[118] The New York Central–Pennsylvania Railroad merger was expected to generate cost savings of roughly 4 per cent after a five-year shakedown period.[119] These are cases in which one would expect unusually large savings because of extensive facilities duplication; normally the opportunities for cost reduction are likely to be much more constrained.

This inference gains support from a study by P. Leslie Cook and associates of mergers in six British industries. It concludes, oddly enough, that plant (and other) economies of scale do arise from mergers, and that scale economies are the most powerful factor leading to concentration.[120] A careful reading of the six case studies discloses few concrete examples of functions eliminated at the plant level as a direct consequence of mergers, and the firms which merged were found to be no more efficient after merger than progressive rivals which had not tread the merger path. One of the few examples cited was the elimination of certain laboratory functions in brewery mergers, but no attempt was made to quantify the savings. To supply this missing

---

[117]C. C. Bosland, "Has Estate Taxation Induced Recent Mergers?" *National Tax Journal*, June 1963, pp. 159–168.

[118]"Why Steelmakers Seek Strength in Merger," *Business Week*, February 15, 1969, p. 104.

[119]"The Big Merger Begins To Click," *Business Week*, May 4, 1968, p. 104; and "Penn Central Sees a Light in the Tunnel," *Business Week*, November 22, 1969, p. 44. For a more general analysis suggesting that large, complex railroad mergers may even have increased costs, see Robert E. Gallamore, "Railroad Mergers: Costs, Competition and the Future Organization of the American Railroad Industry," unpublished Ph.D. dissertation, Harvard University, May 1968.

[120]P. Leslie Cook, *Effects of Mergers* (London: George Allen and Unwin, 1958), especially p. 433.

information, the present author consulted a chemist experienced in brewery laboratory operations in both Germany and the United States. A small brewery, it turns out, can get by fairly well with one analytic chemist; one of the largest brewing plants in New England employs two chemists; and the state-operated central beer chemistry laboratory of Bavaria, supplying specialized analytic services to more than a hundred breweries, employs only 35 chemists and technicians. Census data for the United States show that the average brewery in 1963 employed 222 persons, and that total payrolls were about 20 per cent of the value of shipments. It is obvious from these data that eliminating some duplicating laboratory functions is not apt to confer very great savings. A maximum estimate would be 1 per cent of total costs, and $\frac{1}{4}$ per cent is probably nearer the mark.

What then is the source of the production scale economies alleged by Miss Cook to have resulted from merger? The most important, it appears, was the ability of the acquiring firm to shut down redundant plants in an industry plagued by excess capacity. This is not an economy of scale at all, but an economy of rationalization which we shall consider further in the next two chapters. But passing over this semantic quibble, we must inquire why there was excess capacity. The answer in all cases was that the exit of surplus resources was retarded by monopolistic price-fixing agreements and (in brewing) monopolistic tying agreements which made it possible for inefficient, underutilized plants to survive. According to Miss Cook, mergers were beneficial because they hastened the exit of excess and inefficient capacity. But the same result could have been secured through a healthy dose of competition. Her case for mergers as a source of production economies rests largely upon the assumption that firms will behave monopolistically in any event.[121] Yet this should hardly be a foregone conclusion. It is patently fallacious to argue that monopoly is necessary because the mergers which confer

monopoly power also bring economies, when the economies are realized only because a permissive policy toward monopoly has been adopted.

Given that major changes in plant cost functions cannot be effected as long as the firm is committed to existing physical facilities, the case for plant scale economies rests on the ability of the merged firm to build a bigger new plant. This is definitely possible. But if a new plant must be built, why should the acquiring firm waste its resources buying out a plant of suboptimal scale, instead of proceeding forthwith to the construction of the efficient plant? Again, the answer turns on monopoly elements. The firm may perceive that adding the output associated with a new plant of minimum optimal scale to existing industry output would unduly depress the price —a perception compatible only with a monopolistic or oligopolistic mentality.[122] Or strong product differentiation may prevent the firm from finding customers for its expanded output, unless it reduces its price by an unacceptable amount or acquires (through merger) the brand name and distribution channels of an existing firm. This last factor was crucial to the realization of scale economies in the British calico printing, soap, and brewing industries. The brewing case is especially striking. Breweries depended for sales upon 'tied houses' which sold only their products, and the number of pubs was limited by law. In order to expand production, brewers had to buy out the pubs tied to rivals, and this was done by buying out the rival's whole business. Still there is a much simpler solution obvious to anyone not wedded to restrictive business traditions: Let the government prohibit restrictive tying agreements, permitting the most efficient producers to compete directly and openly for an expanded share of the market.

All this is very negative, and rightly so, for there simply does not appear to be much opportunity to realize plant scale economies through merger, unless an interaction effect with monopoly elements exists. Many European economists who exude enthusiasm over the bene-

[121]On this point, see also Donald Dewey, "Mergers and Cartels: Some Reservations About Policy," *American Economic Review*, May 1961, pp. 258–259.

[122]Cf. Richard B. Heflebower, "Corporate Mergers: Policy and Economic Analysis," *Quarterly Journal of Economics*, November 1963, pp. 554–557.

fits of mergers overlook this point because they take for granted a business environment which has tolerated and even welcomed monopolistic restrictions for nearly a century.

The harvest becomes richer when we cast our net further to include sales promotion and pecuniary economies of scale. In these categories, nearly all the benefits realizable through size generally are attainable also from size achieved via the merger route. The acquired firm can gain the acquirer's advertising discounts; sales forces can be consolidated and streamlined; brand names of the new partners can be pooled in such a way as to maximize product differentiation advantages. A merger which eliminates competition may bring as a fringe benefit a reduction in expenditures on self-cancelling advertising rivalry. Through the centralization of procurement functions, greater leverage may be applied on input suppliers to secure price reductions. Benefits of this nature constituted 93 per cent of the savings Lord Leverhulme projected in 1906 as the result of amalgamating all independent producers in the British soap industry.[123] When, after operating the firms actually acquired as autonomous units for more than 20 years, Lever Brothers did get around to rationalizing its sales promotion functions, impressive savings were evidently realized.[124] The desire to achieve similar savings is undoubtedly an important motive behind many U. S. mergers. Yet as we have been warned earlier, it is not certain that society as a whole benefits from these advantages of increased size. About the only pecuniary economy with indisputable social utility is the elimination of capital market imperfections which previously inhibited the acquired firm's expansion and modernization.

Conglomerate mergers have their own special motivations. One of the most important potential benefits of pure conglomerate diversification, as we have seen, is the reduction of risk. Given a decision to seek this benefit, firms often prefer diversification by merger over the development of new product lines internally. Entering a new market, and especially one unrelated to existing production and marketing operations, demands the accumulation of much new know-how and perhaps also an extensive research and development effort. From the viewpoint of the diversifying firm it is usually safer and easier to gain a foothold by acquiring a small going concern with already developed products, management experienced in the tricks of the trade, established distribution channels, and accumulated product differentiation advantages.[125]

A benefit associated with product line extension mergers but not necessarily confined to them is the generation of so-called *synergetic effects* due to the complementarity of resources possessed by the merging firms. One firm may, for example, have two or three unusually creative research and development engineers, but lack the distribution network needed to derive full commercial benefit from the new products they conceive. Another may have superb distribution channels, but find its laboratories populated with unimaginative clods. Together they can make beautiful music, and numerous mergers are inspired by just such complementarities.[126] Ideas and money may also be brought together through merger. Or the acquiring firm may find the acquired company a suitable outlet for its by-products. In somewhat the same vein are mergers which dissolve vertical pricing stalemates, such as those which arise when the buyer of some input is locked together with its principal supplier in a bilateral monopoly relationship. It must be stressed that all these motives for merger, like others discussed earlier, owe their existence to market imperfections. If creative talent or seasoned management could be bought

[123]Cook, *op. cit.*, p. 223.

[124]*Ibid.*, pp. 257–258.

[125]For illustrations, see J. S. Gilmore and D. C. Coddington, *Defense Industry Diversification: An Analysis with 12 Case Studies* (Washington: U. S. Arms Control and Disarmament Agency, 1966).

[126]See, for example, M. N. Friedman, *The Research and Development Factor in Mergers and Acquisitions*, Study No. 16, U. S. Senate, Committee on the Judiciary, Subcommittee on Patents Trademarks, and Copyrights (Washington: 1958).

and sold like turret lathes, if anyone with a good idea could get the money to develop it, and if distribution channels could be put together effortlessly, the advantage of such mergers would vanish, for the firm lacking some critical complementary resource would simply go out and buy it.[127] However, society is much more likely to benefit from synergetic mergers, for little can be done to eliminate the market imperfections covered in this paragraph, whereas a vigorously enforced antitrust policy would have yielded the same benefits as those attributed by Miss Cook to mergers in several British industries.

We turn now to a different class of advantages for the acquiring firm. Frequently, corporations which have decided to expand their operations find they can obtain the desired production capacity at lower cost by buying out some existing firm than by constructing a completely new plant. The Falstaff Brewing Co., for instance, is said to have implemented its aggressive expansion program by buying out local breweries at half the per-barrel capacity cost of new construction.[128] For acquiring firms to be able to make such attractive deals, two conditions must be satisfied. First, there must be some reason why the owners of the acquired company are willing to sell out at a price lower than the full value of their facilities to the acquiring firm. This might be because they lack some critical resource (such as capable management), or because their firm is too small to advertise on a large scale, or because personal problems compel them to sell out, even though the price is less than the firm's going-concern value. Second, there must be market imperfections which prevent the acquisition price from being bid up to the alternative cost of acquiring comparable assets through new construction. The number of interested buyers is often low, and bidding may be inhibited by uncertainty about the true economic value of the assets. When such imperfections permeate the market for mergers, as they almost always do, the price at which the transaction will occur is indeterminate, in the sense that the buyer and seller would be willing to merge over an often wide range of prices.[129] How good the deal is from the acquiring firm's viewpoint depends then upon its perspicacity in sizing up alternative opportunities and its relative skill and power in bargaining.

The evidence available leads one to believe that the uncertainties in this bargaining process are substantial, and that the acquiring firm fails to strike a favorable bargain with surprising frequency. In one of the largest merger agreements of the 1960s, American Broadcasting Company officials were willing to sell out to International Telephone and Telegraph Corporation at an effective price of $83 per share, but held out in negotiations for a price of $100 per share. Adding insult to injury, I.T. & T. executives expected the merger to supply them with a generous flow of funds for reinvestment in other parts of their company, when a fuller meeting of minds would have shown that ABC was more likely to impose a net drain on the I.T. & T. treasury.[130] More broadly, Bjorksten has estimated from a study of some 5,000 merger histories that one merger in every six ended in failure, in the sense that the acquired firm failed to make a profit within three years, or acquired products had to be changed radically, or the acquired company was subsequently sold.[131] Still the imperfections and uncertainties in the bargaining process probably work more frequently than not in favor of the acquiring firm, making the merger route to corporate growth an attractive one.

[127]Imperfect divisibility of resources is also involved, but market imperfections appear to be more significant.

[128]"How Falstaff Brews New Markets," *Business Week*, July 30, 1966, p. 47.

[129]For a stimulating discussion of this issue, see the papers by Gort and Alberts in Alberts and Segall, *op. cit.*, pp. 31–44, 46–50, and 272–283.

[130]See the reports of the Federal Communications Commission hearing in the *New York Times*, April 13, 14, and 19, 1967. It is worth noting that when the Justice Department announced an antitrust suit to block the merger in July 1967, ABC stock prices fell, while I.T. & T. prices rose! Half a year later, the merger was abandoned.

[131]Testimony of Johan Bjorksten in *Economic Concentration*, pp. 1940–1954.

A further advantage of merger to the acquiring firm is its speed. Internal growth is painstaking, demanding the development of products, markets, and perhaps most important of all, a smoothly running organization. Through merger, a company can obtain all these things almost overnight. The main limit to the rate of growth by merger is the likelihood that too many acquisitions will produce an acute case of managerial indigestion, leaving the acquiring firm unable to coordinate, control, and motivate its new subsidiaries so that their actions harmonize with overall corporate objectives.[132] In general, however, sales can be expanded more rapidly through merger than through internal building, other things (such as managerial capacity) being held equal.

We must be careful not to misinterpret this conclusion. Growth to the individual firm by merger is not necessarily growth to the economy at large. If I.T.&T. increases its sales by $360 million (or 21 per cent) through the acquisition of ABC, gross national product rises not a whit, the gain in I.T.& T.'s sales being cancelled out by the evaporation of ABC's independent sales. This point is so obvious that it hardly seems necessary to state it, were it not for the fact that so many businessmen and journalists apparently have failed altogether to grasp its implications.[133]

The one thing which could cause mergers to have a favorable impact on real economic growth is the existence of complementarities or scale economies which increase the productivity of resources in the consolidated enterprise. What evidence we have on the subject indicates that mergers do not in fact generate strong interaction effects of this type. In an analysis of growth by 448 manufacturing firms drawn from the list of the 500 largest industrial corporations for 1955, the sample was divided into two components: 83 firms which had engaged in numerous or sizeable mergers between 1955 and 1960, and 365 firms which had not.[134] Sales of the 365 firms grew by 24.5 per cent between 1955 and 1959. This growth was achieved almost entirely through internal expansion, implying (when allowance is made for price level changes) commensurate social growth. To put the growth of the merger-prone firms on a comparable basis, sales of acquiring and acquired firms were consolidated for 1955, so that the 1955–1959 growth computation spanned identical starting and ending organizational clusters. Sales growth for the 83 consolidated merger-prone firms proved to be 23.8 per cent! The moral is that the more rapid *private* growth mergers permit may be deceiving, reflecting no commensurate growth to the economy as a whole.

THE EMPIRE-BUILDING MOTIVE

One final motive for merger must be considered. Many business leaders are driven by the urge to build an empire. As we have argued earlier, growth through internal expansion tends to be slow, and if an executive wishes to realize his dreams of empire within a typically short leadership tenure, he is likely to turn to the merger path.

It is conceivable that the attempts of businessmen to increase sales at the highest possible rate, notably through merger, are merely an operational way of maximizing discounted long-run profits. But obversely, growth may be an autonomous management goal, and when there is no strong stockholder group to see that owner interests are advanced, managers may choose to sacrifice a certain amount of profit in order to grow more rapidly. Which of these conjectures is more accurate? To tell, we need evidence on

---

[132]Cf. Penrose, *op. cit.*, pp. 186–192.

[133]An admittedly extreme example is the half-page advertisement for the journal *Mergers and Acquisitions* in the December 3, 1966, *New York Times*. It began, "Have you seen this exciting new business journal that explores the two most dynamic forces leading to profits and wealth—*Mergers and Acquisitions?*" It continued, "Much of today's corporate growth comes through the merger route." To see the absurdity of this statement, we press it to its extreme. If *all* corporate growth came through the merger route, the private economy would not be growing at all—hardly a dynamic situation.

[134]See F. M. Scherer, "Corporate Inventive Output, Profits, and Growth," *Journal of Political Economy*, June 1965, pp. 290–297.

whether profit sacrifices have in fact been accepted by managements striving to grow especially rapidly through mergers.

Such a test has been attempted by Samuel R. Reid.[135] He compiled data on the sales, assets, profits, stock ownership, and mergers of 478 firms on *Fortune*'s list of the 500 largest industrial corporations for 1961. Dividing up the firms into four groups, depending upon the number of mergers consummated between 1951 and 1961, he obtained the following breakdown of 1951–1961 sales and earnings increases:

	48 Firms with No Mergers	214 Firms with 1 to 5 Mergers	142 Firms with 6 to 10 Mergers	74 Firms with 11 or More Mergers
Percentage increase in sales, 1951–1961	160	121	201	341
Percentage increase in price per common stock share, adjusted for splits and dividends	680	230	245	307
Percentage increase in profits per dollar of 1951 assets realized by 1951 stockholders	12.1	3.2	2.3	2.2

While the relationship is not completely consistent, firms which achieved their growth entirely by internal building did relatively poorly in terms of sales growth, but much better than any of the merger-prone groups in increasing the wealth of their original stockholders. The most highly merger-prone firms did best on sales growth and worst on 1961 profits accruing to original stockholders, measured as a percentage of 1951 assets. Similar relations were found when the sample was broken down into major industry groups and in a separate analysis of merger activity and growth covering 165 large commercial banks.

Several caveats must be heeded in evaluating the results of this pioneering study. The analysis covers only a single time period which ended before merger-prone conglomerate firm stocks won investor favor. The variable used to measure profit growth is a curious one, and a mere count of acquisitions does not necessarily tell how important the acquisitions were relative to the acquiring companies' size. One large merger may outweigh many small ones. It is not clear whether the superior stock price and earnings performance of the no-merger corporations were due to the avoidance of mergers per se, or to more deep-seated conditions (such as the enjoyment of richer internal growth opportunities) which restrained their urge to merge. In fact, a study of 75 manufacturing corporations suggests that profitability may have increased with the relative volume of assets acquired between 1952 and 1962, once firm size, industry concentration, and rate of industry growth are taken into account.[136] Even if Reid's results with a much larger sample are more representative, it remains unknown whether the inferior earnings performance of merger-prone firms was due to managerial indigestion, the dilution of original stockholders' equity in financing acquisitions, or some other set of factors. Nor do we know, assuming that profits *were* sacrificed by the merger-prone firms, whether the sacrifice was deliberate or uninten-

[135]*Mergers, Managers, and the Economy* (New York: McGraw-Hill, 1968), pp. 153–264.

[136]Edward J. Heiden, "Mergers and Profitability," paper presented before the December 1968 meetings of the Econometric Society.

tional, and if the former, exactly why it was made. Still the Reid results certainly reinforce our lingering suspicion that an autonomous empire-building motive underlies many corporate acquisitions.

CONCLUSION

No simple summary can do justice to the question of mergers' effects and motives. One can, if he looks hard enough, find facts to support almost any hypothesis. We must content ourselves with a few sweeping generalizations. First, mergers have definitely led to increases in market concentration, although the magnitude of this effect has dwindled over time. Second, businessmen are motivated in a variety of ways to enter mergers, and in most instances multiple motives are at work. The monopoly motive has been declining in relative significance over time; the cost-saving motive increasing. Third, the expectations of private gain which inspire mergers are frequently not backed by prospects of gain to the consuming public. Mergers may instead merely redistribute income, intensify product differentiation, or provide an illusory growth with no counterpart in the national income accounts. While many mergers are unambiguously beneficial, the balance of social advantage in other cases is sufficiently tenuous to warrant a skeptical public policy stance. We shall return to the policy issues in Chapter 20.

THE IMPACT OF GOVERNMENT POLICIES

As framer of the legal environment within which business operates and as the largest single domestic customer for goods and services, the federal government cannot help but shape industrial market structure. Here we examine some areas in which its impact is particularly direct and noticeable.

One important policy tool mentioned already is the whole set of antitrust laws and interpretations. We shall deal with them at length in Chapters 19 through 21, but a few broad comments are appropriate here. Paradoxically, it is possible that passage of the Sherman Act in 1890 actually encouraged the great wave of mergers which followed. After a period of uncertainty, the Supreme Court enunciated a hard line against price-fixing agreements in 1897, but not until 1904 were mergers brought squarely under the law's control. If a group of sellers sought to eliminate competition during this seven-year period, they stood a better chance of avoiding legal difficulties by merging than by engaging in a more loosely structured price-fixing conspiracy. How important this legal imbalance was as a stimulus to the merger movement peaking in 1899 is not known. We do know that the first industrial (as opposed to transportation) price-fixing ring struck down by the Supreme Court was united, after an adverse Court of Appeals decision and only weeks before Supreme Court pleadings commenced, in a merger which placed three fourths of the nation's cast iron pipe manufacturing capacity in the hands of the surviving firm.[137] More recently, there is reason to believe that a similar imbalance in the postwar German antitrust laws spurred a wave of mergers.[138] Nevertheless, American businessmen might have preferred mergers to loose price-fixing arrangements even if both paths had been open, and during the 1890s they were generally contemptuous of the Sherman Act, which had not yet demonstrated its sting. So it is difficult to be sure what the incremental effect of the antitrust laws was at the time. Historical research utilizing legal opinions written for entrepreneurs contemplating late 1890s mergers and the minutes of merger planning meetings could yield valuable new insights into this question.

An attempt to assess subsequent trends in the anti-merger and other antitrust laws would carry us too far afield. The evidence on their effects is at any rate inconclusive. The most widely-accepted interpretation is that they have had a definite but not enormous impact in curbing

[137]Almarin Phillips, *Market Structure, Organization and Performance* (Cambridge: Harvard University Press, 1962), pp. 115–116.

[138]For a suggestion that earlier price-fixing prohibitions had the same effect, see Fritz Voigt, "German Experience with Cartels and Their Control During Pre-War and Post-War Periods," in J. P. Miller, ed., *Competition, Cartels, and Their Regulation* (Amsterdam: North Holland, 1962), p. 204.

latent tendencies toward increased concentration.

Through the grant of patent rights on inventions, the government may facilitate dominance of a market by one or a few firms and make entry into the market by newcomers difficult or impossible. We shall spend a full chapter later analyzing the logic and effects of the patent system. Suffice it to say here that patents have been a major concentration-increasing force, especially in the technologically vigorous electrical equipment and chemicals fields.

With the advent of World War II, the federal government's purchases of goods and services expanded enormously. Since then its voracious consumption has seldom abated as defense expenditures remained at high levels and as it moved into such fields as the development of atomic energy, the control of air traffic, and the exploration of outer space. In 1967, for example, the government spent more than $50 billion for goods and services supplied by private U. S. business firms.

These expenditures have both a direct and an indirect effect on the structure of industry. Directly, the government affects industrial concentration by favoring or discriminating against the largest corporations in awarding orders. In general, orders in the defense sector—generating by far the largest volume of government purchases from industry—tend to be quite concentrated. During World War II, the 100 largest defense prime contractors, ranked by volume of contracts, received nearly 67 per cent of all military prime contract awards by dollar volume. For the Korean war (fiscal years 1951 through 1953) the comparable figure was 64 per cent, and for government fiscal years 1958 through 1968 it ranged between 64 and 74 per cent.[139]

These statistics do not reveal directly the impact of defense procurement on aggregate concentration, since the largest government contractors are not uniformly the largest firms in the private sector, despite the fact that government orders have propelled several defense specialists into the billion-dollar sales category. It is more meaningful to see how well the largest industrial firms, taking both private and government sales into account, fare in the distribution of defense orders. This has been done for the 20 firms leading *Fortune*'s list of the 500 largest industrials in 1961. Those 20 firms accounted for 19 per cent of all 1961 manufacturing industry sales and 23 per cent of the volume of defense prime contracts during fiscal years 1960 through 1962. While fragmentary, the data suggest that defense procurement has exerted modest upward pressure on aggregate concentration. No similar comparisons can be drawn for individual industries, since many industries dominated by prominent defense contractors are so heavily dependent upon government sales, and as a result have unique structural determinants. It is worth noting, however, that the principal identifiable defense and space industries—aircraft, aircraft engines, and military shipbuilding—are more concentrated than the average civilian products industry.[140] Moreover, the tremendous increase in the size of these relatively concentrated industries has, through its effect on the weights, contributed significantly to the observed post-1947 rise in weighted-average indices of market concentration.

Even more important are the indirect effects of government procurement. The pace of technological advance has been extremely rapid in the defense, space, and atomic energy fields. Companies winning major government contracts to develop new concepts and equipment can build a substantial know-how advantage over others in civilian applications of the new technology. Generally, the government has attempted to distribute its orders so that at least several firms gain proficiency in new areas. Boeing's rise to a leadership position in the jet airliner field was based in part upon experience accumulated through the B-47 bomber program, but the Air Force required Boeing to share its B-47 produc-

---

[139]For additional data, see F. M. Scherer, "The Aerospace Industry," in Walter Adams, ed., *The Structure of American Industry* (Fourth ed.; New York: Macmillan, 1970).

[140]Concentration data for the ordnance industries are not published. The Standard Industrial Classification has especially poor definitions for the defense and space electronics industries, so meaningful concentration comparisons are impossible.

tion workload with Douglas and Lockheed—a decision which helped Douglas regain a foothold in the commercial airliner market after its propeller-driven mainstays fell from favor. The widespread diffusion of government research and development contracts in the transistor, integrated circuit, radar, and similar electronics fields contributed to the formation of numerous viable competitors. However, the government's pro-competitive (or at least pro-oligopoly) contracting policy has not always been consistent or successful. IBM's pre-eminence in the electronic computer industry was bolstered by its experience under huge SAGE air defense system contracts. In addition, the military agencies were less than diligent about allowing its smaller rivals a foothold in meeting the government's heavy demands for standard computers.[141] Hughes Aircraft Company's dominant position in communication satellite technology is based upon know-how built up through a long series of missile and space system contracts. And in both the large jet engine and atomic reactor fields, the government initially supported research and development by several contractors, but both industries evolved into near-duopolies after some firms dropped out due to lack of interest and others were denied further support because of unsatisfactory performance.[142]

The federal government has also shaped the structure of important industries through its surplus war plants disposal programs. During World War II rapid expansion of defense production was accomplished partly by the construction of government-owned, contractor-operated plants in key industries. After the war many of these plants, particularly those devoted to raw materials production, were sold to private industry. Some striking inconsistencies materialized. In aluminum, what was once a virtual Alcoa monopoly was transformed into a triopoly through the sale of plants (built at a cost of $300 million and operated during the war mainly by Alcoa) to Kaiser and Reynolds at a total purchase price of $100 million. Alcoa, with an antitrust conviction hanging over its head, was excluded from the bidding.[143] The sale of synthetic nitrogen plants was also arranged in such a way as to increase the number of competing sellers.[144] On the other hand, the wartime synthetic rubber program was run under procedures which gave a few large firms a patent and know-how advantage in the postwar development of that new industry, and because no attempt was made to prevent multi-plant purchases, the sale of 25 plants ended with three firms controlling 47 per cent of industry capacity. For many plants there was only one bidder. In every other case but one, the successful bidder was the firm which had previously operated the plant for the government.[145] Similarly, the sale of a $200 million plant in Geneva, Utah, to its wartime operator, U. S. Steel, high bidder at $47 million, raised U. S. Steel's share of Pacific coast and mountain states ingot capacity from 17 per cent to 39 per cent.

Shifting our concern to still another tentacle of the federal octopus, tax policies influence market structure in a variety of ways. We have already seen that the inheritance tax laws and (to a lesser degree) the capital gains tax work in favor of mergers. The corporate income tax exemption accorded fixed-interest securities was exploited by conglomerate merger promoters of the late 1960s, who bought out the common

---

[141]See "Honeywell's $60-Million Question," *Business Week*, June 3, 1967, p. 40; and "Burroughs Gets Computer Order," *New York Times*, December 21, 1967, p. 55.

[142]In reactors, four firms were hanging on at the fringe with varying degrees of success, but the industry was clearly dominated by Westinghouse and General Electric.

[143]See M. J. Peck, *Competition in the Aluminum Industry* (Cambridge: Harvard University Press, 1961), pp. 11–19.

[144]See Jesse W. Markham, *The Fertilizer Industry: Study of an Imperfect Market* (Nashville: Vanderbilt University Press, 1958), pp. 106–107.

[145]See Robert A. Solo, *Synthetic Rubber: A Case Study in Technological Development Under Government Direction*, Study No. 18 of the Subcommittee on Patents, Trademarks, and Copyrights, U. S. Senate Committee on the Judiciary (Washington: 1959), pp. 115–124; S. E. Boyle, "Government Promotion of Monopoly Power," *Journal of Industrial Economics*, April 1961, pp. 151–169; and (for a more favorable view) C. F. Phillips, Jr., "Market Performance in the Synthetic Rubber Industry," *Journal of Industrial Economics*, April 1961, pp. 132–150.

stock of companies they sought to acquire by issuing tax-deductible debt.[146] According to Professors Lintner and Butters, the corporate income tax laws have also tended to encourage concentration by making it difficult for successful small businesses to retain earnings and attract outside capital to support the rapid growth which would permit them to challenge present industry leaders.[147] This handicap may be partly offset, however, by the favorable treatment given capital gains in the personal income tax structure, making investment in rapidly growing firms attractive to wealthy persons. Turnover or sales taxes on intermediate products, like the one levied in Germany until 1968, create incentives for firm size increases through vertical integration, since by internalizing the various stages of production, a firm can avoid paying the tax which would be levied on inter-firm transactions. The effects of tariffs are more complicated. On one hand, they may foster the development of infant industries to a stage of maturity where they can withstand foreign competition unaided. On the other hand, they may insulate already monopolistic or oligopolistic industries, preserving them in a form which has little or no economic justification and blunting their incentives to adopt efficiency-increasing measures. Since few U. S. industries are in their infancy relative to foreign competitors, the latter of these effects is undoubtedly more prevalent.

Finally, there is a host of special government policies with localized effects on particular industries or segments of the business population. Three illustrations must suffice. By promoting small business investment corporations and making direct loans, the Small Business Administration has fostered small firm growth, exerting downward pressure on concentration, although the effectiveness of its loan program has been limited by a predilection toward low-risk borrowers who in most cases could tap alternative credit sources. Government grants of exclusive off-shore petroleum extraction rights, lumbering rights, and the like to private firms have tended to inhibit the development of competitive market structures. And by limiting entry into such regulated industries as air transport, television broadcasting, and trucking, federal agencies have sometimes denied consumers the benefit of alternative suppliers who could have squeezed into the market without sacrificing scale economies.

STOCHASTIC DETERMINANTS OF MARKET STRUCTURE

Up to this point we have assumed that market structures are the more or less determinate result of tangible variables such as technology, the receptiveness of consumers to advertising, the size of the market, the effectiveness of managerial organization, merger decisions, government policies, etc. Another quite different view of the processes by which market structures emerge has been postulated by some economists. Let us begin by stating the hypothesis in its baldest, most radical form: the market structures observed at any moment in time are the result of pure historical chance.

This idea is best introduced by a concrete illustration. Suppose an industry comes into being with 50 member firms, each with first year sales of $100,000 and hence each with a two per cent starting share of the market. Now suppose the firms begin growing. Each is assumed to have the same average growth prospect as every other firm. But this average is subject to statistical variance; in any given year some firms will be lucky, growing more rapidly than the average, while others are unlucky, growing by less than the average. Let the probability distribution of growth rates confronting each firm be normal, with a mean of 6 per cent per annum and a standard deviation of 16 per cent. These parameters were chosen to reflect the average year-to-year growth actually experienced between 1954 and 1960 by 369 firms on *Fortune's* list of the 500 largest industrial corporations for 1955. To repeat, each firm faces the same distribution of growth possibilities; its actual growth is deter-

146"Mills Squints at Conglomerates," *Business Week*, March 8, 1969, p. 30.
147"Effects of Taxes on Concentration," pp. 274–275.

mined by random sampling from the distribution of possibilities. What will the size distribution of firms look like a number of years hence?

By applying a bit of advanced probability theory it is possible to estimate the parameters of the resulting firm size distribution for any future moment in time. However, insight is enriched by employing an electronic computer to simulate the dynamic properties of the assumed growth process model. Each of 50 firms' growth in each year was determined through random sampling from a distribution of growth rates stored in the computer's memory with a mean of 6 per cent and standard deviation of 16 per cent. The growth history of each firm and the overall size distribution of the industry were then tabulated at 20 year intervals. The results of 16 consecutive simulation runs are summarized in the form of four-firm concentration ratios in Table 4.4.

Contrary to what untutored intuition might advise, the firms do not long remain equal in size and market share, even though their growth prospects are identical *ex ante*. Patterns resembling the concentrated structures of much American manufacturing industry emerge within a few decades. After the growth process has run its course for a century, it is not uncommon to find a single industry leader controlling 25 or 35 per cent of the market while its former equals muddle along with .1 per cent. For the 16 simulation runs at the 100 year mark, the range of leading firm market shares was 10 to 42 per cent, with an average of 21 per cent. The four-firm concentration ratios after a century of growth ranged from 33.5 per cent to 64.4 per cent, with a mean of 46.7 per cent.

The simulation displays a clear tendency for concentration to increase over time, first rapidly

Table 4.4

Four–Firm Concentration Ratios Resulting from 16 Simulation Runs of a
Stochastic Growth Process Model, with Mean Growth of
6 Per Cent Per Annum and a Standard Deviation of 16 Per Cent

	Four–Firm Concentration Ratio at Year:							
	1	20	40	60	80	100	120	140
RUN 1	8.0	19.5	29.3	36.3	40.7	44.9	38.8	41.3
RUN 2	8.0	20.3	21.4	28.1	37.5	41.6	50.8	55.6
RUN 3	8.0	18.8	28.9	44.6	43.1	47.1	56.5	45.0
RUN 4	8.0	20.9	26.7	31.8	41.9	41.0	64.5	59.8
RUN 5	8.0	23.5	33.2	43.8	60.5	60.5	71.9	63.6
RUN 6	8.0	21.3	26.6	29.7	35.8	51.2	59.1	72.9
RUN 7	8.0	21.1	31.4	29.0	42.8	52.8	50.3	53.1
RUN 8	8.0	21.6	23.5	42.2	47.3	64.4	73.1	76.6
RUN 9	8.0	18.4	29.3	38.0	45.3	42.5	43.9	52.4
RUN 10	8.0	20.0	29.7	43.7	40.1	43.1	42.9	42.9
RUN 11	8.0	23.9	29.1	29.5	43.2	50.1	57.1	71.7
RUN 12	8.0	15.7	23.3	24.1	34.5	41.1	42.9	53.1
RUN 13	8.0	23.8	31.3	44.8	43.5	42.8	57.3	65.2
RUN 14	8.0	17.8	23.3	29.3	54.2	51.4	56.0	64.7
RUN 15	8.0	21.8	18.3	23.9	31.9	33.5	43.9	65.7
RUN 16	8.0	17.5	27.1	28.3	30.7	39.9	37.7	35.3
AVERAGE	8.0	20.4	27.0	33.8	42.1	46.7	52.9	57.4

and then more gradually. This has interesting implications. Should similar growth processes operate in real-world manufacturing industries, as some economists have suggested,[148] we should expect aggregate concentration to be higher, the more mature a nation's industrial sector is. We recall from Chapter 3 that we in fact observed a positive association between aggregate concentration in five industrialized nations and the span of time elapsing since those nations entered Rostow's stage of technological maturity.[149] The correspondence of real-world structures to the behavior of the model could be sheer coincidence, but it might also reflect the conformity of actual growth processes to similar dynamic laws.

Why do concentrated firm size distributions arise from initial conditions which seemingly give each firm an equal chance? The answer, in a word, is luck. Some firms will inevitably enjoy a run of luck, experiencing several years of very rapid growth in close succession. Once the most fortunate firms climb well ahead of the pack, it is difficult for laggards to rally and rectify the imbalance, for by definition, each firm—large or small—has an equal chance of growing by a given percentage amount.[150] Furthermore, once a firm has, by virtue of early good luck, placed itself among the industry leaders, it can achieve additional market share gains if it should happen again to be luckier than average (as it will be in roughly half of all cases). In 10 of the 16 simula-

tion runs underlying Table 4.4, the leading firm in Year 140 occupied a position among the top four firms in Year 60, and in four cases the Year 140 leader was also first in Year 60. In Run 13, the leading firm held its leadership position at every single 20 year benchmark, and in Run 5, the leader led at every 20 year point but one.

The simulation experiment reported here was designed to conform to the assumptions of Gibrat's law of proportionate growth.[151] Specifically, the population of firms was fixed, and the distribution of growth rates confronting each firm was the same, being independent of both firm size and the firm's past growth history.[152] Stochastic growth processes adhering to Gibrat's law generate a log normal size distribution of firms—that is, a distribution which is highly skewed when sales are plotted by the frequency of their actual values, one or a few firms realizing high sales while most make low sales, but which is normal and symmetric when the logarithms of firms' sales are plotted.[153] As we have seen in the preceding chapter, the parameters of the log normal distribution have been proposed as indices of market concentration by some economists, and statistical studies reveal that a log normal distribution often (but not always) fits actual firm size data tolerably well.[154] However, the assumptions of Gibrat's law need not be satisfied rigidly to obtain results similar to those of Table 4.4. There is a whole family of stochastic

---

[148]See P. E. Hart and S. J. Prais, "The Analysis of Business Concentration," *Journal of the Royal Statistical Society*, 1956, Part 2, pp. 150–181; and Herbert A. Simon and C. P. Bonini, "The Size Distribution of Business Firms," *American Economic Review*, September 1958, pp. 607–617.

[149]Cf. p. 45 *supra*.

[150]For an analogous illustration concerning runs in coin-flipping, see William Feller, *An Introduction to Probability Theory and Its Applications*, Vol. I (Second ed.; New York: Wiley, 1957), pp. 83–85. See also the testimony of Leonard Weiss in *Economic Concentration*, pp. 729–731.

[151]R. Gibrat, *Les Inegalites Economiques* (Paris: 1931); and Michal Kalecki, "On the Gibrat Distribution," *Econometrica*, April 1945, pp. 161–170.

[152]In one sense Gibrat's assumptions were violated. A "bankruptcy rule" was included, causing a firm to drop out of the industry permanently if its sales dropped to $30,000 or less. There were only three bankruptcies in the 800 company histories simulated.

[153]Proof: Let S_{oj} be the initial sales of the jth firm, and ϵ_i the random growth multiplier (in our numerical example, with mean of 1.06 and σ of .16) in the ith year. Then sales in year t are $S_{tj} = S_{oj} \, \epsilon_1 \cdots \epsilon_i \cdots \epsilon_t$; that is, the cumulative product of initial sales times a string of random growth multipliers. Taking logarithms, we obtain: Log $S_{tj} = \log S_{oj} + \log \epsilon_1 + \cdots + \log \epsilon_i + \cdots + \log \epsilon_t$. By the central limit theorem, the distribution of the sum of T random variables is asymptotically normal when $T \to \infty$.

[154]Cf. Hart and Prais, *loc. cit.*; Simon and Bonini, *loc. cit.*; and (for results suggesting that the lognormal distribution holds in roughly half the industries studied) Irwin H. Silberman, "On Lognormality as a Summary Measure of Concentration," *American Economic Review*, September 1967, pp. 807–831. For an alternative hypothesis attributing log normal firm size distributions to a particular type of oligopoly pricing, see Dean A. Worcester, Jr., *Monopoly, Big Business, and Welfare in the Postwar United States* (Seattle: University of Washington Press, 1967), Chapters 5 and 6.

growth processes which lead to the skewed firm size distributions typical of real-world industries.[155] All have the common feature of making a firm's size in, say, year $t + 1$ proportional, subject to random variation, to its size in year t. Other dynamic processes lacking the proportionate growth property exist, but they typically fail to generate firm size distributions resembling those most frequently encountered in the real world. Reasoning backward from observation to hypothesis, Simon and Bonini argue that industry structures must in fact be determined by some such stochastic growth process, since actual size distributions "show such a regular and docile conformity . . . that we would expect some mechanism to be at work to account for the observed regularity."[156]

We are all so thoroughly imbued in the belief that chance favors the well-prepared that it is difficult to accept a model which makes corporate growth the result of mere chance. Still it is not essential to interpret the stochastic growth models quite so literally. There are certainly aspects of business enterprise in which luck plays a significant role—e.g., in the hiring of key executives, in research and new product development decisions, in legal disputes involving critical patents, in the choice of an advertising campaign theme, or in a thousand and one other decisions among attractive but uncertain alternative courses of action. Given the operation of chance in these elemental decisions, high or low sales growth follows in a more traditionally deterministic manner.

One implication of this milder restatement is the possibility that growth rates for a given firm from year to year will not be independent, as assumed in the Gibrat model. For example, a lucky chief executive choice may affect growth

favorably for a decade or more. Support for this assertion is derived from the study of 369 firms' growth on which the simulation model's parameters were based, for the standard deviation of cumulative growth over the full 1954–1960 period was higher than it would have been had growth rates in each one-year interval been independent. Yet this is not a fatal objection. Ijiri and Simon have demonstrated in a simulation study that size distributions quite similar to those generated by Gibrat models can also be obtained when there is serial correlation in firms' year-to-year growth rates.[157]

The assumptions of the Gibrat model may also be violated if growth rates, or the standard deviation of growth rates, are systematically related to firm size. Independence of size and growth rates implies that small firms operate at neither an advantage nor a disadvantage relative to large firms. If, on the other hand, substantial economies of scale exist, large firms would possess an advantage which might be exploited, *inter alia*, in the form of more rapid sales growth rates. Such a state of affairs, combined with a stochastic growth process, would lead to even more rapid concentration of output in the hands of the largest firms. Conversely, if small firms could grow more rapidly on the average, *ceteris paribus*, or if there were a continuous inflow of small new firms, the tendency toward increasing inequality of firm sizes would be moderated and under certain circumstances checked altogether. Several empirical investigations have been launched to determine whether firm growth rates do vary systematically with firm size. The conclusions have been predominantly negative: no significant correlation between growth rates and size could be found.[158]

There is less support for the Gibrat assump-

---

[155]See especially H. A. Simon, "On a Class of Skew Distribution Functions," *Biometrika*, December 1955, pp. 425–440. In fact, the distributions are sufficiently similar that it is difficult to find statistical tests which will tell which of several alternative stochastic processes generated the observed size distribution. See Richard E. Quandt, "On the Size Distribution of Firms," *American Economic Review*, June 1966, pp. 416–432.

[156]*Op. cit.*, p. 608.

[157]Yuji Ijiri and H. A. Simon, "Business Firm Growth and Size," *American Economic Review*, March 1964, pp. 77–89. See also J. L. Stein, "Oligopoly in Risk-Bearing Industries With Free Entry," *Economica*, May 1963, pp. 159–164.

[158]For a survey of the literature, see Stephen Hymer and Peter Pashigian, "Firm Size and Rate of Growth," *Journal of Political Economy*, December 1962, pp. 565–566. See also C. E. Ferguson, *A Macroeconomic Theory of Workable Competition*, pp. 168–172; (for contrary results) Edwin Mansfield, "Entry, Gibrat's Law, Innovation, and the Growth of Firms," *American Economic Review*, December 1962, pp. 1031–1034; and J. M. Samuels, "Size and the Growth of Firms," *Review of Economic Studies*, April 1965, pp. 105–112.

tion that growth rate standard deviations are independent of firm size. With few exceptions, statistical studies have shown that the variability of growth rates for large firms is lower than for small firms; that is, large firms seem to enjoy more stable growth.[159] Still this qualification is compatible with the hypothesis that observed industry size distributions have been generated by some stochastic process.[160] Indeed, it strengthens the case. Chance will occasionally permit a small firm facing a highly variable distribution of growth rates to be propelled to large size, and such events increase concentration, *ceteris paribus*. But once a firm enters the large size bracket, the variance of its growth rate distribution diminishes, and so the chance that it will fall abruptly to a lower size level is much smaller. Thus, the statistical forces which might cause decreases in concentration, once it has developed, are blunted, while the forces which lead to increasing concentration remain intact. The conjunction of these phenomena may explain why market share turnover tends to be lower in concentrated industries than in atomistically structured industries.[161]

One final point implicit in the discussion thus far should be made explicit. The more variable firm growth rates are, the more rapidly concentrated industry structures will emerge, other things being equal. Two important implications follow.

First, despite its grounding in actual industry growth data, the simulation model of Table 4.4 probably overstates the length of time required for concentrated market structures to emerge as a result of random growth. The growth rate standard deviation of 16 per cent was based on a sample including only the largest firms. For smaller firms—e.g., companies of the size typical

during an industry's infancy—variability of growth rates is likely to be much higher, implying more rapid convergence toward market concentration.

Second, the variability of growth rates is likely to differ from industry to industry, depending upon the nature of the product and the character of competition. We might expect variability to be especially high in industries characterized by a rapid pace of product design change due to technological or styling innovation and also in markets populated by fickle consumers who respond enthusiastically to clever advertising campaigns. The firm with a good design or promotional idea may leap ahead rapidly; the firm which misgauges market sentiments can suffer spectacular market share declines. The hypothesis that concentration should rise especially rapidly in differentiated durable goods industries because of the chance factors permeating design competition has been tested by Weiss.[162] He divided 87 four-digit industries with sales exceeding $500 million into several product characteristic classes. For the 1947–1954 period, he found concentration rising significantly more rapidly on the average in the consumer durables, consumer semidurables, and durable equipment industries—lines which presumably experienced the most vigorous design change competition—than in four other product categories. However, this relationship failed to persist in the 1954–1958 period. New evidence reveals that after a hiatus in 1954–1958, concentration again rose more rapidly between 1958 and 1963 in the differentiated consumer goods industries, although the pattern in the consumer durables subset has not been analyzed.[163]

Unfortunately, the waters are muddied by alternative hypotheses which could also explain

[159]See the sources in note 158. In an analysis of cumulative growth for the years 1953 through 1961 covering 352 firms on *Fortune*'s 1955 list, the author found the standard deviation of growth rates for firms in the quartile of largest companies to be persistently lower than the standard deviation for firms in the smallest-firm quartile. There seemed to be some tendency for the disparity in standard deviations to level off and perhaps to decline over intervals exceeding seven years, which may explain why Hart and Prais found no correlation between size and variability of growth rates in their analysis spanning the exceptionally long 1885–1950 period. The question of very long-run relationships deserves further study.

[160]Cf. Simon, "On a Class of Skew Distribution Functions," *loc. cit.*; his comment in the *Journal of Political Economy*, February 1964, p. 81; and the testimony of Weiss in *Economic Concentration*, pp. 736–739.

[161]Cf. p. 66 *supra*.

[162]Leonard W. Weiss, "Factors in Changing Concentration," *Review of Economics and Statistics*, February 1963, pp. 70–77, summarized and updated in *Economic Concentration*, pp. 731–734.

[163]See the testimony of Willard Mueller in U. S. Senate, Select Committee on Small Business, Hearings, *Status and Future of Small Business*, p. 478; and of John Blair in *Economic Concentration*, pp. 1902–1910.

concentration trends between 1947 and 1963. Notably, the above-average increase in differentiated consumer goods industry concentration may have been due to economies of scale in advertising and other aspects of sales promotion, instead of, or as well as, high growth rate variability due to chance elements in design and promotional rivalry. Further doubts are raised by Gort's finding that market shares tended to be more stable between 1947 and 1954 in industries with highly differentiated products than in industries with moderate or low degrees of differentiation.[164] At present, therefore, the implications of the stochastic growth process hypothesis in this area remain uncertain. What is needed is an attack on the problem which discriminates more effectively between those cases in which product differentiation solidifies existing market positions and those in which it works as a potent but unpredictable vehicle for upsetting the status quo.

To sum up, the random growth hypotheses have considerable appeal, both because chance clearly does play some role in company growth and because firm size distributions observed in the real world often correspond closely to those generated by stochastic process models. It would be unwise, however, to reject more conventional explanations of market structure out of hand. Economies of scale, government policies, and the like are surely influential, and not merely in a random way. Indeed, the fact that many industries remain atomistically structured despite the concentration-increasing forces associated with stochastic growth suggests that static and dynamic managerial diseconomies of large size and rapid growth must frequently retard the rise of firms to dominance. A sophisticated explanation of how industry structures came to be what they are must blend the conventional, more or less static, determinants with the kinds of dynamic considerations introduced by stochastic growth process models. This is where future research on the determinants of market structure is most urgently needed. And since we have gone about as far as we can go on the basis of present knowledge, it is also a suitable ending point for this chapter.

[164]Michael Gort, "Analysis of Stability and Change in Market Shares," *Journal of Political Economy*, February 1963, pp. 58–59. See also Norman Schneider, "Product Differentiation, Oligopoly, and the Stability of Market Shares," *Western Economic Journal*, December 1966, pp. 58–63, who found no systematic relationship between leading firm market share stability and differentiation in eight industries.

Chapter 5

Economic Theories of Oligopoly Pricing

We turn now from market structure to conduct in the market. The two cannot, however, be divorced completely. A paramount task of industrial organization theory is to identify links running from market structure to such aspects of conduct as pricing behavior, decisions concerning product variety and quality, and innovation; and from there to economic performance. In this chapter we begin the endeavor.

We have observed that in the manufacturing sector and in parts of mining, finance, construction, and retailing, a few relatively large sellers commonly supply the lion's share of output in the markets they serve. If then we wish to learn how the real-world price system functions, we must understand oligopoly pricing. This will be our principal concern in the next four chapters. Chapters 5 and 6 review the developments in pure theory which came to associate monopolistic performance with oligopolistic market structures and examine institutions which contribute to the maintenance of monopoly prices. Chapters 7 and 8 then analyze conditions which limit the power of oligopolists to hold prices persistently above cost.

IS OLIGOPOLY PRICING BEHAVIOR DETERMINATE?

Oligopoly pricing is interesting and important not only because it is so prevalent, but also because it poses such difficult problems for the economic theorist. When either pure competition or pure monopoly prevails, there exist clear-cut solutions to the firm's price and output decision problem, assuming only that managers seek to maximize expected profits and that they hold definite (though probabilistic) expectations concerning future cost and demand conditions. With rivalry among the few, however, this is not so. Each firm recognizes that its best choice depends upon the choices its rivals make. The firms are interdependent, and they are acutely conscious of it. Their decisions depend then upon the assumptions they make about rival decisions and reactions, and many alternative assumptions might be entertained.

Economists have developed literally dozens of oligopoly pricing theories—some simple, some marvels of mathematical complexity. This proliferation of theories is mirrored by an equally rich array of behavioral patterns actually observed under oligopoly. Casual observation suggests that virtually anything can happen. Some oligopolistic industries appear to maintain prices approximating those a pure monopolist would find most profitable. Others gravitate toward bitter price warfare. To illustrate the latter extreme, in 1964 the entry of a new supermarket into the New London, Connecticut area touched off a price war in which bread sold at $.05 per loaf (about one fifth the usual price) and milk at $.29 per half gallon (about half the usual price).[1]

Recognizing the wide range of theoretical

---

[1] "Bread 5¢ in New London Price War," *New York Times*, December 5, 1964, p. 33. For other examples, see Ralph Cassady, Jr., *Price Warfare in Business Competition* (East Lansing: Michigan State University, 1963).

predictions and actual behavior, some economists have asserted that the oligopoly problem is
indeterminate.[2] This is correct, in the narrow
sense that one cannot forge unique and compelling mechanistic links from cost and demand
conditions to price equilibria. But it would be
misleading to conclude that we cannot develop
theories which predict oligopolistic conduct and
performance with tolerable precision. A more
constructive interpretation is this: to make
workable predictions we need a theory much
richer than the received theories of pure competition and pure monopoly, including variables
irrelevant to those polar cases. In our quest for a
realistic oligopoly theory we must acquire Professor Mason's "ticket of admission to institutional economics,"[3] at the same time retaining
the more sharply honed tools with which economic theorists have traditionally worked. We
must not expect too much, however. The most
that can be hoped for is a kind of soft deter-
minism: predictions correct on the average, but
subject to occasionally substantial errors.

THE PURE THEORY OF OLIGOPOLY
PRICING

To begin, it is useful to survey briefly a few
landmarks in the development of oligopoly
theory. The first noteworthy attempt to deal
with the oligopoly problem was by Augustin
Cournot, whose work was published in 1838, but
not really discovered by economists until 45
years later.[4] Cournot postulated that each firm
chooses to market that quantity of output which
maximizes its own profits, assuming the quantities marketed by rivals to be fixed. From this
simple assumption, Cournot derived two main
conclusions. First, for any industry, there exists
a determinate and stable price-quantity equilibrium. Second, the equilibrium price depends
upon the number of sellers. With a single seller,

the monopoly price results. As the number of
sellers increases, the equilibrium price declines
until, when there are very many firms, price
approaches equality with marginal cost. Thus,
the Cournot model indicates that competitive
equilibrium is more closely approximated, the
greater the number of sellers is—a prediction
compatible with ordinary observation.

Still Cournot's initial premises were unrealistic in important respects. For one, he assumed
that the quantity of output supplied was the
firm's key decision variable. Firms chose their
outputs and then offered them on the market,
which (through some unarticulated bidding
process) established a price just sufficient to
equate quantity demanded with the total quantity supplied. This assumption was criticized by
later economists, who argued from observation
that price typically is the decision variable of
primary interest to firms with market power.
That is, producers set a price and then let buyers
decide whether and how much to purchase at
that price. This objection can be met while
preserving the heart of the Cournot model if we
assume some degree of product differentiation,
so that different producers are able simultaneously to sell in the same market at different
prices. To illustrate the modified theory, a
numerical example is useful.

We assume an industry with two firms selling
differentiated products. Each company chooses
the price for its product, and buyers respond by
deciding from whom and how much to purchase.
Profits depend upon the price charged and the
amount sold, as well as on costs. Figure 5.1
summarizes the possible results of this duopolistic rivalry from the viewpoint of Firm 1. The
numerical entries give the net profits (in thousands of dollars per month) realized by Firm 1
for any combination of its own price P_1 and rival
Firm 2's price P_2. Three simple but plausible
assumptions underlie the equations generating

---

[2]Cf. K. W. Rothschild, "Price Theory and Oligopoly," *Economic Journal*, September 1947, pp. 299–302; and
R. B. Heflebower, "Toward a Theory of Industrial Markets and Prices," *American Economic Review*, May 1954,
pp. 121–139.

[3]Edward S. Mason, *Economic Concentration and the Monopoly Problem* (Cambridge: Harvard University Press,
1957), p. 60.

[4]*Researches Into the Mathematical Principles of the Theory of Wealth*, translated by N. T. Bacon (Homewood:
Irwin, 1963).

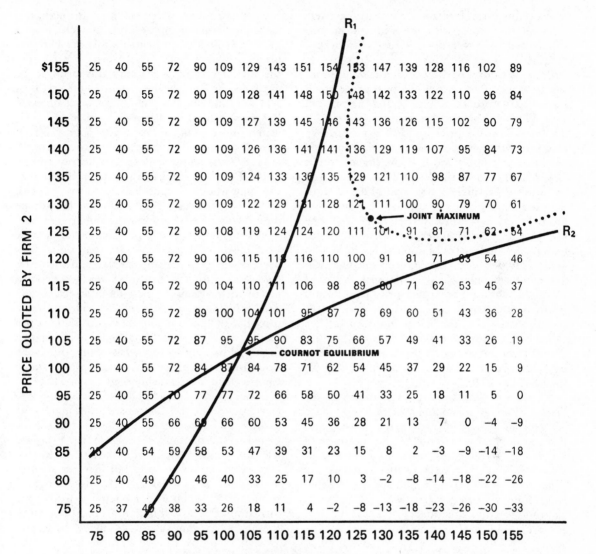

Figure 5.1
Net Profit Matrix for Firm 1

these profit values. First, the two firms share the market equally when their prices are identical, and when their prices are not equal, the high-price firm's market share is smaller, the greater is the percentage difference between its price and its rival's price. Second, the total quantity demanded from the two firms is an inverse linear function of the two prices, weighted by the firms' market shares. No units will be demanded when both firms charge prices of $200 per unit or more, and at a zero price 10,000 units would be demanded monthly. Third, the firms are assumed to have identical U-shaped short-run average total cost functions, with the minimum attainable cost of $65 per unit occurring at an output of 2,250 units per month.[5]

Firm 1's Cournot-type decision-making problem is to pick that value of its own price which maximizes its profits, assuming that the price of rival Firm 2 remains constant. Suppose, for instance, Firm 2's price is $140 per unit. We read across the row of possible payoffs associated with that price until we find the highest profit (about $141,000) attainable by Firm 1, achieved by setting P_1 at slightly less than $120 per unit. This is Firm 1's Cournot-optimal decision when Firm 2's price is $140. But if Firm 2's price should instead be $120 per unit, the best choice under the Cournot assumption is for Firm 1 to quote $110 per unit, earning profits of $118,000 per month. Similar Cournot-optimal values of P_1 can be found for any other price rival Firm 2 might quote. The locus of all these values is traced out by the line R_1 in Figure 5.1. It is called Firm 1's Cournot *reaction function*, because if rival Firm 2 changes its price from, say, $140 to $120, Firm 1 will react by moving along R_1 from $120 to $110.

A similar profit matrix could be drawn up for Firm 2, although it is not shown (to keep Figure 5.1 legible). Assuming symmetry of cost and demand functions, it would be the transpose of Figure 5.1; that is, the profit to Firm 2 with $P_2 = \$80$ and $P_1 = \$100$ is the same as the profit to Firm 1 with $P_1 = \$80$ and $P_2 = \$100$. From Firm 2's profit matrix we can derive its Cournot reaction function, shown by the line R_2 in Figure 5.1.

Now the stage is set to play through the Cournot drama. Suppose Firm 2 is charging a price of $140 per unit (which would maximize its profits as a pure monopolist) when Firm 1 enters the industry. Firm 1 assumes this price to be fixed and makes the best of it, moving to its reaction function R_1 by quoting a price of $119. But now conditions have changed for Firm 2, which must readjust its price policy. Given Firm 1's price of $119, the best price for Firm 2 is $110. (It is found by drawing a horizontal line to the P_2 axis from Firm 2's reaction function at the point where a vertical line from Firm 1's price of $119 intersects.) This alters the conditions initially assumed by Firm 1, which therefore moves along its reaction function to a new Cournot-optimal price of $107 per unit. This process of price-cutting and counter-cutting continues until the two firms reach the point where their reaction functions intersect. There and only there, where each firm is quoting a price of $103 per unit and selling 2,450 units per month, will the two firms find no alternative price yielding higher profits, assuming the rival's price to remain constant. At this point stable Cournot equilibrium is attained.

Given the stipulated behavioral assumptions, convergence to the Cournot equilibrium point follows almost inexorably.[6] But what has happened to the duopolists' profits in the process? At the Cournot equilibrium price, each firm realizes profits of roughly $91,000 per month. This is no bargain for Firm 2, which enjoyed profits of $220,000 as a monopolist before the intrusion of Firm 1. If both firms must remain in the industry, they could do much better by

---

[5]In mathematical form, Firm 1's market share S_1 is given by the exponential decay equations:

$$S_1 = .5 \exp^{-8} \left(\tfrac{P_1 - P_2}{P_2} \right) \text{ when } 200 > P_1 > P_2; \text{ and}$$

$$S_1 = 1 - .5 \exp^{-8} \left(\tfrac{P_2 - P_1}{P_1} \right) \text{ when } P_1 < P_2 < 200.$$

The total quantity X demanded from *both* firms is given by:
$$X = 10,000 - 50 S_1 P_1 - 50 S_2 P_2.$$
The total quantity demanded from Firm 1 is $S_1 X$, and Firm 1's total revenue is $P_1 S_1 X$. Firm 1's total cost function (identical to Firm 2's) is: $C_1 = 50,000 + 20 X_1 + .01 X_1^2$.
Firm 1's profit, given in Table 5.1, is $P_1 S_1 X - C_1$, except in cases when Firm 1's price is so much lower than Firm 2's price that Firm 1 is able to sell such a large quantity that marginal cost rises above price. In such cases, it has been assumed that Firm 1 sells only that quantity at which the price equals marginal cost. This might lead to a diversion of sales to high-price Firm 2, requiring a redefinition of the market share equations, but this complication has been ignored.

[6]For some dynamic complications, see R. E. Quandt and M. McManus, "Comments on the Stability of the Cournot Oligopoly Model," *Review of Economic Studies*, February 1961, pp. 136–139; J. Hadar, "Stability of Oligopoly with Product Differentiation," *Review of Economic Studies*, January 1966, pp. 57–60; and R. E. Quandt, "On the Stability of Price Adjusting Oligopoly," *Southern Economic Journal*, January 1967, pp. 332–336.

raising their quoted prices, moving diagonally northeast in Figure 5.1 until each is quoting a price of $128 per unit and realizing profits of $112,000 per month. Such a move would seem clearly advantageous from the two firms' viewpoints.[7] But if each adheres to the Cournot assumption that its rival's price will remain constant (at the Cournot equilibrium value of $103), neither has an incentive to raise its own price. For if, say, Firm 1 were to increase its price while Firm 2 maintained a price of $103, Firm 1's profits will necessarily fall.

The cause of this paradox is the Cournot stipulation that firms assume their rivals' decision variables (in this case price) to be fixed. Criticism of the assumption appeared as early as 1898:

> . . . no business man assumes either that his rival's output or price will remain constant any more than a chess player assumes that his opponent will not interfere with his effort to capture a knight. On the contrary, his whole thought is to forecast what move the rival will make in response to his own.[8]

Even if the firms' managers were not chess players, the very process of moving toward Cournot equilibrium would demonstrate that their assumptions had been incorrect. For if Firm 1 altered its price, believing that Firm 2's price would remain constant, it could hardly fail to notice that its assumption was contradicted by Firm 2's retaliatory action. By refusing to recognize that rivals will react to its price initiatives, a firm conforming to the Cournot assumption is guilty of myopia. We shall see in later chapters that decision-makers do exhibit myopic tendencies in certain rivalry situations. Nevertheless, economists have come to believe that the Cournot assumption is quite unrealistic when applied to pricing decisions involving only a few firms.

CHAMBERLIN'S CONTRIBUTION

There were many efforts to patch up the Cournot theory by devising more complex reaction assumptions, i.e., by postulating that firms expect their rivals to react to price or output changes in a specific way.[9] All suffer from the objection that an intelligent businessman would find his assumptions contradicted if he tested them thoroughly. A much bolder and more influential step was taken in 1929 by Edward Chamberlin.[10]

Chamberlin asserted that when the number of sellers is small and products are standardized, the oligopolists can scarcely avoid full recognition of their interdependence. Each therefore would be reluctant to take measures which, when countered, would leave all members of the industry worse off. Instead, the firms would set price at the monopoly level:

> If each seeks his maximum profit rationally and intelligently, he will realize that when there are only two or a few sellers his own move has a considerable effect upon his competitors, and that this makes it idle to suppose that they will accept without retaliation the losses he forces upon them. Since the result of a cut by any one is inevitably to decrease his own profits, no one will cut, and although the sellers are entirely independent, the equilibrium result is the same as though there were a monopolistic agreement between them.[11]

When sellers are few in number, Chamberlin emphasized, this result follows from the very structure of the industry. No formal collusion or agreement is necessary. Each firm can make its

---

[7]For a general proof that firms operating at the Cournot equilibrium point could become better off (i.e., move to the contract curve) by raising their prices, see W. J. Baumol, *Business Behavior, Value, and Growth* (New York: Macmillan, 1959), p. 21, note 12, and pp. 23–25.

[8]Irving Fisher, "Cournot and Mathematical Economics," *Quarterly Journal of Economics*, January 1898, p. 126.

[9]For surveys of the literature, see J. R. Hicks, "Annual Survey of Economic Theory: The Theory of Monopoly," *Econometrica*, January 1935, pp. 1–20; and William Fellner, *Competition Among the Few* (New York: Knopf, 1949), pp. 55–119. For an extension, see J. W. Friedman, "Reaction Functions and the Theory of Duopoly," *Review of Economic Studies*, July 1968, pp. 201–208.

[10]E. H. Chamberlin, "Duopoly: Value Where Sellers Are Few," *Quarterly Journal of Economics*, November 1929, pp. 63–100; incorporated with revisions as Chapter III in *The Theory of Monopolistic Competition* (Cambridge: Harvard University Press, 1933). Subsequent references are to the sixth edition of the latter.

[11]*The Theory of Monopolistic Competition*, p. 48.

own price and output decisions without consulting the others. For the monopoly price to emerge, it is essential only that the firms *recognize* their mutual interdependence and their mutual interest in a high price. Indeed, he argued, it would be unreasonable to expect members of a highly concentrated industry to behave otherwise:

> . . . the assumption of independence cannot be construed as requiring the sellers to compete as though their fortunes were independent, for this is to belie the very problem of duopoly itself. It can refer only to independence of action—the absence of agreement or of "tacit" agreement.[12]

This passage, as we shall see much later, had a profound impact on thinking with respect to antitrust policy, for it led economists to recognize that monopoly pricing could occur without explicit collusion if the industry structure is conducive, and that the gatherings in smoke-filled rooms traditionally attacked under the antitrust laws were not an essential ingredient of monopoly behavior.

Chamberlin acknowledged that monopoly prices might not be attained or maintained due to certain complications. Perhaps most obvious, when the number of sellers becomes so large that individual firms begin to ignore their direct or indirect influence on price, an abrupt break toward the competitive price is apt to occur. Second, when substantial time lags intervene between the initiation and matching of price cuts, some firms might undercut the monopoly price, risking future profit sacrifices for the sake of short-term gain. And finally, firms might fail to hold prices at the monopoly level if they are uncertain about the reactions, intelligence, or far-sightedness of their rivals. Despite these qualifications, the main impact of Chamberlin's

analysis was to show that when sellers are few and products standardized, a monopoly price can be established without formal collusion.

COMPLICATIONS DUE TO COST AND DEMAND ASYMMETRIES[13]

Chamberlin's formal theory covered only an especially simple and unrealistic case—duopolists producing at zero cost. Once costs enter the picture, difficulties arise. Notably, the firms may come into conflict over the most favorable monopoly price if they produce under differing cost conditions.

An analytic handle on the problem can be gained by assuming that, in equilibrium, all members of an oligopolistic industry charge the same price for their products. This assumption is almost certain to be satisfied when the products are perfect substitutes, since any firm trying to charge more than its rivals' price would sooner or later suffer the erosion of its entire sales volume. For oligopolies with differentiated products, it serves as a useful first approximation, perhaps modifiable to permit constant price differentials in equilibrium. With price-matching, each firm should normally expect to supply a more or less fixed share of the overall market, whether the price quoted by all is relatively low or relatively high. If so, each producer can estimate from knowledge of the industry demand curve its own individual demand curve. The quantity it sells is simply some constant fraction of the total quantity demanded from all sellers at the common price.[14] The market shares of the several industry members under this price-matching assumption need not be identical; some firms may sell more than others because of minor product quality advantages, a larger sales force, historical ties built up by serving more customers during periods of shortage, etc.

[12]*Ibid.*, pp. 46–47.

[13]For some early approaches to the material in this section, see A. J. Nichol, "Professor Chamberlin's Theory of Limited Competition," *Quarterly Journal of Economics*, February 1934, pp. 317–337; R. H. Coase, "The Problem of Duopoly Reconsidered," *Review of Economic Studies*, February 1935, pp. 137–143; K. E. Boulding, *Economic Analysis* (First ed.; New York: Harper, 1941), pp. 608–613; and William Fellner, *Competition Among the Few*, pp. 198–229.

[14]If, for example, the total quantity demanded from the industry $Q = f(P)$, the quantity demanded from Firm A is $a f(P)$, where a is Firm A's share of the market. At any given price, Firm A's individual demand curve has the same price elasticity as the industry demand curve. Proof: The industry elasticity of demand is $\dfrac{df}{dP}\dfrac{P}{Q}$.

Firm A's elasticity is $\dfrac{d}{dP}\left[a f(P) \right] \dfrac{P}{aQ} = a \dfrac{df}{dP} \dfrac{P}{aQ} = \dfrac{df}{dP} \dfrac{P}{Q}$.

Let us begin, however, by assuming that two firms have identical shares of the market at identical prices in order to focus on the impact of cost asymmetries. For clarity we shall use the same numerical assumptions as those underlying Figure 5.1. The industry demand function is assumed to be $P = 200 - .02 (X_1 + X_2)$, where X_1 and X_2 are the amounts demanded from Firms 1 and 2 respectively. Each duopolist serves half of this demand, so that the demand function of Firm 1 is $P = 200 - .04 X_1$, illustrated by D in Figure 5.2. Its marginal revenue function (identical to Firm 2's) is given by MR in Figure 5.2. We assume initially that each firm operates with the same total cost function: for Firm 1, $TC_1 = 50,000 + 20 X_1 + .01 X_1^2$. Its marginal cost function (shown as MC_1 in Figure 5.2) is $MC_1 = 20 + .02X_1$. If Firm 1 independently sets marginal cost equal to marginal revenue, it will quote a price of $128 per unit and produce 1,800 units. Firm 2, facing identical cost and demand conditions, will do the same. The $128 price maximizes joint profits, as one can see by referring back to Figure 5.1. Thus, by engaging independently in the conventional calculus of profit maximization, duopolists with identical costs and equal price-matching market shares avoid the Cournot dilemma, each choosing that price-output combination which maximizes their collective profits.

Suppose, however, that Firm 2 has the higher marginal cost function MC_2, derived from the total cost function $TC_2 = \$20,000 + 40 X_2 + .02X_2^2$. This might happen because Firm 2 is endowed with poorer natural resources, or because it has chosen to build a plant with low initial (and subsequently fixed) capital costs, but with high and more rapidly rising marginal costs. High-cost Firm 2 will find the price of $147 per unit associated with an output of 1,333 units optimal from its viewpoint, while low-cost Firm 1 (with marginal cost function MC_1) prefers a price of $128 per unit. There is conflict between the companies in their price and output preferences. This result is quite general. Whenever pro-

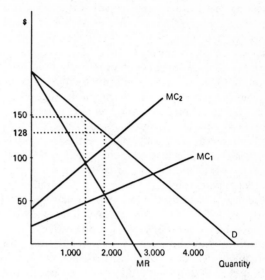

Figure 5.2
Constant-Shares Pricing with Differing Costs

ducers obtaining equal shares of a market at identical prices have disparate marginal cost functions, their individual price preferences differ, except in a special case.[15] The value of a numerical example is that it allows us to compare the profits each firm would earn charging its own preferred price with the profits earned at its rival's preferred price. With the cost functions assumed, individual and combined profits are as follows:

	Firm 1's Profits	Firm 2's Profits	Joint Profits
$P = \$128$	\$112,000	\$ 73,600	\$185,600
$P = \$147$	\$100,950	\$ 86,667	\$187,617

Each firm is worse off at its rival's favored price than at its own, and each therefore would prefer to see its own favored price set on an industry-wide basis.[16]

When homogeneity of products precludes any

---

[15]E.g., when the two firms' marginal cost functions intersect each other where they mutually intersect the common marginal revenue curve.

[16]Combined profits are slightly higher with Firm 2's preferred price of $147 because Firm 2, with more rapidly rising marginal costs, enjoys a greater cost reduction in reducing output from 1,800 to 1,333 units than does Firm 1.

lasting price differential, or when the price differential required for producers of differentiated products to retain their customary market shares is not equal to the difference between favored prices, some means of conflict resolution must be found. One way is for the firms to strike a compromise among their conflicting preferences, i.e., through overt meetings and collusive agreements or more subtle tacit bargaining.[17] But this implies a sacrifice of pricing independence, undermining Chamberlin's argument for the emergence of a monopoly price through purely independent action. An alternative method is for the firm preferring the lowest price arbitrarily to impose its will upon the other producers.[18] Because patronage flocks to the low-price seller, the firm with the lowest price preference has a distinct advantage over its rivals in this regard. If others attempt to hold the price up at the higher levels they favor, they will suffer a severe erosion of sales and market shares. Still this mode of price leadership is not always quite so simple. If firms with higher costs do attempt to maintain their prices despite market share losses, the low-price producer may be forced to satisfy more customers and hence supply more than the quantity of output which maximizes its profits. Or if the high-cost firms are dissatisfied with their profits at the low-cost firm's favored price, they may resort to aggressive pricing tactics, either out of desperation or in the hope of threatening and coercing the low-cost firm into adopting a more cooperative stance. The result can be an uncontrolled war in which the price is driven well below the low-cost producer's preferred level.[19] In short, when the members of an oligopolistic industry operate under significantly divergent cost conditions, attaining a price-quantity equilibrium approximating the monopoly solution through independent action is not always easy or certain.

Analogous problems arise when, due to moderate degrees of product differentiation or differences in capacity, the various members of the industry obtain different shares of the market at identical prices. Figure 5.3 presents the analysis for one case. Two firms are considered, each (for analytic convenience) with the same marginal cost function $MC_{1,2}$. Firm 1, with demand curve D_1 and marginal revenue function MR_1, is assumed normally to sell 60 per cent of the duopoly's output. Firm 2 sells the remaining 40 per cent, so its demand curve D_2 and marginal revenue curve MR_2 lie to the left of Firm 1's corresponding curves. Equating marginal cost with its own marginal revenue, Firm 1 maximizes its profits by producing output OX_1. Reading up to demand curve D_1, we find its preferred price to be OP_1. Firm 2 maximizes its profits individualistically with output OX_2, which calls for a price of OP_2. Again the producers' preferences conflict. The firm with the smaller market share prefers a lower price than its rival with a larger market share.

This conclusion holds only for the special case in which marginal costs rise as output is

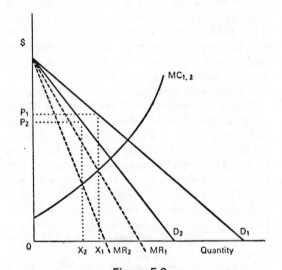

Figure 5.3
Oligopoly Pricing with Disparate Market Shares

[17]Cf. Fellner, *op. cit.*, pp. 23–24.

[18]Cf. Boulding, *op. cit.*, pp. 610–611.

[19]See R. L. Bishop, "Duopoly: Collusion or Warfare?" *American Economic Review*, December 1960, pp. 933–961. For an example from rail freight pricing on the Chicago–New York route during the late 19th century, see Paul W. MacAvoy, *The Economic Effects of Regulation* (Cambridge: M.I.T. Press, 1965), pp. 129–135.

increased. The high-share firm prefers a higher price in this instance because, in the higher output range where it operates, rising marginal costs discourage expansion more than at lower outputs. More generally, three cases exist:

(1) When marginal costs are rising, the lowest price is preferred by the firm with the smallest market share, *ceteris paribus*.

(2) When marginal costs are constant over the relevant range of outputs, differences in market shares do not lead to different price preferences, *ceteris paribus*.

(3) When marginal costs fall with higher output, the lowest price is preferred by the firm with the largest market share, which has an incentive to expand and take full advantage of the low costs associated with high outputs.

One implication of these relationships is that the amount of conflict over preferred price levels may depend upon whether firms price to achieve long-run or short-run objectives. As we have seen in Chapter 4, long-run average and marginal costs tend to be roughly constant in the range of plant sizes most frequently adopted by manufacturing firms. This suggests the prevalence of no-conflict case (2) when pricing is oriented toward long-run goals. On the other hand, short-run cost curves are more likely to fit the case (1) mold, except in output ranges substantially below designed plant capacity, and so considerable conflict might be expected among firms of diverse size pricing to maximize short-run profits.

Obviously, both market shares and cost functions may vary simultaneously from firm to firm; the two problems have been kept separate thus far only for analytic convenience. Disparities in both conditions may render the problem of setting a mutually acceptable price even more difficult, although it is also possible (e.g., when firms with small market shares use less capital-intensive production processes, and hence have higher short-run marginal cost functions) that the opposing forces will tend to cancel out. Since the correlation between market shares and capital intensity is more likely to be inverse than

positive, the net tendency is probably toward some cancelling out of conflicts. Still substantial conflicts do exist, as we shall observe repeatedly in later chapters.

One further complication related to cost conditions must be examined. When fixed costs are high and/or when marginal costs vary substantially among firms, it is conceivable that no set of price-quantity choices consistent with independent action by industry members will maximize collective profits. To see this, we return to our numerical example. Firm 1 is assumed to be a capital-intensive, low-marginal-cost producer, with the total cost function $TC_1 = 50,000 + 20 X_1 + .01 X_1^2$. Firm 2 is a high-marginal-cost producer, with $TC_2 = 20,000 + 40 X_2 + .02 X_2^2$. To find the outputs which yield maximum combined profits, we must set up a joint profit equation, consisting of total revenue from sales of both firms' outputs less total costs of the two separate production operations:

$$\pi_{joint} = (X_1 + X_2) [200 - .02 (X_1 + X_2)] - (50,000 + 20 X_1 + .01 X_1^2) - (20,000 + 40 X_2 + .02 X_2^2).$$

When this function is maximized with respect to the outputs of Firms 1 and 2, the optimal values of X_1 and X_2 turn out to be 2,500 and 750 units respectively. With total production of 3,250 units per month, the price which equates demand with supply is $135 per unit. Joint profits are $215,000—about 15 per cent higher than those attainable if the production burden is shared equally at Firm 2's preferred price of $147. If Firm 1 collects all the revenue from selling its output of 2,500 units and deducts from it the costs of producing that output, its total profits turn out to be $175,000. Firm 2, producing and selling only 750 units per month, realizes profits of only $40,000. Firm 2 could do much better under the equal market shares approach discussed earlier, selling either at its own preferred price of $147 or at Firm 1's preferred price of $128. Firm 2 is therefore not apt to cooperate in this 'rationalization' scheme, despite the higher collective profits, unless a plan for distributing profits on some basis other than individual sales is enforced. And obviously, such profit-pooling agreements are several steps removed from the independent action implied in a naive version of Chamberlin's joint profit maximization theory.

Even higher collective profits could be realized under the applicable numerical assumptions if, by shutting down high-cost Firm 2's plant completely, the fixed costs of $20,000 associated with maintaining that plant could be eliminated. Then low-cost Firm 1 would produce and sell the pure monopoly output of 3,000 units at a price of $140 per unit, realizing profits of $220,000. But again, Firm 2 would surely not consent to such a drastic step unless an iron-clad agreement were reached assuring that it would receive a substantial share of the enhanced industry profits.

One final point must be made clear. "Rationalization" measures such as closing down high-cost Firm 2's plant increase collective industry profits by enforcing a more efficient organization of production. But the consumer does not necessarily benefit from such efficiency-increasing measures. In the example presented, prices are higher and quantities sold lower under either rationalization scheme than they would be if the two firms made their output decisions independently, letting Firm 1 pull the price down to its preferred level of $128. Only when marginal costs are falling continuously over the attainable range of outputs, or when the low-cost firm's marginal cost function is at all relevant outputs below the lowest point on the high-cost firm's marginal cost function, will the consumer benefit directly through lower prices under rationalization schemes accompanied by a pricing policy which maximizes producers' collective profits.

To sum up, when cost functions and/or market shares vary from firm to firm within an oligopolistic industry, conflicts arise which, unless resolved through formal collusive agreements, interfere with the maximization of collective monopoly profits. And if left unresolved, these conflicts may trigger myopic, aggressive behavior which drives the industry far from the joint-profit-maximizing solution of its price-output problem.

THE CONTRIBUTIONS OF GAME THEORY

Because of these complications, it became clear that the conventional tools of microeconomic theory could not provide a full explanation of oligopoly pricing. New hope for a definitive solution arose with the publication by von Neumann and Morgenstern of their *Theory of Games and Economic Behavior*.[20] Or at least, many economists who had not waded through the book's 632 pages of set theoretic proofs added hopeful footnote citations in works applying traditional tools to the oligopoly problem with less than evident success. We shall find that the hopes of the more optimistic were in vain. Nevertheless, game theory is extremely useful as a source of insights into the oligopoly problem, even though it cannot give solutions determinate in any conventional sense.

The most compelling contribution by von Neumann and Morgenstern was their theory of *zero-sum* games, for which they derived solutions which are indeed determinate, assuming rational but conservative behavior on the part of rivals anxious to make the best of their rivalry. The consequences of alternative choices by each rival are represented through a payoff matrix, as in the following illustrative matrix for Player A in a two-person zero-sum game involving A and Player B:

$$
\begin{array}{c}
\text{B's Strategies} \\
\begin{array}{cc}
\begin{array}{c}
\text{A's} \\
\text{Strategies}
\end{array}
\begin{array}{c}
a_1 \\
a_2 \\
a_3
\end{array}
\end{array}
\begin{array}{ccc}
b_1 & b_2 & b_3 \\
\left[\begin{array}{ccc}
8 & -5 & -10 \\
0 & -2 & 6 \\
4 & -1 & 5
\end{array}\right]
\end{array}
\end{array}
$$

Each entry in the matrix is the payoff expected by A associated with a particular pair of strategy

[20]John von Neumann and Oskar Morgenstern, *Theory of Games and Economic Behavior* (Princeton: Princeton University Press, 1944). For a lucid exposition of the central concepts, see Anatol Rapoport, *Fights, Games, and Debates* (Ann Arbor: University of Michigan Press, 1960), pp. 105–242. A more advanced presentation is found in R. D. Luce and Howard Raiffa, *Games and Decisions* (New York: Wiley, 1957). The most ambitious application to oligopoly theory is in Martin Shubik, *Strategy and Market Structure* (New York: Wiley, 1959). See also Alexander Henderson, "The Theory of Duopoly," *Quarterly Journal of Economics*, November 1954, pp. 565–581.

choices by A and B; for example, if A chooses strategy a_2 and B chooses strategy b_3, A's payoff will be $+6$. Rival B's payoffs are the negative of A's; if A gains 6, B must lose 6. All payoff pairs sum to zero, hence the name *zero-sum*. To determine his best strategy, A examines each row of his payoff matrix to find the worst payoff which can occur if he chooses the strategy associated with that row: -10 for a_1, -2 for a_2, and -1 for a_3. The best of these worst outcomes— the *maximum minimorum*—is -1, associated with strategy a_3. Because it makes the best of the worst which can happen, a_3 is A's optimal (though not very lucrative) choice. Rival B follows the same procedure. Since his payoffs are the negative of those in A's matrix, he looks for the best outcome to A (and hence the worst outcome to himself) in each column (representing a strategy choice by B) of A's payoff matrix. These are $+8$ for b_1, -1 for b_2, and $+6$ for b_3. The worst of these best outcomes (*minimum maximorum*) from A's viewpoint, and hence the best of the worst from B's viewpoint, is -1, associated with strategy b_2. This is B's optimal *minimax* strategy. The set of strategies a_3, b_2 turns out to be a stable solution, or saddle point, to the game, since each participant's expectations about its rival's choices are confirmed. That is, B in fact chooses the strategy b_2 which is least favorable to A, given A's choice of a_3. Not all zero-sum games have such simple solutions, but von Neumann and Morgenstern proved that for all two-person zero-sum games there exists a minimax strategy (or set of strategies) which promises each participant higher average payoffs than any alternative set of strategies, assuming that each rival intelligently tries to maximize the expected value of its payoffs.

For our purposes there is only one hitch. As von Neumann and Morgenstern recognized, the kinds of rivalry encountered in oligopoly seldom conform to the zero-sum assumption. Only two exceptions can be found. First, firms might set market share as their sole competitive objective, and one firm's market share gain is necessarily the market share loss of other firms. But to depict oligopolistic rivalry in terms of such simple

objectives is undoubtedly to misrepresent reality. The intense interest in market position displayed by many oligopolists probably reflects the belief that higher profits come hand-in-hand with certain kinds of market share gains, and thus it is profit which the shouting is really about. A second defense of zero-sum oligopoly models is only slightly more plausible: that firms engage in 'games of survival' or 'games of ruin,' the winner enjoying the whole of a profitable market.[21] While some examples can be found in real life and forced into the zero-sum mold, the task is difficult. And as we shall see much later, the authorities in most nations with antitrust laws take a dim view of business tactics explicitly calculated to ruin one's rival.

For a more realistic example of the payoff structure encountered in business rivalry, we refer again to Figure 5.1. It should be evident now that Figure 5.1 is simply a large payoff matrix. To facilitate the analysis, let us consider only two alternative price strategies for each firm. At the price ($105) nearest the Cournot equilibrium point, each firm receives profits of $95,000, and so joint profits are $190,000. If Firm 1 holds its price at $105 while Firm 2 raises its price to $130 (nearest the joint-maximizing point), total profits will be $122,000 (for Firm 1) plus $57,000 (for Firm 2) = $179,000. If both firms quote prices of $130, joint profits will be $222,000. The payoffs in the matrix clearly do not sum to zero, nor is there any simple mathematical transformation (such as subtracting a fixed amount from every payoff) which will make them sum to zero. Games of this sort, in which some outcomes are more favorable to the participants jointly than others, are called non-constant-sum or variable-sum games.

Minimax is an unbeatable strategy in zero-sum games. But it is ill-suited to the typical variable-sum game of oligopolistic rivalry. To see this, let us find the minimax strategy for Firm 1 in Figure 5.1. We scan each column, corresponding to a strategy (price) choice by Firm 1, locating the worst possible outcome if that strategy is chosen. The best of these worst is a profit of approximately $40,000, resulting when Firm 2 quotes a price of $75 and Firm 1 a price of $85.[22] If Firm 2, with symmetrical cost and demand conditions, reasons similarly, both firms will quote minimax prices of $85. As a result they end up with profits of $54,000 each, instead of the $91,000 each they could earn through supposedly myopic Cournot behavior, or the $112,000 attainable if both quote prices of $128 to maximize joint profits subject to no output allocation agreement.

The nature of the pricing problem in oligopoly can be seen still more sharply if we limit our focus to two salient strategy alternatives—e.g., as before, $105 and $130. The profits (in thousands of dollars per month) to Firms 1 and 2 resulting from various strategy combinations are set down in abbreviated game matrix form as follows:

Firm 2's Price Strategies

		$130	$105
Firm 1's Price Strategies	$130	111,111	57,122
	$105	122, 57	95, 95

Because Firm 1's gains are not necessarily Firm 2's losses, we must record two profit outcomes for each strategy pair—the first (before the comma) Firm 1's profit, and the second Firm 2's profit. The worst that can happen from Firm 1's viewpoint if it quotes a price of $130 is a profit of $57,000; the worst if its price is $105 will be $95,000. The lower price is the minimax strategy. Or consider the choice problem from another perspective. If Firm 2 quotes a price of $130, Firm 1 will be better off quoting $105. If Firm 2 quotes $105, Firm 1 will be better off quoting $105. In the language of game theory, the $105 price *dominates* the $130 price. The low-price strategy seems to have an irresistible magnetism. Yet if both rivals engage in mental processes of

this sort, they end up with lower profits than they need to have!

This paradoxical situation is a typical member of the genus called Prisoner's Dilemma games.[23] A digression on the original prisoner's dilemma will provide valuable analogies for subsequent use. Suppose Smith and McAlpin are charged with committing a mail train robbery. The district attorney is unable to prove his case unless he can obtain a signed confession, but he can make lighter charges (e.g., possessing stolen goods) stick. The two suspects are interrogated in separate rooms (after being informed of their constitutional rights) and are confronted with specific alternatives. If McAlpin doesn't confess, both get one year in prison on the minor charge if Smith clams up too, while Smith goes free as state's evidence and McAlpin receives a 10 year sentence if Smith confesses. If McAlpin does confess, Smith gets 10 years and McAlpin goes free if Smith fails to confess, while both get six years if both confess. In game matrix form, with Smith's time in prison listed first, the payoffs are as follows:

McAlpin's Strategies

		Don't Confess	Confess
Smith's Strategies	Don't Confess	−1,−1	−10,0
	Confess	0,−10	−6,−6

Assuming that he dislikes prison and that his safety from McAlpin's revenge is assured, Smith is better off confessing, no matter what McAlpin's choice may be.[24] The same holds true from McAlpin's viewpoint. Confessing is a dominant strategy for both prisoners. If they reason in this way, both end up spending six years in jail, instead of the single year they would serve if somehow they could solve the prisoner's dilemma

---

[22]Actually, because the payoff matrix has been truncated to exclude lower prices, the true minimax strategy involves even lower profits. It should be noted also that a saddle point minimax equilibrium may not obtain.

[23]See Luce and Raiffa, *op. cit.*, pp. 94–102.

[24]By making the assumptions explicit, we see that neither the example nor the analogy has claim to universal applicability. With the Mafia, for example, the 'confess' payoffs are much less favorable because a stool pigeon can be almost certain of early departure from these earthly premises. Bombs thrown into the windows of price cutters' offices, or (to cite a slightly more ethical alternative) penalty clauses in market-sharing agreements can also change the payoff structure of oligopoly games.

and deny their guilt despite the strained circumstances.

In terms of their static, single-play structure, the oligopoly price game presented earlier and the classic Prisoner's Dilemma game are identical.[25] There is a dominant strategy which, if chosen by both parties, leads to an outcome in which both parties are worse off than they need be. Nor are these the only such examples. In the military field, the deterrence of nuclear attack, decisions whether or not to use poison gas, and arms races also tend to have the structure of Prisoner's Dilemma games. And as we shall see in later chapters, advertising and new product rivalry in oligopoly often fit the Prisoner's Dilemma mold.

With similar structures, these games might be expected to tend toward similar outcomes. But this is not the case. We observe, for example, that nuclear deterrence has been remarkably stable and successful over the past two decades. There has been no exchange of nuclear weapons which would leave all nations worse off, even though successful unilateral attack could lead to world domination and being attacked unilaterally would (at least in the average citizen's judgment) be disastrous. On the other hand, nations large and small have had little success in avoiding mutual and therefore self-defeating steps in quantitative and qualitative arms races.[26] Why is it that in some Prisoner's Dilemmas the participants avoid mutually unfavorable outcomes, while in others they do not?

The answer evidently involves more than the static structure of the payoff matrix. Particularly important are the dynamics of the situation, the amount of information available to participants, and the opportunities for communication.

The problem in the classical Prisoner's Dilemma is one of information and communication. If Smith and McAlpin could get together on their stories and remain constantly in touch so that each knows the other is not confessing, both could get off with light sentences. It is a wise district attorney who places the prisoners in separate interrogation rooms to foment uncertainty and distrust. One reason why nuclear deterrence has been successful is that communication is relatively free and rapid. A hostile move is known at least as soon as the first weapon explodes. In addition, nations have invested vast sums in early warning systems to detect attacks before they damage retaliatory capabilities and in 'hot lines' to guarantee that accidents will not be misunderstood. As a result, each nation finds it possible to wait and watch. If all goes well, this process of watchful waiting and abstinence from aggressive (or preemptory defensive) moves will continue indefinitely. We shall find close analogies in oligopoly pricing two chapters hence. In contrast, nations have been unable to resist the development of new weapons partly because of the secrecy in which military agencies enshroud their research and development efforts. Not knowing what is going on in alien laboratories, military leaders have tended to fear the worst (the minimax assumption) and initiated the development of each new, potentially decisive weapon. These actions in turn validate the suspicions of other nations, giving the technological arms race its irresistible momentum.

The existence of lags is a second important determinant. It is possible to retaliate quickly to a massive nuclear attack or to certain kinds of price cuts. In such cases, potential aggressors recognize that they have little to gain and much to lose from aggression, and therefore they refrain. It may take many years, however, to respond fully to a successful new weapon system or the superior new product of an industrial rival. Consequently, aggressive moves may be taken both because initiators believe they can gain an advantage of some duration and because Nervous Nellies fear they must begin now to offset secret rival moves which, if not countered, could lead to a painfully long period of inferiority.

A third factor is the dynamics of the rivalry. Some rivalries are continuous; others are dis-

---

[25]This identity no longer holds, and the character of the solution may change, if sequential and contingent strategies are built into the game's structure. See Anatol Rapoport, "Escape from Paradox," *Scientific American*, July 1967, pp. 50–56.

[26]See F. M. Scherer, "Was the Nuclear Arms Race Inevitable?" *Co-existence*, Spring 1966, pp. 59–69.

continuous or perhaps even 'one-shot' affairs. Maximization of joint benefits is more likely when the rivalry is continuous for two main reasons: repeated experience under stable conditions affords an opportunity for learning to cooperate and trust one another; and when the game will be played continuously or repeatedly, each party can threaten its rivals with damaging retaliation tomorrow if cooperation is not forthcoming today. Indeed, these two elements interact, for rivals can in time be taught to cooperate by the deft use of threats, rewards, and punishments.[27] Thus, a further reason why nuclear deterrence is stable is that the game is replayed day after day. Conversely, it is difficult to avoid qualitative arms races because each new round is different in many details from the prior round. This experience leads us to predict that oligopolists selling an unchanging product under stable demand conditions are more likely to maximize joint profits than oligopolists selling rapidly changing products under variable demand conditions. Supporting evidence will be marshalled in later chapters.

Besides yielding insight through analogy into the nature of real-world rivalries, game theory makes another important contribution. By reducing oligopoly pricing problems to game payoff matrices, it is possible to conduct controlled experiments testing relevant hypotheses. Several fruitful experimental efforts have been reported. L. B. Lave administered numerous repetitions of a Prisoner's Dilemma game to subjects isolated and unable to communicate formally. He found that through repeated experience, three fourths of the players learned to cooperate in choosing the strategy pair which maximized their joint payoff. However, on the last trial (after which punitive retaliation for uncooperative behavior was impossible) double-crossing was common.[28] Fouraker and Siegel observed that repeated bidding served as a means of communication through which participants in bilateral monopoly games were able to reach bargains which were optimal (or, more precisely, Pareto-optimal) in the sense that no further change could be made which increased one player's profits without reducing the other's profits. In another set of experiments, they found that cooperation to maximize joint oligopoly profits is less likely, the larger the number of participants is and the less information participants have on rival prices, outputs, and profits.[29] Repeating the Fouraker-Siegel experiments with a slightly different payoff matrix, J. L. Murphy found that prices and profits were higher when both rivals faced a threat of outright losses due to mutual price-cutting than when they did not.[30] An experiment administered by J. W. Friedman revealed an equilibrium tendency for subjects to reach and adhere to agreements on oligopoly prices roughly 80 per cent of the time, despite the possibility of cheating to increase profits once agreements were concluded. Friedman observed in addition that Pareto-optimal agreements were more likely in symmetric duopoly games—i.e., when both cost curves and market shares were the same—than in asymmetric games.[31] This result underscores the hazards to oligopolistic coordination posed by unequal costs and market shares, as revealed through *a priori* analysis in the preceding section.

In sum, although game theory does not yield compelling mechanistic solutions to oligopoly pricing problems, it does help identify certain very general structural characteristics of situations involving conflict mixed with incentives for cooperation. Armed with these generalizations,

[27]For a superb treatment of this problem, see T. C. Schelling, *The Strategy of Conflict* (Cambridge: Harvard University Press, 1960), Chapter 5. See also Luce and Raiffa, *op. cit.*, pp. 100–101; and Shubik, *op. cit.*, pp. 222–226, 252, 284, and 333.

[28]L. B. Lave, "An Empirical Approach to the Prisoners' Dilemma Game," *Quarterly Journal of Economics*, August 1962, pp. 424–436.

[29]L. E. Fouraker and Sidney Siegel, *Bargaining Behavior* (New York: McGraw-Hill, 1963), especially pp. 50–51, 165–166, and 199. For supporting results from a more elaborate experimental game, see F. T. Dolbear *et al.*, "Collusion in Oligopoly: An Experiment on the Effect of Numbers and Information," *Quarterly Journal of Economics*, May 1968, pp. 240–259.

[30]"Effects of the Threat of Losses on Duopoly Bargaining," *Quarterly Journal of Economics*, May 1966, pp. 296–313.

[31]"An Experimental Study of Cooperative Duopoly," *Econometrica*, July-October 1967, pp. 379–397.

we are better able to understand the conditions facilitating and impeding solution of the pricing problems faced by real-world oligopolists.

THE KINKED DEMAND CURVE AND PRICE RIGIDITY

The minimax strategy of game theory is a strategy of pessimism: it assumes that rivals will take those actions least favorable from one's own viewpoint. It is in fact much too pessimistic to describe most oligopoly behavior realistically. But by making an assumption which meets minimax halfway down the road to pessimism, we encounter the kinked demand curve theory, which has been employed to explain why oligopolistic firms shy away from frequent price-cutting.[32]

The theory asserts that oligopolists face two different subjectively estimated demand curves: one describing the quantities they will sell at various prices, assuming that rivals maintain their prices at present levels (the Cournot assumption); and the other describing the amount of output sold, assuming that rivals exactly match any price changes away from the present level (the price-matching, constant market shares assumption). The latter curve has the same elasticity at any given price as the overall industry demand curve. The first, however, is much more elastic. If Firm 1 raises its price while rivals hold their prices constant, the quantity of output demanded from Firm 1 will fall off much more sharply than it would if all sellers matched the price increase. If Firm 1 lowers its price while rivals do not, it will make inroads into their market shares, and the quantity of output it can sell will be greater than it would be if rivals matched the price reduction. The two curves intersect at the current price level, for if Firm 1 (whose kinked demand curve we shall construct) continues to quote its current price, the alternative assumptions of rival price maintenance

and price-matching imply identical rival prices.

Figure 5.4a illustrates these points, assuming the current price to be *OP* per unit and the quantity supplied by (and demanded from) Firm 1 to be *OX*. *DEF* is Firm 1's demand curve, assuming that rival firms hold their prices at *OP* per unit no matter what Firm 1 does. *GEH* is Firm 1's demand curve, assuming that rivals match Firm 1's prices. *DS* is the marginal revenue curve associated with demand curve *DEF*, and *GR* the marginal revenue curve for demand curve *GEH*.

These curves, to repeat, are defined for two alternative rival reactions to price changes: holding the line, or matching. The key assumption of the kinked demand curve theory is that oligopolists expect rivals to choose the less favorable of these alternatives in response to a price change. The theory does not go as far as minimax, assuming that rivals will *take the initiative* in choosing a damaging strategy, but only that they will *react* unfavorably to one's own price initiatives. Specifically, if Firm 1 raises its price, rivals are expected not to follow the increase, enjoying an increase in market share at Firm 1's expense due to the newly-created price differential. If on the other hand Firm 1 reduces its price, rivals are expected to match the cut promptly in order to ward off incursions into their own market shares. When these pessimistic assumptions are held, only the more elastic demand segment *DE* is applicable for contemplated increases above the current price by Firm 1, while only the less elastic demand segment *EH* is applicable for price cuts by Firm 1. The complete demand curve (as visualized by Firm 1) is composed of these two segments *DE* and *EH*, with a kink at the current price *OP* and output *OX*. The other segments *EF* and *GE* are obliterated by Firm 1's pessimistic assumptions, and so in Figure 5.4b we include only the applicable segments of the kinked demand curve *DEH*. Elimination of the two demand curve segments

---

[32]The kinked demand curve theory was proposed independently and almost simultaneously by R. L. Hall and C. J. Hitch in "Price Theory and Business Behavior," *Oxford Economic Papers*, May 1939, pp. 12–45; and Paul M. Sweezy in "Demand Under Conditions of Oligopoly," *Journal of Political Economy*, August 1939, pp. 568–573. For further extensions and criticisms, see George J. Stigler, "The Kinky Oligopoly Demand Curve and Rigid Prices," *Journal of Political Economy*, October 1947, pp. 432–449. For a discussion of some antecedents, see J. J. Spengler, "Kinked Demand Curves: By Whom First Used?" *Southern Economic Journal*, July 1965, pp. 81–84.

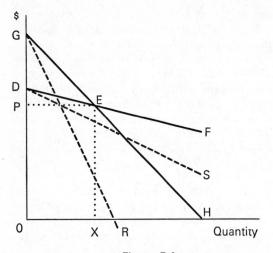

Figure 5.4a
Derivation of the Kinked Demand Curve

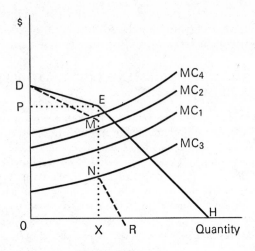

Figure 5.4b
The Effect of Cost Changes

EF and *GE* also requires that we eliminate the associated marginal revenue segments. For the remaining demand curve segment *DE*, only the marginal revenue segment *DM* to the left of the current output level is applicable. For the remaining demand segment *EH*, only the segment *NR* to the right of the current output is relevant. Therefore, the marginal revenue function for the kinked demand curve *DEH* in Figure 5.4b is the discontinuous set of curves *DM* and *NR*.[33] We see that whenever there is a kink in the demand curve, there must be a vertical discontinuity in the associated marginal revenue function. The more the demand curve segments differ in elasticity in the neighborhood of the kink, the greater will be the vertical discontinuity or gap between the associated marginal revenue segments.

We know that to maximize its profits, a producer must equate marginal cost with marginal revenue. Let us see what implications the kinked demand curve has for an oligopolist's maximizing decisions in the face of cost and/or demand changes. Suppose initially that Firm 1 faces cost conditions represented by marginal cost func-

tion MC_1 in Figure 5.4b. Then output *OX* will be optimal, for at a lower output marginal revenue exceeds marginal cost, providing an incentive to expand, while at a higher output marginal revenue is less than marginal cost, so that profits may be increased by reducing the quantity supplied. An important implication of the kinked demand curve theory is that the same output *OX* and price *OP* will be optimal even after a change in cost conditions, as represented by either the higher marginal cost function MC_2 or the lower curve MC_3. In both new situations, the marginal cost function cuts the marginal revenue function in the latter's discontinuity, so there is no incentive either to expand or contract output. Only with a very substantial change in costs—e.g., to MC_4—will there be an incentive to move to a new (in this case lower) output and (higher) price.

The same rigidity of prices (but not outputs) follows for moderate shifts in demand. In Figure 5.5, for example, the original situation is reflected by demand curve *DEH* kinked at the price *OP*, with the corresponding marginal revenue function *DLKR*. Should a recession

---

[33]Many students have trouble understanding the kinked demand curve analysis because they fail to remember that *quantity* is the independent variable in defining marginal revenue, and as a result they do not see that each marginal revenue segment is applicable only up to that quantity of output at which the demand curve kink occurs.

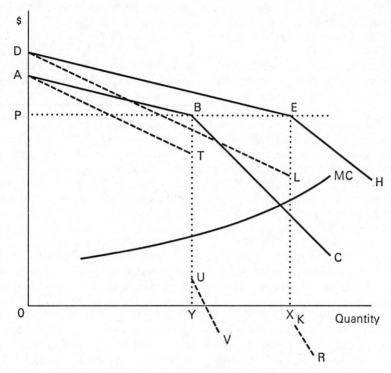

Figure 5.5
Demand Changes under the Kink Assumption

overtake the industry, the demand curve shifts horizontally to the left to *ABC*, and the corresponding new marginal revenue function is *ATUV*. In both cases marginal cost continues to cut the marginal revenue functions through their gaps, and so there is no incentive to change the price, although output will be reduced to *OY* to clear the market in the face of reduced demand.

In sum, the kinked demand curve theory yields two main predictions: (1) When the constant-shares demand curve is relatively inelastic, oligopolists will refrain from price-cutting, since they expect that matching cuts by rivals will nullify any profit gains; and (2) oligopoly prices will tend to be rigid in the face of moderate cost and demand conditions changes. Both predictions are consistent with observed behavior. Interviews with businessmen and the testimony recorded in numerous antitrust investigations reveal that a paramount consideration deterring price-cutting, especially in industries with few sellers and homogeneous products, is the belief that cuts will be matched, forcing all firms onto inelastic segments of their demand curves.[34] There is also evidence that oligopoly prices are adjusted less frequently than prices in atomistically structured industries. Because it can ex-

[34]For examples, see J. W. Markham, *Competition in the Rayon Industry* (Cambridge: Harvard University Press, 1952), p. 143; A. D. H. Kaplan, J. B. Dirlam, and R. F. Lanzillotti, *Pricing in Big Business* (Washington: Brookings, 1958), p. 174 (steel); R. B. Tennant, "The Cigarette Industry," in Walter Adams, ed., *The Structure of American Industry* (Third ed.; New York: Macmillan, 1961), pp. 370–372; Reed Moyer, *Competition in the Midwestern Coal Industry* (Cambridge: Harvard University Press, 1964), pp. 53–54; and (for a case in which the kink was not always effective) E. P. Learned and C. C. Ellsworth, *Gasoline Pricing in Ohio* (Boston: Harvard Business School, 1959), pp. 244–252. Other examples can be found in the records of the Salk vaccine (*U.S.* v. *Eli Lilly et al.*) and tetracycline (*F.T.C.* v. *American Cyanamid et al.*) antitrust cases.

plain significant facets of industrial pricing behavior, the kinked demand curve theory has earned a place in the economist's box of tools.

Nevertheless, there are cases in which the fit between theory and reality is less satisfactory. One problem is that alternative explanations for the rigidity of oligopoly prices can be found. When price structures are complex, cost considerations may discourage frequent price revisions, since a certain amount of administrative toil invariably goes into price-making decisions, and since the costs of printing and disseminating new price lists are not inconsequential. More importantly, oligopolists are aware that frequent price revisions may endanger industry discipline. Cooperation to maximize joint profits is often a fragile thing, particularly, as we have seen earlier, when cost curves and market shares differ among industry members. When formal coordination mechanisms are lacking, price changes may be misinterpreted as aggressive moves, to be met by a vigorous counterattack. Given the risk that price warfare may break out if a price change is misinterpreted, oligopolists may choose not to rock the boat, announcing changes only when cost or demand conditions have altered so clearly as to leave no danger of misinterpretation.

A second limitation is more subtle. Suppose we try to explain, using the kinked demand curve theory, price rigidity in industries which have experienced fair success in maintaining prices which tend to maximize joint oligopoly profits. We assume identical cost conditions and market shares for all industry members, although the same analysis can be applied to individual firms whose low price preferences place a ceiling on the industry price. To maximize collective profits, marginal cost must equal marginal revenue (derived from the constant-shares demand curve) for a representative firm. If the price is set so as to satisfy this condition and then a kink appears, the marginal cost curve must cut the marginal revenue curve gap at the very bottom of that gap—e.g., at point N in Figure 5.4b. This is so because only the segment NR is marginal to the constant-shares demand curve. It follows that prices will now be rigid against upward shifts in the marginal cost function, but even a slight downward shift will induce a price reduction (since any marginal cost curve lower than MC_3 will no longer cut the gap). Yet observation indicates that prices tend to be at least as rigid downward as they are upward in well-disciplined oligopolies. We are forced to conclude either that the kinked demand curve theory is unable fully to explain pricing behavior in industries which achieve joint profit maximization, or that the price must initially have been set below the profit-maximizing level if the subsequent emergence of a kink makes the price rigid against both upward and downward cost curve shifts. We shall find when we study price leadership in the following chapter that both conclusions may be valid.

Finally, the kinked demand curve theory is much better at explaining why prices persist at particular levels than how they attained those levels in the first place. To see this, consider Figure 5.4b once again. Suppose there is a substantial increase in costs, so that Firm 1 now operates with MC_4, cutting the marginal revenue function to the left of the gap MN. A price increase by Firm 1 appears warranted, despite the anticipated loss of market share and sales. Assume also that all other firms in the industry experience the same cost increase (i.e., because of pattern bargaining over wages or because all purchase inflation-prone raw materials in the same markets). Since their position is symmetric to Firm 1's, they too will have an incentive to raise their prices. But if they do, Firm 1's pessimistic assumption that rivals will hold their prices constant—the heart of the kinked demand curve theory—is contradicted. Alternatively, if other firms' cost curves do not shift upward and the rivals adhere initially to price OP, their demand curves must shift to the right (i.e., they enjoy higher sales at price OP) because of Firm 1's new higher price. If this rightward shift is sufficiently large, it may induce a price increase by the rivals, again contradicting the price maintenance assumption. Similar contradictions arise when exogenous demand curve shifts induce at least one firm to change its price.[35] In

---

[35]Cf. Stigler, "The Kinky Oligopoly Demand Curve and Rigid Prices," p. 436.

short, the assumptions of the kinked demand curve theory are violated when incentives for a price change appear either simultaneously or sequentially for several members of the oligopoly. As a result, the theory cannot explain how prices change or how they settle down at new levels when cost or demand conditions alter, even though it can explain why they remain stable once they do settle down. Other mechanisms must be invoked to explain the dynamics of price changes. We shall consider several in Chapter 6.

ORDER BACKLOGS, INVENTORIES, AND OLIGOPOLISTIC COORDINATION

We advance now onto ground which has barely felt the cutting edge of the theorist's plow.[36] All the oligopoly pricing theories surveyed thus far presume that firms select prices and outputs by equating marginal cost with marginal revenue—the latter derived, of course, from the firm's subjectively estimated demand curve. There are two serious problems with all such theories as representations of actual behavior.

First, the demand curve of an oligopolist depends upon the actions and reactions of his fellow oligopolists. The theories examined in this chapter proceed by making specific assumptions about rival reactions. This is a perfectly valid method of theorizing, although uncertainties inevitably arise both in theoretical model-building and on the business firing line as to which assumptions are most plausible. And as we shall see in a moment, in certain instances formidable obstacles to even the theoretical specification of individual firm demand curves arise.

Second, the economic environment within which firms operate is constantly in motion. Population grows; the weather pursues its capricious course; tastes alter; governments with varying economic policies come and go;

military conflicts erupt and (one hopes) ebb; new technologies appear; old business rivals liquidate and new ones enter; etc. As a result, demand and cost functions are seldom stable long enough for firms to settle down into a lasting price-quantity equilibrium. All this means that the businessman faces considerable uncertainty in predicting future cost and (especially) demand conditions. This is not to say that rational decision-making is impossible. Guesses about the future must be made, however difficult the task may be. The main point for our purposes is this: the uncertainties rendering demand curve estimation difficult even under favorable conditions interact with the problems of predicting oligopolistic rival reactions in a manner which undermines the operational utility of the orthodox profit maximization calculus.

To see this, let us examine more carefully two familiar illustrations. We begin with the simpler case: the kinked demand curve theory of output determination under changing demand conditions. Suppose a firm has been operating for some time with demand curve *DEH* in Figure 5.5 when (for any reason) demand begins to taper off. It is easy enough in the classroom to draw a new, leftward-shifted demand curve *ABC*. But how does the businessman know that this is where the new demand curve lies? How does he know that demand in the price-matching segment *BC* is not more elastic, or less elastic? The standard methods of demand elasticity estimation involve either multivariate analysis of past experience, or experimentation, or both. Yet historical experience may be misleading or irrelevant under significantly altered economic conditions. And experimentation with alternative prices is virtually debarred by the assumptions of the kinked demand curve theory, for price rigidity can hardly follow as a logical consequence when flexible experimental prices are needed to render the theory operational. At best, the elasticity estimates must be subjective—the result of the businessman's finely-honed

[36]Some initial steps are taken in Fellner, *op. cit.*, pp. 166–168; R. M. Cyert and J. G. March, *A Behavioral Theory of the Firm* (Englewood Cliffs: Prentice-Hall, 1963), especially p. 12; Markham, *Competition in the Rayon Industry*, Chapters 7 and 8; M. J. Peck, *Competition in the Aluminum Industry* (Cambridge: Harvard University Press, 1961), Chapter 6; and Victor Zarnowitz, "Unfilled Orders, Price Changes, and Business Fluctuations," *Review of Economics and Statistics*, November 1962, pp. 367–394.

intuition. This is not an unacceptable basis for theorizing in general, and it is particularly harmless in the present case, since *pricing* decisions under the kink theory are not highly sensitive to elasticity estimation errors as long as firms consider the *differences* in elasticity at the kink to be large.

However, *production* decisions are very sensitive to estimates of the point B in Figure 5.5, denoting the quantity demanded at the ruling price OP. And of course, such estimates are also uncertain under changing demand conditions. Errors are bound to be made, both by individual firms and by all industry members collectively. What if the errors are, say, optimistic on the average? More output will be produced than the market will absorb at the going price OP. If the conventional static theory is construed literally, price must fall to clear the market, and again the price rigidity prediction is contradicted. But at this point the traditional theory makes things unnecessarily difficult for itself by oversimplification. In fact, firms do not have to sell all they produce in any given period; they can compensate for production scheduling errors by building up or drawing down inventories, or by allowing fluctuations in their unfilled order backlogs. The additional degrees of freedom provided by inventories and order backlogs rescue the kinked demand curve theory from oblivion in the real world of uncertainty. Indeed, they do even more. By keeping a careful running check of order backlogs and finished goods inventories, along with the flow of outgoing shipments from production, the businessman is able continuously to revise his estimate of where his demand curve is located.

For our second illustration, we return to the case discussed earlier in which firms selling homogeneous products at identical prices share an oligopolistic market equally, but have dissimilar cost curves. Each of three firms is assumed to have the same constant-shares demand curve D and marginal revenue curve MR in Figure 5.6, while each has a different marginal cost function. With the lowest costs, Firm 1 prefers the lowest price OP_1.

Let us assume initially that because a low-price seller can always draw business away from high-price sellers, Firm 1 has its way. Its output is OX_1, and so also must be the outputs of the other sellers if total quantity supplied is to equal total quantity demanded at the ruling price OP_1. Will Firms 2 and 3 in fact produce OX_1? Consider Firm 2 first. Since it has been forced to sell at a price lower than the price OP_2 it prefers, should it not view price OP_1 as fixed and beyond its control? If it does, it may attempt to expand output all the way out to P_1E, where its marginal cost has risen to equal the price. This is far too much output to sustain a market equilibrium at price OP_1, and so Firm 2 must either be reined in by its inability to sell all it produces or the price must fall. In these circumstances it will probably recognize its power to drive down the price by dumping a large supply on the market, as well as its inability to charge a price higher than OP_1. Then it will face a kinked demand curve P_1AD and a marginal revenue function $P_1AB\,MR$, with AB being the familiar gap of kinked demand curve theory. If it perceives its environment in this way, Firm 2 will find that its marginal cost function cuts its marginal revenue function at the gap AB, and it will produce the output OX_1 necessary to sustain market equilibrium at price OP_1. This assumes of course that the oligopolists have similar estimates of the shape and location of their constant-shares demand curves. If because of uncertainty they have different estimates (as some almost surely will), there is no guarantee that producers like Firm 2 will produce the amounts needed to let the market clear at price OP_1, and unless inventory and order backlog variations take up the slack, price OP_1 again will not stick.

Consider now the problem facing Firm 3. Here it makes no difference whether Firm 3 views price OP_1 as a parameter unaffected by its output, or whether it considers its demand curve to be the kinked stretch P_1AD. In either case Firm 3 has an incentive to produce only P_1F units of output, for at any greater output marginal cost would exceed marginal revenue (which is equal to the price OP_1). This is too little output to make the total quantity supplied satisfy demand at price OP_1, and so unless something happens to eliminate the deficit FA, price OP_1 cannot be an equilibrium price. By means of an ingenious

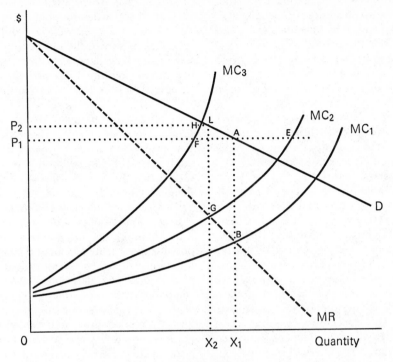

Figure 5.6
Output Determination with Conflicting Price Preferences

geometric construction, Kenneth Boulding has shown for the duopoly case how Firm 1 could readjust its perceived demand schedule and, by changing both its price and quantity offered, attain market equilibrium.[37] This construction cannot be extended to the case of three or more firms without making arbitrary, debatable assumptions concerning the division of the unfilled demand among the firms with lower price preferences. Equally important, it is doubtful whether firms could in practice perform the geometric or mathematical manipulations required to make things turn out correctly. A more plausible inference is that when cost conditions vary from firm to firm and output decisions are made independently, there is no guarantee that the conventional calculus of profit maximization will lead to

an equilibrium stable even temporarily. Additional variables must be introduced to explain the evident absence of instability in most oligopolistic industries.

The situation is only slightly different when, perhaps to avoid a price war triggered by dissatisfied high-cost producers, some compromise price higher than the lowest-cost producer's preferred price OP_1 is established. Suppose the compromise price is OP_2, preferred by Firm 2. For Firm 3, the same output insufficiency problems discussed in the previous paragraph appear. However, Firm 1, in accepting the compromise price, must now abandon the standard output determination rules. If Firm 1 regards OP_2 parametrically, it will produce far too much output for the compromise price to stick. If it

[37] *Economic Analysis* (First ed.), pp. 610–612.

equates marginal cost with its marginal revenue, even assuming a discontinuity LG where P_2L cuts the demand curve, it will produce OX_1. The total supply of the three producers may very well exceed the quantity demanded at price OP_2, if (as in Figure 5.6) Firm 1's surplus contribution X_2X_1 exceeds Firm 3's deficit HL. Firm 1 will limit output to OX_2 in this case only as a sacrifice to preserve group discipline and ward off more serious threats to both its own and the group's profits. There is nothing in the conventional calculus of profit maximization which tells it to produce no more than OX_2.

In short, when oligopolists independently follow the rule of equating marginal cost with estimated marginal revenue, there is a substantial probability that the quantity of output they collectively supply will not clear the market at the price established. This is so partly because future demand conditions are inherently uncertain, and partly because conflicting price-quantity preferences lead firms following the $MC = MR$ rule to choose production levels incompatible with short-run market equilibrium. The consequence, if the textbook analysis is construed literally, can only be disequilibrium, unstable prices, and perhaps even chaotic price warfare. But this is clearly not what we observe in most oligopolistic industries most of the time. The standard theories give inaccurate predictions because they leave out important variables. In particular, no theory of oligopolistic price and output determination is complete if it fails to incorporate inventory and order backlog variables.

Inventories and backlogs contribute in several ways to orderly oligopoly pricing. Two main cases can be identified. First, when there is little conflict among industry members over price and output policies, a price (or price structure) is established by any of the methods considered in detail in the next chapter. Individual firms make their output decisions for the next period conventionally—e.g., by attempting to bring marginal cost and estimated constant-shares marginal revenue into equality. Mistakes will undoubtedly be made. If too much is produced relative to the current flow of customer orders at the established price, the first reaction is a buildup of inventories or the reduction of order backlogs, rather than a cut in price to clear the market. If too little is produced, inventories will be drawn down or delivery times extended. These changes will then be analyzed, along with new order flow data, to project future demand conditions, on the basis of which output and pricing decisions for future periods will be adjusted. Thus, inventory and order backlog changes provide both *buffers* to compensate for production imbalances without price structure tampering, and *feedback signals* to facilitate the adjustment of future production to demand. Only when the signals point strongly to changed demand conditions is a decision to revise the price structure seriously entertained.

Second, when oligopolists taking into account fully their mutual interdependence find it impossible to estimate meaningful marginal revenue functions, or when they recognize that their price-quantity preferences embody strong incompatibilities, they may abandon the conventional profit maximization calculus entirely for purposes of output determination. This does not mean that they are no longer guided by the profit maximization goal. To the contrary, under the circumstances postulated, jettisoning the $MC = MR$ rule is the best way (short of elaborate cartelization) to establish mutually cooperative conduct which maximizes group profits in the large, even though it means some sacrifice of profits in a narrower sense. The behavioral pattern in successfully collusive oligopoly will then be as follows. By one of the methods to be studied in the next chapter, a price (or price structure) is established which approximates the joint profit maximizing level, taking into account cost and demand conditions anticipated over at least the next several months. The price, while perhaps not ideal from any single producer's viewpoint, must be satisfactory to all. Each firm recognizes the group's common interest in orderly pricing, and hence in adherence to the accepted price structure. Each realizes too that output decisions governed by narrow self interest are likely to undermine the structure. Consequently, all adopt a passive output determination policy, adjusting production to demand at the accepted price and abjuring attempts to force upon the market (or withhold) output in a way which will upset the price equilibrium.[38] Substituting this simple passive output determination policy for the $MC = MR$ rule in no way leads to indeterminacy, for changes in order flows, order backlogs, and inventory levels generate ample signals to guide each firm in its production decisions. The system is supremely operational —so much so that it is hard to see how most microeconomists have persistently overlooked it.[39]

We find then that an important contribution of inventory and order backlog variations in an oligopolistic industry is to facilitate maintenance of a particular price or price structure for some substantial period of time. The question remains, why do oligopolists find price stability so desirable? Or conversely, why should they prefer to avoid the continuous price adjustments necessary to equate quantity produced with quantity demanded in every short period? Two considerations are relevant. First, if oligopolists conform to the pessimistic assumptions of the kinked demand curve theory, it is much easier for prices to trend downward than upward. Upward price revisions to correct some temporary imbalance may not be met by rivals, and therefore will be cancelled when the imbalance disappears. Price cuts on the other hand must be countered to protect one's market share, and once a lower price equilibrium is established, the kink makes it difficult to return to the heights. The net result is an erosion of the price level as temporary disequilibria come and go. Since maximization of joint profits over the long run is seldom compatible with such a trend, producers will seek ways of avoiding price changes with no purpose other than correcting a temporary imbalance. Second, as we have observed earlier, oligopolistic coordination is a fragile thing. A

misinterpreted price cut may induce an aggressive reaction which in turn leads firms to abandon their restraint and engage in price warfare. Recognizing this, sellers are well advised to revise their prices only in response to clear-cut changes in long-run demand and cost conditions; that is, only when the signals for change come through loud and clear.

One further potential objection must be cleared away. Why are inventory and order backlog changes essential for oligopolistic markets to clear at an accepted price? Why don't firms simply adjust their production to the flow of demand in order to maintain the desired price structure? The answer is that there are certain natural lags in the production planning process. It takes time to reschedule production. Changes in the production plan are also costly: setup, hiring, and retraining costs increase with frequent production rate alterations; productivity falls with the interruption of routines; and work force morale may suffer. As a result, firms find it undesirable to make hair-trigger changes in production schedules on the basis of only faint demand change signals. They wait for stronger signals. And since the flow of orders is inherently erratic, time is required to distinguish a random short-term aberration from a more persistent demand change. Therefore, decisions to change the level of production tend to lag changes in demand by a sizeable interval. In his pioneering studies of inventory and production cycles, Metzler found the "planning period" between changes in demand and changes in production to be five months on the average.[40] In a more recent analysis of radio and television inventory behavior, Teigen found lags of from nine to 15 months between demand peaks and production peaks.[41] In the interim, at least as a first approxi-

---

[38]This passive policy with respect to price may be accompanied by measures to increase one's share of the market through non-price methods such as advertising, personal selling, and innovation. See Chapter 14 *infra*.

[39]For example, this motive for carrying inventories is not recognized in a leading theoretical and empirical work relating prices and inventories: Edwin S. Mills, *Price, Output, and Inventory Policy* (New York: Wiley, 1962), especially pp. 47–49 and 82–84. Mills gives three main reasons for carrying inventories: the speculative motive (producing quantities which will not be sold in the current period in anticipation of price increases in later periods); the desire to reduce production costs by smoothing production; and the desire to avoid turning down orders when imperfectly predictable demand turns out to be especially strong.

[40]Lloyd Metzler, "Factors Governing the Length of Inventory Cycles," *Review of Economics and Statistics*, February 1947, p. 7.

[41]Ronald L. Teigen, "The Effects of Fiscal Policy on Sales, Inventories, Production, and Employment in the Television and Radio Receiver Industry" (unpublished manuscript, 1966).

mation, the imbalance is corrected by changes in inventories and/or order backlogs.

Actually, however, sellers have two alternative responses open during periods of demand change when production is imperfectly synchronized with orders. Inventories and order backlogs can be permitted to fluctuate, as we have seen, or prices can be adjusted to clear the market. Some incentives exist for absorbing at least a part of the adjustment burden through price changes. Theoretical studies suggest that usually there is some optimal relationship of inventory levels to sales.[42] Too large an inventory causes excessive capital, storage, and deterioration costs; too low an inventory leads to uneconomic production lot sizes and possibly to the loss of sales when items are out of stock. Although less work has been done on order backlog theory, similar relationships undoubtedly exist. Too small a backlog reduces production scheduling flexibility; too large a backlog alienates customers.[43]

Thus, when inventory levels climb sharply or order backlogs fall, an incentive to reduce price materializes; while when inventories decline or order backlogs grow, there is an incentive to choke off some of the excess demand through a price increase. These incentives to limit inventory and backlog fluctuations through price adjustments apply more or less uniformly across all industry structures—atomistic, oligopolistic, and monopolized. But as we have seen, oligopolists attempting to cooperate tacitly in a strategy which maximizes joint profits have compelling reasons for refraining from short-run price adjustments. This motive for avoiding price changes is absent in atomistically structured industries. Therefore, we should expect oligopolistic industries to rely more heavily than atomistic industries upon inventory and backlog variations in adjusting to demand fluctuations, *ceteris paribus*, and less heavily upon price variations. Concretely, prices should be less variable and inventories and backlogs more variable over time in oligopolistic than in atomistic industries. Inventory and backlog variability should be especially pronounced in concentrated industries lacking formal arrangements (such as cartel agreements) for coordinating prices and outputs, but striving nonetheless to take into account mutual interdependence.[44]

This set of conjectures is quantitatively testable. The limited amount of evidence available at present clearly supports the stated hypotheses.[45]

In an unpublished exploratory study, the author collected quarterly inventory and sales data for 23 broadly defined industry groups, spanning most of the manufacturing sector, for the 1955-1961 period.[46] A coefficient measuring the variability over time of seasonally adjusted inventory/sales ratios was computed for each industry. This variability coefficient was found to be positively correlated with the weighted average four-firm concentration ratios of the 23 industry groups, after taking into account also whether the industries produced durable or non-durable goods and consumer or producers' goods. The partial correlation between variability and concentration was .36, which is statistically significant at the 90 per cent confidence level. Thus, the more concentrated the industries were, the more variable over time their inventories were relative to sales, other things being held equal.

---

[42]For an extensive bibliography, see Mills, *op. cit.*, pp. 261–265.

[43]See M. D. Steuer, R. J. Ball, and J. R. Eaton, "The Effect of Waiting Times on Foreign Orders for Machine Tools," *Economica*, November 1966, pp. 387–403.

[44]We should also expect inventories of firms with market power to be larger, as well as more variable, on the average. Firms with downward sloping demand curves are generally uncertain how much they can sell at any given price; while in pure competition, a firm can presumably be confident of selling its whole output at the ruling price. The higher price is relative to marginal cost (and hence, implicitly, the more market power a firm has) the more worthwhile it is to carry high inventories to reduce the probability that sales will be lost in periods of peak demand due to shortages. See Mills, *op. cit.*, pp. 82–83, 96, and 116–117. For a perceptive illustration, see Peck, *op. cit.*, pp. 88 and 92.

[45]Discussion of studies relating price variability to market structure is deferred to Chapter 12.

[46]The source of the inventory and sales data was the Federal Trade Commission – Securities and Exchange Commission series, *Quarterly Financial Reports for Manufacturing Corporations*. Ideally, the analysis should have included only finished goods inventories, which account for only a third of all manufacturing industry inventories by value. But comprehensive data on finished goods inventories broken down by industry have been published only very recently by government statistical bureaus.

As one might expect, the analysis also showed that inventory/sales ratios are more variable in durable goods industries than in nondurables. Basic product characteristics such as perishability and style obsolescence undoubtedly force firms in many nondurable goods industries to avoid large inventory buildups, and consequently make it more difficult to avoid price cuts in response to short-run demand declines. This is an important factor explaining the flexibility of prices and profits in the moderately concentrated meat-packing industry. At least one leading producer—Swift—has consciously attempted to gain more control over prices by integrating into product lines more susceptible to storage.[47]

Using a model which neglected oligopolistic interdependence, E. S. Mills found that production changes could be predicted quite well from inventory behavior, but that the predicted correlations between price and inventory movements failed to emerge. He rationalized the latter result by suggesting that prices were insensitive to short-run changes in demand and inventory levels in the quasi-collusive industries (cement, rubber tires, shoes, and southern pine lumber) analyzed—an explanation consistent with the hypotheses advanced here.[48] In a study of eleven Japanese industries covering the 1950–1955 period, S. Fujino discovered that the more consistently reactions to inventory buildups or drawdowns took the form of production adjustments, the less prices were adjusted. He postulated that differences in these reactions were related to market structure differences, although no explicit tests of the hypothesis were executed.[49]

Order backlogs may also play an important shock absorber role, especially in the durable goods industries, where the value of order backlogs is roughly four times the value of finished goods inventories in a typical year. The only relevant analysis is by Zarnowitz. He observed that the more variable average delivery periods (i.e., the ratio of order backlogs to sales) were, the less variable prices were.[50] He found also that changes in price were more closely correlated with changes in order backlogs than with changes in wages in the relatively unconcentrated paper and textiles industry groups, while changes in wages were by far the more powerful explanatory variable in the relatively concentrated primary metals, machinery, and fabricated metal products groups.[51] These results lend strong support to the hypothesis that oligopolists rely upon order backlog variations rather than price adjustments to adapt to short-term demand changes.

Industry case studies also reveal that the ability and willingness to absorb short-run demand shocks through inventory variation are important to maintaining stable price structures. In the copper industry, for example, firms operating in the atomistically structured scrap smelting segment typically refuse to hold large inventories, and so when scrap supplies are high, the output of smelters exercises a depressing influence on prices. However, primary copper producers Anaconda, Kennecott, and Phelps Dodge, controlling about 75 per cent of total U. S. production, have repeatedly shored up the price structure by taking strong inventory positions. In 1949, Kennecott maintained production but discontinued all open market sales until custom smelter supplies had been exhausted and prices had risen 30 per cent above earlier depressed levels.[52] During the early 1960s the Anglo-American producers held 100,000 tons of copper off the world market to stabilize prices at $.31 per pound over a two-year period.[53]

---

[47]Kaplan, Dirlam, and Lanzillotti, *Pricing in Big Business*, p. 47.

[48]Mills, *op. cit.*, pp. 124–125 and 258–259. See also M. D. Steuer and A. P. Budd, "Price and Output Decisions of Firms—A Critique of E. S. Mills' Theory," *Manchester School of Economic and Social Studies*, March 1968.

[49]S. Fujino, "Some Aspects of Inventory Cycles," *Review of Economics and Statistics*, May 1960, pp. 203–209.

[50]Victor Zarnowitz, "Unfilled Orders, Price Changes, and Business Fluctuations," *Review of Economics and Statistics*, November 1962, pp. 380–381.

[51]*Ibid.*, pp. 390–391.

[52]Kaplan, Dirlam, and Lanzillotti, *op. cit.*, pp. 176–181.

[53]Thomas O'Hanlon, "The Perilous Prosperity of Anaconda," *Fortune*, May 1966, pp. 121 and 235.

Similar inventory policies in the aluminum industry have been analyzed by M. J. Peck. When sales fell off sharply because of the Great Depression, Alcoa in 1931 accumulated inventories equal to six months' output before closing down any of its plants. Although other world producers also found themselves holding large stocks, prices remained firm. As Aluminium, Ltd., of Canada noted in its 1932 annual report, "World stocks of aluminium are not excessively large. They are in firm hands and do not weigh unduly upon the world market."[54] During the postwar period, short-term declines in the demand for aluminum ingot were again absorbed primarily through inventory accumulation rather than price cuts or production shutdowns.[55] The mere desire to avoid disruptive price-cutting was not, however, a sufficient explanation for the willingness of aluminum producers to accept enormous inventory fluctuations, Peck found. The high fixed and low marginal costs of ingot production led firms to prefer building up their inventories to shutting plants down. The wide disparity between marginal costs ($.06 per pound in 1948) and price ($.15) made it worthwhile to incur substantial inventory carrying charges in anticipation of future profitable sales when demand recovered. And of course, aluminum ingots are not subject to physical or style deterioration. Inventories of fabricated aluminum products are allowed to vary much less than ingot inventories, partly because of obsolescence risks and partly because the margin between price and variable cost is smaller. Unfortunately, Peck's analysis does not discern whether the palpably weaker pricing discipline in many fabricated products lines can be traced in part to this inventory policy difference as well as to the larger number of sellers.

Markham's study of the rayon industry prior to 1950 exhibits both similarities and differences.[56] Short-term fluctuations in demand were regularly absorbed through inventory variations and not production adjustments or price changes. Only when sales declines persisted for several months were cutbacks in production initiated, and price changes were resisted even longer. When demand continued to decline, however, industry discipline was not strong enough to ward off downward price revisions, partly because accounting profit margins fell sharply at below-capacity production rates and partly because smaller firms were unwilling to bear the continued burden of high inventory carrying costs. Still these recession-inspired price cuts were not nearly as detrimental to industry profits as they might have been in other industries, for they permitted rayon producers to win back a more than proportionate volume of business from substitute fibers whose prices were highly flexible downward during recessions. Taken together, the price-output-inventory policies pursued by rayon producers appear in general to have contributed positively to the industry's profitability.

Other industries have been less successful in avoiding price competition through their inventory policies. The accumulation of especially large stocks of gasoline in local markets has often triggered price wars,[57] despite efforts by the major integrated producers to keep excess supplies out of the hands of firms prone to price-cutting.[58] Producers in the relatively unconcentrated textiles industry characteristically accumulate finished goods stocks to smooth out production during slack periods, but when demand continues to be weak and carrying charges mount, they tend to dispose of their inventories at distress prices.[59] And in a large retail department store studied by Cyert and March, price

[54]Quoted in M. J. Peck, *Competition in the Aluminum Industry*, p. 88, note 6.

[55]*Ibid.*, p. 42.

[56]*Competition in the Rayon Industry*, Chapters 7 and 8.

[57]See Cassady, *Price Warfare in Business Competition*, p. 52; Learned and Ellsworth, *Gasoline Pricing in Ohio*, pp. 33–48; and R. H. Holton, "Antitrust Policy and Small Business," in Almarin Phillips, ed., *Perspectives on Antitrust Policy* (Princeton: Princeton University Press; 1965), pp. 206–207.

[58]See Joel B. Dirlam, "The Petroleum Industry," in Walter Adams, ed., *The Structure of American Industry* (Third ed.; New York: Macmillan, 1961), pp. 290–293.

[59]Cf. Leonard W. Weiss, *Economics and American Industry* (New York: Wiley, 1963), p. 143.

changes are the standard means of keeping inventories in check.[60]

In sum, the ability of oligopolistic industries to maintain price structures which maximize joint profits evidently depends significantly upon inventory and order backlog policies. By letting inventories and order backlogs fluctuate, producers can adjust to short-term demand shifts in a way which minimizes the threat to industry pricing discipline, although this strategy carries a concomitant risk that under pressure the faint-hearted will dump excessive stocks at disruptive prices. Variations in inventories and backlogs also provide a feedback mechanism to supplant the orthodox profit maximization calculus in guiding production decisions under conditions of oligopolistic interdependence. Much more research is needed on these aspects of oligopoly behavior.

CONCLUSION

Let us try now to tie together the principal lessons emerging from this survey. Any realistic theory of oligopoly must take as a point of departure the fact that when market concentration

[60]*A Behavioral Theory of the Firm*, p. 140.

is high, the pricing decisions of sellers are interdependent, and the firms involved can scarcely avoid recognizing their mutual interdependence. If they are at all perceptive, the managers of oligopolistic firms will recognize too that profits will be higher when cooperative policies are pursued than when each firm looks only after its own narrow self-interest. As a result, we should expect oligopolistic industries to exhibit a tendency toward the maximization of collective profits, approximating the pricing behavior associated with pure monopoly. Still coordination of pricing policies to maximize joint profits is not easy, especially when cost and market share disparities engender conflicting price and output preferences among industry members. Factors conducive to cooperation include free and rapid inter-firm communication, repetitive transactions, the cultivated expectation that price cuts will be promptly countered, the willingness of industry members to substitute inventory and order backlog fluctuations for hair-trigger price adjustments, and reliance upon order and inventory feedback signals instead of myopic marginal rules as guides to output determination.

Chapter 6

Conditions Facilitating Oligopolistic Coordination

Our first approximation to a theory of oligopolistic pricing predicts a tendency toward the maximization of collective industry profits. Yet adoption of joint profit maximizing policies is not automatic or easy, especially when industry members have diverse and conflicting opinions about the most favorable price structure. How do oligopolists arrive at mutually satisfactory prices for their products? What processes of coordination and communication operate to resolve conflicts? In this chapter we examine four important institutions facilitating oligopolistic coordination: overt and covert agreements, price leadership, rules of thumb, and the use of focal points.

OVERT AND COVERT AGREEMENTS

Collusion to secure monopolistic prices and profits is a venerable, if not venerated, institution. It was practiced in ancient Babylon, Greece, and Rome. Adam Smith remarked sagely that "People of the same trade seldom meet together, even for merriment and diversion, but the conversation ends in a conspiracy against the public, or in some contrivance to raise prices." In the United States nearly every form of agreement, open or secret, to fix prices or restrict output is illegal, but dozens of violations are prosecuted each year, and countless others

go undetected. As one executive involved in the electrical equipment conspiracy of the 1950s observed, price-fixing is "a way of life" for many American businessmen.[1] Until recently, European laws were more tolerant of price-fixing arrangements, and as a result cooperative activity on the Continent has been more readily visible to the naked eye. During the early 1930s nearly all raw materials and semifinished goods production and at least a fourth of all finished goods manufacturing in Germany were covered by formal restrictive arrangements.[2] A government commission found 136 formal horizontal price-fixing cartels in force during 1953 in tiny Switzerland.[3] And despite a bias toward secrecy inspired by fear of antitrust prosecution under Article 85 of the European Economic Community treaty, firms doing business in the Common Market had by 1967 registered several hundred horizontal price-fixing cartels with the EEC Commission.

The variety of collusive pricing arrangements in industry is limited only by the bounds of human ingenuity. Some are casual and short-lived, e.g., the spontaneous meetings called to terminate price wars. Others endure for decades, held together by an elaborate organizational web and binding written contracts. Here only the most important species can be identified.

---

[1] R. A. Smith, "The Incredible Electrical Conspiracy," *Fortune*, May 1961, p. 224.

[2] Fritz Voigt, "German Experience With Cartels and Their Control During Pre-War and Post-War Periods," in J. P. Miller, ed., *Competition, Cartels, and Their Regulation* (Amsterdam: North Holland, 1962), p. 183.

[3] Corwin D. Edwards, *Cartelization in Western Europe* (Washington: U. S. Department of State, June 1964), p. 3.

158

Social gatherings are an occasion for one of the least structured, but not ineffective, forms of collusion. A well-known example was the Gary dinners held by Judge Elbert H. Gary, chairman of U. S. Steel's board of directors, during the early years of this century. Judge Gary once explained that the "close communication and contact" developed at these dinners generated such mutual "respect and affectionate regard" among steel industry leaders that all considered the obligation to cooperate and avoid destructive competition "more binding . . . than any written or verbal contract."[4] A more modern variant is the trade association convention held in a resort hotel, where members who have been cutting prices are alternately browbeaten, plied with martinis, and cajoled until they promise to adopt a more 'gentlemanly' stance in the future.

Informal gentlemen's agreements are also reached on a wide range of specific issues and practices. The best-known examples are, of course, agreements to set and abide by particular prices. If this is impractical, emphasis may be placed on securing mutual adherence to pricing formulas or lists of 'representative' prices published by trade associations. When product lines are very complex, firms often find it advantageous to collude on specific product details and on the handling of extras. Until recently, for instance, American steel producers were fairly successful in abjuring price competition on standard products without resorting to formal collusion. But they found it far more difficult tacitly to coordinate prices for the virtually infinite gradations in finish, temper, gauge, packaging, and the like requested on special order by individual customers. As a result, company representatives held covert meetings to agree on uniform standards, specifications, interpretations, and charges for extras.[5] Or to cite a more ludicrous example, the International Air Transport Association, which fixes passenger fares on most of the international airline routes, had to meet in plenary session in 1958 to define "sandwich," and in 1966 many hours of debate preceded the decision to raise the surcharge for in-flight motion pictures. Finally, businessmen may meet in smoke-filled rooms to agree on output limitations, market shares, or specific geographic areas or product lines to be regarded as each firm's exclusive sphere of interest. Spheres of interest agreements have been especially popular among giant international chemical producers as a means of restricting competition.[6]

Nearly all these dimensions of collusion were present in the electrical equipment conspiracy of the 1950s—the most spectacular case of illegal collusion in several decades of American antitrust experience.[7] It involved at least 29 different companies selling turbine generators, transformers, switchgear, insulators, industrial controls, condensers, and other electrical equipment with total sales of roughly $1.5 billion annually. Although agreements to limit competition have been a recurrent feature of the electrical industry since the 1880s, the schemes of the 1950s were given specific impetus when repeated episodes of price warfare proved incompatible with top management demands for higher profits. Several collusive systems evolved, each tailored to the peculiar demands of the particular product line and selling method.

On standardized products such as insulators, standard transformers, and industrial controls, company representatives met and agreed upon prices which each promised to quote in all subsequent transactions until an agreement to change was reached. This was by far the simplest arrangement, but it suffered from the disadvantage of arousing suspicions when all firms sub-

---

[4]From a government antitrust brief cited in Fritz Machlup, *The Political Economy of Monopoly* (Baltimore: Johns Hopkins Press, 1952), p. 87.

[5]"Steel Gets Hit with the Big One," *Business Week*, April 11, 1964, pp. 27–28. Although the accused firms denied their guilt at the time, in July 1965 they pleaded 'no contest,' which in a criminal antitrust case involving large firms is tantamount to an admission of guilt. See also G. W. Stocking, "The Rule of Reason, Workable Competition, and Monopoly," *Yale Law Journal*, July 1955, p. 1132.

[6]Cf. G. W. Stocking and M. W. Watkins, *Cartels in Action* (New York: Twentieth Century Fund, 1946), Chapters 9–11.

[7]Cf. Smith, *op. cit., Fortune*, April and May, 1961; J. G. Fuller, *The Gentlemen Conspirators* (New York: Grove, 1962); and John Herling, *The Great Price Conspiracy* (Washington: Luce, 1962).

mitted identical bids in repeated transactions. A more complex approach was required for products such as turbine generators, since each buyer demands modifications to suit his own special needs, and as a result no two orders are ever exactly alike. Collusion in this case was facilitated by the publication of a pricing formula book half the size of a Sears Roebuck catalogue. By piecing together the prices of each component required to meet a buyer's generator specifications, firms were able to arrive at the 'book price' on which discussions centered.

Some of the most elaborate procedures were devised to handle switchgear pricing. As in the case of generators, book prices served as the initial departure point. Each seller agreed to quote book prices in sales to private buyers, and meetings were held regularly to compare calculations for forthcoming job quotations. Sealed-bid competitions sponsored by government agencies posed a different set of problems, and new methods were worked out to handle them. Through protracted negotiation, each seller was assigned a specified share of all sealed-bid business, e.g., General Electric's share of the high voltage switchgear field was set at 40.3 per cent in late 1958, and Allis-Chalmers' at 8.8 per cent. Participants then coordinated their bidding so that each firm was low bidder in just enough transactions to gain its predetermined share of the market. In the power switching equipment line, this was achieved for a while by dividing the United States into four quadrants, assigning four sellers to each quadrant, and letting the sellers in a quadrant rotate their bids. A 'phases of the moon' system was used to allocate low-bidding privileges in the high voltage switchgear field, with a new seller assuming low-bidding priority every two weeks. The designated bidder subtracted a specified percentage margin from the book price to capture orders during its phase, while others added various margins to the book price. The result was an ostensibly random pattern of quotations, conveying the impression of independent pricing behavior.

There is no question that prices and profits were elevated substantially through the electrical equipment conspiracy when it operated successfully. Yet durable success is by no means assured under informal restrictive arrangements. Indeed, the electrical equipment case illustrates vividly the fragility of non-binding collusive agreements, for parties to the agreements of the 1950s 'cheated' repeatedly, touching off bitter price wars. As one General Electric executive explained his group's decision to go its own independent way in 1953, "No one was living up to the agreements and we . . . were being made suckers. On every job some one would cut our throat; we lost confidence in the group."[8]

Two problems underlie the tendency for informal price-fixing and output-restricting agreements to break down. First, the parties to the conspiracy may have divergent ideas about appropriate price levels and market shares, making it difficult to reach an understanding which all will respect. Second, when the group agrees to fix and abide by a price approaching monopoly levels, strong incentives are created for individual members to cheat—that is, to increase their profits by undercutting the fixed price slightly, gaining additional orders at a price which still exceeds marginal cost. These two problems often interact, for parties dissatisfied with the original agreement may be especially prone to cheat in its subsequent execution.

The first of these difficulties has already been raised in the previous chapter. Hard bargaining lubricated by hard liquor cannot eliminate differences in firms' price and output preferences due to cost and market share disparities; it can only provide a favorable environment for compromise, if compromise is possible at all. Because price-fixing negotiations are usually conducted in secrecy, we have little evidence on the amount of internal stress encountered in establishing agreements. But there are indications that it is considerable. In the electrical equipment conspiracy, for example, there were conflicts over pricing policy between the high- and low-cost producers, and over market shares between the bigger firms and two smaller firms—one a new entrant. Both disputes were resolved only when General Electric and Westinghouse made concessions to

[8]Smith, *op. cit.*, April 1961, p. 172, quoting Clarence Burke.

save the agreement. Some of the richest insights have been provided by Bjarke Fog from interviews with company officials involved in six price-fixing agreements legal under the Danish laws.[9] Fog found that agreements were not easily reached; that negotiations were characterized by "reciprocal suspicion and distrust" concerning others' prices and motives; and that in two cases negotiations broke down completely even though agreement would have been to the mutual benefit of all industry members. Disparities in cost were one source of disagreement, as the pure theory predicts. Fog observed in addition that differences over broad policy—i.e., whether to take a long-run or short-run approach—were an even more important hurdle. In the industries he studied, the smaller firms generally preferred to make the most of short-term possibilities, while larger firms advocated a longer-range pricing perspective.

Given the difficulty of agreeing, there is a propensity for changes to be avoided once agreements are reached. The International Air Transport Association, for example, has been continuously divided into two camps: members preferring low transatlantic fares to encourage high volume, and those favoring high fares. Since the Association by-laws require that fare changes be approved unanimously, the result—at least up to 1969—was a perpetuation of the status quo. Changes were for the most part confined to such peripheral matters as jet surcharges, motion picture fees, and the definition of a sandwich. In his study of Danish cartels, Fog uncovered an extreme case in which a key product's price was left unchanged for a decade, despite rising costs and disappearing profits. Parties to the agreement were reluctant to suggest a price increase for fear of appearing weak to their confederates.

Once agreement has been reached, a different set of problems arises. The very act of fixing the price at a monopolistic level creates incentives to expand output beyond that quantity which will sustain the agreed-upon price. If a firm sells only a modest fraction of the total output, it may consider the price to be truly parametric—that is, not perceptibly affected by its own output decisions. As a result, it may choose to break formally or informally with the agreement, quoting a slightly lower price and expanding output until its marginal cost rises almost to the level of the fixed price. Of course, if every firm were to behave in this manner, the price will descend from the agreed-upon monopoly value to the level of all producers' combined marginal cost, where no further incentive for output expansion remains.[10] However short-sighted such undercutting may be, it has been known to topple many a price-fixing scheme. An additional hazard, to be analyzed in Chapter 8, is the lure a high price holds for new entrants. The added output contributed by such entrants either drives down the price immediately, or it forces parties to the original agreement to restrict their own outputs in defending the price, and this in turn can evoke such dissatisfaction among the original producers that they choose to abandon the agreement. In his study of German cartels, Fritz Voigt found that a combination of cheating, bickering among insiders, and new entry from outsiders caused numerous price-fixing agreements to be short-lived, breaking down after periods of operation as short as a few months.[11]

Despite these difficulties faced by groups seeking to restrict competition, we cannot conclude that explicit collusion is necessarily ineffective or unsuccessful. An agreement successful over even a short period can yield monopoly profits sufficient to make the effort worth while. Furthermore, many businessmen are farsighted enough to recognize that their long-run interests are served best by maintaining industry discipline, and this may be enough to inhibit widespread price-shading. Finally, it is often possible (especially in nations with weak antitrust laws)

---

[9] "How Are Cartel Prices Determined?" *Journal of Industrial Economics*, November 1956, pp. 16–23.

[10] For an ingenious mathematical analysis of pricing strategies by which a cartel can deter specific firms from cheating, see Daniel Orr and Paul W. MacAvoy, "Price Strategies To Promote Cartel Stability," *Economica*, May 1965, pp. 186–197. The main weakness in their analysis is that almost any firm may be a cheater, and if all recognize the symmetric incentive for cheating, deterministic solutions lose their compelling character.

[11] *Op. cit.*, pp. 169–208.

to formalize restrictive agreements in such a way as to reduce greatly the incentives for cheating.

An approach particularly popular because of its effectiveness and compatibility with antitrust policies is the insertion of restrictive provisions into patent licenses. Several types of restriction are possible when one firm or (outside the United States) several firms jointly hold a strong patent position. First, the entry of new sellers can be blocked by refusal to grant licenses. Second, each licensee can be restricted to a specific geographic territory or segment of the market. Third, the price of the patented product can be specified as one of the license terms.[12] And fourth, direct or indirect output restrictions can be incorporated in the licensing agreement. A potent way of damping licensees' incentive to expand output by shading prices is to combine quota restrictions with punitive royalty provisions. For example, during the 1930s Westinghouse's license to General Electric's incandescent lamp improvement patents stipulated a royalty of 2 per cent for sales by Westinghouse up to 25.4421 per cent of the two firms' combined sales, but the royalty rate increased to 30 per cent for sales exceeding this quota.[13] Similarly, du Pont's moistureproof cellophane patent license to Sylvania during the 1930s prescribed a punitive royalty rate of 30 per cent or more for sales exceeding some predetermined share of the total cellophane market.[14]

When patent protection is lacking, output restrictions may be enforced through various other formal cartel agreements. One approach is the so-called compulsory cartel, under which a government agency imposes binding production and marketing restrictions upon individual firms. The first true modern cartels (dating back to the late 18th century) were of this type, and governments (including that of the United States) have over the years continued to encourage output restriction in some industries, particularly for raw materials such as petroleum, tobacco, coal, sugar, tin, tea, coffee, and rubber.[15] If national laws permit, industry members may enter voluntarily into formal cartel agreements prescribing penalty payments when output quotas are exceeded. Excess production penalties were a prominent feature of the European steel and aluminum cartels following World War I.[16] As a third possibility, work week limitations written into labor contracts through collective bargaining may be used as a means of restricting output. This approach was successful in the U. S. flat glass industry during the 1920s.[17] The United Mine Workers have been accused of similar attempts in the bituminous coal industry, although the evidence is disputed.[18]

A cartel tightens its control over member prices and outputs if it can require all members to distribute their output through a central industry sales bureau. During the depression of the 1930s, soft coal producers in the Appalachian Mountain region organized an exclusive selling agency with power to apportion sales and outputs among the 137 member firms.[19] European

---

[12]Patent license restrictions, and particularly price restrictions, lie in a grey area of American antitrust law. See U. S. Attorney General, *Report of the Attorney General's National Committee To Study the Antitrust Laws* (Washington: 1955), pp. 231–246.

[13]See G. W. Stocking and M. W. Watkins, *Cartels in Action*, pp. 304–362; and H. C. Passer, *The Electrical Manufacturers* (Cambridge: Harvard University Press, 1953), pp. 161–164.

[14]G. W. Stocking and W. F. Mueller, "The Cellophane Case and the New Competition," *American Economic Review*, March 1955, p. 43.

[15]G. W. Stocking and M. W. Watkins, *Cartels or Competition?* (New York: Twentieth Century Fund, 1948), Chapter 1.

[16]*Ibid.*, pp. 185–186; and R. F. Lanzillotti, "The Aluminum Industry," in Walter Adams, ed., *The Structure of American Industry* (Third ed.; New York: Macmillan, 1961), p. 192. For an analysis of the statics and dynamics of quota systems, see Fritz Machlup, *The Economics of Sellers' Competition* (Baltimore: Johns Hopkins Press, 1952), pp. 482–488.

[17]G. W. Stocking and M. W. Watkins, *Monopoly and Free Enterprise* (New York: Twentieth Century Fund, 1951), pp. 123–124.

[18]For conflicting views, see Almarin Phillips, *Market Structure, Organization and Performance* (Cambridge: Harvard University Press, 1962), p. 134; and Reed Moyer, *Competition in the Midwestern Coal Industry* (Cambridge: Harvard University Press, 1964), pp. 162–164.

[19]Phillips, *op. cit.*, pp. 125–132.

coal producers continue to distribute much of their output through centralized sales syndicates.[20]

A variant of the central sales bureau method adapted for products sold through 'competitive' bidding is the so-called bidding or tender cartel. The U. S. electrical manufacturers' conspiracy possessed many attributes of a bidding cartel, although it lacked formal, binding agreements and organization. The Water-Tube Boilermakers' Association agreement approved in 1959 by the British antitrust authorities is typical of formally organized bidding cartels.[21] When bids for steam generating boilers were requested by some buyer (such as the nationalized Central Electricity Generating Board), each member firm submitted to the association director a confidential quotation of the price at which it was willing to fill the order. Using a formula which compared recent with historical shares of the market, the director nominated one firm to undertake the job. The firm nominated could then adjust its quotation downward to meet the lowest quotation, and when the revised bids were officially tendered to the buyer, the nominated firm was usually the winner. Since nomination to be low bidder depended upon the past allocation of orders rather than price, there was no incentive for member firms to undercut each other's price quotations.

The ultimate in overt agreement, short of merging all producers into a monolithic monopoly, is the rationalization cartel. Rationalization, or integrated planning of production, is profitable when cost functions differ from firm to firm, or when not all plants in the industry can operate at minimum average cost in producing the output which maximizes joint profits.[22] In the former case profits can be increased by assigning to low-cost firms higher production quotas than high-cost firms. In the latter case it is profitable in the long run to shut down some plants completely. Both points are illustrated by the example presented in Chapter 5, where Firm 1 is a low-cost producer and Firm 2 a high-cost producer. The

outcomes of alternative price-output plans can be reconstructed as follows:

	Firm 1's Profits	Firm 2's Profits	Joint Profits
Each firm produces 1800 units; price = $128 per unit	$112,000	$ 73,600	$185,600
Each firm produces 1330 units; price = $147 per unit	$100,950	$ 86,667	$187,617
Rationalization, with Firm 1 producing 2500 units and Firm 2 750 units at a price of $135	$175,000	$ 40,000	$215,000

Joint profits are higher under a rationalization plan which takes advantage of Firm 1's lower costs than they are when the two firms share the market equally, setting either of the prices preferred from their individual myopic viewpoints. Nevertheless, Firm 2 will not go along with the rationalization scheme unless a profit-pooling agreement is reached, for it would be better off under either equal-shares approach than it would be retaining the profits from selling only its own rationalized production. Still Firm 1 would be well-advised to encourage profit-pooling, since it could transfer to Firm 2 as much as $63,000 of its profits under rationalization and still be as well off as under the equal-shares approach with its preferred price of $128. As a practical matter, a centralized sales bureau is normally required along with profit-pooling to operate a rationalization cartel successfully.

It should be noted further that if the fixed costs of $20,000 per period incurred with Firm 2's plant could be eliminated by shutting down the plant, further rationalization would be profitable. Given the assumed demand and cost conditions, profits of $220,000 would be realized by operating only Firm 1's plant, letting the monop-

[20]Voigt, *op. cit.*, p. 189.

[21]*In re Water-Tube Boilermakers' Agreement*, L.R., 1 R.P. 285 (1959).

[22]See Don Patinkin, "Multiple-Plant Firms, Cartels, and Imperfect Competition," *Quarterly Journal of Economics*, February 1947, pp. 173–205; and William Fellner, *Competition Among the Few* (New York: Knopf, 1949), pp. 191–197.

oly output of 3,000 units be sold at a price of $140 per unit. Again, Firm 2 would agree to this step only if it were assured a share of total profits at least equal to what it could earn by continuing to produce independently.

Yet even when joint profits are increased through rationalization and profit-pooling is feasible, it is by no means certain that high-cost firms will participate willingly. Agreeing to reduce one's output substantially, or to shut down completely, has been likened to disarming.[23] One never knows whether firms producing most of the output under rationalization will take advantage of their position in the future, demanding a higher share of total profits. Maintaining production capabilities intact is a good bargaining counter against such demands. As a result, few cartels have gone very far toward the rationalization of production, even when profit-pooling is accepted.[24]

To sum up, restrictive agreements can take many forms. Some approaches are more effective than others. None is completely free from the risk of breakdown. But the central tendency is to support prices higher than they would be under independent competitive conduct.

PRICE LEADERSHIP

The paramount problem for firms trying to make the best of an oligopolistic market structure is to devise and maintain communication systems which permit behavior to be coordinated in the common interest. The conflicts which inevitably arise must be resolved without resorting to price warfare. Adjustments to changes in demand and cost conditions must be made in a way which elicits unanimous consent and minimizes the risk that actions taken in the group's interest will be misinterpreted as self-seeking aggression. Collusion is communication par excellence, but it is generally illegal in the United States, and the tide of antitrust legislation is running against it in other industrialized nations. Businessmen have an understandable desire to find alternative means of coordinating their behavior without running afoul of the law. One such means (which lies in the grey area of American antitrust law) is price leadership.

Price leadership implies a set of industry practices or customs under which list price changes are normally announced by a specific firm accepted as the leader by others, who follow the leader's initiatives. Wide variations are possible in the stability of the price leader's position, the reasons for his acceptance as leader, his influence over other firms, and his effectiveness in leading the industry to prices which maximize group profits. It is conventional to distinguish three main types of price leadership: dominant firm leadership, collusive leadership, and barometric leadership.[25]

DOMINANT FIRM PRICE LEADERSHIP

The dominant firm case is really a digression from our main concern here, since it involves no problems of oligopolistic interdependence and coordination, at least in a static sense.[26] It is a

---

[23]Fellner, *op. cit.*, pp. 218–220 and 232.

[24]See John A. Howard, "Collusive Behavior," *Journal of Business*, July 1954, pp. 196–204, for an analysis of the degree to which rationalization was carried in certain British industries; and Edwards, *op. cit.*, pp. 6–32, for statistics on the number of profit-pooling and joint production agreements on the Continent. Unfortunately, Edwards' data do not reveal how far rationalization has proceeded in the industries where it has been attempted, although his brief summaries of industry practices suggest very little true rationalization.

An alternative explanation for the paucity of rationalization is that the benefits are modest; e.g., because cost conditions vary little from firm to firm, because long-run cost curves are flat (as suggested in Chapter 4), and because most firms in normal years run their plants at or near the level which minimizes average cost.

[25]This schema was proposed by Jesse W. Markham, expanding on an earlier proposal by George J. Stigler. See Stigler, "The Kinky Oligopoly Demand Curve and Rigid Prices," *Journal of Political Economy*, October 1947, pp. 444–446; and Markham, "The Nature and Significance of Price Leadership," *American Economic Review*, December 1951, pp. 891–905. For critical comments, see Alfred Oxenfeldt, "Professor Markham on Price Leadership," *American Economic Review*, June 1952, pp. 380–384; R. F. Lanzillotti, "Competitive Price Leadership: A Critique of Price Leadership Models," *Review of Economics and Statistics*, February 1957, pp. 55–64; and Joe S. Bain, "Price Leaders, Barometers, and Kinks," *Journal of Business*, July 1960, pp. 193–203.

[26]The dominant firm theory was originally developed by Karl Forchheimer, "Theoretisches zum unvollständigen Monopole," *Schmollers Jahrbuch*, 1908, pp. 1–12; and A. J. Nichol, *Partial Monopoly and Price Leadership* (Philadelphia: 1930).

useful digression, however, since it illustrates the diversity of price leadership forms, and since an examination of its dynamic properties (to be undertaken in Chapter 8) will yield new insight into the long-run pricing problems of cartels and jointly-acting oligopolies. The analysis also has considerable empirical relevance, since it was applicable at one time or another in such important industries as steel, tractors, tin cans, petroleum, rayon, and cigarettes.

Dominant firm price leadership occurs when an industry consists of one firm dominant in the customary sense of the word—i.e., controlling at least 50 per cent of total industry output—plus a 'competitive fringe' of firms, each too small to exert a perceptible influence on price through its individual output decisions. If the industry's product is homogeneous, firms comprising the fringe take the dominant firm's price as given, making the best of it by expanding their output up to the point where short-run marginal cost rises to equal the price. If the product is slightly differentiated, the price at which fringe members can sell as much as they please will be the dominant firm's announced price plus or minus some differential. The dominant firm's problem in either case is to choose the best price from its own viewpoint, taking into account the supply of the competitive fringe at whatever price it sets.

The solution is illustrated in Figure 6.1. The overall market demand curve is D'D. The supply curve for all members of the competitive fringe together is S'S. At the price OS', no output will be supplied by fringe members (because price is less than the minimum average variable cost of every fringe producer). As the dominant firm sets higher prices, firms in the fringe will find it profitable to produce more—at each possible announced price equating that price with their (rising) marginal costs. Knowing the competitive fringe supply curve S'S, the dominant firm knows how much of the market will be served by the fringe at any price, and hence how much is left over for it to serve. At prices of OS' and lower, it has the entire market to itself. At price OG, the competitive fringe supplies all the output the market will absorb at that price, with no residual demand left over for the dominant firm. Inter-

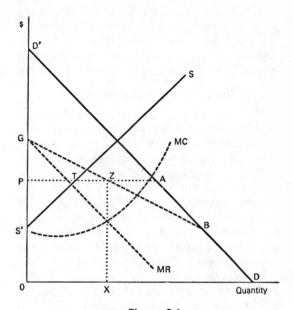

Figure 6.1
Equilibrium under Dominant Firm Price Leadership

mediate quantities of fringe supply are called forth at prices between OS' and OG, so that the dominant firm's own effective demand curve is the kinked curve GBD—found by subtracting from the total quantity demanded at a given price the amount supplied by the competitive fringe.

Given its residual demand curve GBD, the dominant firm derives its marginal revenue function GMR. It now maximizes its profits by producing that output OX where its marginal cost (represented by curve MC) equals marginal revenue, announcing the price OP which brings the quantity it produces into equilibrium with its demand schedule. That is, at the price OP, the dominant firm will produce and sell OX = PZ units, while the competitive fringe produces and sells ZA = PT units. The overall market will be in equilibrium with PA (= PZ + ZA) units supplied and PA units demanded.

This solution is strictly determinate, assuming that the dominant firm seeks to maximize its own profits during the period for which its demand

and cost functions are defined and that it can estimate those functions, however imperfectly, along with the competitive fringe supply functions. In this respect the dominant firm case differs from most oligopoly pricing problems.

COLLUSIVE PRICE LEADERSHIP

We return now to the messier world of oligopoly. The concept of collusive price leadership was formulated by Professor Markham to describe that type of price leadership especially apt to facilitate monopolistic price solutions. He elaborated five structural prerequisites for successful collusive leadership, but his list can be boiled down to two broad characteristics: industry members must recognize that their common interest in cooperative pricing behavior overrides any centrifugal aspirations toward independent behavior, and the principal firms together must have a significant amount of pricing discretion.

The cigarette industry during the 1920s and 1930s affords a classic example of price leadership used to establish a price structure which (barring miscalculations) tended to yield maximum collusive profits.[27] The Big Three, selling from 68 to 90 per cent of industry output, clearly recognized their mutual interdependence. High expenditures on product differentiation and the resultant brand acceptance made new entry difficult. There is no close substitute for cigarettes in the minds of most consumers, and so the cigarette manufacturers enjoyed considerable discretion in choosing the price of their product.

Between 1911 and 1921, conditions in the cigarette industry were unsettled due to several radical changes: the dissolution of the old Tobacco Trust in an antitrust action, the introduction of new tobacco blends, and the initiation of nationwide promotional campaigns. In 1918 American Tobacco tried to lead a price rise, but Reynolds (the largest seller) refused to follow. In 1921, American cut its price and Reynolds retaliated with a further cut, which American and the other sellers were forced to match. This

experience apparently had a profound educational impact on American and the other major brand sellers, none of whom challenged Reynolds' leadership again for a decade. Between 1923 and 1941, virtual price identity prevailed continuously among the 'standard' brands. During this period there were eight list price changes. Reynolds led six of them, five upward and one downward, and was followed each time, in most cases within 24 hours of its announcement. The other two changes were downward revisions during 1933 led by American and followed promptly by the other standard brand vendors. American also attempted to lead a price increase in 1941, but Reynolds again refused to follow and the change was rescinded. Throughout this period, the return on invested capital realized by Reynolds, American, and Liggett & Myers averaged 18 per cent after taxes—roughly double the rate earned by American manufacturing industry as a whole.

The one departure from Reynolds' leadership illustrates further the high degree of coordination displayed by the Big Three. Even the most astute price leaders make mistakes, and Reynolds made one in 1931. In June, as cigarette consumption was declining due to widespread unemployment and as leaf tobacco prices reached their lowest level since 1905, Reynolds announced an increase in the net wholesale price of Camels from \$5.64 to \$6.04 per thousand, or \$.1208 per pack—ostensibly to generate revenue for the promotion of its new moisture-proof cellophane package. The other leading producers followed immediately—American, allegedly, because it saw "the opportunity to make some money" and Liggett & Myers because its officers concluded that "safety lay in imitation."[28] But this increase, combined with the dire financial straits in which many cigarette smokers found themselves, opened up rich market penetration possibilities for firms selling cigarettes of inferior quality. With the standard brands selling at retail prices of up to \$.15 per pack, these "ten cent" brands increased their share of the market from 1 per

---

[27]See William Nicholls, *Price Policies in the Cigarette Industry* (Nashville: Vanderbilt University Press, 1951); and R. B. Tennant, "The Cigarette Industry," in Adams, *The Structure of American Industry*, pp. 357–392, for a more extensive analysis.

[28]Nicholls, *op. cit.*, pp. 84–85.

cent in early 1931 to 23 per cent in late 1932. In response, American cut its Lucky Strikes price from $6.04 to $5.29 per thousand in January 1933, and then to $4.85 per thousand (after wholesale discounts) in February 1933. Reynolds and Liggett followed immediately, this time without undercutting.[29] At the same time the Big Three put intensive pressure on retailers to keep the price differential between standard brands and the $.10 brands below $.03, and in some chain outlets the price of standard brands fell to $.10 per pack. The attack against the intruding ten cent brands was largely successful; their share of the market dropped from 23 per cent in November 1932 to 6 per cent in May 1933. Having recovered much of the lost ground, American and Liggett followed Reynolds' increase to $5.38 per thousand in January 1934.

Following World War II the pattern changed. Efforts by Liggett & Myers and (in 1965) Lorillard to lead price increases were persistently rebuffed. But American successfully led several increases, and thus came to share the leadership role with Reynolds. This change was apparently due in part to shifting patterns in sales volume, partly to the increasing complexity of cigarette product lines, and perhaps also to the antitrust judgment rendered against the Big Three in 1946. American moved into first place in total cigarette sales at about the time of its first successful upward price thrusts, only to fall behind Reynolds again later. Reynolds has typically led price changes for filter tips (which accounted for 70 per cent of its production in 1965), while American has dominated non-filter price-setting, where it is the volume leader. However, the pattern has not been perfectly consistent—possibly because sharp judicial censure of their prewar pricing caused the firms to recognize the political value of some diversity.

Size appears to be the variable most frequently distinguishing firms whose price changes (and especially price increases) are regularly followed from those whose initiatives are rejected. Thus, top sellers Reynolds and American share leadership in cigarettes; U. S. Steel has been the principal steel industry price leader; Alcoa has led most frequently in virgin aluminum; International Harvester in farm tractors and cultivators; American Viscose in rayon; du Pont in nylon and polyester fibers; and Continental Can first challenged American Can's traditional leadership only two years after its corporate sales surpassed those of American. But other influences also play some part. Historical circumstances, such as having been the first to introduce a new product, may permit a smaller firm to be accepted. In automobiles, General Motors is normally recognized as the price leader, but when its new model introduction dates lag those of rivals, Ford or Chrysler may be forced to make the first move—beating a hasty retreat if General Motors' subsequent price schedule contains some surprises.[30] The firm with the lowest costs may also be in an especially favorable position to exercise price leadership, since it has little incentive to follow high-cost firms up to a price higher than what it prefers, while they must follow it down or suffer market share erosion, unless it is operating at maximum capacity. Alcoa, for instance, is said to be the customary aluminum ingot price leader because of its low costs, although it also enjoys market share primacy and acceptance as the industry founder.[31] However, during most of its reign as price leader U. S. Steel was far from the lowest-cost producer. And in the British rubber tire industry, the price leader is Dunlop—the largest seller, but not the lowest-cost producer. Commenting on Dunlop's position, Thomas Wilson has suggested that price leadership will be accepted with less strain and embarrassment

---

[29]There is some inconclusive evidence that outright collusion occurred at this point in time. The night before American's second price cut announcement, the A&P Company's national headquarters telegraphed its 15,000 stores to reduce prices of *all* standard brands to $.10 per pack. In subsequent court testimony, A&P officials denied receiving advance notice, but said their action was based upon "trade rumors." Nicholls, *op. cit.*, pp. 119–120.

[30]U. S. Senate, Committee on the Judiciary, Subcommittee on Antitrust and Monopoly, Report, *Administered Prices: Automobiles* (Washington: 1958), pp. 61–76; "GM Sets Off Rollback in Prices," *Business Week*, October 1, 1966, p. 46; and "All Four Auto Makers End Up Matching Price Boosts," *Business Week*, October 5, 1968, p. 46.

[31]M. J. Peck, *Competition in the Aluminum Industry* (Cambridge: Harvard University Press, 1961), pp. 41–45 and 205–206.

when the price leader itself is a medium-cost producer.[32]

Whatever the reasons for a firm's acceptance as price leader, its leadership must be followed consistently and with near unanimity if the industry is to make the most of its market opportunities. Leadership is a means of communicating, and the process may break down if some messages go unheeded, so that one never knows what the reaction to a new price announcement will be.

The hazards of refusal to follow the leader are illustrated by the experience of the tin can industry during the late 1950s.[33] In September 1958, American Can announced a 6 per cent across-the-board price increase. Continental, which had skirmished with but not directly defied American's leadership in the past, decided not to match the change. Instead, it raised its prices only 3 per cent. American retaliated with price cuts ranging from 2 to 5 per cent, announcing in addition a completely new system of making price quotations. Continental matched the American reductions, and in subsequent months further rounds of price-cutting occurred. Thus, instead of securing higher can prices, as both producers apparently intended originally, the industry found itself in mid-1959 with prices as much as 10 per cent lower than they were a year earlier. The only ray of sunshine in this episode, at least for the can producers, was that the lower prices may have dissuaded some large container users from establishing their own integrated can manufacturing operations.

In recent years the discipline of certain industries with strong price leadership traditions has deteriorated noticeably, raising doubts whether leadership will be as effective an instrument of oligopolistic coordination in the future. The steel industry is the most prominent example.[34] For decades, the industry followed in lock step U. S. Steel's leadership on list prices, although some sub rosa shading off list prices occasionally took place. Then, in 1958, a general wage increase touched off a clamor in industry circles for higher prices, even though the industry as a whole was operating at only 61 per cent of capacity due to a recession. U. S. Steel, under attack from a congressional committee for inflationary wage and price behavior, failed to exercise the expected leadership. Finally Armco, with roughly 4.4 per cent of industry capacity, announced an increase, which was followed by U. S. and the rest of the industry.[35] For nearly four years no further general list price changes were attempted. Then, in 1962, U. S. Steel's announcement of a list price increase averaging $6 per ton drew withering criticism from President Kennedy, and eventually was rescinded. This experience apparently dampened U. S. Steel's zeal for bearing the burden of price leadership. The following year price increases were announced on a product-by-product (as opposed to across-the-board) basis in numerous product lines by several smaller producers. The typical reaction of U. S. was to follow with a slightly smaller increase in its own list prices, causing the original leaders to revise their quotations downward and fall into line. Price revisions through 1968 continued to be made on a piecemeal basis, with the initiative coming from several different companies. When U. S. did exercise leadership, it announced cuts mixed with increases, displaying a "new diplomacy" which contrasted vividly with the "bludgeon" approach employed up to 1962.[36]

---

[32]"Restrictive Practices," in J. P. Miller, ed., *Competition, Cartels, and Their Regulation*, p. 135.

[33]Charles H. Hession, "The Metal Container Industry," in Adams, ed., *The Structure of American Industry*, *op. cit.*, pp. 449–451; James W. McKie, *Tin Cans and Tin Plate* (Cambridge: Harvard University Press, 1959), pp. 280–282; and "Canners Profit from Price War," *Business Week*, February 14, 1959, p. 56.

[34]Other unprecedented breaks in industry pricing discipline occurred in the British steel industry and the U. S. tobacco industry, both during April of 1966.

[35]For a more complete discussion of this episode, see Leonard W. Weiss, *Economics and American Industry* (New York: Wiley, 1961), p. 294.

[36]See "U. S. Steel Lifts Prices on Most Types of Plate But Also Trims Quotes on Some Other Items," *Business Week*, March 5, 1966, p. 44; "Did Prices Rise? Steel Users Ask," *New York Times*, September 2, 1965; "Steel Price Step a 3-Prong Attack," *New York Times*, October 17, 1965, Section 3; "U. S. Steel Proves It's the Leader," *Business Week*, December 16, 1967, p. 34; and "Calling the Shots on Steel Prices," *Business Week*, August 10, 1968, pp. 26–27.

By adopting this new and more subtle approach to pricing, the steel industry has managed to stay out of political hot water. In the process, however, it has acquired new problems. With price leadership being passed from hand to hand and with price changes announced almost monthly in some product line, the danger of coordination breakdowns grew. By 1968 the strains could no longer be suppressed. Lacking strong leadership and under mounting pressure from imports, which had captured nearly 20 per cent of the American market, steel producers began to engage in increasingly widespread sub rosa price cutting. This was not unprecedented, but another development was. As its domestic market share fell to an all-time low of 21 per cent, U. S. Steel abandoned its traditional policy of holding list prices inviolate and joined the 'chiselers,' offering substantial secret concessions to a number of buyers.[37] The once-rigid steel price structure began to crumble.

These developments led headlong into one of the most fascinating episodes in steel industry history.[38] On November 4, 1968, Bethlehem Steel announced a 22 per cent cut in the list price of hot-rolled steel sheets, from $113.50 per ton (excluding extra charges) to $88.50 per ton. Its action, covering a product line accounting for 11 per cent of total industry output, was evidently provoked by an under-the-counter offer U. S. Steel made to a major Bethlehem customer. In its announcement, Bethlehem asserted that the reduction was effected "in spite of rising costs to meet current domestic competition." "Prices should go up, not down," the statement continued, but "Bethlehem must be competitive." Within three days all significant producers had joined in the decrease. Three weeks later

U. S. Steel in effect sued for peace, quoting a new price of $125.00 per ton for fully-processed hot-rolled steel sheet and simultaneously creating a new semi-finished product category, hot-rolled bands, to be priced at $110.00 per ton.[39] Bethlehem, however, waited nine days before responding. On December 6 it matched U. S. Steel's hot-rolled band price but raised its fully-processed product price to only $117.00 per ton. A week later U. S. Steel revised its price schedules to match the lower response. In February of 1969 Bethlehem then led an increase in prices to $124 per ton for hot-rolled bands and $129 per ton (or after adjustment for extra charge changes, $125) for fully-processed sheets. The price war was over. Bethlehem had communicated its message in the most vivid possible terms, and for the time being it apparently achieved its intended goal of restoring industry discipline. In March of 1969, when this chapter was revised, there were reports that sub rosa price cutting had dwindled, although it had not disappeared altogether.[40] The long-term ramifications remain to be seen.

When (under less strained circumstances) an oligopolist wishes to exercise price leadership in such a way as to command substantial compliance, it is likely to employ several time-tested tactics. First, it will not announce list price changes too frequently. Each move carries a risk that the change will be misinterpreted or opposed, with the further risk of a breakdown in industry discipline. Most oligopolists appear willing to forego the modest profit gains associated with micrometer-like adjustment of prices to fleeting changes in demand and costs in order to avoid the risk of more serious losses due to poorly coordinated pricing policies and price warfare. Second, the leader will announce

[37]Cf. "The Hedge Has Fewer Blossoms," *Business Week*, April 27, 1968, p. 40; "U. S. Steel Cuts Prices To Fight Import Boom, Dismaying Other Mills," *Wall Street Journal*, May 9, 1968, p. 1; and "Steel Pricing Shows Some Flexibility," *Business Week*, July 27, 1968, p. 71.

[38]Accounts of key developments include "Bethlehem Cuts Major Price 22%," *New York Times*, November 5, 1968, p. 67; "Steel Industry Hit By Major Price Cut," *Business Week*, November 9, 1968, p. 35; "U. S. Steel Moves To End Price War," *New York Times*, November 28, 1968, p. 75; "New Split Opens in Steel Pricing," *New York Times*, December 7, 1968, p. 73; "Revolution in Steel Pricing?" *Business Week*, December 14, 1968, p. 41; "Bethlehem Cuts Steel Sheet List," *New York Times*, February 5, 1969, p. 47; and "Steel Heads Up Again," *Business Week*, February 8, 1969, p. 27.

[39]The $125.00 price is not directly comparable with the earlier $113.50 price because it included some elements which had previously been priced as "extras." According to the U. S. Steel announcement, the new $125.00 price approximately restored the *status quo ante bellum*.

[40]"Steelmen Pick Up a Boomlet," *Business Week*, March 22, 1969, pp. 40–41. But see "Dr. Bethlehem's New Steel Formula," *Business Week*, November 15, 1969, p. 39.

changes only in response to significant changes in cost and demand conditions recognized throughout the industry. During the 1950s, for example, steel price increases normally coincided with industry-wide wage increases, while list price cuts announced by U. S. Steel during the 1930s were made in response to widespread, depression-induced sub rosa price shading. Third, the leader will prepare other firms for its announcement by directing public attention to the changed demand or cost conditions through executive speeches, interviews with trade publications, and the like. The steel industry's use of this technique prior to its 1958 price rise prompted one government official to suggest that a new form of "conspiracy through newspaper announcements" was underway.[41] Fourth, it may punish firms which challenge its leadership by refusing to follow their price increases and by undercutting their price reductions. This tactic was pursued by Reynolds Tobacco in the early 1920s, by American Can in 1958, and by an unidentified firm studied by Cassady whose practice in price wars was "not to quit promptly when the opponent cried 'uncle' " in order to deter any subsequent challenges to its leadership.[42]

A final question of tactics price leaders must resolve is whether to announce price changes most favorable from their own narrow viewpoints, or to build a price structure which compromises conflicting interests within the industry. A low-cost firm may increase its profits by leading the industry to its preferred low price, but it risks goading dissatisfied rivals into aggressive moves which may drive the price below every producer's preferred level. Little solid evidence is available on what price leaders actually do when such conflicts arise. According to

Peck, Alcoa has tended to impose its low-price preference on other firms in the American aluminum industry.[43] However, Kaplan, Dirlam, and Lanzillotti suggest that price leaders, including Alcoa, temper their price policies in order to suppress intra-industry conflicts.[44]

BAROMETRIC PRICE LEADERSHIP

Although it is difficult to sort actual cases into neat piles, many economists have followed Markham in distinguishing conceptually between collusive and barometric price leadership. The distinction turns on both conduct and performance criteria. In the performance domain, price leadership has been called collusive if it facilitates the attainment of monopolistic prices, while it is barometric if it does not. We shall see that this distinction is not very useful operationally, and it may have negative utility when used carelessly to stereotype market practices as either good (i.e., legal) or bad. Barometric leadership is said also to exhibit certain behavioral characteristics not generally found in the purely collusive case.

For one, the identity of the barometric price leader occasionally changes. In copper, for example, leadership may be exercised at a given time by any of the Big Three—Anaconda, Kennecott, or Phelps Dodge. In rayon yarn, the largest producer, American Viscose, led only about three fourths of all price changes between 1926 and 1949. Du Pont (the second largest seller) accounted for most of the others, including several price increases.[45] Similarly, Armstrong led only about half of all price changes in the hard-surface floor coverings field, the remaining initiatives being distributed among several smaller rivals.[46] By this criterion alone, it should be noted, we would have to classify price leader-

---

[41] *Washington Post*, February 24, 1963, p. E-1, quoting Victor R. Hansen's testimony before the Kefauver committee. See also B. Fog, *Industrial Pricing Policies: An Analysis of Pricing Policies of Danish Manufacturers* (translated by I. E. Bailey; Amsterdam: North Holland, 1960), pp. 139–140.

[42] Ralph Cassady, Jr., *Price Warfare in Business Competition* (East Lansing: Michigan State University, 1963), p. 7.

[43] *Competition in the Aluminum Industry*, pp. 41 and 205–206.

[44] A. D. H. Kaplan, J. B. Dirlam, and R. F. Lanzillotti, *Pricing in Big Business: A Case Approach* (Washington: Brookings, 1958), pp. 269–270.

[45] Cf. J. W. Markham, "The Nature and Significance of Price Leadership"; and *Competition in the Rayon Industry* (Cambridge: Harvard University Press, 1952), pp. 84–86.

[46] See Lanzillotti, "Competitive Price Leadership," pp. 55–64.

ship in the postwar cigarette industry and in steel since 1958 as barometric—a doubtful inference indeed.

Second, barometric price leaders are not always followed, presumably because they lack the power to coerce others into accepting their price decisions. Or if they are followed, acceptance may be delayed while other firms pursue a wait-and-see strategy. In cellophane, for instance, the typical practice is for Avisco to initiate a price increase, with du Pont quoting a smaller increase in response, forcing Avisco to reduce its original quotation.[47] In rayon the average lag between initiation and matching of price increases was ten days, and occasionally lags of three weeks occurred.[48]

Third, it is said that barometric price leaders often exercise leadership only in a *de jure* sense, making known through formal list price announcements changes which have already pervaded the industry through informal departures from the list price. This tendency holds with special force for price decreases. For instance, the practices of Standard Oil of Ohio, considered to be a barometric price leader in its home territory, were described as follows by one of its executives:

> . . . . The major sales executives of all companies watch carefully the number and size of subnormal markets. . . . If the number of local price cuts increases, if the number and amount of secret concessions to commercial consumers increase, if the secret unpublicized concessions to dealers increase, it becomes more and more difficult to maintain the higher prices. . . . Finally, some company, usually the largest marketer in the territory, recognizes that the subnormal price has become the normal price and announces a general price reduction throughout the territory.[49]

Similar practices have been observed in many other industries, such as rayon, copper, and fabricated asbestos products. List price increase announcements by barometric price leaders may also merely formalize *de facto* conditions, as in the copper industry, where list price hikes by the American Big Three typically lag behind developments on the London Metal Exchange and in domestic refined scrap markets during boom periods. More commonly, however, the barometric leader must exercise true leadership in effecting increases. This is brought out clearly in another Standard Oil of Ohio statement:

> On the other hand, in our own interest we must usually take the lead in attempting higher price levels when we believe that conditions will permit. Having a substantial distribution in our market we are confronted with the fact that few marketers, especially those with a lesser consumer acceptance, can take the lead in increasing prices.[50]

The same statement emphasizes that such initiatives may be rejected by the rest of the industry:

> . . . . Upward moves in our market are made by us only when, in our opinion, general prices and the economic pressure from industry costs are such that our competitors in their own interest will follow. It is notorious that when we guess wrong, or when we advance our market too far, immediate market disintegration sets in.

The interpretation given these leadership patterns—lowering the list price when market conditions are depressed, while raising it successfully only when demand and cost conditions support the higher level—is that the leader merely acts as a barometer of market conditions, and not as an instrument of collusion. As Professor Stigler put it, the barometric firm "commands adherence of rivals to his price only because, and to the extent that, his price reflects market conditions with tolerable promptness."[51]

Although more than one economist has earned a high consulting fee by doing so, it

[47]Kaplan, Dirlam, and Lanzillotti, *op. cit.*, p. 101.
[48]Markham, *Competition in the Rayon Industry*, pp. 86–88.
[49]Statement of S. A. Swensrud, quoted by Stigler in "The Kinky Oligopoly Demand Curve and Rigid Prices," p. 445. Copyright 1947 by the University of Chicago.
[50]Edmund P. Learned and Catherine C. Ellsworth, *Gasoline Pricing in Ohio* (Boston: Harvard Business School, 1959), p. 25, quoting a company policy statement. See also pp. 42 and 83 of the same volume.
[51]*Op. cit.*, pp. 445–446.

would be misleading to conclude that any leadership pattern which displays these characteristics is socially harmless. Consider first the matter of price increases. The price an industry can sustain obviously depends upon market conditions, as suggested in the theory of barometric leadership. But under given supply and demand conditions, alternative institutional arrangements may lead to different price levels. And here the institution of price leadership can be important. As the Standard Oil of Ohio statement quoted previously indicates, even when market conditions are firm, producers with weak market positions might be unable successfully to increase price. An accepted price leader like Standard can lead the way to prices higher than those attainable if no such firm existed. This price may not be *much* higher, but there is no guarantee that it will not exceed the competitive level by at least a small amount on the average.

Consider too the classic symptom of barometric price leadership: when the price leader reduces its list price only because sub rosa departures from the list price have permeated the industry. This is also not necessarily harmless. By making a firm and dramatic list price cut, the price leader can often restore industry discipline and discourage further price-cutting. It achieves this result in two ways: by providing a rallying point at which prices can be held, and by raising the implicit threat that further off-list pricing will incite additional list price reductions, constraining even more the opportunities for profitable operation. The latter was no doubt what Bethlehem had in mind with its hot-rolled steel price cut of 1968. Similar actions had been taken by U. S. Steel during the depressed 1930s with the acknowledged intent of ending market deterioration.[52] And in 1965 du Pont decreased its list price for polyester staple fibers by 14 per cent in response to sub rosa price shading by rivals. Industry sources reported that by making this change in one fell swoop, du Pont had placed the price where it was not likely to be undercut again.[53]

The difficulty of distinguishing between collusive and barometric price leadership is illustrated forcefully by events in the aluminum industry. Alcoa has attempted to exercise active price leadership in both ingot and fabricated product lines. It has generally preferred ingot prices lower than the levels favored by its domestic rivals and has several times refused to follow their upward initiatives, but on other occasions, especially when operation at full capacity prevented it from making any incursion into rival market shares, Alcoa followed price increases by the smaller firms. The situation during 1963 and 1964 is particularly interesting. Kaiser announced a price increase in December 1963 and Reynolds one in January 1964, but both times Alcoa refused to go along, stating that higher ingot prices would not be in the best interest of the industry.[54] However, two months later it partially met an increase in the world price by Aluminium, Ltd., of Canada, and after an additional two months it followed Olin-Mathieson in raising the domestic price to the world level. Meanwhile Alcoa was trying hard to increase fabricated aluminum prices—partly because more than 85 per cent of its ingot production is utilized internally for its own fabricated products, and partly because it was under court order from an antitrust judgment to avoid a squeeze between fabricated and ingot prices adversely affecting independent fabricators. After efforts to lead the way to higher fabricated product prices encountered only partial success, Alcoa in December 1963 issued a public statement threatening other members of the industry with across-the-board retaliatory list price cuts unless secret promotional price-shading on individual items ceased.[55] The threat was carried out seven weeks later, and further list price re-

[52]Kaplan, Dirlam, and Lanzillotti, *op. cit.*, pp. 167, 170. See also Weiss, *Economics and American Industry*, p. 295.

[53]"Du Pont Price Cut Sweeps Industry," *New York Times*, January 19, 1965.

[54]"Alcoa Holds Line on Ingot Price, Kaiser Backs Off," *Wall Street Journal*, December 9, 1963. For similar developments in 1969, see "Producers Raise Aluminum Prices," *New York Times*, August 7, 1969, p. 47; and "Aluminum Ingot in Price Rollback," *New York Times*, August 9, 1969, p. 31.

[55]"Trying Hard To Untangle a Price Snarl," *Business Week*, December 7, 1963, p. 81.

ductions were announced by Alcoa in subsequent months.[56] Fabricated and mill product prices in fact firmed up and then were raised in late 1964 and early 1965, although it is difficult to tell whether these developments were due to changes in underlying demand conditions or to Alcoa's aggressive leadership.[57]

At any rate, it is clear that the prices of fabricated aluminum products were not depressed during the early 1960s for want of leadership. Alcoa tried hard to lead the way to higher price and profit levels. If it failed, the failure must be attributed not to the type of leadership exercised, but to underlying structural conditions—that is, to the absence of exploitable market power. This appears to be true more generally for firms described as barometric price leaders. Professor Learned, for example, observed that if Standard Oil of Ohio "had thought it could reasonably get more it would have tried to do so."[58] We are led to conclude that the intent of ostensibly barometric price leadership may be identical to the intent of collusive price leadership: maximization of joint industry profits. What varies is the value at which the maximum lies, dependent in turn on structural and other conditions to be examined further in Chapters 7 and 8.

THE EFFECTS OF PRICE LEADERSHIP IN OLIGOPOLY

To sum up, the effect of both collusive and barometric price leadership in oligopoly tends to be the establishment of prices higher than they would otherwise be, other things (such as market structure and the strength of demand) being held equal. This effect is achieved by sending to other members unambiguous signals indicating the way toward the profit-maximizing price in good times and a rallying point in depressed times. Only two important exceptions must be noted. First, when the price leader in a concen-

trated industry like primary aluminum has lower costs, it may hold the price below levels desired by other firms. And second, strong price leaders may occasionally resist raising prices to the short-run profit-maximizing level during a boom, partly because long-run profits might be reduced by exploiting temporary conditions to the utmost and partly as an act of economic statesmanship (e.g., to cooperate with the government in combatting inflation).[59] Taking this latter qualification into account, we find that price leadership tends both to increase prices on the average and to reduce the magnitude of price fluctuations.

Price leadership also has implications for the kinked demand curve theory. For a firm whose leadership role is solidly established, the kink is eliminated, since the leader can expect its rivals to follow price increases as well as decreases. The kink remains, however, for firms (like Liggett & Myers) whose price increase initiatives are consistently rebuffed. They cannot expect to be followed upward, although they can usually expect their price cuts sooner or later to be matched. Finally, for barometric firms whose leadership is sometimes rejected, the kinked demand curve theory becomes an uncertain engine of analysis.

RULE-OF-THUMB PRICING AS A COORDINATING DEVICE

Another means of maintaining industry discipline when prices are set or changed is the use of pricing rules-of-thumb. These typically involve some variant of the full-cost or cost-plus pricing principle, in which a 'normal' or desired profit margin or percentage return on invested capital is added to estimated unit costs to calculate the product price. If all firms in an industry have similar costs and adhere to similar full cost

---

[56] "Aluminum's Paradox in Prices," *Business Week*, February 1, 1964, p. 21.

[57] For a suggestion that industry attitudes changed under Alcoa's tutelage, see "Metal of the Future Is Getting There," *Business Week*, June 24, 1967, p. 118. However, sub rosa price shading continues to occur. See "Aluminum Expects To Resume Its Climb," *Business Week*, December 16, 1967, pp. 142–144; "Aluminum Gleams with Hope," *Business Week*, December 21, 1968, pp. 24–25; "Where the Price Spiral Gets That Extra Twist," *Business Week*, April 5, 1969, pp. 18–19; and "Sparks Fly in Aluminum War," *Business Week*, May 10, 1969, p. 49. See also "Aluminum Frets Over Another Big Glut," *Business Week*, November 29, 1969, pp. 28–29.

[58] *Gasoline Pricing in Ohio*, p. 158.

[59] See, for example, Kaplan, Dirlam, and Lanzillotti, *op. cit.*, p. 271; and Joel Dean, *Managerial Economics* (Englewood Cliffs: Prentice-Hall, 1951), pp. 435–436. This phenomenon will be analyzed further in Chapters 12 and 13.

formulas, or if a price leader uses the formula and other firms accept its leadership, price-cutting below full cost levels is minimized, the behavior of rivals becomes more predictable than it otherwise would be, and efficient producers are virtually assured of realizing at least 'normal' profits.

Businessmen have apparently been using pricing rules of thumb for a long time, but the concept did not penetrate the main stream of economic analysis until it was discovered (along with the kinked demand curve) by R. L. Hall and Charles J. Hitch through an interview survey of pricing practices in 38 British firms.[60] Since then an enormous literature on the subject has appeared.[61]

Hall and Hitch and later analysts found several reasons why businessmen use cost-based rules of thumb in their pricing decisions. For one, it is a way of coping with (essentially by ignoring) uncertainties in the estimation of demand function shapes and elasticities. Second, many businessmen defend the practice on typically vague grounds of 'fairness.' Under closer scrutiny, this explanation appears sometimes to reflect the belief that a firm's long-run position will be jeopardized by charging too high a price in the short run, and sometimes the belief that all firms in an oligopolistic market benefit if each refrains from charging prices which provide less than a fair margin of profit over cost. Third, calculation and posting of prices are costly, especially for firms selling hundreds or thousands of different products with considerable turnover in the items sold. Adopting rules-of-thumb greatly simplifies the pricing problem in such businesses, of which department stores, automobile repair shops, and metal-working job shops are representative.

All sorts of full cost pricing rules are encountered. Here two examples must suffice. In the retail trades, a conventional pricing approach is to seek some standard percentage margin—e.g., 40 per cent—of price less cost over price. Knowing the wholesale cost W of an item, the indicated price is simply $W/(1 - .4)$. The 40 per cent margin in this case is not pure profit, since all selling and overhead expenses must be covered by the total margin realized from selling a vast array of items priced this way.

A quite different, well known full cost pricing rule is the technique used with evident success by General Motors for more than 40 years.[62] GM begins its pricing analysis with an objective of earning, on the average over the years, a return of approximately 15 per cent after taxes on total invested capital.[63] Since it does not know how many autos will be sold in a forthcoming year, and hence what the average cost per unit (including prorated overhead) will be, it calculates costs on the assumption of *standard volume*—that is, operation at 80 per cent of conservatively rated capacity. A *standard price* is next calculated by adding to average cost per unit at standard volume a sufficient profit margin to yield the desired 15 per cent after-tax return on capital. A top level price policy committee then uses the standard price as the initial basis of its price decision, making (typically small) adjustments upward or downward to take into account actual and potential competition, business conditions, long-run strategic goals, and other factors. During the depressed 1930s the quoted price was reduced below the standard price more frequently than it was raised. No evidence is available on postwar adjustment biases. The actual amount of profit realized also depends, of course, upon the number of vehicles actually sold. Since the end of

---

[60]"Price Theory and Business Behavior," *Oxford Economic Papers*, May 1939, pp. 12–45.

[61]For an excellent survey of the literature up to 1952, see Richard B. Heflebower, "Full Costs, Cost Changes, and Prices," in the National Bureau of Economic Research conference report, *Business Concentration and Price Policy* (Princeton: Princeton University Press, 1955), pp. 361–396.

[62]Cf. Donaldson Brown, "Pricing Policy in Relation to Financial Control," *Management and Administration*, 1924, pp. 195–198, 283–286, and 417–422; Albert Bradley, "Financial Control Policies of General Motors Corporation and Their Relationship to Cost Accounting," *National Association of Cost Accountants Bulletin*, January 1, 1927, pp. 412–433; H. B. Vanderblue, "Pricing Policies in the Automobile Industry," *Harvard Business Review*, Summer 1939, pp. 385–401; U. S. Senate, Committee on the Judiciary, Report, *Administered Prices: Automobiles* (Washington: 1958), pp. 104–130; and Kaplan, Dirlam, and Lanzillotti, *op. cit.*, pp. 48–55 and 131–135.

[63]A 15 per cent return on invested capital yields a return of roughly 20 per cent on GM's net worth. There is reason to believe that the profit target has been adjusted downward, since the Bradley article cited above suggests that the target yield on *total* capital in the 1920s was 20 per cent.

World War II unit sales have exceeded standard volume in most years, and so the realized return on invested capital has averaged well over the 15 per cent target rate.

Case studies reveal that the use of full cost pricing procedures is widespread. Only eight of the 38 firms in the Hall-Hitch sample indicated that they used no such rules. Half of the 20 large U. S. corporations studied by Kaplan, Dirlam, and Lanzillotti used some target return on investment approach to pricing major products.[64] In a study of 139 Danish firms, Fog found that most used some kind of full cost pricing scheme.[65] Cyert, March, and Moore were able with a simple wholesale cost markup rule to predict to the penny the prices actually charged for 188 out of 197 randomly selected items sold by a large department store.[66] At a more aggregative level, empirical studies of corporate income tax shifting provide modest support for the full cost hypothesis. Gordon, for example, found little shifting incompatible with strict profit maximization in manufacturing industry generally, but there was evidence of considerable shifting in the most concentrated industry sectors.[67] However, his and other analyses have suffered from such severe methodological and/or data limitations that the issue remains unsettled.

Most of the economic literature on full cost pricing has been addressed to the question: Does it contradict the profit maximization assumption of microeconomic theory? Since the time of Alfred Marshall, received doctrine has held that both demand and cost must be taken into account by a firm with market power to set the price which maximizes profits. Full cost pricing seems to consider only cost, ignoring the demand half of the Marshallian scissors. Early participants in the debate made their heresy explicit, arguing from observation that companies using full cost rules-of-thumb consciously abjured profit maximization, at least in any conventionally defined sense. According to Hall and Hitch, if maximum profits result at all from the application of full cost pricing, they do so "as an accidental (or possibly evolutionary) by-product."[68] Lanzillotti concluded on the basis of his joint research with Kaplan and Dirlam that profit maximization "is not the *dominant* motive of the firm, particularly the large corporate oligopoly."[69] Defenders of the traditional wisdom argued in reply that although full cost pricing methods appeared superficially to be inconsistent with the profit maximization rules of economic theory, they were in fact a profit-maximizing response to the complexities and uncertainties of business decision-making. Indeed, Kaplan, Dirlam, and Lanzillotti reported in their joint book that the business executives they interviewed doubted whether any change in pricing procedures would lead to higher profits.[70] Similarly, General Motors' stated policy in using its full cost pricing technique is to obtain "over a protracted period of time a margin of profit which represents the highest attainable return commensurate with capital turnover and the enjoyment of wholesale expansion, with adequate regard to the economic consequences of fluctuating volume."[71]

---

[64]*Op. cit.*, p. 130; and Lanzillotti, "Pricing Objectives in Large Companies," *American Economic Review*, December 1958, pp. 923 and 929. Similarly, half of some 88 very small firms interviewed by W. W. Haynes made at least some use of full cost rules. "Pricing Practices in Small Firms," *Southern Economic Journal*, April 1964, p. 320.

[65]B. Fog, *Industrial Pricing Policies*, p. 217.

[66]R. M. Cyert and J. G. March, *A Behavioral Theory of the Firm* (Englewood Cliffs: Prentice-Hall, 1963), pp. 146–147.

[67]Robert J. Gordon, "The Incidence of the Corporation Income Tax in U. S. Manufacturing, 1925–62," *American Economic Review*, September 1967, pp. 731–758. See also Marian Krzyzaniak and Richard A. Musgrave, *The Shifting of the Corporation Income Tax* (Baltimore: Johns Hopkins Press, 1963); and John G. Cragg et al., "Empirical Evidence on the Incidence of the Corporation Income Tax," *Journal of Political Economy*, December 1967, pp. 811–821.

[68]*Op. cit.*, pp. 18–19.

[69]"Pricing Objectives in Large Companies: Reply," *American Economic Review*, September 1959, p. 685 (his italics).

[70]*Pricing in Big Business*, p. 130. See also the review by Jesse W. Markham in the *American Economic Review*, June 1959, p. 474.

[71]Brown, *op. cit.*, p. 197. See also *Administered Prices: Automobiles*, p. 104.

To determine whether full cost pricing rules are compatible with profit maximization, three questions must be considered. First, does the application of the rules take into account differences in demand conditions between products? Second, is their application to a particular product adapted in the short run to changing demand conditions? And third, does the use of a full cost approach permit profit maximization in the long run, even though it might not make the most of market conditions at any moment in time?

A perhaps excessively rigid interpretation of the full cost doctrine implies that the percentage profit margin will be the same, whether demand is elastic or relatively inelastic. Is this consistent with economic theory? Suppose a firm plans to maintain a plant whose average total cost ATC (excluding profit) is minimized at the normal or average output. When profits are maximized, marginal cost MC = marginal revenue MR. It is readily shown that, where P is the price and e the demand elasticity:[72]

$$MR = P - P/e.$$

To maximize profits, we must have $MC = MR = P - P/e$. Rearranging, we obtain: $(P - MC)/P = 1/e$. Since $MC = ATC$ when ATC is at its minimum, we can substitute ATC into this expression, obtaining the equilibrium condition:

$$\frac{P - ATC}{P} = \frac{1}{e}.$$

The first term is the profit margin, expressed as a fraction of price.[73] The more elastic demand is, the lower the profit-maximizing profit margin will be. Firms maximizing their profits must apply lower percentage profit margins in pricing products with close substitutes (i.e., with highly elastic demands) than in pricing products whose demand is relatively inelastic, *ceteris paribus*.

Virtually all the recent evidence on full cost pricing practices shows that firms do not in fact apply rigid profit margins, regardless of demand conditions. They vary the margin to suit the product: the more elastic the demand, the lower the margin.[74] Or in some bizarre cases observed by Fog, they applied fixed margins, but juggled their cost allocations to achieve the same result.[75] In this respect, then, the evidence is consistent qualitatively with the profit maximization assumption.

The problem of short-run price and margin adjustments over the business cycle is more complicated, and a full analysis must be deferred to later chapters. Except under a standard volume rule of the General Motors type, unit *profit margins* will not decline in a recession if full cost pricing is scrupulously practiced, and they can increase under some full cost rules. Likewise, under all but a standard volume regime, we should expect full cost *prices* to rise in a recession, since fixed overhead must be prorated over a smaller unit volume. The evidence related to these predictions is mixed. Twelve of the 38 British businessmen interviewed by Hall and Hitch indicated that they would break away from full cost rules and cut prices in a severe recession, while an equal number insisted that they would adhere to the rules.[76] Fog found only 14 out of 67 firms unwilling to cut below calculated full costs when running at less than capacity.[77] Similarly mixed evidence on the behavior of U. S. firms

---

[72]Proof: Total revenue = $P \cdot Q$. Marginal revenue $MR = P + Q(dP/dQ) = P\left(1 + \dfrac{dP}{dQ}\dfrac{Q}{P}\right)$. Elasticity e is defined as $-\dfrac{dQ}{dP}\dfrac{P}{Q} = -\dfrac{1}{\dfrac{dP}{dQ}\dfrac{Q}{P}}$. Substituting this last expression for e into the expression for MR, we obtain $MR = P(1 - 1/e) = P - P/e$.

[73]The percentage margin over cost can be derived from this. It is $100\{[e \ / \ (e - 1)] - 1\}$. The more elastic demand is, the closer the margin over cost approaches zero.

[74]Fog, *Industrial Pricing Policies*, pp. 101–115 and 204–223; Heflebower, *op. cit.*, pp. 380–382; Cyert and March, *op. cit.*, pp. 138–145; Haynes, *op. cit.*, p. 318; Kaplan, Dirlam, and Lanzillotti, *op. cit.*, p. 173; and Weiss, *op. cit.*, p. 397.

[75]*Op. cit.*, pp. 65 and 98.

[76]*Op. cit.*, pp. 25–27.

[77]*Op. cit.*, p. 120.

during the 1930s and 1950s will be examined in Chapters 12 and 13. Some industrial pricing behavior over the cycle is apparently consistent with the full cost hypothesis; other behavior evidently is not.

One might suppose that observed departures from full cost pricing rules in times of especially weak or strong demand represent a profit-maximizing producer response. But this is true only in a narrow sense. Breaks in time of slack demand could instead reflect price warfare which reduces the profits of all firms (though it is initiated by companies myopically trying hard to increase their individual profits). By adhering rigidly to the rule, a firm no doubt fails to squeeze the most out of its profit-making opportunities at every moment in time.[78] Nor will a group of firms with effective methods of coordinating their prices and outputs maximize joint profits by slavish adherence. But in most real-world oligopolies, and particularly when legal prohibitions inhibit outright collusion, the old Russian adage that "the perfect is the enemy of the good" holds with special force. Poorly coordinated efforts to increase short-run profits under changing and uncertain demand and cost conditions can, through shortsightedness or misinterpretation, deteriorate into moves and countermoves which reduce rather than increase group profits. Faithful application of full cost rules, by improving coordination and discipline, virtually assures at least satisfactory profits over the long pull, even though gains may not be as high as they would be under impossibly perfect coordination. If by employing rules of thumb an industry does the best it can on the average under less than ideal conditions, we must conclude that the rules constitute an instrument of long-run profit maximization.

This conclusion is now widely accepted. It is supported *inter alia* by case study evidence.

Machlup observes that through the application of full cost pricing rules, cartels may "succeed in the maintenance of a monopolistic level of price in spite of strong temptations for competitive price cutting." He adds that "Tacit understandings to observe average-cost rules of pricing sometimes constitute an alternative way of achieving price maintenance in a declining market."[79] Heflebower summarizes several studies which reveal the use of full cost rules as a coordinating device in loose-knit cartels.[80] Hall and Hitch note that full cost pricing is especially prevalent in oligopoly, where the established price, approximating the full cost of a representative firm, "is reached directly through the community of outlook of business men, rather than indirectly through each firm working at what its most profitable output would be if competitors' reactions are neglected."[81] Cyert and March stress the use of rules-of-thumb to eliminate oligopolistic uncertainties:

> Our studies . . . lead us to the proposition that firms will devise and negotiate an environment so as to eliminate the uncertainty. . . . In the case of competitors, one of the conspicuous means of control is through the establishment of industry-wide conventional practices. If "good business practice" is standardized . . . we can be reasonably confident that all competitors will follow it. We do not mean to imply that firms necessarily enter into collusive agreements in the legal sense; our impression is that ordinarily they do not, but they need not do so to achieve the same objective of stability in competitive practices.[82]

Kaplan, Dirlam, and Lanzillotti describe how, by the application of well-known costing rules, members of the steel industry were able independently to make fairly good advance estimates of the price increase announced in 1956 by U. S.

[78]It would be interesting to know just how far rule-of-thumb pricing departs from full profit maximization under representative conditions. W. J. Baumol and R. E. Quandt have taken a few steps in "Rules of Thumb and Optimally Imperfect Decisions," *American Economic Review*, March 1964, pp. 23–46, but their approach covers only a special case. Much more theoretical and empirical work is needed.

[79]*The Economics of Sellers' Competition*, p. 65. See also Alexander Henderson, "The Theory of Duopoly," *Quarterly Journal of Economics*, November 1954, pp. 576–579.

[80]*Op. cit.*, pp. 376–378.

[81]*Op. cit.*, pp. 27–28.

[82]*Op. cit.*, p. 120.

Steel.[83] Haynes' interviews with small business-men disclosed that trade associations attempt to restrict "cutthroat competition" by urging wider adoption of full cost pricing. He found also that full cost prices serve as "resistance points" below which prices are not permitted to fall.[84] Fog claims that firms adhered to full cost pricing rules because they inhibited the inclination to reduce price on myopic grounds and because under standards of "commercial morality" it was considered "unloyal" to deviate from accepted prices.[85] In sum, full cost pricing facilitates oligopolistic coordination by making rivals' decisions more predictable and by providing common guidelines as to appropriate price levels.

When costs vary widely from firm to firm within an industry, coordination through the use of full cost rules becomes more difficult. One escape, although not a very plausible one, is the "representative firm" device discussed by Hall and Hitch. Price leadership appears more workable, with followers drawing upon their knowledge of the leader's costs if they must make independent price calculations. Still more effective, and apparently widespread, is the dissemination by a trade association of industry-wide average cost data by product line, function, or component. This information then becomes, by overt or tacit consent, the basis of price calculations.[86] Coordination of pricing decisions is also aided when a trade association develops standard cost accounting systems for the benefit of its members.

When pricing decisions are based upon some kind of full cost rule, we should expect as a corollary that prices will be more responsive to changes in cost than to changes in demand. Industry-wide cost changes generate, under the rule, a readily understood signal that price changes are in order. As Heflebower observes, ". . . when factor prices fall, the initiator of a selling price reduction is not suspected of trying to enlarge his share. Or, in reverse, the boldness of the firm which moves to reflect higher factor prices in his selling prices is appreciated, particularly when margins have been squeezed sharply."[87] The adjustment problem is different for demand changes. When demand declines, full cost pricing may call for price increases to cover higher overhead allocations, but this may be barred by the very weakness of demand. Still, price-cutting may at least be avoided because it goes contrary to the rule and because retaliation is feared. In boom times, full cost rules dictate little or no increase in prices unless marginal costs have risen sharply due to pressure on capacity, pulling total cost per unit along. Producers may be willing to hold prices below levels supportable by current demand, Heflebower suggests, because this is a good method of cementing long-run relations with customers.[88] Thus, we expect prices to be more rigid over the business cycle than they would be if sensitive marginalist adjustments to demand changes were attempted. There is in fact some evidence that concentrated industries display such pricing rigidity, as we shall see in Chapters 12 and 13.

One further implication must be mentioned briefly. Setting a price which affords only a moderate profit margin over unit costs may not maximize profits during the immediate time period. However, unless an industry enjoys substantial barriers to new entry, a higher price and profit margin policy could attract new entrants, whose additional output will have a depressing impact on future prices and profits. Profits over the long pull may therefore be higher if firms use pricing rules which yield less than the maximum return attainable in any current

---

[83]*Op. cit.*, p. 16.

[84]*Op. cit.*, pp. 317–319.

[85]*Op. cit.*, pp. 78–79 and 152–153.

[86]Cf. Haynes, *op. cit.*, p. 317; and Cyert and March, *loc. cit.*

[87]Richard B. Heflebower, "Toward a Theory of Industrial Markets and Prices," *American Economic Review*, May 1954, p. 135. See also his "Full Costs, Cost Changes, and Prices," pp. 389–390.

[88]"Toward a Theory of Industrial Markets and Prices," p. 137.

period, but at the same time discourage new entry. This important aspect of business pricing strategy will be analyzed further in Chapter 8.

FOCAL POINTS AND TACIT COORDINATION[89]

We have emphasized repeatedly that in the Prisoner's Dilemma game of oligopoly pricing, coordinated action is the key to joint profit maximization. Coordination is only moderately difficult when the oligopolists can communicate freely and openly. But the antitrust laws, which for good reason are concerned with inhibiting monopoly pricing, make overt communication hazardous. Price leadership and adherence to rules of thumb may be adequate substitutes. There are also more subtle ways of coordinating pricing decisions. Insight into these communication methods is provided by Thomas Schelling's theory of focal points.[90]

The theory is introduced most conveniently through a non-economic example. Consider the following problem posed by Schelling:

> You are to meet someone in New York City. You have not been instructed where to meet; you have no prior understanding with the person on where to meet; and you cannot communicate with each other. You are simply told that you will have to guess where to meet and he is being told the same thing and that you will have to try to make your guesses coincide.
>
> You are told the date but not the hour of this meeting; the two of you must guess the exact minute of the day for meeting. At what time will you appear at the chosen meeting place?[91]

Although there are tens of thousands of conceivable meeting places in New York City, a majority of the 36 persons on whom Schelling tried this problem chose the information booth at Grand Central Station, and nearly all chose to meet at 12 noon. The reason is that Grand Central Station (at least for New Yorkers) and noon have a certain compelling prominence; they are focal points. And in a wide variety of problems, when behavior must be coordinated tacitly—that is, without direct communication—there is a tendency for choices to converge on some such focal point. The focal points chosen may owe their prominence to analogy, symmetry, precedent, aesthetic considerations, or even the accident of arrangement; but they must in any event have the property of uniqueness. In economic problems, round numbers tend to be focal points, as do simple rules such as 'split the difference.'

Focal points also play a role in explicit, across-the-table bargaining, when a solution is difficult to reach despite free communication because a concession by one party generates an expectation in the other's mind that further concessions may be extracted. Focal points provide a barrier which each recognizes as a natural place for further concessions to be resisted, and thus they facilitate convergence upon a unique solution. As Schelling observed, the automobile salesman who works out the arithmetic for his rock bottom price of $2,507.63 is almost pleading to be relieved of $7.63.[92] Labor contract agreements often converge on some round number cent or percentage increase, or on a split-the-difference decision. In international relations, prominent natural features such as rivers or mountain ridges provide the most common basis of boun-

[89]A slightly different version of this section appeared as "Focal Point Pricing and Conscious Parallelism" in the *Antitrust Bulletin*, Summer 1967, pp. 495–503.

[90]Thomas C. Schelling, *The Strategy of Conflict* (Cambridge: Harvard University Press, 1960), especially Chapters 2 and 3. On p. 74, Schelling anticipates the application of his theory to price theory: "In economics the phenomena of price leadership, various kinds of nonprice competition, and perhaps even price stability itself appear amenable to an analysis that stresses the importance of tacit communication and its dependence on qualitatively identifiable and fairly unambiguous signals that can be read in the situation itself." Almarin Phillips also suggests that Schelling's insights are relevant, but fails to develop the approach further. *Market Structure, Organization and Performance*, p. 44, n. 25.

[91]*Op. cit.*, p. 56.

[92]*Ibid.*, p. 67.

dary adjustments, followed in second place by round number parallels of latitude.

The great merit of Schelling's general focal point theory is that it permits us to integrate into the main stream of oligopoly theory a number of phenomena which might otherwise be deemed mere curiosities. Several specific ways in which focal points enter into oligopolistic price determination can be identified.

First is the practice of 'price lining,' widespread at the retail level. Even dollar amounts serve as one focal point for pricing decisions. More common in retailing is the use of odd pricing points such as $199.95, which owe their acceptance to tradition. By setting its product price at some such focal point, a firm tacitly encourages its rivals to follow suit without undercutting. Conversely, if one company announces a price which has no such compulsion, a rival is tempted to set its own price just a cent or two below. This leads to a further small retaliatory cut, precipitating a downward spiral which, in the absence of focal points, has no clear-cut stopping point. In setting price at a focal point, one in effect asks rhetorically, If not here, where? implicitly warning rivals of the danger of downward spiraling.[93]

Most consumer goods manufacturers are well aware that adherence to accepted pricing points facilitates coordination and discourages price warfare. They go to considerable pains to preserve the system. The problem of passing along to consumers the benefits of the 1965 excise tax reform was complicated by the desire of many manufacturers to protect their pricing points while making downward adjustments. As a result, the price reductions on some items were less than the tax cut, while on others they were actually greater.[94] Tampering with the accepted pricing point structure always threatens industry discipline and may induce price warfare. Na-

tionally branded men's shirt manufacturers apparently experienced several such conflicts when some firms attempted to shift from pricing points like $4.95 to even dollar points, although in prosperous 1966 the transition was made with the aid of price leadership.[95]

Government agencies may inadvertently facilitate price parallelism by setting ceiling prices, e.g., as part of anti-inflation campaigns. For example, a student of French price controls concluded that official ceiling prices provided a focus for individual quotations which might otherwise have differed.[96] In England it was customary, at least until the last few months before the steel industry was nationalized in 1967, for all producers to quote only the maximum prices announced by the Iron and Steel Board.[97]

Turning to still another class of pricing practices, how does one explain the following experience of the U. S. Veterans Administration? On June 5, 1955, five different producers submitted sealed bids to fill an order for 5,640 100-capsule bottles of the antibiotic tetracycline, each quoting an effective net price of $19.1884 per bottle.[98] The typical purchasing agent's reaction would be that no explanation is needed; the Justice Department should be called in to investigate a clear-cut case of conspiracy. But although one can never be certain, it is probable that there was no direct collusion connected with this transaction. Rather, the bids were influenced by two kinds of focal points. First, there was a past history of price quotations which provided a focal point for the June 5 bids. This facet will be explored more fully in a moment. But second, the curious price of $19.1884 per bottle was arrived at through the application of a series of round number discounts to round number base prices: $19.1884 is the standard trade discount of 2 per cent off $19.58, which

---

[93]*Ibid.*, pp. 111–112.

[94]See "Excise Cut Begins To Trickle Down," *Business Week*, June 26, 1965, p. 36.

[95]"Shirt Prices Up 5¢, But Who Cares," *New York Times*, April 24, 1966.

[96]John Sheahan, "Problems and Possibilities of Industrial Price Control: Postwar French Experience," *American Economic Review*, June 1961, p. 352.

[97]"Steel Price War Rages in Britain," *New York Times*, April 7, 1966. See also M. Howe, "The Iron and Steel Board Pricing, 1953–1967," *Scottish Journal of Political Economy*, February 1968, pp. 43–67.

[98]From exhibit PX-645, *Federal Trade Commission v. American Cyanamid Co., et al.*, FTC docket 7211 (1959).

(after rounding) is 20 per cent off the wholesale price of $24.48, which in turn is 20 per cent off the $30.60 price charged to retail druggists, which is 40 per cent off the prevailing retail list price of $51.00, which in turn reflected an earlier 15 per cent cut from the original list price of $60.00 per 100 capsules.

When price cuts were made by the oligopolistic producers of antibiotics, they nearly always took one of three forms: a cut to a new even dollar price, a round number percentage reduction in the old price, or rounding off the odd fraction of a cent produced when round number discounts led to a figure like $19.1884. Consider, for instance, the history of prices to retailers and hospitals of American Cyanamid's antibiotic aureomycin in bottles of 16 capsules. It was introduced in December 1948 at $15.00 per bottle. In response to the introduction of a competing product, the price was cut to $10.00 in March 1949. In February 1950, the price was cut 20 per cent to $8.00. In May 1950, a 25 per cent reduction to $6.00 followed. In September 1951, the price was cut 15 per cent to $5.10, at which level it stabilized for several years.[99]

This sort of round number discounting is apparently not confined to the drug industry, although we have little information on how widespread it is. It was a prominent feature of plate glass mirror pricing, on which some evidence has been assembled. The Mirror Manufacturers Association published a list price booklet for various mirror sizes, and nearly all wholesale transactions were made at round number discounts—e.g., 80 per cent and then 10 per cent off the list price.[100]

What is the significance of round number discounting and quoting as a coordinating device? When commodities are sold repeatedly in fairly large quantities to well-informed buyers, sellers are anxious to have some means of changing prices once in a while without precipitating a

spiral of retaliatory undercutting. By reducing its price a round percentage amount, the initiator tacitly says to its rivals, 'See here, I'm not trying to touch off a war. I think the price should be lower, and I've quoted a good, clean reduction to which we all should now conform.' A cut which lacks the prominence of a round number percentage discount or a new round number price value is a cut without staying power. There is no magnetic attraction preventing a further change on the next transaction. And since large, well-informed buyers are adept at making prices slide downhill, it is to the interest of sellers to avoid incessant price changes. The way to do so is to ensure that any changes which are made move to a new focal point likely to be respected by rivals.

Focal point pricing may also be used as a coordinating device by *buyers* anxious to avoid driving up the prices of commodities in an oligopsonistic market (i.e., one with few buyers). Bakken and Mueller found that tobacco leaf buyers' adherence to round number quotations in the Wisconsin market discouraged aggressive outbidding of each others' offers.[101]

The notion of round number discounts as focal point barriers to further cutting applies not only to pricing, but also to certain kinds of non-price rivalry. For an example, we return to the antibiotics industry. A common trade practice is to avoid price-cutting, but to compete for hospital and retail pharmacy orders by giving 'free goods' —additional units of a product for which no bill is rendered. One company's analysis of the New York district situation in 1955 revealed that in 46 out of 47 cases, the percentage of free goods to supplies purchased by hospitals was one of three round numbers: 10, 15, or 20. In the same memorandum, the district sales manager reported that "Gradually the (free goods percentage) is at 20 per cent. We back away when it goes beyond because once that barrier is broken, our experience has been that there is no bottom."[102]

[99]U. S. Federal Trade Commission, *Economic Report on Antibiotics Manufacture* (Washington: June 1958), p. 190.

[100]Phillips, *op. cit.*, pp. 177–196.

[101]H. H. Bakken and Willard F. Mueller, *The Market for Wisconsin Binder Leaf Tobacco*, Research Bulletin 181 (Madison: University of Wisconsin Agricultural Experiment Station, June 1953), pp. 34–38.

[102]From exhibit RACX-753A in *FTC* v. *American Cyanamid Co. et al.*, placing in evidence an American Cyanamid inter-office memorandum dated April 18, 1955.

This clearly reflects the spiraling problem encountered once a critical focal point is passed: 'If not here, where?'

The theory of focal points can be extended along dynamic heuristic lines. Even a price which has no particular uniqueness or compulsion in its own right may become a focal point simply by virtue of having been quoted repeatedly. The Veterans Administration tetracycline price history is again illustrative. The first VA order for tetracycline was filled by the Pfizer Company as sole bidder at a price of $19.58 less 2 per cent trade discount. In the next transaction (March 1955), five firms bid $19.58, but three omitted the 2 per cent discount. When all matched the winning bid of $19.1884 net in the third transaction, on June 5, that price obtained the additional prominence of unanimous acceptance. All five firms then adhered to it in responding to four further VA sealed bid requests during the following year. An extensive antitrust investigation has produced no evidence that this pattern of identical bidding was the result of outright collusion, nor were meetings and explicit agreements essential under the circumstances. Given a focal point established through past experience, and given the reluctance of the five tetracycline sellers to initiate a movement to lower price levels by departing from that focal point, everything needed for coordinating *tacitly* on identical bids of $19.1884 net per bottle was in place.

Each year the federal and state governments receive thousands of sets of identical bids in the sealed bid competitions they sponsor.[103] It is probable that many such transactions have a history similar to the tetracycline pricing case. This is not to deny that identical bidding is sometimes due to direct collusion; the repeated identical bids submitted by electrical transformer and insulator manufacturers were, for example, the result of an elaborate price-fixing conspiracy. But overt agreement is not a *necessary* condition for identical bidding. If the participants are inclined toward avoiding undercutting one another, they can coordinate their behavior tacitly by searching for and respecting focal points.

CONCLUSION

In sum, there are several means by which oligopolists can coordinate their pricing decisions to approach the maximization of joint industry profits. Collusion, although under increasing antitrust fire, has not disappeared from the scene. Price leadership facilitates monopolistic pricing when follower firms are willing to cooperate with the leader's decisions. Mutual adherence to full cost pricing rules is not apt to yield profits as high as under ideal collusive conditions, but it helps keep returns higher than they would be under a regime of independent competitive conduct. Finally, firms can reduce the likelihood of competitive price cutting by setting and keeping prices at focal point levels.

[103]For various views on the identical bidding problem, see Vernon A. Mund, "Identical Bid Prices," *Journal of Political Economy*, April 1960, pp. 150–160; J. M. Clark, *Competition as a Dynamic Process* (Washington: Brookings, 1961), pp. 397–406; Paul W. Cook, Jr., "Fact and Fancy on Identical Bids," *Harvard Business Review*, January-February 1963, pp. 67–72; and R. A. Bicks, "The Federal Government's Program on Identical Bids," *Antitrust Bulletin*, November-December 1960, pp. 617–626.

Chapter 7

Conditions Limiting Oligopolistic Coordination

While oligopolists have incentives to cooperate in maintaining prices above the competitive level, there are also divisive forces. In this chapter we examine several conditions limiting the effectiveness of coordination. They include significant numbers of sellers, heterogeneity of products and distribution channels, the interaction of high overhead costs with adverse business conditions, lumpiness and infrequency of product purchases, opportunities for secret price-cutting, and weaknesses in an industry's informal social structure.

THE NUMBER AND SIZE DISTRIBUTION OF SELLERS

One structural dimension with an obvious influence on coordination is the number and size distribution of sellers. Generally, the more sellers a market includes, the more difficult it is to maintain prices above cost, other things being equal. This is so for three main reasons.

First, as the number of sellers increases and the share of industry output supplied by a representative firm decreases, individual producers are increasingly apt to ignore the effect of their price and output decisions on rival actions and the overall level of prices. As a very crude general rule, if evenly matched firms supply homogeneous products in a well-defined market, they are likely to begin ignoring their influence on price when their number exceeds ten or twelve. It is more difficult to generalize when the size distribution of sellers is highly skewed. Then pricing discipline depends more upon the relative concentration of output than upon the mere number of sellers.

Second, as the number of sellers increases, so also does the probability that at least one will be a maverick, pursuing an independent, aggressive pricing policy. And if market shares are sensitive to price differentials, even one such maverick of appreciable size can make it hard for other firms to hold prices near monopoly levels. As Peck observed, "[O]ne Henry Ford could introduce a new price policy, whereas fifteen sellers with conservative styles of business might produce results akin to the most 'static' of monopolies."[1]

Finally, different sellers are likely to have at least slightly divergent notions about the most advantageous price. Especially with homogeneous products, these conflicting views must be reconciled if joint profits are to be held near the potential maximum. The coordination problem clearly increases with the number of firms. Some economists have suggested that the difficulty of coordination rises nearly exponentially with the number of firms.[2] Their reasoning is as follows. Unless there is a central coordinating agency (such as a cartel sales bureau or a well-accepted price leader), each firm must tacitly or overtly communicate with every other firm over a

[1]M. J. Peck, *Competition in the Aluminum Industry: 1945–1958* (Cambridge: Harvard University Press, 1961), p. 207.

[2]See Almarin Phillips, *Market Structure, Organization and Performance* (Cambridge: Harvard University Press, 1962), pp. 29–30; and Oliver E. Williamson, "A Dynamic Theory of Interfirm Behavior," *Quarterly Journal of Economics*, November 1965, p. 600.

modus vivendi in pricing. The number of two-way communication flows required is given by the combinatorial expression $\frac{N(N-1)}{2}$. With two sellers, the number of channels is one; with six, it rises to 15, etc. Breakdown of any single channel can touch off independent actions threatening industry discipline. Although oligopolists may escape the implications of the formula by building in redundancies and creating central coordination institutions, the difficulty of coordination undoubtedly does increase more than proportionately with the number of sellers.

There have been many empirical studies relating profitability (which reflects success in holding prices above cost) to the number of sellers or (more frequently) seller concentration.[3] It is not easy to obtain appropriate measures of profitability and concentration, and different analysts have used widely divergent measures and statistical techniques. Yet with only one significant exception, they have reached the same conclusion: that profitability rises with concentration.

In a pioneering study of 42 meaningfully defined four-digit manufacturing industries, Bain found that producers specializing in lines whose leading eight firms accounted for 70 per cent or more of total industry shipments had 1936–1940 after-tax profits as a percentage of stockholders' equity averaging 11.8 per cent, while profits in industries with eight-firm concentration ratios below 70 per cent averaged only 7.5 per cent.

Using different techniques, Weiss reached similar conclusions for the period following World War II. By computing weighted average four-firm concentration ratios for 22 broad two-digit industry groups, he was able to cover the whole of U. S. manufacturing industry. For the 1949–1958 period, he found average after-tax profits as a percentage of stockholders' equity to be strongly and positively correlated with concentration, with a correlation coefficient of 0.73. Industry groups with average four-firm concentration ratios above 40 per cent achieved average profits of 12.7 per cent, while those with ratios below 30 per cent averaged only 8.8 per cent.

We should not, however, expect highly concentrated industries necessarily to be more profitable than unconcentrated industries at all times. Only in long-run equilibrium need atomistically structured industries earn no more than the minimum return required to attract capital. When disequilibrium prevails—e.g., when demand is pressing hard on capacity which in the short run cannot be expanded sufficiently —profits exceeding the long-run normal level may be earned in competitively structured markets. Such a state of affairs prevailed during the period of readjustment immediately following World War II. Prices rose rapidly in competitive industries unable to keep up with the flood of demand, while producers in some of the more concentrated industries held their prices in check for long-run strategic reasons. And during this period, Weiss's analysis for the years 1948 and 1949 shows, the correlation between profitability and concentration broke down completely. Indeed, the less concentrated industries were somewhat more profitable on the average. But as theory predicts, investment in additional capacity soon drove profits downward in the un-

---

[3]For the manufacturing sector they include, in order of publication, Joe S. Bain, "Relation of Profit Rates to Industry Concentration," *Quarterly Journal of Economics*, August 1951, pp. 293–324; David Schwartzman, "The Effect of Monopoly on Price," *Journal of Political Economy*, August 1959, pp. 352–362; Harold M. Levinson, *Postwar Movement of Prices and Wages in Manufacturing Industries*, Study Paper No. 21, Joint Economic Committee of the U. S. Congress (Washington: 1960); Victor Fuchs, "Integration, Concentration, and Profits in Manufacturing Industries," *Quarterly Journal of Economics*, May 1961, pp. 278–291; Leonard W. Weiss, "Average Concentration Ratios and Industrial Performance," *Journal of Industrial Economics*, July 1963, pp. 237–253; George J. Stigler, *Capital and Rates of Return in Manufacturing Industries* (Princeton: Princeton University Press, 1963), pp. 54–70; William S. Comanor and Thomas A. Wilson, "Advertising, Market Structure and Performance," *Review of Economics and Statistics*, November 1967, pp. 423–440; Norman R. Collins and Lee E. Preston, *Concentration and Price-Cost Margins in Manufacturing Industries* (Berkeley: University of California Press, 1968); and Collins and Preston, "Price-Cost Margins and Industry Structure," *Review of Economics and Statistics*, August 1969, pp. 271–286. For studies relating profits, interest rates paid, and service charge levels to concentration in banking, see Franklin R. Edwards, "The Banking Competition Controversy," *National Banking Review*, September 1965, pp. 1–34; and F. W. Bell and Neil B. Murphy, "Impact of Market Structure on the Price of a Commercial Banking Service," *Review of Economics and Statistics*, May 1969, pp. 210–213. Similar analyses are lacking for other sectors because it is so difficult to measure concentration meaningfully.

concentrated markets, while returns fell hardly at all in the concentrated sectors.

The one study yielding results at variance with the orthodox concentration – profitability hypothesis was by Stigler.[4] His approach departed from others' in two main respects. First, his measure of profitability was the sum of interest payments, dividends on stock, and after-tax additions to retained earnings as a percentage of total assets, including those financed through debt and trade credit. This choice attenuated, but for the years following 1947 did not eliminate, the positive correlation between returns to capital and concentration. Thus, 14 three-digit manufacturing industry groups with weighted average four-firm concentration ratios of 60 per cent or higher had 1951–1957 capital returns averaging 6.64 per cent, compared to 5.22 per cent for 54 industry groups with average four-firm ratios of less than 50 per cent. Second, Stigler discovered that the concentrated industries included a smaller fraction (2 per cent by sales) of firms with assets below $250,000 than unconcentrated industries (13 per cent). Arguing that small firms were more apt to reap their economic profits in the form of high owner-manager salaries, Stigler adjusted his data in a way which almost wiped out the differential between concentrated and unconcentrated industry returns. His adjustment technique has been shown to impart a systematic statistical bias, and when R. W. Kilpatrick used a more defensible adjustment method for a similar industry sample, he found a persistent positive relationship between concentration and profits as a percentage of stockholders' equity for 1950, 1956, and 1963.[5]

A negative implication of the Stigler study is more interesting. It is possible that the high observed returns on stockholders' equity in concentrated industries have been due as much to financial leverage as to greater success in realizing monopoly gains on the total amount of capital employed. That is, firms in concentrated industries may have elected a capital structure with an unusually high ratio of low-cost but inflexible debt obligations, so that returns above interest charges were magnified in relation to the relatively small quantity of equity capital. Stigler found that concentrated industries had significantly more stable returns over time than unconcentrated industries,[6] and this may put them in a better position to accept high leverage without incurring excessive risks. The possibility of interactions among concentration, leverage, and profitability has not yet been subjected to thorough empirical analysis. Further research is clearly needed.

All the studies summarized thus far suffer from the methodological flaw of assigning profits to specific industries on a company-wide basis, whereas concentration indices are computed on an establishment (i.e., plant) basis. Consequently, to cite a typical example, the substantial turbojet engine profits earned by General Electric were lumped together with and recorded as electrical equipment industry profits, since the latter field is General Electric's home base. This deficiency has been avoided in a study by Collins and Preston of percentage margins between prices and estimated costs.[7] As is usually the case, the penalty for avoiding some problems was the acceptance of others, since depreciation and advertising costs could not be deducted in computing the price-cost margins. After correcting for differences in capital/output ratios, to which depreciation is related, Collins and Preston found moderate to strong positive correlations between their price-cost margin index and four-firm concentration ratios for the four-digit industries in six groups: food products; stone, clay, and glass products; primary metals; fabricated metal products; electrical machinery; and miscellaneous manufacturing. In four other groups (textile mill products, apparel, chemicals,

---

[4] *Capital and Rates of Return in Manufacturing Industries, loc. cit.*

[5] Robert W. Kilpatrick, "Stigler on the Relationship between Industry Profit Rates and Market Concentration," *Journal of Political Economy*, May-June 1968, pp. 479–487. Kilpatrick found the relationship to be weakest in 1950, before the postwar readjustment had run its course.

[6] For corroborating evidence, see J. M. Samuels and D. J. Smyth, "Profits, Variability of Profits, and Firm Size," *Economica*, May 1968, pp. 127–139.

[7] *Concentration and Price-Cost Margins in Manufacturing Industries*, especially pp. 79–106.

and non-electrical machinery), the correlations were more often positive than negative, but all were statistically insignificant.

Although doubts remain and more research with better data is needed, the bulk of the evidence supports the hypothesis that profits increase with the degree to which market power is concentrated in the hands of a few sellers. Nevertheless, none of the analyses reveals a perfect correlation between profitability and concentration. A considerable fraction of the inter-industry variance in profitability cannot be explained by simple differences in concentration. For a fuller explanation, we must look to other structural and behavioral variables, such as those to be explored in the remainder of this chapter and subsequent chapters.

One loose end must be tied. Does the presence of numerous small firms operating on the fringe of an otherwise oligopolistic industry affect pricing behavior and profits? It undoubtedly does, though the strength of the effect depends upon the ability of fringe producers to make inroads into the market shares of industry leaders. Oligopolists who take their interdependence seriously are not apt to counter aggressive moves by fringe firms contributing only a tiny fraction of industry output, since even a doubling of the fringe's sales has a modest proportionate effect on their own sales. They are especially unlikely to respond if the retaliatory cut must apply across-the-board because of anti-discrimination laws or because all buyers will demand any price reduction offered to selected customers. Recognizing this, fringe producers will not be deterred by fear of retaliation from initiating independent pricing actions. But over the short run of a few years, the impact of their actions depends upon the relationship between their production capacity and total industry output.

When demand is strong, fringe members will be able to produce at capacity and sell their output at the price preferred by the industry leaders, or at some mutually accepted price differential.

But if a recession occurs, they may find themselves operating well below desired levels if they adhere to the high prices the oligopolistic leaders are attempting to maintain. To remedy this, they will bid for additional orders at reduced prices. This pattern has been observed repeatedly in cement, rayon, tin cans, gasoline, steel, and fabricated aluminum products, among others.[8] The reaction of the leading firms depends then upon the magnitude of the fringe's incursions. If the fringe's capacity is small relative to total industry output, so that the shift in market shares is less than approximately 10 per cent of total industry output, the leading producers are apt to ignore the incursions and persevere in their efforts to hold the price line. But when larger market share transfers appear imminent, defensive price reductions by the leading firms will normally begin. Whether price-cutting will proceed further depends mainly upon three things: the expected duration of the demand slump, the degree to which cost constraints inhibit deeper price shading by the smaller firms, and the responsiveness of fringe producers to the educational message implicit in the leading firms' retaliatory price moves. In general, oligopoly price structure breakdowns are more likely, the higher is the proportion of industry capacity in the hands of competitive fringe producers and the further from desired operating levels industry members find themselves at posted prices.

PRODUCT HETEROGENEITY

Product homogeneity implies that the offerings of rival sellers are alike in all significant physical and subjective respects, so that they are virtually perfect substitutes in the minds of consumers. With perfect homogeneity, there remains only one dimension along which rivalrous actions and counteractions can take place: price. In such cases, oligopolists have a particularly easy task of coordinating their behavior, for they must coordinate along only the one dimension.

[8]Cf. Samuel M. Loescher, *Imperfect Collusion in the Cement Industry* (Cambridge: Harvard University Press: 1959), pp. 120 and 293; Jesse W. Markham, *Competition in the Rayon Industry* (Cambridge: Harvard University Press, 1952), pp. 78 and 127–136; James W. McKie, *Tin Cans and Tin Plate* (Cambridge: Harvard University Press, 1959), pp. 217–218; Edmund P. Learned and Catherine C. Ellsworth, *Gasoline Pricing in Ohio* (Boston: Harvard Business School Division of Research, 1959), pp. 108 and 149; and Peck, *op. cit.*, pp. 66–72.

When products are heterogeneously differentiated, the terms of rivalry become multidimensional, and the coordination problem grows in complexity by leaps and bounds.

Four broad product heterogeneity classes, arrayed in order of ascending dimensionality, can be identified. First, there may be stable inter-firm differences in real or subjectively imputed product quality sufficient to require price differentials in market equilibrium. The coordination problem here is two-dimensional, involving both the price level and the amount of the differential. Judging from the amount of conflict over gasoline price differentials between major brand and independent retailers, it is probably more than twice as difficult to coordinate on these two magnitudes together than it is to reach tacit agreements concerning only a uniform price.[9] Second, when spatial differentiation (sellers located at varying distances from buyers) is present and transportation costs are relatively high, a very complex price structure may be required. Further analysis of this problem is deferred to Chapter 10. Third, product qualities may be dynamically unstable, as in fashion goods industries and fields subjected to rapid technological change. Each product change alters the relative competitive position of every producer and requires either a new set of pricing decisions or the acceptance of a rigid, historically-based price structure which is not likely to maximize profits. Fourth, complex products such as airplanes, electrical power generators, buildings, and non-standardized personal services are sold on a custom-made-to-order basis. When no two orders are ever exactly alike or when there is leeway for deviations from the buyer's product specifications in hundreds of particulars, tacit coordination on joint profit-maximizing strategies becomes virtually impossible to achieve.

Several examples serve to illustrate the range of coordination difficulties associated with static and dynamic product heterogeneity. Perhaps most extreme is the problem of aerospace firms bidding to secure government contracts for the development of new, technologically advanced weapon systems and space vehicles. The choices of government decision-makers are necessarily multi-dimensional; what is sought is the best combination of qualitative design features; time of availability; and expected development, production, and operating costs. A virtual infinity of potential design feature combinations is open to bidders, and each firm's judgment concerning the quality – cost – time tradeoffs most likely to win approval from the customer (itself a bureaucratic maze with internally conflicting preferences) invariably differs from that of its rivals. Effective coordination of bid details under these circumstances is literally impossible, and inter-firm rivalry to win attractive new development program contracts has been vigorously independent even when the number of bidders was only two.[10] Because of this, and given certain other characteristics unique to the environment of advanced weapons and space systems development, competition for new research and development program contracts often has more desirable behavioral effects when the number of rivals is small than when there are numerous bidders.[11]

For nearly a century, the heavy electrical equipment industry has exhibited the pricing patterns associated with complex, multidimensionally differentiated products. During the closing decades of the 19th century spirited competition prevailed with respect to both product quality and price in the electric traction motor, induction motor, and polyphase generator lines, even though there were only two sellers vying for many of the orders. Passer isolated two main reasons for the strenuous duopolistic rivalry in traction motors: complexity of the

[9]See Learned and Ellsworth, *op. cit.*, pp. 133 and 149; Leonard W. Weiss, *Economics and American Industry* (New York: Wiley, 1961), pp. 411–412; and Joel Dirlam, "The Petroleum Industry," in Walter Adams, ed., *The Structure of American Industry* (Third ed., New York: Macmillan, 1961), p. 295.

[10]For a fascinating account of the two-firm TFX aircraft competition, see Richard A. Smith, *Corporations in Crisis* (Garden City: Doubleday, 1963), Chapters IX and X. On another vigorous two-firm competition, see john M. Mecklin, "Why Boeing Is Missing the Bus," *Fortune*, June 1, 1968, pp. 80 ff.; and "Rolls Royce and G. E. Fighting To Win Airbus Engine Orders," *New York Times*, March 6, 1968, p. 61.

[11]Cf. F. M. Scherer, *The Weapons Acquisition Process: Economic Incentives* (Boston: Harvard Business School Division of Research, 1964), pp. 44–49.

product and rapid technological change. Regarding the complexity of railway motors, he observed:

> When a product possesses many features and when the possible variations in these features are numerous, it is hard to see how agreement on the product could be tacit. And the process of reaching explicit agreement on the product would have been lengthy and elaborate, if possible at all.[12]

On the other hand, his analysis shows that after an initial settling-down period, price competition was mild and stable in the electric arc lamp and incandescent lamp fields, where the products were simpler and more readily standardized.[13] Concerning the pace of technical change in motor technology, Passer concluded that:

> Vigorous product competition stimulated price competition. The engineers who labored hard to design a superior product did not want to see it fail to gain a market because the price was too high.[14]

He contrasted behavioral patterns in static to those in technologically dynamic product lines:

> It is probable that continuous and unpredictable change in the technology of a product and its manufacture introduces the element of uncertainty which accounts for the competitive rather than the monopolistic behavior of the oligopolists. . . . If technological change proceeded at a slower pace . . . the traditional duopoly case, with a fairly homogeneous product and a recognition of mutual dependence, may have resulted. Product competition based on a static technology, in which product choices are made from a perfectly well-known and unchanging set of alternatives, may have an effect on duopolistic behavior different from that based on a rapidly advancing technology.[15]

Of the two disruptive influences stressed by Passer, complexity of the product seems to have been more important, for in the absence of explicit collusive agreements, there have been periods of intense price competition in the electrical generator field despite a maturing of the product technology. We recall from Chapter 6 that to facilitate standardized pricing, a General Electric employee developed and published an elaborate pricing formula book with which industry price analysts could build up the prices for thousands of generator component parts into an overall book price. Still because the typical generator order is so complex, there is considerable opportunity for alternative interpretations of customer specifications, and parties to the conspiracies of the 1950s found mere agreement to follow book pricing techniques an insufficient foundation for effective collusion. They had to meet to compare calculations before submitting bids. When the meetings were suspended because some firm refused to participate, the poor coordination of price calculations was one element leading to sharp price reductions, although as we shall see shortly, there were other contributing factors.

Automobile tires present a different set of pricing coordination problems. Tires are fairly simple products and the industry is quite concentrated, with eight firms accounting for 89 per cent of shipments in 1963. One might expect a high degree of tacit cooperation. Yet the price structure in tires has been described as "chaotic"; tire manufacturers have been subjected to "an almost uninterrupted series of price buffetings"; and profits have been lower on the average than those of other industries with comparable market structures.[16] One apparent reason is the great variety of manufacturers' and private-label grades, complicated by the welter of conflicting sales claims, labels, guarantees, and prices. In 1964, when the industry was pressed by the

---

[12]Harold C. Passer, *The Electrical Manufacturers: 1875–1900* (Cambridge: Harvard University Press, 1953), p. 263.

[13]*Ibid.*, pp. 62 and 161–162.

[14]*Ibid.*, p. 264.

[15]*Ibid.*, pp. 352, 353.

[16]A. D. H. Kaplan, J. B. Dirlam, and R. F. Lanzillotti, *Pricing in Big Business* (Washington: Brookings, 1958), p. 280. See also "Automobile Tire Safety," *New York Times*, July 7, 1966, p. 23.

Federal Trade Commission to adopt a uniform system of grading and labelling, the president of the Rubber Manufacturers Association reported that its lawyers had warned against such a step "because of the antitrust questions involved."[17] It would in fact be difficult to agree on standardized grades and labels in such a concentrated industry without facilitating price agreements at the same time. And it is probable that the uniform grading legislation enacted by Congress in 1966, while making rational choice easier for tire consumers, will also pave the way to tacit agreement among producers on a price structure which yields higher profits.

Differentiation in product characteristics has also permitted automobile producers to exercise a modest amount of independence in pricing decisions. Thus American Motors, suffering from declining consumer acceptance in 1965, was able to reduce its 1966 model list prices an average of $60 relative to the Big Three. An even sharper cut of roughly $200 followed in February of 1967.[18] General Motors, Ford, and Chrysler chose not to retaliate because brand loyalties limited the shift of patronage toward American Motors to relatively painless magnitudes. More generally, when inventories are high at the end of a model year, as they were in 1966, the auto makers initiate wholesale price cuts as high as $150 per unit to help dealers dispose of their (stylistically) perishable stocks.

Four more brief examples round out the picture. In the rayon industry, distress sales of yarns made obsolete by technological change were a threat to pricing discipline during the early 1930s. The problem was intensified by the efforts of some producers to dispose of first-line yarns at reduced prices by misbranding them as obsolete remnants.[19] Bituminous coal is a product which varies widely in quality, but which can be priced on a standardized B.T.U. per ton basis. Still some producers have engaged in subtle price shading with unsophisticated buyers by 'blowing up' their guaranteed B.T.U. specifications above those of competitors.[20] In railroading, the Grand Trunk Line provided circuitous and hence slower service than its three major rivals between Chicago and New York City during the 1880s and 1890s. It could attract a substantial volume of perishable commodities like dressed meat only by charging lower rates. Disputes over the size of the rate differential led to two rate wars in which rate levels fell by roughly 50 per cent.[21] And despite a long record of price uniformity among standard brand cigarettes, the introduction of new king size and filter tip cigarettes by the leading producers during the 1950s was followed by several years of widely varying differentials before all firms came together on a uniform price structure.[22]

In sum, when the offerings of rival producers differ over numerous dimensions, the problem of coordinating on a common price structure is much more complex than it is with homogeneous products. Other things being equal, cooperation to maintain high collective profits is less likely to be successful, the more heterogeneous products are. However, some aspects of product differentiation work in the opposite direction. When sellers can build strong brand loyalties, when there are economies of scale in product differentiation, or when (as we shall see in the next chapter) product differentiation erects barriers to the entry of new competition, profits may be higher than they would be with homogeneous products. The net effect of these opposing forces depends in a complex way upon the specific type of product differentiation present and the degree to which other influences conducive to coordinated pricing operate. The type of heterogeneity

---

[17]"FTC Kicks Some Tires," *Business Week*, December 5, 1964, p. 34.

[18]"Rambler Takes a Gamble," *Business Week*, February 25, 1967, p. 39. On a similar 1969 cut by Chrysler, see "Detroit's Cloudy Spring," *Business Week*, May 10, 1969, p. 48.

[19]Markham, *op. cit.*, pp. 75–76.

[20]Reed Moyer, *Competition in the Midwestern Coal Industry* (Cambridge: Harvard University Press, 1964), p. 149.

[21]Paul W. MacAvoy, *The Economic Effects of Regulation: The Trunkline Railroad Cartels and the ICC Before 1900* (Cambridge: MIT Press, 1965), pp. 129–135.

[22]R. B. Tennant, "The Cigarette Industry," in Adams, *The Structure of American Industry*, pp. 376–377.

most likely to disrupt pricing discipline appears to be multidimensionality of a product's technical features.

THE EXTENT OF PRODUCT HETEROGENEITY IN CONCENTRATED MARKETS

How widespread is product heterogeneity as a structural condition limiting inter-firm coordination? To gain some insight into this question, an analysis was made of the 65 manufacturing industry groups defined by Kaysen and Turner as "Type I" oligopolies—those in which the leading eight firms made at least 50 per cent and the leading 20 firms at least 75 per cent of industry shipments.[23] These 65 industries have structures most favorable to oligopolistic pricing. Each industry was given a score of from (1) to (4) on four attributes: multidimensionality of its products, the rate of change in product technology, the degree to which there are physical differences in the quality of rival products, and the degree to which consumers subjectively impute quality differences to products as a result of such influences as advertising. (No attempt was made to take geographic or spatial differentiation into account.) With respect to product dimensionality, the following system of scores was used:

(1) Standardized technical configuration.
(2) Some configuration options.
(3) Complex configuration options.
(4) Very complex configuration options.

On the rate of technological change, physical product difference, and subjective product quality difference attributes, the scores varied from (1) for 'virtually none' to (4) for 'great,' with 'modest' and 'considerable' categories intervening.

The results were as follows. The mean score was 1.85, suggesting a net tendency more toward homogeneity than heterogeneity. Seven of the 65 industries received a score of (1) on all four attributes, connoting virtually complete product homogeneity both statically and dynamically. Thirty-nine industries, or 60 per cent of the total, had no score higher than (2), while 34

per cent had at least two scores of (1) and none higher than (2). Forty per cent of the industries had at least one score higher than (2), indicating a considerable degree of heterogeneity on at least one attribute. There were 46 scores of either (3) or (4) altogether. Thirteen industries had scores of (3) or (4) on the product dimensionality criterion, which probably affects pricing coordination with special force.

Although the analysis is subject to judgmental errors, it seems reasonable to draw three broad conclusions. First, few manufacturing industries conform tightly to the polar case of perfectly homogeneous oligopoly. Second, somewhere between 20 and 40 per cent of all concentrated industries supply products heterogeneous enough to pose fairly difficult obstacles to tacit coordination. Third, the predominant pattern in oligopolistically structured industries is a modest degree of product heterogeneity, engendering slight to moderate coordination problems.

METHODS OF COORDINATING HETEROGENEOUS PRODUCT PRICING

Even modest product heterogeneity might undermine pricing discipline were it not for certain devices which facilitate coordination. One considered in Chapter 6 is focal point pricing. 'Price lining' is especially important in consumer goods fields such as clothing, where style changes occur frequently. Faithful adherence to focal points permits sellers to avoid price competition which physical and subjective product changes would otherwise precipitate. But even when direct price competition is minimized, it is possible for active quality competition to continue as firms attempt to offer the most attractive qualitative features consistent with a fixed, inflexible price. This phenomenon will be considered further in Chapter 14.

Independent pricing behavior may also be headed off through the negotiation of standardization agreements on product features which would seriously complicate tacit collusion if left uncoordinated. In the steel industry, for example, explicit agreements have in the past been

---

[23]Carl Kaysen and Donald F. Turner, *Antitrust Policy* (Cambridge: Harvard University Press, 1959), pp. 27–37 and 275–313. See also p. 60 *supra*.

reached to secure uniform treatment of extras—
e.g., complex differences in finish, temper, packaging, etc.[24] Although the layman might think
that cement is cement, cement trade associations
found it necessary to negotiate standardization
agreements in order to discourage rivalry based
upon claims of superior quality. They also published for the guidance of members standardized
terms of sale, cash discounts, package charges,
refunds for returned bags, and bin testing cost
rules, differences in any of which might undermine a carefully cultivated system of direct and
tacit price agreements.[25] Still another common
practice (until it was condemned in a series of
antitrust decisions) was the development of basing point pricing systems to overcome the intricate problem of quoting transportation charges
in industries where such costs constitute a major
fraction of the total delivered product price. The
basing point system will be examined at greater
length three chapters hence.

OTHER ASPECTS OF HETEROGENEITY

Conflicts over pricing policy may also arise
because of inter-firm differences in distribution
channels, vertical integration, or reliance upon
foreign sources of supply.

For instance, the tire industry's pricing problems, vexing enough due to the tangle of conflicting grades and quality claims, are complicated further by the diversity of middlemen and
retail outlets through which replacement tires
are sold. In 1966, there were 120 'private label'
firms which purchased tires from the regular
manufacturers and marketed them through their
own distribution channels under their private
brand names. Kaplan and his associates found
that the importance of mail order houses, auto
supply chains, and oil companies in imparting

fluidity to the tire price structure was "overwhelming."[26] The tires supplied by these outlets

> . . . have undercut the factory brands and
> necessitated a continuous procession of
> sales and special discounts, allowances, and
> so on—some authorized, some not . . . . In
> addition, private brands have led to a suc-
> cession of changes in tire quality, innova-
> tions that have upset the precarious sta-
> bility of tire "levels" as a framework for a
> price structure.[27]

Professor Mason concluded that the tire industry's distribution channels led to a discount
structure which facilitated price-cutting "on the
slightest provocation."[28] This experience lends
some credence to Clair Wilcox's quip that "The
formula for competition is simple: add one part
of Sears Roebuck to twenty parts of oligopoly."[29]

The drug industry sells its products directly
to all sorts of public and private hospitals and
agencies, offering varying discounts off the list
price to different customer types. To avoid the
confusion which could arise in making quotations
to hospitals whose status is ambiguous, firms
adhere by mutual tacit consent to published
standard hospital classification guides. Even so,
errors sometimes occur, much to the dismay of
industry salesmen.[30]

Differences in degrees of vertical integration
led to pricing policy conflicts among American
copper producers during the 1947–1955 period,
despite nearly perfect product homogeneity and
high market concentration. Anaconda, integrated on a broad scale into fabricated product
lines and heavily dependent upon copper supplies from Chile, desired high primary prices
partly to placate the volatile Chilean government
and partly to maintain an advantage over nonintegrated rival fabricators by keeping their input

[24]Cf. p. 159 *supra.*
[25]Loescher, *op. cit.*, pp. 134–135.
[26]Kaplan, Dirlam, and Lanzillotti, *op. cit.*, p. 203.
[27]*Loc. cit.*
[28]Edward S. Mason, *Economic Concentration and the Monopoly Problem* (Cambridge: Harvard University Press, 1957), p. 68.
[29]"On the Alleged Ubiquity of Oligopoly," *American Economic Review*, May 1950, p. 71.
[30]See exhibit PX-129A in *Federal Trade Commission* v. *American Cyanamid Co., et al.*, FTC docket no. 7211 (1959), offering in evidence a sales manager's report of a rival's bid, apparently "submitted in error" to a state hospital at the prevailing federal agency price.

costs high. Kennecott, on the other hand, was much less integrated vertically. It was anxious to hold the primary price at more moderate levels to maintain demand for its ample primary copper supplies. According to J. L. McCarthy, these conflicts prevented the industry from achieving joint maximization of profits.[31]

Similar pricing conflicts due to varying degrees of vertical integration have been observed in the aluminum[32] and steel industries, although they have not been sufficiently intense to undermine industry discipline. In steel, Adams and Dirlam reported, small nonintegrated fabricators accepted the price structure because they understood "the power and influence of the firms shaping [it]." Yet because of differences in outlook associated with their positions, they represent "a source of potential danger to the structure."[33]

DYNAMIC IMPLICATIONS OF COST STRUCTURES

The ability of oligopolists to cooperate with one another is also affected in a variety of ways by cost conditions. In Chapter 5 this problem was examined from a static viewpoint. Generally, the more cost functions differ from firm to firm, the more trouble the firms will have maintaining a common price policy, and the less likely joint maximization of profits is. Nothing more need be added on this point. Instead, we shall turn to some dynamic implications of industrial cost structure.

A dynamic corollary of the proposition just stated is self-evident and can be treated briefly. The more rapidly producers' cost functions are altered through technological innovation, and the more unevenly these changes are diffused throughout the industry, the more likely con-

flict in pricing actions is. For example, National Steel, after installing new and more efficient continuous strip mills during the 1930s, became an active price cutter, pulling other steel makers with higher costs along.[34] The introduction of mechanized window glass production techniques around the turn of the century touched off a bitter struggle for survival in which prices were driven below cost even for the new and more efficient machine methods. After stability was restored through cartel agreements, a second episode of price warfare between glass makers using new continuous process techniques and those employing obsolete methods arose during the early 1930s.[35] In the sanitary pottery fixtures industry, conflicts attendant to the introduction of tunnel kilns (replacing more costly beehive oven processes) were in part responsible for the failure of producers to eliminate widespread price-cutting despite repeated attempts to reach collusive agreements.[36]

Our main concern will be with a different issue: the dynamic interaction between cost structures and business conditions. There is evidence that industries characterized by high overhead costs are particularly susceptible to pricing discipline breakdowns when a cyclical or secular decline in demand forces member firms to operate well below designed plant capacity. This tendency appears to be especially marked in industries with heavy investments in developed natural resource deposits (like petroleum extraction and underground coal mining) and those using very capital-intensive production processes (such as railroading, petroleum refining, chemicals, steel, aluminum, cement, glass, and paper-making).

To understand this phenomenon, two questions must be answered. First, why do oligopolists with high fixed costs have stronger incen-

[31]"The American Copper Industry: 1947–1955," *Yale Economic Essays*, Spring 1964, pp. 64–130. Unfortunately, McCarthy did not attempt to specify the price level at which industry profits would in fact have been maximized.

[32]Cf. p. 172 *supra*.

[33]Walter Adams and J. B. Dirlam, "Steel Imports and Vertical Oligopoly Power," *American Economic Review*, September 1964, p. 640.

[34]Cf. Weiss, *Economics and American Industry*, pp. 296–297.

[35]G. W. Stocking and M. W. Watkins, *Monopoly and Free Enterprise* (New York: 20th Century Fund, 1951), pp. 121–126.

[36]Cf. Phillips, *op. cit.*, pp. 175–176.

tives to cut prices when demand declines than firms with low fixed costs? And second, if price-cutting does break out, how does the cost structure affect the extent to which it will be carried?

We proceed using diagrams comparing two different (and not necessarily competing) firms: Firm A, with average fixed costs amounting to 15 per cent of average total cost ATC at 85 per cent of designed capacity output (Figure 7.1a); and Firm B with average fixed costs equalling 50 per cent of ATC at 85 per cent of designed capacity output (Figure 7.1b). Since the shape of the cost curves is crucial, we must strive to be as true to life as possible. For both firms, marginal cost is assumed to be constant up to 85 per cent of designed capacity output, after which it rises sharply. This is consistent with most of the statistical evidence on short-run cost functions.[37] To ensure comparability, average total cost is equal in the two cases at designed capacity output (that is, where ATC is at a minimum). Identical linear constant-shares demand curves reflecting three states of the business cycle— prosperity (D_1), a modest recession (D_2), and a severe recession (D_3) are assumed for the two firms. To keep the drawings as simple as possible, each lower demand curve has twice the slope of its higher neighbor, permitting the marginal revenue curve for one demand function to serve also as a demand curve under more depressed conditions. It follows that the demand curves all have the same elasticity at any given price.[38]

Suppose each firm is operating with demand D_1 at 100 per cent of designed capacity, maximizing profits under the assumption of rival price-matching (and hence constant shares) by equating MR_1 with MC, and selling at the highly profitable price OP_1. Now a mild recession shifts demand to D_2. For low fixed cost Firm A, the optimal reaction is a substantial reduction in output to about 65 per cent of capacity, where MR_2 and MC are equated, and a modest reduction in

price to OP_2. A smaller, but still consistent, profit margin is attained. High fixed cost Firm B's marginal cost situation dictates a reduction in output only to 90 per cent of capacity, but a sharp reduction in the profit-maximizing price to OP_2. The previously substantial profit margin is nearly eliminated. Thus, when demand falls below levels which will sustain capacity output, the profit-maximizing enterprise with high fixed costs cuts prices more sharply and suffers more severe erosion of profits than a similarly-inclined firm with low fixed costs. This result is quite general, for marginal costs must fall more steeply with reduced output from the point at which ATC is minimized for a firm with higher fixed and lower marginal costs at below-capacity production levels.

We turn the screw tighter now, letting demand shift from D_2 to D_3. For Firm A, since both MR_2 and MR_3 (derived from demand curves with the same elasticity at given prices) cut MC at the same level, no change in price is induced. For Firm B, with a slight curvature in MC in the neighborhood of its intersection with MR_2, an insignificantly small price reduction is induced. Thus, when marginal costs are roughly constant at below-capacity operation, as statistical studies suggest, and when demand curves shift iso-elastically, the intensification of an already depressed situation will motivate little or no price reduction by oligopolists pursuing joint profit maximization.[39]

Yet it is precisely when business conditions really turn sour that price-cutting runs most rampant among oligopolists with high fixed costs. Something more than the marginal conditions for profit maximization must affect producer behavior. The missing link is profits. With the shift in demand from D_2 to D_3, both firms show losses; P_3 is below ATC at the profit-maximizing output. Firm A's loss is small, by the inflated standards of textbook draftsmanship—about five

[37]For surveys of the literature, see J. Johnston, *Statistical Cost Analysis* (New York: McGraw-Hill, 1960), Chapters 4 and 5; and A. A. Walters, "Production and Cost Functions: An Econometric Survey," *Econometrica* January-April 1963, pp. 39–51.

[38]Cf. note 14, p. 136 *supra*.

[39]Or when elasticities change symmetrically with the shift in demand, equal price changes will result. This case is ignored because the change in price follows from demand conditions, and not from differences in the cost structure.

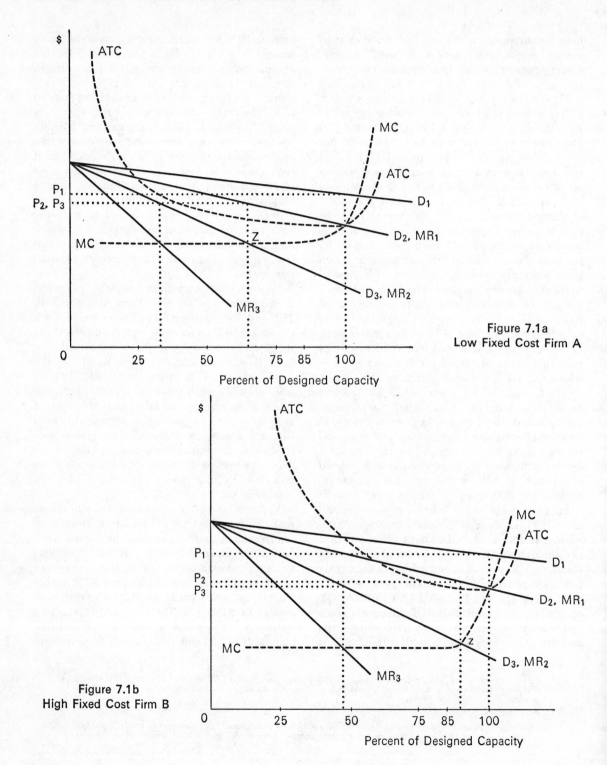

Figure 7.1a
Low Fixed Cost Firm A

Figure 7.1b
High Fixed Cost Firm B

per cent of costs. But Firm B, with its high fixed costs spread over a restricted volume of output, shows an enormous deficit—roughly 27 per cent of costs. With a milder, perhaps more realistic leftward demand shift Firm B would incur substantial losses, while Firm A would find itself in the black. These losses are likely to confront Firm B, or some similarly situated high fixed cost operator in B's industry, with a financial crisis. Unable to meet dividend and interest payments out of earnings, the firm's decision-making horizon shortens. Its managers turn all their attention to immediate remedies, ignoring the risks of diminished profits due to weakened industry discipline in the uncertain future. They see that if additional business could be secured by quietly undercutting joint profit-maximizing price OP_3 slightly and moving off the constant-shares demand curve along a 'rival price constant' curve, operation at higher capacity levels would be possible, overhead could be spread over more units of output, and losses would be reduced or even (if capacity utilization could be increased to 90 per cent) eliminated. Some producers in Firm B's straits will choose to take the chance. As Hall and Hitch summarized their interviews with British businessmen during the depressed 1930s, "Usually one entrepreneur is overcome by panic: 'there is always one fool who cuts'; and the rest must follow."[40] Unless they are imbued with a strong sense of group loyalty, the rest will indeed follow sooner or later as price-cutters make inroads into their sales, and the end result will be a general decline in price away from the joint profit-maximizing level OP_3.

Assuming the persistence of depressed demand state D_3, the limit to which proliferating non-cooperative price-cutting can be carried is where price falls uniformly to the level of marginal cost, at point Z in Figures 7.1a and 7.1b. Here again we find an important difference between industries with high and those with low fixed costs. Price-cutting will be checked at higher price levels when marginal costs are high

and fixed costs low than when marginal costs are low and fixed costs high. The industry characterized by high fixed costs suffers more when demand is depressed both because of stronger inducements toward price-cutting and a lower floor to price declines.

From this analytic conclusion we are tempted to generalize: the higher fixed costs are relative to total costs, the more prone an industry is to serious pricing discipline breakdowns during recessions. Unfortunately, the problem is more complicated. Recognizing the temptations confronting them, firms in high fixed cost industries seem to exercise extraordinary restraint in their pricing actions, and when tacit restraint fails, they have an unusually high propensity to scurry into formal collusive agreements. According to Alfred Neal, when the number of sellers is small:

> Each seller realizes that if every other seller follows his price, all will make smaller profits or greater losses and *no permanent cure to depressed demand will be achieved*, since only the most ruthless price war will eliminate enough capacity to improve the price situation. Under such circumstances, only the most sanguine or the most fool-hardy seller would start an open price war (though none would be averse to making secret concessions up to the point where an open price war threatened to start).[41]

Yet when several firms engage in this sort of brinkmanship, some are likely to lose their footing, pulling the rest along, unless an explicit collusive agreement can be reached quickly to halt the slide. We conclude then that the probability of pricing discipline breakdowns increases with the burden of fixed costs borne by sellers, *ceteris paribus*, but that recognition of this danger may stimulate institutional adaptations which nullify the tendency.

It is hard to say confidently how this tug-of-war between the incentive to look out only for one's own short-run interests and the incentive

[40]R. L. Hall and Charles J. Hitch, "Price Theory and Business Behavior," *Oxford Economic Papers*, May 1939, p. 25. See also Bjarke Fog, *Industrial Pricing Policies: An Analysis of Pricing Policies of Danish Manufacturers* (translated by I. E. Bailey, Amsterdam: North Holland, 1960), p. 34; and Alfred C. Neal, *Industrial Concentration and Price Inflexibility* (Washington: American Council on Public Affairs, 1942), p. 87.

[41]*Op. cit.*, p. 77.

to cooperate will turn out. Some examples show the range of observed behavior.

Railroading is the case *par excellence* of an industry with high fixed costs and an historical propensity toward pricing discipline breakdowns when competition is left unfettered. The capital of railroads as of 1914 has been estimated at 574 per cent of gross operating revenues, compared to 94 per cent for manufacturing companies.[42] Thus, railroading was much more capital-intensive than manufacturing generally, with a heavy component of fixed charges for capital sunk in roadbeds, rails, terminals, and rolling stock; combined with a very low short-run marginal cost for adding an extra freight car or two onto an already scheduled train. Because of these cost conditions, rivalry among railroads in the closing decades of the 19th century was often marked by oscillation between price warfare and collusive agreements. This pattern was most striking on the key Chicago – New York routes.[43] During the early 1870s, only the New York Central and the Pennsylvania offered through service between Chicago and New York City. By concluding explicit price-fixing agreements they managed to maintain eastbound grain rates at roughly $.56 per hundredweight. However, when the Baltimore & Ohio completed its route in 1874, it refused to join the agreement, price-shading developed, and the grain rate fell to $.40 that year, $.20 in 1876, and to $.15 in 1877. Some shipments moved east for as little as $.075 per hundredweight during the summer of 1879—a rate which may not even have covered immediate marginal costs, although the evidence is inconclusive. Subsequent collusive arrangements between the New York Central, Pennsylvania, B & O, and Grand Trunk lines succeeded in raising rates to $.30 under favorable conditions, but the agreements broke down repeatedly until the whole rate structure was subjected to effec-

tive regulation by the Interstate Commerce Commission. The New York – Chicago lines were perhaps extreme in the duration and intensity of their competitive price-cutting, since there were four financially independent trunk lines and several rail-water interlines vying for business, but similar price wars of shorter duration occurred on many other segments of the U. S. railroad network.[44]

Turning now to the manufacturing sector, rayon manufacturing is a capital-intensive industry whose pricing behavior before 1950 has been analyzed thoroughly.[45] Producers had short-run cost relationships similar to Figure 7.1b, with fixed costs amounting to one third of total unit cost at capacity output, and with average total cost rising to 125 per cent of its minimum value for operation at one half capacity. (In Figure 7.1b, the comparable figure is 138 per cent.) The first reaction of producers to a decline in demand was typically to maintain capacity production and build up inventories. If the recession persisted, the larger firms restricted output to maintain the price level, but smaller firms tended to shade prices to keep their plants busy. This approach was successful in preserving a semblance of pricing discipline in mild recessions. But if operations fell much below 75 per cent of capacity, profit margins were wiped out completely, and after this point attempts to maintain stable prices proved "futile."[46] In the depths of the early 1930s depression, when industry leaders American Viscose and du Pont were operating at only 55 per cent of capacity, a formal price-fixing agreement was instituted. Elaborate steps were taken to implement it, but financial pressures on individual firms were so strong that the agreement broke down. Even the largest producers were violating it through off-list selling.[47]

The cement industry has a cost structure simi-

[42] Eliot Jones, "Is Competition in Industry Ruinous?" *Quarterly Journal of Economics*, May 1920, pp. 484–485.

[43] See MacAvoy, *op. cit.*

[44] For a skeptical view of the extent of rate warfare, see C. Emery Troxel, *Economics of Transportation* (New York: Rinehart, 1955), pp. 428 and 656–657. Although railroading has been studied by dozens of scholars, hard evidence on the incidence of price warfare is remarkably meager.

[45] Cf. Markham, *Competition in the Rayon Industry*, pp. 103, 130, and 150–153.

[46] *Ibid.*, p. 161.

[47] *Ibid.*, pp. 76–77 and 135–136.

lar to rayon's.[48] Though the product is essentially homogeneous and the number of sellers in most markets is relatively small, the industry has experienced repeated pricing discipline breakdowns when demand declined generally or locally. Recognizing their inability to collude tacitly with any great success, cement makers have entered into a series of price-fixing arrangements since 1904, but these have tended to collapse under financial stress. From 1930 to 1932, unfettered price-cutting drove down the average realized price per barrel by 30 per cent while unit overhead costs were rising.[49] An antitrust judgment in 1948 deprived the industry of its principal collusive device—the basing point pricing system. Strong demand kept prices on the upswing during the early 1950s, but excess capacity began to appear after 1956, precipitating price-shading and, between 1960 and 1966, a general decline in the price level.[50]

The steel industry is not unlike rayon and cement. Its products are fairly homogeneous, once the 'extras' problem is solved; and the fixed costs associated with its capital-intensive, vertically integrated production processes are relatively high. When account is taken of geographic market bounds, the industry is less concentrated than either cement or rayon. Yet up to 1968 and except for some episodes during the 1929–1938 depression, it was more successful than either cement or rayon in avoiding widespread price deterioration, even when operating at less than 65 per cent of capacity between 1958 and 1962. The main explanation for this record apparently lies in the extraordinary respect industry members exhibited for their mutual interdependence. A price structure which permitted producers to avoid outright losses unless output fell below 40 per cent of capacity was a contributing factor.[51]

High fixed and low marginal costs also played a part in the heavy electrical equipment industry's inability to avoid price warfare without formal collaboration in times of depressed demand. Demand for electrical equipment is a cyclical, feast-or-famine thing, and during the 1950s the industry was burdened by considerable excess capacity.[52] In addition to carrying fixed plant and equipment costs, producers maintained staffs of skilled design and production engineers which they were reluctant to disperse, and so a significant fraction of labor costs was also viewed as fixed. These conditions contributed to the rivalry which on occasion drove prices as low as 40 per cent of book values.

Finally, we consider the petroleum extraction and refining industries, which have their own special fixed cost problems. Much extraction capital is invested in holes in the ground—sunk cost in every sense of the word. Once a well is drilled, the marginal cost of drawing oil from it is practically nil. Refineries are capital-intensive, and to complicate matters, many products emerge from the distillation towers as joint or by-products with a marginal cost that is either low or indeterminate.[53] The industry has also suffered from excess refining capacity, e.g., of some 20 per cent during the late 1950s. Tacit collusion is complicated by disagreements over retail price differentials between major and independent brands and by the perishability (through physical deterioration) of local gasoline inventories. Frequent gasoline price wars at the retail and wholesale levels have been the result. At the crude oil extraction stage, prices fell from an average of $1.19 per barrel in 1930 to $.65 per barrel in 1931, descending to $.25 per barrel in some territories during the summer of 1931 as the onset of the Great Depression and the open-

---

[48]Loescher, *op. cit.*, pp. 59–72.

[49]*Ibid.*, Chapters 4 and 5, especially pp. 181–185.

[50]U. S. Federal Trade Commission, *Economic Report on Mergers and Vertical Integration in the Cement Industry* (Washington: April 1966), pp. 16–17.

[51]See Walter Adams, "The Steel Industry," in Adams, ed., *The Structure of American Industry*, p. 176. On the role of overhead costs in the steel industry during the 1930s, see also C. R. Daugherty, M. G. de Chazeau, and S. S. Stratton, *The Economics of the Iron and Steel Industry* (New York: McGraw-Hill, 1937), vol. 2, p. 1098.

[52]Cf. Richard A. Smith, "The Incredible Electrical Conspiracy," *Fortune*, April 1961, p. 170.

[53]See "Are Gas Price Wars at an End?" *Business Week*, May 29, 1965, pp. 134–144. See also Dirlam, "The Petroleum Industry," in Adams, ed., *The Structure of American Industry*, especially pp. 278, 284, and 288.

ing up of new fields coincided.[54] However, crude prices have displayed remarkable downward rigidity since World War II, mainly because of stringent cartel-like production controls imposed by the leading crude extraction state governments.

·To summarize, some industries (like steel up to 1968) have been fairly successful in avoiding independent pricing despite high fixed costs and depressed demand; some have been successful only when the financial pressures on their members were not strong; and some have been unsuccessful even after engaging in illegal collusion. The explanation for these differences appears to lie largely in the presence or absence of other conditions conducive to cooperative pricing. When other factors such as the size distribution of firms, the degree of product homogeneity, the extent of acceptance accorded the price leader, the ability and willingness of producers to carry sizeable inventories, and deftness in avoiding antitrust action are favorable, pricing discipline may be maintained despite substantial fixed costs. When they are unfavorable, a heavy fixed cost burden makes independent pricing during business downturns all the more probable.

As the federal government develops increased skill in using macroeconomic policy tools to combat general recessions, the interaction of high fixed costs with depressed business conditions will become a less important cause of pricing discipline breakdowns. But when and if recessions do materialize, or when shifts in demand adverse to particular industries occur, fixed costs will be a more pressing problem to businessmen, since the trend is for a growing proportion of all costs to fall into the fixed

category. This is so partly because the work force composition is shifting away from direct laborers and operatives, whose numbers can be varied with demand, to overhead-type employees like managers, salesmen, clerks, and engineers, who are hired to meet longer-term needs and are not laid off as readily in response to short-run production declines. The ratio of production workers to all workers in manufacturing industries declined from 84 per cent in 1947 to 74 per cent in 1963.[55] In addition, unions are increasingly demanding and winning greater job security for direct laborers. This raises the fixed component of cost structures and makes it difficult for producers to absorb demand shocks by maintaining prices and restricting output.[56]

A DIGRESSION ON CUT-THROAT COMPETITION

Thus far, we have implicitly assumed that when a fall in demand induces price competition among oligopolists, society is the gainer, since monopolistic profit margins are wiped out and prices are brought into closer proximity to marginal cost. However, this judgment is not universally accepted. It is sometimes argued that competition among oligopolists burdened with high fixed costs has a tendency to become "cutthroat" or "ruinous," and that it should be restrained through price-fixing agreements or mergers. This view was widespread around the turn of the century, but even in recent years it has been propounded by a few American economists and by many prominent scholars abroad.[57]

The cut-throat competition problem has two principal branches. One pertains to industries

[54]U. S. Bureau of the Census, *Historical Statistics of the United States, Colonial Times to 1957* (Washington: 1960), p. 360; and Clair Wilcox, *Public Policies Toward Business* (Third ed.; Homewood: Irwin, 1966), pp. 748–754.

[55]U. S. Bureau of the Census, *Statistical Abstract of the United States: 1964* (Washington: 1964), p. 221; and Charles L. Schultze, *Recent Inflation in the United States*, Study Paper No. 1, Joint Economic Committee of the U. S. Congress (Washington: 1959), pp. 79–80 and 87.

[56]The striking cyclical price flexibility observed in Japanese industries may be due to the fact that most Japanese workers have virtual lifetime tenure in their jobs. Therefore, most labor costs (with the exception of bonus payments) tend to be fixed. See James C. Abegglen, *The Japanese Factory* (Glencoe: Free Press, 1958), pp. 11–25; Shigeto Tsuru, "Survey of Economic Research in Postwar Japan," *American Economic Review*, Supplement, June 1964, pp. 95–99; and "Executive Scores Spirit of Samurai," *New York Times*, May 23, 1967.

[57]For various views, see Spurgeon Bell, "Fixed Costs and Market Price," *Quarterly Journal of Economics*, May 1918, pp. 507–524; Eliot Jones, "Is Competition in Industry Ruinous?" *Quarterly Journal of Economics*, May 1920, pp. 473–519; J. M. Clark, *Studies in the Economics of Overhead Costs* (Chicago: University of Chicago Press, 1923), especially pp. 434–450; L. G. Reynolds, "Cutthroat Competition," *American Economic Review*, December 1940, pp. 736–747; Fritz Machlup, "Monopoly and the Problem of Economic Stability," in E. H. Chamberlin, ed., *Monopoly and Competition and Their Regulation* (London: Macmillan, 1954), pp. 385–397;

with chronic excess capacity because superior substitutes have appeared on the scene, or as the aftermath of some unique episode such as a surge of wartime orders or the abandonment of tariff protection. The other concerns industries subjected to sharp cyclical or random fluctuations, with vigorous price competition breaking out during troughs of the cycle. Each is worth considering carefully, although in so doing we must depart from the main thread of our analysis.

THE SICK INDUSTRY PROBLEM

First we have the case of the secularly declining or 'sick' industry, of which soft coal mining, ice manufacturing, railroading, some branches of agriculture, and (during the 1920s and 1930s) cotton textile manufacturing are well-known examples. As this range of illustrations suggests, it is not necessary that the market structure be oligopolistic; sick industry problems can also occur in atomistically structured fields. There are two chief prerequisites: capacity substantially in excess of current and probable future demands, and rigidities which retard the reallocation of capital and/or labor toward growing industries. Then unless there is some artificial restraint such as a government price support program (as in agriculture and railroading) or tightly knit cartel agreements, competition is likely to drive prices down to levels which yield investors much less than a normal return on their capital. When firms' cost structures include a high proportion of fixed costs, this profitless existence can continue for years or even (as in railroading and coal mining) for decades, since producers find it preferable to continue operation and cover at least their (relatively modest) variable costs than to shut down and have their investments wiped out completely. The burden of stagnating demand may also fall upon the industry's labor force, for if workers are unable or unwilling to acquire new

skills and/or migrate to new regions offering more abundant job opportunities, unemployment will be acute and wage rates may fall to low levels. Capitalists almost surely suffer, then, in a sick industry, and laborers may suffer if they lack alternative employment opportunities.

It is standard practice for the afflicted, and frequently also for well-meaning outsiders, to urge that such industries be granted immunity from the rigors of competition to ease the pain of adjustment. Through privately or government-sponsored price-fixing programs, prices can be held at levels which let investors realize a 'fair' return on their capital and permit the payment of 'just' wages to laborers during the adjustment period. These proposals have a certain amount of appeal on equitable grounds. But abandoning the discipline of competition carries a distinct cost. However painful, losses serve the economic function of driving out surplus and inefficient production capacity and compelling the reallocation of resources into more remunerative lines. Monopolistic price-fixing schemes protect the inefficient producers who, under competitive pressure, would exit first from an industry. They almost always retard the adjustment of physical capacity to reduced demand, although it is less clear that labor mobility is necessarily enhanced by downward pressure on wages. In some cases price-fixing agreements, by permitting positive monopoly profits to be gained, have actually caused capacity to be increased in industries confronted with stagnating demand, aggravating the resource misallocation problem.[58] This perverse effect is particularly likely in cartels allocating members' sales and profit shares in proportion to physical capacity, for by building additional redundant capacity, a firm can increase its profits.[59]

The policy maker dealing with such situations faces a value judgment: he must weigh the pains associated with competitive pricing against its

S. M. Loescher, *Imperfect Collusion in the Cement Industry*, pp. 191–199; Almarin Phillips, *Market Structure, Organization and Performance*, pp. 16–19 and 221–242; Romney Robinson, "The Economics of Disequilibrium Price," *Quarterly Journal of Economics*, May 1961, pp. 199–233; Kojiro Niino, "The Logic of Excessive Competition," *Kobe University Economic Review*, 1962, pp. 51–62; Edgar Salin, "Kartellverbot und Konzentration," *Kyklos*, 1963, No. 3, pp. 177–202; and G. B. Richardson, "The Pricing of Heavy Electrical Equipment: Competition or Agreement?" *Bulletin of the Oxford University Institute of Economics and Statistics*, May 1966, pp. 73–92.

[58]Cf. Loescher, *op. cit.*, pp. 192–194.

[59]See Kurt Bloch, "On German Cartels," *Journal of Business*, July 1932, pp. 213–222.

superior allocative efficiency. It is well known that politicians opt frequently for a narcotic approach. However, there are compelling arguments for the competitive solution. When demand is price elastic, as is usually the case for products whose secular decline is due to the incursion of substitutes, or when machinery can be substituted readily for labor (as in coal mining and agriculture), keeping prices and wages up through monopolistic restrictions will substantially increase the number of immobile laborers thrown into the ranks of the unemployed, and the higher income enjoyed by those who manage to retain their jobs is not likely to outweigh the losses experienced by those who do not. Moreover, it may be possible to satisfy both goals— equity and efficiency—through programs to retrain and subsidize the relocation of workers employed in or displaced from declining industries. Extending subsidies to investors caught by declining demand, on the other hand, seldom commands much political support. Because, therefore, monopolistic price-fixing schemes do not necessarily ease the lot of workers, because economic efficiency is definitely impaired, and because no premium is placed on avoiding occasional capital losses by investors, most economists are inclined to reject the argument that cut-throat competition in declining industries justifies a deviation from the competitive rule.[60]

CYCLICAL COMPETITION

The case of temporary cyclical or random demand downturns is more complicated. Here by definition capacity is not permanently in excess of demand, and the problem is to avoid the loss or deterioration of capacity needed when demand recovers. Oligopolists operating evenly-matched capital-intensive plants in cyclically sensitive, price inelastic durable goods markets may, in the absence of institutions facilitating collusion, en-

gage in especially bitter competition during recessions, since each company may strive to increase capacity utilization and cover overhead costs by price shading, and none will cease operations, relaxing the pressure of its supply on price, until all are near the brink of collapse.[61] Competition of this character is said to have several potentially undesirable effects.

For one, if the slump persists, some firms can be driven into bankruptcy by their losses. These will not necessarily be the least efficient producers, but those which are weakest financially—i.e., the newer and smaller organizations without well-developed banking connections.[62] This is clearly objectionable on equity grounds, and it might at first glance appear that capacity needed to meet future demands is lost. However, the latter supposition is debatable. The financial reorganization following a bankruptcy plea seldom involves the outright dismantling of technically efficient production facilities. Rather, the plants are normally acquired at bargain prices by another solvent firm, which sooner or later restores them to operation, burdened by much lower capital charges. It must be noted too that major bankruptcies are relatively rare. In 1958, at the trough of the last general business recession of any severity, there were 758 bankruptcy cases filed by manufacturing firms, out of a total population of 329,000 incorporated and unincorporated manufacturing enterprises.

Second, it is claimed that the stop-and-go operation of plants and firms associated with financial reorganization or less drastic intra-firm adjustment to sharp competition causes all sorts of inefficiencies. The maintenance and replacement of machines may be postponed; workers may be laid off; skills deteriorate during layoffs; organizational continuity is lost; and research and development projects may be slowed down or terminated. While all this is possible, it is an empirical question whether the long-run effi-

---

[60]It is also true that the seriousness of the 'sick industry' problem is exaggerated by those who favor monopolistic restrictions on other (typically selfish) grounds. As George Stigler suggests, relatively few industries are really 'sick,' but many are hypochondriacal. *The Theory of Price* (New York: Macmillan, 1952), p. 249.

[61]Conversely, an industry whose members operate numerous plants of widely varying efficiency and with a high variable cost component can adapt more smoothly to demand downturns, since less efficient plants will be closed down long before the most efficient plants (and their controlling firms) are threatened with failure.

[62]Cf. Phillips, *op. cit.*, pp. 104 and 116, for some spectacular if ancient examples.

ciency sacrifices accepted under pressure from temporarily intense price competition are very great. What evidence we have suggests that serious sacrifices are uncommon in ordinary slumps, showing up only during a depression as deep and protracted as that of the 1930s. Indeed, Mueller found that industrial firms adjusted their capital expenditure plans to *favor* long-term research and development projects at the expense of capital replacement and expansion projects during the recession of 1958.[63] Moreover, it is doubtful whether firms would invest more heavily in new equipment and retain more workers on their payrolls under a monopolistic high price policy (which reduces the quantity of output demanded and capacity utilization rates, *ceteris paribus*) than they would in a competitive milieu. We shall return to this last issue in Chapter 13.

An argument heard frequently overseas, but seldom in the United States, is that temporary price-fixing arrangements to control cut-throat competition during recessions prevent permanent increases in market concentration, because otherwise small firms would either fail or head off the inevitable by merging with stronger industry leaders. There is no evidence that small but efficient U. S. firms have been forced in wholesale lots into the arms of their larger rivals during business recessions since the 1930s. However, some reports indicate that a movement toward crisis-induced concentration operated during the relatively mild Japanese recession of 1965 and 1966.[64] The Japanese experience may have differed from that of the United States because small Japanese firms were committed by tradition not to lay off workers and were therefore more vulnerable financially. Alternatively, the explanation might turn on the higher incidence of inefficiently small plants observed by Bain for several foreign countries, including Japan.[65] Yet even if the need of small firms to merge were accepted as inevitable, mergers could be channeled in such a way as to minimize adverse structural effects through a strong antitrust policy (which most nations abroad lack).

One thing is indisputable. When all-out competition does break out during business slumps, driving price below the unit costs of efficient producers, prices *must* rise above full cost during booms if average profits over the complete business cycle are to attract a continuing supply of investment. The more volatile downward prices are in recessions, the more volatile upward they must be in booms. This poses several problems. First, wide fluctuations in prices and profits may have destabilizing macroeconomic effects, making it more difficult to maintain aggregate employment at high levels through fiscal and monetary policy. This is an extremely complex question which we must postpone to Chapter 13. Second, public opinion is often myopic, and attempts by important oligopolistic industries to raise their prices during booms to levels which compensate for recession losses could provoke demands for government price controls and other direct intervention. Recognizing the difficulty of controlling such controls once they are imposed, politicians and entrepreneurs alike may prefer some formal price stabilization scheme to a less structured situation in which tacit collusion yields high boom profits but collapses in recessions. Third, some firms may fail under the burden of losses accumulated during hard times, even though long-run profit expectations are favorable. Fear of this contingency can lead risk-averting investors to demand a return exceeding the return earned in less volatile industries before committing their capital. If so, an industry subjected to alternating periods of highly profitable operation and price warfare might be forced to pay more to attract a given amount of capital than more stable industries, other things being equal. Or alternatively, at a given expected rate of return on invested capital, more capital will be

[63]Dennis C. Mueller, "The Firm Decision Process: An Econometric Investigation," *Quarterly Journal of Economics*, February 1967, pp. 71–73.

[64]See "Big Businesses in Japan Are Growing Bigger," *New York Times*, January 24, 1966; and "MITI May Enforce New Antidepression Cartel," *Japan Times*, February 9, 1966. I am indebted to Robert Fritts, second secretary of the U. S. Embassy in Tokyo during 1966, for information on this point.

[65]Cf. pp. 93–95 *supra*.

attracted into stable-price than unstable-price industries.

This last conjecture seems a persuasive defense of collusive price stabilization measures. At least, it convinced the British Restrictive Practices Court, which approved a price-fixing agreement among cement manufacturers, accepting their argument that the industry, with high overhead costs and cyclically unstable demand, could attract the capital needed to satisfy long-term demand growth at lower costs if prices were collusively stabilized than if they were set independently. With capital costs lower under a formal agreement, the argument continued, prices would also be lower.[66] There is just one difficulty. Theoretical analysis reveals that prices could well be higher, rather than lower, under such a scheme.

A THEORETICAL MODEL OF PRICE STABILIZATION CARTELS

To see this, we hold supply conditions and mean demand conditions equal while comparing three different cases:

Case A: Price and output are competitively determined, and demand is perfectly stable over time.

Case B: Price and output are competitively determined, and demand fluctuates around a mean value identical to Case A.

Case C: Price is stabilized collusively at the level of Case A, and demand fluctuates as in Case B.

Figure 7.2 embodies the simplest assumptions under which these alternatives can be compared.[67] Curve D_0 represents the demand curve of Case A. For the fluctuating demand of Cases

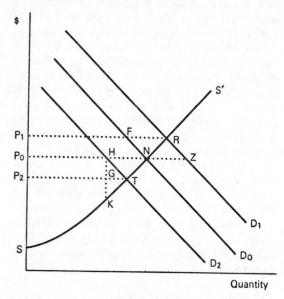

Figure 7.2
Competitive Pricing vs. Cartel Price Stabilization

B and C, we assume two possible states: boom conditions, represented by curve D_1, and slump conditions, represented by curve D_2. The demand curves are drawn parallel to one another and equidistant from the 'normal' curve D_0. By this device and by the further assumption that boom and slump conditions occur with equal frequency, curve D_0 reflects the mean quantity demanded at any given price over the full business cycle, so that Cases B and C differ from Case A only in the variability of demand, and not in its average strength.[68] We assume also that output adjustments to new demand conditions

---

[66] *In re Cement Makers' Federation Agreement*, L.R., 2 R.P. 241 (1961). For various critical views, see A. Beacham, "Some Thoughts on the Cement Judgment," *Economic Journal*, June 1962, pp. 335–343; the comment by J. B. Heath and R. R. Gould and the reply by Beacham, *Economic Journal*, June 1963, pp. 350–355; and A. Sutherland, "Economics in the Restrictive Practices Court," *Oxford Economic Papers*, November 1965, especially pp. 386–398.

[67] For analyses in a similar spirit, see Walter Y. Oi, "The Desirability of Price Instability Under Perfect Competition," *Econometrica*, January 1961, pp. 58–64; Clem Tisdell, "Uncertainty, Instability, Expected Profit," *Econometrica*, January–April 1963, pp. 243–248; Albert Zucker, "On the Desirability of Price Instability: An Extension of the Discussion," *Econometrica*, April 1965, pp. 437–441; and Benton F. Massell, "Price Stabilization and Welfare," *Quarterly Journal of Economics*, May 1969, pp. 284–298.

[68] More complicated variants can be analyzed by assigning variable probability weights to two or more demand states and locating D_0 so that it reflects the expected value of the various demand states. The results are essentially the same.

are made quickly, without significant lags or cobweb effects.[69]

The short-run industry supply function SS' is the horizontal summation of all individual producers' marginal cost functions. Total variable cost at any given level of output is therefore the area under the supply function up to that output. In stable demand Case A, the competitive equilibrium price is OP_0, the equilibrium quantity demanded and supplied P_0N, and the surplus of revenue over total variable cost (e.g., the quasi-rent contribution to profit and the payment of fixed costs) is the area $S N P_0$ per time period.

Under Case B, price drops to OP_2 in the slump. Profits fall short of Case A profits by the trapezoidal area $P_2 T N P_0$. In the boom, profits exceed Case A profits by the area $P_0 N R P_1$. Given linearity of the supply and demand curves within the relevant range and equidistant parallel demand curve shifts, the increase in price relative to 'normal' level OP_0 during the boom is exactly equal to the fall in price relative to OP_0 during the slump. That is, $P_2 P_0 = P_0 P_1$.[70] Since the height of the boom surplus profit trapezoid $P_0 N R P_1$ equals the height of the slump profit deficit trapezoid $P_2 T N P_0$, but since the latter has a smaller base, boom surplus profits necessarily exceed the slump profit deficit as long as the supply curve is positively sloped.[71] Therefore mean profits across the full business cycle in Case B are necessarily higher than mean profits in Case A. Fluctuations in demand accompanied by competitive pricing at all stages of the business cycle make the industry more profitable than it would be under stable demand,

other things (such as the mean level of demand) being held equal. It follows that if entry into the industry is governed solely by average profit expectations untainted by risk aversion, there will be more capital invested in the industry at a given average price, or the capital necessary to sustain a given average supply can be obtained at a lower average price, under fluctuating demand than under stable demand.

We turn now to Case C, assuming price to be stabilized collusively at the 'normal' level OP_0 which would prevail under competitive pricing with mean demand D_0. This implies, as cartels often insist in self-defense, that the producers do not take undue advantage of their monopoly power. In the slump, this arrangement is clearly advantageous to the producers, increasing profits relative to what they would be under competitive recession pricing by the rectangle $P_2 G H P_0$ less the small triangle GTH. In boom times, however, a stabilization cartel operating under the guidelines assumed here exercises restraint, holding its price at OP_0, producing quantity P_0N (since further expansion would require producing units whose marginal cost exceeds marginal revenue), and leaving NZ units of demand unsatisfied.[72] The profits which might be made by raising price to the boom competitive level are foregone. Thus, in the boom the stabilization cartel's quasi-rents amount to $S N P_0$ per time period, and in the slump to $S K H P_0$. In Case A they are continuously $S N P_0$. If booms and slumps occur with equal frequency in Case C, mean profits under the stabilization cartel scheme will be $\dfrac{KNH}{2}$ less than profits in Case A.

---

[69]Otherwise Tisdell's analysis, *op. cit.*, becomes relevant, at least for the case of completely ineffective adjustment to demand changes.

[70]Proof: $HN = FR$, because by assumption D_2 and D_1 are equidistant from D_0. Angle TNH = angle NRF because a straight line intersecting parallel straight lines cuts off equal angles. Angle THN = angle NFR because parallel straight lines intersecting parallel straight lines cut off equal angles. Therefore, triangle TNH is congruent to triangle NRF. It follows that $P_2P_0 = P_0P_1$, since congruent triangles have equal altitudes.

[71]Nonlinearity of the supply function alters this result, but usually in a direction which reinforces the conclusion that profits are higher under fluctuating demand, *ceteris paribus*. For if the supply function rises more steeply in the range analogous to NR in Figure 7.2 than in range TN, the increase in price during the boom will exceed the fall in price during the slump. And since boom output is at least as great as normal output, boom surplus profits will exceed the slump deficit. Unless demand is very elastic, the boom surplus profit will be higher with a convex downward supply function than with a linear supply function.

[72]Should the cartel attempt to satisfy the full boom demand at price OP_0 out of current production, profits would be even lower. Alternatively, production might be stabilized at P_0N over the cycle, with inventory being accumulated during slumps and depleted during booms. In this case mean profits will be equal to profits in Case A, less inventory carrying and spoilage costs. This 'buffer stock' arrangement is more profitable than the Case C approach (unless inventory carrying costs are prohibitive), but less profitable than Case B pricing.

Summing up, profits are higher in fluctuating demand Case B than in static demand Case A, while they are higher in Case A than in stabilization cartel Case C. Thus, under the type of demand fluctuation postulated thus far, profits are higher with competitive pricing than with a cartel which stabilizes price at the mean competitive level! Obviously, such a sacrifice of profits will not be accepted gladly by cartel members, unless they place great weight on being relieved from the risk of fluctuations. It seems almost inevitable that they will try to improve their lot by using their collective market power to stabilize price at a level exceeding the mean competitive level OP_0. And if so, the alleged consumer benefits of the stabilization cartel evaporate.

This result is not, however, completely general. It is sensitive to the stipulation as to how demand fluctuates. The assumption underlying Figure 7.2 that the slump, mean, and boom demand curves are equidistant parallel straight lines implies that demand becomes increasingly elastic at any given price during recessions.[73] An alternative assumption—that the three demand functions are horizontally equidistant straight lines with equal elasticity at any given price—is illustrated in Figure 7.3. In this instance a key property of Figure 7.2 is lacking. Assuming a straight line supply function, the rise in the boom price OP_1 relative to OP_0 is necessarily less than the fall in the slump price OP_2 relative to OP_0, and so the area of the two profit change trapezoids cannot be compared directly merely on the basis of their widths.[74] It is possible for the boom surplus $P_0 N R P_1$ to be less than the slump deficit $P_2 T N P_0$ under competitive Case B pricing. This is more likely, the less elastic the supply function is in the neighborhood of the equilibria. Profits under collusive Case C continue to be lower than profits under Case A by

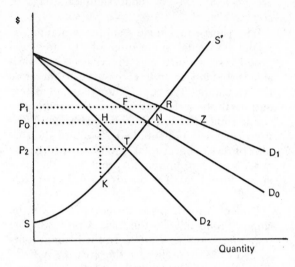

Figure 7.3
A Stabilization Cartel with Constant-Elasticity Demand Shifts

$\dfrac{KNH}{2}$. But since profits under Case B may also fall below those of Case A, Case B competitive profits do not necessarily exceed Case C collusive profits, assuming the Case C price to be stabilized at the 'normal' level OP_0.[75] Examples to the contrary can easily be constructed. Moreover, when demand becomes *less* elastic in recessions than in booms, the possibility of gaining higher profits through stabilization agreements than through competition is even stronger, *ceteris paribus*.

The relative profitability of stabilization cartels hinges therefore on two factual conditions: how inelastic supply is in the neighborhood of normal equilibrium, and whether demand becomes more or less elastic during recessions. Since industries susceptible to cut-throat competition tend to

[73]The elasticity of demand is given by $-\dfrac{dQ}{dP}\dfrac{P}{Q}$. With parallel demand curves, $\dfrac{dQ}{dP}$ is the same in every case. At a given price, elasticity is higher, the smaller the quantity demanded Q.

[74]Proof: $HN = NZ$ by definition. Angle HNT = angle RNZ. But because D_2 is steeper than D_1, angle NZR is smaller than angle NHT, and so triangle NHT is larger than triangle NZR.

[75]The cases are not as fully comparable here as in Figure 7.2, since the average Case B price is lower than the Case A price, and hence lower than the assumed cartel price. If cartel prices were stabilized at the average Case B price, rather than the competitive price for 'normal' demand D_0, the profit comparison again becomes unambiguously favorable to competitive price-setting. Similar difficulties are encountered with the Figure 7.2 demand shift assumptions when supply functions are nonlinear. But again, if cartel prices are stabilized at the mean competitive level, cartel profits are necessarily lower than under competitive pricing, *ceteris paribus*.

have relatively high fixed and low variable costs, marginal cost functions probably resemble the one in Figure 7.1b, and this suggests a bias toward relatively inelastic supply functions. Therefore, stabilization cartels of the Case C type may well have a profit advantage when demand does not become more elastic during recessions. On the crucial question of how elasticity varies over the business cycle, we have no empirical evidence, but only conflicting *a priori* conjectures. In a seminal contribution, R. F. Harrod argued that demand becomes more elastic during the downturn because consumers and industrial buyers are pressed by adversity to search more diligently for cheaper substitutes.[76] However, Professor Heflebower has shown that the problem is more complex.[77] Most of the durable goods purchases made during a recession may be those for which the need is urgent and non-postponable, implying especially low slump price elasticities. Elasticity may decline in recessions for nondurable luxury goods as all but price-insensitive affluent consumers withdraw from the market, while it may rise for inferior substitutes. Increases in recession price elasticity are also more likely when the prices of substitutes have fallen, drawing away patronage which can be recaptured through price cutting.[78] Heflebower's balanced judgment is that price elasticities are more apt to fall than to rise during the downturn, especially for durable goods, but he concedes (no doubt correctly) that sweeping generalizations are extremely difficult to draw.

In view of these complexities, it is impossible to say generally whether cartels stabilizing price at the 'normal' competitive level will be more or less profitable on the average than industries letting price fluctuate competitively, other things being equal. Since demand for at least some commodities surely becomes more elastic during recessions, and since greater stabilization cartel profitability is not assured even when elasticity fails to rise during a recession, it seems clear that there is a substantial subset of cases in which collusive stabilization of prices at the normal demand level reduces mean profits, *ceteris paribus*. For this subset, if not others, there are bound to be pressures to raise prices above the level to which they would gravitate competitively. Indeed, prices *must* be raised in order to attract as much investment as there would be under competition (and hence to have the same supply function, as assumed throughout our analysis), unless risk aversion under competitive pricing is so strong that it offsets fully the mean profitability disadvantage of the cartel. The risk premia needed to lure capital into cyclically volatile industries do not in fact appear to be very large— not more than two or three percentage points on invested capital, and about the same fraction of unit costs for a producer twice as capital-intensive as the average manufacturing firm.[79] Considering the smallness of this margin, it is hard to believe that producers who sacrifice profits by operating a collusive stabilization scheme would not try to attain the best of both worlds—risk avoidance *and* average returns commensurate with what they could earn if they behaved competitively.

This conclusion is reinforced by an accumulation of evidence that the risks of financial failure are not really very high in cyclical industries prone to alleged excesses of cut-throat competition. Eliot Jones studied the financial records of the steel, harvester, sugar refining, tobacco, whiskey, cordage, wallpaper, malt, bicycle, and other manufacturing industries which entered into large-scale consolidations around the turn of the century in a purported effort to escape ruinous competition.[80] He found that although

[76]R. F. Harrod, "Imperfect Competition and the Trade Cycle," *Review of Economic Statistics*, February 1936, pp. 84–88. See also R. F. Bretherton, "A Note on the Diminishing Elasticity of Demand," *Economic Journal*, September 1937, pp. 574–577.

[77]Richard B. Heflebower, "The Effect of Dynamic Forces on the Elasticity of Revenue Curves," *Quarterly Journal of Economics*, August 1941, pp. 652–666.

[78]This seems to have been the case for rayon *vis a vis* other fibers. See Markham, *Competition in the Rayon Industry*, pp. 162–170.

[79]Dynamic risk premium estimates as high as 7 per cent of stockholders' equity are presented by I. N. Fisher and G. R. Hall in "Risk and Corporate Rates of Return," *Quarterly Journal of Economics*, February 1969, pp. 84–88. However, it is probable that their estimates include components properly attributable to monopoly power or to the interaction between capital structure leverage and monopoly power.

[80]"Is Competition in Industry Ruinous?"

many of the firms had experienced some lean years, nearly all managed to remain financially healthy. Loescher concluded that the "quite brutal" competition occasionally breaking out in the American cement industry did not impair the industry's long-run health, and that incentives for price warfare were aggravated by the excessive capacity lured into the industry by earlier attempts to stabilize prices at too high a level.[81] Conduct at all resembling ruinous competition has been extremely rare in the recessions experienced by the United States since World War II. With the possible exception of the electrical turbogenerator industry, from which Allis-Chalmers exited in 1962, leaving inadequate domestic capacity to serve subsequently booming demands,[82] it is hard to find examples of manufacturing industries not declining secularly whose structural or financial health has been significantly impaired by episodes of sharp price competition.

Thus, on the basis of existing theory and evidence, it appears appropriate to adopt a skeptical stance toward claims that competition tends to become cut-throat and destructive. There may be exceptions—i.e., when demand is quite cyclical, turning more inelastic in recessions; when short-run supply functions are highly inelastic; and when for some reason producers are either too weak or too short-sighted to weather storms without serious degradation of quality or efficiency. But such cases appear to be precisely that—exceptions to the broad general rule.

LUMPINESS AND INFREQUENCY OF ORDERS

We return now to our main theme. The effectiveness of oligopolistic coordination also depends upon the size distribution over time of buyers' orders. Profitable tacit collusion is most likely when orders are small, frequent, and regular. It is least likely when requests for price quotations on large orders are received infrequently and at irregular intervals.[83]

Any decision to undercut a price on which industry members have tacitly concurred requires a balancing of probable gains against costs. The gain from cutting turns on the increased probability of securing a profitable order. The cost follows from the increased probability of rival reactions driving down the level of future prices and hence reducing future profits. The gains from cutting are obviously greater when the order at stake is large relative to total sales than when it is small. Expected costs, on the other hand, probably rise less than proportionately with order size. The amount of information a firm conveys concerning its pricing strategy depends more upon the number of transactions in which it quotes independent prices than upon the size of the transactions. A price cut on a large order transmits as much information as one on a small order. To be sure, rivals may weight more heavily the information on cuts involving substantial revenues. But this needn't be true when opportunities to bid for large orders appear only infrequently and irregularly. More typically, competitors will reason, 'Well, this was evidently a special case which can hardly be disregarded, but which is also not necessarily a good indicator of what we have to do to win the next round.' Three or four departures in close succession on $10,000 orders are more apt to trigger rival retaliation than undercutting the established price on a single, unusual million-dollar order.[84] Consequently, the gains-cost balance will often be conducive to price-cutting when a large order is at stake, while it will seldom be so for a small order, other things being equal.

[81]*Imperfect Collusion in the Cement Industry*, pp. 192–194.

[82]See "Allis-Chalmers To Stop Making Some Generators," *Wall Street Journal*, December 21, 1962; and, for a discussion of the subsequent capacity deficit, "Brown, Boveri Invited To Build Big Electric Turbines in U.S.," *New York Times*, December 22, 1967; "Generator Prices Get a Guarantee," *New York Times*, January 16, 1968; and "Swiss Turbine Deal Shorts Out," *Business Week*, May 3, 1969, p. 36. See also Arthur D. Little, Inc., *Competition in the Nuclear Power Supply Industry*, Report to the U. S. Atomic Energy Commission and Department of Justice (Washington: December 1968), pp. 305–314; and "Allis May Resume Building Big Generators," *New York Times*, December 10, 1969, p. 77.

[83]When there is a regular flow of orders from large buyers in addition to the flow of small orders, systematic price discrimination may arise. This case will be considered further in Chapters 9 and 10.

[84]See also the discussion of learning through repeated bidding on pp. 143–144 *supra*.

Occasional large orders are particularly attractive to enterprises with short time horizons or high future discount rates—i.e., those having difficulty covering high overhead costs during a moderate recession. Such a firm will be favorably disposed toward accepting the risk of uncertain future retaliation if the immediate gain is an order sufficiently large to keep operations humming at capacity for several months. Small firms, it should be noted, will have stronger incentives from this standpoint with respect to orders of a given size than large firms.

The history of the cast iron pipe industry during the 1880s and 1890s illustrates these relationships well. The product, purchased mainly by municipalities and gas utilities through competitive bidding, was homogeneous, and the number of sellers in the midwestern market, isolated by high freight costs, was at most 15. Phillips describes the problems faced by firms in bidding as follows:

> Jobs for a large city on which a bid was submitted might be of sufficient magnitude to keep a shop operating for weeks or months. The fine adjustments within each firm which would allow variations in output according to revenue and costs so as to maximize profits were impossible. In the absence of agreement among firms, the outcome of the bidding made the difference between operating and not operating for a substantial period of time. The firm with excess capacity, bidding on a large job, would be prone to submit any price so long as it was in excess of incremental costs of filling the order. And in view of the sporadic and large-sized jobs, some one of the several firms was apt to have the excess capacity created by a few unsuccessful bids.[85]

The result, at least in the absence of formal collusion, was intense price competition, and several bankruptcies occurred. Another consequence was the formation of a bidding cartel to restrain industry members' competitive zeal. This arrangement was the target of a precedent-setting antitrust decision in 1899.[86]

For a second example we return to the 20th century. By far the largest single buyer of the antibiotic tetracycline is the Federal government. As we observed in the preceding chapter, during 1955 and 1956 the five tetracycline producers settled down into a pattern of submitting identical $19.1884 bids per 100-capsule bottle in Veterans Administration transactions, the largest of which involved 30,000 bottles. Then, in October of 1956, the Armed Services Medical Procurement Agency (ASMPA) made its first tetracycline purchase, calling for 94,000 bottles. Partly because of the unprecedented order size and partly because pricing precedents for the agency were unclear, industry discipline broke. Two firms held to the established $19.1884 price, but Bristol-Myers undercut to $18.97 and Lederle cut all the way to $11.00.[87] Even at this reduced price, Lederle secured before-tax profits of at least $750,000, since the marginal cost of producing an additional 100 capsules was less than $3.00. This action touched off a series of rival counter-moves, although the exact form of the retaliation would have been difficult to predict in advance. In the next VA transaction (two weeks later, for 50,400 bottles), four suppliers (including Lederle and Bristol-Myers) quoted $19.1884, apparently because they considered the VA and ASMPA purchases, which differed in delivery details, to be in different classes. But Pfizer cut to $17.63 (10 per cent off the old $19.58 base) less 2 per cent trade discount. Nearly a year later, in the next Armed Services purchase (this time for only 14,112 bottles), Pfizer matched Lederle's previous $11.00 price, but Lederle returned to $19.1884. Seven months later, in the third Armed Services transaction, all bidders returned to the $19.1884 level. The overall picture during the two years following Lederle's $11.00 bid was one of considerable

---

[85]Phillips, *op. cit.*, p. 103.

[86]*U. S.* v. *Addyston Pipe and Steel Co. et al.*, 171 U. S. 614 (1899).

[87]See U. S. Federal Trade Commission, *Economic Report on Antibiotics Manufacture* (Washington: June 1958), pp. 195–197. Although the tetracycline producers were subsequently found guilty of antitrust violations, no specific evidence was offered to prove formal collusion in the transactions described here. Nor is it likely that Lederle would have cut the price as deeply as it did if a prior collusive understanding existed.

disarray in both ASMPA and VA bidding, punctuated by Lederle's persistent adherence to the pre-break price in an apparent effort to signal that it wished to see stability restored at high price levels after it had captured the largest plum.

Lumpiness of orders contributed also to the poor pricing discipline of the electrical equipment industry. In 1965—a boom year for the industry—only 36 big generator units were produced, some on multi-unit orders. A single order was sufficient to keep General Electric or Westinghouse, the industry leaders, busy for a month or more. For Allis-Chalmers, which dropped out of the steam turbogenerator business in 1962 due to mounting losses and its inability to cope with the industry's instability, a single order might mean a half year's successful operation.[88] Similarly, in Great Britain, where electrical equipment purchasing is concentrated in the governmental Electricity Generating Board, a single turbogenerator order could keep one of the three producers busy for more than a year, and a transformer order might amount to three months' backlog. There, too, pricing discipline has been fragile due to the struggle for orders which can fill capacity voids.[89]

SECRECY AND RETALIATION LAGS

The tendency for firms to cut prices to secure orders ensuring capacity operation for a substantial period is a special case of a more general phenomenon. The longer the adverse consequences of rival retaliation can be forestalled, the more attractive undercutting the accepted price structure becomes. A common method of attempting to delay retaliation is to grant price concessions secretly. Whenever price exceeds marginal cost under oligopoly and when it appears feasible to keep special concessions secret, producers have an incentive to engage in secret price shading. If the practice is confined to a small fraction of industry sales, the price-cutters may be able more or less permanently to enjoy a larger volume of profitable business than they could by hewing faithfully to list prices. But when secret price-cutting spreads to more than 20 or 30 per cent of total sales volume, list prices will undoubtedly be reduced openly. If further *sub rosa* shading continues, industry discipline may collapse completely.[90]

Our old friend, the electrical equipment industry, illustrates the latter, more dramatic result. Aggravating all the other disruptive conditions described previously is the propensity of manufacturers to enter into secret deals with major buyers. Thus, the proximate cause of the 1957-1958 'white sale' in switchgear, during which prices plunged to 40 per cent of book values, was an under-the-counter bargain that turned out not to be secret. In 1956 and early 1957 the conspiracy among switchgear sellers was proceeding swimmingly, and prices had been stabilized at high levels. Then Westinghouse offered a secret 4 per cent discount to the president of Florida Power and Light Company on a million-dollar order. General Electric salesmen learned of the deal and offered to match it.

---

[88]Cf. note 82, p. 206 *supra*.

[89]See G. B. Richardson, "The Pricing of Heavy Electrical Equipment: Competition or Agreement?" *Bulletin of the Oxford University Institute of Economics and Statistics*, May 1966, pp. 73–92.

[90]An ingenious theoretical approach to the problem of secret price cutting is taken by George Stigler in "A Theory of Oligopoly," *Journal of Political Economy*, February 1964, pp. 44–61. See also the extensions in R. I. McKinnon, "Stigler's Theory of Oligopoly: A Comment," *Journal of Political Economy*, June 1966, pp. 281–285. However, as is sometimes the case, Stigler's ingenuity outruns his sense of realism. The heart of the theory is the assumption that non-cutters will retaliate only when the cutter's market share expands more than can be explained (at some predetermined level of statistical confidence) by chance transfers of customer loyalty. But most businessmen lack the sophisticated understanding of randomness required to behave in the way Stigler postulates. When market shares change hands, their first impulse is to suspect some underlying causation other than chance. Their first overt reaction is not to sit down and compute the probability that the shift could have been due to chance, but to seek concrete information on the causes of the shift (e.g., by sending salesmen out to pump recently defected customers on the reasons for their defection). In other words, they initiate the search process emphasized by behavioral theorists. And as R. M. Cyert and J. G. March point out, "Search is simple-minded. It proceeds on the basis of a simple model of causality until driven to a more complex one." *A Behavioral Theory of the Firm* (Englewood Cliffs: Prentice-Hall, 1963), p. 121. The type of search assumed by Stigler is anything but simple-minded.

For another theoretical model with some relevance to secret price cutting, see Daniel Orr and P. W. MacAvoy, "Price Strategies To Promote Cartel Stability," *Economica*, May 1965, pp. 186–197.

When Westinghouse executives heard of the leak, they reacted angrily by cutting prices on another buyer's order. Other firms joined in, and the conspiracy broke down in a torrent of price warfare.[91]

A different pattern is found in the steel, fabricated aluminum, and rayon industries. Price shading is usually initiated under adverse business conditions by the smaller firms. They are encouraged to act independently in part by knowledge that the details of their concessions will be kept secret, even though industry leaders typically find out quickly that 'chiseling' is taking place.[92]

Thus, it is not so much secrecy per se as the limited scope of the deviations that inhibits retaliation; secrecy is merely a priming element in the process. If the covert concessions become fairly widespread, however, industry leaders react by announcing formal list price reductions. In aluminum extrusions, for instance, where the independent fabricators entering into secret deals control about half the market, off-list pricing normally leads to a reduction in list prices because the 'chiselers' make serious inroads into primary producer sales. But in aluminum sheet fabrication, the independents account for only about 6 per cent of total sales, and primary producers are inclined to ignore off-list quotations as a minor irritant.[93]

Secret price cutting, whether pursued to the point of a complete breakdown in industry discipline or merely to across-the-board list price reductions, interferes with the maximization of collective profits. Recognizing this, oligopolists have tried to nip the problem at its root by making it difficult to conceal concessions. This they do through some variant of the so-called "open price" policy, pioneered in 1912 by corporate lawyer Arthur Jerome Eddy.[94] In the typical case, an industry trade association is authorized to collect detailed information on the transactions executed by each member. To ensure full compliance, the association or an independent auditing firm is sometimes empowered to audit company records, and fines may be levied for failure to report sales quickly or accurately.[95] The association then publishes at frequent intervals (i.e., weekly) a report describing each transaction, including the name of the seller, the buyer, the quantity sold, and the price. Thus each member knows shortly after the fact who has been shading prices for whom and can take appropriate retaliatory action. The potential price-cutter in turn recognizes that he will be found out quickly, so the incentive for offering concessions in the hope of deferring retaliation through secrecy evaporates. Maximum knowledge of rival actions provides an exceptionally favorable environment for tacit collusion, as one open price agency, the American Hardwood Manufacturers' Association, boasted to prospective members:

> The theoretical proposition at the basis of the Open Competition plan is that . . . *Knowledge regarding prices actually made is all that is necessary to keep prices at reasonably stable and normal levels*. . . . By keeping all members fully and quickly informed of what the others have done, the work of the Plan results in *a certain uniformity of trade practice*. There is no agreement to follow the practice of others, *although members do naturally follow their most intelligent competitors*, if they know what these competitors have been actually doing. . . . The keynote to modern business success is mutual confidence and co-operation. *Co-operative competition, not Cut-throat competition*.[96]

It is worth noting that eliminating opportunities for secret action is an effective cure for

[91]R. A. Smith, "The Incredible Electrical Conspiracy," *Fortune*, April 1961, p. 175.

[92]Cf. Adams, *op. cit.*, p. 147; Weiss, *op. cit.*, pp. 295–298; Markham, *op. cit.*, p. 128; and Peck, *op. cit.*, p. 69.

[93]Cf. Peck, *loc. cit.*

[94]See his book, *The New Competition* (Chicago: McClury, 1912). For a more modern argument in the same spirit, see G. B. Richardson, "Price Notification Schemes," *Oxford Economic Papers*, November 1967, pp. 355–365.

[95]For a summary of several cases, see G. W. Stocking, "The Rule of Reason, Workable Competition, and the Legality of Trade Association Activities," *University of Chicago Law Review*, Summer 1954, pp. 527–619.

[96]Phillips, *op. cit.*, pp. 147–148, quoting from *U. S. v. American Column and Lumber Co. et al.*, 257 U. S. 377, 393–394 (1921) (italics in original).

'cheating' not only in price rivalry, but also in many other conflict situations characterized by a payoff matrix of the Prisoner's Dilemma type. Failure of the United States and Russia to agree on measures for assuring that covert tests were not being conducted was one bottleneck frustrating negotiation of an underground nuclear test ban, just as confidence that atmospheric tests could be detected was vital to the test ban treaty of 1963. The hot line between Washington and Moscow was originally intended to ensure that an accidental nuclear explosion (analogous to a mistaken price cut) was not misinterpreted as the start of real hostilities. And a sense of urgency was instilled into the U. S. atomic and hydrogen bomb development programs by the fear that similar actions were being taken covertly in rival nations' laboratories. Eliminating the secrecy enshrouding new weapons developments is a precondition for slowing down the qualitative arms race.[97]

This message has permeated into governmental economic thinking as slowly as it has into foreign policy. Except in procuring complex, technologically advanced equipment such as **weapon systems** and space vehicles, the federal government and most state and local governments require that purchases of supplies, equipment, etc. be made through sealed competitive bidding. That is, the procurement agency issues a request for bids with detailed specifications of the items desired, and would-be suppliers tender sealed price quotations in response. These are opened publicly on a predetermined date, and the firm submitting the lowest responsible quotation wins the order. (In case of ties, various procedures may be employed, depending upon time pressures. The winner may be chosen by lot, or the order may be split, or negotiations to secure a lower price may be initiated, or all bids may be rejected and new bids requested.) This approach to procurement has the great advantage of minimizing opportunities for bribery and favoritism. But as Paul Cook observes, "It would . . . be hard to find a device less calculated to foster open and aggressive competition among [oligopolistic] sellers."[98] For any firm tempted to cut its price below the prevailing industry level knows its action cannot escape the attention of rivals, and therefore it must fear retaliation on the next round. It will cut then only if the gain appears to outweigh this clear-cut risk. In addition, sellers may be reluctant to cut prices below current levels in a sealed bid competition because other large *buyers* will find out and demand similar price reductions.[99] Aware that oligopolistic suppliers are more willing to make price concessions in secret than openly, and because they are better able to control internal corruption (or are less apt to be the subject of front-page headlines when it is discovered), large industrial buyers typically rely upon secret negotiations rather than sealed bidding in their procurement operations.

INDUSTRY SOCIAL STRUCTURE

We turn last to the relationship between an industry's informal and formal social structure and its ability to coordinate pricing behavior.[100] This set of influences lies beyond the reach of conventional economic analysis, and its effects would be difficult to estimate even with a very rich multi-disciplinary theory. Consequently the economist is forced, without denying their importance, to view variations in industry conduct and performance due to differences in social structure as an unexplained residual or 'noise.'

---

[97]See F. M. Scherer, "Was the Nuclear Arms Race Inevitable?" *Co-existence*, January 1966, pp. 59–69. For other analogies, see Thomas C. Schelling, *The Strategy of Conflict* (Cambridge: Harvard University Press, 1960), especially pp. 20 and 33.

[98]Paul W. Cook, Jr., "Fact and Fancy on Identical Bids," *Harvard Business Review*, January-February 1963, pp. 67–72. See also V. A. Mund, "Identical Bid Prices," *Journal of Political Economy*, April 1960, pp. 150–169.

[99]For example, the "most favored nation" clauses in Salk vaccine procurement contracts, requiring that the seller charge no higher price to that buyer than it does to any other buyer, were a significant deterrent to price cutting. See *U. S. v. Eli Lilly & Co. et al.*, CCH 1959 Trade Cases, para. 69,536.

[100]For a seminal treatment of this problem, see Almarin Phillips, *Market Structure, Organization and Performance*, Chapter 2. See also Richard B. Heflebower, "Stability in Oligopoly," *Manchester School of Economics and Social Studies*, January 1961, pp. 79–93.

We can nevertheless at least identify some conditions which appear either to facilitate or impair collusion.

We have noted repeatedly the strong discipline of American steel producers, who resisted the urge to break from list prices during the late 1950s even when operating at only 60 per cent of capacity. The industry's finely-honed *esprit de corps* can be traced back to the Gary dinners of 1907 through 1911.[101] Differences in social structure undoubtedly have much to do with the contrasting performance observed in different parts of the European steel industry. During the 1960s excess steel capacity began to appear in Europe. Although they serve overlapping market areas and are separated by only moderate transportation costs and tariffs, the British and continental sectors reacted in dissimilar ways. On the Continent prices fell by as much as 25 per cent, while British domestic prices held firm, despite an influx of imports from hard-pressed continental producers.[102] British firms adhered to list prices in part because they shared homogeneous goals and had a close-knit industry organization, and because their directors (many of whom attended the same elite schools and belonged to the same social clubs) held cooperative attitudes.[103] On the other hand, members of the European Coal and Steel Community embodied many diverse backgrounds, styles of doing business, and national goals; and permissive leadership from the ECSC's High Authority was not enough to overcome these obstacles to cooperation.

As suggested in the preceding chapter, informal social contacts made at trade association meetings often lead to bonds of friendship and mutual understanding which facilitate tacit and explicit collusion. This was one foundation of the rayon industry's cooperative pricing policies; another was the fact that the two leading firms occupied adjacent home office buildings in Wilmington, Delaware.[104] American rayon producers also participated, directly or through affiliates, in cartel arrangements in nations where they were legal, and this collaboration abroad engendered cooperative attitudes in the domestic market. Nor is the pattern unique to rayon. Stocking and Watkins found that the three firms dominating the U. S. sulphur industry competed vigorously between 1913 and 1922. However, they then formed an export cartel (legal under the American antitrust laws) which apparently fostered the spirit of cooperation necessary to sustain high prices even during the severe depression of the 1930s.[105]

Still the existence of an industry association institutionalizing frequent business and social contacts does not guarantee cooperation. Personal antagonisms and distrust arising from all sorts of real and imagined causes can shatter organizational harmony. Cassady found that emotional behavior resulting from fear, anger, hatred, or desperation plays a major part "in many if not all" price wars.[106] Testimony from an antitrust case involving southern U. S. mirror manufacturers illustrates vividly the problems which can arise. At a trade association meeting in 1954, several producers got together to negotiate an increase in prices.[107] One participant described his experience as follows:

> . . . . I had never expressed myself to him, my actual feelings at all times. So when we got in this meeting . . . I just decided to tell him, "John, you are the one that started

---

[101]For a fascinating account of how steel makers bring social and other pressure to bear on non-conformists, see Dan Cordtz, "Antiestablishmentarianism at Wheeling Steel," *Fortune*, July 1967, pp. 105 ff.

[102]See "Steel Feels Weight of Global Surplus," *Business Week*, November 27, 1965, p. 31; "Steel Slump Hits Europeans Again," *New York Times*, February 14, 1966; and "The World Battle for Steel," *Business Week*, June 4, 1966, pp. 58–76.

[103]Cf. D. Swann and D. L. McLachlan, "Steel Pricing in a Recession," *Scottish Journal of Political Economy*, February 1965, pp. 81–104.

[104]See Markham, *op. cit.*, pp. 3 and 97–98.

[105]*Monopoly and Free Enterprise*, pp. 126–128.

[106]Ralph Cassady, Jr., *Price Warfare in Business Competition* (East Lansing: Michigan State University Bureau of Business and Economic Research, 1963), pp. 53–55.

[107]Phillips, *Market Structure, Organization and Performance*, pp. 183–193, drawing upon the record of *U. S. v. Pittsburgh Plate Glass Co. et al.*, 260 F. 2d 397 (1958), 360 U. S. 395 (1959).

this price war to begin with." I can't recall just the exact things that took place, but he as much as said I was a damn liar, that I started it. I said, "What do you mean, I started it, Mr. Messer?" He said, "You shipped mirrors into Galax, Virginia. You started it." I said, "I have never shipped a square foot of mirrors into Galax, Virginia, and I want you to retract and quit accusing me of starting this price war, when you are the one that did it." . . . Mr. Messer turned so red I thought he was going to have a stroke.

Another participant recalled:

. . . . I thought they were going to come to blows. The luncheon meeting had been very congenial, but after the first two or three minutes in this meeting . . . it looked like there might be a free-for-all break out at any time.

An agreement was in fact reached by all save Mr. Messer, but during the following month the agreed-upon price was undercut on nearly 70 per cent of all transactions. In his analysis of this case, Phillips concludes that "In a psychological sense, it is doubtful that these men were capable of agreeing on anything."[108] The uniqueness of this aberration is shown by the fact that the western and northern branches of the mirror industry, with similar market structures, managed to avoid price warfare without engaging in known collusion.[109] However, the problem of mutual distrust does not seem to be an unusual one. Fog observes that in Denmark, where formal price-fixing agreements are legal:

Cartel agreements are not always the expression of cordial co-operation among firms. In many cases it is rather a deeply rooted distrust that necessitates the signing of binding agreements, as the firms dare not place confidence in a gentleman agreement.[110]

Similar coordination problems arise when an industry includes a maverick of significant size— i.e., a strong-headed, individualistic entrepre-neur whose values or business methods differ from those of other industry members. Ernest P. Weir, president of National Steel, was such a figure, and during the 1930s his aggressive pricing policies contributed importantly to some of the industry's rare pricing discipline break-downs. Henry Ford played the role during the early decades of the auto industry, as did his friend Harvey Firestone in the rubber tire industry. The emergence of a maverick willing and able to disrupt industry tranquility seems to depend more on chance than on clearly identifiable structural or behavioral preconditions, and this imparts an additional element of randomness into predictions of industrial performance. Nonetheless, really striking cases appear to be rare. Perhaps one reason for their paucity is the fact that large, less aggressive firms will often pay a handsome acquisition price to eliminate small rivals actively promoting price competition. As the president of a cement manufacturing company wrote the head of a rival concern, ". . . the most effective way to cure a bad situation is to buy up the offenders."[111]

SUMMARY

To summarize, cooperation to hold prices above the competitive level is less likely to be successful, the less concentrated an industry is; the larger the competitive fringe is; the more heterogeneous, complex, and changing the products supplied are; the higher the ratio of fixed or overhead to total costs is; the more depressed business conditions are; the more dependent the industry is on large, infrequent orders; the more opportunities there are for under-the-counter price shading; and the more relations among company executives are marred by distrust and animosity. None of these links is strictly deterministic; all reflect central tendencies subject to random deviation. It is in part because of this complexity and randomness that oligopoly poses such difficult problems for the economic analyst.

[108]*Ibid.*, p. 193.
[109]*Ibid.*, p. 192.
[110]*Industrial Pricing Policies*, p. 155.
[111]Loescher, *op. cit.*, p. 120, note 76. See also Moyer, *op. cit.*, pp. 82 and 157.

Chapter 8

The Dynamics of Monopoly and Oligopoly Pricing

To the extent that the profit motive directs business behavior, it is long-run rather than short-run profits which businessmen normally seek to maximize. On this most economists agree. There is less agreement on the theoretical and performance implications. In this chapter we seek to determine how a long-run orientation affects pricing behavior.

Before we begin, one hazard must be anticipated. Long-run profit maximization requires that the consequences of today's pricing decisions on market position and profits be weighed far into an uncertain future. The businessman making decisions of this sort must exercise judgment concerning contingencies and probabilities, and different decision-makers may reach divergent conclusions under identical objective conditions. To avoid framing hypotheses which explain everything but predict nothing, we shall confine our analysis to structure-performance links where the opportunities and

reasons for contradictory outcomes are, if not tightly constrained, at least clearly explicable.

SUBSTITUTION AND LONG-RUN DEMAND FUNCTIONS

One hypothesis with important performance implications is the assertion that demand for the products of a firm or interacting group of firms possessing market power is much more price elastic over the long run than in the short run. This was first argued persuasively by J. M. Clark, who suggested that long-run demand schedules might "in numerous cases approach the horizontal so closely that the slope would not be a matter of material moment, in the light of all the uncertainties involved."[1]

There are two main reasons for the higher postulated elasticity of long-run demand schedules. First, competition among substitute products is more intense over the long run than dur

[1]"Toward a Concept of Workable Competition," *American Economic Review*, June 1940, p. 248. See also Richard B. Heflebower, "Toward a Theory of Industrial Markets and Prices," *American Economic Review*, May 1954, p. 126; and P. W. S. Andrews, *On Competition in Economic Theory* (London: Macmillan, 1964), pp. 73–85.

The very notion of a long-run demand curve, it should be noted, poses theoretical difficulties which most authors ignore. By tradition, demand curves are represented geometrically as two-dimensional schedules relating quantity demanded to the price charged. But what does the price dimension mean in a long-run framework? If the price axis reflects the current price only, the quantity variable (presumably some weighted average of quantities demanded in various periods) is not fully determined, since future demands depend upon future prices as well as the current price. If it represents the price charged in every period, reality is flouted, for even the most cautious oligopolists revise their prices from time to time. If price is viewed merely as an average of current and future values, we are left in the dark about the actual price in any specific period, including the current period, for which decisions must be taken. The essential dilemma, as Clark recognized, is that an orthodox approach to the long-run demand function attempts to compress into two dimensions a multi-dimensional reality. See his "Competition: Static Models and Dynamic Aspects," *American Economic Review*, May 1955, pp. 458–459.

Early attempts to cope with the problem, typically by oversimplifying the dynamic linkages, include M. W. Reder, "Inter-Temporal Relations of Demand and Supply within the Firm," *Canadian Journal of Economics and Political Science*, February 1941, pp. 25–38; William Fellner, *Competition Among the Few* (New York: Knopf, 1949), pp. 162–165; Alfred C. Neal, *Industrial Concentration and Price Inflexibility* (Washington: American

ing any short period; a given percentage change in price will induce greater shifts in purchases between substitutes over the long pull than in the short. Second, efforts by a particular firm or group of firms to hold its price persistently above the level of average total cost may attract new entry which in the long run makes heavy inroads into sales volume. In this section we focus on long-run competition among substitutes. The entry problem will be studied from several angles in later sections.

Competition among substitutes is one of the most universal economic phenomena. Steel, aluminum, magnesium, copper, titanium, high density polyethylene, fiberglass, western pine, bamboo, and dozens of other raw materials are potential substitutes for one another in thousands of fabricated product applications. Which one wins out in any particular application depends *inter alia* upon relative prices. To be sure, some materials have unique advantages, so the choice is multidimensional, but there is nearly always some combination of price and other features at which custom will shift away from one possibility and toward another. The same is true with respect to virtually every good and service; it is only through failure of imagination that we sometimes consider certain lines to have no substitutes.

Competition among substitutes is more intense in the long run than in the short for several reasons, all related to adjustment lags on both the demand and supply sides of the market.

Consumers, for one thing, are creatures of habit. A sharp rise in butter prices will induce only a moderate shift to oleomargarine in the short run, but as housewives reconsider their budgets and by experimentation find acceptable new uses for the substitute, the shift will increase in magnitude. Introductory sales are one way by which producers attempt to break the habit barrier. By inducing consumers to try a substitute product at unusually attractive prices, they build up preferences which make it possible to sell more of their product at any given price in the future.

Not all consumer lags are due to subjective inertia, however. Some shifts in consumption can occur only after modifications in complementary durable goods stocks are accomplished. If, say, the price of fuel oil were to rise by 25 per cent, demand during the current heating season would fall off very little. Short-run demand is price inelastic. But if the higher price persists, consumers will convert their heating systems to use gas, electricity, or coal, and in the long run the price increase is likely to cause a very substantial drop in the quantity of fuel oil demanded. Similarly, the initial impact of a doubling of gasoline prices would be slight but, as European experience suggests, in the long run many more motorists would shift to autos with less voracious gasoline appetites or perhaps even to electrically powered vehicles, and the decline in gasoline demand would become more pronounced.

Comparable rigidities constrain industrial purchasers.[2] Products must often be redesigned and

Council on Public Affairs, 1942), pp. 79–81; and M. J. Peck, *Competition in the Aluminum Industry: 1945–1958* (Cambridge: Harvard University Press, 1961), pp. 54–55. None achieves noteworthy success.

The only really satisfactory approach is to tackle the problem in its full mathematical complexity; geometry simply cannot suffice. Thus, different short-run demand functions may be specified for each future time period, with linkages to the past through past prices as arguments. When a reduction in the current price shifts future demand curves to the right, restraint will be profitable, *ceteris paribus*. In the more unusual case of leftward future demand curve shifts following from current price reductions (i.e., because orders for a durable good are merely shifted forward in time, and not increased in the aggregate), it may prove optimal to charge a price higher than the one which maximizes short-run profits. The system of equations obtained under this approach is sure to be formidably complex, and it may be violently nonlinear. However, analytic solutions might be generated using calculus of variations techniques, and almost any such problem which can be formulated numerically can be solved through dynamic programming methods. See R. E. Bellman and S. E. Dreyfus, *Applied Dynamic Programming* (Princeton: Princeton University Press, 1962).

An even more unorthodox approach has been proposed by Sidney G. Winter and E. S. Phelps in "Optimal Price Policy under Atomistic Competition," in E. S. Phelps, ed., *Microeconomic Foundations of Employment and Inflation Theory* (New York: Norton, 1970). They in effect do away with the conventional demand curve, relating a firm's profit maximization decision to the rate at which its quantity sold changes over time as a function of price changes.

[2]Fuel use is perhaps a poor example here. Moyer found that plants accounting for 64 per cent of all midwestern electricity generating capacity were equipped to interchange fuels, so they could quickly take advantage of shifting market conditions. Reed Moyer, *Competition in the Midwestern Coal Industry* (Cambridge: Harvard University Press, 1964), pp. 57–60.

production processes retooled to substitute one material input for another. Consequently, once production is geared to use a particular input, the demand for that input is inelastic in the short run. But given time and the appropriate incentives, redesign and retooling will take place. For example, in 1966 the American automobile industry began seeking ways to reduce its consumption of copper below the prevailing average of 38 pounds per car after sharp price increases added more than $30 million to annual materials costs.[3] The immediate impact was negligible, but the development of new production processes opened up longer-run prospects for displacing copper even from such traditional uses as in radiators. Moreover, past experience in times of rising copper prices indicates that once such displacements have occurred they have tended to become permanent.[4]

High prices also induce efforts to invent and develop substitute products which, after sometimes substantial lags, provide a powerful new competitive challenge. For instance, during the 1920s natural rubber prices rose as a result of cartel agreements. This triggered intensified research and experimentation on synthetic rubber, which ultimately displaced natural rubber in many applications.[5] Likewise, when the Chilean nitrate cartel drove fertilizer nitrogen prices up during the first two decades of the 20th century, a search for synthetic sources began, and from 1913 to 1918 the share of the world's fixed nitrogen output supplied by synthetic producers soared from 8 to 23 per cent.[6] During the 1950s the aluminum and container industries developed aluminum cans which challenged the sovereignty of costly tin-plated steel in the tin can market. The steel industry fought back with research and development on a steel container stock coated with aluminum (at $.25 per pound) in

place of tin (at $1.90 per pound).[7] More generally, Mrs. Carter, in a comparative analysis of input-output tables for 1947 and 1958, found that rapid developments in technology have made materials increasingly interchangeable, with steel giving way to aluminum and cement, copper to aluminum, natural fibers to synthetics, wood to paper, and paper to plastics.[8]

The net effect of these influences is to make demand more sensitive to price in the long run than in the short run, and because of this to constrain—perhaps severely—the prices which firms or oligopolistic groups can charge without inviting heavy sales losses through substitution. Then if producers strive to maximize long-run profits, prices will depart less from cost than one might expect merely from considering the short-run monopoly power present.

There is considerable evidence that many monopolistic and oligopolistic firms in fact exercise pricing restraint to ward off long-run substitution. During the mid-1960s, for instance, the domestic copper oligopoly held its prices in the neighborhood of $.40 per pound to prevent further inroads by aluminum, while prices of secondary (reprocessed scrap) copper and London Metal Exchange quotations reached as high as $.90 per pound.[9] Peck found that aluminum producers refrained from raising prices to short-run profit-maximizing levels in order to enhance long-term growth. He concluded that the existence of close substitutes made high long-run price elasticity a permanent feature of the aluminum market.[10] According to Markham, strong competition from other fibers limited the control of leading rayon producers over their prices.[11] And although the midwestern coal industry developed through a series of mergers into an oligopoly capable of tacit collusion, Moyer has argued that the possibility of

---

[3]See Thomas O'Hanlon, "The Perilous Prosperity of Anaconda," *Fortune*, May 1966, pp. 118–119; "Copper Keeping Its Share of Market for Metals," *New York Times*, April 24, 1966; and "Aluminum Inroad on Autos is Seen," *New York Times*, May 13, 1966.

[4]Cf. J. L. McCarthy, "The American Copper Industry," *Yale Economic Essays*, Spring 1964, pp. 77–80.

[5]G. W. Stocking and M. W. Watkins, *Cartels in Action* (New York: Twentieth Century Fund, 1964), p. 73.

[6]*Ibid.*, p. 127.

[7]"How Steel May Save an Old Market," *Business Week*, December 5, 1964, p. 33.

[8]Anne P. Carter, "The Economics of Technological Change," *Scientific American*, April 1966, pp. 25–31.

[9]For similar evidence on earlier periods, see McCarthy, *op. cit.*, p. 80.

[10]*Competition in the Aluminum Industry*, pp. 52–62 and 206–207.

[11]Jesse W. Markham, *Competition in the Rayon Industry* (Cambridge: Harvard University Press, 1952), p. 208.

substitution toward alternative fuels put an effective ceiling on the prices coal suppliers could charge.[12]

It is apparent, however, that fear of long-run substitution has not deterred some industries from maintaining prices which pave the way to competitive inroads by alternative products.[13] Steel is the most prominent example. American producers implemented a series of sharp price increases during the 1950s which led to increasing infringement upon traditional steel markets by substitute metals and plastics. This and other pricing policies which encouraged substitution may have been due to upward pressures from cost on prices, short-sightedness, conscious decisions to sacrifice long-term market position for higher immediate profits, or most probably, a combination of all three factors.

The steel experience demonstrates that aversion to long-run substitution is no sure-fire guarantee against excessive prices. But even when producers fail to show restraint, the possibility of turning to substitutes at least gives consumers an escape from severe and extended monopolistic exploitation. And as modern science makes it possible to create substitutes for more and more products, the combination of these two protective mechanisms—the threat of substitution and its actual occurrence—will become an increasingly important check on the social losses attributable to monopoly power.

THE DYNAMICS OF DOMINANT FIRM PRICING

Another check on industrial pricing power is the threat of entry by new competitors. To secure a foothold for our analysis of this phenomenon, which will occupy most of the remaining pages in the present chapter, let us focus on some dynamic implications of dominant firm price leadership.[14]

The static theory was presented in Chapter 6. To recapitulate very briefly, the dominant firm (controlling upwards of 50 per cent of industry output) finds its demand function by subtracting from the total quantity demanded at any given price the quantity supplied by members of the industry's competitive fringe, who choose their outputs by expanding until their short-run marginal cost equals the dominant firm's price. After finding its residual demand function and the derived marginal revenue function, the dominant firm maximizes its profits by adjusting output until marginal revenue equals marginal cost.

There is just one hitch. This solution is perfectly determinate and stable in the short run, since indefinite expansion by the fringe is prevented by rising short-run marginal costs as capacity constraints are encountered. But if the price set by the dominant firm is high enough to confer positive economic profits upon fringe firms, they will as time passes have an incentive to expand their existing plants and/or to build new plants. In addition, new entrants will be attracted into the fringe. This expansion and new entry cause the competitive fringe's supply curve to shift to the right; at any given price set by the dominant firm, more output will be supplied by the fringe. Since its own demand curve is found by subtracting the fringe's output from total demand, the dominant firm's residual demand curve must shift relatively and perhaps even absolutely to the left.[15]

If it conforms to the classic dominant firm profit maximization rule, the dominant firm in effect makes room for the expanded competitive fringe by curbing its own output, and even with growing industry demand, its share of the overall market and hence its share of the market's profit potential declines over time. High prices and profits today set into motion a chain of repercussions which reduce the dominant firm's profits

---

[12] *Competition in the Midwestern Coal Industry*, p. 185.

[13] For a discussion of the Dutch government's decision to "get all they can, while they can" in natural gas pricing, see "All That Gas in the North Sea," *Fortune*, August 1966, p. 115.

[14] The first complete and still definitive analysis of the dynamics of dominant firm pricing is Dean A. Worcester, "Why 'Dominant Firms' Decline," *Journal of Political Economy*, August 1957, pp. 338–347. An earlier treatment is found in Don Patinkin, "Multiple-Plant Firms, Cartels, and Imperfect Competition," *Quarterly Journal of Economics*, February 1947, pp. 200–202.

[15] In a static market the fringe has an incentive to expand while the dominant firm has none. In a growing market both have incentives to expand, but the fringe's incentive is stronger and its relative growth will normally be greater.

the day after tomorrow. In many instances there is only one way for the dominant firm to head off this Greek tragedy: it must abandon its attempt to maximize short-run profits, instead reducing its price to a level at which new entry and the expansion of fringe members are discouraged. Whether this alternative pricing strategy is feasible and attractive, and the consequences of failing to adopt it, depend primarily upon the shape of the cost functions accessible to industry members. Three cases can be identified.

First, when the long-run average total cost function is horizontal—that is, when neither economies nor diseconomies of scale prevail beyond some insignificantly small minimum optimal scale—the unit costs of small and large producers will (assuming correct planning of investments) be identical, and so small competitive fringe members will realize profit margins just as high as the dominant firm's margin. As long as the dominant firm sets a price exceeding minimum unit cost, fringe members will be encouraged by their positive profits to build new plants and outsiders will be tempted to enter the industry. To discourage expansion and new entry, the dominant firm must maintain price at the level of unit cost. Since foregoing all supranormal profits is not a particularly appealing long-run prospect, the dominant firm may decide to raise its price and reap the short-run profits commensurate with its monopoly position. As the competitive fringe expands, the leader's market share will fall steadily until it no longer is dominant and the industry will gravitate toward a more balanced loosely-knit oligopolistic structure.

Second, when the long-run unit cost function is rising (due to diseconomies of scale), smaller fringe firms will earn higher profit margins than the dominant firm at any price set. Existing fringe members have an incentive to expand moderately, and outsiders have a strong incentive to enter at small scales. The dominant firm cannot discourage this new entry unless it cuts price below unit cost. Since this is unattractive, the industry will evolve toward an atomistic structure.

The third case—steadily falling long-run unit costs—is more complicated. If there are very substantial scale economies, the price which maximizes the dominant firm's short-run profits may be lower than the minimum unit cost of small, high-cost fringe producers. New entry on a small scale is improbable, and existing fringe members can be driven out by aggressive pricing. This is a classic natural monopoly setting. It is rare, except among regulated public utilities and in tiny, geographically isolated markets. When its short-run profit-maximizing price is high enough to let fringe members cover their costs, the dominant firm may still drive them out by cutting price below their costs, reducing but not eliminating its own short-run profits. But if it elects to leave a profitable foothold for fringe producers, they will tend to expand their market shares at its expense, for by building larger plants they achieve scale economies and increase their profits. The dominant firm's dominance will gradually wane, until eventually a more evenly balanced tight oligopoly structure results.

We have seen in Chapter 4 that continuously declining long-run cost functions are exceptional in American industry, and that the prevalent case is one in which unit production and distribution costs are roughly constant once a minimum optimal scale considerably smaller than the market size is attained. This evidence, coupled with predictions generated by the theory, suggests that the market shares of dominant firms will commonly display a declining trend.

The facts are consistent with this prediction. There has been a distinct tendency for the market shares of firms which once dominated their industries to decline over time, even when we exclude from examination those industries in which the leading firm's decline was the result of government trust-busting. U. S. Steel, for example, controlled 65 per cent of American ingot capacity in 1901. Its high prices provided an 'umbrella' favoring the entry and expansion of smaller producers. By 1915 its share had fallen to 52 per cent, and it continued to decline to 28 per cent in 1960 and 21 per cent in 1968.[16] In 1919, the American Viscose Company controlled

[16]That U. S. Steel's early pricing strategy was profitable is demonstrated by George Stigler in "The Dominant Firm and the Inverted Umbrella," *Journal of Law and Economics*, October 1965, pp. 167–172. For a discussion of U. S. Steel's more recent attempts to avert a continuing market share decline, see A. D. H. Kaplan, J. B.

100 per cent of the domestic rayon market. Once key patents expired, new entry and the expansion of entrants caused its share to fall to 42 per cent in 1930, after which, according to Markham, it no longer conformed to the dominant firm pricing model.[17] However, it continued to bear the brunt of industry output restriction efforts, and by 1949 its share had fallen further to 26 per cent. American Can controlled 90 per cent of all tin can output at the time of its organization in 1901. Its high price policy encouraged new entry, and its market share fell to 63 per cent in 1913. and to roughly 40 per cent by 1960.[18] Similar histories are observed in corn products refining,[19] farm implements,[20] synthetic fibers,[21] aluminum extrusions,[22] and when dominance in regional markets is taken into account, also in the gasoline industry.[23]

Nevertheless, a few firms have retained dominant positions in their markets for decades. Alcoa virtually monopolized the U. S. primary aluminum industry until 1945, when an antitrust decree and the government war plants disposal program jointly led to the development of an oligopolistic structure. The United Shoe Machinery Corporation controlled from 80 to 90 per cent of the output in its field for more than a half century.[24] Since the 1930s General Motors has managed to retain its 45 to 55 per cent share of the automobile market. The maintenance of a stable dominant or near-dominant position in these and a few other industries can be attributed to a combination of two characteristics, both consistent with the dominant firm theory: the existence of significant scale economies or other barriers to new entry, and the dominant firm's decision to refrain from setting the high prices associated with a short-run profit maximization policy.

Oligopolists who together control the lion's share of their industry's output and who are colluding to maximize joint profits are in much the same position as the classic dominant firm. They too must ponder the reactions of active or potential competitive fringe members. If they set price above the level of fringe producers' unit costs and if barriers to new entry and expansion are modest, the fringe will build new capacity and expand, and the dominant oligopolists' market share will decline accordingly. For instance, the Big Three of the cigarette industry saw the market share of "ten cent" brand manufacturers rise from 1 to 23 per cent in just 20 months when they rendered their positions vulnerable by an ill-timed price increase in 1931. Only by cutting prices again were they able to check the incursion of fringe producers. To preserve the discipline of their covert price-fixing agreements, the leading three electrical switchgear manufacturers found themselves compelled in 1958 to surrender 10 percentage points of their market share to an insistent new entrant and another veteran conspirator anxious to expand.[25] Similar pressures confront formally-organized cartels. As Machlup put it, cartel members often "find themselves 'holding the umbrella' over the outsiders and getting increasingly wet feet."[26] Fritz Voigt found that most of the thousands of

---

Dirlam, and R. F. Lanzillotti, *Pricing in Big Business* (Washington: Brookings, 1958), pp. 166–167; "U. S. Steel Strips for a Fight," *Business Week*, September 28, 1963, pp. 114–119; and "A New Boss at the Corporation," *Business Week*, July 8, 1967, pp. 140–146.

[17] *Competition in the Rayon Industry*, pp. 14–20, 46–47, and 103–104.

[18] C. H. Hession, "The Metal Container Industry," in Walter Adams, ed., *The Structure of American Industry* (Third ed.; New York: Macmillan, 1961), pp. 432–434; and James W. McKie, *Tin Cans and Tin Plate* (Cambridge: Harvard University Press, 1959), pp. 46 and 89.

[19] Simon N. Whitney, *Antitrust Policies*, vol. II (New York: Twentieth Century Fund, 1958), pp. 258–260.

[20] Kaplan, Dirlam, and Lanzillotti, *op. cit.*, p. 69.

[21] "Sagging du Pont Casts Shadow over the Dow," *Business Week*, April 8, 1967, p. 120.

[22] Peck, *op. cit.*, p. 70.

[23] Edmund P. Learned and Catherine C. Ellsworth, *Gasoline Pricing in Ohio* (Boston: Harvard Business School, 1959), pp. 23–24 and 161; and Kaplan, Dirlam, and Lanzillotti, *op. cit.*, pp. 86 and 157.

[24] Carl Kaysen, *United States v. United Shoe Machinery Corporation* (Cambridge: Harvard University Press, 1956), pp. 39–64.

[25] Richard A. Smith, "The Incredible Electrical Conspiracy," *Fortune*, April 1961, p. 180.

[26] Fritz Machlup, *The Economics of Sellers' Competition* (Baltimore: Johns Hopkins Press, 1952), pp. 527–529.

German cartels formed between 1873 and 1933 collapsed quickly, often after only a few months of operation. The reason was that "if they succeeded in raising prices, new firms entered the industry, operating as outsiders, which led to a decline in sales by the cartel members; the cartel collapsed and a price war set in. . . ." Only the cartels with strong patent protection or other effective entry barriers were able to hold prices up while retaining their market shares, but they were the exceptions.[27]

This analysis has several morals. The threat of new entry or competitive fringe growth limits the pricing power of a dominant firm or a group of colluding firms unless steep barriers to entry exist. As a rule, the dominant firm or group can maintain market position only by holding prices below a level which yields positive economic profits to fringe members. If the group choose to restrain their pricing in this way so as to maximize long-run profits, society benefits from the lower prices. If they choose to squeeze the most out of their short-run monopoly position, they must pay the consequences in the form of an eventual fall from power, and the industry will become less concentrated.

Neither alternative ensures that price will be driven, sooner or later, all the way down to the competitive level. It is possible, under certain conditions, for a dominant firm or collusive oligopoly to exclude new entry while retaining some supra-normal profits. The main questions remaining are, how far above costs can price be held without inducing entry? And upon what does this price-cost margin depend?

PRICING TO DETER ENTRY

These questions are tackled under the theory of pricing to deter entry, known also as limit

pricing theory. There is a vast theoretical and empirical literature, and here it is possible to deal only with the central concepts.[28] We shall proceed in five steps: developing a naive 'comparative statics' model of limit pricing with homogeneous products; introducing dynamic complications; exploring the effects of large-scale entry; examining such complications as product differentiation; and reviewing the evidence on the consequences of limit pricing and high entry barriers.

A NAIVE MODEL

We have seen that economies of scale and other barriers to entry affect the profit margin which can be maintained by a dominant firm without attracting new entry. Let us carry this suggestion further. Our problem is to find the optimal price policy for a dominant firm or group of collusively acting oligopolists whose product is sufficiently homogeneous that all sales are made at essentially identical prices. In Figure 8.1, let DD' be the demand curve for the group. If the group supplies all current output, DD' is also the industry demand curve, or if there is a competitive fringe whose presence is tolerated by the dominant group, it is the industry demand curve less the output current fringe members supply. To avoid the complications brought out in the first footnote of this chapter, we assume that demand is expected to be stable over time, so that DD' can also serve to represent long-run industry demand.

Now suppose that existing fringe producers and potential entrants, including both domestic firms and potential importers, are small in size relative to total market volume, so that they view their individual output contributions as having no perceptible influence on price. Suppose furthermore that at this small scale of operation the

[27]"German Experience with Cartels and Their Control during Pre-War and Post-War Periods," in J. P. Miller, ed., *Competition, Cartels and Their Regulation* (Amsterdam: North Holland, 1962), pp. 184, 171–172, and 181.

[28]Seminal works include Nicholas Kaldor, "Market Imperfection and Excess Capacity," *Economica*, February 1935, pp. 33–50; J. M. Clark, "Toward a Concept of Workable Competition," *American Economic Review*, June 1940, especially pp. 247–248; Joe S. Bain, "A Note on Pricing in Monopoly and Oligopoly," *American Economic Review*, March 1949, pp. 448–464; P. W. S. Andrews, *Manufacturing Business* (London: Macmillan, 1949); R. F. Harrod, *Economic Essays* (London: Macmillan, 1952), especially pp. 139–174; H. R. Edwards, "Price Formation in Manufacturing Industry and Excess Capacity," *Oxford Economic Papers*, February 1955, pp. 194–218; Joe S. Bain, *Barriers to New Competition* (Cambridge: Harvard University Press, 1956); Paolo Sylos-Labini, *Oligopoly and Technical Progress* (translated from the Italian by Elizabeth Henderson; Cambridge: Harvard University Press, 1962); Franco Modigliani, "New Developments on the Oligopoly Front," *Journal*

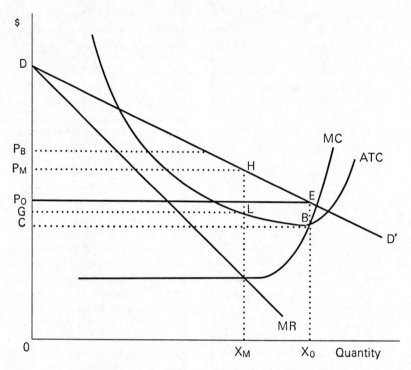

Figure 8.1
Pricing To Deter Small-Scale Entry

lowest attainable average total cost, or unit cost, including normal profits, is OP_0, and that all potential entrants can achieve this cost level (i.e., the long-run competitive supply function is perfectly elastic). Then if the dominant group sets and maintains a price even slightly above OP_0, firms in the competitive fringe realize supra-normal profits. Existing members have an incentive to expand or replicate their plants, and if there are no barriers to entry not subsumed in the cost curves, new firms will enter the industry. The dominant group's demand curve—initially DD'—will not remain stable. It will shift to the left and continue shifting to the left due to the expanded supply of fringe members as long as the price is kept above OP_0. The *long-run* demand curve for the dominant group is not, therefore,

DD'. It does include segment ED'. But when the price is raised and held above OP_0, the quantity demanded from the dominant group falls off more and more as time passes. If the price were held long enough above OP_0, the amount of output demanded from the group (i.e., not supplied by fringe members) will eventually approach zero. P_0E therefore approximates the remaining segment of the dominant group's long-run demand curve, the whole of which is given by P_0ED'. At the price level above which new entry flows in, the dominant group's long-run demand function tends to become perfectly elastic. It is this entry phenomenon, more than long-run substitution between different products, which prompted J. M. Clark, Sir Roy Harrod, P. W. S. Andrews, and others to insist

of Political Economy, June 1958, pp. 215–232; Roger Sherman and Thomas D. Willett, "Potential Entrants Discourage Entry," *Journal of Political Economy*, August 1967, pp. 400–403; and B. P. Pashigian, "Limit Price and the Market Share of the Leading Firm," *Journal of Industrial Economics*, July 1968, pp. 165–177. For other citations, see D. K. Osborne, "The Role of Entry in Oligopoly Theory," *Journal of Political Economy*, August 1964, pp. 396–402.

that the long-run demand curves confronting monopolists and oligopolistic groups tend to be highly elastic, approaching the horizontal.

If it chooses to keep the competitive fringe in check and deter entry, the dominant group must set and maintain the entry-deterring or limit price OP_0 (or, more precisely, some price slightly less than OP_0). Its long-run profit expectations depend upon its costs. The minimum cost per unit for fringe producers, by assumption, is OP_0. If the group members can do no better than this —that is, if there are no economies of scale, or if the limit-pricing firms lack special cost advantages such as particularly favorable ore deposits or patented production processes[29]—they must reconcile themselves to an existence devoid of supra-normal profits if they wish to deter entry. If on the other hand economies of scale or other cost advantages can be realized by dominant group members, or if tariffs and transportation costs put equally efficient foreign producers at a delivered cost disadvantage, supra-normal profits can be earned continuously while holding the price at OP_0. Suppose the group is able to operate on a combined short-run average total cost function ATC, with corresponding marginal costs MC. This cost structure is ideally suited to producing the output OX_0 compatible with price OP_0. Unit costs attain a minimum of $OC = X_0B$ at X_0. The group will then be able to earn total profits of P_0EBC per period while preventing new entry.

Is setting the limit price OP_0 and hauling in, year after year, profits of P_0EBC the most profitable long-run strategy for the original dominant group? The answer depends upon the particular facts. But to explore the logic of a prominent alternative strategy, suppose the group's cost structure continues to be characterized by curves ATC and MC in Figure 8.1.[30] Then the group might elect to set the price OP_M, which yields maximum short-run profits of P_MHLG. This return necessarily exceeds the limit price profit P_0EBC in the current period. But OP_M encourages expansion of actual and potential fringe members, reducing the original group's future profits in three ways.

First, even if a pricing policy which held total *industry* profits at their maximum could be pursued, the original group's share of that total would fall as its share of output declined. Second, if the group reduces its output while remaining committed to plant and equipment suitable for producing the pre-entry output, its profit margin will be squeezed from below by rising unit costs due to underabsorption of fixed overhead charges. Third, the price is not likely to be held for very long at the level which maximizes either original group or overall industry short-run profits. If the first response to an entry-inducing price is the growth of a few fringe members to a size where they recognize their impact on price, the new oligopolists might be willing to work toward joint profit maximization. But the original group, under heavy pressure from underabsorbed fixed costs, may prove uncooperative. The result could be a price war. If the original group continues to maximize its current profits in accord with the dominant firm leadership model, its optimal price will probably fall over time, since fringe expansion usually renders the group's residual demand curve more elastic.[31] Should sufficient pricing discipline be maintained to maximize either industry or group profits for the short run, further entry will be enticed. Eventually there will be so many fringe firms supplying such a large proportion of the total output that the price will be driven to OP_0—the marginal cost of marginal entrants.

In choosing a price policy, the original group must therefore compare the initially lower but persistent profits from an entry-limiting strategy against the initially higher but eventually lower

[29]In principle, cost savings associated with patented processes or favorable ore deposits are rents which should be imputed through capitalization to the patent or leasehold. In practice, accountants refuse to do so in the absence of a market transaction, and such assets are bought and sold too infrequently and in too imperfect a market for imputation to work well.

[30]This is slightly unrealistic, but does no real violence to the analysis. If it were contemplating a more restrictive output policy leading to long-run output declines, the group would undoubtedly invest in less capacity.

[31]A possible exception occurs when marginal costs rise significantly with reduced output. But this enhances cost–push pressures on profits.

profits from the short-run maximization strategy. The decision depends upon the size of P_0EBC as opposed to P_MHLG, the rate at which profits under the short-run maximization strategy are expected to erode due to entry, and the discount rate applied to future earnings. In many cases, the last of these variables can play a decisive role. If companies discount the future heavily, they may place little weight on the future profits foregone due to new entry and strive for maximum profits in the short run. According to standard managerial economics textbooks, high discount rates are especially appropriate when the future is uncertain, as it surely is in planning long-range price policy.[32] However, uncertainty may work in exactly the opposite direction. As Harrod observes:

> All entrepreneurs . . . have in mind the vast uncertainties of a relatively distant future. The best method of insuring against them is to attach to oneself by ties of good-will as large a market as possible as quickly as possible. If one can get a substantially larger market by earning no more than a normal profit than one could get by earning a surplus profit . . . one may well choose to do the former, as an insurance against future uncertainties.[33]

It is well known that some decision-makers are more short-sighted or discount the future more heavily than others. Fog found such differences to be the most important single source of internal conflict and disagreement in Danish price-fixing cartels, with larger firms typically placing more weight on long-run considerations.[34] The pricing policy chosen in any particular situation depends, then, upon both the objective data and the psychology of the decision-makers involved.

One further possibility must be explored. Suppose the cost disadvantages of entering at a small scale are great, i.e., economies of large scale operation are substantial, so that the lowest unit cost attainable by a small new entrant is OP_B in Figure 8.1. Then the original group can charge any price up to OP_B without attracting small new entrants. (Entry on a large, low cost scale might still be feasible, but we will defer this point.) The price OP_M which maximizes short-run group profits is less than OP_B. Now the group can have its cake and eat it: maximizing short-run profits and at the same time deterring new entry. In this situation, entry is said to be *blockaded*.

Following Bain, we define four distinct cases characterizing the relationship between cost advantages and pricing behavior:

(1) *Easy entry.* Existing industry members have no cost or other advantages over potential entrants, so that in the long run they cannot hold price above their minimum average total cost, nor can persistent monopoly profits be earned.

(2) *Ineffectively impeded entry.* The existing dominant group does have an advantage over fringe members or potential entrants, and it could deter new entry while earning sustained supra-normal profits by exercising pricing restraint. However, because the advantage is small or entry lags are expected to be long or discount rates are high, the group finds it preferable to raise price above the entry-deterring level and let new firms enter.

(3) *Effectively impeded entry.* The existing dominant group has an advantage over fringe members or potential entrants and finds it preferable to forego short-run profit maximization in order to deter entry. From electing such a strategy it anticipates a *continuing* stream of supra-normal profits.

(4) *Blockaded entry.* The short-run profit-maximizing price lies below the limit price, so that short-run profit maximization and entry deterrence strategies are identical.[35]

Case (3) implies the most pronounced divergence between long-run and short-run profit-maximizing behavior. If it holds, with price being

---

[32]Cf. Joel Dean, *Managerial Economics* (Englewood Cliffs: Prentice-Hall, 1951), p. 568; and William J. Baumol, *Economic Theory and Operations Analysis* (Second ed.; Englewood Cliffs: Prentice-Hall, 1965), pp. 454–455.

[33]*Economic Essays*, pp. 147 and 174. For a similar view, see Bain, *Barriers to New Competition*, p. 174.

[34]Bjarke Fog, "How Are Cartel Prices Determined?" *Journal of Industrial Economics*, November 1956, pp. 16–23.

[35]*Barriers to New Competition*, pp. 21–22.

set at the entry-deterring level OP_0 in Figure 8.1, two important deviations from predictions generated by the orthodox theory of profit-maximizing monopoly and oligopoly may materialize.

First, it is entirely possible that equilibrium will occur at a point where industry demand is price inelastic. This is true in Figure 8.1, if we assume the absence of a competitive fringe. At the entry-deterring output OX_0 the group (and hence industry) marginal revenue is negative. Nearly all A students of economic theory (and a few B students) have at one time or another written into examination booklets that profit-maximizing monopolists never operate in an inelastic segment of the industry demand function. Yet because *after* entry their private demand function would diverge from the industry demand function, this is not necessarily true.

Second, if a group of oligopolists elects to practice limit pricing, marginalist output determination rules are no longer appropriate. The total amount of output to be produced by the group is perfectly determinate under limit pricing—it is the quantity OX_0 in Figure 8.1. However, there is no simple condition telling individual group members how much to produce.[36] If each member sets output at the level where its marginal cost equals marginal revenue (derived under the price-matching, constant shares assumption), too little will be produced. If each equates marginal cost with the price, too much will normally be produced. Ideally, each firm should produce a predetermined share of the total quantity demanded when the price is set at OP_0. But this requires explicit agreements on market shares, and even that is insufficient in a world of change and uncertainty. When the industry demand function shifts erratically over time (as most demand functions do), member firms could find themselves in the awkward position of planning to produce a known share of an unknown total quantity demanded. As a result, there is no way of ensuring that the

quantities member firms plan either independently or collusively to supply will add up to a total which just clears the market at the limit price OP_0. The limit price can be sustained only if production planning errors are absorbed through fluctuations in finished goods inventories and order backlogs. Changes in orders, backlogs, and inventory levels also provide signals to guide member firm production decisions when collusive output determination institutions are lacking. This feedback system, rather than marginalist rules, must be the main basis of output decisions in tacitly collusive oligopolies practicing limit pricing.

In recognizing these problems, we must become aware also that even when oligopolists mutually prefer to adopt an entry-limiting price policy, the limit price may not be attained or maintained. Through miscalculation, the price may be set too high. But more importantly, if the group's discipline is weak, the actual price may fall persistently below the limit price. In this case entry will be deterred, but member firms will realize lower profits than they would under an effectively coordinated deterrence policy.[37]

One further link between marginalist rules and limit pricing must be considered. As Chapter 6 brought out, since 1939 economists have been debating whether the use of 'full cost' pricing rules, which appear devoid of any attempt to equate marginal revenue with marginal cost, is consistent with profit maximization. The conflict fades in a limit pricing context. Producers pricing to deter entry must set their price slightly below the entrants' minimum average cost. The application of full cost pricing rules is an operational method of achieving this result. When prices of labor and raw materials change, they typically do so more or less uniformly for all industry members, actual or potential. The limit price must therefore change correspondingly, and adjustments based upon a full cost rule will keep actual prices in fairly close step with the

---

[36] I am indebted to Robert T. Smith, a former student, for this observation. In his senior thesis at Princeton University Smith showed, among other things, that the Sylos-Labini model achieves determinate member firm outputs only by assuming rectangular marginal cost functions. Cf. Sylos-Labini, *op. cit.*, p. 43.

[37] In *The Economics of Sellers' Competition*, p. 537, Machlup states that poorly coordinated oligopolists trying to practice limit pricing are caught on the horns of a dilemma. Low prices may induce actual competitors to compete belligerently, while high prices will induce new entry.

altered conditions of entry deterrence.[38] The 'conventional profit margin' applied to accounting cost need not be invariant across industry lines; it may (as case studies have documented) be adjusted to reflect the cost advantage established firms have over potential entrants. Thus, when the most profitable long-run strategy for existing producers is to deter new entry, intelligent application of full cost pricing rules is apt to lead as close to the goal of maximum profits as one can hope to come in a world of change and uncertainty.[39]

OPTIMAL DYNAMIC PRICING STRATEGY

Like most of the limit pricing literature, the analysis thus far has emphasized two main pricing alternatives: setting price at the level which maximizes short-run profits and invites entry (unless it is blockaded), or holding the price at a level which deters *all* entry. There is no reason to believe that producers necessarily behave in this dichotomous fashion.[40] Intuitively, one might expect them more frequently to adopt an intermediate strategy. The rate of entry probably depends upon the size of the gap between the price set and the unit cost of potential entrants. Because information about costs and potential profits is imperfect and because inertia provides protection against mistakes, a small positive margin between price and potential entrants' unit cost may induce the small-scale entry only of the most alert or rash entrepreneurs. As the gap between price and entrants' cost widens,

outsiders learn more rapidly that a profitable entry opportunity exists, and they are stimulated to move more quickly in exploiting it. When the gap is very large, as when ball-point pens costing $.80 each were sold at $12.50 in 1945, a veritable torrent of entry may be induced.[41]

By manipulating the size of the gap, existing producers can influence the *rate* of new entry. It seems entirely plausible that the most profitable policy will be to set the price enough above the strict entry-deterring level to encourage a modest amount of entry, but not so much above it as to precipitate a flood. This policy, which is a sub-case of Bain's "ineffectively impeded entry" case, will lead to a gradually declining market share for the dominant firm or group, and probably also a gradual decline in price to the absolute entry-deterring level.[42] As before, the optimal gap at any moment in time is likely to be higher, the higher is the discount rate of existing producers. The gap will undoubtedly tend also to increase, the slower is the dynamic response of potential entrants to a given profit-making opportunity. Existing producers are more likely to pursue a price policy which strongly discourages entry when their cost advantage over potential entrants is great than when it is small.

The pursuit by real-world firms of this more sophisticated dynamic approach to limit pricing could explain a phenomenon which has puzzled some scholars: the fact that modest amounts of entry occur even in industries observed to have substantial entry barriers.[43] However, we lack

[38]Cf. Sylos-Labini, *op. cit.*, pp. 57–60; and Modigliani, *op. cit.*, pp. 225–228.

[39]For a reconciliation of full cost pricing with the equalization of long-run marginal revenue and marginal cost, see Harrod, *op. cit.*, pp. 161–163.

[40]As Alfred Marshall insisted, *"Natura non facit saltum."*

[41]See R. G. Lipsey and P. O. Steiner, *Economics* (New York: Harper, 1966), pp. 305–307, for a case study.

[42]This approach lends itself well to treatment using the calculus of variations. The heart of the model is a stipulation of some form like: $\frac{dZ}{dt} = k\,[P(t) - C_e]$; where Z is a parameter of the competitive fringe supply function, $P(t)$ is the price trajectory over time, C_e is the cost of the most-favored entrant, and k is a response coefficient. This differential equation can be factored into the discounted profit equation of the dominant firm or group, and the optimal price trajectory can be ascertained. Work on various forms of this model was under way by Darius Gaskins when final revisions to the present manuscript were completed. See his paper, "Dynamic Limit Pricing: Optimal Pricing Under Threat of Entry," presented before the Econometric Society in December 1969.

A virtually identical differential equation was proposed independently by B. P. Pashigian in "Limit Price and the Market Share of the Leading Firm," *Journal of Industrial Economics*, July 1968, especially pp. 168 and 173. However, Pashigian was concerned only with determining the moment in time when the dominant firm moves abruptly from a short-run profit maximizing strategy to a strict limit pricing strategy. He overlooks the possibility of continuous gradations in price to optimize the rate of entry.

A quite different approach to the dynamic entry problem is taken by Dean A. Worcester in *Monopoly, Big*

comprehensive evidence on how frequently producers consciously attempt to control the rate of entry through their pricing decisions. The only well-documented example is Xerox's strategy in pricing its copying machines.[44]

When the Xerox 914 copier was introduced in 1959, sales efforts were initially directed toward penetrating the low and medium volume market segments—i.e., serving customers making fewer than 5,000 copies per machine per month. In the low volume segment, where Xerox had no inherent long-run cost advantage over alternate copying processes, prices were set very close to the short-run profit maximizing level. According to company executives, this decision was taken partly because the company was desperately in need of cash, and therefore discounted the future at a high rate, and also because they realized that Xerox would eventually have to yield the market to substitute copiers—notably, to those using the Electrofax process, which is simpler, but uses expensive coated paper. Actually, 29 firms entered the low volume market with Electrofax machines between 1961 and 1967. In the medium and high volume ranges, xerography had a modest to substantial cost advantage. Xerox prices were set below the short-run profit maximizing level, but above the entry-deterring level, in the expectation that a share of the market would gradually be handed over to Electrofax producers. The entry rate was in fact much less than in the low volume market. In 1967, there were 10 firms offering Electrofax machines designed for medium volume application and only four firms in the high volume range. Finally, in the very high volume field (above 100,000 copies per month), Xerox's comparative cost position was such that entry was blockaded. As it moved into this market by introducing new high-speed machines during the 1960s, it was able to exploit the full profit potential of its impressive xerography patent portfolio.

DETERRING LARGE-SCALE ENTRY

Up to this point we have assumed that new entrants or existing fringe firms enter on such a small scale relative to total market volume that they can reasonably assume their influence on price to be negligible. When there are impressive economies to be realized by entering at a large scale, however, this assumption may be violated. To deal with this case we need a more complicated model developed originally by Bain and Sylos-Labini and extended by Modigliani.

The problem, in essence, is that a firm contemplating entry at a large scale has reason to fear that its incremental output contribution will be absorbed by the market only if the price is reduced. As a result, even though the entrant's costs will be just as low as those of firms presently in the industry, and even though the pre-entry price exceeds the entrant's full expected unit cost, the price after entry may fall below cost, and entry will prove to be unprofitable. If this is anticipated, entry will be deterred.

Now the amount by which price falls after entry depends, *inter alia*, upon the surplus of post-entry over pre-entry output. This depends in turn not only upon the entrant's output, but also upon any output changes effected by the original industry members. Here we run squarely into the problem of oligopolistic interdependence. How will the established firms react? Conceivably, they could restrict their own outputs to make room for the newcomer. If so, the price might not fall at all. At the other extreme, they could hold their production constant or even increase it to make life as difficult as possible for the interloper. Some assumption has to be made by a potential entrant calculating the

Business, and Welfare in the Postwar United States (Seattle: University of Washington Press, 1967), pp. 83–105. Worcester argues that the first firm into a market charges the short-run profit maximizing price and then holds its output constant in the face of successive new entries. The behavioral assumptions on which Worcester builds his model seem rather implausible, but the predictions he derives from them—notably, that a log-normal size distribution of firms will eventuate—have considerable appeal.

[43] See Osborne, *op. cit.*; and Michael Mann *et al.*, "Comment: Entry and Oligopoly Theory," *Journal of Political Economy*, August 1965, pp. 381–383.

[44] This summary is taken from Erwin A. Blackstone, "The Copying Machine Industry: A Case Study," Ph.D. dissertation submitted at the University of Michigan, 1968, pp. 129–160 and 186–196.

profitability of entry. The theorist too must build his theory upon an assumption, hopefully conforming as closely as possible to the thought processes of real-world entrepreneurs.

Both Bain and Sylos-Labini emphasize maintenance of output by established firms as the most likely reaction to new entry. Bain's main defense of output maintenance is that it is a relatively pessimistic assumption from the standpoint of the new entrant.[45] And, of course, a certain amount of pessimism is in order when one is contemplating entering a new industry on a large scale. According to Sylos-Labini, existing firms maintain their output partly in an effort to discourage entry and partly because cost structure rigidities encourage full utilization of capacity.[46] If we provisionally accept the output maintenance assumption, we can derive several generalizations. For simplicity we assume in all cases that new entrants can, by building a plant of minimum optimal scale, produce at unit costs just as low as those of existing firms. The problem is, how much can existing firms elevate prices above their own (minimum) unit costs without attracting new entry?

First, suppose the new entrant chooses to enter at minimum optimal scale; that is, to produce an output volume just sufficient to realize all economies of scale. Then the larger the minimum optimal scale is relative to the overall size of the industry, the more price will be depressed by a new entrant, other things (such as the elasticity of demand) being held equal. Suppose, for example, that demand has unit elasticity in the relevant neighborhood. If entry at minimum optimal scale requires the entrant to produce (and hence dispose of) 10 per cent of the total quantity demanded at the post-entry price, price will be depressed by 9 per cent due to entry. So unless the pre-entry price exceeds the potential entrant's expected unit costs by more than 10 per cent, entry will be unprofitable. A pre-entry price exceeding minimum unit cost by slightly less than 10 per cent will be just sufficient to deter entry. If, alternatively, entry at optimal scale requires the entrant to produce only 5 per cent of the total quantity demanded at the post-entry price, price will fall by only 4.5 per cent upon entry, and existing firms can hold price no higher than 5 per cent above minimum unit cost without encouraging entry. Generalizing, the smaller the minimum optimal scale is relative to the output volume demanded at a price equal to minimum unit cost (i.e., the competitive price), the less price can be held persistently above the competitive level without attracting new entry, *ceteris paribus*.

Suppose now that the scale of entry continues to be 10 per cent of total market volume at the competitive price. If the elasticity of demand is 2 instead of 1, price will fall by only about 4.5 per cent instead of 9 per cent upon entry. If the elasticity is 5, price will fall by only about 2 per cent, and a pre-entry price exceeding minimum unit cost by more than 2 per cent will attract entry. Thus, the more elastic market demand is —e.g., the more readily the market will absorb an increment of supply without a large fall in price—the less price can be held persistently above the competitive level without attracting new entry, *ceteris paribus*.

Finally, we relax the assumption that the new entrant must enter at optimal scale. By entering at a smaller-than-optimal scale, a firm incurs the disadvantage of higher costs, but gains the advantage of adding a smaller increment to the supply of output, and thus precipitates a milder price decline. Consider (in Figure 8.2) two alternative long-run cost functions, C_3C', with its origin or zero output point located at X_3, and C_2C', with its origin at X_2.[47] Each is assumed to have the same minimum unit cost OP_0. The main difference between the two is that costs decline more rapidly to the value X_1C_1 with cost function C_2C_1C' than with C_3C_1C'; X_1C_1 is attained at about one third of minimum optimal scale X_2X_0 with C_2C_1C', but at one half of minimum optimal scale X_3X_0 with C_3C_1C'. Each curve is

[45]*Barriers to New Competition*, p. 105. Bain did explore alternative output behavior assumptions in the course of his analysis.

[46]*Oligopoly and Technical Progress*, p. 43.

[47]This method of presentation is adapted from Modigliani, *loc. cit.*

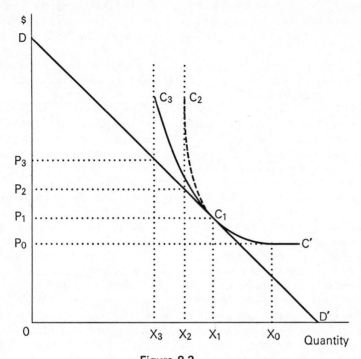

Figure 8.2
Entry at Large But Suboptimal Scales

drawn so that it is tangent to the demand curve DD' at point C_1. This means that if the original firms produce OX_3 and an entrant with cost curve C_3C_1C' produces X_3X_1 units, entry will be just barely profitable. Similarly, if the original firms produce OX_2 and an entrant with cost curve C_2C_1C' produces X_2X_1 units, entry will be barely profitable. Any higher output by the original firms would shift the origins of the potential entrants' cost curves to the right, so that they would at no point touch the demand curve. There would be no output at which entrants (adding their output to the original firms' output) could break even. Thus, an output slightly greater than OX_3 with a corresponding price below OP_3 is just sufficient to deter entry if C_3C_1C' is the entrant's long-run cost curve. An output slightly greater than OX_2 with price below OP_2 will deter entry if C_2C_1C' is the long-run cost curve. Function C_2C_1C', with costs declining rapidly to the intermediate level X_1C_1, has a

lower limit price OP_2 than the more gradually declining curve C_3C_1C', whose limit price is OP_3. Generalizing, the less disadvantaged by above-minimum unit costs an entrant is when operating at some fraction of the minimum optimal scale, the less price can be held persistently above the competitive level without attracting new entry, *ceteris paribus.*

To sum up, when potential entrants expect existing firms to maintain their output in the face of new entry, price can be held persistently above the competitive level without attracting entry by a greater percentage margin: (1) the less elastic demand is; (2) the higher the proportion of total industry output a firm of minimum optimal scale produces; and (3) the more a firm operating at less than minimum optimal scale is disadvantaged by high unit costs. We see then that even when new entrants are physically able to operate just as efficiently as existing firms, the interaction between price and large-scale entry can be a significant deterrent to new entry, and because of this barrier existing firms may command supra-normal profits more or less permanently in the presence of substantial scale economies.

This conclusion depends crucially upon the assumption that existing firms maintain their output in the face of new entry. Will they in fact do so? If, despite pricing at a level calculated to deter new entry under the output mainte-nance assumption, new entry does take place, maintaining output normally will *not* be the most profitable strategy for the original firms. Indeed, if production is maintained, price will fall to the competitive level and the original firms' supra-normal profits will be wiped out altogether. To enforce this outcome when positive profits could be earned by reducing output would be like cutting off one's nose to spite the face. Moreover, output maintenance implies a certain behavioral asymmetry. Before entry, firms can make the strategically determined limit price stick only by adopting a passive, feedback-oriented policy of output determination. After entry, a policy of holding output fixed is supposedly pursued. This is conceivable, but paradoxical. Surely a tightly-knit oligopolistic industry would not shift per-manently from one policy to another because of one new entry. Sooner or later it will return to some kind of cooperative policy aimed at maintaining either the short-run joint profit maximizing price or the limit price (modified, perhaps, to reflect the prior unsuccessful experience).

Now if a potential entrant recognizes that the existing firms have no economic incentive to adopt and persevere in an uncooperative price-output policy following its entry, it will not be deterred by the belief that its addition to industry output will depress price severely. The threat of output maintenance and price-cutting by exist-ing firms lacks credibility, and threats which are not credible do not deter. This is analogous to the classic problem of nuclear deterrence. If the Soviet Union invaded Western Europe, would the United States retaliate massively with nu-clear weapons, knowing that the Soviets would respond in kind against the American homeland? If not, the nuclear deterrent is not credible, and it must be replaced by other barriers to entry— large conventional forces, and/or the French Force de Frappe.

There is more to be learned from the nuclear deterrence analogy. Let us assume that a nuclear response to conventional aggression would be irrational in the normal meaning of the word. If, however, U.S. leaders have committed their reputations to such a response, or if U.S. troops were steamrollered by the aggression, or if emo-tional behavior for any other reason displaced sober analysis, escalation might progress to the large-scale use of nuclear weapons. Fear by the Soviet Union of such an *irrational* response contributes to deterrence. Furthermore, the U.S. has something to gain by cultivating the impression that it will act irrationally or that events will get out of control if aggression occurs, for this too contributes to deterrence. By making irrational actions more likely in a contingency one seeks to avert, one may move nearer the rational goal of averting the contingency. This is the so-called "rationality of irrationality."[48] So also with deterring market entry. There is always a chance that industry discipline will break down when new entry takes place. Oligop-olistic coordination is often a fragile thing, and entry may strain it to the breaking point. If a newcomer captures a significant volume of sales from producers burdened by high fixed costs, those firms may undercut the established price to solve their individual short-run financial problems, touching off a price war. Or some entrepreneurs may be carried away by their irra-tional desires to make life difficult for the inter-loper, even though the punishment also hurts the executor. There is evidence that such behavior sometimes accompanies entry. Cassady found that irrational reactions by established firms to new entry were a common cause of price wars.[49] A Federal Trade Commission study disclosed

---

[48]Cf. Herman Kahn, *On Thermonuclear War* (Princeton: Princeton University Press, 1960), pp. 291–295; and Thomas C. Schelling, *The Strategy of Conflict* (Cambridge: Harvard University Press, 1960), Chapter 8.

[49]Ralph Cassady, Jr., *Price Warfare in Business Competition* (East Lansing: Michigan State University Bureau of Business and Economic Research, 1963), pp. 51–53.

that cement price decreases were much more prevalent in market areas subjected to new entry during the 1960s than in territories without entry.[50] And even if they hope to avoid irrational pricing, established firms can enhance their deterrent by concealing that hope, deliberately conveying the impression that pricing discipline will deteriorate in the event of entry.

Fear of irrational action, then, rather than the expectation of rational pricing responses, may be what deters the potential new entrant from entering on a large scale, if he is deterred at all. But if this is so, why should existing industry members limit their price to the value calculated under the Bain-Sylos output maintenance theory? Assuming that they retain sufficient fighting capacity in reserve to support an expansion of output, why not hold price at the short-run profit-maximizing level, leaving open the possibility of a sharp decrease if someone tries to enter? Alternatively, given that it often takes two years or longer to build and equip new production facilities in industries characterized by substantial scale economies, why not cut to the Bain-Sylos price on the day a potential new entrant first shows definite interest, thereby 'showing the flag' in the most vivid possible way?

Bain's explanation for adherence to a restrained limit price is that "the entrant is likely to read the current price policies of established firms as some sort of a 'statement of future intentions' regarding their policies after his entry has occurred."[51] This is not entirely convincing, given the role bluff, counterbluff, and irrational response play in deterrence. It seems more reasonable to believe that oligopolists anxious to deter entry exercise restraint because, if they held their price at levels which maximize short-run profits except when the threat of large-scale new entry is imminent, entry at inefficient scales

too small to evoke a price response would be encouraged. Recognizing this brings us full circle to our original naive theory of limit pricing. The synthesis which emerges is a twofold strategy of deterrence. Existing firms restrain price just enough to deter entry at inefficient small scales. The more important economies of scale and absolute cost advantages possessed by insiders are, the higher is the margin by which price can exceed the competitive level without attracting such entrants. Implicit or explicit threats of irrational price warfare, on the other hand, are employed to deter entry at large, efficient scales.

This interpretation is consistent with another intermediate form of entry observed frequently: upstream vertical integration by established manufacturers. Major food packers, for example, have repeatedly threatened to enter into tin can manufacturing, and to avoid the loss of these important customers the oligopolistic can manufacturers have been forced to exercise pricing restraint. Only because the can manufacturers enjoy certain economies of scale and specialization has the limit price not been forced to the level of minimum unit cost.[52] For even if entry by a major packer into can manufacturing touched off a price war, the packer would not be adversely affected, since it enjoys a captive internal market affected only indirectly by outside price levels.[53]

If the threat of irrational price warfare is the main deterrent to large-scale entry by firms producing for other than their own use, it is probably less effective when demand is growing rapidly than when demand is stagnant or declining.[54] In a period of vigorous growth, established producers are less likely to engage in price-cutting to help absorb high fixed costs, and capacity constraints may prevent them from carrying a price war very far. This suggests that

[50] U. S. Federal Trade Commission, *Economic Report on Mergers and Vertical Integration in the Cement Industry* (Washington: April 1966), p. 16.

[51] *Barriers to New Competition*, p. 95. For a comparable view, see Wayne A. Leeman, "The Limitations of Local Price-Cutting as a Barrier to Entry," *Journal of Political Economy*, August 1956, especially p. 331.

[52] Cf. McKie, *op. cit.*, especially pp. 110–114. Similar barriers deter the entry of tin can manufacturers into tin plate manufacturing. See *idem.*, pp. 50–54.

[53] If outside suppliers' prices fall after upstream integration, one might say that an opportunity cost has been incurred by not taking advantage of the new, lower price. But the opportunity would not have materialized had the packer not integrated vertically.

[54] Cf. Sylos-Labini, *op. cit.*, pp. 61–62; and Dean, *op. cit.*, p. 423.

more large-scale entry will occur during booms than at other stages of the business cycle.[55]

THE EFFECTS OF OTHER ENTRY BARRIERS

Thus far we have stressed economies of scale in production and distribution as the obstacle permitting established firms to hold price above cost without attracting new entry. Other barriers include absolute cost advantages associated with the control (e.g., through patents or secrecy) of superior production processes or the possession of strategic raw materials; the need to commit large amounts of capital in entering; strong consumer preferences favoring established differentiated products; and tariffs and transportation charges increasing delivered costs for potential foreign competitors.

In his study of barriers to domestic entry in 20 industries, Bain found production scale economies and product differentiation to be of substantial and roughly equal importance, while absolute cost advantages were typically of slight significance.[56] The role of capital investment barriers was less certain. In five industries analyzed by Bain, entry at an efficient scale necessitated a commitment of at least $100 million. The need to raise such a large sum was clearly a major obstacle to the entry of small new enterprises. But a large established corporation seeking diversification outlets would have little difficulty obtaining the requisite funds, and for it heavy capital demands would not be a barrier.[57]

Differentiation barriers also have complicated consequences. Expenditures on advertising and service often have a cumulative effect, so that newcomers starting from scratch face a dilemma: they either have to spend large amounts on promotion per unit of output to overcome their disadvantage, or they must accept a lower unit price for products of comparable quality and cost. Either way, established firms may be able to hold their prices above their own costs by a sometimes substantial margin before making entry attractive to newcomers. Patent protection on superior products is also an important barrier to new entry, especially in the technically vigorous fields such as chemicals, drugs, and electrical equipment (which are underrepresented in Bain's sample).[58]

Nevertheless, product differentiation may also work in the opposite direction. Large, well-established firms can exploit the reputations they have built up in other fields and utilize well-developed distribution channels and service organizations to minimize consumer resistance when diversifying into a new industry.[59] Differentiation also facilitates sequential entry. Thus, a company finds an isolated geographic area or a set of demands for special qualitative product features which has not been served adequately by existing producers, carving out a snug little niche in which operation is profitable. From this base of operations it is possible, with luck, gradually to expand into other geographic areas or to a broader product line. Finally, an outsider who succeeds in developing and building up patent protection on a new product can utilize product differentiation to its own advantage in penetrating a market previously dominated by others. Innovation is probably one of the most common and successful ways of hurdling otherwise formidable barriers to new entry.

How these relationships work out on balance, and hence how severely the threat of new entry

---

[55]Of course, entry decisions made during a boom may not come to fruition until a slump has set in. This is what happened during Olin-Mathieson's ill-starred entry into the aluminum industry. See Richard A. Smith, *Corporations in Crisis* (New York: Doubleday, 1963), Chapter 1. For other examples of entry in boom periods despite seemingly high scale economy barriers, see "Plastics That Come On Strong," *Business Week*, November 8, 1969, pp. 76–78; "Nickel's Newest Crisis," *Business Week*, July 19, 1969, pp. 106–108; and "Magnesium Eyes Lightweight Crown," *Business Week*, May 31, 1969, pp. 52–53.

[56]*Barriers to New Competition*, pp. 142–143, 155, and 169.

[57]*Ibid.*, pp. 165–166. See also Marshall Hall and Leonard W. Weiss, "Firm Size and Profitability," *Review of Economics and Statistics*, August 1967, pp. 319–331.

[58]But see G. C. Hufbauer, *Synthetic Materials and the Theory of International Trade* (Cambridge: Harvard University Press, 1966), pp. 59–60, who argues that synthetic fiber and plastics producers have tended to set new product prices at very high levels which, despite high entry barriers, encouraged entry.

[59]Cf. Howard H. Hines, "Effectiveness of 'Entry' by Already Established Firms," *Quarterly Journal of Economics*, February 1957, pp. 132–150; and Frank J. Kottke, "Market Entry and the Character of Competition," *Western Economic Journal*, December 1966, pp. 24–43.

restricts the pricing freedom of firms in concentrated industries, is an empirical question. We turn now to the evidence.

THE EVIDENCE ON ENTRY BARRIERS AND PRICING BEHAVIOR

The pioneering empirical study in this field has been conducted by Bain.[60] He divided his sample of 20 industries on a judgmental basis into three categories: those with 'very high' overall barriers to entry, those with 'substantial' barriers, and those with 'moderate to low' barriers. He also divided the industries into one group with high concentration (where eight sellers controlled more than 70 per cent of industry output) and another with "moderate to low" concentration (with eight sellers controlling less than 70 per cent of output). Average after-tax profit rates on stockholders' equity for the leading firms in each industry were collected by group for the years 1936–1940 and 1947–

1951. His results, along with results from a similar study of 30 industries covering the 1950–1960 period by H. Michael Mann,[61] are summarized in Table 8.1.

Consistent with the analysis in Chapter 7, industries with high concentration had generally higher average rates of return than those with low or moderate concentration. But in addition, highly concentrated industries with very high entry barriers (in Bain's sample, automobiles, cigarettes, liquor, typewriters, and quality fountain pens; plus chewing gum, ethical drugs, flat glass, nickel, and sulphur in Mann's sample) had higher rates of return than the other highly concentrated industries with lower entry barriers. Among the industries with substantial and moderate to low entry barriers, the relationship was mixed; those with substantial barriers were less lucrative if highly concentrated, but more profitable if moderately concentrated.

Although it is possible to quibble over some

Table 8.1

Average Profit Rates on Stockholders' Equity, by Height of Entry Barriers and Concentration, 1936–40, 1947–51, and 1950–60

	Very High Barriers	Substantial Barriers	Moderate to Low Barriers
1936–1940			
High concentration	$19.0_{(5)}$	$10.2_{(5)}$	$10.5_{(2)}$
Moderate concentration	—$_{(0)}$	$7.0_{(3)}$	$5.3_{(5)}$
1947–1951			
High concentration	$19.0_{(5)}$	$14.0_{(5)}$	$15.4_{(2)}$
Moderate concentration	—$_{(0)}$	$12.5_{(3)}$	$10.1_{(5)}$
1950–1960			
High concentration	$16.4_{(8)}$	$11.1_{(8)}$	$11.9_{(5)}$
Moderate concentration	—$_{(0)}$	$12.2_{(1)}$	$8.6_{(8)}$

Sources: Joe S. Bain, *Barriers to New Competition* (Cambridge: Harvard University Press, 1956), pp. 192–200; and H. Michael Mann, "Seller Concentration, Barriers to Entry, and Rates of Return in Thirty Industries," *Review of Economics and Statistics*, August 1966, pp. 296–307. Subscripts in parentheses indicate the number of industries in each class.

[60]*Barriers to New Competition*, pp. 190–201.

[61]"Seller Concentration, Barriers to Entry, and Rates of Return in Thirty Industries, 1950–1960," *Review of Economics and Statistics*, August 1966, pp. 296–307. See also K. D. George, "Concentration, Barriers to Entry and Rates of Return," *Review of Economics and Statistics*, May 1968, pp. 273–275.

of the classifications made by Bain and Mann, the results show rather forcefully that the ability of firms persistently to earn supra-normal profits is related positively to the height of entry barriers. A question of interpretation remains, however. Industries with very high entry barriers might have higher profits because entry is blockaded, so that members have no need to exercise restraint in their pricing decisions, or because producers have actively tried to limit entry by holding profit margins within the tolerances imposed by the entry barriers. Similarly, profits may be lower in industries with modest entry barriers because new entry has driven prices down, or because existing industry members anxious to maintain their positions found it necessary to keep their prices close to costs. In short, is the variation in profits due to differences in the amount of pricing restraint required to deter entry, or to differences in the actual incidence of competitive entry?

The evidence (and no doubt the reality it reflects) is mixed. That many dominant firms and dominant oligopolies have had their market shares steadily eroded away suggests that no concerted attempt was made to deter entry, or that producers considered it preferable to set prices which slowed entry down, but did not choke it off completely. In other industries, including some with declining dominant firm histories, efforts to limit entry through low prices are evident, at least in recent decades. Whether the apparent change of heart in some of the latter is due to learning from experience, the development of more farsighted professional management, or a technological transition from ineffective to effectively impeded entry is not known. There is a pressing need for more research to determine across a large sample of industries the amount of new entry occurring and the conditions associated with varying rates of entry.[62]

One bit of evidence suggesting restrained pricing is the frequent finding of econometric investigations that demand in concentrated industries is not highly price elastic. For example, it has been estimated that the price elasticity of demand for steel is on the order of 0.3 or 0.4.[63] Yet to maximize joint short-run profits, equilibrium would have to prevail where elasticity exceeds unity. The highest of several automobile price elasticity estimates made during the 1950s was 1.5.[64] If profit-maximizing equilibrium were to occur at this value, marginal cost could not exceed one third of price, but in fact marginal cost apparently runs closer to two thirds of auto wholesale prices.[65] Similarly, in such industries as cigarettes, typewriters, farm machinery, petroleum refining, soap, gypsum products, cement, flour, and rubber tires—all included in Bain's sample—it is probable that industry demand has a price elasticity below unity.

Other evidence of pricing restraint with the threat of entry in mind is provided by industry case studies. We have seen earlier that after the cigarette manufacturers exceeded their limit price and encouraged a flood of entry and fringe expansion in 1931, they quickly shifted and since then have apparently adhered to a policy which keeps the less extensively advertised brands in check. Similarly, Xerox adopted a sophisticated entry-limiting strategy in pricing its copying machines for diverse volume segments. McKie found the threat of upstream vertical integration by major customers to be a potent constraint on the pricing decisions of tin can manufacturers.[66] Kaplan and his asso-

---

[62]One such effort is reported in Edwin Mansfield, "Entry, Gibrat's Law, Innovation, and the Growth of Firms," *American Economic Review*, December 1962, pp. 1023–1051. Mansfield found that the number of firms entering four industries during four time periods was positively correlated with profits and negatively correlated with the size of the capital investment required to establish a firm of minimum optimal size. Unfortunately, his definition of entry includes mergers and changes of ownership, which are largely irrelevant from our present point of view. See also M. A. Alemson, "Demand, Entry, and the Game of Conflict in Oligopoly over Time: Recent Australian Experience," *Oxford Economic Papers*, July 1969, pp. 161–176.

[63]Cf. Leonard W. Weiss, *Economics and American Industry*, (New York: Wiley, 1961), pp. 290–291.

[64]U. S. Senate, Committee on the Judiciary, Subcommittee on Antitrust and Monopoly, Report, *Administered Prices: Automobiles* (Washington: 1958), pp. 144–145.

[65]Cf. Albert Bradley, "Financial Control Policies of General Motors Corporation and Their Relationship to Cost Accounting," *National Association of Cost Accountants Bulletin*, January 1, 1927, pp. 412–433.

[66]*Tin Cans and Tin Plate*, pp. 2' -292

ciates reported that the principal force leading General Foods Corporation to price its specialty products at moderate levels was "a full realization that a high price will restrict the volume and . . . speed up the process of developing competition."[67] W. B. Reddaway found that the ability of British basic chemical producers to exploit their concentrated market positions was limited by the ease with which other firms could enter a product line by converting existing facilities and by the ability of important customers to begin producing their own requirements.[68] Ease of entry is credited for the paucity of monopoly profits in most retail lines. As Holton observes, any merchant eager to charge a high price for some group of items must "anticipate that other retailers, some of whom may be in quite different lines of business, may 'enter' the market in the sense that they will begin to stock the profitable item."[69] It would appear furthermore that pricing to deter entry has been part of the businessman's bag of tricks for a long time. During the 1790s, as the expiration date of its basic patent drew near, the firm of Boulton & Watt began to implement efficiency-increasing measures so that its high steam engine prices could be brought down to competitive levels.[70] A century later, according to Passer, the leading manufacturers of arc carbon and incandescent lamps adopted a low price policy explicitly to deter the entry of new competitors using production techniques not protected by patents.[71]

IMPLICATIONS

Whether or not producers adopt a deliberate policy of pricing to deter new entry, the ultimate beneficiary of low and moderate entry barriers is the consumer. If monopolists or oligopolists strive to hold price well above the competitive level when entry barriers are modest, their efforts will sooner or later be defeated by the entry of new competition. If they choose to defend their market positions, they must hold the margin between price and cost to a level consistent with their advantage over potential entrants. These dual controls play an important role in steering the economy toward more workable performance than it would otherwise achieve. Serious and persistent monopolistic deviations of price from cost are likely only when two conditions co-exist: sufficiently high seller concentration to permit cooperative pricing, and high barriers to the entry of new competition. If Bain's sample is approximately representative of oligopolistic industries, the conditions are satisfied only in a minority of instances. Of the 12 industries in his sample with eight-firm concentration ratios exceeding 70 per cent, only five also had very high barriers to entry—defined as those sufficient to permit established firms to elevate price 10 per cent or more above minimum unit costs while forestalling new entry.[72] In the majority of concentrated industries with lower entry barriers, we should expect long-run competition to have a restraining influence on price.

Furthermore, it is sometimes possible through government action to reduce high barriers to entry, and thus to apply additional pressure on profit margins. Not much can be done to eliminate the advantage associated with economies of scale in production and physical distribution, nor would many policy-makers be inclined to tamper extensively with this source of economic efficiency. But financial aid can be provided to new entrepreneurs, abuses of the patent grant can be inhibited, and practices which artificially tie customers to established sellers can be enjoined. These and other policy measures affect-

---

[67]*Pricing in Big Business*, p. 216.

[68]W. B. Reddaway, "The Chemical Industry," in Duncan Burn, ed., *The Structure of British Industry* (Cambridge: Cambridge University Press, 1958), Vol. I, p. 226. For similar views on the American chemical industry, see Alfred E. Kahn, "The Chemical Industry," in Walter Adams, ed., *The Structure of American Industry*, pp. 240 and 262–263.

[69]Richard H. Holton, "The Role of Competition and Monopoly in Distribution, in J. P. Miller, ed., *Competition, Cartels and Their Regulation*, pp. 302–303. See also P. W. S. Andrews, *On Competition in Economic Theory*, pp. 107–114.

[70]F. M. Scherer, "Invention and Innovation in the Watt-Boulton Steam Engine Venture," *Technology and Culture*, Spring 1965, p. 185.

[71]Harold C. Passer, *The Electrical Manufacturers: 1875–1900* (Cambridge: Harvard University Press, 1953), pp. 163 and 351.

[72]*Barriers to New Competition*, p. 170.

ing freedom of entry will be considered further in later chapters.

PRICING TO MAXIMIZE SALES GROWTH

Our analysis of dynamic pricing strategy has thus far adhered to the assumption that business firms seek to maximize profits over the long pull. An alternate hypothesis has been advanced by a number of economists, with William J. Baumol in the vanguard. In the most complete statement of his proposition, Baumol argued that instead of maximizing profits, either short-run or long-run, firms with market power tend to maximize sales, subject only to the condition that profits not fall below some specified minimum value.[73] He was led to this break from orthodoxy by repeated observation of managers' preoccupation with the level of their firms' sales rather than current profits. He postulated several explanations for this apparent emphasis on sales: banks are less willing to finance companies with declining sales; personnel relations problems increase when falling sales necessitate layoffs; and the power to adopt effective competitive tactics is weakened when sales and market position decline. All of these considerations can be rationalized in terms of a desire to maximize long-run profits. As Richard Heflebower observed in an earlier work:

> . . . management recognizes good market position to be a valuable asset, whose long-term attributes must condition all short-term decisions. Its value is not merely defensive . . . but also is a basic attribute of the firm's ability to make positive moves; that is, to deal with unanticipated developments when they occur. In that sense, market position becomes a means of long-term profit maximization under conditions of uncertainty.[74]

But in addition, Baumol asserted, executives are interested in increasing sales volume *for its own sake* because managerial salaries and prestige are more closely correlated with sales than with profits.[75] Thus, sales maximization is said to be an independent goal of managers, quite apart from its connection with long-run profit maximization.

Still profits also play a role in the pricing decisions of firms interested in maximum sales. In an early version of his theory, Baumol specified that sufficient profits must be achieved "to pay dividends, and to reinvest in such amounts that the combination of dividend receipts and stock price rises can remunerate stockholders adequately."[76] In a later modification he proposed that managers more frequently seek to maximize the rate at which sales grow, and that profits are an instrumental variable for obtaining capital to finance expansion.[77] The need for capital was reflected in Baumol's original static model by the condition that some arbitrary minimum profits constraint be satisfied. In the later, fully dynamic version he envisioned determining the profit constraint in terms of a tradeoff between a low-price policy with a directly stimulating impact on sales and a high-price policy supplying increased profits to support the investment required for higher future sales. Since the models are conceptually similar, we shall examine here only the simpler static version.

Nearly all the diagrams in this volume are presented using average and marginal curves, but the Baumol theory can be represented more conveniently with *total* cost and revenue curves. In Figure 8.3, *TR* is the firm's total revenue or sales curve and *TC* its total cost curve. The shapes assumed are conventional. Profit is the vertical distance between the *TR* and *TC* curves,

---

[73]*Business Behavior, Value, and Growth* (New York: Macmillan, 1959), pp. 45–82; (Rev. ed.; New York: Harcourt, Brace & World, 1967), pp. 45–82 and 86–104.

[74]"Toward a Theory of Industrial Markets and Prices," p. 126. See also the Harrod quotation on p. 222 *supra.*

[75]For references to the evidence, see pp. 32–33 *supra.*

[76]*Business Behavior, Value and Growth,* (First ed.), p. 51.

[77]W. J. Baumol, "On the Theory of Expansion of the Firm," *American Economic Review,* December 1962, pp. 1078–1087, incorporated with revisions as Chapter 10 in the revised edition of *Business Behavior, Value and Growth.* For extensions which differ in significant respects from Baumol's conclusions, see John Williamson, "Profit, Growth and Sales Maximization," *Economica,* February 1966, pp. 1–16; and B. D. Mabry, "Sales Maximization and Profit Maximization: Are They Inconsistent?" *Western Economic Journal,* March 1968, pp. 154–160.

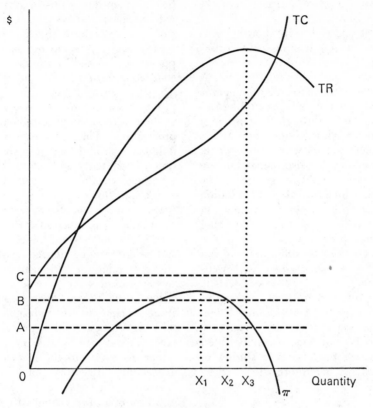

Figure 8.3
Sales Maximization Subject to a Minimum
Profits Constraint

and is shown explicitly by the π curve. Profit is maximized at output OX_1 and sales are maximized at output OX_3. If the firm's managers insist upon earning profits of OC before seeking to satisfy other objectives such as sales maximization, they will not be in a position to increase sales beyond the short-run profit-maximizing level, since the profit objective lies out of reach. To come as close as possible to meeting its profit constraint the firm must produce the profit-maximizing output OX_1. If, however, profits of OB will suffice, the firm's profit goal is over-fulfilled at OX_1. It can increase output to OX_2 while earning at least OB in profits, enjoying higher sales than it would under a (short-run) profit maximization policy. Finally, if its profit

constraint is the still lower magnitude OA, the firm will increase its output all the way to OX_3, which maximizes sales. It will not expand further, even though the profit goal is overfulfilled at OX_3, because additional output would be absorbed in the market only at prices reduced so much as to make total sales fall.

The most important implication of the Baumol analysis is this: if firms with market power in fact strive to increase sales volume for its own sake and if they require less profit to meet capital needs than the maximum amount attainable, they will charge lower prices and produce more than they would under short-run profit maximization. Even if output is not expanded all the way to the competitive level, the net tendency is typically in the direction of superior resource allocation.[78]

No one has yet succeeded in showing conclusively whether or not business enterprises actually behave in the ways and for the reasons postulated by Baumol and other sales maximization theorists.[79] One obstacle to enlightenment is that the behavioral differences between long-run profit maximization (i.e., through limit pricing) and various forms of sales maximization are so subtle that econometric tests with available data are not powerful enough to discriminate among the contending hypotheses. There are, to be sure, some cases in which the sales maximization and limit pricing hypotheses generate conflicting predictions, and in this sense the limit pricing hypothesis would appear to hold an empirical edge, since (unlike sales maximization) it can explain expansion by monopolists and well-disciplined oligopolists into ranges of inelastic market demand. However, no final verdict can be rendered in the present state of knowledge. To resolve the impasse, it is probably necessary to conduct not only much more sophisticated econometric research, but also case studies in greater depth than any heretofore attempted by economists.[80]

OTHER DYNAMIC INFLUENCES AFFECTING PRICE

A few further dynamic considerations affecting price decisions must be mentioned to round out the picture. One is the whole set of influences lumped together conveniently under the caption 'public opinion.' Clear and blatant exploitation of market power leads to a bad press, which most businessmen take pains to avoid. The executive with a concern for his place in the history books can scarcely ignore the fact that William H. Vanderbilt is remembered more for his "The public be damned" outburst than for his substantial entrepreneurial and philanthropic accomplishments. Persistently high prices and profits may also provoke direct government intervention in the form of price controls or antitrust proceedings. The desire to maintain a favorable public image and fear of government intervention undoubtedly induce some firms to avoid squeezing all they can out of a monopolistic market position.

Uncertainty also affects pricing in a variety of ways. We have observed earlier that firms may expand output beyond the level at which short-run profits are maximized in order to cement customer relations and ensure room for maneuvering should some adverse contingency materialize in the future. On such aspects of dynamic strategy economic theory has little to contribute; their significance is an empirical question. However, theoretical analysis provides some interesting insights into the links between demand uncertainty, inventory policy, and pricing behavior.

A firm in a purely competitive market can, by definition, sell as much output as it wishes at the ruling market price. Uncertainty pertains only to the price which will prevail. This is not so for the firm possessing market power. At any given quoted price, the monopolistic firm will be able to sell more if demand turns out to be strong than if it is weak. Unless production to order is practical, the firm must decide how much to produce before it knows how strong demand will

---

[78]It is also possible to overshoot, producing more than the competitive output. See W. G. Shepherd, "On Sales-Maximising and Oligopoly Behavior," *Economica*, November 1962, pp. 420–424. Shepherd shows in addition that the sales-maximizing output may be identical to the monopoly profit maximizing output, if a sales maximizer faces a kinked demand curve.

[79]For one less than spectacularly successful attempt, see Marshall Hall, "Sales Revenue Maximization: An Empirical Examination," *Journal of Industrial Economics*, April 1967, pp. 143–154; with the comment by Leonard Waverman, *Journal of Industrial Economics*, November 1968, pp. 73–80. See also the summary of merger effect studies on pp. 120–122 *supra*.

[80]To do the latter well, it is necessary to interview numerous persons about each pricing decision studied, since the diverse functional specialists in a firm typically emphasize different goals. Fog reported that sales departments tend to stress maximum sales, while production departments hold out for higher profit margins. *Industrial Pricing Policies*, p. 31. It is worth noting that many of the observations reported by Baumol were made as a consultant for a marketing research firm. Conceivably, executives interested in hiring and working with such a firm may have a functional bias toward sales maximization.

be. If it produces too much, it will be left holding a large inventory, incurring higher storage, capital, and possibly obsolescence costs, or else it will have to dispose of its surplus at distress prices. If it produces too little, it will lose sales and perhaps drive disappointed customers permanently into the arms of rival sellers. It must decide then upon an optimal price, production, and inventory policy to make the best of demand uncertainties.

Do price and output decisions differ under these conditions from what they would be in a world of certainty? Pioneering mathematical analyses by Mills, Karlin and Carr suggest that they do, although numerical simulation studies by Nevins show that under plausible assumptions the deviations are not very large.[81]

Unfortunately, few sweeping generalizations are possible. The output of a firm with a downward-sloping demand curve may be either greater or less under uncertainty than under certainty; it depends upon the amount and character of the uncertainties faced, the shapes of cost and demand functions, and the costs and risks of maintaining an inventory position. One fairly general result relates inventory policy to market structure. When errors in predicting demand are symmetrically distributed about their mean, the monopolistic firm will tend to produce and hold more output for inventory (reducing the probability of shortages and dissatisfied customers), the higher the ratio of price to marginal cost is.[82] This is so because the more price exceeds marginal cost, the more profitable it is to satisfy an extra unit of demand from inventory in times of peak demand, amply repaying inventory holding costs. This is one sense in which market power confers some compensating benefits. To keep the phenomenon in perspec-

tive, it should be noted that monopolistic firms will never find it optimal to produce an output which makes marginal cost exceed price—e.g., more than the competitive output—merely to hedge against demand uncertainties.[83]

The dependence of price upon inventory behavior is more complex. As we have seen in Chapter 5, the main function of inventory policy in oligopoly may be to support the price at a value chosen for strategic reasons, and not to maximize profits in any narrower sense. But if we limit our attention to profit maximization efforts which ignore oligopolistic interdependence, mathematical studies of optimal inventory policy become relevant. Mills, Karlin and Carr have demonstrated that when demand is uncertain, firms with market power will set their price at the same value as that which maximizes profit under certainty only by coincidence. Nevins clarified this conclusion by showing that the certainty and uncertainty pricing strategies will be identical, *ceteris paribus*, in the unlikely case of zero time discount rates and inventory carrying costs. Excluding this case, producers must make a complicated tradeoff decision balancing the effects of price changes on expected demand against the effects of the price and inventory variables on the probability of costly shortages or surplus production. The price resulting from this tradeoff may be above or below the price which would be set by a monopolist under certainty; it depends mainly upon the shape of the marginal cost function and the character of the demand uncertainties (i.e., whether the error distribution is additive or multiplicative relative to mean demand expectations). In the case of rising short-run marginal costs, which is most typical of real world conditions when production is not greatly below ca-

---

[81]Edwin S. Mills, "Uncertainty and Price Theory," *Quarterly Journal of Economics*, February 1959, pp. 116–130, and *Price, Output, and Inventory Policy* (New York: Wiley, 1962), Chapters 5–7; Samuel Karlin and Charles Carr, "Prices and Optimal Inventory Policy," in Kenneth Arrow *et al.*, *Studies in Applied Probability and Management Science* (Stanford: Stanford University Press, 1962), pp. 159–172; and Arthur J. Nevins, "Some Effects of Uncertainty: Simulation of a Model of Price," *Quarterly Journal of Economics*, February 1966, pp. 73–87. See also T. M. Whitin, "Dynamic Programming Extensions to the Theory of the Firm," *Journal of Industrial Economics*, April 1968, pp. 81–98.

[82]Mills, "Uncertainty and Price Theory," pp. 121–122. This finding was anticipated by M. J. Peck in "Marginal Analysis and the Explanation of Business Behavior under Uncertainty," in Mary Jean Bowman, ed., *Expectations, Uncertainty, and Business Behavior* (New York: Social Science Research Council, 1958), p. 123.

[83]Mills, *Price, and Inventory Policy*, p. 90.

pacity, the optimal price under uncertainty tends to be less than the certainty price. At the same time, however, production is likely to be restricted so that out-of-stock situations occur more frequently than surpluses.

Much more research on the implications of demand uncertainties for business pricing behavior remains to be done. The theory must be extended, and empirical studies of actual inventory and price policies are needed. Additions to knowledge in this area may have a marked impact on welfare economics. As we have noted, it is possible that prices will be set at lower levels under uncertainty than when demand is known with certainty, *ceteris paribus*. At first glance, this seems to be favorable from the standpoint of allocative efficiency. However, its side effect could be a failure to satisfy demand not because of excessive prices, but because production and inventory levels are inadequate to meet peak demands. How one weighs the welfare losses due to traditional monopolistic resource misallocation against those associated with stochastic out-of-stock conditions is not at all apparent.

CONCLUSION

It is appropriate now to draw together the main conclusions emerging from Chapters 5 through 8. We have seen that when sellers are few in number, there are incentives for them to recognize their interdependence and to cooperate in policies which lead toward maximum group profits. Institutions such as outright collusion, price leadership, pricing by rules of thumb, and focal point pricing facilitate the maintenance of prices above the competitive level. But there are important limits on the ability of monopolists and oligopolists to hold prices at highly profitable levels. Oligopolistic coordination may break down due to conflicts over the most suitable price, heterogeneity of products, the pressure of underabsorbed fixed costs, secret price-cutting, or simple cussedness on the part of some maverick producer. Long-run substitution and the threat or actuality of entry by new competitors place a ceiling—and sometimes a low one—on producers' pricing discretion.

The performance implications of this complicated picture are themselves complex. It is clear that under conditions favorable to the exercise of market power prices may be held substantially above competitive levels for long periods of time. Still this result does not follow automatically from the mere existence of a concentrated market structure. Prices often hover closer to cost than one would predict from an analysis which takes into account only the fewness of sellers, ignoring coordination obstacles and long-run constraints. These more subtle structural and behavioral variables help explain why pricing performance in modern industrial markets has on the whole been fairly satisfactory despite significant departures from the structural ideal of pure theory.

Chapter 9

Market Power on the Buyers' Side

In this chapter we turn to the buyers' side of the market. We proceed more rapidly, partly because previous chapters have prepared the ground, but also because the links from market structure on the buyers' side to conduct and performance are imperfectly understood. The theory is weak; the evidence scant. We must settle for modest gains: identifying the leading hypotheses and exploring their general plausibility.

THE EXTENT OF BUYER CONCENTRATION

Our ignorance begins with the question of how much buyer concentration exists. There are no data analogous to the surveys of seller concentration in manufacturing industry. An overall impressionistic view suggests that concentration on the buyers' side is generally more modest than concentration on the sellers' side, although significant pockets of monopsony or oligopsony power (the power associated with fewness of buyers) can be found.

More than two thirds of the gross national product and some 85 per cent of all goods and services produced and sold through the economy's market sector go ultimately to consumers. Buyer concentration in this vast consumer goods market is patently low, ignoring such oddities as the market for 42 carat diamond brooches. Yet most goods pass through numerous intermediate transactions before reaching the consumer's hands. Consumers buy from retailers, who may obtain their supplies from wholesalers, who buy from consumer goods manufacturers, who secure raw materials, equipment, and parts from other manufacturing and mining firms, who in turn purchase from still other companies, etc. Within manufacturing industry alone, each dollar of final product sales at wholesale generates on the average more than a dollar's worth of additional manufacturers' sales for parts, materials, etc. And at any point in this chain of transactions monopsony (as well as monopoly) power may intrude.

Although local market definitions are appropriate in measuring retail sellers' concentration, retailers as buyers normally purchase all but perishables and bulky, low value commodities in a national market. Until 1964, the largest American retailing corporation was A & P. It made approximately 10 per cent of all U.S. retail grocery sales for three decades. Since it handles a balanced line, its national share as a buyer of most food items, after taking into account restaurant and institutional wholesale demands, must have been on the order of 8 per cent.[1] The next largest chain (Safeway) is only about three fifths A & P's size in terms of sales and purchases. The largest 20 chains together made 35 per cent of all grocery sales in 1965, and

---

[1] Cf. M. A. Adelman, *A & P: A Study in Price-Cost Behavior and Public Policy* (Cambridge: Harvard University Press, 1959), pp. 211 and 275; and "The Giants Put on More Muscle," *Business Week*, July 23, 1966, p. 72.

their share of wholesale purchases was probably on the order of 28 per cent. In groceries, then, the overall pattern is one of modest concentration on the buyer's side.

Sears, Roebuck moved into first place among retailers in 1964, with sales of $5.7 billion. Total U. S. retail sales in the field most closely related to its interests—tires and auto accessories, furniture and appliances, hardware, apparel, and general merchandise—amounted that year to $67 billion.[2] If Sears' share of sales in each product line were the same as its overall share, it would account for roughly 8 per cent of wholesale purchases in each line. But since it is stronger in some fields than in others, its share of wholesale purchases no doubt ranges from as little as 1 per cent in certain clothing lines to as much as 20 per cent on such items as auto accessories and washing machines.

Most other retailing fields are characterized by less concentration. For example, the Walgreen Company's 1967 sales of $559 million represented roughly 5 per cent of all drug store sales. Since about half of all prescription drugs reach ultimate users through hospitals and government agencies, Walgreen's share of the pharmaceutical purchasing market was between 2 and 3 per cent. Its share of candies, toys, and similar purchases was undoubtedly even smaller, given that non-drug retailers also stock those items. The six largest retail shoe chains together owned about 18 per cent of all retail shoe outlets in 1956, and this approximates their share of wholesale shoe purchases.[3] On the whole, the concentration of buying power in retailing (and in the related, often vertically integrated wholesale trades) seems to be moderate, although not negligible.

The degree of buyer concentration among manufacturers purchasing from other manufacturers is harder to assess quantitatively. If each supplying industry specialized in providing inputs to a single buying industry, the concentration of buying power could be estimated directly from seller concentration ratios in the buying industries. This is seldom the case, however. Three complications arise.

First, inspection of input-output tables for the American economy shows that most raw materials and intermediate goods manufacturing industries sell their products to many other using industries and are dependent upon any single class of industrial buyers for only a small fraction of their sales. The steel industry's best customer in 1958, for example, was the auto industry, which directly consumed only 13 per cent of net steel output.[4] This fact in isolation would suggest that because manufacturers' interindustry sales are spread over so many fields, buyer concentration is much lower on the average than end product seller concentration.

But second, industrial firms sometimes possess more buying power in the aggregate than they do in purchasing for particular end product markets. Since General Motors' share of auto output in 1958 was about 46 per cent, we might expect its share of all steel purchases to have been roughly 6 per cent. However, GM buys steel not only for autos, trucks and busses, but also for construction equipment, locomotives, refrigerators, diesel motors, army tanks and (on a very modest scale) missile guidance systems. Its overall share of steel purchases must therefore have been higher than 6 per cent—perhaps as high as 8 per cent. This qualification is not very important, however, since relatively few firms operate in such a diversity of industries, and the kinds of supplies their divisions purchase in common are for the most part general-purpose materials and equipment whose sellers are strongly dependent upon no single using industry.

The third complication is more compelling. The industry definitions in available input-output tables are often too broad to reflect the true amount of seller dependence upon specific buying sectors. The glass industry, for instance, sells only 11 per cent of its output (broadly defined)

---

[2]*Ibid.*, and U. S. Bureau of the Census, *Statistical Abstract of the United States: 1965* (Washington: 1965), p. 824.

[3]See David D. Martin, "The Brown Shoe Case and the New Antimerger Policy," *American Economic Review*, June 1963, p. 342.

[4]In 1967, an auto boom and construction slump year, the figure was 20 per cent.

to the automobile industry, but four auto makers purchase nearly all the output of plants specializing in laminated and tempered window glass. Similarly, auto makers in 1965 consumed roughly half of all cold and hot rolled sheet steel, whose production requires specialized, costly rolling mills. When plant and equipment are specialized to meet the needs of a single concentrated buying industry, the buying firms may possess considerable power over transaction prices. But since a relatively small proportion of all inter-industry transactions involves such a high degree of specialization on the suppliers' side, average concentration on the buyers' side is undoubtedly lower than is seller concentration in end product markets. With existing data, it is difficult to go beyond this crude generalization.

COUNTERVAILING POWER

The best-known conjecture relating market power on the buyers' side to economic performance is J. K. Galbraith's theory of countervailing power.[5] Galbraith advances two main arguments. First, in modern oligopolistically structured industries, the force compelling sellers to conform to consumer wants and to hold prices near cost is not the inter-seller competition traditionally stressed by economists, but countervailing power exercised by strong buyers. As examples, Galbraith cites A & P's deft use of power to extract price reductions from grocery manufacturers; the discounts won from oligopolistic tire makers by Sears Roebuck; the auto industry's reputed success in curbing the pricing power of steel mills; and (on the other side of the market) the ability of strong unions to win large wage and fringe benefit concessions from powerful employer groups. Second, powerful buyers do not just offset the power of concentrated sellers occasionally and haphazardly. Instead, a systematic propensity for power on the buyers' side is

said to emerge whenever power exists on the sellers' side:

> . . . . Power on one side of a market creates both the need for, and the prospect of reward to, the exercise of countervailing power from the other side. . . . The first begets the second. . . . Retailers are required by their situation to develop countervailing power on the consumer's behalf. . . . At the end of virtually every channel by which consumers' goods reach the public there is, in practice, a layer of powerful buyers.[6]

The economics profession seldom reacts complacently to charges that it has backed the wrong horse for 175 years, and a lively debate followed the publication of Galbraith's countervailing power thesis.[7] There was little disagreement over the contention that strong buyers may, under appropriate circumstances, negate the power of oligopolistic sellers. Galbraith's assertion that power begets countervailing power in a spontaneous, self-generating fashion was more sharply attacked. The historical evidence he advanced to support his conjectures—purportedly demonstrating that strong unions and retail chains arose sooner where the corresponding manufacturing industries were powerful—was for the most part debunked. Whether countervailing power currently provides a widespread check on the power of concentrated sellers is also open to doubt. In an analysis of the 65 industries classified as "Type I oligopolies" by Kaysen and Turner[8]—i.e., those in which eight firms contributed at least 50 per cent of industry sales and 20 firms at least 75 per cent—the present author was able to find not more than 20 industries in which concentration on the buyers' side even approached the level of concentration on the sellers' side. (Doubts were resolved in favor of classifying industries in the high buyer concentration group.) In the remaining 45 industries,

[5]*American Capitalism: The Concept of Countervailing Power* (Boston: Houghton Mifflin, 1952; Rev. ed., 1956). Page references are to the revised edition.

[6]*Ibid.*, pp. 113, 111, 117, and 120.

[7]See, for example, George Stigler, "The Economist Plays With Blocs," *American Economic Review*, May 1954, pp. 7–14; and Simon N. Whitney, "Errors in the Concept of Countervailing Power," *Journal of Business*, October 1953, pp. 238–253.

[8]*Antitrust Policy* (Cambridge: Harvard University Press, 1959), pp. 27–37 and 275–313. See also pp. 60 and 190 *supra*.

the dynamics of countervailing power had apparently not operated, or had at least not progressed very far.

A further criticism of the countervailing power thesis may be the most damaging of all: there is no guarantee that price reductions secured by strong buyers will be passed along to consumers in the form of lower retail prices. The result of effectively exercised countervailing power may be merely a redistribution of profits among contending industrial and commercial blocs, with little or no ultimate benefit to the consumer.

Since the available evidence is meager, not much can be gained by debating further whether it supports Galbraith's contention that power inexorably or even typically begets countervailing power. Instead, let us explore the means by which powerful buyers secure price reductions from sellers and the conditions facilitating or inhibiting the transmission of such gains to consumers.

THE EXERCISE OF POWER BY BUYERS

The student with a Teutonic obsession for classifying things into neat categories can identify six main market structure types involving power on the buyer's side, including a single buyer facing a single seller (bilateral monopoly), a single buyer facing many purely competitive sellers (pure monopsony), a few buyers facing a few sellers (bilateral oligopoly), a few buyers facing many sellers (oligopsony), and so on. Only for the first two cases, which are seldom encountered in a pure form in the real world, do we possess much in the way of formal economic theory. Despite its low empirical relevance, the theory of bilateral monopoly does provide a useful point of departure for examining more realistic cases. The standard geometric exposition can become incredibly messy and has led more than one capable economist down the path to error. The reader must therefore be content with (or thankful for) a verbal summary of the principal findings, supplemented by mathematical footnotes and one diagram illustrating central points.[9]

BILATERAL MONOPOLY

The theory of bilateral monopoly is indeterminate with a vengeance. It embodies all the problems we met in our study of oligopoly theory in Chapter 5, i.e., do the parties attempt to maximize their individual profits, ignoring their interdependence, or do they cooperate to maximize joint profits? And unlike oligopoly, even if the parties do collaborate to establish the joint profit-maximizing output, the price is indeterminate within a potentially wide range. Ignoring extremes resulting if the firms try to drive each other out of business, the upper limit of this range coincides with the price set by a monopolist facing a purely competitive buying industry; the lower limit is the price a monopsonistic buyer would impose upon purely competitive sellers. Pure conflict prevails within these extremes. The bargaining power wielded and the tactics employed by the trading partners determine the resolution of this conflict, and on formal theoretical grounds it is possible to say only that almost anything can happen. The price may be either higher or lower than the equilibrium price resulting from bilateral competition under identical cost and demand conditions.

Suppose the price is lower than, or at least not above, the bilaterally competitive equilibrium price. Does this mean that consumers will benefit from lower prices when the monopsonistic buyer resells the product on which he has struck such a good bargain, or (equivalently) uses it as an input in producing some final output? The answer is, 'perhaps, but not necessarily.' Conceivably, the buyer will retain the fruits of his bargain in the form of higher profits and pass no gains on to consumers. Whether or not this happens depends primarily upon whether output of the intermediate good is re-

---

[9]For the most thorough analysis of the problem, see James N. Morgan, "Bilateral Monopoly and the Competitive Output," *Quarterly Journal of Economics*, August 1949, pp. 371–391. The original standard exposition is A. L. Bowley, "Bilateral Monopoly," *Economic Journal*, December 1928, pp. 651–659. For a broader analysis of vertical price relationships, see James McKie, *Tin Cans and Tin Plate* (Cambridge: Harvard University Press, 1959), pp. 10–34.

stricted due to the bilateral monopoly link. If less of the intermediate good is produced than under bilateral competition, less of the final good will be offered to consumers, *ceteris paribus*, and the price of the final product will be higher than it would be under competition.

From the standpoint of consumers, the least favorable outcome is likely to occur under what may be called myopic chain monopoly—that is, when the end product seller, a monopolist in its product market, buys an input from a monopolistic supplier and myopically views the price set by the supplier as given. Then allocative distortions intrude at each stage of the vertical pricing chain, and the cumulative restrictive effect is worse than it would be if all monopoly power were concentrated at one link in the chain, or if the various firms collaborated in a joint profit-maximizing policy. In fact, if cost relationships are unaffected technologically by the industry's vertical organization and if substitution of other inputs is infeasible, the quantity of the monopolized input transferred under joint profit maximization by the bilaterally monopolistic buyer and seller is identical to the quantity which would be transferred if the input supply market were purely competitive. This proposition is best shown mathematically. Since the demonstration is intricate even for a simplified case, we shall relegate it to a footnote.[10]

[10]We assume two vertical stages. Firm A monopolizes the sale of its end product to consumers, while Firm B supplies an intermediate product, one unit of which is required by Firm A to produce a unit of end product. Let X therefore denote the quantity of both the end product and the necessary intermediate product produced. The consumer demand for end product is given by the linear relation $P_A = a - bX_A$. We assume that Firm A incurs a cost of $\$V_A$ per unit in transforming Firm B's intermediate good into end product, and that Firm B incurs a cost of $\$V_B$ per unit in producing its intermediate product. We explore three cases: competitive pricing of the intermediate, two-stage myopic monopoly, and joint monopoly profit maximization.

If the intermediate is sold competitively, its price P_B will in equilibrium be equal to its marginal cost V_B. Firm A's total cost function will be $X_A(V_A + P_B)$. Firm A's profit equation is:

(1) $\pi_A = X_A(a - bX_A) - X_A(V_A + P_B)$.

Setting the first derivative of this function equal to zero, we find that the optimal quantity produced by Firm A is:

(2) $X_A = \dfrac{a - V_A - P_B}{2b}$.

And since $P_B = V_B$ under competitive input pricing,

(3) $X_A = \dfrac{a - V_A - V_B}{2b}$.

Suppose now that Firm B is a monopolist whose price Firm A accepts as a parameter in its maximizing decisions. Solving Firm A's profit-maximizing condition for P_B and substituting in X_B for X_A, we obtain:

(4) $P_B = a - V_A - 2bX_B$,

which is the derived demand function for Firm B's output. Firm B's profit equation is given by:

(5) $\pi_B = X_B(a - V_A - 2bX_B) - V_BX_B$.

Differentiating and setting the result equal to zero, we obtain the maximum condition:

(6) $X_B = \dfrac{a - V_A - V_B}{4b}$.

Recalling our 1:1 production assumption that $X_A = X_B$, and comparing equation (6) with equation (3), we see that when Firm A accepts the price of monopolistic Firm B as given, output is only half as great as it would be if Firm B priced its intermediate good competitively. Nonlinear demand curves, non-constant cost conditions, and the existence of substitutes for X_B can cause this relation to deviate from the one-half figure, but output in the two-stage monopoly case is necessarily less than output when Stage B is competitively structured, other things being equal.

Suppose now that the firms, recognizing their interdependence, attempt to maximize joint profits. The combined profit function is:

(7) $\pi_A + \pi_B = X_A(a - bX_A) - X_A(V_A + P_B) + X_BP_B - X_BV_B$.

Substituting in Firm B's derived demand function $P_B = a - V_A - 2bX_B$ and letting $X = X_A = X_B$, equation (7) can be rewritten:

(8) $\pi_A + \pi_B = X(a - bX) - XV_A - X(a - V_A - 2bX) + X(a - V_A - 2bX) - V_BX$
$= aX - bX^2 - V_AX - V_BX$.

Setting the derivative of (8) equal to zero and solving for X, we obtain:

(9) $X = \dfrac{a - V_A - V_B}{2b}$,

which is the same as the competitive case output of equation (3) and is twice the two-monopoly-stage output of equation (6).

When rents are imputed differently under competitive organization of the intermediate good sector B than under monopolistic organization, or when various pecuniary or physical external economies apply differentially, it is probable that the joint profit-maximizing output will be less than the output under competitive organization of the intermediate good sector. See Morgan, *op. cit.*, pp. 390–391; and McKie, *op. cit.*, pp. 19–20. The reader is warned that there are errors in McKie's Figure 2.

Whether end product output under joint profit-maximizing bilateral monopoly is extended all the way to the level which would be forthcoming if all vertical stages were competitively structured depends in a subtle way upon demand conditions. To see this, a geometric model similar to the mathematical model of note 10 is useful. We assume, to eliminate complications associated with input substitution and diminishing returns, that monopsonistic buyer Firm A immediately resells the product it purchases, without doing anything to the product or incurring any further production costs. The purchased product is its only input. If Firm A is also a monopolist in reselling the product to consumers, the average value of a unit purchased is equal to the price at which that unit can be sold, and so the average value product function AVP in Figure 9.1 is identical to the end product demand curve. Marginal to this curve is the marginal revenue product function MRP, showing the change in Firm A's total revenue

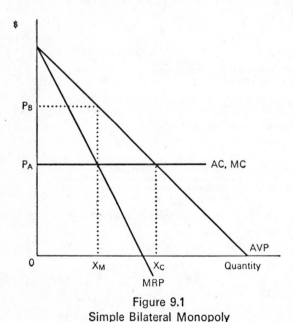

Figure 9.1
Simple Bilateral Monopoly

associated with buying and then reselling an extra unit of the product in question. To avoid complications related to rent imputation and external effects, we assume (with empirical support in Chapter 4) that the product can be supplied to Firm A by Firm B under conditions of constant long-run unit cost. The marginal and average unit cost function of supplier Firm B is therefore the horizontal line AC,MC in Figure 9.1.

Now Firms A and B will maximize their joint bilateral monopoly profits by equating MRP with MC, exchanging OX_M units of the product. Price is indeterminate within the range $P_A P_B$; monopsonist Firm A prefers the low price OP_A and monopolist Firm B the high price OP_B. The point of central interest, however, is the ensuing output OX_M. By way of comparison, what output would result if both sides of the market were competitively structured? Competitive firms on the supply side would increase output whenever price exceeds unit cost, and so the competitive supply curve is the horizontal line $P_A AC,MC$. Firms reselling the product will purchase units for resale up to the point where average revenue (the resale price) equals marginal cost, so AVP is the competitive demand curve. Supply and demand are equated at the competitive output OX_C, which obviously exceeds OX_M. It would appear that bilateral monopoly with joint profit maximization causes output to be less than it would be under fully competitive conditions.

Or does it? Firms A and B jointly restrict output to OX_M because they recognize that any higher output will be absorbed in the end product market only at reduced prices, and after the price reduction is taken into account, marginal revenue product would be less than the cost of the marginal unit. But if Firm A were a competitor in the resale market (even though a monopsonist with respect to Firm B) it could not by definition take into account the effect of its additional sales on the resale price. As a result, if it were powerful enough to hold the input price at OP_A, it would expand purchases (and resales) all the way to OX_C.[11] Under the assumptions stipulated here, Firm A's desire to restrict output can be attributed only to its position as a monopolist in the resale market, and not to its position as a monopsonist. To be sure, if Firm B were a monopolist selling to a purely competitive resale industry (i.e., Firm A broken into 100 pieces), it would view AVP as its demand curve, MRP as its marginal revenue curve, and it would exploit its monopoly power to restrict output to OX_M, selling at the highly profitable price OP_B. The crux of the matter is, however, that *if* the firms (or firm) purchasing from Firm B had sufficient monopsony power to thwart Firm B's efforts and hold the price at OP_A, and if at the same time they had no perceptible power over resale prices, the competitive output OX_C would be achieved.

This result requires an improbable concatenation of assumptions, but it shows that at least in principle, bilateral monopoly does not *necessarily* interfere with reaching the competitive output, and that power on the buyer's side which countervails upstream seller power may actually help. Its main practical significance lies in an extension to the case of bilateral oligopoly. It is entirely conceivable that a few end product sellers could have sufficient power as buyers to hold the prices of intermediate products supplied by upstream oligopolists at or near competitive levels. At the same time, for any of the reasons discussed in Chapters 7 and 8, they might find themselves unable to depart significantly from competitive pricing in the end product market. If so, countervailing power may well lead to an allocation of resources approximating the competitive norm.

BILATERAL OLIGOPOLY

Let us focus now on the ways countervailing power is actually exercised. By what means can a few strong buyers restrain the pricing actions of oligopolistic sellers? How successful are they in doing so?

One possibility was identified in Chapter 7. There we saw that oligopolists are prone to cut prices in order to land an unusually large order, especially when they have excess capacity. Large buyers can exploit this weakness by concentrating their orders into big lumps, dangling the temptation before each seller and encouraging a break from the established price structure. This tactic was employed on occasion to good advantage by the A & P Company. Still it is not always necessary to be one of the largest buyers to play the game, and mere size is insufficient if wielded ineffectively. In the cement industry, for example, the largest buyers were state government agencies procuring supplies for their highway construction programs. But during the depressed 1930s, and even when all requirements of a state were lumped together into a single giant purchase, cement makers refused to undercut each other because when the state purchasing agency announced an aggressive winning bid, as required by law, rival cement makers instituted retaliatory cuts on nongovernmental business. Large construction contractors, who normally purchased less cement than the state governments, were more successful in breaking the producers' pricing discipline because they shopped around and bargained for *secret* concessions before placing their sizeable, irregularly occurring orders. Recognizing this, many states ceased buying cement directly, decentralizing the procurement function to highway contractors.[12]

Large buyers also play one seller off against the others to elicit price concessions. For instance, each of the major automobile manufacturers has a principal tire supplier, but each also spreads its business around to other tire makers so that it can threaten to shift, or actually shift, its distribution of orders in favor of

on price. A bevy of little Firm A's would be of indeterminate size each and might in the long run gravitate toward a monopolistic size distribution.

An alternative and plausible assumption, if the analysis is centered on a single firm, is to postulate that the end product price is held near the competitive level for strategic reasons—i.e., to deter easy entry. Alternatively, a multiplicity of little Firm A's might possess monopsony power if suppliers were tied to them by long-term contracts.

[12]Samuel M. Loescher, *Imperfect Collusion in the Cement Industry* (Cambridge: Harvard University Press, 1959), pp. 54–55, 112–113, and 130–134.

the supplier who offers more attractive terms.[13] Similar practices were reported by McKie in his study of price relationships between the tin can and tin-plated steel manufacturers.[14] A complementary ploy is considered unethical in business circles, but it is still used regularly. When sellers lack confidence in each other's determination to maintain pricing discipline, they are easy prey to the purchasing agent who fabricates convincing but fictitious claims of concessions offered by unnamed rivals. Once a single supplier is taken in by this ruse, his actual quotation (and the favorable shift in patronage with which it was rewarded) provides a lever to extract lower prices from additional sellers.

These tactics are pursued most successfully when demand is slack, so that producers have excess capacity which can be utilized profitably if an increased share of some major buyer's business can be captured through price cuts, or when the loss of business to a price-cutting rival would leave previously favored sellers with a substantial burden of underabsorbed overhead costs. The balance of power is clearly in the hands of the buyer, and especially the large buyer, during a downturn. One might expect a bargaining power reversal during booms, when demand is outracing capacity. Then oligopolistic sellers may be in a position to compensate for past concessions, playing one eager buyer off against the others to bid prices up. On this symmetry conjecture we have little concrete evidence. Galbraith states, without offering much empirical support, that countervailing power "does not function at all as a restraint on market power when there is . . . inflationary pressure on markets."[15] Adelman's rough estimates show that A & P won proportionately larger special price concessions from its suppliers during the depressed early 1930s than in prosperous 1929, and there were faint indications of a decline in concessions as the onset of World War II revived

demand.[16] McKie, on the other hand, found no evidence that tin plated steel manufacturers were able to play one large tin can maker off against others to escalate prices when steel was in short supply following the war. His explanation was that "Sellers hesitate to give buyers their own medicine at such times, fearing the imminent return of a buyer's market. Thus, there tends to be an asymmetry of bargaining power in bilateral oligopoly, other things being equal."[17] As we shall see in a later chapter, oligopolistic industries have tended to show more restraint than competitively structured industries in raising prices during booms, although it is not clear whether this was due to countervailing power, a longer-run perspective in pricing decisions, or the concentrated industries' greater vulnerability to governmental suasion and anti-inflationary measures. Thus, we must return a Scotch verdict. We simply do not know whether strong buyers in a bilateral oligopoly situation forego in booms what they gain during slumps.

Large buyers can also issue credible threats to integrate vertically upstream, producing their own requirements of an input unless prices are held close to cost. Unlike potential outside entrants, they have an assured market, and therefore have no reason to fear the pricing reactions of established producers.[18] When the buyer's demand is substantial enough to permit realization of all scale economies in producing for its own use, it can scarcely lose: either sellers restrain their prices in response to its threat, or if the threat fails, the buyer displaces them and consumes its own low-cost production. Numerous applications of this dual strategy are recorded in industry studies. Although some scale economies are apparently unattainable to firms integrating vertically, tin-plated steel prices have been restrained by the ability of the tin can manufacturers to begin plating their own

[13]"Tire Prospects," *Fortune*, May 1966, pp. 211–212.
[14]*Tin Cans and Tin Plate*, pp. 58–63.
[15]*American Capitalism*, p. 128.
[16]*A & P*, pp. 237 and 242.
[17]*Tin Cans and Tin Plate*, pp. 24–25 and 63.
[18]Cf. p. 229 *supra*.

steel, while tin can prices have been held in check by the threat (and in some cases the actuality) of upstream integration by large food canners.[19] The auto manufacturers have kept downward pressure on glass window, electrical component, fabricated parts, and even cold-rolled steel sheet prices by their demonstrated willingness to produce for their own use whenever the prospect of cost savings becomes attractive.[20] Markham reports that a large fertilizer manufacturer obtained repeated price concessions from a phosphate rock producer by threatening to reopen its dormant mines.[21]

Surprisingly, Adelman found only one clear instance of a successful vertical integration threat by A & P to win price concessions, despite the giant retailer's extensive entry into food manufacturing operations.[22] Whether this reflects inadequacies in the data available to Adelman, or A & P's belief that threats of potential competition would have little effect on suppliers already under heavy competitive pressure from their many peers, is not certain. The A & P history does demonstrate, however, that the desire to countervail oligopoly pricing power is not the only motive for vertical integration into suppliers' fields. Integration may permit significant real (as opposed to pecuniary) economies in transferring goods from one stage to another—i.e., minimization of sales representation and contracting functions, better coordination of production with requirements, streamlining of distribution channels, lower spoilage, etc.[23] It can also be a means of ensuring the availability of supplies in boom periods, or when suppliers are struck by labor union disputes. And given that transfer prices under bilateral oligopoly must be established through bargaining, vertical integration may be a way of avoiding the stalemates (with consequent supply interruptions) otherwise likely to arise.[24]

A further potential advantage of upstream integration merits more extended comment. Some firms, including the automobile and aircraft manufacturers, engage in what is called "tapered integration."[25] That is, they produce a portion of their materials and parts requirements and farm out the remainder to independent specialists. This approach gives the buyer a powerful bargaining position relative to his suppliers, for he can threaten credibly to increase internal production at their expense unless prices are held in check. Internal production also gives the buyer a good 'feel' for costs, which is most useful in bargaining. In addition, the buyer can transfer the risk of demand fluctuations to suppliers. In both good times and bad, internal production lines are kept operating near capacity. Peak requirements are met by loading outside suppliers with orders, while in a slump outside orders are cut back sharply. As a result the outsiders bear nearly all the brunt of output swings, and the percentage variation in their employment over the business cycle is much greater than it would be if they produced the buyer's full requirements. Of course, 'overflow' suppliers will be reluctant to accept this precarious existence without being compensated for their risks, and one might expect them to hold out for high prices in periods of peak demand. The available evidence fails to support this hypothesis, apparently because the suppliers recognize that when the boom ebbs their ability to keep going at all depends upon the good will

---

[19]McKie, *op. cit.*, pp. 50–54, 110–114, and 291–292.

[20]Simon Whitney, *Antitrust Policies* (New York: Twentieth Century Fund, 1958), vol. I, pp. 496–500; and A. D. H. Kaplan, Joel B. Dirlam, and R. F. Lanzillotti, *Pricing in Big Business* (Washington: Brookings, 1958), p. 172.

[21]Jesse W. Markham, *The Fertilizer Industry* (Nashville: Vanderbilt University Press, 1958), p. 113.

[22]*A & P*, pp. 269–271 and Chapter XII generally.

[23]*Ibid.*, pp. 253–258. See also M. J. Peck and F. M. Scherer, *The Weapons Acquisition Process: An Economic Analysis* (Boston: Harvard Business School Division of Research, 1962), pp. 183–185.

[24]Cf. pp. 87–88 *supra*.

[25]For autos, see Whitney, *op. cit.*, pp. 496–498; and "UAW Mounts Campaign Against 'Monopsony,' " *Business Week*, July 24, 1965, pp. 43–44. For aircraft, see Peck and Scherer, *op. cit.*, pp. 386–404; and John S. Day, *Subcontracting Policy in the Airframe Industry* (Boston: Harvard Business School Division of Research, 1956). For a more general analysis, see M. A. Adelman, "The Large Firm and Its Suppliers," *Review of Economics and Statistics*, May 1949, pp. 113–118.

of their customer. The main connection between risk and profits in such cases works through the mechanism of entry. New firms will not enter unless buyers are paying prices sufficiently high to compensate for the risks. If buyers desire to maintain a flow of new outside investment to satisfy their needs, they must refrain from frightening would-be entrants by taking full advantage of their bargaining power over firms whose investments are already committed. If on the other hand they believe there is too much investment in supplier capacity—i.e., because demand is secularly declining, as it was in the military manned aircraft field during the 1950s— they can extract unusually favorable bargains from their overflow suppliers, whose lot is not a happy one.

Thus, large buyers may find it advantageous to integrate vertically upstream for any of several reasons, of which the desire to hold suppliers' prices near competitive levels is only one. Still the fact that U. S. retailing giants do relatively little manufacturing for resale, and that manufacturers spend on the average half of every sales dollar for materials and parts supplied by independent firms, supports either and probably both of two conclusions: (1) that only in a minority of cases does the net financial advantage lie in favor of making rather than buying general-purpose materials and parts; and (2) that supplier prices are usually kept near competitive levels, if not by actual competition, then by fear of new competition through vertical entry. Only when barriers to entry into the suppliers' fields are high do these generalizations break down.

A device short of vertical integration sometimes employed to reduce the risk of bargaining stalemates and the cost of repeated recontracting is the long-term requirements contract, negotiated to cover transactions extending through a period as long as 30 years.[26] Sellers are attracted to these agreements by the assurance that their production capacity will be utilized at predictable levels and perhaps also by selling cost savings. They are typically protected from severe risk by formulas which relate the price in future periods to changes in appropriate cost or price indices. Given these attractions, buyers may be able to secure agreement on prices well below current and expected market levels, at the same time assuring future supplies. A disadvantage for both parties to such agreements is their inflexibility, rendering optimal adaptation to changing needs and opportunities difficult. There is also an important social cost, for new entry into an industry is harder when a significant fraction of the market is preempted under long-term contracts. Because of their entry-foreclosing tendency, long-term requirements contracts have been attacked in a number of antitrust actions. We shall consider their legal status in Chapter 21.

Price concessions won by a large buyer for any of the reasons identified here may or may not spread throughout the buying industry. Three main cases can be distinguished. First, if the concessions reflect real production and distribution economies associated with large scale ordering and production, there is no reason to believe that smaller buyers will receive the same opportunities, at least in the absence of arbitrary legal compulsion.[27] Second, if the concessions are exacted not because of cost differences, but because the buyer has bargaining leverage which smaller buyers lack, the large buyer may (again in the absence of legal intervention) enjoy a persistent price advantage over its less powerful rivals. This is the clearest form of price discrimination, to which we shall return in the next chapter. A striking example was the sale by the Champion Company of identical spark plugs to Ford Motor Company at $.06 per unit for use in original equipment and $.22 for replacement part use, while wholesalers paid $.261 per unit.[28] But third, when several aggressive buyers pur-

---

[26]For examples, see Adelman, *A & P*, pp. 269–273 and 314–321; M. J. Peck, *Competition in the Aluminum Industry* (Cambridge: Harvard University Press, 1961), pp. 134–143; McKie, *op. cit.*, pp. 146–160; Carl Kaysen, *United States v. United Shoe Machinery Corporation* (Cambridge: Harvard University Press, 1956), pp. 214–255; and Reed Moyer, *Competition in the Midwestern Coal Industry* (Cambridge: Harvard University Press, 1964), pp. 130–137.

[27]Such as the Robinson-Patman Act, which will be studied in Chapter 21.

[28]Cf. H. L. Hansen and M. N. Smith, "The Champion Case: What Is Competition?" *Harvard Business Review*, May 1951, pp. 89–103.

chase substantial quantities of an intermediate product, a concession unrelated to cost offered by an oligopolistic supplier to one buyer will sooner or later be found out by other buyers and sellers and, unless discipline in the oligopoly is strong, the concession stands a high probability of spreading. Here what begins as isolated price discrimination touches off a chain of rivalrous reactions which ultimately affects the whole structure of prices.

It is in this last case that countervailing power is most apt to have an effect generally beneficial to consumers. As McKie observes:

> When there is moderate or low concentration among sellers—a "loosely" oligopolistic structure—and there are some large buyers, the result is likely to be a pattern of behavior more effectively competitive than if there were atomistic competition on the buying side.[29]

Similarly, Adelman concluded that:

> A limited degree of monopoly ("substantial bargaining power") on one side of the market can be of great service in maintaining competition on the other. A strong, alert buyer, large enough so that the loss of his patronage is not a matter of indifference, constantly on the watch for a break which he can exploit by rolling up the whole price front, able to force concessions first from one and then from all, and followed by the other buyers, can collapse a structure of control or keep it from ever coming into existence.[30]

As we saw in Chapter 7, the granting of covert price reductions which then spread can have a potent disruptive effect on the discipline of oligopolistic industries. What we do not know is how frequently the bargaining power of large buyers is the catalyst behind such conduct, and therefore it is difficult to be certain how important buyer power is as a check to the power of oligopolistic sellers.

POWERFUL BUYERS FACING WEAK SELLERS

Two further questions on the power relations between buyer and seller are of interest. Do strong buyers obtain lower prices from weak (i.e., atomistic) sellers than from sellers with market power? And are weak sellers more likely to grant discriminatory price concessions?

The theory of bilateral monopoly is useful in attacking the first question. If cost and demand conditions remain the same, the quantity of an intermediate good purchased by a monopsonist from atomistic suppliers will be identical to the quantity purchased under joint profit-maximizing bilateral monopoly. But while the price under bilateral monopoly is indeterminate, the price paid by a monopsonist to competitive sellers will in equilibrium equal the lowest price within the range of indeterminacy under bilateral monopoly. This in turn equals the price which would prevail under pure bilateral competition if the long-run supply function is horizontal. It will be less than the bilateral competition transfer price if the long-run supply function is rising. A similar range of indeterminacy presumably exists under bilateral oligopoly, assuming effective collusion. There is no compelling theoretical ground for predicting that the price when strong buyers confront strong sellers must gravitate to the floor of this range. But if, as McKie argues, there is an asymmetry of bargaining power, the transfer price under bilateral oligopoly will tend closer to the lower than to the upper limit. Unfortunately, the evidence available is too meager to tell whether buyers do on the average strike the better half of the bargain.

A more confident verdict is possible on the second question. Price discrimination is profitable only when the seller enjoys some control over price. Atomistic sellers of a homogeneous product have no such control, and since they can (by definition) sell as much as they wish at the ruling price, they have no incentive to offer discriminatory price reductions. We should therefore expect systematic price discrimination to be practiced only by sellers with some market

---

[29] *Tin Cans and Tin Plate*, pp. 20–21.

[30] M. A. Adelman, "Effective Competition and the Antitrust Laws," *Harvard Law Review*, September 1948, p. 1300. Copyright 1948 by the Harvard Law Review Association.

power. Adelman's evidence on A & P's procurement program supports this prediction. He found that atomistic suppliers of unbranded packaged groceries and fresh produce offered no price reductions not connected with commensurate transfer cost savings. A & P was most successful in obtaining preferential treatment on moderately differentiated products, while sellers of products with strong brand acceptance (such as Crisco and Wheaties) seldom made concessions, since A & P needed their items on its shelves to satisfy its customers just as intensely as they needed A & P as an outlet.[31] Thus, strong buyers are apparently more apt to win discriminatory price concessions from sellers with a modest degree of market power than from those with either no power over price or a great deal of it.

Integrating these two points, we conclude that a strong buyer is not likely to secure lower prices from oligopolistic sellers than he would from competitive sellers, *ceteris paribus*, for he will strike the most favorable bargain consistent with supply conditions in the competitive case. Still he may be able to do nearly as well, playing off one seller against the others to keep the general market price at low levels or encouraging sellers to grant discriminatory price concessions.

ARE THE BENEFITS OF COUNTERVAILING POWER PASSED ON?

It seems clear that countervailing power can and does lead to lower transfer prices, at least in that middle ground of oligopolistic market structure where sellers are few enough to recognize their interdependence, but too weak to maintain a disciplined front against the whipsaw tactics of a strong, shrewd buyer. The question remains, Who benefits: the strong buyer, or the consuming public? Are consumer prices reduced because retailers and consumer goods manufacturers have struck unusually favorable bargains on the procurement side of their operations?

Consumers definitely gain if countervailing power counteracts and eliminates the cumulative distortion of price-output relationships associated with myopic profit maximization at each of two or more vertically linked and monopolistic production stages. In a pioneering critique of emerging antitrust policies, Professor Spengler has singled out vertical integration as a means of achieving this desirable end.[32] His analysis is correct, but the inference sometimes drawn that vertical integration is a uniquely efficacious means of avoiding cumulative pricing distortions is misleading. End product output will indeed be increased if its monopolistic producer, previously accepting as given the price quoted by a monopolistic supplier, begins instead producing its own input requirements under cost conditions identical to those enjoyed by the supplier.[33] However, the same beneficial effect can be achieved if the supplier and the end product seller coordinate their production decisions to maximize joint profits, or if the end product maker can bring to bear its power as a monopsonist to keep the supplier's price near the competitive level. These alternative solutions to the cumulative distortion problem, and especially the countervailing power approach, are often preferable to vertical integration, since powerful sellers may under certain conditions be able to entrench or extend their

---

[31]*A & P*, pp. 207–220.

[32]Joseph J. Spengler, "Vertical Integration and Antitrust Policy," *Journal of Political Economy*, August 1950, pp. 347–352.

[33]Spengler's proof can be summarized by an extension of the demonstration in note 10 *supra*. Suppose Firm A produces its own requirements of the input which would otherwise have been supplied by Firm B. The cost per unit is V_B, as it was assumed to be for Firm B. Firm A will now maximize its monopoly profits:

$$\pi_A = X_A(a - b X_A) - X_A (V_A + V_B).$$

Differentiating, setting the result equal to zero, and solving for X_A, we get:

$$X_A = \frac{a - V_A - V_B}{2b},$$

which is identical to the output produced under competitive organization of input production [equation (3) of note 10], and twice as great as the output when Firm A takes as given monopolistic Firm B's supply price.

monopoly power through vertical integration, foreclosing input supplies or end product markets to actual or potential rivals.[34]

Whether *all* the benefits of countervailing power are passed on to consumers, or whether some gains are trapped within the vertical price structure, depends upon the absence or presence of power on the selling side of the market. If, as we have seen earlier, monopsonistic or oligopsonistic buyers have little control over the prices at which they sell to their own customers, the intermediate product price reductions extracted through countervailing power stand a good chance of being passed along to the ultimate consumer. It is certainly possible to find real-world situations in which firms have market power as buyers but not as sellers, though we do not know how representative they are.

One familiar example is the chain of market relationships involving the humble tin can. McKie found that American Can and Continental Can, because of their strong positions as buyers, were able to restrain the price of the tin-plate oligopolists. The tin can makers were in turn countervailed by larger canners, who could credibly threaten to manufacture their own cans if prices were allowed to depart very far from the competitive level. From that point on, opportunities for retaining as profit the gains from monopsonistic bargaining power were severely constrained by vigorous competition among canners and ultimately among retail food chains.[35]

The essential combination of power on the buying side with lack of it on the resale side appears especially compatible with conditions in the retail trades, suggesting that Galbraith's emphasis on retailing -to illustrate workable countervailing power was not misguided. As buyers, the large mail-order, food, and drug chains and the major department stores can engage in all the bargaining tactics discussed earlier. These do not always work—i.e., against pharmaceutical manufacturers with strong patent protection—but under favorable conditions they can succeed, and the result is a reduction in wholesale prices. The chains in turn are under competitive pressure to pass along their gains. Entry into retailing is not particularly difficult, in part because stores traditionally operating in one field can with a minimum of bother add a whole new line if the prospects are attractive (i.e., E. J. Korvette's entry into prescription drug retailing, or Macy's role as a liquor price-cutter). Incentives for independent pricing behavior are also strong in retailing, since it is virtually impossible with tens of thousands of different products to play the price-matching game characteristic of oligopolists selling a few homogeneous items.[36] Given these conditions, there is a good chance that gains made through the exercise of buying power will sooner or later be squeezed out and passed along to the consumer.

Still the competitive steam roller does not operate flawlessly even in retailing; pockets of monopsony profit may persist for extended periods of time. A & P did not, for instance, pass along to consumers all the gains derived from its superior purchasing power and efficiency during the late 1920s and early 1930s. Because of organizational inertia and internal pricing policy disputes, its prices were adjusted downward more slowly than the fall in its costs, and profits climbed to new peaks. But A & P's very success created incentives for others to imitate its methods and introduce their own innovations (such as the supermarket). As they did, A & P's volume declined, dragging profits along. By "pursuing a policy of making too much

---

[34]Cf. pp. 70 and 87–88 *supra;* and William S. Comanor, "Vertical Mergers, Market Power, and the Antitrust Laws," *American Economic Review,* May 1967, pp. 254–265.

[35]*Tin Cans and Tin Plate,* pp. 303–304 and 234.

[36]For evidence of surprisingly independent pricing of advertised items among Philadelphia retail food chains, see W. J. Baumol, R. E. Quandt, and H. T. Shapiro, "Oligopoly Theory and Retail Food Pricing," *Journal of Business,* October 1964, pp. 346–362.

money," A & P "was slowly drowning in its own good fortune."[37] This slow-acting competition forced A & P to reassess its business policies, and one result was a concerted effort to reduce retail prices and price-cost margins. Ultimately, then, consumers were the beneficiaries of A & P's power as a buyer, but not without substantial delays.

Recognizing this, we can scarcely take an optimistic view of the benefits to consumers when strong buyers also occupy positions of strength as sellers. Such firms are likely to pass on the gains made through countervailing power only if they are adhering for strategic reasons to a full-cost pricing policy (i.e., to deter new entry) and when actual and potential rivals are expected to enjoy equal input cost reductions. Otherwise, the gains will be trapped in the form of monopsony or monopoly earnings.

CONCLUSION

We end up with an agonizingly 'iffy' picture. When power in sellers' markets is countered by power in buyers' markets, almost anything can happen. Buyers *may* be able to exploit their power to secure lower intermediate product prices, and they *may* pass the resultant savings on to consumers. But when suppliers are powerful or when competition in end product markets is weak, monopoly or monopsony gains are likely to be trapped somewhere in the production and distribution pipeline. With presently available evidence we are limited to such statements about *possibilities*; not enough is known to make confident judgments about *probable* patterns. While countervailing power undoubtedly has some favorable effects on prices and resource allocation, the extent of these effects remains unknown.

[37]Adelman, *A & P*, pp. 36 and 45. The first quotation is from A & P president John Hartford; the second is Adelman's interpretation.

Chapter 10

Price Discrimination

Most of the analysis up to this point has assumed that sellers quote a uniform price to all buyers during any short period of time. This is a tolerable first approximation to nearly all retail product pricing in the United States (but not in Asia!) and to much wholesale and intermediate goods pricing. Still many exceptions are encountered. When a seller charges diverse prices to different buyers of products which are essentially identical (in terms of subsidiary services such as packaging and delivery, as well as in the usual physical sense), he is engaging in price discrimination.

No simple, all-inclusive definition of price discrimination is possible. But very tersely, price discrimination is the sale (or purchase) of different units of a good or service at price differentials not directly corresponding to differences in supply cost. Note that this definition includes not only the sale of identical product units to different persons at varying prices, but also the sale of identical units to a single buyer at differing prices (e.g., when electric utilities charge less for additional kilowatt hour blocks), and the execution of transactions entailing different costs at identical prices (i.e., when an airline provides steak dinners to tourist passengers on some flights, but nothing more than coffee and a roll on others).

For a seller profitably to practice price dis-

crimination, three conditions must be satisfied. First, the seller must have some control over price—some market power. A purely competitive firm cannot discriminate profitably. It can of course sell some units at less than the market price (i.e., for altruistic reasons), but it need not do so to sell as much as it wants, and it sacrifices profit in doing so. Second, the would-be discriminator must be able to segregate its customers into groups with different price elasticities of demand, or into discrete classes with varying reservation prices (the highest prices buyers will pay for any specific unit of output). Third, opportunities for *arbitrage*—resale by low-price customers to high-price customers—must be constrained. Reselling personal services such as medical care and transportation to make an arbitrage profit is virtually impossible, and so the service industries lend themselves particularly well to price discrimination. Because most *goods*, on the other hand, can be stored, transported, and resold, arbitrage is more easily practiced with manufacturing industry outputs, so the possibilities for price discrimination are more limited, although by no means negligible.[1]

STANDARD THEORETICAL CASES

It is customary, following the lead of A. C. Pigou, to speak of three main price discrimina-

---

[1] In a classic case, duopolists Röhm & Haas and du Pont charged \$.85 per pound to general industrial users of the plastic molding powder methyl methacrylate, while special mixtures of the same compound were offered for use in denture manufacture at \$22 per pound. The opportunity for making an arbitrage profit attracted firms which bought at the industrial price, incurred moderate conversion costs, and undercut the duopolists' denture price. To thwart the arbitragers, Röhm & Haas considered mixing some arsenic into the industrial

tion classes: first degree, second degree, and third degree.[2] With first degree, or perfect, discrimination, each unit is sold at its reservation price, so that every consumer is milked of the largest outlay he would be willing to commit for the good in question and still consider its purchase worthwhile. In other words, the perfect discriminator leaves no consumers' surplus; he appropriates it all to himself as producer's surplus. Second degree discrimination is similar, only cruder. It is illustrated in Figure 10.1. The standard demand curve is given by DD', the marginal revenue curve by $D\ MR$, and the marginal cost curve by MC. A simple monopolist would equate marginal cost with marginal revenue, setting the uniform price of OP_M for all

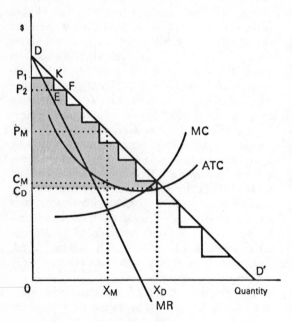

Figure 10.1
Second Degree Price Discrimination

buyers and selling OX_M units. A discriminating monopolist, however, is able to partition demand into ten blocks in order of descending reservation prices. There are consumers willing to buy P_1K units at the highest discernible reservation price OP_1; an additional EF units will be taken at the lower price of OP_2, etc. The seller, charging each block its reservation price, finds it worthwhile to expand output until there are no remaining blocks whose reservation price exceeds marginal cost. Thus, OX_D units will be sold at a total of seven different prices. Total profit is the sum of the declining margins of price over average unit cost OC_D for all units sold. It is shown by the shaded area. This discriminatory profit is considerably larger than the profit realized under simple nondiscriminatory monopoly (shown by the area of the rectangle with height C_MP_M and width OX_M).

Third degree discrimination is quite different. It is assumed that the seller can divide customers into two or more groups, each of which has its own continuous demand function reflecting quantities sold to that group at alternative prices. If these demand functions have different elasticities at common prices, it will pay to discriminate. To see this, suppose the firm charges the uniform price P^* to each of two groups, at which price the demand elasticity for Group A is 2.0 and for Group B 4.0. This strategy does not maximize profits. We recall from Chapter 6 that marginal revenue is related to price by the formula $MR = P - P/e$, where e is the elasticity of demand.[3] Thus, marginal revenue must be one half of price P^* in selling to Group A and three fourths of price P^* in selling to Group B.

It pays to reallocate some output away from Group A and toward Group B, for the marginal revenue from selling an extra unit to Group B customers exceeds the marginal revenue lost from selling one unit less to Group A customers. This reallocation can continue profitably until

powder so it would be unsuitable for oral use. It ultimately rejected the idea, but did plant rumors that the industrial powder had been adulterated. See G. W. Stocking and M. W. Watkins, *Cartels in Action* (New York: Twentieth Century Fund, 1946), pp. 402–404.

[2] A. C. Pigou, *The Economics of Welfare* (London: Macmillan, 1920), pp. 240–256. For additional cases, see Stephen Enke, "Some Notes on Price Discrimination," *Canadian Journal of Economics and Political Science*, February 1964, pp. 95–109.

[3] Cf. p. 176 *supra*.

prices in the two markets have changed by a sufficient amount to make marginal revenue in the two markets equal. Generalizing, a third degree discriminator maximizes profits by charging the highest price in the market whose demand elasticity at the simple monopoly price is lowest and the lowest price in the market with the highest elasticity at the simple monopoly price.

Figure 10.2 presents the conventional geometric analysis of third degree discriminating monopoly for two markets, A and B, whose demand and marginal revenue curves are given in panels A and B. The problem is to ensure that the last unit of output sold in Market A adds the same amount to total revenue as the last unit sold in Market B; that is, to equalize the marginal revenues. To accomplish this, the marginal revenue curves of the two markets are summed horizontally, giving the combined marginal revenue function *CMR* in the far right panel. *CMR* is equated to marginal cost *MC*, indicating the optimal combined output OX_C. To equalize marginal revenue in the separate markets at the profit-maximizing value, we con-

struct a horizontal line from the point where $MC = CMR$. The optimal output in each market is found where this horizontal line intersects the market's *MR* function, and the profit-maximizing price is found (as usual) by reading off the relevant demand function the price at which the optimal quantity is demanded. Thus, the higher price OP_A is optimal in the less elastic Market A and the lower price OP_B in the more elastic Market B.

TYPES OF DISCRIMINATION FOUND IN PRACTICE

So much for the theoretical categories. Although the soporific effect of exhaustive categorization normally outweighs any educational value, a systematic list of ideal types provides useful insight into the tremendous variety of real-world price discrimination practices. We can do no better than follow, with slight modifications, the classification scheme adopted by Professor Machlup.[4] Three main classes are identified: personal discrimination, based upon differences among individual customers; group

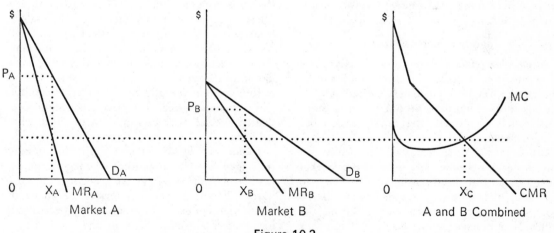

Figure 10.2
Third Degree Price Discrimination

[4]Fritz Machlup, "Characteristics and Types of Price Discrimination," in the National Bureau of Economic Research conference report, *Business Concentration and Price Policy* (Princeton: Princeton University Press, 1955), pp. 400–423. Machlup in turn borrowed some of his categories from Ralph Cassady, Jr., "Techniques and Purposes of Price Discrimination," *Journal of Marketing*, October 1946, pp. 135–150.

discrimination, in which inter-group differences are exploited; and product discrimination, under which different products are priced at divergent and discriminatory levels. For each broad class we list the principal types encountered, appending a brief explanation and example.

PERSONAL DISCRIMINATION

Haggle-every-time. Each transaction is a separately negotiated bargain. Examples include the typical pricing practice in Middle-Eastern bazaars and the sale of used textbooks by students to college bookstores.

Give-in-if-you-must. Secret departures are made from list prices when buyers play one seller off against the others. Examples were given in the preceding chapter.

Size-up-his-income. Wealthier customers with inelastic demand are charged more than the less affluent, who at high prices would restrict consumption disproportionately. Standard examples are the pricing of legal and medical services.

Measure-the-use. Customers who use a good or service more intensively are charged more, even though differences in cost may be negligible. For instance, Xerox machine rentals are based on the number of copies made, and the incremental rental charge more than compensates for maintenance costs.

GROUP DISCRIMINATION

Absorb-the-freight. There are several types of discrimination involving the absorption or over-charging of freight to customers located at varying distances from one's production site. Since these will be analyzed later, we defer a more precise classification.

Kill-the-rival. Prices are systematically reduced, perhaps below cost, only in the market served by a rival the discriminator is trying to drive out of business. The American Tobacco Company engaged in such tactics during the 1890s. Modern examples are harder to find, since the law deals harshly with perpetrators who are caught.

Dump-the-surplus. Goods temporarily in excess supply are offered at reduced prices overseas so as not to depress the domestic price. Although Western nations have signed anti-dumping agreements, allegations of dumping continue, as in the steel industries during the early 1960s. The U. S. Food for Peace program during the early 1960s was a form of dumping (motivated in part, however, by humanitarian considerations).

Get-the-most-from-each-region. Prices are persistently held higher in regions where competition is weak than where it is strong (e.g., European high-fidelity phonograph records were for many years sold at lower prices in the United States than in the countries where they were produced).

Promote-new-customers. New customers are offered prices lower than those paid by established customers in the hope of developing permanent brand loyalty. Magazines are avid practitioners of this art, offering new subscriptions at prices a fraction of what old subscribers pay. The airlines' granting of special discounts to college students is partly motivated by such considerations.

Favor-the-big-ones. Large buyers are granted systematic price concessions exceeding the cost savings associated with volume transactions. Examples were given in the preceding chapter.

Protect-the-middleman. Large retail buyers who incur the cost of performing their own warehousing and distribution functions are charged the same prices as retailers who buy from wholesalers in an attempt to protect the wholesalers from competition through vertical integration. As we shall see in Chapter 21, the Robinson-Patman Act was intended to encourage discrimination of this genre.

Hold-them-in-line. Retailers who fail to comply with a manufacturer's list price suggestions are denied special discounts granted to those who conform.

Divide-them-by-elasticity. Group discrimination may also be practiced whenever groups readily classifiable by age, sex, occupation, etc. have different reservation prices or demand elasticities. For example, lower prices are charged for children's haircuts (despite the higher labor input in shearing a wiggling object) because of stronger 'do-it-yourself' competition. College professors are offered lower room rates at many hotel chains, presumably because their price elasticity of demand is higher than that of businessmen with liberal expense accounts.

PRODUCT DISCRIMINATION

Appeal-to-the-classes. Differences in price more than proportional to differences in cost are associated with premium quality. For example, much higher margins between price and incremental production cost are realized on clothbound as opposed to paperbound books, and railroads exploit the snob appeal of first-class cars by charging fare premiums exceeding the additional cost of parlor car service.

Make-them-pay-for-the-label. Manufacturers distribute a physically homogeneous product under various brands, charging more for the better-known brands. Examples abound on the shelves of any chain supermarket.

Clear-the-stock. Price concessions are granted at special times of the year, or continuously in special sections of a retail store, in order to reduce inventories or increase sales to customers with weak budgets and strong elbows. Filene's basement in Boston is a breathtaking example.

Switch-them-to-off-peak-times. Lower prices are charged for services identical except with respect to time of consumption in order to encourage fuller and more balanced utilization of capacity. Resort prices varying with the season, the $1.00 telephone rate from New York to San Francisco after 8 p.m., and the French green tariff for electricity (charging higher rates for service guaranteed at peak periods) are examples.[5]

Get-the-most-from-each-group. In this final catch-all category we include such practices as charging higher railroad freight rates on commodities valuable relative to their weight; offering additional blocks of electricity at lower rates to encourage homeowners to install electric stoves, water heaters, and heating systems; and the realization by multi-product firms of higher price-cost margins on items for which demand is relatively inelastic than on those in elastic

demand.[6] In this category we might also include *skimming*—introducing a new and superior product at a high price designed to extract the highest possible revenue from persons with high reservation prices, and then gradually reducing the price to penetrate a broader market.[7]

THE IMPLICATIONS OF DISCRIMINATION FOR ECONOMIC WELFARE

With such a diversity of types, it is clearly impossible to reach any simple blanket judgment about the social desirability of price discrimination. We can, however, formulate some guidelines for assessing specific types in terms of three criteria: income distribution effects, efficiency effects, and impact on market structure and the intensity of competition.

INCOME DISTRIBUTION EFFECTS

Price discrimination causes a redistribution of income toward the discriminator and away from his customers. In the absence of legal quirks, no firm with market power *has* to discriminate. It will do so only if a system of discriminatory prices yields higher profits than uniform pricing. Since most firms choose freely whether or not to discriminate, profits must usually be higher with discrimination than without, *ceteris paribus*.[8]

Whether this is a bad thing hinges on value judgments over which reasonable (as well as self-interested) men may disagree. Most academic economists believe that social welfare would be enhanced if the profits gained through price discrimination by monopolistic corporations were redirected into the hands of the consuming public and away from stockholders, the majority of whom (by dollar holdings) are already well off. But this is a subjective evaluation, and there is no way of demonstrating its correctness. Furthermore, the practitioners of price

[5]If there are constant returns to scale in production, price differentials just sufficient to repay the cost of building facilities capable of satisfying peak demands are not strictly discriminatory in a long-run sense. See Peter O. Steiner, "Peak Loads and Efficient Pricing," *Quarterly Journal of Economics*, November 1957, pp. 585–610; and the comment by Jack Hirshleifer, *Quarterly Journal of Economics*, August 1958, pp. 451–468.

[6]See J. F. Wright, "Some Reflections on the Place of Discrimination in the Theory of Monopolistic Competition," *Oxford Economic Papers*, July 1965, pp. 175–187.

[7]See Joel Dean, *Managerial Economics* (Englewood Cliffs: Prentice-Hall, 1951), pp. 419–421.

[8]An exception may occur when secret discriminatory price cuts by oligopolists made with the intention of raising individual profits induce spreading retaliation which reduces *group* profits.

discrimination are not always the great corporations. Physicians are the most highly paid professional class in the United States, with median lifetime earnings estimated at $717,000 by 1960 standards, compared to $415,000 for physicists and $261,000 for high school teachers.[9] The relative affluence of the medical profession is due in part to the high barriers limiting entry into medicine and partly to the widespread exploitation of opportunities for price discrimination.[10] Again, approval or disapproval depends upon one's values and prejudices. It is surely not true, however, that higher physicians' incomes are essential to maintain superior health standards, for in the Soviet Union physicians (choosing their professions under surprisingly free conditions) occupy a much lower stratum in the income hierarchy with no evident adverse effect on mortality rates.

Third degree price discrimination also redistributes income away from consumers in the low price elasticity groups, who normally pay a price higher than under simple monopoly, toward consumers in the high price elasticity groups, who pay lower prices.[11] As in all income redistribution situations, economic analysis provides no hard and fast criteria for evaluating this result, although economists and policy-makers may have strong personal opinions. As Mrs. Robinson has observed:

> ... we may have some reason to prefer the interests of one group above those of the other. For instance, members of the more elastic markets (for whom price is reduced) may be poorer than members of the less elastic markets, and we may consider a gain to poorer buyers more important than a loss to richer buyers. In this case price discrimination must always be considered beneficial. On the other hand, the less elastic market may be at home and the more elastic market abroad, so that the interests of the

members of the stronger market are considered more important than the interests of the weaker market.[12]

EFFICIENCY EFFECTS

Price discrimination is sometimes condemned because it is symptomatic of monopoly, and the exploitation of monopoly power implies a misallocation of resources. This is an inappropriate criticism, if monopoly power would be present whether or not discrimination were practiced. The correct question is, are resources allocated more or less efficiently under discriminating monopoly than under simple (uniform price) monopoly? The answer depends to some extent upon the type of discrimination practiced.

First and second degree discrimination nearly always lead to larger outputs than under simple monopoly, and hence (*ceteris paribus*) to an improved allocation of resources. To see this, consider Figure 10.1 again. The simple monopolist, recognizing that any price reduction made to customers on the margin between buying and not buying must also be offered to customers who would buy even if the price were not reduced, maximizes profits by equating marginal cost with marginal revenue, producing output OX_M. The second degree discriminating monopolist must offer a price reduction *only* to marginal buyers and therefore finds it profitable to expand output all the way to OX_D. Indeed, the discriminating monopolist of Figure 10.1 produces as much as a competitive industry with a short-run supply curve identical to the monopolist's marginal cost function, since price to the last block of customers served is equal to the marginal cost of serving those customers. More generally, first and second degree discriminators produce more than the simple monopoly output in all but trivial cases, and unless adverse income effects associated with their pricing policies are large, their output closely approximates the compet-

---

[9]Herman P. Miller, *Rich Man, Poor Man* (New York: Crowell, 1964), pp. 172–173.

[10]See Reuben A. Kessel, "Price Discrimination in Medicine," *Journal of Law and Economics*, October 1958, pp. 20–59; and Elton Rayack, *Professional Power and American Medicine* (Cleveland: World, 1967), especially Chapters 3, 4, and 5.

[11]If discrimination facilitates an expansion of output permitting the realization of substantial scale economies, it is possible (although not necessary) that the price to consumers in the less elastic market will also be lower than the simple monopoly price.

[12]Joan Robinson, *The Economics of Imperfect Competition* (London: Macmillan, 1933), p. 204.

itive output, *ceteris paribus.* Thus, the inefficiencies of output restriction for which simple monopoly is criticized may disappear altogether under first or second degree discrimination.

As indicated earlier, first degree discrimination is rare in actual practice. But many examples of second degree discrimination can be found. Much personal discrimination conforms to the second degree model—i.e., haggle-every-time, size-up-his-income, and measure-the-use. Other cases include output block pricing by public utilities and 'family plan' rates offered air travelers to encourage them to bring along wives and children. In such instances price discrimination typically permits more output to be supplied than under uniform monopoly pricing.

Third degree discrimination is probably the most widely used of the three main theoretical types. It also has the most ambiguous efficiency implications. If the demand functions for both (or all) markets are linear, as in Figure 10.2, total output under discrimination will be identical to output under simple uniform-price monopoly, assuming that the simple monopolist sells at least some output in the more elastic market and ignoring income effects on the position of the demand curves. For third degree discrimination to increase output above the simple monopoly level, certain conditions involving the geometry of the various market demand functions must be satisfied. Briefly, the demand curve in the more elastic market must be less convex from below (i.e., with respect to the quantity axis) than the demand curve in the less elastic market.[13] We have little evidence on whether this condition occurs more frequently than the converse. Mrs. Robinson has argued on *a priori* grounds that the most likely impact of third degree discrimination will be to increase

output, since the quantity of output demanded by consumers in the low-elasticity market will remain near the satiety point even after price is raised to the discriminatory level, whereas a small reduction in price to high-elasticity customers will induce a large increase in quantity demanded.[14] But we really do not know, and so it is impossible to determine whether on balance third degree discrimination increases output and improves the allocation of resources.

Any of the three main theoretical types may have desirable allocative effects in special situations where demand is too weak to permit profitable operation of a service under simple monopoly pricing. It is possible, for instance, that no physician would be attracted to a small town if he were required to charge the same fee to rich patients as to poor. Since profits can be increased by discriminating, the added revenue attainable through discrimination may be sufficient to make the difference between having a service supplied and not having it.[15] In the same vein, it is probable that railroad service would not have been provided to remote areas of the American frontier during the 19th century, had rate discrimination between high-value and low-value commodities been impossible.

THE SPECIAL CASE OF MULTI-PRODUCT JOB SHOPS

Some important special problems arise in the case of multi-product firms, and particularly for firms which possess an array of equipment and skills readily adaptable to the production of numerous products. Job shops in the fabricated metal products, machinery, plastics, electrical apparatus, and printing industries fit the pattern well.[16] What such enterprises are selling in a sense is not specific products, but their capacity

---

[13]*Ibid.*, pp. 188–195; and E. O. Edwards, "The Analysis of Output Under Discrimination," *Econometrica*, April 1950, pp. 163–172. Mrs. Robinson's "concavity from above" is the same as "convexity from below," as used here.

[14]*Op. cit.*, pp. 201–202.

[15]For a geometric treatment of the problem, see Pigou, *op. cit.*, pp. 950–951; and George J. Stigler, *The Theory of Price* (Third ed.; New York: Macmillan, 1966), pp. 213–214. It should be noted that if price discrimination were not practiced in larger cities, the potential small town physician's opportunity cost would be lower, and he might settle in the small town at a lower profit expectation.

[16]The analysis has little applicability to firms using specialized equipment suitable for producing only a narrow line of outputs. Examples include steel and aluminum refineries, breweries, cigarette plants, cement mills, and automobile assembly lines.

to produce. And when they sell different blocks of capacity at varying price-cost margins, they are engaging in a subtle form of price discrimination.

The standard analysis of this problem has been developed by Eli Clemens.[17] Here we summarize verbally his geometric treatment, appending an algebraic proof in a footnote. The multi-product job shop surveys its market opportunities and defines for each market a peculiar kind of demand function, relating the price received to the number of units of capacity devoted to satisfying demand in that market. It supplies first those markets with the lowest demand elasticities, charging the highest prices (presumably exceeding cost by a substantial margin) there. However, it will continue to invade markets of higher and higher demand elasticity until there are no markets remaining in which the potential contribution to revenue exceeds the marginal cost of devoting a block of capacity to that market. If any such market remains untapped, the most profitable strategy is to reduce the amount of capacity employed in markets already served, increasing the prices charged in those markets, in order to commit at least one unit of capacity to the untapped market.[18]

Now if the last product line served has a high price elasticity, which is entirely plausible, the gap between marginal revenue and price will be small in that line, and since marginal revenue is equated to marginal cost, the gap between price and marginal cost will also be small. Thus the discriminating multi-product firm approaches full (competitive) utilization of its capacity (where marginal cost is equal to price). Indeed, the firm may be only a competitive fringe member in its marginal market, in which case price and marginal revenue are identical, and output will be expanded until price and marginal cost are equal-

ized. This result reflects a kind of efficiency in resource use and is clearly a point in favor of multi-product price discrimination.

Viewed in a different light, however, the efficiency implications are more complicated. Only in the marginal product line is price approximately equal to marginal cost. Consumers of the firm's other products pay a price exceeding marginal cost. They are willing to give up more dollars for an additional unit of these products than the cost of producing the additional unit, and hence the firm's output of 'these intramarginal products is inefficiently low. If this were the whole story, we should have to conclude that misallocation in the accepted sense persists. Still it is conceivable that what to one multi-product firm is an intra-marginal product line (because the firm has a dominant position in the market and/or enjoys special product differentiation advantages) is a marginal line to other multi-product firms specializing in different fields. Each firm or group of firms might then penetrate each others' markets, granting discriminatory concessions in product lines considered marginal.[19] In the resulting equilibrium, price would approximate marginal cost for at least some producers in virtually every product line. This result bears a superficial resemblance to the equilibrium of pure competition. Nevertheless, it is not clear that it approaches the allocative efficiency of competition, since price exceeds marginal cost on the intra-marginal sales of all firms. If this merely reflects efficiency differences in producing for intra-marginal as opposed to marginal markets, a tolerably close approximation to the competitive equilibrium may result. But if it reflects higher prices paid by some consumers for comparable products (or slightly differentiated variants) produced at similar costs, allocation is

---

[17]Eli W. Clemens, "Price Discrimination and the Multiple-Product Firm," *Review of Economic Studies,* 1951, vol. 19, pp. 1–11.

[18]This rearrangement of the product line is profitable for the following reason. Before the new line is taken on, profit maximization requires that marginal revenue in each line be equal to the marginal cost of the last capacity unit utilized. Let MR_i be the marginal revenue of the ith (typical) line in the original equilibrium product array and let MC be the marginal cost of the last capacity unit utilized. Now suppose a new opportunity is found, offering an addition to revenue MR_n exceeding MC. (MR_n will be less than the price in line n, if the market is monopolistic, or equal to it, if the market is perceived to be competitive by the firm in question.) Since $MR_n > MC$ and $MC = MR_i$, $MR_n > MR_i$. The last unit of capacity adds more to revenue when devoted to product line n than to product line i (or any of the other original lines). Therefore it is profitable to take line n on. Output in each previous line should be reduced until marginal revenue in each of these lines rises to equality with MR_n.

[19]Certainly, such tendencies are observed in many fields. See Wright, *op. cit.,* p. 185.

likely to be efficient only if consumers just on the margin between buying and not buying happen to be served by firms offering the lowest prices. There is no reason to believe this will necessarily occur, and so there is also no reason to expect significantly improved resource allocation under the postulated conditions. Still the problem is so complex that no confident generalizations seem feasible.

THE EFFECTS OF DISCRIMINATION ON COMPETITION

Price discrimination can be practiced profitably only if the discriminator possesses some market power. The practice of discrimination can in turn have feedback effects on market structure and the vigor of competition. It may strengthen competition or weaken it, depending upon the type of discrimination and how successful it is.

Discrimination can enhance competition by encouraging more experimentation in pricing. The best way to determine whether the demand for one's products is price elastic is to try out selected price changes. Recognizing that it is often more difficult to raise prices than to lower them, sellers may be reluctant to engage in such experimentation if the changes must be implemented across-the-board—i.e., in every geographic market. They will be much more willing if changes can be tried only in restricted test markets, so that the consequences of an adverse rival or consumer reaction are less serious.

Another important pro-competitive effect is the tendency of unsystematic price discrimination to undermine oligopolistic discipline. The dynamics of this process have already been described in Chapters 7 and 9. In order to utilize capacity more fully, producers grant secret, discriminatory price concessions to a few aggressive buyers. Sooner or later the word leaks out, often through the efforts of buyers to extract similar concessions from additional suppliers, and others match or undercut the cuts. As the price concessions spread, list prices become increasingly unrealistic relative to actual transaction prices and eventually they are reduced, benefitting all buyers and not just those in whose favor the discrimination originally worked. When secret price shading of this sort occurs frequently, sellers may lose all confidence in their rivals' willingness to cooperate toward a common price policy, and the resulting loss of discipline makes joint profit maximization impossible.[20]

For price discrimination to enhance competition, it is vital that the discriminatory concessions be *unsystematic*. Systematic price discrimination is likely to have the opposite effect, weakening competition. This it does in several ways.

For one, it may entrench firms in their positions of power by creating strong buyer-seller ties and raising barriers to the entry of new competitors. The tin can industry illustrates this point.[21] American Can's dominant position was bolstered both by the discriminatory price concessions it received from suppliers of tin-plated steel and the discriminatory price reductions it granted to large canners. As a buyer, American received discounts on the order of 7.5 per cent from tin plate manufacturers until the practice became illegal in 1936. Smaller tin can makers, denied these discounts on an input accounting for roughly 70 per cent of their costs, were at an obvious cost disadvantage. Other things being equal, American could set prices yielding excess profits as high as 5 per cent of costs before smaller competitors could enter and earn a normal return. As a seller, American granted discounts of up to 14 per cent to large customers. These were usually tied in with long-term contracts covering a larger annual volume of cans than smaller can makers could supply. By making it difficult for small producers to secure can orders from large packers, this combination of discriminatory discounts with long-term, high-volume requirements contracts turned "what would have been a fairly innocuous practice into a rather formidable obstacle to open

---

[20]Conversely, MacAvoy concluded that the price discrimination prohibitions of the Interstate Commerce Act of 1887 provided the necessary foundations for successful collusive pricing among railroads. Paul W. MacAvoy, *The Economic Effects of Regulation: The Trunkline Railroad Cartels and the ICC Before 1900* (Cambridge: MIT Press, 1965), p. 204.

[21]James W. McKie, *Tin Cans and Tin Plate* (Cambridge: Harvard University Press, 1959), pp. 58–64 and 160–182.

competition."[22] American also engaged in more subtle forms of discrimination, such as providing special equipment to large customers at nominal rentals, which strengthened its customer ties and raised barriers to entry. The discounts and other preferences granted by American to large canners in turn gave the favored canners a cost advantage over their smaller rivals, although according to McKie, these were "probably not enough to make or break a canning firm."[23]

A further example of systematic discriminatory pricing which strengthened a seller's market power existed in the shoe machinery industry.[24] United Shoe Machinery Corporation successfully defended its 85 per cent market share in part by accepting much lower rates of return on machines which faced competition than on those it supplied exclusively. In this way it could take full advantage of its monopoly power in lines it dominated, while the low prices in lines with competition made it difficult for rivals to gain a foothold. By discouraging the entry and expansion of rivals, United in turn was able to remain the only shoe machinery manufacturer offering a full line—an advantage which strengthened its position with customers.

Accepting lower rates of return on product lines facing competition shades into more predatory kill-the-rival types of price discrimination. In actual situations the line between meeting competition and destroying it is seldom sharp, since a great deal depends upon intent, which is hard to pin down. Kaysen found only one instance in which United Shoe Machinery executives explicitly articulated the expectation that discriminatory pricing would lead to "a gradual elimination of . . . competitors."[25] Clear-cut cases are rare partly because businessmen recognize the danger in reducing an expression of intent to writing, partly because fear of antitrust prosecution deters efforts to drive rivals out of business, and also because predatory tactics usu-

ally entail high costs (the short-run profits foregone) offset only by the uncertain prospect of actually succeeding. It is worth noting that predatory discrimination which is unsuccessful may actually *increase* competition, in the sense that prices are reduced while the rivals are slugging it out to a conclusion which eliminates no one from the arena.

In sum, systematic price discrimination preserves and strengthens monopoly positions by permitting large firms to enjoy imput costs lower than their smaller rivals, by tying buyers together with sellers giving discounts for concentrated purchases, and by making entry into narrow segments of a market difficult or impossible. On the other hand, unsystematic price discrimination can have a pro-competitive effect by undermining oligopolistic discipline.

GEOGRAPHIC PRICE DISCRIMINATION AND THE BASING POINT SYSTEM

Another linkage between price discrimination and the vigor of competition is so important that it warrants a more extended analysis. This is the whole set of freight pricing practices arising in response to differences in the geographic distance separating producers from their customers. The most controversial is the basing point system of pricing, to which we shall devote special attention.

APPROACHES TO THE SPATIAL DIFFERENTIATION PROBLEM

Even when firms produce commodities identical in every physical respect, complete homogeneity is not likely to be attained because of differences in location. From the viewpoint of a consumer in Indianapolis, a ton of cold-rolled steel in Pittsburgh is not the same as a ton of the same cold-rolled steel in Chicago. When producers are located at different points on the

---

[22]*Ibid.*, p. 175.

[23]*Ibid.*, p. 172.

[24]Carl Kaysen, *United States* v. *United Shoe Machinery Corporation* (Cambridge: Harvard University Press, 1956), especially pp. 126–134. Similar allegations were leveled against IBM's computer pricing in a 1969 antitrust suit.

[25]*Ibid.*, p. 132.

map, their products are said to be *spatially differentiated*.[26] Differences in shipping distance imply differences in transportation cost and delivery time. For certain commodities—notably those which are of low value relative to their weight—spatial differentiation is of considerable practical significance. In 1966, for instance, the truck freight charges for transporting steel I-beams from Chicago to Pittsburgh in truckload lots amounted to approximately 8 per cent of the steel's Chicago mill price. Freight charges for shipping a truckload of standard-grade cement from Chicago to Indianapolis were 13 per cent of the cement mill price, and for a shipment from Chicago to Pittsburgh they rose to 23 per cent. To the producer of a spatially differentiated product, the problem is to determine how to handle freight costs in setting prices. For the economist, the problem is to assess the impact of alternative geographic pricing policies on the vigor of competition.

There are several alternative freight pricing methods. One is the so-called 'postage stamp' system, under which a uniform delivered price is charged to every buyer, regardless of distance from the production source. Or in a variant, buyers in a particular zone—i.e., west of the Mississippi—all pay the same delivered price. In each case, the producer absorbs higher freight costs on shipments to distant customers than on shipments to customers near its plant. It therefore discriminates in favor of distant customers. Postage stamp pricing is used most frequently with commodities whose value is high relative to transportation costs and also for items whose price is nationally advertised and must therefore be kept uniform. But some curious exceptions are also encountered. For example, since 1921 aluminum ingots have been sold on a uniform delivered price basis throughout the United States.

An approach better suited to bulky, low-value commodities is uniform F.O.B. mill pricing.[27]

Here producers announce a mill price at which customers may buy, paying their own freight bills. Or if delivery by the producer is preferred, the actual charges for transportation from the producing mill to the buyer's destination will be added onto the mill price. This is the only system which entails no geographic price discrimination, since the price paid by buyers increases in direct relation to shipping costs, while (barring other discriminatory concessions) the seller receives a uniform *mill net price* after outbound freight expenses are deducted from its delivered price.

Some important properties of uniform F.O.B. mill pricing can be illustrated with a simple diagram. In Figure 10.3, the horizontal axis represents geographic distance between points. One mill is assumed to be located at point *C* (Chicago), selling at the announced F.O.B. mill price *CA*. As it sells to customers located to the east, the delivered price rises along the path *AR*, reflecting increasing freight costs for shipment over greater distances. Another mill is located at point *P* (Pittsburgh), selling at the F.O.B. mill price *PB*, with delivered prices rising along the line *BT*. Given these assumptions, customers from Dayton westward enjoy lower delivered prices buying from the Chicago mill, and so (if the product is otherwise homogeneous) they will give all their orders to Chicago. The spatial market segment *CX* is Chicago's *freight advantage territory*, while in the segment *XP* Pittsburgh enjoys a delivered price advantage, capturing all the orders. If each mill adheres strictly to its F.O.B. mill pricing policy, neither can sell in the other's territory.

This seems a curious kind of competition, in which the two mills quote matching prices and vie directly for orders only in Xenia, Ohio (point *X*), 1960 population 20,445. How can the Chicago mill increase its sales, say, by capturing some orders in Columbus?

If a uniform F.O.B. mill pricing system is to be

---

[26]For an excellent introduction to the theory of spatial differentiation and competition, see Kenneth E. Boulding, *Economic Analysis*, vol. I, "Microeconomics" (Fourth ed.; New York: Harper, 1966), pp. 470–475 and 482–486.

[27]F.O.B. means free on board; that is, the price quoted to load a product on board the transporting vehicle, after which the buyer becomes responsible for all freight charges.

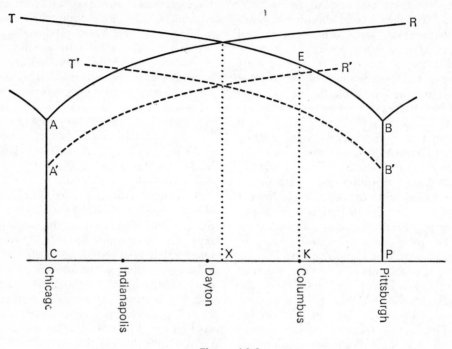

Figure 10.3
F.O.B. Mill Pricing

maintained, there is only one way—cutting the mill price, e.g., to *CA'*. Then the delivered price locus shifts downward to *A'R'*, the Chicago mill's freight advantage territory is expanded roughly to Columbus, and the Pittsburgh mill's territory contracts accordingly. But this approach has two obvious disadvantages. First, the Chicago mill is not apt to be very enthusiastic about cutting price to all the customers between Chicago and Xenia, to whom it can otherwise sell at mill net price *CA*, merely to expand sales between Xenia and Columbus. Second, the Pittsburgh mill will be even less enthusiastic about losing its customers between Columbus and Xenia to the rival in Chicago. If Chicago reduces its mill price to *CA'*, Pittsburgh will probably respond with a matching cut in its own price to *PB'*. With the new F.O.B. Pittsburgh delivered price function *B'T'*, the market division point is once again Xenia. Each seller finds itself serving the same market territory as before the round of

price cuts, but at a lower mill net price. And each will soon recognize that they will not endow many libraries through such uncooperative tactics.

One way around this problem is to shift to a system of F.O.B. mill pricing coupled with unsystematic discrimination through freight absorption. Each mill then quotes its F.O.B. mill price: *CA* for Chicago and *PB* for Pittsburgh. Normally each delivers output at this mill price plus freight, but if an especially attractive sales opportunity arises in Columbus, Chicago may choose to absorb freight and meet or even undercut the Pittsburgh delivered price *KE*. This is discrimination on Chicago's part, since a lower mill net price (after deduction of freight) is realized on the Columbus order than on Chicago, Indianapolis, and Dayton orders. Yet such discriminatory freight absorption may be attractive to Chicago, since if marginal production costs are low relative to the listed F.O.B. mill price *CA*, Chicago can add to its profits by picking up an occasional order outside its territory without having to cut prices to local customers. Of course, two or more can play at this game, and so Pittsburgh is likely to meet or undercut Chicago's prices in Indianapolis and Dayton through its own freight absorption. If the discrimination is unsystematic, both mills will be uncertain how low a price they must quote to win an order in their home territories. As we have seen earlier, such uncertainty can precipitate a breakdown in oligopoly discipline, culminating in a general erosion of the price structure, cuts in the announced F.O.B. mill price, and perhaps even outright price warfare.

Once again, this is not the way to endow libraries and symphony halls. To minimize the temptation toward independent pricing initiatives, the firms may adopt some sort of *basing point system*, as the steel, cement, lead, corn oil, linseed oil, wood pulp, automobile, sugar, and many other industries have at one time or another.[28] Basing point pricing has been used most frequently by oligopolists selling physically standardized products whose transportation costs are high relative to product value and whose marginal production cost is low relative to total unit cost at less than capacity operation, for under these conditions competitive price-cutting through unsystematic freight absorption is probable, unless a collusive disposition of the freight cost problem is worked out.

The most striking variety is the *single basing point system*—i.e., the Pittsburgh-plus system used in the steel industry until 1924. One production point is accepted by common consent as the basing point, and *all* prices are quoted as the announced mill price at that point plus freight (usually rail freight) to destination. Although the geometry is similar, a new diagram (Figure 10.4) will illustrate the system. Pittsburgh is the basing point, at which the announced mill price is *PB*. Delivered prices are quoted according to the Pittsburgh-plus-freight line *BT* not only by Pittsburgh mills, but also by Chicago (as well as Birmingham, Los Angeles, and all other) mills. Thus, the Chicago mill will quote the price *CG* to its local customers, *IL* to Indianapolis customers, and *KE* to Columbus customers—a clearly discriminatory pattern. The farther from Chicago and the nearer Pittsburgh the Chicago mill's customers are, the higher Chicago's freight costs are, but the lower is the price at which it sells. On nearby shipments, Chicago charges customers the high freight from Pittsburgh, whereas its actual freight costs (rising along the path *AR*) are modest. The surplus of billed over actual freight under basing point pricing is called *phantom freight*. At Indianapolis, customers pay phantom freight of *LD* if they buy from a Chicago mill (although no phantom freight emerges if they buy from Pittsburgh, whose mills incur the actual freight costs from Pittsburgh).[29] The Chicago mill's phantom freight in selling to local customers is *GA*. Only when it sells in the territory east of Xenia does Chicago receive no phantom freight. Then its actual freight costs exceed billed freight charges, so that in selling to Columbus customers it absorbs freight equal to *EN* dollars per unit. It will be willing to do this if its marginal cost of producing the units for Columbus is less than *CA* minus *NE*. With sufficiently low marginal costs, Chicago may find it worthwhile to absorb freight and penetrate all the way to Pittsburgh or even further east. Pittsburgh at the same time receives full compensation for its freight when selling at the Pittsburgh-plus price in Chicago and further west. Obtaining the same mill net price on such sales as on sales at home, it has every incentive to seek a share of the Chicago business. Each mill

---

[28]For a more extensive list of industries, see Fritz Machlup, *The Basing Point System* (Philadelphia: Blakiston, 1949), p. 17. Other standard references on basing point pricing include Carl Kaysen, "Basing Point Pricing and Public Policy," *Quarterly Journal of Economics*, August 1949, pp. 289–314; Arthur Smithies, "Aspects of the Basing Point System," *American Economic Review*, December 1942, pp. 705–726; and J. M. Clark, "Basing Point Methods of Price Quoting," *Canadian Journal of Economics and Political Science*, November 1938, pp. 477–489.

[29]There is a certain amount of ambiguity in defining the amount of phantom freight, since the Chicago mill has no announced mill price. To make phantom freight represent the surplus of quoted over actual freight charges, we assume in drawing *AR* that the price *CA* if Chicago were a base equals the Pittsburgh base price *PB*, and that westbound and eastbound freight rate schedules are symmetric. Other writers (e.g., Smithies) have defined *CA* as the marginal cost in Chicago.

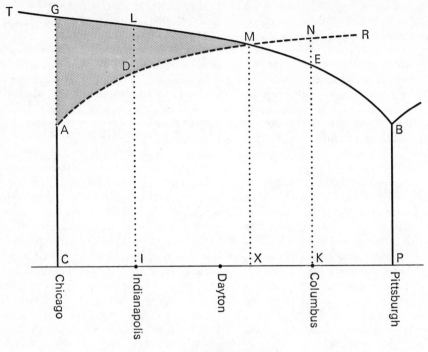

Figure 10.4
Basing Point Pricing

may therefore ship products into the other's home territory, incurring freight charges higher than those required if the order were filled locally. This practice is known as *cross-hauling*.

The incidence of phantom freight is reduced, perhaps greatly, under a *multiple basing point system*. Here more than one producing mill is designated as a basing point, and the delivered price quoted to any given customer reflects the lowest applicable basing point price plus freight to destination. In the steel industry after 1924 there were several basing points (typically including Pittsburgh, Chicago, and Birmingham) for most products. The cement industry had 79 basing point mills and 86 non-basing point mills during 1937.[30] To illustrate the system's operation, suppose in Figure 10.4 that both Chicago and Pittsburgh are designated as basing points, and that *CA* is the Chicago base price and *PB* the

Pittsburgh base price. Then the delivered price *ID* will be quoted on *all* sales to Indianapolis customers, whether made by Pittsburgh or Chicago mills, and *KE* will be quoted to all Columbus buyers. When Chicago sells to Indianapolis it receives no phantom freight if it is its own basing point, and when it sells to Columbus it must absorb freight equal to *NE* dollars per unit. Phantom freight is gained only by non-base mills—i.e., by a mill located at Dayton and selling in its home territory at the delivered price quoted by Pittsburgh or Chicago.

Superficially, the multiple basing point system is similar to F.O.B. mill pricing with discriminatory freight absorption, and it is sometimes difficult to classify actual borderline cases firmly into one category or the other. There are several important differences in principle, however. For one, buyers under any form of F.O.B. pricing

[30]Cf. Machlup, *The Basing Point System*, p. 80.

have the option of paying only the mill price, taking delivery at the producing mill and then providing their own transportation. This is seldom possible under strict basing point systems, since all prices quoted are *delivered* prices. Second, freight absorption may be unsystematic under discriminatory F.O.B. mill pricing. Producers do not necessarily match the rival mill's delivered price to the penny when they seek orders in the rival's home territory; they may match it, undercut it, or try to gain an order at the full list F.O.B. mill price plus freight. But under multiple basing point pricing, producers *systematically* adhere precisely to pricing rules which enable each to quote identical delivered prices to buyers at every destination. Through such adherence, they avoid independent initiatives which could threaten pricing discipline. Third, to achieve perfect uniformity of price quotations, the delivered price quoted under basing point systems nearly always assumes rail freight charges, whereas the delivered price quoted under an F.O.B. mill system is usually the mill price plus most economical freight costs to destination (or the costs of transportation using a mode specified by the buyer), whether the medium be rail, highway, air, or water.

BASING POINT SYSTEMS AND COMPETITION

In a series of Supreme Court decisions during the 1940s, basing point pricing systems were outlawed. They continue to be legal in most European countries,[31] however, and there have been repeated efforts to resurrect them in the United States. It is important therefore to analyze more thoroughly the objections to basing point pricing systems and to assess the relative merits of alternative spatial pricing approaches.

We have seen already that basing point pricing, and especially the single basing point variant, is discriminatory. This may be objectionable in its own right, but even more significant are the effects on competition and efficiency.

Competition is impaired because basing point pricing systems reduce what would be an incredibly complicated price quotation problem, if executed independently, to a relatively simple matter of applying the right formula. As we observed in Chapter 7, cooperation on a joint profit-maximizing policy becomes more difficult, the more heterogeneous the product is. If each producer independently and unsystematically quoted prices to the thousands of destinations it might serve, it would almost surely undercut rivals on some orders, touching off retaliatory price cuts. But common adherence to basing point formulas in effect eliminates discretion and uncertainty, and if each firm plays the game and sticks to the formulas, price competition is avoided. Identical prices are quoted to a given customer by every producer, leaving the division of orders to chance or nonprice variables (such as delivery times, special service, the dryness of martinis provided by salesmen at business luncheons, etc.—bases on which oligopolists often prefer to compete). By following the basing point rules, for example, 11 manufacturers were all able to submit quotations of $3.286854 per barrel in response to a government request for bids on cement delivered to Tucumcari, New Mexico.[32]

This is not to say that determining the right basing-point-plus-freight price is easy. Far from it. Freight rate classifications are maddeningly complex, with dozens of exceptions and considerable room for discretion. But discretion is exactly what one wishes to avoid in a system designed to suppress price competition. Consequently, industry trade associations (such as the American Iron and Steel Institute or the Cement Institute) published elaborate freight rate books listing the rail freight charges between every basing point and every conceivable destination point. Member firms were then expected faithfully to add the listed freight charges to the well-known base price (usually published by a price

[31]See Klaus Stegemann, "Three Functions of Basing-Point Pricing and Article 60 of the E.C.S.C. Treaty," *Antitrust Bulletin*, Summer 1968, pp. 395–432.

[32]Cf. Machlup, *The Basing Point System*, p. 2. It should be stressed that adherence to basing point formulas is not the only possible explanation for identical price quotations. Focal point pricing is an alternative explanation with somewhat less insidious connotations, although in the example cited there is little doubt as to what was happening. The end result—avoiding actions which upset the price structure—is the same in either case.

leader) in computing their delivered price quotations, even when they knew the rate book figure was obsolete or when the shipment would travel by water or truck instead of rail.

To be sure, the collusive purpose of basing point systems might be frustrated if producers chose not to adhere to the formulas. There are always incentives to chisel, especially when business is slack and departures from the formula price can be kept secret. Examples of non-adherence can be found in every industry following a basing point system, particularly for industries like maple flooring, which had so many sellers that recognition of mutual interdependence was weak.[33] Still adherence to formula prices has generally been quite consistent in the industries on which we have fairly complete information, and it seems certain that pricing discipline was much stronger under basing point systems than it would have been in their absence. Analyzing Bureau of Labor Statistics data on steel price-shading during 1939, when producers were operating at only half of rated capacity and discipline was unusually poor, Kaysen found concessions averaging between 3 and 8 per cent of formula prices. He concluded that "the figures . . . speak well for the efficacy of the basing point system as a method of price leadership."[34] After overcoming widespread price-cutting between 1930 and 1932, cement producers exhibited even firmer discipline during the depressed 1930s. A survey of invoices from 1938 showed that in only 6 of the 40 states covered did prices depart from identity in more than 10 per cent of all dealer transactions. On bids to government agencies, nearly perfect uniformity of quotations was sustained.[35]

Multiple basing point systems have built-in institutions to encourage adherence. In cement, for example, other firms imposed upon producers caught shading price on even a single transaction a punitive base price equivalent to the mill net realized in that transaction. All quotations for orders in the offender's home territory were then computed at the punitive base price, so that in effect a price cut made to one customer, if found out, became the ruling basis for quotations to every customer in the future. Not surprisingly, Loescher found that "The usual result of an imposition of a punitive base was the cessation of further price cutting by the offending mill. And the awareness that certain mills were being thus disciplined served to deter other competitors from selective cutting of prices."[36]

Partly because of this feature, basing point systems inhibit the sort of unsystematic price-shading which might otherwise trigger a general reduction in price levels. Incentives to reduce base prices are weak for other reasons too. Under a single basing point scheme, only the base producer is in a position to announce a formal change in the base price. Except when it considers demand so elastic that profits will be increased (in which case a pure monopolist would behave similarly), or unless it seeks to strengthen industry discipline by rallying members around a new price structure,[37] the base mill has little reason to reduce the base price, since all other firms will follow automatically and its market position will not be improved. Under a multiple basing point system, individual base mills likewise recognize that price reductions will be met by others. Their principal incentive for downward adjustments is the hope that, with sales in their home territory made less attractive, outsiders will be less anxious to seek orders there through freight absorption and will therefore leave a larger share of the market to the base mill This is often not a sufficient incentive, and so basing point systems tend to exhibit considerable downward price rigidity even during recessions.

In sum, basing point pricing weakens com-

---

[33]See George Stocking, "The Rule of Reason, Workable Competition, and the Legality of Trade Association Activities," *University of Chicago Law Review*, Summer 1954, pp. 546–567; and Almarin Phillips, *Market Structure, Organization and Performance* (Cambridge: Harvard University Press, 1962), pp. 153–160.

[34]*Op. cit.*, p. 297.

[35]Samuel M. Loescher, *Imperfect Collusion in the Cement Industry* (Cambridge: Harvard University Press, 1959), pp. 162–163.

[36]*Ibid.*, pp. 125–126.

[37]Cf. p. 172 *supra*.

petition and increases price rigidity. The more candid defenders of the system have not denied either charge. Their main defense, in fact, has been to interpret these tendencies as a plus factor, and not a social ill. Among reputable economists the case has been argued most strongly by J. M. Clark.[38] He stressed that when fixed costs represent a high proportion of total cost and when demand fluctuates either cyclically or randomly within local markets (as in cement), price competition among oligopolists often becomes cut-throat or ruinous. The efforts of strong buyers to play sellers off against one another intensify the process, said Clark. Basing point pricing moderates these propensities. "The problems that concern us involve comparisons of different kinds and degrees of competition, and should be faced in the light of the possibility that competition may be unduly strong, in a given industry, as well as unduly weak or unequal in its incidence," according to Clark.[39] Or as a trustee of the Cement Institute put it, ". . . ours is an industry that cannot stand free competition, that must systematically restrain competition or be ruined."[40] Similar arguments have been examined at length and found generally wanting in Chapter 7. There is no reason to modify our views here, so we must conclude that the ruinous competition cry does not save the day for basing point pricing.

Assuming then that a more competitive resolution of the spatial pricing problem is desired, how attractive are the alternatives to basing point pricing? It is doubtful whether uniform F.O.B. mill pricing would induce more competitive behavior when the number of sellers is small. As we have seen, such a system makes producers at each shipping point the sole suppliers of customers within their freight advantage territories, although of course the actual picture may be more complicated than Figure 10.3 suggests due to the different transportation methods used for shipments of varying sizes to diverse destinations.[41] Unless several rivals are located at a single shipping point, there is little inter-firm competitive contact, except in the zones where mill prices plus freight costs are equalized (e.g., Xenia in Figure 10.3). If these zones are densely populated with potential customers, producers may try to extend their territories and win additional sales by reducing mill prices. Small firms are often in an especially favorable position to gain through mill price reductions, since their inroads into the territory of a large rival (or group of rivals) may be so small that the rival will consider an across-the-board retaliatory response (affecting sales in other markets as well) unwarranted.[42] But when most of the plants in an industry are of appreciable size, each firm will expect attempts to extend the area in which it has a delivered price advantage to provoke offsetting price cuts from rivals. If so, it is likely to refrain from aggressive price moves, resting content with the established distribution of territorial advantage.

Both single and multiple basing point systems bring producers at different locations into rivalrous contact with one another over a much broader geographic area than uniform F.O.B. mill pricing. However, the rules of the game prohibit using price as a competitive weapon, and so the greater inter-firm contact leads mainly to more intense non-price rivalry—at best diligence in providing good service; at worst inflated customer entertainment outlays.[43]

F.O.B. mill pricing with unsystematic discriminatory freight absorption appears to be the best compromise between the available extremes when

---

[38]"Basing Point Methods of Price Quoting," pp. 477–478 and 484–489.

[39]J. M. Clark, *Competition as a Dynamic Process* (Washington: Brookings, 1961), p. 361, in a discussion of basing point pricing more cautious than his earlier statements.

[40]Quoted in Loescher, *op. cit.*, p. 85. Loescher presents an excellent analysis of the arguments for basing point pricing in cement, concluding finally that they are unconvincing.

[41]Under uniform F.O.B. mill pricing a Chicago shipper might, for example, be able effectively to compete for large orders in distant Buffalo by water transportation, but not for small orders in nearby Dayton by rail.

[42]This point is stressed by Machlup in *The Basing Point System*, pp. 187–188.

[43]Sixteen per cent of the revenues received by 47 cement manufacturers in 1939 went into distribution and selling costs other than outbound freight. This is extremely high, considering the standardized character of the commodity and the well-informed customers buying it. Cf. Loescher, *op. cit.*, p. 213.

market structures are oligopolistic.[44] Unlike uniform F.O.B. mill pricing, it permits firms to shade mill net prices and invade each others' territories in search of additional business, thereby imparting added flexibility to the price structure and raising the probability that oligopoly discipline will be broken. And unlike multiple basing point pricing, this market interpenetration is achieved through explicit price rivalry, not mere passive acceptance of prices ordained by the system.

BASING POINT SYSTEMS AND EFFICIENCY

We advance now to the efficiency implications of basing point pricing. One clear problem is cross-hauling. On theoretical grounds we should expect single basing point systems to be the worst offender, since mills located at the basing point incur no mill net price disadvantage even when they serve customers located next door to a distant rival's plant. Some cross-hauling is expected under multiple basing point and discriminatory F.O.B. mill pricing. Only a uniform F.O.B. mill pricing approach has negligible cross-hauling. Indeed, Arthur Smithies has shown that because cross-hauling necessarily reduces group profits by increasing costs, oligopolists colluding perfectly would always prefer F.O.B. pricing to a basing point system. He explained the then widespread use of basing point pricing as "a clumsy but automatic device for protecting the competitors from their own self-destructive tendencies."[45]

Evidence on the quantitative magnitude of cross-hauling costs under basing point systems is sparse. One study of the steel industry estimated that in February of 1939 freight absorption, which in a multiple basing point system is a rough indicator of cross-hauling, amounted to between 3 and 5 per cent of delivered prices.[46] Since demand was slack at the time—a condition encouraging unusually high interpenetration of

territories—and since some freight absorption would probably occur under alternative pricing systems, this sets an upper limit on the amount of socially undesirable steel cross-hauling costs. A study of the cement industry found that unnecessary cross-hauling costs during prosperous 1927 approximated 15 per cent of total revenue, though there is reason to believe that this estimate may overstate the true magnitude by as much as a factor of two.[47] In any event, it is clear that cross-hauling costs were not insignificant.

Another inefficiency peculiar to the basing point system is the tendency to employ nonoptimal transportation media. As we have observed, basing point prices were normally quoted under the assumption of rail haulage. This in fact encouraged the use of rail transportation, even when truck or water routings would have been cheaper or more convenient. There were several reasons for this anomaly.[48] If, say, a steel producer shipped by water and saved money, its customers might insist that the savings be shared. Any such concession could disrupt the whole identical price maintenance system. When customers were required to pay full rail costs in any case, they demanded rapid delivery, which placed water transport at a disadvantage. For shipments moving relatively short distances, trucking was usually cheaper and more convenient, but it too was shunned, partly because the lack of any simple, complete published trucking rate tariff rendered mutual adherence to identical delivered price quotations virtually impossible. Recognizing that delivered prices under the basing point system assumed the use of inefficient transportation methods, some cement and steel buyers asked to take delivery at the producer's plant, paying the rail-delivered price minus rail freight and providing their own trucking services. This too was resisted by sellers, because it introduced complications and uncer-

---

[44]This view is held by Kaysen, *op. cit.*, pp. 313–314. For a dissenting opinion, see Machlup, *The Basing Point System*, pp. 249–251, who favors uniform F.O.B. mill pricing in concentrated industries.

[45]"Aspects of the Basing Point System," pp. 714–715.

[46]Cited in Kaysen, *op. cit.*, p. 299. See also McKie, *op. cit.*, p. 71; and Machlup, *The Basing Point System*, pp. 56–57, 72, and 82–83.

[47]Cf. Loescher, *op. cit.*, pp. 208–213; and J. M. Clark, "Basing Point Methods of Price Quoting," p. 482. To keep cross-hauling costs from rising even further, cement firms sometimes swapped orders. For example, a central Ohio producer would have a Cleveland producer fill its orders in northern Ohio, and vice versa. In this way both increased their mill nets. See Loescher, *op. cit.*, pp. 139–141.

[48]Cf. Loescher, *op. cit.*, pp. 102–111; and Machlup, *The Basing Point System*, pp. 200–202.

tainty into the calculation of prices on shipments for which freight was to be absorbed, and because it encouraged a kind of arbitrage. We return to Figure 10.4 to illustrate the arbitrage phenomenon under Pittsburgh-plus pricing. A customer might give a Chicago mill an order allegedly for Indianapolis, ask a freight rebate equal to the delivered price *IL* less the base price *PB*, and then pick up the order in Chicago with its own trucks and deliver it (at a cost much lower than the rebate) to its own plants or those of third parties in Chicago as well as in Indianapolis. To discourage such practices, firms using the basing point system collectively refused to ship orders via customers' trucks, refunded only a fraction of the rail freight component of delivered prices on orders picked up at the mill, or charged a punitive extra fee for loading buyers' trucks. As a result, relatively little use was made of trucks, despite their advantages. When the steel industry shifted from basing point to F.O.B. mill pricing, the share of trucks increased from almost nothing to 53 per cent of total shipments in just five years.[49]

Both excessive cross-hauling and the use of inefficient transportation media increase the cost of products sold under the basing point system, and higher costs tend to be reflected in higher delivered product prices. The basing point system also contributes to high prices by facilitating collusion. Given that prices are higher than they would be under competition, resource misallocation in the conventional sense is an almost certain consequence of basing point pricing.

In addition, basing point pricing engenders a more subtle kind of misallocation—the distortion of industrial location decisions. Industries heavily dependent upon an input supplied by sellers adhering to basing point pricing may build too much of their capacity near basing points and too little near supply nodes not designated as basing points. This problem is especially serious under the single basing point system. To illustrate, suppose in Figure 10.4 that steel mills

in Pittsburgh and Chicago have roughly equal production costs, but that Pittsburgh is designated as the sole basing point. Although steel could be supplied in the Chicago area at a price of approximately *CA*, the actual Pittsburgh-plus price is *CG*. Because they must pay an artificially inflated price for steel in the Chicago area, fabricators to whom steel is an important input have an incentive to locate a disproportionate share of their fabricating capacity in the Pittsburgh area, where the delivered price is only *PB*. The Pittsburgh-plus system is said to have retarded the development of steel fabricating industries in the South and West, though it is difficult conclusively to isolate the effect of the geographic price structure from a variety of other elements affecting industry location decisions.[50] In the cement industry no similar effect has been observed, partially because a multiple basing point system was employed and partly because decisions to locate, say, a highway or parking structure are not very sensitive to spatial differences in input costs.

It is also asserted that basing point pricing biases producers' locational decisions. A firm planning to build new capacity in an industry operating under the basing point system must weigh the advantages of building at a basing point against those of a nonbase location. Favoring the basing point location is the possibility of serving all customers in the relevant territory without having to absorb freight. Nonbase mills benefit from their ability to realize phantom freight on sales near home, but they suffer an increasing freight absorption burden as they try to expand and serve more distant customers. How this tradeoff is resolved depends upon the facts of each case with respect to such variables as the geographic distribution of customers and basing points, the structure of freight rates, the nonprice advantages (such as more rapid delivery) of greater proximity to customers, and the costs of producing at alternative locations. The consensus of most analysts is that the ad-

---

[49]Cf. Louis Marengo, "The Basing Point Decisions and the Steel Industry," *American Economic Review*, May 1955, p. 521. This estimate based on trade sources may be somewhat on the high side. According to census statistics, trucks carried 40 per cent of the steel industry's outbound freight tonnage in 1963. U. S. Bureau of the Census, *Census of Transportation: 1963* (Washington: 1966), vol. III, Part 2, p. 301.

[50]Cf. Leonard W. Weiss, *Economics and American Industry* (New York: Wiley, 1961), pp. 300–303; Machlup, *The Basing Point System*, pp. 237–247; and Kaysen, *op. cit.*, pp. 304–305.

vantage lies more frequently in favor of concentrating production at basing points, although exceptions certainly exist.[51] It is clear that basing point pricing also retards the adjustment of capacity in response to secular demand shifts, for mills located at basing points where demand is declining can, at no cost disadvantage, ship their output into growing nonbase areas whose prices are quoted from the same basing point. Recognizing this threat from afar, producers in rapidly growing nonbase areas are likely to expand their capacity at a rate falling short of the local demand growth rate. In support of these generalizations, Loescher found that basing point pricing retarded a desirable shift of cement production capacity during the late 1930s toward the South, where consumption was increasing more rapidly than in other parts of the country.[52] In steel, there was a distinct acceleration in the rate of capacity growth at Chicago, Birmingham, and California as the industry gradually moved away from Pittsburgh-plus pricing and established new basing points in those areas.[53]

OVERALL ASSESSMENT

To sum up, rigid adherence to a basing point system of pricing has several undesirable effects: the virtual elimination of price competition; inefficiencies with respect to costs, prices, and the choice of locations; and discrimination against customers located near nonbase mills. Some of its disadvantages can be avoided by legal proscription. Still it is doubtful whether any completely satisfactory solution to the spatial differentiation problem can be reached, at least for concentrated industries. Firms are adaptive, and where there is a will to avoid competition, ways will be found even when the most direct route is blocked. In the steel indus-

try, for example, a shift from multiple basing point to F.O.B. mill pricing with (not very) unsystematic freight absorption did not precipitate a breakdown in pricing discipline, though it made the avoidance of independent pricing more difficult.[54] Conversely, the nominal employment of basing point formulas need not have serious anticompetitive consequences if industry members disregard them regularly because other structural conditions encourage independent behavior. Nevertheless, from the standpoint of public policy there is much to be said in favor of raising the highest possible barriers to explicit and tacit collusion in pricing. For this reason, and to minimize the ancillary inefficiencies, legal prohibitions against the use of rigid basing point systems appear warranted.

CONCLUSION

There are so many kinds of price discrimination, with such diverse consequences, that simple generalizations about the economic effects and desirability of discrimination are apt to be misleading. Discrimination always causes a redistribution of income whose merits cannot be assessed without invoking value judgments. Some forms of discrimination increase the efficiency of resource allocation compared to simple monopoly, others are essentially neutral, while still other types such as single basing point systems lead to serious inefficiencies. Unsystematic discrimination can increase the vigor of competition, while systematic discrimination has a tendency to bolster the market power of already powerful firms and to facilitate adherence to a collusive price structure. Given these complexities, it is necessary to judge particular cases of discrimination on their individual merits.

---

[51]Cf. Smithies, *op. cit.*, p. 723; Machlup, *The Basing Point System*, pp. 233–237; Kaysen *op. cit.*, pp. 300–306; and M. L. Greenhut, *Microeconomics and the Space Economy* (Chicago: Scott Foresman, 1963), pp. 130–158. For a slightly dissenting view, see Loescher, *op. cit.*, p. 151 n.

[52]*Op. cit.*, pp. 199–208. For perspective, it is worth noting that the Soviet Union apparently experienced even worse inefficiencies in locating its cement production units through central planning. See A. Abouchar, "Rationality in the Pre-War Soviet Cement Industry," *Soviet Studies*, October 1967, pp. 211–231.

[53]Cf. A. R. Burns, *The Decline of Competition* (New York: McGraw-Hill, 1936), pp. 340–345; Weiss, *op. cit.*, pp. 302–303; and "Billions Build Chicago into a Steel Titan," *Business Week*, November 19, 1966, p. 68. For a more skeptical view, see Walter Isard and W. M. Capron, "The Future Locational Pattern of Iron and Steel Production in the United States," *Journal of Political Economy*, April 1949, especially pp. 131–133.

[54]See Marengo, *op. cit.*, p. 521.

Chapter **11**

Conglomerate Bigness and Pricing Behavior

Our emphasis thus far has been on the relationship between *relative* size—i.e., power in specific markets—and pricing behavior. This is the conventional focus of economic analysis. But absolute size may also matter. The pricing actions of a giant conglomerate firm may differ from those of dispersed independent specialists, each holding a share equal to the giant's share in some market served by the giant. Power in narrowly-defined markets may interact with overall corporate bigness to produce an outcome different from what would occur if the absolute size factor were lacking. In this chapter we explore some of the principal hypotheses: that conglomerate bigness is especially conducive to predatory pricing, 'spheres of influence' agreements among giant rivals, reciprocal dealing, and nonmaximization of profits.[1]

PREDATORY PRICING

One purported trait of large, financially powerful conglomerate firms is their greater ability and willingness to engage in sustained price-cutting with the intent of disciplining smaller competitors or even driving them out of the market. This so-called "deep pocket" hypothesis has been stated most forcefully by Corwin Edwards:

> An enterprise that is big in this sense obtains from its bigness a special kind of power, based upon the fact that it can spend money in large amounts. If such a concern finds itself matching expenditures or losses, dollar for dollar, with a substantially smaller firm, the length of its purse assures it of victory. . . . The large company is in a position to hurt without being hurt.[2]

The most extreme form of predatory pricing takes place when a seller holds price below the level of its rivals' costs (and perhaps also its own) for protracted periods, until the rivals either close down operations altogether or sell out on favorable terms. The predator's motivation is to secure a monopoly position once rivals have been driven from the arena, enjoying long-run profits higher than they would be if the rivals were permitted to survive. Even if it must itself sustain losses during the price war, the predator can afford to do so because it can draw upon profits

[1]We shall limit our analysis to pricing behavior and will not try to cover the whole waterfront of the conglomerate bigness issue—e.g., with respect to economies of absolute scale and advantages in the exercise of political power. For studies with a broader sweep, see Corwin D. Edwards, "Conglomerate Bigness As a Source of Power," in the National Bureau of Economic Research conference report, *Business Concentration and Price Policy* (Princeton: Princeton University Press, 1955), pp. 331–359; John M. Blair, "The Conglomerate Merger in Economics and Law," *Georgetown Law Journal,* Summer 1958, pp. 672–700; Donald F. Turner, "Conglomerate Mergers and Section 7 of the Clayton Act," *Harvard Law Review,* May 1965, pp. 1313–1395; and the Federal Trade Commission's *Economic Report on Corporate Mergers,* presented as Part 8A of the Senate Antitrust Committee hearings, *Economic Concentration* (Washington: 1969).

[2]Edwards, *op. cit.,* pp. 334–335.

earned selling the same product in other geographic territories, or from selling different products. In other words, it subsidizes its predatory operations with profits from other markets until the predation creates conditions which will repay the original subsidy.

For reasons to be elaborated in a moment, it is difficult to be certain that firms have in fact been cutting prices expressly to drive out competitors. Still the annals of antitrust litigation contain some highly probable examples. The old Tobacco Trust eliminated competitors around the turn of the century by selling certain 'fighting brands' at prices below out-of-pocket cost, and during the 1930s the cigarette Big Three repelled an attack on their market shares from 'ten-cent' brands by sharp price cutting.[3] Alcoa's pricing of aluminum sheet below production costs during the late 1920s fits the predatory pattern.[4] Several suspicious incidents were turned up in the antitrust investigation of United Shoe Machinery Corporation's price structure, although in only one case was definite evidence of an intent to eliminate competitors found.[5] The price wars which occasionally occur between national and local milk distributors in some regions appear consistent with the hypothesis, despite the fact that proof of predatory intent on the part of the nationwide distributors has not been established.[6] And at the time of writing, two antitrust suits were in process charging predatory pricing by four ocean freight cartels. In one of the cases, the defendant shipping companies allegedly cut trans-Pacific cement freight rates from $8.95 to $4.96 per ton, forcing four other carriers out of business, after which rates were increased again.[7]

The most famous case of alleged predatory pricing is that of the old Standard Oil Company. It has also been studied more thoroughly than

any other and is therefore worth discussing in greater detail. Under the leadership of John D. Rockefeller, the Standard Oil trust between 1870 and 1899 attained and maintained a 90 per cent share of the petroleum refining market through a vigorous program of mergers, combined with various sharp practices which supposedly animated the willingness of independent refiners to sell out. These included the securing of discriminatory rail freight rates and rebates, foreclosing supplies of crude oil through the control of pipelines, business espionage, price warfare waged both overtly and secretly through bogus independent distributors, and (although never proved) astute placement of an occasional stick of dynamite. Regarding predatory price warfare —our main concern here—the conventional wisdom, handed down from generation to generation of economists, tells us that Standard cut prices sharply in specific local markets where there was competition while holding prices at much higher levels in markets lacking competition. Thereby it presumably softened up its rivals until they were receptive to merger offers. In a precedent-setting opinion, Supreme Court Chief Justice Edward White enumerated the predatory practices of which Standard was accused and cited approvingly the prosecution's contention that "The pathway of the combination . . . is strewn with the wrecks resulting from crushing out, without regard to law, the individual rights of others."[8]

This interpretation stood virtually unchallenged until 1958, when it was attacked by Professor McGee on two main grounds: (1) that there was little evidence to support the contention that Standard achieved its monopoly position through predatory price-cutting; and (2) that such a strategy by Standard would have

---

[3]Cf. pp. 166–167 *supra*.

[4]Cf. Leonard W. Weiss, *Economics and American Industry* (New York: Wiley, 1961), p. 194.

[5]Cf. Carl Kaysen, *United States* v. *United Shoe Machinery Corporation* (Cambridge: Harvard University Press, 1956), pp. 74 and 132.

[6]See U. S. Federal Trade Commission, *In the Matter of Beatrice Foods*, Docket no. 6653, Opinion of the Commission, April 26, 1965, pp. 36–37.

[7]*Pacific Seafarers, Inc. et al. v. Pacific Far East Lines, Inc.*, *et al.*, 404 F. 2d 804 (1968), cert. den. 1969; and *Sabre Shipping Corp. v. American President Lines, Ltd.*, *et al.*, CCH 1968 Trade Cases, Para. 72,493; CCH 1969 Trade Cases, Para. 72,680 and 72,703. The facts are summarized in "4 Steam Ship Conferences Face Antitrust Suits for $68.4 Million," *New York Times*, November 21, 1966, p. 89.

[8]*Standard Oil Company of New Jersey* v. *U. S.*, 221 U.S. 1, 47, 76 (1911).

been irrational because it demanded an excessive sacrifice of profits.[9]

McGee's criticism of the supporting evidence was based solely upon an analysis of the voluminous Standard Oil antitrust case record. It is not convincing, since antitrust investigations labor under such severe evidentiary difficulties that they frequently fail to elicit proof of the main points at issue. Had McGee bothered to cast his net further into historical works drawing upon the Rockefeller papers, he would have found that Standard tried in some instances to drive out its rivals through price-cutting. As Rockefeller wrote to an associate in 1881, "We want to watch, and when our volume of business is to be cut down by the increase of competition to fifty per cent, or less, it may be a very serious question whether we had not better make an important reduction, with a view of taking substantially all the business there is."[10]

McGee's second point is better taken, for the independent evidence suggests that Rockefeller recognized the limitations of local price warfare, engaged in it for the explicit purpose of driving rivals to the wall only infrequently, and instead pursued a much more complex and sophisticated pricing strategy.[11] One problem was that Standard, controlling or attempting to control the lion's share of the markets in which it sold, had to accept profit sacrifices disproportionate to the harm it inflicted upon small rivals when it resorted to price warfare. In the words of another Rockefeller associate, Standard "gained or lost on a titan's scale while its opponents did so on a pygmy's."[12] The profit sacrifices of a sustained local price war were worthwhile only if the postwar situation would be much more favorable once competitors were gone.

But second, this was by no means assured. Except for the difficulty of securing crude oil supplies, barriers to new entry were modest. A refinery of substantial size by 1880s standards could be erected for less than $50,000.[13] Consequently, any attempt by Standard to elevate prices in areas with adequate rail or water transportation from crude oil producing centers could stimulate an influx of new entry. To be sure, the threat of renewed price warfare might deter some potential entrants, but unless Standard repeatedly accepted the profit sacrifices associated with carrying out this threat, it soon lost its credibility. In addition, small-scale refineries closed down during a price war were typically put back into operation when prices were raised unless the facilities were purchased by Standard. And in taking such capacity off the market through acquisition, Standard occasionally created additional troubles for itself, since some entrepreneurs to whom it had paid a handsome liquidation price broke their agreements not to compete in the future, reinvesting the proceeds in new refining capacity![14]

Price warfare to eliminate rivals might also be unprofitable if the liquidation prices at which the victims sold out were not much less than they would have been in a merger agreement entered under less coercive conditions.[15] McGee argues that this was so in the Standard Oil case; that Standard could have acquired rival facilities in any event by paying only a modest premium over their competitive value. But this is doubtful. A successful price war could spell the difference between paying the nuisance value of a firm, which most entrepreneurs opposing Standard believed to be high, and the distress price, which for narrowly-based specialists suffering a liquidity crisis would be quite low.

[9]John S. McGee, "Predatory Price Cutting: The Standard Oil (N.J.) Case," *Journal of Law and Economics*, October 1958, pp. 137–169.

[10]Letter to H. A. Hutchins, quoted in Allan Nevins, *Study in Power: John D. Rockefeller* (New York: Scribner's, 1953), vol. II, p. 65.

[11]*Ibid.*, pp. 62–67.

[12]*Ibid.*, p. 66.

[13]*Ibid.*, p. 54.

[14]Cf. Wayne A. Leeman, "The Limitations of Local Price-Cutting as a Barrier to Entry," *Journal of Political Economy*, August 1956, pp. 329–332.

[15]See Lester G. Telser, "Cutthroat Competition and the Long Purse," *Journal of Law and Economics*, October 1966, pp. 259–277, for an algebraic statement of this argument.

Nevertheless, largely because of the new entry and dormant capacity problem, Rockefeller apparently recognized the futility of trying to drive rivals out of business through predatory pricing in all but exceptional cases. He turned instead to a classic entry-deterring strategy: holding price-cost margins to a value not exceeding Standard's cost advantage, which was modest in territories where Standard's control over low-cost crude oil transportation media was weak. Under this policy efficient competitors were not driven out, but undercutting Standard's price to achieve market share gains at Standard's expense was rendered unattractive, and outsiders' incentives to invest in new refining capacity were weakened. Only where rivals were having trouble getting crude oil supplies did Standard price its products to achieve high profit margins.

To generalize, no matter how deep a large firm's pocket is, price warfare aimed at driving small but equally efficient rivals from the market will not be attractive, and is therefore improbable, unless barriers to new entry can be maintained during the postwar period at levels sufficiently high to permit the realization of profit margins considerably greater than they would be if rivals were permitted to survive. Furthermore, this condition is not apt to be satisfied where giant conglomerates face small specialists in narrow segments of some market, for the very fact that specialists can operate profitably in the absence of predatory pricing or strong product differentiation suggests that entry barriers are not high. Precisely because entry into grocery retailing was easy, for example, M. A. Adelman rejected as unconvincing the government's charges in an antitrust action that the A & P Company engaged in cut-throat pricing during the 1930s to eliminate its competitors in certain localities, subsidizing those operations with profits from areas of less intense competition.[16] Similarly, Fog found in his survey of 139 Danish firms that large companies did not try to cut

prices to the bone because they believed any attempts permanently to drive out small rivals were doomed to failure.[17]

Does this mean there is little empirical support for the deep pocket theory of predatory pricing? It apparently does, at least for a strict construction of the theory. But a looser construction can be rescued by showing that less malevolent decisions to sustain price-cutting are influenced by the availability of compensating profits from unaffected markets. Four main cases can be identified.

First is the classic case of permanently accepting low but supra-normal profit margins to deter new entry and the expansion of rivals. The critical question here is, are large conglomerate firms more likely to engage in limit pricing than companies specializing in a single product or market? Several considerations are relevant. For entry deterrent pricing to be an attractive strategy, the limit price must normally exceed one's average total cost by at least a small margin, so neither type of firm is saddled with the problem of finding funds to subsidize its limit pricing operations. To both the conglomerate and the specialist, limit pricing is profitable if the discounted addition to future profits due to deterring new entry exceeds the loss of current profits due to charging less than the short-run profit-maximizing price. The only conceivable difference with any relevance to the deep pocket hypothesis is the possibility that conglomerates might systematically discount future earnings at a lower rate than specialists, and hence might be more favorably disposed toward entry deterrence. This could be so either because they enjoy lower capital costs due to their size, or because their managers are content with the stream of profits emerging from unrelated markets and therefore assign low marginal utility to additional current profits from markets for which limit pricing is being considered. The former conjecture is consistent with a profit-maximizing

---

[16]M. A. Adelman, *A & P: A Study in Price-Cost Behavior and Public Policy* (Cambridge: Harvard University Press, 1959), p. 14. More recently, the Federal Trade Commission economics staff has argued that barriers to entry into supermarketing are rising, making local predatory pricing a more profitable strategy for nationwide supermarket chains. See the Federal Trade Commission staff report, *Economic Report on the Structure and Competitive Behavior of Food Retailing* (Washington: January 1966), pp. 272–285.

[17]Bjarke Fog, *Industrial Pricing Policies* (Amsterdam: North Holland, 1960), pp. 147–151.

view of the firm; the latter not. Both are empirically plausible, and either could explain Fog's finding that large firms were more inclined to prefer lower, entry-deterring prices than small firms.[18] It is clear that large firms enjoy lower capital costs than small firms, although this advantage seems to be associated more closely with bigness than with conglomerateness.[19] The possibility of behavior which departs from strict profit-maximizing standards cannot be ruled out when firms possess market power. As a result, we must conclude that a deep, well-lined pocket *may* affect sellers' limit pricing decisions, although it does not necessarily do so.

A second case is the reduction of price temporarily, perhaps even below cost, to discipline rivals and teach them that cooperation pays. A well-documented example is the price war Safeway Stores outlets in Texas initiated in 1954 to counter and presumably to discourage the use of trading stamps by rivals. During the ensuing 15 month period the price-cutting stores recorded losses of $4 million on sales of roughly $230 million while profits in other regional divisions remained healthy. At the peak of the war, nearly a fourth of the 2,000 grocery items checked by government antitrust investigators were being sold at less than invoice cost.[20] Such tactics can be viewed as an investment in creating conditions conducive to higher future profits, to which both conglomerate and specialist firms should be equally attracted, unless they discount the future differently. However, there is a further difference when prices are driven below short-run marginal cost so that outright subsidy of the disciplinary effort is required. Small specialists may be reluctant to take the initiative in committing their limited funds to a course of action with such uncertain consequences, while large conglomerates with low-cost or low-utility funds from other operations are in a more favorable position to assume the risk. Below-cost disciplinary pricing nevertheless appears to be a relatively rare phenomenon.

Third, firms may move into a new product line or market, charging a price which fails to cover costs in the hope of building a strong, profitable future market position, and subsidizing the losses with profits derived from other lines. Here again we have an investment made to increase future profits, although in most cases of this sort competition is not adversely affected even when firms already in the invaded market must give ground.[21] There is no *a priori* reason to expect that conglomerates are more apt to behave in this way than are small specialists, unless the specialists are subjected to more stringent capital constraints. Only through its capacity to generate greater quantities of low-cost capital does the conglomerate enjoy an advantage.

Finally, large diversified firms may offer certain products as 'loss leaders' at prices below cost in order to encourage the sale of other products. This is common in retailing, with some items being advertised at low prices to draw in customers who may then buy additional high-margin goods as a matter of convenience or impulse. Its anticompetitive effects are generally modest, since other retailers can retaliate with their own loss leaders, and since the customer is free to purchase nothing more than the loss leader if he so chooses. For an illustration from the manufacturing sector, major drug manufacturers sell certain pharmaceutical preparations at a loss in order to maintain good relations with prescribing physicians. While this policy may injure firms specializing in those items, it is doubtful whether it impairs the vigor of competition, provided there are no compulsory ties between the loss leader items and high-margin products.[22] And as we shall see in Chapter 21,

---

[18]B. Fog, "How Are Cartel Prices Determined?" *Journal of Industrial Economics*, November 1956, p. 20.

[19]Cf. pp. 100–102 *supra*.

[20]See the testimony of Willard Mueller in *Economic Concentration*, pp. 1872–1873 and 2007–2009; and the Federal Trade Commission staff report, *Economic Report on the Structure and Competitive Behavior of Food Retailing*, pp. 121–142.

[21]If the entry is accomplished through merger with a firm already in the market, the impact on competition might be less favorable. See Blair, *op. cit.*, pp. 688–694; and Turner, *op. cit.*, pp. 1362–1386.

[22]For a further discussion, see Turner, *op. cit.*, pp. 1349–1351.

formal tying contracts which injure competition are illegal under the U. S. antitrust laws.

In sum, there are undoubtedly situations in which conglomerate bigness may facilitate pricing behavior which constrains the entry, growth, and independence of smaller rivals. But the cases in which conglomerate size per se leads in this way to serious anti-competitive effects appear to be uncommon.

THE SPHERES OF INFLUENCE HYPOTHESIS

In the previous section we worried whether bitter price-cutting and a struggle for survival are more likely when a conglomerate giant faces a group of small specialists in some market than when specialists alone occupy the market. Now we reverse our field, examining the hypothesis that when conglomerate giants face other conglomerates in a web of markets, they will compete *less* sharply than would specialists occupying the same markets. Putting the two propositions together, when there is an asymmetry of conglomerate power, rivalry is said to be more severe, whereas symmetry blunts the incentives for rivalry. This hypothesis was first advanced by Corwin Edwards, who merits quoting at length:

When one large conglomerate enterprise competes with another, the two are likely to encounter each other in a considerable number of markets. The multiplicity of their contacts may blunt the edge of their competition. A prospect of advantage from vigorous competition in one market may be weighed against the danger of retaliatory forrays by the competitor in other markets. Each conglomerate competitor may adopt a live-and-let-live policy designed to stabilize the whole structure of the competitive relationship. Each may informally recognize the other's primacy of interest in markets im-

portant to the other, in the expectation that its own important interests will be similarly respected. Like national states, the great conglomerates may come to have recognized spheres of influence and may hesitate to fight local wars vigorously because the prospect[s] of local gain are not worth the risk of general warfare.[23]

Edwards' observations on live-and-let-live attitudes among conglomerate giants were influenced by his experience as director of a U. S. mission to investigate Japanese combines following World War II. Before the war, a substantial share of all Japanese business activity was concentrated in the hands of a few giant conglomerate holding companies known as *Zaibatsu* (literally, money cliques). The four largest Zaibatsu— Mitsui, Mitsubishi, Sumitomo, and Yasuda— controlled a fourth of all paid-up capital in prewar Japanese industry and finance.[24] They were far more diversified than any American corporation. Even after a postwar Zaibatsu dissolution program, Mitsui interests ranged into shipbuilding, coal mining, copper mining, iron and aluminum production, synthetic fibers, plastics, fertilizers, basic chemicals, cameras, banking, insurance, and real estate.[25] Each Zaibatsu group was strong in some lines and relatively weak in others. They came into contact in dozens of markets, especially in the heavy industrial sector. In addition, there were frequent social and matrimonial ties among members of the several families dominating the principal Zaibatsu.

Students of Japanese industrial history disagree on the effect this widespread interpenetration of markets had on competitive behavior. Some concur with Edwards that a live-and-let-live attitude was encouraged by the fear that aggressive action in a market where one had an edge would be countered by aggression in markets where rivals had the advantage.[26] Others

---

[23]From Edwards' testimony in *Economic Concentration*, p. 45. His original statement of the hypothesis is in "Conglomerate Bigness as a Source of Power," p. 335.

[24]Cf. William W. Lockwood, "Japan's 'New Capitalism,' " in Lockwood, editor, *The State and Economic Enterprise in Japan* (Princeton: Princeton University Press, 1965), pp. 495–500. See also T. A. Bisson, *Zaibatsu Dissolution in Japan* (Berkeley: University of California Press, 1954), pp. 6–32.

[25]For analyses of postwar Zaibatsu structure and control, see Eugene Rotwein, "Economic Concentration and Monopoly in Japan," *Journal of Political Economy*, June 1964, pp. 265–272; and George C. Allen, *Japan's Economic Expansion* (London: Oxford University Press, 1965), pp. 173–194. See also p. 45 *supra*.

[26]This is Rotwein's view, based on Eleanor M. Hadley, "Concentrated Business Power in Japan," (unpublished dissertation, Radcliffe College, 1949), pp. 7 and 13–14.

found that the principal Zaibatsu were "keen rivals," and that they often refused to cooperate with one another in cartel agreements because of confidence in their own superiority, clique rivalries, prejudice and ignorance, the desire to guard private secrets, and dissatisfaction with prices and output quotas.[27] Perhaps the most balanced view of this complex and conflicting picture is given by Lockwood, who described prewar Japanese enterprise as:

> . . . a rather indeterminate blend of sharp jealousy and mutual solidarity, of rugged individualism and collusive action. If rivalries were keen, they yet operated in a setting characterized by a propensity among the rivals to cooperate in abating the rigors of the free market.[28]

It would appear then that balanced conglomerate power did encourage mutual forebearance and respect for spheres of influence, although it by no means eliminated all traces of independent rivalry among the Zaibatsu.

Do similar proclivities exist among Western conglomerate giants, despite differences in scope and traditions? On this question we have very little evidence. One fragment comes from Professor Kahn's study of inter-firm relations in the international chemicals industry.[29] Among the most conglomerate of Western firms prior to World War II were I. G. Farben in Germany, Imperial Chemical Industries in England, and du Pont in the United States. Their interests touched in hundreds of product lines, and they unquestionably adopted a live-and-let-live policy towards one another, negotiating explicit geographic spheres of influence agreements for products on which they had exclusive patent protection and avoiding aggressive price competition where they did compete directly. The rela-

tionship between du Pont and Farben was summarized as follows:

> Both companies gave heed to strategic considerations favoring some kind of understanding; each either had something the other wanted or could at least harm the other's interests. Both realized the hazards of seriously antagonizing each other, and, above all, the folly of upsetting the market. This was the nature of their gentlemen's agreement: they would cooperate wherever possible, and in any event they would act like gentlemen.[30]

There is reason to believe competition among the three chemical giants intensified in the postwar period after the Farben combine was broken up, du Pont's spheres of influence agreements were attacked by the American antitrust authorities, and other chemical firms began to diversify and expand into product lines formerly dominated by the Big Three.[31] Still competition among chemical makers continues to have a mild quality except in lines where severe overcapacity exists, and it may well be that mutual interpenetration of markets is one of the factors inhibiting aggressive instincts.

Respect for spheres of influence also appears to be a prominent characteristic of pricing relationships among the various international merchant marine cartels. According to an individual connected with one of the conferences, particular ship lines and groups of lines strive to negotiate advantageous freight rate agreements covering the routes they dominate by threatening rival groups with rate warfare over routes in which the rivals' profit stake is greatest. The full story of how the shipping cartels operate has yet to see the light of day. And unfortunately, there is a dearth of evidence on spheres of influence ac-

---

[27]G. C. Allen, *A Short Economic History of Modern Japan: 1867–1937* (New York: Praeger, 1963), p. 135; and W. W. Lockwood, *The Economic Development of Japan* (Princeton: Princeton University Press, 1954), pp. 228–230.

[28]*Ibid.*, p. 231.

[29]Alfred E. Kahn, "The Chemical Industry," in Walter Adams, ed., *The Structure of American Industry* (Third ed.; New York: Macmillan, 1961), pp. 246–252. See also G. W. Stocking and M. W. Watkins, *Cartels in Action: Case Studies in International Business Diplomacy* (New York: Twentieth Century Fund, 1946), Chapters 9 to 11.

[30]Stocking and Watkins, *op. cit.*, p. 489.

[31]See the testimony of Joel Dirlam in *Economic Concentration*, pp. 755–758; and M. J. Gart, "The British Company That Found a Way Out," *Fortune*, August 1966, pp. 104 ff.

cords in other industries, if indeed the phenomenon exists on any widespread basis.

In the present state of knowledge we can conclude only that the spheres of influence hypothesis is provocative and plausible, but that its empirical significance remains unknown. As the trend toward conglomerate diversification continues, there may be rich opportunities for perceptive research on the problem.

RECIPROCAL BUYING

Another business practice with a potentially close connection to conglomerate bigness is reciprocal buying, that is, giving preference in purchasing decisions to firms which are good customers for one's own products. It is also known as 'taking in each other's wash,' or in Hawaiian, *Hoo male male*—literally, You tickle me, I'll tickle you. Even though a majority of company executives responding to a 1953 survey expressed dislike for the practice, most of their firms engaged in it to some extent.[32] A later survey reveals that larger firms are more likely to base purchasing decisions on reciprocity considerations than small firms.[33]

Reciprocal buying is normally associated with the existence of several conditions.[34] First is an oligopolistic market structure, leading industry members to prefer nonprice rivalry over price competition. Second, producers must have excess capacity which they would like to utilize by filling orders won on nonprice grounds. Surveys show, for instance, that pressures to engage in reciprocal buying are stronger during recessions than in booms.[35] Third, there must be a two-way flow of transactions between industries, with Industry A both buying from and selling to Industry B in significant quantities. This is a fairly restrictive condition in many cases, for a

survey of some 300 firms disclosed that the median firm made only from 1 to 3 per cent of its sales to suppliers, and only 6 per cent of the companies sold more than 30 per cent of their output to suppliers.[36] Finally, it is said that asymmetry in size among the firms involved favors reciprocal purchasing, especially when a conglomerate giant towers over rival sellers specializing in one or two narrow lines.

The advantages of conglomerate bigness are best shown by some examples. One of the most striking, which ultimately provoked an antitrust suit, involved the exercise of power not through direct conglomerate diversification, but through the interlocking of financial interests by individual company executives. Two traffic department (i.e., freight routing) officials of the Armour Company bought stock in a small firm manufacturing special draft gears for the railroad industry. They gave preference in routing Armour's huge meat shipment volume to railroads which purchased gears from their company. As a result, the gear-making firm indirectly exploiting Armour's power moved from seventh place in its field, with a 1 per cent market share, to industry sales leadership and a 35 per cent market share in only six years.[37]

In 1963 the Department of Justice brought suit against General Motors in another case turning on reciprocal dealing with respect to freight routings. According to the government complaint, GM attained and maintained its 80 per cent share of the diesel locomotive market in part by giving preference in routing the freight of larger company divisions (notably, the automobile divisions) to railroads buying General Motors locomotives, at the same time reducing or withholding shipments on railroads buying rival locomotives.[38] The suit was abandoned, however, in 1967 because of insufficient evidence.

[32]M. C. Neuhoff and G. G. Thompson, "Reciprocity: Many Practice, Few Favor," *Business Record*, March 1954, pp. 106–109.

[33]Leonard Sloane, "Reciprocity: Where Does the P.A. Stand?" *Purchasing*, November 20, 1961, pp. 70–77.

[34]See G. W. Stocking and W. F. Mueller, "Business Reciprocity and the Size of Firms," *Journal of Business*, April 1957, pp. 73–95; and Joel Dean, "Economic Aspects of Reciprocity, Competition and Mergers," *Antitrust Bulletin*, September-December 1963, pp. 843–852.

[35]Sloane, *loc. cit.*

[36]*Ibid.*, p. 77.

[37]*In re Waugh Equipment Company et al.*, 15 F.T.C. 232, 242–243 (1931).

[38]*U. S.* v. *General Motors Corporation*, complaint issued in 1963, CCH *Trade Regulation Reporter* Para. 45,063.

It is clear that GM's market dominance was not due solely to conglomerate purchasing leverage, for certain of its early rivals were notoriously slow in shifting from steam to diesel models; and another rival, General Electric, was able to carve out only an 8 per cent market share despite its status as the most conglomerate of all American conglomerate giants.

One limitation on conglomerate bigness as a bargaining weapon arises when the conglomerate company sells a variety of products to suppliers in a particular industry. The du Pont Company, for instance, has long placed special stress on reciprocal buying.[39] To win dynamite orders from steel makers vertically integrated into iron ore mining, it allegedly held out as a bargaining counter substantial steel purchases not only for its explosives divisions, but also for its basic chemical, plastics, synthetic fiber, and other divisions. This practice was disadvantageous to specialists Hercules Powder and Atlas Powder, who (at least until they undertook their own diversification programs) could place on the balance only the steel requirements of their explosives operations. Still du Pont's reciprocal buying advantage might be attenuated if steel producers pursued varying policies with respect to different chemical inputs. If, say, Bethlehem Steel bought all of its explosives from Hercules and Atlas, but purchased a substantial portion of the acid for its pickling baths from du Pont, the latter could scarcely reduce its steel purchases from Bethlehem without risking a loss of acid orders. In general, conglomerate leverage is strongest when the giant firm sells only one or a very few narrow segments of its product line to a supplier who in turn is anxious to satisfy the demand for an input employed by all of the conglomerate's divisions. To the extent that this generalization is valid, significant examples of conglomerate leverage are likely to be limited to a small proportion of the typical giant firms's total sales.

The exercise of conglomerate power through reciprocal buying also tends to be less successful when smaller firms offer more attractive sales terms. Most of the 163 corporation executives responding to a 1963 survey stated that their firms' purchases were awarded on the basis of reciprocity only when price, quality, and delivery conditions were equal.[40] A paramount reason for the emphasis on reciprocal purchasing in the railroad and common motor carrier field is the fact that freight rates are equal under the binding scheme of public regulation, and so the distribution of patronage necessarily depends upon nonprice factors.[41] One known exception to the customary *ceteris paribus* rule was the policy of U. S. Rubber Company, which permitted its sales department to absorb any excess costs due to awarding a purchase order to a good customer quoting other than the lowest price.[42] How frequently this latitude was exercised is not known. Another apparent exception is found in the precedent-setting *Consolidated Foods* antitrust case.[43] Consolidated, with extensive food wholesaling operations, acquired Gentry, a manufacturer of dehydrated onion and garlic. It tried to exert leverage from its position as a leading soup wholesaler to induce the purchase of Gentry products by soup makers. In a few instances soup producers yielded to this pressure, despite their belief that the Gentry products were qualitatively inferior to rivals' offerings. But these seem to have been exceptional. For the most part the Consolidated – Gentry amalgamation either failed in its efforts to secure reciprocal favors or gave up trying, and during the seven years following the merger, Gentry's share of the dehydrated garlic market fell from 51 to 39 per cent.

To the extent that reciprocity affects purchasing decisions only when price, quality, service, and the like are all equal, the main effect of the practice may be merely to redistribute sales among the members of an industry, with

[39]Cf. Stocking and Mueller, *op. cit.*, pp. 80–85.
[40]Neuhoff and Thompson, *op. cit.*, p. 107.
[41]Stocking and Mueller, *op. cit.*, pp. 77–78.
[42]*Ibid.*, p. 87.
[43]*Federal Trade Commission* v. *Consolidated Foods Corporation*, 329 F. 2d 623 (1964), 380 U. S. 592 (1965). See also the analysis in Turner, *op. cit.*, pp. 1391–1393.

no adverse incremental effect on allocative efficiency. Unless the power to swap orders is unevenly distributed, the redistributions may tend to cancel out, leaving market structure about the same as it would have been if the practice did not exist.[44] Nevertheless, several side effects of a potentially undesirable character may emerge, especially when the *ceteris paribus* condition is violated or when power is asymmetrically held.

For one, reciprocity may have an indirect impact on the price structure. On the negative side, when firms get into the habit of basing purchasing decisions on reciprocity grounds, their purchasing agents may become less aggressive in searching out and bargaining for price reductions. Consequently, competitive price shading is inhibited.[45] On the other hand, firms in an oligopolistic industry normally unconducive to price competition may combat a loss of sales to rivals with greater reciprocal leverage by cutting prices. If so, reciprocal purchasing might actually invigorate competition.[46] No satisfactory evidence on the relative strength of these opposing possibilities exists.

Second, when companies do buy at above-minimum prices or accept inferior quality in order to secure reciprocal favors, the functioning of the price mechanism as an allocative guide is thwarted, and society is almost surely the loser. Third, when price, quality, and other conditions of sale are identical but bargaining power is asymmetrically distributed, reciprocal buying generally has anticompetitive effects on market structure. It enables large firms to increase their market shares at the expense of smaller specialists, and it increases barriers to entry for new firms lacking substantial purchase orders to trade for a share of potential customers' patronage. The long-run result is increased concentration.

Finally, the manipulation of purchasing decisions to influence sales may deaden price competition when firms are simultaneously competitors in some markets and trading partners in others. The experience of Consolidated Foods—this time on the short end of the purchasing leverage stick—illustrates the dangers. In 1965, Consolidated's seven subsidiary retail supermarkets in the Chicago area launched a price-cutting and advertising campaign to expand their market shares. This effort bit into the sales and profits of National Tea, a nationwide retailing chain with 237 stores in the Chicago area. In retaliation, National ceased purchasing the baked goods of Consolidated's Sara Lee manufacturing subsidiary for a week. Consolidated's supermarkets shortly thereafter abandoned their price-cutting campaign, and later Consolidated announced a decision to leave the supermarketing field altogether because of the "adverse effect on its processing operations."[47]

How typical such cases are is unknown. In all probability, the situations in which reciprocal purchasing is socially harmless outnumber those in which serious anti-competitive effects occur. Still the practice offers few advantages to compensate for its drawbacks, and so it should undoubtedly be discouraged by appropriate public policies.

NONMAXIMIZATION OF PROFITS

Giant conglomerate firms have also been accused, notably by Professor Edwards, of being inordinately slow in responding to changes in demand and in eliminating inefficient or wasteful operations. They may, for example, continue certain lines of business long after they turn unprofitable, subsidizing losses with funds earned in other more profitable branches.[48] They may become sluggish; failing to introduce the most efficient production methods, to lay off unnecessary overhead personnel, and to control

---

[44]Businessmen sometimes argue that reciprocity is a sales-increasing device. But this is true only myopically. As long as price, quality, and the like remain constant, one firm's sales gains must be offset by some other firm's losses, and the net industry-wide gain is zero.

[45]Cf. Sloane, *op. cit.*, p. 79.

[46]This is the view of Joel Dean, *op. cit.*, p. 851.

[47]See the testimony of Willard Mueller in *Economic Concentration*, pp. 1874–1875; and *Moody's Industrial Manual*, June 1966, p. 1930.

[48]See his testimony in *Economic Concentration*, pp. 43–44.

properly the flow of materials through their plants.[49]

Obviously, such conduct conflicts with profit maximization. According to Edwards, conglomerates depart from the profit-maximizing norm partly because their accounting systems provide inadequate information to top management on actual conditions and potentialities in the operating divisions, and partly because operating level managers resist changes incompatible with pursuing their narrow goals (such as plant or divisional survival) even though such changes may benefit the corporation as a whole.

While these conjectures are not wholly implausible, they are open to several qualifications and objections. For one, the chiefs of most modern conglomerate enterprises are acutely aware of their information problem and devote extra attention to developing information systems with built-in checks against concealment and distortion. Whether the effort is completely successful in overcoming the dilemmas of bureaucracy depends, as we have seen in Chapter 4, upon the quality of management. Success is clearly not assured.[50]

Second, prolonged subsidization of unprofitable lines is hardly possible without some degree of monopoly power in profitable lines. Thus monopoly power must be linked with bigness *per se* for nonmaximizing behavior to persist. When the two structural conditions co-exist, it is conceivable that they interact to make profit-maximizing responses more sluggish than they would be if either condition existed in isolation. In this sense conglomerateness could contribute at least marginally to deficient performance.

But finally, it can be argued that conglomerate enterprises allocate capital *more* efficiently than specialists, not less. As long as they avoid becoming locked into an excessively inflexible debt structure (as Ling-Temco-Vought did in 1968 and 1969), they are able quickly to raise new capital for investment in promising opportunities. The managerial orientation which led to their conglomerate growth and the staff resources needed to control widely diffused operations may make them peculiarly sensitive to the appearance of such opportunities. And since neither the health of the corporation nor the status of top management is likely to be impaired when one or two operations out of many are abandoned, conglomerates may be in a particularly favorable position to reallocate capital out of declining fields and into existing or wholly new ventures with more attractive growth prospects. Whether this propensity or the sluggishness stressed by Edwards prevails more frequently remains to be elucidated by careful empirical research.

CONCLUSION

To sum up, there are some grounds for apprehension concerning the economic consequences of conglomerate bigness. Yet the links between bigness and deficient performance are tenuous and uncertain, and in the present stage of U. S. industrial development relatively few serious problems can be traced directly to giant size uncomplicated by more conventional market imperfections. For this reason conglomerate bigness carried a relatively low priority on the industrial organization economist's list of public policy problems, at least up to the late 1960s. However, as the trend toward conglomerate bigness accelerates, concern over the issues it raises will appropriately grow apace.

[49]See the characterization of U. S. Steel on p. 77 *supra*.

[50]For two sobering failure stories, see "Litton Down to Earth," *Fortune*, April 1968, pp. 139 ff.; and "Why Rain Fell on 'Automatic' Sprinkler," *Fortune*, May 1, 1969, pp. 88 ff.

Chapter 12

Administered Prices, Efficiency, and Inflation

The debate over administered prices was one of the less distinguished episodes in the history of economic thought. It was attended by much sound and fury, many attacks by critics who had not bothered to study carefully what they were assailing, and considerable jumping to conclusions based upon ill-conceived or faulty analyses. Yet the ferment also brought to light important questions concerning the relationships between market structure, oligopolistic conduct, and macroeconomic performance. It is on these questions that we shall focus in this and the next chapter, digressing only briefly to illustrate how the quest for knowledge can bog down.

THE ORIGINAL CONCEPT

The term "administered prices" first emerged from the pen of Gardiner C. Means during the depths of the Great Depression.[1] Means observed that prices in certain industries fell very little between 1929 and 1933, despite the sharp decline in demand, while other prices (e.g., in agriculture, crude petroleum, and textile products) fell by as much as 60 per cent. This disparity in results he attributed to differences in methods of price formation, which he grouped into two broad categories: administered prices and market prices. Administered prices were defined as prices "set by administrative action and held constant for a period of time," whereas market prices were said to be "made in the market as the result of the interaction of buyers and sellers."[2]

To identify administered prices, Means devised a rough-and-ready test. Taking 747 commodities in the Bureau of Labor Statistics' wholesale price index, he plotted a distribution according to the frequency of recorded price changes during the 1926-1933 period. The distribution turned out to be U-shaped, with one strong mode for items whose price index changed on the average less than one time every 10 months and another for items whose price index changed nearly every month. This bimodal distribution led Means to conclude that "there are two quite different types of prices"—the administered prices which change infrequently, and the market prices observed to change frequently.[3] He noted in addition a positive correlation between the frequency and amplitude of price changes during the depression. The more frequently prices changed during the 1926-1933 period, the more they tended to fall from 1929 to 1932.

Unfortunately, neither of Means' definitional

[1]*Industrial Prices and Their Relative Inflexibility*, a report to the Secretary of Agriculture published as Senate Document No. 13, 74th Congress, 1st session (January 1935). The body of the report is reproduced in Means, *The Corporate Revolution in America* (New York: Crowell-Collier, 1962), pp. 77-96, to which subsequent citations refer.

[2]*Ibid.*, p. 78.

[3]*Ibid.*, p. 80.

approaches is completely satisfactory. The line between setting a price through "administrative action" as opposed to the "interaction of buyers and sellers" in the market is fuzzy. Even if an arbitrary division could be found, the question remains open of why some prices are administratively determined, while others are not. His empirical test suffers from similar problems. For instance, because of peculiarities in the data, his limiting category of prices recorded as changing from 90 to 94 times during the eight-year period necessarily lumped together items whose prices in fact changed roughly 90 times with those whose prices changed daily or even more frequently—i.e., several thousand times or more. If a complete record of price changes could be compiled, the high-frequency tail of Means' distribution would be greatly extended, suppressing the high-frequency mode and hence the empirical dichotomy between administered and market-determined prices.[4] More important, a classification of commodities or industries into administered and market-determined price categories on the basis of observed price change frequencies continues to leave unanswered the fundamental question: Why does the difference arise?

Means did explore the causes of the administered price phenomenon. In essence, he said, administered prices were the result of market power—the discretionary power over prices associated with fewness of sellers, product differentiation, and/or other market imperfections. The structure-conduct nexus was characterized most cogently in a later elaboration of Means' thesis:

> While many factors influence price insensitivity, the dominant factor making for depression insensitivity of prices is the administrative control over prices which results from the relatively small number of concerns dominating particular markets.[5]

However, in other explanations he sowed the seeds of later controversy by choosing terminology which swam against the tide of standard economic usage, by taking pains to avoid a simplistic model relating market power to any single structural feature (such as measured concentration ratios), and by emphasizing that firms might possess pricing discretion too weak to have socially harmful consequences. Many readers, for example, were led astray by his 1935 statement that

> In general, monopolized industries have administered prices, but so also do a great many vigorously competitive industries in which the number of competitors is small. The bulk of the administered prices . . . are in the competitive industries. . . .

preceded by the suggestion that the automobile industry was highly competitive.[6] While auto producers did (and still do) compete vigorously in certain ways, they did not (and do not) engage in conspicuous rivalry on the price dimension, nor could the industry be characterized as either purely or monopolistically competitive, following the Chamberlinian guidelines which had taken the economics profession by storm during the 1930s. Quibbles over what did and what did not represent a competitive or monopolistic industry underlay many barren exchanges in later years of the administered price debate.

Recognizing these terminological problems, we perpetrate no undue violence to the original ideas of Means by asserting that administered prices are a phenomenon uniquely associated with some degree of market power. The precise character of the phenomenon must now be sketched out in greater detail. At least two interpretations exist.

The narrower one traces a causal chain running from market power to inflexibility of prices. It meshes with the theory of oligopoly pricing

---

[4] Cf. Richard Ruggles, "The Nature of Price Flexibility and the Determinants of Relative Price Changes in the Economy," in the National Bureau of Economic Research conference report, *Business Concentration and Price Policy* (Princeton: Princeton University Press, 1955), pp. 450–452, citing an original critique by Tibor Scitovsky. Ruggles observes in addition that the distributions of commodities by *amplitude* (as opposed to frequency) of price change have tended to be unimodal, casting further doubt on Means' dichotomy.

[5] National Resources Committee, *The Structure of the American Economy*, Part I (Washington: 1939), p. 143.

[6] *The Corporate Revolution in America*, pp. 78–79.

developed in Chapters 5 and 6. When oligopolists adopt the pessimistic expectations of the kinked demand curve theory concerning rival reactions to price changes, prices will display greater rigidity than they would in an industry where consciousness of mutual interdependence is lacking. Price stickiness may also arise from respect for the difficulties of preserving oligopolistic industry discipline. Even an accepted price leader, presumably not subject to the kink mentality, recognizes that every decision to lead a change carries some risk of misinterpretation or rejection by rivals with conflicting preferences or views of market conditions. Since poorly coordinated actions threaten an oligopoly's price structure and profits, price changes will be led only in response to significant alterations in cost or demand conditions widely believed to be more than transitory. This sort of consensus is likely to materialize only intermittently, so actual changes will be attempted with corresponding infrequency.

A second, broader interpretation is simply that firms with market power by definition possess discretion over the prices they will charge, which they may choose to exercise in a variety of ways, including some contrasting sharply with the behavior of more competitive industries.[7] When a depression occurs, they may decide for any number of reasons (all presumably related to the achievement of ultimate company goals) not to reduce their prices or to reduce them only slightly, even though prices plummet in atomistically structured markets. This is consistent with the observation that "administered prices" were inflexible during the early 1930s. But the power to maintain prices when business conditions are bad implies the power to make other, conceivably different, choices at other stages of the business cycle. Specifically, such firms have the power and may have the inclination to effect repeated price increases during more prosperous times. This is the post-World War II analogue of the administered prices doctrine: that the prices charged by sellers with

market power tend to be inflexible downward in depressed times, but disconcertingly flexible upward when overall business conditions are healthy and sometimes even when they are not.

Three important substantive issues follow. First, does the bias of oligopolistic industries toward infrequent price adjustment impair the allocative efficiency of the price system by delaying responses to demand shifts? Second, do groups of firms with collective market power contribute to creeping inflation by their pricing policies in prosperous times? And third, do the so-called administered price industries intensify business slumps and retard recovery by pursuing a policy of price inflexibility despite the waning of demand? The first two questions will be taken up in this chapter; the third in Chapter 13.

PRICE RIGIDITY AND ALLOCATIVE EFFICIENCY

Economists from Adam Smith on have stressed the efficacy of a competitive market economy in keeping supplies of goods and services attuned to consumer demands, which seldom remain fixed for any significant length of time. Assuming upward-sloping supply curves (which is usually the case in the short run, though less frequently in the long) and competitive pricing, a demand shift in favor of some commodity generates a two-fold incentive for supplies to rise. The increased price induces firms to push production further into the stage of diminishing marginal returns in the short run, and over a longer stretch of time to invest in additional production capacity. Conversely, a shift in demand away from some commodity induces both short-run and long-run resource withdrawal responses.

When on the other hand price changes are inhibited or delayed due to the exercise of market power, operation of the classical reallocation mechanism might be frustrated. However, it is singularly difficult to reach firm conclusions on this matter. It is clear that the supply responses of administered price industries to a

[7]For a detailed exposition of this view, see Means' testimony in U. S. Senate, Committee on the Judiciary, Subcommittee on Antitrust and Monopoly, Hearings, *Administered Prices*, Part I, "Opening Phase—Economists' Views" (Washington: 1957), pp. 77–84.

shift in demand are normally in the right direction, and they may even approximate in magnitude the responses of competitive industries. By keeping prices rigid over the short run, monopolistic and oligopolistic sellers almost necessarily adopt a policy of flexible output responses, at least to the extent permitted by physical constraints. If anything, the output response is more pronounced than it would be under a flexible price regime. When demand declines, the quantity supplied must be cut back more than it would be if price were reduced to stimulate additional sales, while failure to increase price following a rightward demand shift means that a powerful rationing effect is foregone. Assuming that output responds sufficiently to clear the market, these effects represent distortions relative to what would occur under flexible competitive pricing. Still the problem is complicated by the fact that when monopoly power exists, the pattern of resource allocation may have been distorted away from the optimum in the first place. The output response necessitated by a rigid price policy in the face of demand shifts may lead either nearer to or farther away from the social optimum. As a first approximation, one would expect the higher supply restoring equilibrium after a demand increase coupled with no price rise to be nearer the social optimum, while the obverse will be true when demand shifts to the left. Further complexities intrude when failure to elevate price in response to a demand increase forces producers to ration their supplies on a nonprice basis (e.g., rationing by historical allotment or by queue) because capacity is insufficient to fill all demands at the price maintained. The welfare implications of rationing by queue vs. price rationing are imperfectly understood, nor is it likely that any clear-cut verdict can be reached, at least for consumer goods, without invoking debatable ethical judgments.

Even if we were to conclude, on the basis of inadequate logical support, that the net short-run allocative effects of price rigidity tend on balance to be unfavorable, there may be broader compensating advantages. For one, changing the prices of products sold in elaborately structured, geographically dispersed markets is costly. There are administrative costs, costs of publishing new price lists, costs of disseminating them to customers, and (as any recipient of 'junk' mail knows) costs to wholesalers, retailers, and ultimate consumers of keeping up with a flood of sales literature. Some tradeoff must be struck between minimizing the information transmission cost of change and minimizing the misallocation costs of price inflexibility. It is by no means certain that the balance will always swing toward frequent revision. Second, it is possible for prices to be too responsive, inducing a lagged 'overshooting' reaction from suppliers, which in turn drives the economic system away from rather than toward stable equilibrium following some shock. The cobweb and corn-hog cycles are familiar examples from agricultural economics. Other more general cases can be identified in theory, although their real-world incidence may be rare.[8] Finally, users of intermediate industrial commodities and perhaps even final consumers seem to place a positive value on price stability, apparently because the costs of deciding whether to shift back and forth between substitutes as prices change are substantial, and also because firms desire to avoid the risk of inventory losses due to price fluctuations. The greater stability of synthetic as apposed to natural fiber prices is said to be an important sales advantage for synthetic fiber manufacturers, and the instability of copper prices in comparison to aluminum prices has reportedly diverted some demand permanently away from the red metal.[9]

Unfortunately, our resolution of this tangle

---

[8] See J. M. Henderson and R. E. Quandt, *Microeconomic Theory: A Mathematical Approach* (New York: McGraw-Hill, 1958), pp. 109–123.

[9] Cf. A. D. H. Kaplan, J. B. Dirlam, and R. F. Lanzillotti, *Pricing in Big Business* (Washington: Brookings, 1958), pp. 145, 166, 176, 178, 181, and 272; Jesse W. Markham, *Competition in the Rayon Industry* (Cambridge: Harvard University Press, 1952), p. 109; E. P. Learned and C. C. Ellsworth, *Gasoline Pricing in Ohio* (Boston: Harvard Business School Division of Research, 1959), p. 251; and R. B. Heflebower, "Conscious Parallelism and Administered Prices," in Almarin Phillips, ed., *Perspectives on Antitrust Policy* (Cambridge: Harvard University Press, 1965), pp. 99–100.

must dissatisfy the reader in quest of certainty. Economic theory does not permit us to assert confidently how seriously oligopolistic price rigidity impairs the allocative functioning of the price mechanism, or indeed whether the effects are necessarily adverse. It seems probable, however, that price rigidity over moderate periods of time (e.g., up to a year) in the face of modest demand and cost changes does little incremental harm in the realm of allocative efficiency.

ADMINISTERED PRICES AND INFLATION: THE THEORY

Avoiding inflation—a general increase in the level of prices with no compensating advance in output quality—stands high on the list of economic goals in the United States, as in most industrial nations. Inflation leads to income redistribution effects which, in the words of the President's Council of Economic Advisers, "are always capricious and often cruel," especially for insurance recipients, elderly pensioners, and other persons in the low income brackets.[10] It distorts the structure of prices and, in large doses, may choke off economic development and growth. It also complicates greatly the problem of maintaining balance in international trade and payments, given rigidities in the international monetary system.

During the 1950s, some economists advanced the thesis that oligopolistic and monopolistic industries pursue wage and price policies which contribute to creeping inflation, especially when the economy approaches (but does not quite attain) the full employment level. The hypothesized phenomenon, if true, poses a dilemma for policy makers. Using fiscal and monetary tools, the federal government can keep the economy operating near the full employment level. But if, as full employment is approached, inflation breaks out in the so-called administered price industries and then spreads to other industries, the government may be forced to sacrifice the attainment of either its price stability goal or its

full employment goal. That is, simultaneous satisfaction of both objectives could prove infeasible, given the alleged wage-price behavior of concentrated industries.

Before examining the relevant evidence, we need a conceptual framework. It is customary to speak of two main types of inflation: demand-pull and cost-push. Each has many possible variants, and real-world inflations often exhibit attributes from both types, interacting with and feeding upon one another, so that attempts to force actual cases into a single mold run the risk of misleading as much as they inform. With these caveats in mind, let us survey briefly the principal variants, devoting special attention to the cost-push types, into which administered price inflation falls.[11]

Until the 1950s, demand-pull theories of inflation dominated economic thought, and most recorded inflations conform more closely to the demand-pull model than to any other. To oversimplify, demand-pull inflation is experienced when too much money chases too few goods. In the classical view, this occurs when the stock of money is expanded more rapidly than real output, with no offsetting change in the velocity of monetary circulation, so that the price level P in the 'quantity theory' equation $MV = PQ$ must rise. Or in Keynesian terms, the price level rises when aggregate demand exceeds aggregate supply at the full employment level. The standard illustration of how demand-pull inflation gets underway is the case in which, under full employment conditions, the government attempts to increase defense or public works expenditures using funds borrowed from the central banking system, without withdrawing equivalent purchasing power from the private sector (e.g., by credit restraints or taxation).

Cost-push inflation arises when, under conditions of less than full employment, some group tries to raise its real income by securing higher money income, and other groups successfully defend their prior positions in the real income distribution by winning comparable money in-

---

[10]*Economic Report of the President* (Washington: January 1962), p. 167. See also Martin Bronfenbrenner and F. D. Holzman, "Survey of Inflation Theory," *American Economic Review*, September 1963, especially pp. 646–652.

[11]For a more comprehensive survey, see Bronfenbrenner and Holzman, *op. cit.*

come gains. For the cost-push inflationary effect to take hold, it is necessary in addition that national authorities pursue fiscal and monetary policies which support the contending groups in their money income-raising efforts.

The most important cost-push sub-case is wage-push inflation. Here labor is presumed to exercise the initiative, winning through collective bargaining wage increases in excess of productivity gains despite the persistence of some aggregate unemployment. If employers then pass along their higher labor costs by raising end product prices in an attempt to defend their profit share, inflation follows, among other things nullifying much of the workers' hoped-for real income gains. For labor to initiate this wage-push process, it must possess some market power—usually through a strong union. However, market power in the employers' product markets may facilitate the process in several ways.[12]

First, union bargaining power is apt to be stronger in oligopolistic industries. When sellers are few, it is easier to organize the whole industry, at least within the institutional environment conducive to unionization which has existed in the United States since the 1930s. And when significant barriers to entry exist, as is often the case in industries which retain oligopolistic structures, it is more difficult for new non-union producers to enter and undermine labor's united front. Second, wage increases are more readily passed along to consumers when the product market structure is monopolistic or oligopolistic, especially in the case of firm-by-firm (as compared to industry-wide) collective bargaining. The competitive firm cannot expect a price increase following a wage increase unless most other members of its industry are in a symmetric position with respect to labor cost changes. The firm possessing market power (and particularly one filling a price leadership role)

is better able to exercise pricing initiatives, even if rivals do not reach exactly the same labor bargain, and recognizing this, it may be more willing to yield wage concessions. Third, sellers with market power tend to earn higher profits than competitive producers, and these profits serve as a bargaining target out of which unions strive, alleging 'ability to pay,' to win above-average wage gains.

Thus, power possessed by labor unions interacts with power in sellers' markets to trigger an upward push on wages and costs. Once substantial wage increases have been won in key industries and the prices of industry products have risen, inflationary pressures spread as other unions attempt to emulate the initial example and as all employee groups try to compensate for increased costs of living by demanding still higher incomes.

The business firm analogue of wage-push inflation is profit-push inflation, where producers raise prices in order to increase profit margins, even though there has been no instigating increase in demand or costs. Clear illustrations are hard to find, although one likely case was the steel industry's effort from 1955 on to change its pricing formulas so as to raise its after-tax profit return on stockholders' equity from the time-honored figure of 8 per cent at 80 per cent capacity operation to 12 per cent—ostensibly to generate a higher cash flow for use in anticipated capital modernization programs.[13] Most economists believe that pure profit-push stimuli are less likely to cause significant inflation than are wage-push pressures for three main reasons: because profits constitute a much smaller share than wages in the national income; because the political and social compulsion to emulate a peer group's gain is less potent among business firms than in organized labor; and because the opportunity for making profit-push gains vanishes

---

[12]For various views, see Harold M. Levinson, "Unionism, Concentration, and Wage Changes: Toward a Unified Theory," *Industrial and Labor Relations Review*, January 1967, pp. 198–205; Martin Segal, "Union Wage Impact and Market Structure," *Quarterly Journal of Economics*, February 1964, pp. 96–114; and Albert Rees, "Union Wage Gains and Enterprise Monopoly," in *Essays on Industrial Relations Research* (Ann Arbor: University of Michigan – Wayne State University Institute of Labor and Industrial Relations, 1961), pp. 125–139.

[13]Cf. John M. Blair, "Administered Prices: A Phenomenon in Search of a Theory," *American Economic Review*, May 1959, pp. 442–443; and Charles L. Schultze, "Recent Inflation in the United States," Study Paper No. 1, *Study of Employment, Growth, and Price Levels*, Joint Economic Committee of the U. S. Congress (Washington: September 1959), pp. 92–93.

once price-cost margins have been raised to the profit-maximizing level.[14]

Producers with market power have also been confronted with the charge that, by engaging in full-cost or cost-plus pricing practices, they facilitate the spread of inflation, even when they do not initiate it.[15] Under the standard assumptions of both monopoly and (assuming rising supply functions) competitive short-run profit maximization, an increase in costs (i.e., due to a new wage bargain) normally leads to a rise in price less than the unit cost increase. Part of the higher costs are borne by the firm, and only part by customers. But when full-cost pricing rules are followed for any of the reasons considered in Chapters 6 and 8, an increase in costs can be transmitted entirely to customers in the form of higher product prices.

A hybrid theory synthesizing elements of both the demand-pull and cost-push models has been advanced by Charles L. Schultze.[16] In his schema, unionization makes wages inflexible downward when demand is weak, but flexible upward when the derived demand for labor is strong. Concern for oligopolistic interdependence and cost-plus pricing practices in the product markets combine to make product prices inflexible downward, but flexible upward in response to cost and perhaps also strong demand increases. Now even when the economy as a whole is operating slightly below the full employment level, demand is apt to be outracing capacity in some sectors while growing slowly or declining in others due to changes in tastes, technology, the population age structure, the war-peace balance, etc. Prices will tend to rise in the high demand sectors, partly due to conventional profit-maximizing responses by producers and partly because wage increases required to attract additional labor are passed along to consumers. If prices are generally more rigid downward than upward, these price increases will not be offset by equivalent decreases in sectors experiencing relatively slack demand. As a result, the *average* price level creeps upward. The more pronounced and frequent the intersectoral demand shifts are, the more rapidly this 'ratchet effect' inflationary process proceeds. Furthermore, the inflationary pressures originating in booming sectors tend after a lag to diffuse throughout the economy, as labor unions in the declining sectors seek to match the pattern-setting wage increases of booming sectors, and as the price increases of overheated sectors raise the cost of living to all employment groups, generating further demands for wage increases. The end result is a new and higher price–wage plateau from which additional ratchet effects exert their upward leverage.

In concluding this reader's guide to the principal inflation theories, it is worthwhile repeating that simple, unambiguous classification of actual cases is often difficult or impossible. Elements of several models may co-exist and interact. In particular, no type of cost-push inflation can be sustained unless validated by government policies which maintain adequate aggregate demand. Both union pressures for higher wages and company efforts to secure higher profits can be choked off by recession or persistent underemployment equilibrium of sufficient severity. To quote Schultze, under these circumstances:

> The difference between the cost-push and demand-pull explanations of inflation thus devolves into a debate about the *degree* of unemployment and excess capacity required to break through the strict cost-determined nature of price and wage decisionmaking. This in turn is really a debate about the compatibility of full employment growth with price stability.[17]

---

[14] See Bronfenbrenner and Holzman, *op. cit.*, p. 622.

[15] *Ibid.*, p. 621; Schultze, *op. cit.*, pp. 55–59 and 90–95; Gardner Ackley, "Administered Prices and the Inflationary Process," *American Economic Review*, May 1959, pp. 419–430; and Walter Adams and R. F. Lanzillotti, "The Reality of Administered Prices," in U. S. Senate, Committee on the Judiciary, Subcommittee on Antitrust and Monopoly, *Administered Prices: A Compendium on Public Policy* (Washington: 1963), pp. 15–20.

[16] "Recent Inflation in the United States," especially pp. 46–59 and 95.

[17] *Ibid.*, p. 30. See also Ackley, *op. cit.*; and Abba Lerner, "Sellers' Inflation and Administered Depression," in *Administered Prices: A Compendium on Public Policy*, pp. 199–201. Another way of making this point is to trace out a "Phillips curve" showing the possibilities for trading off inflation and unemployment. The original Phillips curve was proposed in A. W. Phillips, "The Relation between Unemployment and the Rate of Change of Money Wage Rates in the United Kingdom, 1861–1957," *Economica*, November 1958, pp. 283–299.

PRICE MOVEMENTS FOLLOWING WORLD WAR II

The administered price inflation concept arose from observation, not from *a priori* theorizing. To understand the historical circumstances underlying its genesis and to put the problem of cost-push inflation in perspective, it is useful to review briefly the record of price changes during the period following World War II. We shall concentrate on movements in the wholesale price index, summarized in Table 12.1.

The most intense inflation experienced by the United States followed hard on the heels of World War II. Economists agree that it was of the demand-pull variety. Prices had been kept in check throughout most of the war, despite deficit financing policies which were inherently inflationary, by strict price controls combined with quantity rationing. Both sets of controls were relaxed and then terminated in 1945 and 1946,

with a consequent upsurge in prices. As reconversion began, demand for all types of goods soared, partly reflecting pent-up wants not satisfied during the period of wartime shortage, partly because consumers had accumulated vast hoards of liquid and semi-liquid assets, and partly because industry commenced a massive investment program to meet booming demands and to replace equipment which had been allowed to deteriorate during the depressed 1930s. Prices rose rapidly in all sectors, although the inflation tended to be more severe in atomistically structured sectors (such as agriculture) than in the concentrated sectors. In steel, autos, cement, and other fields, oligopolistic producers failed to raise prices sufficiently to bring limited supplies and booming demand into equilibrium, and as a result steel supplies were rationed to customers on the basis of historical patronage quotas, new autos went to customers with close personal ties to dealers or willing to offer the

Table 12.1

Percentage Changes in the U.S. Wholesale Price Index
During Selected Periods: 1945–1968

Period	All Commodities	Manufactured Commodities	Farm Products	Metals and Metal Products	Machinery and Motive Products
January 1945 to June 1948	+53.5	n.a.	+58.0	+54.8	+39.5
June 1948 to June 1949	− 6.2	− 3.8	−17.0	+ 1.1	+ 7.4
June 1949 to June 1951	+17.2	+16.4	+23.1	+20.4	+11.7
June 1951 to December 1952	− 4.8	− 3.5	−16.9	+ 1.1	+ 2.3
December 1952 to June 1958	+ 7.1	+11.4	− 3.6	+20.0	+23.2
June 1958 to December 1964	− 0.4	+ 1.5	−11.2	+ 6.8	+ 3.2
December 1964 to September 1966	+ 6.1	+ 3.3	+17.2	+ 3.5	+ 3.1
September 1966 to December 1968	+ 2.8	+ 3.9	− 5.0	+ 4.1	+ 6.7

Source: U.S. Bureau of Labor Statistics, monthly report, *Wholesale Prices and Price Indexes;* and files of the Council of Economic Advisers.

largest bribes, black markets appeared, and used cars (traded in a fairly competitive market) were sold at prices exceeding the list prices of new cars.

The postwar boom peaked in mid-1948 and a mild recession followed in 1949, pulling the general price level down slightly. However, prices in the relatively concentrated metals, metal products, machinery, and transportation equipment sectors continued to rise. This forerunner of things to come was soon overlooked as the economy recovered in 1950 and then hurtled into the Korean war boom. Prices increased rapidly in all sectors as defense expenditures were accelerated and panic buying broke out. The consensus again holds the Korean inflation to have been predominantly of the classic demand-pull variety. Price controls initiated early in 1951, stabilization of the conflict at the 38th parallel in mid 1951, and increases in capacity responding to the pull of demand reversed the trend in late 1951, but prices continued to rise slowly in the metals and machinery sectors.

It was during the first extended period of postwar 'normalcy' beginning in 1952 and 1953 that unfamiliar happenings on the price front became noticeable. Despite the gradual accumulation of excess capacity in many areas of manufacturing industry and a progression toward the highest annual unemployment rates experienced since the 1930s—both suggesting the absence of general, persistent demand-pull influences— prices crept upward steadily, with a marked surge from 1955 to 1958. The typically oligopolistic metals, metal products, machinery, and transportation equipment sectors were the leaders in this 'new inflation,' registering price index gains exceeding 20 per cent on the average while farm product prices actually declined. The steel industry's role was particularly spectacular. It raised prices year after year, culminating its performance with a major increase only a few months after the economy began emerging from the 1957–1958 recession, while steel plants were operating at less than two thirds of rated capacity.

This inflationary trend, in apparent defiance of traditional demand-pull prerequisites, precipitated two full-scale congressional investigations and much independent stock-taking by economists. Several explanations emerged. One was Schultze's ratchet-effect theory. The economy did seem to experience unusually rapid changes in the composition of demand between 1955 and 1957.[18] The machinery industry, a leader in the inflationary spiral, enjoyed a sustained demand shift in its favor, while both steel and autos experienced surges followed by even sharper declines.

Still this could not be a complete explanation, since prices in industries such as steel and autos continued to rise long after favorable demand conditions had waned. Attention focused on the possibility that those industries were arbitrarily exercising their market power to raise prices and profits, in the process spreading the virus of inflation to other sectors. If this were so, however, why were prices raised in a series of steps extending over several years? Why hadn't they been raised to the joint profit-maximizing level in one fell swoop and kept there, as one might expect on the basis of orthodox theory?[19] An answer suggested by J. K. Galbraith was that when demand curves are shifting to the right, oligopolists adapt only in "deliberate and discrete steps," leaving at any moment in time "a quantum of unliquidated monopoly gains" which was fully exploited only during the 1955–1958 period.[20] In an elaboration, M. A. Adelman proposed that oligopolists, uncertain of the exact price level at which profits are maximized and fearful that industry discipline will be disrupted if price increases are inadvertently carried beyond the profit-maximizing point, move toward

[18]Cf. Schultze, *op. cit.*, pp. 9–15 and 97–121; W. G. Bowen and S. H. Masters. "Shifts in the Composition of Demand and the Inflation Problem," *American Economic Review*, December 1964, pp. 975–981; and (for a more critical view) Keith Hancock, "Shifts in Demand and the Inflation Problem: Comment," *American Economic Review*, June 1966, pp. 517–521.

[19]See George J. Stigler, "Administered Prices and Oligopolistic Inflation," *Journal of Business*, January 1962, p. 8.

[20]See the Senate Antitrust and Monopoly Subcommittee Hearings, *Administered Prices*, Part I, "Opening Phase —Economists' Views," p. 65.

that level only in a sequence of cautious, probing steps. This point was not reached in the steel industry until 1958, he argued.[21] Both conjectures appear capable of explaining the sluggish price responses of concentrated industries during the late 1940s as well as the continuing increases of the 1950s, and both are consistent with the theoretical argument developed in Chapters 5 and 6 above. Perhaps equally relevant is the fact that in autos and steel, three-year wage contracts with liberal delayed automatic increase provisions were concluded in 1955 and 1956, while demand remained fairly robust. These led to strong cost-push pressures on prices in 1957 and 1958, when demand had stagnated.

After 1958, administered price inflation receded to the status of a potential rather than an actual problem. Between 1958 and 1964 the overall wholesale price index showed no significant change, and in the previously troublesome metals and machinery sectors the changes were modest, though still in a positive direction. Yet most analysts believe this price stability was achieved only by accepting an even more onerous burden: an economy unable to operate at its full potential. Unemployment rates hovered between 6.7 and 5.2 per cent through the 1958–1964 period, leaving sufficient slack to keep inflationary pressures in a dormant state. Two other influences may have helped to hold cost-push propensities in check. Shifts in the composition of demand appear to have been more moderate than during the mid 1950s, limiting the opportunities for ratchet-effect inflation.[22] Also, Presidents Kennedy and Johnson brought their powers of persuasion to bear on the steel, aluminum, auto, and other administered price industries in an attempt to discourage inflationary price and wage increases.

In 1965 the economy began to move nearer the full employment level, at first as a result of tax reductions and then from heightened government spending on the Vietnam war and welfare programs. The wholesale price index moved upward again at a disturbing pace, apparently more because of demand-pull influences related to the government's stimulative fiscal policies and ratchet effects due to structural imbalance than to cost-push factors. During the first 21 months of the inflation price increases were greater in such competitively structured sectors as farm products and lumber, but in 1967 and 1968 the concentrated industries accelerated their own moves on the price and wage front. The most striking inflationary developments of this period, however, fell outside the coverage of Table 12.1. Medical care prices rose by 18 per cent between 1965 and 1968 in response to the increased demand (and decreased elasticity of demand) attributable to new federal and state health insurance programs. Prices of nonmedical services climbed nearly as rapidly due to a combination of rising demand and low productivity growth. Demand-pull pressures must bear most of the blame for inflation in these areas, although the pricing power possessed by individual physicians, hospitals, and service tradesmen undoubtedly played a contributory role.

Overall, the inflation experienced during the Vietnam war boom appears to have been a good deal more complex than that of earlier periods. One further aspect may be of special interest. Pricing restraint in the administered price industries was less evident than it was following World War II and during the Korean war. It will be interesting to see whether those industries lead the pace of price increases in the less turbulent years which will undoubtedly follow, or whether they behave unexceptionally because they have less catching up to accomplish.

TESTS OF THE ADMINISTERED PRICE INFLATION HYPOTHESIS

A feature distinguishing economics from the other social sciences is its concern with variables which are eminently quantifiable: prices, costs, outputs, and profits. Presumably, it should be possible to test the assertion that structural characteristics associated with administered price

---

[21]"Steel, Administered Prices, and Inflation," *Quarterly Journal of Economics*, February 1961, pp. 16–40. See also the comment by W. S. Gramm in the *Quarterly Journal of Economics*, May 1962, pp. 320–327.

[22]Bowen and Masters, *op. cit.*, pp. 980–981; and Hancock, *loc. cit.*

industries lead to inflationary pricing behavior. Most of the administered price literature in fact pursues an empirical, quantitative course.

Nevertheless, the testing job is far from simple. There are several well-known limitations in the data most frequently used to measure price levels and price changes—the Bureau of Labor Statistics wholesale price index (WPI). Quality changes are reflected only imperfectly by the index. The size of the samples taken by the Bureau of Labor Statistics leaves a good deal to be desired.[23] But most important of all, the *list* or *quoted* prices reported in the WPI are not always a faithful representation of what is actually going on, because many sales entail unreported discounts, secret concessions, advertising allowances, the supply of free goods, etc. Comparisons of oligopolistic with atomistic industry pricing behavior over the business cycle may be subject to persistent biases, since oligopolists are more inclined to make secret price concessions when business conditions are unfavorable.[24] In response to these objections, economists defending the use of the WPI for quantitative studies have emphasized two points. First, there simply are no better price statistics available. Second, despite their recognized limitations, quoted prices constitute the foundation of the price structure, and deviations of actual from quoted prices appear to be small on the average, so that gross differences in pricing behavior between industry groups are not obscured through use of the BLS index.[25]

A second pitfall involves stating the administered price hypothesis in testable form. As we have seen, Means held that administered prices were a phenomenon of market power. But he judiciously avoided linking the power to administer prices to any measurable structural variable, such as the four-firm concentration ratio. This left open the problem of distinguishing administered from market price industries in

testing the hypothesis that administered price industries exhibit different pricing behavior. Means' original approach—identifying administered price industries by the observed rigidity of their prices during the 1926–1933 period—is circular, since the distinguishing characteristic is the phenomenon to be tested. Despite Means' objections, investigators have been forced to test not the broad conjecture, "Market power leads to prices rigid downward and flexible upward," but the narrower and more concrete hypothesis, "The more concentrated an industy is, as reflected by its four-firm concentration ratio, the more its prices will tend to be inflexible downward and flexible upward."

OBSERVED PRICING RELATIONSHIPS DURING THE 1930S

There have been several studies of the relationship between concentration and price trends during the Great Depression. Concern in these efforts was with the alleged failure of prices to fall during the 1929–1933 deflation—the depression analogue of inflation.

One analysis was directed by Means.[26] Because of his doubts about the validity of concentration ratios as measures of market power, Means excluded from his original data set all industries producing primarily for local or regional markets and those whose products were not homogeneous. He also deleted industries with high nonmanufactured raw material input ratios (since their costs were heavily dependent upon developments in markets beyond their control) and those for which reliable price data were unavailable. Using these criteria, his final sample was reduced from 282 to only 37 manufacturing industries. For these 37, the correlation between 1929–1933 price changes and concentration turned out to be $+0.385$. The more concentrated an industry was, the less its price tended to fall during the depression. Unfortunately, the

[23]Cf. Stigler, *op. cit.*, pp. 4–5.

[24]*Ibid.*, pp. 5–8; E. S. Mason, *Economic Concentration and the Monopoly Problem* (Cambridge: Harvard University Press, 1957), p. 120; and Ruggles, *op. cit.*, pp. 451–453.

[25]Adams and Lanzillotti, *op. cit.*, pp. 6–10; and John M. Blair, "Means, Thorp, and Neal on Price Inflexibility," *Review of Economics and Statistics*, November 1956, pp. 427–430.

[26]National Resources Committee, *The Structure of the American Economy*, Part I, pp. 138–145.

results of this analysis are no better than the analyst's ability to make valid exclusion decisions, for when additional observations thrown out by Means are included, the correlation coefficient declines.[27] And on this ground, as well as over narrower technical issues, the Means study was sharply criticized.

An opposite tack was steered by W. F. Crowder and W. L. Thorp in a study for the Temporary National Economic Committee.[28] Without trying to exclude or include observations on the basis of market definition adequacy or data reliability criteria, they correlated a synthetic index of 1929–1933 realized price changes (derived from census data on sales volume and physical volume) with concentration ratios for 407 supposedly representative manufacturing product lines. They found no perceptible correlation. This study was criticized both for technical deficiencies in its price change index and its indiscriminate sampling approach.[29] When 190 product lines were deleted from the Crowder-Thorp sample because they failed to satisfy Means' inclusion criteria, a statistically significant positive correlation of 0.178 was obtained for the remaining 217 observations.[30] This is hardly strong, but it is also not negligible, suggesting that some relationship between price flexibility and concentration did exist among the welter of other factors affecting prices during the early 1930s.

Other analyses of depression pricing behavior, among which one by Alfred C. Neal is the best-known, approached the problem in still another way.[31] Neal stressed the common-sense notion that industries whose input costs fall sharply

should reduce their prices more than industries experiencing smaller cost declines, other things (such as market power) being held equal. To test this supposition, he collected data on input utilization and input price changes, from which he computed indices of *expected price changes* for 106 manufacturing industries, assuming that prices would change by the same absolute amount as input costs per unit of output. This expected price change index was highly correlated with actual price changes, the simple correlation coefficient being 0.85 for 1929–1931 and 0.92 for 1929–1933. Neal concluded that "amplitude of price decline in depression is for the most part explained . . . by amplitude of direct cost decline, a matter over which particular industries have little if any discretion."[32] On the strength of this and other evidence, he rejected Means' assertion that market power was the dominant factor affecting depression price responses. Further analysis showed, however, that the concentrated industries in Neal's sample experienced a higher ratio of actual to expected prices, along with smaller declines in the margin of overhead plus profits, than did the more atomistic industries. Neal's work therefore affords the important insight that market power makes more difference with respect to cyclical patterns of price–cost margins than with respect to price per se. Although Neal did not stress the point, it follows that variations in cost conditions add a great deal of 'noise' to analyses of the relationship between price index changes and concentration, so that one should not really expect to find a strong

[27]Jules Backman, "Economic Concentration and Price Inflexibility," *Review of Economics and Statistics*, November 1958, pp. 399–400.

[28]U. S. Temporary National Economic Committee, Investigation of Concentration of Economic Power, Monograph No. 27, *The Structure of Industry* (Washington: 1941), pp. 350–365.

[29]Cf. Blair, "Means, Thorp, and Neal on Price Inflexibility," pp. 430–434.

[30]See Backman, *op. cit.*, p. 404.

[31]*Industrial Concentration and Price Inflexibility* (Washington: American Council on Public Affairs, 1942), especially pp. 90–140. For a critical view, see Blair, "Means, Thorp, and Neal on Price Inflexibility," pp. 434–435. Other studies similar to Neal's include J. T. Dunlop, "Price Flexibility and the Degree of Monopoly," *Quarterly Journal of Economics*, August 1939, pp. 522–533; Ruggles, *op. cit.*, pp. 464–487; and (concerning the postwar period) W. J. Yordon, Jr., "Industrial Concentration and Price Flexibility in Inflation," *Review of Economics and Statistics*, August 1961, pp. 287–394. For a comparison of pricing behavior during the 1890–1897 and 1929–1933 depressions, see John M. Blair, "Economic Concentration and Depression Price Rigidity," *American Economic Review*, May 1955, pp. 566–582.

[32]*Op. cit.*, pp. 124–125.

correlation between the two.[33] Even a weak positive correlation might be indicative of significantly different pricing patterns between concentrated as opposed to unconcentrated industries, assuming that cost changes and concentration are not systematically but spuriously related.

There the matter stood as World War II began. To sum up, it seems fairly clear that concentrated industries did exhibit somewhat less deflationary pricing behavior during the early 1930s, although direct relationships between market power and price were obscured by variations in other variables with a more potent impact on price. The main effect of market power was to minimize downward deviations in that relatively small fraction of price representing profit margins.

CONCENTRATION AND THE POSTWAR INFLATION

Following World War II, attention turned from deflation to inflation. That there existed some relationship between market structure and inflation was suggested by Harold M. Levinson, who found in an analysis of 16 two-digit manufacturing industry groups a positive correlation between year-to-year wholesale price index changes and weighted average concentration ratios in eight periods out of eleven between 1947 and 1958.[34]

A more ambitious study of the 1953–1959 inflation was undertaken by H. J. DePodwin and R. T. Selden.[35] Selden had previously published a paper attributing the observed price level increase to demand-pull influences,[36] and in their joint contribution the authors set out to debunk the claims of the administered price theory proponents. Given this preconception, they naturally succeeded. They constructed 1953–1959 wholesale price change indices for 322 manufactured product groups on which comparable data were available. Simple correlations of + 0.12 between unweighted price changes and four-firm concentration ratios, and + 0.30 between sales-weighted indices and concentration were obtained. These are not very strong, as one might have anticipated from the previous discussion of Neal's results, but the correlation coefficients do differ significantly from zero at the 95 per cent confidence level commonly applied in statistical investigations. Still because the correlations were modest, DePodwin and Selden concluded that "there seems to be no indication that administered prices, as measured by degree of industrial concentration, increased appreciably more in the 1953–1959 period than prices determined under supposedly more competitive conditions," and that "it is time to put the administrative inflation hypothesis to rest."[37]

There were, however, some hitches, as Gardiner Means pointed out in a devastating critique which first appeared as a government document, since it had been rejected by the journal publishing the DePodwin-Selden article.[38] His discussion of biases in the sample and in the measurement of concentration need not detain us. Much more important, Means observed that if the DePodwin-Selden sales-weighted regression equations are used as best estimate predictors of the relationship between concentration and inflation, one finds that prices would not have risen at all on the average in industries with a four-firm concentration ratio approaching zero, while they would have risen by 20 per cent between 1953 and 1959 in industries dominated completely by four or fewer firms. Thus, the DePodwin–Selden results in fact supported the

[33]Another statistical problem in the same vein should be noted. When concentration ratios are used as a surrogate index of market power (the 'true' independent variable), and when errors introduced by using the former to measure the latter are random, the observed correlation will tend to *understate* the true correlation between price changes and market power. See J. Johnston, *Econometric Methods* (New York: McGraw-Hill, 1963), pp. 148–150.

[34]"Postwar Movement of Prices and Wages in Manufacturing Industries," Study Paper No. 21, *Study of Employment, Growth, and Price Levels*, Joint Economic Committee of the U. S. Congress (Washington: 1960), p. 15.

[35]"Business Pricing Policies and Inflation," *Journal of Political Economy*, April 1963, pp. 116–127.

[36]"Cost-Push vs. Demand-Pull Inflation: 1955–57," *Journal of Political Economy*, February 1959, pp. 1–20.

[37]DePodwin and Selden, *op. cit.*, pp. 123 and 126.

[38]"Business Pricing Policies and Inflation: A Comment," in U. S. Senate, Committee on the Judiciary, Subcommittee on Antitrust and Monopoly, Hearings, *Economic Concentration*, Part I (Washington: 1964), pp. 489–497.

original Means conjecture, instead of refuting it.

All the pre- and postwar studies considered thus far employed only the most humble of statistical methods. It remained for Leonard W. Weiss to bring heavy artillery into the breach.[39] Using a sample of 81 four-digit manufacturing industries for which he could get data, Weiss analyzed through multiple regression techniques the relationship between unweighted 1953–1959 price increases and concentration, taking into account as additional independent variables output changes, changes in materials cost per unit of output, changes in unit labor costs, changes in labor productivity (expressed as output per man hour input), and changes in wages. He found that prices had indeed risen more rapidly in the more concentrated industries after the influence of all but the wage change variable was taken into account, and that this relationship had been blurred in the DePodwin–Selden analysis by fluctuations in the excluded cost and output variables. He observed furthermore that concentration and changes in wage rates were highly correlated (with a correlation coefficient of $+ 0.57$), and that the independent effect of concentration was much weaker but still positive when the wage rate change variable was introduced into his regression equations. From this latter result he inferred that "the main occasion (excuse) for increases in margins in concentrated industries in the 1950's was wage-rate increases and that price increases which accompanied these wage increases more than covered the increase in unit labor costs."[40]

One additional result is of considerable importance. Weiss repeated his analysis using data on price, cost, and output changes between 1959 and 1963. For this later period he found that the partial correlation between concentration and price increases had turned negative, but was statistically insignificant. Given this striking difference between periods, Weiss concluded (no doubt correctly) that the administered price inflation of the mid 1950s was a temporary phenomenon not sustained during the early 1960s.

From what we have seen thus far, two explanations of manufactured product pricing behavior over the entire 1953–1963 period remain open. Either the concentrated industries had by 1959 compensated completely for their sluggishness in raising prices during the immediate postwar period, so that on the average no further increases in profit margins were profitable; or they were inhibited from making further gains during the early 1960s by the weapons of persuasion brought to bear by Presidents Kennedy and Johnson. Since application of the Presidential wage-price guideposts was less than a smashing success, the 'catching-up' hypothesis appears more nearly to approximate the truth.[41] If so, profit-push tendencies linked with market power must play only a minor role in explanations of sustained inflation, and over the long run one might expect the sticky profit margin performance of concentrated industries during demand-pull inflation and their aggressive performance following periods of high demand to balance out. However, judgment on the *total* inflationary impact of concentrated industries must be deferred until the relationship between cost changes and concentration is explored.

INFLATIONARY BEHAVIOR IN PARTICULAR INDUSTRIES

Throughout the long debate over administered prices, Gardiner Means continued to argue that his thesis related more to the behavior of specific large industries with clear-cut market power and a significant influence on the national economy than to statistically discernible patterns spanning the whole spectrum of manufacturing industries, large and small. Certain studies of administered pricing have pursued this more selective, qualitative approach.

The group singled out most frequently as a prime villain of administered price inflation was

[39]L. W. Weiss, "Business Pricing Policies and Inflation Reconsidered," *Journal of Political Economy*, April 1966, pp. 177–187.

[40]*Ibid.*, p. 182.

[41]The 'guideposts' approach will be examined further in Chapter 18.

the steel industry.[42] As we have seen earlier, during the 1950s steel makers apparently changed their pricing formulas so as to command higher profit returns at any given level of capacity utilization. In addition to this profit-push, steel companies granted wage increases well in excess of both nationwide average wage rate changes and steel worker productivity gains. These cost and profit margin increases were transmitted to steel users in the form of exceptionally rapid price increases, despite the existence of substantial excess steel-making capacity during the latter half of the 1950s. Between 1953 and 1958 steel prices rose by roughly 34 per cent, while the overall wholesale price index rose by only 8 per cent. One result was an increase in steel imports from 1 per cent of total U. S. consumption in 1955 to 11 per cent in 1965, causing a direct adverse incremental impact on the U. S. balance of payments of $1.3 billion. And since steel is a basic raw material for many manufactured goods, the increases in its price constituted cost increases to many other industries, with an undoubted effect on the prices charged for the end products of those industries. Using an input-output table of the American economy to estimate the secondary effects of steel price increases on the costs and prices of products incorporating steel as a raw material, Otto Eckstein and Gary Fromm concluded that the wholesale price index would have risen by 40 per cent less over the 1947–1958 period had steel prices risen no more rapidly than the wholesale prices of all other goods.[43]

In a broader study, Jesse Markham compared the cyclical and secular pricing behavior of nine important concentrated industries from 1953 through 1959 with that of four major atomistically structured industries.[44] He found that only two of the concentrated industries—steel and autos— exhibited pricing patterns patently

inconsistent with supply and demand movements, with prices remaining constant or even rising during severe recessions as well as in boom periods. In four other concentrated industries (cigarettes, aluminum, glass containers, and tin cans) prices proved to be more flexible upward than downward, but price increases at least occurred only in response to input cost increases or during times of heavy demand pressure upon capacity. In the three remaining concentrated industries (synthetic fibers, petroleum refining, and meat packing) price movements were similar to those in the four relatively competitive industries (milled flour, mixed fertilizer, broadwoven cotton, and paperboard boxes). In view of these inter-industry differences, Markham concluded that the administered price problem is "particular rather than general." Oligopolists *may* disregard short-run demand influences, but they do not necessarily do so.

This conclusion is compatible with the results of the statistical analyses examined earlier. The pricing decisions of oligopolists are certainly influenced by both cost and demand considerations, and relatively few industries attempt or are able to sustain pricing decisions which swim against cost and demand tides. Still some may and do. The conjunction of conventional behavior by the many with abnormal behavior by the few helps explain both the positive correlation between inflationary price increases and concentration in the 1950s and for the weakness of that correlation. In other words, there must be something to the administered price inflation hypothesis, but it by no means explains everything.

CONCENTRATION AND WAGE-PUSH INFLATION

The question remains whether oligopolistic and monopolistic industries contribute dispro-

---

[42]See, for example, Gardiner Means, *Pricing Power and the Public Interest* (New York: Harper, 1962); Walter Adams and Joel B. Dirlam, "Steel Imports and Vertical Oligopoly Power," *American Economic Review*, September 1964, pp. 626–655; and the series of hearings on administered prices in the steel industry conducted by the Senate Subcommittee on Antitrust and Monopoly in 1957.

[43]"Steel and the Postwar Inflation," Study Paper No. 2, *Study of Employment, Growth, and Price Levels,* Joint Economic Committee of the U. S. Congress (Washington: 1959), pp. 1–38. For a pertinent but far from damning criticism, see Bronfenbrenner and Holzman, *op. cit.,* pp. 636–637.

[44]"Administered Prices and the Recent Inflation," in the Commission on Money and Credit compendium, *Inflation, Growth, and Employment* (Englewood Cliffs: Prentice-Hall, 1964), pp. 144–173.

portionately to cost-push inflation through their allegedly greater willingness and ability to yield large wage concessions, which then form a pattern for matching wage increases in other industries. The theoretical possibilities have been outlined earlier: Oligopolists may prove a softer touch in bargaining because of confidence in their ability to pass higher labor costs on to consumers, because their high profits whet the appetites of workers for large wage gains, and because the very compactness of an oligopolistic sellers' group facilitates union solidarity.

The determinants of wage levels and wage increases have been a perennial focus of statistical studies.[45] One would naturally expect labor supply and demand conditions to affect wage gains—a proposition which receives considerable empirical support. The higher the unemployment rate is, either in the economy as a whole or in particular industries, the lower the rate of increase in wages tends to be. Some studies have shown too that wage increase rates are positively correlated with employer profits. This result might at first glance appear to support the hypothesis that labor is better able to make wage gains when a pool of monopolistic profits is waiting to be tapped. However, it is also possible that high profits merely reflect strong demand, and that the true chain of causality runs from the pull of demand through high profits to increased demand for labor to wage gains. To isolate the contribution of monopoly and oligopoly elements, therefore, it is essential to introduce an explicit measure of market power, such as the concentration ratio.

Several such analyses have been reported. In J. W. Garbarino's study of 1923–1940 wage changes in 34 narrowly-defined manufacturing industries, the rank correlation between concentration and wage increases turned out to be +0.67.[46] However, when David Schwartzman recast Garbarino's data series into four coherent time periods, inconsistencies emerged. The correlations for 1921–1923 and 1923–1929 were only +0.02 and −0.02 respectively, while during 1929–1933 and 1933–1937 the correlations soared to +0.51 and +0.45.[47] Schwartzman attributed this evident behavioral change to the rapid spread of unionization in some of the most concentrated industries during the 1930s—a point to which we shall return—although it is also possible that concentrated industries are relatively more generous as employers when business is depressed. (Only in 1921 did unemployment rates during the 1920s even approach those of the 1930s.)

Turning to the period following World War II, we recall that Weiss found a +0.57 correlation between 1953–1959 wage rate increases and four-firm concentration ratios in his sample of 81 four-digit manufacturing industries.[48] Wage behavior in more finely divided segments of the postwar period was analyzed at a more aggregated level by Levinson and Bowen. Using data on 19 two-digit manufacturing industries, Levinson discovered a persistent positive correlation between year-to-year wage changes and an index of seller concentration for all 11 one-year intervals between 1947 and 1958, with much stronger correlations after 1952 than before.[49]

[45]For surveys of the relevant literature, see Bronfenbrenner and Holzman, *op. cit.,* pp. 617 and 630–635; and H. G. Lewis, *Unionism and Relative Wages in the United States* (Chicago: University of Chicago Press, 1963), especially pp. 155–181.

[46]"A Theory of Interindustry Wage Structure Variation," *Quarterly Journal of Economics,* May 1950, pp. 282–305.

[47]"Monopoly and Wages," *Canadian Journal of Economics and Political Science,* August 1960, pp. 428–438. Schwartzman also provides his own analysis of the wage–concentration relationship, comparing 1954 wage *levels* in Canadian vs. American industries of similar and differing degrees of concentration. He found no significant international wage structure differences as a function of differences in concentration. See also Lewis, *op. cit.,* pp. 157–159.

[48]Cf. p. 297 *supra.* For similar results from a different sample, see L. W. Weiss, "Average Concentration Ratios and Industrial Performance," *Journal of Industrial Economics,* July 1963, pp. 237–253.

[49]"Postwar Movement of Prices and Wages in Manufacturing Industries," pp. 3–13. Covering the same sample for the years 1958 through 1966, Elizabeth Rothman in an unpublished paper found a continuation of the previous tendencies. The correlations between concentration and year-to-year wage changes were 0.33 for 1958–1959, 0.33 for 1959–1960, 0.42 for 1960–1961, 0.58 for 1961–1962, 0.27 for 1962–1963, −0.39 for 1963–1964, 0.59 for 1964–1965, and 0.08 for 1965–1966. Seven of the eight partial correlations between concentration and annual wage changes were positive, after taking into account the extent of unionization.

Bowen, grouping virtually identical data for 1947–1959 into six sub-periods corresponding to distinct phases of the business cycle, obtained results different in detail but not in broad substance.[50] For three sub-periods (two characterized by recession and one by recovery), the simple correlation between wage increases and concentration was strongly positive; for three others (two recoveries and one recession) it was weakly negative. On the other hand, Eckstein and Wilson found the partial correlation between wage changes and concentration to be negligible after they grouped their 1948–1960 data into five 'wage round' periods allowing time for pattern-setting wage increases to diffuse to other industries, and after taking into account as additional variables industry profitability and the degree of unionization.[51]

By way of preliminary generalization, the dominant tendency during the 1930s and after the post World War II and Korean war booms seems to have been for wages to increase more rapidly in concentrated than in unconcentrated industries. However, the relationship is not completely stable; it breaks down during certain periods, especially under boom conditions.

Several further complications must be considered before final conclusions can be drawn. For one, labor union strength and seller concentration have been positively associated since industrial unions expanded their representation rapidly following enactment of the National Industrial Recovery Act in 1933 and the National Labor Relations Act in 1935. Bowen found a +0.46 correlation between the percentage of workers employed in manufacturing establishments operating under collective bargaining agreements and weighted average concentration ratios for the 19 industry groups comprising his sample.[52] Given this association, is it possible that the predominantly positive correlations between wage increases and concentration are

spurious, and that the true causal chain runs from union power (which happens to be associated with concentration) to wage increases?

One way to approach this question is to examine the influence on wage level changes of both concentration and extent of unionization as separate independent variables through multiple regression analysis. H. Gregg Lewis proposed in addition that the analysis include a variable reflecting the interaction of concentration with unionization, such as the product of the concentration and unionization variables. Lewis applied this technique to the Garbarino and Bowen-Levinson wage change data.[53] However, his interpretation of the interaction variable's meaning is misleading and his results are presented in such a way as to preclude valid reinterpretation. Therefore, the analyses were recomputed by the present author. For the Garbarino sample, and using only 32 industries on which consistent data were available, the resulting regression equation was:

$$\Delta W = -2.02 + 1.04\ C + .24\ U - .0098\ C \cdot U;$$
$$\quad\quad\quad (.33)\quad\quad (.23)\quad\quad (.0057)$$

where ΔW is the percentage change in wages between 1923 and 1940, C is the 1935 four-firm concentration ratio, and U is an estimate of the percentage of the work force unionized in 1940. Standard errors of the regression coefficients are given in parentheses. The regression equation for the Bowen-Levinson data on 1948–1958 wage changes in 19 two-digit manufacturing industries was:

$$\Delta W = 3.82 + .95\ C + .73\ U - .0108\ C \cdot U.$$
$$\quad\quad (.80)\quad\quad (.44)\quad\quad (.0124)$$

For both data sets, the unionization and concentration coefficients are positive and the interaction term coefficients negative, although most of the coefficients (except the Garbarino con-

---

[50]W. G. Bowen, *Wage Behavior in the Postwar Period* (Princeton: Princeton University Industrial Relations Section, 1960), pp. 55–84. See also Bruce T. Allen, "Market Concentration and Wage Increases: U. S. Manufacturing, 1947–1964," *Industrial and Labor Relations Review*, April 1968, pp. 353–365.

[51]Otto Eckstein and Thomas A. Wilson, "The Determination of Money Wages in American Industry," *Quarterly Journal of Economics*, August 1962, pp. 379–414, especially p. 400. See also the comment by Timothy McGuire and Leonard Rapping in the *Quarterly Journal of Economics*, November 1967, pp. 684–694.

[52]*Wage Behavior in the Postwar Period*, p. 70.

[53]*Unionism and Relative Wages in the United States*, pp. 159–161 and 177–178.

centration coefficient) are not significantly different from zero at the 95 per cent level of statistical confidence.[54]

That the interaction term coefficients are negative does not mean that wage changes necessarily tend to be smaller with increased concentration, holding unionization constant. To visualize the net effect of the interacting variables, it is helpful to examine a two-way table of wage changes predicted by the regression equations for the highest and lowest observed values of the independent variables. For the Garbarino 1923–1940 data, the predictions are as follows:

		Percentage of Work Force Unionized	
		20	90
Four-firm Concentration Ratio	5	+ 7.1%	+20.7%
	81	+71.0%	+32.4%

The Bowen-Levinson regression equation for 1948–1958 yields the following percentage wage change predictions:

		Extent of Work Force Unionization*	
		30	90
Four-firm Concentration Ratio	10	+32.1%	+69.3%
	76	+73.4%	+68.2%

*Specifically, the percentage of workers employed in establishments in which a majority of the workers were covered by collective bargaining agreements.

For industries which were not heavily unionized, wage gains increased unambiguously with higher concentration. For those which were strongly unionized, the concentration effect was positive in the prewar period but negligible in the 1948–1958 period. Unionization seems to be conducive to rapid wage increases in industries of low seller concentration, but exerts a surprisingly negative effect in highly concentrated industries.

On the strength of these findings, it appears reasonable to infer tentatively that there existed a distinct, independent positive relationship between concentration and rates of wage increase, at least for manufacturing industry during the periods covered by the regression analyses, despite the fact that concentration was correlated with unionization, which also had an impact on wage gains.[55]

Moving now to a second complication, we note that all the tests discussed thus far dealt with changes in wage rates over time, and not with the *level* of wages at some moment in time. In view of the predominantly positive correlations between wage increases and concentration reported by Garbarino, Levinson, and Bowen, we might expect employees of concentrated industries to enjoy an increasing *wage level* differential advantage over workers in atomistically structured industries. Yet as M. W. Reder has objected, such a trend is far from evident.[56] One possible explanation is that the differential emerging during the 1930s was whittled away when labor markets were extremely tight during World War II and immediately thereafter. When Lewis related 1940–1947 wage changes in Garbarino's sample of industries to 1935 concentration ratios, the rank correlation was

[54]The standard errors are high mainly because of harmful multicollinearity. Addition of the interaction variables causes an explosion of the standard errors; e.g., the concentration coefficient's standard error increased by 2.6 times in the Garbarino regression and by 5.4 times in the Bowen-Levinson regression. When the interaction terms are deleted, the concentration coefficients are significantly different from zero at the 95 per cent level in both cases.

[55]This relationship may hold *only* for manufacturing industry, for it is clear that in other sectors of the economy some of the most rapid rates of wage increase occurred in relatively unconcentrated industries such as trucking, construction, longshoring, and bituminous coal mining. Harold Levinson attempts to explain this disparity by arguing that union power is most readily maintained in manufacturing when seller concentration is high, whereas in the service and construction industries, spatial isolation of the product and labor markets is equally conducive to strong unionization. In this he implies that the main determinant of wage gains is union power, rather than power in the product market as reflected by concentration ratios. Cf. "Unionism, Concentration, and Wage Changes: Toward a Unified Theory," pp. 201–203. See also Martin Segal, "Union Wage Impact and Market Structure," *Quraterly Journal of Economics,* February 1964, pp. 100–111.

[56]M. W. Reder, "Wage Differentials: Theory and Measurement," in the National Bureau of Economic Research conference report, *Aspects of Labor Economics* (Princeton: Princeton Unversity Press, 1962), pp. 291–296.

—0.56.[57] Similar forces may have operated during the Vietnamese war boom of the late 1960s. The existence of some such catching-up phenomenon does not, however, necessarily rule out all links between concentration and wage-push inflation. Market power on the sellers' side may facilitate a ratchet-effect escalation of labor costs, beginning in the more concentrated industries when the economy is operating below full employment levels and then spreading to the atomistic sectors at a later time when all firms scramble for workers because of unusually full employment.

Even though workers in concentrated industries may not be steadily increasing their earnings advantage, it remains possible that at any moment in time they do command higher average earnings because of incomplete catching-up by workers in atomistic sectors and/or because firms with market power are willing to share the fruits of their power with labor, instead of retaining all monopoly gains in the form of high profits. This hypothesis was tested by Leonard Weiss in a study using comprehensive Census of Population data for the year 1959.[58] He found that total annual earnings were positively and significantly correlated with concentration after unionization and industry characteristics such as changes in industry employment levels, size of plants, durability of products, and broad skill requirements were taken into account. To cite one representative example of his results, male semiskilled workers in highly concentrated industries were found to earn 16 per cent more than their counterparts in atomistic industries when unionization was weak and 11 per cent more when unionization was strong. However, Weiss then introduced a battery of additional variables describing personal characteristics of individuals in his sample. These included weeks worked during 1959, hours worked per week,

age, years of education, family size, region of the country, and race. The partial correlation between earnings and concentration thereupon fell to insignificantly low values for nearly all occupations, and in roughly half of the occupations the net effect of concentration on earnings turned out to be negative. This striking change occurred because concentration was correlated with some of the personal characteristic variables, which captured from the concentration variable much of its explanatory power. Unionization on the other hand continued to exert a generally positive influence on earnings, even after individual worker characteristics were taken into account. Weiss' interpretation is that:

> . . . firms in concentrated industries do pay their employees more, but . . . they get higher "quality" labor in the bargain. . . . The laborers in concentrated industries seem to receive no more for their services than they might in alternative employments for persons with similar personal characteristics. Their earnings contain little or no monopoly rent.[59]

Indirect support for this interpretation can be derived from the results of a study by Ashenfelter and Johnson using a more compelling conceptual framework and more sophisticated econometric techniques than previous efforts.[60] Like Weiss, they found that ordinary least-squares regression analysis showed wages in manufacturing industries to be higher with extensive than with meager union membership, *ceteris paribus*. But this result, they hypothesize, reflects a confounding of distinguishable causal connections. Concretely, they found union strength to be greater in concentrated product markets (where organization is easier) and in industries where the unions were historically successful in achieving high wages. When these relationships were taken into account with a model incorporating three simul-

---

[57] *Unionism and Relative Wages in the United States,* pp. 159–160.

[58] "Concentration and Labor Earnings," *American Economic Review,* March 1966, pp. 96–117. See also the comment by Frank P. Stafford in the *American Economic Review,* March 1968, pp. 174–184, providing support for Weiss' findings with respect to the positive effect of unionization on income levels.

[59] "Concentration and Labor Earnings," pp. 108 and 115. Note that Weiss' use of the word "quality" does not necessarily imply inferiority in a normative sense, but only a difference in measurable attributes.

[60] Orley Ashenfelter and George E. Johnson, "Unionism, Relative Wages, and Labor Quality in United States Manufacturing Industries," Working Paper No. 9, Industrial Relations Section, Princeton University, May 1969.

taneous equations, the net influence of union strength on wage levels dwindled to an insignificant value. One reason, Johnson and Ashenfelter argue, is that when unions have raised the relative wages of their members in some industry, there follows a gradual upgrading of labor force quality as employment in that industry becomes more attractive relative to alternative openings.

By analogy, when wages rise especially rapidly in the more concentrated industries due to greater ability or willingness to pay or stronger unionization, employers in those industries enjoy 'first pick' among potential job candidates. The quality of their work forces gradually increases until the premia paid can be attributed almost entirely to differences in worker characteristics. Whether these characteristics are linked in any meaningful way to differences in productivity is not clear. A pessimistic verdict might be suggested by Weiss' finding that rapid wage gains during the 1950s in the more concentrated manufacturing industries were not fully mirrored by increased labor productivity. Or to the extent that work force quality reallocations with significant productivity implications did occur, there could still have been a net inflationary impact as atomistic producers were forced (when demand conditions became favorable) to match the concentrated industries' wage patterns in order to attract adequate supplies of sufficiently skilled workers.

CONCLUSION

Clearly, the links between market concentration, wage behavior, and the trend of prices over time are not simple. A great deal remains to be learned. In view of the residual uncertainties, it is difficult to reach confident generalizations concerning the administered price inflation thesis. Certainly it involves more than mere sound and fury. On both *a priori* and empirical grounds, there is reason to believe that wages and prices in concentrated industries are relatively inflexible downward, even when business conditions turn sour. During periods of sustained, more or less normal prosperity, producers with market power show an above-average proclivity to yield generous wage concessions. These are passed along to consumers through higher prices, and they form a pattern to be matched in competitive markets when demand conditions permit. This combination of prices rigid downward but flexible upward can cause ratchet-effect inflation even when aggregate demand is in balance with supply. On the other hand, monopolistic and oligopolistic sellers appear to display some short-run price restraint and perhaps also wage restraint during booms. What we do not know is the exact dynamics and the net secular effect of these patterns, and therefore we cannot reach a balanced assessment of how serious the administered price inflation problem is. The author's personal interpretation is that the price-setting and wage bargaining practices of concentrated industries do make it more difficult to maintain overall price stability and full employment simultaneously, but that administered price inflationary stimuli have been of modest importance compared to more traditional influences such as the pull of demand in a superheated economy.

Chapter 13

Rigid Prices and Macroeconomic Stability

Sharp fluctuations in the level of national economic activity and employment are hopefully a thing of the past. Through the use of fiscal and monetary tools it is possible to moderate, if not to eliminate altogether, the business cycle. The incidence and severity of future recessions will depend primarily upon how well those tools are managed. Still differences in market structure and the pricing behavior associated with them also have some bearing on the struggle for stability. Because of lags in the identification and implementation of appropriate fiscal and monetary measures, perfection cannot be achieved in contra-cyclical policy, and downturns will occasionally get under way. Difficulties in maintaining a viable international balance of payments position can also tie the hands of macroeconomic policy makers, preventing them from taking all the steps needed to cope with an emerging recession. It is important therefore to have firms and industries pursue pricing policies which minimize the adverse impact of macroeconomic policy lags, errors, and constraints. Our question in this chapter is, What pricing behavior best carries out this supporting role? Specifically, is it better for prices to remain relatively rigid or to fall flexibly in the face of a business downturn?

PRICE RESPONSES IN RECESSION UNDER VARIOUS MARKET STRUCTURES

Let us begin by resuming the empirical thread of Chapter 12. Market structure does have some

effect on cyclical pricing responses. In booms, prices tend to rise less rapidly in concentrated industries than in atomistically structured industries. In modest recessions, they tend to hold firm or sometimes even to rise in concentrated industries, while competitive prices are falling. In serious depressions like the one of 1929–1933, they tend to fall less in concentrated industries, other things being equal. These relationships, as we have seen, are not strong in a statistical sense. There is a great deal of noise associated predominantly with the differential behavior of input costs. The link between concentration and price changes operates mainly through price – cost margins, a relatively small component of the whole price structure, as Neal's study of 1929–1933 data showed and as Weiss' analysis of the 1953–1959 inflation confirmed. Still those who claim that no such link exists at all appear, on the basis of the evidence now available, to be defending a breached fortress.

Why should monopoly and oligopoly prices be more rigid in a recession? Why should the International Nickel Company (controlling at the time 90 per cent of world nickel production) have held its price constant at $.35 per pound between 1929 and 1932, while its output fell by more than 80 per cent? Why should the Big Three of the cigarette industry have raised their prices by 7 per cent in 1931, as cigarette demand was declining and as leaf tobacco prices were falling to their lowest levels since 1905? Why did Alcoa reduce its aluminum ingot prices by only 4 per cent between 1929 and 1932, while the average prices received by wheat growers (facing similarly high fixed costs and low marginal costs up to capacity operation) fell by some 63 per cent? Can the greater downward rigidity of concentrated industries' prices be explained by the conventional theory of profit maximization, or must alternative explanations be provided?

When the demand function confronting a competitive industry shifts to the left due to a general business downturn, other things (such as the schedule of input costs) remaining equal, the equilibrium price will necessarily fall if the industry supply function is upward sloping.[1] And in the short run of a single recession, the supply function will almost surely be upward sloping, since competitive firms normally expand output into the range of diminishing marginal returns and since the external economies which sometimes cause declining supply curves in competitive industries are a distinctly long-run phenomenon.

With monopoly pricing, matters are more complicated. What happens under the assumptions of the pure theory of monopoly profit maximization depends upon the slope of the marginal cost function, any shifts it may undergo, and changes in demand elasticity. If marginal costs are constant over the relevant range of outputs, the profit-maximizing reaction to a leftward demand shift will be to raise the price if demand becomes less elastic, to reduce it if demand becomes more elastic, and to hold it constant if demand at any given price retains the same elasticity after the downturn.[2] If the marginal cost function is upward sloping, or if it shifts downward due to a recession-induced decline in input costs, the optimal monopolistic reaction will be to reduce price if demand becomes more elastic or retains its pre-recession elasticity, while a price increase may be optimal if demand becomes less elastic and the decline in elasticity outweighs the reduction in marginal costs associated with producing less output. It is clear that increasing price or holding it constant *can* be a profit-maximizing response to a recession, at least under certain conditions, and in this respect monopolistic pricing differs qualitatively from competitive pricing. How frequently these conditions occur is a difficult empirical question. As we have seen in our discussion of cut-throat competition models in Chapter 7, situations in which demand becomes less elastic as a result of a recession are entirely possible, although there is no particular reason to believe that such cases predominate.

Alternate reasons for the rigidity of monopolistic and especially oligopolistic prices in the face of a recession include a kinked demand curve mentality, the fear of price leaders that downward adjustments will endanger industry discipline, and the application of full-cost pricing rules. Several responses are possible in the full-cost pricing case, depending upon the type of rule used. If a standard volume rule like General Motors' is employed, with price set to yield a predetermined return on existing investment at a 'normal' rate of capacity utilization, the price will be invariant (assuming that input prices do not change), but the unit profit margin will fall as unit overhead at reduced recession output levels exceeds standard volume overhead.[3] If a constant dollar margin is added to actual unit costs, the unit profit margin will be invariant, but at reduced outputs the price will be higher (since pro-rated unit overhead costs are higher). If a constant percentage margin is added to actual unit costs, including pro-rated overhead, both the dollar margin and the price will be higher at low outputs than at full employment levels. If the firm attempts to maintain a specified percentage return on its invested capital (fixed in the short run) it must seek higher dollar margins at low outputs than at high, and unless it is prevented from doing so by highly elastic demand, it will attempt to raise its price during a recession. For all four cases, prices will not fall in times of slack

---

[1] Obviously, input costs are more likely to fall than rise in a recession, reinforcing the tendency for price to decline.

[2] To prove this, we need only recall from Chapter 6 that the profit-maximizing margin of price over marginal cost $(P - MC)/P$ under monopoly is equal to $1/e$, where e is the elasticity of demand. With MC constant at various outputs, the price-cost margin will be higher, the lower the elasticity of demand becomes.

[3] Cf. pp. 174–175 *supra*.

demand unless input prices fall, and in three cases they will rise. In all but the standard volume case, there will be no decline in unit profit margins.

To be sure, the deterioration of demand may prevent sellers from implementing the price increases called for by full-cost rules. There is also no guarantee that the use of full-cost rules or adherence to the kink assumption will lead to a joint oligopoly profit-maximizing position. The indicated full-cost response may even be in the wrong direction relative to what is required for profit maximization Yet as we have seen in Chapter 6, the perfect is often the enemy of the good in pricing, and by avoiding hair-trigger adjustments or by sticking as well as they can to rules of thumb, oligopolists minimize the danger of price warfare. Obversely, if industry discipline does break down when recession sets in, prices may plummet spectacularly from joint profit-maximizing heights to competitive depths. For instance, breakdown of the international crude rubber cartel in the late 1920s was accompanied by a decline in New York import prices from a high of $1.03 per pound in 1925 to an average of $.21 per pound in 1929, and the added burden of depression brought the average down to $.03 per pound in 1932. The fact that such divergent responses to a recession—ranging from price increases to price warfare—can appear under oligopoly or monopoly conditions explains in part why the statistical correlations relating price changes to concentration have been weak. Still the central tendency in concentrated industries seems to be more toward price rigidity than toward precipitous declines when demand ebbs.

ANTI-RECESSION CARTELS

The rigidity of monopolistic and oligopolistic prices is viewed as a good thing in some circles.

It is even argued that cartels and other formal price-fixing arrangements ought to be encouraged in time of recession to prevent the fall of prices from healthy normal levels. One basis for this view is the fear that competition in slack times would otherwise become cut-throat or destructive—a proposition we have examined critically and found largely unconvincing in Chapter 7. Recession cartels are also advocated in the belief that recovery can be speeded by preventing a sustained decline in the general price level. This is the argument with which we shall be primarily concerned here.

It was a significant component of the theory implicitly underlying the National Industrial Recovery Act, passed by the U. S. Congress in the spring of 1933.[4] The act in effect suspended antitrust law prohibitions against price agreements in the hope that the economy could be 'reflated' through tandem increases in wages and prices. Under the uncritical supervision of the National Recovery Administration, industry groups formulated nearly a thousand "codes of fair competition," most with some mechanism for controlling or moderating price competition, before the NIRA was declared unconstitutional and allowed to die in 1935.[5] Judgments on the NIRA's efficacy during its short life vary widely, since it is impossible to isolate the act's effect on the economy from a tangle of concurrent influences.[6] The most widely held view is that the rise of prices due to NIRA-sanctioned collusive schemes did more to choke off recovery than to advance it, and after shedding the NIRA the U. S. government slowly reversed its field and adopted (with a few notable exceptions, as in agriculture and coal-mining) a strong anti-cartel policy which has persisted to the present day, in good times and bad.

Outside the United States, public disenchantment with recession cartels is much less preva-

[4]For various contemporary analyses, see L. S. Lyon, P. T. Homan *et al.*, *The National Recovery Administration* (Washington: Brookings, 1935); J. M. Clark, "Economics and the National Recovery Administration," *American Economic Review*, March 1934, pp. 11–25; and Karl Pribam, "Controlled Competition and the Organization of American Industry," *Quarterly Journal of Economics*, May 1935, pp. 371–393. For a balanced retrospective survey, see Ellis W. Hawley, *The New Deal and the Problem of Monopoly: A Study in Economic Ambivalence* (Princeton: Princeton University Press, 1966).

[5]*Schechter Poultry Corp. et al.* v. *U. S.*, 295 U. S. 495 (1935).

[6]Cf. Lyon *et al.*, *op. cit.*, pp. 756–877; and Leonard Kuvin, "Effects of N.R.A. on the Physical Volume of Production," *Journal of the American Statistical Association*, March 1936, pp. 58–60.

lent. As we shall see in Chapter 19, the antitrust laws of many nations explicitly authorize restrictive arrangements designed to cope with business crises. Japan affords the most striking illustration. When the Japanese economy's growth rate dropped from 9 per cent per annum in 1964 to less than 4 per cent in 1965, numerous price-fixing and output-restriction agreements were approved by the central government. These cartels, some seeking to reduce production by as much as 60 per cent, were motivated partly by the desire to maintain favorable terms of international trade by holding export prices up. But several of the commodities cartelized were sold primarily in domestic markets, and there the chief goal was to mitigate industrial pain and to speed recovery.[7] Likewise, the outbreak of macroeconomic difficulties in Germany, France, Italy, and other Western European nations during the middle and late 1960s after a long period of booming recovery from World War II was accompanied by a minor resurgence of cartel arrangements approved by government agencies or studiously ignored by them. However, cartelization in postwar Europe has not spread nearly as widely as it did during the 1930s.

RIGID PRICES AND BUSINESS RECOVERY: A MACROECONOMIC ANALYSIS

Is price rigidity in fact conducive to rapid recovery from a business downturn, or does it destabilize the economy? This is the crux of the recession cartel policy issue. Let us proceed as far as we can toward resolving the question on the basis of theory and evidence.[8]

SOME COMMON FALLACIES

It is useful to begin by examining briefly some common but fallacious approaches.

One typical misconception goes roughly as follows: 'Monopolists produce less output and hire fewer laborers than competitive industries facing identical demand conditions. It follows that monopoly causes unemployment—the hallmark of depression.' The problem here is that the restriction of output in monopolistic industries frees resources to be used in other sectors. It is perfectly possible to have a full employment equilibrium in a world shot through with monopolies, as we saw in Chapter 2, and the mere fact that *individual* monopolists restrict employment by no means implies that *aggregate* unemployment is created. Of course, monopolistic distortions may affect wage rates in such a way as to induce laborers to choose more leisure and less work. But this is not unemployment in the customary sense, since the labor supply restriction is voluntary, in response to distorted price signals.

Monopoly may lead to depression and true unemployment if it aggravates cumulative long-run tendencies toward the stagnation of aggregate demand—i.e., by transferring too much income into the hands of people with high marginal propensities to save. But this problem, of serious concern to economists during the 1930s, is no longer considered very important, since it can be counteracted by appropriate fiscal policies.

At present the principal monopolistic threat to full employment arises when, in response to a

[7]See "Japanese Establish Another Cartel To Combat Recession; Plan for Still More," *Business Week*, September 18, 1965, p. 127; "MITI May Enforce New Antidepression Cartel," *The Japan Times*, February 9, 1966, p. 10; and "Developments in the Field of Restrictive Business Practices: Japan," *Antitrust Bulletin*, Summer 1967, pp. 646–648. For a more general analysis, see Eugene Rotwein, "Economic Concentration and Monopoly in Japan," *Journal of Political Economy*, June 1964, pp. 272–275; and Kozo Yamamura, "Market Concentration and Growth in Postwar Japan," *Southern Economic Journal*, April 1966, pp. 451–464.

[8]For various views, see Oscar Lange, *Price Flexibility and Employment* (Bloomington, Indiana: Principia Press, 1944); the review of Lange's book by Milton Friedman, "Lange on Price Flexibility and Employment: A Methodological Criticism," *American Economic Review*, September 1946, pp. 613–631; Kenneth Boulding, "In Defense of Monopoly," *Quarterly Journal of Economics*, August 1945, pp. 524–542, with comments and a reply in the August 1946 issue, pp. 612–621; Alfred C. Neal, *Industrial Concentration and Price Inflexibility* (Washington: American Council on Public Affairs, 1942), especially pp. 141–162; J. A. Schumpeter, *Capitalism, Socialism, and Democracy* (New York: Harper, 1942), especially pp. 90–91; E. A. G. Robinson, *Monopoly* (London: Nisbet, 1941), Chapter VII; Edward S. Mason, *Economic Concentration and the Monopoly Problem* (Cambridge: Harvard University Press, 1957), pp. 159–166; Fritz Machlup, "Monopoly and the Problem of Economic Stability," in E. H. Chamberlin, ed., *Monopoly and Competition and Their Regulation* (London: Macmillan, 1954), pp. 385–397; and Emile Despres, Milton Friedman, Albert G. Hart, Paul A. Samuelson, and D. H. Wallace, "The Problem of Economic Instability," *American Economic Review*, September 1950, especially pp. 534–538.

macroeconomic shock, the pricing responses of monopolistic industries frustrate the operation of mechanisms which would direct the economy back toward full employment equilibrium. Our concern must therefore be not with the static properties of whatever equilibrium monopoly yields, but with the dynamics of monopolistic industries' adaptation to economic shocks.

Even when this perspective is adopted, it is possible to fall into logical traps. Suppose, for example, that the price in a monopolistic industry remains rigid when demand curves shift to the left as a result of a macroeconomic shock. Then output in that industry will be cut back more than it would have been if the price had been reduced. But despite popular beliefs, it does not necessarily follow that output *in general* will be lower than it otherwise would have been. The incremental reduction in output forthcoming from the monopolistic industry as a direct consequence of price rigidity may be offset by a relative increase in the quantity supplied by and demanded from other industries. This offset is achieved through substitution effects, as the prices of some items fall relative to the price of the monopolized commodity; through a reduction in wages as workers released by the output-restricting industry enter the job market, driving down the equilibrium wage and making additional hiring attractive to all industries; or through some combination of the two. Overall production and employment will of course be lower than they would have been had there been no slump in the first place. But *further* declines in production and employment can be attributed to monopoly only if aggregate demand is further reduced as a direct or indirect result of the monopolistic industry's rigid pricing response. We shall see that it is possible for this to happen, but the link is neither simple nor certain.

It is no more correct to propose, as some economists have, that price decreases are beneficial for stability if product demand is price elastic, since both production and total spending

on the relevant commodity will be increased, while they may impair recovery if demand is inelastic, since spending then will be reduced. Unless the level of aggregate demand for all goods and services changes, prices and elasticities of demand affect only the mix of production, not the overall level of production. Once again, the key issue is whether different pricing responses affect aggregate demand differentially.[9]

Let us therefore focus explicitly on the relationship between pricing responses and incremental changes in the level of aggregate demand. Following neo-Keynesian traditions, we assume a closed economy with three main aggregate demand components: consumption spending, investment spending, and government spending. To concentrate on the private consumption and investment sectors, we take the level of government demand to be exogenously determined. To simplify matters further, we shall analyze only two alternative responses to a general fall in demand: maintaining prices rigid at pre-recession levels (the monopoly or oligopoly case), and letting prices fall as they would under competitive pricing with rising short-run supply functions.

PRICE RIGIDITY AND AGGREGATE CONSUMPTION

The link between prices and aggregate consumption stressed most heavily in the literature of macroeconomic theory is the so-called Pigou effect, also known as the real balance effect or the net claims effect.[10] If, after the onset of a recession, prices fall, the real purchasing power of consumers' cash balances and net fixed claims to future cash payments (e.g., the surplus of fixed-interest securities held over outstanding debts) increases. Consumers may, therefore, consider themselves to be wealthier in a real sense. As a result they may be inclined to consume more and save less, raising aggregate demand. The failure of monopolistic or oligopolistic prices to fall thwarts operation of the Pigou effect and thus chokes off one potential stimulant to economic

---

[9]For a more relevant approach which focuses on the elasticity of demand for investment goods as an aggregate, see Abram Bergson, "Price Flexibility and the Level of Income," *Review of Economics and Statistics*, February 1943, pp. 2–5.

[10]Cf. Arthur C. Pigou, "The Classical Stationary State," *Economic Journal*, December 1943, pp. 343–351; and Don Patinkin, *Money, Interest, and Prices* (Second ed.; New York: Harper & Row, 1965).

recovery. In this respect, price rigidity is detrimental to macroeconomic stability. Nevertheless, what evidence we have on the matter suggests that consumption decisions are not much affected by changes in the real value of cash balances and fixed claims within the range of potential price level variation associated with all but the most severe recessions.[11] It is generally believed, therefore, that the Pigou effect consequences of oligopolistic and monopolistic price rigidity are not very serious.

The failure of prices to fall in industries with market power also has an incremental effect on the distribution of income. As Neal has shown for the early 1930s and as we shall amplify shortly for the 1950s, profit margins tend to fall less in concentrated than in unconcentrated industries at the onset of a recession. To the extent that the higher profits and cash flow associated with price rigidity are paid out as dividends to stockholders or as salaries and bonuses to top management, aggregate consumption will be lower than it would be under flexible pricing, since stockholders and top managers as a group are wealthier and have lower marginal propensities to consume than the average consumer.[12] If corporate earnings are retained rather than paid out, corporate saving rises at the expense of private consumption. This latter adverse effect may be offset if the additional corporate saving is matched by a concomitant increase in investment, but as we shall argue later, it seems more probable that when rigid prices prevent the redistribution of income away from corporations and toward consumers during a recession, hoarding will be increased and aggregate demand diminished. Thus, the redistributive effects of monopolistic and oligopolistic price rigidity appear to be distinctly unfavorable.

Although it would be misleading to say that policy decisions at the time were guided by anything like a coherent body of theory, the passage of the National Industrial Recovery Act was clearly influenced by a belief that recovery from the Great Depression of 1929–1933 might be hastened through a redistribution of income in favor of wage earners as consumers.[13] Price increases were expected as a result of the act's provisions, but it was hoped that wage increases would be implemented even more rapidly. One reason for the subsequent disenchantment with NIRA was the fact that prices actually rose in advance of wages, partly because of speculation and partly because the price-fixing actions of cartelized sellers were more successful in the short run than the wage-raising efforts of labor organizations encouraged under NIRA and concurrent legislation. Thus, the hoped-for redistribution did not ensue. Whether this outcome contributed to the unprecedented persistence of depressed conditions during the 1930s has never been determined conclusively.

A third link between market structure, pricing behavior, and aggregate consumption involves the dynamics of output and employment reallocation. As we have seen, if prices fall less in concentrated or cartelized industries, there must be a reallocation of output, so that the relative shares of output supplied by the concentrated industries fall, other things (such as income elasticities of demand) being equal. If this reallocation took place instantaneously and without friction, or if the recession encroached gradually enough to permit smooth readjustment, the reallocation process per se should cause no further downward spiraling of aggregate demand. But the adjustment process is not in fact frictionless. Labor in particular does not flow easily from one occupation into another; usually workers are at least temporarily unemployed before finding new jobs. Some unemployment is an unavoidable direct effect of the recession. But in addition, the

[11]Cf. Patinkin, *op. cit.*, pp. 651–664; his "Price Flexibility and Full Employment," *American Economic Review*, September 1948, pp. 543–564; and Thomas Mayer, "The Empirical Significance of the Real Balance Effect," *Quarterly Journal of Economics*, May 1959, pp. 275–291.

[12]Robert J. Lampman has estimated that the wealthiest 1 per cent of all individuals in the United States own more than 75 per cent of all personally held corporate bonds and stocks. "Taxation and the Size Distribution of Income," in U. S. House of Representatives, Committee on Ways and Means, *Tax Revision Compendium*, (Washington: 1959), Vol. 3, p. 2237. See also George Katona and John B. Lansing, "The Wealth of the Wealthy," *Review of Economics and Statistics*, February 1964, pp. 1–13.

[13]See Lyon *et al.*, *op. cit.*, especially pp. 756–795 and 871–877.

amount of frictional unemployment is likely to be larger, the more reallocation there is due to divergent price behavior in concentrated as opposed to atomistic industries. If the displaced laborers are without income during the period of readjustment (or if their incomes are not fully replaced by unemployment compensation), they will reduce their consumption, and this decline in consumption implies an *incremental* fall in aggregate demand, intensifying the recession. In this sense layoffs by price-maintaining, output-restricting industries aggravate the recession problem.

Nevertheless, a qualification must be raised. If rigid price industries reduce employment in proportion to output, they will tend to lay off relatively more workers than flexible price industries, *ceteris paribus*. But the proportionality assumption may be invalid. Statistical studies show that output per worker and output per manhour decline during economic downturns and rise in upturns because employers do not adjust their work forces in strict proportion to output changes over short periods of one or two years.[14] During a slump they hold on to workers, and especially overhead personnel, whose services are not immediately needed. They do this partly to avoid the costs of rehiring and retraining when business conditions improve in the future and perhaps also on humanitarian grounds or to preserve work force morale. Some of the shock of a recession is therefore absorbed through underemployment or disguised unemployment, rather than direct unemployment, reducing the drag on aggregate consumption. Only when demand recovers are the workers fully utilized again, and because the expansion of output is accomplished in part by working long-term employees harder, new hirings rise less than proportionately and output per worker increases.

This suggests the question, Is it possible that rigid-price concentrated industries accept more disguised unemployment during a recession than do atomistic, flexible-price industries? It could happen because firms with market power are less likely to experience a liquidity crisis compelling urgent cost reduction measures. That is, such firms can afford to maintain more 'organizational slack.' Or they may discount the future at a lower rate, placing more weight on avoiding future rehiring and retraining costs.

This conjecture is amenable to empirical testing, but the task is not an easy one. Three bits of evidence are available.

C. E. Ferguson collected data on quarterly employment during the 1947–1956 interval for from five to 12 companies in 12 industries of widely varying product characteristics.[15] For each firm he computed a trend-adjusted coefficient of the variability of employment over time. These were consolidated into weighted average industry employment variability indices. He then correlated a ranking of the industries by variability of employment with a ranking of the industries by concentration ratios, obtaining a rank correlation of +0.15, which was not significantly different from zero by conventional statistical tests.[16] The more concentrated the industries were, the more variable their employment seemed to be from quarter to quarter, but the relationship was at best an extremely weak one.

S. H. Masters analyzed changes in sales per employee during 21 recession episodes experi-

[14]Cf. Edwin Kuh, "Cyclical and Secular Labor Productivity in United States Manufacturing," *Review of Economics and Statistics*, February 1965, pp. 1–12; Stanley H. Masters, "The Behavior of Output Per Man During Recessions: An Empirical Study of Underemployment," *Southern Economic Journal*, March 1967, pp. 388–394; and Thor Hultgren and M. R. Pech, *Cost, Prices, and Profits: Their Cyclical Relations* (New York: Columbia University Press, 1965).

[15]"The Relationship of Business Size to Stability: An Empirical Approach," *Journal of Industrial Economics*, November 1960, pp. 43–62; and *A Macroeconomic Theory of Workable Competition* (Durham: Duke University Press, 1964), pp. 91–105.

[16]Ferguson is vague on how his industries were defined, but it is evident that some of the concentration ratios were poor indicators of monopoly power.

Using the same data, he also correlated individual firm employment variability over time with firm size for each industry group, and in every case but one found that stability of employment increased with the size of firms. Unfortunately, his results yield no insight into whether or not this greater stability was merely the result of the statistical averaging associated with size. Specifically, it is not clear whether a group of small independent firms would have exhibited as much stability in their combined employment as a single firm with the same total employment.

enced in 10 broadly-defined industry groups.[17] He found that the recession decline in sales per employee was smaller (that is, work forces were tailored more closely to changes in output), the higher the industries' weighted average four-firm concentration ratios were and the higher profits as a percentage of stockholders' equity were in the year prior to the recession. For both variables, however, the relationships were far from statistically significant. Thus, Masters' results, like Ferguson's, run contrary to the hypothesis that concentrated industries mitigate the adverse aggregate consumption effects of recession by increasing organizational slack, but the observed relationships are extremely weak.

Hoping to escape the stringent data constraints faced by Ferguson and Masters, the author of the present work attacked the problem in a different way. Abundant data on employment and other measures of economic activity for four-digit manufacturing industries are collected in the biennial census of manufactures. As luck would have it, two of the first four postwar censuses occurred in years (1954 and 1958) coinciding with the troughs of pronounced but short-lived recessions. Of the other two years, 1947 fell within the postwar reconversion boom, while 1963 is generally considered a year of moderate prosperity, with production in the manufacturing sector rising by 5.2 per cent despite an overall unemployment rate lingering at the 5.7 per cent level. We have, then, two recession years straddled by a boom year and an almost 'normal' year.

Now if the prices of unconcentrated industries fell relative to the prices of concentrated industries in the recession years, a reallocation of output should have occurred, with the output of the unconcentrated industries rising relative to the output of concentrated industries, other things (such as income elasticities) being held equal. If in addition there was no difference associated with market structure in the adjustment of employment to output changes, we should expect the percentage share of total industrial employment in concentrated industries to have fallen during the recessions. If, on the other hand, concentrated industries absorbed more of the recession shock in the form of disguised unemployment, the tendency for the concentrated industries' employment shares to fall during recessions would be attenuated, and their shares might even have risen if the organizational slack effect were strong enough.

To test these conjectures, data were gathered on 108 four-digit manufacturing industries whose definitions were economically meaningful (in the sense that concentration ratios either provide directly or could be adjusted to provide a good first approximation to the degree of structural market power), and for which census statistics were fully comparable over the 1947–1963 interval.[18] The 108 industries together originated 33 per cent of total manufacturing sector value added in 1963. Each individual industry's share of total manufacturing sector employment and production worker manhours was computed for each of the four census years, and time trends in the shares (due, for instance, to secular growth or stagnation or differential productivity trends) were removed by estimating a linear regression of each industry's share on time. After these operations, two dependent variables were available, defined as follows:

E_{it} = The total employment share of the ith industry in the tth year, expressed as a percentage of the share predicted by the industry's trend adjustment regression equation.

MH_{it} = The total production worker manhours share of the ith industry in the tth year, expressed as a percentage of the share predicted by the industry's trend adjustment regression equation.

[17]"The Behavior of Output Per Man During Recessions: A Study of Underemployment," unpublished Ph.D. dissertation, Princeton University, 1965, pp. 154–155.

[18]More than 100 other industries on which data for the four years were available were excluded because the industry definitions were unsatisfactory. In four cases, two or three four-digit industries were combined to obtain more meaningful definitions. In eight cases, the concentration ratios were adjusted (typically by taking the weighted average of component five-digit product lines) to get more meaningful estimates. Dummy variables were also used for six industries whose markets were local or regional in scope.

The predictions concerning E_{it} and MH_{it} generated by alternative behavioral theories are illustrated by means of Figure 13.1. Suppose line T shows the true trend of some concentrated industry's employment shares over time, averaging out cyclical and random deviations. If there were no differential pricing behavior over the business cycle associated with market structure, the observed employment share for any given year should have the same expected value as the trend value, subject of course to random error. But if prices in concentrated industries fall less during recessions than atomistic industry prices, the 1954 and 1958 employment share observations for concentrated industries will tend to lie below the trend line, as shown in Figure 13.1, *unless* employees made redundant by the reduction in output are absorbed in the form of organizational slack. The unqualified rigid price hypothesis predicts therefore that the 1954 and 1958 employment and manhours shares of concentrated industries will lie below their trend values, while the organizational slack hypothesis predicts that they will be drawn toward the trend line and may even lie above it. Since 1947 was a boom year during which oligopolistic industries tended to exercise pricing restraint, we would expect their employment shares to have exceeded the long-run trend

values (unless output and employment were severely restrained by nonprice rationing, as was evident to some extent). In 1963, the economy was not operating at full steam, but it was also not in the throes of a recession, so we should expect the shares of concentrated industries to lie very close to the true trend line, or perhaps (with no organizational slack differential) slightly below it, as shown in Figure 13.1. Note, however, that since end-point years 1947 and 1963 were not symmetrical in terms of business conditions, the trend line estimated by linear regression may not correspond to the true trend line T. The fitted line is apt to be pulled down slightly, like dotted line T^* in Figure 13.1. Since the observed trend deviations are measured from the fitted and not the true trend line, we would expect the 1954 and 1958 observations for concentrated industries to lie below the fitted trend line and the 1947 and 1963 observations to lie above it, if concentrated industries have more rigid prices *and* if there is nothing to the differential organizational slack hypothesis.

One further point must be made clear. That prices fell less during the 1954 and 1958 recessions in concentrated industries is an assumption. It cannot be verified conclusively because the wholesale price data collected by the Bureau of Labor Statistics are not fully compatible with four-digit census industry data and because the BLS data fail to detect secret recession price shading (which may be more widespread in the concentrated industries). One imperfect test possible with census data is to examine year-to-year changes in price-cost margins, defined as:[19]

$$\pi_{it} = \frac{\begin{array}{c}\text{Value of shipments} - \text{cost of materials} \\ \text{and supplies purchased from other} \\ \text{firms} - \text{payroll expenditures}\end{array}}{\text{Value of shipments}}.$$

Estimates of π_{it} were calculated for each of the four years for 103 of the 108 sampled industries on which data could be obtained. Simple average values of π_{it} were then computed for two groups of industries—those with four-firm concentration

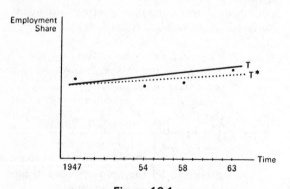

Figure 13.1
Trend Deviations with an Adverse Price Rigidity Effect on Recession Employment

[19]Costs which are not subtracted out in calculating the price-cost margin include depreciation and advertising outlays For a further discussion, see Norman R. Collins and Lee E. Preston, *Concentration and Price-Cost Margins in Manufacturing Industries* (Berkeley: University of California Press, 1968), pp. 54–57 and 119–121.

ratios below 40 and those with ratios of 40 or higher; and the percentage changes in these average margins were derived. The results are as follows:

	1947–54	1954–58	1958–63
Percentage change in π, concentration less than 40	−17.1	+1.9	+12.2
Percentage change in π, concentration above 40	− 2.0	+9.1	+11.9

Evidently, price-cost margins dropped by much less on the average between 1947 and 1954 in the more concentrated industries, and they rose more between 1954 and 1958. While these results do not show conclusively that prices moved in parallel, they at least suggest that inference, which is assumed here to be true.

We proceed now to the central test. For each of the four census years, regression estimates of the relationships between E_{it} and MH_{it} and concentration were computed. To hold other influences constant while testing for the effect of market structure, dummy variables distinguishing durable goods from nondurables, consumer goods from producers' goods and intermediates, and national from local markets were included in the regression equations. Ten industries which seemed likely to have particularly low income elasticities of demand were also assigned special dummy variables.[20] After these influences were taken into account, the net predicted percentage deviations from trend employment and manhours share values associated with an increase in the four-firm concentration ratio from 0 to 100 were as follows (with standard errors of the coefficients given in parentheses):[21]

	1947	1954	1958	1963
Per cent deviation from trend manhours share	+0.04 (2.79)	−0.27 (5.18)	−0.57 (3.43)	+1.14 (2.96)
Per cent deviation from trend employment share	−1.56 (2.68)	+1.20 (4.59)	+1.07 (2.53)	−0.52 (2.70)

The results, we see, are both mixed and extremely weak statistically. Trend-adjusted production worker manhours shares tend to be lower in concentrated than in unconcentrated industries during recession years 1954 and 1958 and higher in 1947 and 1963, *ceteris paribus*, suggesting that the organizational slack shock absorber was either inoperative or insufficiently strong to overpower reallocation effects associated with more rigid prices. But all signs reverse for total employment (which includes a substantial complement of overhead personnel), suggesting that at least some employees may have benefitted from the greater ability and willingness of concentrated industries to increase organizational slack during recessions. However, in no case is the trend deviation in employment or manhour shares significantly different from zero in statistical tests; the standard errors in every instance exceed the concentration coefficients. The only verdict which can legitimately be drawn is a scotch one: there is no significant indication that concentration makes a systematic difference one way or the other in the cyclical behavior of employment and production worker manhours shares.

Concentration does, however, appear to make a difference in another respect. The deviations of actual from trend-adjusted share values showed more *unsystematic* variation in concentrated than in unconcentrated industries. To ascertain this, the sample was divided into two groups—65 industries with four-firm concentration ratios of 40 or more, and 43 industries with concentration ratios of less than 40. A multiple analysis of variance on the ratio of actual to trend-adjusted employment and manhours shares was performed, taking into account as additional independent classes the year (and hence the stage of the business cycle), durability of the product, consumer vs. producer vs. intermediate goods, and special low expected income elasticity cases. For both dependent variables (as well as in other analyses using fewer independent class distinctions) the residual variance of the concentrated

---

[20]They were cereal preparations, chewing gum, cigarettes, cigars (the American-made product being a probable inferior good in pre-Castro days), chewing and smoking tobacco, pharmaceuticals, tin cans, electric lamps, opthalmic goods, and morticians' goods.

[21]The concentration ratios used were the simple average of ratios for the years 1947, 1954, 1958, and 1963.

industry group was higher than that of the un-concentrated industry group, with the following variance (F) ratios:

Analysis of employment
   share (E_{it}) values $F = 3.10$
Analysis of manhours
   share (MH_{it}) values $F = 2.69$

These are highly significant statistically, the 99 per cent confidence F ratio value being 1.43.

This result might have two plausible interpretations. First, the cyclical pricing behavior of concentrated industries may exhibit more diversity, shocks being met in some fields by a rigid pricing response and in others by a breakdown of discipline which allows prices to plummet from the collusive to the competitive level. Second, concentrated industries possess more discretion to cushion employment shocks by increasing organizational slack, but this discretion may be exercised less uniformly than in atomistic industries, where the margin for discretion is slim in any event. Consistent with the latter hypothesis is the fact that the unsystematic variability of actual vs. trend-adjusted share values is greater for total employment, which includes more of the workers susceptible to disguised unemployment under current institutions, than for production worker manhours.

Summarizing the evidence from three studies of the cyclical variability of employment in concentrated as compared to unconcentrated industries, we find that none of the three has succeeded in uncovering a statistically significant systematic link between concentration and employment stability, though there is greater unsystematic variability in the more concentrated industries. This is disappointing, but we learn even from negative results. The absence of strong systematic relationships leads us to conclude tentatively that concentration and the pricing behavior associated with it simply do not make much of a difference in terms of cyclical employment share fluctuations. In this respect oligopolistic industries emerge in a more favorable light than one might expect on the basis of

a priori theorizing. Whether this is so because the differences in price responses are small and erratic, because the output reallocations caused by differential pricing responses are slight, because the employment effects of monopolistic output restriction during recessions are largely offset by increases in organizational slack, or because of other more subtle relations remains an open question.

While the employment destabilization indictment against concentration must therefore be set aside, the charge that oligopolistic price rigidity during a recession has unfavorable Pigou and income redistribution effects on aggregate consumption stands. On balance, then, market power appears more likely to retard the recovery of aggregate demand than to stimulate it, at least on the basis of influences considered thus far. Still we have no reason to believe that these unfavorable effects are very severe.

THE DIRECT EFFECTS OF PRICE RIGIDITY ON INVESTMENT

Most business cycle theories emphasize the role of capital investment as both a triggering element in downturns and (when it recovers) a stimulant to the upturn. In this section we address the question: Does the pricing behavior of monopolistic and oligopolistic industries cushion the fall of aggregate investment when a recession begins and hasten its resurgence as the recession matures, or does it exert a net destabilizing influence? The possibility that differences in market structure affect investment in other ways will be examined in a later section.

It is useful heuristically to assume that investment decisions of both individual firms and the economy as a whole are determined by the interaction of two functions: the marginal efficiency of investment schedule (MEI in Figure 13.2) and the marginal cost of capital schedule (MCC in Figure 13.2). Both may be affected by pricing responses to an economic downturn.

Consider first the capital cost side of the system.[22] The typical business firm consciously or unconsciously estimates its MCC schedule by

---

[22]The approach taken here follows James S. Duesenberry, *Business Cycles and Economic Growth* (New York: McGraw-Hill, 1958), Chapter 5.

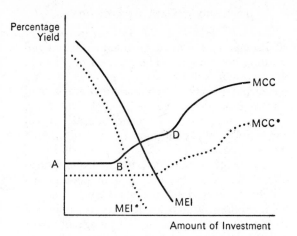

Figure 13.2
The Determinants of Investment Equilibrium

Solid lines denote the situation with flexible prices;
dotted lines the rigid-price case.

arraying all potential sources of investible funds in the order of their cost, from least to most costly. Many firms apparently view the cost of funds generated by depreciation and (after some customary level of dividends has been paid out) retained earnings to be either zero, or (with better theoretical justification) the return attainable by using the funds to buy short-term government securities. These considerations dictate the location of the segment *AB* in Figure 13.2. If additional funds are to be invested, the firm turns first to relatively low-cost borrowing (segment *BD*), whose cost rises with the amount borrowed because of increasing risk, and then to relatively high-cost new equity issues (segment *D-MCC*).

For monopolistic firms able to hold their profits up during a recession, the quantity of low-cost internally generated funds is higher than it would be under more flexible pricing, *ceteris paribus*, and so the *AB* segment of the *MCC* function is extended to the right. The cost of external funds and the opportunity cost of investing internally generated funds in the government securities market may also be af-

fected by pricing responses, but in a more complicated way. If rigid-price firms are able to pay out higher dividends than they would in a flexible-price regime, income is redistributed in favor of wealthy stockholders. Because stockholders have a high marginal propensity to save, they will channel a substantial fraction of these funds back into the securities market, driving interest rates down and pushing the *MCC* schedules of *all* firms downward and to the right. Also, the prices of stock issued by monopolistic firms able to maintain high product prices will continue to be relatively high, permitting the flotation of new issues at relatively low future earnings costs. This too implies a rightward shift in the *MCC* schedule relative to the flexible price situation, although only in the *D-MCC* region, which producers may be reluctant to explore during a recession. On the other hand, the failure of product prices to fall makes it necessary for consumers to hold larger cash balances than they would need if price levels declined, and thus prevents a release of funds from transactions motive holdings into security markets. This implies a general leftward shift in the *MCC* schedule. How these countervailing influences affecting the upper reaches of the *MCC* function net out is uncertain. Perhaps most important, however, is the relative increase in internally generated liquidity associated with rigid prices, suggesting that on balance the effect of price rigidity is to place the *MCC* function further to the right (as shown by the dotted function *MCC** in Figure 13.2) than it would be with flexible pricing.

The position of the *MEI* schedule is also affected by pricing behavior. If the prices of capital goods fail to fall due to the exercise of market power by suppliers, the *MEI* schedule for all firms will lie further to the left than it would under flexible capital goods pricing, since some projects which would have passed a profitability test at bargain machinery and construction price levels will not do so. However, most economists believe that this effect would not be very strong, or that it would be swamped by other effects to be considered in a moment.[23] More important,

---

[23]See the discussion in Neal, *op. cit.*, pp. 156–159; and Mason, *op. cit.*, p. 163.

those firms which maintain prices and profit margins in a recession are likely to do so only by operating well below capacity. Under these circumstances, they will hardly be enthusiastic about adding still more capacity, or even about replacing existing semi-obsolescent but idle equipment. This too implies a leftward displacement of the *MEI* schedule, and probably also substantial inelasticity of the curves with respect to changes in expected yields. From the considerations examined thus far, the impact of price rigidity on the marginal efficiency schedule appears to be unambiguously adverse.

With the *MCC* schedule lying further to the right and the *MEI* schedule further to the left under rigid than under flexible recession pricing, what is the net outcome? Unfortunately, we cannot be sure; the answer depends upon the relative magnitudes of the displacements and on the elasticities of the curves. It does not seem too unreasonable to suppose the result will be a 'damned if we do, damned if we don't' dilemma. Investment is choked off by excess capacity in industries whose high prices generate ample investible funds, while it is discouraged by poor profits in industries which maintain output by letting prices drop.

Conditions in European steel markets during the early 1960s illustrate this kind of dilemma.[24] The industry found itself in the throes of a localized recession as the growth of capacity caught up with and then overtook demand. In the well-disciplined United Kingdom branch, prices held firm, but producers found themselves with considerable excess capacity. On the Continent, prices fell by 25 to 30 per cent while the rate of capacity utilization remained fairly high (mainly because lower prices permitted the successful penetration of overseas markets), but investment was discouraged by the increased intensity of competition and (in 1963) the erosion of profits. The net result was a 93 per cent decline in investment between 1960 and 1963 in *both* the British and Continental industries.

PRICE RIGIDITY AND EXPECTATIONS

Expectations about the future are another vital component of the aggregate investment and consumption pictures. The behavior of prices in the early stages of a recession can affect expectations, and through them both investment and consumption decisions, in a number of ways. Consider first the investment side. If capital goods prices slide continuously downhill when a recession begins, the inclination of producers to defer expansion and replacement expenditures because of excess capacity and/or poor profits will be reinforced by the expectation that by holding off until the price decline has run its full course, they can gain the advantage of lower investment costs and higher returns. This implies a sharp leftward shift in the marginal efficiency of investment function. The resulting decline in investment intensifies the downward spiral through its multiplier effects. Similarly, if raw material and intermediate goods prices are steadily falling, users will draw down their inventories, delaying replenishment until the last minute in order to buy at lower prices. Output and employment in the intermediate goods industries will drop sharply, with further adverse multiplier effects.

These unfavorable expectational effects are much less likely when prices are held rigid through the exercise of market power. They can also be avoided when price reductions inspired by the recession are implemented in such a way as to convey a once-and-for-all impression, so buyers come to believe that the time is ripe for taking advantage of bargains. Creating this impression is exactly what strong price leaders seek when they announce across-the-board list price reductions in a time of deteriorating sub-rosa prices as a means of reestablishing industry discipline around a new rallying point.[25] If buyers are convinced the tactic will succeed, the adverse expectational effect of price erosion is again mitigated.

[24]D. Swann and D. L. McLachlan, "Steel Pricing in a Recession," *Scottish Journal of Political Economy*, February 1965, pp. 95–98.

[25]Cf. p. 172 *supra*.

Rigid prices may be favorable from an expectational standpoint in still another way. A severe recession accompanied by sharply falling prices is apt to precipitate a wave of bankruptcies, with an extremely unsettling effect on business confidence. Loss of confidence in turn means pronounced leftward shifts in the marginal efficiency of investment schedules. Nevertheless, to keep the rate of business failure at normal levels during a recession it might be necessary to accept such widespread cartelization that serious side effects would appear on other dimensions of aggregate demand, and it is not clear that the cure is preferable to the disease.

Similar relationships between pricing reactions and expectations exist in the consumer durables sector, although perhaps in attenuated form, since consumers have less information on current economic conditions and trends. If the prices of durable goods such as automobiles, new housing, cameras, etc. are sliding downward visibly, consumers may choose to defer planned purchases to a more propitious moment. Price rigidity can undermine this ground for delay.

One further potential effect of market power on expectations must be noted. Conceivably, firms with sufficient monopoly power to avoid liquidity crises and weather recession storms handily may have a longer time horizon in planning their investment programs. The classic illustration is General Motors' behavior during the 1953–1954 recession. In January of 1954, the U. S. economy was moving into what was widely viewed as a distinct if moderate recession. Automobile sales were falling, and the Federal Reserve Board index of industrial production had declined by 9 per cent from its July 1953 high, with no sign of changing direction. This was the moment chosen by General Motors to launch a billion dollar capital expansion and modernization program, with $600 million to be spent during calendar year 1954 and the remainder in the following year. To put the decision in perspective, GM capital spending between 1946 and 1953 had amounted to only $2 billion altogether; total capital investment in the automobile and parts industry during 1954 proved to be $732 million, of which GM accounted for roughly 80 per cent; and GM's $600 million capital outlays during 1954 represented about 8 per cent of total manufacturing sector investment, compared to GM's 3.4 per cent share of total manufacturing sector sales that year. Explaining his company's decision, GM president Harlow Curtice announced:

> The fact that we are embarking on an unprecedented expansion program at this time . . . is evidence we have confidence in the immediate future and in the long term growth of the market for our products.[26]

That GM's forecasters were right—1955 proved to be a record year for automobile sales—does not alter the fact that General Motors exhibited foresight and courage which other less well-heeled corporations lacked. And its announcement undoubtedly had favorable repercussions on overall business confidence, with an unmeasurable but probably significant indirect effect on investment and employment.

Whether this case was typical or a fluke is unknown.[27] Nevertheless, the general impact of price rigidity on entrepreneurial and consumer expectations during the opening phases of a recession does appear to be almost unambiguously favorable. Here, at least, monopoly power rates high marks.

A BALANCED ASSESSMENT

Bringing together the pieces of our aggregate demand analysis, we conclude that price rigidity due to oligopoly or monopoly is almost certainly detrimental to aggregate consumption through its Pigou and income distribution effects, possibly detrimental to aggregate investment by compounding excess capacity problems even though it operates favorably on the marginal cost

---

[26]"G.M. Will Expend Billion on Plants in 2-Year Program," *New York Times*, January 20, 1954, p. 1.

[27]Clearly, the macroeconomic power of large corporations can also conflict with stabilization efforts. For example, General Motors increased its capital spending from $80 million in 1968 to $1.1 billion in 1969 to prepare for production of a new small car line, despite federal government pleas for restraint in investment to combat inflationary pressures. See "Top G.M. Officers Reply to Critics," *New York Times*, May 24, 1969, p. 47.

of capital, and almost surely beneficial to aggregate investment in its expectational effects. Since the effects are not all in one direction, and since the empirical evidence is meager, we cannot demonstrate conclusively that monopolistic pricing either contributes to or lessens instability when recessions begin. We are left with a substantial margin of uncertainty. The case for price rigidity is strongest if one believes that expectational effects are what really matter in the business cycle, and this is a premise with considerable appeal. My personal opinion is that moderate price rigidity is more likely to have a stabilizing than a destabilizing influence on the economy. Still for the most part the advantages and disadvantages seem to offset one another, so that on balance it may make little difference whether prices are rigid or flexible within the range of variation encountered in ordinary experience. And it is clear that the intelligent application of fiscal and monetary correctives is much more important to stability than industrial pricing policies. Therefore, if a bias toward price rigidity is a desirable trait of monopoly and oligopoly, the social benefit provided is surely not great enough to constitute an absolute defense.

MARKET STRUCTURE AND THE STABILITY OF INVESTMENT

Let us move now to a different vantage point. A leading cause of business fluctuations is the instability of investment. In the upturn of the cycle, producers scramble to enhance their capacity to meet growing demands, but once capacity has caught up with and perhaps overshot demand, they cut back their investment plans, precipitating unemployment in the capital goods industries, which reduces aggregate consumption and demand, which dampens further the incentive to invest, which carries the economy further down the spiral. All this is well known. What concerns us here is the question, Is there a stronger bias toward overshooting in in-

vestment decisions, followed by recession-inducing cutbacks, under certain market structures than under others?

That there may be is implied by G. B. Richardson's provocative reexamination of the theory of pure competition.[28] Richardson's thesis can be stated succinctly as follows. Suppose a purely competitive industry is in long-run equilibrium when the industry demand curve shifts unexpectedly to the right, say, by 10 per cent. In the short run, prices will rise to clear the market, and each producer will be earning positive economic profits. These profits signal the need for additional investment. But how much investment? And by whom? If each producer is operating one plant of minimum optimal scale, and if each attempts to take advantage of the expansion opportunity by building a second plant, the addition to industry capacity will far exceed what is called for by the demand shift. Indeed, if every producer responds to the opportunity, it would seem that only by the sheerest accident would the expansion of capacity be precisely what is needed to restore a new long-run competitive equilibrium. The result of a demand increase may therefore be a massive investment wave which sows the seeds of later recession. Or alternatively (as Richardson believes will be more likely), if producers recognize this dilemma, they may hold back in a kind of Alphonse and Gaston reaction sustaining too little investment to attain long-run equilibrium. As Richardson argues, a purely and perfectly competitive market structure has no built-in mechanism conveying the information needed to nominate some firms to invest and others to refrain from investing:

> [A] general profit potential, which is known to all, and equally exploitable by all, is, for this reason, available to no one in particular. . . . [T]he conditions supposed to ensure allocative efficiency are in fact such as would prevent purposive economic activity of any kind, for they are incompat-

---

[28] G. B. Richardson, *Information and Investment* (Oxford: Oxford University Press, 1960). An earlier version of the argument appeared under the title "Equilibrium, Expectations and Information," *Economic Journal*, June 1959, pp. 223–237. For an analysis anticipating Richardson's in some respects, see Tibor Scitovsky, *Welfare and Competition* (Homewood: Irwin, 1951), pp. 233–241 and 365–367. See also David McCord Wright, "Some Notes on Ideal Output," *Quarterly Journal of Economics*, May 1962, especially pp. 176–178.

ible with the availability to entrepreneurs of the necessary market information.[29]

From these premises, Richardson goes on to assert that market imperfections are essential if the economy is to respond to demand changes with the correct amount of investment. He distinguishes two kinds of restraints, "natural" and "contrived," which help match investment with demand, observing that they are essentially homogeneous, yielding the same effect in nominating producers to expand capacity.[30] Among the natural restraints, investment may be correctly proportioned to demand if information is imperfect, so that some producers recognize profit-making opportunities more rapidly than others; or capital market imperfections may prevent some firms from obtaining the funds they need to carry out desired investments; or when products are differentiated firms may restrict their investments because they know it will be difficult to win away customers loyal to competitors. Mergers, formal price-fixing agreements and market-sharing cartels, or simply the desire not to compete too strenuously are the "contrived restraints" of Richardson's schema. He asserts that at least in certain cases mergers or price-fixing arrangements may be "the indispensable condition of informed investment decisions and the orderly adjustment of output to demand."[31]

Richardson's work is an exceptionally sophisticated defense of monopolistic restraints. He is correct in his contention that some imperfections are essential if the dynamic flow of investment is to be balanced properly with demand. And although he chooses to emphasize the possibility that purely competitive markets will generate inadequate quantities of investment, it seems equally plausible that such markets may over-react to demand changes with a wave of excessive investment. Nevertheless, it is debatable whether "contrived restraints" will perform the investment nominating function as well as or even better than natural restraints.

In truth, collusive agreements are as apt to destabilize investment as to stabilize it. Richardson implies that under simple price-fixing arrangements, prices will be set at levels providing only a normal return, unless entry into the industry can be blocked.[32] But this is most unlikely. For sellers with little or no cost advantage over potential entrants, long-run profit maximization requires setting a price exceeding the entry-deterring level.[33] And if this is done, instability of investment will follow.[34] In his study of German cartels, Fritz Voigt found that price-fixing schemes caused a "peculiar rhythm" of investment with a significant bearing on the growth rate of the overall economy.[35] When the cartels were working successfully, prices were raised to high levels, outsiders began investing heavily to take advantage of lucrative entry opportunities, and insiders invested in efficiency-increasing techniques to prepare for a forthcoming competitive struggle. Then, as the cartel collapsed because members were no longer willing to bear an increasingly onerous burden of output restriction to compensate for the growing supply of outsiders, prices plummeted and investment declined drastically.

Richardson suggests also that market-sharing agreements are conducive to rational investment planning. But the *sine qua non* of such arrangements is a meeting of minds on how the market will be divided. In Germany during the 1920s and 1930s, shares were allocated on the basis of production capacity. Cartel members therefore raced to increase their sales quotas by building

---

[29]*Information and Investment*, pp. 14 and 124. By permission of the Clarendon Press, Oxford.

[30]*Ibid.*, pp. 68–70 and 128.

[31]*Ibid.*, pp. 67, 94, 130, and 136.

[32]*Ibid.*, pp. 133–136.

[33]See Darius Gaskins, "Dynamic Limit Pricing: Optimal Pricing Under Threat of Entry," paper presented before the Econometric Society, December 1969.

[34]On the relationship between entry barriers, pricing choices, and investment instability, see Joe S. Bain, *Barriers to New Competition* (Cambridge: Harvard University Press, 1956), pp. 36–41 and 189–190.

[35]Fritz Voigt, "German Experience with Cartels and Their Control During Pre-War and Post-War Periods," in J. P. Miller, ed., *Competition, Cartels, and Their Regulation* (Amsterdam: North Holland, 1962), pp. 171–172 and 184.

more capacity, with an effect exactly the opposite of that predicted by Richardson. In the Rhenish-Westphalian coal cartel, for example, production capacity exceeded *peak* demand levels by 25 per cent because of the competition in investment.[36] Even when market shares are not linked formally to capacity, a cartel member's bargaining power depends upon its 'fighting reserves'—the amount of output it can dump on the market, depressing the price, if others hold out for unacceptably high quotas. Recognizing this, companies participating in market-sharing cartels will be tempted to invest in more capacity than they need to serve foreseeable demands at anticipated collusive price levels.

A similar bias toward unstable or excessive capital investment may exist when oligopolists collude only tacitly on price. If price competition is shunned, the distribution of orders among sellers will depend largely upon such non-price considerations as reliability of service and personal buyer-seller ties. The firm with reserve capacity to serve customers in times of peak demand stands a good chance of retaining their loyalty permanently, and this motivates each enterprise to try raising its market share through competition in production capacity.[37] Also, fear of losing market share to more aggressive rivals spurs oligopolists to invest heavily in additional capacity when demand is growing rapidly—frequently at a collective rate exceeding demand growth, so that new investment must be cut back abruptly when excess capacity begins to disrupt pricing discipline. This is what happened in the U. S. plastics and aluminum industries during the late 1950s and in synthetic fibers during the

early 1960s.[38] It was a common phenomenon in postwar Japan, where rapid but erratic industrial growth interacted with the widespread adoption of new, large-scale, lumpy technologies to touch off a "race for rationalization" which ended with excessive capacity in many industries and contributed noticeably to cyclical instability.[39] To combat the problem, the Japanese government began encouraging a new type of cartel arrangement, controlling investment rather than output or prices.

We see then that the investment nomination mechanism may be defective, signalling too much or too little investment in response to a demand change, in oligopolistic as well as purely competitive industries. The question remains, which market structure poses the greater threat to macroeconomic stability?

EMPIRICAL EVIDENCE

In an effort to find out, annual data on capital investment outlays between 1954 and 1963 were collected for a sample of 75 manufacturing industries, all but three defined at the four-digit level.[40] The sample, which substantially overlaps the 108 industry sample analyzed earlier in this chapter, was selected to satisfy two criteria. First, the investment series for the 10 years covered had to be complete or nearly complete. In 53 cases, data for all 10 years were available; in 21 more, one year was lacking; and in a single case investment data for two years were unavailable. Second, the census industry definition had to be such that four-firm concentration ratios could be used either directly or after adjustment

---

[36] Cf. Kurt Bloch, "On German Cartels," *Journal of Business*, July 1932, pp. 213–222.

[37] For a seminal discussion, see Duesenberry, *op. cit.*, pp. 113–133. See also Donald H. Wallace, *Market Control in the Aluminum Industry* (Cambridge: Harvard University Press, 1937), pp. 336–343.

[38] Cf. M. J. Peck, *Competition in the Aluminum Industry* (Cambridge: Harvard University Press, 1961), pp. 146–147, 162–164, and 208; and "Too Many Fibers Spoil the Miracle," *Business Week*, October 29, 1966, pp. 165–170. On similar overexpansion in fertilizer production, see "All That Fertilizer and No Place To Grow," *Fortune*, June 1, 1968, pp. 90 ff.; and "Oil Companies Bail Out of Fertilizer Surplus," *Business Week*, December 13, 1969, pp. 35–36.

[39] Cf. Yamamura, *op. cit.*

[40] This material is adapted from F. M. Scherer, "Market Structure and the Stability of Investment," *American Economic Review*, May 1969, pp. 172–179. In a more qualitative study, James W. Meehan found that capacity expansion in response to demand increases overshot the levels consistent with long-run equilibrium in two atomistically structured industries—soft coal mining and flour milling—and also in two oligopolistic industries—steel and cement manufacturing. Only in the monopolized prewar aluminum industry was there no evidence of over-shooting. "Market Structure and Excess Capacity: A Theoretical and Empirical Analysis," unpublished Ph.D. dissertation, Boston College, 1967.

as a meaningful index of structural market power. Altogether, the 75 industries in the sample accounted for 37 per cent of all new capital investment and 30 per cent of value added in the manufacturing sector during 1963.

What we want to determine is whether investment outlays are less stable over time in concentrated industries as compared to atomistically structured industries. To measure the degree of investment instability, we use the standard error of estimate obtained after regressing the logarithms of annual new capital expenditures between 1954 and 1963 for each sampled industry on a simple time trend variable. Let us call this index of instability V_i. The higher V_i is, the more unstable observed investment outlays were relative to a smooth exponential growth trend.

Our concentration variable C_i is the simple average of the unadjusted or (in 12 industries) appropriately adjusted four-firm concentration ratios for 1954, 1958, and 1963. Because the stability of investment over time is affected by a variety of supply and demand influences, several additional explanatory variables will be employed. They include the following:

Dur_i: A class variable distinguishing durable from nondurable goods.

$Cons_i$: A class variable distinguishing consumer goods from all other commodities.

Int_i: A class variable distinguishing intermediate goods from commodities sold as end items.

VMH_i: An index of demand instability, given by the standard error of estimate derived after regressing the logarithms of annual production worker manhours between 1954 and 1963 on a time trend.

S_i: An index of industry size, given by the simple average of the logarithms of value added in 1954, 1958, and 1963.

$(K/VA)_i$: An index of capital intensity, given by the ratio of December 1957 capital investment at book value to 1958 value added.

The simple correlations between the index of investment variability V_i and the explanatory variables are as follows:

Variable	Correlation Coefficient
C_i	+0.331
Dur_i	+0.354
$Cons_i$	−0.300
Int_i	+0.216
VMH_i	+0.309
S_i	−0.299
$(K/VA)_i$	+0.288

All but the intermediate goods correlation are significantly different from zero at the 95 per cent level of statistical confidence. The relatively strong positive correlation between V_i and C_i lends preliminary support to the view that instability of investment increases with concentration. As one would expect, durable goods producers and industries with large fluctuations in production worker manhours had more unstable investment profiles.[41] Investment was more stable in the larger industries, probably because such industries have more highly diversified product lines and face steeper short-run capital goods supply functions in boom times, and possibly also because the larger industries tend to be less concentrated.

To isolate the net effect of concentration among these various influences, multiple regression analysis must be employed. The linear regression of V_i on all the main independent explanatory variables but VMH_i is as follows, where concentration C_i is measured in ratio form:

$$(13.1) \quad V_i = .181 + .057 \; C_i + .054 \; Dur_i$$
$$ (.029) \quad\quad (.018)$$

$$+ \; .0035 \; Cons_i + .022 \; Int_i$$
$$ (.0186) \quad\quad\quad (.017)$$

---

[41] It is worth noting that concentration is positively correlated with the index of production worker manhours instability VMH_i, with $r = 0.205$, which is significant at the 90 per cent confidence level. This lends additional support to the findings reported on pp. 313–314 *supra*.

$$- .055\ S_i + .056\ (K/VA)_i;$$
$$\quad (.015) \qquad (.023)$$

$$R^2 = .407;\ N = 75.$$

(Standard errors of the regression coefficients are given in parentheses.) The observed positive relationship between investment instability and concentration passes a statistical significance test at the 94 per cent confidence level. When VMH_i is introduced as an additional index of demand instability, the results are as follows:

$$(13.2)\ V_i = .160 + .050\ C_i + .045\ Dur_i$$
$$\qquad\qquad (.029) \qquad (.019)$$

$$+ .0099\ Cons_i + .027\ Int_i$$
$$\ (.0190) \qquad\quad (.017)$$

$$- .054\ S_i + .059\ (K/VA)_i$$
$$\ (.015) \qquad (.023)$$

$$+ .625\ VMH_i;\ R^2 = .424;\ N = 75.$$
$$\ (.437)$$

Here the positive effect of concentration is attenuated somewhat, but it passes a statistical significance test at the 90 per cent confidence level. All in all, the analysis provides moderately strong support for the hypothesis that investment is more unstable relative to its trend in concentrated than in atomistic industries. Raising the four-firm concentration ratio from .10 to .90—that is, moving from an atomistic structure to tight oligopoly—leads to a 40 per cent average increase in the instability of investment, as estimated by equation (13.1) when all other variables are held at their mean values, or to a 34 per cent increase according to equation (13.2).

It remains to be ascertained whether this observed instability is of a cyclical or largely random character. Cyclical instability would prevail if oligopolists increased their capital outlays especially sharply in response to demand spurts, cutting back equally vigorously during slumps. But alternatively, the concentrated industry outlays might be scattered more widely in essentially random fashion across the business cycle,

without notably greater dispersion solely at peaks and troughs.

To shed some light on these alternatives, Durbin-Watson autocorrelation coefficients were computed from the time trend adjustment regressions of the 53 industries on which complete investment data were available. The Durbin-Watson coefficient can vary from a value of zero, when each trend deviation is positively correlated with the next period's deviation, revealing a regular cyclical pattern, to 4.0, when each deviation is negatively correlated with the next year's deviation, implying annual oscillations. The computed Durbin-Watson coefficients were negatively correlated with concentration, suggesting that the degree of cyclical variability rises with concentration. However, the correlation coefficient of -0.13 is not significantly different from zero by standard statistical tests. Similarly negative but statistically insignificant relationships appeared in multiple regression analyses taking the Durbin-Watson coefficient as the dependent variable and concentration as one of several relevant independent variables. This indicates that investment was at best only slightly more volatile cyclically in the more concentrated industries. The observed instability associated with concentration seems instead to have been predominantly of a random character.[42] The reason for this stronger bias toward unsystematic instability is evidently the paucity of independent decision-making centers in concentrated industries, so that surges in spending by one large firm are not always offset (as they might be under the law of large numbers) by declines in other firms' spending. In atomistic industries, on the other hand, investment decisions are so widely dispersed that the random components of individual producers' investment series tend to cancel each other out, reducing variability at the industry-wide level.

INTERPRETATION

These results provide no support to economists who argue for concentration because of its alleged investment stabilization advantages. But the greater observed intertemporal instability of

---

[42]For further supporting evidence, see Scherer, *op. cit.*, pp. 176–177.

concentrated industry capital spending may also do relatively little disservice to the cause of macroeconomic stability, at least to the extent that it is in fact largely of random character, and not synchronized with overall business cycle movements. For although statistical averaging-out may not operate fully within specific concentrated industries, there will be further averaging-out *between* industries. We conclude therefore from the evidence available that the net effect of concentration on investment stability is unfavorable, but only moderately so.

Chapter 14

Product Differentiation, Market Structure, and Competition

After being concerned in the past nine chapters almost exclusively with pricing behavior, we shift our attention to firms' product policies—i.e., the methods by which they strive to differentiate their goods and services from rival offerings. The objective in both pricing and product differentiation decisions is presumably to maximize profits. But there is a difference in the character of the decisions. It is not hard to change a pricing decision once it has been made. Companies can move from a high-profit-margin, entry-encouraging price posture to a low-margin position virtually overnight if they so desire. This is not nearly as true of product differentiation decisions. Once the firm has committed itself to a set of physical and subjective product attributes, months or even years may be required before it can escape that commitment. Although each involves both short-run and long-run considerations, it is not too severe an oversimplification to suggest that pricing decisions epitomize the tactical problems of business enterprise, while product differentiation decisions fall more heavily in the realm of strategy.[1]

Sellers differentiate their products in four main ways. First, they may select plant or store locations which are more convenient (in terms of travel time and/or transportation costs) than rival locations. The locational advantages of the corner drug store and the local stone quarry are illustrations. Second, they may offer exception-ally good (or, alas, bad) service. Some retailers maintain sufficiently large and well-trained staffs to provide prompt, intelligent, and courteous service; others are better known for long checkout lines and grumbling cashiers, mollifying the effect with rock-bottom prices. Some computer manufacturers contribute an array of free programming services to those who use their machines; others do no programming. And so on. Third, there are physical differences in the products supplied. Paints may be more or less mildew-resistant; a suit may incorporate the most finely woven wool worsted or a coarser substitute; the design of an appliance may be mundane or reflect the genius of a Henry Dreyfuss; an automobile may accelerate to 60 m.p.h. in 8 seconds or 14 seconds; a drug may have minimal or serious side effects; an FM tuner may or may not embody drift-free components; etc. Finally, products are differentiated in terms of the subjective image they impress on the consumer's mind. Firms attempt to enhance the image of their products through brand labelling, advertising, direct word-of-mouth sales promotion, and the design of attractive packages.

Much and perhaps most of the product differentiation effort observed in a modern private enterprise economy represents little more than a natural and healthy response to legitimate demands. Peoples' wants are fantastically di-

[1]For similar views, see K. W. Rothschild, "Price Theory and Oligopoly," *Economic Journal*, September 1947, especially pp. 307–319; and Richard B. Heflebower, "Toward a Theory of Industrial Markets and Prices," *American Economic Review*, May 1954, pp. 121–139.

verse, and consumers clearly desire a variegated menu of consumption opportunities. It is a rare consumer who doesn't value convenience in the location of suppliers serving him, and many will pay a price premium for a certain amount of locational convenience. Nearly every consumer prefers good service over poor, though the prices individuals stand willing to pay for extra service vary widely. The diversity of wants with respect to physical design and performance characteristics is especially great. Some men prefer cotton shirts, some silk shirts, some hair shirts, and some no shirt at all. Some want to fly supersonically; others would just as soon walk in the woods. Likewise, different consumers place varying weights on the subjective aura or image accompanying the products they buy.

The relevant question for economic analysis is not, therefore, whether product differentiation is a good thing, but rather, how much product differentiation there should be and whether certain market conditions might lead to excessive or inadequate differentiation. Unfortunately, there are no hard-and-fast answers, partly because we lack data on the costs and benefits of diversity but even more because economic theory has provided no operational calculus for comparing the benefits of diversity with its social costs. There is general agreement that more diversity is preferable to less if the cost is the same; and that consumers are better off if they can choose freely between high-service (or quality or convenience), high-price consumption bundles and low-service (or quality or convenience), low-price bundles than when they face only one possibility. By such weak rules alone, much of all product differentiation is apt to pass the test of social desirability. Thus, if the typical consumer can choose between several well-stocked, price-competitive supermarkets within 15 minutes' driving distance of home and a friendly but high-priced Mom-and-Pop grocery store within five blocks' walking distance, the state of consumer welfare can hardly be said to be seriously amiss. Our task in this chapter is to identify circumstances in which product differentiation efforts lead to outcomes less clearly in harmony with the public interest. Then, in Chapters 15 and 16, we shall attempt to determine which market structures are most conducive to a vigorous flow of technological innovations enhancing the array of available product choices.

Product differentiation activities most often singled out for a vote of public disapproval include image differentiation and those aspects of physical differentiation which entail the most superficial, transitory variations in product style or design. Was the American economy better off for having spent $17 billion on advertising in 1968, or was an appreciable fraction of this sum wasteful or even counter-productive? Were the users of deodorants, pain remedies, hair bleach, and similar products benefited because Bristol-Myers devoted 28 per cent of its 1966 sales revenues to advertising?[2] What are the consequences of the American automobile industry's annual model change cycle, which rapidly renders aging vehicles stylistically obsolete?

THE SOCIAL BENEFITS OF IMAGE DIFFERENTIATION

Perhaps we should continue this line of attack by asking, When did advertising men stop beating their wives? However, the advertising and image differentiation issue is not all that one-sided. Before letting fly a hostile volley, let us examine the confirmed and alleged benefits of image differentiation.[3]

For one, advertising serves an informative function, letting buyers know the available product alternatives and permitting them to make better choices than they might if they had to ferret out information from a host of geographically dispersed sellers. A stock question in the debate over advertising is, How much advertising is beneficially informative, and how much merely persuasive? No clear-cut answer can be given, since it is difficult to draw a sharp line

---

[2] Cf. "Bristol-Myers' Hard Sell," *Fortune*, February 1967, p. 118.

[3] For a recent survey of the literature in this and other areas, see P. Doyle, "Economic Aspects of Advertising: A Survey," *Economic Journal*, September 1968, pp. 570–602.

between informing and persuading. Much advertising exhibits some of each trait. Nevertheless, a crude impression can be obtained by considering the distribution of advertising expenditures by media in 1965, summarized in Table 14.1. Newspaper advertising, accounting for nearly 30 per cent of total outlays, is preponderantly of an informative character, although (as any erstwhile home seller knows) even classified ads are written in persuasive fashion. However unwelcome it may be to the deluged recipient, direct mail advertising plays a largely informative role, as do many of the advertisements in business and farm periodicals. The information content of radio and television commercials is also not zero, despite a seemingly magnetic attraction toward that value. Even outdoor billboards sometimes supply wanted information, as travelers who sought gasoline or lodging in the early sign-less days of the U. S. interstate highways can testify. If a horseback generalization must be hazarded, it would be that half of all advertising expenditures cover messages of a primarily informative character, while the other half serve largely to persuade.

Second, a certain amount of image differentiation helps consumers select products of high quality and reliability and motivates producers to maintain adequate quality standards. If there were no brand names and trademarks, the con-

Table 14.1

U.S. Advertising Expenditures in 1965

Medium	Millions of Dollars		Per cent of Total
Newspapers		4,457	29.2
Classified ads	1,200		
Local display	2,400		
National display and other	857		
Magazines		1,199	7.9
Farm publications		34	0.2
Business and trade publications		671	4.4
Television		2,515	16.5
Network	1,237		
Local	412		
Spot	866		
Radio		917	6.0
Network	60		
Local	589		
Spot	268		
Direct mail		2,324	15.2
Outdoor billboards and signs[a]		180	1.2
Miscellaneous[b]		2,959	19.4
TOTAL		15,256	100.0

Sources: *Printers' Ink,* February 24, 1967, pp. 9–10; Jules Backman, *Advertising and Competition* (New York: New York University Press, 1967), pp. 30 and 161–179; and Neil H. Borden, *The Economic Effects of Advertising* (Chicago: Irwin, 1942), pp. 52–58.

[a]This appears to be an underestimate. In 1966, S.I.C. industry 3993 (signs and advertising displays) had sales of $819 million and value added of $496 million.

[b]A catch-all category, including the estimated cost of corporate advertising departments, art work and engravings, motion picture trailers, car cards, sandwich men, signs and advertising novelties, sky-writers, and perhaps such true miscellanea as the Goodyear blimp.

sumer might never be sure who made an item he consumed, and he would have difficulty rewarding through repeat purchases manufacturers who achieve high quality or cater to his special tastes. This is a lesson which dawned late but forcefully upon Soviet Union economic planners, who found that requiring consumer goods manufacturers to imprint their individual 'production marks' on products helped guard against deteriorating quality standards.[4] Trademarking and brand labelling also contribute in a subtle way to distributional efficiency. Without them, the conscientious housewife would have to make repeated inquiries about products susceptible to quality or taste variations, asking whether a particular product was good, what its distinguishing characteristics were, and perhaps (as in the almost bygone days of the pickle barrel) whether she might try a sample. This takes a great deal of time for both merchants and shoppers, increasing transaction costs significantly. The existence of branded goods whose characteristics vary little from week to week makes it possible to have convenient self-service shopping and hence to realize the efficiencies of supermarkets.

The crucial question is, How far must image differentiation go to achieve these benefits? Is mere trademarking sufficient, or must there also be advertising to bolster the supplier's or the product's image? The answer depends upon the nature of the product. For industrial goods, even trademarking is usually unnecessary, since industrial buyers are skilled at evaluating the products they receive, and they keep records permitting them to trace responsibility for quality deficiencies to specific suppliers. For consumer goods purchased repetitively, trademarking without more is probably sufficient, since a bad experience with one brand will induce a prompt

shift to another, this process of experimentation continuing until some brand proves persistently satisfactory.[5] The best case for additional image differentiation exists for consumer durables complex enough to prevent the buyer from distinguishing through inspection whether they will function effectively, and purchased so infrequently that past experience is insufficient or obsolete as a guide. Here many consumers base their decisions on the manufacturer's reputation for quality and reliability—a reputation built up through advertising as well as actual performance.

However, does proclaiming to the world that one's quality is superior make it true? Not necessarily, but there may be some beneficial spillover from image creation to actual behavior. As Borden observed in his massive study of the economic effects of advertising, the advertised brand usually represents a goodwill asset which has been built up at considerable expense, and injury to it would mean a business loss.[6] The link between image and behavior is perhaps strongest for firms selling a broad line of consumer durable goods. Companies like General Electric and Sunbeam are acutely aware that the poor performance of any single appliance series can, through its adverse reputation effects, impair the sales of many other lines. Though this does not guarantee good performance, it at least increases the probability that the image-conscious producer will try hard to maintain adequate quality standards. This assurance in turn has some value to the consumer, who by purchasing a well-known brand can reduce the risk of being fleeced by a fly-by-night—a species unfortunately not yet extinct. Given that the majority of all small firms strive as diligently as the large to preserve their reputations for quality, this may be a modest benefit, but it is surely not insignificant.

[4]See Marshall I. Goldman, "Product Differentiation and Advertising: Some Lessons from Soviet Experience," *Journal of Political Economy*, August 1960, pp. 346–357; Gilbert Burck, "The Auspicious Rise of the Soviet Consumer," *Fortune*, August 1966, pp. 130 ff.; and (for a more skeptical view) Philip Hanson, *The Consumer in the Soviet Economy* (London: Macmillan, 1969), pp. 204–206. In 1966, Soviet Union advertising expenditures were on the order of $18 million, compared to nearly $16 billion in the United States.

[5]This defense mechanism can break down when there are substantial variations in quality over time for reasons beyond the control of the manufacturer. Winemaking is a prime example. In such cases, no amount of image differentiation is likely to help the consumer much.

[6]Neil H. Borden, *The Economic Effects of Advertising* (Chicago: Irwin, 1942), especially pp. 631–632 and 866.

Another benefit sometimes attributed to advertising is that it permits the realization of production scale economies which might otherwise be unattainable.[7] For this to be true, there must be other market imperfections, such as spatial isolation or the appeal of one's product to only a limited spectrum of tastes, which inhibit expansion of output to the point where long-run average cost is minimized. Advertising, by broadening the firm's market appeal, may facilitate profitable expansion into a range of lower production cost. This effect does not necessarily occur, however. Without detailed quantitative information on the shape of the cost functions, price elasticities of demand, and the response of demand to advertising outlays, economic theory cannot predict unambiguously whether or not output will be increased.[8] What evidence we have is also inconclusive. Borden went further than others in assembling relevant data, but he was forced to end his analysis by admitting that "it is impossible from cost data to trace a clear causal relationship between decreased production costs and advertising."[9]

A related conjecture is that advertising, by making known the availability of new products, enables innovators to tap larger markets more rapidly, enhancing the profits from innovation and hence strengthening incentives for investment in innovation. This point is stressed by Professor Backman in a book commissioned by the Association of National Advertisers.[10] It finds support in the theory of optimal research and development expenditure scheduling, as we

shall see further in the next chapter.[11] However, except for prescription drugs, most of the product lines cited by Backman as fields of innovation accompanied by especially high promotional outlays—e.g., deodorants, frozen dinners, soaps, hair bleaches, cold breakfast cereals, cake mixes, dog foods, and oleomargarine—hardly seem to be those in which human welfare has taken giant strides through technological change.

Advertising is also credited with subsidizing the mass communications media. In recent years the sale of advertising space or time has provided roughly two thirds of the gross revenues of American newspapers and magazines and (excluding educational stations) virtually all the revenue of radio and television broadcasters. Of course, if there were no advertising, newspapers and magazines would be much thinner and publication costs would be lower. Still the best evidence available indicates that advertising revenues yield a net publication subsidy after deducting incremental costs. Borden found the subsidy component to be roughly half of advertising revenues for U. S. newspapers and a fourth of revenues for magazines in 1935.[12] Kaldor's estimate of the net subsidy to British newspapers in 1938 was £20 million out of £90 million advertising revenues.[13] It is not certain, however, that such subsidies are an unambiguous blessing. Subsidies tend to distort the allocation of resources, unless the subsidized commodity generates external economies or is produced under conditions of declining long-run unit cost (in which case it could not be sold profitably if

---

[7]For an interesting but not altogether convincing dynamic conjecture in this vein, stating that advertising freed manufacturers from dependence upon wholesalers, permitting them to tap a mass consumer market, see Nicholas Kaldor, "The Economic Aspects of Advertising," *Review of Economic Studies,* Vol. 18, 1949–1950, pp. 17–21.

[8]Cf. Edward H. Chamberlin, *The Theory of Monopolistic Competition* (Sixth ed.; Cambridge: Harvard University Press, 1950), Chapter VII; Harold Demsetz, "The Nature of Equilibrium in Monopolistic Competition," *Journal of Political Economy,* February 1959, pp. 21–30; *idem,* "The Welfare and Empirical Implications of Monopolistic Competition," *Economic Journal,* September 1964, pp. 623–641; Chamberlin, "Reply to Mr. Demsetz," *Journal of Political Economy,* June 1964, pp. 314–315; and G. C. Archibald, "Chamberlin versus Chicago," *Review of Economic Studies,* Vol. 29, 1961–1962, pp. 2–28; with comments and a reply in Vol. 30, 1962–1963, pp. 68–71.

[9]*Op. cit.,* p. 854.

[10]Jules Backman, *Advertising and Competition* (New York: New York University Press, 1967), pp. 3, 23–27, and 157–158.

[11]See F. M. Scherer, "Research and Development Resource Allocation under Rivalry," *Quarterly Journal of Economics,* August 1967, especially pp. 368 and 388.

[12]*Op. cit.,* pp. 68–71 and 923–933.

[13]*Op. cit.,* p. 6.

priced at marginal cost).[14] Both rationalizations for subsidy apply to some extent in the mass media industries. Yet the very nature of the subsidization process may undermine what might otherwise be an important external benefit of the mass media—the cultivation of a sensitive, informed public. Consumer goods advertisers generally favor media which will transmit their messages to the largest relevant audience, and the media respond by attempting to maximize audience size through an appeal to the lowest common denominator. The result is the scandal sheet and television's "vast wasteland," as Federal Communications Commission chairman Newton Minow described it in 1961. Indeed, many TV programs are of such low intellectual caliber that the commercials stand out as a refreshingly sophisticated interlude.

This last point suggests still another benefit of advertising and image differentiation. Advertising is art, and some of it is good art, with cultural or entertainment value in its own right. In addition, it can be argued that consumers derive pleasure from the image which advertising imparts to products, above and beyond the satisfaction flowing in some organic sense from the physical attributes of the products. There is no simple case in logic for distinguishing between the utility people obtain from what they think they are getting and what they objectively obtain. As Galbraith observed, "the New York housewife who was forced to do without Macy's advertising would have a sense of loss second only to that from doing without Macy's."[15]

Finally, it is sometimes said that advertising has the desirable effect of mitigating the business cycle and stabilizing the economy. On closer scrutiny, this claim can be divided into two propositions: (1) that businessmen hasten recovery from recessions by redoubling their promotional efforts to stimulate lagging sales; and (2) that

advertising has a long-run stabilizing effect on aspirations, making people less willing to reduce consumption when income falls and more anxious to increase it when income rises, thereby minimizing the danger of recessions due to cyclical or secular stagnation of demand. On the first point, the evidence is uniformly unfavorable. Advertising expenditures exhibit a definite procyclical pattern, rising in booms and falling in recessions, contrary to what is required for stabilization.[16] On the second we simply have no evidence. Whatever the merits of the case may be, advertising is obviously not uniquely efficacious as a consumption stabilizer, since the same job can be done through fiscal and monetary policy measures.

THE SOCIAL COSTS OF IMAGE DIFFERENTIATION

Against these benefits, demonstrated and conjectural, we must weigh the social costs of advertising and other image differentiation activities. The most obvious is the cost of the resources used—at least $17 billion, or 2.0 per cent of GNP, for advertising in 1968, plus several billion dollars more for such packaging gimmicks as the injection-molded Yogi Bear plastic containers for children's bubble bath compound. This is no trivial sum, and some of it is demonstrably wasteful. The promotional efforts of pharmaceutical manufacturers are a prime illustration. In 1964, the U. S. drug industry spent an estimated $700 million promoting the prescription products it sold for $2.4 billion. This represents an average outlay of more than $3,000 per prescribing physician, including at least $1,300 per physician for advertising and the remainder for salesmen's compensation, all-expenses-paid trips by doctors to New York City for a round of cocktail parties and musical comedies, and other promotional

[14]Cf. Chapter 22 *infra.*

[15]J. K. Galbraith, *American Capitalism: The Concept of Countervailing Power* (Rev. ed.; Boston: Houghton Mifflin, 1956), p. 98. For conflicting views on the metaphysics of image differentiation, see Jules Henry, *Culture Against Man* (New York: Random House, 1963), Chapters 2 and 3; and Walter Taplin, *Advertising: A New Approach* (Boston: Little, Brown, 1963).

[16]See Borden, *op. cit.*, pp. 725–736 and 865–866; Backman, *op. cit.*, pp. 178–179; and Joel Dean, *Managerial Economics* (Englewood Cliffs: Prentice-Hall, 1951), pp. 375–385.

costs.[17] A sizeable fraction of this effort served some informational purpose, letting physicians know about the newest tools of their art. Yet the diffusion of medical knowledge would surely be advanced more effectively if a much smaller sum were spent to subsidize bringing each physician away from the pressures of his office to an objective two-week-long annual seminar on pharmaceutical advances.

Second, much of the 'information' conveyed in advertisements is something less than a faithful depiction of reality. Outright falsification, although once common, is now kept in check reasonably well by laws against unfair and deceptive trade practices, administered by the Federal Trade Commission and the Food and Drug Administration. But persuasion through partial disclosure persists. The consumer is told, for instance, that Anacin contains twice as much pure pain reliever as other leading headache remedies, but not that the pure pain reliever referred to is plain aspirin. Or a gasoline is touted for containing Platformate, with no explanation that this is merely a brand name for gasoline cracked with a platinum catalyst, which nearly all refiners use. When the government moves in on such practices, as the F T C did for pain remedies in 1967, advertisers invent new and more subtle ways of exaggerating their products' merits, playing a continuous game of brinkmanship with respect to the law. To be sure, many consumers are sophisticated enough to avoid being stampeded into ill-informed purchases by such half-truths.[18] Some must be taken in, however, for advertisers would not try to mislead if they thought they were convincing no one.

Another potential cost of advertising is the contribution it makes toward instilling or entrenching hedonistic values. How much advertising is responsible for whatever ascendance hedonism has enjoyed in Western society is impossible to say. Certainly, other forces have made independent contributions. And to impute any social cost at all is to make a moral judgment over which reasonable men can disagree. We shall therefore not belabor the question, leaving the debate to philosophers, who have comparative advantage at it.

We are on only slightly firmer ground chalking up a negative score for image differentiation on a related ethical dimension. The approach of much advertising and style differentiation is to lead the consumer into making introspective comparisons between his own well-being and that of people he admires or would like to emulate. He is told he stands a better chance of attaining the status to which he aspires if he follows the example of consumption pacesetters or becomes one himself, and in the more blatant assaults, that his current status is endangered by not consuming what the 'right' people consume. Translated into economic jargon, advertising seeks to make the utility of any given consumer depend not merely upon the goods and services he himself consumes, but also upon the consumption decisions of his peers. It renders utility functions interdependent, generating external diseconomies in consumption. To the extent that it is successful in doing this, advertising can destroy utility along with creating it. To be sure, by responding to the stimulus and buying an advertised product the consumer may feel he is gaining something worthwhile. But it is not clear he has done any more than return to the satisfaction level he would have maintained with no attack through persuasion on his preference structure.

Finally, to descend to a less esoteric plane, advertising and other forms of image differentiation confer upon the firms using them some monopoly power. They permit the seller to choose within a more or less restricted range

---

[17]See the testimony of Dr. James L. Goddard, reported in "Goddard Tells of False Drug Ads by a Third of Companies in 1965," *New York Times*, May 26, 1966, p. 1. See also U. S. Department of Health, Education, and Welfare, Task Force on Prescription Drugs, Background Paper, "The Drug Makers and the Drug Distributors" (Washington: December 1968), pp. 27–28.

[18]For the results of a survey of consumer reactions to advertisements of varying degrees of deceptiveness, see Borden, *op. cit.*, pp. 742–767. See also the extensive opinion survey reported in Raymond A. Bauer and Stephen A. Greyser, *Advertising in America: The Consumer View* (Boston: Harvard Business School Division of Research, 1968).

whether to charge a higher or lower price for its product. Presumably, if the differentiation effort has been successful, the price will be higher than it would have been under undifferentiated competition, other things (such as costs) being held equal. Image differentiation can also raise barriers to entry, increasing the likelihood that prices can be maintained continually above cost and perhaps biasing industry structure in an oligopolistic direction. It is with these direct effects of product differentiation and their indirect consequences that we shall be concerned in the remainder of this chapter.

Some evidence is helpful in introducing the discussion. The opportunities for product differentiation are particularly abundant in grocery retailing. The products sold in grocery stores can be differentiated spatially, through differences in service, and through advertising, *inter alia*. An impressionistic but not atypical view of what this means in terms of prices can be obtained by making, as the author did, a quick shopping excursion for a physically standardized product such as 5.25 per cent liquid sodium hypochlorite laundry bleach in two-quart plastic containers. Four stores in Ann Arbor, Michigan, were visited. Store A was a physically decrepit specialty shop in the heart of the student residential district. It carried the broadest line of dark breads and Kosher meats in town and was also distinctive for being open until midnight. Store B was a small, high-quality shop located a half block from the edge of the University of Michigan central campus. Among other things, it made home deliveries. Store C was a large A & P supermarket located on the periphery of town in an industrial neighborhood. Store D was a small A & P store in the heart of the main campus shopping district, where locational rents attain a maximum. Three brands of bleach were encountered: nationally advertised Clorox, the unadvertised product of a Detroit manufacturer, and A & P's private-label brand, advertised only in connection with A & P newspaper displays. The prices per half-gallon were as follows:

Specialty Store A:

Clorox	49¢
Detroit brand	45¢

Specialty Store B:

Clorox	45¢
Detroit brand	43¢

Large Suburban A & P:

Clorox	35¢
Detroit brand	29¢
A & P brand	29¢

Small Downtown A & P:

Clorox	None
Detroit brand	29¢
A & P brand	27¢

The highest prices were found in Store A, which was most convenient to masses of married students, remained open longest, and offered bread products not obtainable elsewhere. Surprisingly, there was no locational premium for the downtown A & P store.[19] The nationally advertised Clorox bleach commanded a price premium of from $.02 to $.06, or from 4.4 to 21 per cent over less heavily advertised products. Locational and service differentials appeared to be larger quantitatively than image differentials, although the latter were by no means negligible.

That consumers will pay a price premium for locational convenience or special service disturbs few observers. It is the differential between products alike in every respect but image which incites the most alarm. Nor is the example chosen unusual in this regard. A staff report of the National Commission on Food Marketing found through a sample survey of ten canned and bottled food products that the price of the most popular nationally advertised brand sold in chain stores was 21.5 per cent higher on the average than the price of private-label items of comparable quality. The price premia for nationally advertised goods ranged from 4 to 35 per cent.[20] In pharmaceuticals, the differentials are even more striking. Walker discovered in an analysis of 656 ethical drugs that the prices of

[19] A year after the survey, the store was closed due to its unprofitability.

[20] U. S. National Commission on Food Marketing, Technical Study No. 10, *Special Studies in Food Marketing* (Washington: June 1966), p. 65.

branded, advertised preparations were two thirds higher on the average than the prices of comparable items sold under their generic chemical names.[21] To some extent these differentials, especially in drugs, may be a payment the consumer is willing to make for the assurance of uniform quality which advertised brands presumably (but not necessarily) convey.[22] But it is hard to avoid concluding that if the housewife-consumer were informed about the merits of alternative products by some medium more objective than advertising and other image-enhancing devices, her readiness to pay price premiums as large as those observed here would be attenuated.

THE EFFECTS OF MARKET STRUCTURE ON PRODUCT DIFFERENTIATION EFFORT

Let us focus more closely on the relationships between differentiation and monopoly power. The chain of causation can run in two directions. Clearly, differentiation can confer power over price. We have yet to explore the full ramifications of this connection. But also, the structure of the market may affect the character and magnitude of sellers' product differentiation activities. This will be our immediate concern.

THE LARGE NUMBERS CASE

Serious thought about product differentiation began with Edward H. Chamberlin's analysis of the case in which numerous firms, each too small to take into account the effect of its price decisions on others, occupied an easily entered market. The analysis is so well known that only two key points need to be summarized. First, cost and demand conditions may be such that sellers find it profitable to differentiate their products. If they do, they will gain some control over price and will set a price which equates marginal cost

with marginal revenue. In the short run, monopoly profits may result. But second, these profits lure additional firms into the industry, leaving less market space for the original participants and hence forcing their demand curves to the left. Long-run equilibrium results when so much entry has occurred that no further opportunities for making a supra-normal profit remain. In the idealized case, each seller ends up with its downward-sloping demand curve tangent to its long-run cost function. For each, average total cost, including promotional costs, is higher than it needs to be, and the equilibrium price is correspondingly higher. Whether unit *production* costs are as low as they might be cannot, as we have seen earlier, be determined without additional facts.

An interesting and important variant case arises when the price charged by monopolistic competitors is fixed and beyond their control—i.e., because the government imposes price controls, because sellers have surrendered their price-making discretion to a cartel authority too bureaucratic or unsure of itself to attempt frequent adjustments, or when manufacturers have enforced resale price maintenance upon firms retailing their products. Again, above-normal profits may be earned in the short run. But two kinds of forces will operate to eliminate those profits.

First, existing industry members will strive to increase the sales they make at the fixed price by escalating advertising, service, etc. This is illustrated graphically in Figure 14.1. The unit cost curve without special promotion is given by ATC, the fixed price by OP, and the quantity sold by a representative firm without special promotion by PA. A generous profit margin AF is earned. As companies intensify their promotional efforts to increase sales, the cost curve rises, e.g., to ATC^*. Sales expand to PB, with the profit margin BG being earned. The amount of the sales increase

[21]Hugh D. Walker, "Market Power and Relative Prices in the Ethical Drug Industry," *Abstracts of Econometric Society Papers*, December 1967 meetings, pp. 73–74.

[22]On the problem of clinical and biological equivalence in drugs, see "Drug Brands Compared by F.D.A.," *New York Times*, July 16, 1968, p. 13; and U. S. Department of Health, Education, and Welfare, Task Force on Prescription Drugs, *Final Report* (Washington: February 1969), pp. 9 and 31–35. The latter finds the lack of clinical equivalence danger to have been "grossly exaggerated."

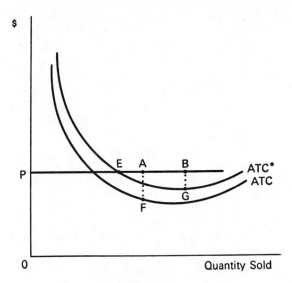

Figure 14.1
Promotional Competition with a Fixed Price

of monopolistic competition when prices are fixed can be too many firms of too small a size spending appreciable sums on promotion and service.

The liquor retailing trade offers an excellent example of these phenomena.[24] In many states, prices are either fixed by a state board or manufacturers are permitted by law to prescribe the prices at which their products can be distributed. Given a tendency for the price to consumers to be set at relatively high levels, liquor stores go all out to provide friendly service, offer speedy home delivery, take large advertisements in the yellow pages and local newspapers, and outdo each other in variety of products. The result is a significant increase in promotional and service costs, squeezing profit margins. It is unlikely, however, that margins will be eliminated for this reason alone. Diminishing returns undoubtedly discourage the expansion of promotional efforts before profits disappear altogether. New entry can complete the task if it is allowed to do so. But in some states entry restrictions are enforced in conjunction with price-fixing. Then supranormal profits may persist indefinitely, or at least until they are transformed into rents as established liquor store owners sell out to newcomers at a high price which capitalizes the scarcity value of their operating permits.

The women's dressmaking trades provide a slightly different manifestation of the same phenomenon. Retail dress prices tend to be set at traditional *pricing points* (such as $9.95 and $14.95) and the discount which manufacturers allow retailers is also confined to certain standard percentage values. This leaves manufacturers relatively little pricing discretion. Competition then takes the form primarily of competition in quality, each producer adding increments of quality through better materials, more careful stitching, more liberal cooperative advertising allowances, etc. so as to make its product as attractive as possible at the anticipated price

will be greater, the more elastic market demand is with respect to promotional expenditures and the less aggressively rival sellers implement offsetting promotions. Unless there are significantly diminishing returns in the winning of additional sales through expanded promotional expenditure, equilibrium profits are likely to be substantially reduced and perhaps even eliminated as a consequence of the promotional rivalry.[23]

Second, if entry is free, new firms will enter the industry to take advantage of the profit-making opportunity. The total quantity demanded will be divided up among more competitors, so that each seller's share of the market shrinks. This process is likely to continue until all opportunities for making a supra-normal profit have been exhausted. Equilibrium will then occur at a point like *E* in Figure 14.1, where the sales volume of the representative firm is too small to allow realization of all production and promotional scale economies. The result, then,

[23]See George J. Stigler, "Price and Non-Price Competition," *Journal of Political Economy*, January-February 1968, pp. 149–154; Robert Dorfman and Peter O. Steiner, "Optimal Advertising and Optimal Quality," *American Economic Review*, December 1954, pp. 835–836; and Lawrence Abbott, *Quality and Competition* (New York: Columbia University Press, 1955), especially pp. 139–170.

[24]Cf. Leonard W. Weiss, *Economics and American Industry* (New York: Wiley, 1961), pp. 427–430.

subject to the constraint that some target profit-margin be realized. With large numbers of firms in the trade and easy entry, this quality competition is frequently so intense that manufacturers find themselves able to realize profit margins yielding on the average no more than a normal return on invested capital.

ADVERTISING UNDER OLIGOPOLY

On *a priori* grounds, there is reason to believe that incentives to advertise will be stronger when the number of sellers is limited than when it is very large. Promotional activity can produce two distinguishable types of private gain. Demand may be shifted in favor of the general product line advertised at the expense of all other products, and it may be shifted in favor of the specific firm doing the advertising at the expense of other firms making similar products. If individual sellers' offerings are capable of image differentiation at all, the second gain can be realized whether the company advertising is one among many or an oligopolist. But the first type is more apt to be significant for monopolists or oligopolists. One firm among many can expect to reap only a very small fraction of the benefits from an overall expansion of market demand through advertising, whereas for an oligopolist the gain will be roughly proportional to its appreciable market share. In other words, the effect of advertising on overall market demand is an externality to the atomistic seller. It can be internalized completely only by a pure monopolist. Whether the amount of advertising undertaken by atomistic sellers is relatively large or small depends then upon the nature of advertising's benefits. Do they accrue predominantly to the industry as a whole or to the specific advertiser? And this no doubt varies from one type of product to the next.

Thus, no individual orange grower has an incentive to advertise on a nationwide basis, since his share of the increased demand for oranges would be minute, and advertising would probably not shift much business toward him from other growers. (Nor would he profit noticeably from the latter shift, since he presumably can sell as much as he pleases at the ruling market price.) But the Florida Citrus Commission, representing many growers, has a definite incentive to promote the sale of oranges generally and Florida oranges (which can be distinguished from the California product) in particular. Similarly, a small mass producer of dresses has little or no incentive to advertise in national fashion magazines. It may, however, undertake cooperative newspaper advertising with retail establishments which feature its wares, since the spillover effects of such advertising are modest. And a small high-fashion garment house may even buy space in the nationwide media, since it can gear its promotional appeal to unique design features.

Although a pure monopolist has the maximum incentive to undertake advertising with broad market-expanding effects, it lacks any incentive for advertising to win sales away from rival sellers. Here oligopolists occupy the best (or worst) of both worlds. They have rivals from whom they can capture sales, and they share significantly in the overall expansion of market demand. As George Washington Hill, swashbuckling president of the American Tobacco Co. from 1925 to 1946, explained his company's advertising philosophy, "Of course, you benefit yourself more than the other fellow . . . but you help the whole industry if you do a good job."[25]

We might expect, therefore, advertising expenditures per dollar of sales to be higher under oligopoly than under either pure monopoly or monopolistic competition, *ceteris paribus*. There is only one hitch. Mutual interdependence is the hallmark of oligopoly. If one firm advertises to draw sales away from its rivals, what is to prevent the rivals from pursuing the same course, with a stalemate as the end result? And if all perceive this, would they not find it preferable to cooperate in spending only that amount on

---

[25]Quoted in W. H. Nicholls, *Price Policies in the Cigarette Industry* (Nashville: Vanderbilt University Press, 1951), p. 60. Nicholls presents an exceptionally interesting analysis of the cigarette Big Three's advertising rivalry. See also Borden, *op. cit.*, pp. 207–249; and Lester G. Telser, "Advertising and Cigarettes," *Journal of Political Economy*, October 1962, pp. 471–499.

advertising which maximizes their collective profits—that is, an amount approximating what would be spent by a pure monopolist?[26]

The static structure of oligopolistic advertising rivalry is similar to that of oligopolistic price rivalry, studied in Chapter 5. For each such rivalry a matrix of payoffs associated with alternative strategy choices can be constructed. Each, within the most interesting range of strategies, is a Prisoner's Dilemma game when the rivals occupy symmetric positions. To illustrate, consider the following hypothetical payoff matrix for an advertising rivalry between companies A and B.[27] We assume symmetry and for simplicity present only two strategy options for each firm— one connected with the Cournot equilibrium outcome and the other with a joint profit-maximizing outcome. Firm A's net profit payoffs (in millions of dollars per year) are given first, and Firm B's after the commas:

Firm B Spends Each Year
on Advertising

		$4 Million	$6 Million
Firm A Spends	$4 Million	10.0, 10.0	6.0, 12.0
	$6 Million	12.0, 6.0	8.7, 8.7

If the rivals match one another with outlays of $4 million, each gets profits of $10.0 million. If they increase the ante to $6 million each, overall sales rise, but these are more than offset by the higher advertising costs, so that each firm realizes net profits of only $8.7 million. If A outspends B, A will increase its take to $12.0 million, while if it is outspent, it will suffer market share losses and realize profits of only $6.0 million. The $6 million spending strategy dominates the $4 million strategy, so there is a compulsion for each company to commit the larger sum. But by so doing, the rivals end up with lower profits than they would earn if they cooperated in limiting expenditures to $4 million each.

In duopolistic price rivalry, we saw in Chapter 5, there is reason to expect, at least as a first approximation, that the sellers will cooperate on joint profit-maximizing strategies. But advertising rivalry appears to be different in several respects.[28] First, price cuts can be matched almost instantaneously unless concessions can be kept secret, whereas it takes weeks or even months to set a retaliatory nationwide advertising campaign in motion. During this interim, the initiator enjoys market share and profit gains at the laggard's expense. The longer the lag between initiation and matching, the stronger the incentive to spend on image differentiation will be.[29] Fear of being left behind by its rivals spurs each oligopolist to anticipate the worst and to initiate campaigns, even if it means provoking an advertising race (not unlike an arms race) which carries expenditures beyond the level maximizing collective profits. Second, success at image differentiation depends at least as much upon the way the appeal is presented as on the amount of money spent. The outcome of an advertising campaign is therefore uncertain. Moreover, any fool can match a price cut, but counteracting a clever advertising gambit is far from easy. In this unpredictable clash of creative power sellers often tend to overestimate their own ability to make market share gains and

[26]If each firm executes a part of the campaign, the joint-profit-maximizing expenditure on advertising under oligopoly may not coincide exactly with the pure monopolist's optimal expenditure. It will tend to be lower if there are economies of scale in promotion which the oligopolists cannot exploit fully in their separate campaigns. It will tend to be higher if the variety of appeals attainable through separate campaigns has a more potent impact on overall market demand than a monopolist's monolithic campaign.

[27]For other examples, see Martin Shubik, *Strategy and Market Structure* (New York: Wiley, 1959), pp. 252–254 and 308.

[28]Cf. William Fellner, *Competition Among the Few* (New York: Knopf, 1949), pp. 183–191; Nicholls, *op. cit.*, pp. 187–203; Alexander Henderson, "The Theory of Duopoly," *Quarterly Journal of Economics*, November 1954, pp. 580–581; and J. M. Clark, *Competition as a Dynamic Process* (Washington: Brookings, 1961), pp. 245–263.

[29]For an ingenious dynamic analysis of differentiation rivalry under Cournot–type assumptions, see Hans Brems, "Response Lags and Nonprice Competition with Special Reference to the Automobile Industry," in Mary Jean Bowman, ed., *Expectations, Uncertainty, and Business Behavior* (New York: Social Science Research Council, 1958), pp. 134–143.

underestimate their rivals' ability to retaliate successfully, exhibiting little concern for mutual interdependence. Third, since price competition is unappealing in oligopoly, businessmen may seek an outlet for their aggressive instincts on nonprice dimensions such as advertising, where the drawbacks are not so obvious. And if prices are held comfortably above marginal production cost, the quest for additional orders through nonprice rivalry is more lucrative than it would be under competitive pricing.

Exactly where this rivalrous behavior will lead is difficult to predict. Cournot-type reactions do not seem improbable, given the lag structure and uncertainties of advertising rivalry. But expenditures may even be pushed higher. To see this, consider the following extension of our example:

Firm B Spends Each Year
on Advertising

		$6 Million	$8 Million
Firm A Spends	$6 Million	8.7, 8.7	6.0, 7.8
	$8 Million	7.8, 6.0	7.4, 7.4

Here a dominant strategy no longer exists. If Firm B is expected to maintain its outlays at $6 million (the Cournot assumption), the best strategy for Firm A is to hold its expenditures at $6 million too. A Cournot equilibrium will be established. If on the other hand Firm A fears the worst, it may elect its minimax strategy of $8 million and advertising outlays will continue to increase until choked off by severely diminishing marginal returns.[30] In either event each firm ends up spending a great deal on advertising messages which merely cancel out rival messages.

There is considerable evidence that oligopolists often fail to coordinate their advertising policies successfully, spend'ng much more than they would under joint profit maximization. In cigarettes, advertising expenditures rose from $4.3 million in 1910 to $13.8 million in 1913 after the American Tobacco Company, with 90 per cent of the market, was broken into several pieces under an antitrust judgment.[31] Further escalation followed during the 1920s as American attempted to regain industry leadership through an all-out promotional assault. Advertising spending settled down during the 1930s and 1940s, only to rise again from 8 per cent of sales in 1947 to 14 per cent in 1959 as new filter-tip and king-size brands were introduced, upsetting the prior market share equilibrium.[32] In the soap industry, it seems certain that the enormous sums spent on advertising (e.g., $250 million, or nearly 13 per cent of U. S. sales, in 1962) do little more than cancel rival messages out, since aggregate soap consumption can hardly be affected much by advertising.[33] Indeed, the principal savings anticipated by Lord Leverhulme in his 1906 proposal to create a soap monopoly in Great Britain were to be realized by eliminating the "frenzied competitive advertising" undertaken by rival producers.[34] In the U. S. automobile industry, an advertising race broke out among the leading manufacturers after supply caught up with demands left unsatisfied during World War II and the Korean war.[35] A study of several small-town motion picture markets found that total display lineage fell significantly when the number of theatres was reduced from two to only one.[36] In his book on the aluminum industry, M. J. Peck observed that the pace of market-

---

[30]The worst outcome if Firm A spends $6 million is a profit of $6.0 million. The worst outcome if Firm A spends $8 million is a profit of $7.4 million. The *maximum minimorum* is to spend $8 million.

[31]Cf. Borden, *op. cit.*, p. 212.

[32]Cf. Telser, "Advertising and Cigarettes"; and "Supply and Demand for Advertising Messages," *American Economic Review*, May 1966, pp. 463–464.

[33]Cf. Backman, *op. cit.*, pp. 17 and 27; and Joe S. Bain, *Barriers to New Competition* (Cambridge: Harvard University Press, 1956), pp. 282–283.

[34]P. Leslie Cook, *Effects of Mergers* (London: George Allen & Unwin, 1958), p. 223.

[35]Weiss, *op. cit.*, pp. 359–363.

[36]Julian L. Simon, "The Effect of the Competitive Structure upon Expenditures for Advertising," *Quarterly Journal of Economics*, November 1967, pp. 610–627. Simon concludes more generally from a novel Cournot-type analysis of optimal advertising strategy that "on most assumptions two sellers will together spend a sum for promotion greater than a monopolist."

ing and sales promotion accelerated when Kaiser and Reynolds entered to challenge Alcoa's monopoly.[37] And although cement manufacturers successfully enforced agreements to limit price and product quality competition, they found themselves "helpless in combatting excessive selling costs" during the 1930s, with outlays covering salesmen's compensation, entertainment and gifts for cement buyers, and other nonfreight distribution costs mounting to 16 per cent of net sales in 1939.[38]

While failure to hold advertising expenditures at joint profit-maximizing levels appears to be the rule in oligopoly, some exceptions can be found. The cigarette manufacturers collectively developed an advertising code discouraging such tactics as making claims with respect to product tar and nicotine content. This undoubtedly had some effect in suppressing advertising appeals exploiting the cancer scare. However, when the sales of its Kent cigarettes began falling, P. Lorillard Co. withdrew from participation in the code.[39] In 1957 the U. S. auto producers agreed to deemphasize horsepower in their advertisements and to refrain from direct participation in auto racing, ostensibly as a public service gesture but no doubt also to slow the growth of advertising outlays. The agreement was subsequently honored more in the breach than the keeping. They experienced somewhat greater success in avoiding competitive advertising of safety features.[40] Whether this reflects a spirit of oligopolistic forebearance, or merely the belief (based upon Ford's experience during the 1950s) that advertising safety features doesn't pay, is not

clear.[41] No other cases of explicit attempts to restrain advertising rivalry are known to the author, although some undoubtedly exist. As Professor Fellner has suggested, nonrivalrous handling of advertising expenditures is most likely to be found only in very mature oligopolies, where the strategy options of member firms have been reduced to a matter of routine and demand is fairly stable. And these, he adds, are not very common in the industrial and commercial world.[42]

Even when cooperation to limit promotional expenditures is weak, stable industry spending patterns eventually emerge.[43] Runaway advertising races, like runaway arms races, are exceptional, since a point must sooner or later be reached at which additional advertising outlays have little marginal impact on sales even if rivals fail to match them. More often than not, this equilibrium entails a great many messages merely cancelling one another out. This is as much as we can safely conclude from the foregoing analysis and evidence. Further inquiry into the relationship between market structure and advertising intensity is deferred to a later section.

TRADING STAMP AND PREMIUM RIVALRY

Another way retailers strive to gain consumer favor is to give premiums, trading stamps redeemable in merchandise, sweepstakes tickets, and the like as a 'free' bonus to purchasers. Expenditures on such giveaways have been estimated at roughly $3 billion per year.[44] In 1963, purchases of trading stamps alone amounted to $754 million.[45] Rivalry in the distribution of this

---

[37]M. J. Peck, *Competition in the Aluminum Industry* (Cambridge: Harvard University Press, 1961), pp. 123, 208.

[38]Samuel M. Loescher, *Imperfect Collusion in the Cement Industry* (Cambridge: Harvard University Press, 1959), pp. 135–136 and 213–216.

[39]"P. Lorillard Co. Withdrawing from Voluntary Code on Ads," *New York Times*, March 29, 1966, p. 53.

[40]"The Race for Safety Is On," *Business Week*, June 11, 1966, pp. 186–190. Asked by a reporter whether Ford would capitalize in its advertising on safety features its rivals lacked, president Arjay Miller responded, "Probably not. It wouldn't be fair because the others are not anti-safety. They'll move as fast as they can. But we plan to compete like hell on the safety features themselves."

[41]As industry wags put it at the time, "McNamara is selling safety, but Chevy is selling cars." See Dan Cordtz, "The Face in the Mirror at General Motors," *Fortune*, August 1966, p. 208.

[42]*Competition Among the Few*, pp. 188–189.

[43]See Roy W. Jastram, "Advertising Outlays under Oligopoly," *Review of Economics and Statistics*, May 1949, pp. 106–109.

[44]"$3 Billion Spent Yearly for Premiums," *Ann Arbor News*, April 27, 1967, from an Associated Press feature citing a premium industry newsletter.

[45]U. S. National Commission on Food Marketing, Technical Study No. 7, *Organization and Competition in Food Retailing* (Washington: June 1966), pp. 437–473.

largesse is similar structurally to advertising rivalry; both can be represented as Prisoner's Dilemma games. Since a detailed example would add little to the previous analysis, let us confine ourselves to a brief glance at the dynamics of trading stamp use.

The outlet which initiates a popular trading stamp program in a market where none existed previously undoubtedly benefits, drawing sales away from its rivals. With overhead costs fixed in the short and medium run, its sales gain is often so large that the contribution to profits from new patronage more than offsets the cost of the stamps. Thus, no price increase is required, and nearly everyone benefits, as the trading stamp redemption companies claim: the innovating store through increased sales volume and higher profits; and the consumer by receiving stamps redeemable for desirable merchandise without any increase in price. The only losers are rival retailers without stamps. But they consider this position intolerable, and many hasten to introduce competing stamp plans or similar premiums. This tends to neutralize the promotional advantage of the innovator, which finds its volume ebbing toward prestamp levels. With unit overhead costs returning to previous heights but burdened now with the cost of stamps, the innovator must either suffer reduced unit profits or raise prices. Since its rivals also incur stamp costs, a price increase joined by other members of the trade is the more likely alternative. A staff group of the National Commission on Food Marketing found that after some 200,000 to 300,000 retail establishments had joined the trading stamp parade, the cost of stamps and other giveaways in food chains was 2.12 per cent of 1960 sales, and prices had been raised by an amount equal to the stamp costs.[46] In the end, therefore, retailers are no better off on the average than they were before stamps were introduced (although some market share shifts will have taken place). Consumers end up paying higher prices covering at least the full economic cost of merchandise received for their stamps— and perhaps more.[47]

Complicating matters and making oligopolistic coordination of such promotional struggles difficult is the fact that the rivalry can spill over into a multiplicity of dimensions. After companies introducing trading stamps found it necessary to raise prices because imitation eroded their advantage, a few competitors discovered that challenging the stamp-givers by offering lower prices and no stamps was a viable strategy, even though it appeared futile in the early stages of the game. This was the tack the A & P Co. tried to pursue during the 1950s, hedging with its own stamp plan in areas where it was unable to maintain its market share merely by holding the price line. In supermarketing and gasoline retailing, some chains reacted to the trading stamp stalemate of the 1960s by initiating sweepstakes promotions. Although most sellers were at first reluctant to become involved, the games spread rapidly until discouraged, first by state antigambling code enforcement authorities and then by the Federal Trade Commission.[48] From observation of these and other promotional experiences a moral emerges: The more dimensions there are along which sellers can exercise their promotional ingenuity, the harder it is to avoid moves ultimately cancelled out by countermoves, despite the most ardent desire to respect mutual interdependence.

STYLE COMPETITION IN THE AUTOMOBILE INDUSTRY

One further illustration will round out the analysis. Differentiation through styling change has much in common with image differentiation. The appeal, to be sure, is embodied physically within the product, not in some separate message. But the incentives and pressures for sellers

---

[46]Ibid., p. 462. See also "Food Stamp Ban Dropped by Panel," New York Times, March 20, 1966, p. 38.

[47]For further analyses of consumer welfare implications, see Roger Sherman, "Trading Stamps and Consumer Welfare," Journal of Industrial Economics, November 1968, pp. 29–40; and Carolyn S. Bell, "Liberty and Prosperity, and No Stamps," Journal of Business, April 1967, pp. 194–202, with the comment by E. Beem and L. Isaacson and the reply by Mrs. Bell in the Journal of Business, July 1968, pp. 340–346.

[48]See "Why Gas Stations Keep Up Games," Business Week, September 21, 1968, pp. 62–66; Thomas O'Hanlon, "Who Wins Marketing Promotion Games?" Fortune, February 1969, pp. 104 ff.; and "F.T.C. Criticizes Giveaway Games," New York Times, January 1, 1969, p. 30.

to shed their oligopolistic restraint are essentially the same.

Automobile style change rivalry is the classic example.[49] In this facet of their operations the leading American producers have been vigorously and independently competitive, though all tend to shun daring departures with uncertain mass consumption appeal. After pent-up World War II demands had been satisfied, a three-year model cycle became the norm during the 1950s. Typically, grille, molding, and other details are altered in a minor facelift a year after some completely new model is introduced; in the second year more extensive changes are implemented; and after three years the cycle begins again as most of the major body parts—fenders, hoods, rear decks, roofs, doors, etc.—are totally restyled. The chief restraint on styling rivalry has been a tacit understanding that this three-year pattern is in some sense 'right.' But even that is not inviolate. On numerous occasions auto makers have broken away to a two-year cycle in the hope of increasing their market acceptance, and wholly new lines (e.g., the Thunderbird, Edsel, Corvette, Corvair, Mustang, and Maverick) are introduced at irregular intervals. Within this broad framework, efforts to be first with new styling features which will capture the consumer's fancy have been aggressive to a fault. Advanced styling plans are kept as secret as they can be in a land which frowns on indentured servitude and cutting out the tongues of employees. Espionage and counterespionage abound. Among other Bondian tactics, auto makers fly observation planes over their rivals' testing grounds, hoping to minimize the risk of being caught off guard by some styling innovation.

Three factors energize the process of auto styling competition. First, consumers are highly sensitive to design differences. The company which comes up with a winning design can make heavy inroads into rival market shares. Second, it takes from 15 to 24 months to produce a new model after a final design commitment has been made. The firm caught in a position of styling inferiority for such a long interval suffers considerably. Therefore, auto makers believe they cannot afford not to cover themselves against rival thrusts. Knowledge that others are preparing new models, coupled with uncertainty over the exact character of their plans, compels each firm to sustain its own style change effort. In other words, the prevailing attitude is that of the minimaxer. Third, the difficulty of predicting how consumers will respond to new designs interacts with the self-confidence auto executives develop from climbing above the pack to a top management position, leading each decision-making group to take an optimistic view of its chances for making market share gains through styling innovation.

The game played in this styling arena is not an inexpensive one. Using 1949 as a benchmark year of normal design modification, Fisher, Griliches, and Kaysen estimated that the extra cost of new dies and tooling attributable to the acceleration of auto styling rivalry in the 1950s averaged $560 million per year between 1956 and 1960, or $102 per automobile produced.[50] In tandem with this style change competition was a steady increase in the length, weight, horsepower, and complexity of the average auto sold. Fisher and his associates estimated that the average cost increase due to these changes was roughly $3.3 billion per year between 1956 and 1960, or $584 per car sold. Whether this latter cost upsurge was a direct result of styling rivalry, or whether it merely reflected a response to exogenously changing consumer wants, is arguable. Since consumers had the option of buying smaller, less high-powered autos, and since the compact cars introduced around 1960 enjoyed strong market acceptance only briefly, the second interpretation seems more compelling. In any event, the costs associated with styling rivalry are far from negligible.

Although the style changes put forward by one auto maker tend on the average to be offset by

[49]For various views, see Weiss, *op. cit.*, pp. 357–371; Robert F. Lanzillotti, "The Automobile Industry," in Walter Adams, ed., *The Structure of American Industry* (Third ed.; New York: Macmillan, 1961), pp. 311–354; and U. S. Senate, Committee on the Judiciary, Subcommittee on Antitrust and Monopoly, Report, *Administered Prices: Automobiles* (Washington: 1958), pp. 77–94.

[50]F. M. Fisher, Zvi Griliches, and Carl Kaysen, "The Costs of Automobile Model Changes Since 1949," *Journal of Political Economy*, October 1962, pp. 433–451.

rival countermoves, it is not clear that the leading producers are worse off due to their competition, since the costs added by rapid change have been passed along to consumers in the form of higher prices. A profit sacrifice would result only if significantly fewer cars were purchased because of the higher unit costs and prices. One's first impulse is to suspect that the opposite is true: overall car demand has been strengthened by a pace of styling change which makes three-year-old models passé. This is probably correct, but for rather subtle reasons. Ignoring short-run variations, the flow of new cars sold each year depends upon the *stock* of autos consumers wish to hold and on the average life of autos comprising that stock. Does rapid styling change affect either of these magnitudes?

No obvious link between style change and average life is evident, for a visit to any junkyard reveals that the vast majority of all autos there are scrapped for other than aesthetic reasons.[51] There is more reason to believe that the size of the equilibrium stock is affected by style changes. Used car prices fall more rapidly in an environment of rapid styling obsolescence. Outmoded cars are therefore sold at relatively low prices long before their physical utility is spent. With large numbers of stylistically obsolescent automobiles available at low prices, many persons (i.e., teen-agers, college students, and other indigents) are able to become car owners when they could not afford to do so if used car prices fell more slowly. Thus, rapid styling change has an output-expanding effect analogous to second-degree price discrimination. The auto makers extract consumers' surplus from buyers affluent and eager enough to pay a high price every two or three years for a vehicle with the latest design gimmicks, simultaneously reaching buyers with low ability or willingness to pay through the used car market. At least up to some point, therefore, styling competition probably increases aggregate industry profits. Whether it is carried

only to the point of joint profit maximization or beyond is difficult to judge. In view of the evident lack of restraint, it is certainly conceivable that the maximum-profit point is overstepped.

For smaller auto producers, a rapid rate of styling change is almost unambiguously disadvantageous.[52] If they match the giants in frequency of change, they must amortize the fixed costs of redesign and retooling over a smaller volume, suffering substantially higher unit costs. If they change models less frequently, recent experience suggests, they will sacrifice market penetration. For them, the styling rivalry game offers little but negative payoffs. And there is no way for them to escape other than leaving the industry (as the smaller companies have done, one by one), since the rules are dictated by producers willing to accelerate the pace.

Finally, how about the consumer? Does he benefit or lose from frequent style changes? Clearly, the new car buyer pays more than he would if model changes were effected less often. Equally clearly, he freely elects to do so, for he has the option of holding on to his present auto longer, or buying last year's model or a Volkswagen-like import. By the stern criterion of consumer sovereignty, styling rivalry would seem to emerge with only minor scars. Still this is not completely convincing. The interdependence of consumer preferences complicates matters. Smith may buy a new model only because he fears that if he does not and neighbor Jones does, his utility will be reduced. Jones perceives the situation symmetrically, and both end up buying new models, though neither might if they could find some way to enforce mutual (and more widespread) buying restraint. This gloomy view may be wrong, imputing to the consuming public values held only by academicians and other malcontents. But it is not necessarily wrong, and therefore one may well harbor qualms about the social desirability of all-out style change rivalry.

[51] If less were spent on styling changes, more might be spent on making cars more durable. An analysis by Lawrence J. White indicates that durability of representative U. S. autos declined during the 1950s and 1960s, although he does not prove that there is any causal connection between the style change and durability phenomena. "The American Automobile Industry in the Postwar Period," Ph.D. dissertation submitted at Harvard University, 1969, Chapter XII.

[52] Cf. p. 98 *supra* and John A. Menge, "Style Change Costs as a Market Weapon," *Quarterly Journal of Economics,* November 1962, pp. 632–647.

ADVERTISING, MARKET STRUCTURE, AND PROFITABILITY

We have seen that product differentiation through advertising can give sellers some pricing discretion. Whether that discretion can be exploited to gain profits persistently exceeding a normal return on invested capital remains to be established. We have observed too that the incentive to advertise is stronger under oligopoly than under pure monopoly. It is less clear *a priori* whether oligopolists spend more than monopolistic competitors. One further possible relationship must be identified before we can address the quantitative evidence on market structure, the intensity of advertising, and profits. Does heavy advertising lead to increased market concentration?

There is reason to think it might, through the mechanism of scale economies and entry barriers. As Chapter 4 brought out, economies of scale often exist in the use of advertising because a certain saturation threshold must be reached for best results and because many media offer discounts to high-volume advertisers. Also, it takes time to build up strong brand preferences, and this gives the established firm which has been advertising a product line for decades an advantage over smaller newcomers. The advertising cost advantages large firms enjoy make it more difficult for small enterprises to survive, *ceteris paribus*. Together with the advantages of accumulated reputation, they constitute a barrier to the entry of newcomers, especially small newcomers.[53] The new entrant into an industry where advertising is important may be forced either to charge a price much lower than established seller prices to compensate for its inferior image or to advertise heavily—much more heavily than present market occupants—in the hope of building an image quickly. In either event, sellers enjoying a well-developed brand reputation can maintain their prices persistently above costs without making entry attractive to newcomers. This in turn can spell the perpetuation of an oligopoly structure once it is achieved.

As always, exceptions can arise. A newcomer may be able to enter an industry with high advertising barriers by offering a superior physically differentiated product, or by operating in only one region of the country at first, concentrating its advertising firepower on local newspaper insertions and spot television commercials. This is what the makers of Lestoil, the first liquid household detergent, did with fair success during the 1950s. However, their position outside New England deteriorated rapidly when Procter & Gamble and then Lever Brothers retaliated on a nationwide scale with heavily advertised imitations. For the most part, the life of a locally advertised brand does not appear to be a bed of roses.

ADVERTISING AND CONCENTRATION

For at least two reasons, then, we might expect to discover a positive relationship between intensity of advertising expenditure and market concentration. Promotional economies of scale will favor the survival of a few relatively large sellers in markets conducive to heavy advertising; and (less certainly) advertising rivalry may be more vigorous among oligopolists than among large numbers of monopolistic competitors.

To see whether such a relationship existed, Telser correlated the ratio of advertising to sales in 42 three-digit consumer goods industry groups for 1947, 1954, and 1958 with the weighted average four-digit 1954 concentration ratios for those groups. The resulting correlation coefficients were all positive but diminutive (on the order of 0.16) and in no case statistically significant by conventional tests.[54]

---

[53]Cf. Kaldor, *op. cit.*, p. 20; Bain, *op. cit.*, pp. 114–143, 216–217, and 262–317; Oliver Williamson, "Selling Expense as a Barrier to Entry," *Quarterly Journal of Economics*, February 1963, pp. 112–128; and William S. Comanor and Thomas A. Wilson, "Advertising, Market Structure and Performance," *Review of Economics and Statistics*, November 1967, pp. 425–427.

[54]Lester G. Telser, "Advertising and Competition," *Journal of Political Economy*, December 1964, pp. 541–546. From this and other tests Telser rejects the hypothesis that advertising is a source of monopoly power. This is a *non sequitur*, since the concentration ratio measures only one dimension of monopoly power. That no correlation exists between advertising and concentration does not prove that atomistic sellers cannot differentiate their products through advertising and gain some control over price.

Two other investigations suggest a somewhat stronger relationship. Concerned that Telser's aggregation of advertising and concentration data into three-digit industry groups might blur the true picture, Michael Mann and associates obtained data for a narrower sample of 42 firms operating primarily in 14 advertising-prone four-digit industries. They observed fairly substantial and statistically significant positive correlations, ranging from 0.41 to 0.72, between the ratio of advertising outlays to sales and four-digit concentration ratios for 1954, 1958, and 1963.[55] In a study of 33 British nondurable consumer goods product lines for the years 1951 and 1954, P. K. Else found that the advertising/sales ratio was negatively correlated with the total sales volume of a product line and positively correlated with the number of specific products within a line.[56] The former relationship suggests that smaller industries must advertise relatively more to achieve the most advantageous level of medium saturation; the latter that variegated, complex product lines require the transmission of more messages to secure an equivalent consumer response. After taking these factors into account, Else found a slight but not completely uniform tendency for the intensity of advertising to increase with a crude index of market concentration.

From this limited evidence, it appears that advertising expenditures may gravitate toward slightly higher levels in oligopolistic than in atomistically structured industries, *ceteris paribus*, but the relationship is weak and erratic. More thorough analyses with better data are needed.

If a positive correlation does exist between concentration and advertising intensity, at least over some range, the direction of causality remains to be established. First, however, a partial digression is in order. In his search for links between advertising and monopoly power, Telser analyzed the stability of recalled market shares of the leading brands in 30 food product, 9 soap

product, and 15 toiletries and cosmetics lines, using data derived from 1948–1959 consumer interview surveys in Milwaukee. His hypothesis was that if advertising fosters monopoly power, the most heavily advertised products (the toiletries and cosmetics) would display more stable market shares than the least advertised products (the food items). In fact, the evidence showed exactly the opposite relationship; recalled market shares were least stable in toiletries and most stable in foods.[57] Telser interpreted this result as support for the view that advertising does not necessarily confer monopoly power, but here his reasoning falters. Presumably, price competition received the greatest relative emphasis in the least advertised food product lines, whereas nonprice competition predominated in the heavily advertised toiletries and cosmetics lines. As we have noted earlier, any fool can match a price cut, but an ingenious promotion campaign is hard to counteract. We should therefore expect to find high market share stability in food products, where advertising expenditures were low because sellers cannot persuade consumers to continue buying a product with no appeal to the palate and where attempts to gain market position by price-cutting are easily countered. Unstable market shares should have been much more likely in toiletries and cosmetics, where a dazzling advertising campaign playing upon consumer ignorance, prejudices, and fears can lead to soaring sales, especially for new products. What Telser's results show, therefore, is that non-price rivalry can be a dynamic, dog-eat-dog affair. They say nothing about whether it lessens or increases the incidence of such monopolistic ills as high profits, misallocated resources, and waste.

From this follows an important insight. If brand market shares are more unstable in product lines with heavy advertising, other things being equal,[58] the market shares of industry members are probably also more unstable.

---

[55]H. Michael Mann, J. A. Henning, and J. W. Meehan, Jr., "Advertising and Concentration: An Empirical Investigation," *Journal of Industrial Economics*, November 1967, pp. 34–45.

[56]P. K. Else, "The Incidence of Advertising in Manufacturing Industries," *Oxford Economic Papers*, March 1966, pp. 88–110.

[57]"Advertising and Competition," pp. 547–551.

[58]The *ceteris paribus* assumption is probably violated, but in a way which reinforces the argument. High advertising outlays are more likely to be accompanied by a high rate of change in physical product characteristics

From our examination of Gibrat's law and related stochastic growth processes in Chapter 4, we know that the more unstable market shares tend to be, the stronger are the forces leading toward a rise in market concentration over time. Or to draw the chain of causation tighter, the more intense advertising is, the more rapidly concentration will tend to grow, *ceteris paribus*.

The evidence relevant to this hypothesis has been laid out in Chapter 4.[59] To recapitulate briefly, concentration exhibited a distinct tendency to rise between 1947 and 1963 in the consumer goods industries, which are particularly susceptible to advertising and other image differentiation practices, while it fell in the producer goods industries. Among industries spending more than $250,000 on television advertising in 1963, the four-firm concentration ratio rose by 6 percentage points or more in 23 cases, while it fell by an equivalent amount in only six cases. Still there are some anomalies in the pattern—notably, Gort's finding that market shares were more stable in industries with highly differentiated products than in those with weak differentiation.

Considerable additional research must be done before we will have a complete picture of how advertising affects concentration and vice versa. It does not seem too farfetched to conclude tentatively that intensive advertising sets into motion forces which tend to increase market concentration, though many other forces are simultaneously at work, so that the net observed effect of advertising on concentration is a weak one, surrounded by considerable variance.[60] It is also not improbable that oligopoly is somewhat more conducive than an atomistic industry structure to intense advertising rivalry. Here, however, the evidence is singularly weak.

ADVERTISING AND PROFITABILITY

The question remains, Does heavy advertising lead to sustained supra-normal profits—a prime manifestation of monopoly power? If entry into advertising-prone industries is easy, the profits gained through image differentiation should be eroded away as newcomers are drawn by the profit lure to play the same game. High advertising may also contribute to the breakdown of oligopolistic pricing discipline by increasing the dimensionality of sellers' rivalry, with a consequent negative impact on earnings.[61] On the other hand, if firms by advertising heavily can erect barriers to new entry, they may be able persistently to earn monopoly returns. Each of these influences undoubtedly operates to some degree. Which is dominant?

Casual observation suggests that successful product differentiation through advertising is an important source of exceptionally high industrial profits. Prominent among the most profitable firms on *Fortune*'s annual list of the 500 largest U. S. industrial corporations have been Avon Products, Alberto-Culver, Gillette, American Home Products, and Bristol-Myers, which owe their success in large measure to massive advertising. All earned after-tax returns on stockholders' equity exceeding 20 per cent between 1964 and 1966.

For a more general perspective, the definitive work is a statistical study by Comanor and Wilson.[62] Using multiple regression techniques, they analyzed the effect of advertising expenditures on the average 1954–1957 after-tax return on stockholders' equity in 41 three-digit consumer goods industry groups, taking into account also the influence of market concentration, production scale economies, the absolute amount of capital required to enter the industry, and the

---

than the opposite. See Dennis Mueller, "The Firm Decision Process: An Econometric Investigation," *Quarterly Journal of Economics*, February 1967, pp. 83–84.

[59]Cf. pp. 99–100 and 129–130 *supra*.

[60]For a similar conclusion, see Borden, *op. cit.*, pp. 859–860.

[61]Cf. pp. 186–190 *supra*.

[62]W. S. Comanor and T. A. Wilson, "Advertising, Market Structure and Performance," *Review of Economics and Statistics*, November 1967, pp. 423–440. See also their "Advertising and the Advantages of Size," *American Economic Review*, May 1969, pp. 87–98; Richard A. Miller, "Market Structure and Industrial Performance: Relation of Profit Rates to Concentration, Advertising Intensity, and Diversity," *Journal of Industrial Economics*, April 1969, pp. 104–118; and Leonard W. Weiss, "Advertising, Profits, and Corporate Taxes," *Review of Economics and Statistics*, November 1969, pp. 421–430.

rate of growth of demand. They discovered a positive and statistically significant relationship between the ratio of advertising to sales and profit returns, other things being held equal. Industries with high advertising outlays were found to command profits roughly 50 per cent higher on the average (i.e., 12 per cent as opposed to 8 per cent) than industries spending modest amounts on advertising, *ceteris paribus*.[63] Their results provide strong support for a conclusion that intensive image differentiation through advertising is an important source of monopoly profits, allowing its practitioners to hold prices above costs without encouraging the competition of new entrants.

POLICY IMPLICATIONS

If all advertising and other image differentiation activity were abolished, society would surely be worse off. Or to put the matter positively, image differentiation definitely confers some social benefits. But it can be overdone, and that is cause for concern. Advertising campaigns can be carried far beyond the point where they are informative or add spice to consumption, serving merely to barrage the consumer with mutually cancelling claims or even to mislead him. Prime offenders in this respect include the soap, proprietary and ethical drug, cosmetic and toilet goods, cigarette, cereal, beverage, automobile and gasoline industries. Intensive advertising can also raise barriers to the entry of new competition, permitting producers to enjoy for extended periods of time monopoly profits

commensurate with their power over price. Thus, high prices, waste, income redistribution in favor of stockholders, and misallocation of resources are the consequences of excessive image differentiation.

Since the market system as such contains no fully satisfactory automatic mechanism for curbing advertising abuses, the burden of corrective action falls largely upon government. There are a number of things which might be done.

First, advertising can be scrutinized to detect and enjoin misleading practices. This is already being done in the United States by the Federal Trade Commission, although the task could be pursued more vigorously if budgetary constraints were less severe. Needless to say, the job is not an easy one, for the line between misleading and merely persuading is fuzzy, and too heavy a hand at the controls could suppress desirable initiative and creativity.

Second, the government might intervene directly to force a reduction of advertising expenditures in industries where they are patently excessive. This has never been seriously attempted in the United States. In England in 1966, the Monopolies Commission recommended a 40 per cent cut in advertising outlays by Unilever, Ltd., and Procter & Gamble, accompanied by a 20 per cent reduction in wholesale prices. However, after the respondents threatened to move some of their operations to the European continent, the government settled in 1967 for a milder compromise under which the two companies agreed to introduce new, less heavily promoted soap and detergent products priced 20 per cent lower than

---

[63]Profits were also correlated positively with concentration, but when concentration ratios, a measure of production scale economies, and a measure of absolute capital requirements were all included with the advertising/sales ratio as independent variables to explain profitability, the concentration variable proved to be statistically insignificant. This was so because concentration is positively correlated with the extent of scale economies and the magnitude of capital requirements. *Ibid.*, pp. 433–435.

Another study of the relationship between advertising and profitability deserves mention partly for its substantive content and partly as an illustration of faulty methodology. Backman, *op. cit.*, pp. 150–152 and 212–216, computed a simple correlation of profit returns on stockholders' equity for the 111 or 114 U. S. corporations spending the largest dollar amounts on advertising in 1964 and 1965 with the advertising/sales ratios of those firms. Correlation coefficients of $+ 0.345$ and $+ 0.315$, highly significant by conventional statistical tests, were obtained. However, Backman dismisses these results as inconsequential because there is considerable dispersion in the observations (which is what statistical significance tests are designed to interpret) and because the data are imperfect (as all economic data are). Along with this logical failure, there is probably a serious bias in Backman's technique. His sample has a definite bias—it includes only the largest advertisers. There are two reasons why a company might be included in this sample: because it is very large, even though its advertising/sales ratio is not unusually high; or because it has a very high advertising/sales ratio despite moderate sales. If there is a positive correlation between firm size and profitability, as we found on pp. 80–82 *supra*, the profit observations for large corporations with low advertising/sales ratios will be biased upward relative to the population of all corporations, and Backman's regression equations must understate the true strength of the relationship between advertising and profitability holding size constant.

existing brands.[64] This experience and the rumblings of conservative members of Congress following threats of similar measures in the United States suggest that stiff political resistance to direct advertising limits can be expected, but the step appears well worth trying.

Another possibility is to impose a progressive excise tax on advertising. The rate of taxation might be steeply graduated with respect to the total volume of a company's advertising expenditures, the ratio of advertising outlays to sales, or some combination of the two. This is a relatively blunt instrument, however, and it might lead to unexpected or even unwanted results. It would no doubt discriminate against conglomerate enterprises, which must advertise relatively more to attain the most advantageous saturation level, and it could encourage such evasion tactics as joint ventures and holding company arrangements. Direct surgery seems a more effective control technique.

Fourth, mergers especially apt to raise advertising barriers to new competition could be discouraged through antitrust action. This approach will be considered more carefully in Chapter 20. Also, quantity discounts given to large advertisers by the leading media might be attacked under the anti-discrimination laws when they impair the competitive position of small firms and potential entrants.

Finally, the adverse effects of advertising might be reduced by making available to consumers additional objective information on the relative qualities of rival sellers' products. Three possibilities come to mind. The wider implementation of uniform quality grading systems, enforced through inspection and supplemented by programs to inform the consumer, can be encouraged. Reports of quality and suitability tests conducted on thousands of consumer items by federal procurement agencies could be published and distributed on a massive scale. And the government might subsidize the activities of such organizations as the Consumers Union, permitting them to conduct more frequent and extensive product tests and to disseminate reports to a broader audience. All three have considerable promise for helping consumers make better-informed, more rational choices, and all deserve sympathetic consideration.

[64] See "Can You Spend Too Much for Ads?" *Business Week*, August 20, 1966, pp. 34–35; and "Britain and 2 Soap Makers End Price Battle with Compromise," *New York Times*, April 27, 1967, p. 65.

Chapter 15

Market Structure and Technological Innovation

Making the best use of resources at any moment in time is clearly important. But in the long run, it is dynamic performance that counts. As we observed in Chapter 2, an output handicap amounting to 10 per cent of gross national product due to static inefficiency is surmounted in just five years if the rate of growth of output can be raised through more rapid technological change from 3 to 5 per cent per annum, or in 20 years if the growth rate can be increased from 3 to 3.5 per cent.

From the time of David Ricardo until well into the 20th century, the main stream of bourgeois (non-Marxian) economic theory exhibited remarkably little sensitivity to this possibility. Emphasis was on the result of combining labor and capital with production functions of an essentially static character. Not until the 1950s did technological change become more than a sideshow attraction. Although there had been earlier, equally well-aimed volleys, the shot which signaled a revolution in economic thought is commonly attributed to Robert M. Solow.[1] He set out to measure the extent to which increases in the amount of capital employed were responsible for the rise of U. S. nonfarm output per manhour of work between 1909 and 1949. To

the surprise of economists mired in static modes of analysis, Solow found that increased capital intensity accounted for only 12.5 per cent (later corrected to 19 per cent) of the measured growth in output per manhour; the rest of the 1.5 per cent annual average productivity advance was evidently due to improvements in production practices and equipment (technological change in the strictest sense) and to increased quality of the labor force. In a subsequent extension, Edward Denison estimated that 42 per cent of the rise in output per worker between 1929 and 1957 could be credited to improved work force education, 36 per cent to the advance of scientific and technological knowledge, and only 9 per cent to increased capital intensity.[2] Some of the assumptions used in reaching these estimates are arbitrary, but it is hard to dispute the main thrust of Solow's and Denison's conclusion: that the growth of output per worker in the United States has come predominantly from the application of new, superior production techniques by an increasingly well-trained work force. Much the same conclusion holds for other industrialized nations.[3]

The introduction of new production methods which raise productivity—i.e., process innova-

---

[1] "Technical Change and the Aggregate Production Function," *Review of Economics and Statistics*, August 1957, pp. 312–320. Earlier works reaching similar numerical conclusions include Jacob Schmookler, "The Changing Efficiency of the American Economy, 1869–1938," *Review of Economics and Statistics*, August 1952, pp. 214–231; and Solomon Fabricant, "Economic Progress and Economic Change," 34th Annual Report of the National Bureau of Economic Research (New York: 1954).

[2] Edward F. Denison, *The Sources of Economic Growth in the United States and the Alternatives Before Us* (New York: Committee for Economic Development, 1962), pp. 271–272.

[3] Edward F. Denison, *Why Growth Rates Differ* (Washington: Brookings, 1967).

tion—is one main arm of technological advance. Another is consumer product innovation—the creation of better things for better living, as the advertisement proclaims. The estimates by Solow, Denison, and others take into account only the effects of process innovation on national output, since no satisfactory way of measuring changes in the quality of consumption has been devised. As a result, the overall impact of technological change on consumer well-being is understated by their estimates. Product innovation may also affect consumers' choices between goods and leisure, stimulating demand for the increasing quantities of output made possible by a productive system of growing efficiency.

The principal consequences of technological change, then, are increases in productivity and increases in the quality of consumption. Several subsidiary effects can also be identified. For one, process innovation may alter the structure of labor demands, most likely strengthening demand for skilled workers and weakening demand for the unskilled, with possibly troublesome income distribution repercussions. Second, international differences in the ability to develop and apply modern technology have an obvious impact on the balance of political and military power. Third, it has been discovered that such differences also affect international trade flows, with the most technologically advanced nations enjoying dominance in the export of sophisticated products such as aircraft, machine tools, drugs, and computers. Europeans in particular have become concerned about an alleged 'technology gap' between themselves and the United States, which saw them paying an estimated $250 million during 1961 for patent license royalties, technical assistance, and the like, while receiving from American firms only $45 million for the use of technology pioneered in Europe.[4] Finally, technological change has effects on market structure, for major innovation often brings new firms to the fore and displaces laggards, defining the structural conditions within which price and other more static forms of rivalry are conducted for decades to come.

Here we shall be concerned largely with a possible causal flow in the opposite direction; from market structure to technological innovation. Is progress faster or slower under monopolistic conditions, or does it make no difference? One of the few influential bourgeois economic theorists who consistently stressed the important role technological change plays in a capitalistic economy was Joseph A. Schumpeter. In a well-known and controversial work, he argued that market structure does make a difference. Despite the restrictive pricing behavior in which they indulge, he asserted, large, monopolistic firms are ideally suited for introducing the technological innovations which benefit all society.

> What we have got to accept is that [the large-scale establishment or unit of control] has come to be the most powerful engine of [economic] progress. . . . In this respect, perfect competition is not only impossible but inferior, and has no title to being set up as a model of ideal efficiency.[5]

Whether or not this is true is the question we tackle in this chapter. More precisely, we shall explore three narrower issues: Are large firms more adept at making technological innovations than small firms, other things being equal? Are highly diversified firms more vigorous engines of technical progress than companies operating in only one or a few product lines? And is monopoly power, e.g., as manifested in high market concentration, a favorable climate for innovation and technical progress?

INDUSTRIAL RESEARCH AND DEVELOPMENT

Before we address these questions, it is useful to pause and examine more carefully what the process of technological change is all about.

Technical innovations do not fall like manna from heaven. They require effort—the creative

---

[4]Cf. William Gruber, D. Mehta, and R. Vernon, "The R & D Factor in International Trade," *Journal of Political Economy,* February 1967, pp. 20–37; Donald B. Keesing, "The Impact of Research and Development on United States Trade," *Journal of Political Economy,* February 1967, pp. 38–48; and F. M. Scherer, "Marktstruktur, Know-How fuer das Marketing, und die Technologische Luecke," *Ordo,* Vol. XIX (1968), pp. 159–170.

[5]Joseph A. Schumpeter, *Capitalism, Socialism, and Democracy* (Third ed.; New York: Harper, 1950), p. 106.

labor of invention, development, testing, and introduction into the stream of economic life. To some extent innovative effort is a haphazard thing, conducted by individuals or firms as a digression from routine workaday activities. But to an increasing degree, the task of creating and developing new products and processes has been institutionalized through the establishment of formal research and development laboratories. It is not clear exactly when this trend began. We know that in the 1770s and 1780s the firm of Boulton & Watt had the equivalent of a research and development laboratory for work on steam engines.[6] The genesis of the modern R & D laboratory in America is commonly traced to 1876, when Thomas Edison opened his famed laboratory in Menlo Park and Alexander Graham Bell established an analogous facility in Boston. Wherever the starting point is placed, the idea spread rapidly until now research and development has come to be big business. In 1966, approximately 13,400 U. S. companies expended $15.5 billion on activities formally designated as research and development. Industrial expenditures on R & D grew at a compounded rate of 9 per cent per year between 1953 and 1966.

Total outlays on R & D conducted by all organizations, private and public, in the United States during 1966 amounted to $22.2 billion, or 3 per cent of the gross national product. Private industry performed the lion's share of this total—roughly 70 per cent. The remaining expenditures were divided among federal government laboratories (15 per cent), universities and colleges (12 per cent), and nonprofit institutions (3 per cent).[7]

Of the $15.5 billion spent for R & D conducted by profit-oriented firms in 1966, 47 per cent was financed by the performing companies. The remaining financial burden was assumed by the federal government, mostly in connection with contracts for goods and services supplied by private industry to the Department of Defense, the National Aeronautics and Space Administration, the Atomic Energy Commission, and other agencies. Under such contracts the government usually accepts most of the financial risk and exercises more or less detailed control over the decisions and actions of its contractor. This activity is therefore far removed from the conventional functioning of the market mechanism. It is only with respect to the 47 per cent privately-financed share of industrial R & D effort, amounting to $7.3 billion in 1966, that the links between market structure and performance analyzed in this chapter are directly relevant.[8]

Within industry, research and development spending is heavily concentrated in a few manufacturing groups enjoying a rich scientific base and/or serving the military-space colossus. Table 15.1 presents data on total R & D spending, federal government sponsorship, and private spending by industry sector (typically at the two-digit level) for 1966. From it, we can calculate that 68 per cent of all industrial R & D activity occurred in the aircraft and missiles, electrical equipment and communications, and chemicals and drugs sectors—of which the first two are heavily involved in meeting the government's defense and space demands. Only 2.7 per cent of total expenditures took place in nonmanufacturing industries—a catchall including mining, public utilities, transportation, retailing, etc. Privately supported spending as a fraction of sales ranged from 4.0 per cent in the instruments sector (which includes measuring devices, optics, photographic equipment, and surgical instruments) down to 0.3 per cent in the food and tobacco products group. The mean level for all industries was 2.0 per cent.

---

[6]F. M. Scherer, "Invention and Innovation in the Watt-Boulton Steam-Engine Venture," *Technology and Culture*, Spring 1965, especially p. 180.

[7]U. S. National Science Foundation, *National Patterns of R & D Resources: Funds and Manpower in the United States, 1953–68* (Washington: 1967).

[8]On structure and performance relationships in federally supported R & D programs, see F. M. Scherer, "The Aerospace Industry," in Walter Adams, ed., *The Structure of American Industry* (Fourth edition; New York: Macmillan, 1970); H. O. Stekler, *The Structure and Performance of the Aerospace Industry* (Berkeley: University of California Press, 1965); and W. L. Baldwin, *The Structure of the Defense Market: 1955–1964* (Durham: Duke University Press, 1967).

Table 15.1

U.S. Industrial Research and Development Expenditures in 1966

Industry Group	Total 1966 Expenditures (millions)	Percentage Government Supported	Private Spending as a Percent of Sales
Food and tobacco products	$ 166	1	0.4
Textiles and apparel	42	small	0.5
Lumber, wood products, and furniture	14	small	0.5
Paper and allied products	85	0	0.7
Chemicals and drugs	1,518	13	3.5
Petroleum refining and extraction	441	13	1.0
Rubber products	182	14	1.7
Stone, clay, and glass products	131	4	1.6
Primary metals	228	3	0.7
Fabricated metal products	164	10	1.2
Machinery	1,301	27	3.0
Electrical equipment and communications	3,570	61	3.4
Motor vehicles and other transportation equipment	1,321	26	2.6
Aircraft and missiles	5,446	86	3.5
Instruments	444	32	4.0
Other manufacturing industries	65	2	0.6
Nonmanufacturing industries	425	70	n.a.
ALL INDUSTRIES	$15,541	53	2.0

Source: U.S. National Science Foundation, *Research and Development in Industry, 1966* (Washington: 1968), pp. 23, 30, and 73.

A survey by the McGraw-Hill Department of Economics reveals that the principal goal of industrial firms in conducting R & D is the development of new and improved products. Forty-five per cent of the firms responding cited new product development as their main objective, 41 per cent the improvement of existing products, and 14 per cent the development of new processes to be used in their manufacturing operations.[9] However, these estimates do not bring out clearly the impact of industrial R & D on the economy, since what is a new product to the developing firm may be a new production process to another company purchasing it. From the laboratories of General Electric, for example, have come new and improved products such as electrical generators and turbofan engines. These are sold to electrical utilities and airlines, for whom they represent processes which raise productivity. The fraction of industrial research laboratory output flowing to other industries to increase productivity, as opposed to raising the quality of consumption for the public at large, is presently unknown. It is undoubtedly large.

[9] "Pouring More Billions into R & D," *Business Week*, May 7, 1966, pp. 164–165.

THE PROCESS OF RESEARCH, DEVELOPMENT, INVENTION, AND INNOVATION

Raw data on research and development spending do not reveal much about the nature of the underlying activities supported. To gain additional insight we must view the process from several additional perspectives.[10]

One approach is to break the expenditure totals into three conventional (but not always easily distinguished) categories. *Basic research*, defined as investigation to gain knowledge for its own sake, consumed 4 per cent of all industrial R & D outlays in 1966. *Applied research*—investigation directed toward obtaining knowledge with specific commercial implications—accounted for 18 per cent of total spending. The remaining 78 per cent went into *development*—the translation of technical and scientific knowledge into concrete new products and processes. Private industry accounts for roughly 20 per cent of all basic research conducted in the United States, 65 per cent of all applied research, and 85 per cent of all development. From these figures it is evident that industry's forte is applications—specific new products and processes—while pure science remains predominantly the domain of the universities and federal government laboratories.

Schumpeter's writings provide another viewpoint.[11] He visualized technological change as occurring in three steps: invention, innovation, and imitation or diffusion. Invention to him was the act of conceiving a new product or process and solving the purely technical problems associated with its application. Innovation involved the entrepreneurial functions required to carry a new technical possibility into economic practice for the first time—identifying the market, raising the necessary funds, building a new organization, cultivating the market, etc. Imitation or diffusion is the stage at which a new product or process comes into widespread use as one producer after another follows the innovating firm's lead.

The trouble with this schema is that it leaves in an ambiguous state the costly technical activities which are the heart of modern research and development programs. It seems more useful to describe the pre-imitation or innovative process in terms of four essential functions: invention, entrepreneurship, investment, and development.[12] Invention then is the act of insight by which a new and promising technical possibility is recognized and worked out (at least mentally and perhaps also physically) in its essential, most rudimentary form.[13] Development is the lengthy sequence of detail-oriented technical activities, including trial-and-error testing, through which the original concept is modified and perfected until it is ready for commercial utilization. The entrepreneurial function involves deciding to go forward with the effort, organizing it, and obtaining financial support for it. Investment is the act of risking funds for the venture. These functions need not be performed by the same person or even by the same organizational entity; in many cases, we shall see later, they are organizationally separate.

All such attempts at conceptualization are little more than empty words until fitted into a meaningful real-world context. Therefore, it is helpful to consider two brief illustrative examples. No case is completely typical; the illustrations presented here were chosen because they reflect unusually important and ambitious technical

[10]For other views, see Edwin Mansfield, *The Economics of Technological Change* (New York: Norton, 1968), Chapters II, III, and IV; Richard R. Nelson, M. J. Peck, and E. D. Kalachek, *Technology, Economic Growth, and Public Policy* (Washington: Brookings, 1967), Chapters 2, 3, 4, and 5; and John Jewkes, David Sawers, and Richard Stillerman, *The Sources of Invention* (New York: St. Martin's Press, 1959).

[11]Joseph A. Schumpeter, *The Theory of Economic Development*, trans. by Redvers Opie (Cambridge: Harvard University Press, 1934), Chapter II; and *Business Cycles* (New York: McGraw-Hill, 1939), especially Chapter III. See also Carolyn Solo, "Innovation in the Capitalist Process: A Critique of the Schumpeterian Theory," *Quarterly Journal of Economics*, August 1951, pp. 417–428; and Vernon W. Ruttan, "Usher and Schumpeter on Invention, Innovation, and Technological Change," *Quarterly Journal of Economics*, November 1959, pp. 596–606.

[12]Cf. Scherer, "Invention and Innovation in the Watt-Boulton Steam-Engine Venture."

[13]'Invention' as used here must be distinguished most emphatically from the mass of trivia which sometimes pass for inventions under the patent system. A higher standard of novelty and insight is implied in this discussion.

changes and because the stages and functions stand out with particular clarity. One, the Watt-Boulton steam engine venture of the 1770s, is ancient; the other, xerography, quite new.

It is generally accepted that James Watt 'invented' his steam engine in 1765, when he repaired a Newcomen steam engine model owned by Glasgow University and perceived that its efficiency could be greatly enhanced by condensing the steam outside the operating cylinder. He wrote later that "In three days, I had a model at work nearly as perfect . . . as any which have been made since that time."[14] But a great deal remained to be done before he could supply a machine useful in industrial practice. Full-scale models had to be built, condenser concepts had to be devised and tested, valves designed, methods of machining and sealing the operating cylinder perfected, etc. All this required time and money, and for want of both financial support and entrepreneurial initiative Watt twice abandoned the venture to work as a salaried engineer. Not until Matthew Boulton appeared to provide these missing ingredients was a full-scale model completed, and the first commercially useful Watt-Boulton steam engine was installed only in 1776, 11 years after the original invention. Expenditures preparing the way for operating the first full-scale engine amounted to the equivalent of at least 60 man-years of skilled labor.

While working as a patent attorney, Chester Carlson was impressed by the difficulty of copying documents efficiently.[15] For several years he spent a good deal of his spare time after work mulling over the problem and browsing in potentially relevant technical literature, eventually (in 1938) conceiving the central idea of xerography. With the assistance of an unemployed physicist, he successfully tested his concept with an extremely crude model. After several fruitless attempts to interest industrial firms in helping him develop a commercially practical copying system, in 1944 he enlisted the cooperation of the Battelle Development Company, a subsidiary of the Battelle Institute. From two years' labor by a Battelle research physicist and his aides came two key inventions building upon Carlson's original principle: the use of a selenium-coated plate to store the electrostatic image, and the corona discharge method for sensitizing the plate and applying ink to the copying paper. With these inventions, the xerography concept began to show distinct signs of practical promise. At this point the Haloid Corporation (later renamed the Xerox Corporation) took over developmental responsibility. By 1950 its engineers had completed a prototype system useful primarily for making offset lithography masters. This was an extremely cumbersome, three-machine contraption, however, with limited market potential. The company then devoted its resources to developing a single-unit console copier—a task which required surmounting a difficult lens design problem along with numerous lesser engineering challenges. The result was the 914 copier, which took the world by storm after its introduction in 1959. During the more than two decades which preceded this event, formulation of the basic xerographic copying concept consumed the inventor's energies part-time for a very few years. The crucial selenium plate and corona discharge inventions came from an only slightly greater increment of effort. After Haloid entered the picture, it expended roughly $4 million on research and development up to 1953, when it redirected attention to developing a console model. To attain that goal, further R & D outlays estimated at $16 million, severely straining the company's financial resources, were committed.

Several generalizations can be extracted from these and the many other case studies now available. First, the initial invention which precipitates a major innovative effort is typically inexpensive, both relatively and absolutely. Its money cost is often so modest that almost any well-prepared imaginative individual thrown into contact with the problem is in a position potentially to achieve the essential insight. The

---

[14]Quoted in Scherer, "Invention and Innovation in the Watt-Boulton Steam-Engine Venture," from which this summary is drawn.

[15]This example is drawn from Jewkes, Sawers, and Stillerman, *op. cit.*, pp. 405–408; and Erwin Blackstone, "The Economics of the Copying Machine Industry," Ph.D. dissertation, the University of Michigan, 1968.

inventive challenge may be recognized as a result of formal work assignments, as a by-product of work or leisure pursuits, or from any of the hundred-and-one experiences a person has each day. If industrial research and development laboratories enjoy some comparative advantage in generating inventions, it is because they are more likely to put together the critical combination of a fertile mind, a challenging problem, and the will to solve it.

Second, there is a high random component in fundamental invention. Thousands of persons may recognize an unsolved problem or unmet need, but only a fraction will be sufficiently intrigued to devote serious thought to it, and of these an even smaller fraction will have the ingenuity and good luck to gain a correct insight by viewing the problem in exactly the right way —that is, in the proper *Gestalt*.[16] After the insight is achieved, the solution may seem obvious, but before the fact invention is largely unpredictable. If this were not so, every problem, once recognized, would be solved quickly.

Third, supporting inventions of greater or lesser creative magnitude may be required before the innovation begins to look technically and economically viable. Once the original insight is attained, however, it forms a *Gestalt* within which these supporting inventions will tend inevitably to emerge if good minds are focused on the problem.

Fourth, when the necessary conceptual advances have occurred and when their essential correctness has been demonstrated, typically through crude model tests requiring only a modest resource investment, the uncertainties associated with innovation are reduced by an order of magnitude. The question, Is there something interesting and technically feasible here? is no longer a serious issue. Uncertainty centers on such questions as: What will the detailed configuration of the mechanism be? How well can it be made to work? How much

will perfecting it cost? How long will it take? At what price can it be sold? What will be the market demand at that price? These are not negligible uncertainties, but usually they are also not overwhelming or outside the bounds of entrepreneurial experience. The vast majority of all industrial R & D projects, it should be noted, begin at this stage, since they either embody no fundamental new concepts or build upon insights achieved elsewhere.

Finally, once the sequence has progressed this far, outlays much greater than those expended during the early conceptual stages are necessitated before an innovation is brought to the point of commercial utility. The investment decision at this juncture entails committing possibly substantial quantities of resources in the face of moderate technological uncertainties. It is quite different from the earlier decision, where the amounts of money involved are small, but the technical uncertainties are great. If inexpensive conceptual work has not reduced the degree of technical uncertainty to tolerable levels, a decision to move into full-scale research and development will be taken only under the most unusual pressures (as in the atomic and hydrogen bomb programs).[17] Normally, conceptual work will be continued at a low spending level until the main technical uncertainties have been resolved.

FIRM SIZE, INVENTION, AND INNOVATION

With this background in mind, let us return to our principal theme. We begin by exploring the links between firm size and technological progressiveness. It is important to recall that bigness and monopoly power are by no means synonymous. Although the two attributes *may* coincide, we shall try here to preserve a sharp distinction. The central issue can be stated as follows: Are large firms in general more effective

---

[16]This interpretation of the inventive act is based upon Abbott P. Usher, *A History of Mechanical Inventions* (Rev. ed.; Cambridge: Harvard University Press, 1954), Chapter IV; N. R. Hanson, Patterns of Discovery (Cambridge, England: Cambridge University Press, 1958); and Thomas S. Kuhn, *The Structure of Scientific Revolutions* (Chicago: University of Chicago Press, 1962).

[17]Cf. R. G. Hewlett and O. E. Anderson, Jr., *The New World: 1939/1946* (University Park: Pennsylvania State University Press, 1962), Chapters 4–7; and F. M. Scherer, "Was the Nuclear Arms Race Inevitable?" *Co-existence*, January 1966, pp. 59–69

than small firms in making technological inventions and introducing them into commercial practice?

A number of *a priori* hypotheses favorable to big business exist. One of the best known is Professor Galbraith's assertion that the costs of technological innovation in modern times are so great that they can be borne only by large corporations:

> There is no more pleasant fiction than that technical change is the product of the matchless ingenuity of the small man forced by competition to employ his wits to better his neighbor. Unhappily, it is a fiction. Technical development has long since become the preserve of the scientist and engineer. Most of the cheap and simple inventions have, to put it bluntly and unpersuasively, been made. . . . Because development is costly, it follows that it can be carried on only by a firm that has the resources which are associated with considerable size.[18]

Furthermore, it is argued, research and development projects are risky as well as expensive. Small firms place themselves in a dangerous position when they invest all their resources in a single innovative project whose prospects for technical and commercial success are far from guaranteed. This, combined with the risk aversion to which businessmen and investors are supposedly prone, is said to discourage technical pioneering by small companies. The large corporation, on the other hand, can afford to maintain a balanced portfolio of R & D projects, letting the profits from those which succeed more than counterbalance the losses from those which fail. The ability to average out losses and gains may lead large firms to consider innovative opportunities on their 'best guess' merits, without being constrained unduly by risk aversion.

Third, there may be economies of scale in the conduct of research and development.[19] A big laboratory can justify purchasing all sorts of specialized equipment—wind tunnels, electron microscopes, heavy-duty strain gauges, etc.—which make experimentation easier. It can employ specialists in many disciplines to cross-fertilize one another and to lend temporary assistance when a team working on some development project becomes bogged down by a technical problem outside its regular sphere of competence. This latter advantage might be minimized if small firms could call freely upon outside specialists (such as university engineering professors) when they run into unfamiliar problems, but it is not clear that outside expertise is tapped as willingly and speedily as internal expertise.

Fourth, research and development projects may benefit from scale economies realized in other parts of the large firm's operations. As we have seen in Chapter 4, large corporations can attract additional capital at lower cost and in larger quantities than their smaller cousins, and thus may be better able to finance ambitious R & D undertakings. They have well-established marketing channels and enjoy certain economies of scale in promotion and physical distribution. Their promotional advantages often permit them to penetrate markets more rapidly with new products, and this affects the profitability of developing a product. Being able to reach 50 per cent of a new product's market potential in two years instead of five may make the difference between profit and loss. There is reason to suspect that this speed of penetration factor is perhaps the most important single advantage enjoyed by large firms in developing new products.[20]

Finally, large producers have an obvious advantage in making process innovations. A new process which reduces costs by a given percentage margin yields larger total savings to the

[18]John Kenneth Galbraith, *American Capitalism* (Rev. ed.; Boston: Houghton Mifflin, 1956), pp. 86–87.

[19]For various views, see Jewkes, Sawers, and Stillerman, *op. cit.*, pp. 158–161; M. J. Peck and F. M. Scherer, *The Weapons Acquisition Process: An Economic Analysis* (Boston: Harvard Business School Division of Research, 1962), pp. 181–188; and Carl Kaysen, *United States* v. *United Shoe Machinery Corporation* (Cambridge: Harvard University Press, 1956), pp. 97–99.

[20]Cf. Scherer, "Marktstruktur, Know-How fuer das Marketing, und die Technologische Luecke," pp. 167–168; and Arthur R. Bright, Jr., *The Electric Lamp Industry* (New York: Macmillan, 1949), p. 346.

company producing a large volume of output than to the firm whose output is small. As a result, the large firm presumably has stronger incentives to develop such improvements.

Against this impressive array of actual and conjectured advantages the disadvantages of size must be weighed.[21] For one, decisions to bear the risks of R & D projects are made by individual managers, not by impersonal organizations, and so the argument on risk-spreading may not hold water. In a small firm, the decision to go ahead with an ambitious project typically involves a very few people who know one another well. In a large corporation, the decision must filter through a whole chain of command—the person with the idea, his section chief, the laboratory manager, the vice president for research, and if substantial financial commitments are required, several members of top management. Each participant is risking his reputation, if not his money, in backing the project. Under these circumstances there is a distressingly high probability that some member of the chain will prove to be what C. Northcote Parkinson has called "an abominable no-man," and that the idea will die from lack of support or from the objections which can always be raised to an untried proposition.[22]

A direct consequence of this problem, which has been noted time and again in case histories and treatises on research management, is a bias away from really imaginative innovations in the laboratories of large firms. But more important, inability to get ideas approved by higher management drives many of the most creative individuals out of large corporation laboratories to go it alone in their own ventures. During the two decades following World War II thousands of research-based new enterprises were founded by frustrated fugitives from the laboratories of such U. S. giants as Sperry-Rand, IBM, Western Electric, Hughes Aircraft, Raytheon, and many others.[23]

A related malady is the propensity for research in large laboratories to become over-organized. If too many people become involved in a project, they spend a disproportionate amount of their time writing memoranda to each other at the expense of more creative endeavor. Also, the quickest and surest path to higher status and pay in a large firm's R & D establishment often lies in giving up actual work at the bench and becoming a member of the management team. Although some firms have tried to combat this tendency by creating well-paid positions for senior research fellows, it is still commonplace to find the most able people in a laboratory devoting nearly all their time to supervising a swarm of drones. This is not the way truly creative work gets done.

THE COSTS AND RISKS OF INDUSTRIAL RESEARCH

How these disadvantages and advantages of bigness balance out cannot be resolved through *a priori* reasoning; the question is an empirical one. Before we turn to the evidence, however, a further comment on the costs and risks of industrial research and development projects is in order.

In his statement on technical change and the small man, Professor Galbraith is guilty of outfictionalizing the fiction writers. The costs of technical development cannot be characterized so simply. To be sure, there are projects whose financial burden is beyond the capacity of any but large corporations. But there are also many opportunities which can be exploited on a small scale. At one extreme is the case of a production engineer known to the author who returned at night to the transistor plant where he worked to devise new transistor designs, producing them in experimental quantities the next day when his production operatives had spare time. Many simple mechanical and electromechanical device developments fit this pattern. At the other ex-

---

[21]Cf. Jewkes, Sawers, and Stillerman, *op. cit.*, pp. 127–146; and Dan Hamberg, "Invention in the Industrial Research Laboratory," *Journal of Political Economy*, April 1963, pp. 95–115.

[22]In the Standard Oil Co. of New Jersey there are reportedly 12 levels of management between R & D scientists and top decision-makers. This is said to have been one reason why Esso had not developed a single major proprietary commercial product in 15 years. "Research and Development," *Forbes*, November 15, 1968, p. 35.

[23]Cf. A. H. Rubenstein, *Problems of Financing New Research-Based Enterprises in New England* (Boston: Federal Reserve Bank, 1958); and Edward B. Roberts, "Entrepreneurship and Technology," *Research Management*, July 1968, pp. 249–266.

treme is the development of extremely complex systems—long-range ballistic missiles, communications satellites, nuclear reactors, supersonic transports, color television, or time-sharing electronic computers—where R & D costs may mount into the tens of millions or even billions of dollars. Because of the limited uses for weapon systems and because it may be the only consumer able to afford such products as a trip to the moon, the U. S. federal government subsidizes and frequently pays the full cost of most projects necessitating multi-million dollar R & D commitments, and in such cases the financial advantages of large company size are less relevant. Still some ambitious projects remain squarely within the private sector. As we saw earlier, the Xerox Corporation invested more than $16 million in perfecting its 914 copier. RCA is said to have spent more than $65 million on color television R & D before anything resembling a mass market materialized. And private investment in the design and development of civilian jet airliners has exceeded the $100 million mark on more than one occasion.

A more fruitful way of considering the technical opportunities confronting small and large firms is to visualize a frequency distribution of development projects, ordered according to their cost. A census would undoubtedly reveal the distribution to be highly skewed. The spectacularly costly projects which receive the most attention in newspapers and trade journals are few in number, forming the distribution's long thin tail. Smaller projects are much more numerous, giving rise to a peak or mode in a spending range somewhere between $50,000 and $300,000.[24] The parameters of this distribution have been shifting over time; that is, the modal R & D project today is more expensive than its counter-

part 30 years ago. But firm sizes have also been rising secularly, so that there continue to be very many technical challenges which can be met successfully by firms defined as small under current standards. If large firms have an advantage, it is primarily in their ability to select among both modest and ambitious projects in building up their R & D project portfolios. Yet small firms are by no means barred from the game, especially if they are willing to bear the risks of incomplete hedging.

It is also likely that the risks and uncertainties of industrial research and development are less formidable than corporate publicists and proponents of the hero theory of invention would have us believe. In an analysis of 70 projects carried out in the central R & D laboratories of a leading electrical equipment manufacturing company, Edwin Mansfield and Richard Brandenburg found that in more than three fourths of the cases, the *ex ante* probability of technical success had originally been estimated at 0.80 or higher, and only two projects had predicted success probabilities of less than 0.50. After the projects were completed, 44 per cent turned out to be fully successful technically, and only 16 per cent were unsuccessful due to unanticipated technical difficulties.[25] This experience is probably representative of industrial R & D generally. The reason has been brought out earlier: Business firms do not as a rule begin new product or process development projects until the principal technical uncertainties have been whittled down through inexpensive research, conducted either by their own personnel or by outsiders.[26]

The sequential character of modern research and development also makes it possible for small enterprises to play a creative role in major technological achievements. As we have seen, the

---

[24]One fragment of supporting evidence comes from a survey of 70 representative projects executed in the central R & D facility of a large, diversified American electrical equipment manufacturing firm during 1963 and 1964. The projects accounted for research expenditures of roughly $5 million per year altogether, and since the average duration of a project was approximately four years, the average cost per project was on the order of $285,000. In a skewed distribution the modal projects will have still lower costs. See Edwin Mansfield, *Industrial Research and Technological Innovation* (New York: Norton, 1968), p. 55.

[25]*Ibid.*, pp. 56–61. For corroborating evidence from studies of chemical, petroleum, and drug company research portfolios, see Mansfield, "Industrial Research and Development: Characteristics, Costs, and Diffusion of Results," *American Economic Review*, May 1969, pp. 65–69. See also Roberts, *op. cit.*, who discovered that four fifths of the new technology-based enterprises founded by fugitives from Boston area industrial and university laboratories survived through the first four or five years of their existence.

[26]See also Peck and Scherer, *op. cit.*, Chapters 2 and 16; W. Paul Strassmann, *Risk and Technological Innovation* (Ithaca: Cornell University Press, 1959); and Strassmann, "The Risks of Innovation in 20th Century Manufacturing Methods," *Technology and Culture*, Spring 1964, pp. 215–223.

earliest, most imaginative steps in the innovative process normally entail only modest resource commitments. The heaviest expenditures do not fall due until full-scale development begins. Neither inadequate size nor insufficient financial capacity necessarily bars small firms from the early stages. Creative thinking power is a scarce resource, but it comes in fairly inexpensive man-sized lumps which can be attracted as easily (and often more easily) by small companies as by large. Crude test models are also not so costly that they cannot be financed by entrepreneurs of modest means, if the will is present. Where trouble may intrude is at the development stage, once creative thought and small-scale testing have pointed the way. Here the small enterprise may find its resources taxed beyond the breaking point, and it may be compelled to yield its position in the race to a larger firm through patent licensing, merger, or default. The chief disadvantage of small firms in the early creative stages is the prospect of deficient bargaining power when and if a transition becomes necessary. They may lack the financial and legal resources to pursue their patent rights against well-heeled infringers, or their inventions may be easily circumvented, rendering patent protection ineffective. But this handicap does not appear seriously to discourage small research-oriented companies from testing their luck, and the combination of a good idea with the zeal and creative talent to develop it has proved an attractive asset in literally hundreds of merger negotiations.

These characteristics of industrial innovation go a long way toward explaining the findings of several recent empirical studies. Jewkes, Sawers, and Stillerman, for example, compiled case histories of 61 important 20th century inventions and learned that less than a third had their origin in industrial research laboratories. More than half were pioneered by men working either completely independent of any formal research organization or as independent investigators in an academic environment.[27] Updating their results, Hamberg investigated 27 major inventions introduced during the 1946–1955 decade. Only seven were originally conceived in large industrial laboratories, while 12 were traced to independent inventors.[28] Using a more selective approach, Mueller studied the 25 most important product and process innovations pioneered in the United States by the du Pont Co. between 1920 and 1950. He discovered that only 10 or at most 11 were initially discovered in du Pont's laboratories; the rest came from other firms or independent researchers.[29]

These and other studies show that small firms, academicians, and even the totally independent inventor (once assumed to be extinct) continue to contribute heavily toward the creation of new products and processes. To stop at this conclusion, however, and by inference to denigrate the role of corporate R & D laboratories, would be to miss a significant part of the whole point. For while a seeming preponderance of the original inventions studied by Jewkes, Hamberg, and Mueller originated outside corporate laboratories, in most cases corporations ended up shouldering the burden of developing the inventions for commercial utilization. Thus, in exploding the myth of du Pont's creative genius, Mueller fails to bring du Pont's real contributions into perspective. He ignores, for example, the fact that the Calico Printers' Association of England, which sponsored the small-scale research producing the idea for Dacron, found itself unable or unwilling to undertake the long and expensive job of developing the fiber for consumer use, licensing development rights instead to Imperial Chemical Industries, Ltd., and to du Pont. He likewise fails to bring out clearly that W. J. Kroll's path-breaking work in refining ductile titanium during the 1930s was just the first step—albeit a crucial one—in the protracted R & D sequence which brought that 'wonder metal' into practical use. Or to cite a

[27] *The Sources of Invention*, pp. 71–85. The authors use a loose and sometimes curious definition of invention; many of the cases studied are better described as systems or conglomerations of inventions.

[28] "Invention in the Industrial Research Laboratory," p. 96. Hamberg began with a sample of 45 inventions. Why he stopped his research after exploring only 27 is not made clear.

[29] Willard F. Mueller, "The Origins of the Basic Inventions Underlying du Pont's Major Product and Process Innovations, 1920 to 1950," in the National Bureau of Economic Research conference report, *The Rate and Direction of Inventive Activity* (Princeton: Princeton University Press, 1962), pp. 323–346.

non-du Pont example, striking increases in the efficiency of diesel engines were made after General Motors bought out two small companies which had pioneered the technology and assigned to the engine problem a development team led by Charles Kettering. And the Eastman Kodak Co. supported work by the originally independent inventors of Kodachrome for 10 years before the new color film was ready for the market. Invention and development are necessary complements in the process of technological advance; neither is sufficient alone if major changes are to be wrought. As Jewkes, Sawers, and Stillerman concede after devoting 196 pages of their book to the inventive step alone:

> Although when this work was started it was not intended to say anything in detail about the development of inventions, it subsequently became increasingly apparent that some comment on it was unavoidable. For even those who are prepared to accept the description and analysis of invention as given in the foregoing pages might well protest that this is, after all, the less important part of the story of technical progress and that the real determinants of the rate of advance will be the scale and the speed of the efforts made to perfect new commodities and devices and to contrive ways of producing them cheaply and in quantity.[30]

In any such attempt to clear up popular misconceptions, we must be wary of overcompensating. From the evidence presented thus far, three main generalizations appear warranted. First, small firms and independent inventors play a prominent and perhaps even disproportionate role in generating the new ideas and concepts upon which technological advances rest. Second, developing these ideas to the point of practical utility normally requires a significant investment of resources. Usually, however, the costs of development are not so high that they cannot be borne by medium-sized and small

companies. Third, there remain a relatively few advances which demand such heavy private developmental investment that they can be undertaken with something approaching equanimity only by very large corporations, or with less than equanimity by medium-sized firms possessing an especially high tolerance for risk.

One conclusion relevant to public policy follows immediately. No single firm size is uniquely conducive to technological progress. There is room for firms of all sizes. What we want, therefore, may be a diversity of sizes, each with its own special advantages and disadvantages.

FIRM SIZE AND THE INTENSITY OF R & D EFFORTS

Granted then, the search for a firm size uniquely and unambiguously optimal for invention and innovation is misguided. Nevertheless, are there broad statistical tendencies for companies in some size categories to be more vigorous than others in advancing technology, even though the pattern may not hold in all cases?

To address this question quantitative evidence is needed. Unfortunately, it is not easy to measure the vigor of firms' inventive and innovative efforts. In recent attempts to do so several measures have been tried: expenditures on research and development, the number of personnel engaged in formal R & D activities, a count of invention patents received, a count of significant innovations pioneered, and estimates of the sales associated with new products introduced. None is completely satisfactory and debate over the relative merits of alternative approaches persists.[31] We shall not prolong that debate here. It suffices to say that each approach has its own peculiar merits, and so the best strategy is undoubtedly to employ a variety of approaches, testing one's conclusions for their sensitivity to the choice of measures. In fact,

[30] *The Sources of Invention*, p. 197.
[31] See Simon Kuznets, "Inventive Activity: Problems of Definition and Measurement," and Barkev S. Sanders, "Some Difficulties in Measuring Inventive Activity," both in *The Rate and Direction of Inventive Activity*, pp. 19–90; U. S. National Science Foundation, *Methodology of Statistics on Research and Development* (Washington: 1959); and C. Freeman and A. Young, *The Research and Development Effort in Western Europe, North America and the Soviet Union* (Paris: Organisation for Economic Co-operation and Development, 1965).

it turns out that different measures yield remarkably similar results in many cases.[32]

One salient relationship is the high concentration of formal R & D effort among the largest manufacturing firms. In 1958, for which the best comparative data are available, U. S. firms with 5,000 or more employees originated 46 per cent of all value added in manufacturing. At the same time they accounted for 88 per cent of all expenditures on R & D performed by manufacturing companies, including 93 per cent of expenditures on federally-supported R & D programs and 83 per cent of the privately-financed effort.[33] Federally-supported expenditures were more highly concentrated than private spending in part because government agencies apparently prefer the convenience of dealing with large firms, but mainly because key tasks in the weapons system development programs contracted out by the federal government were so large that they could be handled only by sizeable firms, even when diligent efforts were exerted to disintegrate the work vertically through subcontracting.

A different pattern emerges when we use a count of invention patents received to assess the relative contributions of large and small producers. A complete count was made of patents issued in 1959 to 463 manufacturing firms included on *Fortune*'s list of the 500 largest U. S. industrial corporations for 1955. This sample, closely overlapping the population of companies with 5,000 or more employees, received 56 per cent of the U. S. invention patents issued to domestic manufacturing corporations in 1959 and accounted for approximately 57 per cent of the 1955 sales of U. S. manufacturing corporations.[34] Thus, the largest firms barely held their own in the receipt of invention patents despite their disproportionate share of both government and private R & D spending.

A possible explanation for this disparity might be that the patented inventions of large firms are in some sense of higher quality than those of smaller companies, reflecting a more intensive technical resource input. However, there is no empirical support for this hypothesis, and what evidence we have points in the opposite direction. Notably, the percentage of patented inventions actually brought into commercial utilization—one indicator of quality—is higher for small firms than for large. Interview studies also reveal that large corporations with an active staff of patent attorneys are less discriminating in their choice of inventions on which patent protection is sought.[35] Two alternative hypotheses appear more plausible. First, the division of labor has not progressed far enough in many smaller firms to permit the establishment of formal research and development programs. Their efforts to advance technology tend more often to be a casual, part-time endeavor not detected in statistics on formal R & D spending. This is consistent with Schmookler's estimate from a random sample of 1953 patented inventions that for every eight inventions flowing from full-time R & D employees, companies obtained five inventions from employees engaged only part-time in innovative activity.[36] Second, as we have suggested in the previous section, small firms may be at their best in the early, most inventive stages of the process of technical advance, while large corporations enjoy a comparative advantage at those types of detailed development which generate relatively few patentable inventions.

---

[32]See Dennis Mueller, "Patents, Research and Development, and the Measurement of Inventive Activity," *Journal of Industrial Economics*, November 1966, pp. 26–37; and W. S. Comanor and F. M. Scherer, "Patent Statistics as a Measure of Technical Change," *Journal of Political Economy*, May-June 1969, pp. 392–398.

[33]U. S. National Science Foundation, *Industrial R & D Funds in Relation to Other Economic Variables* (Washington: 1964), pp. 49–56. Later studies show no marked changes in the concentration of expenditures.

[34]See F. M. Scherer, "Firm Size, Market Structure, Opportunity, and the Output of Patented Inventions," *American Economic Review*, December 1965, pp. 1104–1105; and the testimony in U. S. Senate, Committee on the Judiciary, Subcommittee on Antitrust and Monopoly, Hearings, *Economic Concentration*, Part 3 (Washington: 1965), pp. 1198–1199.

[35]Cf. Barkev Sanders *et al.*, "Patent Acquisition by Corporations," *Patent, Trademark, and Copyright Journal of Research and Education*, Fall 1959, p. 238; and U. S. Federal Council for Science and Technology, Committee on Government Patent Policy, *Government Patent Policy Study*, Volume IV, "Effect of Government Patent Policy on Commercial Utilization and Business Competition" (Washington: June 1968), Part I, pp. 31 and 43.

[36]Jacob Schmookler, "Bigness, Fewness, and Research," *Journal of Political Economy*, December 1959, p. 630.

That formally organized R & D is disproportionately the domain of the larger corporation is shown by additional data from the U. S. National Science Foundation. In 1958 there were approximately 283,000 manufacturing firms with fewer than 1,000 employees. A formal R & D effort was maintained by somewhere between 3 and 20 per cent of those firms.[37] Of the 1,301 manufacturing companies with from 1,000 to 4,999 employees, 56 per cent maintained R & D programs. Of the 378 with 5,000 or more employees, 350, or 93 per cent, had formal programs. Thus, nearly all very large manufacturing firms engage in some formal R & D, while only a small fraction of the smallest companies do.

Among those enterprises which do support organized R & D, differences in the intensity of spending associated with size are apparent. Table 15.2 presents 1963 statistics on privately-financed R & D spending as a percentage of sales for all industries combined and for the seven industrial groups with private outlays of $200 million or more. In every group but petroleum refining (although not in some subsectors of the other listed groups) companies with 5,000 or more employees invested more intensively in R & D than their smaller rivals. The largest disparities are observed in the motor vehicles industry, where differences in size mirror differences in function, smaller firms operating mainly as suppliers of component parts made to specification, and in the machinery industry group, where a considerable amount of product engineering may be done on a casual, part-time basis in the smaller companies.

Although there are exceptions to the pattern, these statistics suggest that there must be certain advantages of size in the execution of research and development, broadly construed, even if not in the vital idea-generating stages of the process.

Table 15.2

Privately Financed Research and Development Expenditures
as a Percentage of Sales: 1963

Industry Group	Companies with Total Employment of		
	Less than 1,000	1,000 to 4,999	5,000 or more
All industries combined	1.5	1.4	2.1
Chemicals and drugs	2.7	3.3	3.7
Petroleum refining and extraction	n.a	1.0	0.9
Machinery	1.5	2.0	4.0
Electrical equipment and communications	3.2	2.5	3.8
Motor vehicles and other transportation equipment	0.8	0.7	2.6
Aircraft and missiles	2.0	2.0	2.6
Professional and scientific instruments	3.1	3.4	5.5

Source: U.S. National Science Foundation, *Basic Research, Applied Research, and Development in Industry, 1963* (Washington: 1966), p. 113. The companies included are only those maintaining a formal R&D program. Similar but less complete data are published annually.

[37]See U. S. National Science Foundation, *Industrial R & D Funds in Relation to Other Economic Variables,* p. 52; *Funds for Research and Development in Industry, 1958* (Washington: 1961), p. 15; and *Science and Engineering in American Industry: Final Report on a 1953-1954 Survey* (Washington: 1956), p. 60. The lower estimate is from a 1958 survey, the higher from a more extensive 1953 survey. The 1953 survey showed sponsorship of research rising from 8 per cent of all firms with from 8 to 99 employees to 42 per cent for firms with from 500 to 999 employees. See also C. R. McConnell and W. C. Peterson, "Research and Development: Some Evidence for Small Firms," *Southern Economic Journal,* April 1965, pp. 356-364.

Concretely, companies with 5,000 or more employees appear more likely to conduct R & D and, if they do so at all, to conduct it somewhat more intensively than smaller enterprises.

Still the employment of 5,000 persons is a modest threshold, as bigness in business goes. In 1967 General Motors had 145 times that number of employees, and there were more than 125 U. S. manufacturing concerns employing at least 25,000 persons. It is important therefore to probe more deeply into the structure of R & D activity among the nearly 500 industrial firms surpassing the 5,000 employee mark. There have been several statistical analyses of this select group.[38] Those which avoided fatal methodo-

logical errors have all come to the same conclusion: Increases in size beyond an employment level of roughly 5,000 are not in general accompanied by a more than proportional rise in innovative inputs or outputs.

To gain a broad perspective on the technical activity of the largest firms, data were collected on the 1955 sales, 1955 R & D employment (including supporting staff members), and 1959 invention patent acquisitions of 352 firms on *Fortune*'s 1955 list of the 500 largest industrial corporations. The companies were ranked in order of sales volume, and cumulative shares of the three variables were computed, with the results displayed in Table 15.3. It is evident

Table 15.3

Concentration of Sales, Patents, and R & D Employment
in a Sample of 352 Large Corporations

Number of Firms Included, Ranked by 1955 Sales	Percentage of Total for All 352 Firms		
	1955 Sales	1955 R & D Employment	1959 Patents
First 4	19.9	9.7	10.4
First 8	27.5	16.4	16.8
First 12	32.8	25.9	24.9
First 20	41.5	36.7	32.9
First 30	49.0	44.7	42.9
First 40	55.0	50.4	45.0
First 50	59.9	57.8	50.8
First 100	75.9	71.9	71.0
First 200	90.8	90.0	89.4
First 300	97.7	97.8	97.6
All 352	100.0	100.0	100.0

Source: F. M. Scherer, "Firm Size, Market Structure, Opportunity, and the Output of Patented Inventions," *American Economic Review,* December 1965, p. 1104.

[38]See James S. Worley, "Industrial Research and the New Competition," *Journal of Political Economy,* April 1961, pp. 183–186; Edwin Mansfield, "Size of Firm, Market Structure, and Innovation," *Journal of Political Economy,* December 1963, pp. 556–576; *idem,* "Industrial Research and Development Expenditures," *Journal of Political Economy,* August 1964, pp. 319–340; D. Hamberg, "Size of Firm, Oligopoly, and Research: The Evidence," *Canadian Journal of Economics and Political Science,* February 1964, pp. 62–75; F. M. Scherer, "Size of Firm, Oligopoly, and Research: A Comment," *Canadian Journal of Economics and Political Science,* May 1965, pp. 256–266; *idem,* "Firm Size, Market Structure, Opportunity, and the Output of Patented Inventions"; W. S. Comanor, "Research and Technical Change in the Pharmaceutical Industry," *Review of Economics and Statistics,* May 1965, pp. 182–191; and *idem,* "Market Structure, Product Differentiation, and Industrial Research," *Quarterly Journal of Economics,* November 1967, pp. 639–657.

that the largest firms account for a considerably smaller share of both R & D employment (reflecting inventive and innovative inputs) and patents (reflecting technical output) than their share of sales.

A similar pattern appears when the data are broken down by two- and three-digit industry groups. Of 14 such groups, only the general chemicals sector exhibited a distinct tendency for R & D employment to rise more than proportionately with sales all the way out to the scale of the largest firm.[39] These results are consistent with those from two studies by Edwin Mansfield, one utilizing a count of major innovations in the petroleum refining, coal mining, and steel industries; the other estimates of R & D spending in the chemicals, petroleum, drugs, steel, and glass industries.[40] As in the author's analysis, only the chemicals industry revealed a propensity toward steadily rising R & D intensity or productivity with increased size. Despite some differences in detail—notably for the chemicals and electrical equipment groups—Comanor's results from a regression analysis of R & D employment covering 387 large firms in 21 industry groups are essentially the same. The dominant pattern was for R & D activity to increase less than proportionately with sales.[41]

The weight of the available quantitative evidence favors a conclusion that among the largest 500 or so U. S. industrial corporations, increases in size do not as a rule contribute positively to the intensification of R & D inputs or inventive outputs, and in more cases than not, giant scale has a slight to moderate stultifying effect. The most technically progressive American firms appear, with the possible exception of chemicals

and petroleum producers, to be those with sales of less than $200 million at 1955 price levels.

IMPLICATIONS

What we find from analyzing the qualitative and quantitative evidence is a kind of threshold effect.[42] A little bit of bigness—up to sales levels of roughly $75 million to $200 million in most industries—is good for invention and innovation. But beyond the threshold further bigness adds little or nothing, and it carries the danger of diminishing the effectiveness of inventive and innovative performance. This conclusion naturally bears all the limitations of a statistical generalization. Exceptions certainly exist. Companies far below the suggested threshold may be extraordinarily prolific in generating new ideas, and they may suffer no handicap in developing relatively uncomplicated new products and processes. Firms above the threshold undoubtedly have an advantage in developing extremely complicated and costly systems, but a tiny firm (as Control Data Corporation was when it led the way to very high speed digital computers for scientific applications) can overcome its inherent disadvantage through a combination of genius, pluck, and luck.[43] Giants may escape the stultifying effects of size through unusually enlightened management, but this too is not easy or even probable. All things considered, the most favorable industrial environment for rapid technological progress would appear to be a firm size distribution which includes a preponderance of companies with sales below $200 million, pressed on one side by a horde of small, technology-oriented enterprises bubbling over with bright new ideas and on the other by a few larger

[39]Scherer, "Firm Size, Market Structure, Opportunity, and the Output of Patented Inventions," pp. 1105–1113; and testimony in the Senate *Economic Concentration* hearings, pp. 1194–1198. There is evidence that chemicals may no longer be an exception. Du Pont's preeminence has faded in recent years as smaller rivals strengthened their R & D programs, and in 1966 chemical producers with from 1,000 to 4,999 employees spent a higher fraction of their sales dollar on R & D than companies with 5,000 or more employees. See "How To Compete by Committee," *Business Week*, September 21, 1968, pp. 82–83; and U. S. National Science Foundation, *Research and Development in Industry, 1966* (Washington: 1968), p. 77.

[40]"Size of Firm, Market Structure, and Innovation," pp. 566–567; and "Industrial Research and Development Expenditures," pp. 333–337. This interpretation of the results from the first article is based in part upon plotting Mansfield's regression equations, which are extremely difficult to interpret otherwise.

[41]"Market Structure, Product Differentiation, and Industrial Research," pp. 642–643.

[42]Cf. Jesse W. Markham, "Market Structure, Business Conduct, and Innovation," *American Economic Review*, May 1965, p. 325.

[43]Cf. "Small, Smart, Sharp," *Business Week*, May 25, 1963, pp. 154–166; "Control Data's Magnificent Fumble," *Fortune*, April 1966, pp. 165 ff.; and "Building Another Giant," *Business Week*, December 7, 1968, p. 38.

corporations with the capacity to undertake exceptionally ambitious developments.

DIVERSIFICATION, RESEARCH, AND INVENTION

Another dimension of market structure with possible relevance to the rate of progress is diversification. The leading hypothesis imputing a potentially beneficial role to diversification has been advanced by Richard R. Nelson.[44] In his view research, and especially basic research, is a venture into the world of uncertainty, yielding inventions and discoveries in unexpected areas. The firm with interests in a diversity of fields will generally be able to produce and market a higher proportion of these unanticipated inventions than a company whose product line is narrow. Therefore, the profitability of speculative research is greater for highly diversified firms, and such firms will tend to support more of it. Diversified enterprises may also have an advantage at research and development because the very breadth of their interests allows particularly effective hedging against the risks of failure on any single R & D project or group of projects.

The Nelson hypothesis applies most directly to the support of basic research. Unfortunately, the National Science Foundation has released only highly aggregated statistics on basic research expenditures from its annual company surveys. What evidence we do have lends little support to the hypothesis. Firms with fewer than 1,000 employees are obviously much less diversified than those of larger size. Yet these relatively small and undiversified companies perform approximately 11 per cent of all U. S. basic industrial research—a contribution far exceeding their 4.9 per cent share of total R & D outlays or their 7.3 per cent share of privately-financed 1966 R & D spending.[45]

It is possible to obtain much richer data on industrial firms' *total* R & D inputs and outputs.

Three studies linking some index of overall inventive or innovative activity to diversification have been reported. Unfortunately, conflicting conclusions materialized.

One study was conducted by the author of the present work.[46] For each of 463 firms on *Fortune*'s list of the 500 largest industrials in 1955, an index of product line diversification was compiled. This measured the number of technologically distinct manufacturing lines (out of some 200 possibilities in total) spanned by each company during 1955. This diversification index was introduced into regression equations relating 1959 patenting to 1955 sales for 14 broad industry groups and into similar equations relating 1955 R & D employment to 1955 sales for seven two-digit industry groups. In the electrical equipment and the combined chemical and drug groups—leaders in conducting privately-financed R & D—the partial correlations between R & D employment or patenting and diversification were *negative* but statistically insignificant. This is the opposite of what we would expect if diversification has a stimulating effect. On the other hand, positive and in some instances highly significant partial correlations were obtained for a number of other industry groups—notably, for those which in general did relatively little privately-financed R & D. This was apparently so because the more diversified firms assigned under a 'principal product line' criterion to two-digit industry groups supporting little private R & D were more likely to have secondary interests in the chemicals and electrical equipment fields, where richer opportunities for pursuing research and new product development existed. Thus, for companies whose home base was a technically unprogressive industry, diversification did not appear to be a stimulus to greater research effort, but rather a structural indicator that the firms were grazing simultaneously in greener research pastures.

Grabowski analyzed total R & D expenditures from 1959 through 1962 for a smaller

[44] "The Simple Economics of Basic Scientific Research," *Journal of Political Economy*," June 1959, pp. 297–306.

[45] U. S. National Science Foundation, *Research and Development in Industry, 1966*, pp. 24, 33, and 82.

[46] Scherer, "Firm Size, Market Structure, Opportunity, and the Output of Patented Inventions," pp. 1114–1116.

sample, including 16 chemical producers, 15 petroleum refiners, and 10 drug manufacturers.[47] For all three industry groups, he found R & D spending as a percentage of sales to rise with the number of five-digit product lines in which the firms operated, taking into account also variables to reflect research productivity and cash flow in earlier periods. His results for the chemicals and drugs groups, which were highly significant statistically, run directly contrary to those obtained by the present author. The reasons for this difference are not clear. It seems unlikely that major structural changes could have occurred in the five years separating the time periods analyzed. The explanation may turn on differences in the variables used—R & D spending for Grabowski's dependent variable, compared to patents and R & D employment for the present author's, or the more narrowly defined diversification index employed by Grabowski as an independent variable. Or alternatively, differences in sample coverage may have been responsible. Grabowski's sample included a total of 41 chemical, drug, and petroleum companies, compared to 71 such firms in the author's analysis. But at this stage we can do no more than speculate.

Diversification fared badly in a more narrowly focused study by Comanor.[48] For a sample of 57 pharmaceutical manufacturers, he found that R & D productivity, measured by total new drug product sales in their first two years after introduction over a six-year period, was inversely correlated with diversification after taking into account also firm size and the intensity of R & D employment. He interpolated from this result that inefficiencies may arise from spreading one's research effort too thinly over many lines, and that it may be better to work exhaustively on a limited number of technical problems.

We must conclude our survey in a slightly perplexed state. Most of the evidence compiled thus far offers little support for the hypothesis that diversification is conducive to especially vigorous research and development activity, but a more favorable verdict is suggested by Grabowski's results. Further tests with the richer data likely to become available in the near future are needed before a more confident judgment can be rendered.

MONOPOLY, CONCENTRATION, AND INNOVATION

Monopoly power is the final variable whose impact on technical progress must be ascertained. There are two ways it might operate. First, the *expectation of achieving a monopoly* with accompanying supra-normal profits through successful invention and innovation may induce firms to invest in creating new products and processes. Here innovation leads to monopoly, and the belief that such a nexus exists is what provides the incentive to innovate. This hypothesis is at the heart of the theory of patent protection, which we shall defer for extended analysis in Chapter 16. Second, the *possession of monopoly power* might provide conditions which make businessmen more willing and able to undertake the burdens of innovation. Here a quite different causal connection is implied: monopoly power already in existence leads to innovation. It reflects a more uniquely Schumpeterian *Weltanschauung*, and to it we shall devote the balance of this chapter.

INNOVATION AND THE AVAILABILITY OF FUNDS

There are a number of sub-hypotheses to the conjecture that a monopolistic market structure favors innovation. One suggested directly by Schumpeter[49] begins with the notion that innovation is costly and risky. Through the profitable exploitation of monopoly power, firms may assemble a pool of funds they are disposed to invest in advancing technology—an investment they would be afraid or unwilling to make if fresh outside capital had to be tapped. Or to put the proposition in more general form, firms with

[47]Henry G. Grabowski, "The Determinants of Industrial Research and Development: A Study of the Chemical, Drug, and Petroleum Industries," *Journal of Political Economy*, March/April 1968, pp. 292–305.

[48]"Research and Technical Change in the Pharmaceutical Industry," p. 184.

[49]*Capitalism, Socialism, and Democracy*, p. 101.

market power are more apt to possess financial and organizational slack which can be used in a variety of discretionary ways, including investment in research and development.

In opposition to this view is the contention that innovation is the result of a conscious search for new and better solutions to pressing problems, and that such search activity is triggered by stress—i.e., by the sort of pressure on profits a competitive market applies.[50] Affluence, on the other hand, might breed complacency and disinterest in change.

It is possible that organizational slack favors certain kinds of innovations while pressure induces a different kind. Still we might hope to discern whether one or the other influence is dominant in a broad statistical sense. There have been three empirical studies in this spirit.

One, my own, tested the hypothesis that corporate innovative inputs and outputs rise as a function of current profitability and liquidity.[51] It covered 463 firms on *Fortune*'s 1955 list. The correlation between 1959 patents per billion dollars of 1955 sales and 1955 profits as a percentage of sales for the full sample turned out to be only $+0.03$. Between patents per billion dollars of sales and the ratio of 1955 liquid assets to total assets the correlation was $+0.06$. Neither correlation is significantly different from zero by standard statistical tests. Negative results also appeared when the data were broken into two-digit industry groups and when R & D employment per billion dollars of sales was used as the index of technical progressiveness. Further analysis suggested that intensive patenting led after a lag of three or four years to a rise in profits

as a consequence of increased sales.[52] But the study afforded no support for the contention that *current* profitability and liquidity affect the vigor of innovative activity one way or the other.

Similar results were obtained by Minasian in an analysis of 18 chemical producers covering the 1947–1957 period.[53] He discovered that R & D expenditures explained subsequent profitability much more powerfully than profitability explained either concurrent or subsequent R & D spending.

Again, however, Grabowski's work sounds a dissonant note. He reported that the ratio of R & D spending to sales for three samples including a total of 41 chemical, drug, and petroleum makers was strongly and positively correlated with the ratio of cash flow (i.e., after-tax profits plus depreciation plus depletion charges) to sales in the preceding year, other things such as diversification and productivity of past research being held equal.[54]

As in our discussion of the diversification phenomenon, there is no obvious explanation for the differences between Grabowski's findings and those of Minasian and the author. We must therefore report a hung jury. None of the studies completed thus far was completely satisfactory methodologically. Further insight is likely to come from analyses using sophisticated distributed lag techniques with richer data.[55]

OTHER HYPOTHESES

This by no means exhausts the list of ways monopoly might affect the pace of invention and innovation.[56] Organizational slack may be associated less with higher profits, cash flow, or

[50]Cf. Richard M. Cyert and James G. March, *A Behavioral Theory of the Firm* (Englewood Cliffs: Prentice-Hall, 1963), pp. 278–279.

[51]Scherer, "Firm Size, Market Structure, Opportunity, and the Output of Patented Inventions," p. 1117.

[52]F. M. Scherer, "Corporate Inventive Output, Profits, and Growth," *Journal of Political Economy*, June 1965, pp. 290–297. Although the results support the conventional wisdom that innovation pays, it is not certain that they are representative, since some peculiar business cycle perturbations evidently affected the data.

[53]Jora R. Minasian, "The Economics of Research and Development," in *The Rate and Direction of Inventive Activity, op. cit.*, especially pp. 118–122.

[54]"The Determinants of Industrial Research and Development," *loc. cit.* For results which might be interpreted as providing limping support, see Dennis C. Mueller, "The Firm Decision Process: An Econometric Investigation," *Quarterly Journal of Economics*, February 1967, pp. 71–73.

[55]At the time final revisions were being made on this book, Ben S. Branch was conducting a dissertation project on this problem at the University of Michigan. His preliminary findings for several industries revealed distinguishable positive relationships between profitability and inventive activity, including profits influencing innovation and vice versa.

[56]For a masterful survey of the *a priori* arguments, see P. Hennipman, "Monopoly: Impediment or Stimulus to Economic Progress?" in E. H. Chamberlin, ed., *Monopoly and Competition and Their Regulation* (London: Macmillan, 1954), pp. 421–456.

liquidity than with ample R & D staffs and high salaries which attract the superior brains.[57] Or companies insulated from short-run competitive pressures may be better able to make long-range plans concerning research projects which must be supported for several years and perhaps even a decade before bearing fruit. And by steadying the ship, monopolistic restrictions may establish a more stable platform for shooting at the rapidly and jerkily moving targets of new technology, to use Schumpeter's metaphor.[58] Producers dominating their markets may be able to internalize most of the benefits from innovations they make, whereas some benefits elude the atomistic innovator, who confers external economies upon imitators learning both the technical shortcuts and the blind alleys from its example.[59] On the other hand, critics charge that a monopoly position breeds lethargy and complacency toward technological pioneering.

These global assertions make no distinction between product and process innovations. From the orthodox profit-maximizing theory of firm behavior it can be deduced that pure competitors often have an edge over monopolistic sellers in developing and installing new production processes, other things (such as the volume of pre-innovation output) being held equal. This is illustrated in Figure 15.1, which is adapted from a more complex analysis by Professor Fellner.[60] Suppose the short-run marginal cost function (excluding investment costs) before innovation is MC_1 and after innovation MC_2. To facilitate comparison, we assume in all cases a pre-innovation output of OX_1: the competitive firm equates MC_1 with its horizontal marginal revenue function MR_C; the monopolistic producer equates MC_1 with its downward-sloping function MR_M. Each then weighs the profitability of introducing a new process characterized by cost function MC_2. After innovation, the monopolist

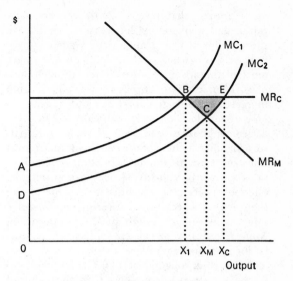

Figure 15.1
Process Innovation by a Monopolist and a Pure Competitor

will equate MC_2 with MR_M, producing output OX_M. It realizes an incremental quasi-rent contribution to profits and the recoupment of R & D and capital equipment outlays of $ABCD$ per period. The competitive firm after innovation expands its output to OX_C, realizing the incremental quasi-rent contribution $ABED$ per unit of time. Because the competitor has an incentive to expand output further following a cost reduction, its quasi-rent increment exceeds that of the monopolistic firm by the shaded area BCE per period, *ceteris paribus*.[61] This extra margin might just tip the balance between innovating and not innovating, and so we should expect competitive producers to adopt new cost-reducing processes more rapidly than firms with market power, other things being equal.

With respect to product innovations, it is

[57]Cf. Schumpeter, *Capitalism, Socialism, and Democracy*, p. 101.

[58]*Ibid.*, pp. 87–88 and 103.

[59]For a related analysis of how vertical integration influenced aluminum producers in making innovations of various kinds, see M. J. Peck, *Competition in the Aluminum Industry* (Cambridge: Harvard University Press, 1961), pp. 198–200.

[60]William Fellner, "The Influence of Market Structure on Technological Progress," *Quarterly Journal of Economics*, November 1951, pp. 560–567.

[61]An oligopolist subject to the kinked demand curve mentality will not increase output at all unless the cost reduction due to innovation is sufficiently large to jump the marginal revenue function's gap. See Oscar Lange, "A Note on Innovations," *Review of Economic Statistics*, February 1943, pp. 23–24.

often argued that progress will be especially rapid under oligopoly for reasons similar to those adduced in explaining the vigor of oligopolistic advertising rivalry.[62] Oligopolists have most of the advantages attributed to a monopolist. Their ability to suppress price competition increases organizational slack and permits a longer-run decision-making horizon. They are large enough relative to their markets to internalize a significant share of the benefits from innovations subsequently imitated. In addition, because sales at tacitly collusive prices are profitable, oligopolists have an incentive to try increasing their market shares by maneuvering on non-price dimensions—i.e., through product innovation. Non-price rivalry may also provide a needed outlet for ingrained aggressive instincts.

As a rule, oligopolists find it difficult to establish a cooperative solution to the game of product innovation. Like price rivalry, new product rivalry tends to have a static payoff structure of the Prisoner's Dilemma type. But each R & D project differs in numerous respects from all previous undertakings, so opportunities for tacit learning, the development of quantitative precedents, and the dynamic use of threats to elicit cooperation are minimal. The sensitivity of outcomes to variations in the participants' skill, creativity, and luck is much higher than in price rivalry, complicating the problem of reaching mutual accommodation.[63] During the early stages of a research and development project, so few persons are typically employed that plans can be kept secret; and uncertainty about what its rivals are brewing in their laboratories compels each seller to fear the worst. Even more important, two to five years of development may be required to bring a complex new product from the concept stage to a point where it is ready for

the market. The firm caught off guard by a rival innovation is condemned to a position of inferiority during this catching-up period, and recognizing this, each company has an incentive to begin development of any important, threatening new product possibility in which rivals have shown interest. For all these reasons, we should not expect oligopolists to be very successful in handling product innovation collusively, though it is possible to find some apparent exceptions to the rule.[64]

A MODEL OF OLIGOPOLISTIC PRODUCT R & D RIVALRY

Further insight into the structural conditions favoring a rapid pace of innovation can be gained by formulating the problem of new product rivalry more rigorously.[65] We start from the standard profit maximization premise: Firms seek to conduct their research and development projects in such a way as to maximize the surplus of expected revenues over expected costs. For simplicity, we assume that imitation in kind is feasible (i.e., that patent barriers can be surmounted); that rivalry takes the form of matching each others' improved qualitative features; and that each participant in the process must carry out its own R & D to market its improved product.

The potential innovator's problem is to decide how rapidly it will proceed in developing its product and introducing it into the market. Development can be carried out at a leisurely pace, as a crash program, or at various speeds in between. Accelerating the pace of development is costly because errors are made when one overlaps development steps instead of waiting for the information early experiments supply, because it may be necessary to support parallel

[62]See especially Galbraith, *American Capitalism*, pp. 88–90; Henry Villard, "Competition, Oligopoly, and Research," *Journal of Political Economy*, December 1958, pp. 483–497; and James W. McKie, *Tin Cans and Tin Plate* (Cambridge: Harvard University Press, 1959), pp. 253–254.

[63]Cf. Fellner, *op. cit.*, pp. 574–576; and (by the same author) *Competition Among the Few* (New York: Knopf, 1949), pp. 185 and 220–221.

[64]The automobile industry's record in developing gas turbine and electric propulsion technology and smog control devices is a probable illustration. See also Alfred E. Kahn, "The Chemical Industry," in Walter Adams, ed., *The Structure of American Industry* (Third ed.; New York: Macmillan, 1961), pp. 246–252 and 272.

[65]The model presented here is developed more fully in F. M. Scherer, "Research and Development Resource Allocation under Rivalry," *Quarterly Journal of Economics*, August 1967, pp. 359–394. See also W. L. Baldwin and G. L. Childs, "The Fast Second and Rivalry in Research and Development;" *Southern Economic Journal*, July 1969, pp. 18–24.

experimental approaches to hedge against uncertainty, and because of conventional diminishing returns in the application of additional scientific and engineering manpower to a given technical assignment. The possibilities for saving time by spending more money to develop a given new product starting in Year 0 are specified by the time-cost tradeoff function C in Figure 15.2. The shorter the development schedule, the more the effort costs, *ceteris paribus*. This represents the cost side of the firm's R & D scheduling problem.

Against the costs of accelerated development a potential innovator must weigh the benefits of proceeding more rapidly. These are reflected in a benefits function like V_1 in Figure 15.2, which indicates the discounted total quasi-rents (i.e., the surplus of sales revenues over production and distribution costs) expected from having the new product ready for commercial introduction at varying dates. It is negatively sloped for two main reasons: because completing the development effort earlier allows the firm to tap the market's profit potential over more units of time, and because earlier completion improves the

firm's competitive position relative to rivals, with possibly lasting implications for its market share and hence its share of the market's total profit potential.

Now the firm's problem is to choose that development schedule which maximizes the surplus of benefits V_1 over costs C. The optimum is found where the slope of the benefits function equals the slope of the time-cost tradeoff function; i.e., at development time OT_1. At the optimum, the marginal benefit from schedule acceleration (e.g., the increase in discounted quasi-rents due to compressing the development by one more unit of time) is equal to the marginal cost of acceleration (the increase in cost due to reducing development time by one more unit).

At any given moment, the shape and position of the time-cost tradeoff function C is largely determined by the state of technology. But the shape of the benefits function depends *inter alia* upon market structure. This is the core of our concern. From the conditions for profit maximization, we know that the pace of innovation will be faster, the steeper the slope of the innovator's benefits function is. Is the slope steeper when the number of firms is large or small? And is it steeper for small firms or relatively large (i.e., dominant) enterprises?

There is no absolutely general, unambiguous answer; it depends upon a number of conditions. There are, however, some most probable answers. If we accept the Cournot-like assumption that firms consider themselves unable to determine rival schedule decisions by their own decisions— an assumption compatible with the many obstacles preventing collusive handling of new product rivalry, and if producers are not restrained from penetrating into the new product's market by capacity bottlenecks, then an increase in the number of rivals or a reduction in the relative size of the innovator accelerates the pace of development.

Concretely, when the number of evenly-matched rivals increases from, say, two to three, *ceteris paribus*, the benefits function faced by a potential innovator will undergo a shift, as from V_1 *to* V_2, and the optimal time of development will be compressed from OT_1 to OT_2. This is so because by introducing its new product ahead

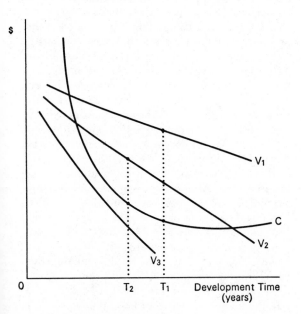

Figure 15.2
Optimizing the Speed of New Product Development

of the others, the innovator enjoys temporarily what would otherwise be the market domain of its rivals. The more evenly-matched rivals there are to carve up the market, the larger will be the portion (which would otherwise go to rivals) the innovator gets to enjoy during its term of leadership. Moreover, by leading the way the innovator may also be able to gain an image or reputation advantage, enabling it permanently to increase its market share at the expense of rivals. The larger the share of the market rivals would achieve if they exactly matched its new product introduction date, the more the innovator has to gain by being first and permanently capturing some of that share, *ceteris paribus*. Or to put the point the other way around, the smaller a company's share of some new product market will be if it fails to lead, the more it has to gain by leading, and hence the more rapidly it will be inclined to proceed in its R & D effort.

It follows obversely that a monopolist or a company which already dominates the market it supplies has little to gain by speeding up the introduction of product improvements as long as other firms refrain from doing so, since there is not much it can take away from others. Dominant firms are not likely to be vigorous innovators. But if their market position is threatened by the intrusion of a smaller innovator, they have a great deal to lose from running a poor second: the larger share they would otherwise enjoy. The theory predicts then that profit-maximizing dominant firms will be potent imitators when their market shares are endangered, and they may even accelerate their development efforts so strongly in response to a challenge that they induce the small challenger to relax its development pace and settle for the smaller market share associated with being second. Still, in this more complex case it is the small firm which wins honors for hastening technological progress, since without its initial challenge, the dominant firm would not have moved so quickly.

We conclude from the analysis thus far that the rapidity of innovation increases with the number of firms, and that sellers with small market shares are more likely to trigger a rapid pace of innovation than dominant firms, though the latter may retaliate vigorously. This suggests that tight oligopoly is less conducive to progress than loose oligopoly and that both are better than pure monopoly. Reinforcing this inference is a point heretofore neglected. The more rivals an industry harbors, the more independent centers of initiative there are, and the more likely it is that some entrepreneur will consider the development of a potential new product worthwhile. Once he does so, he threatens the market shares of other industry members, precipitating a spiral of reactions which ends up with each seller introducing its countervailing new product at an earlier date than would have been the case in the absence of rivalry.

These conclusions rest solely upon analyzing how market structure affects the *slopes* of the benefit functions confronting would-be innovators. There is another side to the picture, however. While an increase in the number of rivals steepens the slope of the benefits function, it also shifts the function down and to the left, reducing the total discounted profit an innovator can expect to realize. This occurs because after imitation takes place, and especially if it comes fairly rapidly, the innovator will find itself dividing up the market's total profit potential with more rivals and enjoying a smaller share itself, other things being equal. Also, if the number of imitating rivals becomes too large, pricing discipline will break down, causing not only the innovator's *share* of the profit pie, but the pie itself, to shrink. If the number of likely imitators is sufficiently large, the benefits function confronting a would-be innovator may lie as far to the left as V_3 in Figure 15.2. Here pioneering a new product development is expected to be downright unprofitable, and if all sellers have similar expectations, none will be willing to take the first step. A kind of Alphonse- and- Gaston dynamics will ensue, each industry member holding back initiating its R & D effort in the fear that rapid imitation by others will be encouraged, more than wiping out its innovative profits. Whether or not this will happen depends largely upon the interrelationship of five variables: the size of the overall market profit potential, the number of actual or potential rivals vying to share that potential, the speed at which rivals are expected to react and imitate, the degree to which being first confers a permanent product differentiation advantage, and the magnitude of anticipated R & D costs. The smaller the new product market's total profit potential is in relation to any single firm's development costs, *ceteris paribus*, the more the presence of a significant number of rivals is apt to discourage early innovation.

What we find then is a clash of structural influences. In terms of the marginal conditions for profit maximization, an increase in the number of sellers is conducive to more rapid innovation. This influence can be called the *stimulus factor*. But in terms of the requirement that expected profits from innovation be non-negative, an increase in the number of firms can, beyond some point, discourage rapid innovation. This influence might appropriately be called the *Lebensraum factor.*[66]

To carry the analysis further we need a broader dynamic conception of the process of technological advance. The profitability of innovation depends in the most fundamental sense upon supply and demand conditions. On the supply side, the costs of carrying out a research and development project are influenced by changes in the stock of knowledge. As scientific and technological knowledge advances, what may be impossible today will be feasible but costly tomorrow and easy the day after tomorrow. That is, there is a tendency for time-cost tradeoff functions, recalibrated periodically in current time, to shift toward the origin of Figure 15.2 (e.g., in a southwesterly direction) as time passes and knowledge accumulates. The benefits function is concurrently affected by changing demand conditions. As population grows, per capita incomes rise, and (less certainly) factor cost ratios vary, the benefits function for a potential innovation may shift in a northeasterly direction. An innovation becomes profitable when, as a result of changes in knowledge and/or demand, the benefits function comes to lie at least partially above the time-cost tradeoff function. Innovations induced primarily by advances in knowledge are called technology-push innovations. Those rendered attractive by rising demand are called demand-pull innovations. Usually both supply and demand conditions are changing, and innovation may be induced by a combination of the two forces.[67]

Suppose now that the advance of knowledge and increases in demand take place smoothly and continuously. At some moment in time, an innovation which was not profitable before will suddenly become profitable for a pure monopolist as the shifting benefits and time-cost tradeoff functions fleetingly come into tangency with one another. At this same moment the development will not yet have become profitable if the market were divided among oligopolists, each anticipating having to share the new product's sales with rivals and hence unable completely to monopolize the fruits of its R & D effort. If innovation is to occur as rapidly as is profitably feasible under the conditions postulated, monopoly is essential!

Of course, a monopolist may choose not to innovate at this first profitable moment. If it can foresee continuing cost and benefit function shifts, it will prefer to wait until it can earn more than a bare normal profit on its development investment.[68] When cost and benefit function shifts are smooth and continuous, a monopolistic structure is superior to others in making the earliest possible innovation date theoretically feasible, but not necessarily in terms of when innovation will actually occur. There can be ample room in the market for profitable innovation by more than one firm—e.g., by oligopolists or monopolistic competitors—when the functions have shifted discontinuously, as in the case of technological breakthroughs, or when there have been lags in the recognition or exploitation

---

[66]For similar views, see Jewkes, Sawers, and Stillerman, *op. cit.*, pp. 173–176; and Hennipman, *op. cit.*, p. 449.

[67]For a brilliant theoretical and empirical investigation of the demand and supply influences inducing technological advance, see Jacob Schmookler, *Invention and Economic Growth* (Cambridge: Harvard University Press, 1966).

[68]See Yoram Barzel, "Optimal Timing of Innovations," *Review of Economics and Statistics*, August 1968, pp. 348–355; and Morton I. Kamien and Nancy L. Schwartz, "Timing of Innovations under Rivalry," Carnegie-Mellon University, mimeo, May 1969.

of profitable new product opportunities. These conditions may be satisfied frequently in practice, since many innovations do follow from breakthroughs, and since evidence of generous prevailing profit returns to R & D investment suggests that the profit potential of new product markets is by no means spread too thinly.[69]

We come out, as is often our lot, with ambiguous theoretical predictions. Monopoly and high concentration are conducive to rapid innovation in certain respects—e.g., through the *Lebensraum* and organizational slack effects; but rivalry among numerous sellers is beneficial in others—notably, in terms of its stimulus effects. Which tendencies dominate in the real world is an empirical question to which we now turn.

QUALITATIVE EVIDENCE

Like the predictions from theory, the qualitative evidence from case studies of technological progress in specific industries presents a mixed picture. One theme which appears repeatedly is the apparent inhospitality of an atomistic market structure to research, development, and innovation. The paucity of significant innovations conceived and developed within the home construction industry, with its thousands of small producers, is well known.[70] A chronicle of the snail's pace at which automated brick-making equipment was developed reveals deficient incentives to innovate when the leading four producers together account for only 12 per cent of nation-wide production, even when substitute materials are eroding industry sales.[71] In the fertilizer industry, with 144 bulk producers in 1963 and a four-firm concentration ratio of 34, vigorous innovative activity has been conspicuously absent. Many of the leading new developments had to be pioneered and demonstrated by the Tennessee Valley Authority—an arm of the federal government.[72] Two book-length studies of the radio industry in the United States and Great Britain reached the common conclusion that small manufacturers did little to advance the underlying technology during the 1920s and 1930s. Instead they concentrated on producing attractively styled products at low cost. Most of the significant research and development contributions came either from powerful firms like A.T. &T., General Electric, and R.C.A. or from independent inventors.[73]

Nevertheless, there are clear exceptions to this pattern. Since World War II an impressive R & D effort has been sustained in both the unconcentrated and concentrated product lines of the electronics industry, with small competitors bearing at least their share of the load. Professor Peck found that most of the innovations in aluminum end product applications came from the 24,000 odd firms engaged in fabricating such products, not from the oligopolistic primary metal refiners. He observed also that the general pace of innovation was accelerated when Alcoa's monopoly position in ingot production was dissolved through the government-sponsored entry of several rivals.[74] And in petroleum refining, where the leading four firms originate only a third of total national output, active R & D programs are supported by the industry leaders and by numerous smaller producers. Phillips, probably the most technically progressive refiner, commands a market share of only 4 per cent.

Some case studies demonstrate too that innovation was retarded when competition has been suppressed. Maclaurin concludes, for example, that technical progress would have been

---

[69]Cf. Mansfield, *Industrial Research and Technological Innovation*, pp. 57, 65, and 75–76.

[70]See Charles Foster, "Competition and Organization in Building," *Journal of Industrial Economics*, July 1964, pp. 163–174.

[71]"Brick Kiln Builds Up Its Speed," *Business Week*, July 15, 1967, pp. 72–74.

[72]See Jesse W. Markham, *The Fertilizer Industry* (Nashville: Vanderbilt University Press, 1958), pp. 164–168 and 212–214; and U. S. Federal Council for Science and Technology, Committee on Government Patent Policy, *Government Patent Policy*, volume III, "Government Promotion of Federally Sponsored Inventions," Section VIII (Washington: June 1968).

[73]W. R. Maclaurin, *Invention and Innovation in the Radio Industry* (New York: Macmillan, 1949), pp. 153–224 and 251–256; and S. G. Sturmey, *The Economic Development of Radio* (London: Duckworth, 1958), pp. 155, 162, and 233.

[74]M. J. Peck, "Inventions in the Postwar American Aluminum Industry," in *The Rate and Direction of Inventive Activity*, pp. 291–298.

faster in the radio field during the 1920s and 1930s if A.T. &T., General Electric, and Westinghouse had not agreed to limit competition among themselves by defining spheres of influence and by forming the Radio Corporation of America to coordinate their patent portfolios.[75] Bright observed that the cartelization of the U.S. electric lamp industry during the same period slowed down the development of fluorescent lighting and other advances.[76] And the general sluggishness which led to a gradual deterioration of Imperial Chemical Industries' position in world markets has been traced to its participation in elaborate cartel and spheres of influence agreements with international rivals.[77]

There is also considerable evidence to support our earlier prediction that companies dominating their markets will be slow innovators but aggressive followers. Gillette's experience in bringing out a stainless steel razor blade during the 1960s,[78] IBM's slow start and fast finish in developing digital electronic computing equipment and time-sharing computers,[79] A.T. &T.'s record in the development of microwave radio relay systems and communications satellites,[80] the reaction of Procter & Gamble and Lever Brothers to the introduction of liquid household detergents by a tiny newcomer,[81] and the United Shoe Machinery Corporation's response to Compo's sole-cementing device innovations are illustrations.[82] Even here, however, the record is not completely uniform. R.C.A.'s almost single-handed struggle to develop and promote color television after the Federal Communications Commission approved its dot-sequential system as the national standard (rejecting the Columbia field-sequential system) suggests that technical pioneering is not a virtue totally foreign to industry leaders. Equally impressive was the invention and development of the float glass technique by Pilkington Brothers, Ltd., supplying 90 per cent of all British flat glass requirements.[83] And before World War II the I. G. Farben combine, which dominated Germany's chemical industry, is said to have been one of the most research-intensive firms in the world.[84]

The main lesson to be drawn from a review of the qualitative evidence is that no simple, one-to-one relationship between market structure and technological progressiveness is discernible. Indeed, it seems reasonable to infer that market structure has less influence on the pace at which innovation occurs than certain other variables.

The most important determinant is undoubtedly the richness of opportunities opened up by advances in science and technical knowledge. It would be myopic to suggest that there are no attractive opportunities for improving fire bricks or the way they are made. But companies producing electronic circuit modules, synthetic hormones, peripheral input and output devices for computers, atomic reactors, artificial kidneys, numerically controlled milling machines, and color film surely face a much more bountiful array of unexploited technical possibilities. The richness of technological opportunity varies widely from one product area to another, giving rise to extensive inter-industry variation in R & D

[75]Maclaurin, *op. cit.*, p. 254.

[76]Arthur A. Bright, Jr., and W. R. Maclaurin, "Economic Factors Influencing the Development and Introduction of the Fluorescent Lamp," *Journal of Political Economy*, October 1943, p. 449.

[77]"The British Company That Found a Way Out," *Fortune*, August 1966, pp. 104 ff.

[78]"How Gillette Has Put on a New Face," *Business Week*, April 1, 1967, pp. 58–60; and "Gillette Hones Its Edge," *Business Week*, October 23, 1965, p. 143.

[79]C. Freeman, "Research and Development in Electronic Capital Goods," *National Institute Economic Review*, November 1965, p. 60; and "I.B.M.'s $5,000,000,000 Gamble," *Fortune*, September 1966, pp. 118 ff., and October 1966, pp. 139 ff.

[80]F. M. Scherer, "The Development of the TD-X and TD-2 Microwave Radio Relay Systems in Bell Telephone Laboratories," unpublished case study, Harvard University Graduate School of Business Administration, October 1960.

[81]"Lestoil: The Road Back," *Business Week*, June 15, 1963, pp. 118–124.

[82]Carl Kaysen, *United States* v. *United Shoe Machinery Corporation*, pp. 77 and 184–189.

[83]G. H. Wierzynski, "The Eccentric Lords of Float Glass," *Fortune*, July 1968, pp. 91 ff.

[84]C. Freeman, "The Plastics Industry: A Comparative Study of Research and Innovation," *National Institute Economic Review*, November 1963, p. 33.

spending, patenting, and the like.[85] Furthermore, some industries are in a better position than others to take advantage of new opportunities. To extend a homely example, the brickmaking industry might benefit from computer control of its production processes, but economies of specialization dictate that the computer be designed by and acquired from an electronics producer. Such specialization is a prominent feature of every industrialized economy. Because of it, companies at home in the electrical and chemical fields, blessed with rich and growing funds of scientific knowledge, have enjoyed a distinct advantage in developing and producing new processes and intermediate materials used by a host of other sectors.[86] For firms surrounded by a more meager knowledge base, progressiveness may demand no more than the ability to recognize their own needs and the willingness to utilize products and processes others develop to satisfy those needs.

A second, more illusive prerequisite for rapid progress is an attitude of receptiveness on the part of entrepreneurs to harnessing modern science for industrial purposes. Opportunities created by the advance of knowledge may not even be recognized unless resources are devoted to identifying them and unless businessmen listen to the people able to identify them. This "research conception," as Maclaurin put it, is much stronger in some U. S. industries than in others.[87] Likewise, Hohenberg observed that differences in technological progressiveness among the German, French, British, and Swiss chemical industries from 1850 to 1914 resulted more from differences in entrepreneurial attitudes than from disparities in scientific opportunity, raw materials endowments, or market structure.[88]

Why a research conception appears in some industries or nations and not in others is unclear. The only conceivable way market structure might affect the process is through a kind of *demonstration effect*, i.e., when some monopolistic firm with organizational slack decides to dabble in research, as du Pont did during the 1920s, and has such good luck that others are inspired to follow suit. But this is only one of many possible precipitating factors. The strikingly successful application of science to warfare during World War II undoubtedly had a much more potent demonstration effect on the electrical instruments, chemicals, and drug industries in the United States, and this in turn may explain the rapid spread of formal R & D program sponsorship to smaller firms in those industries.[89] For our present purposes, it does not seem too great an oversimplification to assume that industries acquire a research conception largely by historical accident. To the extent that this is true, it adds random variation or 'noise' to the relationships observed between market structure and technical progressiveness. If such relationships exist, therefore, we should not expect them to be powerful statistically and certainly not to explain all the inter-industry variation in progressiveness indices.

QUANTITATIVE EVIDENCE

Cautioned against expecting too much, let us see whether any general statistical relationships can be detected.

The first thrusts in this direction were not particularly encouraging. One standard measure of technological progress is the growth of productivity—i.e., of output per worker, preferably adjusted for differences in capital intensity. In 1956 Professors Stigler and Phillips published

[85]Cf. Scherer, "Firm Size, Market Structure, Opportunity, and the Output of Patented Inventions," pp. 1099–1103, in which it is estimated that some 30 per cent of the observed inter-firm differences in patenting can be attributed to inter-industry differences in technological opportunity.

[86]Cf. Schmookler, *Invention and Economic Growth*, pp. 165–178.

[87]W. R. Maclaurin, "Technological Progress in Some American Industries," *American Economic Review*, May 1954, pp. 178–189.

[88]Paul M. Hohenberg, *Chemicals in Western Europe: 1850–1914* (Chicago: Rand McNally, 1967), especially pp. 67–84.

[89]It is conceivable that before World War II had its demonstration effect, the organizational slack associated with market power was a more important basis of technological leadership. This could explain why the performance of such firms as du Pont, I.C.I., I. G. Farben, R.C.A., and A.T.&T. was more impressive relative to that of smaller concerns before the war but not after.

independent studies of the relationship between changes in output per worker from 1899 to 1939 and market structure.[90] They used the same basic productivity change data and their samples overlapped for more than half the industries covered. Yet they came to opposite conclusions, Stigler finding that productivity increased more in industries of low concentration (and even faster in industries of declining concentration), while Phillips reported a positive correlation between productivity gains and concentration. Their results diverged partly because of different concentration measures: Phillips used *plant* concentration ratios and Stigler more meaningful (but less reliable) *firm* ratios. If it were possible to ascertain which sample and data were superior, it is still not clear what we would know. Differences in the capital intensity cf processes introduced, presumably in response to dissimilar production functions and input price relationships, undoubtedly affected the results. Opportunities for achieving productivity gains may have varied widely from industry to industry. And as we have seen earlier, the new processes and materials which raise productivity in an industry are often conceived and developed elsewhere. Less than a fourth of U. S. firms' R & D is directed toward improving their own internal production processes. To the extent that process technology is imported from other industries, productivity growth shortfalls over such a long period attributable to differences in market structure would have to reflect either producers' unwillingness to cooperate with process improvement specialists or reluctance to replace worn-out equipment with the best new techniques available on the market.[91] While pathological cases of refusal to accept what is practically a free lunch may exist, it is dubious whether this is what the Stigler and Phillips studies measure.

Due to the conceptual pitfalls in relating productivity growth to market structure as a test for technological progressiveness, most subsequent studies have focused on some more direct index of intra-industry efforts to advance technology, such as spending on research and development. The pioneering analyses of this genre sought to ascertain the correlation between the ratio of R & D expenditures to sales, obtained for a sample of from 13 to 20 highly aggregated industry groups, and an index of market concentration.[92] In every such instance, a positive correlation coefficient ranging in magnitude from 0.29 to 0.54 was obtained. Consistent with Schumpeter's conjectures, the more concentrated markets were, the more intensely R & D was supported.

One shortcoming of these studies is that they fail to take into account inter-industry differences in technological opportunity. Some industries tap a rich and growing knowledge base; others do not. More light is shed on this problem by three 'second generation' analyses. Each tried to adjust for something corresponding to differences in the potential for making innovations. Although the data and statistical models were quite heterogeneous, all three reached essentially similar conclusions. Phillips analyzed the ratio of privately-financed R & D spending to value added in 1958 for a sample of 11 broadly defined

---

[90]George J. Stigler, "Industrial Organization and Economic Progress," in L. D. White, ed., *The State of the Social Sciences* (Chicago: University of Chicago Press, 1956), pp. 269–282; and Almarin Phillips, "Concentration, Scale, and Technological Change in Selected Manufacturing Industries, 1899–1939," *Journal of Industrial Economics,* June 1956, pp. 179–193. In an article using 1937–53 data, Leonard Weiss found that market concentration had an erratic and statistically insignificant role in explaining productivity growth after the growth of output was taken into account. "Average Concentration Ratios and Industrial Performance," *Journal of Industrial Economics,* July 1963, pp. 250–252. See also Bruce T. Allen, "Concentration and Economic Progress: Note," *American Economic Review,* September 1969, pp. 600–604.

[91]That is to say, the Fellner-Lange analysis discussed in connection with Figure 15.1 has no relevance in a long-run, outside-purchase context.

[92]Ira Horowitz, "Firm Size and Research Activity," *Southern Economic Journal,* January 1962, pp. 298–301; D. Hamberg, "Size of Firm, Oligopoly, and Research: The Evidence," *Canadian Journal of Economics and Political Science,* February 1964, pp. 74–75; and Yale Brozen, "R & D Differences Among Industries," in Richard A. Tybout, ed., *Economics of Research and Development* (Columbus: Ohio State University Press, 1965), pp. 90 and 128. For an analysis which focuses on the *distribution* of innovative activity within industries (rather than the overall *level* of innovative activity between industries), see Oliver E. Williamson, "Innovation and Market Structure," *Journal of Political Economy,* February 1965, pp. 67–73. Using Mansfield's data for three industries, Williamson found that the leading four firms' share of all significant innovations within an industry was inversely correlated with the four-firm concentration ratio.

industry groups. For each group, he made a subjective estimate of an "index of product changeability," reflecting the extent to which contemporary science permitted functional product changes and product differentiation.[93] Using data from the 1960 Census of Population, I have analyzed the ratio of natural scientist and engineer employment to total employment for 56 manufacturing industry groups, some defined broadly and some narrowly, none involved primarily in government contract work. Data were divided into four product technology classes: electrical, chemical, general and mechanical, and traditional (the last class including such industries as sawmills, pottery making, meat packing, rugs and carpets, and apparel).[94] Comanor used data on 1955 and 1960 research and development employment, adjusted for firm size, for a sample of 387 companies classified into 33 two- and three-digit industry groups. To allow for variations in technological opportunity, he separated the industries into two classes according to differences in the possibility of achieving product differentiation through innovation.[95]

One finding common to all three analyses was that the intensity of industries' R & D efforts was strongly correlated with the index of technological opportunity, and that after differences in opportunity were taken into account, the correlation between R & D intensity and concentration continued to be positive but much weaker. In the study of 56 industries, for instance, a simple correlation of +0.46 was obtained between the ratio of scientific and engineering to total employment and the concentration index. However, when differences in product technology were taken into account, the partial correlation between the technological employment index and concentration fell to +0.20. This occurred because concentration is higher on the average in fields of high technological opportunity (notably, electrical equipment and indus-

trial chemicals) than in the traditional technology groups; and the intensity of scientific and engineering employment or R & D spending, while correlated with both differences in opportunity and concentration, is more strongly correlated with the former than the latter.

This raises a delicate question of cause and effect. Is technological opportunity independent of concentration, or is there some causal connection? And if the latter, in what direction does the chain of causation flow: from high opportunity to high concentration, or from high concentration to high opportunity? Observation leads us to believe that the greater progressiveness of the chemicals, electrical, and (in Phillips' sample) aircraft industries is not due primarily to high concentration, since the advance of scientific knowledge has been exceptionally generous to these fields during the past century. Some support can, however, be mustered for the hypothesis that technological innovation associated with opportunity has led to concentration. The high concentration in such fields as synthetic fibers, organic chemicals, telephone equipment, electric lamps, and computing equipment was built in part upon patent and know-how barriers to entry. Also, a very rapid pace of technological change in high-opportunity industries is likely to have increased the variance of member firms' growth rates, with successful innovators growing rapidly and unsuccessful ones being displaced. This would have the effect of raising concentration levels over time under some variant of Gibrat's law.[96] It appears more plausible, therefore, that technological opportunity and concentration are either causally independent or that the observed correlation between them denotes a causal flow from opportunity to concentration. In either event, the inclusion of opportunity indices helps avoid imputing to concentration a stimulative effect which is not in fact warranted.

[93]Almarin Phillips, "Patents, Potential Competition; and Technical Progress," *American Economic Review*, May 1966, pp. 301–310.

[94]F. M. Scherer, "Market Structure and the Employment of Scientists and Engineers," *American Economic Review*, June 1967, pp. 524–531.

[95]Comanor, "Market Structure, Product Differentiation, and Industrial Research," pp. 645–652.

[96]Cf. pp. 129–130 *supra*.

Yet even after differences in opportunity were taken into account, a positive association between intensity of R & D effort and concentration persisted in all three studies. This suggests that the climate for innovation is more favorable in concentrated than in atomistic industries, other things being held equal. To this a vital qualification must be added. In two of the studies, it was possible to analyze the correlation between R & D vigor and concentration by opportunity classes. In both cases, the strongest correlations showed up for the industries facing the least rich innovative opportunities. For the analysis of 56 industries, the correlation between scientists and engineers per 1,000 employees and concentration was +0.47 among the traditional products industries, which on the average employed by far the fewest technical personnel. It was +0.30 for the general and mechanical products group and *negative* for the five industries in the chemicals class.[97] The mean level of scientific and engineering employment predicted by the traditional product class regression equation was 110 per cent higher in industries with a four-firm concentration ratio of 60 than in those with a four-firm ratio of 25; while in the general and mechanical products group, it was only 50 per cent higher in the more concentrated industries. Similarly, Comanor found that size-adjusted R & D employment was roughly twice as high in concentrated as in unconcentrated industries when the opportunities for product differentiation through innovation were meager, but only 10 to 20 per cent higher for the more concentrated industries in high-opportunity fields.

This last set of results is extraordinarily important, for it permits us to tie theory and evidence together in a coherent explanatory framework. The class variables used to measure technological opportunity take into account differences in the rate at which the stock of scientific knowledge and technical concepts is growing. This in turn manifests itself in the rate at which the time-cost tradeoff function *C* moves toward the origin of Figure 15.2. In high opportunity industries, the *C* function shifts more rapidly than in low opportunity industries, *ceteris paribus*. These shifts may occur either smoothly and continuously or in discrete breakthroughs. A breakthrough suddenly opens up room for numerous firms to exploit a new product opportunity profitably, so that consideration of the benefits function's slope dominates firms' development scheduling decisions. Under these circumstances, technological progress is more rapid with many sellers (i.e., low concentration) than with few. The same holds true for smooth and continuous changes if there are more or less uniform lags in the recognition of new opportunities. Suppose it takes five years on the average between the moment when a new R & D effort first becomes potentially profitable under monopolized conditions and the moment when some entrepreneur first recognizes that opportunity.[98] Meanwhile the *C* function is steadily shifting. It will have shifted more in high opportunity fields than in low opportunity fields, and so more room will have been created for profitable development by numerous companies. With either continuous or discontinuous change in the knowledge base, then, fear of market overcrowding is less likely to deter vigorous innovative effort when the knowledge base grows rapidly, as in high opportunity fields.[99] It follows that high market concentration is less essential for heavy R & D investment in high opportunity, rapid shift industries than in low opportunity fields. Or to put the proposition negatively, when the overall profit potential for a recognized new product opportunity is modest in relation to contemplated development costs, investment in development may not take place unless the

[97]For further evidence that the correlation is weak in high opportunity fields, see Scherer, "Firm Size, Market Structure, Opportunity, and the Output of Patented Inventions," pp. 1117–1121.

[98]Of course, speed of recognition may be correlated with market structure. Recognition of opportunities may be faster in atomistic industries simply because there are more independent centers of initiative, or it may be faster in monopolistic industries if monopolists alone maintain staffs of researchers to keep track of outside scientific advances.

[99]The relationship between market room and the rate at which benefit functions shift is analogous. Here, however, there is no direct support in existing empirical results.

number of rivals, and hence the number of likely imitators, is low—that is, unless concentration is high. And this is exactly what the empirical evidence suggests.[100]

Nevertheless, there could be another explanation for the results. In low opportunity fields, technological pioneering may appear to be relatively unprofitable, or it may have only a modest impact on market positions, so that companies come to view innovation as a relatively unimportant strategy option. In this case only firms with considerable organizational slack—e.g., those in the more concentrated industries—will undertake significant R & D programs. In high opportunity industries, on the other hand, firms learn through experience that success in the market comes from innovative leadership, and an attempt by some to move ahead of the pack forces other industry members to mount their own R & D programs. Competition then leads to a high equilibrium level of R & D spending, whether concentration is high or low. By way of empirical support, an analysis of 463 large corporations' 1959 patenting revealed that companies in industries characterized by high technological opportunity matched each others' innovative efforts closely, receiving similar numbers of patents per billion dollars of sales, whereas patenting intensity varied widely from firm to firm in low opportunity fields.[101] This conjecture, it should be noted, is not necessarily incompatible with the market room hypothesis. They may complement one another in describing the complexities of real-world behavior.

It seems clear in any event that market concentration has a favorable impact on technological innovation in certain situations. *How much* concentration is advantageous remains to

be determined. Obviously, there is no general answer; the optimum depends upon the size of the overall market profit potential in relation to the cost of development in any given case. Still the available empirical evidence suggests a very tentative generalization. In the study of 56 manufacturing industries, tests were conducted to determine whether there was a nonlinear pattern in the ratio of scientific and engineering to total employment in the low (traditional) and intermediate (general and mechanical) technological opportunity fields.[102] Each revealed that below a four-firm concentration ratio of 10 to 14, virtually no scientific and engineering effort takes place.[103] The maximum intensity of scientific and engineering employment occurred between concentration ratios of 50 and 55, implying that a modest degree of oligopoly is beneficial in fields of limited technological opportunity. Concentration in excess of this magnitude appears in most instances to be unnecessary for, and perhaps even detrimental to, the vigorous exploitation of opportunities for technical advance.

THE ROLE OF NEW ENTRY AND ENTRY BARRIERS

One further facet must be explored. In his analysis of structural variables affecting research and development, Comanor discovered that industries with "moderate" barriers to new entry —i.e., those with minimum optimal plant scales requiring production of from 4 to 7 per cent of total industry output, and/or a capital investment of from $20 million to $70 million—had much higher R & D employment relative to their size than industries with either high or low entry barriers, *ceteris paribus*.[104] The comparative

---

[100]Whether this interpretation is completely consistent with Comanor's results is less clear. His classification scheme emphasizes opportunities for differentiation more than opportunities opened up by changes in knowledge, although it is possible the two are associated. Also, if a strong product differentiation advantage can be gained by being first on the market with a new product, the force of imitation is blunted, and so the innovator's overall profit potential is greater than it would be with weak differentiation and easy imitation.

[101]Scherer, "Firm Size, Market Structure, Opportunity, and the Output of Patented Inventions," p. 1100, note 6. For similar results, see Nevins Baxter and Henry Grabowski, "Imitation, Uncertainty, and the Research and Development Decision," paper presented at a Conference of the Institute of Management Sciences, April 1967.

[102]Scherer, "Market Structure and the Employment of Scientists and Engineers," pp. 529–530.

[103]See Jewkes, Sawers, and Stillerman, *op. cit.*, p. 171, for a similar conclusion based upon qualitative observation.

[104]"Market Structure, Product Differentiation, and Industrial Research," pp. 652–656.

unprogressiveness of industries with low entry barriers, he speculated, might be due to fear that when entry is easy, rapid imitation would quickly erode the profits from an innovation. In industries with high entry barriers, on the other hand, insulation from the threat of new competition could dull producers' incentive to conduct research and development.

There is abundant evidence from case studies to support the view that actual and potential new entrants play a crucial role in stimulating technical progress, both as direct sources of innovation and as spurs to existing industry members. Established producers often develop physical and psychological commitments to the customary way of doing things. Because they lack such commitments, new entrants contribute a disproportionately high share of all really revolutionary new industrial products and processes. The illustrations are legion: arc lighting (Brush), the incandescent lamp (Edison), alternating current (Westinghouse), electric traction for street cars (Sprague), radio telegraphy (Marconi), radio telephony (Fessenden and de Forest), FM radio (Armstrong), the transistorized radio (Sony), the photoflash lamp (Wabash), the dial telephone (Automatic Electric), the synchronous orbit communications satellite (Hughes), the turbojet engine (Whittle in England, Heinkel and Junkers Flugzeugwerk in Germany), sound motion pictures (Western Electric and Warner Brothers), catalytic cracking of petroleum (Houdry), the electric typewriter (IBM), self-developing photography (Polaroid), and electrostatic copying (Haloid), to name only a few. In several of these cases, well-established firms flatly rejected invitations to collaborate with the inventor of a concept which later revolutionized their industry. Many other cases can be found in which the threat of entry through innovation by a newcomer stimulated existing members to pursue well-known technical possibilities more aggressively. Examples include General Electric's handling of the fluorescent lamp, A.T.&T.'s development of micro-

wave radio relay systems, the automobile industry's reaction to electric and steam propulsion development efforts by Westinghouse, Lear, and others; IBM's response to the Control Data Corporation's electronic computer innovations, and the sudden awakening of old-line aircraft makers' interest in basic research and systems engineering in 1955 when the U. S. Air Force chose the infant Ramo-Wooldridge Corporation to oversee its Atlas ICBM development program.

All-in-all, the record of invention and innovation by new entrants is a most impressive one, lending support to Maclaurin's conclusion (from a study of the radio industry before 1940) that "although some degree of monopoly is desirable, it is equally important to have new firms and rising firms searching for technical developments that may have been overlooked or not pressed by the large companies."[105] Or as Sturmey concluded from a similar study:

> . . . the major economic force leading to innovation is not any particular structural form in the industry, but the conditions regarding entry to that industry. . . .Where the entry of significant competitors appears to be impossible, innovation will be slow; when the entry of significant competitors is possible, innovation will be much faster.[106]

CONCLUSION

We emerge again with a threshold concept of the most favorable industrial climate for rapid technological change. A little bit of monopoly power, in the form of structural concentration, is conducive to invention and innovation, particularly when advances in the relevant knowledge base occur slowly. But very high concentration has a favorable effect only in rare cases, and more often it is apt to retard progress by restricting the number of independent sources of initiative and by dampening firms' incentive to gain market position through accelerated research and development. Likewise, it is vital that barriers to new entry be kept at modest levels,

[105]*Invention and Innovation in the Radio Industry*, pp. 255–256.

[106]*The Economic Development of Radio*, p. 277. See also pp. 267–268 of the same work; Jewkes, Sawers, and Stillerman, *op. cit.*, pp. 219–221; and Hamberg, "Invention in the Industrial Research Laboratory."

and that established industry members be exposed continually to the threat of entry by technically audacious newcomers. Schumpeter was right in asserting that perfect competition has no title to being established as the model of dynamic efficiency. But his less cautious disciples are wrong when they imply that powerful monopolies and tightly-knit cartels have any stronger claim to that title. What is needed for rapid technical progress is a subtle blend of competition and monopoly, with more emphasis in general on the former than the latter, and with the role of monopolistic elements diminishing when rich technological opportunities exist.

Chapter 16

The Economics of the Patent System

Few economic institutions have engendered as much controversy for such a long time as the patent system. Debate over the granting of patent monopolies on inventions has continued ever since the practice was formalized by the Republic of Venice in 1474.[1] In the United States, an interminable procession of blue-ribbon commissions and special legislative committees have been constituted, but from their labors no major substantive reforms have followed. Every attempt to change the system has been drowned in a sea of argument and special pleading. Here we shall explore the logic and paradoxes of the system, seeking to shed light where too frequently there has been only heat.

SOME BACKGROUND ON THE SYSTEM[2]

An invention patent is an exclusive right to one's invention, including the derivative right to prevent others from using it. Patents are issued in the United States under the broad authority of Article I, Section 8 of the Constitution, which gives Congress the power "to promote the progress of science and useful arts, by securing for limited times to authors and inventors the exclusive right to their respective writings and discoveries." The term of a U. S. patent grant is 17 years from the date of issue, although new legislation has been proposed to make the term run 20 years from the date at which an application for patent protection is filed.[3]

Under the applicable U. S. laws, as amended in 1952, a patent can be issued to cover "any new and useful process, machine, manufacture, or composition of matter, or any new and useful improvement thereof."[4] Before a patent can be granted, the application is examined in the Patent Office to ensure that three conditions are satisfied: the invention must be new and nonobvious; it must not have been achieved previously by someone else or known to the public for more than a year before the date of application; and the invention must have practical utility.

The test for utility has in most instances been perfunctory, requiring nothing more than the barest suggestion that some practical use might ensue. However, more stringent standards have

---

[1]For a survey of the early history of patent grants and the controversy which attended them, see Fritz Machlup, *An Economic Review of the Patent System*, Study No. 15 of the Subcommittee on Patents, Trademarks, and Copyrights, U. S. Senate, Committee on the Judiciary (Washington: 1958), pp. 1–5 and 22–44.

[2]There is an enormous literature on patent systems in the United States and abroad. The most comprehensive compact source is the series of studies commissioned by the Senate Subcommittee on Patents, Trademarks, and Copyrights during the late 1950s. Contemporary developments are followed in two journals, the *Journal of the Patent Office Society* and *Idea* (formerly the *Patent, Trademark, and Copyright Journal of Research and Education*).

[3]Senate Resolution 1042, 90th Congress, 1st session (1967).

[4]35 U. S. Code 101.

been applied to chemical inventions. For example, in 1966 the U. S. Supreme Court held that the test could not be satisfied for a chemical compound simply by showing that molecularly related compounds inhibited tumors in mice.[5]

A more critical hurdle in determining patentability is often the test for non-obviousness. The basic rule is that an invention is not patentable if "the subject matter as a whole would have been obvious at the time the invention was made to a person having ordinary skill in the art."[6] More stringent tests have been applied in certain Supreme Court decisions, i.e., that an invention must reveal "the flash of creative genius," and not merely crystallize gradually through trial and error.[7] In an apparent effort to neutralize such precedents, Congress specified in 1952 that "patentability shall not be negatived by the manner in which the invention was made."[8] Nevertheless, in 1966 the Supreme Court declared that it would continue to impose strict criteria of non-obviousness in contested cases and noted disparagingly the "notorious difference between the standards applied by the Patent Office and by the courts."[9]

The criteria implemented by the Patent Office have not in fact been very restrictive, since many gadgets and minute improvements receive patent protection. Picking up at random an issue of the weekly *Official Gazette*, one can find patents covering spring-actuated jumping shoes (No. 3,388,485), "a pillow having a central cavity to permit a person having curlers on their head to rest comfortably on the pillow" (No. 3,388,408), and even a better (?) mousetrap (No. 3,388,497), along with such impressive contributions as a gamma ray detection apparatus for determining the proportion of U-235 contained in a sample of uranium (No. 3,389,254). Approximately 60 per cent of the applications filed with the U. S. Patent Office eventually lead to the issuance of

patents, and during the 1960s the number of patents issued (excluding design and plant patents) ranged between 45,679 and 68,415 per year. Most covered inventions of only modest technological and economic significance, but in any given year there are likely to be a thousand or so inventions patented which are moderately to extremely important.

In principle, a patent can be issued only to the person making the invention, but scientists, engineers, and technicians employed by corporations normally assign all rights in their work-related inventions to their employer. Of the U. S. patents issued during 1967, 58 per cent were assigned to domestic corporations, 15 per cent to foreign corporations and governments, 3 per cent to the federal government, and 24 per cent were issued to individual inventors. As one might suppose, the role of the unaffiliated inventor has been declining both relatively and absolutely over time, while corporate patenting has been on the ascendancy. The share of all U. S. patents issued to individual inventors was 81 per cent in 1901, 72 per cent in 1921, 42 per cent in 1940, and 27 per cent in 1963.[10] Individual inventors received their largest absolute number of patents (30,332) in 1925. During the 1960s, they averaged only 14,250 patents per year.

THE PURPOSES OF THE PATENT GRANT

Governments have elected to grant exclusive patent rights on inventions for three main reasons: to promote invention, to encourage the development and commercial utilization of inventions, and to encourage inventors to disclose their inventions to the public.

Early writers on the patent system seldom defined the term 'invention' carefully, and as a result

[5]*Brenner v. Manson*, 383 U. S. 519 (1966).

[6]35 U. S. Code 103, in effect codifying the rule stated in *Hotchkiss v. Greenwood*, 11 Howard's Reports 248, 267 (1851).

[7]*Cuno Engineering Corp. v. Automatic Devices Corp.*, 314 U. S. 84, 91 (1941).

[8]35 U.S.C. 103.

[9]*Graham et al. v. John Deere Co. et al.*, 383 U. S. 1, 18 (1966).

[10]U. S. Bureau of the Census, *Historical Statistics of the United States, Colonial Times to 1957* (Washington: 1960), p. 607. More recent data were supplied by the Patent Office.

they were vague about how they really perceived the role that patents played in fostering invention. This has led to considerable confusion, for many scholars have assumed that the patent laws were enacted primarily to promote invention, construed narrowly to include only conception and perhaps crude proof-testing. Some infer therefrom that the traditional justification has lost most of its relevance to the modern industrial world, where inventive and developmental activities are often divorced from one another organizationally and where development outlays constitute more than three fourths of all industrial R & D expenditures. Critics seize upon this interpretation by insisting that the system should be abolished; defenders argue in return that the system's rationale has changed over time.

It is questionable whether such a sharp historical dichotomy is empirically tenable. In England, from which the U. S. patent precedents stem, patent rights were granted both before and after the 1624 Statute of Monopolies to protect the domestic exploitation of inventions made abroad as well as to encourage invention. One of the most famous English patents covered James Watt's separate condenser principle for steam engines. In extending that patent's life, Parliament in 1775 recognized that the central invention had already been made, and that what it was doing was encouraging further work by Watt to perfect the engine and to "render the same of the highest utility to the publick of which it is capable." Its decree implied furthermore that this was not an unusual case, calling attention to "the many difficulties which always arise in the execution of such large and complex machines . . . and the long time requisite to make the necessary trials."[11] From this and other cases, it would appear that when early patent grants were made ostensibly to encourage invention, what was meant was the complete spectrum of invention, investment, and development—that is, the whole process of innovating.

At any rate, encouraging developmental investment is clearly not an inherently inappropriate function of the patent grant. It might even carry more weight as a public policy objective than merely fostering invention. As Judge Jerome Frank observed in an *obiter dictum* on the conventional rationale:

> The controversy between the defenders and assailants of our patent system may be about a false issue—the stimulus to invention. The real issue may be the stimulus to investment. On that assumption, a statutory revision of our patent system should not be too drastic. We should not throw out the baby with the bathwater.[12]

Still to formulate the issue in this way is not to resolve it. On whether patent protection is actually necessary and desirable to stimulate investment in development, we must temporarily retain an open mind.

The third purpose of the patent system—encouraging disclosure—can be dealt with more briefly. Supposedly, the prospect of patent protection leads inventors to make public what they otherwise would keep secret. This view has numerous critics, who argue that inventors will conceal whatever they can, with or without a patent system, and that only the inventions which would be found out anyway will be patented.[13] Inventions affecting internal production processes are especially susceptible to secrecy while product inventions are not, since a product can be purchased and inspected by any would-be imitator. The assertion that patent rights make no difference at all in the choice between secrecy and disclosure is nevertheless an oversimplification. Relying on secrecy is always risky. Business espionage is common, and engineers migrate frequently from one job to another, carrying knowledge of trade secrets with them. If there were no patent system, producers would have no alternative to accepting the risk of trying to maintain secrecy. But patent protection *is* an alternative, and it can be sufficiently attractive to

[11]15 George III, c. 61 (1775), cited in F. M. Scherer, "Invention and Innovation in the Watt-Boulton Steam-Engine Venture," *Technology and Culture*, Spring 1965, pp. 184 and 187.
[12]*Picard* v. *United Aircraft Corp.*, 128 F. 2d 632, 643 (1942).
[13]Cf. Machlup, *An Economic Review of the Patent System*, p. 76; and Alfred E. Kahn, "The Role of Patents," in J. P. Miller, ed., *Competition, Cartels and Their Regulation* (Amsterdam: North-Holland, 1962), p. 317.

tip the decision toward disclosure in borderline cases. This interpretation draws support from a statistical study of corporate patenting, which showed that firms deprived of patent rights through antitrust judgments reduced their patenting relative to that of unaffected firms.[14] Thus, the patent system probably does encourage more disclosure than there otherwise would be. How great the difference is, and how it affects the rate at which new technology diffuses throughout industry, are largely unknown.

THE COSTS AND BENEFITS OF THE PATENT SYSTEM

Stimulating the invention and development of new products and processes is without doubt the most important benefit expected of the patent system. For it society pays a price: the monopoly power conferred by patent grants. In simplest terms, the overriding issue of patent policy is whether the benefits of the system outweigh the costs. Or on a more sophisticated plane, the problem is to design a system—i.e., by adjusting the length or strength of patent grants—which will yield the maximum surplus of benefits over costs. As Professor Kahn put it in his admirable survey:

> The issue is not one of principle but of practical social engineering: *how much* protection . . . of what kind is required and worth paying for the optimum rate of innovation in a capitalistic economy.[15]

Inventions and innovations bestow benefits upon society. How beneficial they are depends upon how fully they are utilized. Here one of the patent system's many paradoxes appears. Under the system inventors are given the right to control and restrict utilization of their inventions, so that outputs may be lower and prices higher than they would be if the inventions were utilized under purely competitive conditions. Normally, a patent holder can choose between alternative methods of controlling utilization. He can reserve exploitation of the invention exclusively to himself, calling upon the courts to enjoin anyone who attempts to infringe upon that right. In this way, the profit-maximizing price can be set directly. Or he can license as few or as many firms as he pleases to exploit the invention, charging royalties for the privilege. Through astute determination of the royalty rate, the patentee can in theory achieve the same price-quantity outcome and profits as he could retaining exclusive exploitation, other things (such as the costs of internal vs. licensed production) being held equal.[16] In many nations the patent holder can also solidify his control over licensees by prescribing prices at which the product can be sold, imposing output quotas, and limiting licensees to particular markets or fields of use. Such restrictions have come under increasing attack in the United States, but they have not yet been ruled illegal when enforced unilaterally by the patentee.[17]

That patent owners exercise their power to set prices exploiting whatever monopoly power their patents confer does not mean that society is denied all benefits which might otherwise come from invention and innovation. On the contrary, it gains at the very least from the resources cost-saving innovations release for alternative uses, less the research and development cost of achieving that saving. In addition, consumers other than the patentee benefit directly in two ways. First, after the patent has expired, the patent holder should in principle have no further power to restrict output, competitive pricing will prevail, and consumers will reap the full benefits

---

[14]F. M. Scherer, S. E. Herzstein, A. W. Dreyfoos *et al.*, *Patents and the Corporation* (Second ed.; Boston: 1959), pp. 137–146 and 153–155. Further support was drawn from interviews and a questionnaire survey.

[15]"The Role of Patents," p. 311.

[16]This point is stressed, and a partial proof is provided, in John S. McGee, "Patent Exploitation: Some Economic and Legal Problems," *Journal of Law and Economics*, October 1966, pp. 135–162. To complete the proof, one need note only that the area under the derived demand curve for licensed production is congruent to the area between the product market demand curve and the new supply curve, and therefore the curve marginal to each of these demand curves intersects the relevant marginal cost function at an identical output.

[17]The governing precedent is *U. S. v. General Electric Co.*, 272 U. S. 476 (1926). Two attempts to overturn the doctrine were held back by a 4-4 split among the participating Supreme Court justices. *U. S. v. Line Material Co. et al.*, 333 U. S. 287, 315 (1948); and *U. S. v. Huck Mfg. Co. et al.*, 382 U. S. 197 (1965).

of the invention. Ideally, the life of a patent should be no longer than it needs to be to encourage the optimal amount of invention, so that monopolistic restrictions are terminated as soon as possible.[18]

Second, consumers may also realize immediate gains even when innovations are exploited monopolistically. Several cases in pure theory must be distinguished:

Case 1. A new and superior consumer product is introduced. Although the proof is too elaborate to reproduce here, it can be shown that if a consumer product innovation is profitable to the innovator, it will confer upon society a net consumers' surplus even when priced monopolistically.[19] The one exception occurs when perfect, first degree price discrimination can be practiced, so that the innovator extracts from each consumer the maximum price he would be willing to pay for each unit of output.

Case 2. A new and more efficient production process is introduced by a firm already monopolizing its industry. Here the effect is to shift the monopolist's marginal cost curve downward, inducing a decrease in price if the marginal revenue curve is continuous. Consumers benefit from lower prices and higher consumers' surplus. An exception occurs if the kinked demand curve mentality prevails.

Case 3. A substantially more efficient production process is introduced under patent protection into a previously competitive industry. This is illustrated by the cost curve C_2 in Figure 16.1, where C_1 was the pre-innovation cost function and OP_1 the pre-innovation price. The firm controlling the new process will find it worthwhile to monopolize the industry, computing its marginal revenue MR and setting a price OP_2 which drives existing producers out of business. Or alternatively, it will license the invention at a per-unit royalty equal to the difference between

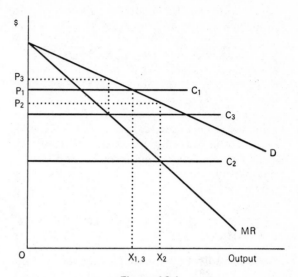

Figure 16.1
Optimal Output with Patented
Cost-Reducing Inventions

the cost of production with C_2 and price OP_2. In either case, consumers benefit from the lower price. This result is more likely, the greater the reduction in cost is, and the more elastic demand is at outputs exceeding the pre-innovation output, *ceteris paribus.*[20]

Case 4. A slightly more efficient production process is introduced under patent protection into a competitive industry. This is illustrated by cost curve C_3 in Figure 16.1. If the patent holder could monopolize the industry without restraint by virtue of its patent, it would like to set price OP_3. But it cannot do this because of competition from the pre-innovation process C_1. It must therefore either set a price slightly below OP_1 and drive others out, or license others at a per-unit royalty slightly less than the difference between C_3 and C_1. Here the reduction in price will be insignificantly small, and consumers will

[18]For a path-breaking treatment of this problem, see William D. Nordhaus, *Invention, Growth, and Welfare* (Cambridge: MIT Press, 1969), pp. 70–90.

[19]Cf. Dan Usher, "The Welfare Economics of Invention," *Economica*, August 1964, pp. 279–287.

[20]See also McGee, *op. cit.*, pp. 143–144; and Kenneth J. Arrow, "Economic Welfare and the Allocation of Resources for Invention," in the National Bureau of Economic Research conference report, *The Rate and Direction of Inventive Activity* (Princeton: Princeton University Press, 1962), pp. 619–622.

benefit little from the innovation until its patent protection has expired.

In three cases out of the four, consumers gain immediately to some extent from the introduction of a patented invention, though they enjoy the full price reduction benefits only after its patent protection has expired. Taking these gains and the net resource savings due to process inventions into account, we conclude that society gains unambiguously from inventions and innovations induced or hastened by the grant of patent rights.

ALTERNATIVE INCENTIVES TO INVENT AND INNOVATE

There is a rub, however. Patents are granted upon all *bona fide* inventions meeting the established standards of novelty and utility. But the exclusionary power provided by patents may not be necessary to induce invention and/or innovation in all cases. There are alternative inducements which can render the patent incentive redundant. If an invention would be conceived and developed without patent protection, no social benefit is correctly attributable to that particular patent grant. Still the inventor is likely to avail himself of the opportunity to secure patent protection, and so the restrictive aspects of the system take their toll. On such inventions, the social benefits of patent rights are zero but the social costs may be positive. In assessing the overall value of the patent system, we must weigh the net benefits associated with inventions which would not have been available without patent protection against the net social losses associated with patented inventions which would be introduced even if no patent rights were offered. This is a difficult and probably impossible task. Still our insight into the problem can be sharpened by trying to determine what kinds of inventions fall into each of these two categories.

If pure and perfect competition in the strictest sense prevailed continuously—e.g., if sellers were numerous, products homogeneous, re-sources highly mobile, entry easy, and knowledge perfect—incentives for invention and innovation would be fatally defective without a patent system or some equivalent substitute. Developing an invention to the point of commercial applicability is costly. The risks of development, while often exaggerated, are also appreciable. To be willing to bear these costs and risks, potential innovators must have some hope of being able to sell their product at a price which exceeds the cost of production, so that they will recoup their development costs plus a premium for risk. But if imitators can swarm in to copy the invention as soon as it has been introduced, post-innovation prices will fall rapidly to the level of production cost, wiping out supra-normal profits for innovators and imitators alike. One would have to be a fool or a philanthropist to invest heavily in invention and development when the imitative steamroller is expected to eliminate profits so quickly and relentlessly. The fundamental argument for a patent system is that patent protection permits the innovator (or inventor) to retard competitive imitation, and hence to anticipate earning supra-normal profits if its contribution in fact proves technically and commercially successful.

However, real-world markets are almost never purely and perfectly competitive. Therefore, the crucial question is, Does imitation actually eliminate innovative profits so rapidly? It may not because of three phenomena: natural imitation lags, the advantages of competitive product leadership, and the existence of non-patent barriers to the emergence of a competitive market structure.

There are several reasons why imitation naturally lags behind the profitable introduction of new products and processes, often by a substantial interval. Secrecy is one. Even when patent protection is sought in exchange for disclosure, the details of an invention may with luck be kept secret until the patent is issued — in the United States, three years on the average after an application is filed.[21] During this interim, the invention's sponsor may be able to secure a

---

[21] In many foreign jurisdictions publication is more rapid, sometimes following shortly after application and before the patent issues.

significant head start preparing its production facilities and marketing channels. According to a statistical survey, roughly 90 per cent of the sampled inventions used commercially were first put into use before the covering patent was issued and, thus, before patent disclosure hoisted a tell-tale flag to potential imitators.[22]

Second, knowledge is almost never perfect. It takes time for entrepreneurs to learn about a new and promising invention, even after its existence has been publicized, and it takes even longer for them to decide it is worth introducing. Some are quicker than others in this regard, but imitation must be widespread before the innovator's profits are wiped out, and for non-trivial inventions the diffusion process often proceeds slowly. For example, the approximate intervals elapsing between first use in the United States and the date when 60 per cent of all relevant producers had imitated for seven innovations studied by Edwin Mansfield were as follows:[23]

Packaging beer in tin cans	1 year
High speed beer bottle filler	7 years
Continuous wide strip steel mill	9 years
By-product coke oven for steel mills	18 years
Continuous annealing of tin-plated steel	20 years
Continuous coal-mining machinery	4 years
Diesel locomotives	11 years

In a statistical analysis of these and other innovations, Mansfield found that the speed of imitation was positively correlated with the profitability of the process or product and inversely related to the magnitude of the investment required. For product innovations in particular, this implies

among other things that the speed of imitation depends upon the innovator's pricing policy. Companies which price their new products to make a quick killing will encourage rapid imitation, while those pursuing a limit-pricing strategy will experience slow imitation. Which strategy is more profitable depends upon the immediate circumstances. Either may suffice to yield substantial profits.

Third, merely knowing that an attractive new product or process exists and examining the patent specifications is often an inadequate basis for imitating successfully. Know-how which can come only from carrying out one's own R & D effort, receiving generous technical assistance from the innovator, or hiring away several of the innovator's key engineers may also be required. The importance of know-how as a barrier to rapid imitation varies widely from field to field. A new garment design or a children's toy can be copied in hours, while it may take years to develop independently the know-how required to produce rayon or synthetic rubber.[24] Moreover, there is probably a positive correlation between the complexity of the original development job and the difficulty of acquiring sufficient know-how to imitate it; so those developments which involve the highest financial risks tend to be the least rapidly imitated.[25] For all these reasons, innovators often enjoy freedom from competitive imitation for a sufficiently long time to recoup their original investment manyfold even without patent protection.

Competition, product differentiation, and natural lags interact to form a second set of incentives for investment in research and innovation. Frequently a company's image is enhanced by being first on the market with a new product,

[22]Barkev Sanders, "Speedy Entry of Patented Inventions into Commercial Use," *Patent, Trademark, and Copyright Journal*, Spring 1962, pp. 87–116. For similar data on inventions made under government contracts but utilized as by-products in civilian markets, see U. S. Federal Council for Science and Technology, Committee on Government Patent Policy, *Government Patent Policy Study*, Vol. I, "Final Report" (Washington: May 1968), p. 46.

[23]Estimated from Edwin Mansfield, *Industrial Research and Technological Innovation: An Econometric Analysis* (New York: Norton, 1968), pp. 134–135.

[24]See Jesse W. Markham, *Competition in the Rayon Industry* (Cambridge: Harvard University Press, 1952), pp. 20–24 and 56–57; and Floyd L. Vaughan, *The United States Patent System* (Norman: University of Oklahoma Press, 1956), pp. 147–148.

[25]An exception might occur when protracted research is required to identify a workable solution, but once that solution is known, it becomes easy to find slightly different but equally effective inventions. Trial and error search for chemical compounds with desired new therapeutic effects, where there is no theory to guide the search toward specific molecular configurations, is a likely example.

and through this product differentiation advantage it may be able to maintain a favorable price differential or retain a sufficiently large share of the market to earn supra-normal profits for some time. The expectation of gaining such a position is a tempting carrot for investment in R & D. There is also a complementary stick. Firms which lag in the innovative race may find their differentiation advantages and market positions eroding, and to avoid this fate they invest in defensive research and development. Competition to be first or at least not to be left behind thus acquires a self-sustaining momentum which needs little or no extra boost from patent rights. That this is commonly the case in American industry is suggested by the results of a questionnaire and interview survey covering 91 large corporations holding approximately 30 per cent of all U. S. corporate patents in 1956. When asked what factors played an important role in their R & D investment decisions, only seven firms selected "patent protection to be secured" as first or second most important of five factors. A preponderant majority indicated that patent protection was least important, emphasizing instead the necessity of maintaining competitive leadership or remaining competitively viable.[26]

Here, however, we must be wary of oversimplifying what are in fact complex relationships. The patent system may affect the competitive struggle for innovative superiority in subtle but important ways. Patent rights constitute one dimension—and in certain industries such as ethical drugs a crucial one—of product differentiation.[27] If there were no patents, the advantages of being first and the disadvantages of being a poor second might be less pronounced, though not vanishingly small. It is also conceivable that the prospect of gaining patent protection serves as a primer in igniting an innovation rivalry which then becomes self-sustaining. That is, some firm decides to pioneer a new field of technology because it believes that

patent barriers to rapid imitation will make the venture profitable. Others react after a lag with countervailing programs to protect their flanks. The threat each firm's program poses to the market positions of rivals becomes in and of itself a sufficient incentive to induce continued R & D investment. Whether there are many actual cases of innovative rivalries which would not have been triggered without an initial patent stimulus, or which would have begun much later, is hard to tell. The development of television is one plausible candidate; the race to introduce new products in the pharmaceuticals industry following World War II is another.[28] But innovative rivalry can and does get under way for reasons unrelated to the expectation of patent rights in many instances, and once it does, it generates its own incentives for continuation.

Another patent-related reason why companies conduct R & D is to guard against being foreclosed from some field of technology by another concern exercising parallel patent rights. By making and patenting appropriate inventions, a firm stakes out its own independent claim in the field and obtains a bargaining counter to deal with others holding complementary inventions. However, few patents are sufficiently basic and broad to 'fence in' a field altogether. Most can be 'invented around,' and a significant amount of industrial R & D is motivated by a desire to avoid infringing or paying royalties upon other firms' patented inventions. The fact that patent rights stimulate this search, and that sometimes the search yields an unambiguously superior new product or process, is frequently cited as a major benefit of the patent system. Yet the sword cuts both ways, for the resources devoted to circumventing patents might, if inventions were made freely available, be allocated instead to alternative activities with higher incremental social payoffs. For instance, Comanor found that while a number of important pharmaceutical improvements were discovered in this way, competitive research also led to a great many prod-

---

[26]Scherer, Herzstein, Dreyfoos *et al., op. cit.,* pp. 107, 118, and 149.

[27]See William S. Comanor, "Research and Competitive Product Differentiation in the Pharmaceutical Industry in the United States," *Economica,* November 1964, pp. 372–384.

[28]See *ibid.*; and W. R. Maclaurin, "Patents and Technical Progress—A Study of Television," *Journal of Political Economy,* April 1950, p. 152.

ucts with therapeutic effects quite similar to drugs already available. He concluded that society would lose relatively little if fewer resources were devoted to highly duplicative "molecule manipulation" R & D.[29] Sturmey observed that British radio manufacturers wasted "a lot of ingenuity" during the 1920s devising circuit arrangements which reduced royalties paid to the Marconi Company, even though radio tube technology advanced in the process.[30] On the other hand, the pace of advance in petroleum cracking technology was almost certainly accelerated by the vigorous efforts of companies to invent around rival processes, and similarly impressive benefits have probably resulted from competitive research on computer memory core devices.[31] All we have to go by at present are examples and counter-examples, and so it is impossible to determine whether, on balance, the benefits of R & D motivated by the hope of circumventing patents exceed the costs of duplication.

The third major reason why firms may find investment in innovation sufficiently profitable despite the absence of patent protection is the existence of non-patent barriers to the emergence of a competitive market structure. Here we tie into the analysis of the previous chapter. For all but those innovations which define a completely new field, the most likely early imitators are companies already operating in the industry to which the innovation pertains. Lack of production facilities, managerial experience, and distribution channels impedes the entry of outsiders. When in addition the market is moderately or heavily concentrated, post-imitation pricing discipline is apt to remain fairly firm, and even

for innovations requiring heavy development outlays there may be sufficient *Lebensraum* for all industry members to imitate without preventing the leader from recovering its development investment. It follows obversely that patent protection will be most important as an inducement to progress when there are large numbers of probable imitators or when development costs are expected to be high in relation to the stream of quasi-rents the innovation could support under favorable (i.e., oligopolistic) pricing conditions.[32]

We find then that businessmen may invest in innovation without patent protection if natural imitation lags are substantial, if there are major competitive differentiation advantages to being first in the market with a new product, and/or if the relevant market is concentrated. All three characteristics are widespread in a modern industrialized economy. Any one of the three can provide a sufficient incentive if the invention is economically important—that is, if it has the potential of yielding market-wide cost savings or premium profits large in relation to the innovator's development costs. In such instances, the prospect of a relatively short lead over imitators —i.e., as little as two or three years—may be attractive enough to induce investment. To cite an extreme example, the Reynolds International Pen Co. earned back its original investment a hundredfold during the 18 months it enjoyed an almost exclusive position, before a host of firms imitated its ball-point pen.[33] It is only when the barriers to widespread and rapid imitation are weak, or when the advantages of competitive leadership are modest, or when the profit potential of the innovation is small, or when there

[29] *Op. cit.*, pp. 381–384.

[30] S. G. Sturmey, *The Economic Development of Radio* (London: Duckworth, 1958), p. 223.

[31] On petroleum cracking, see McGee, *op. cit.*, p. 151; and John L. Enos, "Invention and Innovation in the Petroleum Refining Industry," in *The Rate and Direction of Inventive Activity*, pp. 302–303. In xerographic copying and float glass production, competitive research was apparently discouraged intentionally by decisions of the dominant patent holders to license their patents on favorable terms. See G. H. Wierzynski, "The Eccentric Lords of Float Glass," *Fortune*, July 1968, p. 123; and Erwin Blackstone, "The Copying Machine Industry: A Case Study," Ph.D. dissertation, University of Michigan, 1968, pp. 98–112.

[32] Along analogous lines, Jesse Markham suggests that the patent system has its strongest incentive value when all other means of obtaining a monopoly are foreclosed by law, since then innovation will be the main open route to supra-normal profits. "The Joint Effect of Antitrust and Patent Laws Upon Innovation," *American Economic Review*, May 1966, p. 293. See also the suggestion by Kenneth Arrow that competitive firms have stronger incentives to introduce patented process inventions because, starting from a zero-profit position, they have more to gain than monopolists. "Economic Welfare and the Allocation of Resources for Invention," pp. 620–622.

[33] For a summary, see Richard G. Lipsey and Peter O. Steiner, *Economics* (New York: Harper & Row, 1966), pp. 305–307.

is some adverse combination of the three, that patent protection becomes an important incremental stimulus.

A similar conclusion emerges when one attempts to determine how long the life of a patent must be to induce the socially optimal amount of cost-saving innovation, assuming that no other incentives for innovation exist. Nordhaus has shown that the more important the innovation is—that is, the more it reduces unit costs—the shorter the optimal patent life will be. This is so for two reasons: because an R & D effort which facilitates large cost savings before running into the stage of severely diminishing returns pays for itself quickly, and because the incremental resource misallocation losses attributable to extended patent lives soon begin to outweigh the added induced cost-reduction gains.[34] Making arbitrary but plausible estimates for the parameters of his model, Nordhaus discovered that the optimal life of a patent for inventions reducing costs by roughly 10 per cent ranges between three and seven years for demand elasticities in the neighborhood of 0.7 to 4.0. Only when research yields cost savings grudgingly and in modest amounts—i.e., 1 per cent of unit costs— and when demand is of unit elasticity or less are patent lives of 15 to 20 years optimal.

This perspective on incentives for innovation has profound implications for judging the patent system's value. In most situations, to repeat, natural lags and other advantages permit sponsors to tap an innovation's full profit potential without experiencing severe competition for at least a couple of years, if not more. For the most part, it would appear, only those innovations which offer potentially exploitable benefits small in relation to development costs need the extra lure of patent protection before entrepreneurs will choose to plunge. Important contributions, on the other hand, should pay for themselves in short order. We are led then to ask, would society really lose much at the margin if, by abolishing the patent system, it sacrifices mainly innovations with low benefit/cost ratios? The answer implied by the analysis thus far is negative.

There might, however, be a hitch. It is conceivable that without a patent system some of the most spectacular technical contributions—those which effect a genuine revolution in production or consumption patterns—might be lost or (more plausibly) seriously delayed because their support lends itself poorly to rational benefit/cost calculation. Such innovations may lie off the beaten paths of industrial technology, where no firm or group of firms has a natural advantage, and the innovator may be forced to develop completely new marketing channels and production facilities to exploit them. They may entail greater technological and market uncertainties, higher development costs, and longer inception-to-commercialization lags than the vast bulk of all industrial innovation. Entrepreneurs may be willing to accept their challenge only under highly favorable circumstances—notably, when it is anticipated that if success is achieved, it can be exploited to the fullest through the exercise of exclusive patent rights.

That such cases exist is virtually certain. Black-and-white television and the development of Chester Carlson's xerographic concepts are probable examples.[35] Both would undoubtedly have come to fruition eventually, but patent protection evidently speeded up the process. The most important single gap in our knowledge of patent system economics is how many inventions and innovations fit this pattern, and how long their introduction would have been delayed if there were no patent system. It is the kind of gap which could be narrowed by spending on research sums small in relation to the cost of maintaining the patent system or the social losses incurred when an innovation as important as xerography is delayed by only a single year. The author's best guess is that such cases are rare, occurring perhaps a few times per decade. But this is no more than a stab in the dark.

[34] *Invention, Growth, and Welfare*, pp. 76–82. Nordhaus' analysis stresses only the second reason. He is concerned with the analogue of what we have called the stimulus effect in Chapter 15. However, his model is readily extended to show that relatively short patent lives are sufficient when cost savings are large compared to development costs—that is, when there is ample *Lebensraum*.

[35] Cf. Maclaurin, *loc. cit.*; and Blackstone, *op. cit.*

A closely related question is what kind of reward structure best encourages work in such unexplored, uncertain new technologies. A structure which satisfies orthodox notions of equity, proportioning gains to the investments made, is apt to be the wrong answer. Under the patent system, enormous gains out of all proportion to original investments are occasionally realized. Edwin Land of Polaroid camera fame amassed a fortune estimated at $500 million from his numerous inventive contributions; the market value of securities received by Chester Carlson for his xerography patent rights had mounted to $160 million in 1968; the five companies covered by the tetracycline patent realized collective profits of at least a half billion dollars from selling that antibiotic; and Pilkington Brothers Ltd. was expected to collect $100 million in royalties alone for the use of its float glass patents.[36] Occasional success stories like these may be exactly what best energizes technical risk-bearing, as Schumpeter observed more generally of the capitalist reward system:

> Spectacular prizes much greater than would have been necessary to call forth the particular effort are thrown to a small minority of winners, thus propelling much more efficaciously than a more equal and more "just" distribution would, the activity of that large majority of businessmen who receive in return very modest compensation or nothing or less than nothing, and yet do their utmost because they have the big prizes before their eyes and overrate their chances of doing equally well.[37]

Or as Kaysen and Turner put it, innovation is a lottery, and it is the high prizes that count.[38] Whether the largest prizes need to be as large as some of those cited here is doubtful, but too close a proportioning of gains to costs is sure to discourage investment in the most uncertain technical ventures.

Within this overall incentive framework, is the patent system of more value in stimulating invention and innovation by large firms, small firms, or by independent inventors? In general, it appears to be the small firm and the independent inventor who are affected the most. Small companies commonly lack the distribution channels and market acceptance of their larger rivals. As a result, their rate of penetration into new markets through innovation is likely to be slower and the profit they realize in the first years after innovation lower.[39] Also, their market positions are more vulnerable when large, well-entrenched rivals retaliate with imitating products. The independent inventor occupies an even less tenable position. Patent protection should in principle help offset these disadvantages, permitting the small man to compete in the innovation game on a more equal footing with the giants, who enjoy adequate (or perhaps even excessive) protection against premature imitation by virtue of their established market positions.

Nevertheless, the real-world patent system does not always operate in this ideal fashion. Size confers an advantage not only in promoting new products, but also in waging harassment campaigns. The grant of rights conferred by a patent is not a certain thing. The validity of a patent can be challenged in court, and among the scores of lawsuits fought to completion each year, roughly 60 per cent have ended in invalidation decisions.[40] As one jurist remarked, "A patent is merely a license to bring a lawsuit."[41] In such contests the odds are weighted in favor of the large firm, which has superior legal and financial resources. Therefore, small enterprises whose patents are challenged by powerful rivals

---

[36]See Arthur M. Louis, "America's Centimillionaires," *Fortune*, May 1968, pp. 152–153; and Wierzynski, *op. cit.*, p. 91.

[37]Joseph A. Schumpeter, *Capitalism, Socialism, and Democracy* (Third ed.; New York: Harper, 1950), pp. 73–74.

[38]Carl Kaysen and Donald F. Turner, *Antitrust Policy* (Cambridge: Harvard University Press, 1959), p. 163.

[39]F. M. Scherer, "Research and Development Resource Allocation Under Rivalry," *Quarterly Journal of Economics*, August 1967, pp. 385 and 388–389.

[40]See Scherer, Herzstein, Dreyfoos *et al.*, *op. cit.*, p. 84.

[41]*Guide* v. *Desperak et al.*, 144 F. Supp. 182, 186 (1956).

on either good or spurious grounds often choose to settle out of court, giving up their exclusive position and licensing the challenger to avoid the cost and uncertainty of protracted litigation. Or they may sell out altogether to the challenger. The ability of well-heeled corporations to harass smaller patent holders in this way has been curbed considerably by unsympathetic antitrust judgments, but to the extent that patent validity contests persist, apprehension about them diminishes the incentive value of the patent system for small firms and independent inventors. Still on balance, the system probably does more to stimulate invention and innovation by the small man than by the large corporation, and this is a telling argument in its favor.[42]

One final comment on the benefits of a patent system is appropriate. Our discussion thus far has implicitly been from the perspective of industrialized nations. But what role should patent grants play in underdeveloped lands? Newly emerging nations seldom sustain much of a domestic research and development effort, partly because they lack the necessary human resources and partly because there is such a large backlog of technology developed elsewhere to tap. An indication of this dependence upon external technology sources is given by statistics on the percentage of patents granted to foreigners by various lands between 1957 and 1961. For India, foreigners received 89 per cent of the patents issued; for Ireland, the figure was 96 per cent; and for Trinidad and Tobago, it was 94 per cent. This can be compared with 16 per cent for the United States, 37 per cent in West Germany, 34 per cent in Japan, and 47 per cent in the United Kingdom.[43] Since the amount of domestic inventive activity is modest in underdeveloped nations, one might expect the benefits of a patent system to be particularly small relative to the social costs of granting foreigners patent protection. Indeed, it is surprising that

such countries offer patent rights. Professor Machlup attributes their membership in the International Union for the Protection of Industrial Property to pressures from industrialized nations and to prestige motives, suggesting that newly independent nations seem irrationally eager to "have the honor of paying higher prices for imported products."[44] An alternative rationalization is that foreign firms are more willing to establish a base of operations in underdeveloped lands, importing their know-how in the process, if they can protect their position through patents. But this is not completely convincing, since markets in emerging nations are so imperfect and imitation is so sluggish that an efficient producer should usually be in a favorable position to realize normal and quite possibly even supranormal profits without the fringe benefit of patent protection.

THE SOCIAL COSTS OF THE PATENT SYSTEM

While encouraging some inventions and innovations which would not otherwise be made and hastening the introduction of others, the patent system simultaneously generates social costs. The most obvious cost is the resource misallocation loss attributable to monopolistic pricing of patented inventions which would have been available without patent protection. How much power over price a patent confers varies widely from case to case, depending upon the availability of substitutes and (more generally) the elasticity of demand. Some of the most extreme cases concern the pricing of patented pharmaceutical items, for which consumer demand is typically quite inelastic at moderate prices. From 1956 through the mid 1960s, the Pfizer Company and its four licensees sold the antibiotic tetracycline to druggists at a wholesale price of $30.60 per bottle of 100 capsules. Total sales at

[42]See also John Jewkes, David Sawers, and Richard Stillerman, *The Sources of Invention* (New York: St. Martin's Press, 1959), p. 251, for a similar conclusion.

[43]Fritz Machlup, "Patents," *International Encyclopedia of the Social Sciences,* Vol. 11 (London: Macmillan, 1968), p. 465.

[44]*Ibid.*, p. 471. See also Machlup, *An Economic Review of the Patent System*, pp. 17–19; Edith Tilton Penrose, *The Economics of the International Patent System* (Baltimore: Johns Hopkins University Press, 1951); and Raymond Vernon, *The International Patent System and Foreign Policy*, Study No. 5 of the Senate Subcommittee on Patents, Trademarks, and Copyrights (Washington: 1958).

wholesale to drugstores exceeded a billion dollars during this period. Production costs ranged between $1.60 and $3.80 per bottle, and when doubts about the validity of Pfizer's patent began to mount, several unlicensed firms began producing and selling tetracycline at approximately $2.50 per bottle wholesale. Many similar cases of price – cost margins on the order of 90 per cent for patented drug products have been identified.[45] They are, to repeat, extreme, but it is not at all rare for patent holders to charge prices substantially in excess of full production and distribution costs and to earn handsome profits as a result of their protected market position.

Furthermore, companies have managed through various legitimate and shady practices to extend and pyramid the monopoly power derived from their patents.[46] One way they do this is by 'fencing in' a field of technology. As we have seen earlier, it is usually possible to 'invent around' a single patent, and so the amount of market power conferred by any but the most basic and sweeping patents is constrained, perhaps severely, by the possibility of substitution. However, by accumulating an extensive portfolio of patents producers can solidify their monopolistic domination of a field. When du Pont scientists 'invented' nylon, for instance, they did not rest content with patenting the basic superpolymer composition and processes for producing it. They systematically investigated the whole array of molecular variations with properties potentially similar to nylon, blanketing their findings with hundreds of patent applications to prevent other firms from developing an effective substitute. Similar tactics have been pursued by du Pont and many other corporations in such fields as cellophane, plastics, synthetic leather, synthetic rubber, photo supplies, radio, television, shoe machinery, data processing equipment, electric lamps, telephone equipment,

copying processes, and can-closing machinery, to name just a few. When one company comes to dominate a field by accumulating a massive patent portfolio, it not only prevents rivals from operating except on its acquiescence, but also becomes the logical buyer for related new concepts patented by independent inventors, and so at some point the process of patent accumulation may take on a 'snowball effect.'[47]

Under present U. S. judicial interpretations, all this is perfectly legal when it is unaccompanied by sharp practices. As the Supreme Court commented in one leading case, "The mere accumulation of patents, no matter how many, is not in and of itself illegal."[48] However, firms run the risk of antitrust violation if they build up an impregnable patent portfolio by systematically buying out rival patents, especially when coercive tactics are employed to soften up the sellers. There is reason to believe that an increasingly tough stance will be adopted toward dominant positions achieved through any form of patent acquisition from outsiders.[49] Only domination attained through internal research and development is now reasonably safe from antitrust attack in America.

A dynamic ramification of the pyramiding phenomenon is the extension of one's monopoly power over time by prolonging the effective life of basic patents and by amassing improvement patents once basic patents expire. Since the grant of U. S. patent rights continues for 17 years from the date of issue, applicants have been known to delay a patent's ultimate expiration date by dragging their heels on Patent Office procedural matters while the application is pending. No doubt more important is the prolongation of control achieved through improvement patenting. Electric lighting is the classic illustration. General Electric virtually regimented the domestic incandescent lamp industry from 1892

---

[45]Cf. Henry Steele, "Monopoly and Competition in the Ethical Drugs Market," *Journal of Law and Economics*, October 1962, pp. 131–163; and "Patent Restrictions and Price Competition in the Ethical Drugs Industry," *Journal of Industrial Economics*, July 1964, pp. 198–223.

[46]For a comprehensive catalogue, see Vaughan, *op. cit.*

[47]Cf. Kaysen and Turner, *op. cit.*, p. 166; and Carl Kaysen, *United States* v. *United Shoe Machinery Corporation* (Cambridge: Harvard University Press, 1956), p. 90.

[48]*Automatic Radio Mfg. Co.* v. *Hazeltine Research, Inc.*, 339 U. S. 827, 834 (1950).

[49]See Vaughan, *op. cit.*, pp. 100–103; and Kaysen and Turner, *op. cit.*, pp. 169–171.

through the 1930s, first by acquiring the basic Edison patents; then through patents on the argon-filled lamp and tungsten filaments; and finally through patents on such features as tipless bulbs, internally frosted bulbs, and non-sag filaments.[50]

A further charge against the patent system is that it permits the suppression of inventions from which the public might otherwise benefit. Nearly everyone has heard the recurrent rumor that some shadowy power in the automobile or petroleum industry has obtained and suppressed patents on a carburetor which would let full-sized autos travel 50 miles per gallon of gasoline. Most such rumors, including the present example, prove on investigation to have little or no substance. Still some valid complaints remain. When corporations build up huge patent portfolios to bolster their market positions, they inevitably include many inventions which they do not intend to use directly, patenting them only to prevent others from using them. If decision-makers choose rationally, the inventions left unused will normally be those which are economically inferior to, or at least not superior to, those which are used.[51] Whether this should be called suppression is an empty semantic question. Despite their inferiority, such inventions might well be commercialized to good advantage if the superior invention is priced monopolistically and if the inferior inventions are at least better than the freely available technology. It is also possible that patent holders make mistakes, utilizing inventions inferior to others in their portfolios because they misjudge costs or demand. Abstracting from such situations, there are very few convincingly documented cases of the deliberate suppression of clearly superior inventions. The least ambiguous instances typically involve products which for various reasons could not be priced as profitably as available inferior variants, or inventions whose use could upset the status quo in a delicately coordinated price-fixing scheme.[52]

As noted previously, companies may spend substantial sums inventing around the patent positions of rivals. This cost is offset to an unknown extent by the benefits of superior inventions resulting from the circumventing effort. One firm's patent position may also block another producer from introducing improvements complementary to the original invention. An early example was James Watt's steam engine patent. Access to it was essential if one were to develop high-pressure engines, in which Watt saw little value. Watt's refusal to grant licenses impeded the work of Jonathan Hornblower, Richard Trevithick, and others on high-pressure engines until the patent expired in 1800, and this may in turn have had some small effect in delaying the introduction of steam locomotives and steamboats.[53] Similar blockages occur frequently in modern times—e.g., when the Pfizer Company found that it had to produce aureomycin, patented by the American Cyanamid Company, as an intermediate step in making tetracycline. Nevertheless, in more cases than not, such problems are resolved through purchase of the improvement patents or through a cross-licensing agreement under which each party permits the other to utilize its patents, usually with provisions for the payment of royalties proportionate to the parties' respective patent contributions.

Cross-licensing is a constructive means of avoiding stalemates between complementary patent portfolios. However, it also has enormous potential for abuse. Some of the most blatant price fixing schemes in American economic history were erected on a foundation of agreements

[50]See Arthur A. Bright, *The Electric Lamp Industry* (New York: Macmillan, 1949), pp. 84–104 and 235–302; and G. W. Stocking and M. W. Watkins, *Cartels in Action* (New York: Twentieth Century Fund, 1946), pp. 304–312.

[51]See Machlup, *An Economic Review of the Patent System*, pp. 12 and 41; and McGee, *op. cit.*, pp. 145–148.

[52]One of the best-documented cases is New Jersey Standard Oil's suppression of the Santopour pour-point depressant for lubricating oils. See Stocking and Watkins, *op. cit.*, pp. 497–498. For a more extensive list, see Vaughan, *op. cit.*, pp. 231–238; and for a list which errs on the side of including doubtful cases, see U. S. Senate, Committee on the Judiciary, Subcommittee on Antitrust and Monopoly, Hearings, *Economic Concentration*, Part 6 (Washington: 1967), pp. 3271–3274.

[53]See Charles Singer, E. J. Holmyard *et al.*, *A History of Technology*, Vol. IV, "The Industrial Revolution," (London: Oxford University Press, 1958), pp. 188–197.

to cross license complementary and competing patents. Industries cartelized at one time or another in this way include electric lights, glass bottles, parking meters, eyeglasses, magnesium, synthetic rubber, titanium paint pigments, radio broadcasting equipment, motion picture production, gypsum board, hardboard, machine tools, bathtubs, and a host of other electrical and chemical products.[54] Typically, such arrangements have been implemented by adding to the patent exchange agreement provisions specifying prices, market quotas, membership in the industry, and other aspects of conduct and structure. All attempts reciprocally (e.g., not unilaterally by a single patentee) to extend patent licensing agreements into the realm of price and output determination have been ruled illegal by the American courts, but restrictions of this sort continue to be legal in most other nations. Where they persist, the restrictive effects of a patent system are magnified.

A more subtle practice in the grey area of U. S. law concerns the settlement of patent ownership and validity disputes.[55] It is not unusual for two or more corporations to have conflicting claims to the priority of their employees in making an invention, or they may possess evidence that an invention did not satisfy the criteria for patentability, unknown to the responsible Patent Office examiner. They can fight out their case before the Patent Office and in the courts, but this is costly and it also risks invalidation of the patent, so that no one is able to bar entry into the field. Fearing this, they may simply agree to live and let live, permitting the most advantageously situated firm to receive the patent without opposition and then to license the potential challengers. If there

is an explicit agreement that no other producers are to be licensed, a violation of the antitrust laws exists. But it is difficult to prove this in court, and it may in any event be unnecessary for the companies involved to reach an outright agreement. Recognizing where its interests lie, the patent recipient merely elects unilaterally to license only rivals able to endanger its patent position, restricting the size of the 'club' to sufficiently few sellers that awareness of mutual interdependence makes tacitly collusive pricing likely. Thus, results similar to what would obtain under overt price-fixing are secured. Still it is possible to be tripped up playing this game of legal brinkmanship, as the makers of tetracycline discovered in an antitrust case which led to damage payments of at least $120 million.[56]

We saw earlier that the patent system permits powerful corporations to harass financially weak firms and independent inventors through protracted litigation.[57] This causes obvious inequities, and the legal costs are also not trivial. Between 1900 and 1941, 684 radio patents were involved in a total of 1,567 infringement suits.[58] Inventors like Lee de Forest and Edwin Armstrong were forced to sell out their rights in key patents because, as Armstrong later lamented, he was "in danger of being litigated to death."[59] A single lawsuit over petroleum cracking patents lasted fifteen years, piling up court costs and legal fees exceeding $3 million.[60]

An additional source of inequity arises from the priority system, under which (in the United States) the first person to invent a device or process receives full patent rights, while those who finish second in the race get nothing.[61] Invention is responsive to changes in the state of

---

[54]For a summary of the leading cases, see Vaughan, *op. cit.*, pp. 105–167.

[55]*Ibid.*, pp. 203–210.

[56]*Federal Trade Commission* v. *American Cyanamid Co., et al.*, 363 F. 2d 756 (1966), 3 CCH Trade Regulation Reporter Para. 18,077 (1967); *U. S.* v. *Charles Pfizer & Co., Inc., et al.*, 281 F. Supp. 837 (1968); and "5 Drug Makers Will Settle Price Suits for 120 Million," *New York Times*, February 7, 1969, p. 1. See also *U. S.* v. *Singer Manufacturing Co. et al.*, 374 U. S. 174 (1963).

[57]See also Vaughan, *op. cit.*, pp. 270–274.

[58]W. R. Maclaurin, *Invention and Innovation in the Radio Industry* (New York: Macmillan, 1949), p. 273.

[59]*Ibid.*, pp. 256–257.

[60]McGee, *op. cit.*, p. 153.

[61]Section 102 (g) of the Patent Code mentions three distinct and potentially conflicting criteria for deciding priority contests: "In determining priority of invention there shall be considered not only the respective dates of conception and reduction to practice of the invention, but also the reasonable diligence of one who was first to conceive and last to reduce to practice."

knowledge and demand, and since new oppor-tunities may become evident to many persons at about the same time, it is quite common for two or more inventors to arrive at the same result independently and almost simultaneously. When subsequently a priority contest materializes in the Patent Office, the odds favor the inventor backed by ample resources. An example is the dispute over priority in inventing the laser concept, in which a graduate student unfamiliar with the intricacies of patent procedure and able to work on his ideas only during his spare time lost out to Nobel Prize winner Charles H. Townes and Bell Telephone Laboratories physicist Arthur Schawlow, even though the graduate student seems to have been the first to perceive a correct solution to the problem.[62]

Finally, we must take into account the direct costs of administering a patent system. The budget of the U. S. Patent Office for fiscal year 1968 was $39 million, including salaries for 2,800 authorized employees plus sundry other ex-penses. At the same time the American Patent Bar Association had nearly 3,000 members, all but about 100 of whom worked outside the Patent Office. Assuming salary, clerical support, transportation, and office maintenance costs of roughly $60,000 per practicing patent attorney, we arrive at an estimate of total patent system administration costs of roughly $200 million per year.

THE COSTS AND BENEFITS ON BALANCE

Only in this last category are we able to hazard anything like a numerical estimate of the patent system's costs. The monopolistic restrictions facilitated by the system add costs which are no doubt much higher but unmeasurable. On the opposite side of the balance, the system allows society to realize the benefits of some inventions which would not otherwise be made or which

would become available at a later date without the patent incentive. These benefits are probably confined largely to two categories of inventions: those whose economic value is modest in relation to development costs, and those which represent unusually bold, highly risky departures from known technology. The social gain foregone due to losing an invention in the first category be-cause no patent protection is offered would by definition be slight. How the ledger would stand when all such gains are accumulated—on hun-dreds or perhaps even thousands of borderline inventions per year—is hard to say. My own best guess is that the total would still not be enor-mous. Inventions in the second category repre-sent a horse of a different color. They are few and far between, but even a very few can make a big difference in the efficiency of production or the quality of life. For instance, the introduction of xerographic copying processes permitted business enterprises and government agencies to realize savings of at least a quarter billion dollars per year at 1967 levels of utilization.[63] With-out a patent system, the American economy would probably have been forced to wait at least several years longer for xerography. Recognition that a few such cases exist, offsetting the patent system's substantial costs, is what deters govern-ments from scrapping the system altogether. As Jewkes, Sawers, and Stillerman observed:

> It is almost impossible to conceive of any existing social institution so faulty in so many ways. It survives only because there seems to be nothing better.[64]

PROPOSALS FOR REFORM

This is perhaps too complacent a stance. Even if we concur that the basic system should be preserved, we can try to improve it by making major or peripheral adjustments. Several sub-stantive proposals for reform deserve considera-tion.[65]

[62]*Gould* v. *Schawlow and Townes*, 363 F. 2d 908 (1966). See also "Who Invented the Laser?" *Business Week*, November 27, 1965, pp. 132–137.

[63]Estimated from cost and demand data in Blackstone, *op. cit.*

[64]*The Sources of Invention*, p. 253.

[65]Many other suggestions of a narrowly procedural character were made by the President's Commission on the Patent System. See its report, *"To Promote The Progress of . . . Useful Arts"* (Washington: 1966).

One possibility is to reduce the life of a patent. Obviously, any decision on the duration of the patent grant must be a compromise.[66] Some inventions will be made even if the term of protection is a year, others only if the term runs for 30 years. An ideal patent system would handtailor the life of each patent to the peculiar circumstances of the invention it covers, but this is administratively infeasible. Debate centers, therefore, on the optimal average life. For a special case Nordhaus has shown that terms longer than 15 years are optimal only for inventions yielding very modest cost savings or facing unusually inelastic demand, but his analysis ignores such elements as uncertainty, risk aversion, and alternative incentives to invent and innovate.[67] Making horseback assumptions about relevant but highly aggregated variables, Professor Machlup has concluded that the marginal benefits of the patent system fall short of the marginal costs for terms longer than 15 years.[68] Here again, however, the impact of longer protection on rare but spectacularly novel and ambitious developments is ignored. In the absence of more conclusive support for a shorter term, policy-makers have been reluctant to move away from the *status quo*.

A different way of coping with the optimal life problem is to draw a dichotomy, as the Germans do, granting full-term patents on basic inventions but only petty patents (*Gebrauchsmuster*), with a term of three years, on minor inventions and improvements.[69] This proposal has considerable appeal, especially as a means of preventing the extension of monopoly power for decades on end, as in the incandescent lamp industry. Of course, determining which inventions are basic and which merit only petty patent status requires tedious and sometimes arbitrary administrative judgments. And the system might discourage some improvement work with narrow benefit/cost margins. But it would still appear to be a desirable reform.

There are also alternative ways to prevent patents on minor inventions from clogging the arteries of technological advance. More rigorous standards might be imposed in deciding whether an invention is patentable, so that trivial contributions receive no protection. The American courts have waged a continuing campaign on this front without striking success. Increasing the Patent Office budget and the salaries of overburdened patent examiners may be a prerequisite. Second, to discourage purely defensive patenting, provision can be made for mere registration of inventions, after which the inventions are rendered unpatentable unless another inventor proves priority within a limited period of time. Such a procedure was instituted by the U. S. Patent Office in 1968.[70] Its effectiveness remains to be seen. Third, patents in force could be subjected to an annual tax or renewal fee and cancelled in the event of non-payment, so that patent holders are forced each year to reassess whether it is worth while maintaining their exclusive rights. This is done in many countries outside the United States. In Germany, the annual renewal fee is DM 50 (about $13.65) for the third and fourth years, escalating to DM 1,700 ($464) for the terminal eighteenth year. In order to retain his exclusive rights over the full 18 year term, a German patent holder must pay a cumulative total of $2,800. Under this scheme fewer than 5 per cent of all German patents remain in force for the full term, and the average life of a patent is less than eight years.[71]

---

[66]The 17 year term of United States patents was a compromise between following the British precedent of a 14 year term (originally, time to train two sets of apprentices) and permitting special exceptions to allow a 21 year term.

[67]*Invention, Growth, and Welfare.*

[68]*An Economic Review of the Patent System*, pp. 66–73; and "Patents," p. 471.

[69]See Alfred F. Crotti, "The German *Gebrauchsmuster*," *Journal of the Patent Office Society*, August 1957, pp. 566 ff.

[70]See U. S. Patent Office, *Official Gazette*, May 14, 1968, pp. 337–338.

[71]See P. J. Federico, "Renewal Fees and Other Patent Fees in Foreign Countries," Study No. 17 of the Subcommittee on Patents, Trademarks, and Copyrights, U. S. Senate (Washington: 1958); Rudolf Busse, "Procedures and Practices in the German Patent Office," *Journal of the Patent Office Society*, October 1956, p. 695; and Thomas Dernburg and Norman Gharrity, "A Statistical Analysis of Patent Renewal Data for Three Countries," *Patent, Trademark, and Copyright Journal*, Winter 1961–62, pp. 340–360.

The system is highly effective in weeding out patents with nothing but minor nuisance value. However, neither a defensive registration system nor a renewal fee system can encourage voluntary abandonment of patents which protect important inventions in use or which play a key role in fencing off some area of technology. Thus, they would not do much to reduce the amount of monopoly power based upon patents.

In many nations no patent protection is given for drug compounds, other chemical compounds, and foodstuffs to protect the public from monopolistic exploitation on the purchase of vital staples. Similar exemptions have been urged by advocates of American patent law reform.[72] This notion has an element of paradox. If the patent system is justified at all as a means of encouraging technological progress, one would think the case for patent rights should be at its strongest in fields like medicine, where the public stands to gain the most from innovation. One can logically favor both the patent system generally and medical exemptions from it only if there are peculiar extenuating circumstances—i.e., if pharmaceutical research would be almost as vigorous without patents as with them because it is concentrated in universities and government laboratories; or for underdeveloped countries which have little hope of stimulating significant domestic research but can benefit from the unimpeded importation of foreign medical technology.[73]

A more fundamental reform—the introduction of general compulsory licensing provisions—has been proposed numerous times by commissions and Congressional committees, but every attempt to alter the U. S. law in this direction has been beaten down as a result of determined opposition from industrial groups and the patent bar.[74] Compulsory licensing is an accepted feature of patent laws abroad.[75] Typically, it can be invoked when a patent recipient fails to utilize his invention in the domestic market within a specified period of time, when licensing is essential to bring a complementary invention into use, or when the patent owner abuses his patent position—i.e., by restricting supply excessively. If a potential licensee has been refused a license but can prove that one of the applicable criteria is met, the courts will compel the patent holder to issue the license, intervening further to set a "reasonable royalty" when the parties are unable to come to mutually satisfactory terms. Curiously, these sanctions are not invoked very frequently. In England, for example, 73 applications for compulsory licenses were filed between 1919 and 1939. Sixteen were pursued to the point of final decision, and only five of the petitions were granted. Germany recorded 140 compulsory licensing petitions between 1924 and 1934, of which 61 were carried to a decision, with 17 licenses being granted. The number of cases might be small because inventions worth the cost of a legal battle are too valuable to suppress, because the criteria which must be satisfied before licensing is ordered are stringent, and/or because the very existence of compulsory licensing procedures encourages patent holders and would-be licensees to settle out of court. Whatever the distribution of reasons, compulsory licensing laws clearly serve as a check on the more serious social costs of the patent system.

Still compulsory licensing cannot be a panacea, since it conflicts in some respects with the very logic of the patent grant. If the patent system works, it does so by offering inventors and innovators the prospect of supra-normal returns, and if those who do supply a better mousetrap are promptly stripped of their monopoly gains, the incentives the system is supposed to create are subverted. For inventions which have not been

---

[72] See G. W. Stocking and M. W. Watkins, *Monopoly and Free Enterprise* (New York: Twentieth Century Fund, 1951), p. 488; and Steele, "Patent Restrictions and Price Competition in the Ethical Drugs Industry," pp. 222–223.

[73] Cf. "India's Drug Bill Fought in Italy," *New York Times*, August 9, 1966.

[74] Cf. Catherine S. Corry, *Compulsory Licensing of Patents—A Legislative History*, Study No. 12 of the Senate Subcommittee on Patents, Trademarks, and Copyrights (Washington: 1958).

[75] See Fredrik Neumeyer, *Compulsory Licensing of Patents Under Some Non-American Systems*, Study No. 19 of the Senate Subcommittee on Patents, Trademarks, and Copyrights (Washington: 1959); P. J. Federico, "Compulsory Licensing in Other Countries," *Law and Contemporary Problems*, Spring 1948, pp. 295–309; and Richard Reik, "Compulsory Licensing of Patents," *American Economic Review*, December 1946, pp. 813–832.

suppressed, successful implementation of a compulsory licensing statute hinges on how the responsible authorities determine when supply has been restricted unreasonably. That the patent holder charges monopolistic prices can hardly be an adequate criterion, since the opportunity to do so is what the patent system offers as a carrot. For best results, intervention must be limited to cases in which the patent grant has been abused—i.e., when rival patents are bought out, or when agreements are made with rival patent holders to suppress competition—and perhaps also to those few cases in which the patentee's gains have soared far beyond the level of a merely liberal reward. In cases of the last type there are distinct hazards, for as we have seen, occasional spectacular rewards may have a potent general incentive effect. Analogous dilemmas attend the judicial determination of royalties when licensing is ordered. It is possible on one hand to set royalty rates which yield the patent holder essentially the same return as it would earn exploiting its invention exclusively. On the other hand, judges and economists often display a bias toward cost-oriented royalty standards which permit the patentee to earn little more than a normal return on its development investment, with at best a modest premium for risk-bearing.[76] Widespread application of such rules could have a stultifying impact on incentives for technological pioneering.

We must be equally careful not to overemphasize the dangers of compulsory licensing. Although the American Congress has not seen fit to enact general compulsory licensing laws, compulsory licensing has been specified as a remedy in more than 100 antitrust cases, making available some 40,000 to 50,000 patents at "reasonable" royalties or (in a few instances) royalty-free.[77] In this respect the United States

has outdistanced its European neighbors, whose antitrust bodies have for the most part been chary about intervening in patent matters. By zealously prosecuting predatory practices and attempts to extend monopoly power beyond the limited bounds of specific patent grants, the U. S. antitrust authorities have managed to limit appreciably the social costs of the patent system. This has been achieved without doing serious damage on the benefits side of the equation, for most of the corporations subjected to compulsory licensing orders had alternative incentives to innovate by virtue of natural lags, competitive differentiation, and established market positions. To them the prospect of profits gained by abusing the patent grant apparently had little incremental incentive value, for the effect of compulsory licensing on their R & D efforts appears to have been minute. However, there is reason to believe that firms subjected to tough patent licensing orders have begun to patent fewer of their inventions, resorting to secrecy more often.[78]

It is conceivable that further extensions of antitrust law could have more significant adverse effects. Specifically, it has been proposed that the acquisition of patents from unaffiliated firms be declared illegal when it tends to create a monopoly position.[79] If applied judiciously, such a move might do little harm while providing a wedge into abuses beyond the reach of prior legal precedents. But if corporations gaining market power through the noncoercive purchase of patents from small firms were systematically stripped of those patent rights, the demand of corporations for outside inventions would be sharply curtailed. This in turn could have an unfavorable impact on the risk-bearing incentives of individuals and small firms with resources

---

[76]See Scherer, Herzstein, Dreyfoos *et al., op. cit.,* pp. 91–96. A cost-plus approach was advocated by Carl Kaysen in his proposal for licensing United Shoe Machinery's patents. *United States* v. *United Shoe Machinery Corporation,* p. 284. Kaysen's proposal may have been warranted under the particular circumstances, but it is a poor general precedent for economists to set.

[77]U. S. Senate, Committee on the Judiciary, Subcommittee on Patents, Trademarks, and Copyrights, Staff Report, *Compulsory Patent Licensing Under Antitrust Judgments* (Washington: 1960).

[78]Scherer, Herzstein, Dreyfoos *et al., op. cit.,* pp. 123–128, 137–146, 153–155, and 158–160.

[79]See "Stiff Trust Curb Due for Patents," *New York Times,* November 5, 1966, summarizing a speech by Donald F. Turner, then head of the Justice Department's Antitrust Division, proposing the application of Clayton Act Section 7 to patent acquisitions. For an indication that Turner recognized the dangers of such a policy, see Kaysen and Turner, *op. cit.,* pp. 175–176.

too limited to develop ambitious ideas all the way to the point of commercialization.

Finally, if one despairs of reforming the patent system through halfway measures, there remains the possibility of doing away with it altogether. This is not an alternative favored by the author, but that should scarcely bar considering it seriously. We have no reason to fear that such a step would bring all inventive and innovative activity to a halt, since there are many alternative incentives. Still some contributions would undoubtedly be lost, unless substitute incentives were created. There are two main alternatives.

First, the government might assume an increasingly active role in sponsoring and subsidizing innovation where private initiative proves inadequate. As Chapter 15 brought out, the federal government already supplies funds to support more than half of all U. S. research and development activity. Most of this support is directed toward meeting unique governmental needs, as in the defense and space fields, but roughly 20 per cent of federal expenditures go for work in such civilian areas as agriculture, food products, mining techniques, atomic power, water desalination, civil aviation, and the full spectrum of medical and medicinal technologies. Extension of the government's role would therefore not be a radical departure. Still it has certain drawbacks. A centralized R & D resource allocation process could hardly avoid overlooking promising new opportunities, backing the wrong horse, neglecting unknown young men at the peak of their creative powers, and in general bogging down in red tape. A steady diet of research at the government trough can also dull incentives for efficiency, encouraging those who are subsidized to substitute money for ingenuity. Therefore, while government sponsorship will continue to be a valuable supplement, it holds little promise as a complete alternative to incentive systems which rely as much as possible on private initiative.

The other possibility is to institute a system of governmental awards or bonuses for individuals and firms making significant technological contributions. Such a system was proposed by James Madison at the Constitutional Convention of 1787 as an explicit alternative to the patent system.[80] Something like it was written into the U. S. Atomic Energy Act of 1946, establishing a Patent Compensation Board to confer monetary awards upon individuals making inventions related to military uses of atomic energy, which under the law could not be patented. The award approach is also a standard method of motivating invention by individuals in the Soviet Union, where inventors can apply for "certificates of authorship," and when a certificated invention has been introduced into industrial practice, the inventor is entitled to a share of the cost savings during one of the first three years of use.[81] The award is prescribed by formula, with the inventor's share falling to 2 per cent of marginal savings in the highest savings bracket. Normally a ceiling of 20,000 rubles (equivalent in 1968 purchasing power to roughly $18,000) for any given year is imposed, although an exception may be granted for especially important inventions. Awards of 10,000 rubles are not uncommon.[82]

Despite their evident attractions, award systems of this genre suffer from three main drawbacks. First, estimating the value of inventive contributions is a difficult task, and any bureaucratic council entrusted with the job is bound to make mistakes and perpetrate inequities. When inequity is inevitable, one might prefer that it be the result of an impersonal income distribution mechanism. Second, as the approach has been traditionally interpreted, it pertains only to inventions in the narrow sense. If no provision were made to reward innovative contributions, and if in addition alternative incentive structures were deficient, there might be some danger, to

---

[80]Cf. Machlup, *An Economic Review of the Patent System*, pp. 15–16.

[81]See "Soviet Law on Inventions and Patents," *Journal of the Patent Office Society*, January 1961, pp. 5–96; Francis Hughes, "Soviet Invention Awards," *Economic Journal*, June-September 1945, pp. 291–297; and *idem*, "Incentive for Soviet Initiative," *Economic Journal*, September 1946, pp. 415–425.

[82]See S. Stepanov, "Increasing the Role of Innovators and Inventors in Improving Socialist Production," *Problems of Economics*, August 1958, pp. 75–78.

reiterate Judge Frank's caveat, of throwing out the baby with the bathwater. It is worth noting that a chronic complaint of Soviet inventors is that their inventions all too frequently are not accepted or put into practice by unsympathetic managers.

Third, there is an inherent conservative bias in the prizes granted by administrative and quasi-judicial bodies. Munificence is a rare committee virtue For example, the Atomic Energy Commission's Patent Compensation Board awarded the assignee of Enrico Fermi's basic patent on the production of radioactive isotopes —forerunner of the methods for producing plutonium—a sum of $300,000 when the patent was dedicated to the public. In an analogous case, the federal government agreed to pay $1 million as compensation for utilizing Robert H.

Goddard's basic liquid rocket engine patents. During the life of the Goddard patents, U. S. expenditures on liquid-propelled rockets amounted to roughly $10 billion. Compared to the value of the inventions and the profits which might have been earned if exclusive patent rights could have been enforced, the Fermi and Goddard awards were miserly. They were certainly not what Schumpeter had in mind in describing "spectacular prizes . . . thrown to a small minority of winners." It is doubtful whether a generalized reward system administered in this conservative tradition would motivate as much risk-bearing as the patent system presently does. Still the crucial policy question is how serious the loss of inventions and innovations due to lessened risk-bearing would be. And that, unfortunately, is a subject on which our ignorance is profound.

Chapter 17

Market Structure and Performance: Overall Appraisal

It is time now to stand back and assess what we have learned about the dependence of industrial performance on market structure and conduct. This is best accomplished by addressing the question introduced at the end of Chapter 2: Is competition workable? Or more concretely, how serious are the performance deficiencies resulting from monopolistic structure and conduct in the United States?

No sublime analytic vision is required to discern that industrial performance, viewed broadly and generally, is not at all bad. Professor Galbraith has likened the American economy to the bumblebee.[1] According to aerodynamic theory (as interpreted by Galbraith), the bumblebee cannot fly. Yet it does. Similarly, even though the American economy is shot through with monopolistic and oligopolistic elements which might lead one to predict the direst consequences, performance is in fact rather good.

This exhausts our complacency quota. While performance is good, it is far from perfect. How large are the social losses associated with monopolistic structure and conduct? What keeps performance from departing further than it does from the norm of workability? What can be done to make it still better? These are the questions to which we shall devote the balance of our attention. We must consider several dimensions of performance in our appraisal: allocative effi-

ciency, efficiency of resource use, equity of income distribution, progressiveness, and macroeconomic stability.

THE WELFARE LOSSES DUE TO RESOURCE MISALLOCATION

One adverse consequence of monopoly, the theory of welfare economics instructs, is the misallocation of resources. By raising price above marginal cost, monopolists restrict output, divert resources to less pressing demands, and reduce consumer welfare.

There is considerable evidence to support the assertion that prices are held above cost when monopoly power exists. Statistical studies by Bain, Weiss, Comanor, Wilson, and others reveal that profit returns on stockholder investment in manufacturing industries tend, except during wartime and the boom stages of postwar recovery, to be about half again as high when market concentration and/or expenditures on advertising are high than when they are not.[2] Higher profits in turn imply higher prices and restricted outputs.

By extending the theory developed in Chapter 2 it is possible to obtain a foothold for estimating the social losses caused by monopolistic resource misallocation. Figure 17.1 provides the necessary frame of reference. Suppose the long-run mar-

---

[1] J. K. Galbraith, *American Capitalism* (Boston: Houghton Mifflin, 1952), p. 1.
[2] Cf. pp. 184–186 and 343–344 *supra*.

ginal (and average) cost function is the horizontal line *LRC*, so that the equilibrium price under pure competition would be OP_C and the output OX_C. If the industry were monopolized but without blockaded entry, price would be raised, say, to OP_M, and output would be restricted to OX_M. We recall that at any point on a demand function, the price ordinate reflects in money terms the worth attached to having one more unit of the product purchased by that consumer who is just on the margin between buying and not buying.[3] To the last such customer satisfied by the monopolist, the product is worth OP_M dollars. If, however, the competitive price OP_C prevailed, the consumer would realize a *consumer's surplus* of *AB* dollars in buying that X_Mth unit of output, for he would be willing to pay as much as OP_M dollars but is required to pay only OP_C dollars. Consumers' surplus is gained on all infra-marginal units of output, that is, on every unit sold except the final unit taken by the

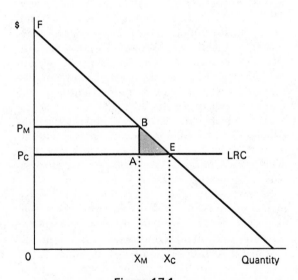

Figure 17.1
The Welfare Loss Attributable to Monopolistic Resource Misallocation

consumer just on the margin between buying and not buying. Total consumers' surplus is therefore measured by the area bounded by the demand curve, a horizontal line reflecting the ruling price, and the vertical axis.

Under competition, the cost of resources used to produce output OX_C—reflecting their opportunity cost, or value in alternative uses—is given by the rectangle $OX_C EP_C$. The total consumers' surplus realized is given by the triangle $P_C EF$. Equilibrium under monopoly differs in several respects. Resources whose cost is given by the rectangle $X_M X_C EA$ are permitted to find employment in alternative uses, yielding (if pricing in the alternative use sectors is competitive) a value commensurate with their cost. At the higher monopoly price and lower output, the total consumers' surplus is only $P_M BF$, falling short of the consumers' surplus under competition by the trapezoidal area $P_C EBP_M$. This is not all dead-weight loss, however. The monopolist receives profits, or a producer's surplus, equal to the rectangular area $P_C ABP_M$. If we assume that the gain to the monopoly's stockholders associated with this producer's surplus is equivalent to the loss in consumers' surplus traced out by the same rectangle, which is tantamount to assuming that those stockholders and consumers in general have the same marginal utility of income, the *dead-weight welfare loss* attributable to monopoly pricing is defined by the shaded triangular area *AEB*.[4] That is, part of the surplus which would have been realized by consumers under competitive pricing in effect vanishes into thin air, being captured by neither consumers nor monopolistic producers. The area of the dead-weight loss triangle is an indicator of society's welfare loss due to monopolistic resource misallocation.

A bit of algebra will help put these geometric results in more useful form. Let ΔP denote the dollar amount by which the monopoly price deviates from the competitive price P and ΔQ the amount (in units of output) by which the

[3]Cf. pp. 15–16 *supra*.

[4]The pioneering article in this vein is Harold Hotelling, "The General Welfare in Relation to Problems of Taxation and of Railway and Utility Rates," *Econometrica*, July 1938, pp. 242–269. Obviously, if the demand function is not linear, the area will not be strictly triangular, but a triangle provides a good approximation in most cases.

monopoly output differs from the competitive output. Since the area of a triangle equals one-half its base times its height, we define the dead-weight welfare loss W by:

$$(1) \qquad W = \tfrac{1}{2} \Delta P \Delta Q.$$

The *relative price distortion* under monopoly, or the ratio by which the monopoly price deviates from the competitive price, is defined as $t = \dfrac{\Delta P}{P}$. Ignoring signs and assuming ΔP and ΔQ to be small, we define the elasticity of demand to be approximately:

$$(2) \qquad \eta = \frac{\dfrac{\Delta Q}{Q}}{\dfrac{\Delta P}{P}} = \frac{\dfrac{\Delta Q}{Q}}{t},$$

which can be rearranged to:

$$(3) \qquad \Delta Q = \eta\, t\, Q.$$

Substituting $P\,t = \Delta P$ and (3) into (1), we obtain:

$$(4) \qquad W = \tfrac{1}{2}\, P\, Q\, \eta\, t^2.$$

Thus, the dead-weight welfare loss due to monopoly rises as a quadratic function of the relative price distortion t and as a linear function of the demand elasticity η.

For fifteen years after these relationships were first worked out theoretically, not much was done with them. Then in 1953 Arnold Harberger attempted, making a number of simplifying assumptions, to estimate in dollar terms the actual dead-weight loss due to monopolistic resource misallocation in American industry.[5] His wedge into the problem was a study of profit returns on capital in 73 manufacturing industries, originating 45 per cent of all manufacturing output, for the more or less normal years 1924–1928. Assuming that equating price with long-run cost

implied earning a profit return neither more nor less than the full sample's average return, he took observed individual industry deviations from the sample profit mean as an estimate of the relative monopoly price distortion t. Using available industry sales (PQ) data, and accepting the further assumption that demand was of unit elasticity in every instance, he possessed all the variables contained in equation (4), plugging them in to arrive at an estimated dead-weight welfare loss of $26.5 million for the industries sampled. Expanding this estimate to cover the whole of manufacturing industry raised the estimated welfare loss to $59 million—about 0.06 per cent of gross national product at the time. Further adjustments to compensate for inadequacies in his data led to a final judgment that eliminating monopolistic resource misallocation during the 1924–1928 period would have increased consumer welfare by slightly less than 0.1 per cent of GNP. At 1968 levels of output, this implies a dead-weight loss of about $800 million per year, or roughly four dollars per capita—enough to treat every family in the land to a steak dinner at a good (monopolistically competitive) restaurant.

Similar results were obtained with quite different data and techniques in a study by David Schwartzman.[6] He based his estimate of monopoly price distortions on a comparison of price/cost ratios for concentrated Canadian industries against unconcentrated U. S. industries, using data for 1954. Assuming the average elasticity of demand to be 2.0 or less, he concluded that the welfare loss did not exceed 0.06 per cent of gross national product.

Several assumptions underlying these estimates are questionable.[7] As we have seen, the estimates depend linearly upon the assumed elasticity of demand. One reason why the price-cost margins observed in monopolistic industries are seldom exorbitant is that long-run price elasticities are often much higher than 1.0 or 2.0 because of substitution between loosely related

[5]Arnold C. Harberger, "Monopoly and Resource Allocation," *American Economic Review*, May 1954, pp. 77–87.

[6]David Schwartzman, "The Burden of Monopoly," *Journal of Political Economy*, December 1960, pp. 627–630; drawing upon an earlier article, "The Effect of Monopoly on Price," *Journal of Political Economy*, August 1959, pp. 352–362.

[7]For a similar critique, see Dean A. Worcester, Jr., *Monopoly, Big Business, and Welfare in the Postwar United States* (Seattle: University of Washington Press, 1967), pp. 210–227.

commodities, i.e., steel, aluminum, and plastics.[8] To the extent that this is so, the welfare losses estimated by Harberger and Schwartzman are biased on the low side.

Second, both studies were limited to the manufacturing sector. This introduces two biases. For one, the average return on capital tends to be lower in agriculture and most divisions of retailing and the service trades than in manufacturing, so that using the average return in manufacturing alone as a surrogate for 'normal' profits leads to an understatement of monopoly price distortions in manufacturing. Correcting for this problem would not increase the welfare loss estimates by much more than 30 or 40 per cent, however. More important, both the Harberger and Schwartzman studies cover only monopolistic misallocations within manufacturing, even though both authors ultimately relate their estimates to overall national income. Monopolistic distortions also exist in other sectors, though they are more difficult to isolate and measure because the data are scarce and because profit figures do not necessarily reflect the magnitude of price–marginal cost deviations in monopolistically competitive markets. The manufacturing sector originated about a fourth of total GNP in the period studied by Harberger and slightly less than a third in 1954. Assuming that the relative incidence of monopolistic distortions is as great outside manufacturing as within it, we must inflate the estimates for manufacturing alone by three or four times to arrive at an economy-wide welfare loss estimate.

The profit data available to Harberger and Schwartzman were typically for quite broadly-defined industries. Excessive aggregation biases dead-weight loss estimates downward by submerging the high monopoly returns of narrow industry lines within broad industry averages. Also, some monopoly gains may have been capitalized as costs rather than profits when, for example, assets changed hands in a merger transaction. And as we shall see in a moment,

there is reason to believe that some of what might have been monopoly profit was actually exploited as cost, so that the departure between price and true marginal social cost was greater than available profit data imply. On the other hand, not all the profit deviations observed in the Harberger study were necessarily the result of monopoly; some may have reflected transient influences or special risks. Harberger made crude adjustments in his estimates to compensate for all but the third of these problems, but it is doubtful whether he eliminated what was undoubtedly a net downward bias.

A more complicated problem overlooked by both authors concerns the transmission of monopoly distortions through vertical price flows.[9] To illustrate, suppose there are two industries, A and B, each with sales of $1 billion per year and constant long-run marginal costs (including a normal return on capital) of $900 million. With $t = 100/900 = 0.11$ in each, and assuming unit demand elasticity, we obtain by applying equation (4) a combined welfare loss estimate of $12 million. However, suppose industry A supplies some of its output as a raw material to industry B—e.g., that half of industry B's $900 million costs are for purchases from A. Then the long-run marginal social cost of B's output is not $900 million, but $450 million + .9 ($450 million) = $855 million. With B's relative price distortion raised to $145/855 = 0.17$, our estimate of the total dead-weight loss increases to $17.9 million ($3.4 million on final goods sales by A plus $14.5 million on sales by B).

Since every dollar's worth of final output sales by business enterprises is supported by an additional dollar of intermediate transactions on the average, one might suppose on *a priori* grounds that the Harberger and Schwartzman loss estimates should at least be doubled to take this bias into account. However, this is probably not a correct approximation. Michael Klass has estimated directly the impact of vertical pricing distortions on allocative efficiency by computing

[8]Cf. pp. 213–216 *supra*; George Stigler, "The Statistics of Monopoly and Merger," *Journal of Political Economy*, February 1956, pp. 33–35; and (for a study which probably assumes excessively high elasticities) David R. Kamerschen, "An Estimation of the 'Welfare Losses' from Monopoly in the American Economy," *Western Economic Journal*, Summer 1966, pp. 221–237.
[9]Cf. pp. 24–25 *supra*.

price distortion ratios for both intermediate and final goods industries and then flowing those distortions through an input-output matrix of the U. S. economy for 1958.[10] It turns out that some major industries with exceptionally low and perhaps even sub-normal profit returns, such as coal mining, transmitted a disproportionate share of their output ultimately to final goods industries like automobile manufacturing with unusually high returns, mitigating to some extent misallocations at the later stages. When price distortion estimation techniques similar to Harberger's are employed, taking vertical distortion effects into account actually *reduces* the final estimate of total welfare losses attributable to monopoly, given the 1958 structure of the economy. When a more sophisticated distortion measurement technique is used, the impact of vertical distortions is to raise welfare loss estimates by roughly 40 per cent compared to the figure obtained with a model which assumes that all outputs satisfy final consumer demands.

Labor is also an intermediate input, and its pricing poses analogous difficulties. As Chapter 12 brought out, there are grounds for believing that except when labor markets are very tight, wage increases and (less confidently) wage levels tend to be higher in the more concentrated industries. If wages rise in monopolistic industries without compensating productivity gains, and if therefore the marginal cost curves confronting producers in those industries are shifted upward, there will be further resource misallocations in both the labor and product markets undetected by the Harberger and Schwartzman techniques. This compels a further upward adjustment, but the size of the effect, if indeed it exists, is too conjectural to permit any informed guess on how large the adjustment should be.

One further complication lurks in the shadows. Any attempt to measure the dead-weight loss due to monopolistic misallocation by estimating the size of the triangle *AEB* in Figure 17.1 rests ultimately upon an assumption that resources are worth no more (and no less) in alternative uses than their marginal cost in the industry scrutinized. This implies a partial equilibrium context in which, among other things, second-best considerations are irrelevant.[11] But in a world of monopolies, the theory of second best *is* relevant, even if non-operational, and so in the strictest sense we operate with a measuring rod (or triangle) of distressingly elastic rubber. In principle we cannot even tell the direction of the measurement error due to neglecting second-best, but it seems more likely to be on the side of exaggerating the welfare losses attributable to monopoly.

Faced with this disconcerting fact, we have two options. We can give up trying to measure the allocative impact of monopoly, or we can cross our fingers and hope the errors from ignoring second-best are not too serious. Leaning toward the second alternative more on faith than on logical grounds, we conclude that the estimates by Harberger and Schwartzman are biased downward. Applying the multiplicative correction factors suggested in our critique of their results, it appears that the dead-weight welfare loss attributable to monopoly in the United States lies somewhere between 0.5 and 2 per cent of gross national product, with estimates nearer the lower bound inspiring more confidence than those on the high side.[12]

OTHER INEFFICIENCIES

Thus far we may have glimpsed only the tip of the iceberg. It is hard to think of realistic circumstances under which the dead-weight loss triangle *AEB* would not be small, for it involves the square

---

[10] "Inter-Industry Relations and the Impact of Monopoly," Ph.D. dissertation, University of Wisconsin, Madison, 1970.

[11] For a rigorous and forceful statement of the dangers of ignoring second-best, see Edward Foster and Hugo Sonnenschein, "Price Distortion and Economic Welfare," forthcoming in *Econometrica*.

[12] A best-guess estimate is derived as follows. Raise Harberger's basic estimate of .06 per cent to .1 to take into account excessive aggregation and the use of too high a 'normal' profit return. Inflate this by a multiplier of 3 to cover the entire economy, by a multiplier of 2.5 to reflect more realistic demand elasticities, and by a multiplier of 1.4 to take into account vertical distortions. The resulting estimate is 1.05 per cent of GNP.

of the relative price distortion ratio t, whose average value was only 0.036 in the Harberger sample and which, common observation reveals, seldom exceeds 0.20 in real-world industries over the long run. More serious consequences follow if monopoly affects costs as well as prices. Then the welfare loss has as its major dimension the whole output of the monopolized industry, not just the change in output associated with an excessive price. Inefficiencies might proliferate to fill or perhaps even overflow the trapezoidal area $P_C EBP_M$ in Figure 17.1, instead of its triangular right-hand extremity. There are several reasons why such losses, which Professor Leibenstein has dubbed "X-inefficiency" to distinguish them from misallocation losses, may accompany the possession and exercise of monopoly power.[13]

In all likelihood the most important, but also the most difficult to verify, management may eat into part or all of its potential monopoly profits—i.e., its 'organizational slack'—by tolerating inefficiency and sheer waste. That is, it operates completely off the production function surface to which profit-maximizing enterprises adhere. Production and office staffs may become bloated and obsolete equipment may be retained in use long beyond the proper time for modernization. The British economy provides a striking case in point. Thoroughly cartelized for several decades, its industries grew increasingly sluggish, failing to adopt new technologies and tolerating low manpower productivity, all of which ultimately had a great deal to do with Britain's economic woes of the 1950s and 1960s.[14] As the chairman of Imperial Chemical Industries, Ltd., Britain's second-largest private industrial firm, explained the almost disastrously high-cost position of his company before a strenuous rebuilding campaign was launched in 1960:

> We had been in existence thirty-four years and had been having a comfortable time. We were doing well without too much exertion and had been favored by a good deal of scientific discovery. Then we ran into competition and had to learn to deal with it.[15]

The most closely comparable U. S. example is the steel industry, whose well-regimented members have with few exceptions compiled a record of notoriously deficient cost reduction and control.[16] Even worse are the aerospace industry, which over-staffed its government-sponsored programs to the tune of at least several billion dollars annually during the late 1950s;[17] and the backward, ailing railroad industry. These two, however, operate within such a jungle of government controls and misdirected incentives that they cannot properly be considered representative of private enterprise. Without casting his net far, Williamson found two clear illustrations of more conventional enterprises incurring substantial discretionary costs which could be cut under the pressure of adversity with no impact on production.[18] Leibenstein presents a number of other impressive examples.[19] How typical it is for firms insulated from competition to operate with copious layers of fat can only be guessed. My own belief is that padding as high as 10 per cent of costs is not at all uncommon.

Promotional outlays represent a second pos-

---

[13] Harvey Leibenstein, "Allocative Efficiency vs. 'X-Efficiency,' " *American Economic Review*, June 1966, pp. 392–415. See also William S. Comanor and Harvey Leibenstein, "Allocative Efficiency, X-Efficiency, and the Measurement of Welfare Losses," *Economica*, August 1969, pp. 304–309.

[14] Cf. Richard Caves *et al.*, *Britain's Economic Prospects* (Washington: Brookings, 1968), especially pp. 12–13, 279–323, and 491–493.

[15] Murray J. Gart, "The British Company That Found a Way Out," *Fortune*, August 1966, pp. 104–105.

[16] Cf. p. 77 *supra*.

[17] Estimated by the author on the basis of 12 case studies and the analysis in M. J. Peck and F. M. Scherer, *The Weapons Acquisition Process: An Economic Analysis* (Boston: Harvard Business School Division of Research, 1962); and F. M. Scherer, *The Weapons Acquisition Process: Economic Incentives* (Boston: Harvard Business School Division of Research, 1964).

[18] Oliver E. Williamson, "Managerial Discretion and Business Behavior," *American Economic Review*, December 1963, pp. 1051–1053.

[19] "Allocative Efficiency vs. 'X-Efficiency,' " *loc. cit.*

sible source of waste, although here we must tread warily for reasons elaborated in Chapter 14. It does not seem too extreme to propose that roughly a fourth of the $16 billion spent on advertising in the United States during 1966, or about 0.5 per cent of GNP, went into messages which served little function but to mislead the consumer or cancel out rival messages. To this sum must be added the amounts spent on disfunctionally elaborate packaging, personal sales calls unsolicited and unwanted by buyers, administering premium give-away programs and sweepstakes, and accelerated styling changes which do nothing more than render last year's model obsolete. The sum of these items is unknown and, because tastes differ, unknowable. In the author's opinion, the total annual expenditure on wasteful promotion could not be less than 1 per cent of gross national product.

Another effect of product differentiation might be operation by firms at scales too small to realize all production and distribution scale economies. Bain's analysis of 20 relatively concentrated manufacturing industries revealed that about 20 per cent of output was produced in plants sufficiently below the optimal scale to elevate unit costs by at least several percentage points.[20] In a more extensive survey using the less reliable survivor technique, Weiss found the average fraction of sub-optimal capacity to be nearer 35 per cent.[21] Although these studies were limited to manufacturing, observation suggests that operation at scales smaller than the minimum-cost size is widespread in such sectors as retailing, mining, construction, banking, and agriculture. If we take Bain's estimate of 20 per cent high-cost production as typical of the economy at large and interpret "at least several percentage points" to mean that unit costs average 5 percentage points higher than at optimal scale, we find the loss due to operation at suboptimal scale to be 1 per cent of gross national product.

Of course, not all of this cost can properly be blamed on monopoly power; some of it reflects natural frictions impeding the withdrawal of obsolete capacity. But the high-cost operations covered by Bain's study appeared for the most part to be persistent, surviving because of locational advantages or specialization in some uniquely differentiated product. Whether the excessive costs attributable to either spatial or physical differentiation can be viewed as a true social loss is debatable. When firms producing specialized product varieties or offering the convenience of spatial proximity remain viable despite relatively high costs and prices, they must be satisfying *bona fide* consumer demands. And as Professor Chamberlin has repeatedly urged, the benefits of such differentiation may compensate or even outweigh the costs.

Nevertheless, differentiation is not the only dimension of market power responsible for inefficiently small-scale operations. From his comparative study of market structures in eight nations, Bain estimated that less than half of all manufacturing employees worked in plants of "reasonably efficient scale" in Sweden, France, Japan, Italy, and Canada.[22] In at least some of these countries, he speculated, such widespread survival of inefficient plants was due to cartelization "performing its historically typical function of controlling or dividing markets in such a way as to create havens for inefficiently small or technologically lagging plants."[23] There is also reason to suspect that restraints on competition encourage the survival of inefficient operations in the United States. Retail trades whose prices and margins are set at generous levels by manufacturers, either through informal suasion or under the aegis of resale price maintenance laws, offer the best illustration. Large numbers of inefficiently small drug stores, liquor outlets, and gasoline stations survive primarily for this reason. It does not seem outrageous to suppose that a fourth of the 1963 sales in these three lines were made by outlets whose costs were 10 per

[20]Joe S. Bain, *Barriers to New Competition* (Cambridge: Harvard University Press, 1956), pp. 184–187; and *Industrial Organization* (New York: Wiley, 1959), pp. 352–354.

[21]Leonard W. Weiss, "The Survival Technique and the Extent of Suboptimal Capacity," *Journal of Political Economy*, June 1964, pp. 257–260; with a correction, *Journal of Political Economy*, June 1965, pp. 300–301.

[22]Joe S. Bain, *International Differences in Industrial Structure* (New Haven: Yale University Press, 1966), p. 65.

[23]*Ibid.*, pp. 146–147.

cent higher than the optimum. Given these assumptions, the estimated cost of inefficiently small-scale operation comes to $775 million, or 0.13 per cent of gross national product. And surely these are not the only trades in which inefficient capacity has been preserved under an umbrella of vertically or horizontally fixed prices.

Further social costs arise when basing point pricing systems and similar methods of handling the spatial differentiation problem collusively encourage cross-hauling and nonoptimal industrial location decisions. Counting only a dozen major industries (such as cement, steel, glass bottles, aluminum, and tin cans) whose pricing systems foster wasteful cross-hauling, and assuming conservatively from the data presented in Chapter 10 that cross-hauling costs amount to 2 per cent of sales,[24] we estimate the costs of cross-hauling to have been roughly $650 million in 1963, or about 0.1 per cent of GNP. The additional losses due to nonoptimal location choices under basing point pricing cannot readily be estimated. They have undoubtedly declined since formal basing point pricing systems were declared illegal, but in such industries as fluid milk production (where geographic pricing relations have been distorted collusively with express government approval) they continue to be substantial.[25]

The cost of chronic excess capacity must also be counted. Its existence can be traced to many factors besides monopoly—i.e., to planning errors and unexpected shifts in demand. Yet there are at least two types of situations in which market power is culpable. First, formal or tacit collusion may protract the survival of capacity in industries (such as coal mining and steam locomotive manufacturing) faced with secularly declining demand. Second, and probably more important, collusive agreements which succeed in

holding price above cost encourage investment in excess capacity if participants' sales depend in any way upon the amount of capacity they possess. This has been a serious problem in Europe, where antitrust sanctions against cartelization were nonexistent until recently, and where cartels often operated by assigning members output quotas proportional to capacity. The most prominent domestic case is the system of *prorationing* under which crude petroleum extraction quotas are assigned to individual wells by state production control agencies (i.e., the Texas Railroad Commission). This stimulates wasteful well-drilling in developed fields and permits inefficient producers to survive while limiting the output of efficient producers. The economic waste caused directly by prorationing was at least $2 billion, or a third of 1 per cent of GNP, in 1962.[26] Despite marked differences in the methods of price-fixing, the cement industry exhibited the same affinity toward excessive investment under the basing point system. Between 1909 and 1946, the fraction of practical production capacity utilized averaged 68 per cent, and in only three years out of 38 did the level of capacity utilization climb above 90 per cent.[27] Races among oligopolistic producers to gain a capacity advantage in the face of expanding demand can have comparable consequences, as we saw in Chapter 13, but we have no good evidence on how widespread or serious this tendency is. Taking into account all these links between monopolistic pricing and the accumulation of excess capacity, it is apparent that fairly significant social losses are involved.

Finally, serious inefficiencies are caused by inadequacies of the regulatory process to which firms with unavoidable monopoly power are subjected when they operate in the so-called public utility fields, such as transportation,

[24]Cf. p. 270 *supra*.

[25]Cf. Reuben A. Kessel, "Economic Effects of Federal Regulation of Milk Prices," *Journal of Law and Economics*, October 1967, pp. 51–78; and Floyd Lasley, *Geographic Structure of Milk Prices, 1964–65* (Washington: U. S. Department of Agriculture Economic Research Service, 1965).

[26]See M. A. Adelman, "Efficiency of Resource Use in Crude Petroleum," *Southern Economic Journal*, October 1964, pp. 101–122. For lower but less comprehensive estimates, see James W. McKie and S. L. McDonald, "Petroleum Conservation in Theory and Practice," *Quarterly Journal of Economics*, February 1962, pp. 98–121; and Alfred B. Kahn, "The Depletion Allowance in the Context of Cartelization," *American Economic Review*, June 1964, p. 310.

[27]Samuel M. Loescher, *Imperfect Collusion in the Cement Industry* (Cambridge: Harvard University Press, 1959), pp. 168–169.

communications, and electric power generation. These will be considered at length in Chapter 22.

Largely because of limitations in the author's knowledge, this cannot pretend to be an all-inclusive tabulation of the social losses attributable to the existence and exercise of monopoly power. Still for whatever it may be worth, let us summarize by attempting to assign explicit numbers to the various loss accounts. This is an inherently 'iffy' and subjective task, so it must be received with the appropriate grain of salt. For each category, there follows a conservative best-guess estimate, expressed as a percentage of 1966 gross national product, of the efficiency losses attributable to collusion, the exercise of market power, and related breakdowns of competitive pricing processes:

	Percentage of GNP, Circa 1966
Dead-weight welfare losses due to monopolistic resource misallocation: unregulated sectors	0.9
Dead-weight losses due to pricing distortions in the regulated sectors[28]	0.6
Inefficiencies due to deficient cost control by market sector enterprises insulated from competition	2.0
Inefficiencies due to deficient cost control by defense and space contractors[29]	0.6
Wasteful promotional efforts	1.0
Operation at less than optimal scale for reasons other than differentiation serving special demands	0.3
Cross-hauling costs and transportation costs associated with distorted locational decisions	0.2
Excess and inefficient capacity due to industrial cartelization and the stimulus of collusive profits[30]	0.6
TOTAL LOSSES DUE TO MARKET POWER	6.2

While each of the individual estimates is subject to a wide margin of error, it seems improbable that the 'true' combined social cost of monopoly,

if it could be ascertained, would prove to be less than half or more than twice the estimated total of 6.2 per cent. Wherever the true figure lies within this range of uncertainty, the static inefficiency burden of monopoly does not appear to be overwhelming. But it is also not so slight that it can be ignored.

Why are the inefficiency costs of market power as moderate as this compilation suggests? From our analysis in foregoing chapters, several explanations emerge. First, a large fraction of the American economy—perhaps as much as a half—consists of industries whose structures, although seldom atomistically competitive, include sufficiently many relatively small firms to permit a vigorous, workable species of competition as long as outright collusion is neither tolerated nor encouraged by the government. Second, many of the industries with oligopolistic structures possess little or no collective power to hold prices substantially above costs for extended periods because barriers to new entry are modest. By the same token, pricing performance is least satisfactory in those concentrated industries sealed off by very high scale economy, product differentiation, or patent barriers to entry. Third, high long-run price elasticities of demand reflecting the threat of product substitution discourage maximum exploitation of short-run monopoly power, even when new entry with a perfect substitute is blockaded. This constraint is becoming increasingly important as industry develops more sophistication in harnessing science to create new and superior synthetic materials. Uncertainty enhances the effect as professional managers strive to protect their firms' market positions against feared but indistinct future threats by avoiding pricing strategies which encourage substitution through innovation. Fourth, the exercise of power by large buyers may countervail the pricing power of sellers, preventing the pyramiding of price distortions through a chain of vertical transac-

---

[28]Cf. Chapter 22 infra.

[29]Given the reciprocally self-defeating character of arms races, one might argue that most of the 3 per cent of GNP devoted to military hardware in 1966 was wasteful. Here we assume a valid demand and consider only the efficiency of producers in serving that demand.

[30]This estimate excludes the substantial excess capacity, inefficient size, and surplus management costs due to price and acreage controls in agriculture, which have a broader (though questionable) social rationale.

tions even when the savings from monopsony are not fully transmitted to consumers. Finally, public policy has played a role. Except in a few 'special case' industries, the United States has since the late 1930s maintained a vigorous anti-trust program, striking down restrictive agreements, punishing abuses of monopoly power, preventing the consolidation of power, and raising legal and financial obstacles in the path of countless monopolistic arrangements.

OTHER EFFECTS OF MARKET POWER

To round out our assessment, we must consider the impact of monopoly power on other dimensions of performance.

One is income distribution. Monopoly profits represent a redistribution of income from the consuming public at large to the stockholders of particular corporations. Through his comparison of Canadian and U. S. price/cost ratios, Schwartzman estimated that monopoly profits in manufacturing amounted to $3.6 billion, or exactly 1 per cent of gross national product, in 1954. This estimate is probably biased downward because of excessive aggregation and the capitalization of monopoly profit earning potential in corporate accounts. And since it includes only the manufacturing sector, it must be doubled or possibly even tripled to reflect economy-wide monopoly gains. Thus, monopoly profits effect an income redistribution on the order of 3 per cent of GNP.

Traditionally economists refrain from imposing their own value judgments on the equity of such redistributions. Still some implications can be pointed out. Many fortunes have been made through monopoly positions, although monopoly in the orthodox sense is by no means the sole path to immense riches. On *Fortune*'s list of the 13 richest Americans in 1968 were four men who rose to the top through oil wildcatting, where shrewdness and luck are as important as government-sponsored output restraints.[31] The others were three members of the Mellon family, which

has maintained long-standing interests in the Aluminum Company of America, Gulf Oil (an early challenger to the Standard Oil trust), and Pittsburgh's dominant bank; Howard Hughes, whose fortune was based on patented oil-well drilling equipment and extended in defense contracting, motion pictures, and the regulated airline industry; Edwin Land of Polaroid Camera fame; the former president and dominant spirit of Minnesota Mining & Manufacturing, with strong patent positions in Scotch tape and other heavily differentiated products; an early stockholder and executive of General Motors; a shipping and shipbuilding tycoon; and an insurance executive.

Typically, those who did gain their fortunes at least in part through market power have for the most part long since diversified their portfolios and no longer dominate the corporations from which they profited. Subsequent stockholders often earn little or no supra-normal profit on their investments, for the expectation of monopoly gains may have been capitalized into the price they paid for their shares. Even so, those who receive most of the profits from corporations with monopolistic market positions occupy a higher stratum in the income distribution than the average American. It is estimated that the wealthiest 1 per cent of all American families control 75 per cent of all privately-held corporate securities.[32] Thus, monopoly profits realized by industrial corporations transfer income from the average consumer to the relatively rich. If one accepts the debatable premise that the marginal utility of income is lower to a rich man than to a poor man, it follows that social welfare is reduced by such transfers.

There is some evidence that the compensation of corporate executives is more generous in companies whose home base is a highly concentrated industry—another transfer of income through monopoly to the relatively affluent.[33] Also, the wage income of rank and file employees is probably higher in concentrated than in un-

---

[31]"The Richest of the Rich," *Fortune*, May 1968, p. 156.

[32]See Robert J. Lampman, "Taxation and the Size Distribution of Income," in U. S. House of Representatives, Committee on Ways and Means, *Tax Revision Compendium*, Vol. 3 (Washington: 1959), p. 2237.

[33]Cf. Williamson, *op. cit.*, pp. 1040–1047; and pp. 35–36 *supra*.

concentrated industries. Redistributions of the latter kind have generally drawn little criticism on equity grounds, although they may have occurred to some extent in conjunction with discrimination against minority group members, which would make the equity implications more disturbing.[34]

Turning to the effects of market structure on the rate of technological progress, it is difficult to make sweeping generalizations. We confine ourselves to four summary observations. First, concentration is much higher and leading firm sizes are much larger in many markets than they need be to support the most vigorous rate of progress. Second, in some atomistic industries concentration is too low and representative firm sizes are too small for ambitious research and innovation efforts to thrive. Whether the technological needs of these industries are adequately served by materials and equipment suppliers operating under structural conditions more conducive to innovation is not certain. Third, some of the most strikingly profitable monopoly positions are the result, not the cause, of successful innovation attended by strong patent protection. The rewards realized in these instances serve an indirect incentive function. However, much corporate inventive and innovative effort does not require a patent stimulus, and abuses and extensions over time of patent positions appear to be unambiguously disfunctional. Fourth, our knowledge is too limited to predict confidently whether the rate of technical progress could be accelerated significantly by structural reforms— i.e., by forcing the deconcentration of highly concentrated industries and permitting a movement toward concentration of atomistic industries. The author's best guess is that such measures, taking the present structure of American industry as a point of departure, would make very little difference.

A similar conclusion applies regarding the effects of market structure on macroeconomic stability. Capital investment may be somewhat more volatile in concentrated than in uncon-

centrated industries, but business expectations are probably affected favorably by the price stability flowing from market power. Given the fiscal and monetary tools we now possess to combat business fluctuations, the consequences of these and other industrial organization variables appear to be of only a second or third order of relative importance.

On the goal of preventing inflation, a less sanguine verdict is required. The principal culprit in inflation is indisputably fiscal and monetary imbalance. Yet two features of concentrated industries—the tendency for their prices to be more flexible upward than downward, and their vulnerability to wage increase demands rationalized on grounds of ability to pay—probably contribute modestly to creeping inflation when aggregate unemployment nears the 4 per cent level. This can create a dilemma for economic policy-makers, forcing them to choose between lower, more acceptable unemployment rates on one hand and price level stability on the other. Admittedly, our knowledge is still too imperfect to be certain that market power definitely affects the inflationary process in this way. If, however, a judgment must be rendered on the basis of the available evidence, it will have to be an unfavorable one.

Finally, there are implications of monopoly power which we must dismiss summarily because they lie outside the conventional domain of economics or because we have failed to find anything perceptive to say about them in the preceding chapters. For instance, one may condemn the possession of market power because it allows economic decisions to be made personally rather than impersonally. Or big business may be faulted because it contributes to the alienation which pervades modern society. Or the sensitivity of oligopolists to the adverse effects of output expansion in their home markets may drive them to search not only for domestic diversification opportunities, but also for investment outlets abroad. However harmless this modern brand of imperialism may seem to Amer-

---

[34]Cf. William G. Shepherd, "Market Power and Racial Discrimination in White-Collar Employment," *Antitrust Bulletin*, Spring 1969, pp. 141–161.

icans, it is a source of great concern in other lands.[35] It may also have subtle and ominous links to the exercise of U. S. military power abroad.[36] On these and other neglected dimensions of industrial performance the reader must make his own evaluations.

CONCLUSION

We return to our original question: Is competition workable? The simpleminded reply must be: If it is results that count, the performance of American industry is surprisingly good, though far from perfect. Nevertheless, this is not a very constructive answer. A more operational approach is to apply Professor Markham's test of workability: Competition is workable when there is no clearly indicated change that can be effected through public policy measures which would result in greater social gains than social losses.[37] From this two further conclusions follow. First, as noted earlier, the standard of performance achieved by U. S. industry is at least in part a result of the public policy measures already adopted to encourage competition. And second, things are not so good that they cannot be improved by new measures and the more intelligent application of existing policies.

Our assignment in the remaining chapters will be to explore the principal policy alternatives, determining where they have succeeded and where their chief weaknesses lie. The ultimate goal is to find a set of policy measures which best channels the energy of industry to serve the public interest. To this task we now turn.

[35]See J. J. Servan-Schreiber, *The American Challenge* (translated from the French by Ronald Steel; New York: Atheneum, 1968).

[36]For two interpretations, see K. W. Rothschild, "Price Theory and Oligopoly," *Economic Journal*, September 1947, pp. 318–319; and Paul A. Baran and Paul M. Sweezy, *Monopoly Capital* (New York: Monthly Review Press, 1966), pp. 178–217.

[37]Jesse W. Markham, "An Alternative Approach to the Concept of Workable Competition," *American Economic Review*, June 1950, pp. 349–361.

Chapter 18

Policy Approaches to the Monopoly Problem

That government should intervene in market processes which go astray is now almost universally accepted. Debate centers not on whether there should be departures from strict *laissez faire*, but on when the government should step in, how vigorous its involvement should be, and what specific policy instruments or mix of instruments it should employ. In this chapter we survey some of the principal policy alternatives. They include taxation, price controls, moral suasion and the glare of publicity, formal public regulation, public ownership, and antitrust policy. Then, in Chapters 19 through 22, we shall explore more intensively antitrust policy and public regulation, the main arrows in the American counter-monopoly quiver.

TAXATION POLICY

The powers of the government to tax and subsidize might be employed to combat monopoly and its effects, although as a practical matter, taxation is generally too blunt an instrument to rely on heavily.

Monopolists restrict output unduly because marginal revenue to them is less than price. One way to remedy this condition is to pay the monopolist a per-unit subsidy equal to the difference between marginal revenue and price at the output which would prevail under pure competition. This subsidy will be just sufficient to

induce an expansion of production to the competitive level. Of course, the adverse income distribution effects associated with monopoly are compounded. In principle, a lump-sum tax equal to the subsidy could be imposed to take back with the left hand what has been given with the right. However, it is extraordinarily difficult to levy lump-sum taxes with the desired neutral effect on output, and it would also be hard to obtain the data needed to set the proper per-unit subsidy rate. Therefore, we must concur in Mrs. Robinson's judgment that this approach is only "an ingenious though unpractical scheme."[1]

A corporation profits tax acts to channel monopoly profits away from relatively wealthy shareholders into lower strata of the income distribution. As a device for combating the effects of monopoly, however, it has two main limitations. First, empirical research suggests that firms with market power are more likely than competitive producers to pass on all or part of a profits tax to consumers by raising prices.[2] If true, the incidence of a profits tax falls relatively more heavily upon competitive than monopolistic firms—the opposite of what is desired. Second, even if this were not true, the corporate profits tax as presently administered in the United States has no special potency with respect to monopoly profits. A firm earning 30 per cent before taxes on its invested capital pays the

[1] Joan Robinson, *The Economics of Imperfect Competition* (London: Macmillan, 1933), pp. 163–164.
[2] See R. J. Gordon, "The Incidence of the Corporation Income Tax in U. S. Manufacturing, 1925–62," *American Economic Review*, September 1967, especially pp. 751–753.

same percentage tax rate as a company earning only 10 per cent, at least after the first $25,000 of income, and therefore ends up about as well off relative to the less profitable firm after taxes as it was before.

When the capture of monopoly profits is a primary goal, it is necessary to implement some kind of excess profits tax which applies especially high marginal rates to income exceeding a normal return on invested capital. Such an approach was pursued in the United States during World Wars I and II and the Korean war, though more as a means of curbing wartime profiteering in general than as an anti-monopoly measure. As the wartime experiences showed, formidable accounting problems arise in administering an excess profits tax, and it is impossible to avoid inequities, whether loopholes are opened up liberally (as has been the case historically) or through a strict, no exceptions policy.[3] Business decisions may also be distorted. For instance, if the tax is applied to profit returns in relation to common stockholders' equity, it can discourage the use of low-cost bonds. More important, it can induce enterprises with market power to make excessively capital-intensive investment choices in a manner analogous to certain effects of public regulation which we will examine fully in Chapter 22. Because of these drawbacks, there has been little enthusiasm in the U. S. for maintaining excess profits taxation during peacetime.

During the 1960s an increasingly popular method of financing mergers was for the acquiring firm to issue new interest-bearing debt in exchange for the common stock of companies it acquired. Although this increased the riskiness of the merged corporation's capital structure, it had significant tax advantages, since income paid out to investors in the form of interest was tax-deductible to the corporation, whereas earnings on common stock were not. Abolishing the tax deduction privilege for interest on convertible debentures issued expressly to consummate a merger, as was enacted by Congress in 1969, will undoubtedly discourage speculative and marginally profitable mergers, particularly those undertaken largely to satisfy an empire-building urge.

The structure of tariffs might also be manipulated to deal with monopoly—i.e., by denying tariff protection to monopolistic industries, thereby intensifying the threat of import competition as a constraint on their pricing freedom. President Grover Cleveland recommended in 1887 that Congress deal with the emerging trust problem in this fashion, and an unsuccessful amendment to the Sherman Antitrust Act of 1890 would have stripped violators of their tariff protection. The Canadian antitrust laws do incorporate such a penalty, honored more in disuse than implementation. The main drawback is that if pricing performance fails to improve after tariff barriers are lowered, imports will rise without any assurance of compensating export growth. For nations acutely concerned, as most are, with their balance of payments position, this may seem too high a risk to run for the sake of promoting competitive domestic pricing.

PRICE CONTROLS

A second general policy option is to enforce price controls, placing binding ceilings on the prices producers can charge. This approach has been used on a broad scale by the U. S. government during wartime. Its extension to peacetime conditions has been advocated by some economists to counter the alleged inflationary propensities of the administered price industries.[4]

Under the orthodox assumptions of monopoly profit maximization, an astute program of price controls can bring about salutary results. To see this, consider Figure 18.1. We assume a monopolist in long-run equilibrium before price controls, charging the price OP_M and operating a plant described by the short-run average total cost curve $SRATC$ best-suited to producing

---

[3]Cf. George Lent, "Excess Profits Taxation in the United States," *Journal of Political Economy*, December 1951, pp. 481–497.

[4]See the statements of Abba Lerner and Gardiner Means in U. S. Senate, Committee on the Judiciary, Subcommittee on Antitrust and Monopoly, *Administered Prices: A Compendium on Public Policy* (Washington: 1963), pp. 208–212 and 232–239.

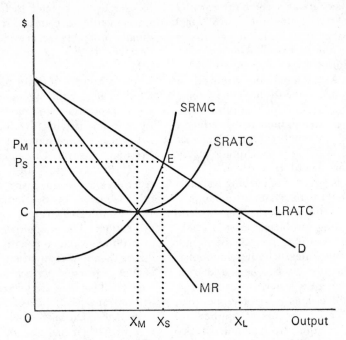

Figure 18.1
Influencing Monopoly Output Through Price Controls

output OX_M. Now the government steps in to impose a ceiling price lower than the monopolist's preferred price. This in effect renders that portion of the demand curve above the ceiling price, along with its corresponding marginal revenue segment, inaccessible. The monopolist's new marginal revenue function is a horizontal line at the level of the ceiling price, at least to the left of the ceiling price line's intersection with the demand function. It follows that by setting the ceiling price OP_S, the government can induce the monopolist to expand its output all the way to OX_S, where price equals short-run marginal cost. Thus, governmental price controls can lead simultaneously to lower prices and increased output—the best of both worlds!

There are, however, some practical hitches. Starting from the assumed cost conditions, a ceiling price of OP_S still permits the firm to earn supra-normal profits. This is sure to upset gov-

ernment price fixers and the legislators who review their accomplishments, so there will be pressure to lower the ceiling. Also, the price controllers never have sufficient knowledge to locate precisely the point E, where the short-run marginal cost function intersects the demand function. In their ignorance, they will be inclined to set a price commensurate with observed unit costs, which again implies undercutting OP_S. Suppose they set the price OC equal to minimum unit costs. Then the firm's optimal response will be to produce the output OX_M— the same as under unconstrained monopoly pricing. At price OC, however, the quantity demanded is OX_L. There will be a shortage of X_MX_L units which can be resolved only by drawing down inventories (at best a temporary expedient), arbitrary customer quota allocations, rationing by queue, the appearance of a black market, or some form of quantity rationing by the government. At ceiling prices intermediate between OP_S and OC there will also be shortages, but they will be smaller than at price OC.[5]

In the long run, the monopolist can probably be persuaded to expand its production capacity along the long-run cost function $LRATC$ if the price ceiling is held slightly above OC, and so eventually the shortage problem will disappear. Its place may be taken, however, by another problem. Given their limited knowledge of cost and demand conditions, government price controllers have little practical alternative but to set a price which covers the observed unit costs of the monopolistic producer or, if the industry has more than one seller producing identical items, of those suppliers who account for the bulk of output. Some sort of cost-plus pricing rule will probably be adopted. This can have debilitating effects on cost control incentives, for if producers recognize that any industry-wide cost increase will compel an upward ceiling price revision, they may strive less vigorously to hold the line against wage concessions exceeding productivity gains, to introduce new and more efficient processes, etc.

Theoretical reasoning suggests, then, that price controls *may* have a favorable impact on the performance of monopolistic industries, but that inevitable mistakes by the price controllers can lead to shortages and disequilibrium in the short run and operating inefficiencies in the long run. Is this consistent with the evidence?

U. S. experience with price controls has been confined almost exclusively to wartime periods, when the intent was to suppress generalized inflation resulting from deficit financing, and not to improve the performance of monopolistic industries. Still some pertinent lessons were learned.

Perhaps most important, price controls tended to be much more successful in oligopolistic and monopolistically competitive industries than in more purely competitive fields. This was no doubt due in part to the fact that price controls can induce producers with market power to increase output, as the theory predicts. The possibility of output expansion was particularly germaine during World War II, which most monopolistic firms entered with abundant reserve capacity. Other contributing factors have been identified by Professor Galbraith, a veteran World War II price controller.[6] It was much easier administratively to deal with oligopolistic industries, whose chief executives could be assembled conveniently around a small conference table. Product differentiation facilitated the allocation of scarce supplies expediently, though not always equitably, as sellers gave preference in shortage situations to buyers with whom they had traditional ties, rationing their output among those buyers on the basis of historical purchasing patterns. And letting prices be unresponsive to short-run changes in demand was a familiar *modus operandi* for oligopolistic producers. Under these circumstances World War II price controls in monopolistic industries were fairly successful, surpassing the expectations of most economists responsible for their administration.

On the other hand, the Office of Price Administration experienced its "most dismal failures" in the more competitive markets, where direct administrative control was impossibly cumbersome and producers responded to distorted price signals in unexpected ways.[7] For example, the price ceilings initially set for clothing permitted higher profit margins to be earned on high-priced items, and so resources surged into expensive clothing lines while shortages of work clothes appeared. To correct this imbalance, the OPA increased the prices of low-end items, but this merely diverted more demand toward high-priced items. Similarly,

---

[5]When the position of the demand curve shifts randomly over time, shortages will arise even when the price is set at OP_S, since an incentive to produce for inventory is eliminated. See Edwin S. Mills, *Price, Output, and Inventory Policy* (New York: Wiley, 1962), pp. 98–99.

[6]J. K. Galbraith, "Reflections on Price Control," *Quarterly Journal of Economics*, August 1946, pp. 475–489; and "The Disequilibrium System," *American Economic Review*, June 1947, pp. 287–302.

[7]Cf. Galbraith, "The Disequilibrium System," p. 300; Seymour E. Harris, *Price and Related Controls in the United States* (New York: McGraw-Hill, 1945); and Harvey C. Mansfield, *A Short History of OPA* (Washington: Office of Price Administration, 1947).

miscalculations in setting meat and grain prices channelled excessive resources toward producing meat, considerable portions of which flowed into black markets, and this eventually forced the government to supplement its food price control program with an elaborate quantity rationing scheme.

In short, as Galbraith concluded, one of the unsuspected virtues of monopoly and oligopoly turned out to be their special vulnerability to wartime price control.[8] Hopefully, this benefit can be rendered unimportant by avoiding new wars. Still, one might extrapolate from the success of price controls in monopolistic industries during wartime similarly favorable prospects for peacetime regulation.

A less sanguine prognosis is implied by the peacetime experience of other countries. Extensive price and output controls were continued in Great Britain through 1950 to cope with postwar readjustments and balance of payments problems. They worked much less well than wartime controls, partly because the objectives of a peacetime economy were more complex than merely achieving victory, and also because producers and consumers were less willing to sacrifice personal interests to make the system work.[9] In his analysis of the French postwar experience, Sheahan concluded that price controls may have improved allocative efficiency and dampened inflationary pressures in the noncompetitive industries, but they distorted resource allocation and lessened efficiency in competitive markets.[10] A less favorable consequence in the concentrated French industries was the tendency for ceiling prices to serve as focal points for tacit collusion —a phenomenon observed also when the British government set ceiling prices for steel producers. There is evidence too that price controls worked disappointingly in India, permitting monopolistic firms to establish prices which a government commission considered "exorbitant."[11] In all three countries, it should be noted, administering a price control system is easier than in the United States because the industrial structures are less complex and because there is a well-accepted business-government 'Establishment.'

Thus, governmental ceiling price-setting is evidently not a certain, foolproof means of improving monopolistic industries' performance. An even dimmer view was taken on general price controls, without distinction as to market power, in the 1968 annual report of the U. S. Council of Economic Advisers:

> While [mandatory controls on prices and wages] may be necessary under conditions of an all-out war, it would be folly to consider them as a solution to the inflationary pressures that accompany high employment under any other circumstance. They distort resource allocation; they require reliance either on necessarily clumsy and arbitrary rules or the inevitably imperfect decisions of Government officials; they offer countless temptations to evasion or violation; they require a vast administrative apparatus. . . . Although such controls may be unfortunately popular when they are not in effect, the appeal quickly disappears once people live under them.[12]

All things considered, the case for price controls seems to be sufficiently tenuous that one is inclined to search for a better alternative, holding the control option in reserve as a last resort.

MORAL SUASION

An approach chosen by the U. S. government to fight inflation during the 1960s was to issue informal, nonbinding guideposts concerning the price and wage behavior of firms and labor unions with market power. As the guideposts

[8]"Reflections on Price Control," p. 480.

[9]D. H. Aldcroft, "The Effectiveness of Direct Controls in the British Economy, 1946–1950," *Scottish Journal of Political Economy*, June 1963, pp. 226–242.

[10]John Sheahan, "Problems and Possibilities of Industrial Price Control: Postwar French Experience," *American Economic Review*, June 1961, pp. 345–359.

[11]See Carl H. Fulda and Irene Till, "An Antitrust Policy for India," *Antitrust Bulletin*, Summer 1968, pp. 379–380 and 389, quoting findings of the Indian Monopolies Inquiry Commission.

[12]*Economic Report of the President* (Washington: February 1968), p. 119.

were articulated in 1962, price reductions were called for when an industry's productivity growth rate exceeded the economy-wide trend rate— later estimated at 3.2 per cent per annum— while price increases could be tolerated in industries whose productivity growth rate fell short of the overall average. Exceptions to take into account special capital needs, the existence of excess capacity, the behavior of material input prices, and excessive monopoly returns were spelled out in broad terms. For wage settlements, a target growth rate equal to the economy-wide productivity growth rate was stated, with deviations from the target being permitted if they reflected unusual labor market conditions. Adherence to the guideposts was encouraged through publicity, conferences between government and business leaders, gentle and sometimes trenchant persuasion by the President and his cabinet, and (in the steel price furor of 1962) thinly-veiled threats of antitrust action.

Opinions on the success of the guideposts vary widely. Statistical analyses predicting industrial prices and wages for the mid 1960s on the basis of economic relationships prevailing during the 1950s suggest that the guideposts did help suppress latent inflationary pressures, particularly during 1964 and 1965.[13] Their influence was especially noticeable in tightly concentrated and strongly unionized industries such as aluminum, steel, copper, and automobiles, which presented compact, highly visible targets for governmental suasion. After 1966, efforts to secure adherence collapsed as a result of pressures generated by inflationary financing of the Vietnam war, and in 1969 the Nixon administration showed little enthusiasm over resurrecting a guidepost policy. The principal lesson that emerges from the experience of World War II and the mid-1960s

is that if suasion from Washington works at all, it has more impact when aimed at concentrated industries than it does in atomistically structured markets.[14]

An even more formally organized suasion approach to concentrated industry pricing was proposed in bills introduced before the U. S. Congress in 1959. One would have required firms with assets exceeding $10 million and among the eight leaders in an industry with an eight-firm concentration ratio of 50 or higher to notify the Federal Trade Commission 30 days in advance of any proposed price increase.[15] Hearings would then be called to explore the justification for the increase, although no binding government action could follow from the hearings. This and related bills died from lack of support—in no small measure because it would be quite costly to investigate an exhaustive sample of concentrated industry price increases and because adversary hearings are seldom capable of clarifying such issues as the justification for a price change.

CONSUMER INFORMATION PROGRAMS

Some of the most serious market performance problems in the contemporary American economy are due more to inadequate knowledge on the consumer's part than to structural imperfections of a traditional sort. Two deficiencies stand out. First, consumers pay unnecessarily high prices for heavily advertised and otherwise differentiated products because they lack the technical knowledge to tell whether a particular gasoline, dentifrice, detergent, pain remedy, vacuum cleaner, weed killer, or fabric is actually better than less expensive unadvertised substitutes. Second, in such fields as home building

---

[13]See John Sheahan, *The Wage-Price Guideposts* (Washington: Brookings, 1967), pp. 79–95; George L. Perry, "Wages and the Guideposts," *American Economic Review*, September 1967, pp. 897–904; and Gail Pierson, "The Effect of Union Strength on the U. S. 'Phillips Curve,'" *American Economic Review*, June 1968, pp. 456–467. For skeptical reactions, see the comments by Paul S. Anderson, M. L. Wachter, and A. W. Throop in the *American Economic Review*, June 1969, pp. 351–369; and Richard Mancke, "The Determinants of Steel Prices in the U. S.: 1947–65," *Journal of Industrial Economics*, April 1968, pp. 147–160.

[14]See also J. T. Romans, "Moral Suasion as an Instrument of Economic Policy," *American Economic Review*, December 1966, pp. 1220–1225.

[15]Some of the smaller European nations enforce a similar program on a more limited scale. See M. A. G. van Meerhaeghe, "Prior Notification of Price Increases as an Instrument of Price-Stabilization Policy," *Kyklos*, No. 1, 1968, pp. 26–42; and "The Belgian Prices Commission," *Weltwirtschaftliches Archiv*, December 1967, pp. 257–270. See also David C. Smith, "Incomes Policy," in Richard E. Caves, ed., *Britain's Economic Prospects* (Washington: Brookings, 1968), pp. 104–139.

and repair services, the consumer can be cheated or exploited because he cannot distinguish honest from dishonest workmanship and because, once he has signed a contract or left his wheezing automobile with a particular businessman, he is in effect locked into a bilateral monopoly relationship conferring considerable pricing power upon the better-informed party. In home construction, builders frequently turn over shoddy workmanship or fail to complete details of a job, leaving the buyer in a typically weak position to take legal action. Or they set inflated prices for contract changes once the buyer has committed himself and cannot secure outside competitive bids.[16] Repairmen charge for work they have not done and fail, through incompetence or deceit, to remedy the problem originally troubling the consumer. The hapless consumer may never find out he has been duped, or he may learn only when the item repaired breaks down anew.

The best strategy for attacking the first set of problems is undoubtedly to provide the consumer with more information on what he is buying. For goods whose purchase is unduly influenced by advertising, this can be done by developing uniform grading systems, publishing government test reports, and subsidizing such independent consumer research organizations as the Consumers Union.

Improving the performance of the repair services and home construction trades demands a different approach. What the consumer in effect buys when he hires a particular repairman or (to a lesser degree) building contractor is reputation. The key to improvement lies in perfecting the consumer's knowledge of how well alternative suppliers have served their customers in the past. This is especially important in large cities, where word-of-mouth communication operates least effectively. A space age solution might operate along the following lines. Each service and building tradesman would be assigned an identification number, which he would publish in telephone directory advertising. After every job exceeding a specified dollar value, he

would be required by law to give the customer two computer cards pre-punched with his identification number. These would be imprinted with questions calling for multiple-choice answers characterizing the consumer's satisfaction with the job done. One would be completed and mailed to a central collection point immediately, the other after a time interval sufficient to let the consumer judge in hindsight how well the job was done. The central data bank's computer would process the information received and store it in summary form. When electronic telephone switching comes into widespread use, consumers could dial the data bank's telephone number plus the identification numbers of prospective vendors, receiving in return an oral summary of the vendors' performance records compared to the average for all vendors in the relevant service category. To be sure, such a system would not be perfect; the information it supplies could be no better than the information originating with fallible consumers. But random aberrations in individual consumer evaluations would average out under the law of large numbers, and the system would surely offer a better foundation for rational consumer choice than the present system, based as it is on total ignorance or fragmentary hearsay.

PUBLIC OWNERSHIP OF INDUSTRY

Public ownership and operation of industry is an option chosen more frequently abroad than in the United States when unfettered private market processes fail to function satisfactorily. It has many variants. It can involve government monopolization of a whole market, or government operations may co-exist and compete with private firms. It can be achieved through the nationalization of existing private firms or the establishment of new government facilities. Its organization can take myriad forms, ranging from operations fully integrated into conventional government departments to public corporations autonomous except with respect to top management appointments. We cannot pos-

[16]Cf. Charles Foster, "Competition and Organization in Building," *Journal of Industrial Economics*, July 1964, pp. 163–174.

sibly do justice to the full range of issues in this brief survey, but let us try to highlight some of the principal fields, objectives, opportunities, and limitations of public ownership.[17]

Activities undertaken on a significant scale by governmental units in the United States include the supply of water, electricity, local transit service, garbage collection service, public housing, and postal service; the operation of hospitals and clinics; the maintenance of schools, universities, and laboratories; the conduct of bank and crop failure insurance programs; the retailing of liquor; and various minor manufacturing endeavors (such as running the Government Printing Office—the world's largest printing establishment). Federal, state, and local government enterprises are credited with originating $8.8 billion in gross national product, or 1.1 per cent of total GNP, in 1967. Since this figure includes only the activities of essentially commercial enterprises selling their products to the general public, it understates somewhat the total scope of government enterprise. In most other industrialized nations, the railroads, airlines, broadcasting networks, electric power and gas utilities, and telephone and telegraph services are typically owned and operated by the government. Public ownership abroad frequently extends also into important manufacturing industries such as steel, automobiles, and aircraft; and into the extraction of coal, crude petroleum, and other basic minerals.

Three broad strategies can be pursued in attempting to improve industrial performance through public ownership. The first is the *yardstick approach*. Under it, only part of an industry's capacity is government-owned. The cost and pricing performance of that segment is held out as a standard for evaluating the comparative performance of privately-owned producers. A good example is the Tennessee Valley Authority, the largest U. S. electrical utility, whose exceptionally low costs have presented a challenge for private utilities, and which demon-

strated to traditionally conservative private firms the advantages of probing the lower reaches of consumer demand curves by reducing prices. Other government yardstick operations include the Naval shipyards and the Army arsenals, but these have been withering away as a result of ideological attacks and pressures from private weapons producers. Aside from their vulnerability to political undermining, the chief disadvantage of publicly-owned yardstick operations is the difficulty of making direct comparisons in dissimilar situations. Citing TVA's costs as a standard, for instance, is criticized by private power interests because the Authority obtains its capital at favorable interest rates, pays no income taxes, and enjoys special cost advantages from using dams built for navigation and conservation purposes. These complaints are well-founded, but valid comparisons *can* be made if appropriate analytic adjustments are introduced—a step private utilities have resisted because, like the squid, they find murky waters an effective defense mechanism.

A second strategy, also requiring only partial government ownership, is to have the government enterprises pursue aggressive policies calculated to compel desired behavioral changes on the part of private operators. This is essentially a second-best approach. Given the market position of the private producers and their probable responses to alternative public enterprise price and output choices, the public firms adopt that pricing policy which induces the most favorable attainable overall industry performance, even though performance will undoubtedly fall short of what it might be under ideal conditions.[18] The public enterprises may, for example, consistently undercut the private producers' prices, or engage in arbitrage to frustrate price discrimination, or threaten to expand their capacity unless price is held at a moderate level. A variant occasionally employed by the U. S. government is the sale of defense stockpile materials to depress inflated prices, although the long-run

---

[17]For more extensive surveys, see Clair Wilcox, *Public Policies Toward Business* (Third ed.; Homewood, Illinois: Irwin, 1966), Chapters 20 through 23; and Ralph Turvey, ed., *Public Enterprise* (Baltimore: Penguin Books, 1968).

[18]For an interesting analysis, see W. C. Merrill and Norman Schneider, "Government Firms in Oligopoly Industries: A Short-Run Analysis," *Quarterly Journal of Economics*, August 1966, pp. 400–412.

leverage attainable with this tactic is limited if the stockpiles must eventually be replenished by purchases from private sellers. Competition may also be waged on nonprice dimensions. For example, the government-owned Renault Company is said to have had a beneficial impact on the French automobile industry's performance by leading the way into low-cost compact car lines in a calculated attempt to facilitate automobile ownership by citizens occupying the lower income strata.[19] In general, however, vigorous competition between public and private enterprises has not been widespread. Political opposition by private firms is one reason, at least in the United States. Also, public enterprise heads frequently display even less zest for the competitive struggle than private entrepreneurs. To avoid complaints about subsidization and to prove their managerial mettle, they may be anxious to show a profit, and vigorous competition could frustrate that ambition. Renault apparently colludes on prices with its private rivals, as do the far-flung divisions of Italy's governmental holding company, the Institute for Industrial Reconstruction.[20] And in England Lord Melchett, the first chairman of the renationalized British Steel Corporation, announced his opposition to letting the individual constituent steel mills compete with one another because "that would be giving the profits to the consumer."[21]

The third main strategy is that of total or virtual public monopoly. It is the dominant approach in all but the service trades and agriculture in communist nations, and it is a common feature of the mass transportation, electric power, and communications sectors of most other countries outside the United States. A spectrum of operating philosophies can be identified. At one extreme is the classic Soviet approach, under which detailed output plans, labor allocations, capital allowances, raw materials quotas, prices, wages, and the like are assigned to each operating unit by central planners. At the other extreme is the approach conceived by 'market socialists' during the 1920s and 1930s, under which prices are set by central planners to reflect supply and demand conditions and then individual enterprise managers expand the output of their products until marginal cost rises into equality with price.[22] In principle, the latter scheme approximates the operation of a purely competitive economy while avoiding such problems as monopoly pricing and inequitable income distribution. In practice, governments representing the various ideological colorations have strayed widely from these pure models, sometimes by design and sometimes by inadvertence, to achieve the results they seek.

Numerous advantages are claimed by the proponents of public monopoly. Perhaps most important from an economic standpoint, it is a way to secure the benefits of size in industries with large minimum optimal scales without suffering the disadvantages of monopolistic pricing. Other alleged advantages include the channeling of returns on capital to the commonwealth rather than to private individuals, the ability to raise capital at no risk premium through governmental risk-pooling, and the reduction of alienation by convincing workers that they ultimately own and control the main branches of industry.

It is hardly necessary to add that certain of these advantages are often more conjectural than real. Moreover, public enterprises face real problems devising operational criteria to guide and motivate decision-makers and workers—something the market system does automatically. Merely telling enterprise managers to act in the public interest is distinctly nonoperational, for such a rule is so vague it could have a dozen plausible interpretations in any given situation.

---

[19] John Sheahan, "Government Competition and the Performance of the French Automobile Industry," *Journal of Industrial Economics*, June 1960, pp. 197–215.

[20] *Ibid.*; S. Moos, "An Experiment in Mixed Enterprise," *Bulletin of the Oxford Institute of Economics and Statistics*, May 1964, p. 200; and "Report from Rome," *Fortune*, November 1968, p. 83.

[21] "Britain's Steel Debate," *New York Times*, March 25, 1967, pp. 31 ff.

[22] See Oskar Lange and Fred M. Taylor, *On the Economic Theory of Socialism* (B. E. Lippincott, ed.; Minneapolis: University of Minnesota Press, 1938).

To ensure that the 'correct' interpretation is chosen and to prevent line managers from advancing their own selfish interests under the discretion a broad criterion allows, countless decisions would have to be passed up the ladder for review and resolution. But this can overload management, causing decision-making breakdowns. Also, excessive centralization of decision-making stifles initiative and responsibility. To make a large organization work at all well, some criterion is needed which is sufficiently tangible and specific to permit decentralized decision-making and to provide a standard against which accomplishments can be judged. Under the traditional Soviet approach the detailed plan attempts to serve this function, but as an economy becomes more complex, difficulties multiply due to the plan's rigidity and its frequent failure to reflect operating level realities. The rule, 'set marginal cost equal to price' is better in theory, but higher echelons may be unable to assure that operating units are following it because marginal cost is so hard to measure; and adherence to the rule may lead, as we shall see in Chapter 22, to losses which upset legislators and treasury officials.

Because of these problems, it has become commonplace in western nations and (more recently) in Soviet satellites to prescribe a profit maximization criterion as the primary guide to decentralized decision-making and accountability. However, government monopolies can increase profits not only by improving their operating efficiency, but also by raising prices or persuading central authorities to raise them. This often happens. Indeed, prices may be raised sufficiently to let the firm pay excessive wages and absorb considerable outright waste while earning what appears to be a satisfactory profit. It is said, for instance, that the worker representatives directing some Yugoslavian industrial collectives quickly learned that by restricting output and exercising what power they had over prices, they could enhance total revenues and the incomes of collective members. So we come full circle. The very pricing distortions which lead nations to embrace public ownership may reappear as a result of attempts to make public enterprise function more efficiently.

To be sure, the incentive to raise prices and restrict output is probably not as strong in public enterprises as it is in private monopolies. Altruism serves as a check, as do controls by the central government and the absence of stock options and other ownership motives. However, the pressure to reduce costs and innovate is also weaker than in all but those private firms most heavily insulated from competition. Political intervention and rigidities introduced by government accountability standards and civil service procedures may impose a further drag on public enterprise efficiency.

How these virtues and drawbacks of public enterprise balance out is an empirical question. Unfortunately, we possess only scattered case study evidence varying widely in both quality and implications. It is possible to find examples of vigorous, efficient, enlightened public enterprises like the Tennessee Valley Authority. One can also find operations such as the U. S. Post Office bogged down in a morass of inefficiency, petty bureaucracy, political influence, and resistance to change. Or within a narrower organizational framework, there are U. S. Army arsenals which have performed extremely well, as the (now revamped) Redstone Arsenal did during the 1950s in developing ballistic missiles and space vehicles, and there are others whose performance records leave a great deal to be desired. Analysis of the British, French, and Italian experiences suggests that differences in performance between nationalized and private firms in the same industries, or in the performance of identical firms before and after nationalization, are not very large.[23] The evidence is presently insufficient to support a sharp choice between the alternatives on straightforward economic performance grounds, and so the decision

---

[23]See, for instance, Moos, *op. cit.*; Sheahan, "Government Competition and the Performance of the French Automobile Industry"; and William G. Shepherd, *Economic Performance under Public Ownership* (New Haven: Yale University Press, 1965).

may perforce continue to be made mainly on the basis of ideology. It does seem plainly desirable to experiment more with various forms of public ownership so that their potential and limitations can be brought into sharper focus.

PUBLIC REGULATION

Occupying a halfway house between public ownership and private enterprise are those industries subjected to more or less thoroughgoing regulation as public utilities. The government's intervention in their activities stops short of outright ownership, but it goes far beyond merely setting ceiling prices. It may include extensive participation in pricing decisions, the control of entry and exit, prescription of service standards, and a host of other controls. Roughly 10 per cent of the U. S. gross national product originates in firms operating under some form of regulation. Further discussion is deferred to Chapter 22, which deals at length with the institutions, theory, and effects of regulation.

ANTITRUST POLICY

Finally, we come to antitrust policy. In the United States, and to an increasing degree in other industrialized nations of the Western world, the enforcement of antitrust laws is the main weapon wielded by government in its effort to harmonize the profit-seeking behavior of private enterprises with the public interest. Antitrust performs this function in two ways: by inhibiting or prohibiting certain undesirable kinds of *business conduct*; and by channeling and shaping *market structure* along competitive lines so as to increase the likelihood that desirable conduct and performance will emerge more or less automatically. Because of its prominence, antitrust policy will be the concern of the following three chapters. We will review the substantive content of the principal U. S. antitrust laws, identify significant differences between American laws and their counterparts in other lands, and explore unsettled policy issues. The remaining pages of the present chapter provide a general introduction and historical backdrop.[24]

EARLY BACKGROUND

Almost the entire edifice of U. S. federal antitrust law rests upon three foundation statutes— the Sherman Act of 1890, the Clayton Act of 1914, and the Federal Trade Commission Act of 1914. These three were virtually the first of their kind in the modern world; they were preceded only by an 1889 addition to the Canadian criminal code similar to the Sherman Act. The legislation establishing antitrust rules in Canada and the United States during the brief span of 25 years represented the reaction of New World dwellers to a concatenation of profound changes in the character of industrial capitalism.

Several things happened during the latter half of the 19th century to set the stage for antitrust. For one, capital-intensive production on a large scale, although by no means unknown previously, enjoyed a rapid rise to prominence in the manufacturing industries. This occurred partly because of technological innovations in metallurgy, industrial chemistry, energy generation and utilization, and the use of interchangeable parts. Also, transportation costs fell, reducing the physical distribution constraint on optimal plant scales. The quest for economies of scale was facilitated by the ascendance of industrial banking houses and the development of modern capital markets able to supply large quantities of venture capital to a single firm. Liberalization of state incorporation laws also contributed, permitting the acquisition of other firms' stock (i.e., in mergers) and the delegation of stockholders' decision-making power to full-time managers.

While production operations were growing in size, so also were markets. The rapid extension of rail networks created for the first time a 'common market' in the United States, with an accompanying intensification of competition. Producers once isolated spatially found their markets penetrated by outsiders. International competition also increased as transatlantic ship-

---

[24]For thorough coverage of the early background, see Hans B. Thorelli, *The Federal Antitrust Policy* (Stockholm, 1954); and William Letwin, *Law and Economic Policy in America* (New York: Random House, 1965).

ping rates fell sharply due to the introduction of iron vessels propelled by efficient compound steam engines.

Two severe business depressions—one international in scope commencing in 1873 and persisting in the United States for six years, the other beginning in 1883 and lasting until 1886, added ferment to the economic broth. The first reaction of large manufacturers, carrying a heavy burden of fixed costs and faced with increasingly intense competition, was to cut prices. This course was viewed with scant enthusiasm by business leaders, whose second reaction was an effort to subdue the forces of competition by entering into restrictive agreements and by consolidating former competitors into a single monolithic firm with control over prices.

In Europe, cartel formation was the prevalent way of coping with the turbulent conditions of the 1870s and 1880s. Fritz Voigt reports that in Germany there were four cartels in 1865, eight in 1875, 70 in 1887, 106 in 1889, and 250 in 1896.[25] American producers also entered into formal and informal price-fixing agreements with their rivals. But the more striking American response—striking both in absolute magnitude and its contrast with what happened in Europe —was the large-scale merger.[26] The pacemaker was the Standard Oil Company. It had many imitators, and the 1880s and 1890s witnessed a wave of mergers and corporate consolidations unequalled in subsequent U. S. history.

The definitive international history of entrepreneurial reactions to the economic changes of the late 19th century remains to be written, and therefore we can only speculate why the U. S. merger wave was so distinctly American, while European businessmen were generally satisfied with their cartel arrangements. One possible explanation is that American entrepreneurs, reflecting the expansive frontier spirit of their times, were more inclined toward corporate empire-building while Europeans preferred operating small, closely-held enterprises in restrictive fashion. Another is that American businessmen, poured from a melting pot of ethnic and economic backgrounds, held such diverse attitudes and goals that they were psychologically unable to cooperate in maintaining nonbinding cartel agreements. Only through a complete surrender of decision-making power to a monolithic consolidation could their maverick impulses be leashed. Europeans, on the other hand, may have shared sufficiently homogeneous cultural traditions to work together amicably in their national markets. Third, mergers tend to be the product of boom times, while cartels are the children of depression. The depressions of the 1870s and 1880s were milder in America than in Europe. The more buoyant expectations of American businessmen may have been conducive to consolidation, while Europeans troubled by the perplexing new forms the business cycle had taken were propelled toward loose confederations. Finally, differences in the legal environment had some bearing. In Germany, at one extreme, cartel agreements were held to be binding contracts. Recalcitrant members could be compelled under the law to honor their restrictive promises. Under American common law and also (with a few qualifications) in England, price-fixing agreements were generally considered unlawful and unenforceable at law. This made it difficult to maintain industry discipline in the face of dissident members' actions, and so, at least in the United States, businessmen turned to the more certain control of trustification.

Although the common law in America took a generally dim view of agreements to restrain trade, it was impotent as a positive preventive force. Restrictive agreements could only be challenged by parties to the agreement, who had little incentive to do so, or by injured private persons, who seldom could sustain the evidentiary and financial burden of proving their case.

---

[25]Fritz Voigt, "German Experience with Cartels and Their Control During Pre-War and Post-War Periods," in J. P. Miller, ed., *Competition, Cartels, and Their Regulation* (Amsterdam: North-Holland, 1962), p. 170.

[26]England also experienced a merger wave at the same time, but it was of much more modest proportions. See Ralph L. Nelson, *Merger Movements in American Industry, 1895–1956* (Princeton: Princeton University Press, 1959), pp. 129–138; and P. L. Payne, "The Emergence of the Large-Scale Company in Great Britain, 1870–1914," *Economic History Review*, December 1967, pp. 519–542.

The pricing practices of trusts lay almost completely beyond the law's grasp. As a result, monopolistic restraints and abuses flourished, stirring in their wake a public hue and cry for corrective action.

Several alleged misdeeds of big business provoked widespread resentment. Through predatory pricing, the trusts were said to have driven thousands of small firms out of business, and it was with these small businessmen that the public's sentiments lay. The trusts engaged in local and personal price discrimination, angering the communities and individuals who lacked competitive alternatives and paid high prices. The fortunes built upon monopoly profits increased the inequality of income distribution, evoking reactions especially bitter because of the way wealth was flaunted then by those who possessed it. And farmers comprising a majority of the voting population in the Middle Western states joined in protest as the industrial consolidations raised manufactured goods prices while farm product prices declined.

About the only group in America other than big businessmen outspokenly unconcerned about the trust problem were the professional economists. Many were captivated by Darwin's theory of biological selection. They saw the growth of big business as a natural evolutionary response consistent with economies of scale, or when scale economies were patently absent from mergers, as a step necessary to eliminate cut-throat competition. But in that unenlightened era, the views of unenlightened economists concerning big business had little influence on public policy.

The public clamor reached a crescendo during the late 1880s. Between 1889 and 1891, no fewer than 18 states (beginning with Kansas) enacted antitrust laws. These, however, were not particularly effective against monopolistic consolidations operating in interstate commerce. At the national level, all the major political parties engaged in the presidential election of 1888 included antitrust planks in their platforms. The initiative in Congress was exercised by Senator John Sherman (Rep.-Ohio), who introduced antitrust bills during the 1888, 1889, and finally, with greater success, 1890 terms. His 1890 bill was debated warmly, subjected to a plethora of amendments, referred to the Judiciary Committee for extensive rewriting, and returned to the Senate to be passed by a 52-1 vote. After House of Representatives concurrence, it was signed into law by President Harrison on July 2, 1890.

SUBSTANCE OF THE BASIC ANTITRUST STATUTES

The resulting statute, bearing little resemblance to Senator Sherman's original proposal, contained two main substantive sections. Section 1 prohibits contracts, combinations, and conspiracies in restraint of trade, prescribing penalties for violators of imprisonment up to one year and/or a fine up to $5,000 (raised to $50,000 in 1955). Section 2 prohibits monopolization, attempts to monopolize, and combinations or conspiracies to monopolize "any part of the trade or commerce among the several States, or with foreign nations," specifying criminal penalties for violation similar to those of Section 1. Of the procedural sections, the most important are Section 4, permitting the Attorney General to institute suits in equity to enjoin illegal practices, and Section 7, permitting private persons injured by actions illegal under Sections 1 or 2 to sue for recovery of three times the amount of actual damages sustained.

Enforcement of the Sherman Act during its first 10 years was unspectacular, to say the least. Several attorneys general entrusted with enforcing the law lacked not only funds and personnel, but also enthusiasm, partly because of prior affiliations as private counsel to leading corporations. The government also suffered significant legal defeats in cases brought against the Whiskey and Sugar Trusts—setbacks traceable in no small measure to careless preparation and unimaginative argumentation. However, government test case victories in 1897 and 1899 set the stage for an invigorated enforcement program after Theodore Roosevelt took office as President in 1901. Roosevelt secured new legislation providing streamlined judicial procedures for civil antitrust cases and creating a special antitrust enforcement division in the Department of Justice. A series of important case decisions (discussed in subsequent chapters) followed, establishing for decades to come the rules by which firms obtaining and exercising market power were required to live.

The remaining two vertices of the U. S. antitrust trinity were framed at the urging of President Woodrow Wilson. The Clayton Act was designed to outlaw specific practices not covered by the Sherman Act and to restrain the growth of monopoly "in its incipiency," before full-blown Sherman Act violations could develop. Section 2, heavily amended in 1936, prohibited price discrimination which substantially lessened competition or tended to create a monopoly. Section 3 outlaws tying clauses and exclusive dealing agreements adversely affecting competition. Section 5 eases the burden of proving antitrust violation for private parties suing to recover treble damages. Section 7, amended in 1950, prohibited certain mergers tending substantially to lessen competition; and Section 8 forbids interlocking directorates among competing firms.

For some time prior to 1914, antitrust advocates saw the need for an agency performing both investigatory and adjudicative functions and possessing special competence in business affairs. To create such an agency was the purpose of the Federal Trade Commission Act, which established a panel of five full-time commissioners invested with substantial quasi-judicial powers and aided by a staff of professional personnel. The FTC Act also, in substantive Section 5, outlaws "unfair methods of competition," leaving to the Commission the task of determining what practices are to be included under this blanket prohibition.

With the passage of the Clayton and Federal Trade Commission Acts, the substantive framework of American antitrust law was basically complete, to be rounded out only by a series of amendments closing loopholes and clarifying exceptions; and the enforcement machinery used ever since 1914 was assembled. Responsibility for enforcing the antitrust laws is presently shared primarily by the Antitrust Division of the Justice Department, which in 1968 spent $7.7 million for the task; and the Federal Trade Commission, whose 1968 budget for antitrust activities (as distinguished from such additional responsibilities as combatting fraud and misrepresentation) was $7.6 million. The Antitrust Division's powers are limited to investigation and enforcement. Cases it initiates are adjudicated before a federal district court, whose decisions in civil (i.e., noncriminal) cases may be appealed on matters of law by either the government or the defendant directly to the Supreme Court. The Federal Trade Commission, on the other hand, investigates industry practices through its Bureau of Industrial Economics, prosecutes complaints through its Bureau of Restraint of Trade, and adjudicates cases in its Office of Hearing Examiners, which can recommend that the five-member Commission issue a cease-and-desist order binding upon respondents. Commission decisions can be appealed (primarily on matters of law) to a federal appellate court, and from there to the Supreme Court. As the jurisdictional provisions of the various statutes have come to be interpreted, both the Justice Department and the FTC may institute civil actions against violations of the Sherman Act and the Clayton Act.[27] This overlapping of responsibilities poses coordination problems which are not always solved successfully. One positive attribute of the dual enforcement approach is a tendency for one agency's oversights to be corrected by actions of the other agency.

EXEMPTIONS FROM ANTITRUST

Over the course of time, a number of exemptions have been written into the antitrust laws and related statutes. Some of the most important relate to labor unions, agricultural cooperatives, export associations, the regulated industries, and the fixing of retail prices by manufacturers.[28]

Section 6 of the Clayton Act exempted from antitrust the activities of labor and agricultural or horticultural organizations whose objective

---

[27]More precisely, Sherman Act violations can be attacked as unfair trade practices under Section 5 of the Federal Trade Commission Act. However, only the Justice Department can institute criminal complaints.

[28]For more comprehensive surveys, see Wilcox, *Public Policies Toward Business*, pp. 669–828; and U. S. Department of Justice, *Report of the Attorney General's National Committee To Study the Antitrust Laws* (Washington: 1955), pp. 261–314.

was the mutual help of members. Price-fixing by agricultural cooperatives was further absolved through the Capper-Volstead Act of 1922, as long as it does not unduly enhance farm product prices. The efforts of laborers to secure higher wages through unionization and collective bargaining were encouraged under the Norris-LaGuardia Act of 1932 and the National Labor Relations Act (Wagner Act) of 1935. The exemptions for agricultural cooperatives have been relatively uncontroversial, since local or regional cooperatives seldom possess much power to affect prices in a national market and since the federal government has maintained direct support and control programs with a far more significant impact on farm product prices. More debate has been stimulated by the labor union exemption, with opponents stressing the inconsistency in permitting sellers of labor services but not sellers of goods or more complex services to join together in a common effort to enhance their economic rewards.[29] Still it is clear that the exemption for collective bargaining has strong political support as a means of balancing more equally the power of employers and employees. The currently binding judicial interpretations have not, however, permitted the exemption to be extended beyond the bounds of particular employer-employee wage and working conditions bargains. Attempts by labor unions to collude with unionized employers in fixing end product prices or driving nonunion firms out of business have been deemed violations of the Sherman Act.[30]

The 1918 Webb–Pomerene Act exemption of price-fixing and other agreements from antitrust prohibitions when they pertain solely to export market sales is a mercantilist throwback common to the antitrust policies of most industrialized nations. Although its intent was partly to permit small domestic firms to penetrate foreign markets more effectively and to secure economies of scale through coordinated marketing, a more fundamental objective has been to alter the terms of trade and to enhance payments balances by allowing domestic producers to exploit whatever power over export prices they might collectively possess. Under Webb–Pomerene Act provisions, American companies are permitted to form and operate associations which restrain the export trade as long as prices of the commodities covered are not intentionally or artificially affected in the United States market. Agreements must be registered with the Federal Trade Commission, which is charged with a continuing supervisory role. In practice, however, the FTC's position is a difficult one, for the mere establishment of a cooperative arrangement affecting overseas markets may facilitate virtually undetectable tacit or explicit collusion with respect to domestic prices. Despite the opportunities it affords, extensive advantage has not been taken of the Webb–Pomerene loophole. In 1965 only 32 Webb–Pomerene associations, originating about 4 per cent by value of U. S. exports, were registered.[31] It is noteworthy that 77 per cent of the export sales made under Webb–Pomerene were by relatively concentrated industries in which the eight industry leaders accounted for 50 per cent or more of domestic sales.

In the early years of American antitrust, the Sherman Act bans on price-fixing agreements and monopolization applied with equal force to regulated and unregulated industries. Gradually, however, grants of immunity were written into

---

[29]For a strong statement of the case for limiting union power, see H. Gregg Lewis, "The Labor-Monopoly Problem: A Positive Program," *Journal of Political Economy*, August 1951, pp. 277–287. For more moderate statements, see Edward S. Mason, *Economic Concentration and the Monopoly Problem* (Cambridge: Harvard University Press, 1957), pp. 196–208; and G. H. Hildebrand, "Economics By Negotiation," *American Economic Review*, May 1959, pp. 399–411.

[30]An important recent Supreme Court decision is *Pennington* v. *United Mine Workers et al.*, 381 U. S. 657 (1965); with the subsequent district court opinion, 257 F. Supp. 815 (1966). It is analyzed by Oliver E. Williamson in "Wage Rates as a Barrier to Entry: The Pennington Case in Perspective," *Quarterly Journal of Economics*, February 1968, pp. 85–116. See also *U. S.* v. *Hutcheson*, 312 U. S. 219 (1941).

[31]See the testimony of Willard F. Mueller in U. S. Senate, Committee on the Judiciary, Subcommittee on Antitrust and Monopoly, Hearings, *International Aspects of Antitrust, 1967* (Washington: 1967), pp. 31–60.

the principal statutes affecting regulated industries. These will be considered further in Chapters 20 and 22.

A final gap in federal antitrust coverage involves the so-called fair trade or resale price maintenance laws, which permit manufacturers to specify the prices at which retailers must sell their branded products as long as the products are in "free and open competition" with substitute products. The original federal statute exempting resale price maintenance agreements from antitrust attack was the Miller–Tydings Act of 1937. It was extended in the McGuire Act of 1952, which permits a manufacturer to specify the prices at which *all* retailers in a state authorizing resale price maintenance must sell its products, as long as any one seller in that state has voluntarily entered into a 'fair trade' agreement. The resale price maintenance laws will be examined further in Chapter 21.

Chapter 19

Antitrust Policy: Price-Fixing Agreements

The Sherman Act, wrote Chief Justice Charles Evans Hughes in 1933, "as a charter of freedom . . . has a generality and adaptability comparable to that found to be desirable in constitutional provisions."[1] Only by studying the trend of actual judicial interpretations can we attach specific meaning to its broad prohibitions. In this chapter we begin the task, focusing on the legal status of price-fixing agreements and similar agreements in restraint of trade.

THE *PER SE* ILLEGALITY OF EXPLICIT RESTRAINTS

Section 1 of the Sherman Act proscribes "every contract, combination . . . or conspiracy in restraint of trade or commerce among the several States." An extended series of court decisions has interpreted this language as making illegal *per se* all agreements among competing firms to fix prices, to restrict or pool output, to share markets on a predetermined basis, or otherwise directly to restrict the force of competition.

It is necessary immediately to distinguish *per se* prohibitions like those applied by the federal courts to price-fixing agreements and 'rules of reason' used in other areas of antitrust law. Under a *per se* rule, a practice is deemed to be illegal whether or not it can be shown in particular circumstances to have a perceptible anti-social effect. The complainant (usually the

Justice Department) must merely establish proof that the defendants in fact engaged in the prohibited act. Under a rule of reason, on the other hand, the prosecution must show not only that the alleged act was perpetrated, but also that the act was unreasonable or contrary to the public interest.

The *per se* rule against overt agreements in restraint of trade was initially articulated in the *Trans-Missouri Freight Association* decision—the first price-fixing case to be appealed to the U. S. Supreme Court. In an effort to eliminate the freight rate wars toward which they were inclined, 18 railroads operating west of the Missouri River entered into formal agreements establishing the rates each line would charge. The U. S. district attorney in Topeka brought suit in 1892 to dissolve the agreements. The railroads advanced two main defenses: that they were exempt from Sherman Act prohibitions by virtue of their status as carriers regulated under the Interstate Commerce Act of 1887, and that the rates they fixed by agreement were in any event legal because they were reasonable. Both defenses were sustained by the lower courts. As the district court judge observed, finding the agreements reasonable and hence not in violation of the Sherman Act:

> . . . when contracts go to the extent only of preventing unhealthy competition, and yet at the same time furnish the public with adequate facilities at fixed and reasonable

---

[1] *Appalachian Coals, Inc. v. U. S.*, 288 U. S. 344, 359–360 (1933).

prices, and are made only for the purpose of averting personal ruin, the contract is lawful.[2]

However, this interpretation, as well as the ruling exempting regulated railroads from Sherman Act jurisdiction, was rejected by the Supreme Court in a 5-4 decision. In its dissent, the Court's minority argued for the application of a rule of reason. But Justice Peckham, speaking for the majority, found that the language Congress used in the Sherman Act could not be construed to admit a test of reasonableness:

> When . . . the body of an act pronounces as illegal every contract or combination in restraint of trade or commerce among the several states, etc., the plain and ordinary meaning of such language is not limited to that kind of contract alone which is in unreasonable restraint of trade, but all contracts are included in such language, and no exception or limitation can be added without placing in the act that which has been omitted by Congress.[3]

He went on to note that while preventing ruinous competition among the railroads might be socially desirable, it would be impossible for the courts to determine whether the rates set through inter-firm agreements were reasonable, and that recognition of this difficulty might have prompted Congress to prohibit *all* agreements in restraint of trade, and not just unreasonable ones His view of the judiciary's role in carrying out the stated intent of Congress is revealed most clearly in this passage:

> It may be that the policy evidenced by the passage of the act itself will, if carried out, result in disaster to the roads. . . . These considerations are, however, not for us.[4]

Through a decision the following year the *per se* prohibition's sweep was limited to con-

tracts "whose direct and immediate effect" was to restrain commerce.[5] In another concurrent case involving six midwestern and southern producers of cast iron water and gas pipe, the rule was reiterated on a new and different logical plane. The six, accounting for about two thirds of total output in the Middle West and West, operated in an industry which gravitated toward bitter price warfare because of sharp fluctuations in orders, the large size of individual orders, and a cost structure characterized by high overhead and low marginal costs at less than full capacity operation. They formed a bidding cartel which rigged the prices quoted to buyers in certain cities, reserved other cities as the exclusive domain of a single seller, and pooled contributions made to a central fund in implementing the scheme. Hearing the case for the Circuit Court of Appeals, Judge (later President and Supreme Court Chief Justice) William Howard Taft went beyond a literal reading of the words used by Congress in Sherman Act Section 1, attempting to build a *per se* prohibition upon the common law prevailing in America and England at the time. He argued that the common law permitted restraints of trade which were merely ancillary to some legitimate cause, but that it voided those contracts whose main object was to restrict competition. Taft insisted that past decisions inconsistent with this view had been erroneous, "set[ting] sail on a sea of doubt" in their attempt to determine how much restraint of competition was in the public interest.[6] Ruling that the pipe producers' agreements were clearly not ancillary, Taft concluded that the reasonableness of the agreements was irrelevant:

> It has been earnestly pressed upon us that the prices at which the cast-iron pipe was sold . . . were reasonable. . . . We do not think the issue an important one, because . . .

---

[2] *U. S. v. Trans-Missouri Freight Association et al.*, 53 Fed. 440, 451 (1892).

[3] *U. S. v. Trans-Missouri Freight Association*, 166 U. S. 290, 328 (1897).

[4] *Ibid.*, p. 340.

[5] *Hopkins v. United States*, 171 U. S. 578, 592 (1898). See also *U. S. v. Joint Traffic Association*, 171 U. S. 505, 568 (1898).

[6] *U. S. v. Addyston Pipe & Steel Co. et al.*, 85 Fed. 271, 284 (1898). Taft's decision has been criticized for reading things into the common law which were not there. See Almarin Phillips, *Market Structure, Organization and Performance* (Cambridge: Harvard University Press, 1962), p. 114.

we do not think that at common law there is any question of reasonableness open to the courts with reference to such a contract. Its tendency was certainly to give the defendants the power to charge unreasonable prices, had they chosen to do so.[7]

He added in the next line that "if it were important, we should unhesitatingly find that the prices charged in the instances which were in evidence were unreasonable." This afterthought muted the force of Taft's decision as a precedent, for while citing the material quoted here approvingly, the Supreme Court on appeal placed more emphasis on the unreasonableness of the prices charged than on Taft's harmonization of the common and statutory law.[8]

The scope of the *per se* prohibition against price-fixing was attenuated and muddied somewhat during the next three decades as the Supreme Court enunciated a rule of reason to apply in Sherman Act monopolization cases (considered in the next chapter) and as decisions were rendered in borderline areas such as patent license restrictions and trade association activities falling short of clear-cut price-fixing. A forceful restatement had to await the *Trenton Potteries* decision in 1927. The defendants, some 23 manufacturers controlling roughly 82 per cent of the bathroom bowl market, published standardized price lists through a trade association committee, discussed prices at frequent association meetings, and exhorted one another not to sell at off-list prices. Evidence compiled through a criminal trial suggested that the exhortations were not very successful. Pricing discipline of the association members was weak, and for many members adherence to list prices was apparently more the exception than the rule. Hearing the case on appeal, the Supreme Court addressed itself directly to the question of whether reasonableness of the prices actually charged was a relevant consideration in determining the defendants' guilt or innocence. It first distinguished price-fixing cases from other cases in

which a rule of reason had been applied, observing that the meaning of reasonableness "necessarily varies in the different fields of the law." It then went on to conclude that:

> The aim and result of every price-fixing agreement, if effective, is the elimination of one form of competition. The power to fix prices, whether reasonably exercised or not, involves power to control the market and to fix arbitrary and unreasonable prices. The reasonable price fixed today may through economic and business changes become the unreasonable price of tomorrow. . . . Agreements which create such potential power may well be held to be in themselves unreasonable or unlawful restraints, without the necessity of minute inquiry whether a particular price is reasonable or unreasonable as fixed and without placing on the Government in enforcing the Sherman Law the burden of ascertaining from day to day whether it has become unreasonable through the mere variation of economic conditions.[9]

The Court's decision has been criticized for neglecting the constraints on the pottery makers' willingness to carry out the agreements they reached, and hence for failing to see that the defendants may well have lacked the very power it condemned.[10] The decision nevertheless represents a clear *per se* prohibition of explicit price-fixing conspiracies, whether carried into effect or not, and it is generally viewed as the basic precedent in price-fixing cases.

Still the courts, like other human organizations, do not always hew faithfully to the rules they have enunciated. A significant break from the *Trenton Potteries* precepts took place only six years later when the economy found itself in the trough of the Great Depression. An industry hit especially hard by the slump was coal mining. Prices of bituminous coal fell by 25 per cent from 1929 to 1933, while output was reduced by 38 per cent. More coal mining firms reported losses than profits. To cope with these conditions, 137

[7]85 Fed. 271, 293.
[8]175 U. S. 211, 235–238 (1899).
[9]*U. S.* v. *Trenton Potteries Co. et al.*, 273 U. S. 392, 396–398 (1927).
[10]See Phillips, *op. cit.*, pp. 171–176.

producers in the Appalachian Mountain region formed in 1931 a new company, Appalachian Coals, Inc., to serve as exclusive selling agent for member firms. Its members accounted for 12 per cent of all soft coal production east of the Mississippi River and 54 per cent of production in the Appalachian territory and immediately surrounding states. The agency was instructed to get the "best prices obtainable" for member output, and if all output could not be sold, to allocate orders among the member mines. In effect, it served as a kind of sales cartel, but with far from complete control over the relevant market. The government brought suit to dissolve the agency. A district court found Appalachian Coals in violation of Sherman Act Section 1, citing the *Trenton Potteries* decision as a precedent.[11] But on appeal the Supreme Court reversed the decision. Chief Justice Hughes, speaking for an eight member majority of the court, pointed to the "deplorable" economic condition of the industry; stated that the purpose of the Sherman Act was to prevent *undue* restraints of interstate commerce; and called for the judiciary to engage in "close and objective scrutiny of particular conditions and purposes . . . in each case" to determine whether or not defendants were merely adopting reasonable measures to protect commerce from injurious and destructive practices.[12] He concluded that Appalachian Coals would not be able to fix the price of coal in consuming markets because of competition from non-members, and that in any event, abuse-correcting measures which had the effect of stabilizing trade and making prices more reasonable were not necessarily an unreasonable restraint of trade. Hughes suggested further that the Appalachian Coals type of selling agency was clearly no worse than a full-blown consolidation of coal producers through merger, which was not likely to be declared illegal under prevailing antitrust law interpretations, and toward which the mines might be driven if not allowed to pursue the less drastic selling agency alternative. As a result, the injunction against Appala-

chian Coals was quashed. But since no concrete experience under the proposed scheme had been accumulated, the Supreme Court ordered the District Court to retain jurisdiction and to take remedial action if Appalachian's operations should in fact prove to impose an undue restraint upon interstate commerce. No review of the association's activities was actually made, since Congress subsequently authorized explicit price restoration measures in the National Industrial Recovery Act of 1933, the Bituminous Coal Conservation Act of 1935, and the Bituminous Coal Act of 1937.

The *Appalachian Coals* decision is widely regarded as an anomaly in antitrust law with no status as a precedent. After disillusion with cartelization as an anti-depression weapon set in during the mid-1930s and after President Roosevelt 'packed' the Supreme Court with five new and more liberal justices during the late 1930s, the Court returned to a clear *per se* rule against explicit price-fixing arrangements. The return came in another case covering depression-inspired pricing practices, this time in the gasoline industry. Independent refiners had been dumping gasoline in the Midwestern market at panic prices, demoralizing the whole price structure. During 1935 and 1936, some 12 to 18 major refining companies organized themselves into a committee and agreed to take surplus gasoline from the independents, disposing of it in a more orderly manner so as not to depress prices. Each major firm chose one or more independent 'dancing partners,' whose surplus it was to acquire. In a subsequent antitrust trial, the defendant firms admitted that their scheme contributed to a rise in prices, but argued that the surplus disposal program's influence on prices was minor compared to the effect of general economic recovery, and that the increase in prices was reasonable in view of the excessively low levels to which prices had fallen during the depression. They were found guilty by a jury, and after review by an appellate court, the Supreme Court on appeal sustained the jury's

[11] *U. S.* v. *Appalachian Coals, Inc., et al.*, 1 F. Supp. 339 (1932).
[12] 288 U. S. 344, 359–360 (1933).

verdict with respect to 12 corporate defendants. Following an unconvincing attempt to rationalize its *Appalachian Coals* opinion, the Court said that:

> . . . for over forty years this Court has consistently and without deviation adhered to the principle that price-fixing agreements are unlawful *per se* under the Sherman Act and that no showing of so-called competitive abuses or evils which those agreements were designed to eliminate or alleviate may be interpreted as a defense. . . . If the so-called competitive abuses were to be appraised here, the reasonableness of prices would necessarily become an issue in every price-fixing case. In that event the Sherman Act would soon be emasculated; its philosophy would be supplanted by one which is wholly alien to a system of free competition; it would not be the charter of freedom which its framers intended. . . . Any combination which tampers with price structures is engaged in an unlawful activity . . . . Congress . . . has not permitted the age-old cry of ruinous competition and competitive evils to be a defense to price-fixing conspiracies.[13]

Ever since 1940, the Supreme Court's blanket condemnation in the gasoline case of all combinations which tamper with price structures has been followed consistently. Included under the *per se* prohibition have been not only express price-fixing agreements, but also conspiracies with a more subtle impact on price, such as agreements to restrict output, to divide up the market into exclusive spheres of influence, to allocate customers by seller, to follow standardized pricing formulas or methods, and to boycott or exclude from the market firms which refuse to abide by industry-pricing norms.[14] The courts have also gone far toward declaring illegal all bilateral or multilateral patent licensing agreements with provisions governing prices to be

charged, markets to be served, and outputs to be produced by parties to the agreement.[15] However, under present interpretations the owner of a valid patent may legitimately include restrictions with respect to price, output, and markets served in the licenses it *unilaterally* grants to other firms. This doctrine has come under sharp attack in recent years, and there is a chance that in the future the Supreme Court will adopt a harder line.[16]

Despite the acceptance of *per se* rules against explicit price-fixing, there remain certain grey areas in which a rule of reason has been applied. We will explore two of the main exceptions a few pages hence. Here one other borderline case deserves brief mention. In 1918, the Supreme Court found that the Chicago Board of Trade was not violating the Sherman Act when it passed a rule requiring that members buy or sell grain when the exchange was not in session (e.g., at night) only at the closing price of the last previous session. The rule clearly affected and in a sense fixed prices. But the Court found it not inconsistent with the Sherman Act, arguing that:

> . . . the legality of an agreement or regulation cannot be determined by so simple a test as whether it restrains competition. Every agreement concerning trade, every regulation of trade, restrains. To bind, to restrain, is of their very essence. The true test of legality is whether the restraint imposed is such as merely regulates and perhaps thereby promotes competition, or whether it is such as may suppress or even destroy competition. To determine that question the Court must ordinarily consider the facts peculiar to the business to which the restraint is applied; . . . the nature of the restraint, and its effect, actual or probable.[17]

Since the Supreme Court in later decisions has shown no disposition to disavow its *Board of*

---

[13] *U. S.* v. *Socony-Vacuum Oil Co. et al.*, 310 U. S. 150, 218–221 (1940).

[14] For an admirable survey of the cases, see A. D. Neale, *The Antitrust Laws of the United States of America* (Cambridge: Cambridge University Press, 1966), pp. 65–80.

[15] *Ibid.*, pp. 261–286.

[16] The governing decision is *U. S.* v. *General Electric Co.*, 272 U. S. 476 (1926). Two attempts to overturn the doctrine were frustrated by 4-4 divisions of opinion among the participating Supreme Court justices. *U. S.* v. *Line Material Co. et al.*, 333 U. S. 287, 315 (1948); and *U. S.* v. *Huck Mfg. Co. et al.*, 382 U. S. 197 (1965).

[17] *Board of Trade of the City of Chicago* v. *U. S.*, 246 U. S. 231, 238 (1918).

Trade opinion, the Court is evidently willing to apply a rule of reason in borderline cases, where it is not obvious whether an agreement merely establishes conditions conducive to competitive trading or whether it actually suppresses competition. The practices prohibited *per se* under existing law are those which fall clearly beyond this line, having the suppression of competition as one of their main purposes.

REMEDIES AND PENALTIES IN PRICE-FIXING CASES

Under the Sherman Act the Justice Department possesses two weapons for attacking price-fixing violations. It can institute a civil suit (e.g., a suit in equity), the end result of which may be a court injunction against illegal practices; or it can seek a criminal indictment leading to punitive fines and/or prison sentences. Because the legal proscriptions against express price-fixing agreements are so clear, and because businessmen engaging in price-fixing cannot help but know they are violating the law, the Justice Department has tended to apply criminal rather than civil sanctions against pricing conspiracies. It may also proceed in tandem, prosecuting a criminal action for punitive purposes and a civil action to secure an injunctive remedy. Between 1956 and 1965, an average of 25 criminal cases per year were initiated against alleged Sherman Act violations, nearly all involving price-fixing and related restrictive practices prohibited under Section 1.[18]

Until 1955, the maximum fine assessable for Sherman Act violations was $5,000 per count. This was so low that it was often more profitable to violate the law and risk being caught than to refrain from violations, although of course, legal costs of presenting a defense and the odium of criminal conviction constituted an additional deterrent. In 1955 Congress raised the maximum fine to $50,000 per count, but the courts have been reluctant to take full advantage of this upper limit. Between 1955 and 1965, the average fine levied on corporations for Sherman Act violations was $12,800.[19] In major cases it is also possible to magnify the bite by imposing fines on multiple counts and by fining not only the guilty corporations, but also executives participating in the conspiracy. A leading example was the criminal case against cigarette manufacturers settled in 1946, before the increase in maximum fines.[20] Three defendant corporations, a subsidiary corporation, and 13 executives were all found guilty on three counts (conspiracy to restrain trade, monopolization, and conspiracy to monopolize) and were fined $5,000 per count, yielding a total fine of $255,000. It is worth noting that neither individual nor corporate fines are tax deductible, nor are legal expenses incurred while defending oneself in a criminal antitrust case ending in conviction. Still the threat of such penalties has obviously been insufficient to deter many violations, as the continuing stream of convictions demonstrates.

A more potent deterrent may be the imposition of prison sentences. This approach was used infrequently at first. Between 1890 and 1940, jail sentences were imposed in only 24 cases, 13 involving trade union leaders and 11 businessmen. All the businessmen imprisoned during this period had perpetrated acts of racketeering accompanied by overt threats, intimidation, and violence.[21] Only since the late 1950s have businessmen been incarcerated for simple price-fixing—most spectacularly in the 1960–1961 electrical equipment conspiracy case, which saw seven executives given 30 day sentences and 24 others suspended sentences.[22] This practice may become more common, for a Justice Department official announced in 1966 that jail sentences would be the Antitrust Division's "normal re-

---

[18]Cf. James M. Clabault and John F. Burton, Jr., *Sherman Act Indictments, 1955–1965* (New York: Federal Legal Publications, 1966), p. 91.

[19]*Ibid.*, p. 104.

[20]*American Tobacco Co. et al.* v. *U. S.*, 328 U. S. 781 (1946).

[21]Cf. Clabault and Burton, *op. cit.*, p. 11, note 18.

[22]*U. S.* v. *Westinghouse Electric Corp. et al.*, CCH 1960 Trade Cases, para. 69,699.

quest . . . at least in the more flagrant cases."[23] Whether this policy will have the anticipated "whopping deterrent" effect remains to be seen.

Another recent development may have an even more potent impact. Sherman Act Section 7 permits persons injured by antitrust law violations to sue for the recovery of three times the amount of damages sustained, and Clayton Act Section 5 permits treble damage plaintiffs to draw upon prior antitrust judgments resulting from government-initiated cases in proving that a violation has occurred. However, these provisions were used infrequently and without much success until after World War II. Then a series of favorable Supreme Court decisions simplified the problems of obtaining evidence and proving damages, and the number of treble damage suits rose sharply. Payments resulting from 1,880 treble damage suits based upon the electrical equipment conspiracy convictions of 1960 have been estimated at between \$400 and \$600 million.[24] The tendency for the courts to view treble damage suits kindly and the ensuing rush of private litigants to take advantage are such new phenomena that their full effect on business behavior remains unclear. Certainly, the stakes of the antitrust game have been raised substantially, and business firms are likely to become more scrupulous in abiding by the law. This is no doubt a good thing, at least insofar as Sherman Act Section 1 is concerned. However, treble damage suits have also proliferated in connection with alleged violations of other antitrust laws, and the effect in some such cases (especially in price discrimination and monopolization cases) may be to encourage generally more conservative, less aggressive business behavior. To prevent this, some students of antitrust law have recommended that the courts be permitted to award only single damages in grey area cases.[25] There is a pressing need for further research on the scope and consequences of increasingly widespread treble damage litigation.

ANTITRUST ABROAD: A CONTRAST

The *per se* prohibition of price-fixing and related agreements in the United States stands in sharp contrast to the situation overseas. While the *per se* rule was emerging in America during the early part of the 20th century, most European nations had no statutory antitrust laws at all, and cartels flourished. The few laws which did exist related only to abuses of individual or collective market power, and they were seldom enforced. After World War II, there was an international antitrust legislation boom. Now nearly every industrialized Western nation (and many a developing nation) has some kind of antitrust law.[26] None, however, adopts what can strictly be called a *per se* rule against price-fixing conspiracies; all embrace a rule of reason tolerating pricing agreements within more or less narrowly circumscribed boundaries.

Examining the approach adopted toward antitrust abroad puts the U. S. laws in perspective and brings out more clearly the underlying philosophy, advantages, and drawbacks of the American system. No nation's laws are completely typical, and a superficial survey of all would be of little value. We shall therefore focus mainly on the British system, which represents one of the tougher, more thoroughgoing codes adopted by a Western nation thus far. The laws

---

[23]Statement of Assistant Attorney General Donald F. Turner, quoted in "Justice Toughens Line on Price Agreements," *Business Week*, October 15, 1966, p. 43.

[24]See "Climbing Toll for the Price-Fixers," *Business Week*, August 29, 1964, pp. 96–102; and "Gadflies Who Put the Bite on Business," *Business Week*, October 14, 1967, pp. 124–130. Exact data on damages are not available, since most of the suits were settled quietly out of court.

[25]U. S. Department of Justice, *Report of the Attorney General's National Committee To Study the Antitrust Laws* (Washington: 1955), pp. 378–385.

[26]An excellent survey and comparison of the laws in 17 nations can be found in two books by Corwin D. Edwards, *Trade Regulation Overseas* (Dobbs Ferry: Oceana, 1966); and *Control of Cartels and Monopolies: An International Comparison* (Dobbs Ferry: Oceana, 1967). A useful continuously-updated loose-leaf compendium is the Organisation for Economic Co-operation and Development's six-volume set, *Guide to Legislation on Restrictive Business Practices in Europe and North America* (Second ed.; Paris: 1962). Surveys and interpretive articles which sweep more widely are found in the Senate Committee on the Judiciary, Subcommittee on Antitrust and Monopoly, hearings, *Antitrust Developments in the European Common Market*, Part I (Washington: 1963), pp. 126–146; and *Economic Concentration*, Parts 7 and 7A (Washington: 1968 and 1969).

of several other leading nations will then be summarized much more briefly to indicate the range of approaches taken.

Prior to World War II, the British had no significant statutory law concerning price-fixing arrangements and cartels. The applicable rules were those of common law, which in the *laissez faire* spirit of the 19th century had gradually given increasing weight to the principle of free contract, permitting businessmen to enter freely into contracts with one another, including those contracts and agreements which restricted competition. In emphasizing this right, the courts implicitly sacrificed another: the right of individual citizens to enjoy the benefits of free and unrestricted competition. Recognizing the antisocial potentialities of restrictive agreements, the British courts refused to provide positive support by enforcing such contracts against parties who breached them. But they also would not intervene to overturn restrictive agreements or to award damages to an injured third party unless some explicitly unlawful act of violence, intimidation, molestation, or fraud was perpetrated in connection with the restriction.[27] It was on this question of balancing producers' rights against the rights of consumers that the U. S. Congress chose a quite different path when it passed the Sherman Act.

Reconciliation of the British and American philosophies toward restrictive business practices did not begin in earnest until 1956, when Parliament approved the Restrictive Trade Practices Act.[28] The act required all agreements in restraint of trade among competing firms to be registered with a Registrar of Restrictive Practices; it authorized the Registrar to challenge any agreements which appear contrary to the public interest; and it established a special Restrictive Practices Court, with streamlined procedures and a membership including both judges and laymen, to determine whether challenged agreements should in fact be prohibited.[29] Parties to a challenged agreement bear the burden of proving to the Court that their agreement provides positive benefits covered under one or more of seven "gateways," and of showing in addition that the benefits from the agreement outweigh the harm. The gateways include such defenses as the following: that the agreement is necessary to protect the public against injury; that it is necessary to counteract measures taken by competitors not party to the agreement; that it is necessary to negotiate fair prices with powerful suppliers; that it is necessary to sustain the level of export earnings; that its removal would have serious and persistent adverse effects on local employment and unemployment; and that its removal would deny the public substantial benefits or advantages. This is clearly a rule of reason approach; the Restrictive Practices Court has broad discretion to determine whether or not an agreement is, on balance, socially desirable or undesirable.

Despite the breadth of certain gateways and legal traditions far from hostile to cooperation among businessmen, the Restrictive Practices Court demonstrated its willingness to adopt a hard line. By the end of 1964, more than 2,400 agreements had been registered and 32 cases had been contested before the Court. Of these 32, only nine led to decisions in favor of the defendants; the other 23 agreements had to be discontinued or substantially revamped. In more than 75 other cases the Court rendered uncontested decisions, typically against the restrictions in question. In its very first contested price-fixing case, the Court accepted as a valid defense the contention of the British Cotton Yarn-Spinners Association that theirs was a declining industry and that painful pockets of localized unemployment would develop if their pricing scheme were

---

[27]A key decision was *Mogul Steamship Co.* v. *McGregor, Gow, and Co.*, 21 Q.B.D. 544 (1888), 23 Q.B.D. 598 (1889).

[28]An extensive literature on the Act and its interpretation has developed. Especially valuable surveys include R. S. Stevens and B. S. Yamey, *The Restrictive Practices Court* (London: Weidenfeld, 1965); the Symposium on Restrictive Practices in *Oxford Economic Papers*, November 1965; and R. C. Bernhard, "The Law and Economics of Market Collusion in Europe, Great Britain, and the United States," *Journal of Industrial Economics*, April 1966, pp. 104–116.

[29]In 1967, an amendment was proposed which would make it unlawful to effect a restrictive agreement unless it is specifically authorized by the Court. Up to then, practices could not be enjoined until the Court had ruled against them.

rejected. But the Court held that the benefits of the agreement were outweighed by the harm— notably, the retention of inefficient and unnecessary capacity in the industry.[30] This ringing (and to most observers unexpected) declaration of faith in competitive market processes, supplemented by hard-line decisions in several subsequent cases, led to the voluntary abandonment of more than a thousand restrictive agreements by other industrial and commercial groups.

Nevertheless, in at least a few cases the Restrictive Practices Court has been willing to accept price-fixing arrangements as reasonable. These decisions are of special interest because they show how far the Court can go in applying the rule of reason. They therefore provide a valuable contrast to the American scene. The first involved a bidding cartel among six steam boiler manufacturers, with facts similar to the *Addyston Pipe & Steel* case of U. S. fame.[31] Overhead costs were high; demand was cyclical; orders often came in substantial chunks; and a single customer (the government's Electricity Generating Board) placed 83 per cent of all domestic orders. One attempted defense, pleading that price-fixing was necessary to maintain industry capacity and support research and development during recessions, was rejected by the Court after an analysis of the facts. Another, emphasizing the necessity of creating countervailing power to deal with the monopsonistic Electricity Generating Board, was struck down on a technicality, although there is reason to believe it influenced the Court's ultimate decision. The Court's approval was formally premised on its acceptance of a defense argument

that cooperation was required in order to compete more effectively in export markets. The decision, applying to both domestic and overseas transactions, is consistent with the approach of the U. S. Webb-Pomerene Act toward export cartels, except that American law prohibits extension of a cartel's influence to the domestic market.

Price-fixing by nut and bolt manufacturers was approved in order to save small-lot purchasers the trouble of shopping around, after a finding that the prices fixed were reasonable.[32] A cement industry agreement was authorized when the Court found that the industry was charging reasonable prices and that it would be able to attract capital at lower costs (and hence charge lower prices) if the uncertainties created by substantial cyclical fluctuations in an environment of high overhead costs were ameliorated through collusion.[33] It is worth noting that the American cement industry, advancing similar arguments in defense of less extensive collusive arrangements, was found to be violating the U. S. antitrust laws.[34] An agreement among magnet manufacturers was endorsed when the Court found that desirable cooperation in research and development would be inhibited unless the firms could also cooperate in pricing.[35] A purchasing cartel among sulphuric acid producers was approved in order to countervail the power of the American sulphur export cartel.[36] Price-fixing by ceramic tile makers was sanctioned to enforce standardization of tile sizes, allowing alleged economies in production.[37] And as one last example, an agreement among steel manufacturers and scrap dealers stabilizing scrap prices was

---

[30]*In re Yarn Spinners' Agreement*, L.R., 1 R.P. 118 (1959). Shortly after the decision, the Conservative government passed a law providing compensation for yarn spinning firms required to close down plants because of price competition.

[31]*In re Water-Tube Boilermakers' Agreement*, L.R., 1 R.P. 285 (1959).

[32]*In re Black Bolt and Nut Association's Agreement*, L.R., 2 R.P. 50 (1960).

[33]*In re Cement Makers' Federation Agreement*, L R , 2 R.P. 241 (1961). For a penetrating criticism, see A. Sutherland, "Economics in the Restrictive Practices Court," *Oxford Economic Papers*, November 1965, pp. 386–398.

[34]*Federal Trade Commission* v. *Cement Institute et al.*, 333 U. S. 683 (1948).

[35]*In re Permanent Magnet Association's Agreement*, L.R., 3 R.P. 119 and 392 (1962).

[36]*In re National Sulphuric Acid Association's Agreement*, L.R., 4 R.P. 169 (1963).

[37]*In re Glazed and Floor Tile Home Trade Association's Agreement*, L.R., 4 R.P. 239 (1963).

authorized because of its presumed effect in reducing the price of finished steel.[38]

Several of the price-fixing agreements approved by the British Restrictive Practices Court would never have survived an American antitrust challenge. Whether these few decisions are sufficient to impart a quite different complexion to British antitrust is difficult to say, given the relatively short history of the British system. Some of the Court's permissive decisions have been sharply criticized for defective economic reasoning, and one commentator has argued that the benefits claimed were dubious at best, so that a *per se* prohibition against all price-fixing arrangements would have caused no serious social losses while saving substantial legal costs.[39] The Court's procedures, too, have been criticized as inefficient, slow and unnecessarily expensive; with too much duplication of testimony, failure to define issues clearly, and boring cross-examination.[40] Still the British have tried harder than most nations to implement an ambitious pro-competitive policy without shutting the door on those restrictions which might conceivably yield net social benefits. And the special adjudication procedures devised to deal with restrictive practices, making it possible to record all the evidence and arguments for a case in from six to 35 hearing days, are clearly more efficient than the comparable U. S. procedures.

We turn now much more briefly to the laws in several other jurisdictions. In Canada, the most recent amendment to its 1889 antitrust code prescribes criminal penalties, among other things, for any one "who conspires, agrees, or arranges with another person . . . to prevent, limit, or lessen, unduly, the manufacture or production of an article, or to enhance unreasonably the price thereof." The words "unduly"

and "unreasonably" suggest a rule of reason approach, but in several leading court cases "unduly" has been interpreted as referring to the manner or degree in which competition is prevented, rather than to the specific consequences of the agreement. The courts have held that the public has a vested interest in the maintenance of competition, and that every agreement which "materially interferes with competition in a substantial sector of trade" is detrimental to the public interest, without proof of actual injury being required.[41] This approaches a *per se* prohibition. However, Canada's enforcement program has probably been insufficiently aggressive to realize the full potential of these stringent interpretations.

The principal German antitrust statute, passed in 1957, generally outlaws price-fixing agreements but permits exceptions to ease the adjustment problems of secularly stagnating industries; to reduce costs through joint research and development, marketing, or production specialization arrangements; to promote exports or facilitate imports; and to cope with "exceptional circumstances" in the general economic situation. Up to 1965 the law was administered and interpreted strictly, though there is considerable sentiment in favor of recession cartels, and the "exceptional circumstances" loophole may be invoked with increasing frequency as the German economy readjusts after emerging from its long reconstruction boom. Enforcement has been hampered to some extent by divisions of opinion at high governmental levels about the efficacy of antitrust, leading to such curiosities as locating the Cartel Office, the principal enforcement agency, in West Berlin, and then tightly limiting its travel budget.

Japan's postwar antitrust laws provide broad exemptions from price-fixing prohibitions for

[38]*In re British Iron and Steel Federation and National Federation of Scrap Iron, Steel, and Metal Merchants' Agreement*, L.R., 4 R.P. 299 (1963).

[39]See Sutherland, *op. cit.*; and J. P. Cairns, "Benefits from Restrictive Agreements: The British Experience," *Canadian Journal of Economics and Political Science*, May 1964, pp. 228–240.

[40]See I. A. MacDonald, "The Restrictive Practices Court: A Lawyer's View," *Oxford Economic Papers*, November 1965, pp. 372–375.

[41]Organisation for Economic Co-operation and Development, *Guide to Legislation on Restrictive Business Practices in Europe and North America*, Canada, "Explanatory Notes on the Legislation," pp. 2–3, and the selection of court decision excerpts in Section 3.0.

small business, "rationalization," depression and export-import cartels, among others. The exemption provisions have been applied liberally, and during the mild recession of 1964–1965, dozens of cartel arrangements were approved by the Fair Trade Commission.

France had a law curbing price-fixing and other restrictive practices as early as 1791, but it was undermined by 19th century pro-cartel legislation. Statutes enacted following World War II prohibit agreements, express or tacit, which encourage the artificial increase of prices. Exemptions are allowed when producers can show that gains in efficiency or technical progress will be achieved as a by-product. Up to the present there has been little zeal in governmental circles for systematic promotion of competitive market processes. Enforcement, carried out in an atmosphere of secrecy by a commission whose membership includes businessmen and bankers, has been lackadaisical.

In many other Western European nations such as Austria, Belgium, Denmark, Sweden, Norway, and Switzerland, cartel arrangements are generally permitted if duly registered with a designated public agency, which is authorized to intervene mainly to prevent abuses.

As a final stop on this Cook's tour of antitrust laws abroad, we consider two codes which span national boundaries. The first is the treaty of the European Coal and Steel Community, adopted in 1951, which under Article 65 prohibits restrictive practices which distort the normal operation of competition. In fact, however, the High Authority of the ECSC has seldom considered competitive conditions in the Community 'normal,' and it has therefore stepped in frequently to set minimum and maximum prices, to assign output quotas for individual firms, and to restrict the free play of competition in a variety of other ways, making private price-fixing schemes somewhat redundant. In addition, the High Authority has been liberal in approving cartel

agreements among firms within particular member nations and general pricing systems (such as the basing point system) which facilitate tacit collusion.[42] As a result, it can hardly be said that there has been a concerted effort in the Coal and Steel Community to adopt a regime of unfettered competition.

The 1957 Treaty of Rome establishing the European Economic Community prohibits, in Section 1 of Article 85, all inter-firm agreements which have the effect of preventing, restraining, or distorting competition within the Common Market, including those agreements which fix prices or restrict output. It then establishes an escape clause in Section 3 of the same article, making it possible to attempt agreements which contribute toward improving the production or distribution of goods or promoting technical or economic progress, while reserving to users a fair share of the resulting profit. This appears to be a rule of reason, although it is not yet clear how strictly it will be interpreted. In 1967, the EEC Commission was buried under an avalanche of paper registering some 38,000 restrictive agreements, including at least several hundred horizontal cartels. Many other cartels have apparently not bothered to register with the Commission, preferring to take a chance on quietly ignoring the law. The Commission had dug its way out far enough to contest only a very few horizontal price-fixing schemes, placing more emphasis on attacking exclusive dealing contracts and other vertical restrictions.[43] Since member nation sentiment is far from unanimously disposed toward a strong antitrust policy, it seems probable that Article 85-3 will eventually be construed as a fairly permissive rule of reason.

THE *PER SE* VS. RULE OF REASON QUESTION REVISITED

We find then that the United States stands virtually alone in applying a *per se* prohibition

---

[42]See Corwin D. Edwards, *Cartelization in Western Europe* (Washington: U. S. Department of State, 1964), pp. 61–82; and Leo Spier, "Restrictive Business Practices and Competition in the European Economic Community," *California Law Review*, December 1965, pp. 1347–1348 and 1356–1358.

[43]On the early record, see Grant W. Kelleher, "The Common Market Antitrust Laws: The First Ten Years," *Antitrust Bulletin*, Winter 1967, pp. 1219–1252. In July of 1969 the first fines for price-fixing violations were levied, against members of quinine and aniline dyestuff cartels. In each case the fines amounted to roughly a half million dollars.

against price-fixing and related restraints of trade. Being a minority of one is always unsettling. Has the U. S. made the best policy choice, or are there superior alternatives?

Given the complexity of the links between market structure, conduct, and performance, it seems almost certain that there are at least some market conditions under which agreements to fix "reasonable" prices will permit better economic performance than unfettered competition. Leading candidates include high overhead cost industries subjected to severe random or cyclical business fluctuations, and industries which would be unable to cooperate in desirable cost-saving programs without some mitigation of price competition. The key question is not whether such cases exist, but how frequently they occur and whether the social benefits attainable through a policy which seeks to allow price-fixing only in those cases exceed the social costs of the policy. Obviously, we have no good quantitative estimates of either benefits or costs; we must resort to rough intuitive judgments. My personal assessment, based on analysis of experience in traditional 'cut-throat competition' industries such as railroading before 1887, cement manufacturing, soft coal mining, and electrical equipment manufacturing, is that the social gains from permitting restrictive agreements on a selective basis would be quite modest. Or to put the point negatively, sharp price competition does not seem to have impaired performance seriously in those industries, and the chief rationale for assertions to the contrary appears to be the natural propensity for those whose oxen are gored to raise the loudest, most persuasive possible cries of distress. It is also doubtful whether the gains from full-blown "rationalization" cartels would be great, for most opportunities to standardize products, pool production or marketing facilities, and cooperate in research and development which would yield high social benefits are sufficiently attractive to appear worth doing even without attendant price-fixing agreements.

Let us nevertheless grant for the sake of argument that the benefits of a selective restriction policy would be finite and positive. If the rule of reason approach required to implement this policy were itself costless, it should be adopted. But it is not costless. There are definite costs in the form of added uncertainty, more complex adjudication, and an enhanced probability of irrational and erroneous choices.

A relatively unimportant cost would be the increased uncertainty businessmen would face as to which agreements are illegal. At least in borderline areas, it would be impossible to proceed with confidence until the enforcement agencies or judiciary had rendered an opinion. This is not a serious problem, however, for companies could always avoid legal uncertainty by refraining from brinkmanship. In so doing, they would be no worse off than under a *per se* rule prohibiting all price-fixing agreements.

Much more impressive would be the costs of adjudicating and enforcing the rule of reason, for each case would become, in the jargon of the antitrust law firms and economic consultants who are its principal financial beneficiaries, 'the big case.' Even with relatively simple *per se* rules, elaborate proceedings are often needed merely to establish whether or not the prohibited act was perpetrated. A rule of reason case would surely have to go further, examining economic and social variables affecting the agreement in question and perhaps analyzing both past industry performance and projecting future trends to reach a balanced judgment on the agreement's reasonableness. A thorough investigation of this sort conducted under traditional antitrust procedures would be so costly that the enforcement agencies would find the number of cases they could initiate sharply limited, unless substantial budget increases were approved by a heretofore reluctant Congress. As Professor Mason has argued, "The demand for a full investigation of the consequences of a market situation or a course of business conduct is a demand for non-enforcement of the antitrust laws."[44]

---

[44]Edward S. Mason, *Economic Concentration and the Monopoly Problem* (Cambridge: Harvard University Press, 1957), p. 398. He goes on to concede that many rule of reason cases might not have to be quite so thorough.

If approval of price-fixing arrangements were made contingent upon the reasonableness of the prices fixed, the antitrust agencies would run squarely into the dilemma perceived by the Supreme Court in its *Trenton Potteries* opinion: "The reasonable price fixed today may through economic and business changes become the unreasonable price of tomorrow."[45] To place upon the enforcement agencies and courts "the burden of ascertaining from day to day whether (the price) has become unreasonable through the mere variation of economic conditions"[46] would be exorbitantly costly, and it might well break the back of an already bowed and groaning camel.

Yet these problems are in part only symptoms of a more fundamental deficiency: the inherent unsuitability of the U. S. judicial process for making balanced judgments on issues as technical and complex as the reasonableness of a price-fixing scheme. This is in turn the consequence of several specific peculiarities and flaws. First, the rules of evidence applied in antitrust cases are cumbersome in the extreme. Nearly every document submitted in evidence and every statement by witnesses is challenged by opposing counsel, and some of the material most relevant to a sensible decision—e.g., statistical analyses of pricing behavior—may not even be admissible. Second, jurists are seldom well-trained in economics, and many lack the knowledge to separate sense from nonsense in the contending parties' briefs or to get a firm analytic handle on the conduct and performance variables at issue. The brightest judges do amazingly well, but the middle ranks turn in performances which could merit no more than a low C on an undergraduate theory examination. Third, the whole adversary process on which the courts operate was designed and is best suited for reaching 'either-or' decisions: Is the defendant guilty, or not? It is much less effective in ascertaining, say, how much competition is optimal out of a continuous spectrum of possibilities.[47] Nor is it well suited for weighing many conflicting considerations to

reach a decision that, on balance, it appears that X best serves the public interest. Indeed, the facts and arguments in antitrust cases are often so complex that they swamp a judge's ability to comprehend and integrate them logically. He may then arrive at his decision on the basis of raw instinct, working backward from that point to develop a line of reasoning which, however strained, supports the predetermined conclusion. It is for this reason, Professor Bok suggests, that one frequently finds antitrust decisions which hold *all* the arguments in a case to support the conclusion taken, though industrial conduct problems are seldom that simple.[48] Decisions reached in this manner by overtaxed jurists will almost surely be erroneous a significant fraction of the time. And those decisions which approve a restrictive agreement when it is, if an accurate balance were to be struck, socially undesirable, constitute an additional cost of the rule of reason approach.

Difficult though the task may be, costs and benefits must be assessed in formulating rational public policies. My opinion, shared by a majority of American economists concerned with antitrust policy, is that in the present legal framework the costs of implementing a rule of reason would exceed the benefits derived from considering each restrictive agreement on its merits and prohibiting only those which appear unreasonable.

Nevertheless, the art of policy design calls for more than merely comparing well-known possibilities in the context of existing institutions. It is equally important to try inventing new, dominant alternatives. Three main alternatives to the conventional rule of reason–*per se* rule dichotomy can be identified.

For one, Almarin Phillips has proposed that the antitrust authorities concern themselves not with whether prices are fixed at reasonable levels —the approach rejected in *Trenton Potteries*, *Socony-Vacuum*, and other decisions—but with whether the organizational characteristics of an

---

[45]273 U. S. 392, 397 (1927).
[46]*Ibid.*, p. 398.
[47]For a superb discussion of this problem, see Derek C. Bok, "Section 7 of the Clayton Act and the Merging of Law and Economics," *Harvard Law Review*, December 1960, pp. 291–299.
[48]*Ibid.*, p. 270.

industry are such that price-fixing would improve economic performance.[49] This approach would require the courts to examine industry structure and conduct, as they relate to performance, but not to exercise continuing surveillance over prices charged and profits realized. On purely logical grounds the Phillips proposal is appealing. But it would demand far more economic sophistication from jurists than the traditional rule of reason, for they would be required to predict the efficacy of performance from observed structural and conduct variables. Even if the theoretical knowledge required to specify all relevant structure – conduct – performance links were available—and it is clear we have not yet reached that utopian state—it is doubtful whether the judiciary, as presently constituted, could display the requisite skill in applying those tools.

A second proposal is credited to Professor S. Chesterfield Oppenheim. He has suggested that instead of holding price-fixing agreements *per se* illegal, they be considered *prima facie* illegal. In order to escape injunction, price-fixers would then bear the burden of proving that their agreements do not constitute an unreasonable restraint of trade. [50] This approach has the merit of forcing the parties with the closest knowledge of internal industry workings to carry forward most of the positive economic analysis. If there is information which might vindicate their conduct, the members of an industry are in a position to. supply it. Conversely, it is much more difficult for a government enforcement agency to obtain evidence needed to prove an agreement's unreasonableness. Yet despite its advantages from an enforcement standpoint, a *prima facie* rule does not solve the problem of continuing surveillance, nor does it overcome the judiciary's inability to deal analytically with the evidence, once it has been assembled.

A third alternative, which could be integrated with either the Phillips or Oppenheim proposals,

is to reform the judicial system, perhaps along lines similar to the British Restrictive Practices Court. A special antitrust court would be established with streamlined procedures, rules of evidence suitable to economic investigations, and a membership which includes judges competent in economics, qualified laymen, or both. The procedures would be designed to get to the heart of the economic issues without tedious quibbling over the admissibility of evidence, argumentative and evidentiary shotgun blasts aimed at covering all conceivable allegations and defenses, etc. One approach, suggested by N. H. Leyland as a means of expediting British restrictive practices cases, would be to have a panel of experts representing the contending parties prepare a common document which defines the issues, advances and criticizes the arguments and counterarguments, and analyzes relevant factual and statistical evidence, going as far as possible toward the point where an intelligent decision on the disputed matters can be rendered.[51] Even without this last feature, impressive gains in adjudicative efficiency might be achieved by streamlining procedures. As an admittedly extreme example, the trial record in the Federal Trade Commission case charging illegal price-fixing by cement manufacturers required three years of hearings to compile and ran to some 49,000 pages of testimony plus 50,000 pages of exhibits.[52] The case dragged on for 11 years between the filing of a complaint in 1937 and resolution by the Supreme Court in 1948. A similar case involving the British cement industry was dispatched after 16 days of hearings before the Restrictive Practices Court. The lag between initial complaint and final judgment was just three and one half years.[53]

To be sure, some sacrifices have to be accepted to reduce the cost of implementing a rule of reason. As noted earlier, it is apparent from the record of the British Restrictive Practices Court that cold economic logic does not always carry

[49]*Market Structure, Organization and Performance*, pp. 235–240.

[50]S. Chesterfield Oppenheim, "Federal Antitrust Legislation: Guideposts to a Revised National Antitrust Policy," *Michigan Law Review*, June 1952, pp. 1158–1161.

[51]N. H. Leyland, "Competition in the Court," *Oxford Economic Papers*, November 1965, p. 465.

[52]*Federal Trade Commission* v. *Cement Institute et al.*, 333 U. S. 683, 687 (1948).

[53]*In re Cement Makers' Federation Agreement*, L.R., 2 R.P. 241 (1961).

the day. But the incidence of mistakes is probably not any higher than it would be under more thorough yet cumbersome (and hence confusing) procedures. More important, the British Restrictive Practices procedures sacrifice certain safeguards by abandoning traditional rules of evidence and by placing strict limits on what can be appealed to higher courts. To make the system work efficiently, a substantial amount of discretion is allowed the court of primary jurisdiction. A rule of men is to some extent substituted for the more plodding rule of laws. It is here that U. S. traditions depart most strongly from those dominating European antitrust.

The difference between nations is summarized perceptively by A. D. Neale, a British observer, in his treatise on American antitrust laws:

> One of the profoundest institutional differences between the two countries is the absence in the United States of anything corresponding to the amorphous but recognizable assemblage of public bodies and personages that we know in Britain as "the Establishment"; and this has much to do, both as cause and effect, with American distrust of authority *per se*. In general the possession of power by established authorities arouses a much lesser degree of anxiety or resentment in Britain, where the emphasis is much more on the use of power. Whereas American institutions often appear to be designed to hamper the exercise of power, ours are designed on the whole to facilitate it, though great importance is attached to protecting minorities against its abuse. . . . It is in line with the same general attitude to power that, if regulation is required, British opinion tends to be more open-minded than American about the choice between judicial enforcement of rules of law and some form of administrative supervision. . . . In the United States administrative decisions (the "government of men") tend to be unpopular as such, and the search is always for a "government of laws." In Britain the choice is more open.[54]

A similar but more complex historical view of the differences in antitrust attitudes on the European Continent is presented by Corwin Edwards:

> Whereas American political institutions were formulated after overthrowing colonial status, under the influence of a philosophy that distrusted concentrated governmental power, and in a setting affected by the individualism of the frontier, European political institutions have evolved gradually from origins of monarchy in the state and hierarchy in the church. . . . The European libertarian movements that expressed distrust of state power and sought to curtail state functions found their program in guarantees of freedom of contract and freedom of association. . . . But as the market economy developed, free association came to mean that businessmen were free to form cartels, and free contract came to include the right to make agreements by which the parties impaired free trade and free competition. Thus the programs that challenged the power of the state tended to strengthen rather than to challenge the power of cartels. It is understandable that as programs to curb cartels developed they tended to accept and rely upon a broad exercise of the regulatory power of the state as a major instrument of control. (These) inherited attitudes . . . have resulted in cartel laws which characteristically grant broad discretion to public officials to amend cartel practices in accord with their own views of the public interest.[55]

The reluctance of the American Congress to discard its cumbersome judicial approach to antitrust problems is undoubtedly the result of a more fundamental unwillingness to place great discretionary power in the hands of a few officials whose decisions are not controlled by rules of law and judicial review. And because the rule of law is cumbersome, a rule of reason approach to price-fixing cases shows up unfavorably in benefit/cost analyses. The policy debate between *per se* rules and the rule of reason turns, there-

---

[54] *The Antitrust Laws of the United States of America*, pp. 475–476.
[55] *Cartelization in Western Europe*, pp. 46–47.

fore, on important questions of political as well as economic philosophy. On such political issues the economist has no special license to prescribe the 'correct' public policy.

OLIGOPOLY PRICING AND THE CONSCIOUS PARALLELISM DOCTRINE

American law on express agreements to fix prices and restrict output is crystal clear: They are illegal *per se*. But what if no definite proof of meetings, discussions, and agreements can be established? What if there is in fact no explicit agreement among rivals in the strict sense of the word, but only an implicitly accepted policy of cooperating to avoid price competition?

Collusion without outright agreement is not very likely when market concentration is low, for sellers producing only a small fraction of a standardized item's total output have strong incentives to secure additional orders by undercutting the established price whenever that price significantly exceeds marginal cost. This must sooner or later pull prices down to the competitive level. The only effective way to eliminate such undercutting is to impose penalties upon price-cutters, and this is hardly possible without some kind of formal agreement. But in oligopoly the incentives are different. When the number of sellers is small, each firm recognizes that aggressive actions such as price-cutting will induce counteractions from rivals which, in the end, leave all members of the industry worse off. All may therefore exercise mutual restraint and prevent prices from falling to the competitive level. And they can do this independently, in the sense that each firm makes its own price and output decisions, without consulting the others in a smoke-filled room. Although product heterogeneity, financial pressures during a slump, opportunities for secret price-cutting, low entry barriers, and plain human cantankerousness may prevent oligopolists from playing the Chamberlinian joint profit maximization game with com-

plete success, it is clear that collusion without formal agreement is both feasible and tempting in many oligopolistically structured industries. Its status under the antitrust laws is therefore an important issue.

The relevant principle is the so-called *conscious parallelism* doctrine, whose implications are best discovered by analyzing the key decisions through which it evolved.[56] To keep what is a messy development in clearer perspective, it must be pointed out immediately that the doctrine has at various times been related to two rather different problems: first, with the behavioral problem of oligopolists acting independently but noncompetitively; and second, with the evidentiary problem of proving illegal collusion where only circumstantial evidence, and not hard direct evidence, can be offered.

In the earliest applicable cases, the emphasis was on evidentiary matters. One of the first involved a retail lumber dealers' trade association which published a list of wholesalers who sold at retail (and hence competed with members of the association).[57] Once the list was issued, many retail dealers ceased purchasing from those wholesalers. The Justice Department, charging the retailers with an illegal conspiracy, could produce no evidence of an explicit agreement to boycott the blacklisted wholesalers. Nevertheless, the Supreme Court upheld the charge, observing that:

> . . . [I]t is said that in order to show a combination or conspiracy within the Sherman Act some agreement must be shown under which the concerted action is taken. It is elementary, however, that conspiracies are seldom capable of proof by direct testimony and may be inferred from the things actually done, and when in this case, by concerted action the names of wholesalers . . . were periodically reported to the other members of the associations, the conspiracy to accomplish that which was the natural consequence of such action may be readily inferred.[58]

---

[56]For analyses of additional decisions, see Phillips, *op. cit.*, pp. 47–73; and Neale, *op. cit.*, pp. 81–94.
[57]*Eastern States Retail Lumber Dealers' Association* v. *U. S.*, 234 U. S. 600 (1914).
[58]234 U. S. 600, 612 (1914).

A reiteration and modest extension occurred in another boycott case 25 years later.[59] The manager of the Interstate Circuit and another motion picture exhibition chain with a large share of the Texas market wrote identical letters to eight motion picture distributors (e.g., Paramount, Metro-Goldwyn-Mayer, and RKO), each letter naming all eight distributors, and each demanding that the distributors not release their first-run films to theaters competing with Interstate which charged less than $.25 admission or which used the films in double features. Interstate's motive was obviously to reduce competition with its own theaters. The eight distributors could also benefit by realizing higher exhibition fees, as long as all eight adhered to the Interstate plan. After the letter was sent out, independent low-price exhibitors in fact found it impossible to secure first-run films, and many reacted by raising their prices to the $.25 minimum. When a district court ordered an end to the boycott, the defendants appealed to the Supreme Court, arguing *inter alia* that no evidence was found to show an agreement or conspiracy among the eight distributors. The Supreme Court rejected the appeal, noting the "singular unanimity of action on the part of the distributors" in carrying out the proposed restraint:

> It taxes credulity to believe that the several distributors would . . . have accepted and put into operation with substantial unanimity such far-reaching changes in their business methods without some understanding that all were to join, and we reject as beyond the range of probability that it was the result of mere chance.[60]

As proof of illegal conspiracy, the Court said,

> It was enough that, knowing that concerted action was contemplated and invited,

the distributors gave their adherence to the scheme and participated in it.[61]

Thus, the distributors (along with the two exhibition chains) were found to have violated Sherman Act Section 1 without proof of express agreement, and without even initiating the message which brought about their behavioral change. Yet it is important to see that in both this and the lumber dealers' case, there was an overt act (the publication of a blacklist or the receipt of a letter) to which the restraint of trade could be traced.

This requisite seemed to disappear in the 1946 *Tobacco* decision, which was said by one observer to constitute "a legal milestone in the social control of oligopoly" by "permitting the inference of illegal conspiracy from detailed similarity of behavior" and nothing more.[62] To recapitulate the well-known facts briefly, the Big Three of the cigarette industry—American Tobacco, Reynolds, and Liggett & Myers—for two decades exhibited a pattern of strikingly parallel pricing. Especially noteworthy were the prompt matching of Reynolds' price increase in June 1931, in the depths of the depression, when tobacco leaf prices and labor costs were falling; and the sharp, concerted price cuts effected 18 months later to recapture the ground gained by rivals after the 1931 action made it possible for 'ten cent' brands to sell at an attractive price differential. In addition, the Big Three brought pressure to bear on retailers to ensure that their products sold at the same price; they declined to participate in leaf tobacco auctions unless buyers from all three were present; they conducted their bidding so that all ended up paying the same price per pound; and each refrained from buying tobacco grades in which the others had a special interest. Although some suspicious incidents came to light,[63] the Justice Department was unable to

[59]*Interstate Circuit, Inc., et al.* v. *U. S.*, 306 U. S. 208 (1939).

[60]306 U. S. 208, 223 (1939).

[61]306 U. S. 208, 226 (1939).

[62]William H. Nicholls, "The Tobacco Case of 1946," *American Economic Review*, May 1949, p. 296. The Supreme Court decision is *American Tobacco Co. et al.* v. *U. S.*, 328 U. S. 781 (1946).

[63]Notably, the night before American Tobacco initiated a list price reduction in February of 1933, the A&P Company sent out a telegram to its 15,000 stores instructing them to reduce the price of *all* Big Three brands. A&P officials denied receiving advance notice of the price change, insisting that their action was based upon "trade rumors," but it seems more plausible that all members of the Big Three were aware in advance exactly when American would announce a price change, and that they communicated this to A&P.

present any concrete evidence of meetings, messages, or explicit agreements among members of the Big Three. The evidence was entirely circumstantial, centering on the parallelism in pricing and purchasing behavior. Nevertheless, a jury found the defendants guilty of price-fixing and other Sherman Act violations, and in reviewing the case, the Sixth Circuit Court of Appeals found the purely circumstantial evidence sufficient to sustain the criminal charges.[64] On appeal, the Supreme Court refused to review the Appellate Court's decision on the price-fixing count, thereby approving it implicitly. It also issued a more general pronouncement on the problem of proving guilt in Sherman Act conspiracy cases:

> No formal agreement is necessary to constitute an unlawful conspiracy. Often crimes are a matter of inference deduced from the acts of the person accused and done in pursuance of a criminal purpose.... The essential combination or conspiracy in violation of the Sherman Act may be found in a course of dealings or other circumstances as well as in an exchange of words....Where the circumstances are such as to warrant a jury in finding that the conspirators had a unity of purpose or a common design and understanding, or a meeting of minds in an unlawful arrangement, the conclusion that a conspiracy is established is justified.[65]

The *Tobacco* decision was viewed by many antitrust aficionados as a dramatic new precedent bringing, as Nicholls speculated, "wholly tacit, nonaggressive oligopoly fully within the reach of the conspiracy provisions of the Sherman Act."[66] From a more distant perspective, it appears that the courts were not going quite as far as Nicholls believed, but were only extending the possibilities of finding guilt on the basis of circumstantial evidence where there is good reason to believe that outright collusion occurred. It is likely also that the *Tobacco* decision implicitly applied a

rule of reason to oligopoly behavior: the firms were found guilty despite weak evidence because their conduct during the 1930s was so flagrantly anti-social.

Were the law against tacitly collusive oligopoly pricing to follow as strict a line as many persons saw in the *Tobacco* decision, a dilemma would arise. How should oligopolists change their behavior so as to avoid breaking the law? Must they begin ignoring their interdependence in pricing decisions, when to do so would be irrational? As Liggett & Myers attorneys asked rhetorically in their brief before the Court of Appeals, "Is everything the appellants do illegal, or evidence of illegality, if done by more than one of them?" When restraint in pricing is the natural consequence of high concentration, legal injunctions against such behavior are virtually impossible to enforce. To be effective, the remedy may have to deal with the basic cause—market structure—and not just with its behavioral symptoms. The dilemma is a real one, but we must leave it unresolved until we deal with other aspects of antitrust policy in the next chapter. It suffices here to note that after fines of $255,000 were levied upon the tobacco firms and their executives, there was little observable change in their conduct.

Following the *Tobacco* case, additional decisions involving the cement and steel industries carried the conscious parallelism doctrine further, outlawing adherence by mutual tacit consent to a *common system* of pricing—the basing point system.[67] The problem in both cases was characterized succinctly in the Court of Appeals' rigid steel conduit decision:

> ... each conduit seller knows that each of the other sellers is using the basing point formula; each knows that by using it he will be able to quote identical delivered prices and thus present a condition of matched prices under which purchasers are isolated and deprived of choice among sellers so far

---

[64]147 F. 2d 93 (1944).

[65]328 U. S. 781, 809–810 (1946).

[66]"The Tobacco Case of 1946," p. 285.

[67]*Federal Trade Commission* v. *Cement Institute et al.*, 333 U. S. 683, 712–721 (1948); and *Triangle Conduit and Cable Co. et al.* v. *Federal Trade Commission*, 168 F. 2d 175 (1948).

as price advantage is concerned. . . . Each seller . . . in effect invites the others to share the available business at matched prices in his natural market in return for a reciprocal invitation.[68]

And this, the court said, was a violation of Federal Trade Commission Act Section 5, which had been stretched in the prior *Cement Institute* decision to cover combinations in restraint of trade as unfair methods of competition. In a subsequent staff memorandum, the Federal Trade Commission pointedly expressed its belief that parallel pricing had become fair game for attack:

> [W]hen a number of enterprises follow a parallel course of action in the knowledge and contemplation of the fact that all are acting alike, they have, in effect, formed an agreement. . . .The obvious fact [is] that the economic effect of identical prices achieved through conscious parallel action is the same as that of similar prices achieved through overt collusion, and, for this reason, the Commission treated the conscious parallelism of action as a violation of the Federal Trade Commission Act.[69]

As events transpired, 1948 proved to be a high water mark in the legal construction of conscious parallelism. Erosion took place in still another boycott case.[70] Nine film distributors all refused to grant first-run status to a new theater in a suburban Baltimore shopping center, giving preference instead to established downtown theaters, three of which were owned by the distributors. No evidence was adduced to prove express agreement among the distributors. Judgment was rendered for the distributors in a jury trial. In its sustaining decision, the Supreme Court found that the distributors' decisions to deny first-run status could have been taken independently and based upon "individual business judgment motivated by the desire for maximum revenue"[71]—e.g., because of the theater's inadequate drawing power, the paucity of its newspaper display advertising compared to downtown theaters, and the fact that giving it first-run status would adversely affect rentals to existing customers. The Court went on to administer a rude jolt to those who had construed its *Tobacco* decision broadly:

> The crucial question is whether respondents' conduct toward petitioner stemmed from independent decision or from an agreement, tacit or express. To be sure, business behavior is admissible circumstantial evidence from which the fact finder may infer agreement. . . . But this Court has never held that proof of parallel business behavior conclusively establishes agreement or, phrased differently, that such behavior itself constitutes a Sherman Act offense. Circumstantial evidence of consciously parallel behavior may have made heavy inroads into the traditional judicial attitude toward conspiracy; but "conscious parallelism" has not yet read conspiracy out of the Sherman Act entirely.[72]

Two drug industry cases round out the picture. In 1954, the National Foundation for Infantile Paralysis licensed six pharmaceutical firms to produce the Salk polio vaccine.[73] During a two-and-one-half year period beginning in March of 1955, there were only two significant price changes which were matched promptly, with virtual identity of price quotations prevailing in the sealed bids submitted to state and local government purchasing offices at almost all

---

[68]168 F. 2d 175, 181. The appellate court's decision was upheld only by a 4-4 tie vote in the Supreme Court. 336 U. S. 956 (1949).

[69]"Notice to the Staff: In RE: Commission Policy Toward Geographic Pricing Practices," October 1948, cited in U. S. Department of Justice, *Report of the Attorney General's National Committee To Study the Antitrust Laws*, p. 38.

[70]*Theatre Enterprises, Inc.*, v. *Paramount Film Distributing Corp. et al.*, 346 U. S. 537 (1954). See also *Peveley Dairy Co.* v. *U. S.*, 178 F. 2d 363 (1949), cert. den. 339 U. S. 942 (1950), in which two St. Louis dairies pursuing parallel pricing policies were found innocent of criminal conspiracy, since the Circuit Court of Appeals was convinced that their behavior could be explained as the result of uniform changes in fluid milk and labor input costs.

[71]346 U. S. 537, 542 (1954).

[72]*Ibid.*, at pp. 540–541.

[73]*U. S.* v. *Eli Lilly & Co. et al.*, CCH 1959 Trade Cases, para. 69,536.

times. There was no direct evidence of price-fixing agreements, but the Justice Department alleged that there was "a continuing agreement, understanding, plan and concert of action" to "submit uniform price quotations" and to "adopt uniform and noncompetitive terms and conditions" on sales to public authorities. After the government had presented its case, defense attorney (and former presidential candidate) Thomas E. Dewey made an eloquent plea for acquittal. The court accepted his motion and dismissed the case. It held that a reasonable alternative hypothesis existed for explaining the defendants' pricing behavior on the basis of "independent business considerations only." Notably, the firms had accepted "most favored customer" clauses in their contracts with government agencies, requiring them in effect to reduce the price of vaccine to all customers if they reduced it for one. This disincentive to price-cutting was deemed sufficient to cause the observed price identity and stability without collusion.

That the conscious parallelism doctrine had not been completely emasculated by these setbacks was demonstrated in a second major drug industry case, decided at the district court level in 1967.[74] The facts are complex, and interpretation is complicated by the way various allegations were scrambled in the government's complaint. Essentially, however, there were two main charges: that the defendants (Pfizer, American Cyanamid, and Bristol-Myers) had during the mid-1950s settled conflicting claims over rights to the tetracycline antibiotic patent by entering a cross-licensing agreement with the explicit or implicit understanding that further entry into the field would be restricted; and that from 1953 to 1961 the three defendants plus two additional licensees conspired to fix identical and noncompetitive prices. No direct evidence of illegal agreements was produced, and executives of the companies vehemently denied any wrong-doing. However, documents were introduced showing that the defendants were acutely aware that failure to settle their patent dispute might encourage a flood of new entries, with adverse effects on

price. The government also showed that prices were stabilized for several years at $30.60 per bottle of 100 capsules to druggists and $19.1884 per bottle to the Veterans Administration, despite unit production costs of only $3 per bottle. In masterful instructions to the jury, District Judge Marvin Frankel observed that the evidence was entirely circumstantial, and that:

> ... whether the prosecution has sustained its burden of proving a conspiracy must frequently be judged by what the jury finds the parties actually did rather than from the words they used. The unlawful agreement may be shown if the proof establishes a concert of action, with all the parties working together understandingly with a single design for the accomplishment of a common purpose. ... It is not sufficient to show that the parties acted uniformly or similarly or in ways that may seem to have been mutually beneficial. If such actions were taken independently as a matter of individual business judgment, without any agreement or arrangement or understanding among the parties, then there would be no conspiracy.[75]

A key point of contention was the large disparity between prices and production costs. Judge Frankel repeatedly cautioned the jury that the reasonableness or unreasonableness of prices charged was irrelevant in a direct sense. But it was relevant indirectly as part of the circumstantial evidence:

> ... I think you will find it helpful to translate the word "unreasonable" to mean "unusual" or "artificial" or "extraordinary." By these suggested definitions I am trying to convey the thought that the idea of unreasonableness in the present context is meaningful only if it is understood to refer to kinds of price behavior or price levels which appear to be divorced from variations and differences in available supply or demand or cost or other economic factors that may normally be expected to cause variations or changes in the prices charged in a competitive market. To put the thought

---

[74]*U. S. v. Charles Pfizer & Co., Inc., et al.,* 281 F. Supp. 837 (1968).

[75]From pp. 6200–6201 of the trial record. In April 1970 the decision was reversed by the appellate court and a new trial was ordered.

in another and slightly shorter way, the charge of unreasonableness in this case is material only insofar as it poses the issue whether the prices involved exhibited qualities or peculiarities of a type that could be deemed evidence that such prices resulted from agreement rather than from competition. . . . Unreasonably or extraordinarily high prices or profits charged uniformly by competing sellers over a substantial period of time may be evidence, taken with all the other circumstances of the case, supporting an inference that the parties had an agreement rather than a competitive situation with respect to prices.[76]

The jury found the defendants guilty on all counts, and maximum fines were imposed. Assuming that the convictions are upheld by higher courts, it is probable that substantial treble damage settlements will follow, since the volume of tetracycline sales involved exceeded a billion dollars.[77]

To say that there now exists a sharply enunciated, readily transferable conscious parallelism doctrine would be to read more consistency into the leading case decisions than they actually exhibit. Still some broad generalizations appear warranted. Mere parallelism of behavior is definitely insufficient. To make conspiracy charges stick, the antitrust enforcement agencies must identify some behavioral pattern which goes beyond mere recognition of mutual interdependence, or they must show that the observed conduct could not credibly have occurred if each firm independently tended to its own self interest. It is likely also that judges and juries will be more inclined to infer a violation when the firms' decisions, however independent, led to prices deviating especially far from competitive norms, even though this rule of reason has never been formally and explicitly incorporated into the law. These are significant limitations, but the conscious parallelism doctrine does provide a wedge into certain oligopoly pricing problems, particularly where performance is

patently deficient or where industry discipline is so fragile that cooperation can occur only if given a slight helping hand.

PRICE LEADERSHIP

One of the most important institutions facilitating tacitly collusive pricing behavior is the existence of a well-established system of price leadership. The legality of price leadership was considered by the Supreme Court in cases involving U. S. Steel and the International Harvester Co. The most succinct statement of the Court's viewpoint is found in its *Harvester* decision:

. . . [International Harvester] has not . . . attempted to dominate or in fact controlled or dominated the harvesting machinery industry by the compulsory regulation of prices. The most that can be said as to this, is that many of its competitors have been accustomed, independently and as a matter of business expediency, to follow approximately the prices at which it has sold its harvesting machines; but one of its competitors has habitually sold its machines at somewhat higher prices. The law, however, does not make the mere size of a corporation, however impressive, or the existence of unexerted power on its part, an offense, when unaccompanied by unlawful conduct in the exercise of its power. . . . And the fact that competitors may see proper, in the exercise of their own judgment, to follow the prices of another manufacturer, does not establish any suppression of competition or show any sinister domination.[78]

This has continued to be the basic law on price leadership, though other points of the *U. S. Steel* and *Harvester* decisions have since been overturned. Price leadership is not apt to be found contrary to the antitrust laws unless the leader attempts to coerce other producers into following its lead, or unless there is an express agreement among members of the industry to use the leader-

---

[76]From pp. 6270–6271 and 6275–6276 of the trial record.

[77]Cf. "5 Drug Makers Will Settle Price Suits for 120 Million," *New York Times*, February 7, 1969, p. 1.

[78]*U. S. v. International Harvester Co.*, 274 U. S. 693, 708–709 (1927).

ship device as the basis of a price-fixing scheme. As long as firms exercise their own independent judgment in choosing to follow the leader, i.e., "because they ma[k]e money by the imitation,"[79] they remain on relatively safe ground.

There is a certain logic in this rule, which avoids making one party's guilt (the price leader's) hang on the autonomous actions of other parties (the followers). Still the rule, in combination with limits written into the conscious parallelism doctrine during the 1950s, makes it difficult for the antitrust agencies to deal effectively with oligopolists quietly but firmly refraining from price competition. We shall be concerned with this problem further in the next chapter.

TRADE ASSOCIATION PRICE AND COST REPORTING ACTIVITIES

Trade associations have often performed functions which run afoul of the antitrust laws. Their meetings are superb vehicles for getting together and agreeing on prices, outputs, market shares, etc. This is *per se* illegal, however difficult it may be to detect, and need not detain us further. But what if the trade association, through its central office staff, merely collects and then distributes to members detailed information on the prices quoted in recent sales transactions, or detailed comparative breakdowns of member production costs?

It might seem paradoxical that there could be anything harmful about information dissemination activities, which at first glance appear only to perfect the market. However, perfect information is unambiguously beneficial only in the context of purely competitive markets. When the market is oligopolistic, it may impair rather than invigorate rivalry. As we have learned in Chapter 7, one important hindrance to collusive oligopoly pricing is secret price-shading. If price cuts can be kept secret, a firm may be able to capture additional orders while avoiding the

adverse repercussions—retaliatory price cuts—for at least a while. Yet when many sellers begin behaving in this way, sub rosa competition can become fierce, and it will be difficult to hold prices at anything approximating monopolistic levels. If on the other hand every transaction is publicized immediately, all members of the industry will know when one has made a price cut, and each therefore can retaliate on the next transaction. Knowledge that retaliation will be swift serves as a powerful deterrent to price-cutting and therefore facilitates the maintenance of a tacitly collusive price structure.

One of the first persons to recognize this and do something about it was Arthur Jerome Eddy. His solution to the secret price-shading problem, advocated in *The New Competition*,[80] was the formation of "open price associations" which would supply rapid and complete information on all sales transactions to all members of an industry. A few quotations convey the flavor of his approach. On the book's frontispiece is the theme, "Competition Is War, and War Is Hell." The analysis runs along the following lines:

> Of all the rivalries in which man engages, brute competition in the production and distribution of wealth is the most contemptible, since it is the most sordid, a mere money-making proposition, unrelieved by a single higher consideration. . . . Cooperation, whether voluntary or involuntary, . . . is the only regulator of prices. Competition, free and unfettered, is absolutely destructive to all stability of prices.[81]

And now the essence of his message:

> The theoretical proposition at the basis of the open price policy is that, Knowledge regarding bids and prices actually made is all that is necessary to keep prices at reasonably stable and normal levels.[82]

Eddy preached his open price gospel widely and persuasively, and soon open price associations became a prominent feature of the American

[79] *U. S. v. United States Steel Corp. et al.*, 251 U. S. 417, 447 (1920).

[80] A. J. Eddy, *The New Competition* (First ed.; Chicago: McClury, 1912). Subsequent references are to the fourth (1917) edition.

[81] *Ibid.*, pp. 18, 29.

[82] *Ibid.*, p. 126.

industrial landscape. In 1921, there were at least 150 open price associations in operation, and possibly as many as 450.[83] After a sharp decline during the late 1920s, the movement thrived again under federal government auspices between 1933 and 1935, when 422 industrial "fair competition" codes including open price reporting provisions were approved by the National Recovery Administration.

Eddy was an able corporation lawyer. He designed his open price system to stay within the bounds of antitrust law, as he perceived them at the time. On this he was at least partly successful. The law on trade association price and cost reporting activities is one of the most subtle (and some would add the most confused) branches of antitrust law. The courts have adopted a rule of reason approach, examining each set of industry practices on its merits.[84] Typically the cases cover such a complex admixture of activities that case-by-case comparison breaks down, and on specific practices some of the judicial pronouncements are downright contradictory.

The first test case to reach the Supreme Court was a defeat for advocates of "the new competition."[85] The American Hardwood Manufacturers' Association, whose members produced roughly a third of the nation's hardwood lumber, instituted an open price scheme which required each member firm to submit to a central office price lists, a detailed daily report on all sales and shipments (with copies of each invoice), monthly production and stock reports, and various other documents. The central office in turn forwarded to members weekly reports listing each transaction, the price at which it was made, the buyer, the seller, etc. Special attention was drawn to list price departures. In addition, meetings were held frequently to discuss market conditions, and at both the meetings and in newsletters the association's Manager of Statistics exhorted members to restrict their output and maintain prices. The Supreme Court, finding the system an illegal conspiracy in restraint of trade, observed in its opinion that:

> Genuine competitors do not make daily, weekly, and monthly reports of the minutest details of their business to their rivals, as the defendants did; they do not contract . . . to submit their books to the discretionary audit . . . of their rivals for the purpose of successfully competing with them; and they do not submit the details of their business to the analysis of an expert, jointly employed, and obtain from him a "harmonized" estimate of the market as it is and as, in his specially and confidently informed judgment, it promises to be. This is not the conduct of competitors, but is so clearly that of men united in an agreement, express or implied, to act together and pursue a common purpose under a common guide. . . .[86]

Nevertheless, the seeds of subsequent dilution were sown in dissenting opinions by three members of the Court, including Justice Brandeis' suggestion that the Sherman Act did not require business rivals to compete blindly and without the aid of relevant trade information.

Following a second decision striking down an open price plan in the linseed oil industry,[87] the Supreme Court seemingly reversed its field in a case involving the Maple Flooring Manufacturers' Association.[88] Disposition of the case may have been affected by inadequate preparation on the Justice Department's part, but there were also certain characteristics distinguishing the facts from those of previous cases. In particular,

[83]See L. S. Lyon and Victor Abramson, *The Economics of Open Price Associations* (Washington: Brookings, 1936), pp. 15–23, for an historical analysis of the movement.

[84]For a more thorough review of the leading cases, see George W. Stocking, "The Rule of Reason, Workable Competition, and the Legality of Trade Association Activities," *University of Chicago Law Review*, Summer 1954, pp. 527–619.

[85]*American Column and Lumber Co. et al.* v. *U. S.*, 257 U. S. 377 (1921). See also the discussion in Phillips, *op. cit.*, pp. 138–160.

[86]257 U. S. 377, 410 (1921).

[87]*U. S.* v. *American Linseed Oil Co. et al.*, 262 U. S. 371 (1923).

[88]*Maple Flooring Manufacturers' Association* v. *U. S.*, 268 U. S. 563 (1925).

evidence of relatively low and nonuniform prices charged by association members was presented; the members supposedly ceased discussing prices in their association meetings after the Supreme Court found the Hardwood Lumber and Linseed Oil operations illegal; the association's weekly report to members stopped linking transactions with specific sellers after the government filed a complaint; and in general, the association made an obvious effort to stay within the letter, if not the spirit, of the antitrust laws. Given these apparent differences, the Supreme Court countermanded a district court decision, showing its willingness to permit trade association activities which went little further than the dissemination of detailed information:

> We decide only that trade associations ... which openly and fairly gather and disseminate information as to the cost of their product, the volume of production, the actual price which the product has brought in past transactions, stocks of merchandise on hand, approximate cost of transportation from the principal point of shipment to the points of consumption [e.g., a basing-point system freight rate book], as did these defendants, and who, as they did, meet and discuss such information and statistics without however reaching or attempting to reach any agreement or any concerted action with respect to prices or production or restraining competition, do not thereby engage in unlawful restraint of commerce.[89]

In another decision handed down on the same day, the Court lent its seal of approval to price reporting activities of a cement industry trade association, despite its awareness that they tended to bring about uniformity of prices.[90]

The next major case involving open price policies was a victory for the antitrust enforcement agencies, but only because the defendants —15 sugar refining companies—had entered into an explicit agreement to adhere to the prices they quoted until they publicly announced changes.[91] While condemning this agreement, the Supreme Court went on to observe that:

> ... competition does not become less free merely because of the distribution of knowledge of the essential factors entering into commercial transactions. The natural effect of the acquisition of the wider and more scientific knowledge of business conditions on the minds of those engaged in commerce, and the consequent stabilizing of production and price, cannot be said to be an unreasonable restraint or in any respect unlawful.[92]

During the late 1930s and 1940s the Federal Trade Commission launched a series of attacks against open price associations which had continued reporting programs originated under National Industrial Recovery Act auspices. All but one led to cease and desist orders. However, in most of the cases, the trade associations had gone further than merely disseminating price information—for example, by hiring a consultant who contacted individual firms and lectured them on the irrationality of price cutting,[93] or by encouraging and facilitating rigid adherence to a basing point pricing system.[94] The sole defeat came in a case against the Tag Manufacturers Institute.[95] The 31 firms who formed the Institute accounted for 95 per cent of the output of price tags, pin tickets, and similar devices used to mark consumer goods. Member firms agreed to file their price lists with the Institute, to submit duplicate copies of every shipment invoice, and to report within 24 hours any sales which deviated from the list price. Financial penalties were assessed against members who failed to

---

[89] 268 U. S. 563, 586 (1925).

[90] *Cement Manufacturers Protective Association* v. *U. S.*, 268 U. S. 588 (1925).

[91] *Sugar Institute* v. *U. S.*, 297 U. S. 553 (1936).

[92] *Ibid.*, at p. 598.

[93] *Salt Producers' Association* v. *Federal Trade Commission*, 34 F.T.C. 38 (1941), 134 F. 2d 354 (1943); and *United States Maltsters Association* v. *Federal Trade Commission*, 35 F.T.C. 797 (1942), 152 F. 2d 161 (1945).

[94] *Federal Trade Commission* v. *Cement Institute et al.*, 333 U. S. 683 (1948).

[95] *Tag Manufacturers Institute et al.* v. *Federal Trade Commission*, 43 F.T.C. 499 (1947), 174 F. 2d 452 (1949).

submit the agreed-upon information on time. The Institute in turn circulated to all members copies of each member's price lists, periodic summaries of the invoice data (which did not identify specific sellers), and daily reports listing each off-list transaction, the name of the seller, the state in which the buyer operated, the seller's list price, and the price actually quoted. There was no express agreement among Institute members to adhere to list prices and the Institute's director scrupulously avoided encouraging members to respect their list prices. Emphasizing the absence of such agreements or encouragement, and noting that 25 per cent of the tag manufacturers' sales were made at off-list prices, the Court of Appeals reversed a prior FTC decision and found that the tag makers had not acted illegally. The decision was not appealed to the Supreme Court, apparently because of the tag industry's diminutive size.

In 1969 the Supreme Court returned to the open price battlefield, reversing a district court decision which had absolved the price reporting activities of 18 firms supplying 90 per cent of the cardboard cartons used in southeastern United States.[96] No systematic centralized price reporting organization had been formed. Instead, the producers supplied to one another upon request (as often as a dozen times per month, for one firm which kept records) information on prices currently or last quoted to particular customers. Once a company had received this information from a rival, it usually quoted the same price to that customer, and it was common for buyers to divide orders among producers offering identical quotations. Sometimes, however, lower prices were quoted, and there was evidence of considerable shifting by purchasers from one supplier to others. Although entry into carton production was easy, the market structure was oligopolistic, with six producers contributing 60 per cent of total sales. The industry showed signs of excess capacity despite rapidly growing demand. Prices were said to be trending downward between 1955 and 1963, but only gradually and within a narrow band of fluctuation. Speaking for a majority of the Supreme Court, Justice Douglas observed

that the facts fit none of the earlier precedents readily. In a brief opinion which addressed itself only to the immediate circumstances, he concluded that the defendants' information exchange practices had tended to stabilize prices and that this was an anti-competitive effect illegal under Sherman Act Section 1. Three members of the Court dissented, arguing that the government had not provided sufficient evidence of intent to restrain competition or actual anticompetitive effect to support the majority's conclusion.

The majority position in the cardboard carton case seemingly represents a somewhat tougher line than earlier decisions, but it was too narrowly drawn to offer clean guidelines for future cases. More generally, it is possible to extract from the leading decisions only a statement of probabilities concerning the legality of price reporting practices. Few certainties exist, except where express agreements to adhere to reported prices have been made. With caution and a bit of luck, producers may be able to stay within the law in maintaining a reporting system sufficiently elaborate to reduce, if not to eliminate altogether, the temptation toward price-shading in an oligopolistic market. However, an open price arrangement is less likely to pass legal muster if it provides that extra margin of active encouragement needed to establish well-disciplined pricing when the industry structure is ill-suited to tacit collusion—e.g., when the number of sellers is relatively large or the product is not homogeneous. The chances of withstanding antitrust attack are also impaired when price reporting is carried to extremes of detail.

This is not the worst of all possible worlds, but it is also not the best. Tacitly collusive oligopoly pricing could be combatted more effectively if the law on trade association information dissemination activities were strengthened. Specifically, the cause of competition would be served if, in addition to prohibitions commonly applied in the past, the courts were to take a uniformly dim view of price reporting schemes which identify the buyers and/or sellers in individual transactions and which impose penalties for failure to

---

[96]*U. S. v. Container Corporation of America et al.*, 273 F. Supp. 18 (1967), 393 U. S. 333 (1969).

report transactions.[97] It would also be desirable to limit the frequency with which detailed market conditions reports are issued, but here a rule of reason is definitely needed. Weekly reports are probably harmless when transactions are small and occur with great frequency, but they may enhance collusion significantly in industries with large, infrequent transactions.

One final comparative note is in order. Price reporting schemes are by no means a uniquely American phenomenon. When the British Restrictive Practices Court handed down its first decisions prohibiting overt price-fixing arrangements, there was a rush to adopt open price agreements, which did not have to be registered under the 1956 Restrictive Practices Act. According to one observer, more than 150 such agreements had already been reached by 1960.[98] The Restrictive Practices Court later managed to strike down an open price agreement in the rubber tire industry on a technicality, but there was no general deterrent.[99] In 1967 a formal effort to extend the law's coverage to open price associations was initiated. Its fate had not been decided at the time of writing.[100]

CONCLUSION

In sum, the United States, unlike nearly all other industrialized Western nations, has adopted an antitrust policy which holds explicit price-fixing and output-restricting agreements *per se* illegal, without regard to their reasonableness. But the law is more permissive with respect to subtler forms of conduct which could have the same effect as explicit agreements. Oligopolists refraining from price competition because they recognize the likelihood of rival retaliation do not violate the law as long as their decisions are taken independently. And by avoiding any suggestion of encouraging or compelling rivals to cooperate, they may also facilitate uniform and non-aggressive pricing through such devices as price leadership and open price reporting systems. These limitations in the law prevent the reign of competition from being carried as far as it might conceivably be.

[97]For a further discussion of possible criteria, see Carl Kaysen and Donald F. Turner, *Antitrust Policy* (Cambridge: Harvard University Press, 1959), pp. 150–152.

[98]J. B. Heath, "Some Economic Consequences," *Economic Journal*, September 1960, pp. 74–84. See also D. P. O'Brien and D. Swann, "Information Agreements—A Problem in Search of a Policy," *Manchester School of Economic and Social Studies*, September 1966, pp. 285–306.

[99]"Darker and Deeper," *The Economist*, June 25, 1966, p. 1449.

[100]For a survey of open price activities and laws in Europe, see the Organisation for Economic Co-operation and Development report, "Report by the Committee of Experts on Restrictive Business Practices on Information Agreements," excerpted in the *Antitrust Bulletin*, Spring 1968, pp. 225–260.

Chapter 20

Antitrust Policy: The Control of Market Structures

In addition to rules governing pricing, the antitrust arsenal contains substantive provisions designed to channel industrial structure in competitive directions. The main weapons are Section 2 of the Sherman Act and Section 7 of the Clayton Act.

MONOPOLY AND MONOPOLIZATION

Sherman Act Section 2 reads in part:

> Every person who shall monopolize, or attempt to monopolize, or combine or conspire with any other person or persons, to monopolize any part of the trade or commerce among the several states, or with foreign nations, shall be deemed guilty of a misdemeanor ...

The language suggests concern primarily with structural conditions rather than conduct. But why did Congress choose the word "monopolize" to describe what it condemned, and not some more conventional phrase such as "obtain or possess monopoly power"? When does a firm monopolize? How large a share of the market must it control? Is it illegal to dominate an industry merely because a firm is so much more efficient than its rivals that they all disappear in the face of its competitive efforts? These are questions which cannot be answered merely by reading the statute. We must analyze the original intent of Congress and the interpretations rendered by the courts.

Unfortunately, the historical record provides only limited insight into what Congress had in mind in enacting Section 2.[1] The original bill proposed by Senator Sherman was debated briskly on the floor of the Senate, but it was changed in major respects by the Judiciary Committee, and passage of the amended bill was preceded by only a cursory debate. It appears probable, however, that the choice of the unconventional word "monopolize" reflected the mixed emotions of legislators toward big business. They were acutely aware of abuses by the "trusts." But they also believed that many combinations brought economies of large scale production, benefitting the consumer. This ambiguity is reflected superbly in Peter Finley Dunne's characterization, through the voice of Mr. Dooley, of Theodore Roosevelt's attitude a decade later:

> "Th' trusts," says [T.R.], "are heejous monsthers built up be th' enlightened intherprise iv th' men that have done so much to advance progress in our beloved country .... On wan hand I wud stamp thim undher fut; on th' other hand not so fast."[2]

As a way out of this dilemma, the Sherman Act draftsmen wrote into the law a prohibition only

---

[1] For various views see Hans B. Thorelli, *The Federal Antitrust Policy* (Stockholm: 1954), pp. 166–210; William Letwin, *Law and Economic Policy in America* (New York: Random House, 1965), pp. 88–99; and Robert H. Bork, "Legislative Intent and the Policy of the Sherman Act," *Journal of Law and Economics*, October 1966, pp. 7–48.

[2] Cited in Letwin, *op. cit.*, p. 205.

of monopolizing, which they apparently intended to mean an active process of securing to oneself a monopoly, going beyond the mere possession of monopoly power as a consequence of superior efficiency.

EARLY LITIGATION

The executive branch and the judiciary did not in fact proceed very rapidly to stamp the monopolistic trusts under foot. An early action against the Whiskey Trust was dismissed at the district court level, first because of a procedural error and then on various substantive grounds.[3] A case involving the sugar refining trust was fought all the way to the Supreme Court, only to be thrown out on the technical question of what constituted interstate commerce.[4] An indictment against the notorious cash register trust was sustained by a district court on four out of 18 counts, but then the case was dropped by the government.[5]

The first real government victory over a close-knit combination came in 1904, when the Supreme Court struck down the Northern Securities Co., formed in 1901 to consolidate the joint control of J. P. Morgan, James Hill, and other contemporary tycoons over the Northern Pacific and Great Northern railroads.[6] The government's attack was based both on Sherman Act Section 1, alleging an illegal combination in restraint of trade, and Section 2, charging an attempt and conspiracy to monopolize rail transportation in northern states west of the Mississippi River. Its relevance as a judicial precedent has been confined mainly to merger cases, on which we shall have more to say later. It is also not a paragon of legal consensus. The Supreme Court justices were so far at odds in their five-four split decision that they found it necessary to render two separate majority opinions along with two dissents. As newly-appointed

Justice Oliver Wendell Holmes prefaced his dissent, implicitly objecting to the grandstand tactics pursued by President Roosevelt and his attorney general in focusing public attention on the case's all-star cast of entrepreneurs:

> Great cases like hard cases make bad law. For great cases are called great, not by reason of their real importance in shaping the law of the future, but because of some accident of immediate overwhelming interest which appeals to the feelings and distorts judgment.[7]

EMERGENCE OF A RULE OF REASON

A more important step followed in 1911, when the Supreme Court held that the Standard Oil Company of New Jersey had illegally monopolized the petroleum refining industry.[8] "The Standard" had been organized as an Ohio corporation in 1870 by the Rockefeller Brothers. It pioneered the trust form of monopolistic consolidation during the 1880s and then, after a skirmish with the Ohio antitrust laws, was incorporated as a New Jersey holding company in 1899. From its inception, it seemed determined to dominate the refining and sale of petroleum products—notably, in that pre-horseless carriage era, kerosene and lubricating oil. It managed to maintain a 90 per cent share of those markets throughout most of the 1880s and 1890s. This it accomplished by acquiring more than 120 former rival firms, securing discriminatory rail freight rates and rebates, foreclosing crude oil supplies to competitors by buying up pipelines, conducting business espionage, and allegedly waging predatory price warfare to drive rivals out of business or soften them up for a takeover. Whether Standard actually engaged in widespread predatory pricing has been disputed. Careful analysis suggests that more frequently it pursued a highly sophisticated region-by-region

---

[3] *U. S. v. Greenhut et al.*, 50 Fed. 469 (1892); 51 Fed. 205 (1892); 51 Fed. 213 (1892); and *In re Greene*, 52 Fed. 104 (1892). See also Letwin, *op. cit.*, pp. 111–113 and 145–149.

[4] *U. S. v. E. C. Knight Co. et al.*, 60 Fed. 306 (1894); 60 Fed. 934 (1894); 156 U. S. 1 (1895).

[5] *U. S. v. Patterson et al.*, 55 Fed. 605 (1893).

[6] *U. S. v. Northern Securities Co. et al.*, 120 Fed. 721 (1903); 193 U. S. 197 (1904).

[7] 193 U. S. 197, 400 (1904).

[8] *U. S. v. Standard Oil Co. of New Jersey et al.*, 173 Fed. 177 (1909), 221 U. S. 1 (1911).

limit pricing strategy.[9] This subtlety, however, eluded contemporary jurists and economists.

Sustaining a district court's finding of guilt, the Supreme Court stated that the crime of monopolization involves two elements: the acquisition of a monopoly position, and the intent to acquire that position and exclude rivals from the industry. The court went on to articulate a rule of reason for ascertaining whether or not actions by accused firms exhibited the essential element of intent: if the acts were unreasonable, going beyond normal business practice, intent could be inferred. Specifically, it ruled that Standard's:

> ...intent and purpose to exclude others... was frequently manifested by acts and dealings wholly inconsistent with the theory that they were made with the single conception of advancing the development of business power by usual methods, but which on the contrary necessarily involved the intent to drive others from the field and to exclude them from their right to trade and thus accomplish the mastery which was the end in view.[10]

To remedy matters, the courts ordered that the Standard Oil holding company be dissolved, its controlling shares in 33 geographically dispersed operating subsidiaries to be distributed on a pro-rata basis to Standard Oil of New Jersey stockholders. At first this led to no appreciable increase in competition, for a controlling interest in the 33 fragments remained in the hands of John D. Rockefeller and associates who had managed the original Standard Oil trust. But as the dominant stockholders distributed their shares among numerous heirs and gave substantial blocks to non-voting philanthropic institutions, as expansion to meet growing gasoline demands necessitated issuing new stock to a broader base of investors, and as some of the fragments merged with Standard competitors, competition among the surviving entities gradually developed, and each interpenetrated markets dominated by its former affiliates.[11]

Two weeks after the Supreme Court handed down its *Standard Oil* decision, it reinforced the rule of reason doctrine in a decision against the American Tobacco Company, also called the Tobacco Trust.[12] American was found guilty of monopolizing the cigarette trade through such unreasonable business practices as excluding rivals from access to wholesalers, engrossing supplies of leaf tobacco, buying out some 250 former rivals, and predatory price competition. In the cold light of hindsight, its pricing behavior appears more swashbuckling than Standard Oil's. It frequently established 'fighting brands' which were sold in rivals' local markets at less than cost and on at least one occasion at an effective after-tax price of zero, forcing the hapless competitors to sell out. In many cases the plants of firms so acquired were promptly closed down. The Supreme Court found these practices to be clear evidence of illegal monopolistic intent. A district court subsequently ordered that the Tobacco Trust be split into 16 pieces, including a successor American Tobacco Company, Liggett & Myers, P. Lorillard, Reynolds (which at the time had no cigarette brand), and the American Snuff Co. (which even today dominates its sadly declining field).

During the next few years, the government scored further but less spectacular victories against the Powder Trust,[13] the glucose and cornstarch trust,[14] Eastman Kodak Company,[15]

---

[9]Cf. pp. 274–276 *supra*.

[10]221 U. S. 1, 76 (1911).

[11]An interesting aftermath of the case is the inability of Standard fragments to use the 'Standard' or 'Esso' trademarks except in their traditional home territories. As a result, many companies maintain two or more trademarks, one for home use and one for "export." E.g., Standard of Indiana sells under the Standard trademark in Illinois, Indiana, and Michigan, but sells elsewhere under the American, Amoco, and other trademarks.

[12]*U. S.* v. *American Tobacco Co.*, 221 U S. 106 (1911).

[13]*U. S.* v. *E. I. du Pont de Nemours & Co. et al.*, 188 Fed. 127 (1911).

[14]*U. S.* v. *Corn Products Refining Co. et al.*, 234 Fed. 964 (1916).

[15]*U. S.* v. *Eastman Kodak Co. et al.*, 226 Fed. 62 (1915).

the Thread Trust,[16] and a group of railroads dominating the anthracite coal industry.[17] The next important step by way of precedent occurred, however, when the government was defeated in its suit against the United States Steel Corporation.[18]

U. S. Steel was formed through a billion dollar merger in 1901, consolidating control over 65 per cent of domestic iron and steel output. It added to its holdings in 1907 by acquiring, with the express permission of President Roosevelt, the Tennessee Coal and Iron Corporation. In that same recession-impacted year Judge E. H. Gary, its chairman, initiated the four-year series of dinners with rival firm leaders which did so much to solidify the industry's pricing discipline. Unlike Standard Oil and American Tobacco, U. S. Steel did not try to drive rivals from the industry through cut-throat pricing and other predatory practices. Instead it adopted a passive price leadership policy, setting prices at levels sufficiently high to encourage the entry and growth of other steel makers. Partly because of this, its share of the market had fallen to 52 per cent in 1915, despite the sizeable Tennessee Coal and Iron merger, and was continuing to fall steadily into 1920.

After winning the *Standard Oil* case, the government brought suit in 1911 to dissolve U. S. Steel. A district court, applying the *Standard Oil* rule of reason, found in favor of the steel company in 1915. The Justice Department appealed to higher authority. With two justices abstaining because they had criticized or prosecuted U. S. Steel in the past, a four member majority of the Supreme Court ruled for the respondent. They argued that since U. S. Steel felt compelled to meet with competitors in order to fix and control steel prices (a practice discontinued before the suit was initiated), and in

view of the decline in its market share, U. S. Steel had not in fact attained monopoly power. They noted further that a multitude of witnesses representing competitors, dealers, and customers had paraded before the district court, and none had anything but good to say about U. S. Steel's conduct. Competitors in particular had testified that they were in no way restrained by the corporation's pricing policies. From this evidence, the majority concluded that U. S. Steel had not monopolized in the Sherman Act sense, and that even if the corporation did possess monopoly power, it had certainly not exercised that power. There followed the famous *obiter dictum* that:

> ... the law does not make mere size an offense or the existence of unexerted power an offense. It ... requires overt acts ... It does not compel competition nor require all that is possible.[19]

Thus, despite the vigorous dissent of a three justice minority, the greatest consolidation in contemporary U. S. industrial history escaped antitrust censure. Moreover, it became settled that dominant firms would subject themselves to telling antitrust attack only if they behaved in a predatory or aggressive manner toward rivals.

This doctrine was cemented in three parallel cases. Two years earlier, the Supreme Court held in a similar four-three decision that the United Shoe Machinery Corporation was innocent of monopolization.[20] It found *inter alia* that the major five-firm merger underlying United's formation in 1899 involved producers of complementary and hence non-competing machines; that 59 subsequent acquisitions were "justified by exigencies or conveniences of the situation," and that United's 80 to 95 per cent share of the relevant markets had been maintained largely

[16]*U. S.* v. *American Thread Co.*, settled by consent decree in 1913.

[17]*U. S.* v. *Reading Co. et al.*, 253 U. S. 26 (1920); and *U. S.* v. *Lehigh Valley Railroad Co. et al.*, 254 U. S. 255 (1920).

[18]*U. S.* v. *United States Steel Corporation et al.*, 223 Fed. 55 (1915), 251 U. S. 417 (1920).

[19]251 U. S. 417, 451 (1920).

[20]*U. S.* v. *United Shoe Machinery Co. of New Jersey et al.*, 247 U. S. 32 (1918). An earlier criminal case against United's officers was also unsuccessful. *U. S.* v. *Winslow et al.*, 195 Fed. 578 (1912), 227 U. S. 202 (1913).

through superior efficiency and the legitimate exploitation of valid patent rights. The government had also suffered a 1916 defeat at the district court level in its suit against the American Can Company. The facts were strikingly similar to those of the *U. S. Steel* case. American Can had been formed through a 1901 merger of some 120 independent entities, but competitors thrived under the umbrella of its high prices, eroding its market share from 90 per cent in 1901 to roughly 50 per cent in 1913. The district court observed that American "had done nothing of which any competitor or any consumer of cans complains, or anything which strikes a disinterested outsider as unfair or unethical," adding that it was "frankly reluctant to destroy so finely adjusted an industrial machine."[21] After the Supreme Court rendered its *U. S. Steel* decision, the Justice Department dropped its appeal of the *Can* judgment along with a number of other pending and planned monopolization suits. It persevered in prosecuting only one other major monopolization case, seeking to extend the modest divestiture program ordered in an earlier court judgment against the International Harvester Company.[22] Here again it was rebuked by the Supreme Court, which reiterated its *U. S. Steel* rule that mere size unaccompanied by unlawful conduct was not illegal.[23] Discouraged by these defeats, the Justice Department for more than a decade gave up trying to attack consolidations of monopoly power under Sherman Act Section 2.

THE ALCOA CASE AND ITS AFTERMATH

The next important development came in the *Alcoa* case, resolved 25 years after the *U. S. Steel* decision.[24] The Aluminum Company of America, or Alcoa, was formed in 1888 to exploit the Hall electrolytic reduction patents. It bought out the competing Bradley patents in 1903. There were several attempts to enter the industry after the basic patents expired in 1909, but none

was successful until 1940. Reasons for the dearth of new entry included the difficulty of obtaining conveniently located high-grade bauxite reserves, most of which Alcoa controlled; plain bad luck by two would-be entrants; and the general unattractiveness of entering at a cost disadvantage while Alcoa practiced moderation in pricing.

Over the years Alcoa had been in and out of the courts frequently in patent disputes and on antitrust charges concerning mergers, international cartel agreements, and price discrimination, but it was never seriously discommoded. However, as interest in antitrust revived following disenchantment with the depression-born National Recovery Administration, the Justice Department in 1937 charged the firm with illegal monopolization. Culminating a district court trial lasting 358 hearing days, Alcoa was absolved on all counts, with the *U. S. Steel* and *International Harvester* cases stressed as precedents. The government appealed, but because four Supreme Court justices had participated in the earlier litigation, a quorum could not be obtained, and so the case was heard by a three-member panel of Circuit Court judges, with Learned Hand presiding, as a court of last resort. Its decision, in March of 1945, reversed the lower court and found Alcoa guilty of monopolization. The opinion focused on two central issues: whether Alcoa possessed a monopoly, and whether it had exhibited the intent essential to find monopolization.

The first question turned on how the market in which Alcoa operated was defined. As we have seen in Chapter 3, framing meaningful market definitions can sometimes be quite difficult. In the *Alcoa* case, unlike most of its Section 2 predecessors, this proved to be so. There was no problem of local vs. national market definitions, for aluminum was sold nationally on a uniform delivered price basis. Substitution on the production side—i.e., the possibility that companies producing other materials might convert

[21] *U. S.* v. *American Can Company et al.*, 230 Fed. 859, 861, 903 (1916).

[22] *U. S.* v. *International Harvester Co. et al.*, 214 Fed. 987 (1914), with settlement effected in a 1918 consent decree.

[23] *U. S.* v. *International Harvester Co.*, 10 F. 2d 827 (1925), 274 U. S. 693 (1927).

[24] *U. S.* v. *Aluminum Co. of America et al.*, 44 F. Supp. 97 (1941), 148 F. 2d 416 (1945).

their plants to produce aluminum—was also no problem, since aluminum refining facilities are highly specialized and durable. The key issue was, what substitutes on the demand side shall be included as part of the relevant market?

Because of aluminum's unique properties, other metals such as steel, copper, and magnesium were summarily excluded, though aluminum and other metals are viewed by users as feasible substitutes in many applications, and though the cross elasticity of demand between aluminum and steel is apparently on the order of 2.0, with even higher cross elasticities with respect to copper prices.[25] Judge Hand limited his analysis to the following three alternative definitions of Alcoa's aluminum ingot market share, where the numerator denotes the output credited to Alcoa and the denominator the output attributed to all sources of supply in the market:

$$S_1 = \frac{\text{Alcoa's output of primary ingots less the primary metal Alcoa used internally to fabricate end products}}{\text{All primary ingot production plus all secondary ingot production plus aluminum ingot imports}}$$

$$S_2 = \frac{\text{Alcoa's output of primary ingots}}{\text{All primary ingot production plus all secondary ingot production plus aluminum ingot imports}}$$

$$S_3 = \frac{\text{Alcoa's output of primary ingots}}{\text{All primary ingot production plus aluminum ingot imports}}$$

Under the first definition, which was accepted as correct by the district court, Alcoa is found to have possessed only a 33 per cent share of the market during the 1930s; under the second, its share would be calculated at 64 per cent; and under the third, 90 per cent. Judge Hand rejected the first definition, which deducts from

the ingot production of Alcoa the metal used internally by Alcoa to fabricate aluminum sheets, panels, pots and pans, etc., because "all intermediate, or end, products which 'Alcoa' fabricates and sells, *pro tanto* reduce the demand for ingot itself."[26] This makes good analytic sense, although one might have nagging doubts, given evidence that Alcoa was forced to stimulate the demand for aluminum by pioneering many fabricated product applications. The only difference between definitions S_2 and S_3 is the inclusion of secondary (i.e., reprocessed scrap) metal, accounting for roughly 40 per cent of all domestic aluminum metal supplies, in the denominator of S_2 but not S_3. Judge Hand favored the third definition, arguing that since Alcoa at one time or another in the past had produced the metal which reappears as reprocessed scrap, it would have taken into account in its output decisions the effect of scrap reclamation on future prices, and hence it exerted effective monopolistic control over the supply of secondary metal. As an exercise in pure theory, this decision is unassailable; the production decisions of a profit-maximizing monopolist with perfect foresight would indeed have been influenced in the way Judge Hand postulated. As a practical matter, however, it seems unlikely that Alcoa's output could have been much influenced by so uncertain and remote a contingency. It is worth noting also that the scrap reappearance problem typifies the kind of variational calculus problem mathematical economists learned to solve operationally only a decade after Judge Hand wrote his decision.[27]

Thus, the Appellate Court's definition of the relevant market and Alcoa's share thereof is plainly debatable. And this choice played a key role in the decision, for Judge Hand stated that 90 per cent "is enough to constitute a monopoly; it is doubtful whether sixty or sixty-four per cent would be enough; and certainly thirty-three per cent is not."[28]

---

[25]M. J. Peck, *Competition in the Aluminum Industry* (Cambridge: Harvard University Press, 1961), pp. 31–34.

[26]148 F. 2d 416, 424 (1945).

[27]A pioneering work was Richard Bellman, *Dynamic Programming* (Princeton: Princeton University Press, 1957).

[28]148 F. 2d 416, 424 (1945).

Having concluded that Alcoa did possess a monopoly of the aluminum market, the court went on to determine whether or not it had exhibited the intent to achieve that position which proof of monopolization under Section 2 demands. In his opinion, Judge Hand acknowledged that Alcoa's profits had not been extortionate, but he added that whether or not profits were "fair" was irrelevant to proving monopolization. He admitted also that Alcoa would be well within the bounds of legality if its monopoly position had merely been "thrust upon" itself by the failure of rivals to enter the market, or because it had outlasted its rivals due to superior skill, foresight, and industry. "The successful competitor," he warned, "having been urged to compete, must not be turned upon when he wins.[29] But he found that Alcoa had gone further. He pointed to Alcoa's building up of ore reserves and electric power sources and production capacity in advance of demand:

> It was not inevitable that it should always anticipate increases in the demand for ingot and be prepared to supply them. Nothing compelled it to keep doubling and redoubling its capacity before others entered the field. It insists that it never excluded competitors; but we can think of no more effective exclusion than progressively to embrace each new opportunity as it opened, and to face every newcomer with new capacity already geared into a great organization, having the advantage of experience, trade connections and the elite of personnel.[30]

And this, said the court, was sufficient to show the intent to maintain a monopoly position:

> ... "Alcoa" meant to keep, and did keep, that complete and exclusive hold upon the ingot market with which it started. That was to "monopolize" that market, however innocently it otherwise proceeded.[31]

This decision, broadly endorsed by the Supreme Court a year later in the *Tobacco* case,[32] in effect overthrew the *Standard Oil* and *U. S. Steel* precedents, making it possible to infer illegal monopolization without evidence of predatory or otherwise unreasonable practices driving competitors from the market. It did not exactly make the possession of monopoly power by means other than the receipt of valid patents *per se* illegal, but it came close. And it is possible to read into the decision, with its references to "fair" profits and expanding capacity to meet demand, a condemnation of dominant market positions maintained merely through limit pricing.

Remedial action in the *Aluminum* case was deferred until the disposition of war plants built with government funds and operated by Alcoa could be settled. Alcoa was barred from bidding to buy the plants, and as a result the primary ingot supply industry was transformed from a monopoly to a triopoly through the sale of integrated facilities to Reynolds Metals and Kaiser Aluminum. This, a district court later concluded, was almost sufficient, so Alcoa was not fragmented.[33] The principal further remedy ordered was the divestiture of joint stockholdings in Alcoa and Aluminium, Ltd., of Canada by the Davis, Hunt, and Mellon families, to eliminate the possibility that these potential competitors would be jointly controlled.

A series of cases following on the heels of the *Alcoa* decision contributed to the strengthening of Section 2. Three deserve special mention.

Shortly after bringing suit against Alcoa, the Justice Department also moved against several motion picture exhibition chains, charging them with monopolizing first-run film exhibition. Some were said to have threatened not to exhibit certain producers' films in towns where they operated the only theaters unless the producers gave

---

[29]*Ibid.*, p. 430.

[30]*Ibid.*, p. 431. There is reason to believe that the court's conclusion on this crucial issue of fact was incorrect. In his definitive study of the aluminum industry, Professor Donald H. Wallace found to the contrary that Alcoa's capacity had *lagged behind demand* on numerous occasions. *Market Control in the Aluminum Industry* (Cambridge: Harvard University Press, 1937), pp 252, 259–260, 291–292, 307–308, and 331.

[31]*Ibid.*, p. 432.

[32]*American Tobacco Co. et al. v. U. S.*, 328 U. S. 781, 813–814 (1946).

[33]*U. S. v. Aluminum Co. of America et al.*, 91 F. Supp. 333 (1950).

them first-run preference in cities where they faced competition. In every such instance the Supreme Court found that illegal monopolization existed.[34] This was no large step beyond *Standard Oil* of 1911. However, speaking for a six-to-one majority upholding the government's case against a chain absolved of making such threats, Justice Douglas stated that specific intent to achieve monopoly need not be proved if monopoly has in fact resulted from the defendant's conduct, and that "monopoly power, whether lawfully or unlawfully acquired, may itself constitute an evil and stand condemned under Section 2 even though it remains unexercised."[35] That the old *U. S. Steel* doctrine had now been overturned could scarcely have been reaffirmed more pointedly.

In 1946 the A & P Company, several subsidiaries, and various company executives were convicted on criminal charges of conspiracy to monopolize the food retailing industry, and in 1949 the conviction was upheld by a circuit court of appeals.[36] The prosecution charged, and the courts accepted, that A & P had engaged in abusive practices—notably, by refusing to purchase from suppliers who would offer no special preferential discounts, by threatening to extend its own internal manufacturing operations and compete with recalcitrant suppliers, and by reducing retail grocery prices in cities where it faced "rough competition" while retaining high prices (or supposedly, although implausibly, even raising prices) in those markets where competition was less intense. These conclusions have been severely criticized, mainly on the ground that A & P's conduct did not go beyond what one would expect of a vigorous rival seeking

to minimize costs and maintain its market position, and that consumers benefitted from the purchasing methods pioneered by A & P and imitated by other grocery chains.[37] Alcoa and A & P seemingly share the dubious distinction of having been found guilty of competing too vigorously and successfully. The *A & P* case is different, however, in the sense that only conspiracy to monopolize and not outright monopolization was inferred, since A & P's share of nationwide retail grocery sales was less than 10 per cent, and its share of local markets exceeded 40 per cent in only 23 relatively small cities. As a result of its conviction, A & P was fined $175,000, and subsequently it was required to dissolve its food brokerage subsidiary.

A third decision paralleling *Alcoa* came in a renewed attack against the United Shoe Machinery Corporation. This time United was found guilty of monopolization because certain of its business policies, although not objectionable *per se*, tended to prevent new entry and to perpetuate United's dominance.[38] These included the refusal to sell machines, which were instead only leased for long (e.g., 10 year) terms; a price structure which accepted lower profit margins on machines exposed to competition than on those shielded by United's formidable patent portfolio; and pricing, service, and machine replacement provisions which made it advantageous for shoe manufacturers to employ the full line of United machines. This array of practices appears to stray further from orthodox business conduct than Alcoa's "embracing each new opportunity," and so the *United Shoe Machinery* decision cannot be considered as daring a departure from earlier precedents.

---

[34] *U. S.* v. *Crescent Amusement Co.*, 323 U. S. 173 (1944); *U. S.* v. *Griffith Amusement Co.*, 334 U. S. 100 (1948); and *Schine Chain Theatres* v. *U. S.*, 334 U. S. 110 (1948).

[35] *U. S.* v. *Griffith Amusement Co.*, 334 U. S. 100, 105, 107 (1948).

[36] *U. S.* v. *the New York Great Atlantic and Pacific Tea Co. et al.*, 67 F. Supp. 626 (1946); 173 F. 2d 79 (1949). The case was not appealed to the Supreme Court.

[37] See especially M. A. Adelman, *A & P: A Study in Price-Cost Behavior and Public Policy* (Cambridge: Harvard University Press, 1959); and Donald F. Turner, "Trouble Begins in the 'New' Sherman Act," *Yale Law Journal*, May 1949, pp. 969–982.

[38] *U. S.* v. *United Shoe Machinery Corporation*, 110 F. Supp. 295 (1953), affirmed by the Supreme Court in 347 U. S. 521 (1954). Later the case was reopened when the Justice Department insisted that the remedies ordered in 1954—compulsory licensing of patents and divestiture of minor subsidiary operations—had been insufficient to restore competition. After a Supreme Court decision approving further action, a divestiture program was agreed upon in a consent decree. 391 U. S. 244 (1968); and CCH 1969 Trade Cases Para. 72,688.

MONOPOLIZATION THROUGH VERTICAL
INTEGRATION

While a new hard line was emerging in cases concerned with horizontal aggregations of monopoly power, precedents were also being developed to cope with market power arising through vertical integration. The first sharply focused Supreme Court pronouncement came in the *Yellow Cab* opinion of 1947.[39] Officers of the Checker Cab Manufacturing Co. (CCM) of Kalamazoo, Michigan, had between 1929 and 1932 gained control of taxicab operating companies in several cities. By the mid 1940s their firms operated 86 per cent of all taxis in Chicago, 58 per cent of Minneapolis cabs, and all taxis in the Pittsburgh area. The operating companies purchased their cabs only from the parent CCM Co. The Justice Department brought suit, charging conspiracy in restraint of trade and monopolization because, among other things, the purchasing relationships foreclosed a substantial market to alternative taxi manufacturers. After a district court dismissed the complaint, the Supreme Court on appeal ruled that such foreclosure might indeed be a Sherman Act violation:

> By excluding all cab manufacturers other than CCM from that part of the market represented by the cab operating companies under their control, the appellees effectively limit the outlets through which cabs may be sold in interstate commerce. . . . In addition, by preventing the cab operating companies under their control from purchasing cabs from manufacturers other than CCM, the appellees deny those companies the opportunity to purchase cabs in a free, competitive market. The Sherman Act has never been thought to sanction such a conspiracy to restrain the free purchase of goods in interstate commerce.[40]

When the case was remanded for reconsideration, the district court concluded that the 1929–1932 acquisitions had not in fact been made with the intent of foreclosing taxi markets to other manufacturers, and that the operating companies purchased Checker cabs not because of parent company pressure, but because they were the best-suited products available. Therefore, a decision was entered in favor of CCM. The Justice Department appealed again, but the Supreme Court refused to overturn the lower court's findings of fact, allowing the decision to stand.[41]

Further clarification followed in 1948. The Justice Department sued to prevent U. S. Steel, which controlled 39 per cent of Pacific and Mountain states steel ingot capacity, from acquiring (through its Columbia Steel Division) the Consolidated Steel Corporation, a specialist in structural steel and plate fabrication accounting for roughly 11 per cent of such products in the 11 state market it served. The government charged in part that the merger would foreclose competitors of U. S. Steel from selling rolled steel products, and especially steel plates and shapes, to Consolidated. Consolidated consumed 3 per cent of all rolled steel output in the eleven state Pacific and Mountain area. It purchased roughly 13 per cent of the steel plates and shapes manufactured in that area. In a five-to-four split decision, the Supreme Court ruled that the share of the market foreclosed was not sufficient to strike down the merger under the Sherman Act. It went on to state a rule of reason guiding such cases:

> Exclusive dealings for rolled steel between Consolidated and United States Steel, brought about by vertical integration or otherwise, are not illegal, at any rate until the effect of such control is to unreasonably restrict the opportunities of competitors to market their product. . . . It seems clear to us that vertical integration, as such without more, cannot be held violative of the Sherman Act. . . . In determining what constitutes unreasonable restraint, . . . we look rather to the percentage of business controlled, the strength of the remaining competition, whether the action springs from business

[39] *U. S. v. Yellow Cab Co. et al.*, 332 U. S. 218 (1947). Yellow Cab was one of the Chicago operating affiliates of Checker Manufacturing.
[40] 332 U. S 218, 226–227 (1947).
[41] *U. S. v. Yellow Cab Co. et al.*, 338 U. S. 338 (1949).

requirements or purpose to monopolize, the probable development of the industry, consumer demands, and other characteristics of the market.[42]

Although the Justice Department suffered defeat under the concrete facts of these two leading cases, precedents were established for attacking vertical links which foreclose a large share of the market and which manifest some intent to foreclose. In other cases where vertical foreclosure was combined with additional unambiguously illegal restraints, the courts have ordered severance of the offending relationships. For instance, after being convicted of monopolizing the sleeping-car manufacturing and operating business, the Pullman Company was required in 1944 to sell off its car operating branch.[43] Likewise, the five leading American motion picture producers were ordered to sell 1,197 theaters to independent exhibition companies because they had violated the Sherman Act through a multitude of horizontal and vertical ties.[44]

ATTENUATION OF THE ATTACK ON HORIZONTAL MARKET POWER

In hindsight, the *Alcoa*, *A & P*, and motion picture exhibition chain decisions of the late 1940s appear to have been a high water mark in judicial willingness to infer monopolization without proof of oppressive business practices, just as the conscious parallelism doctrine under Sherman Act Section 1 reached its zenith in nearly contemporaneous decisions. Any illusion that the courts had shifted to a uniformly hard line against firms dominating their markets was shat-

tered in 1956, when the Supreme Court found du Pont innocent of monopolizing cellophane production.[45] Once again, the crucial issue was definition of the relevant market. The Justice Department, emphasizing cellophane's unique properties and the substantial price differences between cellophane and other packaging materials, argued for a narrow definition embracing only cellophane sales, which du Pont clearly dominated by virtue of patents it acquired from a French company, patents it secured on its own improvement inventions, and licensing arrangements it worked out with an American firm challenging its patent claims.[46] Attorneys for du Pont argued that there was a high cross elasticity of demand between cellophane and other flexible packaging materials, and therefore that cellophane ought to be considered only a part of that broader market, in which its share was roughly 18 per cent. A Wilmington, Delaware, district court accepted the broader market definition, acquitting du Pont. In a four-three split decision, the Supreme Court affirmed the lower court's judgment, concluding that:

> While the application of the (market definition) tests remains uncertain, it seems to us that du Pont should not be found to monopolize cellophane when that product has the competition and interchangeability with other wrappings that this record shows.[47]

Since 1956 there has been little judicial action on the Section 2 front involving charges of horizontal market domination untainted by other prohibited practices.[48] Several potentially spec-

[42]*U. S.* v. *Columbia Steel Co. et al.*, 334 U. S. 495, 524, 525, 527 (1948).

[43]*U. S.* v. *Pullman Co.*, 50 F. Supp. 123 (1943); 53 F. Supp. 908 (1944); 55 F. Supp. 985 (1944); and 64 F. Supp. 108 (1945).

[44]*U. S.* v. *Paramount Pictures, Inc., et al.*, 334 U. S. 131 (1948); 85 F. Supp. 881 (1949); and *Loew's, Inc.* v. *U. S.*, 339 U. S. 974 (1950).

[45]*U. S.* v. *E. I. du Pont de Nemours and Co.*, 118 F. Supp. 41 (1953), 351 U. S. 377 (1956). See also the critical article by G. W. Stocking and W. F. Mueller, "The Cellophane Case and the New Competition," *American Economic Review*, March 1955, pp. 29–63.

[46]Also at issue was the question of whether the patent practices through which du Pont maintained its dominance justified an inference of illegal intent to monopolize. The district court thought not, but the Supreme Court, having concluded that du Pont had no monopoly, did not consider the question.

[47]351 U. S. 377, 404 (1956).

[48]The principal government victories were *U. S.* v. *International Boxing Club of New York*, 358 U. S. 242 (1959), 171 F. Supp. 841 (1959); and *U. S.* v. *Grinnell Corporation et al.*, 236 F. Supp. 244 (1964); 384 U. S. 563 (1966). Noteworthy defeats included *U. S.* v. *National Malleable & Steel Castings Co. et al.*, CCH 1957 Trade Cases, Para. 68,890; and *U. S.* v. *General Motors Corporation* (the diesel locomotive case), dropped by the Justice Department in 1967 due to insufficient evidence.

tacular actions were initiated by the Department of Justice, but these were typically settled not with a bang but a whimper through *consent decrees*—remedial agreements negotiated out of court by the adversaries in a case. A consent decree leaves unresolved the question of guilt vs. innocence, but it is binding upon the parties once the decree has been approved by a federal court. A suit alleging monopolization of color film processing by Eastman Kodak Company, for example, was settled with an agreement that Eastman reduce its share of the processing market to below 50 per cent within seven years, helping new firms enter the industry by licensing its patents and conveying its know-how to them.[49] A consent decree with similar provisions affecting tabulating card production ended the suit against IBM charging monopolization of the key punch and related mechanical (but not electronic) data processing equipment industry.[50] The Radio Corporation of America emerged from a suit challenging its domination of television technology by agreeing to license large numbers of patents on a royalty-free basis.[51] Western Electric, the manufacturing arm of A.T. & T., consented to a program of patent licensing and the divestiture of minor subsidiary operations, escaping the major three-way structural break-up originally sought by the government.[52] In 1958 the United Fruit Corporation agreed to relinquish a part of its banana barony by establishing and 'spinning off' a new firm capable of handling 35 per cent of all U. S. banana imports.[53] And in an action attacking General Motors' 85 per cent share of the domestic inter-city bus manufacturing industry, the consent settlement specified several actions by GM to enhance the viability of existing competitors, plus the possibility of future divestiture if any existing rival failed or if GM retained its dominant share despite market growth.[54]

The willingness of companies to yield concessions in settling these monopolization suits without protracted litigation was no doubt influenced by the presence of the *Alcoa*, *A & P*, *Griffith*, and *United Shoe Machinery* precedents in the background, just as fear of another defeat like cellophane motivated the enforcement agencies to settle for remedies weaker than those asked in their initial pleas. Both businessmen and trust-busters are risk-averters. Still it is clear that, on balance, Section 2 enforcement during the 1950s and 1960s has been disappointing to those who saw the *Alcoa* decision opening up vast new horizons for the dissolution of monopolistic market structures.

It is equally apparent, however, that the existence of Section 2 and the court decisions interpreting it has a potent but unmeasurable impact on the behavior of firms with substantial market shares, especially in view of the courts' sympathetic attitude toward treble damage suits against violators. Harassment through patent litigation, predation on weaker rivals through local price warfare, sales policies which needlessly impede entry, and the like are recognized to be extremely dangerous, and few producers with dominant market positions are willing to risk them.

On the less favorable side of the balance, it is possible that fear of Section 2 and related treble damages attacks has led firms with substantial market shares to restrain their competitive efforts so as not to exceed that magic 60 to 64 per cent share identified by Judge Hand as the threshold of legally vulnerable monopoly. That General Motors is so inhibited in pricing its automobiles has been claimed repeatedly, though the charge is denied with equal frequency by GM's management.[55] According to executives of the Xerox Corporation, their company's patent licensing and pricing policies have been significantly influenced by fear that full and unilateral exploita-

---

[49] *U. S. v. Eastman Kodak Co.*, CCH 1954 Trade Cases, Para. 67,920; CCH 1961 Trade Cases, Para. 70,100.

[50] *U. S. v. International Business Machines Corp.*, CCH 1956 Trade Cases, Para. 68,245; CCH 1963 Trade Cases, Para. 70,628.

[51] *U. S. v. Radio Corporation of America*, CCH 1958 Trade Cases, Para. 69,164.

[52] *U. S. v. Western Electric, Inc., et al.*, CCH 1956 Trade Cases, Para. 68,246.

[53] *U. S. v. United Fruit Corporation*, CCH 1958 Trade Cases, Para. 68,941.

[54] *U. S. v. General Motors Corporation*, CCH 1965 Trade Cases, Para. 71,624.

[55] See, for example, Simon Whitney, *Antitrust Policies* (New York: 20th Century Fund, 1958), vol. I, pp. 482–483; and Martin Shubik, *Strategy and Market Structure* (New York: Wiley, 1959), pp. 304–307.

tion of their xerography patent portfolio would provoke an antitrust suit.[56] Paradoxically, General Electric and Westinghouse executives reportedly participated in electrical equipment price-fixing schemes during the 1950s partly to prevent the demise of weaker rivals, which might have led to monopolization charges.[57] Officials of several large corporations reported in interviews that they prefer to concentrate their energy on invading new markets instead of building legally vulnerable dominant positions in traditional markets.[58] There is more than a grain of truth in the adage, 'The ghost of Senator Sherman sits at the board table of every large corporation.'

PROPOSALS TO REFORM SHERMAN ACT SECTION 2

By and large, concentrated market structures have been vulnerable to attack under Sherman Act Section 2 only in extreme cases, and it cannot be said that the enforcement of Section 2 has caused much observable movement toward an economy of genuinely competitive market structures. This much is obvious from our brief chronology of the leading Section 2 cases. It is supported by analysis of existing market structure patterns and by Bain's finding that concentration in American manufacturing industries is often much higher than it needs to be to support all known production and physical distribution economies of scale.[59]

Some students of antitrust policy, disappointed by the record of Section 2 enforcement and adjudication, have advocated a substantial strengthening of the antitrust laws to cope more

effectively with market concentration. The most influential of these proposals has been offered by Carl Kaysen and Donald F. Turner.[60] Their argument merits detailed scrutiny.

Kaysen and Turner suggest that Sherman Act Section 2 be replaced by a statute which declares "unreasonable market power" to be injurious to trade and commerce.[61] The existence of market power would be conclusively presumed if for five years or more one firm has accounted for 50 per cent or more of annual sales in a relevantly defined market, or if four or fewer companies have collectively made 80 per cent or more of sales. Upon such a conclusive showing by an antitrust enforcement agency, a *prima facie* case for liability would exist. The defendants might rebut it by proving that their power was created and maintained entirely or almost entirely because of scale economies, superior efficiency or innovativeness, and/or the ownership of valid patents, not abused. If they cannot sustain this burden of proof, the remedy normally prescribed would be structural fragmentation.

Kaysen and Turner build their case for taking this bold step on three main propositions.[62] The first is a value judgment: Reliance on self-regulating competitive market processes is preferred to either of its chief alternatives—private monopoly control or control by a governmental bureaucracy. Second is an analytical judgment: that there is some minimum level of structural competition which must be achieved if the market sector is to remain market-regulated rather than government-regulated. And this quantum is said not to be self-sustaining; in the absence of effective antitrust, market concentration will tend to

[56]Erwin A. Blackstone, "The Copying Machine Industry: A Case Study," Ph.D. dissertation, University o Michigan, 1968, pp. 90–96.

[57]"Antitrust and Organization Man," *Wall Street Journal*, January 10, 1961, p. 12.

[58]A. D. H. Kaplan, J. B. Dirlam, and R. F Lanzillotti, *Pricing in Big Business* (Washington: Brookings, 1958), p. 268.

[59]See Joe S. Bain, "Economies of Scale, Concentration, and the Condition of Entry in Twenty Manufacturing Industries," *American Economic Review*, March 1954, pp. 15–39. See also pp. 83–85 and 91–92 *supra*.

[60]Carl Kaysen and Donald F. Turner, *Antitrust Policy: An Economic and Legal Analysis* (Cambridge: Harvard University Press, 1959). Kaysen is presently director of the Institute for Advanced Studies in Princeton, N. J.; Turner is professor of law at Harvard University, and between 1965 and 1968 was Assistant Attorney General for Antitrust Enforcement. An earlier but similar proposal was made by the Twentieth Century Fund's Committee on Cartels and Monopolies. See G. W. Stocking and M. W. Watkins, *Monopoly and Free Enterprise* (New York: Twentieth Century Fund, 1951), pp. 553 and 563–564. See also the *Report of the White House Task Force on Antitrust Policy* (Washington: July 5, 1968), Section II and Appendix A, which advocates legislation along Kaysen-Turner lines.

[61]Kaysen and Turner, *op. cit.*, pp. 98–99, 112–119, and 266–270.

[62]*Ibid.*, pp. 4–5, 14–16, 44–45, and 94–97.

rise above the tolerable ceiling. Their third proposition also involves an analytic judgment: Present antitrust policies are not able to cope effectively with market power as it exists in the contemporary American economy.

This last judgment rests in turn partly upon economic and partly upon legal premises. Put succinctly, they argue that "The principal defect of present antitrust law is its inability to cope with market power created by jointly acting oligopolists."[63] Or as Professor Edward Mason wrote in his introduction to the Kaysen and Turner work, "The critical problem—and the chief difficulty confronting anyone who wishes to reassess antitrust policy—is presented by oligopoly."[64]

On the economic side, Kaysen and Turner begin their study with a detailed reexamination of market structures in the American economy. From it they conclude that more than half of all manufacturing industry, strategic to overall economic performance in many ways, is oligopolistic. Following Chamberlin and Fellner, they argue that the principal sellers in a structurally oligopolistic market "have a share of the market sufficient to make it likely that they will recognize the interaction of their own behavior and their rivals' response in determining the values of the market variables."[65] And when mutual interdependence is thus taken into account, "the members of the industry behave nonrivalrously for mutual benefit."[66] In other words, an approximation to monopoly pricing will emerge in a substantial fraction of the economy, even though there is no single firm with 65 to 90 per cent of the market, and even though no explicit collusive agreements of the type illegal *per se* under Sherman Act Section 1 are attempted.

On the legal side, Kaysen and Turner recognize that the conscious parallelism doctrine has not been carried sufficiently far by the courts to prohibit oligopoly pricing which is merely restrained and non-aggressive. Moreover, one of the most convenient devices for coordinating pricing decisions—price leadership—lies within the bounds of the law. And even if guilt could be inferred from Chamberlinian behavior under the conscious parallelism doctrine, it is doubtful whether merely attacking pricing policies would accomplish much. As we have seen in our discussion of the *American Tobacco* case, it is futile to tell firms in a tightly oligopolistic industry to stop taking their interdependence into account.[67] Only by altering the *structural* conditions—i.e., the fewness of sellers—can the basic problem be solved.

It should be noted that there is another line of development in antitrust law which might make it possible to bring tight-knit oligopolies within the grasp of Sherman Act Section 2 as well as Section 1. In the 1946 *American Tobacco* decision, the Big Three were found guilty not only of a price-fixing conspiracy, but also of monopolization and conspiracy to monopolize. None of the three had a sufficiently large share of the market alone to cross the 60 to 64 per cent line drawn by Judge Hand, but together they maintained an 85 per cent share. And given evidence that they acted with "a unity of purpose or a common design and understanding," the three were found to be guilty of collective monopolization.[68] Similarly, the leading five motion picture producers during the 1940s controlled 70 per cent of the first-run theaters in cities with population exceeding 100,000, as well as being linked together through a variety of horizontal and vertical agreements, both express and tacit. In its instructions to the trial court, the Supreme Court observed that the collective actions of the defendants and the share of the large-city market they controlled might be viewed as evidence of monopolization.[69] Taking the hint, the district court ruled that:

> In respect to monopoly power, we think it existed in this case. As we have shown, the

[63]*Ibid.*, p 110.
[64]*Ibid.*, p. xix.
[65]*Ibid.*, p. 27.
[66]*Ibid.*, p. 44.
[67]Cf. p. 465 *supra*.
[68]*American Tobacco Co. et al. v. U. S.*, 328 U. S. 781, 810 (1946).
[69]*U. S. v. Paramount Pictures, Inc., et al.*, 334 U. S. 131, 166–175 (1948).

defendants were all working together. There was a horizontal conspiracy as to price-fixing, runs, and clearances. The vertical integrations aided such a conspiracy at every point. In these circumstances, the defendants must be viewed *collectively* rather than independently as to the power which they exercised over the market by their theatre holdings.[70]

On the basis of this monopolization finding, divestiture of 1,197 theaters was ordered. Still in both the *American Tobacco* and the *Paramount* cases, there was a good deal more than mere recognition of mutual interdependence, and so the cases do not lay a foundation for the kind of attack on oligopoly structure and conduct Kaysen and Turner consider warranted.

Even if it were possible by modest extension of existing doctrines to rule tacitly collusive oligopoly behavior illegal under Sherman Act Sections 1 and 2, it is not clear that the courts would be willing, without further guidance from Congress, to undertake the radical surgery required to atomize market structures and make recognition of mutual interdependence unlikely. Between 1890 and 1955, the courts have ordered corporate dissolution, divestiture, or divorcement (called the three D's of antitrust) in only 24 litigated Sherman Act cases, and between 1955 and 1968 there were only two additions to the list.[71] A few of these orders have been quite drastic—i.e., the division of New Jersey Standard Oil into 33 pieces; the dissolution of the Tobacco Trust; the splitting of du Pont into three separate powder manufacturing firms; the divorcement of the Pullman manufacturing and car-operating activities; and the separation of 1,197 theaters from the motion picture producing Big Five. But most have been mild, such as the order requiring du Pont to end its joint ventures with Imperial Chemical Industries, Ltd., or the 1954 decree requiring that United Shoe Machinery

Corp. divest its tack, nail, and eyelet manufacturing subsidiaries.

The reasons for this restraint were stated by the Supreme Court when it refused to require the Timken Roller Bearing Co. to sell its controlling interests in foreign firms:

> Since divestiture is a remedy to restore competition and not to punish those who restrain trade, it is not to be used indiscriminately, without regard to the type of violation or whether other effective methods, less harsh, are available.[72]

Or as Judge Wyzanski cautioned in his United Shoe Machinery decision:

> In the anti-trust field the courts have been accorded . . . an authority they have in no other branch of enacted law. . . . They would not have been given, or allowed to keep, such authority in the anti-trust field, and they would not so freely have altered from time to time the interpretation of its substantive provisions, if courts were in the habit of proceeding with the surgical ruthlessness that might commend itself to those seeking absolute assurances that there will be workable competition.[73]

In part, this reticence is due to a natural fear that, through incomplete knowledge of an industry's technology and economics, the courts might impair industrial efficiency and make matters worse than they were before the divestiture decree. Firms operating technically complex production processes and/or carrying out ambitious programs of research and new product development are especially apt to escape judicial fragmentation. The courts are more willing to tamper structurally with a motion picture exhibition chain or a railroad car manufacturer mired in 19th century technology than with a digital computer maker or with the company which introduced cellophane, nylon, teflon, and

---

[70] *Ibid.*, 85 F. Supp. 881, 894 (1949) (emphasis added).

[71] For a listing, see U. S. Department of Justice, *Report of the Attorney General's National Committee To Study the Antitrust Laws* (Washington: 1955), p. 354 n. A few minor cases seem to have been overlooked. The cases since 1955 are *U. S. v. International Boxing Club of New York*, 358 U. S. 242 (1959); and *U. S. v. Grinnell Corporation*, 384 U. S. 563 (1966). See also note 38, p. 461 *supra*.

[72] *Timken Roller Bearing Co. v. U. S.*, 341 U. S. 593, 603 (1951).

[73] *U. S. v. United Shoe Machinery Corp.*, 110 F. Supp. 295, 348 (1953). It is worth noting that Kaysen was Judge Wyzanski's "clerk" on this case.

synthetic rubber to the American public. If we could probe into the deepest recesses of the judicial psyche, we might discover that this, rather than the esoterica of market definition, was the real basis of the Supreme Court's 1956 *Cellophane* decision. Recognition that the courts dread surgery on technically progressive firms no doubt affected the government's readiness to settle monopolization suits against IBM, Eastman Kodak, Radio Corporation of America, and A.T. & T. with moderate consent decrees.

The dearth of dramatic dissolution orders is also attributable to judicial recognition that in some cases structural fragmentation cannot proceed very far without imposing palpable efficiency sacrifices. This was clearly so in the *Alcoa* case, for at the time Alcoa owned only two plants for reducing bauxite ore to alumina, and it would have been impossible to split its operations into more than two efficient integrated pieces. Similarly, United Shoe Machinery Corporation conducted nearly all of its machine production in a single plant, making it difficult to implement the government's proposed plan of breaking United into three competing parts. In the telephone equipment field, it might have been feasible to divide up Western Electric's production operations among three new firms independent of each other and A.T. & T., as the government suit originally asked, though certain modest scale economies might have been lost. But the plan for breaking off Bell Telephone Laboratories from Western Electric, putting what *Fortune* called "the world's greatest industrial laboratory" under the wing of A.T. & T., reflected a completely inadequate understanding of industrial research and innovation.[74] The vast bulk of BTL's activity comprised not the basic research which wins Nobel prizes, but detailed equipment engineering and design work which requires intimate coordination with production divisions. And in the suit concerning General Motors'

domination of inter-city bus manufacturing, the Justice Department settled for less than divestiture because all of GM's output was produced in a single plant, and it recognized that the market at the time was too small to absorb an additional entrant of minimum efficient scale.

To admit that these problems sometimes exist is not to say that they always intrude. There are many concentrated industries in which the leading firms operate numerous self-sufficient plants, and from Bain's research, it does not seem likely that atomization of such operations would cause a significant loss of production and physical distribution economies. U. S. Steel, for instance, could surely be broken into three or four pieces without any efficiency sacrifice, and Bethlehem could be cleaved into two parts (centered on its large Sparrows Point, Maryland, and Burns Harbor, Indiana complexes). Paradoxically, the national concentration ratio for the steel industry, which probably needs structural reorganization more acutely than any other American manufacturing industry, is too low to qualify for automatic inclusion under the Kaysen-Turner unreasonable market power criterion! Other oligopolistic industries in which considerable divestiture could probably be effected without serious efficiency losses include copper mining and refining, electric lamps, flat glass, gypsum products, synthetic rubber, tires, storage batteries, cement, industrial gases, soaps and detergents, tin cans, glass bottles, explosives, petroleum refining, cigarettes, and synthetic fibers. In automobiles, which is absent from this list, the most that could be accomplished under existing conditions is a two-way split of General Motors, for GM has only two production complexes for certain high-scale-economy components, and one fragment of a similarly divided Ford Motor Company is not likely to be viable. It is doubtful whether such a reorganization would have much impact on auto industry per-

[74]Cf. Francis Bello, "The World's Greatest Industrial Laboratory," *Fortune*, November 1958. The importance of BTL's vertical integration with Western Electric was stressed by A. T. & T. in its fight to stave off divestiture, but the tactics of the battle bordered on the scandalous. See U. S. House of Representatives, Committee on the Judiciary, Antitrust Subcommittee, Report, *Consent Decree Program of the Department of Justice* (Washington: 1959), pp. 29–120. A more rational approach would have been to split up Bell Telephone Laboratories into three pieces and to give each Western Electric fragment a piece, but at the time most of BTL's non-military work was concentrated in one set of buildings at Murray Hill, New Jersey. It is arguable what fragmentation would do to BTL's innovative productivity.

formance. Still the main implication is that a structural attack of the sort proposed by Kaysen and Turner would be feasible for many oligopolistic industries, even if not for all.

Thus, infeasibility of divestiture is not a fatal flaw in the Kaysen-Turner scheme, though it would limit the scope of the program to a subsample considerably smaller than the population of all oligopolistic industries. To this caveat one further qualification must be appended. The economic basis of the proposal, as we have seen, is the assumption that oligopolists' behavior conforms to the Chamberlinian tacit collusion model. This in turn embodies an unstated assumption that products are homogeneous, for recognition of mutual interdependence can break down if products are heterogeneous, and especially if the offerings of rival sellers vary widely over numerous technical and physical dimensions.[75] It is probable, for example, that price competition in the computer, electrical switchgear, and jet aircraft engine fields is a good deal more vigorous than one might suppose merely from examining those industries' high concentration ratios. From the survey of oligopolistic industries reported in Chapter 7, this objection would appear to apply with some force in at least a fifth of the 65 industries characterized by Kaysen and Turner as "Type I oligopolies."[76] The existence of moderate or low barriers to new entry might also ensure satisfactory long-run performance. We are left with the impression that the Kaysen-Turner proposal is more limited in utility than their analysis implies. Yet for those industries to which the analysis does apply without qualification—and they clearly account for an appreciable share of all industrial output— a greatly strengthened antitrust attack along the Kaysen-Turner lines deserves the most sympathetic consideration.

MERGER POLICY

Besides breaking up consolidations of monopoly power already in existence, there is another way to help maintain structural competition: by curbing the dynamic process of concentration before it goes too far. This is the task of merger policy.

Around the turn of the century, we have observed, a merger wave of massive proportions contributed dramatically to the concentration of American manufacturing industry. Scores of firms controlling more than half the production capacity of their home industries were created through the amalgamation of numerous formerly independent entities. At the time, the Sherman Act had not yet been extended judicially to stop such mergers, and it may even have encouraged them by denying businessmen the opportunity lawfully to restrict trade through loose price-fixing agreements while leaving open the path to monopolization through structural consolidation

Since then there have been two major merger waves, one spanning the 1916–1929 period and another the prosperous quarter century following World War II. These have also affected industrial structure, but their contribution to the increase of concentration in specific markets has for the most part been modest. It is possible that the strengthening of anti-merger policy between 1904 and 1914 had some effect in slowing down the merger movement. But that is surely not the whole explanation, for as we shall see, the law governing mergers was not very potent at first. Also, there might be alternative explanations for the declining importance of mergers as a concentration-increasing force. The most attractive opportunities for gaining monopoly power through merger may have been exhausted during the first great merger wave. Or businessmen may have learned from the many disappointing mergers of the 1890s that they were unable to manage a giant consolidation successfully, or that lasting monopoly power could be achieved through merger only if it was possible to erect substantial barriers to new entry. Whatever the mix of reasons, there was a marked change in the structural consequences of mergers.

[75]The implications of the assumption and its violation are nowhere treated explicitly in the Kaysen-Turner book. Professor Turner does recognize the problem in "Conglomerate Mergers and Section 7 of the Clayton Act," *Harvard Law Review*, May 1965, p. 1355.

[76]Cf. pp. 186–190 *supra*.

THE MOTIVES FOR AND EFFECTS OF MERGERS

In order to formulate an intelligent policy, we must weigh the harmful against the socially beneficial effects of mergers. This leads us to examine the motives for merger, for businessmen will what they expect to achieve. The analytic job has been done in Chapter 4, but a brief review will be helpful.

Most modern mergers involve the acquisition by one firm of one or more (typically smaller) companies. Motives peculiar to the heads of firms willing to be acquired include the desire to preserve organizational continuity or to salvage the enterprise when it is in danger of failing; the desire of elderly owner-managers lacking suitable successors to escape the burden of management by selling out; and the desire of small, closely-held company owners to minimize the adverse tax impact of passing on ownership of their wealth to heirs.

Acquiring firms are influenced by the expectation of many different effects. We list 10 here, appending a brief comment on the desirability of each from the standpoint of public policy.

(1) *To reduce competition and gain monopoly power.* Here the acquiring firm realizes higher profits once competition is eliminated, but the public suffers from poorer resource allocation and all the other detriments of monopoly. This motive is less important now than it was in the 1890s, but from the accumulation of many small mergers may follow a substantial lessening of competition.

(2) *To realize promotional profits.* This strictly private benefit is achieved most readily when monopoly can be established through merger, or when it is possible to engage in stock-watering by disseminating misleading information to unwary securities purchasers. It is less important now than in the 1890s and 1920s, but opportunities to profit still exist both for insiders with stock options and for outside merger brokers.

(3) *To utilize complementary resources more effectively.* Both private and social benefits may accrue when a good research department is married to an affluent would-be research sponsor, when a firm with sound physical facilities but weak management merges with a company rich in managerial talent, or when transaction and planning costs can be reduced through vertical integration of processes. On the other hand, competition may be reduced if a vertical merger forecloses some substantial market.

(4) *To secure production and physical distribution scale economies.* To the extent that such economies are realized through merger, society will benefit. But these benefits are seldom substantial, since scale economies normally result from building larger new plants, not from combining more existing plants. If new plants are to be constructed, it can be done through internal expansion, without merging.

(5) *To secure promotional and pecuniary economies of scale.* An increase in size may confer such private benefits as input price discounts and more effective advertising medium saturation. Whether they are matched by social benefits is debatable. Pecuniary benefits merely redistribute income. Promotional economies may entrench monopoly positions, so that cost savings are not necessarily passed along to consumers.

(6) *To 'rationalize' existing production operations.* Surplus, high-cost production facilities may be closed down, affording savings to the merged entities. The balance of remaining production operations may also be improved. But rationalization opportunities are normally the result of already monopolistic conditions, for vigorous competition would drive out inefficient surplus capacity. Furthermore, theoretical analysis shows that monopolistic rationalization leads to lower end product prices only in special cases.[77]

(7) *To spread risks or move from declining to expanding fields.* Diversification mergers may yield high utility to company managers and staff. Their social benefits are more dubious. Stockholders can spread their risks by acquiring a balanced portfolio of specialized securities. Merger is also not the only available path to diversi-

---

[77]Cf. pp. 139–140 and 163–164 *supra*.

fication. The internal development and promotion of new products may serve as well.

(8) *To build an empire.* Because it is possible for a firm to increase its sales more rapidly through merger than through the patient cultivation of internal growth opportunities, mergers have been a favorite device of entrepreneurs driven by the desire to build an industrial empire. It is doubtful whether such mergers provide any social benefits in addition to those already listed. We must be careful to avoid the common fallacy of confusing growth from the viewpoint of an acquiring firm with growth from the standpoint of society as a whole.

(9) *To pick up new capacity at bargain prices.* The benefits here are almost exclusively private, since wealth is merely redistributed. This is a common motive for mergers mainly because the market for mergers is imperfect.

(10) *To expand production without depressing prices.* The gains here are solely private, stemming from the restrictionist mentality of sellers possessing market power. Only if real output is increased, e.g., by building new production capacity rather than buying out existing capacity, does expansion from the standpoint of society take place.

FORMULATING AN OPTIMAL POLICY TOWARD MERGERS

Clearly, there are many motives for and effects of merger, some salutary, others of dubious or negative social utility. Given the complexity of the problem, what should public policy be?

In an ideal world, the best policy would be a rule of reason which discourages only the undesirable mergers—those whose social costs, in terms of stifled competition and all it connotes, outweigh their social benefits, such as lower costs or higher real economic growth.[78] Unfortunately, the world we live in is far from ideal. It is extremely difficult to assess motives and to predict the effects of a given merger into the uncertain future. Businessmen called into court to explain their motives may have incentives to be less than completely candid. Nor is faulty testimony necessarily the result of deliberate concealment. Due to the inherent uncertainties pervading business decisions and the frequently muddled state of business thinking on mergers, executives may not foresee clearly the effects of alternate actions.

For instance, a high Bethlehem Steel Corporation official, explaining his firm's motives for acquiring the Youngstown Sheet and Tube Co., testified that East-Coast-bound Bethlehem could not construct an integrated steel plant in the Chicago area unless it was permitted to take advantage of Youngstown's existing position in that market.[79] Four years after the merger was prohibited, Bethlehem began constructing a $500 million integrated plant at Burns Harbor, Indiana; while Youngstown committed $255 million to expand and modernize its Chicago area facilities.[80] Similarly, officials of the International Telephone and Telegraph Co. and the American Broadcasting Corporation entered into a merger agreement in 1965 with totally inconsistent expectations. I.T. &T. directors expected ABC to generate a net cash flow of $100 million by 1970 to finance I.T. &T.'s diversification into other fields, while ABC expected I.T. &T. to finance its entry into color television with a net contribution of $140 million during the same period. This incompatibility became known only after the agreement was sealed. I.T. &T. also learned later that ABC would have sold out at an effective price of $83 per share, but held out in negotiations for a $100 price.[81] The sigh of relief heaved by I.T. &T. executives when the Justice Depart-

---

[78]For a formal model comparing the costs and benefits of mergers, see Oliver E. Williamson, "Economies as an Antitrust Defense: The Welfare Tradeoffs," *American Economic Review*, March 1968, pp. 18–34. Williamson finds that a relatively modest cost reduction is usually sufficient to offset the allocative efficiency losses of relatively large merger-related price increases.

[79]See Willard F. Mueller, *The Celler-Kefauver Act: Sixteen Years of Enforcement*, Staff Report to the Antitrust Subcommittee, Committee on the Judiciary, U. S. House of Representatives (Washington: 1967), p. 17 n.

[80]"Billions Build Chicago into a Steel Titan," *Business Week*, November 9, 1966, p. 71.

[81]See the reports of the Federal Communications Commission hearing in the *New York Times* April 13, 14, and 19, 1967.

ment made graceful exit feasible by suing to prevent the merger could be heard as far away as the San Francisco Stock Exchange (still open at the time of the Department's public announcement), where I.T. &T. stock prices rose and ABC prices fell sharply.

Flooded with such misinformation, the courts would make many bad decisions in applying a rule of reason to merger cases. If the antitrust enforcement agencies were required to bear the burden of proving unreasonableness, the bias in decisions would probably fall on the side of permitting doubtful acquisitions, since government economists and attorneys seldom have as much information about the effects of a proposed merger as the merging firms. The end result might well be a gradual decline in competition as one merger after another slipped through the judicial net.

Recognizing this danger, many students of antitrust policy have urged the adoption of stronger rules.[82] One might be to establish a *prima facie* case against certain mergers—i.e., those involving substantial shares of the relevant market—to be rebutted only if the prospective partners can offer convincing evidence that the social benefits of the merger outweigh the injury to competition. Or still tougher, all mergers involving a substantial share of the market might be declared *per se* illegal, without regard to benefits. Several arguments for taking a hard line can be advanced.

First, antitrust prohibitions affect only a small but vital proportion of all actual and potential mergers—notably, those in which an adverse impact on competition is especially likely. Only 1 to 2 per cent of all recorded mergers in recent years have been challenged by the government. Of the 923 manufacturing and mining mergers consummated between 1951 and 1966 in which

the acquired entity had assets of $10 million or more, only 94, or 10 per cent, were attacked.[83] To be sure, many others were thwarted before conception by the realization that a government challenge could not be avoided, but the fact remains that relatively few mergers would come under attack even with stringent rules.

Second, what evidence we have on the matter suggests that the social gains from mergers, and especially from sizeable horizontal mergers, are typically not very great. A firm denied the possibility of merging almost always has the alternative of expansion through internal building, which is more beneficial socially unless industry capacity is already excessive. Since the mergers attacked would be those with the highest probable social costs, and since the social benefits are seldom large, we should expect the net balance of costs vs. benefits under a strict policy to be relatively favorable or at worst not decisively unfavorable.

Third, it is much easier to check the development of market concentration in the bud through a hard line against mergers than it is to correct abuses or to atomize market structures once monopoly or oligopoly has emerged. To stop a merger before it is consummated means at most quenching an opportunity, while tampering with an already integrated monopolistic organization is sure to cause considerable pain and might even lessen efficiency. Once the eggs are scrambled, it is hard to unscramble them.[84]

For these reasons, many economists lean toward erring on the side of a hard stand against mergers, accepting the risk that occasionally mergers offering substantial efficiency benefits will be struck down because the judicial system is such an imperfect screen.

A different rationalization for a tough anti-merger policy is sometimes heard in the halls of

---

[82]See, for example, George J. Stigler, "Mergers and Preventive Antitrust Policy," *University of Pennsylvania Law Review*, November 1955, pp. 176–184; Kaysen and Turner, *Antitrust Policy*, pp. 132–133; and Derek C. Bok, "Section Seven of the Clayton Act and the Merging of Law and Economics," *Harvard Law Review*, December 1960, pp. 271–274 and 299–321.

[83]Cf. Mueller, *op. cit.*, pp. 5–8.

[84]This is not to say that divestiture is always easy in merger cases. When the litigation drags on for years, which is not uncommon, a considerable amount of scrambling may take place. However, those who integrate their organizations in the face of an anti-merger suit surely do so with fair warning and at their own risk. It may also be hard to find suitable customers willing to pay a non-confiscatory price for a divested acquisition. See "Finding Homes for Merger Orphans," *Business Week*, December 9, 1967, pp. 154–160; and "U. S. To Oppose Bids for Pipeline," *New York Times*, September 19, 1967, p. 61.

Congress. This is the populist argument: that bigness in business is bad on social and political grounds, irrespective of its economic merits. Occasionally, even stronger variants are encountered: i.e., that mergers lead to big firms more efficient than their smaller rivals, able therefore to drive the small man out of business. And elimination of the small man is deemed undesirable, whether or not efficiency is enhanced. This sentiment is reflected in a *dictum* from Judge Hand's *Alcoa* opinion:

> Throughout the history of these statutes it has been constantly assumed that one of their purposes was to perpetuate and preserve, for its own sake and in spite of possible cost, an organization of industry in small units which can effectively compete with each other.[85]

We shall meet it again when we examine some of the leading merger decisions.

Those who oppose a strong anti-merger rule on grounds other than narrow self-interest generally do so because their cost-benefit calculations yield answers different from those suggested here. For instance, the editors of *Fortune*, among the most forceful advocates of a soft line, argue that mergers which lead to oligopoly have little or no deleterious effect on competition in a world of dynamic technological change and high cross elasticities of demand among obvious and not-so-obvious substitutes.[86] Indeed, they assert, many mergers increase competition by replacing a lethargic management with an energetic one. At the same time, the soft line advocates impute a higher value to both the private and social benefits of mergers, even when they avoid (as they often do not) the trap of confusing private sales growth with social growth.

Such arguments cannot simply be dismissed out of hand. Whether the efficiency-increasing and progress-inducing effects of mergers are substantial or modest on the average is a factual

question, and the evidence available is less than conclusive. Until more abundant facts are available, the policy-maker must determine which alternative policy poses the smaller risk of serious social loss should its underlying premises prove incorrect. Because no one has been able to produce convincing evidence that mergers convey large social benefits unattainable through internal growth, because most of the evidence points in the opposite direction, and because oligopoly once achieved is hard to eliminate, most economists are inclined to err on the side of a tough policy. But again, the chance of error is there.

EARLY MERGER LAW

Having considered how merger policy ought to be formulated, let us see what has actually been done.

Mergers were originally attacked as illegal combinations in restraint of trade under Section 1 of the Sherman Act and as attempts to monopolize or (when carried far enough) outright monopolization under Section 2. The first government victory came in 1904, in the *Northern Securities* decision discussed earlier. It was followed by successful attacks on other railroad consolidations, including the Union Pacific's acquisition of a dominant stock interest in the Southern Pacific and the Southern Pacific's control of the Central Pacific. During the 1920s and 1930s, however, Sherman Act suits against mergers were attempted only infrequently. Whether this was because there were few mergers deemed to have restrained trade sufficiently, because the 1920 *U. S. Steel* rule was so permissive, or because of a general lack of interest and enthusiasm within the enforcement agencies, is not entirely clear. As we have seen, the government suffered defeat in 1948 when it invoked the Sherman Act to prevent U. S. Steel from acquiring Consolidated Steel. New life was breathed into the law when a merger between

---

[85]*U. S. v. Aluminum Co. of America et al.*, 148 F. 2d 416, 429 (1945).

[86]See Max Ways, "Antitrust in an Era of Radical Change," *Fortune*, March 1966, pp. 128 ff.; the rebuttal by Donald F. Turner, "The Antitrust Chief Dissents," *Fortune*, April 1966, pp. 113–114; an editorial counter-rejoinder, "A New 'Worst' in Antitrust," *idem*, pp. 111–112; and "Antitrust in a Coonskin Cap," *Fortune*, July 1, 1966, pp. 65–66. For a defense of mergers emphasizing the need to keep the largest possible number of firms on the buyers' side of the market to take over faltering corporations, see Henry G. Manne, "Mergers and the Market for Corporate Control," *Journal of Political Economy*, April 1965, pp. 110–120.

two Lexington, Kentucky, banks—one with 40 per cent of local banking assets and the other with 13 per cent—was successfully challenged in 1964. In that case the Supreme Court summarized its position as follows:

> . . . where merging companies are major competitive factors in a relevant market, the elimination of significant competition between them, by merger or consolidation, itself constitutes a violation of Section 1 of the Sherman Act. That standard was met in the present case in view of the fact that the two banks in question had such a large share of the relevant market.[87]

Use of the Sherman Act to deal with mergers has one important limitation. The statute cannot be applied successfully unless the merging firms are on the verge of attaining substantial monopoly power, and this may already be too late if the objective is to maintain competitive market structures. To remedy this and related deficiencies, Congress in 1914 passed the Clayton Act, whose stated purpose was "to arrest the creation of trusts, conspiracies and monopolies in their incipiency and before consummation."[88] The principal provision concerning mergers was Section 7, which read in part:

> That no corporation engaged in commerce shall acquire, directly or indirectly, the whole or any part of the stock or other share capital of another corporation engaged also in commerce where the effect of such acquisition may be to substantially lessen competition between [the two firms] or to restrain such commerce in any section or community or tend to create a monopoly of any line of commerce.

Unfortunately, this choice of language left a gaping loophole through which able corporation lawyers could navigate their clients. It banned only *stock* acquisitions—the dominant large-scale consolidation method of the times. By shifting to the outright purchase of a competitor's *assets*, companies could escape the bite of the law. Direct asset acquisition is not always easy, but the loophole was opened even wider through subsequent Supreme Court interpretations. In three 1926 cases the court ruled that a merger could not be broken up if the acquiring firm first bought its rival's stock, but liquidated the stock and transformed its position to one of asset ownership before the antitrust enforcement agencies brought suit.[89] Then, in 1934, the court found that a merger was safe if converted to the asset ownership form before a Federal Trade Commission order barring the merger was issued.[90] These decisions left Section 7 with few teeth. To make matters worse, the Supreme Court decided in 1930 that in proving a Section 7 violation, the government had to show nearly as substantial a lessening of competition as in Sherman Act cases.[91] The cumulative effect of these decisions was complete emasculation. Between 1926 and 1950 the Federal Trade Commission initiated 31 anti-merger complaints in carrying out its Section 7 enforcement responsibilities. Only five cease-and-desist orders were issued, all between 1926 and 1934, and all were subsequently overturned or evaded.[92] Altogether, only 15 mergers were ordered dissolved as a result of antitrust actions initiated between 1914 and 1950, and 10 of the dissolutions were accomplished through the Sherman Act rather than Clayton Act proceedings.

PASSAGE OF A STRENGTHENED SECTION 7

Two events provoked Congress to take corrective action. One was the government's defeat

---

[87] *U. S. v. First National Bank & Trust Co. of Lexington et al.*, 376 U. S. 665, 671–672 (1964).

[88] Senate Report No. 698, to accompany H.R. 15,657 (63rd Congress, 2d session, 1914), p. 1.

[89] *Thatcher Mfg. Co. v. Federal Trade Commission, Swift & Co. v. Federal Trade Commission*, and *Federal Trade Commission v. Western Meat Co.*, 272 U. S. 554 (1926).

[90] *Arrow-Hart & Hegeman Electric Co. v. Federal Trade Commission*, 291 U. S. 587 (1934).

[91] *International Shoe Co. v. Federal Trade Commission*, 280 U. S. 291 (1930). On the development of Clayton Act Section 7 interpretations during this period, see David Dale Martin, *Mergers and the Clayton Act* (Berkeley: University of California Press, 1959), especially pp. 104–147.

[92] Martin, *op. cit.*, pp. 148–163; and Jesse W. Markham, "The Effectiveness of Clayton Act Section 7, " in Almarin Phillips, ed., *Perspectives on Antitrust Policy* (Cambridge: Harvard University Press, 1965), pp. 167–169.

in its attempt to stop the U. S. Steel – Consolidated Steel merger. The other was publication of a report by the Federal Trade Commission viewing with alarm the increase in merger activity following World War II and suggesting that if nothing were done, "the giant corporations will ultimately take over the country."[93] The report was soon subjected to withering criticism for making inferences unsupported by the actual evidence, but that did not deter Congress from passing the Celler-Kefauver Act of 1950. The Act amended original Clayton Act Section 7, removing the asset acquisition loophole and making several changes in wording to bring non-horizontal mergers within the reach of the law, to eliminate a previously split infinitive, and to make clear Congress' desire to see a more vigorous anti-merger program implemented. Its principal substantive paragraph provides:

> That no corporation engaged in commerce shall acquire, directly or indirectly, the whole or any part of the stock or other share capital and no corporation subject to the jurisdiction of the Federal Trade Commission shall acquire the whole or any part of the assets of another corporation engaged also in commerce, where in any line of commerce in any section of the country, the effect of such acquisition may be substantially to lessen competition, or to tend to create a monopoly.

This new mandate was taken seriously by the enforcement agencies and the courts. From December 29, 1950, when the Celler-Kefauver amendment was signed, through December 31, 1965, the Federal Trade Commission and the Justice Department initiated a total of 173 anti-merger complaints under the new law—more than twice as many as they attempted during the 36 year life of old Section 7. As of July 1, 1967, the box score in these proceedings stood as follows:[94]

Cases won by the government:

Final court or Commission orders barring the merger	23
Consent decrees restraining past or future mergers	75
Merger voluntarily abandoned after challenge	12

Cases won by the respondents:

Final judgment in favor of the merger	18
Case dropped by the government	5*

Cases pending on July 1, 1967:

On appeal after prior government victory	12
On appeal after prior respondent victory	7
No preliminary decision rendered	21

*Two of these were the result of legislative action, when the Bank Merger Act of 1966 retroactively exempted three mergers attacked under Section 7.

Of the 133 actions which had progressed to final resolution as of July 1967, 110 must be called government victories—an 82 per cent batting average. Not all of these 110, however, were total victories; many ended in less than complete divestiture. Mrs. Bock found that of the 62 merger consent decrees filed between 1951 and 1965, 17 either barred the acquisition or required total divestiture; 38 required only partial divestiture of acquired assets; and the remaining seven required no divestiture.[95] Fifty-five of the 62 consent orders included provisions forbidding certain future mergers without express government approval.

Impressive though this record may be, the batting average of the enforcement agencies in appealing cases to the Supreme Court is even more remarkable. As of March 1968, the Supreme Court had written substantive opinions on 12 Section 7 case appeals.[96] In 11 it either struck down the merger directly or couched its decision in language which gave the lower court little alternative on remand but to prohibit the merger. Nine of these 11 were reversals of lower

---

[93]U. S. Federal Trade Commission, *The Merger Movement: A Summary Report* (Washington: 1948), p. 68. See also p. 108 *supra*.

[94]This summary was prepared from the compilation in Mueller, *op. cit.*, pp. 44–67.

[95]Betty Bock, *Mergers and Markets* (Fifth ed.; New York: National Industrial Conference Board, 1966), pp. 10, 39.

[96]In another case, the merger was prohibited after the Supreme Court rendered a jurisdictional opinion, and in two others the Court ruled against the mergers without writing an opinion. Excluded from the count are regulated industry merger decisions in which the Supreme Court limited the Celler-Kefauver Act's applicability on procedural grounds.

court decisions permitting the mergers—the most vivid possible way of communicating that a tough line was to be followed. In only one of the twelve cases was the merger allowed to stand, after the Supreme Court split four-four on whether or not to overturn a lower court's findings of fact.

JUDICIAL RULINGS: HORIZONTAL AND VERTICAL MERGERS

To see what rules have been applied by the courts in interpreting the new Section 7, we must examine the leading decisions.

Before beginning, however, we digress briefly to consider one more case brought under old Section 7. To the surprise of nearly everyone concerned, the government in 1957 was sustained by the Supreme Court on a 1949 suit to require divestiture of du Pont's 23 per cent stock interest in General Motors.[97] The Court found that the financial ties between du Pont and GM foreclosed du Pont's competitors from the opportunity to serve a substantial portion of the automobile industry's demand for synthetic lacquers and fabrics. Besides breaking a long chain of government defeats, the case was distinctive in three respects: as the first successful Section 7 action against a vertical acquisition; because of the 32 year delay between the stock acquisition attacked and initiation of a suit; and in the magnitude of the divestiture problems it posed. On the last point, Congress in 1962 passed a special act allowing du Pont stockholders to pay only capital gains tax rates on the General Motors shares distributed to them under the divestiture decree, instead of the higher regular income tax rates normally applicable.

The first major government victory under new Section 7 came, fittingly enough, in another steel industry merger case.[98] Bethlehem Steel Corporation, the nation's second largest producer, with 16.3 per cent of total U. S. ingot capacity, sought to acquire the Youngstown

Sheet & Tube Co., the sixth largest producer, with 4.6 per cent of ingot capacity. When challenged by the Justice Department, the companies argued that Bethlehem sold most of its output in the East, while Youngstown was primarily active in the Midwest, so that only about 10 per cent of their combined output was shipped to customers in overlapping geographic territories. This defense was rejected in 1958 by the district court, which held that steel transportation costs were sufficiently small in relation to product costs that competition in a nationwide market was practical, and that a merger combining 16.3 and 4.6 per cent of national capacity exemplified the substantial lessening of competition which Congress sought to outlaw under new Section 7. It also found the combined market shares excessive for several narrowly-defined product lines (such as cold-rolled sheet) and in certain geographic sub-markets (such as the Ohio-Michigan territory). The court was unimpressed by the defendants' argument that through the merger they could compete more effectively with U. S. Steel. It concluded to the contrary that the merger would make "even more remote than at present the possibility of any real competition from the smaller members of the industry who follow the leadership of United States Steel."[99] The respondents chose not to appeal, and as we have seen earlier, Bethlehem soon launched an ambitious program of building its own independent capacity to serve the Midwestern market.

New Section 7 withstood its first substantive Supreme Court test in 1962, when a lower court decision against the Brown Shoe Company's merger with the G. R. Kinney Co. was affirmed.[100] The merger had both horizontal and vertical ramifications. Brown was the fourth largest U. S. shoe manufacturer in 1955, producing approximately 4 per cent of national output. Kinney was the twelfth largest manufacturer, with 0.5 per cent of output. Brown was vertically integrated into shoe retailing, owning 470, or 2.1 per cent,

---

[97] *U. S. v. E. I. du Pont de Nemours and Co. et al.*, 353 U. S. 586 (1957); 366 U. S. 316 (1961).

[98] *U. S. v. Bethlehem Steel Corp. et al.*, 168 F. Supp. 576 (1958).

[99] 168 F. Supp. 576, 604 (1958)

[100] *Brown Shoe Co.* v. *U. S.*, 370 U. S. 294 (1962). See also David Dale Martin, "The Brown Shoe Case and the New Antimerger Policy," *American Economic Review*, June 1963, pp. 340–358; with a comment by B. J. Jones and a reply by Martin in the *American Economic Review*, June 1964, pp. 407–415.

of the nation's 22,000 outlets specializing in retail shoe sales, and managing through a subsidiary 190 department store shoe outlets. Kinney owned and operated more than 350 stores, selling 1.6 per cent of all non-rubber shoes in the U. S.

There was no contention that the merger posed a threat to horizontal competition in shoe manufacturing. Debate centered on competition in shoe retailing. The Supreme Court supported the lower court's finding that the relevant markets were individual cities with a population exceeding 10,000 and their environs, rejecting Brown's plea for detailed analysis of spatial buying patterns in particular cities. The combined unit sales shares of the two firms exceeded 20 per cent of the local market in 32 cities for women's shoes and in 31 cities for children's shoes; and this, said the Court, was sufficient to find a substantial lessening of competition under new Section 7. On the merger's vertical dimension, the relevant market was said to be nationwide in scope, with no distinction as to price ranges within which manufacturers and retailers specialized. The Court noted a trend in the shoe industry toward increasing vertical integration, with manufacturers becoming increasingly important sources of supply to their captive retail outlets. In the two years following the merger, Brown moved from supplying no shoes to Kinney stores to producing 8 per cent of their needs. The tendency of the merger was thus to foreclose other shoe manufacturers from a substantial share of the market, the Court concluded. And so the merger was struck down for its probable effects on competition both horizontally and vertically.

Subsequent decisions reinforced the impression that a hard line was to be taken. The *Von's – Shopping Bag* case is particularly significant.[101] Von's Grocery Co., third largest retail grocery chain in the Los Angeles area, with a 4.7 per cent share of the market in 1958, ac-

quired Shopping Bag Food Stores, the sixth largest retailer, whose elderly president and principal stockholder sought a merger to ensure managerial continuity of the chain he had built. Together they accounted for 7.5 per cent of all grocery sales in the area, second only to Safeway Stores, with 8 per cent of the market. Between 1950 and 1961 the number of independent single-unit grocery stores in the area had declined from 5,365 to 3,818. The market share of the top 20 chains had risen from 44 per cent in 1948 to 57 per cent in 1958, although the combined share of the leading five chains had fallen. A six-to-two majority of the Supreme Court reversed a lower court decision in favor of the merger. They stressed the trend toward increasing concentration in grocery retailing and the contribution the Von's – Shopping Bag merger made toward further concentration:

> It is enough for us that Congress feared that a market marked at the same time by both a continuous decline in the number of small businesses and a large number of mergers would slowly but inevitably gravitate from a market of many small competitors to one dominated by one or a few giants, and competition would thereby be destroyed. Congress passed the Celler-Kefauver Act to prevent such a destruction of competition.[102]

In a dissenting opinion, Justices Stewart and Harlan argued that the decline in the number of single-unit stores was the result of "transcending social and technological changes" and that competition in Los Angeles grocery retailing remained "pugnacious," with successful new entry at modest intitial investment levels perceptibly eroding the market shares of leading firms.[103] Still the majority carried the day, providing a powerful precedent for future antimerger actions. Immediately after the decision Assistant Attorney General Turner announced

---

[101]*U. S. v. Von's Grocery Co. et al.,* 384 U. S. 270 (1966).

[102]384 U. S. 270, 278 (1966).

[103]*Ibid.,* p. 300. The dissenting justices might also have noted that, given the multidimensional character of a supermarket's product line, pricing which pays close heed to mutual interdependence among 20 or so rivals is rather unlikely. For supporting evidence, see W. J. Baumol, R. E. Quandt, and H. T. Shapiro, "Oligopoly Theory and Retail Food Pricing," *Journal of Business,* October 1964, pp. 346–363.

that "Whenever we find any merger between healthy substantial competitors with 4 per cent or so of the market each, in an industry that tends toward concentration, we'll sue."

MARKET DEFINITION PRECEDENTS

As in Sherman Act monopolization cases, merger case decisions often hinge on how the relevant market is defined. There are two main sub-problems: defining the relevant geographic market and defining the product line. The Celler-Kefauver Act allows considerable scope for defining geographic markets, since it prohibits mergers which may "in any section of the country" substantially lessen competition. Given this broad mandate, the courts have been inclined to strike down mergers whenever a reasonable argument could be supported for delimiting markets in such a way as to show substantial anticompetitive effects. In the *Bethlehem – Youngstown* case, for example, both national and single-state definitions were accepted. In the *Brown Shoe – Kinney* case, a national definition was chosen for the vertical facets and a single-city definition for the horizontal effects. The Supreme Court found the State of Wisconsin and also the three-state Wisconsin – Michigan – Illinois territory to be relevant markets in considering the merger of Pabst Brewing Company with the Blatz Brewing Co. The two firms together accounted for 24 per cent of Wisconsin beer sales—enough to hold the merger illegal —but only 4.5 per cent of sales in the United States as a whole.[104] And in a bank merger decision, the Supreme Court concluded that even though certain large potential customers reached out hundreds of miles to secure banking services, a local definition was appropriate because:

> Individuals and corporations typically confer the bulk of their patronage on banks in their local community; they find it impractical to conduct their banking business at a distance. . . . The factor of inconvenience localizes banking competition as effectively as high transportation costs in other industries. . . . (T)hat in banking the relevant geographical market is a function of each separate customer's economic scale means simply that a workable compromise must be found: some fair intermediate delineation which avoids the indefensible extremes of drawing the market so expansively as to make the effect of the merger upon competition seem insignificant, because only the very largest bank customers are taken into account . . . or so narrowly as to place appellees in different markets, because only the smallest customers are considered.[105]

Similarly broad scope has been allowed in defining the relevant product line or "line of commerce." This is best seen by comparing two cases decided by the Supreme Court in the Spring of 1964.

One concerned acquisition of the Rome Cable Corporation by the Aluminum Company of America.[106] Alcoa produced various types of aluminum electrical conductor cable—a product line it pioneered and in which it was still the U. S. sales leader, though its share of the market had declined due to the entry of new competitors. Rome specialized in copper conductor cable, but about 10 per cent of its cable output was of aluminum. In defining the relevant market, the courts had to decide whether to view aluminum and copper conductors separately or in common, and whether or not to break down the market into narrower insulated and uninsulated cable subclasses. Estimates of Alcoa's and Rome's 1958 market shares for alternative definitions included the following:

	Alcoa	Rome
Bare aluminum conductor wire and cable	32.5%	0.3%
Insulated aluminum conductor wire and cable	11.6%	4.7%
Combined aluminum conductor wire and cable	27.8%	1.3%
All bare conductor wire and cable, including both aluminum and copper	10.3%	2.0%
All insulated conductor wire and cable	0.3%	1.3%
Combined insulated and bare wire and cable, all metals	1.8%	1.4%

---

[104]*U. S.* v. *Pabst Brewing Co. et al.*, 384 U. S. 546 (1966). The case was remanded to a district court for rehearing on other issues. See note 110 *infra*.

[105]*U. S.* v. *Philadelphia National Bank et al.*, 374 U. S. 321, 358, 361 (1963).

[106]*U. S.* v. *Aluminum Co. of America et al.*, 214 F. Supp. 501 (1963), 377 U. S. 271 (1964).

In choosing among these possibilities, a great many facts had to be weighed. The use of aluminum was clearly on the ascendancy, especially for overhead utility lines, due in part to the fact that copper prices had risen more rapidly than aluminum prices in the postwar period. Between 1950 and 1959, aluminum's share of new bare high-voltage transmission line installations rose from 74 to 94 per cent, and its share of all new overhead transmission and distribution line installations rose from 25 to 80 per cent. Copper fared better in insulated than in bare applications, although insulating machines could coat either aluminum or copper wire interchangeably.

The litigants agreed that bare aluminum cable was a distinct line of commerce, but the district court found Rome's share (0.3 per cent) under this definition to be too small to threaten any substantial lessening of competition when added to Alcoa's 32.5 per cent share. The Justice Department conceded that combined insulated and bare aluminum and copper wire and cable represented a relevant market, but there again the market shares were too small to impute illegality. Reversing a district court decision permitting the merger, a six-to-three majority of the Supreme Court held that the combined (insulated plus bare) aluminum wire and cable market definition, with all copper products excluded, could also be applied. It defended this choice by observing that the price of aluminum conductors was generally lower than the price of comparable copper conductors, and that copper conductor prices had not changed over time in response to changes in aluminum conductor prices or vice versa. Having reached this judgment, the Court went on to find that the addition of Rome's 1.3 per cent share to Alcoa's 27.8 per cent share constituted a substantial lessening of competition, since Rome served as an important source of independent action in an otherwise oligopolistic industry:

> The record shows indeed that Rome was an aggressive competitor. It was a pioneer in aluminum insulation and developed one of the most widely used insulated conductors. . . . Preservation of Rome, rather than its absorption by one of the giants, will keep it "as an important competitive factor," to use the words of S. Rep. No. 1775. . . . Rome seems to us the prototype of the small independent that Congress aimed to preserve by Section 7.[107]

In the second case, the Supreme Court struck down a merger between the Continental Can Company, second largest maker of tin cans in the United States, and the Hazel-Atlas Glass Co., the third largest bottle manufacturer.[108] Continental sold roughly 33 per cent of all tin cans; Hazel-Atlas 10 per cent of all glass bottles. A district court found cans and bottles to be separate lines of commerce and hence concluded that competition was not substantially reduced by the merger. But on appeal, the Supreme Court emphasized that tin cans and glass bottles were closely competitive in such applications as beer, soft drink, and baby food packaging, each product challenging and sometimes winning away trade from the other. Representing a majority of the Court, Justice White wrote that:

> In defining the product market . . . we must recognize meaningful competition where it is found to exist. . . . (T)hough the interchangeability of use may not be so complete and the cross-elasticity of demand not so immediate as in the case of most intraindustry mergers, there is over the long run the kind of customer response to innovation and other competitive stimuli that brings the competition between these two industries within Section 7's competition-preserving proscriptions. . . . That there are price differentials between the two products or that the demand for one is not particularly or immediately responsive to changes in the price of the other are relevant matters but not determinative of the product market issue. . . . Where the area of effective competition cuts across industry lines, so must the relevant line of commerce.[109]

---

[107]377 U. S. 271, 281 (1964).

[108]*U. S. v. Continental Can Co. et al.*, 217 F. Supp 761 (1963); 378 U. S. 441 (1964).

[109]378 U. S. 441, 449, 455, 457 (1964).

The Court therefore defined the relevant market as metal cans and glass bottles combined. In this market, Continental occupied second place with a 22 per cent share, and Hazel-Atlas sixth place with a 3 per cent share. This, the Court ruled, was too much; the merger had to be undone.

These two decisions are logically inconsistent. The long-run cross elasticity of demand between aluminum and copper in cable applications is undeniably high, just as it is between bottles and cans. If anything, copper cable and aluminum cable are more perfect substitutes within an appropriate price range, as the massive market share shifts between 1950 and 1959 testify. Only by assuming that copper prices will never again come close enough to aluminum prices to challenge aluminum in overhead conductor cable applications can one reconcile the Supreme Court's *Alcoa – Rome* decision with its *Continental – Hazel-Atlas* opinion. While this is possible and perhaps likely, it is not inevitable. Even then, an opportunity cost check on aluminum prices would remain, for by reducing the aluminum/copper price ratio, the aluminum cable producers can make further inroads into the many electrical conductor applications still dominated by copper. Nevertheless, the *Alcoa – Rome* and *Continental – Hazel-Atlas* decisions exhibit a different sort of consistency: the consistent willingness of the courts to accept market definitions which resolve inherent doubts on the side of preventing mergers with possible anticompetitive effects. This in turn may be no more than faithful stewardship to the will of Congress.

IS A PER SE RULE AGAINST HORIZONTAL AND VERTICAL MERGERS IN FORCE?

What appears to be emerging from the leading Celler-Kefauver Act court interpretations is a virtual *per se* prohibition of horizontal mergers between firms with substantial shares of the market and of vertical mergers likely to foreclose an appreciable share of some market. We need the modifier "virtual" to indicate that there may be occasional exceptions—notably, when one of the merger partners is on the brink of financial failure, or when the boundaries of the relevant market are particularly difficult to delineate.[110] The courts may also consider special extenuating circumstances which ensure competitive conduct despite high structural concentration, but normally the emphasis will be on structure, as the Supreme Court pronounced in a key bank merger decision:

> This intense congressional concern with the trend toward concentration warrants dispensing, in certain cases, with elaborate proof of market structure, market behavior, or probable anticompetitive effects. Specifically, we think that a merger which produces a firm controlling an undue percentage share of the relevant market, and results in a significant increase in the concentration of firms in that market, is so inherently likely to lessen competition substantially that it must be enjoined in the absence of evidence clearly showing that the merger is not likely to have such anticompetitive effects.[111]

How large the combined market share must be before it becomes "undue" cannot be stated precisely, but an upper tolerance limit is recognizable in the decisions. In the *Philadelphia National Bank* case, the Supreme Court concluded that a 30 per cent share would be clearly excessive. For the horizontal aspects of the *Brown Shoe – Kinney* case, a 20 per cent share of local markets was stressed. In the *Pabst – Blatz* case, a combined 24 per cent share of the Wisconsin beer market was "amply sufficient to show a violation," as were smaller shares of more broadly

---

[110]Fluidity of market boundaries may have saved the Ling-Temco acquisition of the Chance-Vought Aircraft Corporation, approved in a 1961 district court decision; while the 'failing firm' defense undoubtedly explains why the massive 1967 merger between McDonnell Aircraft and tottering Douglas Aircraft, at the time the nation's sixth and eighth largest aerospace specialists, was allowed to go through.

In *U. S.* v. *Pabst Brewing Co. et al.*, CCH 1969 Trade Cases Para. 72,723, a district court restricted the 'failing firm' defense to cover only *acquired* firms. It ruled that Pabst, as the acquiring company, could not cite its own financial difficulties as a defense. It is hard to believe that this interpretation will be supported by the Supreme Court.

[111]*U. S.* v. *Philadelphia National Bank et al.*, 374 U. S. 321, 363 (1963).

drawn markets. The *Bethlehem – Youngstown* merger was struck down for putting together a 21 per cent share of the national steel market, and the *Continental Can – Hazel-Atlas* merger for achieving a 25 per cent share of the combined glass and metal container market. These decisions together suggest that when one firm acquires a competitor with 3 per cent or more of sales in some relevant market, and when the combined market share exceeds 20 per cent, the probability of judicial disapproval approaches unity. And mergers may be prohibited when they involve much smaller market shares, as in the *Von's* case and the vertical aspects of *Brown Shoe*, if the industry has a history of rising concentration.

Furthermore, mergers stepping beyond the tolerable market share limits will not be rescued by showing that compensating efficiencies will result. The courts have been reluctant to weigh efficiency benefits against the social losses associated with reduced competition, as a full-blown rule of reason approach would require. This unwillingness is expressed most forcefully in the Supreme Court's *Philadelphia Bank* decision:

> We are clear . . . that a merger the effect of which "may be substantially to lessen competition" is not saved because, on some ultimate reckoning of social or economic debits and credits, it may be deemed beneficial. A value choice of such magnitude is beyond the ordinary limits of judicial competence, and in any event has been made for us already, by Congress when it enacted the amended Section 7. Congress determined to preserve our traditionally competitive economy. It therefore proscribed anticompetitive mergers, the benign and the malignant alike, fully aware, we must assume, that some price might have to be paid.[112]

Similarly, in its *Brown Shoe* opinion, the Court conceded that vertical integration of Brown with Kinney would yield certain economies.

> But we cannot fail to recognize Congress' desire to promote competition through the protection of viable, small, locally owned businesses. Congress appreciated that occasional higher costs and prices might result from the maintenance of fragmented industries and markets. It resolved these competing considerations in favor of decentralization. We must give effect to that decision.[113]

Or as it stated flatly in still another opinion, "Possible economies cannot be used as a defense to illegality."[114]

If any such balancing of costs against benefits is to occur, it must evidently take place when the antitrust enforcement agencies decide which potential anti-merger suits they will use their limited resources to prosecute. There is reason to believe that some such 'rule of reason' approach was employed at least occasionally during the informal investigations and meetings which precede Justice Department and Federal Trade Commission prosecution decisions. However, even this element of discretion was seemingly eliminated in 1968, when the Justice Department published formal "guidelines" it expected to apply in deciding whether to challenge acquisitions.[115] For horizontal mergers in industries with four-firm concentration ratios of 75 per cent or more, the Department announced that ordinarily it would challenge mergers involving the following market shares:

Acquiring Firm	Acquired Firm
4%	4% or more
10%	2% or more
15% or more	1% or more

[112]374 U. S. 321, 371 (1963).

[113]370 U. S. 294, 344 (1962).

[114]*Federal Trade Commission* v. *the Procter & Gamble Co. et al.*, 87 S. Ct. 1224, 1231 (1967). For a sharply critical view of these decisions, see Robert H. Bork, "The Supreme Court versus Corporate Efficiency," *Fortune*, August 1967, pp. 92 ff.

[115]U. S. Department of Justice, *Merger Guidelines*, May 30, 1968 (mimeograph). By mid 1968, the Federal Trade Commission had issued similar guidelines affecting the dairy, cement, and grocery products industries.

In industries with four-firm concentration ratios of less than 75 per cent, its challenges would be directed toward mergers with the following market shares:

Acquiring Firm	Acquired Firm
5%	5% or more
10%	4% or more
15%	3% or more
20%	2% or more
25% or more	1% or more

And in industries displaying a trend toward increasing concentration, it planned to challenge any merger in which one of the leading eight producers acquired a company with 2 per cent or more of the market. For vertical mergers, a 10 per cent share of the market for the supplying firm and purchases of 6 per cent or more by the buyer were identified as danger points. The guidelines stated further that the Department would not accept as a justification for horizontal or vertical mergers the claim that economies would be realized unless "exceptional circumstances" intervened. Thus, the Justice Department in effect announced clear-cut *per se* rules for an important class of cases.

POLICY TOWARD CONGLOMERATE MERGERS

Conglomerate mergers—mergers between companies operating in separate and distinct markets—pose especially knotty antitrust policy problems. Diversification into numerous fields or markets might conceivably alter behavior in a variety of subtle ways. Conglomerates may be more inclined to wage predatory price warfare against specialist firms; or they may refrain from competing vigorously with fellow conglomerates, entering into tacit or explicit agreements to respect each others' spheres of influence; or they may promote the sale of their products by offering reciprocally to purchase potential customers' products. Of these three alleged abuses, predatory pricing and reciprocal dealing have been successfully attacked in actual merger cases.[116]

Conglomerate mergers take many shapes and forms. It is customary to distinguish three main varieties: market extension mergers, in which the partners sell the same products in spatially isolated markets; product line extension mergers, which add to the acquiring firm's product list new items related in some way to existing production processes or marketing channels; and 'pure' conglomerate mergers, which have no discernible functional link with prior operations. All three types have now been challenged under the Celler-Kefauver Act.

One of the most important weapons for attacking conglomerate mergers of all types is the doctrine that such mergers violate new Section 7 if they reduce *potential* competition. This precedent was established firmly in a case involving acquisition of the Pacific Northwest Pipeline Corporation, a concern tapping extensive natural gas reserves in New Mexico and Western Canada, by the El Paso Natural Gas Co., which supplied natural gas to California users.[117] Pacific Northwest had no pipeline into California and had never sold its gas in that state, but the trial record showed that it had repeatedly considered entering the California market and had in fact bid unsuccessfully to supply California electrical utilities. The Supreme Court ordered the merger dissolved because it eliminated a substantial potential competitor, noting that "We would have to wear blinders not to see that the mere efforts of Pacific Northwest to get into the California market, though unsuccessful, had a powerful influence on El Paso's business attitudes within the state."[118] The potential competition doctrine has since been applied in numerous cases. Typical examples during the mid-1960s involved some nationwide dairy products chain or retail supermarket chain moving into a new territory by acquiring a local firm, where there was evidence that the chain had shown sufficient interest in that market to be considered a serious candidate for entry by building its own facilities.

The only defeat suffered up to 1968 by the antitrust enforcement agencies in appealing ad-

---

[116]For the leading analysis of early cases, see Donald F. Turner, "Conglomerate Mergers and Section 7 of the Clayton Act," *Harvard Law Review*, May 1965, pp. 1313–1395.
[117]U. S. v. El Paso Natural Gas Co. et al., 376 U. S. 651 (1964).
[118]376 U. S. 651, 659 (1964).

verse Celler-Kefauver Act decisions to the Supreme Court on substantive grounds came in an attempt to extend the potential competition doctrine to cover situations in which neither of the parties served the market in question before their fusion. It concerned a joint venture, the Penn-Olin Chemical Co., formed by the Pennsalt Chemicals Corporation and the Olin Mathieson Corp. to produce sodium chlorate, a paper pulp bleaching agent, in southeastern United States.[119] Pennsalt had built its own sodium chlorate plant in Oregon. Olin Mathieson operated related chemical processes and used sodium chlorate purchased from others as an intermediate product. Each of the parties had seriously considered entering the rapidly growing southeastern market independently during the 1950s, but they rejected the idea or deferred it because of disappointing profitability calculations. In 1960 they formed Penn-Olin to enter jointly, building a plant with 28 per cent of all southeastern U. S. sodium chlorate production capacity as of 1961. The Justice Department brought suit to dissolve the consortium, but a district court dismissed the complaint, concluding that competition was not substantially lessened because it was extremely unlikely that *both* firms would have entered the market independently. On appeal, the Supreme Court in 1964 vacated this judgment, ruling that the relevant question was whether one of the two firms would have entered, with the other remaining "at the edge of the market, continually threatening to enter," and hence keeping pressure on the oligopolists actually operating sodium chlorate plants.[120] Reconsidering the facts under these new instructions, the district court decided that independent entry by either of the two firms was improbable.[121] After a second ap-

peal, the Supreme Court divided four-to-four on overturning the lower court's decision, so the joint venture was allowed to stand. Despite losing this battle on specific questions of fact and probability, the Justice Department won its war, since the Supreme Court's 1964 *Penn-Olin* opinion provides a strong precedent for preventing mergers and joint ventures consummated by potential entrants into oligopolistic markets.

In March of 1969 the Justice Department sought to extend the potential competition doctrine still further to cover the pure conglomerate acquisition of the Jones & Laughlin Steel Corporation by Ling-Temco-Vought. It charged *inter alia* that any such merger between two very large corporations reduces the number of firms capable of entering concentrated markets more or less loosely related to those already supplied by the partners. Also, such mergers were said to reduce the number of independent companies with the capability and incentive for competitive innovation. This approach stretches Clayton Act Section 7 well beyond previous precedents, and the LTV – Jones & Laughlin case or some similar action will undoubtedly go to the Supreme Court for final resolution.

Another argument advanced against conglomerate mergers, especially in Federal Trade Commission actions, is that the intrusion of conglomerate power into a market previously occupied by small independent sellers increases the likelihood of predatory pricing, which in turn could drive small firms out of business or make them more docile because they fear punishment. This was a major point in an appellate court opinion affirming the Federal Trade Commission's order that Reynolds Metals Co., the nation's leading producer of aluminum foil, dis-

---

[119]*U. S.* v. *Penn-Olin Chemical Co. et al.*, 217 F. Supp. 110 (1963); 378 U. S. 158 (1964); 246 F. Supp. 917 (1965); 88 S. Ct. 502 (1967).

[120]378 U. S. 158, 173 (1964).

[121]A simple fact leads one to suspect that the district court erred in its judgment. Pennsalt's Oregon sodium chlorate plant and all three of the southeastern U. S. plants of Penn-Olin's rivals were built initially to produce between 15,000 and 16,000 tons of output per year. This uniformity suggests that the minimum optimal scale lies somewhere near that output range, or at least, that plants built to a 15,000 ton capacity do not sacrifice much in the way of cost savings attainable by building at larger scales. The Penn-Olin plant, however, was built to produce 26,500 tons per year. It seems incredible that if the two firms considered it profitable to enter jointly at that large scale, and if there were no serious cost disadvantages to entering at the 15,000 ton scale, one of the firms would not have entered such a rapidly growing market independently, for the 'percentage effect' of small-scale entry would have been less damaging to prices and profits. Promotional and distributional costs were also a consideration, especially to Pennsalt, which had no sales force in the Southeast. But the cost disadvantage of having to organize a new sales force to sell a homogeneous product to a small group of industrial buyers could hardly have been great.

solve its merger with a small firm specializing in florists' foil (a decorative wrapping for flowers):

> The power of the "deep pocket" or "rich parent" for one of the . . . suppliers in a competitive group where previously no company was very large and all were relatively small opened the possibility and power to sell at prices approximating cost or below and thus to undercut and ravage the less affluent competition.[122]

Similarly, the Commission found in a decision establishing guidelines for dairy products industry mergers that:

> A firm strongly entrenched in a number of markets may thereby be able to engage in deep, sustained, and discriminatory price cutting in selected markets to the detriment of weaker competitors.[123]

While such conduct is forbidden by the price discrimination laws, the Commission continued, a conglomerate could legally meet the equally low price of a rival, and . . .

> In the hands of a powerful firm, able to sustain selective price cuts for so long as may be necessary to ensure against a loss of trade, such price cutting may be a potent weapon for repulsing new competition and preventing entry into concentrated markets.[124]

This view was reiterated in a Supreme Court decision concerning Procter & Gamble's acquisition of the Clorox Co. "There is every reason to assume," the Court said, "that the smaller firms would become more cautious in competing due to their fear of retaliation by Procter."[125]

Whether conglomerate enterprises actually engage in predatory pricing more frequently than others, as implied in these judgments, is debatable.[126] Distinguishing price cutting with predatory intent from price cutting in good faith to meet tough local competition is singularly difficult. In the cases cited here, the evidence was insufficient to support such a distinction. It is fair to say that the predatory pricing doctrine is one of the shakiest pillars of existing anti-merger law. Its absence would not be mourned by lovers of competition and/or logic.

A few conglomerate mergers have been challenged successfully, and with more compelling factual support, because they led to the creation and exercise of reciprocal purchasing leverage. The leading case concerns the acquisition of Gentry, Inc., a specialist in the manufacture of dehydrated onion and garlic, by the Consolidated Foods Corporation, which had far-flung interests in food products wholesaling, manufacturing, and retailing.[127] The record shows that Consolidated brought reciprocal buying pressure to bear on some of its suppliers, especially those making soups and related products on which Consolidated affixed its own brand labels for retail distribution, to use Gentry onion and garlic. Although the Gentry products were qualitatively inferior to those of a leading competitor, the reciprocal buying campaign had modest success, and Gentry's average share of the combined onion and garlic market rose from 32 to 35 per cent in the 10 years following the merger, increasing in onions while falling in garlic. Climaxing eight years of litigation, the Supreme Court rejected the decision of an appellate court that the reciprocity program had no substantial effect on competition, and it ordered that Consolidated divest itself of Gentry. It went on to assert that it was neither necessary nor desirable to wait many years until evidence on the actual effects of a merger become available before rendering judg-

---

[122]*Reynolds Metals Co.* v. *Federal Trade Commission*, 309 F. 2d 223, 229 (1962), affirming 56 F.T.C. 743 (1960). The opinion was delivered by Judge (and later Supreme Court Chief Justice) Warren Burger.

[123]*In re Beatrice Foods Co.*, CCH Trade Regulation Reporter, Federal Trade Commission Complaints and Orders, Para. 17,244, p. 22,334 (1965).

[124]*Loc. cit.*

[125]*Federal Trade Commission* v. *Procter & Gamble Co. et al.*, 87 S. Ct. 1224, 1230 (1967).

[126]Cf. pp. 273–278 *supra*; and Turner, "Conglomerate Mergers and Section 7 of the Clayton Act," pp. 1339–1352.

[127]*Federal Trade Commission* v. *Consolidated Foods Corp. et al.*, 380 U. S. 592 (1965).

ment; rather, mergers should be judged by their *probable* effects. Framing a general rule for reciprocal buying cases, the Court stated that not all mergers offering reciprocity opportunities should be prohibited, but where "the acquisition is of a company that commands a substantial share of a market, a finding of probability of reciprocal buying . . . should be honored, if there is substantial evidence to support it."

We have noted earlier that the courts have been unwilling to absolve mergers with probable anti-competitive effects merely because economies would be achieved. This is not an ideal policy, but it may be the best one can do in a world of imperfect knowledge and cumbersome procedures. In a few conglomerate merger cases, however, the courts *have* taken prospective cost savings into account, adopting the view that merger-related economies might actually *harm* competition.

This was one of the central issues in the *Procter & Gamble – Clorox* case, resolved by the Supreme Court in 1967. Procter & Gamble was the nation's largest producer of soaps, detergents, dentifrices, and related products, with sales of $1.1 billion in 1957, when it consummated a product line extension merger with the Clorox Company. Clorox was by comparison a midget, with sales of $40 million, but it dominated the household liquid bleach (sodium hypochlorite) field, its specialty, with a 49 per cent market share. One feature which drew antitrust attention to the bleach industry was its high concentration. The leading six firms accounted for 80 per cent of total sales in 1957, despite the fact that 200 more firms operated on the industry's fringe. Another was the success some producers experienced building up cumulative brand preferences for their products through advertising and related promotional efforts. Clorox often commands a 10 to 20 per cent price premium over lesser-known rival prod-

ucts, even though the active ingredients are chemically identical. As a result of the merger, Clorox bleach could be put on supermarket shelves through Procter & Gamble's far-flung merchandising channels, with undoubted cost savings. More important, Clorox would be able to take advantage of the alleged advertising discounts received by Procter & Gamble by virtue of its $80 million annual expenditures.[128] This combination of Clorox's market power with Procter & Gamble's marketing power led the Federal Trade Commission to question the merger.

In its decision opposing the acquisition, the FTC conceded that advertising and sales promotion economies might in some cases be as beneficial as economies in production and physical distribution. It went on, however, to state:

> . . . [T]here does reach a point "at which product differentiation ceases to promote welfare and becomes wasteful, or mass advertising loses its informative aspect and merely entrenches market leaders." We think that point has been reached in the household liquid bleach industry. . . . Price competition, beneficial to the consumer, has given way to brand competition in a form beneficial only to the seller. . . . [C]ost advantages that enable still more intensive advertising only impair price competition further; they do not benefit the consumer.[129]

Procter & Gamble appealed, and an appellate court reversed the FTC's decision, arguing that:

> The Supreme Court has not ruled that bigness is unlawful, or that a large company may not merge with a smaller one in a different market field. Yet the size of Procter and its legitimate, successful operations in related fields pervades the entire opinion of the Commission, and seems to be the

---

[128]The assumption of the FTC and the courts at the time was that Procter & Gamble received impressive discounts from the television networks, where it concentrated its advertising outlays. This view is debunked in David M. Blank, "Television Advertising: The Great Discount Illusion, or Tonypandy Revisited," *Journal of Business*, January 1968, pp. 10–36.

[129]*In re Procter & Gamble Co.*, CCH Trade Regulation Reporter, Federal Trade Commission Complaints and Orders, Para. 16,673, p. 21,586 (1963). The internal quotation is from Joel B. Dirlam, "The Celler-Kefauver Act: A Review of Enforcement Policy," in U. S. Senate, Committee on the Judiciary, Subcommittee on Antitrust and Monopoly, *Administered Prices: A Compendium on Public Policy* (Washington: 1963), p. 103.

motivating factor which influenced the Commission to rule that the acquisition was illegal.[130]

The Federal Trade Commission thereupon appealed to the Supreme Court, which reversed the lower court's decision and ordered the merger dissolved. Its opinion stressed three grounds for holding the merger illegal: the fact that Procter & Gamble had considered entering the liquid bleach market independently, and hence was a potential competitor; the possibility of predatory pricing supported by Procter & Gamble's enormous financial resources, making smaller producers more timid in their competition; and the tendency of the merger to raise entry barriers by bolstering Clorox's advertising power.[131]

In its brief substantive analysis the Supreme Court dealt with the Clorox problem as a special case, offering no general guidelines for determining when economies realized through merger might be harmful to competition. Certain decisions of the Federal Trade Commission go much further, suggesting that *any* economies realized through merger in an industry harboring small, vulnerable firms should be regarded unfavorably. This attitude emerges most clearly in a dairy products chain merger decision which was not appealed to the Supreme Court:

> . . . the necessary proof of violation of [Section 7] consists of . . . evidence showing that the acquiring firm possesses significant power in some markets *or* that its over-all organization gives it a decisive advantage in efficiency over its smaller rivals.[132]

This, as former Assistant Attorney General Turner has said, is not only bad economics but bad law.[133] It interprets the purpose of the Celler-Kefauver Act as that of protecting existing *competitors*, especially small ones, rather than protecting *competition*. Whether it will be supported in Supreme Court pronouncements, with

a consequent bias against mergers which do no more than increase efficiency, remains to be seen.

In general, the law on conglomerate mergers is much less settled than the law concerning horizontal and vertical mergers. As of 1969 there were several precedents under which market extension and product line extension mergers had been successfully challenged, but all required more conclusive evidence of tangible or probable injury to competition (or to competitors) than the typical horizontal merger case. Under this approach, which amounted to a weak rule of reason, the vast majority of all conglomerate mergers escaped censure.

Whether or not this is a desirable policy has been the subject of vigorous debate. Resolution is difficult in part because there is so little hard evidence on the economic consequences of conglomerate mergers and partly because one's choice may turn on a basic value judgment regarding the social and political acceptability of bigness untainted by more familiar manifestations of monopoly power. Up to 1968 even the enforcement agencies had divided views, with the Justice Department seeing little harm in relatively pure conglomerate mergers while the Federal Trade Commission sought new precedents to combat them.

However, the enormous surge of conglomerate acquisitions during 1968 and the early months of 1969—many carried out largely for empire-building or speculative reasons—shocked a new Justice Department administration into adopting a tougher policy line. A test suit stretching the potential competition and reciprocal buying doctrines was initiated to block Ling-Temco-Vought's acquisition of Jones & Laughlin Steel. More such test cases were expected to follow. Indeed, Attorney General John N. Mitchell announced in June of 1969 that any merger between two companies large enough to be included among the 200 largest industrial corporations would probably be challenged, as would mergers

---

[130] *Procter & Gamble* v. *Federal Trade Commission*, 358 F. 2d 74, 84 (1966).

[131] *Federal Trade Commission* v. *Procter & Gamble*, 87 S. Ct. 1224, 1231 (1967).

[132] *In the matter of Foremost Dairies, Inc.*, 60 F.T.C. 944, 1084 (1962) (emphasis added).

[133] "Conglomerate Mergers and Section 7 of the Clayton Act," pp. 1323–1328.

between one of the 200 largest and another smaller enterprise among the sales leaders in some concentrated industry.[134] The Federal Trade Commission concurrently announced a program requiring corporations with assets of $250 million or more to notify the Commission in advance and submit a detailed report on any planned acquisitions of companies with assets exceeding $10 million. Similar reports were required for any merger creating a firm with consolidated assets exceeding $250 million.[135] These steps, which signify movement toward a policy actively discouraging all sizeable conglomerate acquisitions by large corporations, will undoubtedly be tested before the Supreme Court. The outcome is difficult to predict, since the Court's membership will have changed substantially as a result of new Nixon administration appointments. Should the Court find that the Celler-Kefauver Act's language cannot be construed to strike down significant but relatively pure conglomerate mergers, it seems likely that a hue and cry for new and stronger legislation will be heard.

MERGERS IN REGULATED INDUSTRIES

One further aspect of merger policy—the status of mergers in regulated industries—must be treated with a brevity inversely proportional to its complexity. The Celler-Kefauver Act stated in part:

> Nothing contained in this section shall apply to transactions duly consummated pursuant to authority given by the Civil Aeronautics Board, Federal Communications Commission, Federal Power Commission, Interstate Commerce Commission, the Securities and Exchange Commission . . ., the United States Maritime Commission, or the Secretary of Agriculture . . . .

It went on to assign authority for enforcing compliance to these and other regulatory agencies, qualifying the delegation by establishing procedures under which the Attorney General could intervene in merger proceedings conducted by the regulators. This combination of language in effect legalized regulated industry mergers *duly approved* by the regulatory agencies. What was left unclear was whether the stringent anti-merger presumption of new Section 7 was to apply for regulated industry mergers as forcefully as for mergers of unregulated firms. Much litigation followed. Through the ensuing Supreme Court interpretations the competitive aspects of mergers were relegated to a position of secondary importance in certain industries, while in others they remain a paramount consideration. The precedents developed for railroad and banking mergers will illustrate the extremes.

As we have seen earlier, several railroad mergers were struck down under the Sherman Act during the first two decades of this century. Then, under the Transportation Act of 1920, mergers which rationalized railroad systems while preserving competition "as fully as possible" were expressly encouraged, and those approved by the Interstate Commerce Commission were exempted from antitrust prosecution. This exemption for mergers found by the ICC to be "consistent with the public interest" was continued in the Transportation Act of 1940. In a key test case, the Supreme Court in 1944 held that when it considered mergers among regulated carriers:

> . . . the Commission must estimate the scope and appraise the effects of the curtailment of competition which will result from the proposed consolidation and consider them along with the advantages of improved service, safer operation, lower costs, etc., to determine whether the consolidation will assist in effectuating the over-all transportation policy.[136]

In other words, a broad rule of reason was to be applied, benefits being weighed against the costs

---

[134]"U. S. Serves Notice Curbs Are Likely on Giant Mergers," *New York Times*, June 7, 1969, p. 1. See also the *Report of the White House Task Force on Antitrust Policy*, Section III, which recommended similar changes.

[135]"Federal Trade Commission Announces Merger Notification Program as Mergers Hit Record Peak," FTC news release dated April 13, 1969.

[136]*McLean Trucking Co. v. U. S.*, 321 U. S. 67, 87 (1944).

of diminished competition. After the Celler-Kefauver Act was passed, there was reason to suppose that a more stringent standard might apply. Additional test cases were brought, and in one an appellate court held that the Interstate Commerce Commission had not given the intent of new Section 7 sufficient weight. However, the Supreme Court ruled on appeal that anti-competitive effects were but one factor, and not a crucial one, to be taken into account:

> It matters not that the merger might otherwise violate the antitrust laws; the Commission has been authorized by the Congress to approve the merger of railroads if it makes adequate findings . . . that such a merger would be "consistent with the public interest."[137]

As a result of these interpretations, the Justice Department can successfully attack a railroad or trucking merger only by showing that the Interstate Commerce Commission's benefit vs. cost evaluations were grossly defective. And in general, the Supreme Court has been unwilling to overrule the ICC and other regulatory agencies on findings of fact and probable effect, since the regulators presumably have more special competence than judges in such matters. Consequently, even though the Justice Department opposed the massive merger of the New York Central and Pennsylvania railroads in hearings before the ICC, it refrained from challenging in court the Commission's April 1966 decision permitting the merger. But in 1968 it did contest a consolidation of the Great Northern, Northern Pacific, and Chicago, Burlington & Quincy railroads, hoping to upset an ICC authorization which would have undone the *Northern Securities* decision of 1904. Its plea was denied by the Supreme Court in 1970.

Bank mergers approved by the Comptroller of the Currency were not expressly exempted from Celler-Kefauver Act coverage and responsibility for the Act's enforcement was left in an uncertain state. To clarify matters Congress passed a special Bank Merger Act in 1960, directing the Comptroller to consider "the competitive factor" as well as other points in approving or disapproving national bank mergers. This failed to settle the issue, however, and in 1963 the Supreme Court ruled that Celler-Kefauver Act standards were fully applicable to bank mergers.[138] In response Congress, after chaotic hearings, passed the Bank Merger Act of 1966, which gave the Comptroller of the Currency authority to approve mergers after finding:

> . . . that the anticompetitive effects of the proposed transaction are clearly outweighed in the public interest by the probable effects of the transaction in meeting the convenience and needs of the community to be served.

The Justice Department was permitted to challenge mergers approved by the Comptroller within 30 days of their approval, and it soon exercised this option. Each of its early challenges was dismissed at the district court level, but in 1967 the Supreme Court reversed these decisions, holding that Celler-Kefauver Act criteria were still applicable in deciding whether competition would be substantially lessened in bank merger cases, and that the burden of proving that anticompetitive effects were *clearly* outweighed by public advantages of the merger rested upon the merger partners.[139] Thus, the benefit of doubt was again resolved in favor of prohibiting bank mergers. The Court also ruled that Comptroller of the Currency findings, unlike the opinions of such agencies as the Interstate Commerce Commission, were to be accorded no special stature in challenge cases; the evidence in bank merger suits initiated by the Justice Department was to be considered *de novo* by district court judges.

Mergers in most other strongly regulated industries are governed by rules more like those in railroad cases than bank cases, although there are exceptions, and the precise weight placed on anticompetitive effects as opposed to other con-

[137]*Seaboard Airline Railroad Co. et al. v. U. S. et al.*, 382 U. S. 154, 156–157 (1965). See also *Minneapolis & St. Louis Railroad Co. v. U. S.*, 361 U. S. 173 (1959).

[138]*U. S. v. Philadelphia National Bank et al.*, 374 U. S. 321 (1963).

[139]*U. S. v. First City National Bank of Houston et al.*, 386 U. S. 361 (1967).

siderations depends upon the language of the applicable regulatory statutes. The one common denominator of regulated industry merger cases is sharp conflict between the Justice Department, with its concern for enforcing a regime of competition, and the regulators, who are more inclined to believe that competition is not an unmitigated blessing. This in turn reflects an unresolved issue of regulatory policy: the optimal balance between competition and direct control in industries singled out for regulation. We shall return to it in Chapter 22.

THE EFFECTS OF THE ANTI-MERGER LAWS

To sum up, the United States has since 1950 possessed an anti-merger law with teeth. It is difficult to say what difference in market structures it has made, for one never knows what might have occurred under an alternative policy. A few observations are warranted, however.

First, there is not much evidence that the overall level of merger activity has been sharply curtailed. The number of manufacturing and mining mergers recorded by the Federal Trade Commission rose steadily from 219 in 1950 to a record high of 2,442 in 1968. Perhaps there might have been even more activity without the Celler-Kefauver Act, but of that we simply do not know.

Second, the law has definitely affected the kinds of mergers consummated. Up to 1968, stronger precedents had been developed to combat horizontal and vertical mergers than the conglomerate varieties, and the brunt of enforcement fell upon the first two types. Of the 923 large manufacturing and mining mergers recorded between 1951 and 1966—i.e., those in which the acquired entity had assets of $10 million or more—94 were challenged by the antitrust enforcement agencies. Of these 94, 53 per cent were horizontal mergers, 25 per cent vertical, 11 per cent market extension, 11 per cent product line extension, and none was of the pure conglomerate type. Twenty-seven per cent of all horizontal mergers in the group of 923

and 17 per cent of the vertical mergers were challenged, but only 3 per cent of the conglomerates came under attack.[140] Presumably because of this enforcement emphasis, there has been a distinct trend away from horizontal mergers and toward the conglomerate types. This is shown by the following data on the distribution of assets acquired in large manufacturing and mining mergers for three periods, 1951–1954, 1963–1966, and 1967–1968.[141]

	Percentage of All Assets Acquired in Period		
	1951–54	1963–66	1967–68
Horizontal mergers	40	14	8
Vertical mergers	9	15	7
Product extension mergers	43	43	46
Market extension mergers	4	13	4
Pure conglomerates	5	16	35

By far the largest decline was in the horizontal category, where antitrust flak was heaviest. Both absolutely and proportionately, the greatest growth occurred in the pure conglomerate category, where there were no antitrust challenges during the 1951–1966 period.

This relative decline in horizontal merger activity should presumably have had a favorable impact on market concentration trends. Unfortunately, our data and measurement techniques are too imperfect to isolate such an effect from among the many other factors which affect concentration. Between 1958, when the *Bethlehem – Youngstown* decision showed that a tough line would be adopted, and 1966, the value-added-weighted average four-firm concentration ratio for all manufacturing industry rose from 37.0 to 39.0.[142] But it would be absurd to infer from this that anti-merger policy has been ineffective. Case studies of individual industries such as shoe manufacturing, steel, and dairy products suggest that there were fewer concentration-increasing mergers during the 1960s than there would have been under a weak policy, and so it seems more reasonable to conclude that as a result of the Celler-Kefauver Act, market concentration has

---

[140]Mueller, *The Celler-Kefauver Act: Sixteen Years of Enforcement*, pp. 5–10.
[141]Cf. p. 110 *supra*.
[142]Cf. p. 63 *supra*.

risen less than would otherwise have been the case.[143]

What we know least about is whether frustration of the urge to merge horizontally led to fewer mergers altogether or merely caused businessmen to redirect their efforts along safer acquisition lines; and if the former, how the rate and direction of firms' internal growth investments were affected. One-to-one redirection of merger activity from horizontal to conglomerate types would mean that although the rise in market concentration was impeded, aggregate concentration could have continued to increase. On this point we have fragments of evidence. Analyzing all recorded acquisitions of firms with assets exceeding $10 million, Mueller found that between 1950 and 1960 the 200 largest manufacturing corporations accounted for 70 per cent of the dollar volume of assets acquired, whereas in the 1961-1966 period their acquisition share fell to 54 per cent. To the extent that this was a consequence of merger law, it implies a slight retarding effect on the growth of aggregate concentration.[144] Using a Markov process analysis of 1950-1960 data, McGowan estimated that a complete ban on mergers for the 100 largest industrial corporations during the 1960s would reduce their predicted 1970 aggregate asset share from the 44.9 per cent value associated with a policy of permitting all mergers like those attempted during the 1950s to 40.1 per cent. A policy similar to what had evolved by 1965, preventing all horizontal mergers by the four leaders in each industry and all mergers involving more than 20 per cent of some market, would hold the 100 largest corporations' share at 44 per cent.[145]

These comparisons suggest that the effect of the Celler-Kefauver Act on aggregate concentration has not been overwhelming. Yet great leaps in concentration by small steps grow, and the long-run effect of the act will no doubt be sub-stantial. Furthermore, since Sherman Act anti-merger precedents were sufficient to discourage mergers with the most extreme impact on market concentration even before 1950, it seems probable that the anti-merger laws have played a significant role in suppressing latent tendencies toward increasing market and aggregate concentration.

STRUCTURAL ANTITRUST ABROAD: A CONTRAST

To put American structural antitrust policy in perspective, it is useful to compare it with analogous policies in other industrialized nations. This can be done quickly, for there is not a lot to compare.

Indeed, structural antitrust has been one of the United States' less successful postwar exports. At the end of World War II the U. S. occupation forces imposed upon defeated Germany and Japan stringent antitrust laws, including deconcentration measures directed toward breaking up such market power consolidations as the Krupp and I. G. Farben empires and the Japanese Zaibatsu. The deconcentration program had two purported objectives: to punish the industrial power groups for their support of the war, and to weaken the industrial bases of Germany and Japan so they would be less able to pursue militaristic adventures again.[146] The second objective, although not accepted as logically valid by some occupation policy-makers, implies a curious contradiction of the conventional American wisdom. If we break up monopolistic concentrations to weaken industrial power, what should be done to strengthen it? Contributing to the paradox was the fact that when the United States reversed its field and resolved to build up West German and Japanese industry as bulwarks against commu-

---

[143]Mueller, op. cit., pp. 15 19.

[144]Ibid., p. 33 note. The observed decline was in part spurious, showing only that corporations not among the top 200 have grown large enough to swallow relatively more $10 million asset acquisitions.

[145]John J. McGowan, "The Effect of Alternative Antimerger Policies on the Size Distribution of Firms," Yale Economic Essays, Fall 1965, p. 468.

[146]The German ordinance stated explicitly that its objective was in part "to destroy Germany's economic potential to wage war." Gesetz Nr. 56. "Verbot der uebermaessigen Konzentration Deutscher Wirtschaftskraft," February 1947.

nism, one of the first occupation policies to be relaxed was the deconcentration program. These developments did not escape the attention of businessmen and economists enthusiastic about monopolistic restrictions, who drew support for their views from the U. S. policies. And in general, the postwar structural antitrust serum inoculations engendered a reaction of hostility to such measures after the occupation pressures were relaxed.

This, of course, is not the whole story, since national sympathy for relative and absolute bigness in business extends far beyond the borders of Germany and Japan. National markets outside the United States are typically small, and if all economies of scale are to be realized, market concentration must be higher than it needs to be (although for many industries, not necessarily higher than it actually is) in the United States. Bain's international comparisons study suggests that for reasons which are imperfectly understood, the incidence of plants too small to capture all production scale economies is much higher in Japan, England, France, Italy, Canada, Sweden, and India than in the United States.[147] Recognizing this, policy-makers abroad look favorably toward gaining efficiency through larger plant and firm sizes, and most stand ready to sacrifice deconcentrated market structure at the altar of scale economies. This attitude has been strengthened by the belief that there are major advantages to large company size and high concentration for the conduct of technological research and innovation, and that European nations lagged behind the U. S. in many fields of technology during the 1950s and 1960s partly because their firms were too small to match the efforts of American counterparts. There is some truth in these perceptions, but there is also a great deal of exaggeration, and the scale economy argument is sometimes used as a smokescreen to cloak a deep-seated distaste for hard competition.[148] At any rate, for good reasons or bad, concentrated market structures are commonly viewed sympathetically outside the United States.

There is also less of a philosophical bias toward solving the economic problem through the impersonal operation of competitive markets and more willingness to entrust regulatory functions to some central authority. Consequently, provisions like Sherman Act Section 2 designed to combat structural monopoly are almost nonexistent. The emphasis instead is on preventing *abusive conduct* by firms or groups of firms with monopoly power. This 'abuse doctrine' permeates the antitrust laws of every non-American nation with any provisions at all concerning concentrations of economic power.[149]

Article 86 of the European Economic Community treaty, for instance, prohibits "any improper exploiting . . . of a dominant position" affecting Common Market trade, singling out the imposition of unfair prices, limiting production, discrimination, and tying contracts as abuses to be avoided. No attempt to enforce the article had been made as of 1968. Germany's 1957 restraint of competition law, as amended in 1965, prohibits abusive practices by firms which dominate their industries. Little has been done under it.[150] Since 1948 the United Kingdom has had a Monopolies Commission empowered to investigate industries in which one firm controls a third or more of output. The Commission determines whether conditions in the industry are contrary to the public interest and recommends corrective measures to the British Board of Trade, which in turn must secure Parliamentary approval of formal orders. The remedies recommended by the Commission and approved by the

---

[147]Joe S. Bain, *International Differences in Industrial Structure* (New Haven: Yale University Press, 1966), pp. 55–66 and 144–148.

[148]See F. M. Scherer, "Marktstruktur, Know-How fuer das Marketing und die technologische Luecke," *Ordo*, volume XIX (1968), pp. 159–170.

[149]For a collection of interpretive papers, see U. S. Senate, Committee on the Judiciary, Subcommittee on Antitrust and Monopoly, Hearings, *Economic Concentration*, Parts 7 and 7A (Washington: 1968 and 1969). For a more encyclopaedic treatment, see Corwin Edwards, *Trade Regulation Overseas* (Dobbs Ferry: Oceana, 1966), and *Control of Cartels and Monopolies: An International Comparison* (Dobbs Ferry: Oceana, 1967).

[150]For a discussion of two path-breaking cases, see Hans-Heinrich Barnikel, "Abuse of Power by Dominant Firms: Application of the German Law," *Antitrust Bulletin*, Spring 1969, pp. 221–247.

Board of Trade have for the most part been concerned with narrow facets of conduct, and in all but three cases up to 1966 the firms involved had complied voluntarily. Unlike most European antitrust agencies, the Monopolies Commission has the power to recommend structural reorganization, but the Commission has shown no inclination to do so.

This list of examples could be extended, but it would not alter a general conclusion that monopolization law abroad is much weaker than it is in the United States. Abuses as flagrant as those condemned in the 1911 *Standard Oil* and *Tobacco* cases may be vulnerable,[151] but there is nothing like the *Alcoa* and *United Shoe Machinery* decisions, and structural divestiture is even rarer than it has been in U. S. experience.

The contrast is even sharper in the realm of merger policy. Mergers are promoted by national governments abroad, not discouraged. The antitrust sections of the European Economic Community treaty have no provisions dealing directly with mergers, and in a 1966 policy memorandum the EEC Commission stated that mergers which fall short of entrenching a single firm's dominance in some market would be actively encouraged.[152] One step contemplated by the Commission is the development of a unified Common Market incorporation law, facilitating consolidations among firms presently operating under disparate national laws into truly 'European' corporations. The architects of the first German antitrust law originally included in their draft a provision requiring advance government approval of any merger combining more than 20 per cent of a market, but it came under heavy

attack and was deleted from the final version, which requires only that such mergers be registered with the Cartel Office. The Office has no power to act unless abuse of a dominant position can be shown. France also had no anti-merger statute as of 1968. The French government has provided both financial and moral support for mergers which substantially increased concentration in such fields as steel, nonferrous metals, electronics, chemicals, aircraft, and automobiles. Its attitude is reflected in the assertion of Industry Minister Raymond Marcellin that "the consolidation of French industry has become a national priority. . . . We must form enterprises that are capable of standing up to foreign groups."[153] In England, the Labour government in 1966 created an Industrial Reorganization Corporation with capital of £ 150,000 to encourage and help finance mergers, with the aim of making British firms larger and better able to compete in world markets with U. S. giants. Its record includes acting as broker to the merger of Britain's two largest domestic auto makers (British Motor Corporation and Leyland Motor Corp.); aiding the formation of Europe's third largest electrical equipment manufacturer through the merger of English Electric and Elliott Automation; and financing the creation of Europe's largest computer maker through the merger of International Computers and Tabulators with English Electric Computers, Ltd.[154] The effect of such policies in England, on the Continent, and in Japan has been a merger wave of proportions matched only by the U. S. experience of the 1890s and early 1900s.[155]

A few countries do have anti-merger provisions

[151]Indeed, the leading decision under Canadian law, which prohibits monopolies operating against the public interest, is remarkably similar to the *Standard Oil* and *Tobacco* cases, featuring the use of predatory discrimination, fighting brands, business espionage, mergers, and the like. *Rex v. Eddy Match Co., Ltd.*, 104 C.C.C. 39 (1951), 109 C.C.C. 1 (1953).

[152]Cf. Grant W. Kelleher, "The Common Market Antitrust Laws: The First Ten Years." *Antitrust Bulletin*, Winter 1967, pp. 1250–1252; and "Pragmatic Prophet of a Federalist Europe," *Business Week*, September 16, 1967, p. 74. For an indication of possible changes, see "Common Market Set To Enforce a More Rigid Antitrust Policy," *New York Times*, January 27, 1969, pp. 41 and 49.

[153]"Merging To Survive," *Fortune*, February 1967, pp. 74–79. See also the excerpts from reports of the French Technical Commission on Agreements and Dominating Positions published in the *Antitrust Bulletin*, Fall 1968, pp. 1035–1037.

[154]Cf. "Britain and Mergers," *New York Times*, February 1, 1968; "Britain Links Up Two for the Road," *Business Week*, January 27, 1968, p. 143; and "Computer Giants Wed in Britain," *Business Week*, March 30, 1968, p. 62.

[155]See "Merger Wave Hits Europe," *Business Week*, February 26, 1966, pp. 153–160; "The Bigness Kick in Europe," *Fortune*, September 15, 1967, p. 213; "Europe's Merger Boom Thunders a Lot Louder," *Business Week*, November 23, 1968, pp. 53–56; " 'Business Alliance' Between Toyota and Hino Starts Talk of More Auto Mergers in Japan," *Business Week*, October 22, 1966, p. 108; and "Japan Forges a Colossus in Steel," *Business Week*, April 5, 1969, pp. 92–96.

in their competition policy laws. It is instructive to see how they have been applied.

On a multi-national plane, the European Coal and Steel Community treaty of 1951 requires that mergers be expressly authorized by the Community's High Authority if they might bring about concentration in the coal or steel industries. Approval is mandatory unless the High Authority finds that the merger will convey the power to fix prices, control production, or prevent competition, and if these restrictive possibilities exist, the Authority has considerable discretion for deciding whether or not to grant its blessing. Up to January of 1962, some 136 cases had been considered. None ended in an outright refusal of authorization, although in three cases mergers may have been abandoned voluntarily due to the High Authority's display of reticence.[156] Several of the mergers approved during this period resulted in combined national market shares exceeding 20 per cent. Since 1962 many more larger mergers have been approved, including one between August Thyssen Huette (with 1966 sales of $1.7 billion) and Huettenwerk Oberhausen (with sales of $252 million), creating the world's fourth largest steelmaking concern, with more than 10 per cent of total ECSC capacity.

In 1965 Great Britain passed a Monopolies and Mergers Act which assigned to the Monopolies Commission responsibility for reviewing mergers involving a third or more of some market or acquired firm assets exceeding £ 5 million and for determining whether they are consistent with the public interest. Special, tougher criteria were established for newspaper mergers. In the first 18 months of the Act's life, the Monopolies Commission examined seven mergers, disapproving two. The first merger formally approved by the Commission illustrates the differences between British and American policy. British Motor Corporation, the leading auto producer, with a 25 to 30 per cent share of total passenger car output, sought in 1965 to acquire Pressed Steel Co., Ltd., the largest British body stampings specialist. At the time Pressed Steel sold 60 per cent of its output to BMC, which lacked internal stamping capacity, and the remainder to BMC's competitors. Such a merger creates obvious vertical foreclosure dangers. A price squeeze might be imposed on outsiders, or supplies might be denied to rivals during periods of peak demand, when each foregone body stamping means the loss of a car sale. However, BMC management assured the Commission that outside customers would continue to be served on a nondiscriminatory basis. Satisfied that this promise would be honored throughout the foreseeable future, the Monopolies Commission approved the merger. Under U. S. law, the merger would surely have been struck down to maintain structural conditions which impersonally and automatically minimize the risk of foreclosure. In Britain, the authorities were willing to rely upon *personal* assurances (from other Establishment members) that the same end would be achieved.[157]

Under Canadian law, mergers can be barred if they are found to operate against the public interest. The leading cases reveal that a softer line has been taken than in the United States. In one, Canadian Breweries, Ltd., raised its share of Ontario beer sales from 12 per cent in 1931 to 61 per cent in 1958 through a series of 23 mergers. The mergers were then challenged, but Canadian Breweries won acquittal, mainly on the court's finding that the Ontario Liquor Control Board set all beer prices, so that price competition did not exist and therefore could not have been impaired by the mergers.[158] In another case, the British Columbia Sugar Refining Co. controlled all sugar refining capacity in British Columbia, Alberta, and Saskatchewan. It then acquired the only Manitoba refiner, securing a complete monopoly of refining operations in Western Canada. After a challenge, the merger was permitted by the court, which found that there was

---

[156]Corwin D. Edwards, *Cartelization in Western Europe* (Washington: U. S. Department of State, 1964), pp. 76–79. For a survey of more recent developments, see Hans Mueller, "The Policy of the European Coal and Steel Community Towards Mergers and Agreements by Steel Companies," *Antitrust Bulletin*, Summer 1969, pp. 413–448.

[157]It is conceivable that in Britain the sense of fair play is so finely cultivated and Establishment ties are so strong that harmful foreclosure would be unlikely, despite the pull of profit incentives. But one cannot avoid entertaining doubts.

[158]*Regina* v. *Canadian Breweries, Ltd.*, 126 C.C.C. 133 (1960).

still some competition from Eastern refiners in the sale of sugar to Manitoba and Eastern Saskatchewan and that the prosecution had not established beyond a reasonable doubt that the merger would operate to the detriment of the public interest.[159]

Examination of these and the handful of other anti-merger cases on record outside the United States suggests that a horizontal or vertical merger will be prohibited only if those opposing it bear the burden of proving tangible injury to the public interest. In the United States, the burden of proof lies on the other side: If a substantial share of the market is encompassed, the courts assume that the merger runs contrary to the public interest and hence is illegal, and they may not even weigh evidence to the contrary. Thus, in the sweep and toughness of its anti-merger policy, the United States stands alone among its fellow nations.

Isolation often leads to feelings of self-consciousness and doubt. It does not necessarily follow, however, that U. S. policy is misguided because it is unique. The observed policy differences reflect more deep-seated differences in national economic conditions and attitudes toward competition. European governmental and industrial leaders today have views on competition policy not unlike those of Theodore Roosevelt and American businessmen 70 years ago. It is probable that attitudes in Europe will change, just as they did in the United States. The Europeans have begun to take faltering steps toward encouraging competitive market processes, and they will no doubt make further progress as a new generation of businessmen more accustomed to competing takes the helm. Eventually we may hear a chorus, and not just one powerful but nervous voice, singing the praises of structural competition.

[159]*Regina v. British Columbia Sugar Refining Co., Ltd.*, 32 W.W.R. (New Series) 577 (1960).

Chapter 21

Antitrust Policy: Other Restrictions on Conduct

We return now to some further aspects of business conduct and their status under the antitrust laws. In this chapter we explore the law on price discrimination, tying contracts, requirements contracts, exclusive dealing, resale price maintenance, and unfair methods of competition. All but the last two fall primarily under the jurisdiction of Clayton Act provisions originally framed by Congress to "arrest the creation of . . . monopolies in their incipiency." Whole books have been written on each of these practices. Here we can do no more than hit the highlights, overlooking many intricacies which delight antitrust aficionados.

PRICE DISCRIMINATION

In simplest terms, price discrimination is the sale (or purchase) of different units of a good or service at price differentials not directly related to differences in the cost of supply. There are many varieties of price discrimination, and the diversity of economic effects is equally great. Discrimination can affect allocative efficiency, the equity of income distribution, and the vigor of competition. It may improve the efficiency of resource allocation by permitting monopolistic producers to serve, at prices approaching marginal cost, certain markets they would shun if forced to charge a uniform price; or it can have adverse allocative effects. Some forms of discrimination permit the poor to pay lower prices than the rich—an income redistribution many observers might approve. Nearly all forms tend to increase the incomes of producers with monopoly power, and some benefit large firms more than small—effects which elicit widespread disapproval. Systematic discrimination and discrimination pursued successfully with predatory intent can raise barriers to new entry and entrench established firms in positions of power. Unsystematic discrimination can undermine oligopoly discipline and contribute to the emergence of competitive price–cost relationships.

With such a complex array of effects, a suitable price discrimination law must be sophisticated and discerning to encourage desirable practices and discourage undesirable ones. Unfortunately, the principal anti-discrimination provisions presently applicable in the United States fall visibly short of this ideal. Enacted with the intent of curbing discrimination which adversely affects the fortunes of small businessmen, they frequently inhibit competitive pricing and impede the attainment of efficiency. For these and other shortcomings, they have earned the criticism of economists and businessmen alike.

The first statutory pronouncement on price discrimination for U. S. industries other than railroading was Section 2 of the 1914 Clayton Act. It outlawed price discrimination between different purchasers where the effect "may be to substantially lessen competition or tend to create a monopoly." However, discrimination on account of differences in the grade, quality, or quantity of the commodity sold was exempted, as was discrimination which merely made due allowance for differences in cost or which was carried out in good faith to meet competitive pressures. The quantity loophole proved to be a gaping one, for many discriminatory price structures could be rationalized in terms of quantity differences. Because of this flaw and others, enforcement of the law was not particularly successful. Between 1914 and 1936 the Federal Trade Commission, with primary enforcement responsibility, initiated only 43 complaints charging illegal price discrimination. Only eight of these led ultimately to cease-and-desist orders not overturned on appeal to the courts.[1]

Recognition of these problems played some role in stimulating enactment of a much tougher law. However, other considerations had a more direct and potent influence. During the 1920s and 1930s chain stores like A & P began to rise to the forefront of retail distribution, displacing small independent retailers. A 1934 Federal Trade Commission report on the chain store movement stated that one reason for the decline of independent retailers was the ability of giant chains to wrest discriminatory price concessions from their suppliers. These savings were then passed along to consumers, and because of the chains' low prices, sales were drawn away from smaller retailers. The investigation also revealed that pecuniary gains from induced price discrimination accounted for only about 15 per cent of the chains' selling price advantage over independents; the rest could be traced to direct operating cost efficiencies.[2] But to eliminate whatever advantage the chains derived from exerting purchasing leverage, the Commission's report recommended that Clayton Act Section 2 be strengthened.

Congress was receptive. Under heavy pressure from independent grocer and drug store lobbies and expressing special concern over the buying power allegedly wielded by A & P, it passed the Robinson-Patman Act, substantially amending Clayton Act Section 2, in 1936.[3] The attendant reports and debates made it clear that Congress was anxious to protect small independent enterprises from the price competition of large firms discriminating in both their sales and purchasing functions. As Representative Wright Patman, the bill's co-sponsor, later observed, the law was designed "to give the little business fellows a square deal."[4] There is virtual unanimity among students of the Act that, in sharp contrast to the other antitrust laws, its motivation was a desire to limit competition, not to enhance it. In this respect the Robinson-Patman Act was not inconsistent with the spirit of the times, for in 1936, with recovery from the Great Depression not yet in sight, there were serious doubts afoot concerning the efficacy of unfettered competitive market processes.

The Robinson-Patman Act was enforced much more vigorously and successfully than the original Section 2. Between 1936 and December 1957, the Federal Trade Commission decided 429 cases in which price discrimination had been challenged under the new law. In 311, or 72 per cent, cease-and-desist orders were issued.[5] Only four of the 23 Commission orders appealed to higher courts during this 21 year period were reversed.

The core of the Robinson-Patman Act is embodied in Sections 2(a) and 2(b). They prohibit charging different prices to different purchasers of "goods of like grade and quality" where the effect "may be substantially to lessen competition or tend to create a monopoly in any line of commerce, or to injure, destroy, or prevent competition with any person who either grants or knowingly receives the benefit of such discrimination, or with customers of either of them." Three potential escape routes are then specified. Discrimi-

---

[1]See Corwin D. Edwards, *The Price Discrimination Law* (Washington: Brookings, 1959), p. 6.

[2]U. S. Federal Trade Commission, *Final Report on the Chain Store Investigation* (Washington: 1934), p. 55.

[3]For further background, see Edwards, *op. cit.*, Chapter 2; and Frederick M. Rowe, *Price Discrimination Under the Robinson-Patman Act* (Boston: Little, Brown, 1962), Chapter 1. Many of the criticisms of A & P have since been shown to have been distorted or erroneous. See M. A. Adelman, *A & P: A Study in Price-Cost Behavior and Public Policy* (Cambridge: Harvard University Press, 1959).

[4]"Robinson-Patman: Dodo or Golden Rule?" *Business Week*, November 12, 1966, p. 66.

[5]See Edwards, *op. cit.*, pp. 66–91. Nearly 60 per cent of these cease-and-desist orders pertained to firms operating in the food products industry, with which Congress had been particularly concerned. By 1966, the number of orders issued had risen to a cumulative total of more than 1,100.

nation may be justified if (1) it is carried out to dispose of perishable or obsolescent goods, or under a close-out or bankruptcy sale; (2) it merely makes due allowance for differences in "the cost of manufacture, sale, or delivery resulting from the differing methods or quantities" in which the commodity is sold or delivered; or (3) it is effected "in good faith to meet an equally low price of a competitor." The most prominent change in language from old Section 2 was the provision specifying the requisite character of injury to competition. It seemed to embrace a wider class of cases than the clause, "where the effect . . . may be to substantially lessen competition or tend to create a monopoly," contained in old Section 2 and two other substantive sections of the original Clayton Act. We shall return a few pages hence to analyze its interpretation and the construction of other especially controversial provisions.

The Robinson-Patman Act also reached out to deal with a number of practices ignored in the original Section 2. Section 2(c) of the newer law flatly prohibits the payment of brokerage commissions or any allowance or discount in lieu thereof except to middlemen actually performing services as independent brokers. No defenses— i.e., on the basis of cost differences or good faith meeting of competition—are permitted. Some historical background is essential to understand its significance. During the 1920s and 1930s, and to a lesser degree more recently, many small manufacturers and processors marketed their output through independent sales brokers who contacted potential customers, solicited orders, dispatched the orders to the producer, and collected a commission for their services. Firms like A & P large enough to seek out producers and deal with them directly insisted that they be paid the customary brokerage fee or given a

commensurate price discount for eliminating the brokerage function. Through Section 2(c) Congress sought to thwart this practice. The prohibition has been stringently enforced; 145 of the 311 cease-and-desist orders issued by the FTC between 1936 and 1958 hinged solely on violations of Section 2(c).

The brokerage payment provisions are open to objection on both economic and legal grounds. For one, Section 2(c) implicitly encourages either the preservation of possibly uneconomic brokerage functions or the retention by producers of savings ("phantom brokerage") from eliminating such middlemen, since buyers may not under the letter of the law take advantage of any savings effected from streamlining this aspect of the distribution system. Indeed, the law tends to enforce price discrimination *against* direct buyers, who must pay for services not rendered, even when they incur internal costs carrying out some of the tasks otherwise performed by brokers.[6] Second, to enforce the section it is necessary to make delicate distinctions between brokerage commissions, which are illegal if received by a firm buying for its own needs, and wholesalers' functional discounts, which in certain instances can be justified under Robinson-Patman Sections 2(a) and 2(b).[7] In the early days of Robinson-Patman Act enforcement the distinction was often obvious from industry traditions. But as marketing institutions changed it became increasingly vague, particularly with respect to firms serving as agents for buyers as well as for sellers and for enterprises simultaneously purchasing goods to be distributed through their own retail outlets and performing middleman services for other retailers. Some of the most intricate hair-splitting in antitrust law has occurred in Section 2(c) contests of this type.[8] As the interpretations have evolved,

[6]See Adelman, *op. cit.*, especially pp. 160–161.

[7]See *Federal Trade Commission v. Standard Oil Co. of Indiana et al.*, 355 U. S. 396 (1958). At an earlier stage in this and other cases, firms performing both wholesaling and retailing functions were allowed by the FTC to secure a wholesaler's discount on goods they purchased for sale to independent retailers, but not on purchases made for resale in their own outlets. For an analysis of the contradictions and distortions to which this policy led, see Edwards, *op. cit.*, pp. 286–348; and U. S. Department of Justice, *Report of the Attorney General's National Committee To Study the Antitrust Laws* (Washington: 1955), pp. 202–209.

[8]*Central Retailer-Owned Grocers, Inc.* v. *Federal Trade Commission*, 319 F. 2d 410 (1963); *in re E. J. Hruby*, 61 F. T. C. 1437 (1962); and *Empire Rayon Yarn Co.* v. *American Viscose Corp. et al.*, 354 F. 2d 182 (1965), superseded in 364 F. 2d 491 (1966).

middlemen are likely to be classified as whole-salers if they customarily take title over the goods being distributed, assume the risks of price fluctuations and granting credit, and maintain warehouses and inventories. If they perform none of these functions, a payment for middleman's services is apt to be called a brokerage fee. But the line between these poles is hard to draw, and there is certainly no compelling case in logic for drawing it at one point rather than another. Finally, large companies have managed to escape Section 2(c) by purchasing the entire output of their suppliers, or by purchasing only from sup-pliers who employ no brokers, or through other such dodges. In this respect Section 2(c) may operate to the disadvantage of medium-sized buyers who have less flexibility in choosing sources of supply. Because of these and other shortcomings, there is widespread sentiment for the repeal of Section 2(c).

Section 2(d) of the Robinson-Patman Act prevents sellers from making payments (such as advertising allowances) to buyers for promotional and other services rendered by the buyer, unless the payment is available to all buyers "on pro-portionally equal terms." Section 2(e) prohibits sellers from providing services (such as the use of special display racks, or the supply of inven-tories on a consignment basis) unless the service is made available to all customers on propor-tionally equal terms. These rules were intended to prevent discrimination on non-price as well as price dimensions. In enforcing them it has not always been easy to determine when buyers of widely varying characteristics have in fact been accorded "proportionally equal" treatment.

Section 2(f) makes it illegal for a buyer "know-ingly to induce or receive a discrimination in price" prohibited by other parts of the law. It reflects the belief of Congress that powerful buyers were mainly to blame for the discrim-inatory practices inspiring the Robinson-Patman Act's passage. However, its enforcement has not been consistent with this apportioning of respon-sibility. In a key test case, the Supreme Court interpreted the phrase "knowingly to induce" as meaning that to prove a violation, it must be shown not only that the buyer received illegal price concessions, but that he had good reason to believe the concessions were illegal.[9] This is a heavy burden of proof for the antitrust enforce-ment agencies to sustain, since in practice buyers can seldom obtain the detailed information on supplier operations needed to discern whether a concession is justified by cost savings. Because of this difficulty and others, only 30 cease-and-desist orders out of the more than 1,100 Robin-son-Patman orders issued between 1936 and 1966 were brought under Section 2(f).[10]

SOME INTERPRETATIONS OF SECTION 2(A)

We return now to Section 2(a), under which many of the most important Robinson-Patman Act cases have been brought. The basic prohibi-tion covers charging different prices to different customers. Quoting the same price to different customers served at diverse unit costs—i.e., when there are differences in order processing and delivery costs between customers—is gener-ally not illegal, even though it is discriminatory in a meaningful economic sense.

Actionable discrimination can be inferred only if the goods sold at different prices are of "like grade and quality." The principal point of con-tention under this clause concerns price differen-tials between products unlike only in terms of brand name or some other aspect of image differ-entiation. The issue came to a head in 1966, when the Supreme Court ruled that the Borden Company had engaged in price discrimination by selling physically homogeneous canned evaporated milk at two prices, one for cans sold under the Borden label and a lower price for milk to which buyers affixed their own brand labels.[11] This opinion provoked a cry of protest from those who feared that the competitive chal-lenge of low-price, high-quality unbranded con-sumer products might be blunted. However, the

[9]*Automatic Canteen Co.* v. *Federal Trade Commission*, 346 U. S. 61 (1953).

[10]See "Robinson-Patman: Dodo or Golden Rule?" *Business Week*, November 12, 1966, p. 66; and Edwards, *op. cit.*, p. 72.

[11]*Federal Trade Commission* v. *Borden Co.*, 383 U. S. 637 (1966).

case was shorn of its potentially revolutionary impact when an appellate court ruled on remand that no injury to competition resulted if "a price differential between a premium and nonpremium brand reflects no more than a consumer preference for the premium brand," since it merely represents "a rough equivalent of the benefit by way of the seller's national advertising and promotion which the purchaser of the more expensive branded product enjoys."[12]

One of the most complex and controversial features of the Robinson-Patman Act is the Section 2(a) condition that price discrimination, to be declared illegal, must injure competition in some manner. There are two main issues: upon whom the burden of proving injury rests, and what constitutes the requisite injury. On the first, the Second Circuit Court of Appeals held in early decisions that a *prima facie* presumption of injury existed when the mere presence of price discrimination had been shown.[13] This placed upon respondents the difficult burden of proving that competition had *not* been injured. However, appellate courts for the other circuits have adopted the opposite rule, requiring the enforcement agency or party seeking damages to present affirmative evidence of competitive injury before the burden of defending itself passed to the discriminator. This view has been accepted by the Federal Trade Commission, so the controversy has faded.[14]

Injury to competition under Robinson-Patman Act Section 2(a) may be shown at any of three levels: the primary line, the secondary line, and the tertiary line. A primary line injury involves competition among firms directly competing with the seller practicing discrimination. A secondary line injury involves firms competing with buyers to whom a discriminatory price has been granted.

A tertiary line injury involves firms competing with customers of the buyer to whom a discriminatory price has been granted. Somewhat different standards have evolved for handling primary as opposed to secondary and tertiary line injuries. We will focus on the leading primary and secondary line rulings.

The central issue is whether the injury essential for a violation is injury to the *vigor of competition* or to particular *competitors*. These are usually not synonymous, although they might be, e.g., when individual competitors have been injured so lethally that they withdraw from the market, leaving fewer firms competing more cautiously. In primary line decisions something more than incidental injury to competitors has been required, but the courts have been willing to infer actionable injury when rivals were not literally driven from the market. Two recent cases illustrate the line drawn.

Through sequential price reductions in January and June of 1954, the Anheuser-Busch Co. (AB) completely eliminated the price differential which had customarily prevailed in the St. Louis area between its Budweiser beer and other locally-brewed beers. Prices were not reduced in other markets, and as a result the St. Louis price of Budweiser was considerably below prices AB charged elsewhere. AB's share of St. Louis beer sales rose from 12.5 per cent in December 1953 to 39.3 per cent in February of 1955. Then, in March of 1955, AB raised its St. Louis wholesale price $.45 per case to $2.80, restoring a substantial price differential relative to competing local beers. Its share of the market dropped to 21 per cent within four months and to 17 per cent in 1956. Testimony revealed that AB had initiated its price-cutting program in response to severe Midwestern market sales losses during

---

[12]*Borden Co.* v. *Federal Trade Commission*, 381 F. 2d 175, 181 (1967). The appellate court also noted approvingly that Borden offered all buyers the opportunity to buy unlabeled milk at the lower price. Some evidently chose not to do so only because the differential was not sufficiently large to overcome consumers' preference for branded milk. This emphasis on the efficacy of subjective consumer preferences molded through advertising as a justification for price differentials, it might be added, appears logically inconsistent with the Supreme Court's condemnation of such differentials in the Clorox merger case. *Federal Trade Commission* v. *Procter & Gamble Co. et al.*, 87 S. Ct. 1224 (1967). But Robinson-Patman Act interpretations have never been distinguished for their consistency with the other antitrust laws.

[13]See especially *Samuel H. Moss, Inc.*, v. *Federal Trade Commission*, 148 F. 2d 378 (1945); and *Federal Trade Commission* v. *Standard Brands, Inc.*, 189 F. 2d 510 (1951).

[14]Cf. *Minneapolis-Honeywell Regulator Co.* v. *Federal Trade Commission*, 191 F. 2d 786 (1951), cert. dismissed 344 U. S. 206 (1952); and *in re General Foods Co.*, 50 F.T.C. 885 (1954).

1953; that its St. Louis rivals continued to earn positive profits during the period of reduced Budweiser prices; and that part of the market share gain by AB was attributable to rival quality control and merchandising difficulties. After the Supreme Court found that AB had in fact engaged in price discrimination as defined under the Robinson-Patman Act, the Seventh Circuit Court of Appeals ruled that competition had not been injured sufficiently to find a violation, since the Budweiser price cuts were experimental, temporary, and necessitated by competitive conditions; and since the shift in sales volume among competitors was only temporary.[15] It observed that the Robinson-Patman Act is "not concerned with mere shifts of business between competitors" and that "AB used restraint in its competitive efforts," refraining from "the predatory misconduct" condemned in other cases.

In late 1957 the Utah Pie Company, a tiny family-owned and operated firm, began producing and marketing frozen dessert pies in the Salt Lake City area. Its principal rivals were three large nationwide concerns—Continental Baking, Pet Milk, and the Carnation Company. All had entered the frozen pie business before Utah, shipping their products into Salt Lake City from plants in California. Utah enjoyed a significant transportation cost advantage over the three, and through aggressive price competition it was able to build its Salt Lake City area market share to 67 per cent in 1958. Each of the three cut prices sharply in response to Utah's gains, selling pies in Salt Lake City at prices below average total cost (including overhead allowances) and below the levels quoted in markets nearer their production plants. Utah's share of the market thereupon fell to 34 per cent in 1959, rising to 45 per cent in 1961. Its absolute volume of frozen pie sales expanded steadily in the rapidly growing market, however, and it operated profitably throughout the period. Utah sued the three rivals for damages resulting from their alleged price discrimination. After Utah appealed an adverse lower court decision, the Supreme Court found that sufficient injury to

competition had been shown, stressing the sales of the three rivals below cost, the fact that Pet Milk management had identified Utah Pie as an "unfavorable factor" which "dug holes in our operation," and the fact that Pet had sent a spy into Utah's plant to obtain evidence of quality deficiencies.[16] Recognizing in a footnote the possible claim that Pet, Continental, and Carnation were only displaying "fierce competitive instincts," the Court nevertheless argued that:

> Actual intent to injure another competitor does not . . . fall into that category, and neither . . . do persistent sales below cost and radical price cuts themselves discriminatory. . . . We believe that the Act reaches price discrimination that erodes competition as much as it does price discrimination that is intended to have immediate destructive impact.[17]

What the differences between these two cases seem to say is that discriminatory price cuts cannot legally be aimed directly at undermining the market position of a primary line rival, especially if the discriminating seller is careless enough to drop some additional hint of predatory intent. This is a defensible standard, for oligopolistic price discipline can be upset and (in less concentrated markets) competition can be vigorous without carrying discriminatory price shading to extremely aggressive limits. Still these interpretations reflect only the position of the Supreme Court and one appellate court. In a number of primary line cases the Federal Trade Commission has been less circumspect about drawing a distinction between injury to competition and injury to competitors. Its less subtle view is reflected, for example, in a 1965 opinion on discriminatory pricing by the Dean Milk Company:

> It is the Commission's opinion that a finding of possible substantial competitive injury on the seller level is warranted in the absence of predation where the evidence shows significant diversion of business from the discriminator's competitors to the dis-

---

[15]*Federal Trade Commission* v. *Anheuser-Busch, Inc.*, 363 U. S. 536 (1960), 289 F. 2d 835 (1961).

[16]*Utah Pie Co.* v. *Continental Baking Co. et al.*, 386 U. S. 865, 697 (1967).

[17]*Ibid.*, at pp. 702–703.

criminator or diminishing profits to competitors resulting either from the diversion of business or from the necessity of meeting the discriminator's lower prices, provided that these immediate actual effects portend either a financial crippling of those competitors, a possibility of an anticompetitive concentration of business in large sellers, or a significant reduction in the number of sellers in the market. . . . (I)f a large national firm enters a new market with the intent of merely securing a foothold in the market or of wresting a share of the market from another competitor, either smaller or larger, but, in carrying out this legitimate purpose, utilizes a price discrimination which actually lessens or which may lessen the ability of local firms to compete with it, the requisite statutory injury has occurred.[18]

To the extent that such interpretations survive the scrutiny of higher judicial authority—and in Robinson-Patman Act cases appeals are infrequent, since it is often easier to amend one's price structure than to fight a case to the Supreme Court—competitive expansion by established firms into new markets and other practices which increase competition might well be discouraged.

In secondary line cases a perceptibly tougher stance has been adopted. This reflects the desire of the courts to respect Congress' avowed goal of discouraging discrimination which adversely affects the fortunes of small buyers. The Supreme Court's 1948 opinion in the *Morton Salt* case set the standard. Morton systematically sold its table salt at $1.60 per case in less-than-carload lots, at $1.50 per case for carload purchases, and at still lower prices when larger quantities were purchased over the span of a year. Observing that the discounts permitted large buyers to set retail prices below those of smaller rivals, the Court found an illegal injury to competition, supporting its conclusion as follows:

The legislative history of the Robinson-Patman Act makes it abundantly clear that Congress considered it to be an evil that a large buyer could secure a competitive advantage over a small buyer solely because of the large buyer's quantity purchasing ability. . . . (I)n enacting the Robinson-Patman Act Congress was especially concerned with protecting small businesses which were unable to buy in quantities, such as the merchants here who purchased in less-than-carload lots. . . . That respondent's quantity discounts did result in price differentials between competing producers sufficient in amount to influence their resale price of salt was shown by evidence. This showing in itself is adequate to support the Commission's appropriate findings that the effect of such discriminations "may be substantially to lessen competition . . . and to injure, destroy and prevent competition." . . . Congress intended to protect a merchant from competitive injury attributable to discriminatory prices on any or all goods sold in interstate commerce, whether the particular goods constituted a major or minor portion of his stock.[19]

This statement of the law was amplified in subsequent secondary line cases to indicate that actionable injury will not be found when the price differentials are too small to have any significant effect on sales and market shares, or when they exist for too short a period to affect industry member positions significantly. Still the general emphasis on possible injury to specific competitors or classes of competitors remains, as a 1965 appellate court opinion reveals:

[I]t seems well-established that where the record indicates a price differential substantial enough to cut into the purchaser's profit margin and discloses a reduction which would afford the favored buyer a significant aggregate saving that, if reflected in a resale price cut, would have a noticeable effect on the decisions of customers in the retail market, an inference of injury may properly be indulged.[20]

From these and related decisions it is clear that the courts and the Federal Trade Commission

---

[18]*In re Dean Milk Company*, CCH Trade Regulation Reporter, Federal Trade Commission Complaints and Orders, Para. 17,357 (1965).

[19]*Federal Trade Commission* v. *Morton Salt Co.*, 334 U. S. 37, 43, 47, 49 (1948).

[20]*Foremost Dairies, Inc.*, v. *Federal Trade Commission*, 348 F. 2d 674, 680 (1965).

are more inclined to err on the side of protecting competitors than protecting competition when the two goals are not congruent. And in this respect, the criteria applied in enforcing the Robinson-Patman Act are at odds with the broader pro-competitive objectives of antitrust.

THE DISCRIMINATOR'S DEFENSES

Affirmation that competition has been injured through price discrimination does not complete a Robinson-Patman Section 2(a) proceeding. The burden of proving that its prices were legally justifiable then shifts to the discriminator. This is normally attempted under either the cost or 'good faith meeting of competition' defenses.

Price differentials which merely reflect differences in the costs of serving particular customers are clearly unobjectionable, and to forbid them would be to encourage reverse discrimination. The Robinson-Patman Act permits firms to justify such differentials by showing that they "only make due allowance for differences in the cost of manufacture, sale, or delivery resulting from the differing methods or quantities in which . . . commodities are . . . sold or delivered." However, attempts to sustain a cost defense have encountered several obstacles. For one, the FTC and the courts have insisted that the differential be justified in terms of *full costs*, including prorated overhead, and not merely the marginal costs upon which rational decision-makers base their price structures. This approach has the debatable advantage of setting high standards for legality. If price differentials could be justified on marginal cost bases, only the most aggressive predatory and promotional discrimination would fail to pass the test. Still the imposition of a full-cost rule leads to inherently arbitrary judgments, since there is no uniquely correct way of prorating fixed and joint costs, and any convention adopted necessarily affects the cost comparison and perhaps the case

outcome. Second, the FTC and courts have imposed heavy documentation demands upon sellers attempting to sustain a cost defense. Informed guesstimates have not been accepted and the kinds of data generated routinely under normal accounting procedures have typically been found wanting. Rather, companies have been forced to conduct special cost studies, pinpointing the amount of order-taking, packaging, delivery, maintenance, and other effort associated with serving specific classes of customers. General Electric is said to have spent $100,000 developing the data needed to justify its radio and television tube discount structure, and this is apparently not atypical.[21] Even when special cost studies have been made, firms' customer classifications have been rejected—sometimes for valid reasons, but in other cases because the judge or hearing examiner lacked an adequate understanding of the underlying probability theory and statistical methodology.[22] Finally, the FTC has insisted that price differentials be *fully* cost-justified before it will accept the defense as valid. If a respondent shows that 90 per cent of a price discount can be traced to cost savings, but cannot account for the remaining 10 per cent, its cost defense fails completely. Partly because of these problems, but also because the cost defense is inapplicable in many price discrimination situations, only 11 attempts were made to employ the cost defense in cases contested before the Federal Trade Commission between 1936 and 1954. Of these, only two were fully successful.[23] However, companies have been able more frequently to head off impending FTC complaints at the informal investigation stage by presenting convincing cost data to justify their price differentials.[24]

When discrimination injurious to competition has been found, Section 2(b) of the Robinson-Patman Act permits a seller to rebut the *prima facie* presumption of illegality by showing that

---

[21]Cf. *Business Week*, November 12, 1966, p. 68. See also James W. McKie, *Tin Cans and Tin Plate* (Cambridge: Harvard University Press, 1959), pp. 165–171.

[22]Compare *U. S. v. Borden Co.*, 370 U. S. 460 (1962); with *Federal Trade Commission v. Standard Motor Products, Inc.*, 371 F. 2d 613 (1967). In the latter case, the Second Circuit Court of Appeals displayed considerable statistical sophistication in overturning a FTC decision.

[23]See the *Report of the Attorney General's National Committee To Study the Antitrust Laws*, p. 171.

[24]Edwards, *op. cit.*, pp. 587–591.

its lower price was "made in good faith to meet an equally low price of a competitor." Interpretation of this "good faith meeting" defense presents a tangle of legal and economic problems. For the most part, the Federal Trade Commission has taken a dim view of discriminators' attempts to use the defense. Some of its decisions have been rebuffed by higher courts, but many issues remain unsettled and controversial.[25]

A few of the earlier contested decisions involved the use of basing point pricing systems. In the leading case, A. E. Staley Co., a central Illinois producer of glucose and corn syrup, systematically matched the delivered prices set from a Chicago basing point by its principal rival. For sales in the Chicago area Staley quoted lower delivered prices than in downstate Illinois, even though its shipping costs were higher on Chicago orders. Staley argued that its discrimination was justifiable, since it merely met in good faith the prices of its Chicago rival. Sustaining an FTC cease-and-desist order, the Supreme Court ruled that the good faith meeting of competition defense could not apply when the prices met were themselves illegal, stemming from an illegal discriminatory system.[26]

In a related case appealed twice to the Supreme Court, the FTC argued that the Standard Oil Company of Indiana could not plead good faith meeting of competition when it granted $.015 per gallon functional discounts to four Detroit gasoline jobbers who took delivery in rail carload lots (instead of the much smaller truckload lots accepted by retailers) and then sold the gasoline in their own retail outlets as well as to independent retail gas stations. Stressing the *Staley* precedent, the Commission insisted that Standard's functional discounts to jobbers were made pursuant to a discriminatory pricing system, and

therefore did not qualify as a good faith meeting of "individual competitive situations." The Supreme Court rejected this inference, noting that Standard had lost three of its jobbers by not meeting competitors' discounts during a price war and that it granted the jobber's discount to one distributor only after prolonged haggling. It found that "Standard's use of . . . two prices, the lower of which could be obtained under the spur of threats to switch to pirating competitors, is a competitive deterrent far short of the discriminatory pricing of Staley," and that Standard's good faith meeting of competition could therefore serve as an absolute defense to the charge of illegal discrimination.[27] This "Detroit Gas" case is distinctive in two main respects: for demonstrating that the 'good faith meeting of competition' defense could be used successfully despite the FTC's reticence; and because 17 years of litigation were required to acquit a practice which reflected nothing more than a rational competitive response to secure the valuable services of gasoline jobbers.

Some of the more exotic Section 2(b) deliberations have focused on the discriminator's knowledge of the existence and legality of rival prices. When firms vie for orders through secret price-shading, it is not always clear to the would-be discriminator whose prices it must meet, nor can one always be sure that a customer is telling the truth in reporting competitive offers. Also, the rival price a seller must meet to secure some order may itself be illegally discriminatory—i.e., because it cannot be justified on the basis of cost savings. In some instances the Federal Trade Commission has demanded that respondents show diligence in ascertaining the existence and even the cost justification of rival price offers.[28] Although extreme versions of this doctrine have

[25]For a survey of recent decisions, see Robert W. Steele, "Section 2(b) of the Robinson-Patman Act—Rules for Meeting Competition in the Past and the Present," *Antitrust Bulletin*, Winter 1968, pp. 1223–1269.

[26]*Federal Trade Commission* v. *A. E. Staley Manufacturing Co. et al.*, 324 U. S. 746 (1945). See also *Corn Products Refining Co.* v. *Federal Trade Commission*, 324 U. S. 726 (1945); and *Federal Trade Commission* v. *Cement Institute et al.*, 333 U. S. 683 (1948). In *Safeway Stores, Inc.* v. *Oklahoma Retail Grocers Association, Inc.*, 360 U. S. 334 (1959), the Supreme Court held that a firm cannot in good faith discriminate to meet competitor prices which it believes violate state laws prohibiting sales below cost.

[27]*Federal Trade Commission* v. *Standard Oil Co.*, 355 U. S. 396, 404 (1958). See also the earlier opinion at 340 U. S. 231 (1951).

[28]See *Forster Mfg. Co.* v. *Federal Trade Commission*, 335 F. 2d 47 (1964), 361 F. 2d 340 (1966); *in re Tri-Valley Packing Association*, 60 F.T.C. 1134 (1962); and *Standard Oil Co.* v. *Brown*, 238 F. 2d 54 (1956).

been rejected by higher courts, there is a dilemma in the whole approach. For buyers, a certain amount of secrecy may be essential to extract the best possible bargain. This limits the seller's ability to verify rival offers through its contacts with buyers. And if a salesman checks with rivals alleged to have offered a concession, he runs the risk of violating Sherman Act Section 1's prohibition against price-fixing conspiracies.

Equally baffling questions arise in determining what it means to "meet" a competitor's price. A literal reading of the statutory language suggests that firms practicing discrimination may exactly match rival prices but not undercut them. Widespread seller adherence to such a rule, which has been embraced in some decisions,[29] could smother the forces which undermine oligopoly price structures. Matters become even more complicated when one firm's product customarily commands a premium price because of image differentiation. In gasoline retailing, for instance, the lesser known brands must charge roughly $.02 less per gallon than nationally advertised brands to maintain their market positions, though tacit agreement on the 'correct' differential is difficult to obtain and price wars often begin when some company tries to alter the differential. Against this circumstantial background, the Federal Trade Commission and the courts have in certain cases ruled that "good faith meeting" of competition for nationally branded gasoline sellers consists of maintaining the traditional two cent price differential and that the defense cannot be sustained when a refiner squeezes the differential.[30] While this position makes a certain amount of sense, rigid adherence to it could discourage innovation in marketing and freeze price structures into increasingly archaic molds.

One further illustration completes our survey. The Federal Trade Commission has consistently held that sellers can escape under the "good faith meeting" clause only when they discriminate in self defense to retain existing customers, but not to attract new customers. This interpretation was rejected by the Seventh Circuit Court of Appeals in a case concerning the pricing of Sunshine Biscuit's Krun-Chee potato chips in Cleveland. The court noted that the Robinson-Patman Act permits sellers to meet rival price offers to "any purchaser," and not just to old customers. It observed further that the FTC approach was unworkable, since it is hard to distinguish in practice between new and old customers, and economically unsound, since "competition for new customers would be stifled and monopoly would be fostered."[31] However, in another case the Second Circuit Court of Appeals approved the FTC's position, and so in this respect too the question of how aggressively sellers can compete for new customers remains unsettled.[32]

CONCLUSION

The Robinson-Patman Act has on occasion been called a jungle, a hodgepodge of inconsistencies, and worse. The appellations are well deserved. The statute itself, however, is not so hopeless that it could not, with sensible administration, be used to support a rational public policy toward discriminatory pricing. Much of the problem stems from the Federal Trade Commission's populist zeal in taking seriously Congress' desire, expressed during the depression-ridden 1930s, to protect small business against the ravages of competition and to preserve existing modes of retail distribution. Fortunately, the good sense of the courts has deflected some Commission policies which might otherwise have straightjacketed competition. But the present situation leaves much to be desired. A fresh legislative start may be needed to secure a policy

[29] See *Samuel H. Moss, Inc.,* v. *Federal Trade Commission,* 148 F. 2d 378, 379 (1945); *in re Champion Spark Plug Co.,* 50 F.T.C. 30 (1953); and (for a case in which the FTC's finding that a seller had undercut its rivals was rejected by the appellate court) *Callaway Mills Co.* v. *Federal Trade Commission,* 362 F. 2d 435 (1966).

[30] *In re American Oil Co.,* 60 F.T.C. 1786 (1962), set aside on other grounds at 325 F. 2d 101 (1963); and *Continental Oil Co.* v. *Frontier Refining Co.,* 338 F. 2d 780 (1964), whose facts are summarized in *Business Week,* December 5, 1964, p. 38.

[31] *Sunshine Biscuits, Inc.,* v. *Federal Trade Commission,* 306 F. 2d 48, 52 (1962).

[32] *Standard Motor Products, Inc.,* v. *Federal Trade Commission,* 265 F. 2d 674, 677 (1959).

which discourages systematic and predatory discrimination with adverse effects on the vigor of competition, encourages unsystematic discrimination undermining oligopolistic pricing discipline, and permits the transmission to consumers of *bona fide* savings attainable through large scale ordering, production, and distribution.[33]

TYING CONTRACTS, REQUIREMENTS CONTRACTS, AND EXCLUSIVE DEALING

Section 3 of the Clayton Act prohibits contracts for the sale or lease of commodities which impose a condition that the purchaser or lessee "shall not use or deal in the goods, . . . supplies, or other commodities of a competitor . . . of the lessor or seller" where the effect "may be to substantially lessen competition or tend to create a monopoly." It applies to three main types of practices: tying contracts, requirements contracts, and exclusive dealing arrangements. Under a tying contract, the purchaser of some article—e.g., a machine—agrees as a condition of purchase to buy the seller's supplies of some other commodity—i.e., raw materials processed by the machine. The agreement in effect forecloses competing sellers from the opportunity of selling the 'tied' commodity to that purchaser. A requirements contract is an agreement by the buyer to purchase all of its requirements of some commodity from a particular seller. Here again, competing sellers are foreclosed for the duration of the contract. Exclusive dealing is a special subcase, under which some firm (typically a retailer or wholesaler) agrees to sell only the products of a particular manufacturer, and thus implicitly or explicitly agrees not to handle the products of competing producers. The law on

these practices has developed along divergent lines, so we shall examine each separately.

TYING CONTRACTS

Businessmen have various reasons for attempting to tie the sale of one product to that of another. First, a firm may have monopoly power over one product by virtue of patent protection, strong product differentiation, or scale economies, and it may try to exploit this leverage in a second market where, without the tie, it could earn no more than a normal profit return.[34] Thus it adds to its monopoly profits in the tying good market the profits it can earn by exercising power over price in at least part of the tied good market. Second, the profits attainable from coordinated monopoly pricing of two goods which, for example, are complements in use, will generally be higher than those realized by setting a monopoly price for each commodity separately.[35] This is so because, by ignoring interdependence between the demand functions of complementary products, a producer in effect fails to adjust for all the variables which affect its profit maximum, just as oligopolists producing the same product maximize joint profits only when they take into account fully the interdependence of their demand functions.[36] Third, tying is sometimes a convenient way of discriminating in price according to intensity of use. Suppose, for instance, that one copying machine user makes 3,000 copies per month, while another makes 10,000 copies per month. It would be difficult for a company selling only copying machines to price its machines in such a way as to extract more revenue from the more intensive user. But if the machine maker can tie the purchase of special copying paper to the purchase of its machine, and if it can wield sufficient leverage in the paper market to realize a supra-normal profit margin

---

[33]See, for instance, the draft bill proposed by Carl Kaysen and Donald F. Turner in *Antitrust Policy* (Cambridge: Harvard University Press, 1959), pp. 184–185.

[34]For diverse views, see Ward S. Bowman, Jr., "Tying Arrangements and the Leverage Problem," *Yale Law Journal*, November 1957, pp. 19–36; M. L. Burstein, "A Theory of Full-Line Forcing," *Northwestern University Law Review*, March-April 1960, pp. 62–95; and W. L. Baldwin and David McFarland, "Tying Arrangements in Law and Economics," *Antitrust Bulletin*, September-October 1963, pp. 743–780.

[35]For a proof, see Martin J. Bailey, "Price and Output Determination By a Firm Selling Related Products," *American Economic Review*, March 1954, pp. 82–93.

[36]The effect of vertically integrating successive monopolized stages of production and distribution is analogous. See p. 250 *supra*.

there, it will indeed be able to draw additional profits from the high-volume user.[37] Fourth, the producer of a technically complex machine may engage in trying to control the quality of materials and supplies used with its machine, so that the reputation of its product is not sullied by breakdowns caused by the use of faulty supplies. Fifth, certain economies may be realized by producing or distributing the tied and tying goods together. For example, supplies of special copying machine paper or ink may be delivered by maintenance personnel in the course of routine service visits, saving separate delivery costs. It is doubtful, however, whether the savings realized in this way are very substantial. Finally, tying contracts may be employed to evade governmental price controls—i.e., when a firm supplying some commodity such as gas or telephone service whose price is regulated requires customers to buy from it fixtures and attachments whose prices are not effectively controlled.

In early tying case decisions, companies requiring purchasers of their patented machines also to purchase unpatented supplies were allowed to enforce their tying contracts and secure injunctions against the use of competing supplies.[38] However, these precedents were overturned after the Clayton Act was passed.[39] From then on, tying arrangements have been dealt with severely not only in Clayton Act Section 3 cases, but also in Sherman Act Section 1 and patent infringement actions.[40] In a decision setting forth general guidelines for the interpretation of Clayton Act Section 3, the Supreme Court observed that "Tying agreements serve hardly any purpose beyond the suppression of competition."[41] In a nearly contemporaneous case tried under both Clayton and Sherman Act charges, the Court ruled that it is "unreasonable, *per se*, to foreclose competitors from any substantial market" by means of tying contracts.[42]

These statements have the ring of a flat *per se* prohibition, but the presumption against tying arrangements is not quite as strong as the *per se* rule against price-fixing conspiracies. Violation will not be found unless there is monopoly power in the tying market or unless a substantial volume of sales is foreclosed in the tied good market, and for relatively small firms producing unpatented products, these conditions are not likely to be satisfied.[43] Small companies attempting to break into a new market under the protection of tying contracts may also escape censure.[44] And the courts have been willing to consider extenuating circumstances such as the need to exercise control over complementary goods or services to ensure satisfactory operation of the tying product. This was the central issue in a case involving the International Business Machines Corporation's requirement that its unpatented tabulating cards be used exclusively in the key punch, card sorting, and other mechanical data processing equipment it leased. IBM argued that the use of faulty cards could cause machine jams and processing errors, damaging its reputation. The Supreme Court rejected this contention after studying the evi-

---

[37]For an analysis of this and other complementary goods pricing practices in the copying machine industry, see Erwin A. Blackstone, "The Copying Machine Industry: A Case Study," Ph.D. dissertation, University of Michigan (1968), especially pp. 119–127 and 198–216.

[38]*Heaton Peninsular Button-Fastener Co.* v. *Eureka Specialty Co.*, 77 F. 288 (1896); and *Henry* v. *A. B. Dick Co.*, 224 U. S. 1 (1912).

[39]The turning point was *Motion Picture Patents Co.* v. *Universal Film Manufacturing Co.*, 243 U. S. 502 (1917). An important Section 3 decision outlawing tying agreements imposed by firms dominating some market was *United Shoe Machinery Corp.* v. *U. S.*, 258 U. S. 451 (1922).

[40]Key patent infringement decisions include *Carbice Corp.* v. *American Patent Development Corp.*, 283 U. S. 27 (1931); and *Morton Salt Co.* v. *G. S. Suppiger Co.*, 314 U. S. 488 (1942).

[41]*Standard Oil Co. of California et al.* v. *U. S.*, 337 U. S. 293, 305–306 (1949).

[42]*International Salt Co.* v. *U. S.*, 332 U. S. 392, 396 (1947). See also *Northern Pacific Railway Co.* v. *U. S.*, 356 U. S. 1, 5–6 (1958).

[43]The courts may also strain economic logic beyond the breaking point to acquit practices which seem reasonable by finding that the necessary structural tests are not satisfied. This is apparently what happened in *Times-Picayune Publishing Co.* v. *U. S.*, 345 U. S. 594 (1953), where the Supreme Court found New Orleans' largest newspaper publisher innocent of violating Sherman Act Section 1 when it required persons desiring to advertise in the morning *Times-Picayune* also to take identical insertions in its evening paper, *The States*. Notwithstanding the Supreme Court's arguments to the contrary, this was a clear-cut tying arrangement. But it did have the merit of permitting typesetting and composition cost savings.

[44]See especially the *dictum* in *Brown Shoe Co.* v. *U. S.*, 370 U. S. 294, 330 (1962).

dence. It found that other suppliers were capable of manufacturing cards conforming to IBM's specifications, and that IBM was not prevented under the law from "proclaiming the virtues of its own cards" or even from making its leases conditional upon the use of cards which met the necessary quality standards.[45] In a later case a slightly more tolerant judgment was rendered. The Jerrold Electronics Corporation, a pioneer in the development and installation of community antenna television systems, at first required purchasers of its system also to accept five-year maintenance contracts. This was done to avoid breakdowns which could result if the complex, delicate equipment were serviced by inadequately trained personnel. In a decision broadly endorsed by the Supreme Court, a district court ruled that the service tying arrangement was not unreasonable at the time of its inception, but that it came to violate Sherman Act Section 1 as the "industry took root and grew."[46]

The law also does not reach tying arrangements which are purely voluntary and informal —i.e., when customers habitually buy a machine producer's special supplies in the belief that the machine will thereby function more effectively, or because it is more convenient, and not because the machine maker refuses to sell or lease machines without a supplies contract. There were many informal ties of this type in the segment of the electrostatic copying machine industry requiring specially coated paper during the early 1960s. However, the ties were gradually weakened as newcomers entered the paper coating trade, offering their products at substantially reduced prices. Some machine suppliers reacted to this emerging competitive threat by attempting to formalize their ties, but they were soon dissuaded by the threat of antitrust suits. They then accepted their fate stoically, raising the price of their machines because machine

sales could no longer be counted upon to generate a profitable stream of subsequent paper sales.[47] Such a pricing reaction is common when a tie between complementary products is severed.

The effects on competition of a legal ban against tying contracts vary from field to field, depending upon the degree to which producers can sustain informal ties through product differentiation. On one hand, the 1936 decree requiring IBM to end its tying contracts had very little effect, for data processing machine users continued to buy their tabulating cards from IBM. Twenty years later IBM still accounted for roughly 90 per cent of greatly expanded tabulating card production.[48] On the other hand, an attack on tying practices appears to have had a major impact on the tin can industry. Prior to 1950 the American Can Company tied the sale of tin cans to the lease of its patented can-closing machines by arranging to have the expiration dates of machine leases and long-term can requirements contracts coincide, and by refusing to conclude new machine lease contracts unless the canner also accepted a can requirements contract. After the courts found this subterfuge illegal, American was required to offer its machines for sale at attractive prices and to limit the life of its can supply contracts to one year.[49] Similar injunctions bound Continental Can, its leading rival. Within four years, customers responsible for 75 per cent of the two firms' machine leases had taken advantage of the opportunity to own their can-closing machines. Price competition in the industry has intensified, and the market share of non-Big Four can sellers increased from 20 per cent in 1954 to 29 per cent in 1966.[50]

REQUIREMENTS CONTRACTS

Under a requirements contract, the buyer agrees to purchase all its requirements for some commodity or group of commodities from a

---

[45]*International Business Machines Corp.* v. *U. S.*, 298 U. S. 131, 139–140 (1936).

[46]*U. S.* v. *Jerrold Electronics Corp.*, 187 F. Supp. 545, 557; affirmed *per curiam* 363 U. S. 567 (1961).

[47]See Blackstone, *op. cit.*, especially pp. 126–129 and 202–216.

[48]*U. S.* v. *International Business Machines Corp.*, CCH 1956 Trade Cases, Para. 68,245. See also p. 464 *supra*.

[49]*U. S.* v. *American Can Co. et al.*, 87 F. Supp. 18 (1949).

[50]See James W. McKie, "The Decline of Monopoly in the Metal Container Industry," *American Economic Review*, May 1955, pp. 499–508; Charles H. Hession, "The Metal Container Industry," in Walter Adams, ed., *The Structure of American Industry* (Third ed.; New York: Macmillan, 1961), pp. 430–467; and p. 168 *supra*.

particular seller. Such arrangements have the undesirable effect of foreclosing a market to competing sellers during the life of the contract. They also offer a number of potential advantages, however, as the Supreme Court acknowledged in its 1949 *Standard Stations* opinion:

> In the case of the buyer, they may assure supply, afford protection against rises in price, enable long-term planning on the basis of known costs, and obviate the expense and risk of storage in the quantity necessary for a commodity having a fluctuating demand. From the seller's point of view, requirements contracts may make possible the substantial reduction of selling expenses, give protection against price fluctuations, and—of particular advantage to a newcomer to the field to whom it is important to know what capital expenditures are justified—offer the possibility of a predictable market. . . . They may be useful, moreover, to a seller trying to establish a foothold against the counterattacks of entrenched competitors.[51]

After listing these possibilities, the Court went on to observe that jurists are seldom in a good position to weigh the anticompetitive effects of specific requirements contracts against their economic advantages. It therefore ruled that contested contracts should be judged primarily in terms of their structural impact, and that a violation of Clayton Act Section 3 should be found when there is proof "that competition has been foreclosed in a substantial share of the line of commerce affected."[52] In the case at bar, the Standard Oil Company of California had entered into requirements contracts with 5,937 independent franchised Standard gasoline retailers, comprising 16 per cent by number of all gas stations in a seven-state Western United States area and making 6.7 per cent of all 1946

gasoline sales in that area. Some contracts required the stations to purchase only their gasoline supplies exclusively from Standard; others covered tires, batteries, and other products in addition to gasoline. Emphasizing the 6.7 per cent market share and the fact that annual gasoline sales of roughly $58 million were at issue, the Supreme Court held that a substantial share of commerce had in fact been foreclosed and that the contracts were therefore illegal.[53] This decision served not only to constrain the use of requirements contracts in many fields, but also established a tough structural test of anticompetitive effects upon which subsequent merger decisions were based.

Requirements contracts negotiated by sellers possessing a very small share of the relevant market do stand a good chance of escaping challenge, and not all challenged contracts have been found illegal. In another case carried to the Supreme Court, the Nashville Coal Company contracted to supply at predetermined prices the total coal requirements of a new Tampa Electric Co. generating station for a period of 20 years. Nashville then tried to back out of the agreement. When Tampa sued for breach of contract, Nashville defended itself by arguing that the contract violated Clayton Act Section 3 and was therefore unenforceable. Specifically, the contract was said to foreclose a substantial market, since Tampa's requirements equalled the total volume of coal purchased in the state of Florida before the contract's inception. After two lower courts accepted this defense, the Supreme Court reversed and ruled in favor of Tampa.[54] It defined the relevant market as the *supply* market in an eight-state area, noting that mines in that coal-producing region were eager to sell more coal in Florida. When the market was so defined, the share foreclosed by the Tampa-Nashville contract amounted to less than

[51] *Standard Oil Co. of California et al.* v. *U. S.*, 337 U. S. 293, 306–307 (1949).

[52] *Ibid.*, p. 314.

[53] See also *Richfield Oil Corp.* v. *U. S.*, 343 U. S. 922 (1952), in which a similar arrangement involving even smaller market shares was struck down. In "Exclusive Dealing in the Petroleum Industry: The Refiner-Lessee Dealer Relationship," *Yale Economic Essays,* Spring 1963, pp. 223–247, Richard A. Miller argues that the elimination of formal requirements contracts in gasoline retailing has had little effect on industry conduct, since refiners can bring to bear a number of informal pressures to induce retail outlets to stock their products. These range from the threat of cancelling station leases to negligence in refilling a station's storage tanks.

[54] *Tampa Electric Co.* v. *Nashville Coal Co. et al.,* 365 U. S. 320 (1961).

1 per cent. And this, the Supreme Court said, was not enough to find a Section 3 violation.

EXCLUSIVE DEALING AND EXCLUSIVE DEALER FRANCHISES

Somewhat more extensive treatment is merited by two special classes of restrictions promulgated by manufacturers in association with the retailers or wholesalers who distribute their products. They are quite distinct legally, but since they are often used in tandem, they are best analyzed together.

An exclusive dealing agreement, which falls under the coverage of Clayton Act Section 3, is a special type of requirements contract. The wholesaler or retailer agrees to devote its efforts exclusively to distributing the product line of a particular manufacturer. Handling the products of competing manufacturers is explicitly or implicitly disavowed, and so the dealer in effect agrees to purchase from the manufacturer its full requirements.

As a *quid pro quo* for an outlet's willingness to deal exclusively and sometimes without any such pledge, manufacturers frequently grant their dealers *exclusive franchises*. These generally place some limit on the amount of competition the franchised dealer will have to face from other concerns distributing the manufacturer's line—i.e., by restricting the number of dealers franchised, or by confining dealers to particular territories or customer classes. The legality of such arrangements is governed by Sherman Act Section 1.

Three main sets of interests are affected by the restrictions connected with exclusive dealing and exclusive franchise agreements: the dealer's, the manufacturer's, and the public's. The dealer given an exclusive franchise presumably derives some benefit from having to face less competition from other dealers handling the same product line, especially when the line enjoys a product differentiation advantage. This will be reflected in price – wholesale cost margins higher than they would be under an unrestricted entry policy.

The dealer may also find it advantageous to deal exclusively in the products of a single manufacturer, although the benefit from contract provisions which *compel* it to specialize is dubious, since more freedom of action is almost always preferable to less, if other dimensions of the *quid pro quo* are unaffected. Indeed, the fact that dealers have occasionally sued to recover damages attributed to such restrictions suggests that exclusivity is not always desirable from the dealer's standpoint.

For manufacturers exclusive dealing arrangements are often appealing because they ensure that their products will be merchandised with the full energy and enthusiasm of dealers, since the dealer confined to a single manufacturer's line can scarcely be indifferent as to whose brand consumers purchase.[55] By granting exclusive franchises and restricting competition among its dealers, the manufacturer may benefit in several ways, all related to the possibility of letting dealers earn generous profit margins. Offering the prospect of supra-normal returns may permit manufacturers to attract dealers of superior ability. Also, once a businessman has taken on a profitable dealership, he will be reluctant to lose his franchise, and he will therefore be responsive when the manufacturer suggests changes in his methods of operation. If the margin between price and wholesale cost is ample, dealers have an incentive to carry larger inventories, and they can spend more money on advertising and other promotional activities, enhancing the manufacturer's market penetration. The dealer with a profitable franchise may also be better able and more willing to provide high-quality maintenance and repair services. This is especially important in the sale of complex durable goods, for shoddy service by some distributor out to make a quick killing can permanently damage the manufacturer's reputation.

From the viewpoint of the consuming public, the effects of restrictions on dealer activities are mixed. We have seen that exclusive franchising can limit competition among the dealers han-

---

[55]Obviously, distribution through exclusive dealers is attractive only for specialty and shopping goods. For convenience goods, the manufacturer's best strategy is to get its product into as many retail outlets as it can, even though competing brands are also carried.

dling a particular brand and strengthen product differentiation. Stronger product differentiation can be either good or bad, depending upon its responsiveness to consumer wants. More advertising which merely cancels out rival messages is of little utility to consumers; better service is generally desirable, especially when consumers retain the option of buying the same brand or equivalent products with less service at lower prices.[56] The blunting of intra-brand competition does not necessarily arouse concern as long as inter-brand competition remains vigorous. Whether this condition is satisfied depends mainly upon how entry opportunities are affected. The use of exclusive franchises can invigorate competition if it facilitates the entry of small, struggling manufacturers by permitting them to secure the services of capable dealers and to build a favorable image. But when franchising and exclusive dealing together raise barriers to new entry, serious anti-competitive effects can follow.

The automobile industry provides the clearest example of this last case.[57] There are moderate economies of scale in automobile retailing. Established manufacturers with substantial market penetration are able to have a good-sized exclusive dealership even in relatively small towns, and the opportunity to sell a well-accepted make is attractive to would-be dealers. Therefore, the largest producers have first pick among candidates and can engage the most able ones. This in turn gives General Motors and Ford a lasting product differentiation advantage, for auto buyers flock in disproportionate numbers to the better dealers, and the prospect of obtaining factory-authorized parts and service in both large cities and small may influence the car purchase decisions of mobile consumers. Lack of an extensive first-rate sales and service network is

one of the reasons why Studebaker-Packard was forced to discontinue passenger automobile production, why foreign cars have a difficult time penetrating the U. S. market, and why American Motors and to a lesser degree Chrysler have not found it easy to build up and sustain their sales volume. If all formal and informal pressures toward exclusive dealing in autos could be eliminated and if a sufficient number of dealers were willing to take on additional makes, the growth of competition from smaller and foreign automobile producers would be greatly stimulated.[58]

The limits to which firms may legally go in using exclusive dealing agreements have been progressively narrowed through a series of court decisions. In a 1922 opinion, the Supreme Court found an exclusive dealership arrangement illegal under Clayton Act Section 3 when it encompassed 40 per cent of all dress pattern outlets in the United States.[59] Subsequent pronouncements in related requirements contract cases such as *Standard Stations* shifted the margin of structural tolerance to much lower levels. However, smaller manufacturers are not likely to run afoul of the law when they urge exclusive dealing without actually coercing their dealers to eschew competitive products. For instance, the J. I. Case Company, selling roughly 7 per cent of all U. S. farm machinery in 1948, avoided censure when a district court found that it had not made exclusive dealing an inviolable condition of its franchises, that 2,600 of its 3,738 dealers handled at least some competitive products, and that other farm machinery manufacturers experienced no demonstrated difficulty obtaining outlets for their products.[60] Similarly, an appellate court found that the Hudson Motor Company was within its rights in refusing to renew a dealer's contract because the dealer diffused its efforts

---

[56]For a more skeptical view, see William S. Comanor, "Vertical Territorial and Customer Restrictions: White Motor and Its Aftermath," *Harvard Law Review*, May 1968, pp. 1419–1438.

[57]See also B. P. Pashigian, *The Distribution of Automobiles: An Economic Analysis of the Franchise System* (Englewood Cliffs: Prentice-Hall, 1961).

[58]Even now, automobile distribution is not completely exclusive in the United States, although it appears to be more exclusive than in Europe. Many U. S. dealers carry more than one brand of the same manufacturer, and during the early 1950s about 7 per cent of General Motors' dealers simultaneously sold non-GM cars. See Pashigian, *op. cit.*, pp. 118–123; and the Senate Committee on Small Business Hearings, *Planning, Regulation, and Competition in the Automobile Industry—1968* (Washington: 1968), pp. 627 and 712.

[59]*Standard Fashion Co. v. Magrane-Houston Co.*, 258 U. S. 346 (1922).

[60]*U. S. v. J. I. Case Co.*, 101 F. Supp. 856 (1951).

over too many competing automobile makes.[61] It is doubtful whether the Big Three of the auto industry would emerge as favorably from such a test, and they studiously avoid treading too close to the brink. Still they can and do apply many informal pressures to encourage exclusive dealer loyalty, and thus far, the antitrust agencies have taken no positive steps to foster the spread of multi-make auto retailing.

Frequently, the manufacturers of complex vehicles and equipment have insisted that their dealers refrain from selling or installing repair parts produced by competing firms. This practice is essentially a tying arrangement, since it makes the dealer's ability to buy complete vehicles or machines for resale contingent upon agreement to buy only the franchisor's spare parts. Unlike most tying contracts, it has withstood antitrust attack with fair success, though the defenses may be crumbling. In a 1936 decision the Supreme Court affirmed a lower court opinion approving General Motors' requirement that GM dealers install only GM replacement parts. It accepted the argument that installation of inappropriate or defective parts could impair an automobile's functioning and thereby damage the manufacturer's reputation.[62] Five years later the Federal Trade Commission ordered General Motors to cease insisting that dealers stock and sell only GM supplies and accessories, but it permitted exclusive dealing agreements for "parts necessary to the mechanical operation of an automobile, and which are not available, in like quality and design, from other sources of supply."[63] Following the tightening of Clayton Act Section 3 criteria in the *Standard Stations* decision, the early General Motors parts decisions were criticized by some courts,[64] and in 1959 the Sixth Circuit Court of Appeals ruled that attempts by Ford Motor Company to force its dealers to deal exclusively in Ford-made or approved parts might be found illegal if they substantially lessened competition.[65] However, no definitive Supreme Court reinterpretation has been rendered, so the boundaries of tolerance are not completely clear.

Exclusive franchise agreements which restrict competition among a manufacturer's outlets are not covered by Clayton Act Section 3. They can, however, be challenged as illegal contracts in restraint of trade under Sherman Act Section 1 in some situations. At present a manufacturer is fully within the law in limiting the number and location of outlets to which franchises are granted, and this may be sufficient to protect dealer profit margins when the product line enjoys significant differentiation advantages. But in some cases manufacturers have gone further, delineating the territories within which particular dealers might sell and the customers they might serve. In so doing they run a risk of violating the Sherman Act. There are two main sub-cases.

When the dealers agree *among themselves* not to interpenetrate each others' markets or to solicit the same customers, or when they induce the manufacturer to impose upon them such restrictions, the law is clearly violated. Indeed, in a case involving a collective attempt by Los Angeles Chevrolet dealers and GM officials to prevent some dealers from bootlegging cars to unfranchised automobile supermarkets, the Supreme Court ruled that such horizontal agreements constitute "a classic conspiracy" in restraint of trade.[66]

Purely vertical restrictions—those imposed unilaterally by the manufacturer upon its dealers —have recently been viewed with only slightly greater tolerance. In 1963, a five-to-three majority of the Supreme Court refused to condemn

[61] *Hudson Sales Corporation* v. *Waldrip*, 211 F. 2d 268 (1954).

[62] *Pick Manufacturing Co.* v. *General Motors Corp. et al.*, 80 F. 2d 641 (1935), affirmed *per curiam*, 299 U. S. 3 (1936).

[63] *In re General Motors Corp. and General Motors Sales Corp.*, 34 F.T.C. 58, 86 (1941).

[64] *Dictograph Products, Inc.*, v. *Federal Trade Commission*, 217 F. 2d 821, 828 (1954).

[65] *Englander Motors, Inc.*, v. *Ford Motor Corp.*, 267 F. 2d 11 (1959). The case was remanded to the district court for a finding as to whether the facts warranted a conclusion that competition was lessened, but apparently the suit was settled out of court. See also *Alles Corp.* v. *Senco Products, Inc.*, 329 F. 2d 567 (1964).

[66] *U. S.* v. *General Motors Corp. et al.*, 384 U. S. 127 (1966). See also *White Motor Co.* v. *U. S.*, 372 U. S. 253, 263 (1963); and *U. S.* v. *Sealy, Inc., et al.*, 87 S. Ct. 1847 (1967).

out-of-hand the territorial and customer restrictions placed in dealer franchise contracts by the White Motor Company, a truck manufacturer with sales exceeding half a billion dollars at the time. The Court acknowledged that it did not "know enough of the economic and business stuff out of which these arrangements emerge" to be certain whether they merely stifle competition, or whether they may be "the only practicable means a small company has for breaking into or staying in business."[67] It therefore remanded the action to the district court for a thorough exploration of the facts, i.e., for the application of a rule of reason. However, the case was settled through a negotiated consent decree in which White agreed to terminate the restrictive provisions in its dealer franchises.[68] Four years later the Supreme Court returned to the problem in a case concerning restrictions placed upon the distributors of Schwinn bicycles. At an early stage of its five-to-two opinion, the Court stated that it must "look to the specifics of the challenged practices and their impact on the marketplace" in order to judge their legality—in other words, that it must apply a rule of reason.[69] But a few pages later it announced and then reiterated, without supplying anything to bridge the logical chasm, that manufacturers selling their products subject to territorial and other restrictions upon resale commit *per se* violations of the Sherman Act.[70] It is conceivable that the Court meant to confine this rule to producers like Schwinn which dominate their industry and which are neither failing nor trying to break into some field, but if this was its intent, it was not adequately expressed.

Whatever the Supreme Court's position, a strict *per se* approach to purely vertical restrictions in franchise arrangements would appear to be unsound, since such restrictions may yield tangible economic benefits without choking off competition under at least some circumstances —notably, when the product market is unconcentrated at the manufacturing stage and differentiation is weak; or when the producer restricting its distributors' spheres of operation would otherwise have difficulty gaining or maintaining a foothold in the market. Consequently, a rule of reason approach—albeit a hard-boiled one—seems preferable.

RESALE PRICE MAINTENANCE

Resale price maintenance—the specification by manufacturers of prices below which their products cannot be sold by retailers—is in some respects analogous in effect to franchise restrictions. However, its legal status in the United States is different. Whereas even before the *Schwinn* decision the law at best only tolerated vertical restrictions which went beyond mere franchising (and then only when their reasonableness could be shown), resale price maintenance schemes have been granted special legislative exemption from antitrust attack at the federal level and in a majority of the states.

THE LEGAL BACKGROUND

This was not always so. In the early days of American antitrust, vertical price-fixing agreements were condemned in a series of decisions from which the *Schwinn* opinion is a lineal descendant.[71] In response, retailer and some manufacturer groups banded together for a lobbying campaign they euphemistically entitled the 'Fair Trade Movement.' They received in-

---

[67] *White Motor Co.* v. *U. S.*, 372 U. S. 253, 263 (1963). Territorial limitations were subsequently approved in *Snap-On Tools Corp.* v. *Federal Trade Commission*, 321 F. 2d 825 (1963); and *Sandura Co.* v. *Federal Trade Commission*, 339 F. 2d 847 (1964).

[68] CCH 1964 Trade Cases, Para. 71,195.

[69] *U. S.* v. *Arnold, Schwinn & Co. et al.*, 388 U. S. 365, 374 (1967).

[70] *Ibid.*, at pp. 379 and 382. Most of Schwinn's distributional restrictions were nonetheless absolved on the basis of a technicality—the fact that Schwinn distributed its bicycles largely on consignment, so that title did not pass to wholesalers and retailers.

[71] The first was *Dr. Miles Medical Co.* v. *John D. Park and Sons Co.*, 220 U. S. 373 (1911). For an excellent survey of subsequent extensions, see A. D. Neale, *The Antitrust Laws of the United States of America* (Cambridge, England: Cambridge University Press, 1960), pp. 336–363. Authoritative works on resale price maintenance include B. S. Yamey, *Economics of Resale Price Maintenance* (London: Pitman, 1954); and a symposium edited by Yamey, *Resale Price Maintenance* (Chicago: Aldine, 1966).

tellectual support from such eminent figures as Supreme Court Justice Louis Brandeis, an arch-foe of big business but friend of the small merchant.[72] Bills were introduced in every session of Congress from 1914 to 1936, but none was enacted. The movement experienced its first legislative success in 1931, when the State of California passed a statute authorizing 'fair trade.' By 1935 nine other states had enacted resale price maintenance laws, and within five years after a 1936 Supreme Court decision upholding the California and Illinois statutes, every state but Texas, Missouri, and Vermont had climbed aboard the fair trade bandwagon.

The state laws, however, were effective only with respect to goods sold in intrastate commerce. The retail merchants' lobby, led by the druggists, continued to exert pressure, and in 1937 Congress passed the Miller-Tydings Resale Price Maintenance Act, appending it as a rider to the District of Columbia appropriations bill in order to avert a Presidential veto. It amended Section 1 of the Sherman Act, exempting from antitrust prohibition contracts prescribing minimum prices for the resale of trade-marked or branded commodities "in free and open competition with commodities of the same general class produced or distributed by others" where such contracts were authorized under state laws.

Given this permissive mandate, vertical price fixing thrived in the consumer goods industries. Nevertheless, there was one loophole in the law. Not all retailers were interested in adhering to the manufacturer's specified minimum prices. Those who preferred to seek high sales volume through rock-bottom markup policies refused to sign "R.P.M." contracts with their suppliers. To bring these intransigents into line, most states added "non-signer clauses" to their "fair trade" laws, making adherence to a manufacturer's price

floors binding upon *all* retailers in the state if *any single* retailer signed a resale price maintenance contract with the manufacturer. However, the Supreme Court ruled in 1951 that the Miller-Tydings Act exempted only express contracts to prescribe minimum prices on goods in interstate commerce and that the exemption did not cover non-signing retailers.[73] The retail lobby again went to work, and in the following year Congress passed by overwhelming majorities the McGuire Act, amending Section 5 of the Federal Trade Commission Act. It reiterated the Miller-Tydings policy and extended it to permit the enforcement of resale price maintenance upon non-signing sellers where state laws permit. A challenge to the constitutionality of the new law was rejected by two of the three judges on a Fifth Circuit Court of Appeals panel; and the Supreme Court, reluctant to interfere when Congress had expressed its intent so forcefully, chose not to review the decision.[74] As a result, resale price maintenance enforced unilaterally by manufacturers on both willing and non-signing retailers is immune from federal antitrust attack in states with non-signer clauses. On the other hand, any attempt by retailers collectively to enforce price maintenance among themselves is strictly illegal, like all other horizontal price-fixing conspiracies.

THE ECONOMIC CASE FOR AND AGAINST 'FAIR TRADE'

With this legal backdrop in view, let us turn to the economic issues in the resale price maintenance debate. The advocates of R.P.M. are adept at inventing new arguments to support their position, but they boil down to three main propositions.[75] First, resale price maintenance protects the margin between retail and wholesale prices from being eroded by competition (or by

---

[72]See his article (written before he ascended the bench), "Cut-Throat Prices: The Competition That Kills," *Harper's Weekly*, November 15, 1913.

[73]*Schwegmann Bros. et al.* v. *Calvert Distillers Corp.*, 341 U. S. 384 (1951).

[74]*Schwegmann Bros. Giant Super Markets et al.* v. *Eli Lilly & Co.*, 205 F. 2d 788 (1953), certiorari denied 346 U. S. 856 (1953). See also *Hudson Distributors, Inc.* v. *Eli Lilly & Co.*, 377 U. S. 386 (1964), in which the Supreme Court did explicitly review the legality of non-signer clauses and bowed to the will of Congress.

[75]For some of the most sophisticated defenses, see P. W. S. Andrews and Frank A. Friday, *Fair Trade: Resale Price Maintenance Re-Examined* (London: Macmillan, 1960); and P. W. S. Andrews, *On Competition in Economic Theory* (London: Macmillan, 1964), pp. 127–138. The literature is surveyed more extensively in the two works by Yamey cited in note 71 *supra*.

cut-throat competition, as the fair trade lobby puts it). In this respect it is analogous to franchising restrictions. The effects are also similar. The retailers are supposedly better off economically—a fate to which they can hardly be unsympathetic. The manufacturer may also benefit, since dealers have more funds to spend on advertising and service, which in turn can have a favorable impact on the manufacturer's brand acceptance. Second, resale price maintenance prevents the sale of a manufacturer's products as 'loss leaders'—items sold by a retailer at sharply reduced prices, and perhaps even below cost, in order to attract customers who, once they have entered the store, will buy other goods at standard prices. Loss leader sales are said to injure the manufacturer by detracting from its reputation for quality (since consumers allegedly judge quality from price) and limiting its access to the market (since many retailers will be reluctant to stock an item being sold at much lower prices by others). They may also endanger the survival of small retailers who specialize in an item diversified stores use as a loss leader. Third, and no doubt most important in the Washington political equation, resale price maintenance tends to protect the small, locally-owned retail establishment from the competition of big, more efficient chain stores and discount houses seeking to achieve high volume at low markups. Survival of small retail businesses is valued both as a derivative of the populist ideology and as a well-disciplined source of votes on Election Day.

It is impossible to quarrel analytically with this last argument, for it rests largely on value judgments over which reasonable men may disagree. Against it and other tenets of the case for fair trade, however, several objections can be counterposed.

For one, the loss leader conjecture is neither convincing nor firmly supported by the evidence.[76] It is hard to believe that many consumers are gullible enough to downgrade their estimates of a product's quality simply because some merchant is selling the item at a reduced price, or that they are bamboozled into switching their patronage to a particular store because it offers a few items as loss leaders. It is also doubtful whether manufacturers suffer reduced access to retail outlets because their product is used as a loss leader. Sales below wholesale cost —the most extreme though less common form of loss leader pricing—are likely to be only temporary, and even if other retailers reduce their stocks of the affected commodity temporarily, they bounce back rapidly when the price-cutting ends.

To be sure, specialty shops find survival more difficult when the merchandise they stock is offered permanently at positive but thin profit margins by supermarkets, discount houses, and other diversified outlets. The same is true more generally of small, relatively inefficient retail establishments. But here the sword cuts two ways. If consumers flock to the low-margin discount houses and shun the small, high-margin shops, they must do so because that is what they prefer. To prevent large retailers from pursuing a low-margin strategy, which at bottom is what the fair trade laws seek, is to frustrate the adaptation of distribution channels to meaningful changes in consumer wants and to encourage the perpetuation of obsolete, inefficient channels. Indeed, the experience of European countries suggests that resale price maintenance has retarded the spread of supermarketing, and the pace of innovation in retailing has accelerated perceptibly when legalized R.P.M. was abolished.[77]

Moreover, the widespread adoption of resale price maintenance tends to deprive consumers of a choice between buying on the basis of service and buying at the lowest possible price. The latter alternative is eliminated unless a substantial segment of the output in each industry is not fair-traded. If there is a genuine consumer demand for service and the other amenities

[76]See especially the contribution by L. A. Skeoch in Yamey, ed., *Resale Price Maintenance*, pp. 41–53.

[77]See, for example, the analysis of developments in Sweden by U. af Trolle in Yamey, ed., *Resale Price Maintenance*, pp. 134–140.

which accompany a high-margin policy, the market will normally support without the coercion of R.P.M. the survival of retailers who satisfy that demand, co-existing with other retailers who cater to the (no doubt much larger) mass of price-conscious consumers.

Three further drawbacks of resale price maintenance can be treated more briefly. First, as the discussion thus far has implied throughout, when R.P.M. attains its primary goals it tends in all but special cases to raise retail prices and margins.[78] This has sometimes been denied by advocates, but the data they have marshalled to back up their claims are seriously deficient and the bulk of the available evidence more clearly supports a conclusion that R.P.M. does raise prices.[79] For instance, a 1956 Justice Department survey revealed that the prices of 132 widely fair-traded products were 19 per cent lower than the fair-trade minimum on the average in eight cities not bound by R.P.M. laws.[80] Second, vertical price-fixing not only eliminates price competition among retailers selling a particular manufacturer's product, but may also dampen inter-brand price competition. It gives oligopolistic producers firmer control over the prices at which their products are ultimately sold, thereby permitting them to prevent retail price-shading which might induce retaliatory wholesale price cuts by rival manufacturers. Finally, it is doubtful whether R.P.M. really benefits the small retailer as much as one might at first suppose. Unlike the situation under restrictive franchising, entry into the retailing of specific fair-traded goods is usually easy. If retailers are earning supra-normal profits due to R.P.M., additional sellers will enter, squeezing the sales volume of the original outlets until unit merchandising costs have risen to wipe out the surplus. The representative retailer ends up operating at less than an optimal scale, but earning no more than a normal return.

OPPOSITION AT HOME AND ABROAD

The U. S. fair trade laws do not owe their existence to a careful balancing of economic costs and benefits. Vested interest and influence group politics call the tune. Of the numerous economists and marketing experts who have studied the problem, all but a very few believe that the benefits of resale price maintenance are not sufficiently large to offset such detriments as higher prices, reduced consumer choice, and the suppression of marketing innovation.

This view is widely shared in other industrialized nations. In fact, the retail lobbies have been less successful overseas than in the United States. Resale price maintenance has been either outlawed or subjected to stringent legal limitations in most of the leading industrial nations abroad, including some with much weaker policies toward other restrictive practices than the United States. Canada passed an unconditional ban on R.P.M. in 1951, although it was amended in 1960 to allow exceptions when loss leader pricing or other abuses can be proved.[81] France has had a law against R.P.M. since 1953, but its enforcement has apparently not been vigorous. In 1964 the British after long debate passed a Resale Prices Act. It adopts a *prima facie* presumption that vertical price-fixing is illegal, to be relaxed only if the producer can bear the burden of proving before the Restrictive Practices Court that the benefits of R.P.M. outweigh the detriments. The Court's initial decisions took a tough line, and when cigarette producers abandoned an attempt to defend their practices in 1968, retail cigarette prices dropped sharply.[82] Other nations which permit resale price maintenance only when its reasonableness

[78]For a theoretical analysis of conditions under which prices might be reduced, see J. R. Gould and L. E. Preston, "Resale Price Maintenance and Retail Outlets," *Economica*, August 1965, pp. 302–312.

[79]For a survey of the U. S. evidence, see the contribution by S. C. Hollander in Yamey, ed., *op. cit.*, pp. 93–98; and Marvin Frankel, "The Effects of Fair Trade: Fact and Fiction in the Statistical Findings," *Journal of Business*, July 1955, pp. 182–194.

[80]See the testimony of Robert Bicks in U. S. House of Representatives, Committee on Interstate and Foreign Commerce, Hearings, *Fair Trade: 1959* (Washington: 1959), pp. 506–507.

[81]For a survey of the various national policies, see Yamey, ed., *Resale Price Maintenance*.

[82]"Cigarette Price To Dip in Britain," *New York Times*, September 24, 1968, p. 63.

can be positively demonstrated include Sweden, Denmark, Holland, and Italy. Of the leading Western European nations, only Germany and Belgium have not enacted prohibitions.

In the United States, resale price maintenance has also not experienced completely smooth sailing, despite the hospitable reception accorded it in the halls of Congress. A process of erosion is evident. Two main undermining forces have been at work: legal setbacks at the state level and the inexorable pressures of competition.

R.P.M. laws were never passed in Texas, Missouri, Vermont, and the strategically located District of Columbia. In several additional states, including Alabama, Utah, Montana, Wyoming, Virginia, and Ohio, state courts have ruled the applicable fair trade statutes inconsistent with state constitutions and/or legally unenforceable. In more than a dozen other jurisdictions, the non-signer provisions of state laws were ruled unconstitutional, typically on the ground that they deprived non-signers of property without due process of law. These developments created a number of islands where it was possible to ignore manufacturers' prescribed minimum prices. Entrepreneurs took advantage by locating mail order houses in non-fair-trade areas, building a lively business of shipping branded merchandise at reduced prices to customers in fair trade states. This practice was encouraged by federal court decisions in 1957 holding that such shipments could not be enjoined under the fair trade statutes of the states into which the merchandise was shipped.[83] And even where retailers were clearly bound by state R.P.M. laws, some of the more aggressive outlets chose to ignore them. Faced with this challenge, manufacturers often decided not to initiate the legal proceedings available for enforcing compliance, in part because the burden of proving actionable departure from the stipulated price floor is difficult and costly, and partly because producers were reluctant to alienate important high-volume retailers.

When a significant fraction of the transactions in some product line began taking place at prices which undercut the fair trade minimum, the whole R.P.M. system in that line has tended to crumble. Manufacturers who did enforce their minima found themselves losing sales to those who did not or who refused altogether to play the fair trade game. Some abandoned R.P.M. altogether. Others, like the Sunbeam Corporation (one of the staunchest defenders of fair trade in the electrical appliance industry) brought out new product lines to be sold at uncontrolled retail prices alongside their fair-traded items. When enforcement is weak and retailers stock competing products of comparable quality, some fair-traded and others not, one of the most serious objections to resale price maintenance is defused, for consumers are no longer deprived of the opportunity to choose which mix of price and product differentiation attributes they prefer. Only in those fields where adherence to R.P.M. is widespread—e.g., in drugs, cosmetics, perfumes, photographic supplies, and (for a declining number of states) liquor—does the problem of restricted choice continue to be vexing.

Advocates of fair trade have not exactly been overjoyed about these developments eroding the foundations of the system. They have continued their lobbying activities, urging upon the U. S. Congress a "Quality Stabilization" bill which would permit manufacturers to bypass state laws and specify minimum resale prices on a nationwide basis, using the federal courts to enforce compliance. In 1964, however, the bill was defeated in a Senate Commerce Committee vote—at least partly because of the strong opposition voiced by large numbers of professional economists.[84] Still the fair trade lobby is a hardy and determined species, and it can be expected that further efforts will be exerted in the future to secure legislative support for a strengthened vertical price-fixing system.

---

[83]*Bissell Carpet Sweeper Co.* v. *Masters Mail Order Co. of Washington*, 240 F. 2d 684 (1957); and *General Electric Co.* v. *Masters Mail Order Co. of Washington*, 244 F. 2d 681 (1957), cert. den. 355 U. S. 824.

[84]Cf. Henry H. Villard, "Opposition to the Quality Stabilization Bill," *American Economic Review*, June 1965, p. 683.

UNFAIR METHODS OF COMPETITION

To conclude this survey of the antitrust laws, a few words must be said about Section 5 of the Federal Trade Commission Act and related legislation. In its original 1914 form, the section stated a simple blanket prohibition against "unfair methods of competition," leaving to the newly-created Federal Trade Commission and to the courts the task of determining what specific practices would be proscribed. Through the Wheeler-Lea amendment of 1938, the section's reach was extended to include "deceptive acts or practices in commerce." Subsequent interpretations have made Section 5 an extremely flexible instrument for correcting abusive conduct.

The scope of the "unfair methods of competition" phrase has been construed to cover acts which violate Sherman and Clayton Act provisions and also practices which conflict with the basic policies of those laws, even though they do not go far enough to constitute an outright violation.[85] Among the practices vulnerable under Section 5 are price-fixing, boycotts, exclusive dealing and tying agreements, price discrimination, mergers, bribing the employees of vendors and customers, exerting reciprocal purchasing leverage, business espionage, disseminating derogatory information about rival products, harassing competitors through protracted patent and other litigation with predatory intent, selling products below cost with predatory intent, selling merchandise by means of lotteries, and luring large numbers of rival employees to break their employment contracts.

Since the passage of the Wheeler-Lea amendment, the FTC has been charged with combating deception and misrepresentation, especially in the promotion of consumer goods. In recent years about half of its budget has been allocated toward this end. Practices challenged include misrepresentation of product ingredients or their quality, the presentation of misleading television advertisements (such as one implying that sandpaper could be shaved with Rapid-Shave lather, when in fact what was shaved was plexiglas sprinkled with sand), making unfounded claims concerning the therapeutic properties of patent medicines, marking products with prices higher than those normally charged so the consumer believes he is getting a bargain when the price is marked down, packaging food products in half-filled containers, and billing book and record club members for selections they have not ordered.

Complementing the work of the FTC's Bureau of Deceptive Practices is the Food and Drug Administration, located organizationally in the Department of Health, Education, and Welfare. It is responsible for enforcing the pure food and drug laws, first enacted in 1906 and amended and strengthened intermittently since then. It sets standards for the labeling of food, drug, and cosmetic products; imposes controls on the inclusion of dangerous adulterants; and most recently, oversees testing programs to insure that drug products are medically effective and that harmful side effects are discovered and thoroughly publicized.

The activities of the Federal Trade Commission and the Food and Drug Administration serve an important role in helping keep trade honest and protecting consumers from unscrupulous dealers. The success they have achieved has been limited somewhat by the paucity of enforcement resources entrusted them relative to the enormous number of constantly changing products, producers, and promotional gimmicks with which they must contend. Yet unlimited resources would also not solve the problem completely, for too dense an overlay of controls could sap business initiative and impede genuine progress in product technology and marketing methods. What is needed is the ability to distinguish the truly harmful practice or product from that which is innocuous or even beneficial, plus the judgment to know when to intervene and when to leave well enough alone. This deft touch undoubtedly hinges as much upon the quality of the personnel employed as on the absolute quantity of resources committed to enforcement.

---

[85]See *Federal Trade Commission* v. *Cement Institute et al.*, 333 U. S. 683 (1948); and *Federal Trade Commission* v. *Brown Shoe Co.*, 384 U. S. 316 (1966).

Chapter 22

Public Regulation in Theory and Practice

Thus far our focus has been on means of maintaining competition. An alternative way of attempting to harmonize private business conduct with the public interest when monopoly elements intrude is to designate the firm or industry as a public utility, and then to subject its decisions and actions to the surveillance of a governmental regulatory commission. Normally, the primary concern of public utility regulation is the level and structure of prices charged, though regulation often covers such additional matters as entry into and exit from the industry, mergers, the quality of service provided, safety rules, the financial structure of the regulated firms, and accounting practices. Our goal here must for brevity's sake be a limited one: to survey the theory and practical problems of public utility price regulation. A discussion of other regulatory agency functions, along with a much more comprehensive description of institutions, can be found in any of several excellent treatises.[1]

Table 22.1 lists the principal industries subjected to more or (in finance) less comprehensive public regulation in the United States and shows the approximate share of gross national product each originated in 1965. In all, somewhere between 7 and 11 per cent of GNP is generated

in the regulated industries, depending on how tightly the definitional net is drawn.

Regulatory control is exercised by local, state, and federal agencies. Every state has one or more special commissions with regulatory authority over the intrastate operations of electric power and gas companies, telephone companies, motor carriers, banks, insurance companies, and the like. The first steps in this direction were taken during the 1830s, when a few states established railway commissions with limited powers. In the 1870s there was a substantial increase in the number and power of the state regulatory commissions. State regulation of electric power was initiated in Wisconsin and New York in 1907, spreading rapidly to other states in subsequent years.

At the federal level, control over interstate utility operations is vested in several agencies. The path-breaker was the Interstate Commerce Commission, created in 1887 to regulate the nation's railroads. Its jurisdiction was extended to include common and contract motor carriers in 1935 and interstate water carriers in 1940. Transoceanic water carriers are regulated by the Federal Maritime Board, reorganized in its modern form in 1940, while airline operations are supervised by the Civil Aeronautics Board,

---

[1]Cf. Martin G. Glaeser, *Public Utilities in American Capitalism* (New York: Macmillan, 1957); Charles F. Phillips, Jr., *The Economics of Regulation* (Homewood: Irwin, 1965); James C. Bonbright, *Principles of Public Utility Rates* (New York: Columbia University Press, 1961); Clair Wilcox, *Public Policies Toward Business* (Third ed.; Homewood: Irwin, 1966); Dudley F. Pegrum, *Public Regulation of Business* (rev. ed.; Homewood: Irwin, 1965); D. Philip Locklin, *Economics of Transportation* (Fifth ed.; Homewood: Irwin, 1960); and William G. Shepherd and Thomas G. Gies, eds., *Utility Regulation: New Directions in Theory and Policy* (New York: Random House, 1966).

Table 22.1

The Position of the Principal Regulated Industries
in the U.S. Economy: 1965

Industry	Percentage of Total 1965 GNP	
Transportation industries:		
Railroads	1.3%	
Common and contract motor carriers	1.2	
Local, suburban, and highway passenger lines	0.3	
Water carriers (regulated segments only)	0.1	
Airlines and airfreight carriers	0.5	
Natural gas pipelines	0.1	
Subtotal		3.5%
Local and communications utilities:		
Electric, gas, water, and sanitary services	2.4%	
Telephone and telegraph services	2.0	
Radio and television broadcasting	0.2	
Subtotal		4.6
Financial industries:		
Banks and finance institutions	1.6%	
Insurance carriers	0.9	
Securities and commodities brokers	0.3	
Subtotal		2.8
Total share of GNP in regulated industries		10.9%

Source: U.S. Department of Commerce, Bureau of the Census, *Survey of Current Business*, April 1967, pp. 21–22; and July 1967, p. 17. Deductions to exclude exempted activities are approximate.

established in 1938. Since its formation in 1920, the Federal Power Commission has gradually gained increasing regulatory power over interstate electric power and natural gas operations. The Federal Communications Commission, formed in 1934, regulates radio and television broadcasting, interstate telephone and telegraph service, and the domestic facets of international telecommunications, including activities of the Communications Satellite Corporation. Regulatory powers in the banking and finance fields are shared by the Comptroller of the Currency (under the Treasury Department), the Federal Reserve system, the Federal Deposit Insurance Corporation, the Federal Home Loan Bank Board, the Securities and Exchange Commission, and various state banking and insurance commissions.

THE RATIONALE OF PUBLIC REGULATION

Under present interpretations of the U. S. Constitution, an industry can be subjected to public regulation when its actions are found to be "clothed with a public interest." The standards evolved in applying this criterion have been sufficiently broad to suggest that no industry is immune from regulatory control if there is a sufficiently strong mandate for its regulation.[2] However, the electric power, gas, telephone, and railroad industries share certain economic characteristics which have historically made them prime targets for regulation.

For one, such industries tend to be 'natural monopolies' or 'natural oligopolies.' That is, the minimum optimal scale of production is so large

[2] See *Munn* v. *Illinois*, 94 U. S. 113 (1877); and *Nebbia* v. *New York*, 291 U. S. 502 (1934).

that there is room in a given market for only one or at most a very few firms realizing all production and distribution economies of scale. In other words, the long-run unit cost function declines continuously out to a scale of output which saturates potential market demand. A monopolist therefore can enjoy lower unit costs than a group of small-scale competitors could. To secure the advantages of size while preventing the firm from raising prices to levels which exploit its monopoly position, regulation is imposed.

In railroading, the tendency toward natural monopoly is ascribable to the indivisibility of the right-of-way and the coordination difficulty of having more than one carrier use a given set of tracks. Once a right-of-way has been acquired and the roadbed has been graded, an enormous volume of traffic can be transported before duplication of the right-of-way investment becomes necessary. In electric power, there are impressive scale economies in both production and distribution. Unit production costs decline for coal-fired steam turbine generating plants up to designed plant sizes of at least 750,000 kilowatts—a capacity sufficient to serve an average community with a population of one half million persons. The minimum optimal scale is even larger for nuclear and hydroelectric generating stations. On the distribution side, doubling the capacity of a power distribution network is said to require an investment increase of only 40 to 50 per cent on the average.[3] Likewise, building duplicating telephone, water, or residential gas distribution networks within a given urban area would lead to significantly higher unit costs. Economies of scale from the centralization of message switching and (to a lesser degree) from unified long-distance transmission facilities also contribute to A.T.&T.'s status as a natural monopolist of interstate telephone service.

A different technical rationale exists for regulating the radio and television industries. The minimum optimal scale of operation for local broadcasting may be quite modest. Yet broadcasters utilize a scarce natural resource—the radio frequency spectrum. Regulatory control of entry is needed to prevent the interference which would occur if anyone desiring to use a portion of the spectrum at the zero price currently charged were permitted to do so.[4] Also, given that the right to use a particular radio frequency channel is a restricted and valuable privilege, there has been some tendency to extend the scope of regulation to ensure that program quality does not sink to deplorably low levels. However, federal radio and television regulation does not cover broadcasters' pricing and profits.

Certain industries have also been singled out for regulation because their cost structures encourage pricing behavior considered detrimental to the public interest. Companies in the archetypal regulated industries employ much more capital per dollar of sales than manufacturing and merchandising firms, as the following data, drawn from *Fortune*'s 1965 lists of the largest U. S. corporations, show:

Industry Category	1965 Assets as a Percentage of 1965 Sales Volume
The 50 largest merchandising firms	40%
The 500 largest industrial firms	85%
The 20 largest railroads	310%
The 50 largest electric, gas, and communications utilities	320%

The typical railroad, communications, or electric utility corporation employed nearly four times as much capital per dollar of sales as a representative industrial firm. High capital intensity in turn means that fixed costs are high relative to variable costs at less than capacity operation. And when this is so competition, even am ng

[3]See Marcel Boiteux, "Electric Energy: Facts, Problems, and Prospects," in James R. Nelson, ed., *Marginal Cost Pricing in Practice* (Englewood Cliffs: Prentice-Hall, 1964), p. 25.

[4]An alternative approach advocated by many economists would be to auction off channel allocations to the highest competitive bidder.

oligopolists, may take the form of relatively un-inhibited price cutting.

This, at least, is what happened in segments of the railroad industry during the last quarter of the 19th century.[5] Up to 1874, for example, only two lines—the New York Central and the Pennsylvania—offered through service between Chicago and New York City. Eastbound grain freight rates hovered near $.56 per hundred-weight during the early 1870s. But then the Baltimore & Ohio established through service, and because it sought to increase its market share in the face of combined excess capacity, it refused to join the collusive rate-fixing arrangement in force at the time. In the ensuing wave of secret and overt price-cutting, Chicago – New York grain freight rates fell to roughly $.20 per CWT in 1876 and to $.15 in 1877. Some shipments moved east for as little as $.07 per CWT during the summer of 1879. The rate war was ended through a collusive understanding, but the agreement broke down repeatedly in subsequent years as other lines with less direct rail and water connections to the East Coast tried to obtain a share of the traffic. The prices received for many shipments did little more than cover short-run marginal costs.

Whether this rivalry endangered the financial health of the railroads is not altogether clear. Aggregate railroad earnings as a per cent of capitalization hovered below the yield on government securities during the 1880s, but the railroads were still able to attract new capital and expand. Serious financial setbacks were avoided in part because the rival lines usually managed to work out some kind of collusive rate-making agreement whenever their competition became unacceptably intense. Furthermore, freight rates between cities lacking competitive routes were maintained at highly remunerative levels. In fact, the rates for short non-competitive hauls often exceeded those charged for much longer

hauls of the same commodity over competitive routes.

The net result of these and other developments was a highly discriminatory railroad freight rate structure. Towns lacking competitive rail service found themselves discriminated against relative to cities served by two or more lines. Large shippers were more successful in wresting secret rate cuts than small shippers. Widespread discontent over this discrimination was one of the main factors contributing to the creation of the Interstate Commerce Commission. The implementing Act To Regulate Commerce reflected this discontent by requiring that rates be "just and reasonable," by prohibiting personal discrimination, and by making it illegal to charge more for short hauls than for long under substantially similar conditions. Still those who had been subjected to discrimination were not the only beneficiaries. The railroads also gained, for the Act required that all rates be published, in effect prohibiting secret price-cutting. Between 1887 and 1893 this provision helped curb tendencies toward rate warfare, and as a result freight rates on the more competitive routes rose and aggregate railroad profits were stabilized. In recent years a 'revisionist' school of economic historians has argued that this result was not unintended, and that the framers of the Interstate Commerce Act were motivated as much by the desire to protect the oligopolistic railroads from themselves as to protect consumers from the railroads' exercise of monopoly power.[6] Some of their theses have been contested by orthodox interpreters, but it is clear that the ICC's policies did facilitate tacit and overt collusion in rate-making. On such paradoxes is the tradition of public regulation in the United States built.

In the early days of public utility regulation, welfare economics was in its infancy and had little influence on policy debates. As time went

---

[5]See Paul W. MacAvoy, *The Economic Effects of Regulation: The Trunkline Railroad Cartels and the Interstate Commerce Commission Before 1900* (Cambridge: MIT Press, 1965).

[6]Cf. MacAvoy, *op. cit.*; Gabriel Kolko, *Railroads and Regulation, 1877–1916* (Princeton: Princeton University Press, 1965); and G. W. Hilton, "The Consistency of the Interstate Commerce Act," *Journal of Law and Economics*, October 1966, pp. 87–113. The standard orthodox history of the Interstate Commerce Act and the early years of railroad regulation is I. Leo Sharfman's five volume work, *The Interstate Commerce Commission* (New York: Commonwealth Fund, 1931–37).

on, however, the view gained currency (at least among economists) that utility prices should be set equal to marginal cost for the purpose of maximizing social welfare.[7] This, however, poses a problem in naturally monopolistic industries, as we can discern from Figure 22.1a. If the long-run average total cost curve $LRATC$ is falling, the long-run marginal cost curve must lie below it. Straightforward application of the marginal cost pricing rule requires that price be set at the level OP_M in Figure 22.1a, with the output OX_M being supplied. But then average cost $X_M C = OB$ exceeds the price, and the enterprise incurs a deficit equal to the rectangular area $P_M ECB$. Marginal cost pricing turns natural monopolies into persistent money losers, and no investor will want to sink his funds into them, unless some way out of the dilemma is found.

One possible solution is to abide by the marginal cost pricing rule, letting the govern-ment subsidize the utility's periodic deficit out of general tax revenues. This has the advantage of satisfying the proximate allocative efficiency criterion. It has several offsetting disadvantages, however. First, to subsidize the deficit it may be necessary to increase personal income taxes, and this can introduce new and more subtle allocative distortions, since an income tax makes work relatively less attractive at the margin. Second, the subsidies represent redistributions of income from the general tax-paying public to a narrower class of consumers using the utility's services, and such redistributions may be op-posed on a variety of selfish or principled grounds. Third, subsidy programs of this sort can seldom be implemented without the de-tailed authorization of legislators, and this can readily degenerate into a pork-barrelling process in which the original allocative efficiency goal disappears from sight. For these reasons, among

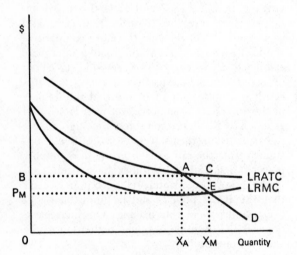
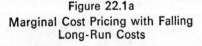

Figure 22.1a
Marginal Cost Pricing with Falling
Long-Run Costs

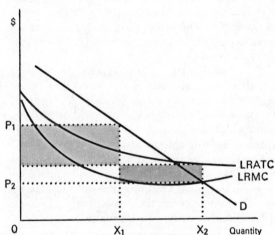

Figure 22.1b
Discriminatory Marginal Cost Pricing with Falling
Long-Run Costs

[7]Arguments in favor of marginal cost pricing for utilities date back to an article by French engineer Jules Dupuit in 1844. See "On the Measurement of the Utility of Public Works," published in translation in *International Economic Papers*, No. 2 (London: 1952), pp. 83–110. Crucial modern contributions include Harold Hotelling, "The General Welfare in Relation to Problems of Taxation and Railway and Utility Rates," *Econometrica*, July 1938, pp. 242–269; and Marcel Boiteux, "Sur la Gestion des Monopoles Publics Astreints a l'Equilibre Budgetaire," *Econometrica*, January 1956, pp. 22–40. For a survey of the literature, see Nancy Ruggles, "Recent Developments in the Theory of Marginal Cost Pricing," *Review of Economic Studies*, vol. 17, 1949–50, pp. 107–126.

others, there has been no deliberate effort by U. S. regulatory agencies to implement a pricing policy for natural monopolies which requires outright subsidies.

Price discrimination offers a second way out. Through discrimination it may be possible to squeeze additional revenue out of eager or affluent buyers while selling to buyers on the margin at a price approximating marginal cost. Figure 22.1b provides an illustration. One block of output OX_1 is sold to customers with high reservation prices at the price OP_1, while a second block X_1X_2 moves at the marginal cost price OP_2. On the second block, accounting losses shown by the solidly shaded rectangle occur, but these are more than offset by the profits earned from the first block (diagonally hatched rectangle). This form of second-degree or block-pricing discrimination is frequently sanctioned by electrical utility regulators. Residential consumers are charged a high price per unit for the first few kilowatt hours monthly, which perform functions such as illumination, for which no good substitutes exist. Lower rates are quoted for additional kilowatt hours serving less vital needs, and still lower rates are charged for the electric power which displaces natural gas cooking and heating. Industrial buyers receive even more favored treatment, since they may react to high prices by generating their own power or by moving to a new location where another power company offers more generous terms. In rail and motor carrier freight rate schedules, price discrimination more closely resembling the third-degree market segmentation type abounds. From the earliest days of railroading, rates have been geared to what the traffic will bear.[8] Shippers of high-value commodities such as machinery have historically paid freight rates higher both absolutely and in relation to marginal transportation cost than firms shipping low-value raw materials. This 'value of service' approach to rate discrimination has been practiced with the blessing of the Interstate Commerce Commission. It contributed to the expansion of rail service during the 19th century, although as we shall see later, in the past three decades it has created more resource allocation problems than it now solves.

Finally, regulators may not try to enforce equality between price and marginal cost, imposing instead a rule under which the price, if uniform, is set equal to average total cost, as at the output OX_A in Figure 22.1a. Or they may permit a discriminatory structure of prices, but insist that the *average* price level equal average total cost, including normal profit. Treatises on public utility regulation draw a dichotomy between this *rate level* problem—i.e., determining the average relationship of prices to costs—and the *rate structure* problem, dealing with the extent to which discrimination is practiced. Although both problems command attention, *rate level* matters are commonly considered the most basic of a regulatory agency's concerns, and it is on this aspect that we shall focus exclusively in the next section.

"FAIR RETURN ON FAIR VALUE"

The legal precepts governing regulatory agency rate level decisions manifest a decidedly 'full cost' flavor. Rates should, said the Supreme Court in a landmark 1898 opinion, be set so as to yield the regulated firm "a fair return upon . . . the fair value of the property being used by it."[9] In applying this rule, regulators concentrate on two quantitative values: the *rate base*, which presumably reflects the fair value of the capital in use; and the *allowed rate of return* on that rate base.

On the operational question of how one actually determines what the rate base should be and what a 'fair' rate of return represents, neither Congress nor the courts have been particularly instructive. The shotgun approach pursued in 1898 by the Supreme Court in setting forth fair value criteria was distinguished

---

[8] A mathematical theory of value-of-service pricing for railroads was published by civil engineer Charles Ellet, Jr., in 1839. It is reprinted as *An Essay on the Laws of Trade* (New York: Kelley, 1966). As consultant to the early railroads, Ellet apparently had a significant influence on the adoption of the value-of-service pricing system.

[9] *Smyth* v. *Ames et al.*, 169 U. S. 466, 546–547 (1898).

more by its confusion and illogic than by its practicality. The Court proposed among other things that fair value be related to the amount and market value of the regulated firm's bonds and stocks without realizing that the value of the company's stocks depends upon expected future earnings, which are what the regulators are supposed to be determining through their valuation decisions. After later court decisions swept aside such obvious fallacies, the search for fair value narrowed to two measures: the reproduction value of assets employed (i.e., what it would cost to replace the assets at current capital goods price levels); and the original or book cost, adjusted for depreciation, of assets in use. Each has merits and shortcomings. The reproduction value criterion tended to dominate regulatory commission decisions up to the 1930s, after which original cost rules came into vogue. In determining a rate base under the original cost approach, regulatory commissions dwell at length on such questions as the proper rate of depreciation, whether facilities under construction should be a part of the base, and whether an investment in World's Fair bonds might be included (i.e., in a New York Consolidated Edison rate case). Participants in the proceedings often become so engrossed in details and precedents that they lose sight of the fact that valuation judgments are inherently arbitrary. Neither accounting practice nor economic theory provides hard and fast solutions to such questions as the 'correct' rate of depreciation. Nor does emphasis on the slippery concept of fairness contribute to enlightenment. Because of these arbitrary elements, and because too high a rate base can easily be countered by reducing the allowed rate of return, Judge Jerome Frank was not far off the mark when he remarked in a railroad valuation case dissent that "the conclusions of the ICC might well be but the conjurations of mystagogues."[10]

What is conspicuously absent from many public utility rate level determination proceedings is an ability to rise above nit-picking and ceremonial arm-waving in order to deal with the central issue: what function profit serves in a regulated industry. Three functions can be identified. First, profit as conventionally defined in the regulatory context is a payment for the supply of capital inputs. It must therefore be set at a level which allows the regulated concern to attract sufficient new capital to satisfy consumer demands with an economically efficient plant. Second, profit performs an incentive function. To exploit its incentive potentialities, the regulators must set rates of return so as to reward efficiency and punish inefficiency. And third, profit serves an income distribution function, high profit rates channeling income from the enterprise's customers to its stockholders, and low profits having the opposite effect. It is only with respect to this third function that standards of fairness have any meaning, and here economic analysis has virtually nothing new or useful to contribute. We shall therefore confine our analysis to how the regulatory price-setting process implements the first and second functions of profit.

ATTRACTING SUFFICIENT NEW CAPITAL

Gradually, the courts and regulatory agencies have come to place increasing stress on the capital attraction function. In 1944 the Supreme Court in effect rejected past precedents compelling rigid adherence to a "fair return on fair value" standard, concluding that:

> Rates which enable the company to operate successfully, to maintain its financial integrity, to attract capital, and to compensate its investors for the risks assumed certainly cannot be condemned as invalid, even though they might produce only a meager return on the so-called "fair value" rate base.[11]

The need to set rates which attract sufficient capital was very much on the collective mind of the Federal Communications Commission in 1965 when it launched an extraordinarily ambitious investigation of the American Telephone

[10] *Old Colony Bondholders et al.* v. *New York, New Haven & Hartford Railroad Co.*, 161 F. 2d 413, 450 (1947).
[11] *Federal Power Commission et al.* v. *Hope Natural Gas Co.*, 320 U. S. 591, 605 (1944).

and Telegraph Company's interstate service rate level and structure. The inquiry was stimulated in part by the observation that A.T.&T. common stock, traditionally a paragon of blue-chip stability, had come to be regarded as a growth stock, with share values appreciating by more than 65 per cent between 1959 and 1965. The Commission was led to reconsider whether its controls on telephone rates had been too lax, permitting A.T.&T. to realize an after-tax return of 7.6 per cent on overall invested capital and 9.3 per cent on stockholders' equity between 1960 and 1965. Testimony on the rate of return required to attract new capital and meet growing telephone service demands was heard from a parade of distinguished academic and industrial witnesses, and among other things, several econometric models of the financial markets were entered into evidence. A.T.&T. took the position that it needed a return of from 7.5 to 8.5 per cent on overall capital to carry out its responsibilities. Recognizing that "a return which is too low could impair the ability of the respondents to raise additional needed capital and also imperil the integrity of existing investment," but cautioning that "it would not be in the public interest . . . to encourage or to facilitate . . . speculative profits," the Commission concluded that an allowed return of 7 to 7.5 per cent was warranted.[12] In reaching this decision, it was influenced heavily by its belief that A.T.&T. could reduce its cost of capital by increasing the leverage built into its capital structure—that is, by issuing relatively more bonds and fewer common stocks.

The 1965–1967 A.T.&T. rate of return inquiry was as sophisticated an example of enlightened regulatory surveillance as one can find. Nevertheless, one conceptual blind spot was present. Pervading many of the arguments was an implicit assumption that there is some single ideal rate of return, and that what the FCC had to do was to find the magic number.[13]

While this view has some merit, it oversimplifies the problem.

To see this, let us consider a hypothetical extreme case. In terms of the capital attraction function, what is the correct rate of return for a regulated firm—say, a railroad—facing stagnating demand? It needs to raise no new capital in the securities market, since it can generate whatever gross investment funds it requires out of depreciation allowances. Clearly, *no* return is necessary as long as angry stockholders and bondholders can be prevented from ousting management and sacking the enterprise in an attempt to salvage their original investments. This point often eludes utility regulators, who intuitively believe, perhaps because they over-stress equity criteria, that a fair return must be allowed if there is any system of prices which will yield that return. Only in the most extreme situations, such as that of the East Coast commuter railroads facing demand too weak relative to costs for any profitable price structure to exist, are the regulators inclined to aim for a rate of return much below the prime rate on corporate securities.

What this illustration suggests is that there may be at least some cases in which regulators have appreciable leeway in setting the allowed rate of return without endangering the utility's ability to attract necessary capital. Is this true more generally? In particular, is it true also for growing firms which must tap the securities market for new capital?

A numerical example will serve to bring out the essential relationships. Suppose the Astoria Edison Co. (AE) employs capital of $100 million in Period 1. Ignoring accounting technicalities, we assume its rate base also to be $100 million. For simplicity, we postulate further that the firm is financed entirely by common stock and retained earnings, with one million shares outstanding, and that there are no capital market imperfections (such as ignorance or risk aver-

---

[12]*In the matter of American Telephone & Telegraph Co. et al.*, 70 Public Utilities Reports (3rd series) 129, 158, 160, and 196 (1967).

[13]But see the concurring opinion of Commissioner Loevinger in *idem*, p. 232: "I think the record before us shows that a fairly wide range of rates might be held reasonable, that on each side of this range there is another range that is not clearly reasonable or unreasonable . . . and that it is only rates considerably beyond the range found reasonable by the commission that are clearly unreasonable."

sion) to differentiate its stock from claims to the earnings of other corporations. We assume throughout that the general market rate of return on common stocks is eight per cent.

Suppose now that in Period 1, the firm is allowed an 8 per cent return on its rate base. Total earnings will be .08 × $100 million = $8 million per year, and earnings per share will be $8.00. If this condition is expected to persist indefinitely, the market value of a share of AE stock in this simple case can be calculated by the formula:

$$V = \frac{\text{Annual Earnings per Share}}{\text{Market Rate of Return}} = \frac{\$8.00}{.08} = \$100.00$$

In Period 2, the regulatory commission unexpectedly reduces the allowed rate of return permanently to 7 per cent. If nothing else changes, annual earnings will be expected to be .07 × $100 million = $7 million, and earnings per share will be $7.00. To equalize the attractiveness of AE's stock with other securities yielding 8 per cent, the market price per share must fall to $\frac{\$7.00}{.08}$ = $87.50. The immediate consequence of the regulatory commission's action is to impose capital losses of approximately $12.5 million on AE stockholders. If nothing else is expected to change in the future, this equilibrium will persist.

Suppose, however, that AE must raise $10 million of new capital to meet growing demands in Period 3. Can it do so? Yes, but not without further adverse effects upon its stockholders. To float a new stock issue netting $10 million, AE must offer new buyers the going market rate of return—8 per cent. This means that it must price the new shares so that the new stock holders supplying $10 million expect to receive earnings of $800,000 annually on their investment. With an allowed rate of return of 7 per cent, the addition of $10 million to the rate base permits AE to realize an additional $700,000 in profits per year, raising the total profit take to $7.7 million. With $0.8 million demanded by new investors, this leaves $6.9 million, or $6.90 per share, for the original stockholders. When the allowed rate of return is less than the market cost of capital, floating new capital issues dilutes the equity of present shareholders. Stock prices must fall to $\frac{\$6.90}{.08}$ = $86.25, signifying further capital losses for pre-expansion shareholders. To raise the needed $10 million, AE must issue 115,942 new shares at the new equilibrium price of $86.25.

Thus, new capital can be raised by a public utility allowed to earn less than the market rate of return on its invested capital, but the expansion injures the financial position of existing stockholders. If despite this injury the utility carries out its expansion programs, the capital losses imposed on original stockholders will be greater, the more rapidly the rate base is expected to grow.[14] When the expected rate of growth of the rate base equals the allowed rate of return, the value of shares held by original

[14]Let K be the rate base at the present moment in time ($t = 0$); s the allowed rate of return; r the market cost of capital; and g the rate at which the rate base is expected to grow over time. Then the size of the rate base in year t will be $K e^{gt}$, and the allowed earnings in year t will be $sK e^{gt}$. Earnings attributable to year 0 stockholders will be total earnings, less the earnings which must be paid (at the market rate) to attract new capital. The cumulative amount of new capital in year t will be $(K e^{gt} - K)$, and the payments to it will be $rK (e^{gt} - 1)$. Discounting all magnitudes to present value at the market rate of return and integrating over all time, we find the present value of year 0 stockholders' claims on earnings to be:

$$P = \int_0^\infty s K e^{(g-r)t} \, dt - \int_0^\infty r K (e^{gt} - 1) \, e^{-rt} \, dt$$

$$= \int_0^\infty r K e^{-rt} \, dt - (r - s) K \int_0^\infty e^{(g-r)t} \, dt.$$

To avoid making the last term infinite, it is necessary that $r \gtrless g$. Given this restriction, the definite integral is:

$$P = K + (r - s) K \left(\frac{1}{g - r} \right) = \left(1 + \frac{r - s}{g - r} \right) K.$$

Given $r > g$, the denominator of $(r - s)/(g - r)$ is negative. When the allowed rate of return s is less than the market cost of capital r, the whole expression $(r - s) / (g - r)$ is negative, and so $P < K$. The greater g is ($g < r$), the *less* P will be. When the allowed rate of return exceeds the cost of capital, $(r - s) / (g - r)$ is positive, and so $P > K$, the more so, the higher g is.

stockholders will (assuming perfect expectations) shrink to zero.[15] Obversely, when the allowed rate of return is set at a level exceeding the market cost of capital, capital gains are conferred upon original stockholders. The more rapid future growth of the rate base is expected to be in this latter case, the higher will be the equilibrium market value of original stockholders' shares.

To be sure, when the allowed rate of return is held persistently below the market cost of capital, existing stockholders will oppose expansion measures because of their earnings dilution effect, and if possible they will try to liquidate the firm's assets completely. Neither step may be feasible, however, since regulatory commissions typically set minimum service standards as well as profit ceilings, and they may insist that earnings be retained and new capital acquired to supply growing demands. We must nevertheless expect a sharp conflict between the investment preferences of the regulatory agency and those of stockholders when the allowed rate of return is held below the market cost of capital. A further ramification of this problem will be taken up later.

Summing up, letting the allowed rate of return depart from the market cost of capital does not necessarily bar attraction of new capital needed in a public utility's operations, assuming that the regulated firm can be compelled to meet service demands. It merely affects the market values of outstanding common stock shares, a generous rate of return conferring capital gains upon stockholders and a miserly policy imposing capital losses.

INCENTIVES FOR COST CONTROL

Why should regulators tamper with the fortunes of utility investors in this way? Why not keep the allowed rate of return for non-declining utilities as close as possible to the market cost of capital? Only one possible reason seems to have any compelling validity: to implement a system of incentives for efficiency.

If the utility is virtually guaranteed a fair return on its invested capital, all the drawbacks of a non-competitive cost-plus pricing arrangement materialize. Should costs rise due to managerial negligence, the regulatory agency authorizes an increase in prices so that profits are restored to the fair level. Recognizing this, management will hardly be motivated to exert its best efforts in controlling and reducing costs.

If, on the other hand, the allowed rate of return is systematically correlated with the regulated firm's operating efficiency, incentives for cost control are created. Inefficiency would be penalized by allowing a rate of return below the cost of capital, imposing capital losses on stockholders and prodding them to bring pressure to bear on management either to improve matters or get out. Above-average efficiency would be rewarded with an allowed rate of return exceeding the market rate. The stockholder pressure on management encouraged by this scheme might even be enhanced by a well-designed stock option plan permitting management to share directly in the capital gains from superior achievement.

At present, no such thing is consciously and systematically attempted by utility regulators.[16] Allowed rates of return may occasionally be adjusted downward because regulatory board members believe a producer's costs are too high, and specific costs (such as entertainment outlays and in some jurisdictions advertising expenditures) may be disallowed so that they reduce profits dollar for dollar. But such actions are taken only sporadically. They lack the consistency essential for an effective system of incentives under which utility executives confidently expect good performance to be rewarded and poor performance penalized.[17]

---

[15]$P = 0$ when $(r - s) / (g - r) = 1$ and $r > s$. This occurs when $s = g$.

[16]For a review of early experiments, see Irvin Bussing, *Public Utility Regulation and the So-Called Sliding Scale* (New York: Columbia University Press, 1936). See also Harry M. Trebing, "Toward an Incentive System of Regulation," *Public Utilities Fortnightly*, July 18, 1963, pp. 22–37.

[17]The problems of structuring incentives for efficiency in the bilaterally monopolistic environment of defense contracting are similar to those of public utility regulation. See F. M. Scherer, *The Weapons Acquisition Process: Economic Incentives* (Boston: Harvard Business School Division of Research, 1964), especially Chapters 1, 9, and 12.

It is not clear that such a system could be implemented in the existing institutional environment of public utility regulation. Determining whether or not costs are excessive is difficult; it takes technical knowledge and sound judgment. All too frequently, especially at the state level, members of the regulatory boards are political hacks with neither the experience nor the interest to exercise their responsibilities imaginatively. Their staffs, upon whom they must rely heavily for guidance, are generally small and poorly paid. Moreover, the will to administer a tough-minded system of performance rewards and penalties may be absent. There is a propensity in public regulation for the regulators to be co-opted by those they regulate, coming to share their values and growing wary of boat-rocking.[18] This is in part the result of living with common problems year after year. But in addition, regulatory boards often depend upon the firms they regulate for political support, and to punish inefficiency too harshly could endanger that support.

The technical difficulty of adjusting public utility rates to penalize inefficiency is illustrated by hearings held in 1967 before the New York State Public Service Commission concerning a proposed $32 million rate increase for the Consolidated Edison Company. Among the witnesses was a consultant hired by the City of New York. He compared Consolidated Edison's costs with those of the five most efficient privately owned U. S. electrical utilities, concluding that the New York concern had excessive costs of at least $58 million.[19] Consolidated Edison officials argued in return that the comparison was meaningless, since their company faced higher construction and fuel costs, served relatively fewer large industrial users, experienced much lower per-capita domestic consumption levels from urban apartment-dwellers, and was forced by the city to incur the expense of burying much of its distribution cable. This defense was successful, for the Public Service Commission approved the rate increase, noting that Consolidated Edison was beset by unique problems and that "if costs are high . . . the rates will be correspondingly high; these are the simple facts of our economy."[20]

Without a detailed investigation, it is impossible to say whether this decision was appropriate or not. But that is precisely the point. If modern tools of analysis were brought to bear, regulators would not have to make their judgments lacking solid evidence on efficiency and besieged by incommensurables and imponderables. For instance, through the use of multiple regression analysis it might be possible to adjust for the effect of such factors as market size, population density, per-capita consumption, fuel costs, construction costs, the age of the capital stock, the percentage of the distribution system buried underground, peak vs. off-peak load variance, and the like, determining how efficient the firm in question is relative to the average after these variables are taken into account. Several exploratory studies of this genre have been carried out.[21] Without doubt, one of the great untapped opportunities for improving the regulatory process lies in applying such methods (bolstered by considerable technical expertise and experienced judgment) to relate allowed rates of return to the efficiency of the firms regulated. As matters presently stand, the principal cost

[18]See Marver H. Bernstein, *Regulating Business by Independent Commission* (Princeton: Princeton University Press, 1955); and Grant McConnell, *Private Power and American Democracy* (New York: Knopf, 1966).

[19]"Con Ed Accused of Wasting $58 Million in 1965," *New York Times*, March 15, 1967, p. 34; and "Tempers Aroused at Con Ed Hearings," *New York Times*, May 17, 1967, p. 3.

[20]*In the matter of Consolidated Edison Co. of New York*, 73 Public Utilities Reports (3rd series) 417, 424, 477–484 (March 1968). The New York City government's reaction was highly critical. See "Mayor Seeks Control of Utilities," *New York Times*, May 2, 1968, p. 1.

[21]Most relevant to the present discussion is William Iulo's multiple regression analysis of unit electricity costs for 186 firms, covering the period 1952–1957. "The Relative Performance of Individual Electric Utilities," *Land Economics*, November 1962, pp. 315–326. Although several variables pertinent to the New York situation were not included, it is worth noting that Iulo found Consolidated Edison to be one of the 32 least efficient power companies in his sample. For similar analyses of railroad and trucking costs, see John R. Meyer, M. J. Peck, John Stenason, and Charles Zwick, *The Economics of Competition in the Transportation Industries* (Cambridge: Harvard University Press, 1959), Chapters 2, 3, and 4; and for air transport, see Robert J. Gordon, "Airline Costs and Managerial Efficiency," in the National Bureau of Economic Research conference volume, *Transportation Economics* (New York: Columbia University Press, 1965), pp. 61–94.

reduction incentive generated by regulation in naturally monopolistic industries comes from a phenomenon called 'regulatory lag.' Conventional regulatory procedure is to set prices or rates which will yield the approved rate of return on capital, given either current cost and demand conditions or some best estimate of future costs and demand. Changing rates once they have been authorized takes time; from several months to two years may elapse between filing of a proposal for change and its implementation with the regulatory body's blessing. If unit costs rise for any reason—within or beyond management's control—the regulated enterprise usually hastens to propose a compensating rate increase, but until the increase is approved, the utility bears the full brunt of the higher costs as a deduction from its profits. If on the other hand unit costs can be reduced below original estimates, the utility retains the full savings as enhanced profit until a rate adjustment is declared in order. Here, however, initiative by the regulated firm to propose a price change is commonly absent, and it may take the regulatory commission one or two years to perceive that new cost conditions warrant an adjustment. Thus, the very cumbersomeness of the regulatory process has the redeeming merit of making cost reduction at least temporarily profitable. Whether the incentives for cost control created through regulatory lag are strong enough to keep regulated firms at fighting weight is arguable. It seems likely that greater efficiency would be achieved if a more pervasive and consistent system of incentives could be maintained.

REGULATION AND THE CHOICE OF THE OPTIMAL CAPITAL INTENSITY

Implicitly, our conception thus far of the public utility's efficiency problem has been the layman's notion that sheer waste should be avoided. This way of looking at the problem is eminently appropriate. Now, however, we turn to a special efficiency problem involving the profit-maximizing responses of regulated firms to their peculiar economic environment.

One classic task of management is to choose the most profitable combination of inputs— capital, labor of various grades, raw materials, etc.—for producing the desired output. Although the typical public utility operation may for fundamental technological reasons be inherently more capital-intensive than manufacturing and retailing activities, opportunities for substitution between capital and other inputs definitely do exist. Buildings can be constructed of durable, maintenance-free materials at relatively high initial capital cost or of less expensive materials which demand more frequent attention Microwave radio relay stations can be designed with complicated automatic failure detection and channel-switching systems, or a man can be assigned to each station to monitor and correct trouble on the spot. Steam for turbogenerators can be produced by a nuclear plant, with relatively high initial investment in shielding and a reactor core, or by coal-fired boilers which require lower initial outlays but a high continuing stream of expenditures on fuel. Railway roadbeds can be built to minimize grade variations, saving the subsequent cost of extra pusher engines and fuel, or more substantial grades may be accepted to avoid the high capital cost of cuts, fills, and tunnels. And so on. The choice made in any given case depends critically upon the cost of capital relative to the prices of other inputs.

Enter the villain. It is possible that the "fair return on fair value" pricing technique employed by regulatory agencies will alter the effective input price conditions confronting regulated firms, in turn distorting the choices taken by those firms.[22] Specifically, if the allowed rate of return set by the regulators exceeds the current cost of capital, incentives are created for excessively capital-intensive operation. If the

[22]This problem was first explored systematically by Harvey Averch and L. L. Johnson in "Behavior of the Firm Under Regulatory Constraint," *American Economic Review*, December 1962, pp. 1052–1069. A special case was studied almost concurrently by Stanislaw H. Wellisz in "Regulation of Natural Gas Pipeline Companies: An Economic Analysis," *Journal of Political Economy*, February 1963, pp. 30–43. For extensions, see Fred M. Westfield, "Regulation and Conspiracy," *American Economic Review*, June 1965, pp. 424–443; and Alvin K. Klevorick, "The Graduated Fair Return: A Regulatory Proposal," *American Economic Review*, June 1966, pp. 477–484.

allowed rate of return is less than the cost of capital, there will be a tendency toward insufficiently capital-intensive operation, if investment is forthcoming at all.

To demonstrate fully the logic underlying this proposition requires some fairly intricate mathematics. Since many readers are barred from that temple, let us proceed as far as we can with plain English, plane geometry, and a numerical illustration. A full mathematical proof is provided in the appendix to this chapter.

Suppose, as did Averch and Johnson, the first to analyze the problem formally, that the rate of return on capital allowed by the regulatory body exceeds the current cost of capital. Concretely, let us assume that the market cost of new capital is 8 per cent, no matter how much capital the utility obtains, and that the regulators allow a 10 per cent rate of return. We ignore such complications as capital market imperfections, the optimal mix of bonds vs. stocks, depreciation, and the effect of inflation on the rate base. With this assumed disparity between the cost of capital and the allowed rate of return, the utility will perceive its true or implicit cost of capital to be less than the market cost. Each million dollars in new capital raised requires an annual commitment of $80,000 in interest, dividends or the appreciation of stockholders' equity, but it simultaneously expands the rate base so that prices and output can be adjusted to yield additional returns to capital of $100,000 annually. Prior stockholders in effect receive a $20,000 bonus for each million dollars in new capital raised. According to Averch and Johnson, under these conditions the "private cost (of capital) is less than the market cost by an amount equal to this difference."[23] Using their rule, the private cost of capital is found to be 6 per cent; that is, 8 per cent less 2 per cent. We shall see later that this is not strictly correct, but it will do for a first approximation.

To produce some desired level of output, the utility faces a set of long-run input substitution possibilities described by an isoquant like curve Z in Figure 22.2. The socially optimal (minimum cost) input combination for producing output

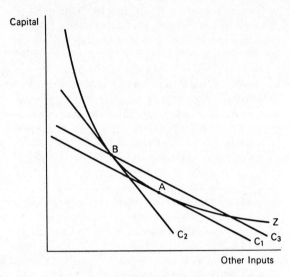

Figure 22.2
The Efficiency Loss under Excessively Generous Rate of Return Regulation

Z is found at point A, where isoquant Z is tangent to an isocost line C_1 having the equation:

$$\text{Total Outlay} = \\ (\text{Amount of Capital Used}) \cdot \\ (\text{Market Cost of Capital}) \\ + (\text{Amount of Other Inputs Used}) \cdot \\ (\text{Market Price of Other Inputs}).$$

Its slope is the ratio of the price of other inputs to the market cost of capital. If, however, the firm perceives its private cost of capital to be less than the market cost, it will make its input proportions decision on the basis of an isocost line like C_2, which is steeper than C_1 because capital is implicitly cheaper relative to other inputs. It will then opt for input combination B, using relatively more capital and relatively less of other inputs than at combination A.

This choice is clearly inefficient. It does not minimize the cost of production, calculated in terms of market prices. The *social cost* of producing output Z with the excessively capital-intensive combination B is shown by the isocost line C_3, drawn parallel to C_1 to reflect the fact that

[23]*Op. cit.*, p. 1053.

market prices are assumed. Since C_3 lies above C_1, the market cost of producing output Z with input combination B necessarily exceeds the market cost of producing that output with combination A.

Now in order to operate at B and cover both its inefficiently high costs and the 2 per cent surplus return to capital, the regulated firm must charge a higher price than it would need to charge if it were operating efficiently. With a higher price, less output will be demanded and the utility will move to a lower isoquant. Thus, costs, prices, and outputs are all adversely affected when the allowed rate of return is set at a level exceeding the market cost of capital. Analogous efficiency-reducing, price-increasing distortions occur when the allowed rate of return is set below the market cost of capital.

To see these effects more clearly, a numerical illustration may be helpful. Let us assume a company producing electricity with the following Cobb-Douglas production function:

$$MWH = 50\ K^{.27}\ L^{.73},$$

where MWH is megawatt (thousand kilowatt) hours of output per year, K is the amount of capital used (measured in thousands of dollars),

and L is the number of labor man–years used. We assume only one complementary input, labor, purely for simplicity; it in no way affects the generality of the analysis. The capital exponent .27 was based on actual capital share data for U. S. electrical utilities in 1962. The market cost of capital was assumed to be 8 per cent, or $80 per $1,000; and the market wage was set at $10,386 per year. These assumptions conveniently permit the cost per kilowatt hour to be exactly $.10 when electricity is generated with the most efficient input combination. The capital stock, assuming efficient production, is 3.38 times annual sales at competitive prices. This corresponds closely to the capital/sales ratio actually observed for U. S. power companies.

Table 22.2 presents the results of solving the utility's profit maximization problem for three cases differing only with respect to the price elasticity of demand. Each case assumes the allowed rate of return to be 10 per cent, and for each the output is 100,000 megawatt hours at the 'competitive' price of $.10 per kilowatt hour yielding a 'normal' 8 per cent return. From this common competitive equilibrium point three linear demand curves were extended, demand being most elastic in Case I and least

Table 22.2

Profit-Maximizing Choices of a Regulated Public Utility
Able To Obtain Capital at Eight Per Cent and Allowed
a Ten Per Cent Return on Its Invested Capital

	Demand Case I $P=150-.0005\ MWH$	Demand Case II $P=200-.0010\ MWH$	Demand Case III $P=250-.0015\ MWH$
Elasticity of demand at competitive output (100,000 MWH)	2.00	1.00	0.67
Most Profitable Output under Regulation	66,950 MWH	64,000 MWH	62,450 MWH
Most Profitable Price under Regulation	11.65¢	13.60¢	15.63¢
Elasticity of Demand at the Regulated Optimum	3.48	2.13	1.67
Social Cost per Kilowatt Hour	10.53¢	11.92¢	13.45¢
Economic Profit under Regulation	$749,700	$1,073,500	$1,361,700
Profit If the Firm Were an Unregulated Monopoly	$1,250,000	$2,500,000	$3,750,000
Implicit Marginal Cost of Capital under Regulation	4.00%	2.29%	1.61%

elastic in Case III.[24] For each case, the utility was assumed to maximize the surplus remaining after all workers are paid the market wage and investors receive the market return of 8 per cent, subject to the constraint that the overall return on invested capital (including the market return plus the premium) be exactly 10 per cent.

One significant insight afforded by Table 22.2 is that the amount of distortion stimulated by an overly generous allowed rate of return is inversely related to the elasticity of demand. The less elastic demand is, the more the capital/labor ratio is distorted away from its socially optimal value, and the higher social cost per kilowatt hour will be.

Elasticity of demand plays a crucial role in preventing the regulated utility from expanding its capital base indefinitely, despite the temptation created when each dollar of investment adds more to allowed earnings than to capital costs. As costs and prices rise due to employing increasingly inefficient quantities of capital, more and more elastic segments of the utility's demand function are entered. Sooner or later the quantity demanded is restricted so sharply by rising prices that total revenues prove insufficient to yield maximum profits. This can be seen most vividly by contemplating an extreme case. Suppose demand is perfectly inelastic, the quantity demanded being constant, no matter how high the price is set. Each inefficient addition to the capital stock requires a price increase to cover the increased cost of production plus the allowed premium return on capital. The profit margin per dollar of cost must rise as the ratio of capital to other inputs increases, and with a rising profit margin on rising unit costs, total profits increase more rapidly than costs. Adding to capital must therefore be profitable until costs are infinite, with an infinite profit sum tacked on! Obviously, this cannot happen, if not because regulators would become uneasy about infinite prices, then certainly because demand is never perfectly price inelastic. It is the rising elasticity of demand with increases in price which checks tendencies toward mounting inefficiency.

The last line of Table 22.2 provides another useful insight. From the marginal productivity of capital in profit-maximizing equilibrium, it is possible to compute the implicit marginal private equilibrium cost of capital to the firm. Contrary to the naive assumption made in introducing Figure 22.2, the implicit private cost of capital is *not* the market cost less the premium return. Rather, it depends in a complex way upon several variables, including the equilibrium elasticity of demand. The less elastic demand is, the lower the implicit marginal cost of capital is, *ceteris paribus*. In least elastic demand Case III it sinks to the remarkably low value of 1.61 per cent.

Equally surprising is the calculated magnitude of the cost inefficiencies resulting from the firm's adaptation to its regulatory environment. In the least elastic demand case, unit costs at market prices exceed the cost of efficient operation by 34.5 per cent. Indeed, the distortions are so large that one cannot avoid entertaining doubts about the realism of the illustration, despite an attempt to base it on real-world data. One assumption undoubtedly helped bias the distortion estimates on the high side. The Cobb-Douglas production function used in this illustration has an elasticity of substitution of unity, i.e., its curvature is such that as one moves along an isoquant, letting the isoquant slope change by a given percentage magnitude, the capital/labor ratio changes in the opposite direction by an exactly equal magnitude. With lower elasticities of substitution, the opportunity for moving to higher capital/labor ratios is constrained, and so also is the size of resultant cost inefficiencies. In the limiting case of zero substitution elasticity (associated with L-shaped isoquants) there will be no departure from the socially optimal capital/labor ratio and no increase in unit costs. However, the possibilities for substituting capital for other inputs in public utility operations are so patently abundant that this extreme case can be ruled out. Also, there is reason to believe that even when the elasticity of substitution is low, a utility may take advantage of an allowed rate of return premium by piling up completely non-

---

[24]On estimates of the elasticity of demand for electric power, see Harry M. Trebing, ed., *Performance under Regulation* (East Lansing: Michigan State University, 1968), pp. 94 and 147.

functional capital (in effect operating off the surface of its production function) or by willingly paying inflated prices to capital goods suppliers.[25] In view of these complications, it is hard to tell how well the distortions quantified in Table 22.2 reflect real-world possibilities. Still it is clear that in principle, excessively generous rate of return regulation can lead to significant cost inefficiencies.

A further surprise emerges when the demand conditions faced by the firm are held constant while the gap between the allowed rate of return and the cost of capital is allowed to vary. For the demand conditions assumed in Case II of Table 22.2, some representative results are as follows, assuming as before that the market cost of capital is 8 per cent:

Allowed Rate of Return	Social Cost per KWH	Implicit Capital Cost
10.0 per cent	11.92¢	2.29 per cent
9.0 per cent	12.47¢	1.99 per cent
8.3 per cent	12.94¢	1.74 per cent
8.0 per cent	10.00¢*	8.00 per cent

*At an allowed rate of return exactly equal to the cost of capital an indeterminacy arises, since it is possible to realize normal profits with inefficient input combinations too.

The smaller the gap between the allowed rate of return and the cost of capital, the more the utility's capital hiring decisions are distorted! This relationship is no fluke; it is verified more generally in the mathematical appendix. Its intuitive foundations are not entirely clear. Apparently, when there is any disparity at all between the allowed and market rates of return, the utility must, to take full advantage, distort its choices more violently when the disparity is small than when it is large. For regulatory agencies this phenomenon would seem to pose a genuine dilemma. Assuming that perfection is

seldom attainable, it in effect says that the better job regulators do in equalizing allowed returns with the current cost of capital, the more they impair investment efficiency! Indeed, the implications are so paradoxical it is difficult to take them seriously.

ARE THE AVERCH-JOHNSON POSTULATES CONSISTENT WITH REALITY?

Even before this paradox was brought to light, there was heated debate over the realism of the Averch-Johnson model's predictions. Public utility executives denied vehemently that they behaved in any such way, while students of public utility economics searched with equal ardor for evidence of so-called A-J investment biases.[26] Nailing down conclusive support for either side of the argument is far from easy, since regulated companies may try to implement only those distortions subtle enough to escape damaging criticism. At present it is possible to do little more than advance impressionistic and not necessarily representative qualitative observations.

The model probably applies poorly to those regulated industries in which price levels are set through joint actions encompassing a number of firms. Railroading is the prime example. The most important Interstate Commerce Commission rate of return determination decisions are addressed to broad commodity groups and geographic territories, and these decisions are commonly implemented by changes affecting many carriers. A particular carrier must be wary of letting its costs rise through excessive capital investment, for if other carriers fail to behave symmetrically, it may obtain no price relief from the ICC, and this fear blunts its incentive to distort its investment.[27] Obversely, the companies most certain to secure price relief when costs rise are those who have no direct or close competitors and whose rates of return and prices are determined on a case-by-case basis. Prime candidates include the electric power and natural

[25]See Westfield, *op. cit.*

[26]See especially the views expressed in two conference reports: Trebing, ed., *Performance under Regulation, op. cit.*; and William Capron, ed., *Technological Change in the Regulated Industries* (Washington: Brookings, forthcoming).

[27]This qualification applies in equal measure to incentives for the control of non-capital costs.

gas utilities, the telephone companies, and private urban transit lines.

It seems almost certain that latent or active incentives for investment decision distortion exist within this latter group. Allowed rates of return vary widely from state to state. In 1966, net income after taxes as a percentage of stockholders' equity among the 50 largest U. S. electric, gas, and communications utilities ranged as high as 19 per cent from a mean of 10.2 per cent, with 17 companies earning returns of 12 per cent or more.[28] Utilities allowed to earn returns exceeding their cost of new capital should tend to operate more capital-intensive processes than less privileged compatriots, *ceteris paribus*. And since the implications of the distortion model are symmetric, we should expect firms allowed a rate of return *below* the cost of capital to adopt processes which are less than optimally capital-intensive. This hypothesis is eminently testable. Unfortunately, no quantitative tests had been published at the time of writing. We are forced to fall back upon qualitative observations.[29]

Crude and plainly tenuous support for the Averch-Johnson hypothesis might be drawn from observing the office and factory buildings of the American Telephone & Telegraph Co. They tend to be unusually massive, durable structures, with lavish reinforced brickwork—the kind of thing erected only when one's discount rate (reflecting the implicit cost of capital) is low. Indeed, they may be among the few 20th century industrial artifacts surviving into the 30th century—a source of wonder to economic anthropologists of that (hopefully) enlightened era.

However, we should not expect all A.T.&T. investments to exhibit this bias. Because intrastate telephone service rates are set on a state-by-state basis, the Bell System's allowed rate of

return varies with the local regulatory climate. In a private communication, an A.T.&T. financial executive indicated that state-by-state variation in returns has a definite impact on the outcome of decisions to build certain facilities. To illustrate one case cited, suppose two coaxial cables are needed, one immediately and the other only in 10 years. The two can be buried simultaneously for an outlay of $25,000 per mile.[30] Alternatively, one cable can be buried today at a cost of $20,000 per mile and then the trench can be re-opened 10 years hence to bury the second cable at an incremental cost of $10,000 per mile. Which alternative is more economical? It depends upon the discount rate, as the following comparison shows:

Discounted Value of the
Cost per Mile of Cable

Discount Rate	Bury Both Cables Simultaneously	Bury One Today, One in Ten Years
0%	$25,000	$30,000
2%	25,000	28,203
4%	25,000	26,756
6%	25,000	25,584
7%	25,000	25,084
8%	25,000	24,632
10%	25,000	23,855

At discount rates of seven per cent and less, burying both cables simultaneously is the low-cost alternative; the opposite is true over 7 per cent. According to the A.T.&T. executive, there is a tendency in states with low allowed rates of return (and hence high implicit capital cost) to choose the sequential strategy, though company officials believed that the simultaneous cable-laying alternative would more often be optimal if evaluated at true capital cost rates. Of

[28]"The 50 Largest Utilities," *Fortune*, June 15, 1967, pp. 224–225.

[29]One new fragment of quantitative evidence became available too late to incorporate in the text. Extending William Iulo's analysis, Joe D. Pace found that U. S. electric power utilities which exhibited unusually high costs (after adjustments were made to correct for cost-influencing variables not subject to managerial discretion) had significantly higher capital/output ratios than more efficient producers. He also discovered less conclusive indications of a relationship between costs and profitability consistent with the predictions developed in the mathematical appendix to this chapter. "Relative Efficiency in the Electric Utility Industry," Ph.D. dissertation, University of Michigan, 1970.

[30]Although the example is a real one, the figures presented here are hypothetical.

course, the socially optimal choice depends upon cost and demand conditions which vary from case to case. It is possible (although this variant was not stressed by the A.T.&T. executive) that in states allowing generous rates of return, the simultaneous strategy might be chosen when the sequential strategy would entail lower costs at correctly imputed market discount rates.

In a less speculative vein, there is solid evidence that A.T.&T. favored coaxial cable over much less capital-intensive microwave radio relay systems to transmit television signals between major cities during the first few years following World War II. But when several other firms began developing potentially competing microwave relay networks, A.T.&T. accelerated its microwave program and cut back its planned coaxial cable installations by 33 per cent.[31] This example suggests that competitive pressures may serve as a check against Averch-Johnson investment biases.

A further possibility on which we can do no more than speculate concerns the introduction of nuclear power. It is conceivable that the rapid growth of nuclear-fueled electricity generating facilities during the 1960s was stimulated in part by the desire of regulated electric utilities to bias their choices in favor of capital-intensive equipment. Should this conjecture be true, it would provide an interesting illustration of an inadvertent second-best solution. Nuclear power might not pass a *private* profitability test in borderline cases, were it not for the distortion introduced by allowed rates of return exceeding the cost of capital. However, because of the external air pollution diseconomies associated with coal-fired generating equipment, nuclear

power might well be the optimal *social* choice.[32]

That regulated utilities are acutely sensitive to opportunities for expanding their rate base is demonstrated by events in the communications satellite field. During 1965 and 1966 there was intense behind-the-scenes fighting over ground relay station ownership rights between the Communications Satellite Corporation (Comsat), created in 1962 by a special act of Congress to develop American interests in international satellite communications, and companies such as A.T.&T. and RCA Communications, which traditionally operated overseas message service facilities. Each sought ownership of the stations relaying messages to and from satellites, since the investment could be added to its rate base as a justification for higher earnings. For Comsat the incentive to enter the ground relay station business was particularly compelling. Its initial capital of $200 million had been raised in the expectation that a system of from 30 to 50 randomly orbiting medium-altitude satellites would be necessary to provide world-wide communications capabilities. But then the synchronous orbit satellite concept was shown to be technically feasible, making it possible to serve the entire globe with only three or four high-altitude satellites at a much lower capital investment. This left Comsat in 1966 with surplus funds of $175 million invested in Treasury bills and time deposits not subject to inclusion in its rate base. By investing the funds in ground relay stations, Comsat could add substantially to its rate base and allowed earnings. The ownership conflict was settled temporarily through a 1966 Federal Communications Commission decision allocating 50 per cent ownership rights to Com-

[31]See William G. Shepherd, "Communications: Regulation, Innovation, and the Changing Margin of Competition," in Capron, ed., *Technological Change in the Regulated Industries*, drawing upon an unpublished study of microwave radio relay system development by the author of the present work. At the time, A.T.&T. planners expected the capital cost of coaxial cable to be approximately $2,300 per channel mile, compared to $1,250 per channel mile of microwave relay. Current operating (non rate base) costs were higher for microwave, but microwave appeared to have a slight economy edge when total (i.e., current plus capital) costs were weighed.

It is sometimes asked why electrical power companies allowed generous rates of return do not go all-out in burying their presently unsightly distribution cables if they are susceptible to A-J investment biases. See the comment by William R. Hughes in Trebing, *Performance under Regulation*, pp. 82–84. The explanation may be that widespread burying would raise costs and hence prices by so much that demand would be choked off enough to reduce net profits despite the rate base expansion. It is significant that electrical utilities do appear willing to do some burying on a restricted, piecemeal basis—and at charges to customers clearly below the costs of burying.

[32]That is, unless there are presently unknown or underestimated external diseconomies associated with disposing nuclear fuel wastes.

sat and 50 per cent to traditional carriers.[33] Meanwhile A.T.&T. and other carriers petitioned the FCC to approve their investment of $90 million in an additional underwater cable to Europe, providing new message transmission capacity at a cost considerably above the satellite technique's cost.[34] At the same time Comsat pressed the development of increasingly sophisticated satellites whose deployment would, among other things, eliminate its meager rate base problem.

A less obvious but extremely important prediction of the Averch-Johnson analysis is that regulated firms allowed a rate of return exceeding the cost of capital have an incentive to diversify into relatively unprofitable ancillary activities—i.e., those which earn less than the market rate of return but more than the implicit cost of capital.[35] This adds to the rate base, and as long as the regulatory agency is unable to segregate investment accurately by fields of operation, it permits the utility to increase prices in fields where it has substantial monopoly power and hence to realize the full allowed rate of return for its combined operations. That A.T.&T. behaves in this way was suggested by a study revealing that the telephone company during 1964 realized only a 0.3 per cent return on capital allocated to its TELPAK multi-channel business service and 2.9 per cent on its TWX (Teletype) service, both offered in competition with Western Union service and privately owned data transmission systems, while earning a 10 per cent

return on its interstate telephone operations.[36] Again, however, the evidence is ambiguous, for the rates of return are estimated on the basis of "fully allocated costs," which include arbitrary overhead cost allocations.[37] Since the TELPAK and TWX rates probably covered at least short-run marginal costs, it is impossible to reject the alternative hypothesis that A.T.&T.'s rate structure was nothing more than a straightforward discriminatory response to varying demand elasticities in different markets, demand being more elastic in the business data transmission field, where competition exists, than in long-distance telephony.

Finally, a variant of the Averch-Johnson model pioneered by Wellisz predicts that regulated utilities may expand their capacity to serve peak-load customers at prices below the long-run marginal cost of providing that service while charging off-peak users excessively high prices.[38] Here again, however, concrete empirical verification is lacking.

What emerges from this review is cause for concern, though no really conclusive evidence of Averch-Johnson-Wellisz investment biases has yet been marshalled. It is possible that serious distortions have been thwarted by the exercise of regulatory oversight. Still the technical competence of most regulatory agencies is much too limited to cope with more subtle distortions. Public utilities may also have refrained from excessively capital-intensive investments out of a concern for the public interest, or because there

---

[33]5 FCC Reports (2nd series) 812 (December 1966). Provision was made to reopen the question in 1969.

[34]The petition was approved in 13 FCC Reports (2nd series) 235 (May 1968), with a vigorous dissent from Commissioner Nicholas Johnson.

[35]Averch and Johnson, op. cit., pp. 1057–1059.

[36]70 Public Utilities Reports (3rd series) 129, 143 (November 1967).

[37]By using different cost allocation assumptions, the Bell System was later able to raise the indicated rates of return on TELPAK and TWX service.

[38]Wellisz, "Regulation of Natural Gas Pipeline Companies: An Economic Analysis." In "The Graduated Fair Return: Comment," American Economic Review, March 1968, pp. 170–173, Alfred E. Kahn argues that this seeming vice is a virtue in disguise because it offsets the natural propensity of monopolistic utilities to restrict the amount of service they offer.

Another objection to the Wellisz conjecture should be noted. If in fact utilities have an incentive to invest in excessive peak load capacity, some critics have asked, why did U. S. power companies find themselves with insufficient capacity to meet peak loads during the 1960s? What is overlooked in citing this experience as a refutation of the Averch – Johnson – Wellisz postulate is that the optimal adaptation to an excessively generous rate of return involves not only building excessive peak load capacity, but also reducing prices to peak period customers so that the capacity is actually utilized. And of course, once a utility has committed itself to such a price structure, it may find that it has underestimated peak demand. However, one might expect producers allowed generous rates of return to build in unusually high safety margins against chance demand peaks. This aspect of the Averch – Johnson – Wellisz theory has not yet been properly developed.

is subjective satisfaction in running a taut ship. Nevertheless, this is at best only faint reassurance, and one may well consider intolerable a set of institutions under which the power to accept or reject inefficient choices is vested solely or primarily in management's hands, without independent checks.

POLICY ALTERNATIVES

What can regulatory agencies do to guard against these actual or potential distortions encouraged by the "fair return on fair value" system? One possibility might be to replace assets with some more neutral measure such as value added in defining the regulated firm's rate base. The divorce from a capital orientation could not be complete, however, since the investment attraction function of profit is inexorably linked to the amount of capital on hand and needed. Merely trying harder to keep the allowed rate of return as close as possible to the cost of capital may not work either, given that the profit-maximizing amount of distortion appears in a wide class of cases to be inversely related to the difference between the two parameters. Still the theory may be spuriously precise on this point; perhaps there is some tolerable margin of error within which firms' investment decisions are insensitive to imperfect matching of allowed rates of return with the cost of capital.

Alternatively, regulators might intervene more vigorously in public utility operating and investment decisions, exercising close control to ensure that producers do not choose excessively capital-intensive processes or cross-subsidize unprofitable lines. Yet this is hard to do well, given the talent limitations plaguing regulatory commissions.[39] Too much intervention can also deaden remaining incentives for good performance, since utility executives would be able to blame the regulators for their complicity in mistakes, and since the sense of frustration evoked when one's decisions are constantly second-guessed

would drive out the most able and energetic managers. In addition, the operation of a large business enterprise, particularly one dealing in sophisticated nuclear, electrical, and electronic technologies, is sufficiently complicated that the companies might always stay two jumps ahead of their regulators in finding ways to extract maximum profits from their predicament.

The most promising solution would appear to lie in developing more effective measures of efficiency and using them to adjust allowed rates of return. 'Yardstick' operations by municipally and federally owned enterprises could be used as a basis for evaluating the costs of private regulated utilities, after appropriate differences in operating conditions and capital costs are taken into account; or multivariate statistical analyses of private utility costs could be developed to identify those producers which are doing well and those which are not. Unlike all other reasons for letting the allowed rate of return depart from the cost of capital, authorizing premium returns explicitly to reward superior efficiency would not stimulate distorted investment decisions, for excessive capitalization would lead to rising costs, a decline in relative efficiency, and an enforced reduction in the future rate of return. Only by continuing to operate efficiently could an enterprise continue to earn high profits.

THE INTERFACE BETWEEN REGULATION AND COMPETITION

The Supreme Power who conceived gravity, supply and demand, and the double helix must have been absorbed elsewhere when public utility regulation was invented. The system is cumbersome, vulnerable to incompetence, and prone toward becoming ingrown and co-opted. In some respects it is directly conducive to inefficiency; in others, it may be merely ineffective in altering the behavior of the companies regulated.[40]

---

[39]The same limitation flaws Alvin Klevorick's proposal to reduce the rate of return allowed as the utility hires more capital, since the staffs of regulatory agencies are unlikely to know how much capital is needed for efficient operation, and hence would be unable to design a correct schedule of gradation. Cf. "The Graduated Fair Return," p. 481.

[40]In a statistical analysis of regulated vs. non-regulated electrical power rates between 1912 and 1937, George Stigler and Claire Friedland conclude that regulation had no effect on average rate levels. "What Can Regulators Regulate? The Case of Electricity," *Journal of Law and Economics*, October 1962, pp. 1–16. However,

Aware of its imperfections, economists and policy-makers continue to search for a better solution. An answer proposed with increasing frequency is to restore market forces as a regulator, at least for those industries like transportation, radio communications, and banking where some semblance of competition is feasible. Only where the cost structure compels monopoly, as in electric power supply and local telephone service, is the competitive solution clearly ruled out, leaving only regulation or nationalization as acceptable alternatives.

At present the transportation industries pose the most interesting and important problems in choosing a balance between regulation and competition. Let us therefore survey briefly some of the leading issues.[41]

The language of the Act To Regulate Commerce in 1887 was vague about the role competition was to play in the railroad industry. Formal freight and profit 'pools' were banned, but nothing was said about other modes of price-fixing. Consequently, rival railroads believed they were within the law in forming collusive rate-making associations, and they were allowed to do so by the Interstate Commerce Commission. However, these were declared illegal in the first substantive Supreme Court interpretations of the Sherman Antitrust Act.[42] Under subsequent revisions of the Interstate Commerce Act and with the encouragement of the ICC cooperative rate-making revived, but it was again found illegal in a 1945 Supreme Court decision.[43] In response, Congress in 1948 passed, over the veto of President Truman, the Reed-Bulwinkle Act, which expressly exempted the collective rate-setting practices of common carriers from antitrust prohibitions, as long as the rates decided upon are approved by the ICC. Consequently, railroad and common carrier truck freight rates are presently fixed cooperatively through regional rate-making bureaus.

Transportation firm mergers approved by the ICC, we observed in Chapter 20, have also gained exemption from antitrust after a harsh line was initially taken in the *Northern Securities* decision of 1904. Furthermore, the Commission exercises strict control over the entry of new firms into common carrier service and over the expansion of existing firms into new routes. Especially in trucking, new entry into a route linking two or more cities is seldom allowed if it will adversely affect the fortunes of a carrier already serving the route or unless there is compelling evidence that the present carriers are offering seriously inadequate service. As a consequence, operating rights obtained under 'grandfather clauses' or through later ICC grants are now sold at prices which reflect the capitalization of substantial scarcity rents.[44]

Despite governmental willingness to accept monopolistic restrictions in transportation, the forces of competition have had a habit of bursting the regulatory fetters. Technological change is one reason. The advent of the motor truck, pipelines, containerization, and 'piggyback' operations has repeatedly threatened to upset the *status quo*.[45] A characteristic response has been

---

this conclusion depends upon the arbitrary application of a 95 per cent statistical confidence rule. In seven tests covering the years 1922, 1932, and 1937, rates were found to be uniformly lower in states with regulation, *ceteris paribus*. The differences were significantly different from zero at better than the 90 per cent confidence level in four of these seven tests. When the independent variables in Table 2 of the Stigler-Friedland work are held at their means, regulation is found to reduce the average price per kilowatt hour sold by between 2 and 20 per cent.

[41]For a fuller treatment, see Meyer, Peck, Stenason, and Zwick, *op. cit.*; Merton J. Peck, "Competitive Policy for Transportation?" in Almarin Phillips, ed., *Perspectives on Antitrust Policy* (Cambridge: Harvard University Press, 1965), pp. 244–272; and the papers in the National Bureau of Economic Research conference volume, *Transportation Economics*, especially Merrill J. Roberts, "Transport Costs, Pricing, and Regulation," pp. 3–42.

[42]*U. S. v. Trans-Missouri Freight Association et al.*, 166 U. S. 290 (1897); and *U. S. v. Joint Traffic Association*, 171 U. S. 505 (1898).

[43]*Georgia v. Pennsylvania Railroad Co. et al.*, 324 U. S. 439 (1945).

[44]See James C. Nelson, "The Effects of Entry Control in Surface Transport," in *Transportation Economics*, pp. 381–422.

[45]Television, microwave radio relay, community antenna TV systems, communications satellites, and most recently long distance computer links have had the same effect in the communications field.

pressure—often successful—to extend or tighten the regulatory net. Transportation regulation was broadened to include common and contract motor carriers as the construction of good highways made trucks a potent competitive force in the 1930s, and in 1938 the airlines came under control. More recently, the regulated motor carriers have unsuccessfully urged the spread of control to exempted sectors of trucking (such as trucks hauling raw agricultural produce for hire, and perhaps even those used by manufacturing and retailing firms to carry their own freight), claiming that these competitors have captured much of the 'gravy' while leaving relatively unprofitable shipments to be handled by the common carriers. In short, there has been a tendency for regulation to spread and embrace fields competing with those currently regulated.

With a variety of transportation modes available, economic efficiency requires that a price structure be established which permits each mode to carry the freight on which it has a natural cost or service advantage. But the pricing system under regulation has not worked in this way. As noted previously, in the early days of railroading a "value of service" discriminatory pattern was adopted. Freight rates were much higher relative to marginal cost for high-value commodities than for low-value commodities. This was a profitable strategy, and it may have improved the allocation of resources in the era when railroads faced little competition from other media. However, when trucks arrived on the scene in large numbers, they captured much of the highly-rated traffic. This they did essentially by imitating the railroads' value of service rate structure. By quoting rates which more or less matched the railroad rates, but by providing quicker service, especially on less-than-carload shipments, the trucks offered shippers a more attractive total transportation package. The more highly valued the commodity was, the greater was the trucks' advantage in this inter-modal competition, since goods in transit constitute an inventory for either the shipper or his consignee,

and the inventory financing costs of slow railroad delivery rise in proportion to both the value of the commodity and the length of the delay.

At first, the railroads' sole reaction to this new competition was to demand regulation of trucking rates. But as their share of the highly rated commodities continued to erode, pulling profits down in tandem, they then began an effort to recover their position through rate adjustments. Here, however, they were frustrated by the regulatory system. The Interstate Commerce Commission has generally taken a dim view of vigorous price competition, intramodal or intermodal, and it has used its power over minimum rates to prevent competitive undercutting. In some cases it permitted the rails to do no more than match the rates quoted by truckers, leaving the trucks in a winning position because of their service advantage. In other situations it opposed railroad rate reductions which left insufficient revenue per ton-mile to cover fully allocated costs, including a substantial overhead component, even though marginal costs would have been more than covered. Similar difficulties were experienced by the railroads in their attempts to meet pipeline and water carrier competition.[46] The net result has been a significant decline of the railroads' share of inter-city ton-mile traffic carried—from 74 per cent in 1930 to 44 per cent in 1960— with highly-rated commodities bearing the brunt of the loss.[47]

That one means of transportation loses out to others in the competitive struggle is not in itself undesirable; it might merely be a symptom of progress. However, the utilization pattern encouraged by the intermodal freight rate structure developed under Interstate Commerce Commission regulation has been enormously deficient from the standpoint of efficient resource allocation. Meyer, Peck, Stenason, and Zwick conducted a thorough study of costs for railroads, trucks, piggyback operations, and other carriers. They found that as a broad rule of thumb, trucks have a comparative long-run marginal cost advantage over rails only on hauls of less than

---

[46]For a recent Supreme Court ruling against competitive marginal cost pricing, see *American Commercial Lines., et al.* v. *Louisville & Nashville R. Co. et al.,* 392 U. S. 5971 (1968).

[47]Cf. Peck, *op. cit.,* p. 250.

roughly 100 miles.[48] Yet 97 per cent of all manufactured goods ton-miles transported by common motor carriers in the early 1950s were on hauls of more than 100 miles—where railroads could have done the job at lower marginal cost.[49]

To illustrate what this implies, suppose that both the truck and rail rates for carrying a certain commodity between two points are $.80 per hundredweight. Because of their delivery time advantage, trucks get the job. Skirting some difficult problems of delimiting the long run, let us assume that the long-run marginal cost of carrying the commodity is $.70 per CWT by truck and $.50 (including in-transit delay costs) by rail. Suppose also that the short-run marginal cost of rail carriage (covering only the extra fuel, handling, and maintenance costs associated with running additional available engines and boxcars, plus delay costs to shippers) is $.35 per CWT. Then in the long run every hundredweight reallocated from the prevailing truck mode to rail would save society $.20. And since short-run trucking costs do not differ much from long-run costs, the short-run saving from such a reallocation of resources would be nearer $.35 per CWT.[50]

Extrapolating from comparative cost and traffic distribution data collected in his joint study with Meyer and others, Professor Peck has estimated that the annual social loss due to rail-truck misallocations of this sort was on the order of several billion dollars during 1963.[51] Nor is the problem confined to relationships between the railroads and common motor carriers. By imitating the railroads' value of service

pricing scheme, the motor carriers have rendered themselves vulnerable to exempted media. Manufacturing companies, for instance, have achieved impressive monetary savings by transporting their highly-rated products in their own trucks, even though common carriers (with better assurance of a back-haul load) could often carry the freight at lower social cost. Oi and Hurter have estimated the misallocation losses from this source alone to have been between $375 and 500 million per year as of 1962.[52] Complicating matters are the ICC restrictions on routes a carrier can use. For example, truckers are often required to haul a load between two authorized points by a circuitous route because they have no operating rights to use the most direct route.[53] In short, while one may quibble over whether the annual social loss due to faulty transportation service pricing is $2 billion, $6 billion, or some figure in between, it is clear that the present system of rate-setting and entry control has made a mess of things.[54]

The remedy proposed in the Meyer-Peck-Stenason-Zwick study and approved by many other economists is a major de-escalation of transportation regulation, combined with increased reliance on the forces of competition. Meyer and associates would eliminate rate regulation completely for truck, water, and air carriers. Interstate Commerce Commission control of minimum rail freight rates would be ended to permit marginal cost pricing of services on which the railroads have a comparative advantage, while maximum rate regulation would be con-

---

[48]Meyer et al., op. cit., pp. 188–194. Obviously, this dividing line is crude; it varies with such factors as the value of the commodity, the condition of the rail and highway arteries connecting the points, whether or not the shipper and consignee have efficient rail sidings, the amount of urban street congestion, etc.

[49]Ibid., pp. 194–195. Ninety-one per cent of the truck traffic was carried more than 200 miles.

[50]A high proportion of total truck costs consists of labor, gasoline, tire, and maintenance expenditures, which are variable in the very short run. Over-the-road equipment wears out in roughly six years, so the long run for most trucking capital is not very long. Terminal buildings often have attractive alternative uses, so their long-run opportunity cost is small. Of course, highways are provided by the government and financed through user charges which are a short-run variable cost to truck operators but which may not entail correspondingly high short-run marginal *social* costs.

[51]Cf. Peck, op. cit., p. 247; and Meyer et al., op. cit., pp. 159–165. Peck's estimates are apparently made in terms of a "medium run" horizon of five to ten years, although his assumptions are not clearly specified.

[52]Walter Y. Oi and Arthur P. Hurter, *Economics of Private Truck Transportation* (Dubuque: Brown, 1965), p. 353. See also M. L. Burstein et al., *The Cost of Trucking: Econometric Analysis* (Dubuque: Brown, 1965).

[53]See Nelson, "The Effects of Entry Control . . . ," pp. 389–395.

[54]While it is unfashionable to temper one's criticism of either the American railroads or the ICC, it is worth noting that other nations have had their fair share of rail vs. truck allocation problems. See "Blitzing Trucks off the Highway," *Business Week*, November 11, 1967, pp. 104–109, for a discussion of German and British difficulties.

tinued to prevent the abuse of whatever monopoly power the railroads retain. To speed the convergence of transportation service prices toward long-run marginal cost, collusion in rate-making would once again be subjected to Sherman Act Section 1 prohibitions.

One risk in such a change is that the transportation industry could not endure it financially, reverting to seizures of all-out price-cutting with much greater potential for financial ruin than those which motivated the imposition of regulation during the 1880s. In reply, Meyer and associates argue that the number of railroads competing for traffic on any given route is so small, and the instinct of cooperation among rail executives so well-developed, that recognition of mutual interdependence would prevent carriers from engaging in destructive intramodal price warfare. Peck has estimated in addition that a reduction in rail rates to attract high-return traffic away from the other media would enhance, or at least would not reduce, presently meager profits.[55] This assumes, however, that the elasticity of demand faced by the railroads for such commodities, taking into account feasible reactions in trucking rates, is well in excess of unity—an assumption on which it is difficult to be altogether sanguine.[56] Should demand prove to be inelastic, it might be necessary to provide government subsidies in order to achieve allocative efficiency while averting widespread bankruptcy.

How a deregulated trucking industry would perform is also not certain. Meyer and associates believe it would adjust easily. It is different from railroading in several vital respects: the minimum optimal scale of operation appears to be much smaller; many high volume routes are served by dozens of rival lines; and fixed costs are modest relative to total costs, with virtually all costs being fully avoidable over a span of more than six years. As a result, the industry could adjust its capacity to major shifts in demand over a fairly short (but painful) period. Nevertheless, trucking does have some attributes conducive to instability, especially on routes with too little

volume to support more than two or three lines. The companies sell a service which cannot be stored; an empty truck is an opportunity lost forever. Also, because the commodities transported are extremely heterogeneous, each with its own cost-of-hauling characteristics, recognition of mutual interdependence is likely to be weak and incentives for independent pricing strong. Yet marginal costs place a relatively high floor under the level to which price warfare can be carried, and the pricing and service instability which does appear on low-volume routes is likely to be but a moderate and transitory blemish in the overall picture.

Thus, much more extensive reliance on competition as an impersonal regulator of the transportation industries appears on balance to be a sound policy. The main roadblock to a new legislative and administrative start is fear of the unknown, cultivated by the self-interested opposition of some carriers and the Interstate Commerce Commission. The latter, like any bureaucracy, is naturally reluctant to support abolition of its assigned responsibilities or to admit that the tasks to which its staff has devoted countless years are socially disfunctional.

Up to the time when this chapter was written, neither Congress nor the Executive Branch had taken any truly bold steps toward changing the mix of competition vs. regulation in the transportation industries. However, in 1967 a new Department of Transportation was created. Its long-run mission is the development of a coordinated transportation system. The Interstate Commerce Commission, Civil Aeronautics Board and Federal Maritime Board continue to be independent of the Department, and in its infant years the Department trod warily, studiously avoiding an all-out confrontation with the regulators. Still all concerned recognize that conflict is inevitable, given the inadequacies of the U. S. transportation system and its regulatory environment. It does not seem unduly optimistic to expect that greatly improved policies will emerge from such a confrontation and to hope that the initiative is exercised before long.

---

[55] Cf. Peck, *op. cit.*, pp. 261–265; and Meyer *et al.*, *op. cit.*, pp. 194–202.

[56] For a skeptical view, see Roberts, *op. cit.*, pp. 20–28.

CONCLUSION

We have come full circle. We began our analysis 21 chapters ago by developing the case in economic theory and social policy for competitive market processes. In the classic public utility sectors it is difficult or impossible to achieve fully competitive market structures without unacceptable scale economy sacrifices. Yet he instruments of direct public regulation evolved to compensate for the absence of work able competition have created so many new problems that we are drawn once again toward relying upon competitive forces, perhaps in attenuated or hybrid forms, whenever it is at all feasible. This is a clear indication that the road map we have used in our quest for good industrial performance, although imperfect, is basically sound. And this is as good a note as any on which to close.

Appendix to Chapter 2

The purpose of this appendix is to demonstrate some central points in the welfare economics of competition and monopoly. It does not pretend to be an exhaustive exposition of general equilibrium theory or welfare economics. The reader with sufficient mathematical background and with a desire to penetrate further is urged to consult one of the more ambitious standard expositions.

For our present purposes the optimal tradeoff between simplicity of notation and richness calls for analyzing an economy with three consumption goods, X, Y, and leisure (which is the difference between the number of hours available per time period and hours worked L); along with one input, homogeneous labor hours L. There can be as many or as few consumers and producing firms as the analysis requires. The total quantity of output consumed or labor supplied is the sum of the quantities consumed or supplied by individual members of society. Thus, where x_i is the quantity of good X consumed by the ith consumer, the total quantity consumed $X = \sum_i x_i$. Similarly, $Y = \sum_i y_i$ and $L = \sum_i l_i$.

We begin with the seemingly innocuous but in fact powerful criterion of Pareto optimality in consumption. Social welfare cannot be at a maximum if it is possible through reallocation to make some consumer better off without making any other consumer worse off. To see what this entails, let $U^i(x_i,y_i,l_i)$ be the utility function of the ith consumer and $U^j(x_j,y_j,l_j)$ the utility function of the jth consumer. Where U^i_X is the first derivative of the ith consumer's utility function with respect to X and U^i_{XX} the second derivative, we assume that $U^i_X > 0$; $U^i_{XX} < 0$; $U^i_Y > 0$; $U^i_{YY} < 0$; $U^i_L < 0$; and $U^i_{LL} < 0$. We maximize U^i subject to the condition that consumer j's utility U^j be held constant at U^{j*}, and subject to the further condition that the two individuals' consumption and labor supplies sum to the amounts X, Y, and L, assumed provisionally to be fixed:

(1) $\text{Max } \Gamma = U^i(x_i,y_i,l_i) - \gamma_1[U^j(x_j,y_j,l_j) - U^{j*}] - \gamma_2(x_i + x_j - X)$
$\qquad\qquad - \gamma_3(y_i + y_j - Y) - \gamma_4(l_i + l_j - L).$

Differentiating with respect to the quantities consumed by individuals i and j, we obtain the following first order conditions for a maximum:

(2a) $\dfrac{\partial \Gamma}{\partial x_i} = U^i_X - \gamma_2 = 0;$

(2b) $\dfrac{\partial \Gamma}{\partial y_i} = U^i_Y - \gamma_3 = 0;$

(2c) $\dfrac{\partial \Gamma}{\partial l_i} = U_L^i - \gamma_4 = 0;$

(2d) $\dfrac{\partial \Gamma}{\partial x_j} = \gamma_1 U_X^j - \gamma_2 = 0;$

(2e) $\dfrac{\partial \Gamma}{\partial y_j} = \gamma_1 U_Y^i - \gamma_3 = 0;$ and

(2f) $\dfrac{\partial \Gamma}{\partial l_j} = \gamma_1 U_L^j - \gamma_4 = 0.$

Rearranging and dividing through by the conditions for Y as the numeraire commodity, we obtain:

(3a) $\dfrac{U_X^i}{U_Y^i} = \dfrac{\gamma_2}{\gamma_3} = \dfrac{U_X^j}{U_Y^j};$ and

(3b) $\dfrac{U_L^i}{U_Y^i} = \dfrac{\gamma_4}{\gamma_3} = \dfrac{U_L^j}{U_Y^j}.$

A Pareto-optimal allocation of consumption goods requires that the ratio of the marginal utilities of any two goods—i.e., the marginal rate of substitution—for any given consumer equal the marginal rates of substitution of the same commodity pair for all consumers and for all commodity pairs. If this set of ratio equalities does not hold, it is possible to make at least one consumer better off (increasing his utility) without making any other consumer worse off, and so welfare cannot be at a maximum.

Many different consumption goods allocations will undoubtedly satisfy this set of conditions, although only one may be consistent with a given real income distribution and/or set of initial resource endowments. To go from conditions like (3a) and (3b) to specifying a global welfare optimum, it is necessary somehow to combine the utility functions of individual consumers into an aggregate social welfare function. No useful purpose would be served by plunging into the many difficulties any such attempt involves. We shall simply assume that a social welfare function

(4) $\underset{x_i, y_i, l_i}{U = U(X,Y,L) = \text{Max } \mathcal{U}[U^i(x_i, y_i, l_i)]}$

can in fact be defined. The reader may, if he wishes, interpret U in any of at least three ways: as reflecting the preferences of some representative consumer with whom we are uniquely concerned; as reflecting the preferences of some central authority, democratically or dictatorially selected; or as reflecting a social consensus approving the existing distribution of income or the distribution with which individuals enter the market after various redistributive measures have been effected. The third approach is most realistic and most closely compatible with the spirit of Chapter 2, but it has no unique claim to scientific or moral validity. What is crucial here is only one point. However the social welfare function is put together, it cannot attain a maximum for society as a whole unless the Pareto-optimal conditions (3a) and (3b) for individual consumers are satisfied.

The production opportunities open to society with a given state of technological knowledge can be represented by a transformation function defined in implicit form $T(X,Y,L) = 0$. Society's objective is to maximize social welfare $U(X,Y,L)$ subject to the limitations imposed by the transformation function. We define the Lagrangian function:

(5) $\text{Max } \Lambda = U(X,Y,L) - \lambda [T(X,Y,L)].$

First order conditions for a maximum include:

(6a) $\dfrac{\partial \Lambda}{\partial X} = U_X - \lambda T_X = 0; \dfrac{U_X}{T_X} = \lambda;$

(6b) $\dfrac{\partial \Lambda}{\partial Y} = U_Y - \lambda T_Y = 0; \dfrac{U_Y}{T_Y} = \lambda;$ and

(6c) $\dfrac{\partial \Lambda}{\partial L} = U_L - \lambda T_L = 0; \dfrac{U_L}{T_L} = \lambda.$

In view of the common equalities with λ, these can be reduced to:

(7a) $\dfrac{U_X}{T_X} = \dfrac{U_Y}{T_Y};$ so $\dfrac{U_X}{U_Y} = \dfrac{T_X}{T_Y};$ and

(7b) $\dfrac{U_L}{T_L} = \dfrac{U_Y}{T_Y};$ so $\dfrac{U_L}{U_Y} = \dfrac{T_L}{T_Y}.$

The ratios U_X/U_Y and U_L/U_Y are marginal social rates of substitution directly analogous to the individual marginal rates of substitution in (3a) and (3b). The ratio T_X/T_Y is a marginal rate of transformation, equal except in sign to the slope of a familiar transformation curve like $t\,t'$ in Figure 2A.1, assuming some given quantity of labor and other inputs. To see this, we differentiate the transformation function implicitly to obtain $T_X\,dX + T_Y\,dY + T_L\,dL = 0$. If L is held constant, $dL = 0$. We have then:

(8) $T_X\,dX + T_Y\,dY = 0.$

Rearranging, we obtain:

(9) $-\dfrac{T_X}{T_Y} = \dfrac{dY}{dX},$

where dY/dX is obviously the slope of the transformation curve.

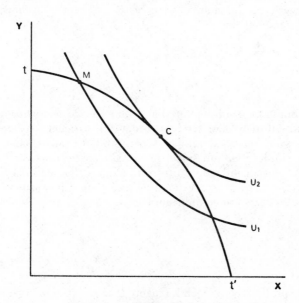

Figure 2A.1
Maximizing Social Welfare

The social welfare function can be represented by a field of social indifference curves like U_1 and U_2 in Figure 2A.1. By analogous manipulation, it can be seen that their slope at any point is the ratio $-U_X/U_Y$, or the marginal social rate of substitution. For social welfare to be at a maximum (as at point C in Figure 2A.1) a social indifference curve must be tangent to the transformation curve. This means that their slopes must be equal, and so $U_X/U_Y = T_X/T_Y$, as equation (7a) states. The conditions implied by equation (7b) could be represented by a similar though less familiar figure.

All this preliminary groundwork is necessary to specify what conditions an optimal (social welfare-maximizing) allocation of resources must satisfy. Concretely, we look for the satisfaction of global conditions (7a) and (7b) and at a more disaggregated level individual consumer conditions (3a) and (3b). Do competitive and monopolistic market processes in fact meet these standards? To find out, we must investigate the role prices play in the market economy.

Consider first the behavior of any representative consumer i with utility function $U^i(x_i, y_i, l_i)$ confronted with parametric prices P^X, P^Y, and W for good X, good Y, and his labor services respectively. The consumer maximizes his utility subject to the constraint that his expenditures on consumption $P^X x_i + P^Y y_i$ equal his income from work $W l_i$. Thus, we have:

(10) $\text{Max } \Theta = U^i(x_i, y_i, l_i) - \theta (P^X x_i + P^Y y_i - W l_i).$

Differentiating with respect to x_i, y_i, and l_i and rearranging the necessary first order conditions for a maximum, we obtain:

(11a) $\dfrac{U^i_X}{U^i_Y} = \dfrac{P^X}{P^Y}$; and

(11b) $\dfrac{U^i_L}{U^i_Y} = \dfrac{-W}{P^Y}.$

Since similar conditions must hold for every consumer and since (in an idealized world) each consumer faces the same set of prices P^X, P^Y, and W, it must be true that for any consumers i and j that:

(12a) $\dfrac{U^i_X}{U^i_Y} = \dfrac{P^X}{P^Y} = \dfrac{U^j_X}{U^j_Y}$; and

(12b) $\dfrac{U^i_L}{U^i_Y} = \dfrac{-W}{P^Y} = \dfrac{U^j_L}{U^j_Y}.$

Therefore, Pareto optimum conditions (3a) and (3b) are satisfied when all consumers purchase goods and sell their labor services at identical parametric prices. Since each consumer has the same marginal rate of substitution for any commodity pair in utility-maximizing equilibrium, and since the social welfare function is simply some weighted aggregation of all individual utility functions, the marginal social rates of substitution must be equal to the corresponding price ratios in consumer equilibrium. Thus, we have as a condition of equilibrium:

(13a) $\dfrac{U_X}{U_Y} = \dfrac{P^X}{P^Y}$; and

(13b) $-\dfrac{U_L}{U_Y} = \dfrac{W}{P^Y}.$

Now suppose the production of X and Y using L as an input is organized competitively. To avoid notational complexity, let us assume that X is produced by a representative competitive firm with the production function $X = \mathcal{X} (L^X)$ and that Y is produced by a representative firm with the production function $Y = \mathcal{Y} (L^Y)$. The firm producing X maximizes:

(14) $\quad \pi^X = P^X \mathcal{X} (L^X) - WL^X.$

Differentiating with respect to L^X, we obtain the first order maximum condition:

(15) $\quad \dfrac{d\pi^X}{dL^X} = P^X \dfrac{dX}{dL^X} - W = 0.$

Likewise, the firm producing Y maximizes:

(16) $\quad \pi^Y = P^Y \mathcal{Y}(L^Y) - WL^Y.$

Differentiating, we obtain:

(17) $\quad \dfrac{d\pi^Y}{dL^Y} = P^Y \dfrac{dY}{dL^Y} - W = 0.$

Assuming that all producers pay the same wage W, equations (15) and (17) solve to the equilibrium condition:

(18) $\quad \dfrac{P^X}{P^Y} = \dfrac{\dfrac{dY}{dL^Y}}{\dfrac{dX}{dL^X}}.$

From (17) we have also:

(19) $\quad \dfrac{W}{P^Y} = \dfrac{dY}{dL^Y}.$

But as long as there are no external effects in production, the right hand sides of (18) and (19) are merely microscopic replications of the transformation ratios T_X/T_Y and T_L/T_Y respectively. To see this, we recall that $T_X \, dX + T_Y \, dY + T_L \, dL = 0$. Holding X constant, we have $T_Y \, dY + T_L \, dL = 0$. This solves to:

(20) $\quad -\dfrac{T_L}{T_Y} = \dfrac{dY}{dL},$

which is the aggregate analogue of the right hand side of (19). Holding Y constant, we obtain $- T_L/T_X = dX/dL$. Using this and (20), it follows that:

(21) $\quad \dfrac{\dfrac{dY}{dL}}{\dfrac{dX}{dL}} = \dfrac{-\dfrac{T_L}{T_Y}}{-\dfrac{T_L}{T_X}} = \dfrac{T_X}{T_Y},$

which is the society-wide analogue of (18).

Introducing into competitive profit maximization conditions (18) and (19) equations (20) and (21) and consumer equilibrium conditions (13a) and (13b), we obtain our final set of competitive equilibrium conditions:

(22a) $\quad \dfrac{\dfrac{dY}{dL^Y}}{\dfrac{dX}{dL^X}} = \dfrac{T_X}{T_Y} = \dfrac{P^X}{P^Y} = \dfrac{U_X}{U_Y};$ and

(22b) $\dfrac{dY}{dL^Y} = -\dfrac{T_L}{T_Y} = \dfrac{W}{P^Y} = -\dfrac{U_L}{U_Y}.$

Thus, equations (7a) and (7b) necessary for a welfare maximum are satisfied under competition as consumers and producers equate their respective marginal rates of substitution and marginal rates of transformation to the common price ratios P^X/P^Y and W/P^Y. In this way competitive market processes provide the basis for achieving an efficient allocation of resources.[1]

Suppose now that the sector producing good X is monopolized. No longer can the producer of good X consider the price P^X to be a parameter unaffected by its output decisions. Rather, it must take into account its demand function $P^X = D^X(X) = D^X [\mathfrak{X}(L^X)]$. Its total revenue $R^X = D^X [\mathfrak{X}(L^X)] \cdot \mathfrak{X}(L^X)$. It maximizes $\pi^X = R^X - W L^X$, with the first order maximum condition:

(23) $\dfrac{d\pi^X}{dL^X} = \dfrac{dR^X}{dX} \dfrac{dX}{dL^X} - W = 0.$

If Y continues to be produced competitively, equation (17) still holds as the profit maximization condition for sector Y. Combining equations (17) and (23) and introducing transformation relations (20) and (21), we obtain the production equilibrium conditions:

(24a) $\dfrac{\dfrac{dY}{dL^Y}}{\dfrac{dX}{dL^X}} = \dfrac{T_X}{T_Y} = \dfrac{\dfrac{dR^X}{dX}}{P^Y};$ and

(24b) $\dfrac{dY}{dL^Y} = -\dfrac{T_L}{T_Y} = \dfrac{W}{P^Y}.$

Note that (24a) differs from the left hand side of (22a) in the replacement of P^X by dR^X/dX. Since $dR^X/dX < P^X$ under monopoly, $\dfrac{dR^X}{dX} \Big/ P^Y$ in (24a) is necessarily less than P^X/P^Y. Consumers meanwhile make the best of the price ratio P^X/P^Y. Equilibrium occurs in a mixed monopolistic and competitive economy where:

(25) $\dfrac{T_X}{T_Y} = \dfrac{\dfrac{dR^X}{dX}}{P^Y} < \dfrac{P^X}{P^Y} = \dfrac{U_X}{U_Y}.$

Clearly, condition (7a) necessary for a welfare maximum is violated. The slope of the social indifference curve attained when X is sold monopolistically and Y competitively exceeds the slope of the transformation curve—i.e., at a point like M in Figure 2A.1. Society ends up on the lower social indifference curve U_1, with relatively less X and relatively more Y produced than at the competitive and optimal equilibrium position C.

One way to try escaping this unhappy state of affairs is to enforce a 'world of monopolies' solution, letting industry Y be monopolized too. Suppose that $dR^X/dX = k P^X$ in equilibrium, where $k = \left(1 - \dfrac{1}{\eta_X}\right) < 1$ when η_X is the price elasticity of de-

---

[1]We ignore certain other conditions necessary for a welfare maximum—notably, the absence of corner equilibria in which none of some good is consumed or produced, and the satisfaction of various market clearing equations. To derive a full set of sufficient conditions for a maximum would carry us beyond the objectives of this appendix.

mand for good X.[2] If by chance (due to identical equilibrium price elasticities) or coercion it is possible to make the marginal revenue dR^Y/dY to producers of Y equal $k\,P^Y$, equilibrium of the goods markets will occur with the following conditions:

$$(26)\quad \frac{\dfrac{dY}{dL^Y}}{\sqrt{\dfrac{dX}{dL^X}}} = \frac{T_X}{T_Y} = \frac{\dfrac{dR^X}{dX}}{\dfrac{dR^Y}{dY}} = \frac{k\,P^X}{k\,P^Y} = \frac{P^X}{P^Y} = \frac{U_X}{U_Y}.$$

In this case welfare maximum condition (7a) is again satisfied. However, now problems arise in satisfying condition (7b.) With production of Y monopolized, the profit-maximizing condition is $\dfrac{dR^Y}{dY}\dfrac{dY}{dL^Y} = W$. We assume as before that $dR^Y/dY = k\,P^Y$. Rearranging and using (20), we obtain:

$$(27)\quad \frac{dY}{dL^Y} = -\frac{T_L}{T_Y} = \frac{W}{k\,P^Y}.$$

Clearly, $W\,/\,k\,P^Y > W\,/\,P^Y$. By (13b) consumers as labor suppliers react to their market environment by setting $-\,U_L/U_Y = W/P^Y$. Equilibrium occurs where:

$$(28)\quad -\frac{T_L}{T_Y} = \frac{W}{k\,P^Y} > \frac{W}{P^Y} = -\frac{U_L}{U_Y},$$

which fails to satisfy welfare maximum condition (7b). The ratio of the price of leisure to the price of good Y as perceived by consumers *qua* labor suppliers is lower than the ratio $W/k\,P^Y$ guiding producer decisions. Unless the labor supply is perfectly inelastic (i.e., $U_L = -\,\infty$), equilibrium occurs with relatively more leisure and relatively fewer goods being consumed than under that set of choices which maximizes social welfare. In effect, the transformation curve $t\,t'$ in Figure 2A.1 is shifted inward, though the goods market equilibrium continues to occur at a tangency point like *C*. To restore the equality between T_L/T_Y and U_L/U_Y required by (7b), it would be necessary somehow either to reduce the wage producers perceive themselves to pay by the factor k or to increase the wage consumers as labor suppliers perceive themselves to receive by the factor $1/k$. Although this might conceivably be achieved through a system of subsidies, the scheme hardly seems practical.

The other leading alternative is to strive for a second-best optimum. There are various possible formulations. Here we present only the most general approach taken by Lipsey and Lancaster.[3] We assume that monopoly in the production of good X prevents society from satisfying welfare maximization conditions (7a) and/or (7b). To bar the attainment of a first-best world of monopolies solution there must also be some sector—i.e., the labor-leisure market—whose behavior cannot effectively be diverted from competitive rules. Thus, we begin with the assumption that it is impossible to bring the marginal rate of substitution between X and L into equality with their marginal rate of transformation. Concretely,

$$(29)\quad \frac{T_X}{T_L} = k\,\frac{U_X}{U_L},$$

where $k = (1 - 1/\eta_X) < 1$. This condition acts as a constraint upon society's ability to maximize its welfare. To secure a second-best optimum it is necessary to

[2] A proof is given in footnote 72, p. 176 *infra*.
[3] "The General Theory of Second Best," *Review of Economic Studies*, 1956–57, vol. 24, no. 1, pp. 26–27.

manipulate outputs and prices in controllable sectors—in this case, in sector Y only—
so as to maximize $U(X,Y,L)$ subject to $T(X,Y,L) = 0$ *and* to (29) as a further constraint. We set up the Lagrangian function:

$$(30) \quad \text{Max } \Phi = U(X,Y,L) - \lambda[T(X,Y,L)] - \phi\left[\frac{T_X}{T_L} - k\frac{U_X}{U_L}\right].$$

The first order conditions for a maximum include:

$$(31a) \quad \frac{\partial \Phi}{\partial X} = U_X - \lambda T_X - \phi\left[\frac{T_L T_{XX} - T_X T_{XL}}{(T_L)^2} - k\frac{U_L U_{XX} - U_X U_{XL}}{(U_L)^2}\right] = 0;$$

$$(31b) \quad \frac{\partial \Phi}{\partial Y} = U_Y - \lambda T_Y - \phi\left[\frac{T_L T_{XY} - T_X T_{YL}}{(T_L)^2} - k\frac{U_L U_{XY} - U_X U_{YL}}{(U_L)^2}\right] = 0; \text{ and}$$

$$(31c) \quad \frac{\partial \Phi}{\partial L} = U_L = \lambda T_L - \phi\left[\frac{T_L T_{XL} - T_X T_{LL}}{(T_L)^2} - k\frac{U_L U_{XL} - U_X U_{LL}}{(U_L)^2}\right] = 0.$$

Rearranging to a form comparable with (7a), this means that the behavior of firms
producing Y must be altered so as to satisfy second-best equilibrium conditions like:

$$(32) \quad \frac{U_X}{U_Y} = \frac{P^X}{P^Y} = \frac{T_X + \dfrac{\phi}{\lambda}\left[\dfrac{T_L T_{XX} - T_X T_{XL}}{(T_L)^2} - k\dfrac{U_L U_{XX} - U_X U_{XL}}{(U_L)^2}\right]}{T_Y + \dfrac{\phi}{\lambda}\left[\dfrac{T_L T_{XY} - T_X T_{YL}}{(T_L)^2} - k\dfrac{U_L U_{XY} - U_X U_{YL}}{(U_L)^2}\right]}.$$

This, as the saying goes, plus $.30 will get you a ride on the New York subway. There
is no way short of having detailed information on tastes and technology to evaluate
the signs of such cross-partial derivatives as U_{XY} and T_{YL}, and even if the signs of all
derivatives were known, the signs of the complete bracketed terms could be determined only if the exact magnitudes of all their components were ascertained. Without
knowing the bracketed terms' signs, it is impossible to tell whether the production of
good Y should be extended until the value of labor's marginal product $P^Y \dfrac{dY}{dL^Y}$ falls
below the wage or whether it should be stopped short of the competitive optimum.
Thus, without detailed information one cannot even provide rough qualitative guidance
on how a second-best solution is to be implemented.

There may be an escape from this dilemma under certain circumstances. We
examine only the one first suggested by Davis and Whinston.[4] If the welfare and
transformation functions are *separable*, all cross-partial derivatives such as U_{XY} and
T_{YL} equal zero. This occurs when a consumer's marginal utility from good X is
unaffected by changes in the amount of good Y consumed, or when the marginal
physical product in producing Y is unaffected by changes in the total amount of labor
employed. If both the welfare and transformation functions are separable, then for a
commodity whose production is susceptible to second-best manipulation the bracketed
expression in its first order maximum condition (i.e., equation 31b) has a zero value
and first-best behavior rules may (ignoring certain numeraire problems) continue to
be optimal. However, it seems probable that this requirement is seldom satisfied widely
in a world of extensive complementarity and substitution in consumption and production.

[4]Otto A. Davis and Andrew B. Whinston, "Welfare Economics and the Theory of Second Best," *Review of
Economic Studies*, January 1965, pp. 2–3.

Appendix to Chapter 22[1]

The behavior of a firm subjected to "fair return on fair value" regulation can be analyzed as follows. Let K be the amount of capital (measured in dollar units) used and included in the rate base. Let L be the number of labor man years employed. We assume for simplicity only two inputs. The market wage of labor is w, the market cost of capital r, and the allowed rate of return on capital $r + \delta$, where the premium δ is assumed to be positive. The production function is given by:

(1) $\quad Q = Q(K, L)$.

The firm's demand function as a monopolist is:

(2) $\quad P = P(Q) = P(Q(K, L))$.

The rate of return on capital is defined as $\dfrac{Q \cdot P(Q) - wL}{K}$; i.e., the surplus of revenues less non-capital costs over the dollar value of the capital stock. We assume that the allowed rate of return $r + \delta$ is less than the rate of return which the firm would earn as an unregulated monopolist. Thus, the utility is bound by the constraint on its profits:

(3) $\quad \dfrac{Q \cdot P(Q) - wL}{K} = r + \delta$,

which can be rewritten in the implicit form:

(4) $\quad Q \cdot P(Q) - wL - (r + \delta)K = 0$.

The utility's problem is to maximize its net profits $Q \cdot P(Q) - wL - rK$ subject to equation (4) as a regulatory constraint. We form the Lagrangian function:

(5) $\quad \text{Max } \Lambda = Q \cdot P(Q) - wL - rK - \lambda[Q \cdot P(Q) - wL - (r + \delta)K]$,

where λ is an undetermined multiplier. Note that if $\lambda = 0$, the regulatory constraint is not binding. The firm can in effect choose the pure monopoly outcome unimpeded. If $\lambda = 1$, equation (5) reduces to:

(6) $\quad \text{Max } \Lambda = \delta K$,

which implies that every dollar of capital hired adds to profits by δ dollars, suggesting the implausible result that infinite amounts of capital will be hired. We expect therefore that $0 < \lambda < 1$.

---

[1] I am indebted to William J. Baumol for suggesting the approach taken in equations (14) and (15) and to Darius Gaskins for many valuable suggestions and criticisms. A similar approach leading to some of the conclusions presented here was taken by Akira Takayama in "Behavior of the Firm under Regulatory Constraint," *American Economic Review*, June 1969, pp. 255–260.

For a constrained profit maximum, equation (5) must be differentiated with respect to K, L, and λ; and the derivatives set equal to zero:

(7) $\dfrac{\partial \Lambda}{\partial K} = R_K - r - \lambda R_K + \lambda(r + \delta) = (1 - \lambda)R_K - (1 - \lambda)r + \lambda\delta = 0$;

(8) $\dfrac{\partial \Lambda}{\partial L} = R_L - w - \lambda R_L + \lambda w = (1 - \lambda)R_L - (1 - \lambda)w = 0$;

(9) $\dfrac{\partial \Lambda}{\partial \lambda} = R - wL - (r + \delta)K = 0$;

where R is total revenue $P \cdot Q$, R_K is the marginal revenue product of capital, and R_L is the marginal revenue product of labor.

Rearranging (8), we find that:

(10) $R_L = w$;

which means that the marginal revenue product of labor is equal to the wage, as in any profit-maximizing monopoly. However, equation (7) rearranges to:

(11) $R_K = r - \dfrac{\lambda\delta}{1 - \lambda}$.

When $0 < \lambda < 1$ and $\delta > 0$, $\dfrac{\lambda\delta}{1 - \lambda} > 0$, and so capital is hired until its marginal revenue product falls *below* the market cost of capital. The right hand side of (11) is the implicit cost of capital, as reported in Table 22.2. The term $\dfrac{\lambda\delta}{1 - \lambda}$ can be called the *distortion factor*, since it measures the amount by which the ratio of R_K to R_L (and hence the ratio of the marginal physical product of capital to the marginal physical product of labor) is prevented from coming into equality with r/w, as efficiency in production requires.

The combination of equations (10) and (11) shows that too much capital is hired relative to the amount of labor when the rate of return constraint is binding; that is, the capital/labor ratio is too high for efficiency in production. Now, does this problem worsen or improve as δ is increased, raising the gap between the allowed rate of return and the market cost of capital? Does K/L rise or fall as δ increases? Differentiating K/L with respect to δ, we obtain:

(12) $\dfrac{d(K/L)}{d\delta} = \dfrac{L\dfrac{dK}{d\delta} - K\dfrac{dL}{d\delta}}{L^2}$.

If the K/L distortion falls with increases in δ, the numerator of the right hand side must be negative. Dividing through by L and K, we rearrange the numerator of (12) to:

(13) $\dfrac{dK}{d\delta}/K - \dfrac{dL}{d\delta}/L$,

which must be negative for the K/L distortion to fall as δ increases.

To find out whether this occurs, we differentiate (8) and (9) implicitly:

(14) $(1 - \lambda)R_{KL}dK + (1 - \lambda)R_{LL}dL + (w - R_L)d\lambda = 0$; and

(15) $(R_K - r - \delta)dK + (R_L - w)dL - Kd\delta = 0$;

where R_{KL} is the cross partial derivative of the revenue function, R_{LL} is the second derivative of R with respect to labor, etc. Note that by (10), the $(w - R_L)d\lambda$ term of (14) and the $(R_L - w)dL$ term of (15) drop out. Rearranging (15), we obtain:

(16) $\dfrac{dK}{d\delta} = \dfrac{K}{R_K - r - \delta}.$

By (11), $R_K < r$. Therefore $(R_K - r - \delta) < 0$, and so $dK/d\delta$ is necessarily negative. As δ rises, the equilibrium quantity of capital declines. This alone does not necessarily imply that the degree of distortion falls as δ increases. It is conceivable that the rising production cost associated with an increasing distortion might lead to price increases which so curtail the quantity of output demanded that less capital is used even though K/L rises.

After cancelling the $(1 - \lambda)$ terms, equation (14) can be solved for:

(17) $dK = -\dfrac{R_{LL}dL}{R_{KL}}.$

Substituting (17) into (15), we obtain:

(18) $(R_K - r - \delta)\left(-\dfrac{R_{LL}dL}{R_{KL}}\right) - Kd\delta = 0.$

This can be rewritten:

(19) $\dfrac{dL}{d\delta} = -\dfrac{R_{KL}K}{R_{LL}(R_K - r - \delta)}.$

Normally we should expect R_{LL} to be negative, reflecting the customary negative slope of the marginal revenue product function. Since $(R_K - r - \delta) < 0$, $R_{LL}(R_K - r - \delta) > 0$. If then $R_{KL} < 0$, $dL/d\delta > 0$. This, combined with the negativity of $dK/d\delta$, would mean that K/L falls as δ increases. However, there is no *a priori* reason why R_{KL} must be negative. Written out fully,

(20) $R_{KL} = \dfrac{\partial R}{\partial Q}\dfrac{\partial^2 Q}{\partial K \partial L} + \dfrac{\partial Q}{\partial K}\dfrac{\partial Q}{\partial L}\dfrac{\partial^2 R}{\partial Q^2};$

where $\dfrac{\partial^2 R}{\partial Q^2} = 2\dfrac{\partial P}{\partial Q} + \dfrac{\partial^2 P}{\partial Q^2}.$ It is possible that an increase in the quantity of one input will raise the marginal physical product of the other input, making the first term of (20) positive, and this need not be offset due to the typically (but with convex downward or irregularly shaped demand curves, not necessarily) negative value of $\dfrac{\partial^2 R}{\partial Q^2}.$

Should both $dK/d\delta$ and $dL/d\delta$ be negative, the effect of changes in δ on the amount and direction of Averch-Johnson distortion must depend upon the *relative* rates of change of K and L. In view of these complexities, it is evident that no completely general conclusions can be drawn.

However, concrete conclusions can be reached for an important special case: the generalized Cobb-Douglas production function combined with a linear demand function. Let the production function be:

(21) $Q = gL^\alpha K^\beta,$

and the demand function:

(22) $P = a - bQ.$

Differentiating and substituting to satisfy (20),

(23) $R_{KL} = (a - 2bQ)(\alpha\beta g L^{\alpha-1}K^{\beta-1}) + (\beta g L^{\alpha}K^{\beta-1})(\alpha g L^{\alpha-1}K^{\beta})(-2b)$

$$= (a - 2bQ)\left(\frac{\alpha\beta Q}{KL}\right) - 2bQ\left(\frac{\alpha\beta Q}{KL}\right) = (a - 4bQ)\left(\frac{\alpha\beta Q}{KL}\right).$$

Clearly $\left(\dfrac{\alpha\beta Q}{KL}\right) > 0$. Therefore, $R_{KL} < 0$ and so KL falls with increases in δ for all outputs exceeding $Q = a/4b$; that is, for all outputs in excess of half the output at which marginal revenue is zero, or at all price elasticities of demand lower than 3.0.[2]

At lower outputs, $R_{KL} > 0$ and so $\dfrac{dL}{d\delta} < 0$. For the distortion to continue falling with increases in δ, it is necessary, following (13), that:

(24) $\dfrac{dK}{d\delta}/K - \dfrac{dL}{d\delta}/L < 0.$

Incorporating (16) and (19), this requires that:

(25) $\dfrac{\dfrac{K}{R_K - r - \delta}}{K} + \dfrac{\dfrac{R_{KL}K}{R_{LL}(R_K - r - \delta)}}{L} < 0.$

Rearranging, cancelling, and recalling that $(R_K - r - \delta) < 0$, this condition simplifies to:

(26) $-\dfrac{R_{KL}K}{R_{LL}L} < 1.$

We note that in its most general form:

(27) $R_{LL} = \dfrac{\partial R}{\partial Q}\dfrac{\partial^2 Q}{\partial L^2} + \left(\dfrac{\partial Q}{\partial L}\right)^2\dfrac{\partial^2 R}{\partial Q^2}.$

Substituting in the appropriate derivatives of (21) and (22):

(28) $R_{LL} = (a - 2bQ)(\alpha - 1)\alpha g L^{\alpha-2}K^{\beta} + (\alpha g L^{\alpha-1}K^{\beta})^2(-2b)$

$$= (a - 2bQ)(\alpha - 1)\alpha\left(\frac{Q}{L^2}\right) - 2b\alpha^2 Q\left(\frac{Q}{L^2}\right)$$

$$= \left(\frac{\alpha Q}{L^2}\right)[\alpha(a - 4bQ) - (a - 2bQ)].$$

Substituting (23) and (28) into (26):

(29) $-\dfrac{R_{KL}K}{R_{LL}L} = -\dfrac{K\left(\dfrac{\alpha\beta Q}{KL}\right)(a - 4bQ)}{L\left(\dfrac{\alpha Q}{L^2}\right)[(a - 4bQ) - (a - 2bQ)]}$

$$= -\frac{\beta(a - 4bQ)}{\alpha(a - 4bQ) - (a - 2bQ)}.$$

[2] At $Q = \dfrac{r}{4b}$, $\eta = -\dfrac{dQ}{dP}\dfrac{P}{Q} = -\left(-\dfrac{1}{b}\right)\dfrac{\left(\dfrac{3a}{4}\right)}{\left(\dfrac{a}{4b}\right)} = 3.$

When $Q > \dfrac{a}{4b}$, $(a - 4bQ) < 0$, and so (29) is negative, satisfying (26) and confirming the result obtained following equation (23). When $Q < a/4b$ and $\alpha \lessgtr 1$; $(a - 4bQ) > 0$; $\alpha(a - 4bQ) > 0$; $\alpha(a - 4bQ) < (a - 2bQ)$; and so (29) is positive. To satisfy (26), the absolute value of the denominator must exceed the absolute value of the numerator. As Q approaches $a/4b$ from below, $(a - 4bQ) \to 0$ and $(a - 2bQ) \to a/2$. Thus, $-\dfrac{R_{KL}K}{R_{LL}L} < 1$ for Q slightly below $a/4b$. At what value of Q does this condition cease to hold? To find out, we solve for that value of Q at which $-\beta(a - 4bQ) = \alpha(a - 4bQ) - (a - 2bQ)$. The solution is:

$$(30) \quad Q = \frac{a(1 - \alpha - \beta)}{2b(1 - 2\alpha - 2\beta)}.$$

With a production function characterized by constant returns to scale, as in the numerical example of Chapter 22, $\alpha + \beta = 1$, and so the numerator of (30) is zero. It follows t'' it the K/L distortion falls with increases in δ over all relevant positive values of Q. This is not necessarily true, however, when there are increasing returns to scale. If the two-thirds rule holds,[3] $\alpha + \beta = 1\frac{1}{2}$. Then the value of Q below which K/L begins to rise with increases in δ is $(\frac{1}{4})\left(\dfrac{a}{2b}\right)$, or one fourth the output at which marginal revenue is zero. At this output, the price elasticity of demand is 7. More generally, the more the production function exhibits increasing returns to scale, and the more elastic demand is in the neighborhood of the Averch-Johnson equilibrium, the less likely it is that increases in δ will lead to the paradoxical decline in the K/L distortion observed in our Chapter 22 numerical example.

[3] Cf. p. 73 *supra*.

Author Index

Law Case Index*

*The dates in parentheses generally refer to the latest significant substantive court decision.

Subject Index